ASP.NET 4.5

(Covers C# 2012 and VB 2012 codes)

Black Book™

Authored by:

DT Editorial Services

Published by:

dreamtech PRESS

ISBN: 978-93-5119-080-6

Reprint: 2020

Printed at: Nisha Enterprises

Contents at a Glance

Bonus chapters available with the book for download

Table of Contents

Bonus chapters available with the book for download

Bonus chapters available with the book for download

Introduction

Congratulations on buying the *ASP.NET 4.5 Black Book, Platinum Edition*! This book endorses our continued commitment towards delivering quality IT books based on intensive research on the requirements of our readers. The book is the result of rich implementation of instructional acumen and technical precision of the authors and editors at Kogent Solutions Inc. and Dreamtech Press; and promises to offer an affluent solution to students and IT professionals who want to outshine in ASP.NET 4.5 domain. This book further extends our philosophy to present comprehensive and easily understandable reference material on emerging technologies. The book has been written considering the diverse audience of ASP.NET 4.5, and promises an exceptional learning experience by presenting relevant, appropriate, and real-life examples. In addition, the book also includes code snippets and executable applications to demonstrate the implementation of various concepts related to ASP.NET 4.5.

We've designed this book to grow with you, providing the reference material you need as you move towards software proficiency.

ASP.NET is a Web application framework developed by Microsoft. C# and VB programmers can use this framework for developing dynamic websites. Many companies are using ASP.NET 4.5 along with C# or VB 2012 to build robust, reliable, and scalable Web applications. The influence of ASP.NET 4.5 is spreading fast, and there's no stopping or looking back! We hope that your learning experience with this book will prove as irresistible to you as it has proved to us while authoring and editing the book.

NOTE

The book provides the Online Travel Agency portal, which requires Visual Studio 2012 IDE, SQL Server 2008 R2, and Windows 7 operating system to be executed.

The Audience

This book is equally beneficial for those people who want to learn ASP.NET from scratch or who are already involved in developing applications in ASP.NET 4.5. Therefore, *ASP.NET 4.5 Black Book, Platinum Edition* serves as an excellent guide in true sense—introducing the fast-changing world of ASP.NET and various programming techniques related to it.

About this book

This book consists of seven parts, which are as follows:

- **Part I**—Introduction to ASP.NET 4.5: Describes the essentials and basic concepts of ASP.NET 4.5.
- **Part II**—ASP.NET 4.5 Controls: Discusses about the controls supported by ASP.NET 4.5 in detail.
- **Part III**—Accessing Data in ASP.NET 4.5: Explains how to work with data in ASP.NET 4.5.

- **Part IV**—Building ASP.NET 4.5 Enterprise Applications: Describes how to build interactive and advanced applications.
- **Part V**—Administering ASP.NET 4.5: Explains how to track and manage ASP.NET applications.
- **Part VI**—Security in ASP.NET 4.5: Explores different aspects of securing ASP.NET 4.5 applications.
- **Part VII**—Miscellaneous Topics: Describes various miscellaneous topics such as mobile applications, and deployment of Web applications.

Moreover, there are hundreds of topics covered in this book, and each of them is explained by applications showing how it works. This book is divided into separate and easily accessible topics, each addressing a different programming issue. Here are just a few of those topics:

- ASP.NET 4.5 Essentials
- Developing a Web application
- Applications Structure and State
- Web Forms and Standard Controls
- Navigation Controls such as TreeView, Menu, and SiteMapPath
- Validation Controls
- Web Parts Controls
- Accessing data using ADO.NET objects
- Working with LINQ
- ADO.NET Entity Framework
- Working with files and streams
- Building ASP.NET Dynamic Data Applications
- Developing ASP.NET AJAX applications
- Using master pages and themes in an ASP.NET application
- Caching in ASP.NET 4.5
- Implementing application globalization
- Creating ASP.NET 4.5 Web services
- Creating WCF services
- ASP.NET MVC Framework
- Understanding Login Controls
- Understanding User Profiles
- Securing Web Applications
- Developing Mobile Applications
- Deploying and Packaging Web Application

How to Use

In this book, all the applications have been developed using Visual Studio 2012 Integrated Development Environment. Visual Studio 2012 provides built-in templates for developing Console, Windows, WPF, WCF, WF, Silverlight, and Web applications.

Conventions

We have used standard conventions throughout this book. This section helps you get acquainted with these conventions to ensure a superior learning experience.

Listing 9.2: Showing the Code for the Code-Behind File of the Default.aspx Page

In VB

```
Partial Class _Default
    Inherits System.Web.UI.Page
    Protected Sub Page_Load(sender As Object, e As EventArgs) Handles
Me.Load
        Dim dc As New MyClassesDataContext()
        Dim query = dc.Products
        For Each item As Product In query
            ListBox1.Items.Add(item.ProductID.ToString() & "       " & item.ProductName)
        Next item
    End Sub
End Class
```

In C#

```
using System;
using System.Collections.Generic;
using System.Linq;
using System.Web;
using System.Web.UI;
using System.Web.UI.WebControls;
public partial class _Default : System.Web.UI.Page
{
    protected void Page_Load(object sender, EventArgs e)
    {
        MyClassesDataContext dc = new MyClassesDataContext();
        var query = dc.Products;
        foreach (Product item in query)
        {
            ListBox1.Items.Add (item.ProductID.ToString() + “ “+item.ProductName);
        }
    }
}
```

The reserved words, properties, methods, events, classes, interfaces, namespaces (used in the code snippets), exceptions, etc. are shown distinctly using a different font within the text.

Each figure has a caption to help you understand the figure better.

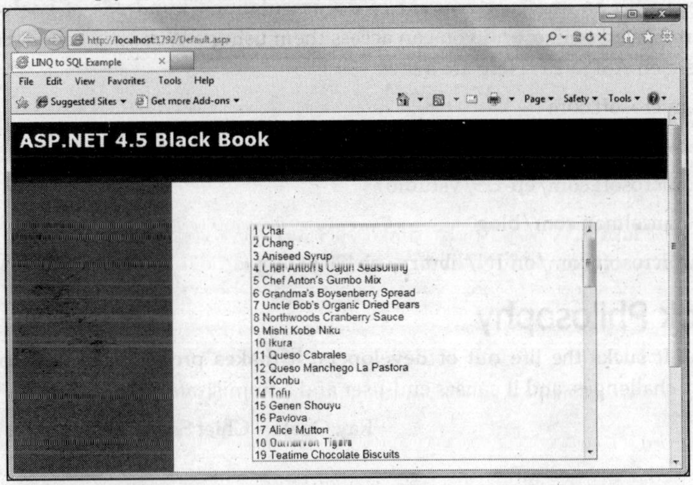

Figure 9.5: Displaying the Output using LINQ to SQL

Notes are represented in the following format:

NOTE

The applications in this chapter are created using the ASP.NET Empty Web Site template in the New Web Site dialog box. After creating the application, you need to add the Default.aspx page to the application.

The tables are numbered and are placed just below their references in the chapters, as shown below:

Table 9.1 lists all the standard query operators used in LINQ:

Table 9.1: Standard Query Operators

Operator	Description
Filtering Operators	Restricts the result set to contain those elements that satisfy a specific condition that are returned
Projection Operators	Transforms an object into a different type of new object
Sorting Operators	Changes the order of elements of sequence returned by the query
Join Operators	Combines collections
Grouping Operators	Puts the data into groups
Quantifier Operators	Checks whether an element of a sequence satisfies a condition
Partitioning Operators	Returns a subset of collection
Set Operators	Returns a result set which is in the form of a collection
Element Operators	Returns just one element
Aggregate Operators	Computes a single value from a collection
Conversion Operators	Converts the collection to an array
Generation Operators	Returns a new sequence of values

Other Resources

ASP.NET 4.5 comes with an immense amount of documentation—hundreds of books worth referring to. The documentations are hosted online, and you can access them using a Web browser. Of course, there are plenty of Web pages out there on ASP.NET. Here are a few:

- http://msdn.microsoft.com
- http://www.asp.net/vnext/overview/aspnet/whats-new
- http://msdn.microsoft.com/en-US/vstudio/
- http://www.hanselman.com/blog
- http://msdn.microsoft.com/en-IN/library/hh420390.aspx

The Black Book Philosophy

"Complexity kills. It sucks the life out of developers, it makes products difficult to plan, build and test, it introduces security challenges, and it causes end-user and administrator frustration."

Ray Ozzie – Chief Software Architect at Microsoft Corporation

Whichever language or platform you might be learning or working on, being a prolific programmer and administrator is fraught with challenges, complications, complexities, and frustrations. We at Kogent Learning Solutions, Inc. and Dreamtech Press realize this veracity seamlessly; and ensure that our **Black Book** series comes as an accomplished and dexterous solution to these complexities. The unique structure of Black Books ensures that complex topics are chunked into appropriate sections and presented in a more comprehensible manner, employing diagrams, code, and real-life examples for further simplicity. In addition, Black Books ensure a learning path replete with adequate practice avenues of the concepts learned by means of code examples, listings, executable programs and applications. Each Black Book is designed to grow with its readers, providing all the guidance and reference material they need as they move towards software proficiency. In summation, the Black Book philosophy extends beyond simple pedagogy; and seeks to decipher the practical challenges imbibed in the professional roles of its readers, whether students or professionals – that is why we call it a "Indispensable Comprehensive Reference"!

Whichever language or platform you might be learning or working on, being a prolific programmer and administrator is fraught with challenges, complications, complexities and frustrations. We at Kogent Learning Solutions Inc. and Dreamtech Press realize this very fact acutely and ensure that our **Black Book** series comes as an accomplished and dexterous solution to these complexities. The unique structure of Black Books ensures that complex topics are chunked into appropriate sections and presented in a more comprehensible manner employing diagrams, code and real-life examples for further simplicity. In addition, Black Books ensure a learning path replete with adequate practice avenues of the concepts learned by means of code examples, listings, executable programs and applications. Each Black Book is designed to grow with its readers, providing all the guidance and reference material they need as they move towards software proficiency. In summation, the Black Book philosophy extends beyond simple pedagogy, and seeks to decipher the practical challenges implied in the professional roles of its readers, whether students or professionals; that is why we call it a "Indispensable Comprehensive Reference".

1

ASP.NET 4.5 Essentials

If you need an Information on:	See page:
Evolution of .NET	2
Benefits of .NET Framework	2
Overview of .NET Framework 4.5	3
Exploring New Features of .NET Framework 4.5	20
Exploring New Features of Visual Studio 2012 IDE	25
Some Miscellaneous Features of Visual Studio 2012	39
Exploring the Visual Studio 2012 IDE	40
Exploring New Features of ASP.NET 4.5	56
The ASP.NET Technologies	61
The ASP.NET Life Cycle	62
Exploring a Sample ASP.NET 4.5 Web Application	66
Creating a Sample ASP.NET 4.5 Website	68
Web Parts Framework	75
LINQ	75
ADO.NET Entity Framework	75
ASP.NET Dynamic Data Applications	75
ASP.NET AJAX	75
Silverlight Technology	76
ASP.NET Web Services	76
The WCF Services	76
ASP.NET MVC Framework	76

Section I – Introduction to .NET

.NET Framework is a development platform under Windows operating system for creating applications by integrating different programming languages, such as C#, Visual Basic, F#, and Visual C++. This Framework consists of a virtual execution system called the Common Language Runtime (CLR) and a set of class libraries. CLR is a Microsoft product of the Common Language Infrastructure (CLI), which is an international standard and a basis for creating execution and development environments in which languages and libraries work together. Microsoft introduced .NET Framework to not only bridge the gap but also to ensure interoperability between applications created in different languages. The .NET Framework is used to integrate the business logic of an application implemented in various programming languages and services. Consequently, it induces significant improvements in code reusability, code specialization, resource management, development of applications, security, deployment, and administration of programs developed in multiple programming languages.

This chapter introduces us to .NET, ASP.NET, and the Visual Studio 2012 Integrated Development Environment (IDE). This chapter also provides the snapshots of .NET-related technologies discussed in various chapters of this book. Let's start with the evolution of .NET.

Evolution of .NET

Around 1995, Java was gaining popularity because of its platform-independent approach and Sun Microsystem's open source policy. Later in 2002, Sun Microsystems released the enterprise edition of Java, that is, Java 2 Enterprise Edition (J2EE), which is a Java Platform to develop and execute distributed Java applications (which implies that the functioning of an application is distributed on several computers) based on the N-tier architecture. The advent of J2EE eventually led to the decline of Microsoft's market share. Consequently, Microsoft started a project called Next Generation Windows Services (NGWS) to regain the market share. It took more than three years to develop the product, which is now known as .NET.

Microsoft released the first version of .NET with the name .NET Framework 1.0 on February 13, 2002, along with the Visual Studio.NET 2002 IDE. The second revised version of .NET took nearly an year to release and was known as .NET Framework 1.1. Microsoft Visual Studio .NET, better known as Visual Studio .NET 2003, was also a part of the second release on 24 April, 2003. The next version, .NET Framework 2.0, was released with Visual Studio .NET 2005 on November 07, 2005. .NET Framework 3.0, formerly called WinFX, was then released on November 06, 2006. .NET Framework 3.5 was released with Visual Studio .NET 2008 on November 19, 2007. The .NET Framework 4.0 version, was announced by Microsoft on September 29, 2008 and on April 12, 2010, the final version of .NET Framework 4.0 was released. Microsoft announced the latest version, .NET Framework 4.5, on February 29, 2012 and on August 15, 2012, the final version of the .NET Framework 4.5 was released.

Benefits of .NET Framework

The following are the benefits of .NET Framework:

- **Consistent Programming Model**—Provides a consistent object-oriented programming model across different languages. You can use this model to create programs for performing different tasks, such as connecting to and retrieving data from databases, and reading and writing in files.
- **Cross-platform Support**—Specifies that any Windows platform that supports CLR can execute .NET application, that is, .NET application enables interoperability between multiple Windows operating systems.
- **Language Interoperability**—Enables code written in different languages to interact with each other. This allows reusability of code and improves the efficiency of the development process. For example, in an ASP.NET application created using Visual Basic language, you can inherit a C# class in the application. The CLR has a built-in support for language interoperability. However, there is no assurance that the code written can be utilized by other developers using another programming language. Therefore, to ensure multi-language code interoperability, a set of language features and rules for using them, called the Common Language Specification (CLS), is defined. Any component that follow these rules and expose only CLS features are said to be CLS-compliant.

- **Automatic Management of Resource**—Specifies that in .NET, you do not need to manually free the application resources, such as files, memory, network, and database connections. .NET Framework provides a feature called CLR that automatically tracks the resource usage and helps you in performing the task of manual resource management.
- **Ease of Deployment**—Specifies that the .NET Framework installs applications or components that do not affect the existing applications. In most cases, to install an application, you need to copy the application along with its components on the target computer. In .NET, applications are deployed in the form of assemblies. Therefore, registry entries are not required to store information about components and applications. In addition, assemblies store information about different versions of a single component used by an application. Therefore, the version problem is also eliminated in .NET Framework.

Overview of .NET Framework 4.5

The new version of .NET provides a Framework that helps in designing portable, scalable, and robust applications. The applications developed in .NET Framework 4.5 can be executed in a distributed environment. Therefore, you can say that the .NET Framework 4.5 is designed to address the latest needs of the developers.

In addition to few enhancements, the architecture of .NET Framework 4.5 mainly consists of components of .NET Framework 4.0, as shown in Figure 1.1:

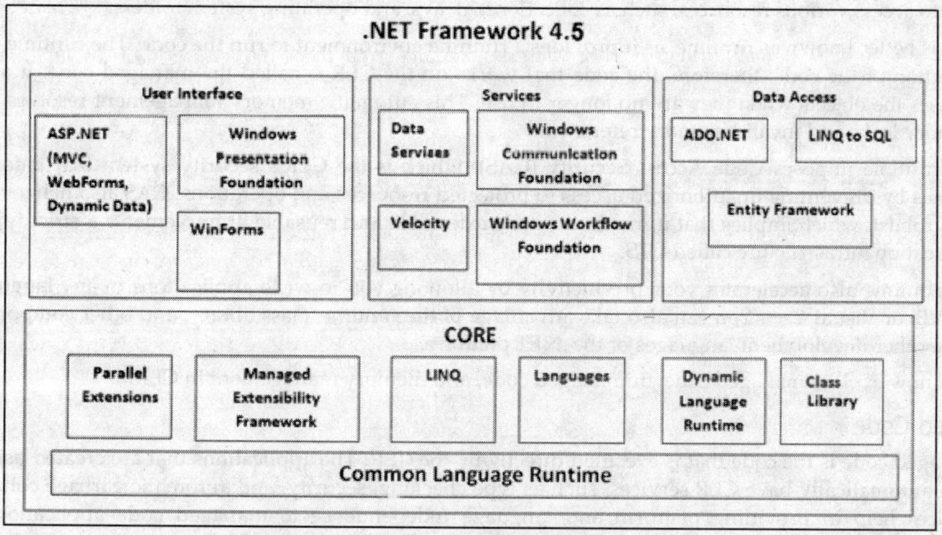

Figure 1.1: .NET Framework 4.5 Architecture

As shown in Figure 1.1, .NET Framework 4.5 consists of the Common Language Runtime (CLR), .NET Framework Class Library(FCL), Base Class Library(BCL), Windows Forms, ASP.NET, Console applications, ActiveX Data Objects for .NET (ADO.NET), CLS, Common Type System (CTS), and .NET languages, such as C# and Visual Basic. .NET Framework 4.5 also comprises of Windows Workflow Foundation (WF), Windows Presentation Foundation (WPF), Windows Communication Foundation (WCF), and Windows CardSpace. .NET Framework 4.5 also has components, such as Language Integrated Query (LINQ), ADO.NET Entity Framework and Data services, ASP.NET AJAX, new compilers for C#, Visual Basic, and C++. Therefore, the components of .NET Framework 4.5 architecture are as follows:

- CLR
- CTS
- Metadata and Assemblies
- FCL
- BCL

- Windows Forms
- ASP.NET and ASP.NET Asynchronous JavaScript and XML (AJAX)
- ADO.NET
- Windows Workflow Foundation(WF)
- Windows Presentation Foundation(WPF)
- Windows Communication Foundation(WCF)
- Windows CardSpace(WCS)
- LINQ

Let's discuss about each of them in detail.

Common Language Runtime

CLR is one of the most important components of .NET Framework. It provides various services, such as memory management, exception handling, debugging, security, thread execution, code execution, code safety, verification, and compilation, to develop an application easily. CLR also supports versioning to any language that it interacts with. This implies that CLR can host a variety of languages and provides common tools to these languages; thereby, ensuring interoperability between the codes. CLR also supports services that an application uses to access various resources, such as collections, arrays, and operating system folders.

CLR is better known as runtime, as it provides a runtime environment to run the code. The runtime manages the execution of the code; therefore, the code that works on the CLR is called the managed code. It automatically releases the objects when they are no longer in use. This automatic memory management resolves the issues of memory leaks and invalid memory references.

The runtime imposes Code Access Security (CAS), which is the CLR's security system that enforces security policies by preventing unauthorized access to protected resources and operations. CAS also helps in making the code robust, which implies that it makes the code extensible and reusable. It implements a strict type and code-verification infrastructure called CTS.

The runtime also accelerates your productivity by allowing you to write applications in any language, such as C#, VB, or Visual C++. You can also take advantage of the runtime, class library, and other components written in the other development languages of the .NET platform.

Let's now explore managed code, unmanaged code, and memory management in CLR.

Managed Code

Managed code is the code that is executed directly by the CLR. The applications that are created using managed code automatically have CLR services, such as type checking, security, and automatic garbage collection. These services help in providing platform and language independence to managed code applications. The CLR compiles the applications to Intermediate Language (IL) or Microsoft Intermediate Language (MSIL), but not the machine code. This IL along with the metadata, which describes the attributes, classes, and methods of the code, reside in an assembly. The compilation takes place in the managed execution environment, which assures the proper working of the code.

The process of executing a piece of managed code is as follows:

1. Selecting a language compiler
2. Compiling the code to IL
3. Compiling IL to native code
4. Executing the code

The benefits provided by the CLR can be used by selecting one or more language compilers, such as VB, C#, Visual C++, or J#, or any third party compiler, such as COBOL, Perl, or Eiffel. The language compiler determines the syntax that must be used by the code.

When you compile the code into managed code, the compiler converts the source code into IL, which is CPU-independent. Before the execution of the code, IL must be converted into CPU-specific code by the Just-in-Time (JIT) compiler. When you compile your source code into IL, the required metadata is generated. The metadata contains the definition of types, member signature, the members in the code, and other details that the code uses at the time of execution. The runtime locates and extracts the metadata from the file during execution. While executing the application, a JIT compiler translates the IL into native code. After compiling, the code is passed through a verification process that examines the IL and metadata to check whether the code is safe, that is, it should be able to access only those memory locations, which it is authorized to access.

NOTE

The native code is a CPU-specific code, which is nothing but the output of the JIT compiler, that is, the machine code that actually runs in the runtime.

The runtime also supports another method of compilation called install-time code generation. It converts IL into native code in a single shot by taking a larger unit of code at a time. Using the install-time code generation, the entire assembly is converted into native code that results in loading the code file more rapidly. By default, the runtime takes care of other assemblies referred in this assembly. It stores the resulting native code in a file for use when the assembly is loaded and run.

The CLR provides the environment to execute the code safely. Throughout the execution, the managed code receives the services, such as garbage collection, security, interoperability with unmanaged code, cross-language debugging support, and enhanced deployment and versioning support. The process of compilation and execution of the code by the JIT compiler, which is repeated until the execution is complete, is shown in Figure 1.2:

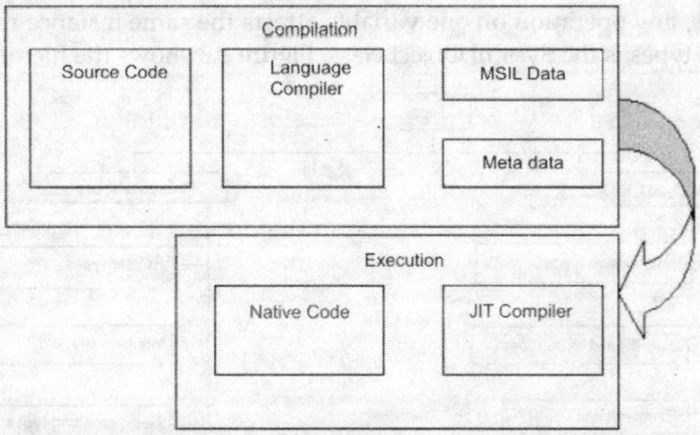

Figure 1.2: Displaying the Compilation and Execution by the JIT Compiler

Figure 1.2 demonstrates the process the IL goes through before the application code is actually executed. When the code is compiled by the JIT compiler, the CLR examines the code to make sure that the IL is correct. The rules that the CLR uses are stated in CLS and CTS.

Unmanaged Code

In contrast to the managed code, unmanaged code directly compiles to the machine code and runs on the machine where it has been compiled. Unmanaged code does not have services, such as security or memory management, which are provided by the runtime. If your code is not secure, then it can be directly interpreted (or manipulated) by any user, which can prove harmful.

Memory Management

One of the most important services that the CLR provides during managed execution is the automatic memory management. The CLR uses the garbage collector to manage the allocation and release of memory for an application. It is one of the advantages of CLR, which is beneficial for developers, as CLR reduces the burden of writing codes to manage memory while developing managed applications. Automatic memory management removes common problems, such as forgetting to free an object, which may result in memory leak, or attempting to access memory for an object that is already free.

Common Type System

The CTS specifies certain guidelines for declaring, using, and managing types at runtime. It is an integral part of the runtime for supporting cross-language communication. The functions performed by the CTS are as follows:

- Helps in cross-language communication, type safety, and high-performance execution of code by establishing a Framework
- Supports object-oriented model for implementation of different programming languages
- Specifies guidelines for different languages to follow; thereby, ensuring proper interaction between objects of different languages
- Supports primitive data types, such as Boolean, Byte, Char, and Int32, which are used in the process of development of an application

The CTS can be classified into two data types: value types and reference types. In the managed code, values can have their memory allocated either on the stack managed by the CLR or on a CLR-managed heap. Variables allocated on the stack are typically created when a method is called or when a running method creates them. The garbage collector manages the memory allocated to these types by releasing the memory space of variables when they are no longer in use. An instance of a value type, such as a string, has its value allocated on the stack; whereas, an instance of a reference type, such as an array, has only a reference to its actual value allocated on the stack.

Variables declared as value types have their own copy of the data; therefore, any operation on one variable does not affect another variable. On the other hand, variables that are declared as reference types always point to the same object; in this case, any operation on one variable affects the same instance referred to by another variable. The base class of all the types is the System.Object class. Figure 1.3 shows the hierarchy of the types:

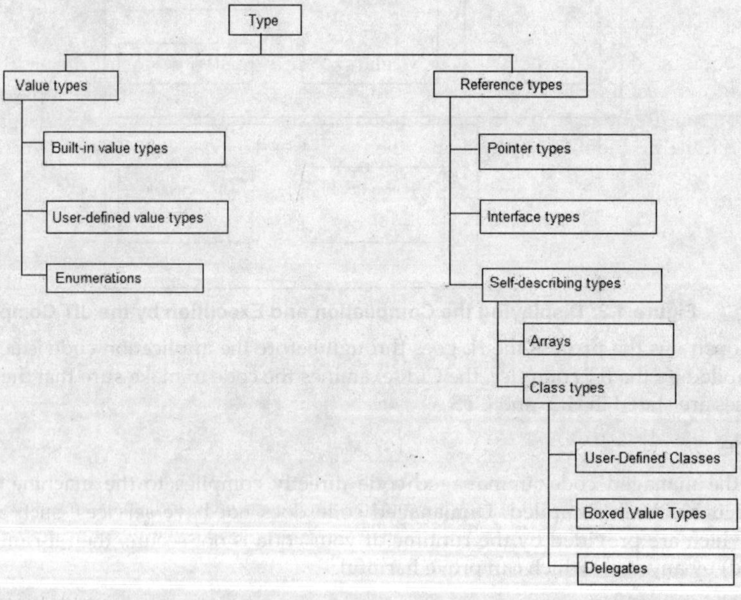

Figure 1.3: Displaying the Hierarchical Representation of Different Data Types

Metadata and Assemblies

A metadata is binary information that describes a program, stored in a CLR Portable Executable (PE) file or memory. When the compilation of the code takes place in a PE file, the metadata is inserted into one part of the file, while the code is converted into IL and then inserted into the other part of the file. The metadata describes every type and member. When the code is in the run mode, the CLR loads the metadata into the memory and finds information about the code's classes and members.

A metadata describes information about the code in a language-neutral manner. The metadata contains the following:

- Assembly information, which includes the metadata identity that can be name, version, culture, public key, the types of assemblies, other referenced assemblies, and security permissions
- Information about types, such as name, visibility, base class, interfaces used, and members (methods, fields, properties, events, and nested types)
- Attribute information that modifies the types and members of a class

After providing the listed information, CLR is able to create objects, access data, and call member functions.

Assemblies are packaged into units containing programs and libraries. An assembly contains a self-describing binary file that can be either Dynamic Link Library (DLL) or Executable (EXE). It also contains a collection of types, such as classes, interfaces, and structures. A single assembly can contain multiple code files or a single code file can have more than one assembly. An assembly contains code that the CLR executes.

Assemblies can be of two types: static or dynamic. Static assemblies include interfaces, classes, and resources. These assemblies are stored in the PE files on a disk. On the other hand, dynamic assemblies run directly from the memory without being saved to a disk before execution. However, after execution, dynamic assemblies can be saved on the disk.

Assembly Contents

Typically, an assembly is a logical unit that consists of four elements—the manifest, type metadata, IL code that implements the types, and a set of resources. As discussed earlier, you can group all these elements in a single file as well as in multiple files.

Assembly Manifest

Every assembly contains data that describes how elements are related to each other within the assembly. The manifest, also known as assembly manifest, contains the assembly metadata needed for providing the assembly's version requirements and security identity. The manifest can be stored either in a PE file with the IL code or in a standalone PE file that contains only the manifest information. Table 1.1 lists the information stored in the assembly manifest:

Table 1.1: Information Stored in the Assembly Manifest

Information	Description
Assembly name	Specifies the name of the assembly.
Version number	Indicates a major version number, a minor version number, and a revision and build number. CLR uses these numbers to enforce the version policy.
Culture	Provides information about the culture or language that the assembly supports.
Strong name information	Indicates a public key from the publisher if the assembly contains a strong name.
List of all files in the assembly	Contains an alphanumeric string that is generated as per the contents of a file or hash of each file contained in the assembly and a file name. Note that all the files that make up the assembly must be in the same directory as the file containing the assembly manifest.
Type reference information	Contains the information required to map a type reference to the file that contains its declaration and implementation. Types exported from the assembly use the type reference information.
Information on referenced assemblies	Provides a list of assemblies, which are used as a reference by an assembly. The reference of the assembly contains the complete details of dependent assembly, such as name, assembly metadata, and public key, if the assembly is strongly named.

The information in the assembly manifest can be modified by using the assembly attributes. You can also change the version, information, and attributes, such as Trademark, Product, Company, and Copyright.

Global Assembly Cache

Global Assembly Cache (GAC) is the central place for registering assemblies, so that different applications on the computer can use it later on. CLR is installed on the cache in a computer. Note that the assemblies must be made sharable by registering them in the GAC, only when needed; otherwise, they must be kept private. Further, it is not mandatory to install the assemblies in the GAC to make them accessible to the Component Object Model (COM) interop or unmanaged code. COM interop is a service that enables .NET Framework objects to communicate with COM objects.

You can deploy an assembly in the GAC by using:

- An installer that is designed to work with the GAC
- The GAC tool known as `Gacutil.exe`
- The Windows Explorer to drag assemblies into the cache

Strong Name Assemblies

A strong name contains the assembly's identity, that is, the information about the assembly's name, version number, culture, public key, and digital signature. Using the private key, the assembly file containing the manifest generates the strong name. You can provide a strong name to an assembly by using the Microsoft Visual Studio .NET and other development tools.

By providing strong names to the assembly, you can ensure that an assembly is globally unique. Using strong names for assemblies has the following benefits:

- Provides uniqueness to the assembly names by generating a private key
- Ensures that a version of the assembly you are using comes from the same publisher that created the version the application was built with
- Facilitates integrity check, which ensures that the contents of the assembly do not change since its last build

Private and Shared Assemblies

When a single application uses an assembly, then it is called a private assembly. For example, if you have created a DLL assembly containing information about your business logic, then the DLL can be used by your client application only. Therefore, to run the application, the DLL must be included in the same folder in which the client application has been installed. This makes the assembly private to your application.

Shared assemblies are those assemblies that are placed in the GAC so that they can be used by multiple applications. Suppose the DLL needs to be reused in different client applications. In this scenario, instead of providing a separate copy of the DLL to every client application, the DLL can be placed in the GAC by using the Gacutil.exe tool, from where it can be accessed by any client application.

Side-by-Side Execution

The process of executing multiple versions of an application or assembly is known as side-by-side execution. Support for side-by-side storage and execution of different versions of the same assembly is an integral part of creating a strong name for an assembly. A strong name of .NET assembly is used to provide unique assembly identity by using the sn.exe command utility. Since the strong-named assembly's version number is a part of its identity, the runtime can store multiple versions of the same assembly in the GAC and can load these assemblies at runtime.

.NET Framework Class Library

.NET Framework consists of classes, interfaces, and value types that help in speeding up the application development process and provide access to system functionality. To facilitate interoperability between languages, .NET Framework should be CLS-compliant so that the code developed in a programming language can be used from another programming language whose compiler conforms to the CLS.

The .NET applications, components, and controls are built on the foundation of .NET Framework types. These types perform the following functions:

- Represent base data types and exceptions
- Encapsulate data structures
- Perform input/output operations
- Access information about loaded types
- Call .NET Framework security checks
- Facilitate data access, rich client-side Graphical User Interface (GUI), and server-controlled client-side GUI

The FCL is a huge library of reusable types meant to be used by managed codes. It is an object-oriented library that is used in component-based applications. The FCL is made up of a hierarchy of namespaces that expose classes, structures, interfaces, enumerations, and delegates. The namespaces are logically defined by their functionality. For example, the System.Data namespace contains the functionalities available for accessing databases. This namespace is further broken down into the System.Data.SqlClient and System.Data.OleDb namespaces. The System.Data.SqlClient namespace exposes the functionality specific to SQL Server; whereas, the System.Data.OleDb namespace exposes a specific functionality for accessing Object Linking and Embedding Database (OLEDB) data sources. Specific assemblies within the FCL do not define the bounds of a namespace; instead, they are focused on functionality and logical grouping. There are more than 20,000 classes in FCL, all logically grouped in a hierarchical manner. In other words, you can write applications that make use of objects in the FCL to read files, display windows, and perform various tasks. However, to exploit the true potential of classes, you can extend the FCL according to the requirements of your application and then write your application code. The following points need to be remembered while using the FCL:

- The classes, interfaces, structures, and enumerated values are collectively referred as types.
- The different types in the framework are arranged in a hierarchy of namespaces. This solves the problem faced in name collisions. Namespaces are arranged in a hierarchy that has words separated by Dots (.). Therefore, we can include namespaces, such as `System.IO.Stream` and `System.Windows.Forms.Form`, for a code that uses a `Stream` class or a `Form` class, respectively.
- The `System` namespace is a parent of all the types available in the .NET FCL. It contains base data type's classes, such as Object, Int, Array, and Short.
- All the types must have a base class. The exception to this rule is the `System.Object` type, which acts as the base type for all the types in .NET Framework. This implies that if you create a class that does not explicitly declare a base class, then the compiler explicitly declares its base class to the `Object` class.

Sometimes, FCL is referred to as BCL, which is incorrect. Actually, FCL is a superset of BCL. Let's discuss BCL in the next section.

BCL

The BCL is the library that contains some common set of functionalities, such as reading from and writing in files, designing graphics, and interacting with databases, for all the .NET Framework languages. Microsoft has upgraded the BCL with every release of .NET Framework. Following are the improvements made in the .NET Framework 4.5 BCL:

- **Simplified asynchronous programming**—In the earlier versions of .NET Framework, the use of asynchronous programming was quite tough. Asynchronous programming is used to prevent the blockage of User Interface (UI) and decrease the number of threads used by the operating system; therefore, it is simplified in .NET Framework 4.5 by adding some new methods in BCL. The asynchronous methods that are added in some header files are as follows:
  - **System.IO.Stream**—ReadAsync, WriteAsync, FlushAsync, and CopyToAsync
  - **System.IO.TextReader**—ReadAsync, ReadBlockAsync, ReadLineAsync, and ReadToEndAsync
  - **System.IO.TextWriter**—WriteAsync, WriteLineAsync, and FlushAsync

- **Read-only collection interfaces**—As the name suggests, these interfaces cannot be modified. Moreover, read-only collection interfaces cannot throw the NotSupportedException exception in case of those methods that do nothing in a program. In the .NET Framework 4.5, the IReadOnlyList<T> and IReadOnlyDictionary<T> collection interfaces are added as the read-only collection interfaces. These are compatible with Windows Runtime (WinRT) because it also provides the read-only version of collection types.
- **Support for .zip archives**—The .NET Framework 3.0 and later versions support the feature of reading and writing archive files according to the Open Packaging Convention (OPC). However, they do not support reading and writing of every type of archive file. Therefore, the .NET Framework 4.5 provides support for reading and writing of every type of archive file by using System.IO.Compression.ZipArchive.

In addition to this, Microsoft has resolved the issues regarding performance and compression quality in the DeflateStream class. This class provides methods and properties to compress and decompress the streams by using the deflate algorithm. In the .NET Framework 4.5, the DeflateStream class uses the zlib library; thereby, providing better implementation of the deflate algorithm during the compression of files. Moreover, the class generates smaller compressed files as compared to the previous versions of .NET Framework.

NOTE

OPC is a container-file technology developed by Microsoft to combine XML and non-XML files and form a single unit known as the Open XML Paper Specification (OpenXPS) document.

Some other miscellaneous improvements in the .NET Framework 4.5 BCL are given as follows:

- **AssemblyMetadataAttribute**—This class allows the association of a string-based key-value pair with an assembly in the .NET Framework 4.5. This helps in navigating to the home page of a website or to the version control label that points to the source from which an assembly is built.
- **WeakReference<T>** —In the earlier versions of .NET Framework, the WeakReference<T> class had the following two issues:
  - Design errors, which make the class exposed to race conditions
  - Compels consumers to cast when the target (or actual) object needs to be accessed

  In the .NET Framework 4.5, the race condition is removed from the WeakReference<T> class by adding the TryGetTarget Application Programming Interface (API). This API performs two operations: checking whether the object is alive and getting the target object. In the earlier versions of .NET Framework, separate APIs were used for each operation, which leads to race conditions. In other words, the WeakReference<T> class allows claiming of an object by garbage collector.
- **Comparer<T>.Create(Comparison<T>)**—In the earlier versions of .NET Framework, BCL provides two ways to compare collections: the IComparer<T> interface and the Comparison<T> delegate. In the .NET Framework 4.5, a static Create method is added on Comparison<T> to compare the collections, as Comparison<T> provides an implementation for IComparer<T>. This method eliminates the need of converting IComparer<T> to Comparison<T>, which takes place during the comparison.
- **ArraySegment<T>**—This structure allows you to represent a subset of an array by not copying it. In the earlier versions of .NET Framework, the ArraySegment<T> structure did not contain any collection interface, which prevents you from passing the structure to methods that can operate over the collection interface. This limitation is removed in the .NET Framework 4.5, as the ArraySegment<T> structure now implements the IEnumerable, IEnumerable<T>, ICollection<T>, IList<T>, IReadOnlyCollection<T>, and IReadOnlyList<T> interfaces.
- **SemaphoreSlim.WaitAsync**—In the .NET Framework 4.5, the SemaphoreSlim class contains a new WaitAsync method that returns a task, which is completed when the semaphore has been successfully waited or entered.
- **ReadOnlyDictionary<TKey, TValue>**—In the .NET Framework 4.5, this collection is added for dictionaries. It cannot be changed by a consumer and is based on the ReadOnlyCollection<T> collection present in the .NET Framework 2.0.

- **BinaryReader, BinaryWriter, StreamReader, StreamWriter**—In the .NET Framework 4.5, these classes contain options to prevent disposing of underlying streams, such as reader and writer. However, this was not possible in the earlier versions of .NET Framework. The disposing of streams is fine until there is only a single reader stream and a single writer stream. In the .NET Framework 4.5, the reader and writer constructors can take a parameter, named leaveOpen, where you can specify that the deposition of stream must not be done.
- **Console.IsInputRedirected, Console.IsOutputRedirected, and Console.IsErrorRedirected**—In the .NET Framework 4.5, these properties help in identifying whether any of the standard output and input is redirected. This is helpful when you want a different behavior of standard input and output on redirection.
- **Console.OutputEncoding and Console.InputEncoding can now be set to Encoding.Unicode**—In the .NET Framework 4.5, you can set Console.OutputEncoding and Console.InputEncoding to Encoding.Unicode. This allows writing of those characters by a program that cannot be represented in the Original Exception Manufacturer (OEM) code page related to console. Moreover, this feature makes easier to show text in multiple scripts on the console.
- **ExceptionDispatchInfo**—In the .NET Framework 4.5, the ExceptionDispatchInfo class captures a current exception object and throws it again, but without losing the valuable information stored in the exception object. However, in the earlier versions of .NET Framework, this valuable information was lost, as throwing of the same object again overwrites the already existing information.
- **Regex.Timeout**—Regular expressions are the best way for validating a user input but they have the exponential time complexity or constraint, which matters a lot in the client-server environment. Therefore, it is important for a regular expression to provide a constraint that how much time the Regex engine will keep on trying to match a given input. In the .NET Framework 4.5, several new APIs, such as Regex.IsMatch, Regex.Match, Regex.Matches, Regex.Split, and Regex.Replace, are provided for Regex to manage time constraint.

Windows Forms

Windows Forms is a graphical representation of any window displayed in an application. It is included as a part of Microsoft's .NET Framework. You can create an application using Windows Forms in any CLR-supported language. Windows Forms is used to either accept input from or display information to a user. In Windows Forms, you can add controls and raise events, such as a mouse-click, which are handled by event handlers in an application.

ASP.NET and ASP.NET AJAX

ASP.NET is a Web development model, which is used to deliver interactive, data-driven applications over the Internet. It consists of a large number of controls, such as text boxes, buttons, and labels, for assembling, configuring, and manipulating code to create Hyper Text Markup Language (HTML) pages. You can create an ASP.NET application by using any CLR-compliant language, such as VB, C#, Visual C++, and J#. The main features of ASP.NET are as follows:

- **Better performance**—Specifies that when you request a Web page for the first time after compiling the ASP.NET code, the CLR compiles the code and stores the cached copy of the result. Now, for any subsequent calls to the same page, the cached copy of the result is retrieved instead of going back to the server.
- **Improved security**—Refers to various methods of authentication included in ASP.NET, which are as follows:
  - **Forms**—Allows an ASP.NET application to use its own custom business logic for authentication.
  - **Windows**—Checks the identity of a user against the Windows user accounts that are stored on the Web server. If the credentials of a user match with that of a Windows user account, then the user is authenticated.

- **Greater scalability**—Specifies that the session states in ASP.NET are maintained in a separate process on a different machine or database. This enables cross-server sessions to occur, solving the problem of Web forms when more Web servers need to be added as the traffic grows.
- **Cookie-less sessions**—Specifies that ASP.NET stores a session state even when the cookies in a Web browser are disabled. In such case, the session ID is passed as a part of the Uniform Resource Locator (URL).

AJAX is used as an extension for ASP.NET to develop and implement the AJAX functionality. ASP.NET AJAX has both client-side and server-side components to develop the Web applications that can update the information on a Web application without reloading the page completely. The following are the advantages of using AJAX:

- **Asynchronous**—Enables asynchronous calls to a Web server without making the users wait for the data.
- **Minimal transfer of data**—Helps in sending only a part of the modified data to a Web server to minimize the network traffic and perform the operations quicker. This feature is useful in sites where restricted pipes are allowed for data transfer resulting in improved network performance.
- **Minimal processing on a Web server**—Helps in minimizing the processing on a Web server, as only the necessary data is sent to it. Moreover, the Web server is not required to send a full page back to the user.
- **Context**—Helps in reducing the burden on a Web server by sending a request back to the server through the client-side script. AJAX-based applications implement partial-page post backs instead of full-page post backs, which reduce the data traffic between the client and the server.

ADO.NET

ADO.NET is a technology used for working with data and databases of all types. It provides access to data sources, such as Microsoft SQL Server, data sources exposed through Object Linking and Embedding Database (OLE DB), and Extensible Markup Language (XML). You can use ADO.NET to connect to data sources for retrieving, manipulating, and updating data.

Some features of ADO.NET are as follows:

- **Disconnected data architecture**—Implies that applications connect to the database only when data needs to be retrieved or modified. After the database operation has been performed, the connection to the database is closed. To perform any database operation again, the connection with the database needs to be re-established. Applications that do not follow the disconnected data architecture waste a lot of valuable system resources and time, as these applications need to maintain a connection with the database even when it is not required.
- **Cached data in datasets**—Implies that datasets follow a disconnected architecture for accessing or modifying data. Therefore, it is not required for the applications to connect to the database for processing each record. As a result, the data is accessed and later stored in the datasets. A dataset is a cached set of database records that is independent of data source. Even when you are disconnected from the database on which you are working, you can make modifications in the database to update the database.
- **Scalability**—Reduces the traffic on the database and saves the resources to make the database more efficient in meeting the demands of a user. ADO.NET helps in attaining scalability while working with datasets. All the database operations are performed on the dataset instead of on the database.
- **Transfer of data in the XML format**—Indicates that XML is the standard format used for transferring of data from a database to a dataset and from the dataset to another component in ADO.NET. You can also use an XML file as a data source and store the data from it into a dataset. A user need not know XML, as the data conversion from and to XML is abstracted from the user.
- **Interaction with the database through data commands**—Specifies that database operations are performed by executing the data commands. All the operations on a database, such as retrieving, modifying, or updating of data, are performed using data commands. A data command is either a Structured Query Language (SQL) statement or a stored procedure.

Windows Workflow Foundation(WF)

WF is a technology, which is introduced by Microsoft, to provide a programming model for building workflow-based applications on Windows. It is a part of .NET Framework 3.0, 3.5, 4.0, and 4.5. The most important feature of WF is the separation between the business process code and the actual implementation code. WF consists of the following parts:

- **Activity** – Receives some parameters from a developer, executes the actions specified in the parameters, and then transfers the flow to the next activity.
- **Workflow designer** – Helps in designing workflows by placing activities within the workflow model. One interesting feature of the Workflow designer is that it can be re-hosted within any Windows Forms application.
- **Workflow runtime** – Executes the activities in a workflow. It is a lightweight and extensible engine that resides within a .NET process. This facilitates a developer to bring workflow to anything from a Windows Forms application to an ASP.NET website or a Windows Service.
- **Rules engine** – Enables declarative, rule-based development for workflows and any .NET application to be used.

WF follows a layered architecture within any application in which it is integrated. Figure 1.4 shows the WF architecture:

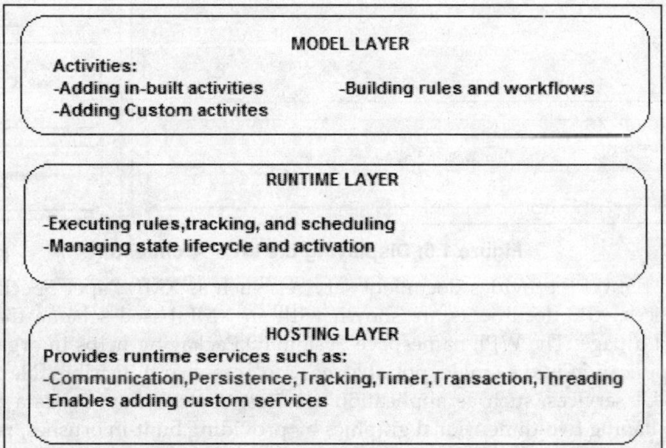

Figure 1.4: Displaying the WF Architecture

As shown in Figure 1.4, the top layer is the Model layer where the developers build their code to run in the workflow. This layer allows a developer to add built-in activities, create custom activities, and enable the engine to build rules. It also connects the activities together.

The second layer in the architecture is the Runtime layer. It ensures that the processes, such as execution of rules, tracking, scheduling, and managing state lifecycle and activation, take place.

The last layer in the architecture is the Hosting layer, which connects the engine and the process that is being executed. It also provides a set of services, such as persistence, timer, tracking, communication, transactions, and threading, required for managing and controlling the workflow. WF also contains built-in services that provide the interfaces required to work with the .NET Framework 2.0 and later versions.

Windows Presentation Foundation (WPF)

Microsoft's WPF (formerly code-named as Avalon) provides the base for building applications and a clear separation between the UI and the business logic. WPF helps in building interfaces that include documents, media, two- and three-dimensional graphics, animations, and Web-like characteristics. It helps in creating Windows client applications with visually stunning user experiences. You can use WPF for creating both standalone and browser-hosted applications. Examples of WPF applications are Yahoo Messenger, New York Times Reader, and Contoso Healthcare Sample Application. WPF introduces a new language called Extensible Application Markup Language (XAML), which is a language based on XML that is used to design interfaces of WPF applications. Even Microsoft comes with Expression Studio that uses XAML for developing UI for any Web- or Windows-based application. Figure 1.5 shows the architecture of WPF:

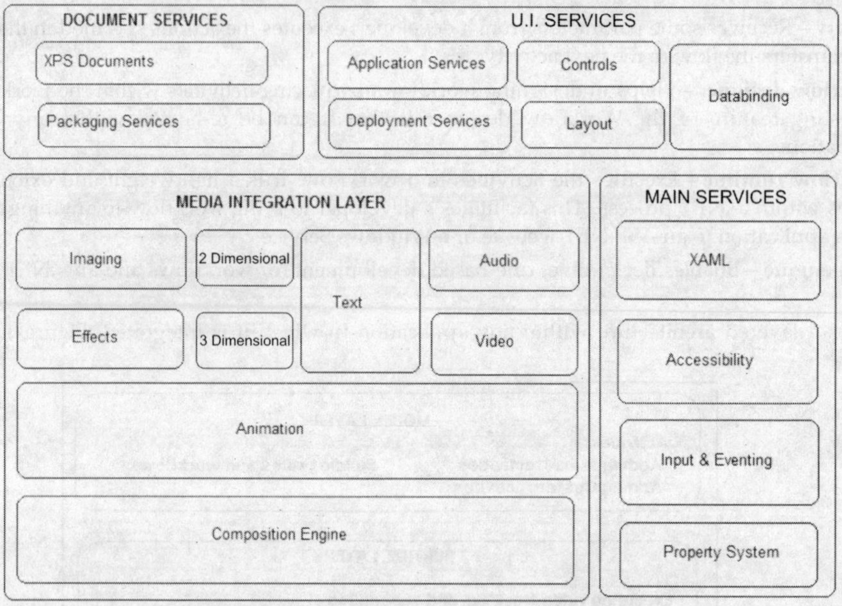

Figure 1.5: Displaying the WPF Architecture

As shown in Figure 1.5, WPF provides document services, such as XML Paper Specification (XPS) documents, and packaging services. XPS documents are shown with an XML-based schema that defines the layout and visual appearance of a page. The WPF namespace System.IO.Packaging helps in organizing data, content, and resources of your application into a single, portable, easy to access, and distributable .zip document. WPF aims at unifying several UI services, such as application services, controls, layout, data binding, and deployment services. It helps in shaping two-dimensional graphics by providing built-in brushes, pens, and geometries. WPF supports various video formats, such as Windows Media Video (WMV), Moving Picture Experts Group (MPEG), and some Audio Video Interleave (AVI) files. It also supports audio files, some common image formats, and animations. In addition, WPF provides some basic services, such as accepting input and raising events, property system, and accessibility.

Windows Communication Foundation (WCF)

WCF (formerly known as Indigo) is one of the new technologies introduced by Microsoft in the .NET Framework 3.0 for building and running connected systems. It is a service-oriented technology for developing applications in a distributed system, which provides services to the client applications. If you are familiar with the concepts, such as Web services, remoting, distributed transactions, and message queuing, then you can easily understand WCF, as it is simply an enhanced technology for providing the same functions in a better way.

WCF applications are interoperable with any process as these communicate through the Simple Object Access Protocol (SOAP) messages. When a WCF process connects with a non-WCF process, it uses XML-based encoding for SOAP messages, but when it connects with another WCF process, the SOAP messages are encoded into a binary format. WCF makes use of a pluggable encoding system, which allows developers to write their own encoders.

JavaScript Object Notation (JSON) was released with the .NET Framework 3.5 for supporting the serialization format in WCF. JSON helps WCF service end points to process service requests from AJAX-powered Web pages.

The enhancements of WCF as compared to the previous technologies, such as Web services and remoting, are as follows:

- Merges technologies, such as Web services, remoting, distributed transactions, and message queuing, at a single place and reduces development time
- Consists of many powerful enterprise features
- Integrates easily with other technologies; and consequently, enables greater interoperability

Figure 1.6 shows the WCF architecture:

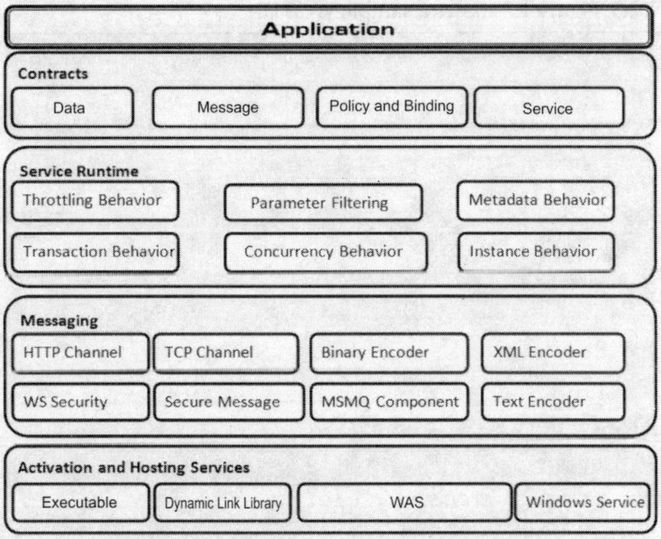

Figure 1.6: Displaying the WCF Architecture

The WCF architecture is composed of the following five layers:

- **Application**—Represents the location of the application.
- **Contracts**—Consists of services, data, and message contracts as well as bindings and policies. The Contracts layer gives you information about various aspects of the message system. For example, the data contract informs about every parameter used while creating a message that a service can consume. The message system involves sending and receiving the messages from one end to another.
- **Service Runtime**—Gives information about different behaviors that take place at runtime. This layer loads all the WCF services.
- **Messaging**—Gives information about different channels that are required at the time of processing a message. This layer deals with the message content that needs to be communicated.
- **Activation and Hosting Services**—Refers to the final layer of the WCF. In this layer, any service can be hosted using the Internet Information Services (IIS) or Windows Activation Service. You can also deploy the services manually in an executable form.

The WCF programming model combines Web services, .NET remoting, distributed transactions, and message queues into a single service-oriented programming model for distributed computing. It runs in a sandbox (a security mechanism for running programs safely) and provides the enhanced security model that all the .NET applications provide. To support distributed computing, WCF is designed in accordance with service-oriented architecture principles where services are used by clients. Services typically have a Web Services Description Language (WSDL) interface, which is used by the clients to utilize the services. WCF implements several advanced Web service standards, such as WS-Addressing, WS-ReliableMessaging, and WS-Security.

Windows CardSpace

WCS (formerly named as InfoCard) is a client software provided by Microsoft that improves the safety of accessing resources and helps in sharing personal information on the Internet. It helps developers in developing websites and software that are less prone to identity-related attacks, such as phishing. WCS helps in reducing the problems of traditional online security mechanisms by relying on separate desktop and cryptographically strong authentication rather than on usernames and passwords. It facilitates secure online transactions during online shopping, banking, and bill payment.

WCS only works with websites that accept the CardSpace logins. When a user tries to access the resources on the website, which accepts CardSpace, the CardSpace selection window appears. The user can then select the required card and access the resources on the website. You can create a card by using the WCS utility present in the .NET Framework 4.5. Figure 1.7 shows a sample WCS UI:

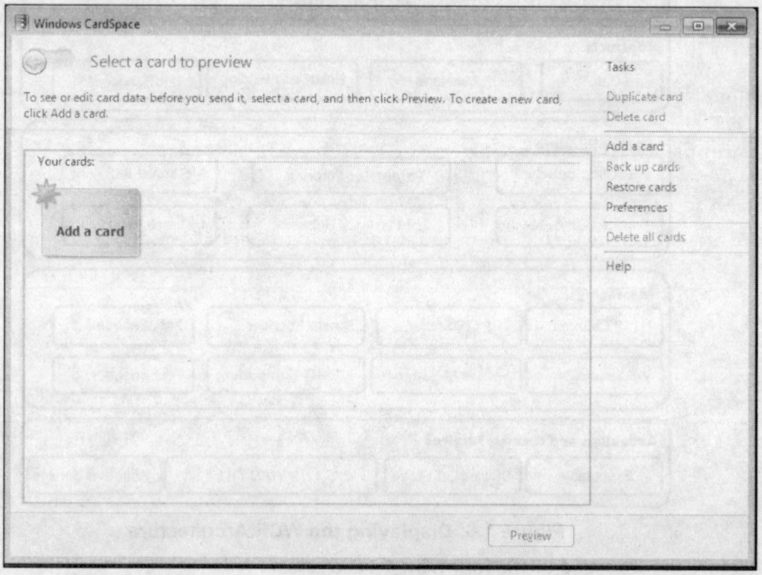

Figure 1.7: Displaying the WCS UI

Now, the user needs to remember only the card instead of multiple usernames and passwords. For using the WCS utility, a provider is required, which would help in converting an identity into a card. For this conversion, some organizations provide their own identity providers to create a card. Even WCS comes with its own self-issued identity providers, which are accepted by websites for validating a user using the card. These cards avoid the use of passwords. WCS is based on the identity meta system, which allows you to use different digital identities across different platforms. There are two types of cards available:

- **Personal cards**—Refer to the card that is based on the self-issued identity providers
- **Managed cards**—Refer to the card that is based on identity providers provided by vendors other than Microsoft

Suppose a CardSpace-enabled website wants to retrieve the personal information of a user (or identity) and for that, demands a particular type of card. The CardSpace then represents the stored identities as virtual information cards. The user selects the card to use and the CardSpace software contacts the identity provider to get the digitally signed token that contains the required information. WCS is built with an open set of XML-based protocols, which includes WS-Security, WS-Trust, WS-MetadataExchange, and WS-SecurityPolicy. With these set of protocols, any technology or platform can integrate with the CardSpace.

The overall process of CardSpace contains issuing, acquiring, and using digital identities that can be defined by the following three distinct roles:

- **User**—Refers to an entity containing a digital identity.
- **Identity provider**—Refers to a provider that provides a digital identity to a user. The digital identity is used to provide information about the username and password of the user. Digital identities created by the identity providers may contain different information and provide different levels of assurance to identify the actual user.
- **Relying party**—Refers to an application that relies on a digital identity. The application can use the identity to authenticate a user and then make authorization decision, such as allowing or disallowing the user to access information.

LINQ

LINQ is one of the important components of the .NET Framework 4.5 that adds native data querying capabilities to .NET languages by using syntax similar to SQL.

The following is a simple LINQ query in VB:

```
Dim query = From s In Students _
   Where s.Gender = "M"
select s.Name
```

The following is a simple LINQ query in C#:

```
var query = from s in Students where s.Gender = "M" ;
select s.Name;
```

When you execute any of the preceding query, it returns the names of all the male students that are stored in the variable query. To print the list, you have to write the following lines of code:

In VB:

```
For Each name In query
   Response.Write(name)
Next
```

In C#:

```
foreach(var name in query)
{
   Response.Write(name);
}
```

In the preceding code, you can notice that the syntax of the query is similar to the SQL, which we normally follow for accessing relational data. It is important to note that even if it looks similar to SQL, the LINQ query is not an SQL statement; instead, it is purely a C# language.

Though LINQ queries resemble SQL, they are not restricted to accessing only relational databases. LINQ-enabled data access components are as follows:

- **LINQ to ADO.NET**—Includes two options: LINQ to SQL and LINQ to DataSet. LINQ to SQL translates a query into an SQL query, and then issues it against the tables specified in the query in an SQL Server database; whereas, LINQ to DataSet executes a query on the contents of a dataset.
- **LINQ to Objects**—Allows querying objects in a collection. LINQ to Objects is not dynamic. After creating and using the result set, any changes made to the source collection do not automatically update the result set.
- **LINQ to XML**—Allows querying of XML data. In addition, it helps in creating and manipulating XML data This option has a different syntax; however, the basic LINQ query remains the same.

LINQ also provides other operators for queries, such as `OrderBy`, `GroupBy`, and `Sum`.

Tools in the .NET Framework 4.5

.NET Framework 4.5 contains a number of tools that are used in creating, managing, and deploying applications and components. Most of the tools are installed implicitly at the time of installation of Visual Studio 2012. All the tools are generally run from the command line window except the Assembly Cache Viewer tool. You can also run the tools by using the Visual Studio Command Prompt, which is provided in Visual Studio 2012. In addition, the Windows SDK Command Prompt or the CMD shell can be used to run the tools. Table 1.2 lists the tools provided by the .NET Framework 4.5:

Table 1.2: Tools in the .NET Framework 4.5

Tool	Type of Tool	Description
Al.exe (Assembly Linker)	Build	Creates a file that contains assembly manifest from a single or multiple files. These files are generally modules or resource files.
Aximp.exe (Windows Forms ActiveX Control Importer)	Interop	Transforms type definitions for an ActiveX control into a Windows Forms control. Type definitions are present in a COM type library.
Caspol.exe (Code Access Security Policy Tool)	Security	Allows you to change the security policy for different policy levels, such as the user policy level, the machine policy level, and the enterprise policy level.
Cert2spc.exe (Software Publisher Certificate Test Tool)	Security	Builds a Software Publisher's Certificate from single or multiple X.509 certificates. It is used only for testing purposes.
Certmgr.exe (Certificate Manager Tool)	Security	Manages certificates, certificate revocation lists and certificate trust lists.
Clrver.exe (CLR Version Tool)	Configuration	Informs about all the installed versions of the CLR on a computer.
CorFlags.exe (CorFlags Conversion Tool)	Configuration	Allows you to configure the CorFlags section of the PE image's header.
Fuslogvw.exe (Assembly Binding Log Viewer)	Debugging	Displays information regarding assembly binding that helps in identifying why the .NET Framework cannot find an assembly at runtime.
Gacutil.exe (GAC Tool)	Configuration	Allows you to display and modify the contents of GAC and download cache.
Ilasm.exe (MSIL Assembler)	Build	Creates a PE file from MSIL. You can execute the PE file to know whether the MSIL is performing according to the expectation or not.
Ildasm.exe (MSIL Disassembler)	Build	Acts as a companion tool to the Ilasm.exe tool. It uses a PE file containing the MSIL code to generate a text file, which acts as an input to the Ilasm.exe tool.
Installutil.exe (Installer Tool)	Deployment	Helps you to install and uninstall the resources of a server by running the components of an installer in the specified assemblies.
Lc.exe (License Compiler)	Build	Reads text files containing licensing information and generates a binary file that can be inserted in a CLR executable as a resource.
Mage.exe (Manifest Generation and Editing Tool)	Configuration	Supports the creation and manipulation of application and deployment manifests.
MageUI.exe (Manifest Generation and Editing Tool, Graphical Client)	Configuration	Functions similar to the Mage.exe tool on the Windows-based UI. The tool helps you in creating, editing, and signing deployment and application manifests.

Table 1.2: Tools in the .NET Framework 4.5

Tool	Type of Tool	Description
Makecert.exe (Certificate Creation Tool)	Security	Builds X.509 certificates for testing purposes only. It creates public and private key pair for digital signatures in a certificate file.
MDbg.exe (.NET Framework Command-Line Debugger)	Debugging	Allows tools vendors and application developers in finding and fixing bugs in tools and applications to make them run in the CLR.
Mgmtclassgen.exe (Management Strongly Typed Class Generator)	Interop	Allows you to create an early-bound managed class for a specified Windows Management Instrumentation (WMI) class quickly. The created class simplifies the code written for accessing an instance of the WMI class.
Mpgo.exe (Managed Profile Guided Optimization Tool)	Build	Optimizes the native image assemblies that are created by the Native Image Generator (Ngen.exe) tool by using the common end-user scenarios. This tool executes training scenarios that generate profile data.
Ngen.exe (Native Image Generator)	Build	Enhances the performance of managed applications.
Peverify.exe (PEVerify Tool)	Security	Helps programmers in determining whether the created MSIL code and related metadata are meeting the type safety requirements.
Regasm.exe (Assembly Registration Tool)	Interop	Reads an assembly metadata and adds the essential entries to the registry to allow COM clients to build .NET Framework classes.
Regsvcs.exe (.NET Services Installation Tool)	Build	Loads and registers an assembly. It also generates, registers, and installs a type library into a mentioned COM+ application. Moreover, it can configure services that have been added programmatically in a class.
Resgen.exe (Resource File Generator)	Build	Transforms text and XML-based resource format files into CLR binary resource files that can be attached with a runtime binary executable or compiled into a satellite assembly.
SecAnnotate.exe (.NET Security Annotator Tool)	Security	Finds the SecurityCritical and SecuritySafeCritical areas of a single or multiple assemblies.
SignTool.exe (Sign Tool)	Security	Signs files, verifies signatures in files, and time-stamps files.
Sn.exe (Strong Name Tool)	Security	Helps in signing assemblies using strong names. This tool also provides choices for key management, signature generation, and signature verification.
SOS.dll (SOS Debugging Extension)	Debugging	Debugs the managed programs in Visual Studio and in the Windows debugger (WinDbg.exe) tool by giving details about the internal CLR environment.
SqlMetal.exe (Code Generation Tool)	Development	Produces code and mapping for the LINQ to SQL components in the .NET Framework.

Table 1.2: Tools in the .NET Framework 4.5

Tool	Type of Tool	Description
Storeadm.exe (Isolated Storage Tool)	Configuration	Saves or deletes all the existing stores for the current user.
Tlbexp.exe (Type Library Exporter)	Interop	Produces a type library that defines the types described in a CLR assembly.
Tlbimp.exe (Type Library Importer)	Interop	Transforms the type definitions present in a COM type library into corresponding definitions in a CLR assembly.
Wincv.exe (Windows Forms Class Viewer)	Development	Searches information rapidly about a class or series of classes depending upon on a search pattern.
Winmdexp.exe (Windows Runtime Metadata Export Tool)	Configuration	Converts a .NET Framework module into the Windows runtime metadata file.
Winres.exe (Windows Forms Resource Editor)	Configuration	Allows localization experts in localizing the resources of Windows Forms UI that forms use.

Let's now explore new features of .NET Framework 4.5.

Exploring New Features of .NET Framework 4.5

As already learned, .NET Framework 4.5 provides a consistent object-oriented programming environment to its developers. Several new features are introduced in .NET Framework 4.5 to provide minimum software deployment and avoid conflicts of versions. New features of .NET Framework 4.5 are as follows:

- .NET for Windows Store Apps
- Portable Class Libraries
- Core New Features and Improvements
- Managed Extensibility Framework (MEF)
- Asynchronous File Operations
- Tools
- Parallel Computing
- Improvements in Web Application Development
- Networking
- Improvements in WPF
- Improvements in WCF
- Improvements in WF

Let's learn about each of them in detail.

.NET for Windows Store Apps

The Windows Store apps are included in the .NET Framework 4.5 to design particular form factors, such as docking, anchoring, and touch screen, and to enhance the strength of the Windows operating system. These apps are designed using the languages, such as VB.NET or C#. Windows Store apps provide a simplified view of the .NET Framework class libraries and contain only the types and members that can be used to build these apps and Windows runtime components.

Portable Class Libraries

The Portable Class Library project included in Visual Studio 2012 allows you to create managed assemblies that can be executed on multiple .NET Framework platforms. You can choose multiple platforms, such as Windows Phone or .NET, to develop Windows Store apps by using the Portable Class Library project. The available types and members in an application are automatically constrained to the common types and members across multiple platforms.

Core New Features and Improvements

The new features and improvements added to the CLR and the .NET Framework classes in the .NET Framework 4.5 are as follows:

- Reduces the system restarts after detecting and closing the applications of .NET Framework 4.5 at the time of deployment.
- Provides the support for arrays that are larger than 2 gigabytes on 64-bit system.
- Provides better performance by running background garbage collection for servers. The background garbage collection is automatically enabled in the .NET 4.5 Framework.
- Provides background JIT compilation, which can be optionally executed on multi-core processors to enhance the performance of an application.
- Limits the time taken by the regular expression engine in resolving regular expressions.
- Defines the default culture for an application domain.
- Supports console for Unicode (UTF-16) encoding.
- Provides the support for versioning of cultural string ordering and comparing data.
- Provides better performance while reclaiming resources.
- Includes improvements in the Zip compression to decrease the size of a compressed file.
- Customizes a reflection context to override the behavior of default reflection through the CustomerReflection class.
- Provides the support for the Internationalized Domain Names in Applications (IDNA) standard with version 2008 when the System.Globalization.IdnMapping class is used on Windows 8.
- Provides the support for allocating string comparison data to an operating system, which implements Unicode 6.0, when the .NET Framework is installed on Windows 8. While running on other operating systems, the .NET Framework uses its own string comparison data, which implements Unicode 5.x.
- Computes the hash codes for strings on a per application domain basis.
- Provides support for type reflection, which allows a split between the Type and TypeInfo classes.

MEF

MEF is a library to create lightweight and extensible applications. In other words, it helps in simplifying the creation of extensible applications. MEF was first introduced in the .NET Framework 4.0. The System.ComponentModel.Composition namespace provides classes that constitute the core of MEF.

Till now, before creating an application that needed a plug-in model, a developer had to create the infrastructure of the application. The disadvantage of this was that the created plug-in is application-specific and cannot be reused across multiple applications. Therefore, in .NET Framework 4.5, Microsoft has introduced some new features in the MEF library to provide extensions that can be reused in multiple applications. New features included in the MEF are as follows:

- Support for generic types
- Support for convention-based programming model, which allows a developer to build modules on the basis of naming conventions and not on the basis of attributes
- Support for multiple scopes
- Support for creating Metro style applications

Asynchronous File Operations

In the .NET Framework 4.5, new asynchronous features, such as async and await for C# as well as Async and Await for VB, are introduced. These features are used to add a task-based model in an application to perform asynchronous operations for files. You can use this new model by using the asynchronous methods, such as ReadAsync and WriteAsync, which are available in the I/O classes.

Tools

The Resource File Generator (Resgen.exe) tool is introduced in the .NET Framework 4.5. This tool allows you to create a .resw file from a .resources file, which is available in the .NET Framework assembly. The .resw file is used in the Windows Metro style applications. In addition to this, .NET Framework 4.5 has introduced the Managed Profile Guided Optimization (Mpgo.exe) tool. This tool allows you to enhance the application startup time, memory utilization (working set size), and throughput by using the native image assemblies. The profile data for native image application assemblies is generated by the command-line tool.

Parallel Computing

.NET Framework 4.5 provides several new features, such as increased control and a new dataflow library, for parallel computing. In addition to this, it provides some improvements in the existing features, such as asynchronous programming, parallel debugging, and performance analysis, for parallel computing.

Improvements in Web Application Development

The new features included for the Web application development in the .NET Framework 4.5 are as follows:

- Provides the support for new HTML5 form types
- Includes model binder that provides support for binding data controls directly with data-access methods, and automatically converts user input to and from .NET Framework data types
- Provides the support for JavaScript to write client-side validation scripts
- Provides improved handling of client scripts through bundling and minification for enhancing the page performance
- Provides integrated encoding routines from the AntiXSS library to safeguard from cross-site scripting attacks
- Provides the support for the WebSockets protocol
- Provides the support for asynchronous reading and writing of HTTP requests and responses
- Provides the support for asynchronous modules and handlers
- Provides the support for the Content Distribution Network fallback in the ScriptManager control

Networking

.NET Framework 4.5 provides the following enhancements and new features in the area of networking:

- Includes a new programming interface for HTTP applications. The .NET Framework 4.5 also includes the support for a new user-defined interface by using the existing HttpListener and related classes for accepting and interacting with a WebSocket connection.
- Provides the support for RFC-compliant uniform resource identifier.
- Provides the support for parsing Internationalized Domain Name.
- Provides the support for Email Address Internationalization.
- Improves the support for IPv6.
- Provides the support for dual-mode socket.

Improvements in WPF

.NET Framework 4.5 provides the following improvements in WPF:

- Includes the new Ribbon control for implementing ribbon UI that hosts Quick Access Toolbar, Application Menu, and tabs.
- Includes the new INotifyDataErrorInfo interface, which supports synchronous and asynchronous data validation.
- Includes new features for the VirtualizingPanel and Dispatcher classes.
- Provides improved performance while displaying large sets of grouped data and retrieving collections on non-UI threads.
- Provides binding of data with static properties, binding of data to custom types that implement the ICustomTypeProvider interface, and fetching of data binding information from a binding expression.
- Provides repositioning of data whenever the values change, which is also known as live shaping.
- Provides the facility to check if the data context for an item container gets disconnected or not.
- Provides the facility to fix the amount of time that should be consumed between property changes and data source updates.
- Provides the support for implementing weak event patterns. Moreover, events are now capable to accept markup extensions.

Improvements in WCF

.NET Framework 4.5 provides the following new features and enhancements to make development and maintenance of WCF applications simpler:

- Simplifies the generated configuration files.
- Provides the support for contract-first development.
- Provides the ability to configure ASP.NET compatibility mode more easily.
- Includes the changes in default transport property values to decrease the possibility of setting them explicitly.
- Includes the enhancements in the XmlDictionaryReaderQuotas class to decrease the possibility of configuring quotas explicitly for the readers of XML dictionary.
- Validates the WCF configuration files during the build process of an application, so that you can detect configuration errors before you execute your application.
- Provides the support for new asynchronous streaming.
- Includes the new Hypertext Transfer Protocol Secure (HTTPS) protocol mapping to make the exposure of an endpoint over HTTPS with IIS.
- Provides the ability to produce metadata in a single WSDL document by attaching **?singleWSDL** at the end of the service URL.
- Supports WebSockets to permit true bidirectional communication over port numbers 80 and 443 having performance characteristics equivalent to the TCP transport.
- Provides the support to configure services within code.
- Provides XML Editor tooltips.
- Provides the support for ChannelFactory caching.
- Provides the support for binary encoder compression.
- Provides the support for a User Datagram Protocol (UDP) transport that allows you to create services that use "fire and forget" messaging. In these types of services, a client sends a message to a service and expects no reaction from the service.

- Provides the ability to support multiple authentication modes while using the HTTP transport and transport security on a single WCF endpoint.
- Provides the support for those WCF services that use Internationalized Domain Names.

Improvements in WF

The .NET Framework 4.5 includes the new features in WF, which are as follows:

- State machine workflows include enhancements in several new classes and activities, which are as follows:
  - Provides the facility to set breakpoints on states
  - Provides the facility to copy and paste transitions in the Workflow designer
  - Provides the designer support for creating shared trigger transition
  - Provides the activities for creating state machine workflows, which includes StateMachine, State, and Transition
- Enhancements in the features of Workflow designer are as follows:
  - Includes the capabilities, such as **Quick Find** and **Find in Files**.
  - Creates a Sequence activity automatically to include a child activity and a container activity when a second child activity is added to the container activity.
  - Supports panning, which allows the visible portion of a workflow to be modified without using the scroll bars.
  - Includes a new **Document Outline** view, which displays the components of a workflow in a tree-style outline view, and allows you to choose a component from the **Document Outline** view.
  - Provides the capability to add annotations to activities.
  - Provides the capability to define and consume activity delegates by using the Workflow designer.
  - Includes the properties, such as Auto-connect and Auto-insert, for activities and transitions in the state machine and flowchart workflows.
- Includes the capability of storing the view state information in a single element in the XAML file of a workflow, so that you can easily find and manipulate the view state information.
- Includes a NoPersistScope container activity to prevent persistence of child activities.
- Workflow projects provide the following support for expressions in languages, such as C# and VB:
  - Workflow projects that are developed in VB will use VB expressions; and in the similar manner, C# workflow projects will use C# expressions.
  - C# workflow projects that were developed in Visual Studio 2010 containing VB expressions have compatibility with C# workflow projects containing C# expressions.
- Supports the following enhancements in versioning:
  - Includes the WorkflowIdentity class that provides mapping between a persisted workflow instance and its workflow definition.
  - Provides the facility of side-by-side execution of multiple versions of workflow in the same host, including WorkflowServiceHost.
  - Includes the capability to change the definition of a persisted workflow instance in dynamic updation.
- Includes the contract-first workflow service development for generating activities to match an already existing service contract automatically.

Let's move on to explore the Microsoft Visual Studio 2012 IDE. It provides a single environment for developing all types of .NET applications and provides many options and rich features to create interactive Web applications by using ASP.NET 4.5.

Section II – Introduction to Visual Studio 2012 IDE

Microsoft Visual Studio is an Integrated Development Environment (IDE) provided by Microsoft to create and develop Windows-based, Web-based, console-based, and mobile-based applications in .NET Framework. These applications might be created by using different languages, such as Visual Basic, C#, and Visual C++. You can use Notepad as a text editor to create these applications. For this, you need a compiler that could convert the programming language into machine language. Now, you might be wondering that if a Notepad can create all these applications, why we need Visual Studio as an editor. Notepad takes more time in building applications as compared to Visual Studio. This is because Microsoft Visual Studio provides various development tools to design and create the applications in comparison Notepad. For example, you need to memorize all the language syntaxes if you are using a Notepad. In case of Visual Studio, you do not need to remember all the syntaxes. You need to type the first few letters of a command and Visual Studio would prompt you with the available options for the command using IntelliSense.

The following are some of the benefits of using Visual Studio 2012:

- Helps in minimizing the application development time
- Simplifies the process of testing applications
- Provides different toolsets for integrating graphic designers into the overall development process
- Supports multiple versions of the .NET Framework
- Enhances data retrieval and data binding
- Helps in finding sections of code that need refactoring
- Provides support for Web, mobile, client, Vista, and Office application development
- Integrates with the .NET Framework 4.5

Now, let's explore Visual Studio 2012 and its new features.

Exploring New Features of Visual Studio 2012 IDE

Visual Studio 2012 is an IDE designed for writing, compiling, and debugging the code in a much easier way as compared to the previous versions of Visual Studio. It contains a complete set of development tools for building ASP.NET Web applications, Web services, desktop applications, and mobile applications.

The following are some of the new features and enhancements introduced in Visual Studio 2012:

- Project compatibility
- Configuration changes in ASP.NET 4.5 Website templates
- Native support in Internet Information Services (IIS) 7.5 for ASP.NET routing
- HyperText Markup Language (HTML) editor
- JavaScript editor
- Cascading Style Sheet (CSS) editor
- The Page inspector tool
- Publishing
- Support for developing Windows Store app
- Enhanced cloud capability
- New tabs in Start Page
- Application Lifecycle Management (ALM) and Team Foundation Server (TFS)
- Managing the application lifecycle
- Modeling applications

- Developing application and better communication in a team
- Automating and debugging builds
- Microsoft Test Manager

Let's learn about these in detail one by one.

Project Compatibility

Earlier, when a project created in the older version of Visual Studio is opened in the newer version of Visual Studio, Visual Studio automatically opens the Conversion wizard, which upgrades and converts the project to the newer version of Visual Studio. After the conversion, the project can be easily opened in the newer version of Visual Studio; however, the same project cannot be opened in the older version of Visual Studio from which it was derived. This backward compatibility issue is removed to some extent in Visual Studio 2012. This implies that after the conversion, the Visual Studio 2010 project can be opened in Visual Studio 2012 as well as in Visual Studio 2010. This feat is achieved in Visual Studio 2012 by adding some backward compatibility properties in the converted file, which are given as follows:

- **FileUpgradeFlags**—Sets a flag for file upgrade. The upgrade process of the project file utilizes this property, which has no impact on working with the project in Visual Studio 2010 or Visual Studio 2008.
- **UpgradeBackupLocation**—Upgrades the backup location.
- **OldToolsVersion**—Stores the version of Visual Studio for the older version project.
- **VisualStudioVersion**—Stores the version of Visual Studio for the newer version project.
- **VSToolPath**—Uses the path of MSBuildExtensionsPath32 to find the target file that needs to be imported.

In addition, you should also change the import element so that the compatibility of various versions of Visual Studio is maintained. Note that if a project is shared between Visual Studio 2010 and Visual Studio 2012 in two different computers and uses local database in the App_Data folder, then the same version of SQL Server must be installed in both the computers.

Configuration Changes in ASP.NET Website Templates

Visual Studio 2012 introduces some changes in the default Web.config file to create ASP.NET websites by using the ASP.NET Website templates. The following are the configuration changes in the ASP.NET Website templates:

- The encoderType attribute of the <httpRuntime> element is set to the default value of AntiXssEncoder type to incorporate core encoding routines. These encoding routines are incorporated in ASP.NET 4.5 due to the popularity of the AntiXSS library. The encoding routines are present in the System.Web.Security.AntiXSS namespace. You can use the AntiXssEncoder type directly either by calling its methods or by configuring it in the Web.config file to use the AntiXssEncoder class by default. When you set the encoderType attribute to AntiXssEncoder, all the output encodings in ASP.NET use the new encoding routines automatically.
- The requestValidationMode attribute of the <httpRuntime> element is set to the default value of 4.5, which indicates deferred or lazy validation for the request validation. In contrast, the previous versions of ASP.NET perform request validation by default to defend against potential cross-site scripting attacks by throwing exceptions if it finds some requests to look for markup or script in headers or cookies. ASP.NET 4.5 introduces two features that allow you to work with unvalidated data. These two features are deferred or lazy request validation and access to unvalidated request data.
- The runAllManagedModulesForAllRequests attribute is removed from the <modules> element present in the <system.webServer> section. However, the removal of runAllManagedModulesForAllRequests might cause some issues in routing and generate routing errors.

Native Support in IIS 7.5 for ASP.NET Routing

Visual Studio 2012 introduces the native support in IIS 7.5 for ASP.NET routing. Prior to the changes in Visual Studio 2012 templates, the Web.config file is configured to support routing, as shown in Figure 1.8:

```
<?xml version="1.0"?>
<configuration>
  <system.webServer>
    <modules runAllManagedModulesForAllRequests="true">
      <!-- some code -->
    </modules>
  </system.webServer>
</configuration>
```

Figure 1.8: Displaying the Web.config File for ASP.NET Routing

As shown in Figure 1.8, the runAllManagedModulesForAllRequests attribute is set to true; however, this setting adds unnecessary processing overhead to the requests. Therefore, this attribute is removed in ASP.NET 4.5, which implies that the setting is false by default. In case you use Windows 7 without using Service Pack 1, errors may occur during routing. In such situation, you need to manually set the runAllManagedModulesForAllRequests attribute to true, but some overhead will occur.

HTML Editor

Visual Studio 2012 introduces some new features in the HTML editor that help in easing the tasks of a programmer. The following are the new features added in the HTML editor:

- **Smart Tasks**—Adds a small glyph just below a server tag when the insertion point is inside the server element. The Smart Tasks menu is displayed when the glyph is clicked or the Ctrl +. key combination is pressed from the keyboard. Smart Tasks was already available in the previous versions of Visual Studio, but can be used through the Design view only. However, in Visual Studio 2012, Smart Tasks can also be used though the Source view. Figure 1.9 shows the Smart Tasks menu associated with the Calendar tag in the Source view:

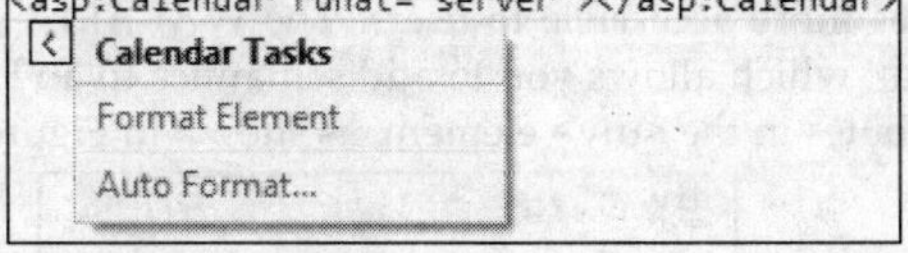

Figure 1.9: Displaying Smart Tasks in the Source View

In Figure 1.9, Smart Tasks contains the Calendar Tasks options, such as Format Element and Auto Format. Selecting one of the options from the context menu performs the task associated with it. For example, if you choose the Auto Format option, then the AutoFormat dialog box appears, as shown in Figure 1.10:

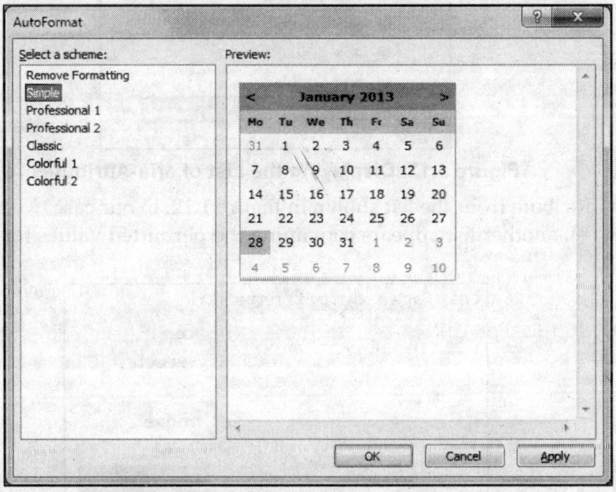

Figure 1.10: Displaying the AutoFormat Dialog Box

You can select any of your preferred settings in the dialog box; for example, you can select the Simple option from the Select a scheme list box present in the left pane of the dialog box and then click the OK button. The code snippet for the selected scheme is appended to the code containing the server tag (in our case, the Calendar tag). Figure 1.11 shows the appended code snippet:

```
<asp:Calendar runat="server" BackColor="White" BorderColor="#999999" CellPadding="4" DayNameFormat="Shortest"
    Font-Names="Verdana" Font-Size="8pt" ForeColor="Black" Height="180px" Width="200px">
    <DayHeaderStyle BackColor="#CCCCCC" Font-Bold="True" Font-Size="7pt"></DayHeaderStyle>

    <NextPrevStyle VerticalAlign="Bottom"></NextPrevStyle>

    <OtherMonthDayStyle ForeColor="#808080"></OtherMonthDayStyle>

    <SelectedDayStyle BackColor="#666666" Font-Bold="True" ForeColor="White"></SelectedDayStyle>

    <SelectorStyle BackColor="#CCCCCC"></SelectorStyle>

    <TitleStyle BackColor="#999999" BorderColor="Black" Font-Bold="True"></TitleStyle>

    <TodayDayStyle BackColor="#CCCCCC" ForeColor="Black"></TodayDayStyle>

    <WeekendDayStyle BackColor="#FFFFCC"></WeekendDayStyle>
</asp:Calendar>
```

Figure 1.11: Displaying the Appended Code Snippet

- **WAI-ARIA suite**—Stands for Web Accessibility Initiative – Accessible Rich Internet Applications. It is introduced in Visual Studio 2012 to increase the accessibility of a Web page. The WAI-ARIA suite defines a methodology to design and develop Web applications so that they can be made accessible to people with disabilities. The suite uses various advanced technologies, such as JavaScript and HTML, to create dynamic content and advanced User Interface (UI) controls. Visual Studio 2012 fully supports the WAI-ARIA standard to make websites more accessible to users. The WAI-ARIA standard introduced some attributes that are prefixed with aria-, which allows you to add semantics to an HTML 5 document. For example, you can use various aria- attributes in the <div> element, as shown in Figure 1.12:

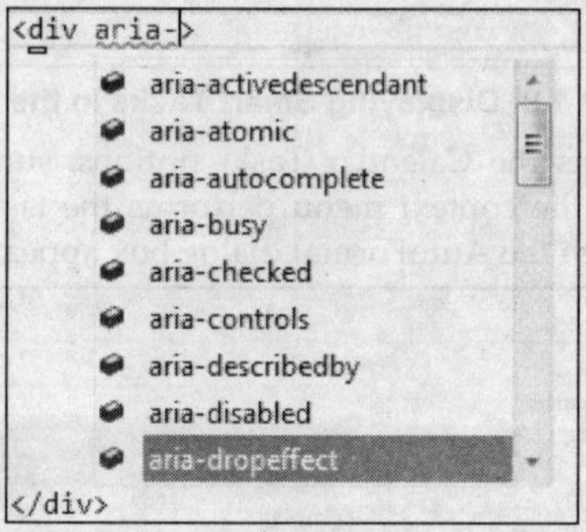

Figure 1.12: Displaying the List of aria-Attributes

You can select any aria- attribute from the list shown in Figure 1.12; in our case, we have selected aria-dropeffect. After typing equal sign (=), another list appears containing the permitted values for the aria-dropeffect attribute, as shown in Figure 1.13:

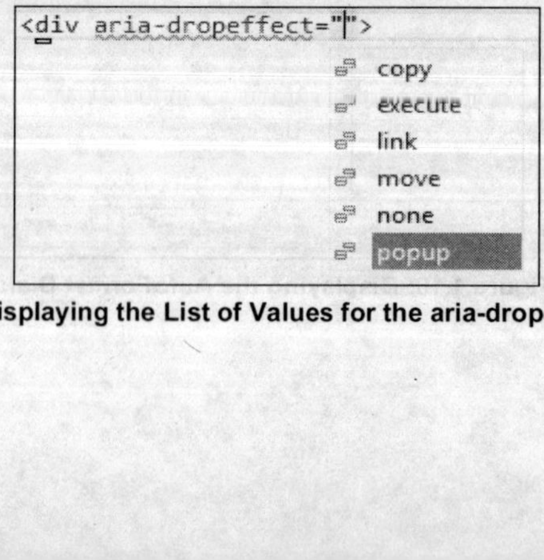

Figure 1.13: Displaying the List of Values for the aria-dropeffect Attribute

The selected value is added to the aria-dropeffect attribute that can be used for creating a pop-up for drop effect.

- **New HTML 5 snippets**—Refers to a feature that adds code snippets to commonly used HTML 5 markups, which can be customized to suit the programming needs. These code snippets make the work of a programmer easier and faster. To invoke the code snippet for any HTML 5 element, you need to press the Tab key twice on the keyboard after selecting the element from the IntelliSense. For example, the <video> element is selected from the IntelliSense, as shown in Figure 1.14:

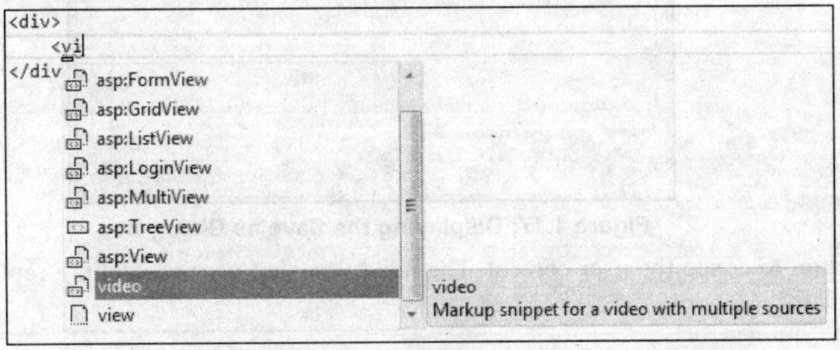

Figure 1.14: Displaying the IntelliSense for the <video> Element

When you press the Tab key twice after selecting the <video> element, you get the corresponding code snippet for that element, as shown in Figure 1.15:

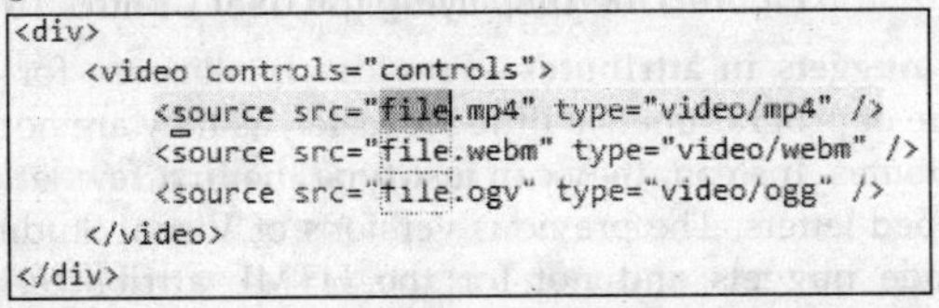

Figure 1.15: Displaying the Automatically Generated Code

- **Extract to user control:** Allows programmers to move individual pieces of a Web page content that can be grouped together into a logical unit, such as user controls. This helps in refactoring the page, increases the readability of the page, and simplifies the page structure. To use this feature while editing Web Forms in the Source view, select the text that can be moved into a user control and then right-click the selected text to display the context menu. Further, select the Extract to User Control option from the context menu, as shown in Figure 1.16:

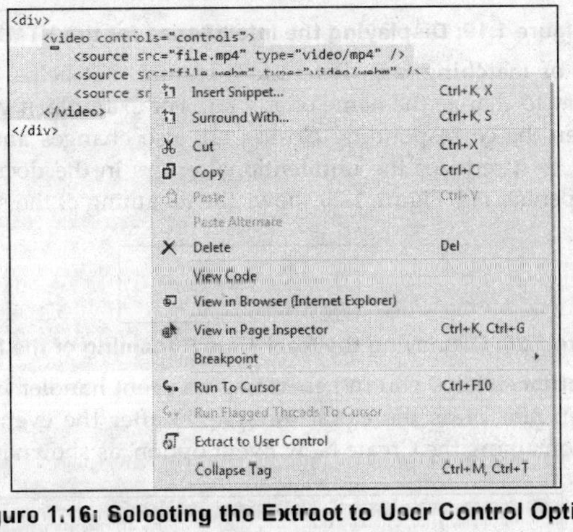

Figure 1.16: Selecting the Extract to User Control Option

The Save as dialog box appears (Figure 1.17). Type the file name in the File name text box; in our case, we have typed VideoControl.ascx, as shown in Figure 1.17:

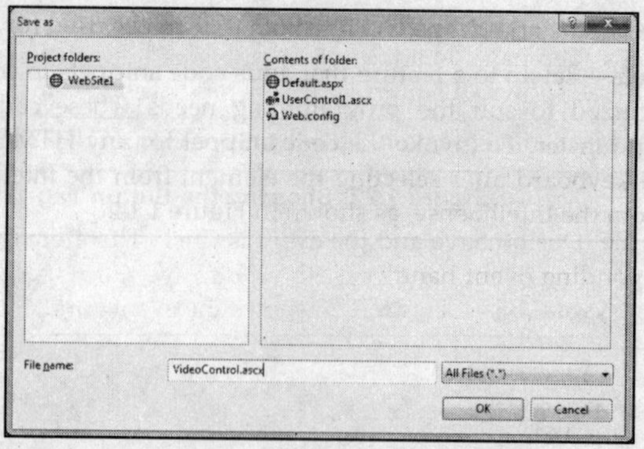

Figure 1.17: Displaying the Save as Dialog Box

Click the OK button to create the user control. The newly created user control tag replaces the selected text, as shown in Figure 1.18:

```
<div>
    <uc1:VideoControl runat="server" ID="VideoControl" />
</div>
```

Figure 1.18: Displaying the User Control Tag

- **IntelliSense for code nuggets in attributes**—Provides IntelliSense for code nuggets in HTML attributes; thereby, making the life of programmers a little bit easier, as they are not required to remember name of the complex tags and attributes. Instead, they can just type the first few letters to get the required list of items beginning with the typed letters. The previous versions of Visual Studio do provide IntelliSense, but only for the server-side code nuggets and not for the HTML attributes. However, in Visual Studio 2012, IntelliSense is provided for both server-side code nuggets and HTML attributes. Figure 1.19 shows the IntelliSense for the value attribute of the <input> element:

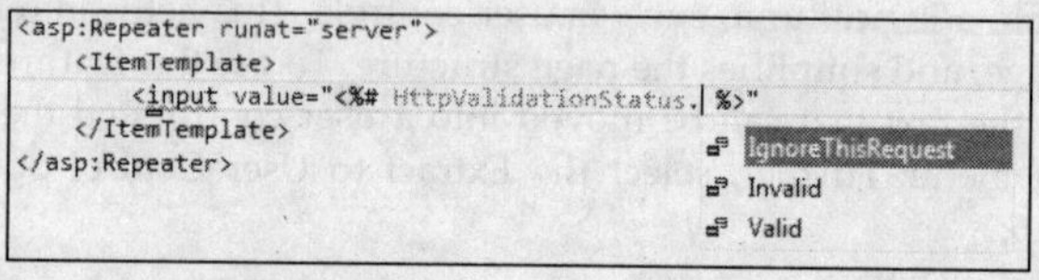

Figure 1.19: Displaying the IntelliSense for the HTML Attribute

- **Automatic renaming of matching tag**—Refers to a feature that helps you in renaming the matching tag automatically if you try to change the name of any tag. For example, if you rename the HTML <div> tag to the <header> tag, then the corresponding closing tag also changes automatically at the same time. This feature is very useful as it reduces the unintentional errors in the document if you forget to rename the matching closing or opening tag. Figure 1.20 shows the renaming of the <div> tag to the <header> tag:

```
<header>
    <!-- some code -->
</header>
```

Figure 1.20: Displaying the Real Time Renaming of the Matching Tag

- **Event handler generation**—Helps you in generating an event handler in the Source view and binding the event manually. When you press the equal to sign (=) after the event name, the IntelliSense for event handler is displayed containing the Create New Event option, as shown in Figure 1.21:

Figure 1.21: Displaying the IntelliSense for Event Handler

To generate an event handler, you need to select the <Create New Event> option. The event handler is generated with a correct signature on a Web page. In addition, the name of the event handler's method is derived by using the name of the control's ID, as shown in Figure 1.22:

```
<asp:Button runat="server" ID="btnSave" OnClick="btnSave_Click" />
```

Figure 1.22: Showing the Button Tag

As shown in Figure 1.22, the ID is btnSave and the event is Click. Therefore, by appending the Click word to the btnSave word, the corresponding event handler method, btnSave_Click, is generated in the .cs file in case of C# and in the .vb file in case of Visual Basic. Figure 1.23 shows the event handler method in C#:

```
protected void btnSave_Click(object sender, EventArgs e)
{

}
```

Figure 1.23: Displaying the Event Handler Method in C#

- **Smart indent**—Puts the insertion point automatically at the correct place after you press the Enter key while inside the empty HTML element. Suppose the insertion point is inside the empty <header> element, as shown in Figure 1.24:

```
<header></header>
```

Figure 1.24: Displaying the Insertion Point inside the <header> Element

When you press the Enter key, you get the insertion point indented to its correct position, as shown in Figure 1.25:

```
<header>

</header>
```

Figure 1.25: Displaying the Smart Indentation of the Insertion Point

The smart indentation will make the document more readable and aesthetically pleasing.

- **Auto-reduce statement completion**—Displays only the relevant list of options in the IntelliSense that matches the letters, which you type. The individual words matching with the title case are also displayed in the IntelliSense. The advantage of the auto-reduce statement completion feature is that it makes statement completion faster for known elements. For example, if you type **bl,** then the IntelliSense contains the options that matches with the title case (in our case, asp:BulletedList) as well as with the relevant letters (in our case, blockquote), as shown in Figure 1.26:

Figure: 1.26: Displaying the IntelliSense List

JavaScript Editor

Visual Studio 2012 has also introduced the JavaScript editor, which is a completely new feature that improves the working experience with JavaScript in Visual Studio. The editor provides the following features:

- **Code outlining**—Outlines all the functions present in the JavaScript code, which can be collapsed or expanded according to the need for setting focus on a particular function.
- **Brace matching**—Highlights the corresponding brace if the insertion point is placed on an opening or closing brace; thereby, easing the debugging process.
- **Go to Definition**—Allows you to jump to the source for a variable or function by using the Go to Definition command; thereby, decreasing the search overhead.

- **ECMAScript5**—Supports the syntax and Application Programming Interfaces (APIs) present in the ECMAScript5 standard, which is the latest standardised version of the JavaScript language.
- **DOM IntelliSense**—Improves the IntelliSense for the APIs of Document Object Model (DOM) by supporting HTML 5 APIs, such as DOM storage, querySelector, canvas, and cross-document messaging. DOM IntelliSense is executed by a single JavaScript file rather than through native library definitions; thereby, making it easier to extend or replace.
- **VSDOC signature overloads**—Uses the <signature> element to declare the comments of the IntelliSense for the separate overloading of JavaScript functions.
- **Implicit references**—Allows you to include JavaScript file to the central list; thereby, making its content available to the IntelliSense without explicitly referencing it.

CSS Editor

Visual Studio 2012 has introduced the CSS editor for dealing with CSS. The CSS editor provides the following features:

- **Auto-reduce statement completion**—Displays a list of options in the IntelliSense for CSS that matches with the letters typed in the .css file. The individual words matching with the title case of the typed words are also displayed in the IntelliSense list. The advantage of the auto-reduce statement completion feature is that it makes statement completion faster for known properties and values. For example, if you type **mw** in the body property, then the IntelliSense list shows the options, max-width and min-width, as shown in Figure 1.27:

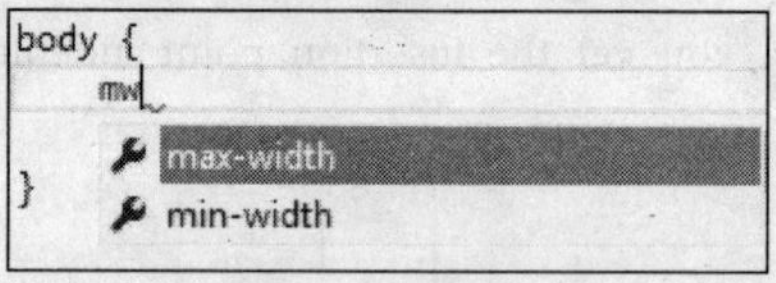

Figure 1.27: Displaying the CSS IntelliSense List

- **Hierarchical indentation**—Indents the content of a CSS file in a hierarchical manner to depict the logical organization of cascading rules. The advantage of hierarchical indentation is that it provides a visual representation of the cascading styles that are applied on a Web page. Note that the indentation of a child rule is determined by its parent rules. When you end a child rule with a brace, Visual Basic 2012 automatically indents the content according to its parent rules. For example, "#list" is a parent rule and "#list a" is its child rule, which is indented hierarchically in a .css file, as shown in Figure 1.28:

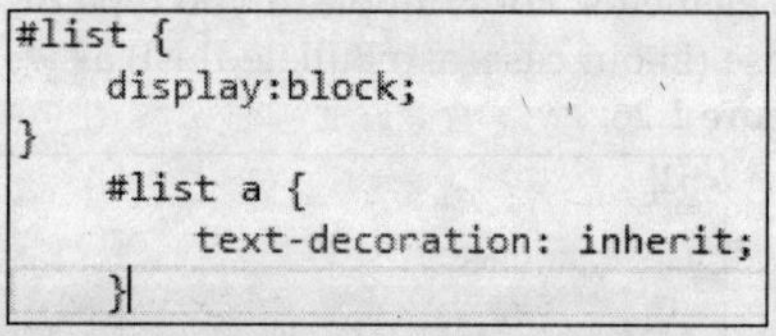

Figure 1.28: Displaying the Hierarchical Indentation

Visual Studio 2012 IDE provides tools to manage the hierarchical indentation. You can open the **Options** dialog box from **TOOLS → Options,** present in the Menu Bar of the IDE, to enable or disable the hierarchical indentation. By default, the hierarchical indentation is enabled; however, you can disable it by deselecting the **Hierarchical indentation** check box (Figure 1.29). The check box can be accessed by selecting the **Text Editor → CSS→Formatting** option from the left pane of the **Options** dialog box, as shown in Figure 1.29:

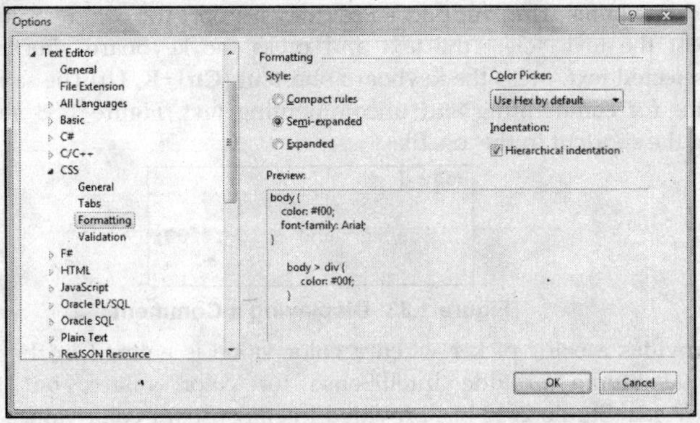

Figure 1.29: Diplaying the Options Dialog Box

- **CSS hacks support**: Provides the most prevalent CSS hacks, such as validation of star (*) and underscore (_) hacks. The feature uses the IntelliSense and performs validation. Figure 1.30 shows the IntelliSense for the validation of * and _ property hacks:

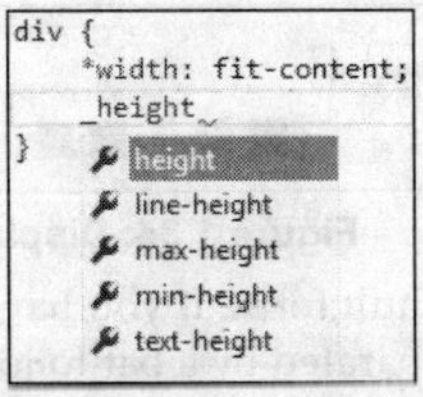

Figure 1.30: Displaying the * and _ Property Hacks

Moreover, the selector hacks are supported to maintain the hierarchical indentation even if they are applied. A common way to apply a selector hack is to prepend a selector with ***:first-child + html**, which maintains the hierarchical indentation. Figure 1.31 shows the selector hack:

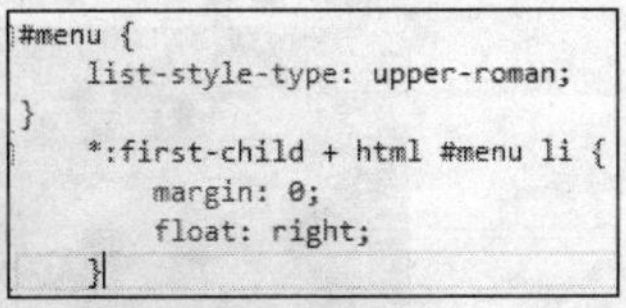

Figure 1.31: Displaying the Selector Hack

- **Vendor-specific schemas**—Supports the use of browser-specific CSS properties in the IntelliSense. Different browsers are created by different vendors and have their own vendor-specific schemas. Due to this, developers had to code for browsers according to their vendor-specific syntax. CSS3 has resolved this issue by providing CSS properties that are specific to a browser, such as Mozilla (-moz), Microsoft Internet Explorer (-ms), Opera (-o), and Webkit (-webkit). The browser-specific properties can be displayed in the IntelliSense by typing hypen (-) followed by the initial letter of the specific browser, as shown in Figure 1.32:

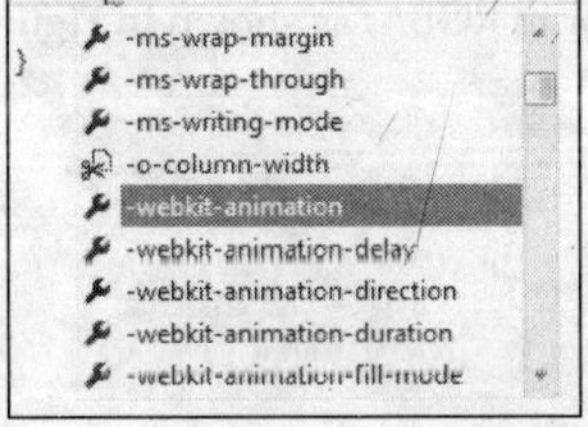

Figure 1.32: Displaying the IntelliSense for Browser-Specific Properties

- **Commenting and uncommenting support**—Provides support for commenting and uncommenting of CSS rules. To comment the text, select the text and press the keyboard shortcut (**Ctrl+K, C**); whereas, to uncomment the selected text, press the keyboard shortcut (**Ctrl+K, U**). The same shortcuts can also be used in the Code editor for commenting and uncommenting text. Figure 1.33 shows the selected text being commented using the shortcut in the .css file:

```
body {
    /*color:#b6ff00;*/
    background-color:#f00;
}
```

Figure 1.33: Displaying a Comment

- **Color picker**—Provides a color picker when a color value is entered in the CSS property. The previous versions of Visual Studio provide IntelliSense for color values, but that was in the form of a drop-down list. Visual Studio 2012 has provided IntelliSense for color values in the form of a color picker, which is displayed automatically, and shows a list of colors that can be selected using a keyboard or mouse. For the keyboard selection, press the down arrow key to access the color picker, the right or left arrow key to navigate the color picker, and the Enter key to select the color value. Figure 1.34 shows a color picker in its contracted form:

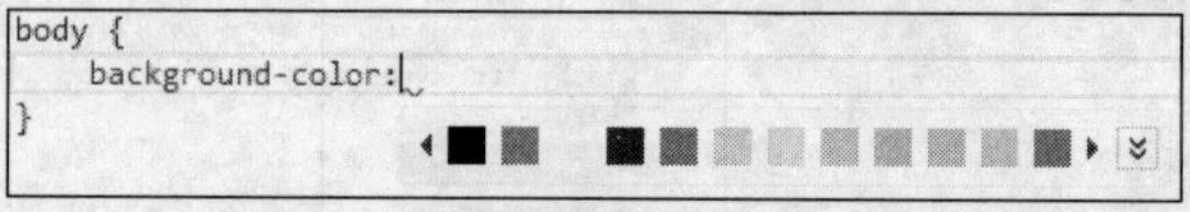

Figure 1.34: Displaying a Color Picker

Figure 1.34 shows a color picker in the default form. If you have already used some colors, then the color picker also displays the previously used colors separated by a bar followed by the default color palette. The color picker also contains a small double-downward-arrow button on the extreme right that can be clicked to display the color picker in its expanded form, as shown in Figure 1.35:

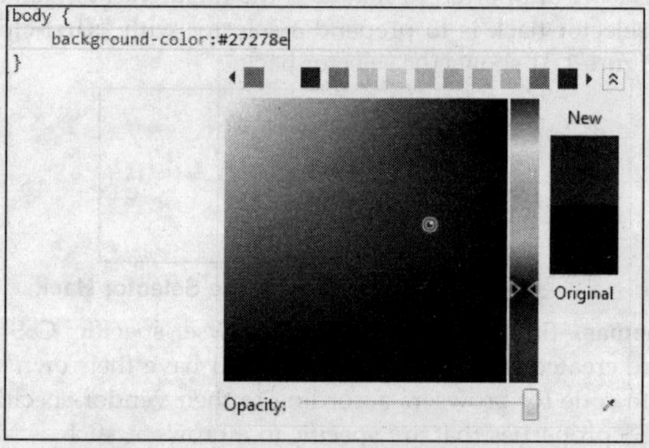

Figure 1.35: Displaying a Color Picker in the Expanded Form

You can also press the downward arrow key twice on the keyboard to display the expanded form of the color picker. This expanded form contains an opacity slider, a color picker button on the bottom left to select a color, a strip containing the colors, and a color viewer. The opacity slider can be moved to control the alpha channel to automatically convert the selected color in RGBA, as shown in Figure 1.36:

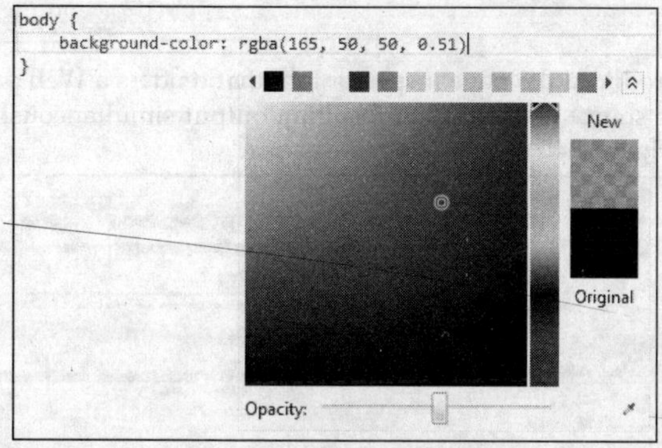

Figure 1.36: Displaying the Color Picker Using Opacity Slider

- **Snippets**: Supports the use of browser-specific CSS properties in the form of snippets. Snippets help a programmer in creating cross-browser styles quickly and easily. Visual Studio 2012 provides CSS snippets that can be generated through IntelliSense. You can type the @ symbol to generate the IntelliSense list, as shown in Figure 1.37:

Figure 1.37: Displaying the IntelliSense using the @ Symbol

You can select any one option from the IntelliSense at a time; in our case, we have selected the **@keyframes** element. Then, press the Tab key twice to get the corresponding snippet, as shown in Figure 1.38:

```
@keyframes name {
    from {
        background: red;
    }

    to {
        background: yellow;
    }
}

@-moz-keyframes name {
}

@-webkit-keyframes name {
}
```

Figure 1.38: Inserting the Snippet in the Editor

- **Custom regions**: Helps you in grouping the related style blocks into the named custom regions, which can be expanded or collapsed. The custom regions feature was already present in the Code editor. Now, Visual Studio 2012 has introduced the custom region feature in the CSS editor as well. When the region is collapsed, it displays only the name of the region followed by ellipses indicating that there is more content in the region, as shown in Figure 1.39:

Figure 1.39: Displaying the Custom Region

Page Inspector

Visual Studio 2012 has introduced the page inspector tool that renders a Web page in the Visual Studio IDE and allows you to examine the source code and the resulting output simultaneously. Moreover, page inspector is a great tool for debugging. Figure 1.40 shows a page inspector:

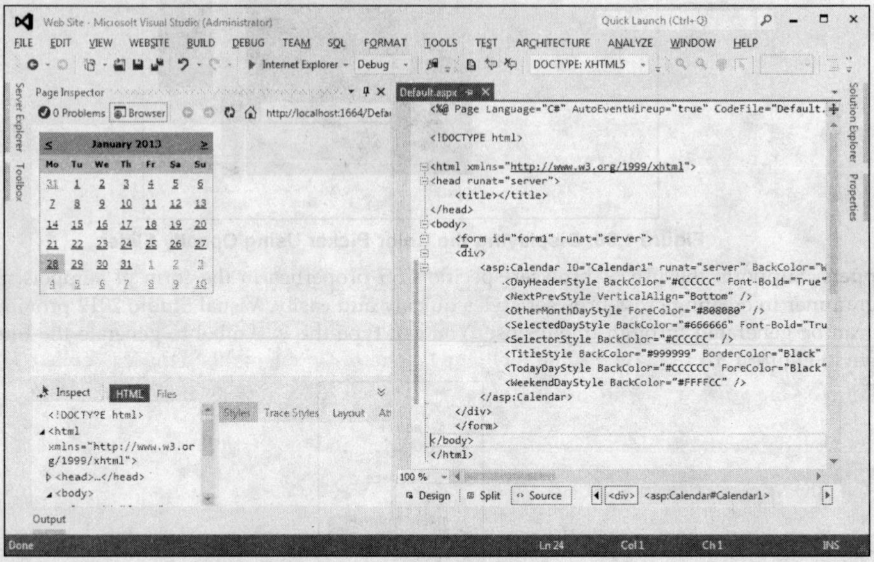

Figure 1.40: Displaying a Page Inspector

For an ASP.NET page, page inspector helps you to determine which server-side code has produced the markup that is rendered in the browser. You can get the page inspector in two ways. One way is to right-click the Website project from the Solution Explorer window and then select the **View in Page Inspector** option from the context menu, as shown in Figure 1.41:

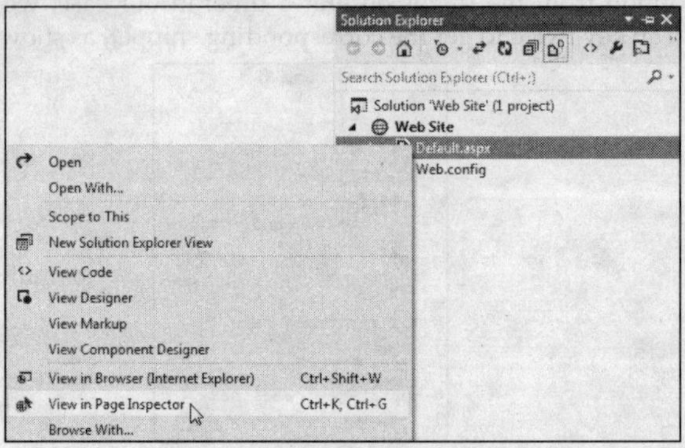

Figure 1.41: Displaying the View in Page Inspector Option

Another way is to select the Page Inspector option from the Standard toolbar, as shown in Figure 1.42:

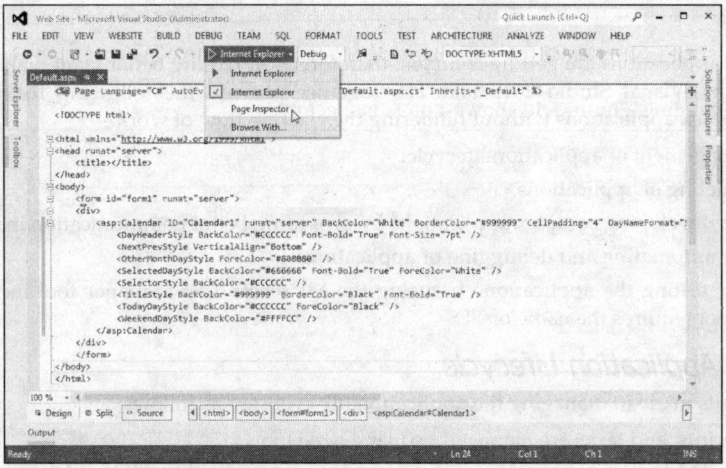

Figure 1.42: Displaying the Page Inspector Option in the Standard Toolbar

Publishing

In publishing, the executable files of a website are compiled and then written to a specified folder. Visual Studio 2012 has introduced the following publishing features:

- **Publish profiles**—Allows you to publish profiles of your Web application project in a specified location. In Visual Studio 2012, it is now easy to leverage a profile from builds, which are based on MSBuild. Publish profile is an MSBuild file and is stored in the PublishProfiles folder. Web application project's MSBuild file imports the publish profiles during publishing. You can also keep all your customizations in a publish profile; thereby, ensuring that the customizations will be used only for that profile.
- **ASP.NET precompilation and merge**—Allows you to precompile and merge your application's content while you publish or package your Web application projects.

Support for Developing Windows Store Apps

A Windows Store app is a kind of application that runs on Windows 8 operating system. You can develop apps that can take input from different sources, such as pen, touch, and keyboard. You can also develop apps that can establish communication among devices. Visual Studio 2012 supports designing, development, debugging, customization, and publishing of the useful Windows Store apps. These apps require Windows Runtime environment and .NET languages, such as Visual Basic and C#, for their developement. The designing of these apps can be done by using several Web technologies, such as HTML5, CSS3, and JavaScript. After desgining and development of the Windows Store apps, you can sell these apps to millions of customers by ensuring their availability on Windows Store, which eases the distribution, updation, and selling of the apps in the worldwide market.

Enhanced Cloud Capability

In Visual Studio 2012, the cloud capability has been enhanced to provide more storage and computing power. In this version, some enhancements have been made that allow applications to be executed on the Windows Azure platform smoothly. This platform provides new templates, publishing options, and distributed caching support for developing an application.

New Tabs in Start Page

The Start Page in Visual Studio 2012 includes new tabs, such as HOW TO VIDEOS (STREAMING) and GET STARTED. The Data link that was present in the GET STARTED tab in Visual Studio 2010 has been omitted from the Start Page in Visual Studio 2012. The Guidance and Resources tab has been replaced with the HOW TO VIDEOS (STREAMING) tab, which explains the ASP.NET 4.5 concepts using videos.

ALM and TFS

In today's time, applications are getting complex; therefore, you require better team management for developing such applications. Visual Studio 2012 and TFS together provide the following functionalities that help in developing complex applications without hindering the existing flow of work:

- Proper management of application lifecycle.
- Proper modeling of applications.
- Support for developing complex applications by providing better communication in a team.
- Support for automating and debugging of applications.
- Support for testing the applications by using the Microsoft Test Manager tool included in Visual Studio 2012. The tool requires the name of TFS.

Managing the Application Lifecycle

The enhancements made in managing the application life cycle are as follows:

- Backlog, sprints, and tasks are managed by using agile tools
- Allows stakeholders to record action scripts, annotations, screenshots, and video or audio recordings
- Allows you to illustrate the requirements with the help of storyboards, and then link those storyboards to work items
- Enterprise projects are managed by using Microsoft Project and Project Server

Modeling Applications

The enhancements made in the modeling of applications are as follows:

- Allows you to visualize your code more rapidly and easily
- Allows you to read, edit, and rearrange items in the dependency graphs more easily
- Allows you to open and view linked model elements in work items
- Allows you to produce C# code from Unified Modeling Language (UML) class diagrams
- Allows you to create UML class diagrams from existing code

Developing Applications and Building Communication in a Team

The enhancements to develop an application and build better communication in a team during the project development in Visual Studio 2012 are as follows:

- Allows you to identify tasks and improve the productivity by using an enhanced interface
- Allows you to work more proficiently in a version-controlled codebase
- Allows you to conduct and get code reviews with the help of new tools
- Allows you to perform unit testing of your code
- Allows you to find duplicate code for refactoring
- Allows you to compare code versions by using an enhanced diff tool
- Allows you to work offline
- Allows you to easily debug code that was produced from text templates

Automating and Debugging Builds

The enhancements made in automating and debugging builds in Visual Studio 2012 are as follows:

- Allows you to execute, track, and manage builds by using an improved interface
- Allows you to execute automated builds by using Team Foundation Service
- Allows you to define gated check-in build processes that support multiple check-ins
- Allows you to execute native and third-party framework unit tests in your build process
- Allows you to debug your build process more easily

Microsoft Test Manager

The Microsoft Test Manager feature in Visual Studio 2012 allows you to do the following tasks:

- Allows you to perform manual testing to identify the bugs in Windows Store apps
- Allows you to conduct exploratory testing to a test script or set of predetermined steps
- Allows you to include multiple lines and rich text in your manual test steps
- Allows you to retrieve the status of your test plans, available in a report, within Microsoft Test Manager
- Allows you to work more easily on different releases in parallel by cloning tests

Some Miscellaneous Features of Visual Studio 2012

The following are some of the miscellaneous features and enhancements introduced in Visual Studio 2012:

- **LightSwitch**—This feature allows you to do the following tasks:
    - Connect the LightSwitch applications to any Open Data Protocol (OData) data source
    - Expose the application data as an OData data source
    - Assign roles and permissions to security groups
    - Limit data that the server returns
    - Improve the appearance of your screen with new controls
    - Customize the formatting of numbers and dates
    - Treat URLs and percentages as data types
- **Data Application Development**—This feature allows you to do the following tasks:
    - Work with database objects in SQL Server Object Explorer
    - Define tables in the new Table Designer
    - Develop and test database applications in SQL Server Express LocalDB
- **Graphic Tools**—This feature allows you to do the following tasks:
    - Add, edit, and compile High Level Shading Language (HLSL) shaders more easily
    - View and modify image assets more efficiently
    - Work with three-dimensional models
    - Create advanced pixel shaders
- **Parallel Computing**—This feature allows you to do the following tasks:
    - Use C++ Accelerated Massive Parallelism (AMP) to make your code run faster
    - Debug your parallel apps more effectively
    - Customize the data that you use to examine how well your parallel apps perform
    - Use Task Parallel Library (TPL) dataflow to make your concurrency-enabled apps more robust
- **SharePoint Development**—This feature allows you to do the following tasks:
    - Create lists and content types by using designers
    - Create site columns for SharePoint sites
    - Add Silverlight Web parts to your SharePoint projects
    - Publish SharePoint solutions to remote SharePoint sites
    - Increase SharePoint performance by using profiling tools
    - Create sandboxed visual Web parts
    - Debug JavaScript more easily
    - Develop SharePoint projects more easily by using streamlined project templates
    - Test your code by using the Microsoft Fakes Framework

- **Office Development**—This feature allows you to do the following tasks:
  - Create apps for Office. You can use Web technologies and cloud services to create office documents, meeting requests, appointments, and email messages
  - Develop solutions for Office 2013
  - Develop solutions targeting .NET Framework 4.5 by downloading and installing Microsoft Office Developer Tools for Visual Studio 2012
- **.NET Framework 4.5**—This feature allows you to do the following tasks:
  - Build managed assemblies that work on multiple .NET Framework platforms
  - Reduce system restarts while installing the .NET Framework
  - Improve file input/output performance by using asynchronous operations
  - Improve startup performance on multi-core processors
  - Develop and maintain Windows Communication Foundation (WCF) applications more easily
  - Improve the scalability of WCF applications
  - Manage workflows more easily
  - Create state machine workflows
  - Add a ribbon UI to your Windows Presentation Foundation (WPF) application
  - Display large sets of grouped data in WPF applications more quickly
  - Create modern Hypertext Transfer Protocol (HTTP) applications more efficiently by using the new programming interfaces

Exploring the Visual Studio 2012 IDE

Visual Studio 2012 provides an IDE, which consists of toolbars and windows that help the Web developers in creating an application. The windows are dockable; therefore, you can rearrange them on the IDE as per your requirements. The IDE can also be used for detecting and correcting the errors in your application. The following are the different parts of the Visual Studio 2012 IDE:

- Start Page
- Menu Bar
- Toolbar
- Toolbox
- Code Editor
- IntelliSense
- Designers
- Solution Explorer
- Properties Window
- Object Browser
- Class View
- Server Explorer
- Component Tray
- Output Window
- Task List
- Error List
- Command Window
- Dynamic Help Window
- Manage Style Window

Start Page

When you open Visual Studio 2012, the very first window displayed is the Start Page, as shown in Figure 1.43:

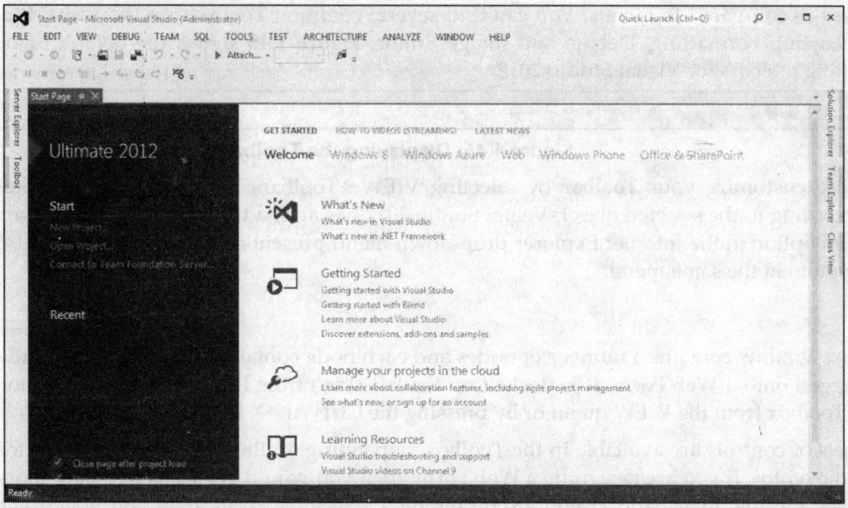

Figure 1.43: Displaying the Start Page of Visual Studio 2012

Start Page displays various sections that are as follows:

- **Command section** – Displays the New Project, Open Project, and Connect to Team Foundation Server links as well as a Recent. In the Recent pane, a list of the most recent projects you have opened in Visual Studio 2012 appears. You can open a project by clicking the hyperlink having the project's name. In Figure 1.43, you can see the New Project, Open Project, and Connect to Team Foundation Server links – one is for opening an existing project, the other is for creating a new project, and the last link is for connecting with TFS.
- **Content area** – Contains the GET STARTED, HOW TO VIDEOS (STREAMING), and LATEST NEWS tabs. It acts as a browser window for displaying resources related to Microsoft's products and technologies when connected to the Internet. In this area, you can see the news related to Visual Studio, the supported languages, articles, and other interesting information.
- **Display options** – Contains two check boxes that determine when the Start Page is displayed. If the Close page after project load check box is selected, then the Start Page closes when a project is opened. Similarly, if the Show page on startup check box is selected, then the Start Page is displayed when Visual Studio 2012 starts.

Menu Bar

Menu Bar of the Visual Studio IDE provides different menus for different Visual Studio commands, as shown in Figure 1.44:

Figure 1.44: Displaying the Menu Bar

Most of the menus are displayed as Toolbars. However, not all the options provided in the menus are available at all times. This is because the options that cannot be applied to the current state of the IDE are made either invisible or disabled.

Toolbar

Toolbar is the shortcut to the most frequently performed actions. The options provided in the Toolbar can be quickly used as compared to menus. You can find several common Toolbars on the Visual Studio IDE, such as Standard, Layout, Formatting, Debug, and Image Editor. Figure 1.45 shows the default Standard and HTML Source Editing toolbars for Visual Studio 2012:

Figure 1.45: Displaying the Toolbars

You can also customize your Toolbar by selecting VIEW→Toolbars→Customize. Visual Studio displays the Toolbar according to the selected object. Visual Studio 2012 has added the multiple browser support through the Browse With option in the Internet Explorer drop-down menu present in the Toolbar. It has also added the Page Inspector option in the same menu.

Toolbox

The Toolbox window contains a number of nodes and each node contains a list of controls and components that can be dragged onto a Web Form. It is docked on the left side of the IDE; however, if it is not visible, you can access the Toolbox from the VIEW menu or by pressing the Ctrl+Alt+X keys.

Different sets of controls are available in the Toolbox, depending on the type of the designer that is active in the Visual Studio editor. If you are designing a Web Form, then you would get a specific set of tools that works with Web controls. On the other hand, if you are designing a Windows Form, then you would get a specific set of tools in the Visual Studio IDE for Windows controls. If you are designing an XML document, then there will be some other controls available within the Toolbox window. You can also add other customized tabs to the Toolbox window where you can place your favourite controls and components. A Toolbox window is shown in Figure 1.46:

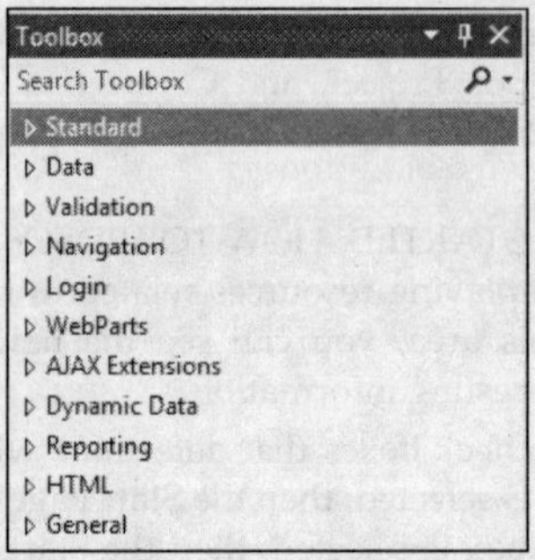

Figure 1.46: Displaying the Toolbox Window

Visual Studio 2012 has introduced the Search Toolbox text box to search a particular control in the Toolbox. The pin icon on the title bar of the Toolbox window is also available to auto hide or pin down the window.

Code Editor

The Code Editor window allows you to write and edit your code. You can use either the F7 key or the Shift+F7 key as a toggle to switch from the Web Forms designer to Code editor. Alternatively, you can switch to Code editor by selecting the VIEW → Code option and to the designer by selecting the VIEW → Designer option. You can also use the Code editor to create different types of files, such as text files and XML documents. Therefore, this window is also known as Text Editor. Figure 1.47 shows the Code editor:

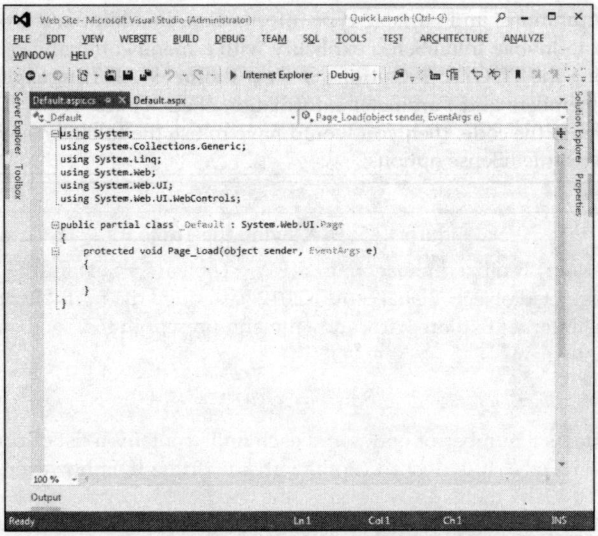

Figure 1.47: Displaying the Code Editor

Using the Code editor, you can set breakpoints for debugging your application and collapse the sections of code to increase readability. The Code editor also contains the IntelliSense feature that makes programming easier.

IntelliSense

IntelliSense is an extremely useful feature of Visual Studio. As you type the code in the Code editor, IntelliSense provides a list of options for making language references easily accessible and helps you in finding the information you need. Intellisense automatically completes typing for you. Now, you can directly enter a member function or a variable by using the list of options. For example, when you type TextBox1 and then a period operator (.), IntelliSense displays a list of options, as shown in Figure 1.48:

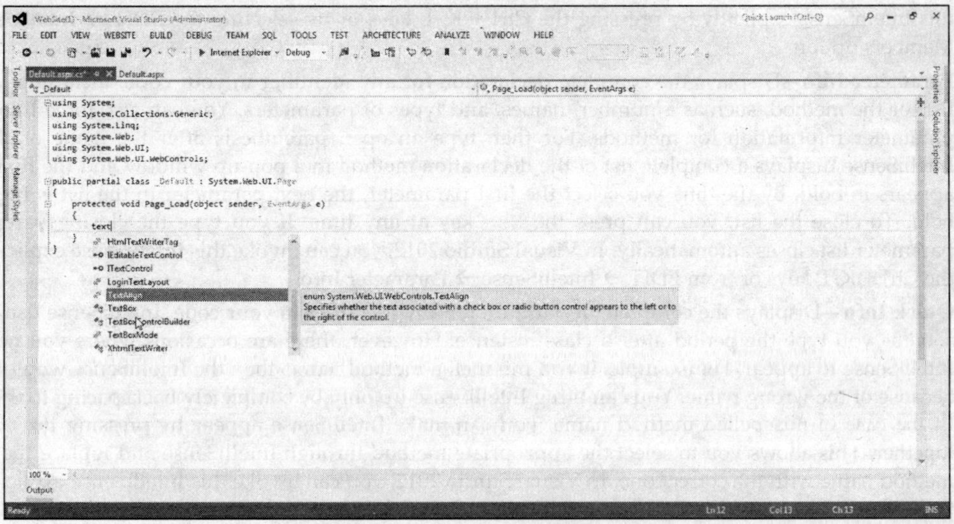

Figure 1.48: Using IntelliSense

The IntelliSense technology makes the writing of code easier and is less prone to errors. It provides quick access to valid member functions or variables, including global variables through the Members list. You can select these member functions and variables from the list and use it in your code. IntelliSense is also used to view code comments, function declarations, and variable type information. In addition, it works automatically, by default. However, if you prefer to invoke IntelliSense explicitly with a menu command or a key combination, disable it by turning it off selecting the **TOOLS → Options → Text Editor → All Languages → General** option and then deselect the Auto list members and Parameter information check boxes. Now, if you want to incorporate the IntelliSense functionality in the code, then you would have to use the IntelliSense menu item in the EDIT menu. Figure 1.49 shows various IntelliSense options:

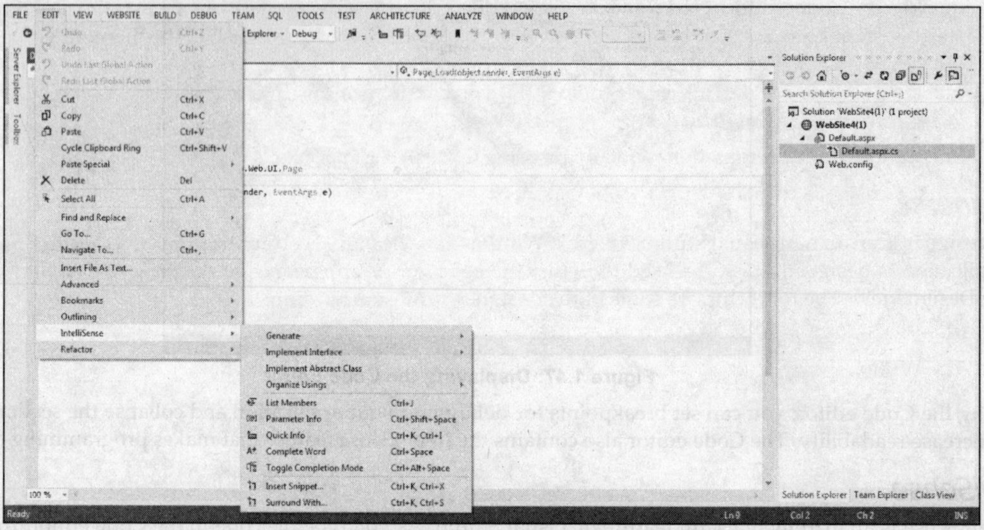

Figure 1.49: Showing the IntelliSense Options

The explanation of some of the most commonly used options available in IntelliSense is as follows:

- **List Members**—Displays a list of valid member variables or functions for the selected class or structure. You can select a member variable from the list to insert it into your code. In Visual Studio 2012, you can invoke this IntelliSense explicitly by pressing the Ctrl + K, L keys or by selecting the EDIT → IntelliSense → List Members option.
- **Parameter Info**—Displays the complete declaration for any identifier in your code, including a parameter list for the method, such as a number, names, and types of parameters. You can also force IntelliSense for parameter information for methods. For that, type an open parenthesis after the name of the method. IntelliSense displays a complete list of the declaration method in a pop-up window and the first parameter appears in bold. By the time you select the first parameter, the next parameter in the list is highlighted in bold. To close the list, you can press the `Esc` key at any time. If you type the closing parenthesis, the parameter list closes automatically. In Visual Studio 2012, you can invoke this IntelliSense explicitly through the Ctrl + K, P keys or from EDIT → IntelliSense → Parameter Info.
- **Quick Info**—Displays the complete declaration for any identifier in your code. IntelliSense usually runs as soon as you type the period after a class instance. However, there are occasions where you need to force IntelliSense to appear. For example, if you misspell a method name, then the IntelliSense would not appear because of the wrong name. You can bring IntelliSense up only by completely backspacing to the period (.). In the case of misspelled method name, you can make IntelliSense appear by pressing the `Ctrl+J` keys together. This allows you to select the appropriate method through IntelliSense and replace the misspelled method name with the correct one. In Visual Studio 2012, you can invoke this IntelliSense explicitly through the Ctrl + K, I keys or from **EDIT → IntelliSense → Quick Info.**

- **Complete Word**—Shows the rest of a variable or function name after you have entered sufficient initial characters. When you start typing a word and typed sufficient initial characters so that it uniquely identifies a given word in your current file, try pressing the Ctrl+ Spacebar keys together. The usual IntelliSense drop-down list will be displayed by the specified starting characters. Select the appropriate word to complete the word quickly. If the series of starting letters uniquely identifies a single word in the IntelliSense list, then the complete word will be inserted automatically. For example, to make the FontFamily property appear quickly on Code editor, type Font on Code editor. An IntelliSense drop-down list appears with options starting from Font, such as Font, FontConverter, FontFamily, and FontHeight. The moment you enter F, the selected item becomes FontFamily and you can press the Enter key to make the FontFamily word appear quickly on Code editor. In Visual Studio 2012, you can invoke this IntelliSense explicitly through Ctrl + K, W or from **EDIT → IntelliSense → Complete Word.**

You can also toggle the completion mode by pressing Ctrl + Alt + Spacebar.

Designers

A designer is an area in Visual Studio, where a Windows application, Web application, or Windows presentation application is designed. It can be used to define the behavior or appearance of the components and controls in the Design view. The following are some of the designers in Visual Studio:

- The Windows Forms designer
- The WPF designer
- The Web Forms designer

Let's explore each of these in detail.

Windows Forms Designer

When you create a Windows Forms application in Visual Studio, a form is automatically added to the project. This form element is considered as the very basic unit of any Windows Forms application and is used to accept input from a user and perform some actions based on the specified input. The Windows Forms designer is shown in Figure 1.50:

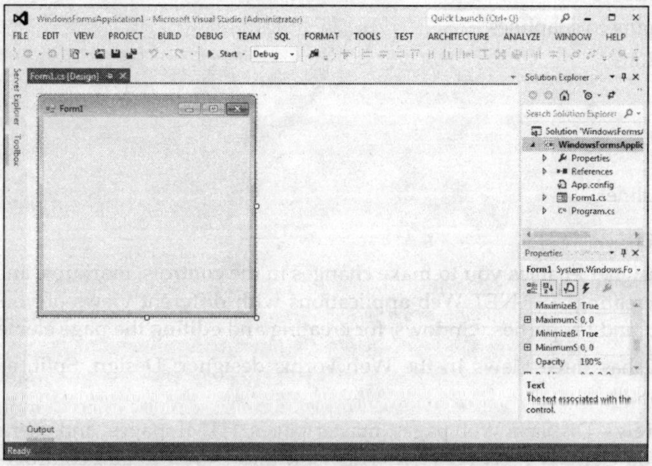

Figure 1.50: Displaying the Windows Forms Designer

The Windows Forms designer enables you to add controls to the form, arrange them, and write code for essential events of the control.

WPF Designer

WPF is a presentation system for developing Windows client applications with graphically rich user experiences. Using WPF, you can create a wide range of both standalone and browser-hosted applications. Figure 1.51 shows the WPF designer window:

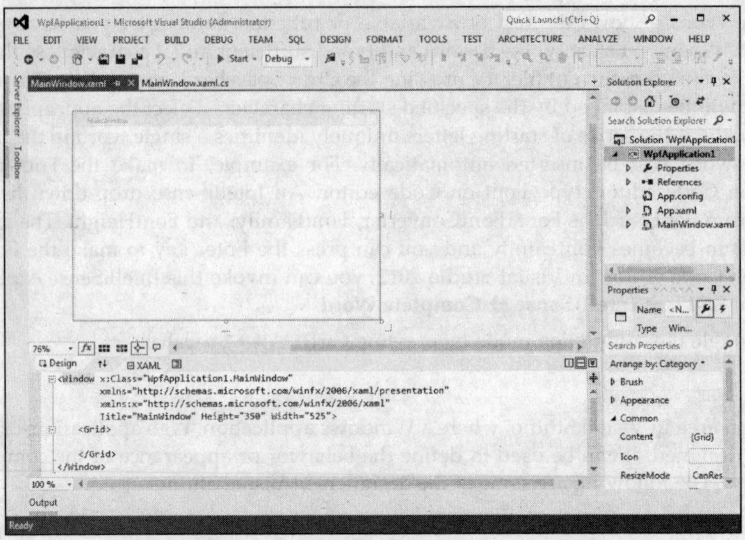

Figure 1.51: Displaying the WPF Designer Window

The WPF designer window allows you to make changes in the XAML file of your application. In other words, the changes made in the WPF designer window are automatically reflected in the XAML file.

The WPF designer window provides the following options:

- Zoom
- Turn off rendering of effects
- Show snap grid
- Snap to gridlines
- Turn off snapping to snaplines
- Show annotations
- Design
- Swap Panes
- XAML
- Document Outline

Web Forms Designer

The Web Forms designer enables you to make changes in the controls, markups, and scripts of Web Forms. This designer helps in creating ASP.NET Web applications with different views of your pages and provides tools, such as the Toolbox and Properties windows, for creating and editing the page elements.

Visual Studio 2012 has three views in the Web Forms designer: Design, Split, and Source. These views are described as follows:

- **The Design view**—Displays Web pages, master pages, HTML pages, and user controls using the What You See Is What You Get - WYSIWYG view. This view allows you to add controls in a Web Form and set their properties.
- **The Split view**—Enables you to view both the Source view and the Design view at the same-time. Figure 1.52 shows the Web Forms designer in the Split view:

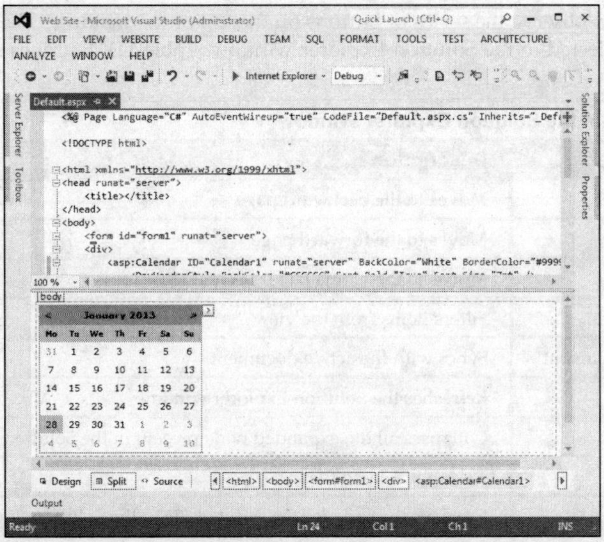

Figure 1.52: Displaying the Split View in Web Forms Designer

- **The Source view**—Displays the markup view of your page, which includes HTML elements, ASP.NET controls, and client script. In case you are working with a single-file page, the Source view also displays the server code for the page.

You can easily switch between the three views of the Web Forms designer using the Design, Split, and Source tabs at the bottom of the currently selected page. You can also open the code-behind page of any selected page in Solution Explorer by right-clicking the page and selecting the View Code option from the context menu.

By default, when you open a Web page, it is always displayed in the Source view. If you want your pages to be opened in a different view other than the Source view, then you need to select TOOLS → Options. Further, select the HTML Designer node and then set your preferred view on the General tab.

Solution Explorer

A solution is defined as a set of projects that is a part of the same application in Visual Studio. The Solution Explorer window displays every project with its references and components. If you wish to activate Solution Explorer in the IDE, then select VIEW→Solution Explorer or press the Ctrl+Alt+L keys or Ctrl+W, S keys together. When you create your application, components may consist of forms, classes, modules, and any other file types. You can edit these components within the IDE by double-clicking them.

The Solution Explorer window gives you a graphical representation of all the files included in your website. Figure 1.53 shows the Solution Explorer window:

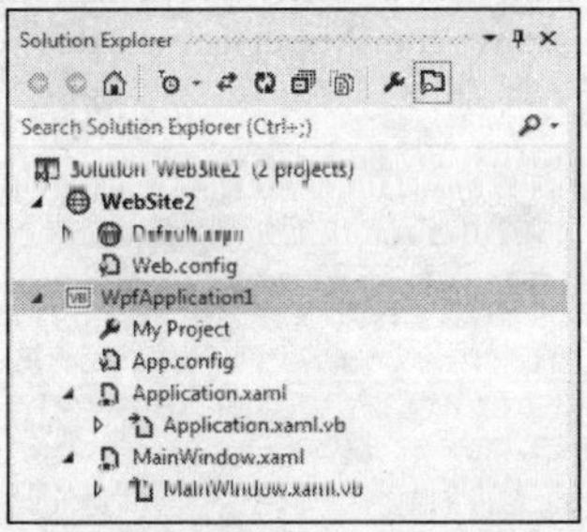

Figure 1.53: Displaying the Solution Explorer Window

In Figure 1.53, you can observe the series of buttons on the top of the window. These buttons change on the basis of the components selected in the Solution Explorer window. Table 1.3 describes some of these buttons starting from left to right:

Table 1.3: Buttons in the Solution Explorer Window

Buttons	Description
Back	Moves to the backward page
Forward	Moves to the forward page
Home	Moves to the Home page
Pending Changes Filter	Filters items from the view
Sync With Active Document	Syncs with the active document
Refresh	Refreshes the Solution Explorer window
Collapse All	Collapses all the expanded node present in the Solution Explorer Window
Nest Related Files	Nests the related files
View Code	Displays the code for the selected file in the Solution Explorer Window
Properties	Opens the Properties window that is used to display the properties of the selected file or control
Preview Selected Items	Previews the selected items

From the Solution Explorer window, you can open a file by double-clicking the file's icon or name. To rename, copy, or delete a file, you need to right-click the file and select the desired action from the context menu that appears. By using Solution Explorer, you can also create folders and move files. Visual Studio 2012 also introduces the Search Solution Explorer text box to search items from the Solution Explorer Window.

Properties Window

As the name suggests, the Properties window in Visual Studio IDE is used to set the properties for various objects at the time of designing a website. When you are working with classes, such as TextBox and Web Form, you need to change certain attributes of these classes as per your requirements. When you select a component or object in the Solution Explorer window or designer, the properties associated with the selected component are displayed in the Properties window. You can view and edit the properties of a file, folder, project, or solution by using the Properties window. In addition, you can modify the properties of projects' components and solutions.

You can view the Properties window by selecting the VIEW → Properties Window option in the Menu Bar, or by pressing the F4 key or the Ctrl+W, P keys together. When the Properties window is displayed, you can either view the list of properties alphabetically or categorize it by the attributes. You can change the font, font size, back color, fore-color, name, text, enabled, and other properties that appear on any control, such as Button or TextBox, in this window. Figure 1.54 shows the Properties window of a Calendar control:

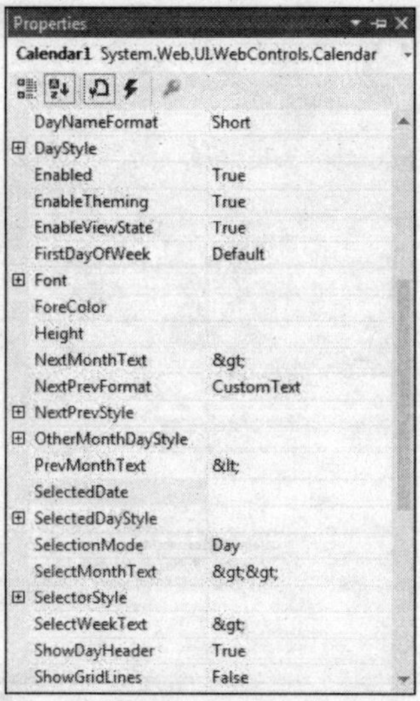

Figure 1.54: Displaying the Properties Window

If you want to view and modify the properties of controls, such as Button or Label, then drag the control, whose properties you want to modify, on the Web Form. After dragging the control, press the F4 key to open the Properties window of the associated control.

The properties displayed in the Properties window are different for different components or controls. In other words, the properties associated with a Button control are different from the properties associated with a Label control. Note that some properties in the Properties window appear in the gray text to indicate that these are the read-only properties.

The Properties window also displays a toolbar containing various buttons, which are explained as follows:

- **Categorized**—Enables you to group the properties for a control into categories. For example, when you select a Button control and click the Categorized button on the toolbar, the properties for the Button control are grouped into categories, such as Accessibility, Appearance, Behavior, Data, Layout, and Miscellaneous.
- **Alphabetical**—Arranges the properties of a control alphabetically.
- **Properties**—Displays the properties of a control.
- **Events**—Displays various events for a control.
- **Property Pages**—Displays the Property Pages dialog box for the selected component. You can use the Property Pages dialog box to view and edit the properties related to the configuration of a project.

The Properties window is a simple tool that provides you with several benefits. You can save time while programming by using new components because information about each component is readily available and graphically configurable in the Properties window. You can change the properties of the components and projects at the design time using the Properties window. Alternatively, you can set the properties of components by right-clicking them in the Solution Explorer window and selecting the desired properties from the context menu.

Object Browser

The Object Browser window is used to examine and find out objects, such as namespaces, classes, structures, types, interfaces, and enums, along with their members, including properties, methods, events, variables, constants, and enum items. To view the Object Browser window, select VIEW → Object Browser or press the Ctrl+Alt+J or Ctrl+W, J keys together. Figure 1.55 shows the Object Browser window:

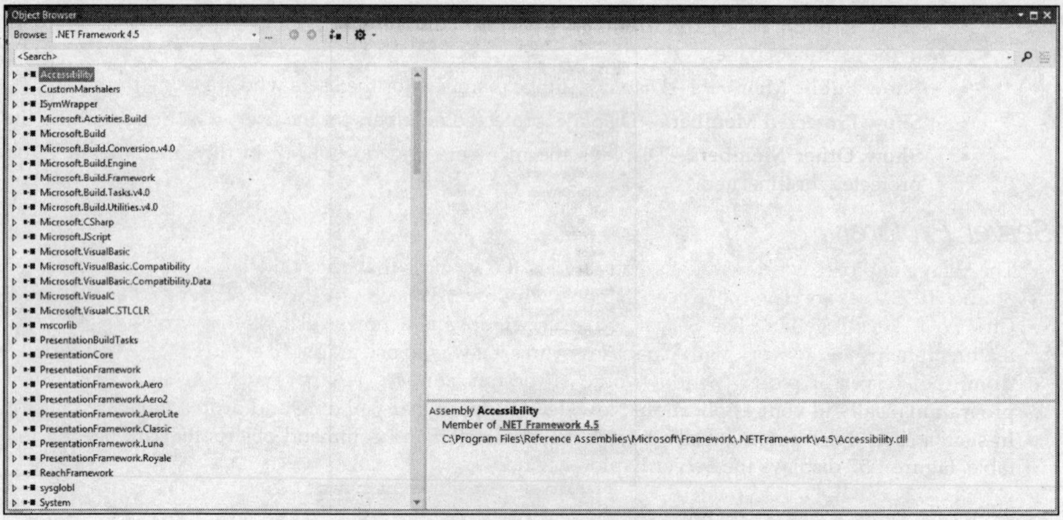

Figure 1.55: Displaying the Object Browser Window

Class View

The Class View window contains a hierarchical tree view representing projects at the top-level node and displays the classes, methods, and properties associated with a particular project. It helps in finding a member of a class that we want to work with. You can view the Class View window by selecting VIEW → Class View or pressing the Ctrl+Shift+C or Ctrl+W, C keys together. Figure 1.56 shows the Class View window:

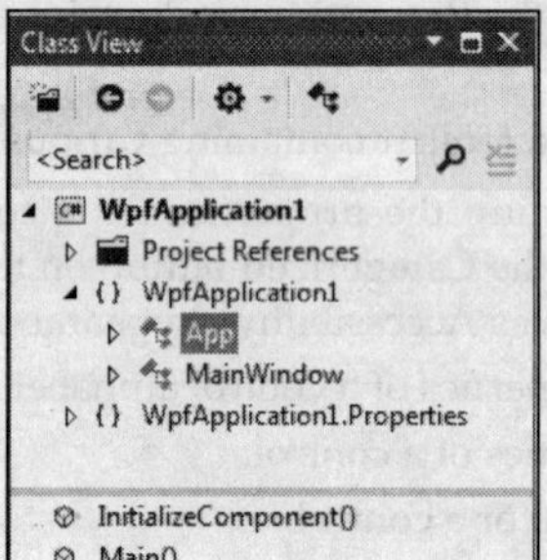

Figure 1.56: Displaying the Class View Window

You can notice that there are two panes in the Class View window. The upper half is the Objects pane and the lower half is the Members pane. In the Objects pane, an expandable tree of symbols is displayed whose top-level nodes represent projects. This hierarchical view specifies the symbolic structure within your code. The Class View toolbar allows you to navigate within the Objects and Members panes. Various buttons available in the Class View toolbar are described as follows:

- **Class View New Folder**—Creates a new folder or subfolder into which you can drag symbols for easy access
- **Back**—Allows you to navigate to the previously selected items until you reach the first item
- **Forward**—Allows you to navigate to the next selected item until you reach the most recently selected item
- **Class View settings**—Allows you to make different settings by using various commands, which are as follows:

- **Show Hidden Types and Members**—Displays hidden types in the Objects pane and hidden members in the Members pane
- **Show Public Members**—Displays public members for the users who are using the classes
- **Show Protected Members**—Displays protected members for the users who are extending the classes
- **Show Other Members**—Displays the members that do not fall in the categories of public, private, protected, or inherited

Server Explorer

The Server Explorer window allows you to view the services that are available on a particular server. In Visual Studio 2012, you can view the Server Explorer window by selecting VIEW → Server Explorer or by pressing the Ctrl+W, L keys together. The Server Explorer window is a powerful tool that provides the drag and drop feature. It helps you to work with databases in an easy way to use graphical environment. You can drag a service from the Server Explorer window onto a design surface, so that you can interact with the service programmatically in your application. Now, let's suppose that you drag and drop a database table onto a form. In such a case, .NET automatically creates the connection and command objects that are needed to access that table. Figure 1.57 displays the Server Explorer window:

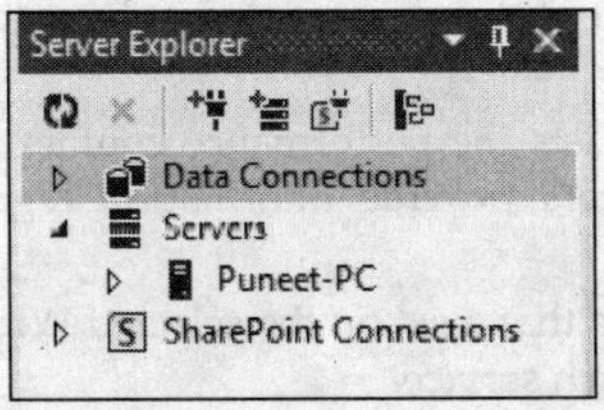

Figure 1.57: Displaying the Server Explorer Window

The Server Explorer window is the server management console for Visual Studio. You can view and retrieve information from all the databases you are connected to. Moreover, you can use Server Explorer to list database tables, views, stored procedures, and functions. You can also expand individual tables to list their columns.

The Server Explorer window provides access to a number of resources. For example, if you have Crystal Reports installed, then you can create a report directly from Server Explorer. Using Server Explorer, you can view and manipulate data links, database connections, and system resources on any server, which is connected to the network. You can perform the following tasks by using Server Explorer:

- Open the data connections and commands.
- Log on to servers and display their databases and system services, including event logs, message queue, performance counters, system services, and SQL databases.
- View information about available Web services and the methods and schemas that the services make available.
- Make data connections to SQL Servers and other databases.
- Store database projects and references.
- Drag nodes from Server Explorer into your Visual Studio projects; and therefore, create data components that reference the data resource or monitor its activity.
- Interact with data resources by connecting them to the data components created in your Visual Studio projects.

There are two primary nodes in the Server Explorer Window:

- **Data Connections**—Provides a list of data connections that are created by the users to the server. You can establish the connections to different types of databases, such as SQL Server and Oracle. Various child nodes available in the Data Connections node are as follows:
  - Database diagrams
  - Tables

- Views
- Stored procedures
- Functions

- **Servers**—Lists the currently connected servers that are available for use. It is categorized as the top-level node. You can use the databases and server resources in your applications that are under each server node. Dragging nodes from the Servers node onto Visual Studio Designer creates new components that are preconfigured to reference the dragged item. Various child node types available in the Servers node are described as follows:
  - **Event Logs**—Lists the Application, Security, and System event logs on the selected Microsoft Windows 2000 server or Windows NT version 4.0, and any custom logs present on the server.
  - **Management Classes**—Enables a developer to browse and modify Windows Management Instrumentation (WMI) data and call methods.
  - **Management Events**—Enables a developer to register for WMI events.
  - **Message Queues**—Lists the message queues, along with the messages that each queue contains on the selected server. This implies that this node helps providing an asynchronous communication protocol. The sender and the receiver of the message do not have to interact with the messages in the queue until the recipient receives it.
  - **Performance Counters**—Lists the performance counters on the selected Windows 2000 or Windows NT 4.0 server. The counters provide information regarding the functioning of an application or website.
  - **Services**—Lists the services that exist on the selected Windows 2000 or Windows NT 4.0 server. It also lists the current status of each service.

Component Tray

The component tray acts as a placeholder that contains the components, such as the Timer control, added at the design time. It allows a user to set the properties of the components at design time. Figure 1.58 shows the component tray:

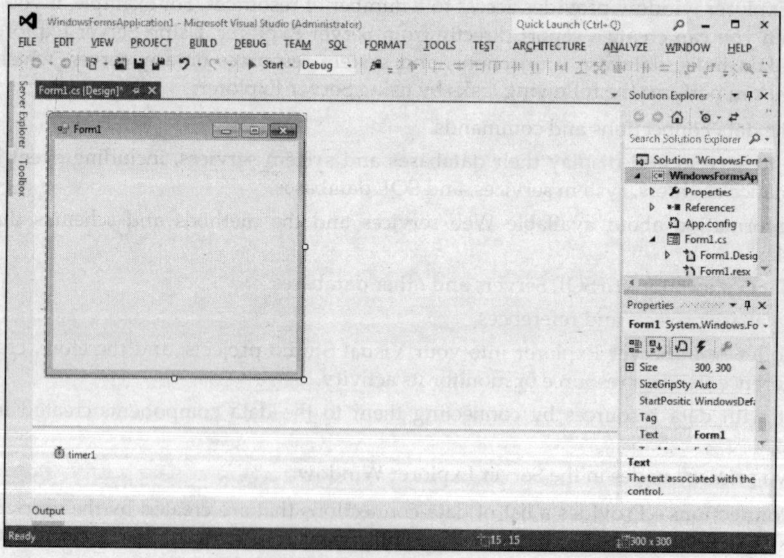

Figure 1.58: Displaying the Component Tray

The components, such as Timer and HelpProvider, do not have a UI and appear as icons in the component tray. As you can see in Figure 1.58, the component tray is a rectangular region located at the bottom of the Design view. The component tray appears only when any component is added to the Windows Form.

Output Window

The Output window displays the result of building and executing applications. You can view the Output window by selecting the VIEW→Output option. Alternatively, you can press the Ctrl+Alt+O keys together to open the Output window. Figure 1.59 displays the Output window:

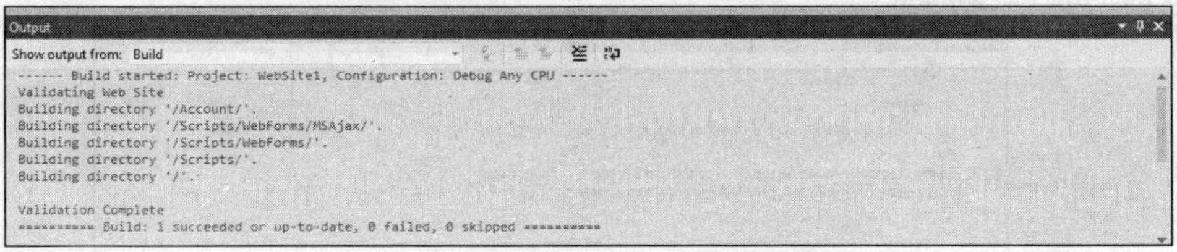

Figure 1.59: Showing the Output Window

The following are the functions that we use in the Output window:

- **Build**—Displays the progress and error messages from the compiler and linker
- **Debug**—Displays the output from the debugger

You can notice various lists and buttons in the Output window, which are given as follows:

- **Show Output from**—Allows one or more output panes to view that might be available, depending on which tools in the IDE have used the Output window. For example, when you run your application, it shows the output for build and if any error, then it shows the output for debugging. You can select either the Build option or the Debug option from the Show Output from drop-down list.
- **Find Message in Code**—Moves the insertion point to the line that contains the selected build error in Code editor.
- **Go to Previous Message**—Moves the insertion point in Code editor to the line that contains the previous build error.
- **Go to Next Message**—Moves the insertion point in Code editor to the line that contains the next build error.
- **Clear All**—Removes all the texts from the Output pane.
- **Toggle Word Wrap**—Toggles the Word Wrap feature on and off in the Output pane. When this button is selected, the text that extends from the viewing area is displayed on the line that follows it.

Task List

The Task List window displays all the tasks that you still have to finish in your application. It helps you to create and manage a list of pending programming tasks. You can view the Task List window by selecting **VIEW → Task List** or by pressing the Ctrl+T keys together. Figure 1.60 displays the Task List window:

Figure 1.60: Displaying the Task List Window

The Task List window also displays syntax and other errors that are normally encountered during coding. Using this window, you can display the task comments that link to the lines in your code files where work must be done. You can also enter notes on the work that remains to be completed as User Tasks.

Error List

The Error List window helps you to accelerate application development by displaying all the errors in a single window. In the Error List window, you can find syntax errors noted by IntelliSense. When you edit and compile code, the errors, warnings, and messages produced are displayed in the Error List window. In addition, you can find Deployment errors, Static Analysis errors, and errors detected while applying Enterprise Template policies. You can open the file, where the error has occurred by double-clicking any error message entry. You can also view the Error List window by selecting VIEW → Error List or by pressing the Ctrl+E keys together. Figure 1.61 shows the Error List window:

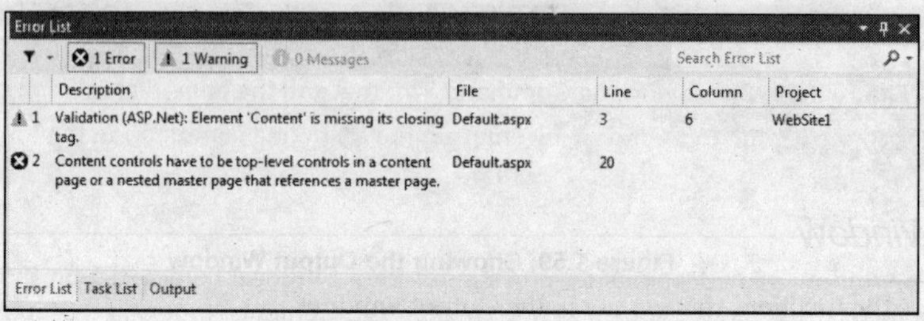

Figure 1.61: Displaying the Error List Window

The Error List toolbar consists of the following buttons:

- **Errors**—Displays the number of errors in the list
- **Warnings**—Displays the number of warnings in the list
- **Messages**—Displays the number of messages in the list

Various UI elements present below the toolbar are as follows:

- **Category**—Displays a list of the type of error list entry
- **Default Order**—Displays the order number in which an entry was generated.
- **Description**—Displays the description of the error, warning, or message entry. Lengthy descriptions are wrapped into additional lines.
- **File**—Shows the file name only or the full path of the file along with the file name.
- **Line**—Shows the line number in the code where the error occurred.
- **Column**—Shows the column number in the line where the error occurred.
- **Project**—Shows the project name in which the error occurred.

Command Window

In the Command window, you can perform operations, such as adding a new item to the project. You can view the Command window by selecting VIEW→Other Windows→Command Window or by pressing the Ctrl+Alt+A keys together.

This window is used to execute commands directly in the Visual Studio IDE. The greater than symbol (>) appears at the left edge of the Command window as a prompt for new lines. You can use the UP arrow or the Ctrl+UP arrow keys to scroll up the window and use the DOWN arrow or the Ctrl+DOWN arrow keys to scroll down the window.

Now, consider a case where your application is in the Debug mode and you need to check the value of the variable varMessage. To do so, type the following command in the Command window:

```
>Debug.Print varMessage
```

(Or)

```
>? varMessage
```

Both the commands display the value of the variable `varMessage`. The question mark (?) is an alias for the `Debug.Print` command that is used to evaluate any expression. Therefore, using both the commands would return the same result.

Enter the following command in the Command window without the greater than sign (>) to switch to an Immediate window, as shown in Figure 1.62:

```
>immed
```

Figure 1.62: Displaying the Command Window and the Immediate Window

You can switch back to the Command window by entering the following command in the Immediate Window:

```
>cmd
```

Dynamic Help Window

The Dynamic Help window provides links to information found in local help based on the portion of the IDE that is currently in focus. It includes the usual HELP menu with Contents, Index, and Search items. In addition, the Dynamic Help window automatically searches things on the Internet. You can see the Dynamic Help window by selecting the HELP →View Help option from the Menu Bar. The Dynamic Help window opens in the Internet Explorer, as shown in Figure 1.63.

Figure 1.63: Displaying the Dynamic Help Window

Manage Styles Window

Visual Studio 2012 consists of a tool called Manage Styles, which shows all the CSS files for the Web page. You can also call it as CSS Style Manager. The Manage Styles tool can be used at the Design view as well as at the Source view. You can open the CSS Style Manager by selecting the VIEW → Manage Styles option. However, before that, you need to first add a style sheet file to your project and then add a reference of it to the Web page, where the styles need to be applied by selecting FORMAT → Attach Style Sheet. Now, open the Manage Styles window, as shown in Figure 1.64:

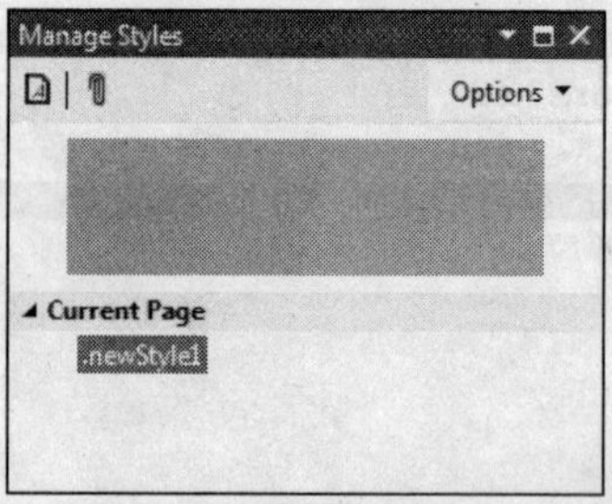

Figure 1.64: Displaying the Manage Styles Window

Figure 1.64 shows a style in the Manage Styles window. It indicates that the specified style is in use within the current Web page. You can modify the CSS rule by right-clicking the name of the style and selecting the Modify Style option from the context menu to open the Modify Style dialog box. You can also attach a style sheet by using the Manage Styles window.

Since this book is on ASP.NET, let's now explore the relation between ASP.NET and .NET Framework. ASP.NET, as we know, is a technology to develop content-rich dynamic and personalized websites. The fundamental component of ASP.NET is the Web form. A Web form is a Web page that users view in the browser. Now, let's discuss it in more detail.

Section III – ASP.NET 4.5 Overview

Since the release of .NET Framework 1.0, Microsoft has put in consistent effort in developing and improving ASP.NET, which is a part of .NET Framework for building rich Web applications. This first release brought a radical change over the older Microsoft technology to build websites using a server-side script engine, called Active Server Pages (ASP). Despite many advantages of ASP.NET over ASP, new programmers found it difficult to start with ASP.NET because of its complexity and the knowledge needed to build applications.

After the initial release in 2002, another version of .NET Framework named .NET 1.1 was released with Visual Studio 2003. Most people considered this release as a mere service pack for the initial release, though it also had new improvements in both the Framework and the development environment.

Later in November 2005, Microsoft released Visual Studio 2005, which integrated ASP.NET 2.0. Again, Microsoft made drastic improvements in this version and reduced the complexity of the initial version. This new version had many new wizards and controls that reduced the amount of code required in building applications, thus increasing productivity.

Now, Microsoft's latest release is ASP.NET 4.5, which includes new features for creating Web-based applications.

Exploring New Features of ASP.NET 4.5

ASP.NET 4.5 was released along with Visual Studio 2012 on September 12, 2012. It uses the same engine as that of ASP.NET 4.0, with some additional features. ASP.NET 4.5 has simplified the process of building websites, making it easier than ever. Now, let's discuss the following new features added to ASP.NET 4.5:

- ASP.NET core services
- ASP.NET Web Forms
- ASP.NET Web Pages 2
- General Enhancements for Web Development
- Data-Related Enhancements for Web Development
- IIS Express for Web Development
- ASP.NET Web API
- ASP.NET MVC 4, Web API, and ASP.NET Web Pages (Razor) are now Open Source

ASP.NET Core Services

ASP.NET 4.5 core services include features, such as Bundling, Integrated Anti-XSS encoding routines, and Minification. The important ASP.NET core services are as follows:

- **Asynchronously reading and writing Hypertext Transfer Protocol (HTTP) requests and responses**—Specifies the capability of reading and writing an HTTP request entity asynchronously. ASP.NET 4.5 also allows double buffering of the HTTP request entity that integrates downstream HTTP handlers with .aspx page and ASP.NET MVC controllers.
- **New ASP.NET request validation**—Allows you to read unvalidated request data even when the request validation is enabled. ASP.NET 4.5 introduces two features to work with invalidated request data: lazy request validation and access to unvalidated request data. In ASP.NET 4.5, all the requests are validated by default. However, you can configure your application to accept request validation before accessing the actual requested data. This validation is referred as the lazy request validation and can be enabled by adding the following code snippet in the Web.config file:

```
<httpRuntime requestValidationMode="4.5" ... />
```

  ASP.NET 4.5 also allows access to unvalidated request data. For this, a new Unvalidated collection property in the HttpRequest class is introduced in ASP.NET 4.5 to provide access to the requested data, such as Form, QueryString, and Cookies. To use this property, first you need to set requestValidationMode = "4.5" in the httpRuntime element of the Web.config file. After that, you can use the HttpRequest.Unvalidated property to read the unvalidated form value through the following code snippet:

```
var s = context.Request.Unvalidated.Form["forum_post"];
```

- **Support for the WebSockets protocol**—Enables you to create a secure real-time bidirectional communication between a client and a server over HTTP. The WebSockets protocol is supported not only by browsers but also by clients. The WebSockets protocol contains enough resources, such as HTML and JavaScript, to be supported on both the client and the mobile operating system. The advantage of using the WebSockets protocol is that it supports large long-running data transfers between the client and the server. ASP.NET 4.5 and Internet Information Services 7.5 (IIS 7.5) provides low-level WebSockets support for asynchronously reading and writing both string and binary data with the help of managed Application Programming Interfaces (APIs). ASP.NET 4.5 includes the System.Web.WebSockets namespace that contains classes, such as AspNetWebSocket, AspNetWebSocketContext, and AspNetWebSocketOptions, for using the WebSockets protocol.
- **Bundling**—Allows you to create bundles of individual JavaScript and .css files by combining them. These bundles are generated by using the Bundle class or by using its child classes, such as ScriptBundle and StyleBundle. After configuring an instance of the Bundle class, the instance is added to the global collection of a Web application so that the JavaScript and .css files can be made available to incoming requests. The BundleConfig file performs bundle configuration in default templates for creating bundles of core scripts and .css files used by the default templates. After the bundling of files, files are sorted alphabetically and then arranged in a way so that libraries and their custom extensions are loaded first.

  Bundles are referenced by using the Render() helper method, which generates markup element for each resource in a bundle in the debug mode. On the other hand, Render() generates a single markup element for the whole bundle in the release mode. You can set these modes in an application by using the Web.config file.
- **Minification**—Shrinks JavaScript and .css files by removing whitespaces and other characters that are not required. Both bundling and minification are used with Web Forms, ASP.NET MVC, and Web pages.
- **Support for asynchronous modules and handlers**—Allows you to write asynchronous HTTP modules and HTTP handlers in Web applications. Some properties are introduced in the classes of the System.Web namespace to write asynchronous HTTP modules and HTTP handlers effectively. These properties are given as follows:
  - **ClientDisconnectedToken**—Refers to a property that is added in the HttpResponse class. It notifies an application when a client gets disconnected from the Web server.

- **TimedOutToken**—Refers to a property that is added in the HttpRequestWrapper class. It notifies an application when a client request has taken more time than the allowed request time out value.
- **ThreadAbortOnTimeout**—Refers to a property that is added in the HttpContextBase class. It allows you to control the behavior of timed out requests by setting the value of the ThreadAbortOnTimeout property to False.
- **Abort**—Allows you to terminate the available TCP connection of a request.

❒ **Integrated Anti-XSS encoding routines**—Allows you to perform anti cross-site scripting. Cross-site scripting is one of the major security threats in Web sites. Due to the lack of security mechanisms in browsers, attackers can inject the client-side script from a Web page to a database to access vital information. In the earlier versions of ASP.NET, the routines were available as external DLLs; however, in ASP.NET 4.5, they are available in its core functionality. Routines are implemented by using the AntiXssEncoder class, which is available in the System.Web.Security.AntiXss namespace. You can call the static methods of the AntiXssEncoder class directly in an application. The best way for using the new anti-XSS encoding routines is to configure an ASP.NET application to use the AntiXssEncoder class by default.

❒ **Support for OAuth and OpenID**—Allows you to create Web sites that give permissions to the users to log in with the credentials created on other sites, such as Google, Yahoo, Facebook, Twitter, and Windows Live. OAuth is an open standard for authorization that provides a method to the users to access server resources using credentials, such as username and password. OpenID is an open standard to authenticate users. A user can create an account with OpenID identity providers, and use the account to access any Web site that supports OpenID authentication.

ASP.NET Web Forms

The Web Forms are the integral part of ASP.NET applications. These have been enhanced several times since the release of ASP.NET. In ASP.NET 4.5, the following new features are introduced for Web Forms:

❒ **Model Binders**—Allows you to bind data controls directly with data-access methods. This feature is similar to model binding that is used in ASP.NET MVC.

❒ **Strongly typed binding expressions in data controls**—Allows you to write strongly typed, two-way data-binding expressions for data controls, in place of using Eval or Bind expression. In this manner, you can use the complex properties of data controls. You can also use these expressions with the new model binding feature.

❒ **Unobtrusive JavaScript for client-side validation**—Moves the client-side validation code into a single external JavaScript file, which reduces the page size and loads the page faster. In addition, this feature provides better caching of files.

❒ **HTML encoded data-binding expressions**—Allows you to encode the data binding expressions in the HTML format by adding colon at the end of the <%# prefix, which marks the start of data binding expressions.

❒ **Fallback support for Content Distribution Networks (CDNs) in the ScriptManager control**—Tests whether the script was loaded successfully from a CDN by using the EnableCdn property of the ScriptManager control. If the script was not loaded successfully from the CDN, then it tries to load the script from the alternate local location.

❒ **Support for HTML5 form types**—Specifies the enhancements done in the Web Forms controls to take advantage of the new features of HTML5. Following are some of the improvements done in the controls of Web Forms:

- The TextBox control now supports new HTML5 input types, such as email and date time, as the TextMode property of the control has been updated.
- The FileUpload control has been updated to support multiple files upload from browsers.
- Validator controls in HTML5 allow validation of HTML5 input elements

- The attributes of HTML5 elements that contain a Uniform Resource Locater (URL) now include the runat=server attribute. Therefore, you can use the ~ operator to display the application root.
- The UpdatePanel control has been modified to support the posting of HTML5 input fields.

- **Improved paging in the GridView control**—Specifies the improvement in the paging functionality by using the AllowCustomPaging and VirtualItemCount properties of the GridView control. These two properties eliminate the need for the GridView control to fetch all the rows from the database every time a new page is loaded.
- **Enhancements to Web Forms compilation**—Specifies the following improvements that have extended the Web Forms compilation system:
  - Includes a ControlBuilderInterceptor class that allows you to customize Web Forms page and control compilation output.
  - Includes a TemplateParser.ParseTemplate method that allows you to create an ITemplate instance from a string of ASPX markup

ASP.NET Web Pages 2

ASP.NET Web Pages 2 allows you to easily combine the server code with the HTML code to create lightweight dynamic Web content. It also allows you to easily connect to a database and add videos and links for social networking sites to develop Web sites according to the modern standards.

Following are the new features and enhancements of ASP.NET Web Pages 2:

- **New and enhanced site templates**—Specifies the inclusion of personal site templates, starter site templates, and upgradation of Web Pages 1 templates to run on Web Pages 2. The personal site templates provide Web pages for a blog, photo gallery, and Twitter. On the other hand, the starter templates have been updated to allow users to sign in to Web sites by using their Facebook, Twitter, or Windows Live account.
- **Razor syntax improvements**—Provides conditional HTML attributes, which reduce the complexity to render the attributes based on the values that you mention in your code. For example, the ~/ syntax allows you to render links of dynamic path information and URLs.
- **Validation**—Refers to a feature that is used for validating user input to improve the performance of a Web site. Two new validation classes, ValidationHelper and Validator, are introduced that help in specifying the validation rules by writing few lines of code.
- **Side-by-side support**—Allows you to execute the Web Pages 1 applications and Web Pages 2 applications on the same computer.
- **Membership and authentication**—Includes two new authentication providers, OAuth and OpenID, which allow users to sign in with external sites, such as Facebook, Twitter, and Windows Live, using their credentials.
- **Map helper**—Allows you to use already existing search engines, such as Bing, Google, and Yahoo, and extract map on your Web site.
- **Mobile display modes**—Allows you to create device-specific Web pages, which render automatically on a mobile device.

General Enhancements for Web Development

The general enhancements done in the area of Web development include various new features that allow you to:

- **Use the most recent Web standards**—The HTML editor in ASP.NET 4.5 supports HTML 5 elements and snippets. Moreover, the CSS editor allows you to work with CSS3, CSS hacks, and vendor-specific CSS extensions.
- **Test the same page, application, or site in a variety of browsers**—You can create and test an application or a website in different browsers, such as Internet Explorer, Netscape, and Mozilla Firefox.
- **Quickly find the source of rendered markup**—Whenever you select a rendered element, the new Page Inspector feature of ASP.NET 4.5 opens the file in which the markup was generated and highlights the source.

- **Find snippets and code elements quickly by using improved IntelliSense**—Whenever you enter any text in the editor, such as CSS editor and HTML editor, the Intellisense feature displays a list of options on the basis of the typed text.
- **Select markup and extract it to a user control**—You can create a markup and reuse it at different locations simultaneously.
- **Create and edit code and markup more easily**—Renaming a tag automatically renames the corresponding tag. For example, if you rename the HTML <div> tag to the <header> tag, then the corresponding closing tag also changes automatically at the same time.
- **Create CSS more efficiently**—ASP.NET 4.5 provides new features, such as expansion and collapse of new sections, color selector, and use of hierarchical indentation to create CSS in an organized manner. You can also comment and uncomment blocks of code in the CSS editor.
- **Write JavaScript in the JavaScript editor**—The JavaScript editor in ASP.NET 4.5 includes various new features that improve the working experience with JavaScript in Visual Studio. Some of these features are code outlining, brace matching, Go to Definition, ECMAScript5, DOM IntelliSense, VSDOC signature overloads, implicit references, set a breakpoint within a single line of code, control objects available in global scope, and View statement completion for identifiers.
- **Deploy Web application projects more easily**—You can import publish settings from hosting providers, such as specification of transformations of Web.config file for a publish profile, storage of encrypted credentials in the publish profile, specification of the build configuration in the publish profile, and preview of updates related to deployment of Web application. It also helps you to deploy your Web applications easily.

Data-Related Enhancements for Web Development

The data-related enhancements made in ASP.NET 4.5 for Web application development allow you to:

- **Automate validation for frequently used data types**—ASP.NET 4.5 supports automatic validation for commonly used data types. For example, you can use DataAnnotation attributes in order to automate data types, such as e-mail address, telephone number, and so on.
- **Deploy incremental database updates**—The database schema deployed with a project gets updated automatically.

IIS Express for Web Development

IIS Express is provided as a default Web server for testing Web-based projects. It is a lightweight, independent version of IIS that includes all the essential abilities of the IIS Web server role. However, IIS Express is still an option to be used as a local Web server during Web development, *that is, you can run your applications in either IIS or IIS Express.*

ASP.NET Web API

ASP.NET Web API is a framework that allows you to build HTTP services, such as browsers and mobile devices. It provides an ideal platform for developing Representational State Transfer (RESTful) applications by using the .NET Framework. The new features of ASP.NET Web API allow you to:

- **Easily build and consume HTTP services that reach a broad range of clients**—The HTTP services can be easily accessed and used by a broad range of clients; software, such as browsers, mobile applications; and hardware, such as tablets and similar kind of devices. These services also come with an inbuilt support for negotiation of content to determine the correct format of data.
- **Directly access and manipulate HTTP requests and responses by using a modern HTTP programming model**—You can directly access and manipulate HTTP requests and responses with the help of modern HTTP programming model that is supported both at the server's and client's end. The Web APIs can be called from any .NET Framework application by using new HttpClient API.
- **Easily extract data from an HTTP request**—You can retrieve data from different sections of an HTTP request by using model binders. This feature is similar to model binding that is used in ASP.NET MVC.

- **Enjoy a full set of routing capabilities**—ASP.NET Web APIs support complete routing capabilities in ASP.NET MVC and ASP.NET. The routing capabilities include route parameters and constraints.

ASP.NET MVC 4, Web API, and ASP.NET Web Pages (Razor) are now Open Source

The Apache 2.0 license is now used by ASP.NET MVC 4, ASP.NET Web API, and ASP.NET Web Pages v2 (Razor syntax). The important points of this development model are as follows:

- **Source code location**—Specifies the location of the source code available on CodePlex. You can access the code by using the URL such as http://aspnetwebstack.codeplex.com/.
- **View check-ins and provide feedback**—Allows the community to view and give feedback on developer check-ins.
- **Community contributions**—Allows developers to contribute by submitting patches and code. The developers may or may not belong to the Microsoft community.
- **Check-ins are evaluated**—Reviews every check-in against the existing standards of the Microsoft development team.
- **Community code is included in Visual Studio**—Includes the approved community code in ASP.NET and Visual Studio.
- **Microsoft development and support continue**—Specifies that Microsoft reserves the right of development of ASP.NET MVC, Web API, and Razor. The development is done according to the Microsoft support policy.

NOTE

Microsoft has not made ASP.NET Web Forms open source as they use System.Web.dll assembly on which Windows server platform is dependent.

The ASP.NET Technologies

In ASP.NET 4.5, some of the technologies have been integrated that make the task of developing websites easier for developers. The combination of these technologies provides a common platform to Web developers by enabling them to handle complicated databases in an easier manner. These integrated technologies are as follows:

- MVC Framework
- ADO.NET Entity Framework
- ADO.NET Data Services Framework
- The Silverlight Technology
- Dynamic Data Framework

Let's learn about these technologies in detail.

MVC Framework

The MVC Framework is an architectural pattern that is used in software engineering. In programming, it is very general to split an application into separate layers such as presentation (UI), logic, and data access layers that run on different computers. The presentation layer is further separated into two parts: view and controller.

ADO.NET Entity Framework

ADO.NET Entity Framework enables users to design models and mappings of databases, tables, and views by using Visual Studio 2012 and .NET Framework 4.5. Every business application has a conceptual data model that has to deal with data represented in relational form. Even if higher level of conceptual model is used, you have to first convert it into relational form and then apply it to logical database schema or relational model. This is done because conceptual model is not directly executable. Entity Framework provides capability to program conceptual model. The goal of introducing Entity Framework is to raise the level of abstraction for data programming and help developers to increase productivity.

ADO.NET Data Services Framework

ADO.NET Data Services Framework consists of a combination of patterns and libraries that enables the creation and consumption of data services for the Web so that it can be consumed by Web clients within a corporate network or across the Internet. The objective of ADO.NET Data Services Framework is to facilitate the creation of flexible data services that are naturally integrated with the Web.

The Silverlight Technology

Silverlight is a technology that allows designers and developers to stretch the boundaries of Web application development. It was formerly known as Windows Presentation Foundation/Everywhere (WPF/E). Silverlight can work in a cross-platform, cross-browser, and cross-device environment. It is an integration of the rich user interface of desktop applications and the transparency of other Web languages, such as HTML and JavaScript. Silverlight enables you to develop Web applications containing high multimedia content and eye-catching visual effects.

Dynamic Data Framework

ASP.NET Dynamic Data is a Framework that allows you to easily build data-driven Web applications based on the foundation of the Entity Framework data model or the LINQ to SQL data model. The purpose of a data model is to represent the information about the items present in a database. It also depicts the relation between different items of the database.

Next, let's understand the ASP.NET life cycle.

The ASP.NET Life Cycle

The ASP.NET life cycle starts when a client requests a page from the Web Server. The ISAPI.dll assembly resides in the Web Server that checks the requested file extension to allow the right ISAPI extension to handle the request. The ISAPI.dll forwards the request to IIS where it runs inetinfo.exe to create an instance of the ASP.NET worker process, aspnet_wp.exe. The HttpRuntime class instance is used by the worker process to process the request. If the file extension mapped successfully, then the ApplicationManager class is called that creates an application domain for the application.

The ASP.NET life cycle shows you how ASP.NET processes the Web pages to produce dynamic output. It also shows you how the application and individual pages are instantiated and processed, and how ASP.NET compiles the pages dynamically. Let's look at these aspects in detail in the following sections:

- Life cycle of ASP.NET application on IIS 7.5
- Life cycle of an ASP.NET Web page

Life Cycle of ASP.NET Applications on IIS 7.5

In this section, let's take a look at the complete application life cycle of ASP.NET applications running on integrated mode of IIS 7.5. IIS 7.5 also supports Classic mode, which works similar to any ASP.NET application running in IIS 6.0.

In an integrated mode of IIS 7.5, the application resource request process is similar to the one in IIS 6.0. However, in IIS 7.5, the `MapRequestHandler`, `LogRequest`, and `PostLogRequest` events are raised during the request process in addition to the events in IIS 6.0. Additionally, IIS 7.5 uses a unified request-processing pipeline for the entire application resource request that was not there in IIS 6.0.

NOTE

IIS 6.0 uses two separate pipelines for processing an application resource request. One pipeline is for unmanaged code filters and extensions; other is for managed code components.

The following are the benefits of using the integrated pipeline in IIS 7.5:

- Raises all the events of the `HttpApplication` class to enable ASP.NET modules in IIS 7.5.
- Enables the configuration of both managed code and unmanaged code modules. In addition, by using the integrated pipeline, developers can enable or disable the managed code modules for all the requests, even if a user requests for an ASP.NET Web page.
- Enables a Web site to call the managed code modules at any stage of the pipeline, such as prior to the processing of a user request, after the request is processed, or in the middle of processing a user request.
- Enables a Web site to be registered in IIS and then either enable or disable the modules by using the `Web.config` file.

Table 1.4 lists different phases of the life cycle of ASP.NET applications on IIS 7.5 integrated mode:

Table 1.4: Phases of the Life Cycle of ASP.NET Applications on IIS 7.5 Integrated Mode

Phase	Description
User requests for an application resource	Refers to the phase in which application resource is requested by a user on the Web server. This request passes through the unified pipeline that calls the ASP.NET modules. Now, even if a page has `.htm` extension and is not explicitly mapped with ASP.NET, still this request can take benefits of the ASP.NET features, such as authentication and authorization processes, which are embedded in the managed-code. In IIS 6.0, these processes require manual configuration due to two separate pipelines.
The unified pipeline receives the first user request	Specifies that when a request for an application resource is received for the first time, an application domain is created by using the object of the `ApplicationManager` class. The application domain is a process that isolates applications from each other and enables the processing of the user requests. In this phase, the information about an application can also be accessed when the `HostingEnvironment` object is created within the application domain.
For each user request, response objects are created	Refers to the phase in which the response objects, such as `HttpContext`, `HttpRequest`, and `HttpResponse`, are created. The `HttpContext` class has objects, such as `HttpRequest` and `HttpResponse`. These objects are valid only for the current user request. The `HttpRequest` object holds information about the current request; whereas, the `HttpResponse` object holds information that is sent to the user, such as cookies and the final output.
An object of the `HttpApplication` class is created and allocated to the request	Refers to the phase in which the application is started when an object of the `HttpApplication` class is created. However, if a `Global.asax` file exists, then an object of the `Global.asax` class is created instead of the `HttpApplication` class. The `Global.asax` class derives from the `HttpApplication` class and represents an ASP.NET application. The modules that need to be invoked depend on the parent application's managed code modules. In addition, it also depends on which modules are configured in the `Web.config` file. You can add or remove modules by specifying the module names in the `Web.config` file within the modules element of the `system.webServer` section.
The `HttpApplication` class processes the user request.	Specifies that the `HttpApplication` class performs the following tasks to process the user request: 1. Validates the user request to confirm that it does not contain any malicious markup. 2. Performs URL mapping to confirm whether any URL is specified in the UrlMappingsSection section of the Web.config file. 3. Invokes the following events and methods in the same order as displayed: • BeginRequest

Table 1.4: Phases of the Life Cycle of ASP.NET Applications on IIS 7.5 Integrated Mode

Phase	Description
	• AuthenticateRequest • PostAuthenticateRequest • AuthorizeRequest • PostAuthorizeRequest • ResolveRequestCache • PostResolveRequestCache • MapRequestHandler • PostMapRequestHandler • AcquireRequestState • PostAcquireRequestState • PreRequestHandlerExecute • Calls the `ProcessRequest()` method of the IHttpHandler class for the request • PostRequestHandlerExecute • ReleaseRequestState • PostReleaseRequestState • Performs response filtering only if the Filter property for the HttpResponse class is defined • UpdateRequestCache • PostUpdateRequestCache • LogRequest • PostLogRequest • EndRequest • PreSendRequestHeaders • PreSendRequestContent

Life Cycle of an ASP.NET Web Page

When a user requests for an ASP.NET Web page, the page passes through a number of stages that is collectively called the life cycle of an ASP.NET Web page. For example, the life cycle of a page begins when a user requests for a Web page and ends when the page is rendered completely to the browser. When you want a specific action to take place at a particular stage of a page, you should completely understand the page life cycle. Moreover, if you are creating any custom control for your project, then you should have a thorough knowledge of the page life cycle as a control's life cycle depends on the page's life cycle.

Let's now understand about the different stages involved in a page's life cycle.

Different Stages of an ASP.NET Page

In general, an ASP.NET Web page passes through seven stages. Table 1.5 lists the stages:

Table 1.5: Different Stages of an ASP.NET Web Page

Stage	Description
Page request	Specifies that the page's life cycle begins when a user requests for a Web page. When the user requests for the page for the first time, ASP.NET ascertains whether the request is new or an old one. If the request is a new one, then the page is compiled and executed. However, if the request is an old one, then a cached copy of the page is sent without executing the page.

Table 1.5: Different Stages of an ASP.NET Web Page

Stage	Description
Start	Refers to the stage in which the `Request` and `Response` properties of the page are configured. The page also ascertains whether the request is an old or a new one by using the `IsPostBack` property. At this stage, the page's `UICulture` property is also configured.
Page initialization	Refers to the stage in which each control on the page is assigned a unique ID by setting the `UniqueID` property. At this stage, if there are any themes, then they are added to the page. If the request is an old one, then the postback data is not loaded and the control property values are still required to be restored to the view state values.
Load	Refers to the stage in which if the current request is an old one, then the properties of controls on the page are loaded with data from the view state and the control state.
Postback event handling	Specifies that if the request made is an old one, then any event handler can be invoked. After that, the validation controls used on the page invoke the `Validate()` method.
Rendering	Determines that prior to rendering the page, the view state and all the controls on the page are saved. While rendering the page, ASP.NET runtime environment invokes the `Render()` method for each control on the page and writes the output of the rendering stage to the `OutputStream` object of the page's `Response` property.
Unload	Refers to the stage where the `Response` and `Request` properties of the page are unloaded and any cleanup operation, if required, is performed.

ASP.NET Pages Life Cycle Events

At each stage of the life cycle of a page, the page raises some events that you can handle by running your own code. For handling control events, you bind the event handler to the specified event by using declarative attributes, such as `onclick` or `handle`, within the code.

ASP.NET Web pages also support automatic event wire-up. This implies that when certain events are raised, ASP.NET searches for methods that correspond to that event and automatically executes those methods. If the `AutoEventWireup` attribute of the `@ Page` directive is `True`, then the page events are automatically bound to the methods used to handle these events. The following are the most common page events:

- **PreInit**—Refers to the first event that occurs during the life cycle of an ASP.NET Web page. It is used to check the `IsPostBack` property of the page to determine whether the page is being processed for the first time. It also creates or recreates dynamic controls. It sets the `Theme` property and the master page dynamically. In addition, it gets and sets the profile property values.
- **Init**—Refers to the event that is raised after the initialization of all the controls and applying skin settings. It is used to read or initialize control properties.
- **Load**—Refers to the `OnLoad()` event method that is called to set the properties of controls and establish database connections. The `Page` class first calls the `OnLoad()` event method on the Web page and then calls the event for each child control, until the page is loaded.

NOTE

We have explained some of the main events. However, ASP.NET life cycle also supports InitComplete, PreLoad, LoadComplete, PreRender, SaveStateComplete, Render, and Upload events.

After understanding the concepts of ASP.NET 4.5, let's learn how to create a simple Web Application.

Exploring a Sample ASP.NET 4.5 Web Application

In ASP.NET 4.5, you can create both Web applications and Websites with each having its own advantages. For example, MVC and some tools for automation of Web deployment works only with Web application projects. The Dynamic Data feature of ASP.NET, works with both Web sites and Web application projects. Before you start creating an ASP.NET project, you should understand and select the appropriate project type.

Table 1.6 summarizes the main difference between a Web application and Web site project:

Table 1.6: Difference between Web application and Web site project

Area	Web Application	Web Site
Structure of project file (.csproj or .vbproj)	Stores information about the list of files that are included in the ASP.NET project.	Consists of no project file. The files are included automatically in the Web site.
Compilation	Requires you to build the project in Visual Studio. In the process of compilation of the application, the class and standalone class files are complied into a single assembly and placed in the Bin folder.	Does not require you to manually compile the project. The Web site is complied dynamically by ASP.NET, which produces multiple assemblies.
Namespaces	Is added to pages, controls and classes by default.	Needs to be added manually are they are not added by default to pages, controls, and classes.
Deployment	Requires you to copy the assembly that is created while compiling the project in an IIS server.	Requires you to copy the project source to an IIS server.

Now, let's create a Web application by following these steps:

1. Select the Start → All Programs → Microsoft Visual Studio 2012 → Visual Studio 2012 option to open Visual Studio 2012.
2. Select the FILE→New→Project option in Visual Studio 2012 IDE, as shown in Figure 1.65:

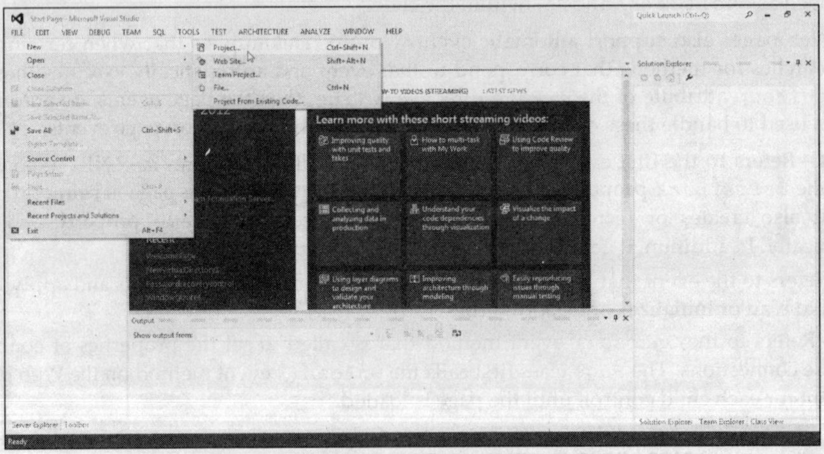

Figure 1.65: Showing the Start Page of Visual Studio 2012

The New Project dialog box appears (Figure 1.66).

3. Select Web → ASP.NET Web Forms Application in the middle pane (Figure 1.66).
4. Enter a name of the application in the Name text box. In our case, we have entered `SampleWebApplication` (Figure 1.66).

5. Enter a location to save the application in the Location combo box (Figure 1.66).
6. Click the OK button, as shown in Figure 1.66:

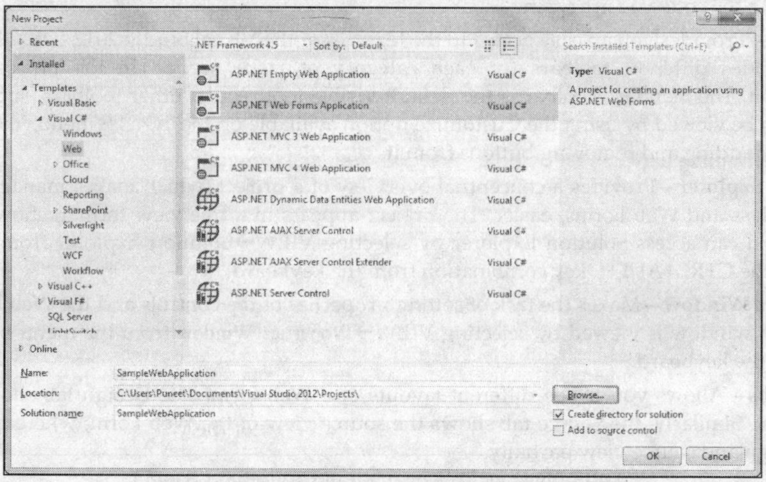

Figure 1.66: Showing the New Project Dialog Box

The SampleWebApplication Web application with the Default.aspx file, also known as the source file, appears, as shown in Figure 1.67:

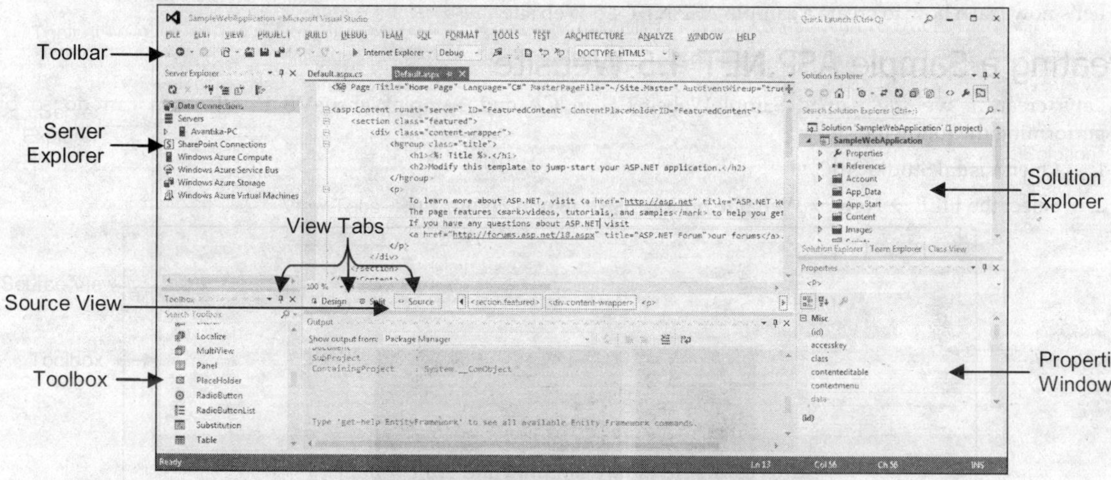

Figure 1.67: Showing the Visual Studio 2012 IDE

Different components of the Visual Studio 2012 IDE are explained as follows:

- **Toolbox**—Contains a number of tabs where each tab contains a list of controls that can be dragged and used on a Web Form. The Toolbox is docked on the left side of the Visual Studio 2012 IDE; however, if it is not visible, then you can access the Toolbox by selecting VIEW→Toolbox from the menu bar or by pressing the CTRL+ALT+X keys together to open it in the Visual Studio 2012 IDE.
- **Server Explorer**—Displays a list of available servers from which data can be accessed through the network. The Server Explorer window is viewed by selecting VIEW→Server Explorer from the menu bar or by pressing the CTRL+ALT+S key combination from the keyboard.
- **Code Editor Window**—Helps you recognize keywords and identifiers of the programming language. It also checks syntax errors, incorrect initialization of variables, invalid declarations, and unrecognized calling of procedures by highlighting them. You can access the Code Editor window by double-clicking the control or

the Web Form or pressing the F7 key in the design mode. The Code Editor window also provides the IntelliSense feature, which provides you a list of options that help in writing code easily and automatically completing the code you are typing.

- **Toolbars**—Provides you an easy access to the features of the Visual Studio 2012 IDE. The Visual Studio 2012 IDE provides different toolbars for each category of tasks needed in the process of developing an application. The Standard toolbar is the default visible toolbar; the other toolbars, such as Formatting and Build, can be viewed by using the Customize option available on the TOOLS menu. You can customize this toolbar by adding and removing buttons from it.
- **Solution Explorer**—Provides a conceptual overview of a project, which makes managing project elements, such as class and Web Forms, easier. The project appears in a tree view format, showing nodes and child nodes. You can access Solution Explorer by selecting VIEW→Solution Explorer from the menu bar or by pressing the CTRL+ALT+L key combination from the keyboard.
- **Properties Window**—Makes the task of setting properties of the controls and the Web Forms very easy. The Properties window is viewed by selecting VIEW→Properties Window from the menu bar or pressing the F4 key from the keyboard.
- **View Tabs**—Allows you to see different layouts of a Web form. The Design tab shows the design of the Web Form. Similarly, the Source tab shows the source view of the Web Form; whereas, the Split tab shows both design and source view partially.

NOTE

Throughout this book, we are creating ASP.NET Web sites and referring them as Web applications interchangeably.

Let's now learn how to create a sample ASP.NET 4.5 Web site.

Creating a Sample ASP.NET 4.5 Website

Let's create a website named SampleWebsiteCS in C# and SampleWebsiteVB in VB. You can do so by performing the following steps:

1. Open Visual Studio 2012.
2. Select the FILE → New → Web Site option, as shown in Figure 1.68:

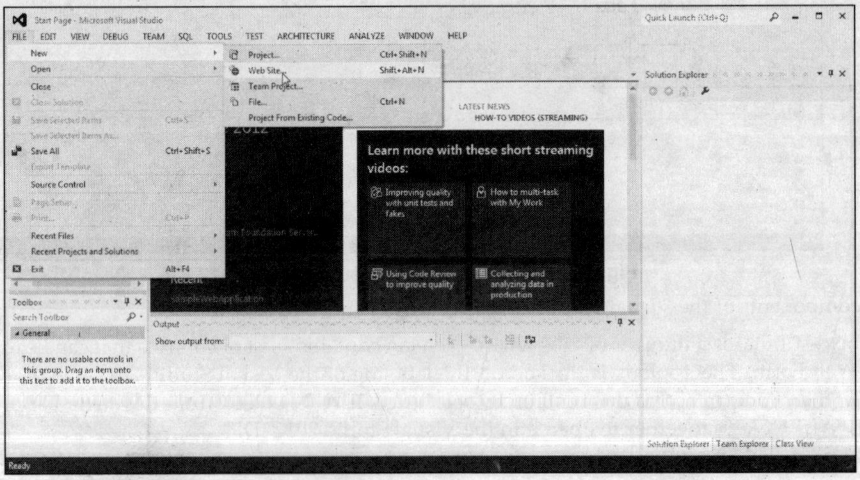

Figure 1.68: Showing the First Step to Create a Web Site

The New Web Site dialog box appears (Figure 1.69).

3. Select the Installed → Templates → Visual C# option from the left pane (Figure 1.69).
4. Select the ASP.NET Web Forms Site option from the middle pane (Figure 1.69).

5. Enter a location and name in the Web location combo box to save the Web site (Figure 1.69).
6. Click the OK button, as shown in Figure 1.69:

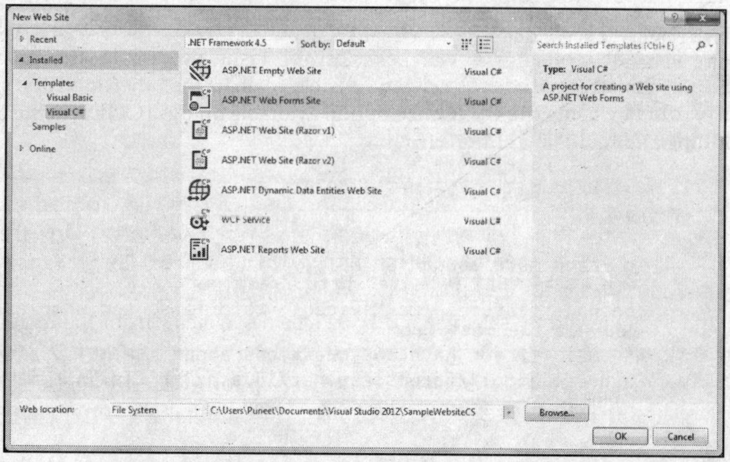

Figure 1.69: Showing the New Web Site Dialog Box

As you can see in Figure 1.69, in ASP.NET 4.5 allows you to create either the empty projects or the projects where some common layouts and functionalities are included. This implies that in the New Web Site dialog box, two new options are also available, which are as follows:

- **ASP.NET Web Site**—Creates a new Web site, which includes the following components:
  - Different folders that contain the membership pages, images, client script files, and .css files
  - A data folder
  - A master page file
  - Three Web pages: Default.aspx ,About.aspx, and Contact.aspx
  - A global application file, Global.asax
  - A Web.config file
- **ASP.NET Empty Web Site**—Creates a new Web site that includes only the Web.config file and no other file or folder. You need to manually add pages, files, and folders required to create a simple Web site.
- **ASP.NET Web Site (Razor v1) & ASP.NET Web Site (Razor v2)**—Helps to create sites using Microsoft's Web Pages framework.

After you click the OK button, the Default.aspx file opens in Visual Studio 2012 IDE, as shown in Figure 1.70:

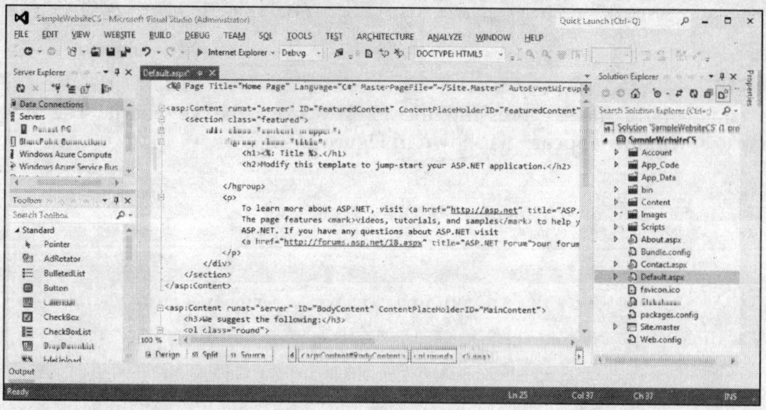

Figure 1.70: Showing the Default.aspx File in the Visual Studio 2012 IDE

Replace the code for the Default.aspx page with the highlighted code given in Listing 1.1:

Listing 1.1: Showing the Code for the `Default.aspx` Page

```
<%@ Page Title="Home Page" Language="C#" MasterPageFile="~/Site.Master"
  AutoEventWireup="true" CodeFile="Default.aspx.cs" Inherits="_Default" %>
<asp:Content runat="server" ID="FeaturedContent" ContentPlaceHolderID="FeaturedContent">
    <section class="featured">
        <div class="content-wrapper">
            <hgroup class="title">
                <h1><%: Page.Title %>.</h1>
                <h2>Welcome to ASP.NET 4.5</h2>
            </hgroup>
            <p>
                To learn more about ASP.NET, visit <a href="http://asp.net"
                 title="ASP.NET Website">http://asp.net</a>.
                The page features <mark>videos, tutorials, and samples</mark> to help
                 you get the most from
                ASP.NET. If you have any questions about ASP.NET visit
                <a href="http://forums.asp.net/18.aspx" title="ASP.NET Forum">our
                 forums</a>.
            </p>
        </div>
    </section>
</asp:Content>
<asp:Content runat="server" ID="BodyContent" ContentPlaceHolderID="MainContent">
    <h3>We suggest the following:</h3>
    <ol class="round">
        <li class="one">
            <h5>Getting Started</h5>
            ASP.NET Web Forms lets you build dynamic websites using a familiar drag-and-
                drop, event-driven model.A design surface and hundreds of controls and
                components let you rapidly build sophisticated, powerful UI-driven
                sites with data access.<a
                href="http://go.microsoft.com/fwlink/?LinkId=245146">Learn
                more…</a></li>
        <li class="two">
            <h5>Add NuGet packages and jump start your coding</h5>
            NuGet makes it easy to install and update free libraries and tools.<a
                href="http://go.microsoft.com/fwlink/?LinkId=245147">Learn
                more…</a></li>
        <li class="three">
            <h5>Find Web Hosting</h5>
            You can easily find a web hosting company that offers the right mix of
                features and price for your applications.<a
                href="http://go.microsoft.com/fwlink/?LinkId=245143">Learn
                more…</a></li>
    </ol>
</asp:Content>
```

7. Open the code-behind file by pressing the F7 key from the keyboard. The default code-behind file (Default.aspx.cs) window appears, as shown in Figure 1.71:

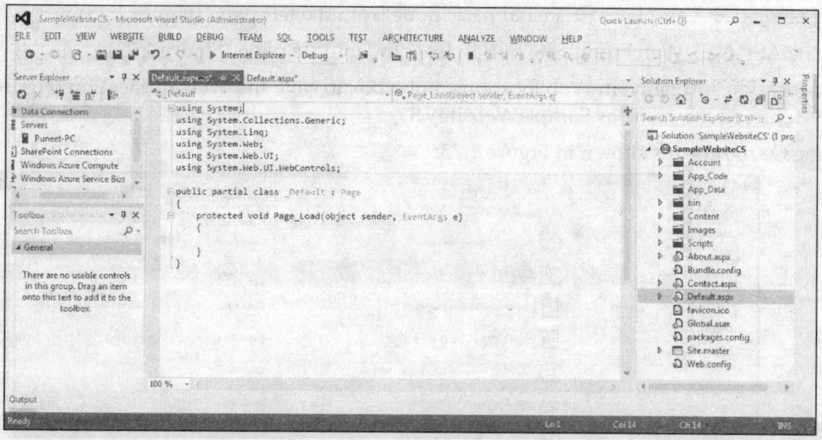

Figure 1.71: Showing the Code-Behind File of the Default.aspx Page

8. Add the highlighted code, shown in Listing 1.2, in the code-behind file of the Default.aspx page:

Listing 1.2: Showing the Code for the Code-Behind File of the Default.aspx Page

```
using System;
using System.Collections.Generic;
using System.Linq;
using System.Web;
using System.Web.UI;
using System.Web.UI.WebControls;
public partial class _Default : System.Web.UI.Page
{
    protected void Page_Load(object sender, EventArgs e)
    {
        Response.Write("Hello World!");
    }
}
```

9. Press the F5 key from the keyboard to get the output, as shown in Figure 1.72:

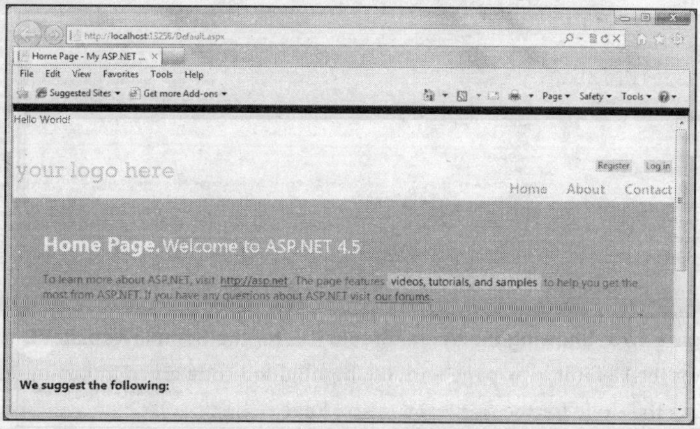

Figure 1.72: Showing the Output of the SampleWebsiteCS Application

In Visual Basic (VB), you can perform the same function for creating an ASP.NET Web site with the help of the following steps:

1. Open Visual Studio 2012.
2. Select the FILE→New→Web Site option from the menu bar. The New Web Site dialog box appears (Figure 1.73).

3. Select Installed → Templates → Visual Basic node from the left pane (Figure 1.73).
4. Select the ASP.NET Web Forms Site option from the middle pane (Figure 1.73).
5. Enter a location and name in Web location combo box to save the Web application (Figure 1.73). In our case, we have entered the name as SampleWebsiteVB.
6. Click the OK button, as shown in Figure 1.73:

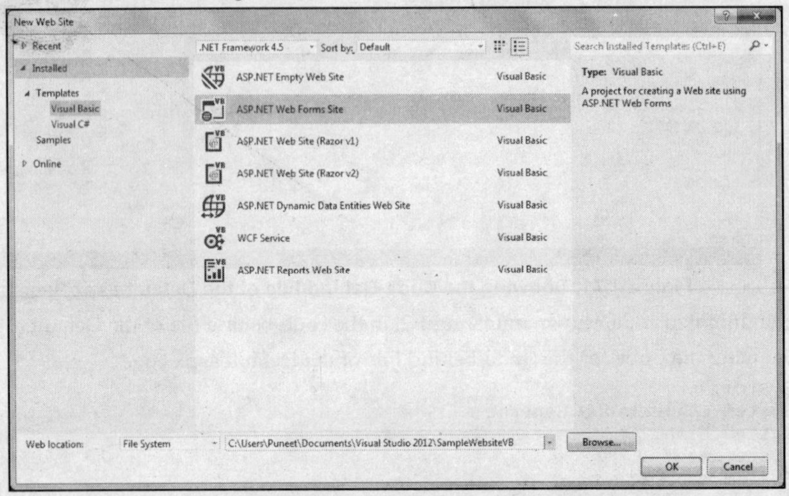

Figure 1.73: Showing the New Web Site Dialog Box

The Visual Studio 2012 IDE with the Default.aspx file appears, as shown in Figure 1.73:

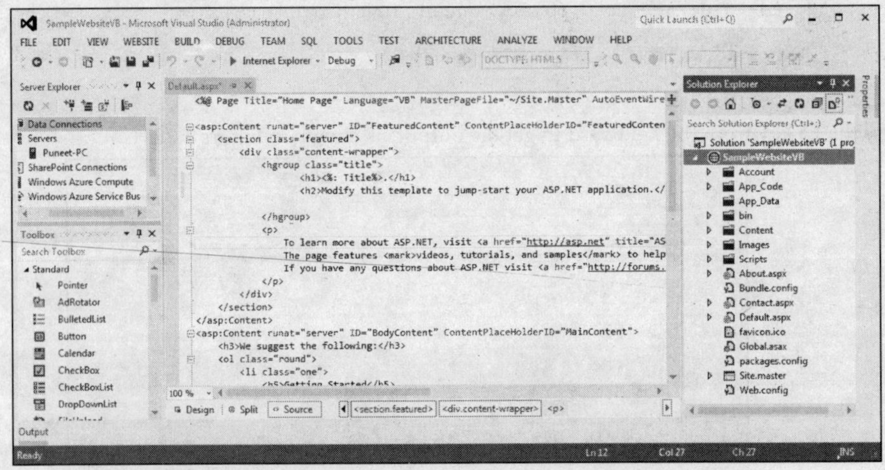

Figure 1.73: Showing the Visual Studio IDE for the SampleWebsiteVB Application

Replace the code for the Default.aspx page with the highlighted code given in Listing 1.3:

Listing 1.3: Showing the Code for the `Default.aspx` Page

```
<%@ Page Title="Home Page" Language="VB" MasterPageFile="~/Site.Master"
  AutoEventWireup="true" CodeFile="Default.aspx.vb" Inherits="_Default" %>
<asp:Content runat="server" ID="FeaturedContent" ContentPlaceHolderID="FeaturedContent">
    <section class="featured">
        <div class="content-wrapper">
            <hgroup class="title">
                <h1><%: Page.Title %>.</h1>
```

```
                <h2>Welcome to ASP.NET 4.5</h2>
            </hgroup>
            <p>
                To learn more about ASP.NET, visit <a href="http://asp.net"
                 title="ASP.NET Website">http://asp.net</a>. The page features
                 <mark>videos, tutorials, and samples</mark>to help you get the most
                 from ASP.NET. If you have any questions about ASP.NET visit <a
                 href="http://forums.asp.net/18.aspx" title="ASP.NET Forum">our
                 forums</a>.
            </p>
        </div>
    </section>
</asp:Content>
<asp:Content runat="server" ID="BodyContent" ContentPlaceHolderID="MainContent">
    <h3>We suggest the following:</h3>
    <ol class="round">
        <li class="one">
            <h5>Getting Started</h5>
            ASP.NET Web Forms lets you build dynamic websites using a familiar drag-and-
                drop, event-driven model.A design surface and hundreds of controls and
                components let you rapidly build sophisticated, powerful UI-driven
                sites with data access.<a
                href="http://go.microsoft.com/fwlink/?LinkId=245146">Learn
                more…</a></li>
        <li class="two">
            <h5>Add NuGet packages and jump start your coding</h5>
            NuGet makes it easy to install and update free libraries and tools.<a
                href="http://go.microsoft.com/fwlink/?LinkId=245147">Learn
                more…</a></li>
        <li class="three">
            <h5>Find Web Hosting</h5>
            You can easily find a web hosting company that offers the right mix of
                features and price for your applications.<a
                href="http://go.microsoft.com/fwlink/?LinkId=245143">Learn
                more…</a></li>
    </ol>
</asp:Content>
```

7. Open the code-behind file by pressing the F7 key from the keyboard. The default code-behind file (Default.aspx.vb) window appears, as shown in Figure 1.74:

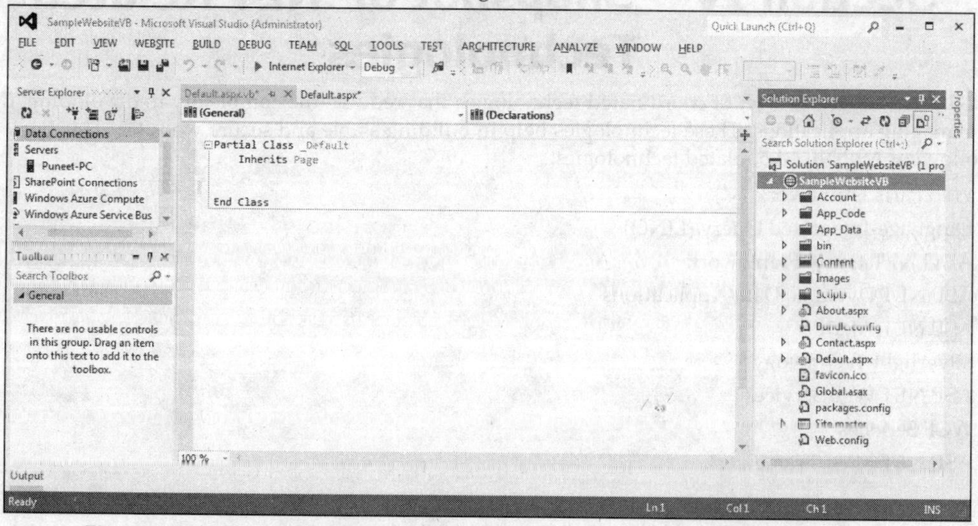

Figure 1.74: Showing the Code-Behind File for the SampleWebsiteVB Application

8. Add the code in the code-behind file of the Default.aspx page, as shown in Listing 1.4:

Listing 1.4: Showing the Code for the Code-Behind File of the Default.aspx Page

```
Partial Class _Default
    Inherits Page
    Protected Sub Page_Load(sender As Object, e As EventArgs) Handles Me.Load
        Response.Write("Hello World!")
    End Sub
End Class
```

9. Press the F5 key from the keyboard to get the output, as shown in Figure 1.75:

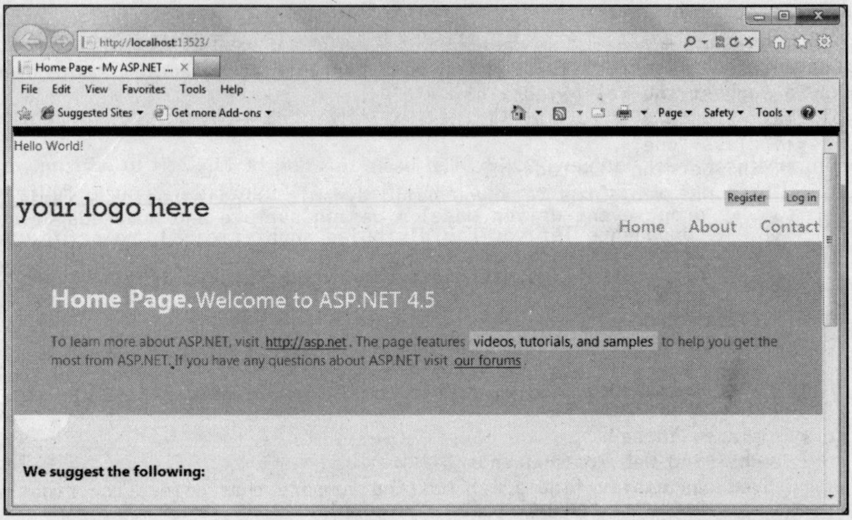

Figure 1.75: Showing the Output of the SampleWebsiteVB Application

From Figure 1.72 and Figure 1.75, it is clear that the output remains the same whether the Web application is developed using C# or VB.

Section IV – Snapshot of .NET Related Technologies

ASP.NET 4.5 integrates a set of coordinated technologies that reduces the complexity in developing, deploying, and managing applications. These technologies help in building stable and secure websites. This book discusses the following ASP.NET 4.5 related technologies:

- Web Parts Framework
- Language-Integrated Query (LINQ)
- ADO.NET Entity Framework
- ASP.NET Dynamic Data Applications
- ASP.NET AJAX
- Silverlight Technology
- ASP.NET Web Services
- WCF Services
- ASP.NET MVC Framework

Web Parts Framework

The Web Parts Framework provides an environment to create Web pages that can be customized according to the requirement of the user. Nowadays, websites have become quite comprehensive as they incorporate a plethora of functionalities for the user. In such situations, there arises a need for a Framework that provides the user with the functionality to display and work with only required parts of a Web page. For example, if you visit a Web page regularly to get the local weather report, then it would be cumbersome for the user to click two or three hyperlinks to display the required information every time. As an alternative, if the Web page supports some sort of personalization mechanism that enables the user to permanently display the local weather report on the home page, then the user's precious time can be saved.

Chapter 15, *Inside Web Parts Framework*, discusses the concept that is used in Web applications to provide the users with the liberty of modifying a Web page as per their needs.

LINQ

LINQ is a component of .NET Framework 4.5. The basic function of LINQ is to add native data-querying capabilities to .NET Framework by using syntax similar to SQL. LINQ allows you to define statements that interrogate a data source to yield a requested result set. In addition, it allows you to obtain and manipulate the data in a consistent manner.

Chapter 9, *LINQ Queries*, discusses the basic LINQ queries and the query operators used to query data from data source. You also learn to retrieve the data from LINQ to Object, LINQ to ADO.NET, and LINQ to XML data sources.

ADO.NET Entity Framework

ADO.NET Entity Framework is designed to support data-centric applications and services, and provides a platform for programming against data that raises the level of abstraction from the logical relational level to the conceptual level.

Chapter 10, *ADO.NET Entity Framework*, discusses features and components supported by Entity Framework, such as Entity Data Model, Object Services, Entity SQL, Client provider, and mapping between conceptual and storage schema.

ASP.NET Dynamic Data Applications

ASP.NET Dynamic Data is a Framework that enables you to easily build the data-driven Web applications based on Entity Framework data model or LINQ to SQL data model. A data model is used to represent the information about the items in a database. In addition, it depicts the relation between these items of the database. ASP.NET Dynamic Data is used to create data-driven Web applications with very less code but complete functionality.

Chapter 12, *Building ASP.NET Dynamic Data Applications*, discusses the data model, dynamic data page templates, and dynamic data field templates.

ASP.NET AJAX

ASP.NET AJAX is a new approach that works on the concept of **Page Update** rather than **Page Replacement.** It provides two ways to developers to build rich server-centric and client-centric Web applications. The server-centric development approach enables a part of the Web page to be refreshed without posting the entire page to the server. This is done by using the UpdatePanel server control. The client-centric approach allows developers to use control extenders to add pre-defined client-side behavior to the new and existing ASP.NET controls. The extenders use a block of JavaScript code to add new and enhanced capabilities to ASP.NET.

Chapter 13, *Developing ASP.NET AJAX Applications*, discusses ASP.NET AJAX along with its components and ASP.NET technology that uses the AJAX approach for Web development.

Chapter 3(online resources), *ASP.NET AJAX Control Toolkit*, discusses the use of sample extenders through a separate download – AJAX Control Toolkit (ACT).

Silverlight Technology

Silverlight is a Web-based technology that allows Web designers and developers to integrate rich user interface of desktop applications and the transparency of other Web languages, such as HTML and JavaScript. Silverlight allows you to develop Web applications that contain high-fidelity multimedia content and eye-catching visual effects. Web designers and developers have already embraced Silverlight for building high-quality interactive Web applications.

Chapter 4(online resources), *Developing Rich-Interactive Applications with Silverlight 5*, discusses the main features and the architecture of Silverlight.

ASP.NET Web Services

A Web service is an entity that can be programmed to provide a particular functionality to any number of applications over the Internet. The functionality provided by the Web service can be used by any application, irrespective of the programming language in which the application is created or the hardware platform and operating system on which the application is running. A Web service does not have any user interface. It just provides specific services to its consumers.

Chapter 18, *ASP.NET Web Services*, discusses how to create and deploy a Web service.

The WCF Services

WCF is a set of .NET technologies that is used to develop and deploy services on Windows. It acts as a platform for creating and distributing connected applications. In addition, it provides a unified Framework for rapidly building service-oriented applications.

Chapter 19, *WCF Services*, discusses the layered architecture and features of WCF. This chapter also covers the important aspects of addresses, bindings, contracts, hosting, and security with WCF.

ASP.NET MVC Framework

In ASP.NET MVC Framework is an architectural pattern that is generally used in software engineering. ASP.NET MVC Framework is not a substitute for the ASP.NET Web forms pattern. It just provides an alternative choice to the developer, when designing and developing a Web application. ASP.NET MVC Framework is a lightweight, extremely testable presentation Framework that is incorporated in ASP.NET features, such as master pages and membership-based authentication.

Chapter 20, *ASP.NET MVC Framework*, discusses the features of the MVC applications, Controller class, URL routing, and MVC templates.

Summary

This chapter has been divided into four sections. Section I discusses the evolution of .NET—explaining the benefits, architecture, and components of .NET Framework. Section II discusses the Visual Studio 2012 IDE and the new features in Visual Studio 2012. Section III of the chapter focuses on creating sample Web applications and sample websites. Section III also provides you with an overview of ASP.NET, new features in ASP.NET 4.5, ASP.NET technologies, and ASP.NET life cycle. Section IV provides an overview of .NET-related technologies covered in this book and also discusses the need for each of these technologies.

2

Developing a Web Application

Earlier, we used to work only on desktop applications that were accessible to a single computer. Desktop applications can be installed on all the computers but not hosted on the Internet. Web applications came into existence to overcome these shortcomings. A Web application refers to an application, which always accessed through a Web browser, such as Internet Explorer or Mozilla Firefox. Now-a-days, the usage of Internet for business has gained immense popularity due to various features and benefits, such as the ease of making transactions from home or office. Therefore, it becomes quite crucial for businesses to make their presence felt over the Internet so that the services provided by them can be easily accessed by their respective customers. These Web applications help the companies in reaching out to prospective clients and conducting businesses online. A very good example of such a scenario is an online shopping website, where you can perform transactions related to buying or selling a product. Another feature that makes Web applications more popular is the convenience of updating and maintaining the application on a single server.

In this chapter, you learn about the basic concepts required to create a Web application, such as specifying a location for a Web application, file types, Web pages, and the coding models used in ASP.NET 4.5. You also get acquainted with the page directives, server controls, and provider model used to create a simple ASP.NET 4.5 application. In addition, you explore how to implement code sharing and simple and dynamic compilation of a Web application in ASP.NET 4.5.

Let's first learn to specify a location for a Web application.

Specifying a Location for a Web Application

After a Web application is developed, it needs to be stored in a particular location in a network. After that, we can open the application from that location and work on it. Visual Studio allows you to create a Web application with a virtual directory mapped to the Internet Information Services (IIS) server or a stand-alone application outside the boundaries of the IIS server. Visual Studio 2012 allows you to store Web applications in the following three locations:

- File System
- HyperText Transfer Protocol (HTTP)
- File Transfer Protocol (FTP)

File System

Visual Studio allows you to keep the files of a Web application or website in a folder in the local hard drive or shared location on the local area network. These websites, known as File System websites, are not associated with any IIS application, unless you create an Internet Information Service (IIS) virtual directory. You can run these websites by using the built-in Web server, which is executed at the runtime. The built-in Web server allows you to run Web applications, even if the IIS server is not configured on your system. You can also verify the existence of the built-in Web Server by selecting the New→Web Site option in the Visual Studio Integrated Development Environment (IDE). In Windows 7, the default location for your Web applications is `C:\Users\Puneet\Documents\Visual Studio 2012\Projects`, as shown in Figure 2.1:

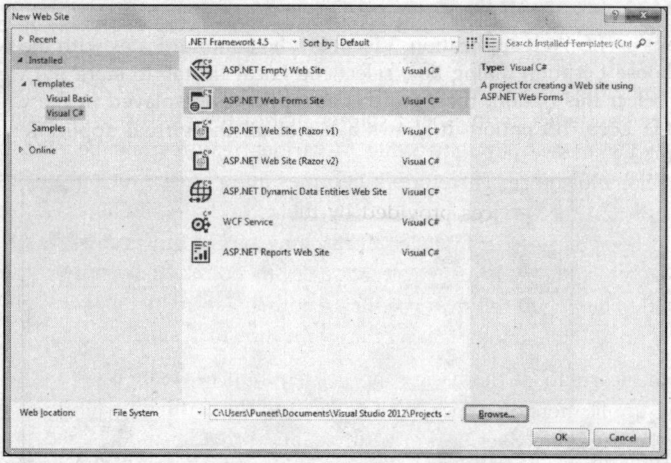

Figure 2.1: Default Path of a Website

NOTE

In this case, Puneet is the Windows user name. You should note that Windows user name varies from system to system.

However, you can also store your Web application at any other location. When you are using a Web server, the location of your Web application is not constrained to any particular folder.

NOTE

You can change the default path of the Web application according to the need of your project by clicking the Browse button. The Choose Location dialog box appears, with the File System tab selected, as shown in Figure 2.2:

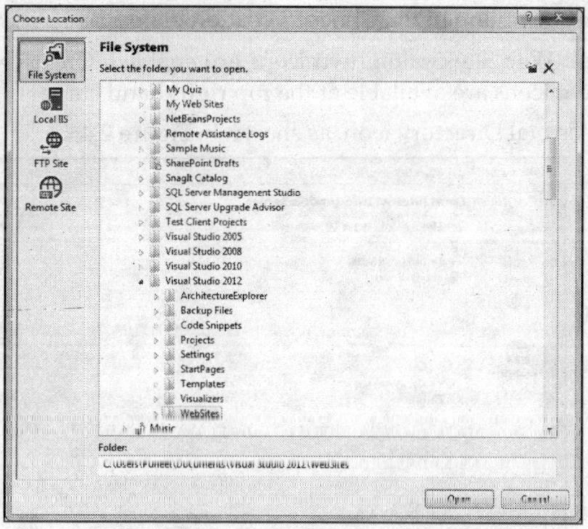

Figure 2.2: Selecting a Different Location

HTTP

Visual Studio allows you to develop and store your Web application on the IIS server through the HTTP option. This option can also be used to develop and store your Web application on the following servers:

- Local IIS Server
- Remote IIS Server

Local IIS Server

A local IIS website is an IIS Web application. Visual Studio communicates with the website by using the HTTP protocol. In the Choose Location dialog box, select the Local IIS tab to store the website files on the local IIS server. When you select this option, the `IIS Sites` option is displayed in the Choose Location dialog box. When you select the Local IIS option, it shows a list of all the virtual application roots on your system, as displayed in Figure 2.3:

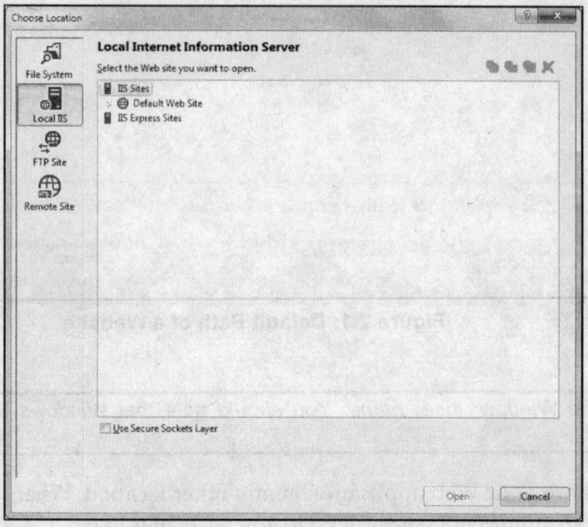

Figure 2.3: Local IIS Option Selected

You can also create a new virtual directory for your Web applications. Let's perform the following steps to create a new virtual directory for your Web application:

1. Select the Local IIS tab in the Choose Location dialog box (Figure 2.4).
2. Select the Default Web Site option in the Choose Location dialog box (Figure 2.4).

When you select the Default Web Site option, two icons are enabled: Create New Web Application and Create New Virtual Directory. These icons are available at the top right-hand corner of the Choose Location dialog box.

3. Click the Create New Virtual Directory icon, as shown in Figure 2.4:

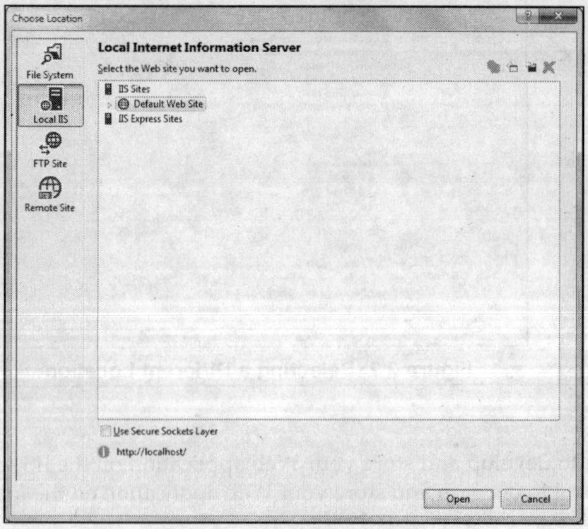

Figure 2.4: Selecting Option to Create Virtual Directory

The New Virtual Directory dialog box opens, as shown in Figure 2.5.

4. Enter a name for the new virtual directory in the Alias name text box (Figure 2.5).
5. Enter a location, where you want to save the new virtual directory in the Folder text box (Figure 2.5).
6. Click the OK button, as shown in Figure 2.5:

Figure 2.5: Providing Name and Location of the New Virtual Directory

The new virtual directory is added to the location provided by the Choose Location dialog box (Figure 2.6).

7. Click the Open button in the Choose Location dialog box, as shown in Figure 2.6:

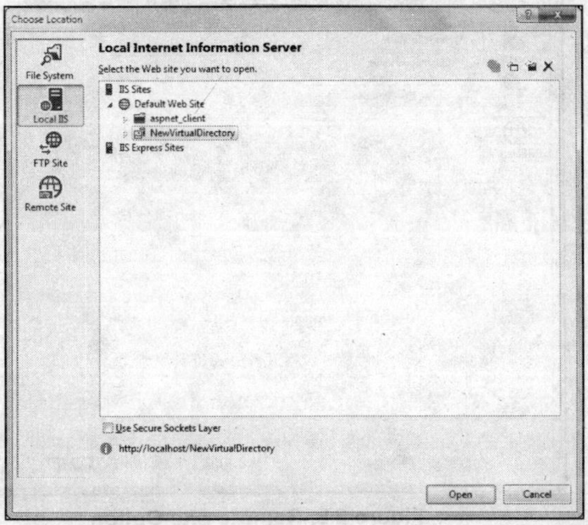

Figure 2.6: Displaying the NewVirtualDirectory Directory

The new directory is selected in the New Web Site dialog box (in the text box beside the Browse button), as shown in Figure 2.7:

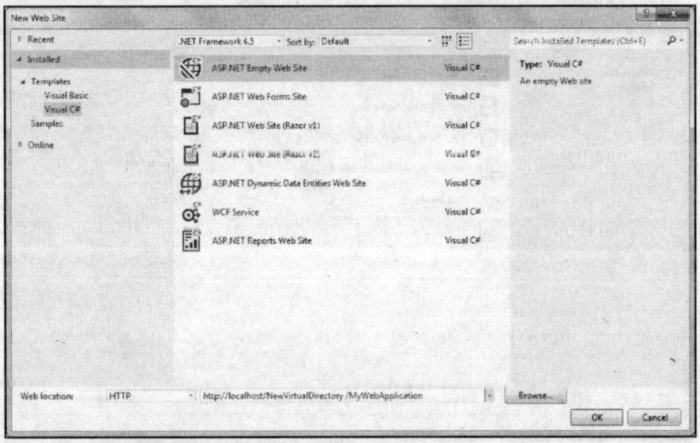

Figure 2.7: NewVirtualDirectory Selected in New Web Site Dialog Box

8. Click the OK button in the New Web Site dialog box to create a new Web application (Figure 2.7).

When you invoke your Web application, the URL `http://localhost/NewVirtualDirectory/Default.aspx` appears which shows that the Web application is using the IIS server.

Remote IIS Server

The Remote Site option stores files on a remote server that is accessible over a local network. A remote IIS website is an IIS Web application linked with a copy of the IIS server that is running on another computer. Visual Studio uses the HTTP protocol to host the remote website on the remote IIS server (the server that is running on another computer). You can store Web applications on a remote server by performing the following steps:

1. Select the Remote Site tab in the Choose Location dialog box (Figure 2.8).
2. Enter the location of website in the Web site location text box (Figure 2.8).
3. Click the Open button, as shown in Figure 2.8:

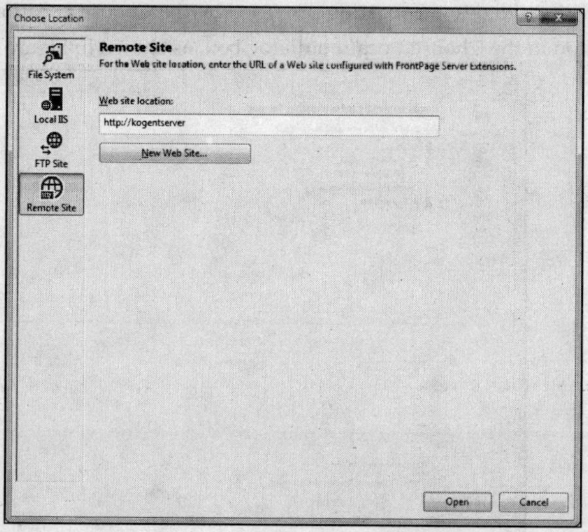

Figure 2.8: Remote Site Option

The remote server location is added to the New Web Site dialog box (in the text box besides the Browse button), as shown in Figure 2.9:

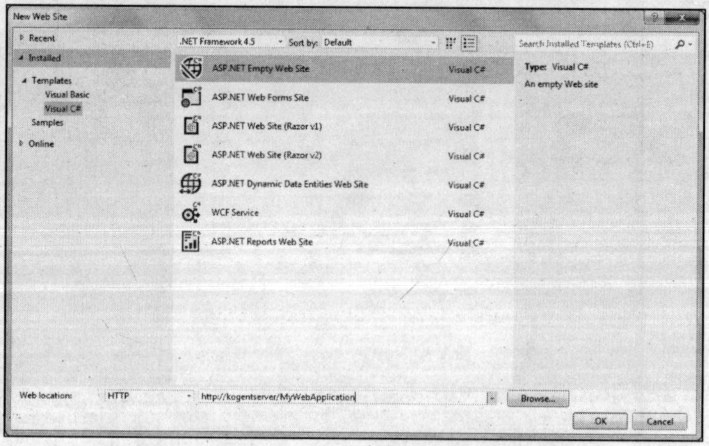

Figure 2.9: Remote Site Using HTTP Location

FTP

FTP enables you to not only store but also code your applications, which reside on a server. For that, you must have the credentials to attach to the FTP server and permissions to read and write to the FTP location. You can also use the FTP features, such as exchanging and manipulating files over any Transmission Control Protocol (TCP) based computer network, to work on different locations within the same server. You have to provide information regarding Server name, Port to use, Directory, and other credentials, if required, to create your application on the remote server using FTP, as shown in Figure 2.10:

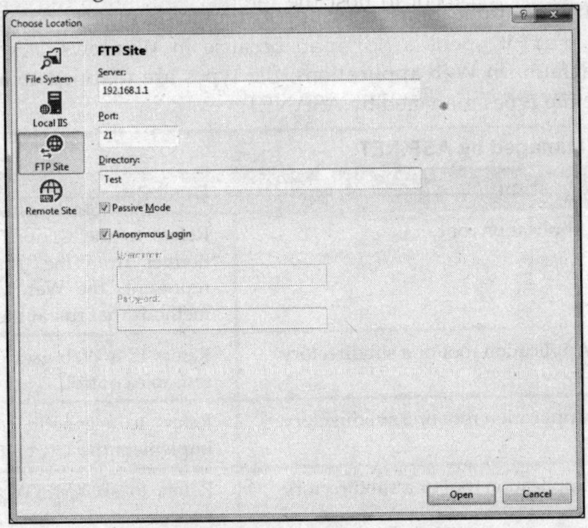

Figure 2.10: FTP Site Option

If you provide the correct information, Visual Studio accesses the remote server and creates the appropriate files required for your application, as shown in Figure 2.11:

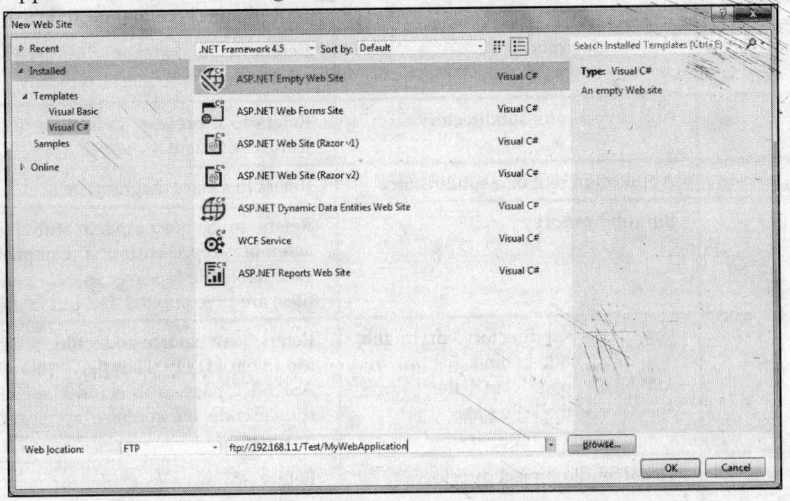

Figure 2.11: FTP Site Option Using FTP Location

NOTE

While creating an ASP.NET website on FTP location, you need to ensure that the virtual directory on FTP server is mapped to virtual directory on IIS web server.

After understanding the various options to store Web applications (websites) at different locations, let's understand the file types supported by ASP.NET 4.5.

File Types in ASP.NET 4.5

Web applications contain numerous file types, which is supported and managed by either the ASP.NET 4.5 or the IIS server. Most of the ASP.NET 4.5 file types can be automatically generated using the Add New Item dialog box in Visual Studio 2012.

File types are mapped to Web applications using application mappings. For example, if you double-click a `.txt` file in `Windows Explorer`, it opens a `Notepad` because in Windows `.txt` file types are mapped to the `Notepad.exe` file by default. In Web applications, file types are mapped to application extensions in the IIS server. Table 2.1 lists the file types managed by ASP.NET:

Table 2.1: File Types Managed by ASP.NET

File Type	Location	Description
`.asax`	Application root	Refers to the `Global.asax` file containing code that derives from the `HttpApplication` class. This file represents the Web application and contains optional methods that run at the start or end of the application.
`.ascx`	Application root or a subdirectory	Refers to a Web user control file that defines a custom, reusable control.
`.ashx`	Application root or a subdirectory	Refers to a generic handler file that contains code to implement the `IHttpHandler` interface.
`.asmx`	Application root or a subdirectory	Refers to an XML Web services file containing classes and methods that are available to other Web applications through Simple Object Access Protocol (SOAP).
`.aspx`	Application root or a subdirectory	Refers to an ASP.NET Web forms containing Web controls and presentation and business logic.
`.axd`	Application root	Refers to a handler file used to manage website administration requests, typically `Trace.axd`.
`.browser`	`App_Browsers` subdirectory	Refers to a browser definition file used to identify the features of client browsers.
`.cd`	Application root or a subdirectory	Refers to a class diagram file.
`.compile`	Bin subdirectory	Refers to a precompiled stub file that points to an assembly representing a compiled website file. The executable file types (`.aspx, ascx, .master`, theme files) are precompiled and put in the Bin subdirectory.
`.cs, .js, .vb`	`App_Code` subdirectory, or in the case of a code-behind file for an ASP.NET page, in the same directory as the Web page	Refers to a source-code file, which can be an HTTP Module, HTTP Handler, code-behind file for an ASP.NET page, or a stand-alone class. In other words, source code file contains application logic compiled at runtime.
`.csproj`, `.vbproj`, `.vjsproj`	Visual Studio project directory	Refers to a project file for a Visual Studio client-application project.
`.disco`, `.vsdisco`	`App_WebReferences` subdirectory	Refers to an XML Web services discovery file, which is used to help in locating available Web services.

Table 2.1: File Types Managed by ASP.NET

File Type	Location	Description
.dsdgm, .dsprototype	Application root or a subdirectory	Refers to a distributed service diagram file that can be added to any Visual Studio solution. It provides or consumes Web services so that the architectural view of the Web service interactions can be analyzed to build a copy of the solution or improve the existing solution.
.dll	Bin subdirectory	Refers to a compiled class library file (assembly). Instead of placing compiled assemblies in the Bin subdirectory, you can put source code for classes in the App_Code subdirectory.
.licx, .webinfo	Application root or a subdirectory	Refers to a license file. Licensing helps authors protect intellectual property by checking whether the user is authorized to use the property or not.
.master	Application root or subdirectory	Refers to a master page that defines the layout for other Web pages in a Web application.
.mdb, .ldb	App_Data subdirectory	Refers to an Access database file.
.mdf	App_Data subdirectory	Refers to an SQL database file to use with SQL Server Express.
.msgx, .svc	Application root or a subdirectory	Refers to an WCF Messaging Framework (MFx) service file. The MFx service file helps in providing direct access to ports, messages, channels, and services
.rem	Application root or a subdirectory	Refers to a handler file, which implements remoting in Web applications.
.resources, .resx	App_GlobalResources or App_LocalResources subdirectory	Refers to a resource file containing resource strings that refer to images, localizable text, or other data.
.sdm, .sdmDocument	Application root or a subdirectory	Refers to a system definition model file.
.sitemap	Application root	Refers to a site-map file containing the structure of the website. ASP.NET comes with a default site-map provider that uses site-map files to easily display a navigational control in a Web page.
.skin	App_Themes subdirectory	Refers to a skin file containing property settings to apply to Web controls for consistent formatting.
.sln	Visual Web Developer Studio project directory	Refers to a solution file for a Visual Web Developer Studio project.
.soap	Application root or a subdirectory	Refers to a SOAP extension file.

NOTE

File types that are managed by ASP.NET are mapped to the aspnet_isapi.dll handler in the IIS server.

Table 2.2 lists the file types managed by the IIS server:

Table 2.2: File Types Managed by the IIS server

File Type	Location	Description
.asa	Application root	Refers to a Global.asa file containing optional methods that run at the start or end of the ASP session or application lifetime
.cdx	App_Data subdirectory	Refers to a compound index file structure, in which one file structure is able to track all the tags in the file
.cer	Application root or a subdirectory	Refers to a certificate file used to authenticate a website
.idc	Application root or a subdirectory	Refers to a Internet Database Connector file mapped to httpodbc.dll
.shtm, .shtml, .stm	Application root or a subdirectory	Refers to an HTML File Containing Server Side Directives, which is mapped to ssinc.dll

Now, let's move on to explore ASP.NET 4.5 Web pages, which are required to create such applications.

Exploring ASP.NET 4.5 Web Pages

ASP.NET 4.5 Web pages are files with the .aspx extension and contain the code to implement a Web application. Now, the question is where are these pages stored? Well, these Web pages are stored on the IIS virtual directory. When a client request is received by the IIS server, the requested page is searched for and information is sent back in a Response object to render the HTML markup on to the client browser. The rendered HTML markup defines everything about a Web page, including its content, layout, and appearance.

Generally, a Web application developed in any programming language is first compiled and then converted into its intermediate code. This code is also known as Microsoft Intermediate Language (MSIL) code. The process of first compiling and then converting the code into MSIL is applicable for an ASP.NET Web application. This ASP.NET intermediate code is processor-independent and obtained by compiling the source code written in any .NET compatible language. Some of the .NET compatible languages for ASP.NET applications are Visual Basic (VB), C#, and F#.

When the request for a Web page is received for the first time, its corresponding .aspx file is compiled to generate the class file. After that, the class file is used to process the request. However, when a request for the same Web page is received subsequently, its class file is referenced directly to process the request. This enhances the performance and reduces the response time of processing a request.

The code used to develop an ASP.NET Web page is similar to the code used in an HTML file. For instance, the code in Listing 2.1 shows a simple ASP.NET Web page displaying a welcome page on the browser. You need to first create an application, WelcomePageVB for VB and WelcomePageCS for C# to display a welcome page on the browser. You have already learned to create an application in *Chapter 1: ASP.NET 4.5 Essentials* of the book.

NOTE

The applications in this chapter are created by selecting the ASP.NET Empty Web Site template in the New Web Site dialog box. After creating the application, you need to add a Default.aspx file, by performing the following steps:

Right-click the project name in the Solution Explorer and Select the Add→Add New Item dialog box. In our case, the project name is WelcomePageCS, as shown in Figure 2.12:

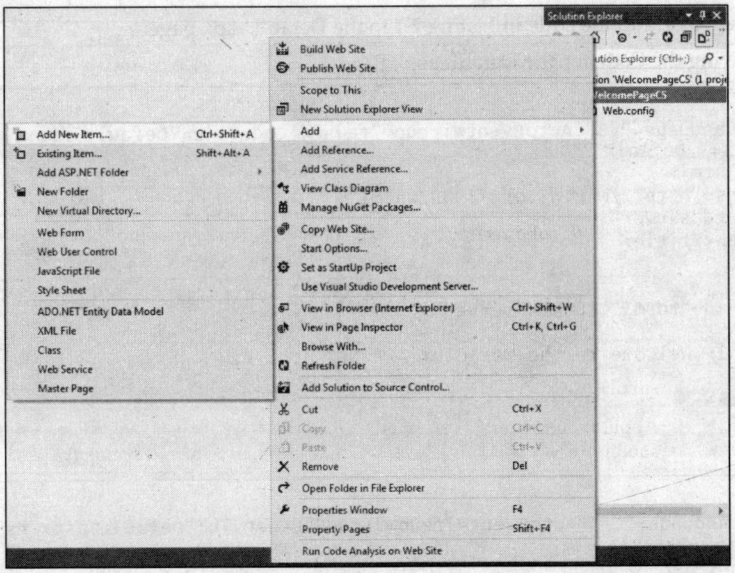

Figure 2.12: Adding New Item

NOTE

The Add New Item dialog box appears, as shown in Figure 2.13

1. *Select Web Form from the middle pane, as shown in Figure 2.13.*
2. *Enter a name for the Web form in the name text box, as shown in Figure 2.13. In this case, we are providing the default name Default.aspx.*
3. *Click the Add button, as shown in Figure 2.13:*

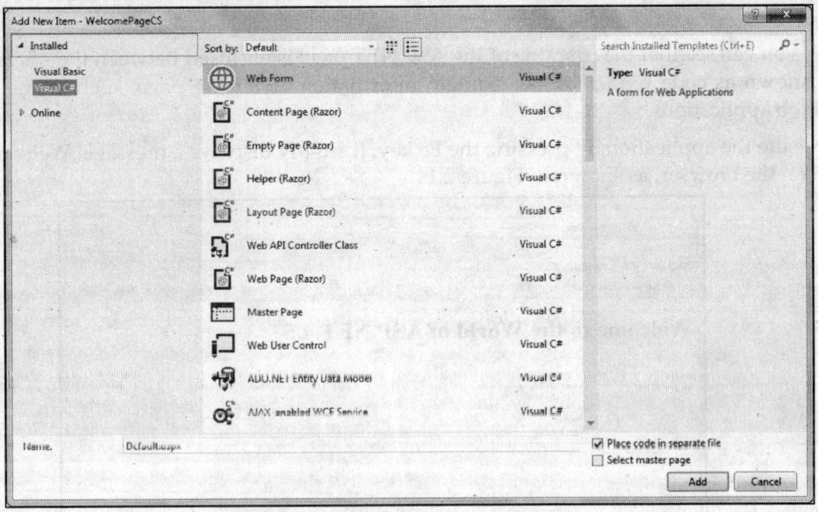

Figure 2.13: Adding Default.aspx File

This adds the Default.aspx file to your WelcomePageCS application.

After creating the page, add the code in Listing 2.1 to the Default.aspx page:

Listing 2.1: Showing the Code for the Default.aspx Page

In VB

```
<%@ Page Language="VB" AutoEventWireup="false" CodeFile="Default.aspx.vb"
  Inherits="_Default" %>
<!DOCTYPE html>
<html xmlns="http://www.w3.org/1999/xhtml">
<head runat="server">
    <title></title>
</head>
<body>
    <form id="form1" runat="server">
    <div>
        <h1> Welcome to the World of ASP.NET 4.5</h1>
    </div>
    </form>
</body>
</html>
```

In C#

```
<%@ Page Language="C#" AutoEventWireup="true" CodeFile="Default.aspx.cs"
  Inherits="_Default" %>
<!DOCTYPE html>
<html xmlns="http://www.w3.org/1999/xhtml">
<head runat="server">
    <title></title>
</head>
<body>
    <form id="form1" runat="server">
    <div>
        <h1> Welcome to the World of ASP.NET 4.5</h1>
    </div>
    </form>
</body>
</html>
```

In Listing 2.1, you can see that the first line of the ASP.NET page is enclosed between the <% and %> tags. These blocks, also known as code render blocks, contain information about the page, such as the language used in developing Web applications.

Now, let's execute the application by pressing the F5 key. It simply displays a message, Welcome to the World of ASP.NET 4.5 on the browser, as shown in Figure 2.14:

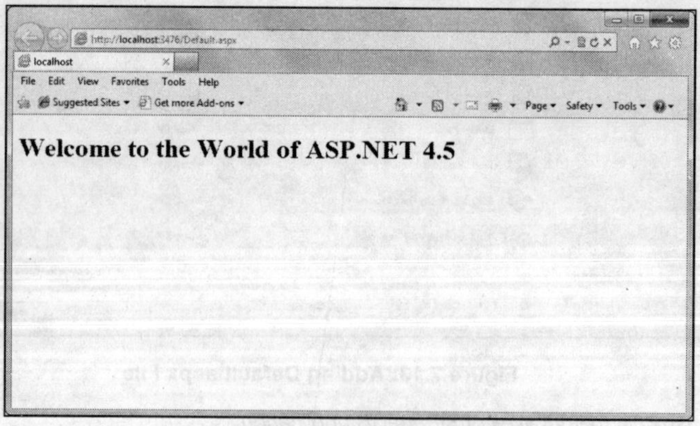

Figure 2.14: The Welcome Page

Now, let's learn about the code render blocks in detail.

Code Render Blocks

Code render blocks define the inline code or inline expressions that are executed when a Web page is rendered. This inline code is then executed by the server and the output is displayed on the client browser that is requested for the page. The code render blocks are capable of displaying information on the client browser without calling the `Write` method. The code render blocks are represented on a page by the `<% and %>` symbols. The code present inside these symbols is executed in the top-down manner. Now, let's put the concept of code render blocks into use by creating an application, `CodeRenderBlock`. This application uses a code render block to implement a loop used for changing the text size. This code can be found as CodeRenderBlockVB for VB and CodeRenderBlockCS for C#. You can find the code for the Default.aspx page for code render blocks in Listing 2.2:

Listing 2.2: Showing the Code for the Default.aspx Page

In VB

```
<%@ Page Language="VB" AutoEventWireup="false" CodeFile="Default.aspx.vb"
  Inherits="_Default" %>
<!DOCTYPE html>
<html xmlns="http://www.w3.org/1999/xhtml">
<head runat="server">
    <title></title>
</head>

<body>
    <form id="form1" runat="server">
    <div>
        <% Dim I As Int64 ,
                For I = 0 To 6 Step 1%>
                <font size="<%=I%>"> Welcome to ASP.NET 4.5</font> <br/>
                <% Next %>
    </div>
    </form>
</body>
</html>
```

In C#

```
<%@ Page Language="C#" AutoEventWireup="true" CodeFile="Default.aspx.cs"
  Inherits="_Default" %>
<!DOCTYPE html>
<html xmlns="http://www.w3.org/1999/xhtml">
<head runat="server">
    <title></title>
</head>

<body>
    <form id="form1" runat="server">
    <div>
    <% for (int i = 0; i <= 6; i++)
        { %>
        <div></div>
        <font size="<%=i%>">Welcome to ASP.NET 4.5</font>
        <%} %>
    </div>

    </form>
</body>
</html>
```

Now, let's execute the application by pressing the F5 key. The output is as shown in Figure 2.15:

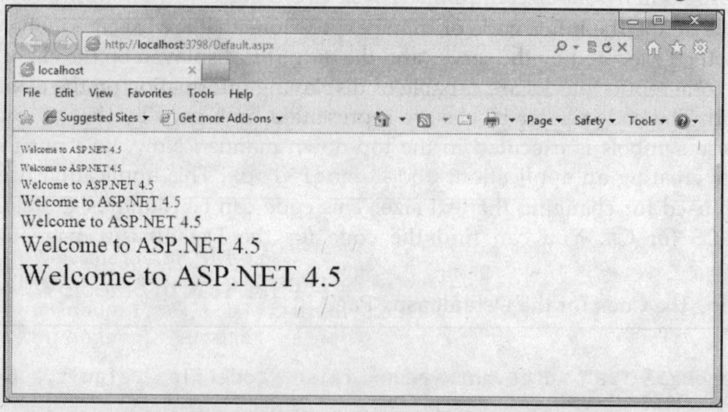

Figure 2.15: Output of CodeRender Application

ASP.NET 4.5 Coding Models

Generally, a Web form consists of controls, such as Label, Button, Hyperlink, and business logic. You can use ASP.NET coding techniques to manage these controls and business logic. ASP.NET 4.5 coding techniques refer to the methodologies used for writing code in a Web application. ASP.NET 4.5 provides two types of coding techniques, `Single-File page model` and `Code-Behind page model`. In the single-file coding approach, developers write code directly in the `.aspx` page of the application. A major drawback of the single-file code model is that writing code in a single file results in difficult-to-read Web pages that mix presentation (HTML) with functionality (code). This drawback is specifically evident while developing complex applications. To deal with the drawback of the single-file page model, ASP.NET has introduced the code-behind page model. In this model, you need to maintain separate code files for each Web page. One file stores the code to implement the functionality of a Web page written in some programming languages, such as VB and C#; and the other file stores the HTML markup of the Web application.

Single-File Page Model

In the single-file page model, the functionality of a Web application and the HTML markup are implemented in the same file. The programming code is in a `script` block that contains the attribute `runat="server"` to mark it as code that ASP.NET should execute. Now, let's understand the single-file page model through an application named as `SingleFileModelExampleVB` in VB and `SingleFileModelExampleCS` in C#. You can find the code for the `Default.aspx` page for the single-file page model in Listing 2.3:

Listing 2.3: Showing the Code for the Default.aspx Page

In VB

```
<%@ Page Language="VB" AutoEventWireup="false" %>
<!DOCTYPE html>
<script runat="server">
  Protected Sub Button1_Click(sender As Object, e As EventArgs)
       Label1.Text = "Clicked at " & DateTime.Now.ToString()
  End Sub
</script>
<html xmlns="http://www.w3.org/1999/xhtml">
<head runat="server">
   <title>Single File Page Model</title>
</head>
<body>
  <form id="form1" runat="server">
  <div>
  <asp:Label ID="Label1"
```

```
            runat="server"></asp:Label>
            <asp:Button ID="Button1"
                    runat="server" Text="Click Me!">
            </asp:Button>
    </div>
    </form>
</body>
</html>
```

In C#

```
<%@ Page Language="C#" AutoEventWireup="true"%>
<!DOCTYPE html>
<script runat="server">
void Button1_Click(Object sender, EventArgs e)
{
  Label1.Text = "Clicked at " + DateTime.Now.ToString();
}
</script>
<html xmlns="http://www.w3.org/1999/xhtml">
<head runat="server">
  <title>Single File Page Model</title>
</head>
<body>
  <form id="form1" runat="server">
  <div>
  <asp:Label id="Label1"
          runat="server"></asp:Label>
          <asp:Button id="Button1" runat="server" OnClick="Button1_Click" Text="Click Me!">
          </asp:Button>
  </div>
  </form>
</body>
</html>
```

In Listing 2.3, we have placed the button's click-event code inside the `<script>` tag at the beginning. It should be kept in mind that the `runat="server"` attribute is mandatory within the `<script>` tags, because it will post the page to the Web server.

Now, let's execute the application by pressing the F5 key. The output of the application is shown in Figure 2.16:

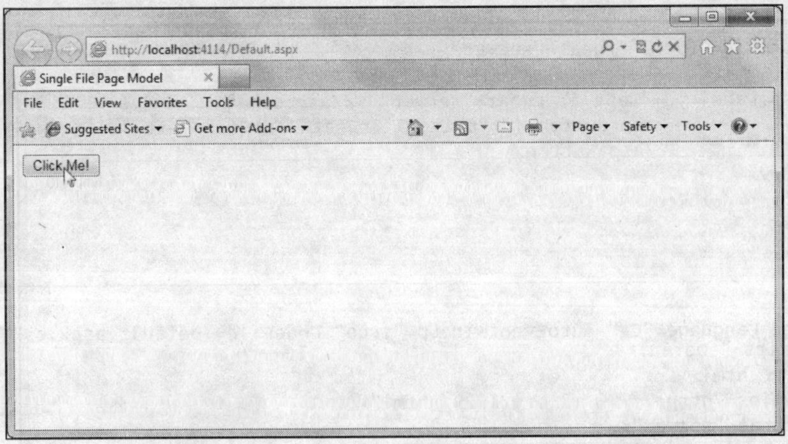

Figure 2.16: Showing the Output of the Application

Now, click the Click Me! button (Figure 2.16). The result of the `click` event is shown in Figure 2.17:

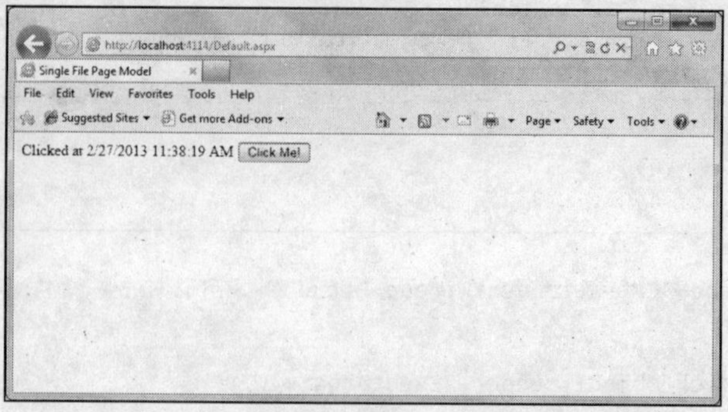

Figure 2.17: Result of Clicking the Click Me! Button

Code-Behind Page Model

In the code-behind page model, there are two separate files, `Default.aspx` and either `Default.aspx.cs` (for C# application) or `Default.aspx.vb` (for VB application). The `Default.aspx` file is used for ASP.NET presentation tags and the `Default.aspx.cs` or `Default.aspx.vb` file is used as the programming logic to implement the functionality of a Web application. These two files are then linked together to run the Web application. All the different versions of ASP.NET support this model, by default.

The code-behind file uses the partial class rather than the main class and it does not inherit the `.aspx` file, whereas both the files are combined together during compilation to implement the complete application.

Now, let's understand the code-behind model through an application named as `CodeBehindExampleVB` in VB and `CodeBehindExampleCS` in C#. You can find the code for the `Default.aspx` page for the code-behind page model in Listing 2.4:

Listing 2.4: Showing the Code for the `Default.aspx` Page

In VB

```
<%@ Page Language="VB" AutoEventWireup="false" CodeFile="Default.aspx.vb"
  Inherits="_Default" %>
<!DOCTYPE html>
<html xmlns="http://www.w3.org/1999/xhtml">
<head runat="server">
    <title>Code Behind Page Model</title>
</head>
<body>
    <form id="form1" runat="server">
    <div>
    <asp:Label id="Label1" runat="server" ></asp:Label>
                 <asp:Button id="Button1" runat="server" Text="Click Me!">
                 </asp:Button>
    </div>
    </form>
</body>
</html>
```

In C#

```
<%@ Page Language="C#" AutoEventWireup="true" CodeFile="Default.aspx.cs"
  Inherits="_Default" %>
<!DOCTYPE html>
<html xmlns="http://www.w3.org/1999/xhtml">
<head runat="server">
    <title>Code Behind Page Model</title>
</head>
```

```
<body>
    <form id="form1" runat="server">
    <div>
    <asp:Label id="Label1" runat="server" ></asp:Label>
     <asp:Button id="Button1" runat="server" OnClick="Button1_Click" Text="Click Me!" >
   </asp:Button>
    </div>
    </form>
</body>
</html>
```

Now, add the code in the code-behind file of the `Default.aspx` page for the code-behind page model, as shown in Listing 2.5:

Listing 2.5: Showing the code for the Code-Behind File of the `Default.aspx`

In VB

```
Partial Class _Default
    Inherits System.Web.UI.Page
    Protected Sub Button1_Click(sender As Object,e As EventArgs)
  Handles Button1.Click
        Label1.Text = "Clicked at " & DateTime.Now.ToString()
    End Sub
End Class
```

In C#

```
using System;
using System.Collections.Generic;
using System.Linq;
using System.Web;
using System.Web.UI;
using System.Web.UI.WebControls;
public partial class _Default : System.Web.UI.Page
{
    protected void Button1_Click(object sender, EventArgs e)
    {
        Label1.Text = "Clicked at " + DateTime.Now.ToString();
    }
}
```

The output of this listing is the same as shown in Figure 2.16 and Figure 2.17.

Understanding ASP.NET 4.5 Directives

ASP.NET directives are instructions to specify optional settings, such as registering a custom control and page language. These settings are used to describe how ASP.NET Web form(.aspx) or User control (.ascx) are processed by.NET Framework.

Page directives can be placed anywhere in a `.aspx` or `.ascx` file; although the standard practice is to include them at the top of the file.

The syntax to use a directive is as follows:

```
<%@ directive {attribute=value}* %>
```

ASP.NET treats any directive block `(<%@ %>), which` does not contain an explicit directive name, as a `@ Page` directive (for a page) or as a `@ Control` directive (for a user-control). ASP.NET 4.5 pages consist of the combination of following directives:

- @ Page
- @ Control
- @ Import
- @ Implements

- @ Register
- @ Assembly
- @ Master
- @ PreviousPageType
- @ MasterType
- @ OutputCache
- @ Reference
- @WebHandler

The @ Page Directive

The @ Page directive defines page-specific attributes used by the ASP.NET page parser and compiler. It can be included only in `.aspx` files.

The syntax for the `@ Page` directive is as follows:

```
<%@ Page attribute="value" [attribute="value"...] %>
```

The @ Page directive is the most important directive in an ASP.NET page. In ASP.NET 4.5, six attributes for the @ Page directive are available, which are shown in Table 2.3:

Table 2.3: Attributes in ASP.NET 4.5 in the @Page Directive

Attribute	Description
`ClientIDMode`	Sets the method used by ASP.NET page while generating ClientID values for the server controls on that page. The values that can be assigned to this attribute are: AutoID, Predictable, Static, and Inherit. The AutoID value is the default value for this attribute.
`ClientTarget`	Specifies the browser capabilities that the ASP.NET engine should target while rendering the page.
`MetaDescription`	Specifies the page description in the meta tag for the purpose of Search Engine Optimization (SEO).
`MetaKeywords`	Specifies a page keyword in the meta tag for the purpose of SEO.
`TargetSchema`	Specifies the name of the schema that validates the content of the page.
`ViewStateMode`	Specifies whether the ViewState property of the page is the default mode or not.

NOTE

Among the preceding six new attributes introduced in the @ Page directive, the MetaDecription and MetaKeywords attributes are included mainly to improve the optimization of ASP.NET site for SEO. This is done because numerous users visit a site through search engines.

The @ Control Directive

The @ Control directive defines control-specific attributes used by the ASP.NET page parser and compiler. It can only be used in `.ascx` files (user controls).

The syntax for the `@ Control` directive is as follows:

```
<%@ Control attribute="value" [attribute="value"...] %>
```

The @ Import Directive

The @ Import directive explicitly imports a namespace into ASP.NET application files, such as a Web page, user control, master page, or `Global.asax` file. It also makes all classes and interfaces of the imported namespace available to application files.

The syntax for the `@ Import` directive is as follows:

```
<%@ Import namespace="value" %>
```

The @ Implements Directive

The @ Implements directive indicates that the Web page, user control, or master page must implement the specified .NET Framework interface.

The syntax for the `@ Implements` directive is as follows:

```
<%@ Implements interface="ValidInterfaceName" %>
```

The @ Register Directive

The @ Register directive creates an association between tag prefix and custom controls. This association helps you to refer to custom controls in ASP.NET Web pages and user controls.

The syntax for the `@ Register` directive is as follows:

```
<%@ Register tagprefix="tagprefix"
  namespace="namespace"
  assembly="assembly" %>
<%@ Register tagprefix="tagprefix"
  namespace="namespace" %>
<%@ Register tagprefix="tagprefix"
  tagname="tagname"
  src="pathname" %>
```

The @ Assembly Directive

The @ Assembly directive links an assembly to the ASP.NET application files, such as a Web page, user control, master page, or a `Global.asax` file during compilation. It also helps in making all the classes and interfaces of an assembly available for use to the application.

The syntax for the `@ Assembly` directive is as follows:

```
<%@ Assembly Name="assemblyname" %>
<%@ Assembly Src="pathname" %>
```

The @ Master Directive

The @ Master directive defines attributes of a master page (`.master` file), which are used by the ASP.NET page parser and compiler.

The syntax for the `@ Master` directive is as follows:

```
<%@ Master attribute="value" [attribute="value"...] %>
```

The @ PreviousPageType Directive

The @ PreviousPageType directive provides the means to get strong typing against the previous page as accessed through the `PreviousPage` property.

The syntax for the `@ PreviousPage` directive is as follows:

```
<%@ PreviousPageType attribute="value" [attribute="value"...] %>
```

The @ MasterType Directive

The @ MasterType directive provides a way to create a strongly typed reference to the ASP.NET master page when the master page is accessed from the `Master` property.

The syntax for the `@ MasterType` directive is as follows:

```
<%@ MasterType attribute="value" [attribute="value"...] %>
```

The @ OutputCache Directive

The @ OutputCache directive controls the output caching policies of a Web page or a user control.

The syntax for the `@ OutputCache` directive is as follows:

```
<%@ OutputCache Duration="#ofseconds"
  Location="Any | Client | Downstream | Server | None |
```

```
    ServerAndClient "
    Shared="True | False"
    VaryByControl="controlname"
    VaryByCustom="browser | customstring"
    VaryByHeader="headers"
    VaryByParam="parametername"
    CacheProfile="cache profile name | ''"
   VaryByContentEncoding="encodings"
    NoStore="true | false"
    SqlDependency="database/table name pair | CommandNotification"
     ProviderName="Provider Name"
%>
```

The @ Reference Directive

The @ Reference directive dynamically compiles and links the user control, page source file, or arbitrary file located at some virtual path.

The syntax for the `@ Reference` directive is as follows:

```
<%@ Reference Page="path to .aspx page"
    Control="path to .ascx file"
    virtualPath="path to file" %>
```

The @ WebHandler Directive

The @ Webhandler directive defines attributes and compilation options for HTTP handler(.ashx) files.

The syntax for the `@ Webhandler` directive is as follows:

```
<%@ WebHandler attribute="value" [attribute="value"...] %>
```

Working with Server Controls

In addition to HTML and programming code, an ASP.NET Web page also contains server controls, such as the `TextBox` and `Image` controls. Server controls are programmable objects that act as User Interface (UI) elements on a Web page. For instance, a typical example of a server control can be a `TextBox` control, which takes data from the user as input and displays the output at the click of a `Button` control. The code for a server control is executed and compiled at the server; therefore, these controls are also known as server-side objects. Working with server controls is a great experience as you can define their complete behavior by setting their properties. You can set the properties of server control by either explicitly writing properties in the server control tag or defining properties in the `Properties` window.

You can use server control tags or intrinsic HTML tags containing the `runat="server"` attribute to declare server controls in a Web application. The server controls declared within the intrinsic HTML tags are executed with the help of the `System.Web.UI.HtmlControls` namespace.

Now, let's develop an application that uses various server controls, such as Label, TextBox, DropDownList, and Button. This code can be found as ServerControlVB for VB and ServerControlCS for C#. Listing 2.6 shows the `Default.aspx` page for server controls:

Listing 2.6: Showing the Code for the `Default.aspx` Page

In VB

```
<%@ Page Language="VB" AutoEventWireup="false" CodeFile="Default.aspx.vb"
    Inherits="_Default" %>
<!DOCTYPE html>
<html xmlns="http://www.w3.org/1999/xhtml">
<head runat="server">
    <title>Server Controls</title>
</head>
<body>
    <form id="form1" runat="server">
    <div>
```

```
        <asp:Label ID="Label1" runat="server" Text="Select
        Title"></asp:Label> <asp:DropDownList ID="DropDownList1" runat="server">
            <asp:listitem >Mr</asp:listitem>
            <asp:listitem >Mrs</asp:listitem>
            <asp:listitem >Miss</asp:listitem>
            </asp:DropDownList>
               <asp:Label ID="Label2" runat="server" Text="Enter Name"></asp:Label>
            <asp:TextBox ID="TextBox1" runat="server"></asp:TextBox><br />
            <br />
               <br />
               
            <asp:Button ID="Button1" runat="server" Text="Submit" Width="60px" />
        </div>
        </form>
    </body>
    </html>
```

In C#

```
    <%@ Page Language="C#" AutoEventWireup="true" CodeFile="Default.aspx.cs"
      Inherits="_Default" %>
    <!DOCTYPE html>
    <html xmlns="http://www.w3.org/1999/xhtml">
    <head runat="server">
        <title>Server Controls</title>
    </head>
    <body>
        <form id="form1" runat="server">
        <div>
        <div>
            <asp:Label ID="Label1" runat="server" Text="Select
              Title"></asp:Label> <asp:DropDownList ID="DropDownList1" runat="server">
            <asp:listitem >Mr</asp:listitem>
            <asp:listitem >Mrs</asp:listitem>
            <asp:listitem >Miss</asp:listitem>
            </asp:DropDownList>
               <asp:Label ID="Label2" runat="server" Text="Enter Name"></asp:Label>
            <asp:TextBox ID="TextBox1" runat="server"></asp:TextBox><br />
            <br />
               <br />
               
            <asp:Button ID="Button1" runat="server" Text="Submit" onclick="Button1_Click" />
        </div>
        </form>
    </body>
    </html>
```

Now, add the code in the code-behind file of the `Default.aspx` page for server controls, as shown in Listing 2.7:

Listing 2.7: Showing the code for the Code-Behind File of the `Default.aspx`

In VB

```
    Partial Class _Default
        Inherits System.Web.UI.Page
        Protected Sub Button1_Click(sender As Object, e As EventArgs)
          Handles Button1.Click
            Dim str As String = "Welcome  " & DropDownList1.SelectedValue & " " &
             TextBox1.Text
            Button1.Visible = False
            DropDownList1.Visible = False
            TextBox1.Visible = False
            Label1.Visible = False
            Label2.Visible = False
```

```
            Response.Write(str)
        End Sub
    End Class
```

In C#

```
    using System;
    using System.Collections.Generic;
    using System.Linq;
    using System.Web;
    using System.Web.UI;
    using System.Web.UI.WebControls;
    public partial class _Default : System.Web.UI.Page {
        protected void Page_Load(object sender, EventArgs e) {
        }
        protected void Button1_Click(object sender, EventArgs e) {
            String str = "Welcome " + DropDownList1.SelectedValue + " " + TextBox1.Text;
            DropDownList1.Visible = false;
            TextBox1.Visible = false;
            Label1.Visible = false;
            Label2.Visible = false;
            Button1.Visible = false;
            Response.Write(str);
        }
    }
```

Now, press the F5 key to execute the Web application, as shown in Figure 2.18:

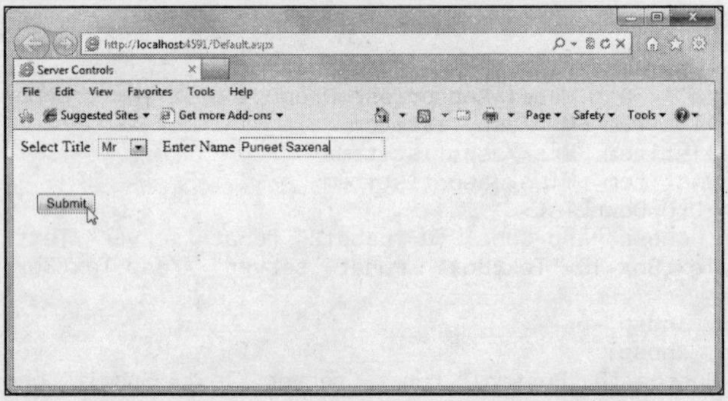

Figure 2.18: Output of Server Control Application

As shown in Figure 2.18, the Web page contains one `DropDownList`, one `TextBox`, two Label, and one `Button` control that allow you to enter your name. Click the Submit button after selecting the title from the Select Title field and entering text in the Enter Name field. Figure 2.19 shows the output:

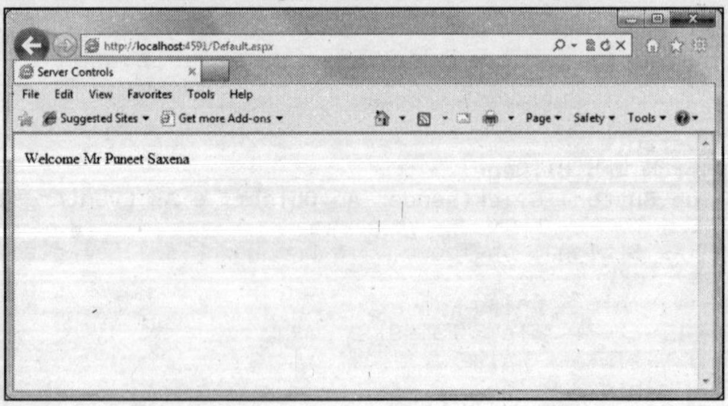

Figure 2.19: Output Generated after Clicking the Submit Button

After learning how to create a Web application in ASP.NET, let's now discuss the ASP.NET 4.5 provider model.

Understanding the Provider Model in ASP.NET 4.5

After the development and release of ASP.NET 2.0, the .NET development team received multiple requests from the users for the development of ways of storing session information, other than `InProc`, `StateServer`, and `SQLServer`. One of the requests was, to develop a provider for ASP.NET that helped in storing sessions in an Oracle database. Instead of developing a provider model for each and every type of database, .NET development team created provider models that enabled the users to add any provider they wanted such as membership, role management and so on. Henceforth, the later versions of the ASP.NET included the provider model. In ASP.NET 4.5, the provider model illustrates the position of providers, which work as a bridge between `Data Stores`, such as `SQL Server`, and `ASP.NET Services`, such as `Membership` in ASP.NET applications. You can best visualize the ASP.NET provider model by looking at Figure 2.20:

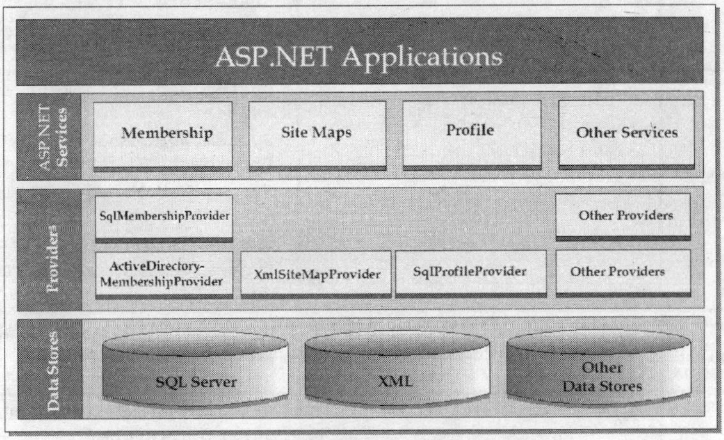

Figure 2.20: ASP.NET 4.5 Provider Model

As shown in Figure 2.20, providers act as communication channels for data sources. To elaborate more on the concept of providers, let's take the example of an online banking website, which allows its customers to access and modify their account information. In such a situation, the bank needs to maintain the records of each customer in a storage media, such as `Oracle` or `DB2` databases. Whenever a user tries to access the information through a website, an appropriate provider is selected, which retrieves or updates the information in the data source. The type of provider selected depends on the type of data source used. The functionality of providers is similar to the device drivers that extract data from the hardware devices, such as floppy disc and CD.

Providers can be of two types, namely Membership and Roles providers, based on the type of services they provide. The Membership provider stores the user names and passwords, and the Roles provider stores the user roles. By default, ASP.NET 4.5 uses the `AspNetSqlMembershipProvider` provider. You can change the default provider by using the `Web Site Administration Tool` or the `Microsoft Management Console` (MMC), which provides various management tools called snap-ins.

Table 2.4 lists the different types of service providers:

Table 2.4: Different Types of Service Providers

Provider Type	Default Provider(s)	Built-in Provider(s)
Membership	`System.Web.Security.SqlMembershipProvider`	`System.Web.Security.ActiveDirectoryMembershipProvider` `System.Web.Security.SqlMembershipProvider`
Role management	`System.Web.Security.SqlRoleProvider`	`System.Web.Security.AuthorizationStoreRoleProvider` `System.Web.Security.SqlRoleProvider`

Table 2.4: Different Types of Service Providers

Provider Type	Default Provider(s)	Built-in Provider(s)
		System.Web.Security.WindowsTokenRoleProvider
Site map	System.Web.XmlSiteMapProvider	System.Web.XmlSiteMapProvider
Profile	System.Web.Profile.SqlProfileProvider	System.Web.Profile.SqlProfileProvider
Session state	System.Web.SessionState.InProcSessionStateStore	System.Web.SessionState.InProcSessionStateStore System.Web.SessionState.OutOfProcSessionStateStore System.Web.SessionState.SqlSessionStateStore
Web events	N/A	System.Web.Management.EventLogWebEventProvider System.Web.Management.SimpleMailWebEventProvider System.Web.Management.TemplatedMailWebEventProvider System.Web.Management.SqlWebEventProvider System.Web.Management.TraceWebEventProvider
Web Parts personalization	System.Web.UI.WebControls.WebParts.SqlPersonalizationProvider	System.Web.UI.WebControls.WebParts.SqlPersonalizationProvider
Protected configuration	N/A	System.Configuration.DPAPIProtectedConfigurationProvider System.Configuration.RSAProtectedConfigurationProvider

All the providers are derived from a common base class known as `ProviderBase`, which is defined in the `System.Configuration.Provider` namespace.

Implementing Code Sharing

Code sharing is a mechanism through which a common code is shared among different pages of a Web application. It is particularly beneficial when you want to make the code, with specific functionality, accessible to all the pages in a Web application. The following three methods are used to implement code sharing:

- Using the `Code` Directory
- Using the `Bin` Directory
- Using the Global Assembly Cache

Using the Code Directory

ASP.NET 4.5 provides a directory known as `App_Code` to store code files accessible to all the Web pages of a Web application. When you add files such as a class or `.wsdl` files, inside the `App_Code` folder, the files are automatically detected and compiled. After compilation, any page in your Web application can access those files or classes. You need to right-click the project name in the Solution Explorer and select the Add ASP.NET Folder→App_Code option from the context menu to create the App_Code folder. It adds the `App_Code` folder in the Solution Explorer. Now, right-click the `App_Code` folder and select the Add New Item option. The Add New Item dialog box appears, as shown in Figure 2.21:

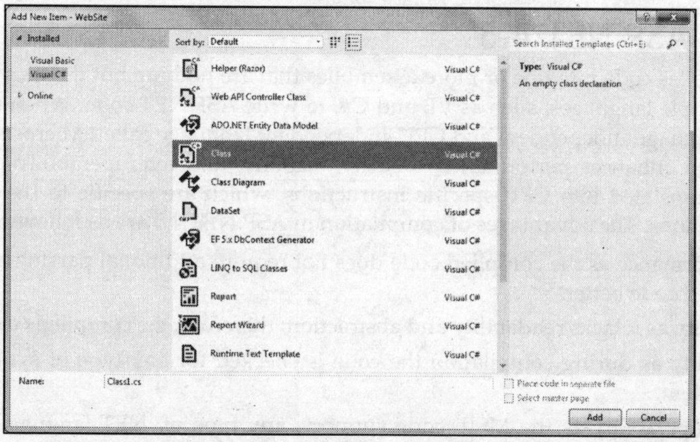

Figure 2.21: Add New Item Dialog Box

Figure 2.21 shows the different classes and files that you can add to the `App_Code` folder so that they can be accessed from all the pages in the Web application. You can add any class or file by first selecting its icon and then clicking the Add button. Figure 2.22 shows the Solution Explorer, with a Class1.cs, added to the `App_Code` folder:

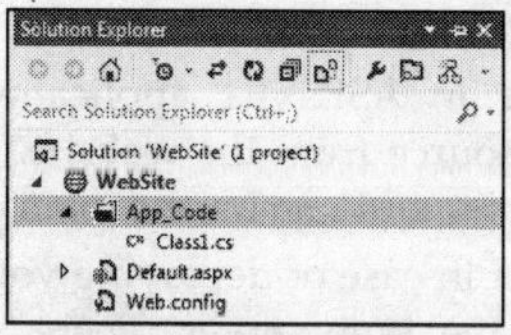

Figure 2.22: Displaying Solution Explorer

Using the Bin Directory

The code for a specific functionality in a Web page of a Web application can be made accessible to all the Web pages by storing the code file in the `Bin` directory. Since the introduction of first version of ASP.NET, the `Bin` directory is used for sharing the code. The `Bin` directory is similar to the `App_Code` directory except that it stores the precompiled assemblies of the code files that are required by all the Web pages of a Web application. You can use this method when you need to reuse the code written in other Web applications. In this case, you need to include the executable or the `DLL` file in the `Bin` directory.

Using the Global Assembly Cache

You can use the global assembly cache to implement a specific functionality to all the Web pages of a Web application. .NET Framework provides various assemblies that are stored in the global assembly cache. These assemblies can be accessed by all the Web pages of the Web application. You need to write the following code in the `Web.config` file of a Web application to register or add the required assemblies in the global assembly cache:

```
<configuration>
  <system.web>
        <compilation>
              <assemblies>
                    <add assembly="System.Data, Version=1.0.2411.0,
                    Culture=neutral,
                    PublicKeyToken=b77a5c561934e089"/>
              </assemblies>
        </compilation>
  </system.web>
</configuration>
```

Now, let's learn about compilation in ASP.NET 4.5.

Compilation in ASP.NET 4.5

ASP.NET first compiles code into one or more assemblies that are nothing but the files with the extension `.dll`. You can select multiple languages, such as VB and C#, to write ASP.NET code. When the code is compiled, it is converted into a language-independent and CPU-independent language called Microsoft Intermediate Language (MSIL). Compilation enhances performance, security, stability, and interoperability of a Web application. At runtime, MSIL is translated into CPU-specific instructions, which are specific to the processors of computers running the applications. The advantages of compilation in ASP.NET 4.5 are as follows:

- Improves performance as the complied code does not require additional parsing as the system can identify the precompiled code better.
- Provides security as it lacks readability and abstraction; therefore, the compiled code cannot be reversed.
- Provides stability as during compilation the code is checked for any type of syntax errors, type safety, or any other problem.
- Provides interoperability as the MSIL code supports any type of .NET language. This implies that in an ASP.NET page created in C#, you can add reference of .dll file, which is created using Visual Basic.

The compilation architecture of ASP.NET 4.5 includes numerous features, which are as follows:

- **Multiple language support**—Specifies that you can use different langauges in a single ASP.NET application. In an ASP.NET 4.5 application, multiple assemblies are created and each assembly supports each langauge used in the application. Therefore, for the code stored in the App_Code folder, you can specify a subfolder for each language.
- **Automatic compilation**—Complies an ASP.NET application and any dependent resource, at the first instance when a user requests a resource from the website. As a rule, an ASP.NET application creates an assembly for each application directory and one for the main directory.
- **Flexible deployment**—Specifies that in case of deploying your ASP.NET application, you can just copy the source code of the application to the Web server. There are two precompilation options provided by ASP.NET. First, you can compile the website before deploying it, or second you can compile it after is has been deployed, but before a user sends a request to the website. The ASP.NET Merge tool (Aspnet_merge.exe) enables you to combine and manage assemblies that are created by the ASP.NET Compilation tool (Aspnet_compiler.exe). This tool enables you to compile an ASP.NET Web application for deployment to a target location, such as a production server. The ASP.NET Merge tool works on assemblies that have been created by using ASP.NET version 2.0 or advanced versions. It creates one assembly for either each content folder in the target website or content file. It also gives you additional flexibility for deployment. The Merge tool enables you to do the following tasks:
  - Creates one assembly for the whole website
  - Creates an assembly for each website folder and adds a prefix to the assembly name
  - Creates a single assembly for just the website UI elements, such as pages and controls

The syntax for using the Merge tool is as follows:

```
aspnet_merge     [-?]
                 applicationPath
                 [-keyfile filename [-delaysign]]
                 [-o assemblyname | -w assemblyname | -prefix prefix]
                 [-copyattrs [assemblyfile]]
                 [-debug]
                 [-nologo]
                 [-errorstack]
                 [-r]
                 [-xmldocs]
                 [-a]
                 [-logfile logfile]
                 [-allowattrs textfile]
```

- **Extensible build system**—Refers to the customization of ASP.NET build system to compile custom resources. The BuildProvider class is used by ASP.NET applications to bulid .aspx pages (ASP.NET Web pages), .ascx files (Web User Control file), and global resources.

Dynamic Compilation in ASP.NET 4.5

When you create an ASP.NET page, the entire content of the page is compiled into a class, which is an instance of the System.Web.UI.Page class. When a user requests for the page, the ASP.NET Framework first searches for the .NET class to execute it. If the class is not located, then it can be compiled into a new .NET class, which is stored in a temporary ASP.NET folder.

If a request is send to the same page again, then the page is not complied again. The .NET class, which has already been compiled, is executed. This process of not compiling the same page again is called ASP.NET dynamic compilation. If any modification is done in the ASP.NET page, the .NET class is delegated automatically. In other words, dynamic compilation helps in modifying the source code and recompiling the files, without compiling the code, before deploying a Web application.

The following topics help you to familiarize with dynamic compilation in ASP.NET 4.5:

- Compiling on First Request
- Recompiling on Change
- Compilation Dependencies
- Compilation Output
- Multiple Language Support
- Optimizing Dynamic Compilation
- Disadvantages of Dynamic Compilation

Compiling on First Request

In ASP.NET, Web pages and code files are compiled dynamically by default when users first request a resource. A resource can be an ASP.NET page (`.aspx` file), which the user requests from a website. ASP.NET supports the dynamic compilation of ASP.NET pages (`.aspx` files), ASP.NET Web services (`.asmx` files), ASP.NET `HTTP handlers` (`.ashx` files), and ASP.NET application files (`Global.asax`), as well as other files, such as source code and class files.

Recompiling on Change

If you make any changes to a dynamically compiled ASP.NET file, it automatically invalidates the file's cached compiled assembly and triggers recompilation of all the affected resources, such as `.dll` files. Now, when the request to the application is made again, ASP.NET recognizes that the code has been changed and recompiles the affected resources of the Web application. This process enables you to quickly develop applications with a minimum of compilation overhead. The decision to compile a single page or the entire website depends on the percentage of changes made to resources.

Compilation Dependencies

ASP.NET compiles files in a particular order when a request is made to an application. The items to be compiled first are referred as the top-level items. After the first request, the top-level items are recompiled only if dependency changes. Top-level items include the `App_GlobalResources` folder, `App_WebResources` folder, profile properties, `App_Code` folder, and `Global.asax` file. After compiling the top-level items, ASP.NET compiles additional items. These items include the `App_LocalResources` folder, individual ASP.NET pages (`.aspx` files), ASP.NET user controls (`.ascx` files), ASP.NET HTTP Handlers (`.ashx` files), ASP.NET HTTP modules (`.asmx` files), themes, master pages, and other source files.

Compilation Output

After the code is complied, the generated assemblies are cached in a floder on the server. This folder is the deafult Temporary ASP.NET Files folder, which is the subdirectory of the location where you have installed the .NET Framework. For example, if you have installed the .NET Framework 4.5 in the C:\ drive of your computer, the location of Temporary ASP.NET Files folder is as follows:

```
C:\Windows\Microsoft.NET\Framework\v4.0.30319\Temporary ASP.NET Files
```

The Temporary ASP.NET Files folder is created by deault when you install .NET Framework and the installation process assigns permissions on this folder to the ASP.NET local user account. In the Temporary ASP.NET Files folder, a discrete subfolder is created for each ASP.NET application. The root location of this subfolder can be configured in an ASP.NET application by using the tempDirectory attribute of the compilation section of the configuartion file.

Multiple Language Support

In the earlier versions of ASP.NET , the App_Code folder was compiled into a single assembly. Therfore, all the files in the App_Code folder should be in the same programming language, that is either VB or C#.

However, the multiple langauge support feature of dynamic compilation in ASP.NET 4.5 helps you to use different lanagauges in a single ASP.NET 4.5 application. You can use different languages in a single ASP.NET 4.5 application by configuring the Web application to treat the subfolders of the App_Code folder as separate compilable units. The codeSubDirectories element of the compilation element in the Web.config file helps you to implement the multiple langauge support feature, in which each folder can contain source code of different programming langauge. For example, you can configure subfolders named VB and CS to compile into separate assemblies, by using the following code snippet in the Web.config file:

```
<compilation debug="false">
    <codeSubDirectories>
        <add directoryName="VB" />
        <add directoryName="CS" />
    </codeSubDirectories>
</compilation>
```

In the preceding code snippet, the reference to the VB and CS subfolders does not require any information about the programming langauge.

Optimizing Dynamic Compilation

As you know, if you make any changes to a dynamically compiled ASP.NET file, it automatically invalidates the file's cached compiled assembly and triggers recompilation of all the affected resources, such as `.dll` files. However, in case of large applications, this process of recompilation may make the application unavailable for a long duration, even if the change is a small one.

You can avoid such a situation by setting the optimizeCompilations attribute to true in the Web.config file. This implies that after setting this attribute to true, when you implement any change, only the files in which changes are made are recompiled.

Disadvantages of Dynamic Compilation

The disadvantages of dynamic compliation in an ASP.NET application are as follows:

- Slow response time for the users as the ASP.NET pages and codes must be complied the first time they are requested
- No means to identify any compile-time bugs, before a user accesses the site
- No provision of creating a compiled version of the site that can be deployed on the production server, without the source code

Summary

In this chapter, we have covered some important aspects of developing a Web application, such as how to specify the location of a Web application by using the File System, HTTP, and FTP options. Further, this chapter also focused on coding models, page directives, server controls, and provider model. It also described the concepts of code sharing and compilation, required for developing Web applications. The new concept of dynamic compilation in ASP.NET 4.5 is also discussed in the chapter.

In the next chapter, we discuss about the structure and state management concepts related to an ASP.NET Web application.

3

Application Structure and State

If you need an Immediate Solution to:	See page:

In Depth

The structure of a Web application includes application domain, application lifetime, and application directory structure. Apart from them, a Web application also contains the `Global.asax` file, which file handles the events or methods that are raised when the application is executed. Therefore, the structure of an ASP.NET Web application comprises files, pages, handlers, and executable code, which are invoked from the virtual directories of a Web server.

Another concept that is discussed in the chapter is the state of a Web application, which is associated with its runtime. The state of a Web application refers to the status of a Web application at any instant of time. Preserving application state ensures that the changes made by a user (such as the products selected and saved in the shopping cart in a case of any online shopping website) persist whenever a page is reloaded. States are further categorized into several types, such as application state, session state, and view state, depending on the nature of information they preserve.

In this chapter, we describe the structure of a Web application and explain the concept of states. We also get to know about the `Global.asax` file, which is used to implement application-level and session-level events. In addition, we learn how to add objects to the `Global.asax` file. The chapter concludes with a detailed discussion about HTTP Handlers that are used to handle user requests for Web application resources, and postbacks, which are used for sending data back to the server for processing.

Structure of an Application

As already stated, the structure of an ASP.NET Web application includes the concepts of application domain, application lifetime, and application directory structure. Application domain is a virtual boundary inside which an application runs, while application lifetime is the span of time for which an application domain exists. Application directory structure, on the other hand, specifies the directory structure that organizes the various entities associated with an application, such as references, resources, and code files, in separate directories. Each directory possesses a well-qualified name that reflects what is stored inside it. Now, let's explore all these concepts one by one.

The Application Domain

To understand the concept of domain, we first need to understand how a Web application works after it is deployed. We deploy a Web application created in ASP.NET on a Web server, such as the Internet Information Services (IIS), and Windows Process Activation Services (WAS). The client browser sends a request for the Web application to the Web server, which further passes the request to the ASP.NET worker process. The worker process then separates the code execution into different application domains with the Web services and Web pages hosted on the same virtual directory. These Web services and Web pages execute in the same application domain, whereas, the Web services and Web pages hosted on different virtual directories executes in different application domains. An application domain is actually implemented by Common Language Runtime (CLR), and the prime objective of the application domain is to prevent concurrently running applications from entering into each other's domain.

Therefore, application domains provide an isolation boundary for applications, which is required to ensure that the code running in one application does not affect any other or unrelated applications.

NOTE

ASP.NET runs within a process known as ASP.NET worker process, which allows ASP.NET Web applications to run on the Web server. It enables different assemblies of a program to work in conjunction with each other.

What do we gain from the concept of the application domain? The most vital benefit of application domains is the independent execution of Web applications. None of the applications can access the in-memory resources of other simultaneously running applications. The main component that helps in the independent execution of applications is a virtual directory. In case of an Internet Information Services (IIS) Web server, the virtual directory with all its subdirectories is created in the IIS console. Some of the primary application entities that are stored in the virtual directory are:

- **Web pages**—Files that are used as Web Form pages in the Microsoft .NET environment. The extension of these files is .aspx.
- **Web services**—Files that enable you to share information with applications on other computers and platforms using XML Web services. These files have the .asmx extension.
- **Code-behind files**—Source code files that contain code for an ASP.NET page in a separate class file. The source code files have the .cs extension if the files are coded in C# and .vb extension if the files are coded in VB.
- **Configuration files**—Configuration files, such as Web.config which stores the configuration settings of a Web application and machine.config which stores the configuration settings of the machine on which the Web application is running.
- **Global.asax files**—Files that contain event handlers to respond to events, such as starting of an ASP.NET Web application for the first time.

In addition, there are other resources in the virtual directory, such as images and XML files. The virtual directory encapsulates all these resources of an ASP.NET Web application and forms an application domain whenever the application is called for the first time.

The Application Lifetime

Application lifetime refers to the time span for which an application domain persists. Now, this does not mean that application lifetime is equivalent to the time span for which an application runs. In fact, an application domain can shut down in several circumstances, including specific error conditions, configuration changes, or Web server shut-down. Therefore, an application's runtime might encounter repeated restarting of the application domain. The application domain might require a restart under the following circumstances:

- Excess requests in the queue
- Excess memory usage by an application
- Lengthy lifetime of the application
- Modifications in the Web.config file
- Replacement of existing Dynamic Link Libraries (.dll files) or Web files

It is not that the shut-down of an application domain is bad on any count. As a matter of fact, developers deliberately include specific settings in the machine.config file to ensure that the application domain is recycled at specific time intervals. This helps in monitoring the performance of the application.

The Application Directory Structure

An efficiently designed directory structure plays a key role in Web application development. It segregates all the code and resources used by an application among different directories, thereby enhancing the productivity of developers. Let's take an example to illustrate this. Suppose you are developing a Web application, the code for which has been divided under different modules, with each module handled by different team members. In such a scenario, it will be easier for you to just put the code, developed by your team members, in different directories and run the application. In this way, the debugging process can also be performed in a more structured manner. Another advantage of using a directory structure is that it enhances the reusability of an application. It becomes easy for you to upgrade the application in the long run because of its structured code files and application resources.

In the 1.x version of ASP.NET and earlier, there was only one default directory and bin for an application and you had to create your own custom directories, if any. However, in ASP.NET 4.5, there is support for a default directory structure, which provides several built-in directories for Web applications. These directories are as follows:

- **Bin**—Contains compiled .NET assemblies, containing precompiled Web service classes. You can directly use these assemblies in your application, thereby reducing the amount of code that needs to be written for an ASP.NET Web application.
- **App_Code**—Contains source code files, compiled dynamically, to be used in the ASP.NET Web application.
- **App_GlobalResources**—Contains the resources that can be used in all Web pages as well as the controls of the ASP.NET Web application.
- **App_LocalResources**—Contains the resources that are accessible only to a specific Web page of the ASP.NET Web application.
- **App_WebReferences**—Contains the references to the Web services used by the ASP.NET Web application.
- **App_Data**—Contains the database and XML files of the ASP.NET Web application.
- **App_Browsers**—Contains browser definition files that identify browsers for different ASP.NET Web applications.
- **App_Themes**—Contains the themes used by the ASP.NET Web application. The themes can be applied to a control or a Web page, or to the entire ASP.NET Web application.

Next, let's discuss the Global.asax application file, which is also known as the ASP.NET application file.

The Global.asax Application File

The `Global.asax` file resides in the root directory of an ASP.NET Web application and is also called the ASP.NET application file. This file contains the code that is executed when certain events, such as start of an application or error in an application, are raised by an ASP.NET Web application.

Events and states, such as session state and application state, which are specified in the `Global.asax` file, are applied to all the resources of the Web application. For example, if an application state variable is defined in the `Global.asax` file, then all the `.aspx` files within the root directory can access the variable. Application state variable is accessible everywhere.

The code in the `Global.asax` file is written in the same way as in Web forms; the only difference is that the code written in the `Global.asax` file does not contain HTML or ASP.NET tags. Instead, the code in this file contains methods with predefined names.

The `Global.asax` file added to the ASP.NET Web application contains empty event handlers for the commonly used application events, such as the start and end of an application. The code for the event handlers is inserted in the appropriate method of the `Global.asax` file. The name of the method for which an event handler is created should be similar to the name of the event occurring in the Web application. For example, the `Application_Start()` method is called when the `Application_OnStart` event occurs in the ASP.NET Web application.

The various methods corresponding to the events that occur in the `Global.asax` file are invoked in the following order when an ASP.NET Web application starts:

- **BeginRequest()**—Invoked when a request for the Web application is received.
- **AuthenticateRequest()**—Invoked just before the authentication of user credentials is performed. You can use this method to specify your own authentication logic before the authentication process begins.
- **PostAuthenticateRequest()**—Invoked just after the authentication of user credentials is performed.
- **AuthorizeRequest()**—Invoked when the current user's credentials are successfully validated. You can use this method to assign special permissions to the user.
- **PostAuthorizeRequest()**—Invoked when the AuthorizeRequest() gets successfully executed.

- **ResolveRequestCache()**—Invoked when the ASP.NET Page framework completes the execution of authorization request. This method is mainly used to handle the output caching of the application that renders the cached HTML without executing the code again.
- **PostResolveRequestCache()**—Invoked after the successful execution of ResolveRequestCache() event().
- **PostMapRequestHandlerevent()**—Invoked when ASP.NET has mapped the current request to the appropriate event handler.
- **AcquireRequestState()**—Invoked just before the session information is retrieved for the current client request.
- **PostAcquireRequestState**()—Invokes when the request state (for example, session state) that is associated with the current request has been obtained.
- **PreRequestHandlerExecute()**—Invoked before the ASP.NET page framework begins to run the HTTP Handler to handle a request.
- **PostRequestHandlerExecute()**—Invoked after the HTTP Handler has finished executing the request.
- **ReleaseRequestState()**—Invoked just before the session information is serialized from the Session collection for the next request.
- **UpdateRequestCache()**—Invoked just before the information for handling the request is added to the output cache of the Web page.
- **EndRequest()**—Invoked at the end of the request.
- **PreSendRequestHeaders()**—Invokes just before ASP.NET sends HTTP headers to the client.
- **PreSendRequestContent()**—Invokes just before ASP.NET sends content to the client.

The methods corresponding to the events that are not invoked with each user request are:

- **Application_Start()**—Invoked when an ASP.NET Web application starts and an application domain is created. An ASP.NET Web application starts when any resource in the application is requested.
- **Session_Start()**—Invoked when a session is started. A new session starts each time a new user requests a page.
- **Application_Error()**—Invoked when an error occurs. You can use this method to handle errors on the ASP.NET Web application instead of using the Web.config file.
- **Session_End()**—Invoked when a user's session expires.
- **Application_End()**—Invoked when an application ends or terminates. The application terminates when there are no more active sessions.
- **Application_Disposed()**—Invoked when an application is destroyed.

The `Global.asax` file is also used to declare the data that is available across different browser sessions. This process is known as application state and session state management.

There are some similarities between an ASP.NET Web page and the `Global.asax` file. Similar to an ASP.NET page, the `Global.asax` file is compiled when a request for any resource in an ASP.NET Web application is made for the first time. Another similarity is that when changes are made to the `Global.asax` file, ASP.NET detects the changes and recompiles the file. New requests are then directed to the recompiled `Global.asax` file.

Now that you are familiar with the `Global.asax` application file, let's discuss about the states of an application.

Using States

State is quite an innovative concept in Web development because it eliminates the drawback of losing state data due to reloading of a Web page. By using states in a Web application, you can preserve the state of the application either at the server or client end. The state of a Web application helps you to store the runtime changes that have been made to the Web application. For example, as already described earlier, a change in the data source of the Web application might be initiated by a user when he/she selects and saves some products in the shopping cart. If you are not using states, these changes are discarded and are not saved. You may think that the whole concept of storing states is optional. However, under certain circumstances, using states with applications is imperative. For example, it is necessary to store states for Web applications, such as an e-commerce shopping site or an Intranet site of a company, to keep track of the requests of the users for the items they have selected on the shopping site or the days requested for vacation on the Intranet site.

There are various methods for storing state information. These include the following:

- **Hidden fields**—Refers to the control that is not visible when a Web application is viewed in the browser. The content of the control is sent in the HTTP Form collection control along with the values of other controls to the server on page reloads. This control acts as a storage area for any page-specific storing information.
- **Cookies**—Refers to the text files that store data, such as user ID and preferences at the client end. When a browser requests a Web page again, the cookie is sent along with the request. The Web server then retrieves the information from the cookie.
- **Query strings**—Refers to the information strings added at the end of a URL to maintain the state of a Web application. However, using query strings is not secure because their values are exposed to the Internet through the URL.

In all these methods, state information is stored at the client end. However, the state of an ASP.NET Web application can also be on a Web server. The following are some of the methods used to save state information on the Web server:

- **Application state**—Stores application data not frequently modified by users. An object of the HttpApplicationState class is used to store the state of an ASP.NET Web application.
- **Session state**—Stores information specific to a user session. User session refers to the duration for which a user uses a website. An object of the HttpSessionState class is used to store the session state for each ASP.NET Web application that is executed.
- **Profile properties**—Stores a user specific data in a persistent form.

Now, let's discuss the various state types: application state, session state, and view state.

Application State

Application state is used to store data corresponding to all the variables of an ASP.NET Web application. The data in application state is stored once and read several times. Application state uses the `HttpApplicationState` class to store and share the data throughout the application. You can access the information stored in an application state by using the `HttpApplication` class property. Data stored in application state is accessible to all the pages of the application and is the same for all the users accessing the application. The `HttpApplicationState` class provides a lock method, which you can use to ensure that only one user is able to access and modify the data of an application at any instant of time.

Session State

Each client accessing a Web application maintains a distinct session with the Web server, and there is also specific information associated with each of these sessions. Session state is defined in the `<sessionState>` element of the `Web.config` file. It also stores the data specific to a user session in session variables. Different session variables are created for each user session. In addition, session variables can be accessed from any page of the application. When a user accesses a page, a session ID for the user is created. The session ID is transferred between the server and the client over the HTTP protocol using cookies.

View State

View state stores page-specific information, when a page is posted back to the server. When a page is processed, the current state of the page and its controls is hashed (transforming a sequence of characters into a fixed-length value) into a string and saved as a hidden field on the page. Such a state of the page is called view state.

The `ViewState` property is used to save the view state of each control used in a page. If the `ViewState` property is not used, then the values written in the controls are not retained when the page is reloaded.

The hidden field of a view state is placed at the top of each page. The source code to maintain a ViewState contains an input tag with three attributes: type, name, and value. The value of the type attribute is set to hidden. The name attribute contains the name of the controls for which the `ViewState` property is used, and the value attribute specifies a string value, which is not in readable format. The string value is a combination of control values that are used in a Web page. When the Web page is reloaded, the server reads the values in the value attribute and restores them when the page is sent back to the client.

View state is maintained in a Web page by default. You can include the following directive at the top of the Web page to disable its view state:

```
<%@ Page EnableViewState = "False"%>
```

To disable the view state of a Web control, add the following attribute to the control:

```
Page.EnableViewState ="false"
```

Next, we discuss the concept of HTTP Handlers in Web applications.

HTTP Handlers

HTTP Handlers, as the name suggests, handle user requests for Web application resources. They are the backbone of the request–response model of Web applications. For each user request type, there is a specific event handler to handle the request and send back the corresponding response object.

Each user request to the IIS Web server flows through the HTTP pipeline, which refers to a series of components (HTTP Modules and HTTP Handlers) to process the request. HTTP Modules act as filters to process the request as it passes through the HTTP pipeline. The request, after passing through the HTTP Modules, is assigned to an HTTP Handler that determines the response of the server to the user request. The response then passes through the HTTP Modules once again and sends back to the user.

You can define HTTP Handlers in the `<httpHandlers>` element of a configuration file. The `<add>` element tag is used to add new handlers and the `<remove>` elements tag is used to remove existing handlers. To create an HTTP Handler, you need to define a class that implements an `IHttpHandler` interface. The method of the `IHttpHandler` interface is:

- **ProcessRequest()** – Invoked when a user request is received. It processes the request using the HttpContext object, which is passed as a parameter.

The property of the `IHttpHandler` interface is:

- **IsReusable** – Determines whether the HTTP Handler object, accessed using the ProcessRequest() method, can be reused. The HTTP Handler object can only be reused if the IsReusable() method returns a true value. The object is discarded when the HTTP Handler object returns a false value.

After understanding the concept of HTTP Handlers, we now move on to know postback.

Postback and Cross-Page Posting

Postback is the process of sending the data back to the server for processing. This is done to authenticate the login and password of a client or other such tasks that a client cannot perform on its own. ASP.NET provides a rich framework for handling postbacks from ASP.NET Web pages. Postback includes cross-page posting, which is the name given to the process of receiving the response of a request by the server on another page.

Immediate Solutions

Using the Global.asax File

The `Global.asax` file is created either in Notepad or as a compiled class, which is deployed as an assembly in the ASP.NET Web application. Now, let's learn to use the `Global.asax` file. For this, we have created an application, Global, in Visual Studio 2012 (available as GlobalVB in VB and GlobalCS in C#), which uses the `Global.asax` file to display the date and time.

NOTE

The applications in this chapter are created by selecting the ASP.NET Empty Web Site template in the New Web Site dialog box. After creating the application, you need to add a Default.aspx file, by performing the following steps:

1. Right-click the website name in Solution Explorer and select Add→Add New Item option from the context menu.
2. The Add New Item dialog box appears.
3. Select Web Form from the middle pane.
4. Enter a name, which in this case is Default.aspx, for the Web form in the Name text box.
5. Click the Add button.
6. This adds the `Default.aspx` file to your application.

After creating the application and adding a Web form, you need to add a `Global.asax` file to an application. For this, perform the following steps:

1. Right-click the name of the website in the Solution Explorer
2. Select the Add→Add New Item option from the context menu to open the Add New Item dialog box
3. Select the Global Application Class option and click the Add button.
4. Add the highlighted code in the Global.asax file.

Listing 3.1 shows the code of the `Global.asax` file:

Listing 3.1: Showing the Code for the `Global.asax` File

In VB

```
<%@ Application Language="VB" %>
<script runat="server">
    Sub Application_OnEndRequest(sender As Object, e As EventArgs)
        Response.Write("This page was executed on:" & DateTime.Now.ToString)
    End Sub
    Sub Application_Start(ByVal sender As Object, ByVal e As EventArgs)
        ' Code that runs on application startup
    End Sub
    Sub Application_End(ByVal sender As Object, ByVal e As EventArgs)
        ' Code that runs on application shutdown
    End Sub
    Sub Application_Error(ByVal sender As Object, ByVal e As EventArgs)
        ' Code that runs when an unhandled error occurs
    End Sub
```

```
    Sub Session_Start(ByVal sender As Object, ByVal e As EventArgs)
        ' Code that runs when a new session is started
    End Sub

    Sub Session_End(ByVal sender As Object, ByVal e As EventArgs)
        ' Code that runs when a session ends.
        ' Note: The Session_End event is raised only when the sessionstate mode
        ' is set to InProc in the Web.config file. If session mode is set to
              StateServer
        ' or SQLServer, the event is not raised.
    End Sub

</script>
```

In C#

```
<%@ Application Language="C#" %>

<script runat="server">
    protected void Application_OnEndRequest()
    {
        Response.Write("This page was executed on: " + DateTime.Now.ToString());
    }

    void Application_Start(object sender, EventArgs e)
    {
        // Code that runs on application startup
    }
    void Application_End(object sender, EventArgs e)
    {
        //  Code that runs on application shutdown
    }
    void Application_Error(object sender, EventArgs e)
    {
        // Code that runs when an unhandled error occurs
    }
    void Session_Start(object sender, EventArgs e)
    {
        // Code that runs when a new session is started
    }
    void Session_End(object sender, EventArgs e)
    {
        // Code that runs when a session ends.
        // Note: The Session_End event is raised only when the sessionstate mode
        // is set to InProc in the Web.config file. If session mode is set to
              StateServer
        // or SQLServer, the event is not raised.
    }
</script>
```

Running the application with the preceding listing opens a Web page that displays the date and time, using the `Global.asax` file, as shown in Figure 3.1:

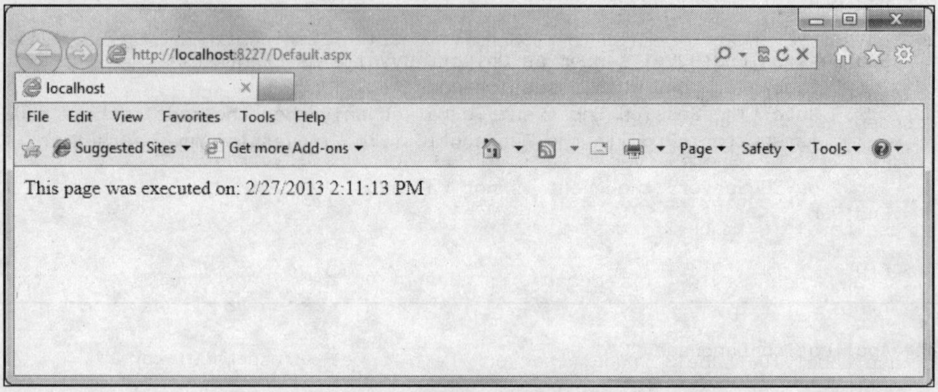

Figure 3.1: Output of the Global.asax File

Using Application State, Session State, and View state

Let's create a sample Web application, `StateImplementation` (available as `StateImplementationVB` in VB and `StateImplementationCS` in C#), which uses all the three state types--application, session, and view. After creating an empty Web site, follow these steps:

1. Add the Default.aspx file in the Web application.
2. Add the code in the `Default.aspx` page, as shown in Listing 3.2:

Listing 3.2: Showing the Code for the `Default.aspx` Page

In VB

```
<%@ Page Language="VB" AutoEventWireup="true" CodeFile="Default.aspx.vb"
  Inherits="_Default" %>
<script runat="server">
    Sub Page_Load(sender As Object,e As EventArgs)
        Label2.Text = Application("visits").ToString()
        Label3.Text = Session("mytext").ToString
    End Sub
    Protected Sub btnSubmit_Click(sender As Object, e As System.EventArgs)
        Dim txtvalue As String = txtName.Text
        ViewState.Add("item", txtvalue)
        Dim item As String = ViewState("item").ToString
        Label1.Text = item
    End Sub
</script>
<!DOCTYPE html>
<html xmlns="http://www.w3.org/1999/xhtml">
<head runat="server">
    <title>Implementing States</title>
</head>
<body bgcolor="#FFFFFF">
    <form id="form1" runat="server" action="default.aspx" method="post">
    <div>
    <strong><span style="text-decoration: underline">View State</span></strong><br />
  <br />
  Enter Your Name:
  <asp:TextBox ID="txtName" runat="server" />
```

```
    <br />                     
               <br />         
                          
       
    <asp:Button ID="btnSubmit" Text="Submit" OnClick="btnSubmit_Click" runat="server" />
    <br />
    <asp:Label ID="Label1" runat="server" Text="Label"></asp:Label><br />
     <br />  <br />  <br />
    <span style="text-decoration: underline"><strong>Application State<br />
    <br />
    </strong></span>Number of last visits:
    <asp:Label ID="Label2" runat="server" Text="Label"></asp:Label><br />
    <br /><br />
    <strong><span style="text-decoration: underline">Session State<br />
    </span></strong>
    <br />
    <asp:Label ID="Label3" runat="server" Text="Label"></asp:Label><br />
      </div>
      </form>

  </body>
  </html>
```

In C#

```
  <%@ Page Language="C#" AutoEventWireup="true" CodeFile="Default.aspx.cs"
     Inherits="_Default" %>
  <script runat="server">
    protected void Page_Load(object sender, EventArgs e)
    {

          Label2.Text = Application["visits"].ToString();
          Label3.Text = (string)Session["mytext"];
    }
    protected void btnSubmit_Click(object sender, EventArgs e)
    {
          string txtvalue = txtName.Text;
          ViewState.Add("item", txtvalue);
          string item = (string)ViewState["item"];
          Label1.Text = item;
    }

  </script>
  <!DOCTYPE html>
  <html xmlns="http://www.w3.org/1999/xhtml">
  <head runat="server">
      <title>Implementing States</title>
  </head>

  <body bgcolor="#FFFFFF">
      <form id="form1" runat="server" action="default.aspx" method="post" >
      <div>
      <strong><span style="text-decoration: underline">View State</span></strong><br />
    <br />
    Enter Your Name:
    <asp:TextBox ID="txtName" runat="server" />
```

```
<br />                     
           <br />        
                      
   
<asp:Button ID="btnSubmit" Text="Submit" OnClick="btnSubmit_Click" runat="server" />
<br />
<asp:Label ID="Label1" runat="server" Text="Label"></asp:Label><br />
 <br />  <br />  <br />
<span style="text-decoration: underline"><strong>Application State<br />
<br />
</strong></span>Number of last visits:
<asp:Label ID="Label2" runat="server" Text="Label"></asp:Label><br />
<br /><br />
<strong><span style="text-decoration: underline">Session State<br />
</span></strong>
<br />
<asp:Label ID="Label3" runat="server" Text="Label"></asp:Label><br />
  </div>
  </form>
</body>
</html>
```

NOTE

You should note that while writing the code in the Default.aspx file, you should set the AutoEventWireup property in the Page directive to true so that the Web application calls the page events, such as Page_Init and Page_Load, automatically.

3. Add the `Global.asax` file in the Web applications and add the code in the `Global.asax` file, as shown in Listing 3.3:

Listing 3.3: Showing the Code for the `Global.asax` File

In VB

```
<%@ Application Language="VB" %>
<script runat="server">
    Sub Application_Start(ByVal sender As Object, ByVal e As EventArgs)
        Application("visits") = 0
    End Sub
    Sub Application_End(ByVal sender As Object, ByVal e As EventArgs)
        ' Code that runs on application shutdown
    End Sub
    Sub Application_Error(ByVal sender As Object, ByVal e As EventArgs)
        ' Code that runs when an unhandled error occurs
    End Sub
    Sub Session_Start(ByVal sender As Object, ByVal e As EventArgs)
        Application("visits") = Int(Application("visits") + 1)
        Session("mytext") = "I am the user!!"
    End Sub
    Sub Session_End(ByVal sender As Object, ByVal e As EventArgs)
        ' Code that runs when a session ends.
        ' Note: The Session_End event is raised only when the sessionstate mode
        ' is set to InProc in the Web.config file. If session mode is set to StateServer
        ' or SQLServer, the event is not raised.
    End Sub
</script>
```

In C#

```
<%@ Application Language="C#" %>
<script runat="server">
    void Application_Start(object sender, EventArgs e)
    {
        Application["visits"] = 0;
    }
    void Application_End(object sender, EventArgs e)
    {
        //  Code that runs on application shutdown
    }
    void Application_Error(object sender, EventArgs e)
    {
        // Code that runs when an unhandled error occurs
    }
    void Session_Start(object sender, EventArgs e)
    {    Application["visits"] = (int)Application["visits"] + 1;
        Session["mytext"] = "I am the user!!";
    }
    void Session_End(object sender, EventArgs e)
    {
        // Code that runs when a session ends.
        // Note: The Session_End event is raised only when the sessionstate mode
        // is set to InProc in the Web.config file. If session mode is set to
                StateServer
        // or SQLServer, the event is not raised.
    }
</script>
```

4. Run the application in browser such as Google Chrome. Figure 3.2 shows the output of the StateImplementation Web application:

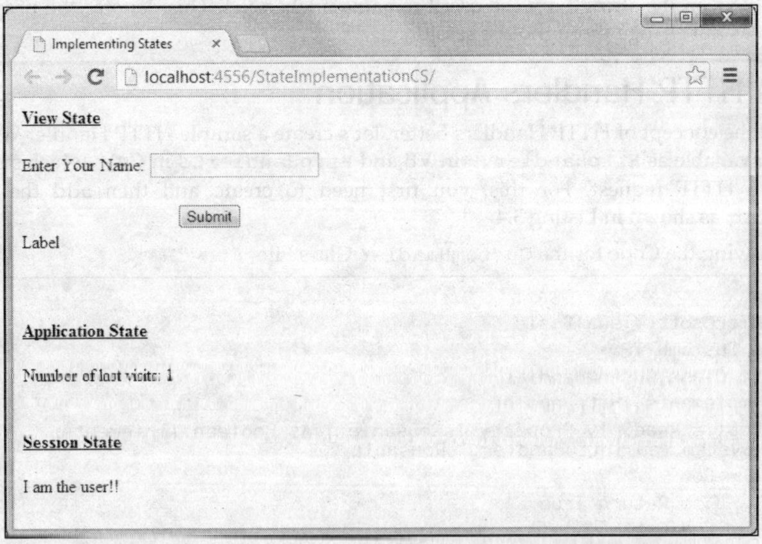

Figure 3.2: Output of the StateImplementationCS Web Application

Now, open the application in another browser such as Internet Explorer. The Number of last visits changes to 2.

5. Enter a name in the Enter Your Name text box and click the Submit button. This displays the name in the Label control.
6. Refresh the page to reload it. The number of visits remains the same. It changes whenever the application is opened in the new browser. Figure 3.3 shows the output after reloading the page:

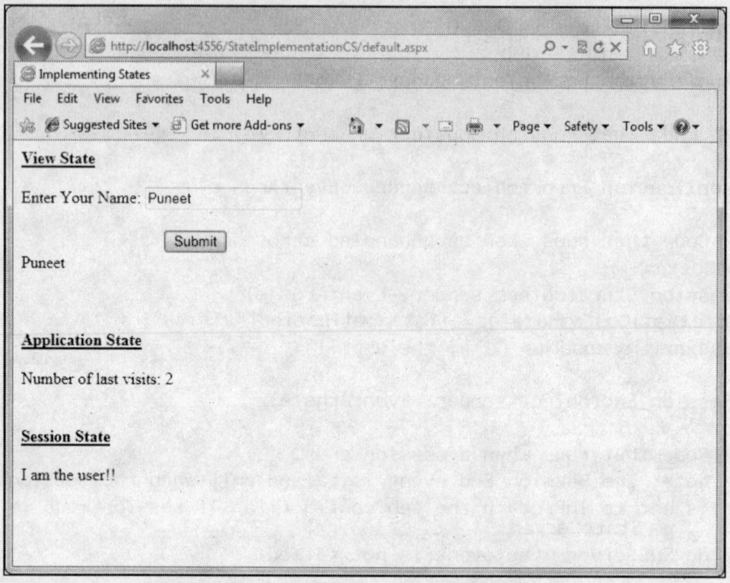

Figure 3.3: Output after Refreshing the Page

As shown in Figure 3.3, the name that you entered in the text box appears as a label, indicating that view state is maintained. The Number of last visits value also increases by 1, indicating that the application state is maintained. However, the string I am the user!! remains unchanged. This denotes the property of session state, whose value does not change throughout a session.

Creating an HTTP Handlers Application

To understand the concept of HTTP Handlers better, let's create a sample HTTP Handler Web application, called HttpHandler (available as `HttpHandlerVB` in VB and `HttpHandlerCS` in C#), which sends a test message in response to an HTTP request. For this, you first need to create and then add the code to a class file `CustomHandler`, as shown in Listing 3.4:

Listing 3.4: Showing the Code for the `CustomHandler` Class File

In VB

```
Imports Microsoft.VisualBasic
Namespace CustomHTTP
    Public Class CustomHandler
        Implements IHttpHandler
        Public ReadOnly Property IsReusable() As Boolean Implements
         System.Web.IHttpHandler.IsReusable
            Get
                Return True
            End Get
        End Property
        Public Sub ProcessRequest(ByVal context As System.Web.HttpContext) Implements
         System.Web.IHttpHandler.ProcessRequest
            Dim Response As HttpResponse = context.Response
            Response.Write("<html><body><H2>Sample HTTP Handler</H2></body></html>")
```

```
        End Sub
    End Class
End Namespace
```

In C#

```
using System;
using System.Collections.Generic;
using System.Linq;
using System.Web;

/// <summary>
/// Summary description for CustomHandler
/// </summary>

namespace CustomHTTP
{
    public class CustomHandler : IHttpHandler {
    public bool IsReusable {
        get
        {
            return true;
        }
    }

    public void ProcessRequest(System.Web.HttpContext context) {
        HttpResponse Response = context.Response;
        Response.Write("<html><body><H2>Sample HTTP Handler</H2></body></html>");
    }
}
}
```

Next, modify the code in the `<system.web>` element of the `Web.config` file, as shown in Listing 3.5:

Listing 3.5: Showing the Code for the `Web.config` File

In VB and C#

```
<?xml version="1.0"?>
<!--
  For more information on how to configure your ASP.NET application, please visit
  http://go.microsoft.com/fwlink/?LinkId=169433
  -->
<configuration>
  <system.web>
    <compilation debug="false" strict="false" explicit="true" targetFramework="4.5" />
    <authentication mode="Windows"/>
    <httpHandlers>
      <add verb="*" path="CustomHttp.test" type="CustomHTTP.CustomHandler"/>
    </httpHandlers>
    <httpRuntime targetFramework="4.5" />
  </system.web>
</configuration>
```

In the preceding listing, we have specified the path of the file that launches the HTTP Handler, as `CustomHttp.test`. Now, let's run the application. When you run the application, the `Default.aspx` page opens in the browser. You need to type the `CustomHttp.test` file name at the end of the URL and press the ENTER key to initiate the custom HTTP Handler, as shown in Figure 3.4:

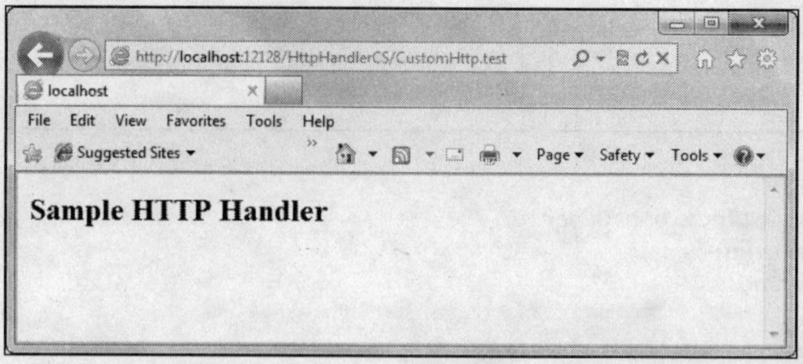

Figure 3.4: Output of the HttpHandlerCS Application

NOTE

You should note that before running the preceding application, you should set the Default.aspx as the start page by right-clicking the Default.aspx page and select the Set As Start Page option from the context menu.

Creating Generic Handlers Application

HTTP Handlers were somewhat tough to understand and create in the previous versions of Visual Studio, such as 2002 and 2003, because these versions did not provide any user-friendly methods for creating the handlers. However, in Visual Studio 2012, this has been made easier. All you need to do is simply add the Generic Handler file type in your application. Creating a Generic Handler is the easiest way to create a new HTTP Handler.

Let's now create an application, named `GenericHandler`, (available as `GenericHandlerVB` in VB and `GenericHandlerCS` in C#), to understand the use of Generic Handlers.

After creating the application, open the Add New Item dialog box by right-clicking the application name in Solution Explorer and select the Add→Add New Item from the context menu. In the Add New Item dialog box, select the Generic Handler template from the middle template pane, enter the name `GenericHandler.ashx` in the name field, and finally click the Add button, as shown in Figure 3.5:

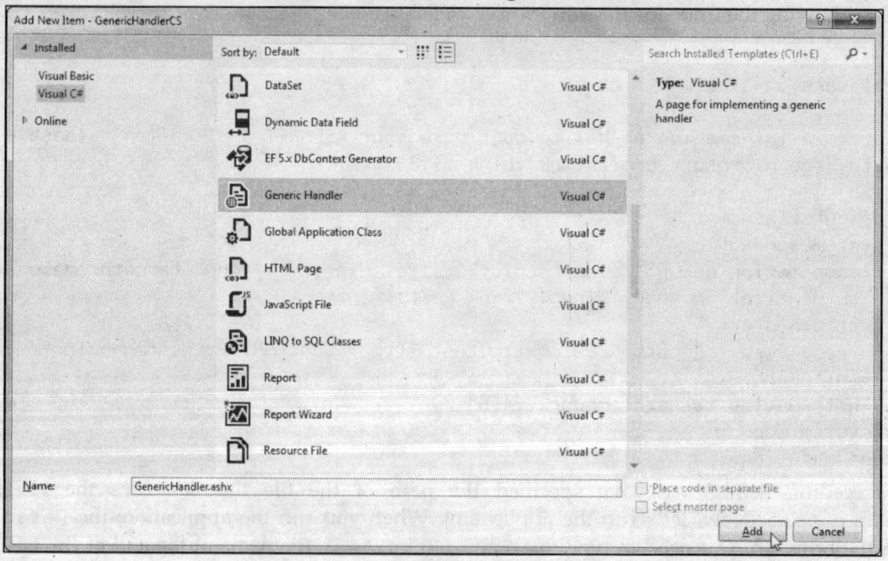

Figure 3.5: The Add New Item Dialog Box

The file is added to Solution Explorer. Now, add the code in the `GenericHandler.ashx` file, as shown in Listing 3.6:

Listing 3.6: Showing the Code for the `GenericHandler.ashx` File

In VB

```
<%@ WebHandler Language="VB" Class="GenericHandler" %>
Imports System
Imports System.Web
Public Class GenericHandler : Implements IHttpHandler
    Public Sub ProcessRequest(context As HttpContext) Implements
        IHttpHandler.ProcessRequest
        ManageForm(context)
    End Sub
   Public Sub ManageForm(context As HttpContext)
        context.Response.Write("<html><body><form>")
        If context.Request.Params("Feature") Is Nothing Then
        context.Response.Write("<h2>Hello there. Select your Favorite Feature of ASP
        .NET 4.5 </h2>")
        context.Response.Write("<select name='Feature'>")
        context.Response.Write("<option> ASP.NET AJAX</option>")
        context.Response.Write("<option> LINQ </option>")
        context.Response.Write("<option> Silverlight </option>")
        context.Response.Write("<option> WCF </option>")
        context.Response.Write("</select>")
        context.Response.Write("<input type=submit name='Lookup'
        value='Lookup'></input>")
        context.Response.Write("</br>")
        End If
        If context.Request.Params("Feature") IsNot Nothing Then
                context.Response.Write("Hi, you picked: ")
                context.Response.Write(context.Request.Params("Feature"))
                context.Response.Write(" as your favorite feature.</br>")
        End If
        context.Response.Write("</form></body></html>")
  End Sub
    Public ReadOnly Property IsReusable() As Boolean Implements IHttpHandler.IsReusable
        Get
            Return False
        End Get
    End Property
End Class
```

In C#

```
<%@ WebHandler Language="C#" Class="GenericHandler" %>
using System;
using System.Web;

public class GenericHandler : IHttpHandler {
    public void ProcessRequest (HttpContext context) {
        ManageForm(context);
    }
     public void ManageForm(HttpContext context)
     {
        context.Response.Write("<html><body><form>");
        if (context.Request.Params["Feature"] == null)
        {
                context.Response.Write("<h2>Hello there. Select your Favorite Feature
                of ASP .NET 4.5 </h2>");
```

```
                context.Response.Write("<select name='Feature'>");
                context.Response.Write("<option> ASP.NET AJAX</option>");
                context.Response.Write("<option> LINQ </option>");
                context.Response.Write("<option> Silverlight </option>");
                context.Response.Write("<option> WCF </option>");
                context.Response.Write("</select>");
                context.Response.Write("<input type=submit name='Lookup'
                value='Lookup'></input>");
                context.Response.Write("</br>");
            }
            if (context.Request.Params["Feature"] != null)
            {
                context.Response.Write("Hi, you picked: ");
                context.Response.Write(context.Request.Params["Feature"]);
                context.Response.Write(" as your favorite feature.</br>");
            }
            context.Response.Write("</form></body></html>");
        }
        public bool IsReusable {
            get {
                return false;
            }
        }
    }
```

Run the application after adding the code shown in Listing 3.6 in the `GenericHandler.ashx` file. Figure 3.6 shows the output of the GenericHandlerCS application:

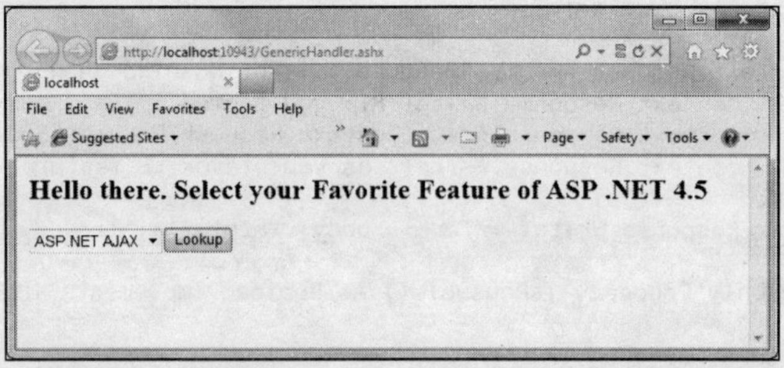

Figure 3.6: Output of the GenericHandlerCS Application

In the Web browser, shown in Figure 3.6, when you click the drop-down list, you see a list of ASP.NET 4.5 features. Select a feature of ASP.NET 4.5 from the drop-down list and click the Lookup button. In our case, we have selected the WCF option, as shown in Figure 3.7:

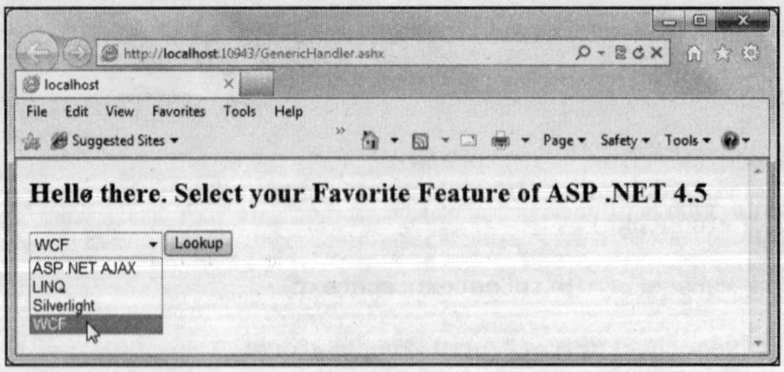

Figure 3.7: Selecting the Feature of ASP.NET 4.5

This displays the selected feature, as shown in Figure 3.8:

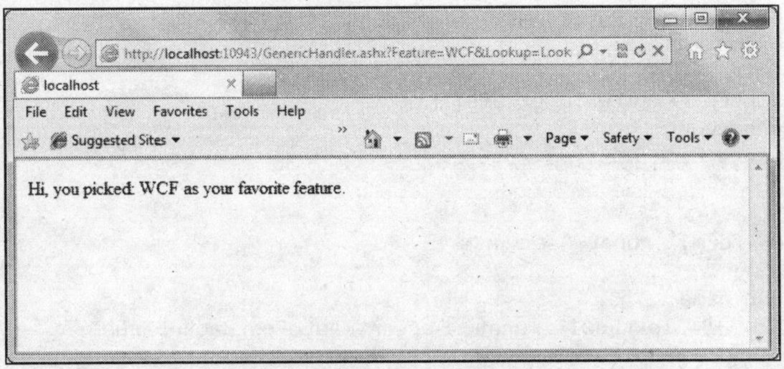

Figure 3.8: Output After Selecting the Feature

Working with Postback and Cross-Page Posting

Normally, when we post back data to the server, the server sends the response back to the same page. If we want to receive the response on another page, we use the concept of cross-page posting.

Let's create an application named `CrossPagePostbacksCS` (available as `CrossPagePostBacksVB` in VB and `CrossPagePostbacksCS` in C#), to understand the working of cross-page posting, and follow these steps:

1. Add the code in the `Default.aspx` file of the `CrossPagePostbacks` Web application, as shown in Listing 3.7:

Listing 3.7: Showing the Code for the `Default.aspx` Page

In VB

```
<%@ Page Language="VB" AutoEventWireup="false" CodeFile="Default.aspx.vb"
  Inherits="_Default" %>
<!DOCTYPE html>
<html xmlns="http://www.w3.org/1999/xhtml">
<head runat="server">
    <title>Cross-Page Posting</title>
</head>
<body>
    <form id="form1" runat="server">
    <div>
    Enter your name:
  <asp:TextBox ID="TextBox1" runat="server" AutoPostBack="True"
   Width="150px"></asp:TextBox>
   <br /><br />
  <asp:Calendar ID="Calendar1" runat="server"></asp:Calendar>
  <br />
    </div>
    <asp:Button ID="Button1" runat="server" Text="Same Page Post Back"
   OnClick="Button1_Click" />
   <asp:Button ID="Button2" runat="server" Text="Cross Page Post Back"
   PostBackUrl="~/Default2.aspx" />
  <p>
  <asp:Label ID="Label1" runat="server"></asp:Label>
  </p>
    </form>
</body>
</html>
```

In C#

```
<%@ Page Language="C#" AutoEventWireup="true" CodeFile="Default.aspx.cs"
   Inherits="_Default" %>
<!DOCTYPE html>
<html xmlns="http://www.w3.org/1999/xhtml">
<head runat="server">
    <title>Cross-Page Posting</title>
</head>
<body>
    <form id="form1" runat="server">
    <div>
    Enter your name:
  <asp:TextBox ID="TextBox1" runat="server" AutoPostBack="True"
   Width="152px"></asp:TextBox>
   <br />  <br />
  <asp:Calendar ID="Calendar1" runat="server"></asp:Calendar>
  <br />
    </div>
    <asp:Button ID="Button1" runat="server" Text="Same Page Post Back"
   OnClick="Button1_Click" />
   <asp:Button ID="Button2" runat="server" Text="Cross Page Post Back"
   PostBackUrl="~/Default2.aspx" />
  <p>
         <asp:Label ID="Label1" runat="server"></asp:Label>
  </p>
    </form>
</body>
</html>
```

In the preceding listing, we have added a TextBox control, a Calendar control, two Button controls, and a Label control. The `Butttonl` control is used to postback the data on the same page and the `Button2` control is used to postback the data on another page (cross page). After adding the code in the `Default.aspx` file, the design view of the page appears, as shown in Figure 3.9:

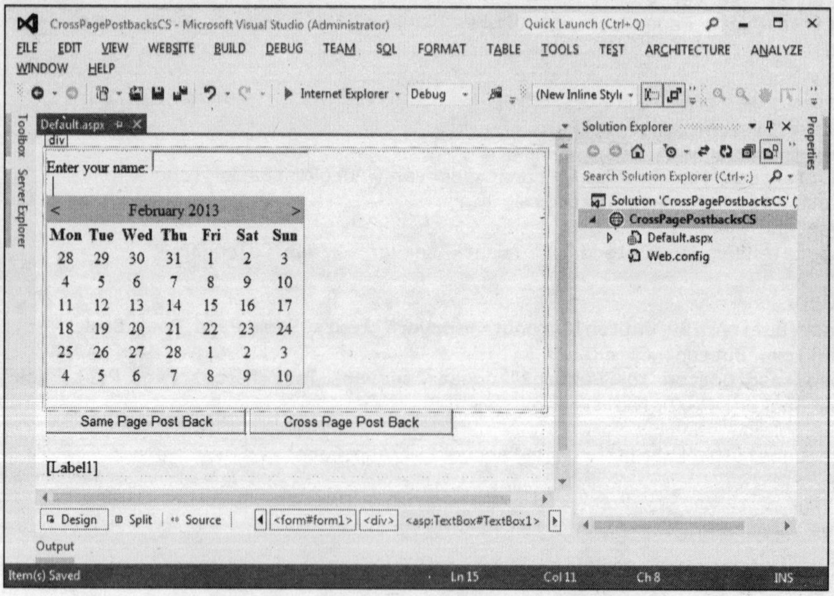

Figure 3.9: The Design View of the Default.aspx File

Instead of adding the code, you can also add the controls with the help of the Toolbox.

2. Add another page named `Default2.aspx` in the application, and add the code in it, as shown in Listing 3.8:

Listing 3.8: Showing the Code for the `Default2.aspx` Page

In VB

```
<%@ Page Language="VB" AutoEventWireup="false" CodeFile="Default2.aspx.vb"
  Inherits="Default2" %>

<!DOCTYPE html>
<html xmlns="http://www.w3.org/1999/xhtml">
<head runat="server">
    <title>Untitled Page</title>
</head>

<body>
    <form id="form1" runat="server">
    <div>
    <asp:Label ID="Label1" runat="server"></asp:Label>
    </div>
    </form>

</body>
</html>
```

In C#

```
<%@ Page Language="C#" AutoEventWireup="true" CodeFile="Default2.aspx.cs"
  Inherits="Default2" %>
<!DOCTYPE html>

<html xmlns="http://www.w3.org/1999/xhtml">
<head runat="server">
    <title>Untitled Page</title>
</head>

<body>
    <form id="form1" runat="server">
    <div>
    <asp:Label ID="Label1" runat="server"></asp:Label>
    </div>
    </form>
</body>
</html>
```

3. Add the code shown in Listing 3.9, in the code-behind file of the `Default.aspx` page:

Listing 3.9: Showing the Code for the Code-Behind File

In VB

```
Partial Class _Default
    Inherits System.Web.UI.Page
   Protected Sub Button1_Click(sender As Object, e As System.EventArgs)
  Handles Button1.Click
        Label1.Text = "Hi " + TextBox1.Text + ", here is the output of the Same Page
         Post
         Back Button: " + Calendar1.SelectedDate.ToString()
    End Sub
End Class
```

In C#

```
using System;
using System.Collections.Generic;
using System.Linq;
using System.Web;
using System.Web.UI;
using System.Web.UI.WebControls;
public partial class _Default : System.Web.UI.Page
{
    protected void Page_Load(object sender, EventArgs e)
    {
    }
    protected void Button1_Click(object sender, EventArgs e)
    {
        Label1.Text = "Hi " + TextBox1.Text + ", here is the output of the Same Page
        PostBack Button: " + Calendar1.SelectedDate.ToString();
    }
}
```

4. Add the code shown in Listing 3.10, in the code-behind file of the `Default2.aspx` page:

Listing 3.10: Showing the Code for the Code-Behind File of the `Default2.aspx` Page

In VB

```
Partial Class Default2
    Inherits System.Web.UI.Page
   Protected Sub Page_Load(sender As Object, e As System.EventArgs) Handles
  Me.Load
        Dim Calendar1 As Calendar
        Dim TextBox1 As TextBox
        Calendar1 = CType(PreviousPage.FindControl("Calendar1"), Calendar)
        TextBox1 = CType(PreviousPage.FindControl("TextBox1"), TextBox)
        Label1.Text = "Hi " + TextBox1.Text + ", here is the output of the Cross Page
        Post Back Button: " + Calendar1.SelectedDate.ToString()
    End Sub
End Class
```

In C#

```
using System;
using System.Collections.Generic;
using System.Linq;
using System.Web;
using System.Web.UI;

using System.Web.UI.WebControls;
public partial class Default2 : System.Web.UI.Page
{
    protected void Page_Load(object sender, EventArgs e)
    {
        Calendar Calendar1 = new Calendar();
        TextBox TextBox1 = new TextBox();
        Calendar1 = (Calendar)(PreviousPage.FindControl("Calendar1"));
        TextBox1 = (TextBox)(PreviousPage.FindControl("TextBox1"));
        Label1.Text = "Hi " + TextBox1.Text + ", here is the output of the Cross Page
        Post Back Button: "+ Calendar1.SelectedDate.ToString();
    }
}
```

5. Run the application and see the output. However, before you do that, set the `Default.aspx` page as your start up page; otherwise, some errors may occur in the application at runtime. When you run the application, the first page appears in your browser, as shown in Figure 3.10:

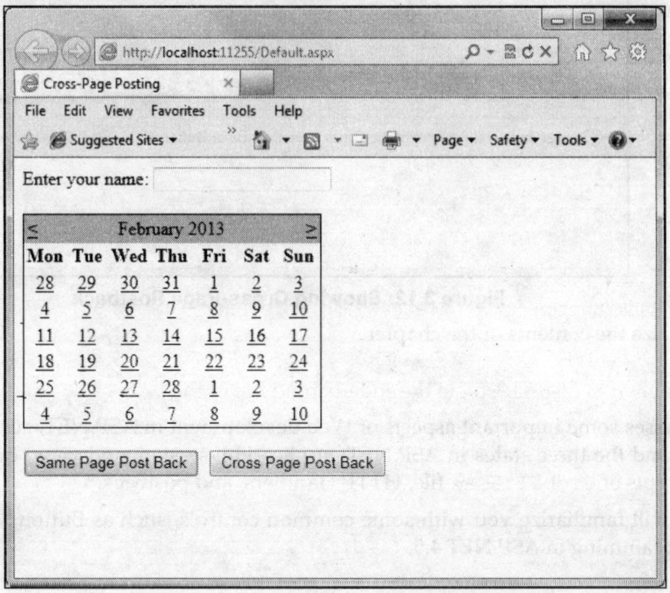

Figure 3.10: First Page of the Application

6. Enter your name in the TextBox control and select the date in the calendar that you want to display. When you click the Same Page Post Back button, the name and the selected date displays on the same page, as shown in Figure 3.11:

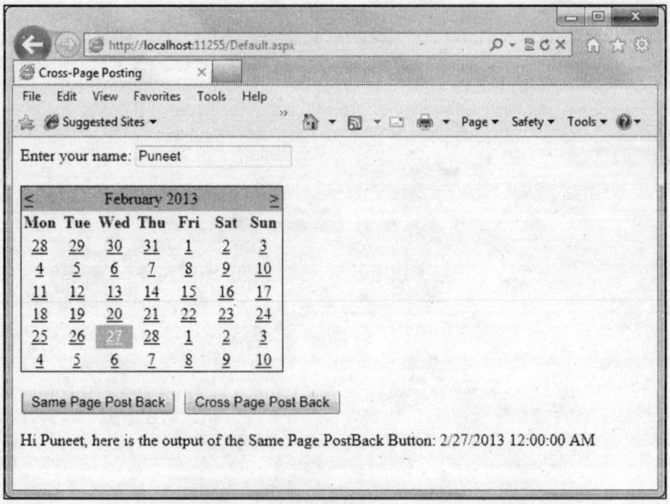

Figure 3.11: Showing Postback on the Same Page

7. Enter your name, select a date, and click the Cross Page Post Back button, to demonstrate cross-page postback. The name and selected date displays on another page, as shown in Figure 3.12:

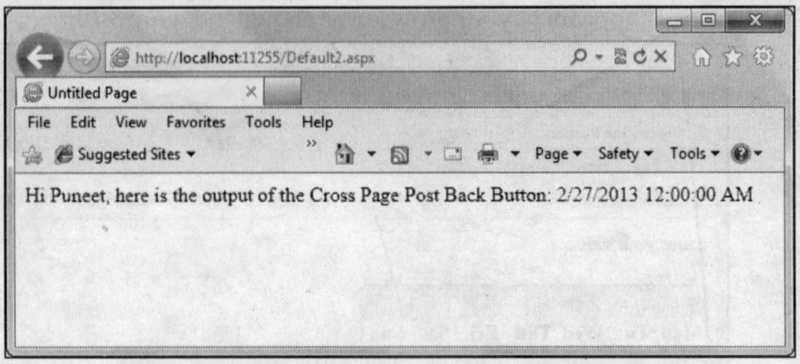

Figure 3.12: Showing Cross-Page Postback

Let's now summarize the contents of the chapter.

Summary

This chapter discusses some important aspects of Web development in ASP.NET, such as the directory structure of an application and the three states in ASP.NET: application, session, and view. In addition, this chapter also describes the concepts of `Global.asax` file, HTTP Handlers, and postback.

The next chapter will familiarize you with some common controls, such as Button, Textbox, Label, and Literal, used for Web programming in ASP.NET 4.5.

4

Web Forms: Standard Controls (I)

If you need an Immediate Solution to:	See page:

In Depth

In the previous chapters, you have already learned how to create Web applications. Now, let's discuss about Web form controls. The Web form controls are designed to resemble standard Visual Basic Windows forms controls. These controls are used to design the interface of any Web application, for example, when you visit the website of Google, you type your search query in a text box, which is a control. ASP.NET provides a standard set of controls that can be used to develop Web applications. You can access all these controls from the Toolbox present in Visual Studio Integrated Development Environment (IDE). These controls can easily be used by just dragging and dropping them at any desired location on a Web form. Based on the tasks performed by them, these controls are grouped under various categories known as tabs. For example, controls for validating the data are placed under the Validation tab and controls used for logging on to websites are placed under the Login tab. Similarly, controls for common use are placed under the Standard tab and are known as Standard controls. All these controls come under the Control class. The Web server controls are based on the `WebControl` class, which in turn, is based on the Control class. In other words, the `WebControl` class is derived from the Control class.

In this chapter, you learn about the inheritance hierarchy, public properties, public methods, and public events of the `Control` and the `WebControl` classes. You also learn about the various controls, such as `Label`, `Button`, `TextBox`, `Literal`, `PlaceHolder`, `HiddenField`, and `FileUpload` that originate from the `WebControl` class, along with their implementations.

Let's start by learning about the `Control` class.

The Control Class

The `System.Web.UI.Control` class is the base class for all Web server controls. This class is derived from the `Object` class, which resides in the `System` namespace. The hierarchy of the `Control` class is as follows:

```
System.Object
  System.Web.UI.Control
```

The noteworthy public properties of the `Control` class are listed in Table 4.1:

Table 4.1: Noteworthy Public Properties of the Control Class

Property	Description
`AppRelativeTemplateSourceDirectory`	Obtains or specifies the application-relative virtual directory of the `Page` instance or `UserControl` that contains the current server control
`BindingContainer`	Obtains the control that contains the server control data binding
`ClientID`	Obtains the control ID for HTML markup that is generated by ASP.NET
`ClientIDMode`	Obtains or specifies the algorithm that generates the value of ClientID property
`Controls`	Obtains a `ControlCollection` object that represents the child controls for a specified server control in the User Interface (`UI`) hierarchy
`DataItemContainer`	Obtains a reference to the naming container if the container implements the IDataItemContainer property
`EnableTheming`	Obtains or specifies a value indicating whether or not themes apply to a server control
`EnableViewState`	Obtains or specifies a value indicating whether or not the server control persists its view-state and the view-state of any child controls it contains
`ID`	Obtains or specifies the programmatic identifier assigned to the server control

Table 4.1: Noteworthy Public Properties of the Control Class

Property	Description
`NamingContainer`	Obtains a reference to the server control's naming container, which creates a unique namespace to differentiate between server controls with the same `System.Web.UI.Control.ID` property value
`Page`	Obtains a reference of the `Page` instance that contains the server control
`Parent`	Obtains a reference of the server control's parent control in the page control hierarchy
`RenderingCompatibility`	Obtains the value that specifies the ASP.NET version, which is compatible with the Hypertext Markup Language (HTML) code
`Site`	Obtains information about the container that hosts the current control when rendered on a design surface
`SkinID`	Obtains or specifies the style to apply to a server control
`TemplateControl`	Obtains or specifies a reference of the template that contains a server control
`TemplateSourceDirectory`	Obtains the virtual directory of the `Page` instance or `UserControl` that contains the current server control
`UniqueID`	Obtains the unique, hierarchically-qualified identifier for the server control
`ViewStateMode`	Obtains or specifies the view-state mode of a server control
`Visible`	Obtains or specifies a value that indicates whether or not a server control is rendered as `UI` on a Web page

Table 4.2 lists the noteworthy public methods of the `Control` class:

Table 4.2: Noteworthy Public Methods of the Control Class

Method	Description
`ApplyStyleSheetSkin`	Applies the style properties defined in the page style sheet to a server control
`DataBind`	Helps in binding a data source to the invoked server control and all its child controls
`Dispose`	Helps in enabling a server control to perform final clean up before it is released from memory
`FindControl`	Helps in searching the current naming container for the specified server control
`Focus`	Helps in setting input focus to a control
`HasControls`	Helps in determining whether or not the server control contains any child controls
`RenderControl`	Stores tracing information about the control if tracing is enabled
`ResolveClientUrl`	Helps in getting a Uniform Resource Locator (URL) that can be used by a browser
`ResolveUrl`	Helps in converting a URL into the desired format
`SetRenderMethodDelegate`	Helps in assigning an event handler delegate to render the server control and its content into its parent control

The noteworthy public events of the `Control` class are listed in Table 4.3:

Table 4.3: Noteworthy Public Events of the Control Class

Event	Description
`DataBinding`	Occurs when a server control is attached to a data source
`Disposed`	Refers to the last stage of the life cycle of a server control and occurs when a server control is released from memory
`Init`	Refers to the first step in the ASP.NET Web page life cycle and occurs when a server control is initialized
`Load`	Occurs when a server control is loaded into the `Page` object
`PreRender`	Occurs when a server control is about to render to its containing `Page` object
`Unload`	Occurs when a server control is unloaded from memory

After discussing the major properties, methods, and events of the Control class, let's move on to discuss the WebControl class, as it is the class on which all the controls directly depend.

The WebControl Class

All Web server controls exist within the System.Web.UI.WebControls.WebControl namespace and can be used on any Web form. The hierarchy of `WebControl` class is as follows:

```
System.Object
  System.Web.UI.Control
       System.Web.UI.WebControls.WebControl
```

The noteworthy public properties of the `WebControl` class are listed in Table 4.4:

Table 4.4: Noteworthy Public Properties of the WebControl Class

Property	Description
`AccessKey`	Obtains or specifies the access key that allows you to quickly navigate to the Web server control.
`Attributes`	Obtains the collection of arbitrary attributes (for rendering only) that do not correspond to properties on a server control.
`BackColor`	Obtains or specifies the background color of the Web server control.
`BorderColor`	Obtains or specifies the border color of the Web server control.
`BorderStyle`	Obtains or specifies the border style of the Web server control.
`BorderWidth`	Obtains or specifies the border width of the Web server control
`ControlStyle`	Obtains the style of the Web server control.
`ControlStyleCreated`	Obtains a value indicating whether or not a `Style` object has been created for the `ControlStyle` property. This property is primarily used by control developers.
`CssClass`	Obtains or specifies the Cascading Style Sheet (CSS) class rendered by the Web server control on the client.
`Enabled`	Obtains or specifies a value indicating whether or not the Web server control is enabled
`EnableTheming`	Obtains or specifies a value indicating whether or not themes apply to the Web server control
`Font`	Obtains the font properties associated with the Web server control

Table 4.4: Noteworthy Public Properties of the WebControl Class	
Property	**Description**
`ForeColor`	Obtains or specifies the foreground color (typically the color of the text) of the Web server control
`HasAttributes`	Specifies a value indicating whether or not attributes are set for the Web server control
`Height`	Obtains or specifies the height of the Web server control
`SkinID`	Obtains or specifies the skin to apply to the Web server control
`Style`	Obtains a collection of text attributes that will be rendered as a style attribute on the outer tag of the Web server control
`TabIndex`	Obtains or specifies the tab index of the Web server control
`ToolTip`	Obtains or specifies the text displayed when the mouse pointer hovers over the Web server control
`Width`	Obtains or specifies the width of the Web server control

Table 4.5 lists the noteworthy public methods of the `WebControl` class:

Table 4.5: Noteworthy Public Methods of the WebControl Class	
Method	**Description**
`ApplyStyle`	Copies any non-blank elements of the specified style to the Web control. It also overwrites any existing style elements of the control.
`CopyBaseAttributes`	Copies the properties that are not encapsulated by the `Style` object from the specified Web server control to the Web server control that this method is called from. This method is used primarily by control developers.
`MergeStyle`	Copies any non-blank elements of the specified style to the Web control, but will not overwrite any existing style elements of the control. This method is used primarily by control developers.
`RenderBeginTag`	Writes the HTML opening tag of the specified markup element to the output stream.
`RenderEndTag`	Writes the HTML closing tag of a markup element to the output stream.

Some of the basic standard controls included in the WebControl class are as follows:

- The Label control
- The Button control
- The TextBox control
- The Literal control
- The PlaceHolder control
- The HiddenField control
- The FileUpload control

Let's discuss these controls in detail.

The Label Control

The Label control is used to display the text that cannot be edited by a user. This control exists within the `System.Web.UI.WebControls` namespace. The class hierarchy of the Label class is as follows:

```
System.Object
   System.Web.UI.Control
         System.Web.UI.WebControls.WebControl
                System.Web.UI.WebControls.Label
```

The noteworthy public properties of the `Label` class are listed in Table 4.6:

Table 4.6: Noteworthy Public Properties of the Label Class

Property	Description
`AccessKey`	Obtains or specifies the access key that allows you to navigate to the Web server control
`AssociatedControlID`	Obtains or specifies the identifier for a server control with which the `Label` control is associated
`BackColor`	Obtains or specifies the background color of the Label control
`BorderColor`	Obtains or specifies the border color of the Label control
`BorderStyle`	Obtains or specifies the border style of the Label control
`BorderWidth`	Obtains or specifies the border width of the Label control
`Font`	Specifies the font properties
`ForeColor`	Obtains or specifies the foreground color
`Height`	Obtains or specifies the height of the Label control
`Text`	Obtains or specifies the text to be displayed in the `Label` control
`Width`	Obtains or specifies the width of the Label control

The Button Control

The Button control is used to create a button that sends a request to a Web page. This control exists within the `System.Web.UI.WebControls` namespace. It posts data to the server when it is clicked.

The class hierarchy of the Button class is as follows:

```
System.Object
   System.Web.UI.Control
           System.Web.UI.WebControls.WebControl
                     System.Web.UI.WebControls.Button
```

Table 4.7 lists the noteworthy public properties of the `Button` class:

Table 4.7: Noteworthy Public Properties of the Button Class

Property	Description
`CausesValidation`	Obtains or specifies a value indicating whether or not validation is performed when the `Button` control is clicked
`CommandArgument`	Obtains or specifies an optional parameter passed to the Command event along with the associated CommandName
`CommandName`	Obtains or specifies the command name associated with the Button control that is passed to the Command event
`OnClientClick`	Obtains or specifies the client-side script that executes when a Button control's Click event is raised
`PostBackUrl`	Obtains or specifies the URL of the page to post when the Button control is clicked
`Text`	Obtains or specifies the text to be displayed on the Button control
`UseSubmitBehavior`	Obtains or specifies a value indicating whether the `Button` control uses the client browser's submit mechanism or the ASP.NET postback mechanism to submit data to a server
`ValidationGroup`	Obtains or specifies the group of controls for which the `Button` control causes validation when it posts back to the server

The noteworthy public events of the `Button` class are listed in Table 4.8:

Table 4.8: Noteworthy Public Events of the Button Class

Event	Description
`Click`	Occurs when the `Button` control is clicked.
`Command`	Occurs when the `Button` control is clicked. This event helps you to create multiple Button controls on a Web page and then it programmatically determines which Button control has been clicked.

The Button controls are also used to create push buttons on a Web page. Push buttons can be either Submit buttons or Command buttons. By default, a Button control is a Submit button. A Submit button does not have a command name element, which you need to specify by using the CommandName property, associated with the Button control. You can provide an event handler with the Click event to programmatically control the actions performed when the Submit button is clicked.

A Command button has a command name associated with the button, which you need to specify by using the CommandName property, such as Sort. This allows you to create multiple Button controls on a Web page and programmatically find out that which of the Button control is clicked. You can provide an event handler for the Command event to programmatically control the actions performed when the Command button is clicked.

The TextBox Control

The TextBox control is an input control, which allows you to enter text. It exists within the `System.Web.UI.WebControls` namespace. The class hierarchy of this class is as follows:

```
System.Object
  System.Web.UI.Control
       System.Web.UI.WebControls.WebControl
             System.Web.UI.WebControls.TextBox
```

You can set the style of the TextBox control by using the `TextMode` property. By default, the `TextMode` property is set to `SingleLine` to create a single-line HTML text field but it can also be set to `MultiLine` for a multiline text box.

You can convert a mode of TextBox control to a Password control, where the text that you type is masked with special symbols, such as asterisks (`*`).

The display width of a text box is set with its `Columns` property and if it is a multiline text box, the display height is set with the `Rows` property. Table 4.9 lists the noteworthy public properties of the `TextBox` class:

Table 4.9: Noteworthy Public Properties of the TextBox Class

Property	Description
`AutoCompleteType`	Obtains or specifies a value that indicates the AutoComplete behavior of the TextBox control
`AutoPostBack`	Obtains or specifies a value that indicates whether or not an automatic postback to the server occurs when the TextBox control loses focus
`CausesValidation`	Obtains or specifies a value indicating whether or not validation is performed when the TextBox control is set to validate the client or server on the occurrence of a postback event
`Columns`	Obtains or specifies the display width of a text box in characters
`MaxLength`	Obtains or specifies the maximum number of characters allowed in a text box
`ReadOnly`	Obtains or specifies a value indicating whether or not the contents of the TextBox control can be changed
`Rows`	Obtains or specifies the number of rows displayed in a multiline text box

Table 4.9: Noteworthy Public Properties of the TextBox Class

Property	Description
`Text`	Obtains or specifies the text of the TextBox control
`TextMode`	Obtains or specifies the behavior mode (single-line, multiline, or password) of the TextBox control
`ValidationGroup`	Obtains or specifies the group of controls for which the TextBox control causes validation when it posts back to the server
`Wrap`	Obtains or specifies a value indicating whether or not the text wraps within a multiline text box

The public event of the `TextBox` class is listed in Table 4.10:

Table 4.10: Noteworthy Public Event of the TextBox Class

Event	Description
`TextChanged`	Occurs when a user changes the text of a TextBox control

The Literal Control

Similar to a `Label` control, the `Literal` control is another Web server control used to display text on a Web page. In ASP.NET, you can add HTML code in a Web page with the help of `Literal` control, without switching to the `.aspx` page. The Literal control exists within the `System.Web.UI.WebControls` namespace. The class hierarchy of this class is as follows:

```
System.Object
  System.Web.UI.Control
      System.Web.UI.WebControls.Literal
```

Table 4.11 lists the noteworthy public properties of the `Literal` class:

Table 4.11: Noteworthy Public Properties of the Literal Class

Property	Description
`Mode`	Obtains or specifies an enumeration value that specifies how the content in the Literal control is rendered
`Text`	Obtains or specifies the caption displayed in the Literal control

You can set the text by using the `Text` property of the `Literal` control. This control does not have any visual appearance in a Web page.

The PlaceHolder Control

The PlaceHolder control is used as a container to store server controls that are added to a Web page at runtime. This control does not produce any visible output and is used only as a container for other controls on the Web page. The class hierarchy for the `PlaceHolder` class is as follows:

```
System.Object
  System.Web.UI.Control
      System.Web.UI.WebControls.PlaceHolder
```

A noteworthy public property of the `PlaceHolder` class is listed in Table 4.12:

Table 4.12: Public Property of the PlaceHolder Class

Property	Description
`EnableTheming`	Obtains or specifies a value indicating whether or not themes apply to the `PlaceHolder` control

The HiddenField Control

The `HiddenField` control is used to store a value that needs to persist across posts to the server. Normally, view-state, session-state, and cookies are used to maintain the state of a Web page. In case, if these methods are disabled or are not available, you can use the `HiddenField` control to store state values. The class hierarchy for the `HiddenField` class is as follows:

```
System.Object
   System.Web.UI.Control
        System.Web.UI.WebControls.HiddenField
```

Table 4.13 lists the noteworthy public properties of the HiddenField class:

Table 4.13: Public Properties of the HiddenField Class

Property	Description
`EnableTheming`	Obtains or specifies a value indicating whether or not themes apply to the `HiddenField` control
`SkinID`	Obtains or specifies the skin to apply to the `HiddenField` control
`Value`	Obtains or specifies the value of the hidden field

The FileUpload Control

The `FileUpload` control displays a text box and a Browse button that enable you to browse a file from the local or remote machine to upload it on a Web server. You can upload a file on the Web server by specifying the full path of the file to be uploaded (for example, `D:\MyFiles\Test.txt`) in the text box of this control. Alternatively, you can select the file by clicking the Browse button and then locating it in the Choose File dialog box. The class hierarchy of the `FileUpLoad` class is as follows:

```
System.Object
   System.Web.UI.Control
        System.Web.UI.WebControls.WebControl
                  System.Web.UI.WebControls.FileUpload
```

Table 4.14 lists the noteworthy public properties of the `FileUpload` class:

Table 4.14: Noteworthy Public Properties of the FileUpload Class

Name	Description
`FileBytes`	Obtains an array of the bytes in a file that is specified by using the `FileUpload` control
`FileContent`	Obtains a Stream object that points to a file to upload using the `FileUpload` control
`FileName`	Obtains the name of a file to upload on a client using the `FileUpload` control
`HasFile`	Obtains a value indicating whether or not the `FileUpload` control contains a file
`PostedFile`	Obtains the underlying `HttpPostedFile` object for a file that is uploaded by using the `FileUpload` control

The noteworthy public method of the `FileUpLoad` class is listed in Table 4.15:

Table 4.15: Noteworthy Public Method of the FileUpload Class

Name	Description
`SaveAs`	Saves the data of an uploaded file to a specified path on a Web server

After learning about the different Web form controls, let's now move to the *Immediate Solutions* section of the chapter to learn how to use them in ASP.NET applications.

Immediate Solutions

Using CSS in Web Applications

CSS helps in giving a better and consistent look to applications. In ASP.NET, CSS has been improved to include significant enhancements that are according to the latest HTML standards. The changes in CSS are mainly targeted toward its better working with the Web server controls. CSS now includes a set of tools to create, apply, and manage styles, which are as follows:

- **Apply Styles**—Enables you to create, modify, and apply styles to a Web page. With the help of this tool, you can also use external CSS in your Web applications. It helps you to identify the style types, and displays whether or not the style is used in the current Web page.
- **Manage Styles**—Lists all the style rules defined in CSS. It also enables you to move styles within a style sheet.
- **CSS Properties**—Displays the styles that are currently selected in a Web page, in a priority order. It also displays the list of all CSS properties and helps you to add properties to an existing style, modify properties of already set styles, and build new inline styles.
- **Direct Style Application**—Helps you to remove or apply styles that are based on class-ID. It helps you to create or apply new styles. It also controls styles that are generated by an ASP.NET application.

Now, let's learn the procedure to create CSS in a Web application.

NOTE

The applications in this chapter are created using the ASP.NET Empty Web Site template in the New Web Site dialog box. After creating the application, you need to add the Default.aspx page to the application.

Let's perform the following steps to create a CSS:

1. Open Visual Studio 2012 and create a new Web application, CSSApplication.
2. Right-click the Web application's name in Solution Explorer and select the Add→Add New Item option from the context menu, as shown in Figure 4.1:

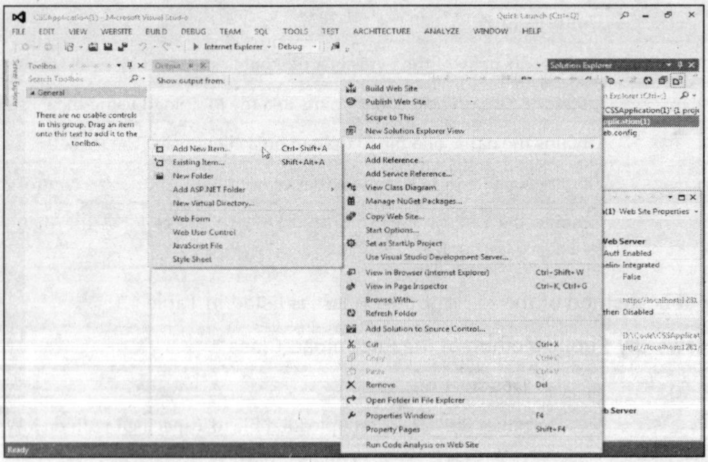

Figure 4.1: Selecting the Add New Item Option

The Add New Item dialog box appears (Figure 4.2).

3. Select the Style Sheet template from the list of given templates and its name appears as StyleSheet.css in the Name text box (Figure 4.2).
4. Click the Add button, as shown in Figure 4.2:

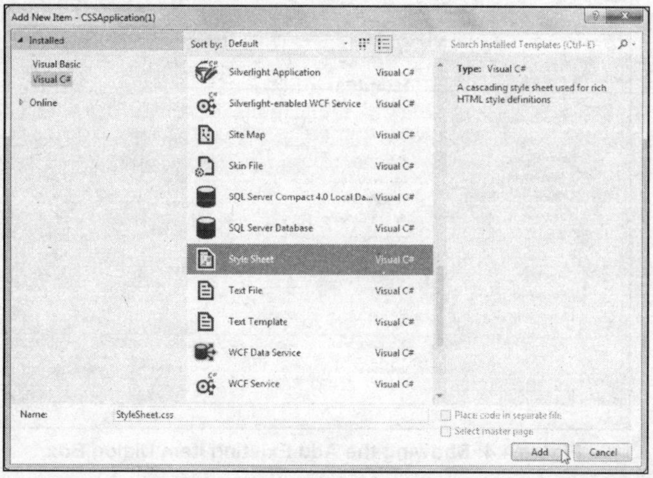

Figure 4.2: Showing the Style Sheet Template in the Add New Item Dialog Box

The CSS file, StyleSheet.css, is added to your Web application.

NOTE

You can also create the CSS file by performing the following steps:

1. *Create a file with the .css extension using a text editor, such as Notepad.*
2. *Add the code (provided in Listing 4.1 later) to the .css file and save it as StyleSheet.css.*
3. *Create a new Web application or open an existing one.*
4. *Right-click the application name in Solution Explorer and select the Add→ Existing Item option, as shown in Figure 4.3:*

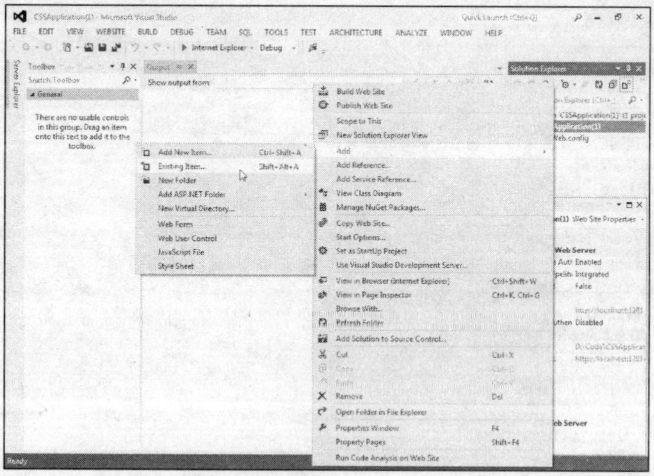

Figure 4.3: Displaying the Existing Item Option

The Add Existing Item dialog box opens.

5. *Browse the CSS file you have created and click the Add button, as shown in Figure 4.4:*

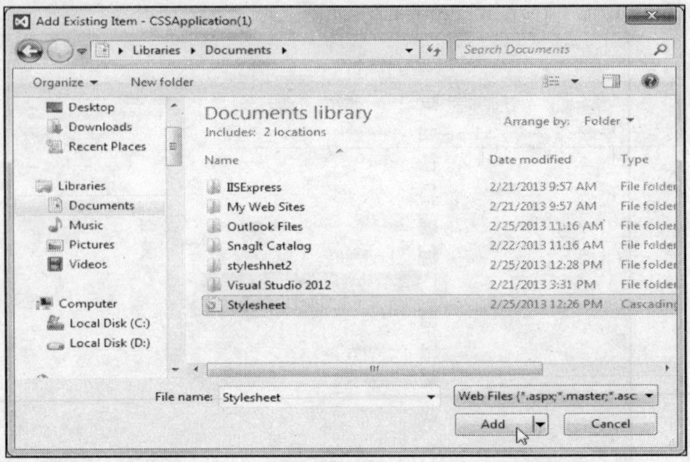

Figure 4.4: Showing the Add Existing Item Dialog Box

The CSS file has been added to application.

Now, you can see this file (`StyleSheet.css`) in Solution Explorer. Listing 4.1 shows the code of StyleSheet.css file:

Listing 4.1: Showing the Code of the `StyleSheet.css` File

```
html, body {
   background-color:Maroon;
   color: #000000;
   font: normal 90%/1.8em 'Lucida Grande', Verdana, Geneva, Lucida, Helvetica, Arial,
    sans-serif;
   margin: 0;
   height: 100%;
}
h1 {
   font-size: 1.8em;
   font-weight: bold;
   margin-top: 0em;
   margin-bottom: 0em;
   color: #a83930;
}
h2 {
   font-size: 1.6em;
   margin: 1.0em 0em 1.0em 0em;
   font-weight: bold;
   color: #a83930;
}
h3 {
   font-size: 1.2em;
   margin: 1.0em 0em 1.0em 0em;
   font-weight: bold;
   color: #a83930;
}
p {
   font-size: 1.1em;
   line-height: 1.8em;
   margin: 1.1em 0em 1.1em 0em;
```

```
  text-align: left;
}
ul
{
  font-size: 1.1em;
}
a:link, a:visited {
  color: #cc3300;
  text-decoration: underline;
}
a:hover {
  text-decoration: none;
}
a:active {
  color: #ff9900;
  text-decoration: underline;
}
title {
  color: #a83930;
}
#header {
  height: 67px;
  padding: 0 0px 0 0px;
  color: #a83930;
  background-color: #000000;
  border-bottom: 8px solid #d30a1a;
}
#header h1 {
  padding: 10px 0 0 0;
  margin: 10px 0 0 0px;
  color: #FFFFFF;
  margin-left: 10px;
  margin-bottom: 10px;
}
#logo {
  background-color: #000000;
  background: url(images/logo.gif);
  background-position: top left;
  background-repeat: no-repeat;
  height: 100px;
  width: 100px;
  border: 0;
  float: left;
}
#content {
  margin-left: 210px;
  padding: 0 20px 1.8em 10px;
  background-color: #fff;
]
.code {
  color: #a83930;
  background-color: #fdea12;
  font: 0.9em/1.4em verdana, arial, helvetica, sans-serif;
  float: right;
  border: solid 1px #a83930;
  padding: 10px;
}
#sidebar {
  float:left;
  padding: 0 10px 10px 10px;
```

```
    background-color: #656565;
    /*background-image: url(images/bg_2.gif);*/
    background-repeat: repeat-y;
    background-position: top left;
    border-top: 2px solid #656565;
    border-bottom: 2px solid #656565;
    width: 168px;  /* ds */
    height:500px;
}
html>body #sidebar {
   width: 180px;
}
#sidebar h3 {
   font-weight: bold;
   padding-bottom: 0.5em;
   border-bottom: 1px dashed #fdea12;
   color: #fdea12;
}
#nav a:link, #nav a:visited {
   /*display: block;*/
   width: 99.99%; /* for IE5 */
   color: #FFFFFF;
   text-decoration: none;
   padding: 0.25em 0.5em 0.25em 0.5em;
   font-weight: bold;
}
#nav a:hover {
   text-decoration: none;
   color: #FFFFFF;
   /*background-color: #fdea12;  */
}
.title {
   color: #a83930;
   font: bold 1.0em/1.0em verdana, arial, helvetica, sans-serif;
   text-align: center;
   padding-bottom: 5px;
   border-bottom: #a83930 thin solid;
   margin-bottom: 5px;
}
#footer {
   /*margin-left: 210px; */
   padding: 0 20px 1.8em 10px;
   border-top: 1px solid #000000;
   clear: both;
}
#footer p {
   font: normal 0.8em/0.9em verdana, arial, helvetica, sans-serif;
   color: #666;
}
#footer p.left {
   float: left;
   clear: left;
}
#footer p.right {
   float: right;
   clear: right;
}
.spacer {
   clear: both;
}
```

```
dd, dt {
  font-size: 0.95em;
}
#mainTitle {
  font-size: 2.0em;
  font-weight: bold;
  visibility: hidden;
}
.pageTitle {
  font-size: 1.5em;
  font-weight: bold;
}
.itemTitle {
  border-bottom: 1px solid #a83930;
  font-size: 1.5em;
}
.itemContent {
  padding-bottom: 1.8em;
}
.box {
  border: solid 1px #a83930;
}
.boxFloat {
  /* border: solid 1px #a83930; */
  float: left;
}
.boxFloatRight {
  border: solid 1px #a83930;
  float: right;
}
.floatRight {
  /* border: solid 1px #a83930; */
  float: right;
}
```

Now, let's link this CSS file to the Web page. You need to add the following code snippet in the `<head>` element of the `Default.aspx` page to link the CSS file to the Web page:

```
<link href="StyleSheet.css" rel="stylesheet" type="text/css" />
```

Listing 4.2 shows the code of `Default.aspx` page:

Listing 4.2: Showing the Code of the `Default.aspx` Page

```
<%@ Page Language="C#" AutoEventWireup="true" CodeFile="Default.aspx.cs"
  Inherits="_Default" %>
<!DOCTYPE html>
<html xmlns="http://www.w3.org/1999/xhtml">
<head id="Head1" runat="server">
    <title>Linking CSS File</title>
    <link href="StyleSheet.css" rel="stylesheet" type="text/css" />
</head>
<body>
    <form id="form1" runat="server">
    <div id="header">
    <h1 align="center">
         ASP.NET 4.5 Black Book
         </h1>
    </div>
<div id="sidebar">
                <div id="nav">
                        
                </div>
```

```
            </div>
            <div id="content">
                    <div class ="itemContent">
                            <div id="footer">
                            <p class="left">
                            All content copyright &copy; Kogent Learning Solutions Inc.</p>
                            </div>
                    </div>
            </div>
        </form>
    </body>
    </html>
```

Now, run the application, CSSApplication, by pressing the F5 key. The output appears, as shown in Figure 4.5:

Figure 4.5: Displaying the CSS File Attached with the Web Page

Let's now learn to work with control properties.

Working with Control Properties

Let's create applications named ControlsCS and ControlsVB in C# and VB, respectively, to show how to use the properties of Web server controls, such as enabling or disabling controls and adding tool tips to these controls in a Web form. In this application, you can see three `Button` controls, one `CheckBox` control, two `TextBox` controls, and four `Label` controls. Listing 4.3 shows the code of the `Default.aspx` page:

Listing 4.3: Showing the Code of the `Default.aspx` Page

In VB

```
<%@ Page Language="VB" AutoEventWireup="false" CodeFile="Default.aspx.vb"
  Inherits="_Default" %>
<!DOCTYPE html>
<html xmlns="http://www.w3.org/1999/xhtml">
<head runat="server">
    <title></title>
</head>
<body>
    <form id="form1" runat="server">
    <div>
```

```
        <asp:Label ID="Label1" runat="server" Font-Bold="True" Font-Names="Verdana" Font-
            Size="Large" Text="Controls Example"></asp:Label>
    </div>
        <p>
            <asp:Button ID="Button1" runat="server" Text="Enable /Disable Text Box"
                ToolTip="Button Tooltip" />
        </p>
        <asp:Button ID="Button2" runat="server" Height="26px" Text="Show / Hide Text
                Box" />
        <p>
            <asp:Button ID="Button3" runat="server" Text="Change Text Box Style" />
        </p>
        <asp:Label ID="Label2" runat="server" Text="First textbox associated with button
                clicks:"></asp:Label>
        <asp:TextBox ID="TextBox1" runat="server" AccessKey="T"></asp:TextBox>
        <asp:Label ID="Label3" runat="server" Text="Label"></asp:Label>
        <p>
            <asp:CheckBox ID="CheckBox1" runat="server" AutoPostBack="True" Text="Select
                Me" />
        </p>
        <p>
            <asp:Label ID="Label4" runat="server" Text="Second textbox associated with
                checkbox"></asp:Label>
        </p>
        <p>
    <asp:TextBox ID="TextBox2" runat="server" style="margin-bottom: 19px"
                Width="228px"></asp:TextBox>
        </p>
        </form>
</body>
</html>
```

In C#

```
<%@ Page Language="C#" AutoEventWireup="true" CodeFile="Default.aspx.cs"
  Inherits="Default" %>
<!DOCTYPE html>
<html xmlns="http://www.w3.org/1999/xhtml">
<head runat="server">
    <title></title>
</head>
<body style="height: 361px; width: 505px">
    <form id="form1" runat="server">
    <div>
        <asp:Label ID="Label1" runat="server" Font-Bold="True" Font-Names="verdana"
                Font-Size="Large" Text="Controls Example"></asp:Label>
    </div>
        <asp:Button ID="Button1" runat="server" OnClick="Button1_Click" Text="Enable
                /Disable Text Box" ToolTip="Button Tooltip" />
        <p>
            <asp:Button ID="Button2" runat="server" OnClick="Button2_Click" Text="Show /
                Hide Text Box" />
        </p>
        <asp:Button ID="Button3" runat="server" OnClick="Button3_Click" Text="Change
                Text Box Style" />
        <p>
            <asp:Label ID="Label2" runat="server" Text="First textbox associated with
                button clicks:"></asp:Label>
            <asp:TextBox ID="TextBox1" runat="server" AccessKey="T"></asp:TextBox>
            <asp:Label ID="Label3" runat="server" Text="Label"></asp:Label>
        </p>
        <p>
```

```
            <asp:CheckBox ID="CheckBox1" runat="server" AutoPostBack="True"
                OnCheckedChanged="CheckBox1_CheckedChanged" Text="Select Me" />
        </p>
        <asp:Label ID="Label4" runat="server" Text="Second textbox associated with
                checkbox"></asp:Label>
        <p>
        <asp:TextBox ID="TextBox2" runat="server" Width="228px"></asp:TextBox>
        </p>
    </form>
</body>
</html>
```

At design-time, the `Default.aspx` page looks similar to the Web page shown in Figure 4.6:

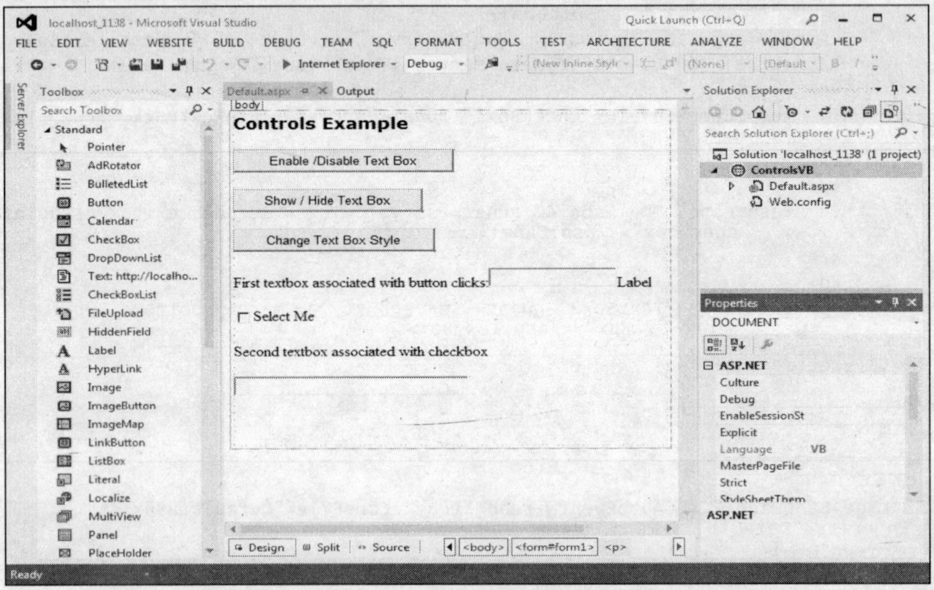

Figure 4.6: Displaying the Controls at Design-time

Now, add the code, shown in Listing 4.4, in the CodeFile of the `Default.aspx` page:

Listing 4.4: Showing the Code of the CodeFile of the `Default.aspx` Page

In VB

```
Partial Class _Default
    Inherits System.Web.UI.Page
Protected Sub Page_Load(sender As Object, e As EventArgs) Handles Me.Load
        Label3.Text = ""
    End Sub
    Protected Sub Button1_Click(sender As Object, e As EventArgs) Handles Button1.Click
        TextBox1.Enabled = Not TextBox1.Enabled
        If TextBox1.Enabled = True Then
            Label3.Text = "TextBox is enabled"
        Else
            Label3.Text = "TextBox is disabled"
        End If
    End Sub
    Protected Sub Button2_Click(sender As Object, e As EventArgs) Handles Button2.Click
        TextBox1.Visible = Not TextBox1.Visible
        If TextBox1.Visible = True Then
            Label2.Text = "TextBox is visible"
```

```
        Else
            Label2.Text = "TextBox is hidden"
        End If
    End Sub
    Protected Sub Button3_Click(sender As Object, e As EventArgs) Handles Button3.Click
        TextBox1.Style("BACKGROUND-COLOR") = "aqua"
    End Sub
    Protected Sub CheckBox1_CheckedChanged(sender As Object, e As EventArgs) Handles
         CheckBox1.CheckedChanged
        If CheckBox1.Checked = True Then
            TextBox2.Text = "CheckBox is selected"
        Else
            TextBox2.Text = "CheckBox is not selected"
End If
    End Sub
End Class
```

In C#

```
using System;
using System.Collections.Generic;
using System.Linq;
using System.Web;
using System.Web.UI;
using System.Web.UI.WebControls;
public partial class Default : System.Web.UI.Page
{
    protected void Page_Load(object sender, EventArgs e)
    {
        Label3.Text = "";
    }
    protected void Button1_Click(object sender, EventArgs e)
    {
        TextBox1.Enabled = !(TextBox1.Enabled);
        if (TextBox1.Enabled == true)
        {
            Label3.Text = "TextBox is enabled";
        }
        else
        {
            Label3.Text = "TextBox is disabled";
        }
    }
    protected void Button2_Click(object sender, EventArgs e)
    {
        TextBox1.Visible = !(TextBox1.Visible);

        if (TextBox1.Visible == true)
            Label2.Text = "TextBox is Visible";
        else
            Label2.Text = "TextBox is hidden";

    }
    protected void Button3_Click(object sender, EventArgs e)
    {
        TextBox1.Style["BACKGROUND-COLOR"] = "aqua";
    }
    protected void CheckBox1_CheckedChanged(object sender, EventArgs e)
    {
```

```
        if (CheckBox1.Checked == true)
            TextBox2.Text = "Check Box selected";
        else
            TextBox2.Text = "Check Box is not selected";
    }
}
```

In Listing 4.4, we have used the `Enabled` property to enable and disable the controls. When you click the Enable/Disable Text Box button, it displays a Label control showing the status of `TextBox` control.

The following code snippet shows the code of `Default.aspx.vb` file for the `Click` event of `Button1` in VB:

```
Protected Sub Button1_Click(sender As Object, e As EventArgs) Handles Button1.Click
        TextBox1.Enabled = Not TextBox1.Enabled
        If TextBox1.Enabled = True Then
            Label3.Text = "TextBox is enabled"
        Else
            Label3.Text = "TextBox is disabled"
        End If
 End Sub
```

The following code snippet shows the code of `Default.aspx.cs` file for the `Click` event of `Button1` in C#:

```
protected void Button1_Click(object sender, EventArgs e)
{
  TextBox1.Enabled = !(TextBox1.Enabled);
  if (TextBox1.Enabled == true)
  {
        Label3.Text = "TextBox is enabled";
  }
  else
  {
        Label3.Text = "TextBox is disabled";
  }
}
```

Now, run the application by pressing the F5 key. You can see the output, as shown in Figure 4.7, where the `TextBox` control has been disabled, after you click the Enable / Disable Text Box button:

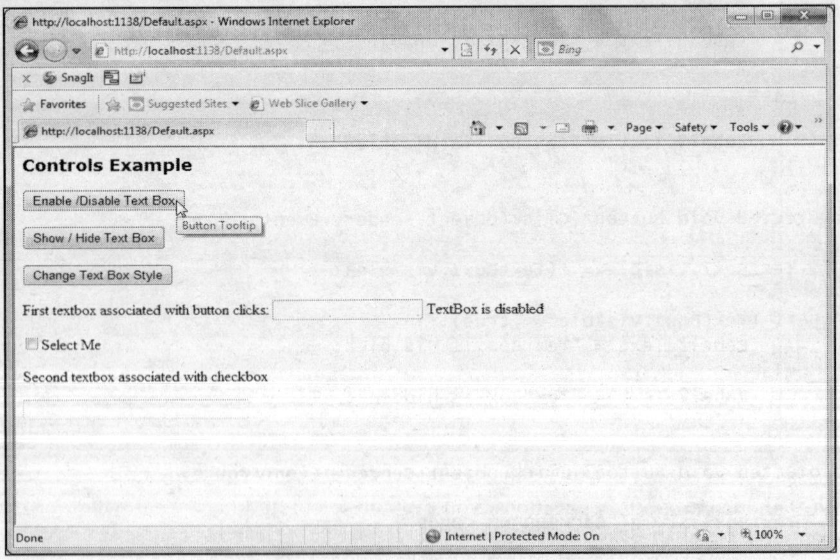

Figure 4.7: Disabling a TextBox Control

NOTE

The output of ControlsCS and ControlsVB applications would be same.

As shown in the ControlsCS and ControlsVB applications, you can make a `TextBox` control visible and invisible, through the `Visible` property. All Web server controls support this property. When you click the Show/Hide Text Box button in these applications, the code toggles the `Visible` property of the `TextBox` control.

The following code snippet shows the code of the `Click` event of `Button2` in `VB`:

```
Protected Sub Button2_Click(sender As Object, e As EventArgs) Handles Button2.Click
        TextBox1.Visible = Not TextBox1.Visible
        If TextBox1.Visible = True Then
            Label2.Text = "TextBox is visible"
        Else
            Label2.Text = "TextBox is hidden"
        End If
 End Sub
```

The following code snippet shows the code of the `Click` event of `Button2` in C#:

```
protected void Button2_Click(object sender, EventArgs e)
    {
        TextBox1.Visible = !(TextBox1.Visible);
 if (TextBox1.Visible == true)
            Label2.Text = "TextBox is visible";
        else
            Label2.Text = "TextBox is hidden";

    }
```

Now, run the application by pressing the F5 key. You can see the output, as shown in Figure 4.8, where the `TextBox` control is hidden:

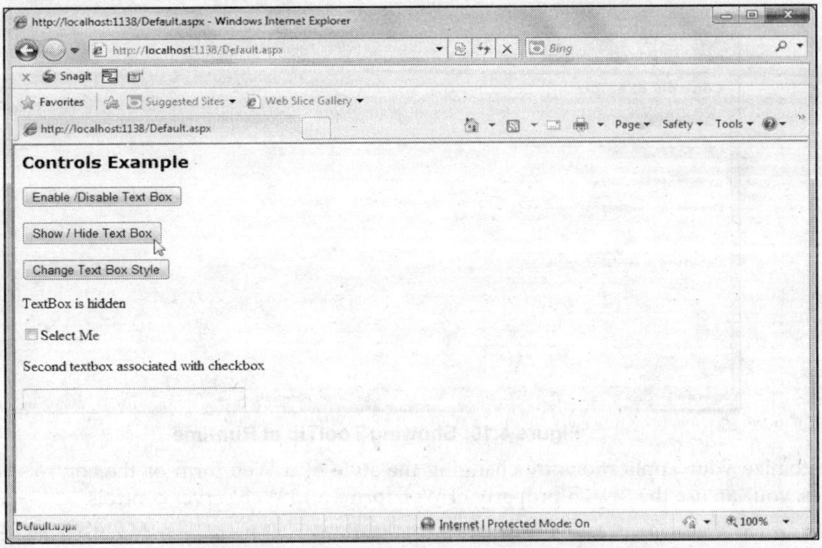

Figure 4.8: Making a TextBox Control Invisible

In the ControlsCS and ControlsVB applications, you can add a tool tip to a control with the `ToolTip` property. In these applications, we have set the `ToolTip` property of `Button1` to `Button ToolTip` through the Properties window, as shown in Figure 4.9:

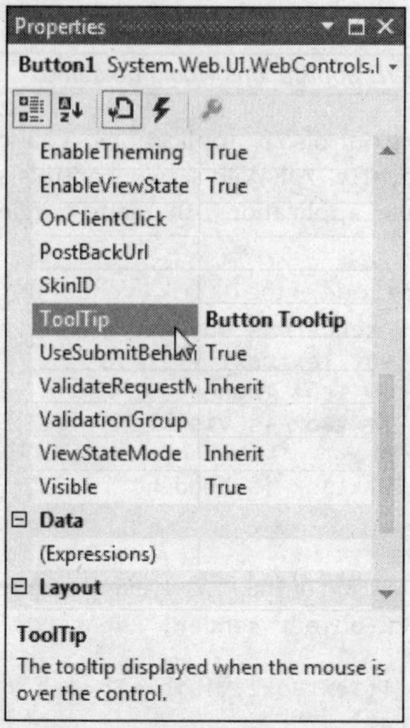

Figure 4.9: Setting the ToolTip Property through Properties Window

The following code snippet shows the code to set the `ToolTip` property in the `Default.aspx` page:

```
<asp:Button ID="Button1" runat="server" Text="Enable /Disable Text Box" ToolTip="Button
   ToolTip" OnClick="Button1_Click" />
```

At runtime, this tool tip is visible, as shown in Figure 4.10:

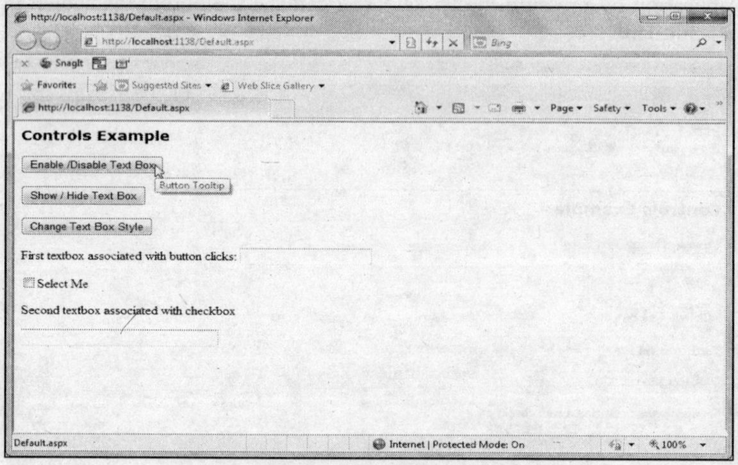

Figure 4.10: Showing ToolTip at Runtime

You can customize your applications by changing the style of a Web form or the controls that it contains. To change styles, you can use the `Style` property of Web forms and Web server controls.

For example, in the ControlsCS and ControlsVB applications, we have changed the background color of the `TextBox` control by setting the `TextBox1.Style(BACKGROUND-COLOR)` property.

The following code snippet shows the code of `Default.aspx.vb` of `Button 3`:

```
Protected Sub Button3_Click(sender As Object, e As EventArgs) Handles Button3.Click
        TextBox1.Style("BACKGROUND-COLOR") = "aqua"
End Sub
```

The following code snippet shows the code of `Default.aspx.cs` of `Button 3`:

```
protected void Button3_Click(object sender, EventArgs e)
{
  TextBox1.Style["BACKGROUND-COLOR"] = "aqua";
}
```

Now, run the application by pressing the F5 key. The output is as shown in Figure 4.11:

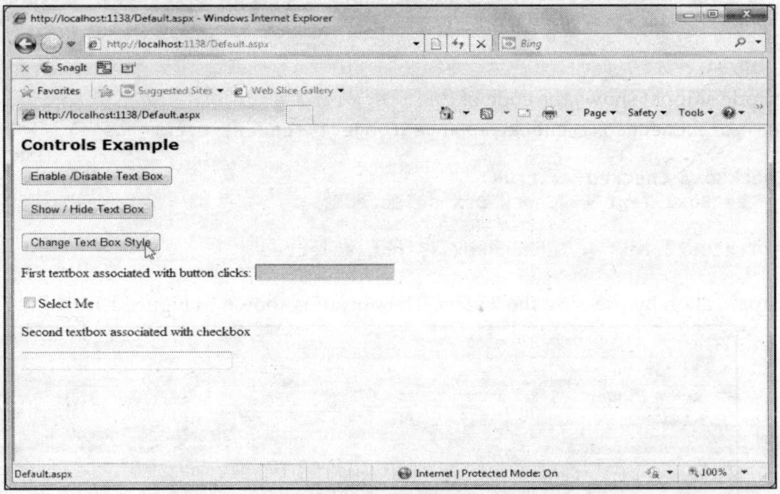

Figure 4.11: Changing a TextBox Control's Style

In the ControlsCS and ControlsVB applications, you can also set the `AutoPostBack` property with some Web server controls, such as `CheckBox`, as shown in Figure 4.12:

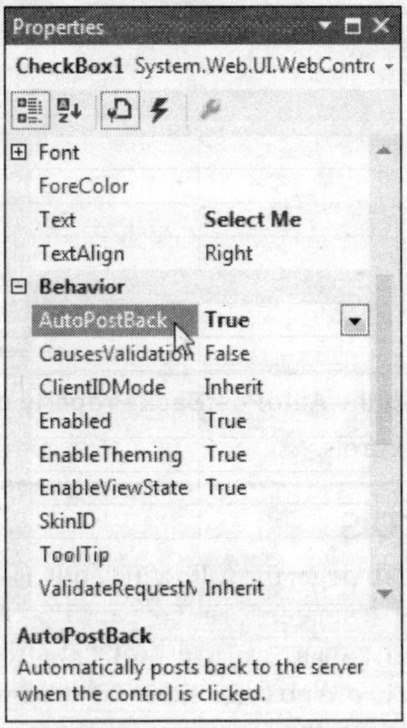

Figure 4.12: Setting the AutoPostBack Property

In these applications, we have set the text of the `TextBox` control based on the state of the `CheckBox` control, once it has been selected or cleared by the user

The following code snippet shows the code of `CheckBox1` in VB:

```
Protected Sub CheckBox1_CheckedChanged(sender As Object, e As EventArgs) Handles
   CheckBox1.CheckedChanged
        If CheckBox1.Checked = True Then
            TextBox2.Text = "CheckBox is selected"
        Else
            TextBox2.Text = "CheckBox is not selected"
        End If

    End Sub
```

The following code snippet shows the code of `CheckBox1` in **C#:**

```
protected void CheckBox1_CheckedChanged(object sender, EventArgs e)
{
   if (CheckBox1.Checked == true)
         TextBox2.Text = "Check Box selected";
   else
         TextBox2.Text = "Check Box is not selected";
}
```

Now, run the application by pressing the F5 key. The output is shown in Figure 4.13:

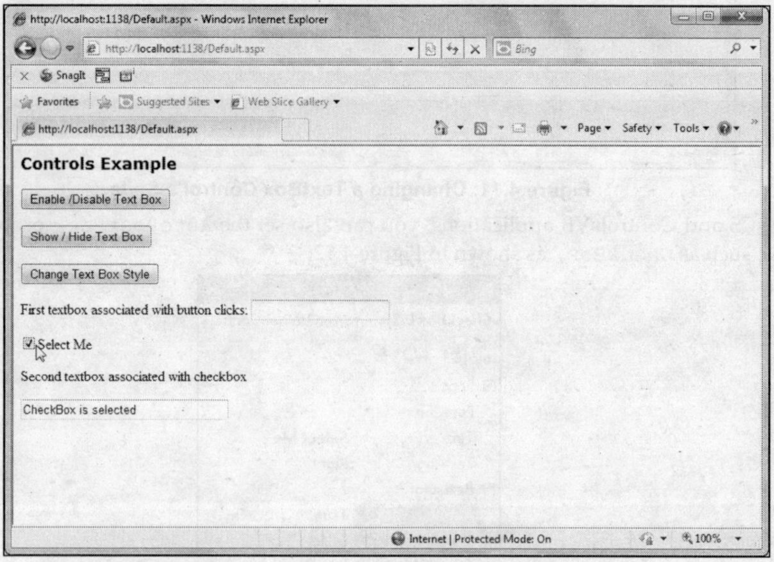

Figure 4.13: Using the AutoPostBack Property of the CheckBox Control

Let's now learn to work with Label controls.

Working with Label Controls

When you add a Label control on a Web page, the following code is added to the source code of the Web page:

```
<asp:Label ID="Label1" runat="server" Text="Label"></asp:Label>
```

Now, let's create applications named LabelCS in C# and LabelVB in VB to show the working of the Label control. You can add a `Label` control to a Web page either by dragging and dropping it from the Standard tab of the Toolbox or by double-clicking it in the Toolbox. In these applications, we are setting the `Text` and `BackColor` properties of a Label control at the `Page_Load` event. Listing 4.5 shows the code of `Default.aspx` page for the Label controls:

Listing 4.5: Showing the Code of the `Default.aspx` Page

In VB

```
<%@ Page Language="VB" AutoEventWireup="false" CodeFile="Default.aspx.vb"
  Inherits="Default" %>

<!DOCTYPE html>

<html xmlns="http://www.w3.org/1999/xhtml">
<head runat="server">
    <title></title>
</head>
<body>
    <form id="form1" runat="server">
    <div>

        <asp:Label ID="Label1" runat="server" Font-Bold="True" Font-Underline="True"
          Text="Example showing some of the properties of the Label Control"></asp:Label>
          <br />
          <br />
   </div>
          <p>
          <asp:Label ID="Label2" runat="server" Text="Label"></asp:Label>
          </p>
          <p>
          <asp:Label ID="Label3" runat="server" Text="Label"></asp:Label>
          </p>
           </form>
</body>
</html>
```

In C#

```
<%@ Page Language="C#" AutoEventWireup="true" CodeFile="Default.aspx.cs"
  Inherits="Default" %>

<!DOCTYPE html>

<html xmlns="http://www.w3.org/1999/xhtml">
<head runat="server">
    <title></title>
</head>
<body>
    <form id="form2" runat="server">
        <div>
             <asp:Label ID="Label1" runat="server" Font-Bold="True" Font-
                 Underline="True" text="Example showing some of the properties of the
                 Label Control"></asp:Label>
            <asp:Label ID="Label2" runat="server" text="Label"> </asp:Label>
        <p>
             </p>
        <asp:Label ID="Label3" runat="server" Text="Label"></asp:Label>
    </div>
          </form>
</body>
</html>
```

Now, add the code, shown in Listing 4.6, in the CodeFile of the `Default.aspx` page:

Listing 4.6: Showing the Code of the CodeFile of the `Default.aspx Page`

In VB

```
Partial Class Default
    Inherits System.Web.UI.Page
    Protected Sub Page_Load(sender As Object, e As EventArgs) Handles Me.Load
        Label2.Text = "Welcome to the World of ASP.NET 4.5"
        Label3.Text = "I have Olive Color"
        Label3.BackColor = System.Drawing.Color.Olive
    End Sub
End Class
```

In C#

```
using System;
using System.Collections.Generic;
using System.Linq;
using System.Web;
using System.Web.UI;
using System.Web.UI.WebControls;
public partial class _Default : System.Web.UI.Page
{
    protected void Page_Load(object sender, EventArgs e)
    {
        Label2.Text = "Welcome to the World of ASP.NET 4.5";
        Label3.Text = "I have Olive Color";
        Label3.BackColor = System.Drawing.Color.Olive;

    }
}
```

Now, run the application by pressing the F5 key. The output is shown in Figure 4.14:

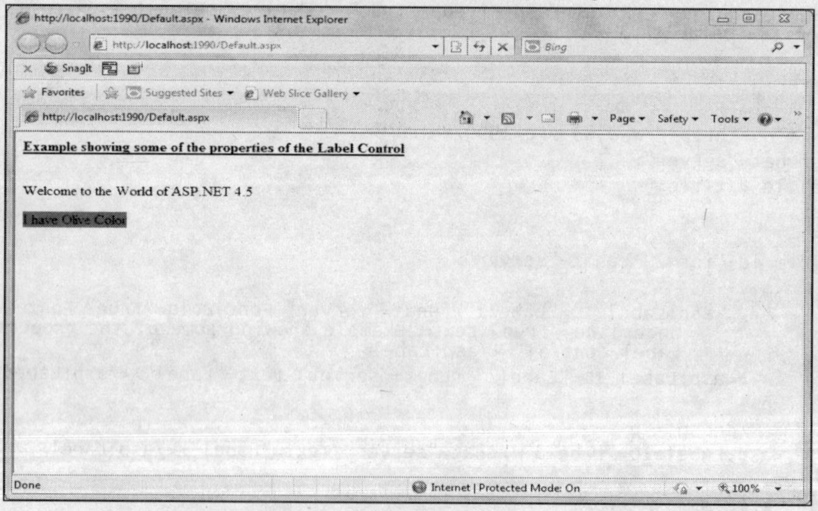

Figure 4.14: Showing the Label Control Properties at Runtime

Let's now learn to work with a Button control.

Working with Button Controls

When you add a Button control on a Web page, the following code is added to the source code of the Web page:

```
<asp:Button ID="Button1" runat="server" Text="Button" />
```

Now, let's create applications named ButtonCS in C# and ButtonVB in VB to show the working of the Button control. You can add a Button control to a Web page either by dragging and dropping it from the Standard tab of the Toolbox or by double-clicking it in the Toolbox. In these applications, we are setting the `Text` and `ForeColor` properties of a Label control at the `Click` event of the `Button` control. Listing 4.7 shows the code of `Default.aspx` page of the Button controls:

Listing 4.7: Showing the Code of the `Default.aspx` Page

In VB

```
<%@ Page Language="VB" AutoEventWireup="false" CodeFile="Default.aspx.vb"
  Inherits="_Default" %>
<!DOCTYPE html>
<html xmlns="http://www.w3.org/1999/xhtml">
<head runat="server">
    <title></title>
</head>
<body>
    <form id="form1" runat="server">
        <asp:Label ID="Label1" runat="server" Font-Bold="True" Font-Underline="True"
         Text="Button control example showing text on button click event"></asp:Label>
        <p>
             </p>
        <p>
             </p>
        <p>
        <asp:Button ID="Button1" runat="server" Text="Click me, I will welcome you!!!"
         Font-Bold="True" Font-Underline="False" />
        </p>
        <p>
            <asp:Label ID="Label2" runat="server" Text="Label"></asp:Label>
        </p>
    </form>
</body>
</html>
```

In C#

```
<%@ Page Language="C#" AutoEventWireup="true" CodeFile="Default.aspx.cs"
  Inherits="Default" %>

<!DOCTYPE html>

<html xmlns="http://www.w3.org/1999/xhtml">
<head runat="server">
    <title></title>
</head>
<body>
    <form id="form1" runat="server">
    <div>

    </div>
        <asp:Label ID="Label1" runat="server" Font-Bold="True" Font-Underline="True"
         Text="Button control example showing text on button click "></asp:Label>
        <p>
            <asp:Button ID="Button1" runat="server" Font-Bold="True"
                OnClick="Button1_Click" Text="Click Me, I will Welcome You !!!" />
```

```
        </p>
        <asp:Label ID="Label2" runat="server" Text="Label"></asp:Label>
    </form>
</body>
</html>
```

Now, add the code, shown in Listing 4.8, in the CodeFile of the `Default.aspx` page

Listing 4.8: Showing the code for the CodeFile of the `Default.aspx Page`

In VB

```
Partial Class _Default
    Inherits System.Web.UI.Page
     Protected Sub Button1_Click(sender As Object, e As EventArgs) Handles Button1.Click
        Label2.Text = " Welcome to the World of ASP.NET 4.5"
        Label2.ForeColor = System.Drawing.Color.RosyBrown
    End Sub
End Class
```

In C#

```
using System;
using System.Collections.Generic;
using System.Linq;
using System.Web;
using System.Web.UI;
using System.Web.UI.WebControls;
public partial class Default : System.Web.UI.Page
{
    protected void Page_Load(object sender, EventArgs e)
    {
    }
    protected void Button1_Click(object sender, EventArgs e)
    {
        Label2.Text = " Welcome to the World of ASP.NET 4.5";
        Label2.ForeColor = System.Drawing.Color.RosyBrown;
    }
}
```

Now, run the application by pressing the F5 key. The output is shown in Figure 4.15:

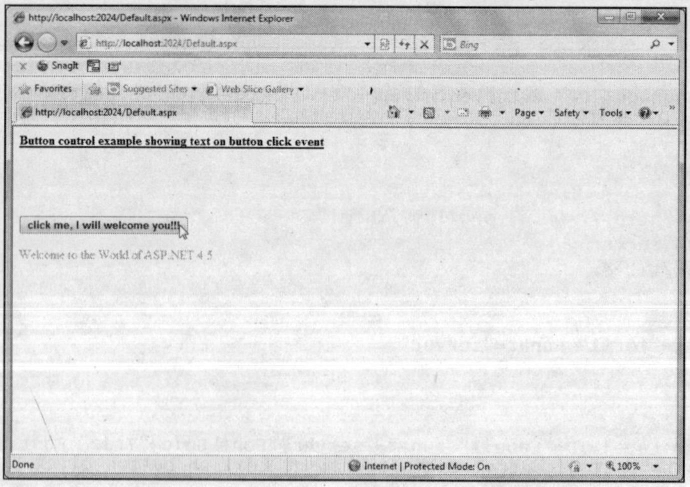

Figure 4.15: Showing Output Text after Clicking the Button Control

Let's now learn to work with a TextBox control.

Working with TextBox Controls

When you add a TextBox control on a Web page, the following code is added to the source code of the Web page:

```
<asp:TextBox ID="TextBox1" runat="server"></asp:TextBox>
```

Now, let's create applications named TextBoxCS and TextBoxVB. These applications show how to work with single-line and multiline TextBox controls, as well as TextBox showing masked text (password). When you click the Button control in these applications, the message, You have clicked the button, appears in a single-line `TextBox` and a multiline `TextBox` shows the message, This is a multiline textbox, which is repeated four times. In addition, the masked text (password) in a `TextBox` control is copied in another `TextBox` control which is below that control. Listing 4.9 shows the code of `Default.aspx` page for the TextBox controls:

Listing 4.9: Showing the Code of the `Default.aspx` Page

In VB

```
<%@ Page Language="VB" AutoEventWireup="false" CodeFile="Default.aspx.vb"
  Inherits="Default" %>

<!DOCTYPE html>

<html xmlns="http://www.w3.org/1999/xhtml">
<head runat="server">
    <title></title>
</head>
<body>
    <form id="form1" runat="server">
    <div>
        <asp:Label ID="Label1" runat="server" Font-Bold="True" Font-Underline="True"
         Text="TextBox example showing types of TextBox controls"></asp:Label>
    </div>
        <p>
            <asp:Button ID="Button1" runat="server" Text="Click Me" Width="125px" />
        </p>
        <p>
            <asp:TextBox ID="TextBox1" runat="server" Width="262px"></asp:TextBox>
        </p>
        <p>
            <asp:TextBox ID="TextBox2" runat="server" Rows="10"
                TextMode="MultiLine"></asp:TextBox>
        </p>
        <p>
            <asp:Label ID="Label2" runat="server" Text="Enter Password"></asp:Label>
        </p>
        <p>
            <asp:TextBox ID="TextBox3" runat="server" TextMode="Password"
                Width="167px"></asp:TextBox>
        </p>
        <p>
            <asp:TextBox ID="TextBox4" runat="server" Width="173px"></asp:TextBox>
        </p>
    </form>
</body>
</html>
```

In C#

```
<%@ Page Language="C#" AutoEventWireup="true" CodeFile="Default.aspx.cs"
  Inherits="Default" %>

<!DOCTYPE html>

<html xmlns="http://www.w3.org/1999/xhtml">
<head runat="server">
    <title></title>
</head>
<body>
    <form id="form1" runat="server">
    <div>
    </div>
        <asp:Label ID="Label1" runat="server" Font-Bold="True" Font-Underline="True"
         Text="TextBox example showing types of TextBox controls"></asp:Label>
        <p>
            <asp:Button ID="Button1" runat="server" Text="Click Me" Width="125px"
                 OnClick="Button1_Click" />
        </p>
        <asp:TextBox ID="TextBox1" runat="server" Width="262px"></asp:TextBox>
        <p>
            <asp:TextBox ID="TextBox2" runat="server" Rows="10"
                 TextMode="MultiLine"></asp:TextBox>
        </p>
        <asp:Label ID="Label2" runat="server" Text="Enter Password"></asp:Label>
        <p>
            <asp:TextBox ID="TextBox3" runat="server" TextMode="Password"
                 Width="172px"></asp:TextBox>
        </p>
        <asp:TextBox ID="TextBox4" runat="server" Width="173px"></asp:TextBox>
    </form>
</body>
</html>
```

NOTE

The SingleLine TextMode property is a default property of the TextBox control and does not appear in the Default.aspx page.

Now, add the code, shown in Listing 4.10, in the CodeFile of the `Default.aspx` page for the TextBox controls:

Listing 4.10: Showing the Code for the CodeFile of the `Default.aspx Page`

In VB

```
Partial Class Default
    Inherits System.Web.UI.Page
    Protected Sub Button1_Click(sender As Object, e As EventArgs) Handles Button1.Click
        TextBox1.Text = "You have clicked the button"
        TextBox2.Text = "This is a multi line textbox. This is a multi line textbox.This
         is a multi line textbox. This is a multi line textbox. "
        TextBox4.Text = TextBox3.Text
    End Sub
End Class
```

In C#

```
using System;
using System.Collections.Generic;
using System.Linq;
using System.Web;
```

```
using System.Web.UI;
using System.Web.UI.WebControls;
public partial class Default : System.Web.UI.Page
{
    protected void Page_Load(object sender, EventArgs e)
    {
    }
    protected void Button1_Click(object sender, EventArgs e)
    {
        TextBox1.Text = "You have clicked the button";
        TextBox2.Text = "This is a multi line textbox. This is a multi line textbox. 
        This is a multi line textbox. This is a multi line textbox. ";
        TextBox4.Text = TextBox3.Text;
    }
}
```

Now, run the application by pressing the F5 key. The output after clicking the Click me button is shown in Figure 4.16:

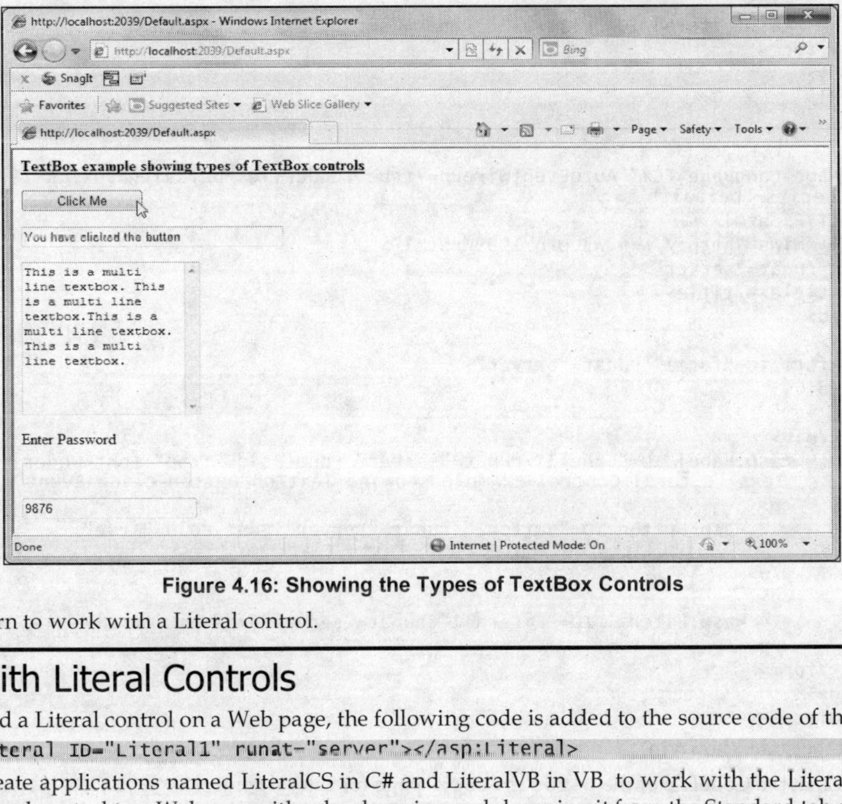

Figure 4.16: Showing the Types of TextBox Controls

Let's now learn to work with a Literal control.

Working with Literal Controls

When you add a Literal control on a Web page, the following code is added to the source code of the Web page:

```
<asp:Literal ID="Literal1" runat="server"></asp:Literal>
```

Now, let's create applications named LiteralCS in C# and LiteralVB in VB to work with the Literal control. You can add a Literal control to a Web page either by dragging and dropping it from the Standard tab of the Toolbox or by double-clicking it in the Standard tab of the Toolbox. When you click the Button control in these applications, the code (CodeFile) inserts the HTML text on a Web page. The Literal control does not have any visual appearance in a Web page. You just set the `Text` property and the specified text is inserted into the Web form, when you click the Button control on the Web page. In this case, we will insert the HTML code for the `<h1>` header and `<marquee>` tag into the Button `Click` event of a Web form by using a `Literal` control. Listing 4.11 shows the code of `Default.aspx` page for the Literal controls:

Listing 4.11: Showing the Code of the `Default.aspx` Page

In VB

```
<%@ Page Language="VB" AutoEventWireup="false" CodeFile="Default.aspx.vb"
  Inherits="Default" %>
<!DOCTYPE html>
<html xmlns="http://www.w3.org/1999/xhtml">
<head runat="server">
    <title></title>
</head>
<body>
    <form id="form1" runat="server">
    <div>
    </div>
        <asp:Label ID="Label1" runat="server" Font-Bold="True" Font-Underline="True"
         Text="Literal Control Example showing Text on Button Click Event"></asp:Label>
        <p>
         <asp:Button ID="Button1" runat="server" Font-Bold="True" Text="Click Me!!" />
        </p>
        <asp:Literal ID="Literal1" runat="server"></asp:Literal>
    </form>
</body>
</html>
```

In C#

```
<%@ Page Language="C#" AutoEventWireup="true" CodeFile="Default.aspx.cs"
  Inherits="Default" %>
<!DOCTYPE html>
<html xmlns="http://www.w3.org/1999/xhtml">
<head runat="server">
    <title></title>
</head>
<body>
    <form id="form1" runat="server">
    <div>

    </div>
        <asp:Label ID="Label1" runat="server" Font-Bold="True" Font-Underline="True"
         Text="Literal Control Example showing Text on Button Click Event"></asp:Label>
        <p>
            <asp:Button ID="Button1" runat="server" Font-Bold="True"
                OnClick="Button1_Click" Text="Click Me!!" />
        </p>
        <p>
            <asp:Literal ID="Literal1" runat="server"></asp:Literal>
        </p>
    </form>
</body>
</html>
```

Now, add the code, shown in

Listing 4.12, in the CodeFile of the `Default.aspx` page for Literal controls:

Listing 4.12: Showing the Code for the CodeFile of `Default.aspx`

In VB

```
Partial Class Default
    Inherits System.Web.UI.Page
   Protected Sub Button1_Click(sender As Object, e As EventArgs) Handles Button1.Click
        Literal1.Text = "<h1><marquee>Welcome to ASP.NET 4.5</marquee></h1>"
    End Sub
End Class
```

In C#

```
using System;
using System.Collections.Generic;
using System.Linq;
using System.Web;
using System.Web.UI;
using System.Web.UI.WebControls;
public partial class Default : System.Web.UI.Page
{
    protected void Page_Load(object sender, EventArgs e)
    {

    }
    protected void Button1_Click(object sender, EventArgs e)
    {
        Literal1.Text = "<h1><marquee>Welcome to ASP.NET 4.5</marquee></h1>";
    }
}
```

Now, run the application by pressing the F5 key. The output after clicking the Click Me!! button is shown in Figure 4.17:

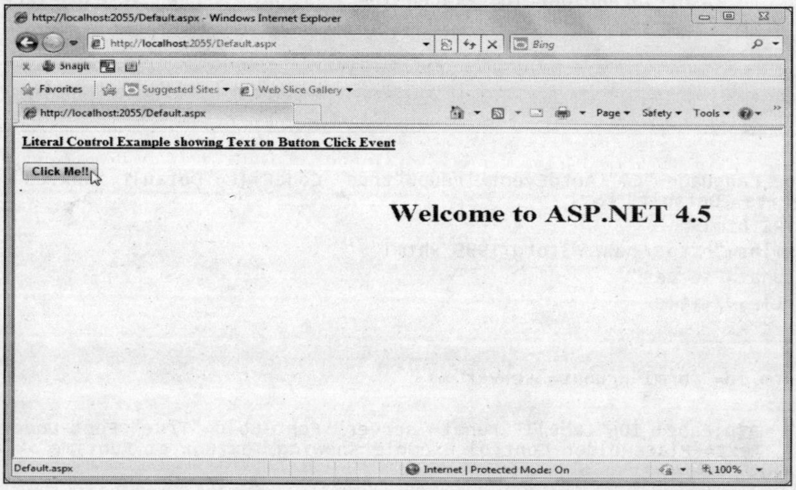

Figure 4.17: Showing HTML Functioning on Button Click Event

Let's now learn to work with PlaceHolder control.

Working with PlaceHolder Controls

When you add a `PlaceHolder` control on a Web page, the following code is added to the source code of the Web page:

```
<asp:PlaceHolder ID="PlaceHolder1" runat="server"></asp:PlaceHolder>
```

A control can act as a container for other controls. For example, the Control class acts a container for the Page class, so you can add controls to a Web form by using the `Controls.Add()` method. The `PlaceHolder` controls are designed in a way that they do not insert any HTML code into a Web page by themselves. You can add controls to them by using the `Controls.Add()` method.

Now, let's create applications named PlaceHolderCS in C# and PlaceHolderVB in VB. When you click the `Button` control in these applications, one `TextBox` control is added to the Web form at runtime within the `PlaceHolder` control. Listing 4.13 shows the code of `Default.aspx` page for the PlaceHolder controls.

Listing 4.13: Showing the Code of the `Default.aspx` Page

In VB

```
<%@ Page Language="VB" AutoEventWireup="false" CodeFile="Default.aspx.vb"
   Inherits="Default" %>
<!DOCTYPE html>
<html xmlns="http://www.w3.org/1999/xhtml">
<head runat="server">
    <title></title>
</head>
<body>
    <form id="form1" runat="server">
    <div>
         <asp:Label ID="Label1" runat="server" Font-Bold="True" Font-Underline="True"
         Text="PlaceHolder Control Example showing TextBox at Runtime "></asp:Label>
    </div>
         <p>
         <asp:Button ID="Button1" runat="server" Font-Bold="True" Text="Click Me!!" />
         </p>
         <p>
             <asp:PlaceHolder ID="PlaceHolder1" runat="server"></asp:PlaceHolder>
         </p>
    </form>
</body>
</html>
```

In C#

```
<%@ Page Language="C#" AutoEventWireup="true" CodeFile="Default.aspx.cs"
   Inherits="Default" %>
<!DOCTYPE html>
<html xmlns="http://www.w3.org/1999/xhtml">
<head runat="server">
    <title></title>
</head>
<body>
    <form id="form1" runat="server">
    <div>
         <asp:Label ID="Label1" runat="server" Font-Bold="True" Font-Underline="True"
         Text="PlaceHolder Control Example showing TextBox at Runtime"></asp:Label>
    </div>
         <p>
             <asp:Button ID="Button1" runat="server" Font-Bold="True"
                 OnClick="Button1_Click" Text="Click Me!!" />
         </p>
         <p>
             <asp:PlaceHolder ID="PlaceHolder1" runat="server"></asp:PlaceHolder>
         </p>
    </form>
</body>
</html>
```

Now, add the code, shown in Listing 4.14, in the CodeFile of the `Default.aspx` page for PlaceHolder controls:

Listing 4.14: Showing the Code for the CodeFile of the `Default.aspx Page`

In VB

```
Partial Class Default
    Inherits System.Web.UI.Page
    Dim Textbox1 As New System.Web.UI.WebControls.TextBox
    Protected Sub Button1_Click(sender As Object, e As EventArgs) Handles Button1.Click
        Textbox1.Text = "This is TextBox inside the placeholder "
```

```
        Textbox1.Style("width") = "280PX"
        PlaceHolder1.Controls.Add(Textbox1)
    End Sub
End Class
```

In C#

```
using System;
using System.Collections.Generic;
using System.Linq;
using System.Web;
using System.Web.UI;
using System.Web.UI.WebControls;
public partial class Default : System.Web.UI.Page
{
    TextBox Textbox1 = new TextBox();
    protected void Page_Load(object sender, EventArgs e)
    {
    }
    protected void Button1_Click(object sender, EventArgs e)
    {
        Textbox1.Text = "This is TextBox inside the placeholder";
        Textbox1.Style["width"] = "280PX";
        PlaceHolder1.Controls.Add(Textbox1);
    }
}
```

Now, run the application by pressing the F5 key. The output after clicking the Click Me!! button is shown in Figure 4.18:

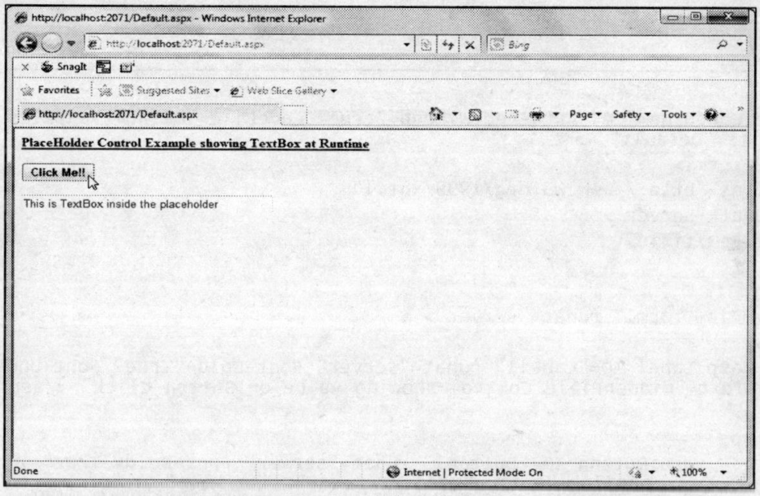

Figure 4.18: Showing TextBox at Runtime in the PlaceHolder Control

Let's now learn to work with a HiddenField control.

Working with HiddenField Controls

When you add a `HiddenField` control on a Web page, the following code is added to the source code of the Web page:

```
<asp:HiddenField ID="HiddenField1" runat="server" />
```

Now, let's create applications named HiddenFieldCS in C# and HiddenFieldVB in VB to show the working of HiddenField control. You can add a HiddenField control to a Web page either by dragging and dropping it from the Standard tab of the Toolbox or by double-clicking it in the Toolbox. When you click the `Button` control in these applications, it displays the value stored in the `HiddenField` control in the `Label` control. Listing 4.15 shows the code of `Default.aspx` page for the HiddenField controls:

Listing 4.15: Showing the Code of the `Default.aspx` Page

In VB

```
<%@ Page Language="VB" AutoEventWireup="false" CodeFile="Default.aspx.vb"
  Inherits="Default" %>
<!DOCTYPE html>
<html xmlns="http://www.w3.org/1999/xhtml">
<head runat="server">
    <title></title>
</head>
<body>
    <form id="form1" runat="server">
    <div>
        <asp:Label ID="Label1" runat="server" Font-Bold="True" Font-Underline="True"
         Text="HiddenField Control showing value on Button click"></asp:Label>
    </div>
        <asp:Button ID="Button1" runat="server" Font-Bold="True" Text="Click Me!!" />
        <p>
            <asp:Label ID="Label2" runat="server" Text="Label"></asp:Label>
        </p>
        <asp:HiddenField ID="HiddenField1" runat="server" />
    </form>
</body>
</html>
```

In C#

```
<%@ Page Language="C#" AutoEventWireup="true" CodeFile="Default.aspx.cs"
  Inherits="Default" %>
<!DOCTYPE html>
<html xmlns="http://www.w3.org/1999/xhtml">
<head runat="server">
    <title></title>
</head>
<body>
    <form id="form1" runat="server">
    <div>
        <asp:Label ID="Label1" runat="server" Font-Bold="True" Font-Underline="True"
         Text="HiddenField Control showing value on Button click"></asp:Label>
    </div>
        <p>
            <asp:Button ID="Button1" runat="server" Font-Bold="True"
                 OnClick="Button1_Click" Text="Click Me!!" />
        </p>
        <p>
            <asp:Label ID="Label2" runat="server" Text="Label"></asp:Label>
        </p>
        <asp:HiddenField ID="HiddenField1" runat="server" />
    </form>
</body>
</html>
```

Now, add the code, shown in Listing 4.16, in the CodeFile of the `Default.aspx` page for the HiddenField controls:

Listing 4.16: Showing the Code for the CodeFile of the `Default.aspx Page`

In VB

```
Partial Class Default
    Inherits System.Web.UI.Page
    Protected Sub Page_Load(sender As Object, e As EventArgs) Handles Me.Load
        HiddenField1.Value = "Welcome to the World of ASP.NET 4.5"
    End Sub
   Protected Sub Button1_Click(sender As Object, e As EventArgs) Handles Button1.Click
        Label2.Text = HiddenField1.Value
    End Sub
End Class
```

In C#

```
using System;
using System.Collections.Generic;
using System.Linq;
using System.Web;
using System.Web.UI;
using System.Web.UI.WebControls;

public partial class Default : System.Web.UI.Page
{
    protected void Page_Load(object sender, EventArgs e)
    {
        HiddenField1.Value = "Welcome to the World of ASP.NET 4.5";
    }
    protected void Button1_Click(object sender, EventArgs e)
    {
        Label2.Text = HiddenField1.Value;
    }
}
```

Now, run the application by pressing the F5 key. The output is shown in Figure 4.19:

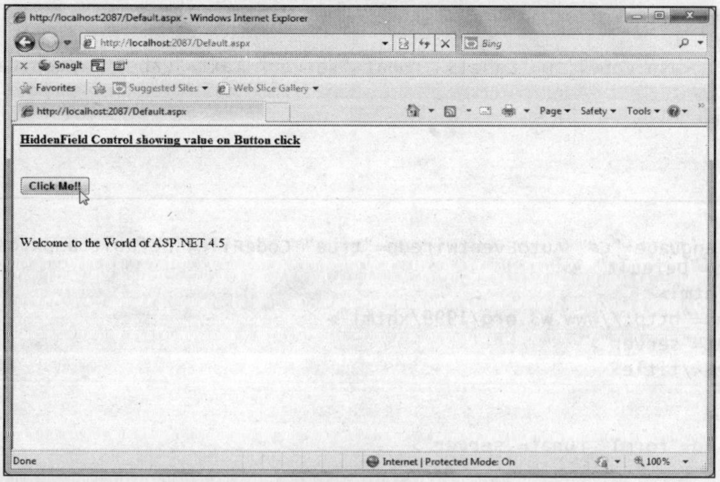

Figure 4.19: Showing a Value of the HiddenField Control on the Button Click Event

Let's now learn to work with a FileUpload control.

Working with the FileUpload Control

When you add a `FileUpload` control on a Web page, the following code is added to the source code of the Web page:

```
<asp:FileUpload ID="FileUpload1" runat="server" />
```

Now, let's create applications named FileUploadCS in C# and FileUploadVB in VB to show the working of the FileUpload control. You can add a FileUpload control to a Web page either by dragging and dropping it from the Standard tab of the Toolbox or by double-clicking it in the Standard tab of the Toolbox. In this case, we are using a `FileUpload` control to browse a file and upload it on the server using the `SaveAs()` method on the `Click` event. Listing 4.17 shows the code of `Default.aspx` page for the FileUpload controls:

Listing 4.17: Showing the Code for the `Default.aspx` Page

In VB

```
<%@ Page Language="VB" AutoEventWireup="false" CodeFile="Default.aspx.vb"
  Inherits="Default" %>
<!DOCTYPE html>
<html xmlns="http://www.w3.org/1999/xhtml">
<head runat="server">
    <title></title>
</head>
<body>
    <form id="form1" runat="server">
    <div>
        <asp:Label ID="Label1" runat="server" Font-Bold="True" Font-Underline="True"
         Text="FileUpload Control Example"></asp:Label>
        <br />
    </div>
        <p>
            <asp:Label ID="Label2" runat="server" Text="Please select a file to
                upload"></asp:Label>
        </p>
        <asp:FileUpload ID="FileUpload1" runat="server" style="height: 22px" />
        <p>
            <asp:Button ID="Button1" runat="server" Font-Bold="True" Height="26px"
                Text="Click to Upload" Width="144px" />
        </p>
        <p>
            <asp:Label ID="Label3" runat="server" Text="Label"></asp:Label>
        </p>
    </form>
</body>
</html>
```

In C#

```
<%@ Page Language="C#" AutoEventWireup="true" CodeFile="Default.aspx.cs"
  Inherits="Default" %>
<!DOCTYPE html>
<html xmlns="http://www.w3.org/1999/xhtml">
<head runat="server">
    <title></title>
</head>
<body>
    <form id="form1" runat="server">
    <div>
        <asp:Label ID="Label1" runat="server" Font-Bold="True" Font-Underline="True"
         Text="FileUpload Control Example"></asp:Label>
    </div>
        <p>
```

```
            <asp:Label ID="Label2" runat="server" Text="Please select a File to
                 Upload:"></asp:Label>
        </p>
        <p>
            <asp:FileUpload ID="FileUpload1" runat="server" Height="22px" />
        </p>
        <p>
            <asp:Button ID="Button1" runat="server" Font-Bold="True" Height="26px"
                 OnClick="Button1_Click" Text="Click to Upload" Width="144px" />
</p>
        <p>
            <asp:Label ID="Label3" runat="server" Text="Label"></asp:Label>
        </p>
    </form>
</body>
</html>
```

Now, add the code, shown in Listing 4.18, in the CodeFile of the `Default.aspx` page for the FileUpload controls:

Listing 4.18: Showing the Code for the CodeFile of the `Default.aspx Page`

In VB

```
Partial Class Default
    Inherits System.Web.UI.Page
  Protected Sub Page_Load(sender As Object, e As EventArgs) Handles Me.Load
        If Not Page.IsPostBack Then
            Label3.Text = ""
        End If
    End Sub
Protected Sub Button1_Click(sender As Object, e As EventArgs) Handles Button1.Click
        If (FileUpload1.HasFile) Then
            FileUpload1.SaveAs("D:/" + FileUpload1.FileName)
            Label3.Text = "File " + FileUpload1.FileName + " is Uploaded"
        Else
            Label3.Text = "No uploaded file"
        End If
    End Sub
End Class
```

In C#

```
using System;
using System.Collections.Generic;
using System.Linq;
using System.Web;
using System.Web.UI;
using System.Web.UI.WebControls;

public partial class Default : System.Web.UI.Page
{
    protected void Page_Load(object sender, EventArgs e)
    {
        if (!Page.IsPostBack) Label3.Text = "";
    }
    protected void Button1_Click(object sender, EventArgs e)
    {
        if (FileUpload1.HasFile)
        {

            FileUpload1.SaveAs("D:/" + FileUpload1.FileName);
```

```
            Label3.Text = "File " + FileUpload1.FileName + " is Uploaded";
        }
        else
            Label3.Text = "No uploaded file";
    }
}
```

Now, run the application by pressing the F5 key. The output is shown in Figure 4.20:

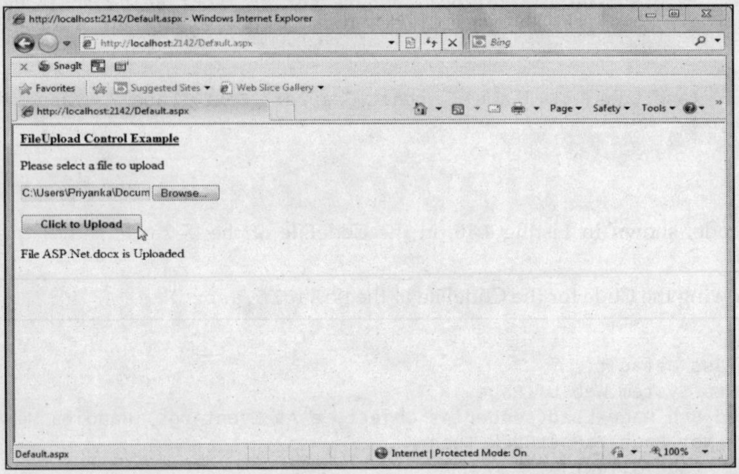

Figure 4.20: Uploading a File on the Server Using the FileUpload Control

NOTE

On clicking the Button control, the text box in the FileUpload Control, showing path of the uploaded file, gets empty.

With this, we come to the end of the chapter. Let's now summarize the main points of the chapter.

Summary

In this chapter, you have learned about various Standard Web controls, such as the Button control, TextBox control, Label control, Literal control, and FileUpload control. These controls are mostly used for designing user interfaces for ASP.NET Web applications. You have also learned how to set properties of the controls.

In the next chapter, we explore few more controls that appear under the Navigation tab of the Toolbox and are used for navigational purpose; such as Treeview, Menu, and SiteMapPath.

5

Navigation Controls: TreeView, Menu, and SiteMapPath

In Depth

Navigation controls allow users to navigate through the Web pages. For example, if your Web site is composed of multiple pages, you need navigation controls that help in making the navigation of pages easier. Navigation controls, such as the `TreeView` control, `Menu` control, and `SiteMapPath` control, make it simple to add page hierarchies, quick links, and provide advanced navigational capabilities to your application. The Navigation controls display data in a consistent manner, thereby enabling the users to comprehend the application structure. These Navigation controls are the most recently introduced controls, and provide several features, such as consistent and easily managed navigation, to developers as well as users.

In this chapter, we explored three Navigation controls - TreeView control, Menu control, and SiteMapPath control, and also discusses about the base class of each of these Navigation controls. This chapter also discusses about the various properties, methods, and events of the Navigation controls, and shows you the practical implementation of using these Navigation controls.

Using the TreeView Class

The `TreeView` class enables you to manage the TreeView control. The `TreeView` class can be used to create a tree-based hierarchical structure in the Web page at runtime.

The class hierarchy of the `TreeView` class is as follows:

```
System.Object
   System.Web.UI.Control
      System.Web.UI.WebControls.WebControl
         System.Web.UI.WebControls.BaseDataBoundControl
            System.Web.UI.WebControls.HierarchicalDataBoundControl
               System.Web.UI.WebControls.TreeView
```

The `TreeView` class contains a `Node` property that can be used to create the nodes of the `TreeView` control. The `Nodes` collection contains the `Add` method that can be used to add a text item or a `TreeNode` object in the `TreeView` class. It can further have child nodes and consists of properties, such as `ExpandAll` and `CollapseAll`, which expand and collapse the tree view nodes. You can also insert check boxes against the nodes and obtain the selected information dynamically by using the `TreeView` class.

Table 5.1 lists the noteworthy properties of the `TreeView` class:

Table 5.1: Noteworthy Properties of the TreeView Class

Property	Description
`AutoGenerateDataBindings`	Obtains or specifies a value that indicates whether the `TreeView` control automatically generates tree node bindings
`CheckedNodes`	Obtains a collection of `TreeNode` objects, which represent the nodes in the `TreeView` control that displays a selected check box
`CollapseImageToolTip`	Obtains or specifies the `ToolTip` for the image that is displayed for the collapsible node indicator
`CollapseImageUrl`	Obtains or specifies the Uniform Resource Locator (URL) to a custom image for the collapsible node indicator
`DataBindings`	Obtains a collection of `TreeNodeBinding` objects that define the relationship between a data item and the node to which the object is binding
`EnableClientScript`	Obtains or specifies a value that indicates whether the `TreeView` control renders client-side script to handle expanding and collapsing events

Table 5.1: Noteworthy Properties of the TreeView Class

Property	Description
ExpandDepth	Obtains or specifies the number of levels that are expanded when a TreeView control is displayed for the first time
ExpandImageToolTip	Obtains or specifies the ToolTip for the image that is displayed for the expandable node indicator
ExpandImageUrl	Obtains or specifies the URL to a custom image for the expandable node indicator
HoverNodeStyle	Obtains a reference to the TreeNodeStyle object that allows you to set the appearance of a node when the mouse pointer is positioned over it
ImageSet	Obtains or specifies the group of images to use for the TreeView control
LeafNodeStyle	Obtains a reference to the TreeNodeStyle object that allows you to set the appearance of leaf nodes
LevelStyles	Obtains a collection of Style objects that represent the node styles at the individual levels of the tree
LineImagesFolder	Obtains or specifies the path to a folder, which contains the line images that are used to connect child nodes to parent nodes
MaxDataBindDepth	Obtains or specifies the maximum number of tree levels to bind to the TreeView control
NodeIndent	Obtains or specifies the indentation amount (in pixels) for the child nodes of the TreeView control
Nodes	Obtains a collection of TreeNode objects that represent the root nodes in the TreeView control
NodeStyle	Obtains a reference to the TreeNodeStyle object that allows you to set the default appearance of the nodes in the TreeView control
NodeWrap	Obtains or specifies a value that indicates text wraps in a node when the node runs out of space
NoExpandImageUrl	Obtains or specifies the URL to a custom image for the non-expandable node indicator
ParentNodeStyle	Obtains a reference to the TreeNodeStyle object that allows you to set the appearance of parent nodes in the TreeView control
PathSeparator	Obtains or specifies the character that is used to delimit the node values that are specified by the ValuePath property
PopulateNodesFromClient	Obtains or specifies a value that indicates whether node data is populated on demand from the client
RootNodeStyle	Obtains a reference to the TreeNodeStyle object that allows you to set the appearance of the root node in the TreeView control
SelectedNode	Obtains a TreeNode object that represents the selected node in the TreeView control
SelectedNodeStyle	Obtains the TreeNodeStyle object that controls the appearance of the selected node in the TreeView control
SelectedValue	Obtains the value of the selected node
ShowCheckBoxes	Obtains or specifies a value that indicates which node types will display a check box in the TreeView control

Table 5.1: Noteworthy Properties of the TreeView Class	
Property	**Description**
`ShowExpandCollapse`	Obtains or specifies a value that indicates whether expansion node indicators are displayed on the Web page
`ShowLines`	Obtains or specifies a value that indicates whether lines connecting child nodes to parent nodes are displayed on the Web page
`SkipLinkText`	Obtains or specifies a value that is used to render alternate text for screen readers to skip the content for the control
`Target`	Obtains or specifies the target window or frame in which the Web page content that is associated with a node is to display
`Visible`	Obtains or specifies a value that indicates whether the control is rendered as UI on the page

Table 5.2 lists the noteworthy methods of the `TreeView` class:

Table 5.2: Noteworthy Methods of the TreeView Class	
Method	**Description**
`CollapseAll`	Collapses every node in the tree
`ExpandAll`	Expands every node in the tree
`FindNode`	Find the TreeNode object in the TreeView control at the specified path

Table 5.3 lists the noteworthy events of the `TreeView` class:

Table 5.3: Noteworthy Events of the TreeView Class	
Event	**Description**
`SelectedNodeChanged`	Occurs when a node is clicked in the `TreeView` control.
`TreeNodeCheckChanged`	Occurs when a check box in the `TreeView` control changes the state between posts to the server. This implies that whenever this event is generated, a custom routine, such as updating of database, is performed.
`TreeNodeCollapsed`	Occurs when a node is collapsed.
`TreeNodeDataBound`	Occurs when data is bound to a node in the `TreeView` control.
`TreeNodeExpanded`	Occurs when a node is expanded.
`TreeNodePopulate`	Occurs when the `PopulateOnDemand` property of a node is set to true. This event helps in populating the node at run time, when the node is expanded.

The TreeView Control

The `TreeView` control is used for logically displaying the data in a hierarchical structure, similar to Windows explorer. You can use this control when you need to display the navigation menu for displaying the files and folders on the Web page. You can display an Extensible Markup Language (XML) document and database records in a tree structure. To work with the `TreeView` control at runtime, you can programmatically access the `TreeView` Web server control.

The `TreeView` Web server control is used to create tree-based hierarchical structure, set properties, and populate nodes. The `TreeView` control consists of the `TreeView` container and `TreeNode` properties. There can be multiple nodes in the tree view structure, which can be nested. The `TreeNode` property has a `Text` property that displays the text for the node.

In addition to the `Text` property, there is also an `Expanded` property for the TreeNode, which is used to expand and collapse the nodes. The default value of this property is `False`. However, if you set it to `True`, the control will be displayed in the expanded view every time it is loaded.

You can access the `TreeView` control directly from the Navigation tab in the Toolbox. You can add the `TreeView` control to your Web page simply by either double clicking the `TreeView` control in the Toolbox or by dragging the control from the Toolbox to the Design view of the Default.aspx page. Figure 5.1 shows the default tree view node when the `TreeView` control is placed on the `Default.aspx` Web page of the TreeViewControl example:

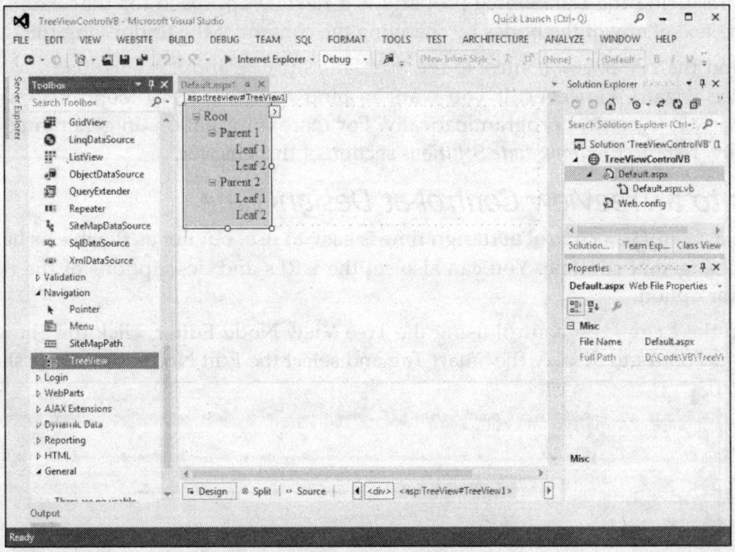

Figure 5.1: Displaying the TreeView Control

You can also add the `TreeView` control on the Web page by adding the following code snippet in the `<form>` element of your Web page:

```
<asp:TreeView ID="TreeView1" runat="server">
  </asp:TreeView>
```

NOTE

The TreeView control supports the AutoFormat feature, which allows you to select from the already existing formats. AutoFormat option can be selected from the Smart Tag of the TreeView control.

The `TreeView` control is a powerful server control that is used to render the tree view UI. It has many properties, such as `CheckedNodes`, `DataBindings`, `NodeIndent`, `Nodes`, and `NodeStyle`, that are served by means of the `TreeView` class. For more information about the `TreeView` control class, refer to the *Immediate Solutions* section of this chapter. The contents for the `TreeView` control can be added in the following ways:

- By adding programmatically at runtime
- By dynamically loading from an external data source, such as an XML file
- The `TreeView` control can also be added while designing an application.

Adding Nodes to a TreeView Control Dynamically

The `TreeView` control can load the data dynamically at runtime. For this, you have to set the properties of the `TreeView` nodes dynamically. The `TreeView` control has a `Nodes` property known as `TreeView.Nodes`. You can add nodes to the `TreeView` control by using the `add` method of the `TreeView.Nodes` property. Refer to the *Immediate Solutions* section of this chapter for more information on the `TreeView` class.

Adding Nodes to a TreeView Control Using the DataSource Property

You can also add data to the `TreeView` control by using the `DataSource` property. In fact, this is a more flexible and easy-to-use property for binding data. By setting the `DataSourceID` property of the `TreeView` control to the desired file, you can load the content of the `TreeView` control from the specified file. The target file can be an XML file, a sitemap, or you can even populate a tree view from the database, such as SQL (Structured Query Language) Server's database or MS (Microsoft) -Access's database.

After an appropriate data source is set for the `TreeView` control, the `TreeView` control displays the information in a tree structure. Using the DataSource property is a flexible approach for the `TreeView` control as you can easily change the text of any of the nodes by changing the content of the underlying file.

You can only bind the `Treeview` control to the `XmlDataSource` and `SiteMapDataSource` controls using the Add Data Source wizard. However, if you want to bind the `TreeView` control to a database, you need to generate the `TreeView` control programmatically. For more information on generating the `TreeView` control programmatically, refer to the *Immediate Solutions* section of this chapter.

Adding Nodes to a TreeView Control at Design Time

Adding node to a `TreeView` control at design time is easy to use, but not as flexible as hardcoding of properties, and cannot be changed at runtime. You can also set the URLs and descriptions of the nodes by using the Tree View Node Editor option.

To add nodes to the `TreeView` control using the Tree View Node Editor, click the Show Smart Tag at the top-right corner of the control to display the Smart Tag and select the Edit Nodes option, as shown in Figure 5.2:

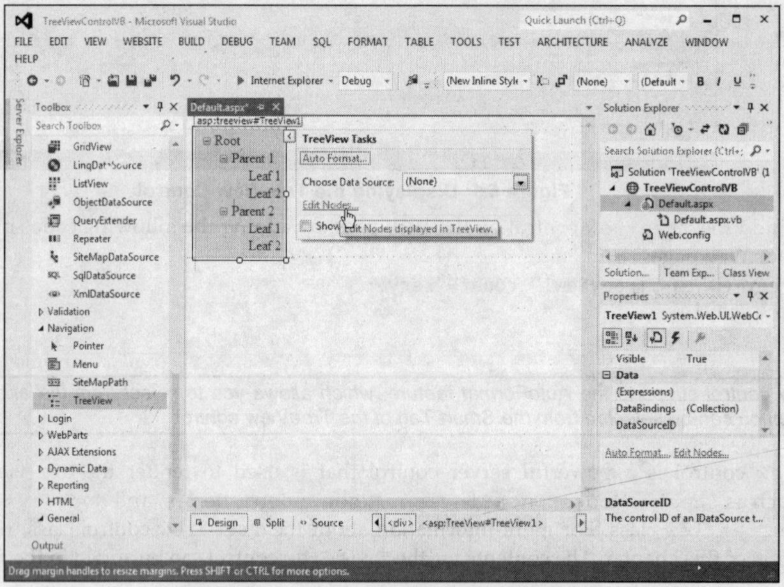

Figure 5.2: Selecting the Edit Nodes Option

The TreeView Node Editor dialog box opens, and allows you to add and delete nodes and set their properties, as shown in Figure 5.3:

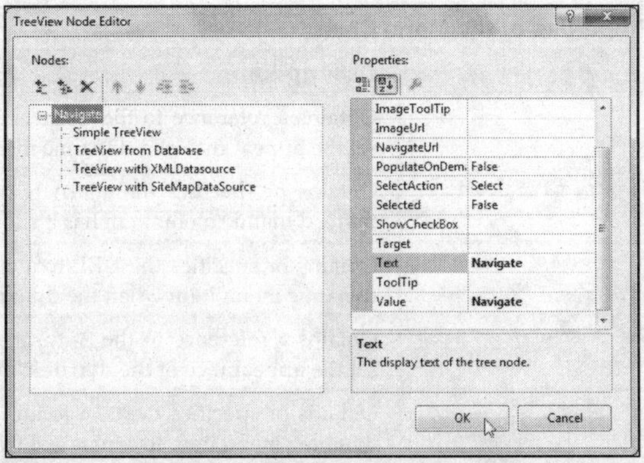

Figure 5.3: Displaying theTreeView Node Editor Dialog Box

Using the Menu Class

The `Menu` class provides various properties, methods, and events that provide a greater flexibility while displaying data using the `Menu` control.

The inheritance hierarchy for the `Menu` class is as follows:

```
System.Object
   System.Web.UI.Control
       System.Web.UI.WebControls.WebControl
           System.Web.UI.WebControls.BaseDataBoundControl
               System.Web.UI.WebControls.HierarchicalDataBoundControl
                   System.Web.UI.WebControls.Menu
```

Table 5.4 lists the noteworthy properties of the `Menu` class:

Table 5.4: Noteworthy Properties of the Menu Class

Property	Description
`DataBindings`	Obtains a collection of `MenuItemBinding` objects that define the relationship between a data item and the menu item to which the object is bound
`DisappearAfter`	Obtains or specifies the duration for which a dynamic menu is displayed after the mouse pointer is no longer positioned over the menu
`DynamicBottomSeparatorImageUrl`	Obtains or specifies the `URL` to an image to display at the bottom of each dynamic menu item to separate it from other menu items
`DynamicEnableDefaultPopOutImage`	Obtains or specifies a value that indicates whether default pop-out image is displayed in the dynamic part of the menu or not
`DynamicHorizontalOffset`	Obtains or specifies the number of pixels that a dynamic menu item is shifted relative to its parent menu item
`DynamicHoverStyle`	Obtains a reference to the `Style` object that allows you to set the appearance of a dynamic menu item when the mouse pointer is positioned over it
`DynamicItemFormatString`	Obtains or specifies additional text shown with all menu items that are dynamically displayed on the Web page
`DynamicItemTemplate`	Obtains or specifies the template that contains the custom content to render for a dynamic menu
`DynamicMenuItemStyle`	Obtains a reference to the `MenuItemStyle` object that allows you to set the appearance of the menu items within a dynamic menu

Table 5.4: Noteworthy Properties of the Menu Class

Property	Description
DynamicMenuStyle	Obtains a reference to the MenuItemStyle object that allows you to set the appearance of a dynamic menu
DynamicPopOutImageTextFormatString	Obtains or specifies the alternate text for the image used to indicate that a dynamic menu item has a submenu
DynamicPopOutImageUrl	Obtains or specifies the URL to a custom image that is displayed in a dynamic menu item when the dynamic menu item has a submenu
DynamicSelectedStyle	Obtains a reference to the MenuItemStyle object that allows you to set the appearance of the dynamic menu item selected by the user
DynamicTopSeparatorImageUrl	Obtains or specifies the URL to an image to display at the top of each dynamic menu item to separate it from other menu items
DynamicVerticalOffset	Obtains or specifies the number of pixels that a dynamic menu item is shifted relative to its parent menu item
Items	Obtains a MenuItemCollection object that contains all menu items in the Menu control
ItemWrap	Obtains or specifies a value that indicates whether the text for menu items should wrap
LevelMenuItemStyles	Obtains a MenuItemStyleCollection object that contains the style settings that are applied to menu items based on their level in a Menu control
LevelSelectedStyles	Obtains a MenuItemStyleCollection object that contains the style settings that are applied to the selected menu item based on its level in a Menu control
LevelSubMenuStyles	Obtains a MenuItemStyleCollection object that contains the style settings that are applied to the submenu items in the static menu based on their level in a Menu control
MaximumDynamicDisplayLevels	Obtains or specifies the number of menu levels to render for a dynamic menu
Orientation	Obtains or specifies the direction in which to render the Menu control
PathSeparator	Obtains or specifies the character used to delimit the path of a menu item in a Menu control
ScrollDownImageUrl	Obtains or specifies the URL to an image displayed in a dynamic menu to indicate that the user can scroll down for additional menu items
ScrollDownText	Obtains or specifies the alternate text for the image specified in the ScrollDownImageUrl property
ScrollUpImageUrl	Obtains or specifies the URL to an image displayed in a dynamic menu to indicate that the user can scroll up for additional menu items
ScrollUpText	Obtains or specifies the alternate text for the image specified in the ScrollUpImageUrl property
SelectedItem	Obtains the selected menu item
SelectedValue	Obtains the value of the selected menu item
SkipLinkText	Obtains or specifies the alternate text for a hidden image read by screen readers to provide the ability to skip the list of links
StaticBottomSeparatorImageUrl	Obtains or specifies the URL to an image displayed as the separator at the bottom of each static menu item

Table 5.4: Noteworthy Properties of the Menu Class	
Property	**Description**
StaticDisplayLevels	Obtains or specifies the number of menu levels to display in a static menu
StaticEnableDefaultPopOutImage	Obtains or specifies a value, which indicates whether the built-in image is displayed to indicate that a static menu item has a submenu
StaticHoverStyle	Obtains a reference to the MenuItemStyle object that allows you to set the appearance of a static menu item when the mouse pointer is positioned over it
StaticItemFormatString	Obtains or specifies additional text shown with all static menu items
StaticItemTemplate	Obtains or specifies the template that contains the custom content to render for a static menu
StaticMenuItemStyle	Obtains a reference to the MenuItemStyle object that allows you to set the appearance of the menu items in a static menu
StaticMenuStyle	Obtains a reference to the MenuItemStyle object that allows you to set the appearance of a static menu
StaticPopOutImageTextFormatString	Obtains or specifies the alternate text for the pop-out image used to indicate that a static menu item has a submenu
StaticPopOutImageUrl	Obtains or specifies the URL to an image displayed to indicate that a static menu item has a submenu
StaticSelectedStyle	Obtains a reference to the MenuItemStyle object that allows you to set the appearance of the menu item selected by the user in a static menu
StaticSubMenuIndent	Obtains or specifies the amount of space, which is in pixels, to indent submenus within a static menu
StaticTopSeparatorImageUrl	Obtains or specifies the URL to an image displayed as the separator at the top of each static menu item
Target	Obtains or specifies the target window or frame in which the Web page content associated with a menu item is to display

Table 5.5 lists the noteworthy methods of the Menu class:

Table 5.5: Noteworthy Methods of the Menu Class	
Method	**Description**
FindItem	Retrieves the menu item at the specified value path
RenderBeginTag	Adds tag attributes and writes the markup for the opening Tag of the control to the output stream emitted to the browser or device
RenderEndTag	Performs final markup and writes the HyperText Markup Language (HTML) closing tag of the control to the output stream emitted to the browser or device

Table 5.6 lists the noteworthy events of the Menu class:

Table 5.6: Noteworthy Events of the Menu Class	
Event	**Description**
MenuItemclick	Occurs when a menu item in a Menu control is clicked
MenuItemDataBound	Occurs when a menu item in a Menu control is bound to data

The Menu Control

The Menu control is another Navigation control, which is also used to display site navigation information. The Menu control can, however, display the site structure vertically as well as horizontally. It can be used as a databound control, for example, binding the menu control with a SiteMapDataSource control. It can also retrieve the data to be displayed from the items that are added to the Items collection of the Menu control at runtime. The Menu control supports binding data with hierarchical data source, such as XML files. You can also add the database items to the Menu control at runtime using the Items collection of the Menu control. The Menu control consists of one or more MenuItems properties displayed at different levels of hierarchy. Each MenuItem, in turn, consists of properties to set the style of the individual MenuItem. The Menu control contains two types of menus:

- **Static menu**—Refers to the type of menu that is displayed completely on the screen with all the menu options on the screen. The entire structure of the static menu, including the parent menu items and their sub menus, is visible.
- **Dynamic menu**—Refers to the type of menu that contains static part, which is displayed on the screen, as well as the dynamic part, which appears when user passes the mouse pointer over the static part of the menu.

Figure 5.4 shows a simple Menu control from the MenuControl example:

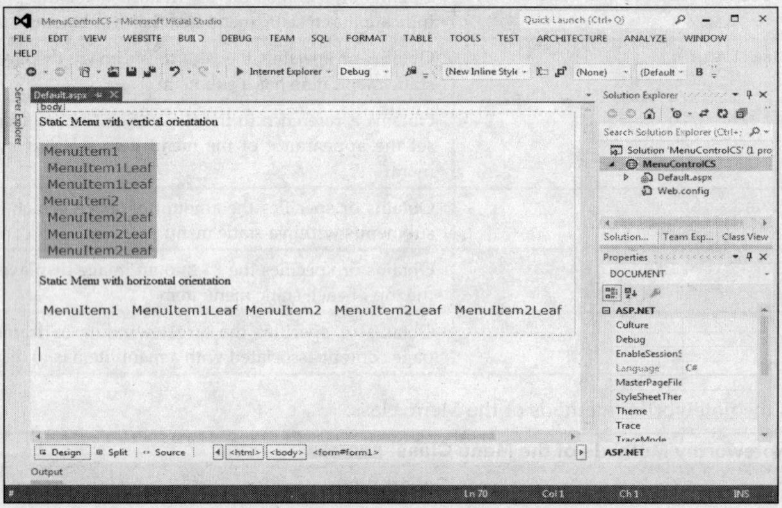

Figure 5.4: Showing the MenuControl Example

Menu Display Properties

You can change the look of the Menu control by setting the following properties:

- **Orientation**—Means that you can set this property to horizontal to display menu either at the top or at the bottom of the page. The default orientation value is Vertical.
- **StaticItemFormatString**— Means that you can set this property to display the value for the static menus.
- **DynamicItemFormatString**— Means that you can set this property to display the value for the dynamic menus.
- **StaticPopOutImageUrl**— Means that you can set the replacement image for StaticPopOutImage. This means that the menu items can be hovered over to display all of its child items. The default image will appear dynamically and continue to be used for menu items.

Menu Styles

The `Menu` control supports various styles at different levels, such as on individual menu items, menu levels, or menu sub levels. You can set styles for all menu levels and menu items that appear as both statically and dynamically on a Web page. The following are the different style properties:

- **Static/DynamicMenuStyle**—Controls properties for all MenuItem property. It also controls properties such as HorizontalPadding and VerticalPadding.
- **DynamicMenuItemStyle**—Controls the style of the individual MenuItems property. It also includes style properties such as ItemSpacing, VerticalPadding, and HorizontalPadding.
- **DynamicSelectedStyle**—Sets the style of the individual nodes in the TreeView control that are currently selected. In other words, it can be described as a collection of style properties for the selected menu item. It also includes style properties such as HorizontalPadding, VerticalPadding, and ItemSpacing.
- **DynamicHoverStyle**—Sets the style properties of the individual MenuItem property that is currently selected. In other words, it can be set for the selected MenuItem while you hover your mouse over a MenuItem property. It also includes properties such as ItemSpacing, HorizontalPadding, and VerticalPadding.

Using the SiteMapPath Class

The `SiteMapPath` class displays a set of text or image hyperlinks that enable the users to easily navigate a Web site.

The inheritance hierarchy for the `SiteMapPath` class is as follows:

```
System.Object
   System.Web.UI.Control
      System.Web.UI.WebControls.WebControl
         System.Web.UI.WebControls.CompositeControl
            System.Web.UI.WebControls.SiteMapPath
```

Table 5.7 lists the noteworthy properties of the `SiteMapPath` class:

Table 5.7: Noteworthy Properties of the SiteMapPath Class

Property	Description
`CurrentNodeStyle`	Obtains the style used for displaying text for the current node
`CurrentNodeTemplate`	Obtains or specifies a control template to use for the node of a site navigation path that represents the currently displayed page
`NodeStyle`	Obtains the style used for the display text for all nodes in the site navigation path
`NodeTemplate`	Obtains or specifies a control template to use for all functional nodes of a site navigation path
`ParentLevelsDisplayed`	Obtains or specifies the number of levels of parent nodes that the control displays relative to the currently displayed node
`PathDirection`	Obtains or specifies the order of the links displayed by the SiteMapPath control. Possible value is `RootToCurrent` (default) or `CurrentToRoot`
`PathSeparator`	Obtains or specifies the string that delimits `SiteMapPath` nodes in the rendered navigation path
`PathSeparatorStyle`	Obtains the style used for the `PathSeparator` string
`PathSeparatorTemplate`	Obtains or specifies a control template to use for the path delimiter of a site navigation path
`Provider`	Obtains or specifies a `SiteMapProvider` control that is associated with the Web server control

Table 5.7: Noteworthy Properties of the SiteMapPath Class

Property	Description
`RenderCurrentNodeAsLink`	Indicates whether the site navigation node that represents the currently displayed page is rendered as a hyperlink
`RootNodeStyle`	Obtains the style for the root node display text
`RootNodeTemplate`	Obtains or specifies a control template to use for the root node of a site navigation path
`ShowToolTips`	Obtains or specifies a value that indicates whether the `SiteMapPath` control writes an additional hyperlink attribute for hyperlinked navigation nodes. Depending on client support, when the mouse pointer is moved over a hyperlink that has the additional attribute set, a tool tip is displayed
`SiteMapProvider`	Obtains or specifies the name of the `SiteMapProvider` used to render the site Navigation control
`SkipLinkText`	Obtains or specifies a value that is used to render alternate text for screen readers to skip the control's content

Table 5.8 lists the noteworthy methods of the `SiteMapPath` class:

Table 5.8: Noteworthy Methods of the SiteMapPath Class

Methods	Description
`DataBind`	Binds a data source to the `SiteMapPath` control and all its child controls

Table 5.9 lists the noteworthy events of the `SiteMapPath` class:

Table 5.9: Noteworthy Events of the SiteMapPath Class

Event	Description
`ItemCreated`	Occurs when a `SiteMapNodeItem` is created by the `SiteMapPath` and is associated with its corresponding `SiteMapNode`. This event is raised by the `OnItemCreated` method.
`ItemDataBound`	Occurs after a `SiteMapNodeItem` has been bound to its underlying `SiteMapNode` data by the `SiteMapPath`. This event is raised by the `OnItemDataBound` method,

The SiteMapPath Control

The `SiteMapPath` control is also known as the breadcrumb Navigation control. Breadcrumb allows you to display the current page's context within the entire structure of a Web site. It also allows you to display links as a path back to the home page. It displays information regarding the user's current page along with the entire hierarchy of the pages, thereby enabling the user to navigate back to some other pages in the hierarchy.

However, the `SiteMapPath` control does not allow you to move forward from the current page to the next page deeper in the site hierarchy. The `SiteMapPath` control does not use the `SiteMapDataSource` control to display data. It relies on a `SiteMapProvider` to retrieve the data. The `SiteMapProvider` contains an XML file `Web.sitemap`, which contains URLs and other information about the pages to be displayed. The `SiteMapPath` control can be localized by adding attributes to the `Web.sitemap` file. Figure 5.5 shows a `SiteMapPath` control on the Web form of the `SiteMapPathControl` example:

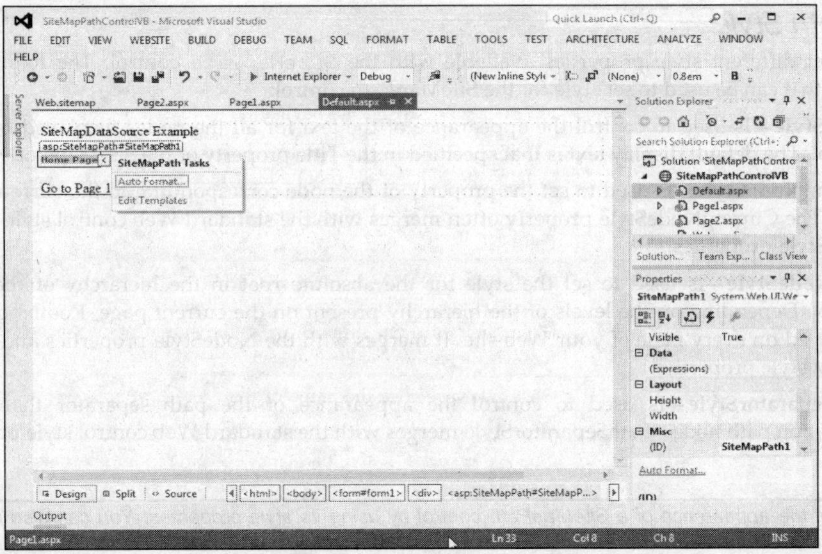

Figure 5.5: Showing the SiteMapPath Control

Data Retrieval Using the SiteMapPath Control

The `SiteMapPath` control uses the `SiteMapProvider` to fetch the data and display it on the Web form. As you have seen earlier, both the `Menu` and `TreeView` controls rely on the `SiteMapDataSource` control The `SiteMapPath` control displays only the data whose URL is present in the specified `SiteMapProvider`. You should always check that there is no typing error in the `Web.sitemap` file; otherwise, the `SiteMapProvider` will not be able to display the desired output.

SiteMapPath Behaviors

The `SiteMapPath` control displays various common properties to change the display behavior. Table 5.10 lists the noteworthy properties of the `SiteMapPath` class, which are used to change the display behavior:

Table 5.10: Noteworthy Properties of the SiteMapPath Class

Property	Description
`ParentLevelsDisplayed`	Specifies to `-1 by default`, which means that all parent levels in the XML file are displayed. You can set it to any integer values, such as `1`, `2`, or `3`, to indicate the N-level of the hierarchy along with the current page.
`PathDirection`	Specifies the order in which the nodes of the navigation path are rendered. The default setting is such that it starts from the highest node in the current XML file and goes up to the current page. By setting this property, the links will be displayed in the opposite direction, which means that the nodes will be displayed starting from the current page and ending on the root page or first page
`PathSeparator`	Specifies this property to `:` (Semicolon) as path separator. Its default value is >.
`RenderCurrentNodeAsLink`	Specifies this property to true, so that the current node text on the Web page will appear as hyperlink and not as plain text.
`ShowToolTips`	Specifies this property to false, so that the description text from the `SiteMapProvider` control is not displayed automatically.

SiteMapPath Style

You can set different style properties available with the `SiteMapPath` control. The following is the list of properties that can be used to set style for the SiteMapPath control:

- **NodeStyle**—Is used to control the appearance of the text for all the nodes displayed by the SiteMapPath control. The default display text is that specified in the Title property of the SiteMapNode.
- **CurrentNodeStyle**—Is used to set the property of the node corresponding to the currently displayed Web page. The CurrentNodeStyle property often merges with the standard Web control style properties and the NodeStyle properties.
- **RootNodeStyle**—Is used to set the style for the absolute root in the hierarchy of the SiteMapProvider control. Depending on the levels of the hierarchy present on the current page, RootNodeStyle may not be displayed on every page of your Web site. It merges with the NodeStyle properties and the standard Web control style properties.
- **PathSeparatorStyle**—Is used to control the appearance of the path separator that appears between navigation path nodes. PathSeparatorStyle merges with the standard Web control style properties.

NOTE

You can set the appearance of a SiteMapPath control by using its style properties. You can also use skin and theme files for setting the appearance.

SiteMapPath Templates

In addition to the style properties discussed earlier, the `SiteMapPath` control also offers templates, which can be used with a better flexibility to set the view of the control. The templates control the HTML rendering for the specific part of the control. Note that if you define a template for a particular node, it will override the previous style setting defined for this node. To set the appearance of the `SiteMapPath` control, you can use the following templates:

- `NodeTemplate`—Applies on all the nodes in the hierarchy, irrespective of their node type.
- `CurrentNodeTemplate`—Sets the appearance of the node corresponding to the current page displayed. `CurrentNodeTemplate` takes precedence over the `NodeTemplate`.
- `RootNodeTemplate`—Sets the appearance for the root node of the site hierarchy. `RootNodeTemplate` takes priority over `NodeTemplate` and `CurrentNodeTemplate`. This means that if the current page is the root page according to the site hierarchy, then only `RootNodeTemplate` will be used for the root node.
- `PathSeparatorTemplate`—Uses to separate the nodes with a separator between the nodes that are currently rendered on the Web page. It replaces the `PathSeparator` text value in your application.

Immediate Solutions

Creating the TreeView Control

The `TreeView` control can be easily created in Visual Studio 2012 (VS 2012). For this, simply drag and drop the control onto the Web page. The `TreeView` control is available under the Navigation tab in the Toolbox of VS 2012.

NOTE

The applications in this chapter are created using the ASP.NET Empty Web Site template in the New Web Site dialog box. After creating the application, you need to add the Default.aspx page to the application. For the proper functioning of the TreeViewControl application, you should set the Default.aspx page as the Start Page.

We have used the `TreeView` control in the `TreeViewControlVB` in VB and `TreeViewControlCS` in C# examples, as discussed in the *In Depth* section of this chapter. You can find the code for the `Default.aspx` page in Listing 5.1:

Listing 5.1: Showing the Code for the `Default.aspx` Page

In VB

```
<%@ Page Language="VB" AutoEventWireup="false" CodeFile="Default.aspx.vb"
  Inherits="_Default" %>
<!DOCTYPE html>
<html xmlns="http://www.w3.org/1999/xhtml">
<head runat="server">
    <title>TreeView Control Example</title>
</head>
<body>
    <form id="form1" runat="server">
    <div>
        <asp:Label ID="Label1" runat="server" Font-Bold="True" Font-Size="Medium"
         Text="Static TreeView"></asp:Label>
        <br />
        <asp:TreeView ID="TreeView1" runat="server">
            <Nodes>
                <asp:TreeNode Text="Navigate" Value="Navigate">
                    <asp:TreeNode Text="Simple TreeView" Value="Simple TreeView"
                        NavigateUrl="~/SimpleTreeView.aspx"></asp:TreeNode>
                    <asp:TreeNode Text="TreeView from Database" Value="TreeView from
                        Database" NavigateUrl="~/TreeViewDatabase.aspx"></asp:TreeNode>
                    <asp:TreeNode Text="TreeView with XMLDatasource" Value="TreeView
                        with XMLDatasource"
                        NavigateUrl="~/TreeViewXMLData.aspx"></asp:TreeNode>
                    <asp:TreeNode Text="TreeView with SiteMapDataSource" Value="TreeView
                        with SiteMapDataSource"
                        NavigateUrl="~/TreeViewSiteMapDataSource.aspx"></asp:TreeNode>
                </asp:TreeNode>
            </Nodes>
        </asp:TreeView>
    </div>
        <p>
             </p>
        <p>
             </p>
    </form>
</body>
</html>
```

In C#

```
<%@ Page Language="C#" AutoEventWireup="true" CodeFile="Default.aspx.cs"
  Inherits="_Default" %>
<!DOCTYPE html>
<html xmlns="http://www.w3.org/1999/xhtml">
<head id="Head1" runat="server">
    <title>TreeView Control Example</title>
</head>
<body>
    <form id="form1" runat="server">
    <div>
        <asp:Label ID="Label1" runat="server" Font-Bold="True" Font-Size="Medium"
         Text="Static TreeView"></asp:Label>
        <br />
        <asp:TreeView ID="TreeView1" runat="server">
            <Nodes>
                <asp:TreeNode Text="Navigate" Value="Navigate">
                    <asp:TreeNode Text="Simple TreeView" Value="Simple TreeView"
                        NavigateUrl="~/SimpleTreeView.aspx"></asp:TreeNode>
                    <asp:TreeNode Text="TreeView from Database" Value="TreeView from
                        Database"
                        NavigateUrl="~/TreeViewDatabase.aspx"></asp:TreeNode>
                    <asp:TreeNode Text="TreeView with XMLDatasource" Value="TreeView
                        with XMLDatasource"
                        NavigateUrl="~/TreeViewXMLData.aspx"></asp:TreeNode>
                    <asp:TreeNode Text="TreeView with SiteMapDataSource" Value="TreeView
                        with SiteMapDataSource"
                        NavigateUrl="~/TreeViewSiteMapDataSource.aspx"></asp:TreeNode>
                </asp:TreeNode>
            </Nodes>
        </asp:TreeView>
    </div>
        <p>
             </p>
        <p>
             </p>
    </form>
</body>
</html>
```

It can be seen in the preceding listing that we have placed a `TreeView` control on the Web page. It contains a navigation structure for this application. The output of the preceding listing is as shown in Figure 5.6:

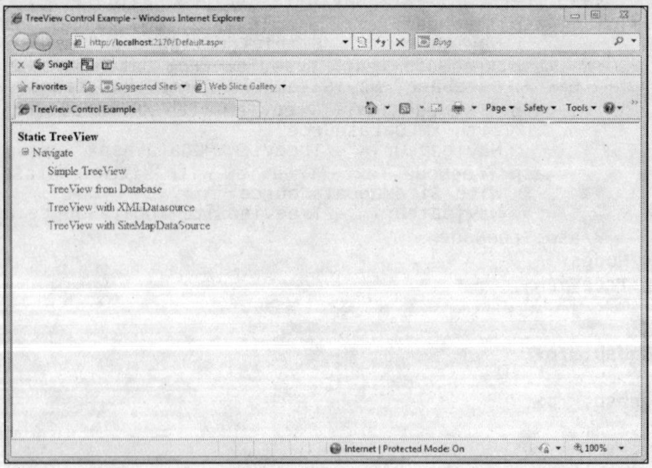

Figure 5.6: Showing the Simple TreeView Example

To add the nodes of the `TreeView` control at design time, choose the `Edit Nodes` option from the Smart Tag of the TreeView Control. Once you click the Edit Node option, a TreeView Node Editor dialog box appears (shown earlier in Figure 5.3).

You can now add nodes by clicking the Add a root node button on the Toolbar of the TreeView Node Editor dialog box, as shown in Figure 5.7:

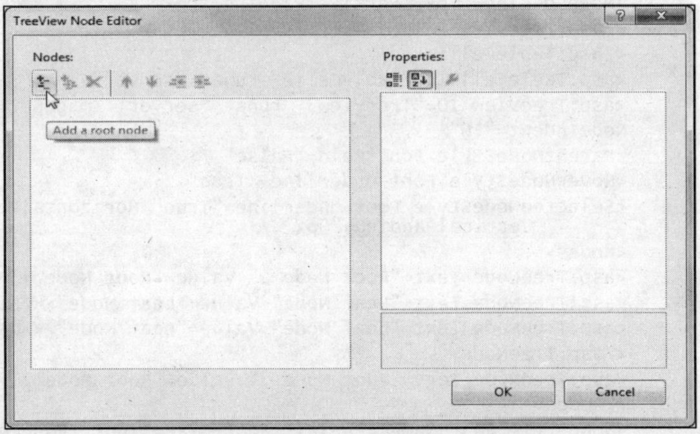

Figure 5.7: Adding a Node in TreeView

You can now add root or parent nodes by clicking the first button (Add a root node), and the child nodes by clicking the second button (Add a child node). Set the `Text` property for the nodes under the Properties panel.

After creating the navigation structure for the application, we have created six different TreeView controls, each one with different styles of formatting. For this, we have added a new page, that is, `SimpleTreeView.aspx` page of the application. You can find the code for the `SimpleTreeView.aspx` page of the `TreeViewControl` application in Listing 5.2.

Listing 5.2: Showing the Code for the `SimpleTreeView.aspx` Page

In VB

```
<%@ Page Language="VB" AutoEventWireup="false" CodeFile="SimpleTreeView.aspx.vb"
  Inherits="SimpleTreeView" %>
<!DOCTYPE html>
<html xmlns="http://www.w3.org/1999/xhtml">
<head id="Head1" runat="server">
    <title>TreeView Control Example</title>
</head>
<body>
    <form id="form1" runat="server">
    <div>
        <asp:Label ID="Label1" runat="server" Font-Bold="True" Font-Size="Medium"
        Text="Example of a Simple TreeView Control"></asp:Label>
    <asp:Table ID="Table1" runat="server" Height="91px" Width="594px">
                <asp:TableRow ID="TableRow1" runat="server">
                <asp:TableCell ID="TableCell1" runat="server">
                <asp:TreeView ID="TreeView2" runat="server" ImageSet="Arrows">
                <Nodes>
                <asp:TreeNode Text="Root Node 1" Value="Root Node 1">
                <asp:TreeNode Text="Leaf Node"  Value="Leaf Node"></asp:TreeNode>
                <asp:TreeNode Text="Leaf Node" Value="Leaf Node"></asp:TreeNode>
                </asp:TreeNode>
                <asp:TreeNode Text="Root Node 2"  Value="Root Node 2"></asp:TreeNode>
                </Nodes>
                <ParentNodeStyle Font-Bold="False" />
```

```
<HoverNodeStyle Font-Underline="True" ForeColor="#5555DD" />
<SelectedNodeStyle Font-Underline="True" ForeColor="#5555DD"
HorizontalPadding="0px"
 VerticalPadding="0px" />
<NodeStyle Font-Names="Verdana" Font-Size="8pt" ForeColor="Black"
        HorizontalPadding="5px"
 NodeSpacing="0px" VerticalPadding="0px" />
</asp:TreeView>
</asp:TableCell>
<asp:TableCell ID="TableCell2" runat="server">
<asp:TreeView ID="TreeView3" runat="server" ImageSet="News"
NodeIndent="10">
<ParentNodeStyle Font-Bold="False" />
<HoverNodeStyle Font-Underline="True" />
<SelectedNodeStyle Font-Underline="True" HorizontalPadding="0px"
        VerticalPadding="0px" />
<Nodes>
<asp:TreeNode Text="Root Node 1" Value="Root Node 1">
<asp:TreeNode Text="Leaf Node" Value="Leaf Node"></asp:TreeNode>
<asp:TreeNode Text="Leaf Node" Value="Leaf Node"></asp:TreeNode>
</asp:TreeNode>
<asp:TreeNode Text="Root Node 2" Value="Root Node 2"></asp:TreeNode>
</Nodes>
<NodeStyle Font-Names="Arial" Font-Size="10pt" ForeColor="Black"
        HorizontalPadding="5px"
 NodeSpacing="0px" VerticalPadding="0px"/>
</asp:TreeView>
</asp:TableCell>
<asp:TableCell ID="TableCell3" runat="server">
<asp:TreeView ID="TreeView4" runat="server" ShowCheckBoxes="All"
        ShowLines="True">
<Nodes>
<asp:TreeNode Text="Root Node 1" Value="Root Node 1">
<asp:TreeNode Text="Leaf Node" Value="Leaf Node"></asp:TreeNode>
<asp:TreeNode Text="Leaf Node" Value="Leaf Node"></asp:TreeNode>
</asp:TreeNode>
<asp:TreeNode Text="Root Node 2" Value="Root Node 2"></asp:TreeNode>
</Nodes>
</asp:TreeView>
</asp:TableCell>
</asp:TableRow>
<asp:TableRow ID="TableRow2" runat="server">
<asp:TableCell ID="TableCell4" runat="server">
<asp:TreeView ID="TreeView6" runat="server" ImageSet="Contacts"
        NodeIndent="10">
<ParentNodeStyle Font-Bold="True" ForeColor="#5555DD" />
<HoverNodeStyle Font-Underline="False" />
<SelectedNodeStyle Font-Underline="True" HorizontalPadding="0px"
        VerticalPadding="0px" />
<Nodes>
<asp:TreeNode Text="Root Node 1" Value="Root Node 1" Expanded="False">
<asp:TreeNode Text="Leaf Node" Value="Leaf Node"></asp:TreeNode>
<asp:TreeNode Text="Leaf Node" Value="Leaf Node"></asp:TreeNode>
</asp:TreeNode>
<asp:TreeNode Text="Root Node 2" Value="Root Node 2"></asp:TreeNode>
</Nodes>
<NodeStyle Font-Names="Verdana" Font-Size="8pt" ForeColor="Black"
        HorizontalPadding="5px"
 NodeSpacing="0px" VerticalPadding="0px"/>
</asp:TreeView>
```

```
                    </asp:TableCell>
                    <asp:TableCell ID="TableCell5" runat="server">
                    <asp:TreeView ID="TreeView5" runat="server" ShowLines="True">
                    <Nodes>
                    <asp:TreeNode Text="Root Node 1" Value="Root Node 1" Expanded="True">
                    <asp:TreeNode Text="Leaf Node" Value="Leaf Node"></asp:TreeNode>
                    <asp:TreeNode Text="Leaf Node" Value="Leaf Node"></asp:TreeNode>
                    </asp:TreeNode>
                    <asp:TreeNode Text="Root Node 2" Value="Root Node 2"></asp:TreeNode>
                    </Nodes>
                    <LeafNodeStyle BackColor="#FFC0C0" BorderColor="Blue"
                    BorderStyle="Solid"
                    Font-Bold="True"
                     Font-Italic="True" />
                    </asp:TreeView>
                    </asp:TableCell>
                    <asp:TableCell ID="TableCell6" runat="server">
                    <asp:TreeView ID="TreeView7" runat="server" ShowCheckBoxes="All">
                    <Nodes>
                    <asp:TreeNode Text="Root Node 1" Value="Root Node 1" Checked="True"
                         Expanded="False"
                     ShowCheckBox="True">
                    <asp:TreeNode Text="Leaf Node" Value="Leaf Node"></asp:TreeNode>
                    <asp:TreeNode Text="Leaf Node" Value="Leaf Node"></asp:TreeNode>
                    </asp:TreeNode>
                    <asp:TreeNode Text="Root Node 2" Value="Root Node 2"></asp:TreeNode>
                    </Nodes>
                    </asp:TreeView>
                    </asp:TableCell>
                    </asp:TableRow>
                    </asp:Table>
        </div>
        </form>
</body>
</html>
```

In C#

```
<%@ Page Language="C#" AutoEventWireup="true" CodeFile="SimpleTreeView.aspx.cs"
  Inherits="SimpleTreeView" %>
<!DOCTYPE html>
<html xmlns="http://www.w3.org/1999/xhtml">
<head runat="server">
    <title>TreeView Control Example</title>
</head>
<body>
    <form id="form1" runat="server">
    <div>
        <asp:Label ID="Label1" runat="server" Font-Bold="True" Font-Size="Medium"
         Text="Example of a Simple TreeView Control"> </asp:Label>
    <asp:Table ID="Table1" runat="server" Height="91px" Width="594px">
                    <asp:TableRow ID="TableRow1" runat="server">
                    <asp:TableCell ID="TableCell1" runat="server">
                    <asp:TreeView ID="TreeView2" runat="server" ImageSet="Arrows">
                    <Nodes>
                    <asp:TreeNode Text="Root Node 1" Value="Root Node 1">
                    <asp:TreeNode Text="Leaf Node"  Value="Leaf Node"></asp:TreeNode>
                    <asp:TreeNode Text="Leaf Node" Value="Leaf Node"></asp:TreeNode>
                    </asp:TreeNode>
                    <asp:TreeNode Text="Root Node 2"  Value="Root Node 2"></asp:TreeNode>
```

```
</Nodes>
<ParentNodeStyle Font-Bold="False" />
<HoverNodeStyle Font-Underline="True" ForeColor="#5555DD" />
<SelectedNodeStyle Font-Underline="True" ForeColor="#5555DD"
HorizontalPadding="0px"
 VerticalPadding="0px" />
<NodeStyle Font-Names="Verdana" Font-Size="8pt" ForeColor="Black"
       HorizontalPadding="5px"
 NodeSpacing="0px" VerticalPadding="0px" />
</asp:TreeView>
</asp:TableCell>
<asp:TableCell ID="TableCell2" runat="server">
<asp:TreeView ID="TreeView3" runat="server" ImageSet="News"
NodeIndent="10">
<ParentNodeStyle Font-Bold="False" />
<HoverNodeStyle Font-Underline="True" />
<SelectedNodeStyle Font-Underline="True" HorizontalPadding="0px"
       VerticalPadding="0px" />
<Nodes>
<asp:TreeNode Text="Root Node 1" Value="Root Node 1">
<asp:TreeNode Text="Leaf Node" Value="Leaf Node"></asp:TreeNode>
<asp:TreeNode Text="Leaf Node" Value="Leaf Node"></asp:TreeNode>
</asp:TreeNode>
<asp:TreeNode Text="Root Node 2" Value="Root Node 2"></asp:TreeNode>
</Nodes>
<NodeStyle Font-Names="Arial" Font-Size="10pt" ForeColor="Black"
       HorizontalPadding="5px"
 NodeSpacing="0px" VerticalPadding="0px"/>
</asp:TreeView>
</asp:TableCell>
<asp:TableCell ID="TableCell3" runat="server">
<asp:TreeView ID="TreeView4" runat="server" ShowCheckBoxes="All"
       ShowLines="True">
<Nodes>
<asp:TreeNode Text="Root Node 1" Value="Root Node 1">
<asp:TreeNode Text="Leaf Node" Value="Leaf Node"></asp:TreeNode>
<asp:TreeNode Text="Leaf Node" Value="Leaf Node"></asp:TreeNode>
</asp:TreeNode>
<asp:TreeNode Text="Root Node 2" Value="Root Node 2"></asp:TreeNode>
</Nodes>
</asp:TreeView>
</asp:TableCell>
</asp:TableRow>
<asp:TableRow ID="TableRow2" runat="server">
<asp:TableCell ID="TableCell4" runat="server">
<asp:TreeView ID="TreeView6" runat="server" ImageSet="Contacts"
       NodeIndent="10">
<ParentNodeStyle Font-Bold="True" ForeColor="#5555DD" />
<HoverNodeStyle Font-Underline="False" />
<SelectedNodeStyle Font-Underline="True" HorizontalPadding="0px"
       VerticalPadding="0px" />
<Nodes>
<asp:TreeNode Text="Root Node 1" Value="Root Node 1" Expanded="False">
<asp:TreeNode Text="Leaf Node" Value="Leaf Node"></asp:TreeNode>
<asp:TreeNode Text="Leaf Node" Value="Leaf Node"></asp:TreeNode>
</asp:TreeNode>
<asp:TreeNode Text="Root Node 2" Value="Root Node 2"></asp:TreeNode>
</Nodes>
<NodeStyle Font-Names="Verdana" Font-Size="8pt" ForeColor="Black"
       HorizontalPadding="5px"
```

```
                     NodeSpacing="0px" VerticalPadding="0px"/>
                    </asp:TreeView>
                    </asp:TableCell>
                    <asp:TableCell ID="TableCell5" runat="server">
                    <asp:TreeView ID="TreeView5" runat="server" ShowLines="True">
                    <Nodes>
                    <asp:TreeNode Text="Root Node 1" Value="Root Node 1" Expanded="True">
                    <asp:TreeNode Text="Leaf Node" Value="Leaf Node"></asp:TreeNode>
                    <asp:TreeNode Text="Leaf Node" Value="Leaf Node"></asp:TreeNode>
                    </asp:TreeNode>
                    <asp:TreeNode Text="Root Node 2" Value="Root Node 2"></asp:TreeNode>
                    </Nodes>
                    <LeafNodeStyle BackColor="#FFC0C0" BorderColor="Blue"
                    BorderStyle="Solid"
                    Font-Bold="True"
                     Font-Italic="True" />
                    </asp:TreeView>
                    </asp:TableCell>
                    <asp:TableCell ID="TableCell6" runat="server">
                    <asp:TreeView ID="TreeView7" runat="server" ShowCheckBoxes="All">
                    <Nodes>
                    <asp:TreeNode Text="Root Node 1" Value="Root Node 1" Checked="True"
                            Expanded="False"
                     ShowCheckBox="True">
                    <asp:TreeNode Text="Leaf Node" Value="Leaf Node"></asp:TreeNode>
                    <asp:TreeNode Text="Leaf Node" Value="Leaf Node"></asp:TreeNode>
                    </asp:TreeNode>
                    <asp:TreeNode Text="Root Node 2" Value="Root Node 2"></asp:TreeNode>
                    </Nodes>
                    </asp:TreeView>
                    </asp:TableCell>
                    </asp:TableRow>
                    </asp:Table>
        </div>
        </form>
    </body>
    </html>
```

Run the application and browse the `SimpleTreeView.aspx` page by selecting the `Simple TreeView` node from the `TreeView`. Figure 5.8 shows the output of the `SimpleTreeView.aspx page`:

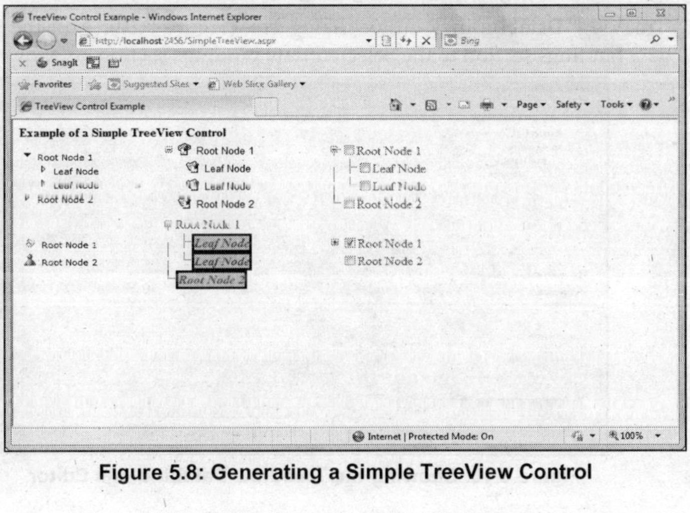

Figure 5.8: Generating a Simple TreeView Control

Creating the TreeView nodes using the TreeView Node Editor dialog box is the simplest form of `TreeView` you can generate with the help of code. You can also generate `TreeView` based on the XML file, `SiteMapDataSource`, or even with databases such as SQL Server.

Now it's time to extend the example to generate the `TreeView` based on the XML data. To do so, we now add a new Web form named `TreeViewXMLData.aspx` to our solution. To generate a `TreeView` from the XML data, we need to bind the TreeView control to an `XmlDataSource control`. First, add an `XmlDataSource` control to the Web form as follows:

```
<asp:XmlDataSource ID="XmlDataSource1" runat="server"
DataFile="~/Navigation.xml"></asp:XmlDataSource>
```

NOTE

You will learn about the XmlDataSource control in detail in Chapter 8: Working with Database Controls of the book.

In the preceding code, we are using an XML file named `Navigation.xml` as the data file for the `XmlDataSource` control. Add the code in the `Navigation.xml` file as follows:

```
<?xml version="1.0" encoding="utf-8" ?>
<application>
  <homepage title="Home Page" value="default.aspx">
    <subpage title ="TreeView From Database" value="treeviewdatabase.aspx"/>
    <subpage title ="TreeView with XMLDataSource" value="treeviewxmldata.aspx"/>
    <subpage title ="TreeView with SiteMapDataSource"
value="treeviewsitemapdatasource.aspx"/>
  </homepage>
</application>
```

After configuring the `XmlDataSource` control, a `TreeView` control is added to the Web form and configure it. Once you placed a `TreeView` control on the Web form, you need to configure it to work with the XML data. To configure our `TreeView` control, first select `XmlDataSource` as its data source in the Smart Tag of the TreeView control and then click the Edit TreeNode Databindings in Smart Tag, as shown in Figure 5.9:

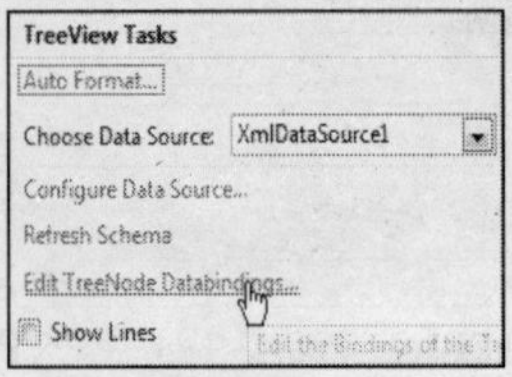

Figure 5.9: Configuring the TreeView Control

This will open the TreeView Databindings Editor dialog box (Figure 5.10). Add the `homepage` and `subpage` from the Available data bindings section to the Selected data bindings section, as shown in Figure 5.10:

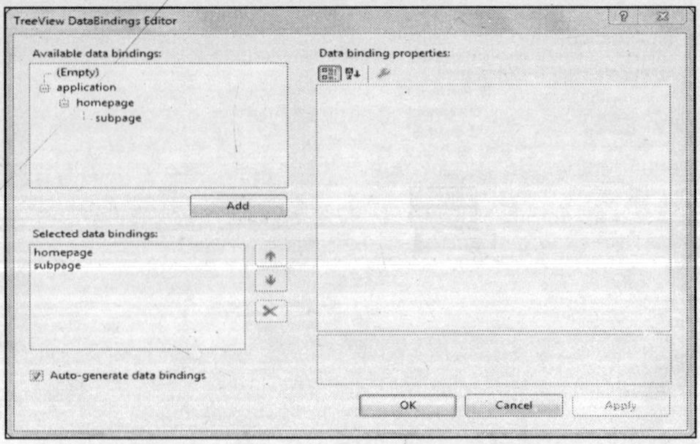

Figure 5.10: Showing the TreeView Databindings Editor

After selecting all the required data bindings, it is time to configure them. In other words, we will now define the structure of our `TreeView` control. Select one of your databinding; in this case, we are first selecting the `homepage` item and then setting the properties for it, as shown in Figure 5.11:

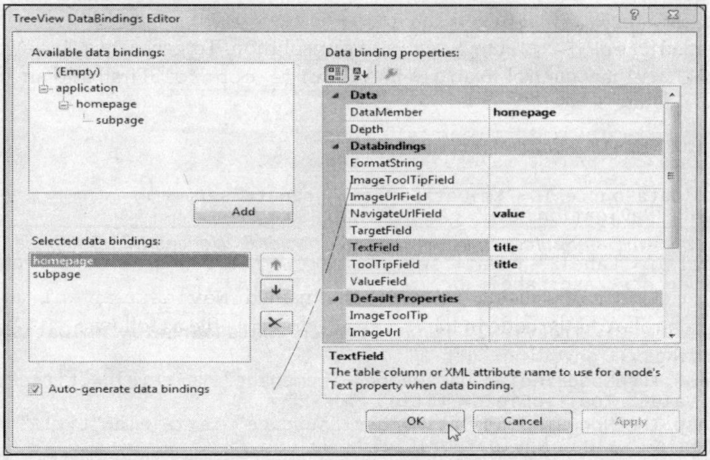

Figure 5.11: Configuring DataBindings

Repeat the same steps for the `subpage` item as well and the process is completed. This complete process generates the `TreeView` controls based on the `XmlDataSource`. We are using the `TreeViewXMLData.aspx` page for displaying the data as per the preceding requirement. You can find the code for the `TreeViewXMLData.aspx` page of the `TreeViewControl` application in the Listing 5.3:

Listing 5.3: Showing the Code for the `TreeViewXMLData.aspx` Page

In VB

```
<%@ Page Language="VB" AutoEventWireup="false" CodeFile="TreeViewXMLData.aspx.vb"
  Inherits="TreeViewXMLData" %>
<!DOCTYPE html>
<html xmlns="http://www.w3.org/1999/xhtml">
<head runat="server">
    <title>TreeView Control Example</title>
</head>
<body>
    <form id="form1" runat="server">
    <div>
    <asp:XmlDataSource ID="XmlDataSource1" runat="server"
         DataFile="~/Navigation.xml"></asp:XmlDataSource>
  <br />
  <asp:Label ID="Label2" runat="server" Text="TreeView generated from
         XMLDataSource"></asp:Label><br />
  <br />
  <asp:TreeView ID="TreeView2" runat="server" DataSourceID="XmlDataSource1">
  <DataBindings>
         <asp:TreeNodeBinding DataMember="homepage" TextField="title" NavigateUrlField
         ="value" ToolTipField="title" />
         <asp:TreeNodeBinding DataMember="subpage" TextField="title"
  ToolTipField="value" NavigateUrlField="value" />
  </DataBindings>
  </asp:TreeView>
    </div>
    </form>
</body>
</html>
```

In C#

```
<%@ Page Language="C#" AutoEventWireup="true" CodeFile="TreeViewXMLData.aspx.cs"
  Inherits="TreeViewXMLData" %>
<!DOCTYPE html>
<html xmlns="http://www.w3.org/1999/xhtml">
<head id="Head1" runat="server">
    <title>TreeView Control Example</title>
</head>
<body>
    <form id="form1" runat="server">
    <div>
    <asp:XmlDataSource ID="XmlDataSource1" runat="server"
  DataFile="~/Navigation.xml"></asp:XmlDataSource>
  <br />
  <asp:Label ID="Label2" runat="server" Text="TreeView generated from
  XMLDataSource"></asp:Label><br />
  <br />
  <asp:TreeView ID="TreeView2" runat="server" DataSourceID="XmlDataSource1">
  <DataBindings>
        <asp:TreeNodeBinding DataMember="homepage" TextField="title" NavigateUrlField
        ="value" ToolTipField="title" />
        <asp:TreeNodeBinding DataMember="subpage" TextField="title"
  ToolTipField="value" NavigateUrlField="value" />
  </DataBindings>
  </asp:TreeView>
    </div>
    </form>
</body>
</html>
```

Again run the application and browse the `TreeViewXMLData.aspx` page by selecting the `TreeView` with `XmlDataSource` node from the `TreeView`. Figure 5.12 shows the output of `TreeViewXMLData.aspx` page:

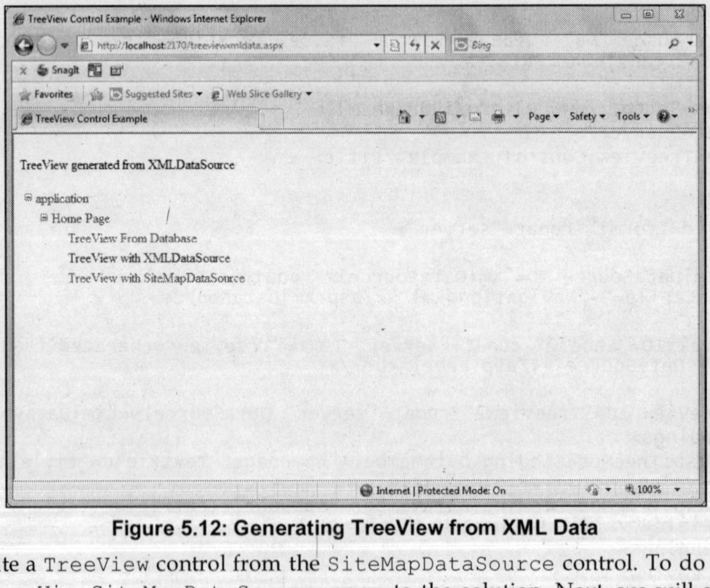

Figure 5.12: Generating TreeView from XML Data

We will now generate a `TreeView` control from the `SiteMapDataSource` control. To do this, first add a new Web form named `TreeViewSiteMapDataSource.aspx` to the solution. Next, we will add a sitemap file to our solution by right-clicking the solution name and selecting the Add New Item option from the context menu in Solution Explorer. In the Add New Item dialog box, select the Site Map Template from the list of available templates and name it as `Web.sitemap`, as shown in Figure 5.13:

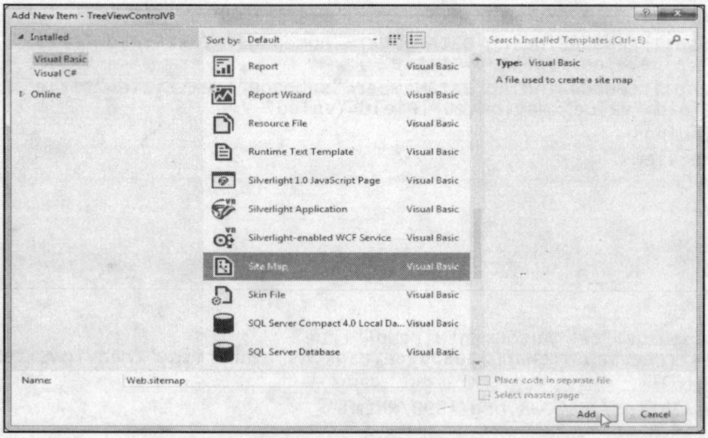

Figure 5.13: Adding a Site Map to Solution

Click the Add button of the Add New Item dialog box. This will open the `Web.sitemap` file; then replace the contents of the file with the following code:

```
<?xml version="1.0" encoding="utf-8" ?>
<siteMap xmlns="http://schemas.microsoft.com/AspNet/SiteMap-File-1.0" >
  <siteMapNode title="TreeView Control Example" url="~/Default.aspx" >
    <siteMapNode title="TreeView from database" url="~/Treeviewdatabase.aspx"/>
    <siteMapNode title="TreeView with XMLDataSource" url="~/Treeviewxmldata.aspx"/>
    <siteMapNode title="TreeView with SiteMapDataSource"
  url="~/TreeViewSiteMapDataSource.aspx"/>
  </siteMapNode>
</siteMap>
```

Now add the following line of code in the `TreeViewSiteMapDataSource.aspx` page to add a `SiteMapDataSource` control:

```
<asp:SiteMapDataSource ID="SiteMapSource1" runat="server" />
```

The `SiteMapDataSource` control automatically links itself to the `Web.sitemap` file that we have added in this application. Let's add a `TreeView` control that will be populated based on this `SiteMapDataSource` control. You can find the code for the `TreeViewSiteMapDataSource.aspx` page of the `TreeViewControl` application in Listing 5.4:

Listing 5.4: Showing the Code for the `TreeViewSiteMapDataSource.aspx` Page

In VB

```
<%@ Page Language="VB" AutoEventWireup="false" CodeFile="TreeViewXMLData.aspx.vb"
  Inherits="TreeViewXMLData" %>
<!DOCTYPE html>
<html xmlns="http://www.w3.org/1999/xhtml">
<head runat="server">
    <title>TreeView Control Example</title>
</head>
<body>
    <form id="form1" runat="server">
    <div>
    <asp:XmlDataSource ID="XmlDataSource1" runat="server"
  DataFile="~/Navigation.xml"> </asp:XmlDataSource>
  <br />
  <asp:Label ID="Label2" runat="server" Text="TreeView generated from
  XMLDataSource"></asp:Label><br />
  <br />
  <asp:TreeView ID="TreeView2" runat="server" DataSourceID="XmlDataSource1">
```

```
    <DataBindings>
            <asp:TreeNodeBinding DataMember="homepage" TextField="title" NavigateUrlField
            ="value" ToolTipField="title" />
            <asp:TreeNodeBinding DataMember="subpage" TextField="title"
    ToolTipField="value" NavigateUrlField="value" />
    </DataBindings>
    </asp:TreeView>
      </div>
      </form>
  </body>
  </html>
```

In C#

```
  <%@ Page Language="C#" AutoEventWireup="true"
    CodeFile="TreeViewSiteMapDataSource.aspx.cs" Inherits="TreeViewSiteMapDataSource" %>
  <!DOCTYPE html>
  <html xmlns="http://www.w3.org/1999/xhtml">
  <head runat="server">
       <title>TreeView Control Example</title>
  </head>
  <body>
      <form id="form1" runat="server">
      <div>
      <asp:Label ID="Label2" runat="server" Text="TreeView generated from
           SiteMapDataSource"></asp:Label><br />
           <br />
           <asp:SiteMapDataSource ID="SiteMapSource1" runat="server" />
           <asp:TreeView ID="TreeView2" DataSourceID="SiteMapSource1" runat="server">
           <DataBindings>
           <asp:TreeNodeBinding TextField="Title" NavigateUrlField="Url" />
           </DataBindings>
           </asp:TreeView>
      </div>
      </form>
  </body>
  </html>
```

You can see the output of the preceding listing in Figure 5.14:

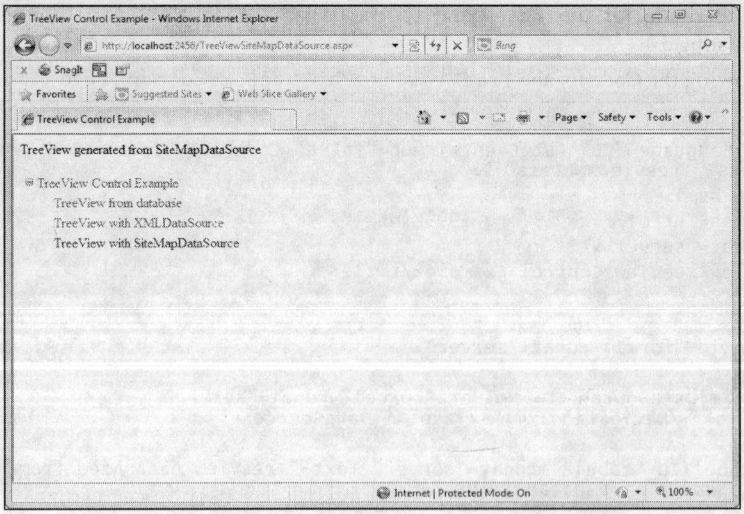

Figure 5.14: Generating TreeView from SiteMapDataSource

Generating TreeView from a Database

In case you want to generate `TreeView` control based on the database, such as SQL Server, you need to generate the `TreeView` control programmatically by using the `TreeView` class, since no wizard is available for this.

We will extend our `TreeViewControl` application for the current example. Just add a new Web form named `TreeViewDataBase.aspx` to the application. We are using Northwind database of the SQL Server. In this application, we will display the categories from the Categories table and their respective products from the Products table of the Northwind database in the `TreeView` control. You can find the code for the `TreeViewDataBase.aspx` page of the `TreeViewControl` application in Listing 5.5:

Listing 5.5: Showing the Code for the `TreeViewDataBase.aspx` Page

In VB

```
<%@ Page Language="VB" AutoEventWireup="false" CodeFile="TreeViewDataBase.aspx.vb"
  Inherits="TreeViewDataBase" %>
<!DOCTYPE html>
<html xmlns="http://www.w3.org/1999/xhtml">
<head runat="server">
       <title>TreeView Control Example</title>
</head>
<body>
    <form id="form1" runat="server">
    <div>
    <asp:Label ID="Label2" runat="server" Text="TreeView Control bind to SQL Server
         NORTHWIND database" Font-Bold ="true"></asp:Label><br />
         <br />
         <asp:TreeView ID="TreeView2" runat="server" MaxDataBindDepth="2" Width="261px">
         <Nodes>
         <asp:TreeNode PopulateOnDemand="True" Text="Categories and their products"
                Value="namesofCustomer">
         </asp:TreeNode>
         </Nodes>
         </asp:TreeView>
  </div>
  </form>
</body>
</html>
```

In C#

```
<%@ Page Language="C#" AutoEventWireup="true" CodeFile="TreeViewDataBase.aspx.cs"
  Inherits="TreeViewDataBase" %>
<!DOCTYPE html>
<html xmlns="http://www.w3.org/1999/xhtml">
<head runat="server">
      <title>TreeView Control Example</title>
</head>
<body>
  <form id="form1" runat="server">
  <div>
  <asp:Label ID="Label2" runat="server" Text="TreeView Control bind to SQL Server
        NORTHWIND database" Font-Bold ="true"></asp:Label><br />
        <br />
        <asp:TreeView ID="TreeView2" runat="server" MaxDataBindDepth="2" Width="261px"
        ontreenodepopulate="TreeView2_TreeNodePopulate" >
        <Nodes>
        <asp:TreeNode PopulateOnDemand="True" Text="Categories and their products"
        Value="namesofCustomer">
        </asp:TreeNode>
        </Nodes>
```

```
        </asp:TreeView>
    </div>
    </form>
</body>
</html>
```

Now, add the code in the CodeFile of the `TreeViewDataBase.aspx` page, as shown in Listing 5.6:

Listing 5.6: Showing the Code for the Code File of the `TreeViewDataBase.aspx` Page

In VB

```
Imports System.Data
Imports System.Data.SqlClient
Partial Class TreeViewDataBase
    Inherits System.Web.UI.Page
    Sub GetCategories(ByVal node As TreeNode)
        Dim sqlQuery As New SqlCommand( _
            "Select CategoryName, CategoryID From Categories")
        Dim ResultSet As DataSet
        ResultSet = PopulateDataFunction(sqlQuery)
        If ResultSet.Tables.Count > 0 Then
            Dim row As DataRow
            For Each row In ResultSet.Tables(0).Rows
                Dim NewNode As TreeNode = New  _
                    TreeNode(row("CategoryName").ToString(), _
                    row("CategoryID").ToString())
                NewNode.PopulateOnDemand = True
                NewNode.SelectAction = TreeNodeSelectAction.Expand
                node.ChildNodes.Add(NewNode)
            Next
        End If
    End Sub
    Sub GetProducts(ByVal node As TreeNode)
        Dim sqlQuery As New SqlCommand
        sqlQuery.CommandText = "Select ProductName From Products " & _
            " Where CategoryID = @categoryid"
        sqlQuery.Parameters.Add("@categoryid", SqlDbType.Int).Value = _
            node.Value
        Dim ResultSet As DataSet = PopulateDataFunction(sqlQuery)
        If ResultSet.Tables.Count > 0 Then
            Dim row As DataRow
            For Each row In ResultSet.Tables(0).Rows
                Dim NewNode As TreeNode = New  _
                    TreeNode(row("ProductName").ToString())
                NewNode.PopulateOnDemand = False
                NewNode.SelectAction = TreeNodeSelectAction.None
                node.ChildNodes.Add(NewNode)
            Next
        End If
    End Sub
    Function PopulateDataFunction(ByVal sqlQuery As SqlCommand) As DataSet
        Dim dbConnection As New SqlConnection("Data Source=KDT-9;Initial
         Catalog=Northwind;uid=sa;pwd=radix")
        Dim dbAdapter As New SqlDataAdapter
        dbAdapter.SelectCommand = sqlQuery
        sqlQuery.Connection = dbConnection
        Dim resultsDataSet As DataSet = New DataSet
        Try
            dbAdapter.Fill(resultsDataSet)
        Catch ex As Exception
```

```
        End Try
        Return resultsDataSet
    End Function
    Protected Sub TreeView2_TreeNodePopulate(ByVal sender As Object, ByVal e As
         System.Web.UI.WebControls.TreeNodeEventArgs) Handles TreeView2.TreeNodePopulate
        If e.Node.ChildNodes.Count = 0 Then
            Select Case e.Node.Depth
                Case 0
                    GetCategories(e.Node)
                Case 1
                    GetProducts(e.Node)
            End Select
        End If
    End Sub
    Protected Sub Page_Load(sender As Object, e As EventArgs) Handles Me.Load
        TreeView2.ExpandDepth = 1
    End Sub
End Class
```

In C#

```
using System;
using System.Collections.Generic;
using System.Configuration;
using System.Data;
using System.Linq;
using System.Web;
using System.Web.Security;
using System.Web.UI;
using System.Web.UI.HtmlControls;
using System.Web.UI.WebControls;
using System.Web.UI.WebControls.WebParts;
using System.Xml.Linq;
using System.Data.SqlClient;
public partial class TreeViewDataBase : System.Web.UI.Page
{
    protected void Page_Load(object sender, EventArgs e)
    {
        TreeView2.ExpandDepth = 1;
    }
    public void GetCategories(TreeNode node)
    {
        SqlCommand sqlQuery = new SqlCommand("Select CategoryName, CategoryID From
         Categories");
        DataSet ResultSet = null;
        ResultSet = PopulateDataFunction(sqlQuery);
        if (ResultSet.Tables.Count > 0)
        {
            foreach (DataRow row in ResultSet.Tables[0].Rows)
            {
                TreeNode NewNode = new TreeNode(row["CategoryName"].ToString(),
                row["CategoryID"].ToString());
                NewNode.PopulateOnDemand = true;
                NewNode.SelectAction = TreeNodeSelectAction.Expand;
                node.ChildNodes.Add(NewNode);
            }
        }
    }
    public void GetProducts(TreeNode node)
    {
```

```
        SqlCommand sqlQuery = new SqlCommand();
        sqlQuery.CommandText = "Select ProductName From Products " + " Where CategoryID=
         @categoryid";
        sqlQuery.Parameters.Add("@categoryid", SqlDbType.Int).Value = node.Value;
        DataSet ResultSet = PopulateDataFunction(sqlQuery);
        if (ResultSet.Tables.Count > 0)
        {
         foreach (DataRow row in ResultSet.Tables[0].Rows)
            {
                TreeNode NewNode = new TreeNode(row["ProductName"].ToString());
                NewNode.PopulateOnDemand = false;
                NewNode.SelectAction = TreeNodeSelectAction.None;
                node.ChildNodes.Add(NewNode);
            }
        }
    }
    public DataSet PopulateDataFunction(SqlCommand sqlQuery)
    {
       SqlConnection dbConnection = new SqlConnection("Data Source=KDT-9;Initial
         Catalog=Northwind;uid=sa;pwd=radix");
        SqlDataAdapter dbAdapter = new SqlDataAdapter();
        dbAdapter.SelectCommand = sqlQuery;
        sqlQuery.Connection = dbConnection;
        DataSet resultsDataSet = new DataSet();
        try
        {
            dbAdapter.Fill(resultsDataSet);
        }
        catch (Exception ex)
        {
        }
        return resultsDataSet;
    }
    protected void TreeView2_TreeNodePopulate(object sender,
    System.Web.UI.WebControls.TreeNodeEventArgs e)
    {
        if (e.Node.ChildNodes.Count == 0)
        {
            switch (e.Node.Depth)
            {
                case 0:
                    GetCategories(e.Node);
                    break;
                case 1:
                    GetProducts(e.Node);
                    break;
            }
        }
    }
}
```

To understand the preceding code, we will now discuss the code step by step. In the first step, we will add the code for the `TreeView2_TreeNodePopulate` method, as shown in Listing 5.7:

Listing 5.7: Showing the Code for the `TreeView2_TreeNodePopulate` Method

In VB

```
Protected Sub TreeView2_TreeNodePopulate(ByVal sender As Object, ByVal e As
   System.Web.UI.WebControls.TreeNodeEventArgs) Handles TreeView2.TreeNodePopulate
        If e.Node.ChildNodes.Count = 0 Then
```

```
            Select Case e.Node.Depth
                Case 0
                    GetCategories(e.Node)
                Case 1
                    GetProducts(e.Node)
            End Select
        End If
    End Sub
```

In C#

```
protected void TreeView2_TreeNodePopulate(object sender,
  System.Web.UI.WebControls.TreeNodeEventArgs e)
    {
        if (e.Node.ChildNodes.Count == 0)
        {
            switch (e.Node.Depth)
            {
                case 0:
                    GetCategories(e.Node);
                    break;
                case 1:
                    GetProducts(e.Node);
                    break;
            }
        }
    }
```

The preceding listing checks the existence of the `TreeView2` control. If it is found that there does not exist any node in the `TreeView2` control, the `GetCategories` function is called to generate the first-level nodes containing the categories names. In the `GetCategories` function, we query the database to retrieve the records and generate the first-level tree nodes by using the `node.ChildNodes.Add` method, as shown in Listing 5.8:

Listing 5.8: Showing the Code for Generating the First-Level Tree Node

In VB

```
Sub GetCategories(ByVal node As TreeNode)
        Dim sqlQuery As New SqlCommand( _
            "Select CategoryName, CategoryID From Categories")
        Dim ResultSet As DataSet
        ResultSet = PopulateDataFunction(sqlQuery)
        If ResultSet.Tables.Count > 0 Then
            Dim row As DataRow
            For Each row In ResultSet.Tables(0).Rows
                Dim NewNode As TreeNode = New _
                    TreeNode(row("CategoryName").ToString(), _
                    row("CategoryID").ToString())
                NewNode.PopulateOnDemand = True
                NewNode.SelectAction = TreeNodeSelectAction.Expand
                node.ChildNodes.Add(NewNode)
            Next
        End If
    End Sub
```

In C#

```
public void GetCategories(TreeNode node)
{
        SqlCommand sqlQuery = new SqlCommand("Select CategoryName, CategoryID From
         Categories");
```

```
            DataSet ResultSet = null;
            ResultSet = PopulateDataFunction(sqlQuery);
            if (ResultSet.Tables.Count > 0)
            {

                foreach (DataRow row in ResultSet.Tables[0].Rows)
                {
                    TreeNode NewNode = new TreeNode(row["CategoryName"].ToString(),
                    row["CategoryID"].ToString());
                    NewNode.PopulateOnDemand = true;
                    NewNode.SelectAction = TreeNodeSelectAction.Expand;
                    node.ChildNodes.Add(NewNode);
                }
            }
        }
```

After generating the authors' `names`, the code again checks for the `TreeView2_TreeNodePopulate` event, and this time, the `GetProducts` function is called to generate the second-level nodes containing the products in the respective categories whose names have been retrieved from the database by using the `GetCategories` function, as shown in Listing 5.9:

Listing 5.9: Showing the Code for Retrieving the Product Names from the Database

In VB

```
    Sub GetProducts(ByVal node As TreeNode)
            Dim sqlQuery As New SqlCommand
            sqlQuery.CommandText = "Select ProductName From Products " & _
                " Where CategoryID = @categoryid"
            sqlQuery.Parameters.Add("@categoryid", SqlDbType.Int).Value = _
                node.Value
            Dim ResultSet As DataSet = PopulateDataFunction(sqlQuery)
            If ResultSet.Tables.Count > 0 Then
                Dim row As DataRow
                For Each row In ResultSet.Tables(0).Rows
                    Dim NewNode As TreeNode = New _
                        TreeNode(row("ProductName").ToString())
                    NewNode.PopulateOnDemand = False
                    NewNode.SelectAction = TreeNodeSelectAction.None
                    node.ChildNodes.Add(NewNode)
                Next
            End If
        End Sub
```

In C#

```
    public void GetProducts(TreeNode node)
        {
            SqlCommand sqlQuery = new SqlCommand();
            sqlQuery.CommandText = "Select ProductName From Products " + " Where CategoryID=
             @categoryid";
            sqlQuery.Parameters.Add("@categoryid", SqlDbType.Int).Value = node.Value;
            DataSet ResultSet = PopulateDataFunction(sqlQuery);
            if (ResultSet.Tables.Count > 0)
            {

                foreach (DataRow row in ResultSet.Tables[0].Rows)
                {
                    TreeNode NewNode = new TreeNode(row["ProductName"].ToString());
                    NewNode.PopulateOnDemand = false;
                    NewNode.SelectAction = TreeNodeSelectAction.None;
                    node.ChildNodes.Add(NewNode);
```

```
            }
        }
    }
```

In the preceding listing, we have used a parameterized query to get the product names only for those categories whose names have already been retrieved from the database. This generates the complete tree view. The output of the TreeViewControl application is shown in Figure 5.15:

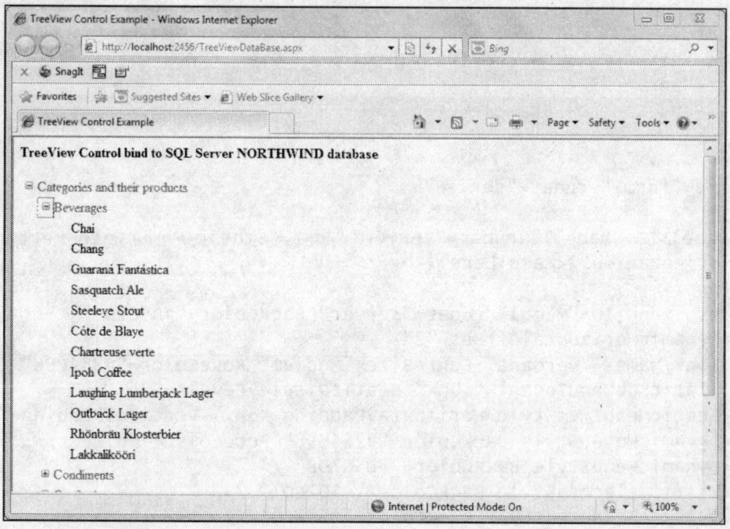

Figure 5.15: Generating TreeView from the Database

Creating Static Menus

The menus in ASP.NET 4.5 can be easily created by simply dragging and dropping the `Menu` controls from the Toolbox to the designer. You can find this as `MenuControlVB` in VB and `MenuControlCS` in C#.

You can also add the Static Menus by double-clicking the `Menu` control in the Toolbox. The `Menu` control is added automatically to the designer. Click the smart tag to select Edit Menu Items in the list. A Menu Item Editor dialog box will appear. Insert nodes at different levels according to your requirements. You can also set the text for the nodes by setting the `Text` property in the Properties pane, as shown in Figure 5.16:

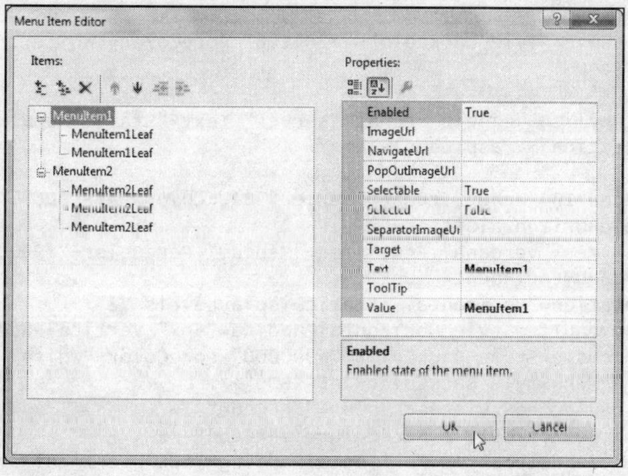

Figure 5.16: Showing the Menu Item Editor Dialog Box

After inserting the nodes, click the OK button. Replace the code of the `Default.aspx` page of the `MenuControlCS` application with the code given in Listing 5.10:

Listing 5.10: Showing the Code for the `Default.aspx` Page

In VB

```
<%@ Page Language="VB" AutoEventWireup="false" CodeFile="Default.aspx.vb"
  Inherits="_Default" %>
<!DOCTYPE html>
<html xmlns="http://www.w3.org/1999/xhtml">
<head runat="server">
    <title>Menu Control Example</title>
</head>
<body>
    <form id="form1" runat="server">
    <div>
    <asp:Label ID="Label1" runat="server" Text="Static Menu with vertical
         orientation"></asp:Label><br />
        <br />
        <asp:Menu ID="Menu1" runat="server" BackColor="#B5C7DE"
         DynamicHorizontalOffset="2"
         Font-Names="Verdana" Font-Size="Medium" ForeColor="#284E98"
         StaticSubMenuIndent="10px" StaticDisplayLevels="2">
        <StaticMenuItemStyle HorizontalPadding="5px" VerticalPadding="2px" />
        <DynamicHoverStyle BackColor="#284E98" ForeColor="White" />
        <DynamicMenuStyle BackColor="#B5C7DE" />
        <StaticSelectedStyle BackColor="#507CD1" />
        <DynamicSelectedStyle BackColor="#507CD1" />
        <DynamicMenuItemStyle HorizontalPadding="5px" VerticalPadding="2px" />
        <Items>
        <asp:MenuItem Text="MenuItem1" Value="MenuItem1">
        <asp:MenuItem Text="MenuItem1Leaf" Value="MenuItem1Leaf"></asp:MenuItem>
        <asp:MenuItem Text="MenuItem1Leaf" Value="MenuItem1Leaf"></asp:MenuItem>
        </asp:MenuItem>
        <asp:MenuItem Text="MenuItem2" Value="MenuItem2">
        <asp:MenuItem Text="MenuItem2Leaf" Value="MenuItem2Leaf"></asp:MenuItem>
        <asp:MenuItem Text="MenuItem2Leaf" Value="MenuItem2Leaf"></asp:MenuItem>
        <asp:MenuItem Text="MenuItem2Leaf" Value="MenuItem2Leaf"></asp:MenuItem>
        </asp:MenuItem>
        </Items>
        <StaticHoverStyle BackColor="#284E98" ForeColor="White" />
        </asp:Menu>
        <br />
        <asp:Label ID="Label2" runat="server" Text="Static Menu with horizontal
         orientation"></asp:Label><br />
        <br />
        <asp:Menu ID="Menu2" runat="server" BackColor="#FFFBD6"
         DynamicHorizontalOffset="2"
         Font-Names="Verdana" Font-Size="Medium" ForeColor="#990000"
         StaticSubMenuIndent="10px"
         Orientation="Horizontal" StaticDisplayLevels="2">
        <StaticMenuItemStyle HorizontalPadding="5px" VerticalPadding="2px" />
        <DynamicHoverStyle BackColor="#990000" ForeColor="White" />
        <DynamicMenuStyle BackColor="#FFFBD6" />
        <StaticSelectedStyle BackColor="#FFCC66" />
        <DynamicSelectedStyle BackColor="#FFCC66" />
        <DynamicMenuItemStyle HorizontalPadding="5px" VerticalPadding="2px" />
        <Items>
        <asp:MenuItem Text="MenuItem1" Value="MenuItem1">
```

```
            <asp:MenuItem Text="MenuItem1Leaf" Value="MenuItem1Leaf"></asp:MenuItem>
            </asp:MenuItem>
            <asp:MenuItem Text="MenuItem2" Value="MenuItem2">
            <asp:MenuItem Text="MenuItem2Leaf" Value="MenuItem2Leaf"></asp:MenuItem>
            <asp:MenuItem Text="MenuItem2Leaf" Value="MenuItem2Leaf"></asp:MenuItem>
            </asp:MenuItem>
            </Items>
            <StaticHoverStyle BackColor="#990000" ForeColor="White" />
            </asp:Menu>
        </div>
        </form>
    </body>
    </html>
```

In C#

```
<%@ Page Language="C#" AutoEventWireup="true" CodeFile="Default.aspx.cs"
  Inherits="_Default" %>
<!DOCTYPE html>
<html xmlns="http://www.w3.org/1999/xhtml">
<head id="Head1" runat="server">
    <title>Menu Control Example</title>
</head>
<body>
    <form id="form1" runat="server">
    <div>
    <asp:Label ID="Label1" runat="server" Text="Static Menu with vertical
          orientation"></asp:Label><br />
         <br />
         <asp:Menu ID="Menu1" runat="server" BackColor="#B5C7DE"
          DynamicHorizontalOffset="2"
          Font-Names="Verdana" Font-Size="Medium" ForeColor="#284E98"
          StaticSubMenuIndent="10px" StaticDisplayLevels="2">
         <StaticMenuItemStyle HorizontalPadding="5px" VerticalPadding="2px" />
         <DynamicHoverStyle BackColor="#284E98" ForeColor="White" />
         <DynamicMenuStyle BackColor="#B5C7DE" />
         <StaticSelectedStyle BackColor="#507CD1" />
         <DynamicSelectedStyle BackColor="#507CD1" />
         <DynamicMenuItemStyle HorizontalPadding="5px" VerticalPadding="2px" />
         <Items>
         <asp:MenuItem Text="MenuItem1" Value="MenuItem1">
         <asp:MenuItem Text="MenuItem1Leaf" Value="MenuItem1Leaf"></asp:MenuItem>
         <asp:MenuItem Text="MenuItem1Leaf" Value="MenuItem1Leaf"></asp:MenuItem>
         </asp:MenuItem>
         <asp:MenuItem Text="MenuItem2" Value="MenuItem2">
         <asp:MenuItem Text="MenuItem2Leaf" Value="MenuItem2Leaf"></asp:MenuItem>
         <asp:MenuItem Text="MenuItem2Leaf" Value="MenuItem2Leaf"></asp:MenuItem>
         <asp:MenuItem Text="MenuItem2Leaf" Value="MenuItem2Leaf"></asp:MenuItem>
         </asp:MenuItem>
         </Items>
         <StaticHoverStyle BackColor="#284E98" ForeColor="White" />
         </asp:Menu>
         <br />
         <asp:Label ID="Label2" runat="server" Text="Static Menu with horizontal
          orientation"></asp:Label><br />
         <br />
         <asp:Menu ID="Menu2" runat="server" BackColor="#FFFBD6"
          DynamicHorizontalOffset="2"
          Font-Names="Verdana" Font-Size="Medium" ForeColor="#990000"
```

```
            StaticSubMenuIndent="10px"
            Orientation="Horizontal" StaticDisplayLevels="2">
           <StaticMenuItemStyle HorizontalPadding="5px" VerticalPadding="2px" />
           <DynamicHoverStyle BackColor="#990000" ForeColor="White" />
           <DynamicMenuStyle BackColor="#FFFBD6" />
           <StaticSelectedStyle BackColor="#FFCC66" />
           <DynamicSelectedStyle BackColor="#FFCC66" />
           <DynamicMenuItemStyle HorizontalPadding="5px" VerticalPadding="2px" />
           <Items>
           <asp:MenuItem Text="MenuItem1" Value="MenuItem1">
           <asp:MenuItem Text="MenuItem1Leaf" Value="MenuItem1Leaf"></asp:MenuItem>
           </asp:MenuItem>
           <asp:MenuItem Text="MenuItem2" Value="MenuItem2">
           <asp:MenuItem Text="MenuItem2Leaf" Value="MenuItem2Leaf"></asp:MenuItem>
           <asp:MenuItem Text="MenuItem2Leaf" Value="MenuItem2Leaf"></asp:MenuItem>
           </asp:MenuItem>
           </Items>
           <StaticHoverStyle BackColor="#990000" ForeColor="White" />
           </asp:Menu>
      </div>
      </form>
  </body>
  </html>
```

The output of the MenuControl application is as shown in Figure 5.17:

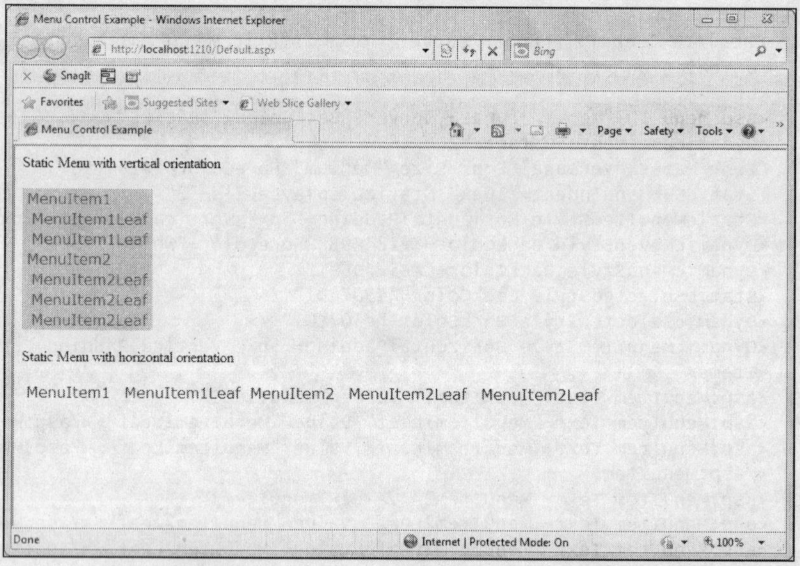

Figure 5.17: Showing the Output of the MenuControlCS Example

Creating Dynamic Menus

In this section, we are going to use the `Menu` control with the XML and `SiteMapDataSource` to create dynamic menus, as we did in the `TreeViewControl` example earlier. We have created an application named `DynamicMenuVB` in VB and `DynamicMenuCS` in C#. Add the code shown in Listing 5.11 in the default page of the `DynamicMenu` application:

Listing 5.11: Showing the Code for the `Default.aspx` Page

In VB

```
<%@ Page Language="VB" AutoEventWireup="false" CodeFile="Default.aspx.vb"
  Inherits="_Default" %>
<!DOCTYPE html>
<html xmlns="http://www.w3.org/1999/xhtml">
<head runat="server">
    <title>DynamicMenu Control Example</title>
</head>
<body>
    <form id="form1" runat="server">
    <div>
    <asp:XmlDataSource ID="XmlDataSource1" runat="server"
         DataFile="~/Data.xml"></asp:XmlDataSource>
                <br />
                <asp:SiteMapDataSource ID="SiteMapDataSource1"  runat="server" />
                <asp:Label ID="Label1" runat="server" Text="Menu using
                XMLDataSource"></asp:Label><br />
                <br />
                <asp:Menu ID="Menu1" runat="server" BackColor="#FFFBD6"
                DataSourceID="XmlDataSource1" DynamicHorizontalOffset="2" Font-
                Names="Tahoma" Font-Size="Medium" ForeColor="#990000"
                 StaticSubMenuIndent="10px" Orientation="Horizontal">
                <StaticMenuItemStyle HorizontalPadding="5px"
                 VerticalPadding="2px" />
                <DynamicHoverStyle BackColor="#990000" ForeColor="White" />
                <DynamicMenuStyle BackColor="#FFFBD6" />
                <StaticSelectedStyle BackColor="#FFCC66" />
                <DynamicSelectedStyle BackColor="#FFCC66" />
                <DynamicMenuItemStyle HorizontalPadding="5px"
                 VerticalPadding="2px" />
                <DataBindings>
                <asp:MenuItemBinding DataMember="setction"
                 NavigateUrlField="value" TextField="title" ValueField="value" />
                <asp:MenuItemBinding DataMember="subpage"
                 NavigateUrlField="value" TextField="title" ToolTipField="title"
                ValueField="value" />
                </DataBindings>
                <StaticHoverStyle BackColor="#990000" ForeColor="White"/>
                </asp:Menu>
                <br />
                <asp:Label ID="Label2" runat="server" Text="Menu using
                 SiteMapDataSource"></asp:Label>
                <br />
                <br />
                <asp:Menu ID="Menu2" runat="server" BackColor="#FFFBD6"
                 DataSourceID="SiteMapDataSource1"
                 DynamicHorizontalOffset="2" Font-Names="Tahoma" Font-Size="Medium"
                ForeColor="#990000" StaticSubMenuIndent="10px">
                <StaticMenuItemStyle HorizontalPadding="5px"
                 VerticalPadding="2px" />
                <DynamicHoverStyle BackColor="#990000" ForeColor="White" />
                <DynamicMenuStyle BackColor="#FFFBD6" />
                <StaticSelectedStyle BackColor="#FFCC66" />
                <DynamicSelectedStyle BackColor="#FFCC66" />
                <DynamicMenuItemStyle HorizontalPadding="5px" VerticalPadding="2px" />
                <DataBindings>
                <asp:MenuItemBinding DataMember="setction"
                 NavigateUrlField="value" TextField="title" ValueField="value" />
```

```
                <asp:MenuItemBinding DataMember="subpage"
                 NavigateUrlField="value" TextField="title"
                 ToolTipField="title" ValueField="value" />
                </DataBindings>
                <StaticHoverStyle BackColor="#990000" ForeColor="White" />
                </asp:Menu>
        </div>
        </form>
    </body>
    </html>
```

In C#

```
    <%@ Page Language="C#" AutoEventWireup="true" CodeFile="Default.aspx.cs"
      Inherits="_Default" %>
    <!DOCTYPE html>
    <html xmlns="http://www.w3.org/1999/xhtml">
    <head id="Head1" runat="server">
        <title>DynamicMenu Control Example</title>
    </head>
    <body>
        <form id="form1" runat="server">
        <div>
        <asp:XmlDataSource ID="XmlDataSource1" runat="server"
             DataFile="~/Data.xml"></asp:XmlDataSource>
                <br />
                <asp:SiteMapDataSource ID="SiteMapDataSource1" runat="server" />
                <asp:Label ID="Label1" runat="server" Text="Menu using
                XMLDataSource"></asp:Label><br />
                <br />
                <asp:Menu ID="Menu1" runat="server" BackColor="#FFFBD6"
                DataSourceID="XmlDataSource1"
                DynamicHorizontalOffset="2" Font-Names="Tahoma" Font-Size="Medium"
                ForeColor="#990000" StaticSubMenuIndent="10px" Orientation="Horizontal">
                <StaticMenuItemStyle HorizontalPadding="5px"
                 VerticalPadding="2px" />
                <DynamicHoverStyle BackColor="#990000" ForeColor="White" />
                <DynamicMenuStyle BackColor="#FFFBD6" />
                <StaticSelectedStyle BackColor="#FFCC66" />
                <DynamicSelectedStyle BackColor="#FFCC66" />
                <DynamicMenuItemStyle HorizontalPadding="5px" VerticalPadding="2px" />
                <DataBindings>
                <asp:MenuItemBinding DataMember="setction"
                 NavigateUrlField="value" TextField="title" ValueField="value" />
                <asp:MenuItemBinding DataMember="subpage"
                 NavigateUrlField="value" TextField="title"
                 ToolTipField="title" ValueField="value" />
                </DataBindings>
                <StaticHoverStyle BackColor="#990000" ForeColor="White" />
                </asp:Menu>
                <br />
                <asp:Label ID="Label2" runat="server" Text="Menu using
                 SiteMapDataSource"></asp:Label>
                <br />
                <br />
                <asp:Menu ID="Menu2" runat="server" BackColor="#FFFBD6"
                 DataSourceID="SiteMapDataSource1"
                 DynamicHorizontalOffset="2" Font-Names="Tahoma" Font-Size="Medium"
                ForeColor="#990000" StaticSubMenuIndent="10px">
                <StaticMenuItemStyle HorizontalPadding="5px" VerticalPadding="2px" />
                <DynamicHoverStyle BackColor="#990000" ForeColor="White" />
```

```
                <DynamicMenuStyle BackColor="#FFFBD6" />
                <StaticSelectedStyle BackColor="#FFCC66" />
                <DynamicSelectedStyle BackColor="#FFCC66" />
                <DynamicMenuItemStyle HorizontalPadding="5px" VerticalPadding="2px" />
                <DataBindings>
                <asp:MenuItemBinding DataMember="setction"
                 NavigateUrlField="value" TextField="title" ValueField="value" />
                <asp:MenuItemBinding DataMember="subpage"
                 NavigateUrlField="value" TextField="title"
                 ToolTipField="title" ValueField="value" />
                </DataBindings>
                <StaticHoverStyle BackColor="#990000" ForeColor="White" />
                </asp:Menu>
        </div>
        </form>
    </body>
    </html>
```

Add an XML file to your Web application, say, `Data.xml`, and add the code, shown in Listing 5.12,in the `Data.xml` file:

Listing 5.12: Showing the Code for the `Data.xml` File

```
<?xml version="1.0" encoding="utf-8" ?>
<application>
  <setction title="Section 1" value="default.aspx">
    <subpage title ="Page 1" value="page1.aspx"/>
    <subpage title ="Page 2" value="page2.aspx"/>
    <subpage title ="Page 3" value="page3.aspx"/>
  </setction>
  <setction title="Section 2" value="default.aspx">
    <subpage title ="Page 1" value="page1.aspx"/>
    <subpage title ="Page 2" value="page2.aspx"/>
    <subpage title ="Page 3" value="page3.aspx"/>
  </setction>
  <setction title="Section 2" value="default.aspx">
    <subpage title ="Page 1" value="page1.aspx"/>
    <subpage title ="Page 2" value="page2.aspx"/>
    <subpage title ="Page 3" value="page3.aspx"/>
  </setction>
</application>
```

Add a `Web.sitemap` file to your Web application and add the code shown in Listing 5.13 in the `Web.sitemap` file:

Listing 5.13: Showing the Code for the `Web.sitemap` File

```
<?xml version="1.0" encoding="utf-8" ?>
<siteMap xmlns="http://schemas.microsoft.com/AspNet/SiteMap-File-1.0" >
  <siteMapNode url= "Default.aspx" title= "Section 1"  description="">
    <siteMapNode url="Page1.aspx" title="Page 1"  description="" />
    <siteMapNode url="Page2.aspx" title="Page 2"  description="" />
    <siteMapNode url="Page3.aspx" title="Page 3"  description="" />
  </siteMapNode>
</siteMap>
```

The output is displayed in Figure 5.18, where we have generated two menus from `XmlDataSource` and `SiteMapPathDataSource applications`, respectively:

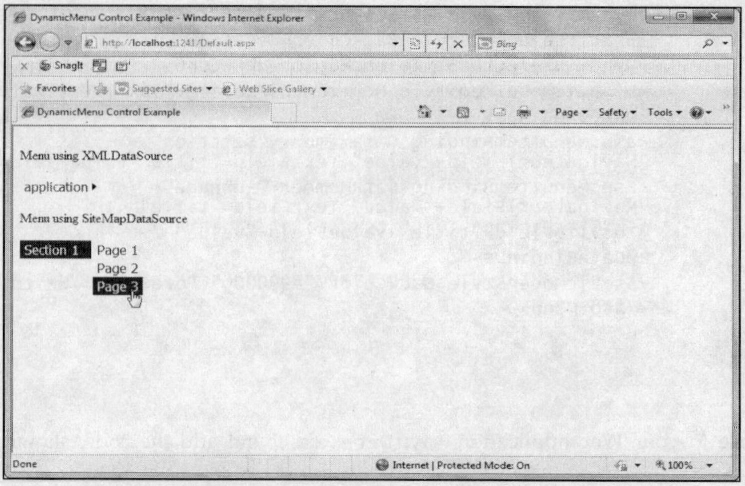

Figure 5.18: Displaying the DynamicMenu Control Example

Creating SiteMapPath

We have aforementioned in the *In Depth* section of this chapter, that the `SiteMapPath` control can be automatically configured to the `SiteMapDataSource` control, which, in turn, can read the `Web.sitemap` file to display the data on the application. We have created an application named `SiteMapPathControl`. You can find this application as `SiteMapPathControlVB` in VB and `SiteMapPathControlCS` in C#.

To create `Web.sitemap` in the `SiteMapPathControl` application, right-click the Project name. A context menu appears. Select the Add New Item option from the context menu. The Add New Item dialog box appears, shown earlier in Figure 5.14. Select Site Map from the options available. This will create a new `Web.sitemap` file in the project.

NOTE

Before running the application, set the Default.aspx page as the Start Page.

The `Web.sitemap` file consists of navigational details for an application. You can set the title, URL, and other information for each page by using the `Web.sitemap` file. Add the code shown in Listing 5.14 in the `Web.sitemap` file:

Listing 5.14: Showing the Code for the `Web.sitemap` File

```
<?xml version="1.0" encoding="utf-8" ?>
<siteMap xmlns="http://schemas.microsoft.com/AspNet/SiteMap-File-1.0" >
  <siteMapNode url="default.aspx" title="Home Page"  description="">
    <siteMapNode url="page1.aspx" title="Section 1"  description="" />
    <siteMapNode url="page2.aspx" title="Section 2"  description="" />
  </siteMapNode>
</siteMap>
```

You also need to add the code shown in Listing 5.15 in the `Default.aspx` page of this application:

Listing 5.15: Showing the Code for the `Default.aspx` Page

In VB

```
<%@ Page Language="VB" AutoEventWireup="false" CodeFile="Default.aspx.vb"
  Inherits="_Default" %>
<!DOCTYPE html>
<html xmlns="http://www.w3.org/1999/xhtml">
<head runat="server">
```

```
    <title>SiteMapPath Control Example</title>
  </head>
  <body>
      <form id="form1" runat="server">
      <div>
      <asp:Label ID="Label1" runat="server" Text="SiteMapDataSource
                    Example"></asp:Label><br />
                   <br />
                   <asp:SiteMapPath ID="SiteMapPath1" runat="server" Font-Names="Verdana"
                    Font-Size="0.8em"
                    PathSeparator=" : " PathDirection="CurrentToRoot">
                   <PathSeparatorStyle Font-Bold="True" ForeColor="#5D7B9D" />
                   <CurrentNodeStyle ForeColor="#333333" />
                   <NodeStyle Font-Bold="True" ForeColor="#7C6F57" />
                   <RootNodeStyle Font-Bold="True" ForeColor="#5D7B9D" />
                   </asp:SiteMapPath>
                   <br />
                   <br />
                   <asp:HyperLink ID="HyperLink1" runat="server"
                    NavigateUrl="~/Page1.aspx">Go to Page 1</asp:HyperLink>
                   <asp:HyperLink ID="HyperLink2" runat="server"
                    NavigateUrl="~/Page2.aspx">Go to Page 2</asp:HyperLink><br />
      </div>
      </form>
  </body>
  </html>
```

In C#

```
  <%@ Page Language="C#" AutoEventWireup="true" CodeFile="Default.aspx.cs"
    Inherits="_Default" %>
  <!DOCTYPE html>
  <html xmlns="http://www.w3.org/1999/xhtml">
  <head id="Head1" runat="server">
    <title>SiteMapPath Control Example</title>
  </head>
  <body>
      <form id="form1" runat="server">
      <div>
      <asp:Label ID="Label1" runat="server" Text="SiteMapDataSource
           Example"></asp:Label><br />
          <br />
          <asp:SiteMapPath ID="SiteMapPath1" runat="server" Font-Names="Verdana"
           Font-Size="0.8em" PathSeparator=" : " PathDirection="CurrentToRoot">
          <PathSeparatorStyle Font-Bold="True" ForeColor="#5D7B9D" />
          <CurrentNodeStyle ForeColor="#333333" />
          <NodeStyle Font-Bold="True" ForeColor="#7C6F57" />
          <RootNodeStyle Font-Bold="True" ForeColor="#5D7B9D" />
          </asp:SiteMapPath>
          <br />
          <br />
          <asp:HyperLink ID="HyperLink1" runat="server"
           NavigateUrl="~/Page1.aspx">Go to Page 1</asp:HyperLink>
          <asp:HyperLink ID="HyperLink2" runat="server"
           NavigateUrl="~/Page2.aspx">Go to Page 2</asp:HyperLink><br />
      </div>
      </form>
  </body>
  </html>
```

Now, add two Web forms, named `Page1.aspx` and `Page2.aspx`, in the project and add the code shown in Listing 5.16 in the `Page1.aspx` page of the `SiteMapPathControl` application:

Listing 5.16: Showing the Code for the `Page1.aspx` Page

In VB

```
<%@ Page Language="VB" AutoEventWireup="false" CodeFile="Page1.aspx.vb" Inherits="Page1" %>
<!DOCTYPE html>
<html xmlns="http://www.w3.org/1999/xhtml">
<head runat="server">
     <title>SiteMapPath Control Example</title>
</head>
<body>
    <form id="form1" runat="server">
    <div>
    <asp:Label ID="Label1" runat="server" Text="SiteMapDataSource
         Example"></asp:Label><br />
         <br />
         <asp:SiteMapPath ID="SiteMapPath1" runat="server" Font-Names="Verdana"
          Font-Size="0.8em" PathSeparator=" : ">
         <PathSeparatorStyle Font-Bold="True" ForeColor="#5D7B9D" />
         <CurrentNodeStyle ForeColor="#333333" />
         <NodeStyle Font-Bold="True" ForeColor="#7C6F57" />
         <RootNodeStyle Font-Bold="True" ForeColor="#5D7B9D" />
         </asp:SiteMapPath>
          <br />
         <br />
         <asp:HyperLink ID="HyperLink2" runat="server"
          NavigateUrl="~/Page2.aspx">Go to Page 2</asp:HyperLink><br />
    </div>
    </form>
</body>
</html>
```

In C#

```
<%@ Page Language="C#" AutoEventWireup="true" CodeFile="Page1.aspx.cs" Inherits="Page1" %>
<!DOCTYPE html>
<html xmlns="http://www.w3.org/1999/xhtml">
<head id="Head1" runat="server">
     <title>SiteMapPath Control Example</title>
</head>
<body>
    <form id="form1" runat="server">
    <div>
    <asp:Label ID="Label1" runat="server" Text="SiteMapDataSource
          Example"></asp:Label><br />
         <br />
         <asp:SiteMapPath ID="SiteMapPath1" runat="server" Font-Names="Verdana"
          Font-Size="0.8em" PathSeparator=" : ">
         <PathSeparatorStyle Font-Bold="True" ForeColor="#5D7B9D" />
         <CurrentNodeStyle ForeColor="#333333" />
         <NodeStyle Font-Bold="True" ForeColor="#7C6F57" />
         <RootNodeStyle Font-Bold="True" ForeColor="#5D7B9D" />
         </asp:SiteMapPath>
          <br />
         <br />
         <asp:HyperLink ID="HyperLink2" runat="server"
          NavigateUrl="~/Page2.aspx">Go to Page 2</asp:HyperLink><br />
    </div>
```

```
        </form>
    </body>
    </html>
```

Now, add the code shown in Listing 5.17 in the `Page2.aspx` page of the `SiteMapPathControl` application:

Listing 5.17: Showing the Code for the `Page2.aspx` Page

In VB

```
<%@ Page Language="VB" AutoEventWireup="false" CodeFile="Page2.aspx.vb" Inherits="Page2" %>
<!DOCTYPE html>
<html xmlns="http://www.w3.org/1999/xhtml">
<head runat="server">
    <title>SiteMapPath Control Example</title>
</head>
<body>
    <form id="form1" runat="server">
    <div>
    <asp:Label ID="Label1" runat="server" Text="SiteMapDataSource
         Example"></asp:Label><br />
         <br />
         <asp:SiteMapPath ID="SiteMapPath1" runat="server" Font-Names="Verdana"
         Font-Size="0.8em" PathSeparator=" : ">
         <PathSeparatorStyle Font-Bold="True" ForeColor="#5D7B9D" />
         <CurrentNodeStyle ForeColor="#333333" />
         <NodeStyle Font-Bold="True" ForeColor="#7C6F57" />
         <RootNodeStyle Font-Bold="True" ForeColor="#5D7B9D" />
         </asp:SiteMapPath>
         <br />
         <br />
         <asp:HyperLink ID="HyperLink1" runat="server"
          NavigateUrl="~/Page1.aspx">Go to Page 1</asp:HyperLink> <br />
    </div>
    </form>
</body>
</html>
```

In C#

```
<%@ Page Language="C#" AutoEventWireup="true" CodeFile="Page2.aspx.cs" Inherits="Page2" %>
<!DOCTYPE html>
<html xmlns="http://www.w3.org/1999/xhtml">
<head id="Head1" runat="server">
    <title>SiteMapPath Control Example</title>
</head>
<body>
    <form id="form1" runat="server">
    <div>
    <asp:Label ID="Label1" runat="server" Text="SiteMapDataSource
         Example"></asp:Label><br />
         <br />
         <asp:SiteMapPath ID="SiteMapPath1" runat="server" Font-Names="Verdana"
         Font-Size="0.8em" PathSeparator=" : ">
         <PathSeparatorStyle Font-Bold="True" ForeColor="#5D7B9D" />
         <CurrentNodeStyle ForeColor="#333333" />
         <NodeStyle Font-Bold="True" ForeColor="#7C6F57" />
         <RootNodeStyle Font-Bold="True" ForeColor="#5D7B9D" />
         </asp:SiteMapPath>
         <br />
         <br />
```

```
            <asp:HyperLink ID="HyperLink1" runat="server"
             NavigateUrl="~/Page1.aspx">Go to Page 1</asp:HyperLink> <br />
        </div>
        </form>
    </body>
    </html>
```

Now, execute the fully functional `SiteMapPath` control. The output is shown in Figure 5.19:

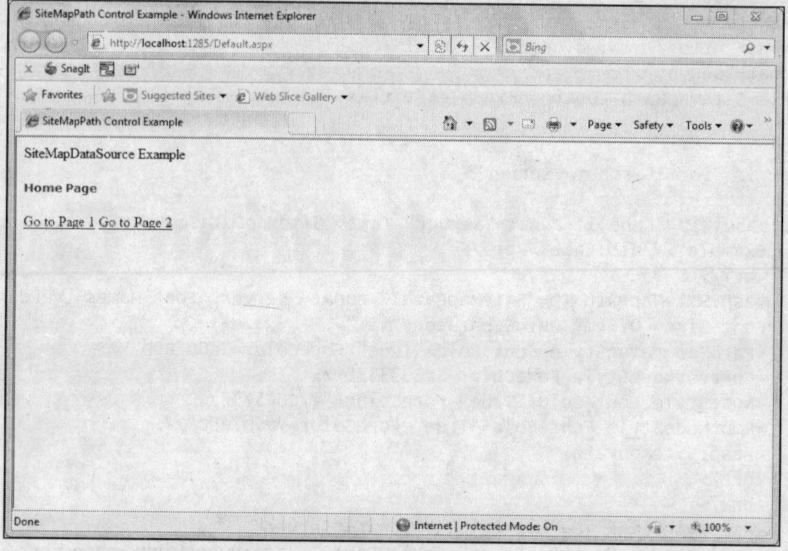

Figure 5.19: Displaying the SiteMapPath Control Example

Summary

In this chapter, three Navigation controls -- the `TreeView` control, `Menu` control, and `SiteMapPath` control of ASP.NET 4.5, have been described. You have learned about the base classes of the Navigation controls along with its properties, methods, and events. In addition, you have also learned about the implementation of these Navigation controls in the *Immediate Solutions* section.

In the next chapter, we will discuss about validation controls available in ASP.NET 4.5.

6

Validation Controls

In Depth

The `Validation controls` are the controls used for validating the data entered in an input control, such as the TextBox control of a Web page. These Validation controls, in turn, helps in reducing the load on the server by eliminating the need to send every piece of data to the server for validation.

When a user enters data on a Web page and submits the page to the server, the Validation controls are invoked to check the data entered by the user. If any of the data is invalid data, the Validation control displays an error message on the screen. The error message is defined as a property value of the Validation control. The data being entered is validated each time it is entered by the user, and the error message disappears only when the data is valid. Validation controls help save time and enhance the efficiency of the applications by validating the data. The following Validation controls are discussed in this chapter:

- The RequiredFieldValidator control
- The RangeValidator control
- The RegularExpressionValidator control
- The CompareValidator control
- The CustomValidator control
- The ValidationSummary control

Let's explore these controls in detail, starting with the `BaseValidator` class, which is the base class of all the Validation controls.

The BaseValidator Class

The `System.Web.UI.WebControls.BaseValidator` class provides basic implementation required for all the Validation controls. The inheritance hierarchy of the BaseValidator class is:

```
System.Object
   System.Web.UI.Control
        System.Web.UI.WebControls.WebControl
              System.Web.UI.WebControls.Label
                    System.Web.UI.WebControls.BaseValidator
```

Noteworthy public properties of the `BaseValidator` class are given in Table 6.1:

Table 6.1: Noteworthy Public Properties of the BaseValidator Class

Property	Description
`ControlToValidate`	Handles an input control, such as the `TextBox` control, which needs to be validated
`Display`	Handles the behavior of the error message in a Validation control
`EnableClientScript`	Handles a value indicating whether or not client-side validation is enabled
`Enabled`	Handles a value that indicates whether or not the Validation control is enabled or not
`ErrorMessage`	Handles the text for the error message displayed in a `ValidationSummary` control when validation fails
`ForeColor`	Handles the color of the message displayed when validation fails
`IsValid`	Handles a value that indicates if the associated input control passes validation or not

Table 6.1: Noteworthy Public Properties of the BaseValidator Class	
Property	**Description**
`SetFocusOnError`	Handles a value that indicates if the focus is set on the control or not, specified by the `ControlToValidate` property when validation fails
`Text`	Handles the text displayed in the Validation control when the validation fails
`ValidationGroup`	Handles the name of the validation group to which this Validation control belongs

NOTE

The ValidationGroup property, when set, validates only the Validation controls within the specified group when the control is posted back to the server

Noteworthy public methods of the `BaseValidator` class are listed in Table 6.2:

Table 6.2: Noteworthy Public Methods of the BaseValidator Class	
Method	**Description**
`Validate`	Helps in performing validation on the associated input control and updates the `IsValid` property
`GetValidationProperty`	Helps in determining the validation property of a control, if it exists

Now, let's discuss the Validation controls one by one in detail.

The RequiredFieldValidator Control

The `RequiredFieldValidator` control is the simplest control, and is used to ensure that the user has entered the data into the input control, such as `TextBox` to which it is bound. For example, if you are entering data, for buying a T-shirt, in an input control, it is necessary to enter the size of the T-shirt that you want to buy. If you do not enter a value, the Validation control displays an error message. The inheritance hierarchy for the `RequiredFieldValidator` class is:

```
System.Object
  System.Web.UI.Control
      System.Web.UI.WebControls.WebControl
          System.Web.UI.WebControls.Label
              System.Web.UI.WebControls.BaseValidator
                  System.Web.UI.WebControls.RequiredFieldValidator
```

The RequiredFieldValidator class has no non-inherited methods or events and it inherits many of the properties and methods of the `BaseValidator` class that are listed in Tables 6.1 and 6.2. Noteworthy public property of the `RequiredFieldValidator` class is listed in Table 6.3:

Table 6.3: Noteworthy Public Property of the RequiredFieldValidator Class	
Property	**Description**
`InitialValue`	Handles the initial value of the associated input control

The RangeValidator Control

The `RangeValidator` control checks whether or not the value of an input control is inside a specified range of values. It has the following three properties:

- **ControlToValidate** – Contains the input control to validate
- **MinimumValue** – Holds the minimum value of the valid range
- **MaximumValue** – Holds the maximum value of the valid range

If one of these properties is set, then the other property must also be set.

Do not forget to set the `Type` property to the data type of the values. The following data types can be used for the values:

- **String** – A string data type
- **Integer** – An integer data type
- **Double** – A double data type
- **Date** – A date data type
- **Currency** – A currency data type

The inheritance hierarchy for the RangeValidator class is:

```
System.Object
  System.Web.UI.Control
       System.Web.UI.WebControls.WebControl
             System.Web.UI.WebControls.Label
                   System.Web.UI.WebControls.BaseValidator
                         System.Web.UI.WebControls.BaseCompareValidator
                               System.Web.UI.WebControls.RangeValidator
```

Noteworthy public properties of the `RangeValidator` class are listed in Table 6.4:

Table 6.4: Noteworthy Public Properties of the RangeValidator Class

Property	Description
`MaximumValue`	Obtains or specifies the maximum value of the validation range for the controls specified in the `RangeValidator` control
`MinimumValue`	Obtains or specifies the minimum value of the validation range for the controls specified in the `RangeValidator` control

The RegularExpressionValidator Control

Regular expressions are used to check whether or not the text matches a certain pattern. The `RegularExpressionValidator` control validates whether the value in the input control (`text box`) matches the format specified by the regular expression, such as a US telephone number or a date format. The `RegularExpressionValidator` control exists within the `System.Web.UI.WebControls` namespace.

In general, regular expressions are made up of text with an embedded code listing that starts with a backslash (`\`) as well as other control code listings. The following is an example:

```
\b[A-Za-z]+\b
```

The code for a word boundary (where a word ends or starts) is `\b` and a `character` class is a set of characters surrounded by `[` and `]`. This allows you to specify what characters you want to accept. Therefore, this regular expression matches a word consisting of uppercase or lowercase letters only. The + sign matches the previous character or the subexpression one or more times, so we are matching one or more uppercase and/or lowercase letters here.

NOTE

The + sign in the RegularExpressionValidator Control helps in matching the previous character or the subexpression one or more times. For example, the expression zo+ will match zo and zoo but not z.

For example, the regular expression to determine if the text matches a valid `e-mail address` is:

```
\w+([-+.]\w+)*@\w+([-.]\w+)*\.\w+([-.]\w+)*
```

In the preceding expression, `\w` stands for a word character (such as letters, and underscores) and `*` sign matches the previous character or subexpression zero or more times. For example, the expression zo* will match z and zoo.

ASP.NET 4.5 includes some pre-built regular expressions that you can use to match well-known sequences of characters, such as a French phone number, P.R.C. social security number, US social security number, e-mail address, and Internet URL address. Regular expressions are complex to understand, as they require in-depth knowledge of the character relations required during custom expression definition.

The inheritance hierarchy for the `RegularExpressionValidator` class is:

```
System.Object
  System.Web.UI.Control
        System.Web.UI.WebControls.WebControl
               System.Web.UI.WebControls.Label
                      System.Web.UI.WebControls.BaseValidator
                             System.Web.UI.WebControls.RegularExpressionValidator
```

The class has no non-inherited methods or events. Noteworthy public property of the `RegularExpressionValidator` class is listed in Table 6.5:

Table 6.5: Noteworthy Public Property of the RegularExpressionValidator Class

Property	Description
`ValidationExpression`	Obtains or specifies the regular expression that you want to match data for validation

The CompareValidator Control

The CompareValidator control is used to compare the value entered by a user into one input control with the value entered into another input control or with an already existing value. The `CompareValidator` control exists within the `System.Web.UI.WebControls` namespace. Table 6.6 lists the various `Operator` property types, specifying the different types of comparisons:

Table 6.6: Operator Properties of the CompareValidator Control

Type	Description
`Equal`	Checks whether the compared values are equal
`NotEqual`	Checks that controls are not equal to each other
`GreaterThan`	Checks for a greater than relationship
`GreaterThanEqual`	Checks for a greater than or equal to relationship
`LessThan`	Checks for a less than relationship
`LessThanEqual`	Checks for a less than or equal to relationship
`DataTypeCheck`	Compares data types between the value entered into the data-entry control being validated and the data type specified by the Type property

The `Type` property is used to specify the data type of both the comparison values, where `String` is the default type. Both values are automatically converted to the String data type before the comparison operation is performed. The different data types that can be used are as follows:

- **String**—A string data type
- **Integer**—An integer data type
- **Double**—A double data type
- **Date**—A date data type
- **Currency**—A currency data type

Noteworthy public properties of the CompareValidator class are given in Table 6.7:

Table 6.7: Noteworthy Public Properties of the CompareValidator Class

Property	Description
ControlToCompare	Obtains or specifies the data entry control, which has to be compared with the data-entry control being validated
Operator	Obtains or specifies the comparison operation to perform
ValueToCompare	Obtains or specifies a constant value to compare with the value entered by a user in the data entry control being validated

The CustomValidator Control

The CustomValidator control is used to customize and implement data validation as per your requirement. Occasionally, you might need to validate your data in a way that is not possible directly with the help of existing Validation controls. For example, if you want to find out whether a number is odd or even, you cannot use an existing Validation control for doing that because this functionality is not included in any of the Validation controls. To solve this problem, you need a Validation control that can be customized to solve this problem. The CustomValidator control exists within the System.Web.UI.WebControls namespace. The inheritance hierarchy for the CustomValidator class is:

```
System.Object
  System.Web.UI.Control
        System.Web.UI.WebControls.WebControl
               System.Web.UI.WebControls.Label
                      System.Web.UI.WebControls.BaseValidator
                             System.Web.UI.WebControls.CustomValidator
```

The CustomValidator control checks whether or not the input you have given, such as prime, even, or odd number, matches a given condition. Noteworthy public properties of the CustomValidator class are listed in Table 6.8:

Table 6.8: Noteworthy Public Properties of the CustomValidator Class

Property	Description
ClientValidationFunction	Obtains or specifies the name of the custom client-side script function used for validation
ValidateEmptyText	Obtains or specifies a Boolean value indicating whether empty text should be validated or not

To use the CustomValidator control in a Web application, first create a function using a scripting language, such as JavaScript or VBScript (both are supported by Internet Explorer), in the source file of the Web page. You can then set the ClientValidationFunction property of the CustomValidator control to the name of the function you have created. The CustomValidator control validates the data entered by the user in the data entry control at the runtime based on the code written inside this function.

A noteworthy public event of the CustomValidator class is listed in Table 6.9:

Table 6.9: Noteworthy Public Event of the CustomValidator Class

Event	Description
ServerValidate	Occurs when validation takes place on the server

The ValidationSummary Control

The ValidationSummary control collects all the Validation control error messages (known as summary) and displays it collectively on the screen. The display of the summary, which can be a list, a bulleted list, or a single paragraph, can be set by using the DisplayMode property. You can also specify whether the summary should be displayed in the Web page or in a message box by setting the ShowSummary and ShowMessageBox properties, respectively. The ValidationSummary control exists within the System.Web.UI.WebControls namespace.

The inheritance hierarchy for the ValidationSummary class is:

```
System.Object
   System.Web.UI.Control
         System.Web.UI.WebControls.WebControl
                System.Web.UI.WebControls.ValidationSummary
```

Noteworthy public properties of the ValidationSummary class are listed in Table 6.10:

Table 6.10: Noteworthy Public Properties of the ValidationSummary Class

Property	Description
DisplayMode	Obtains or specifies the display mode of the ValidationSummary control
EnableClientScript	Obtains or specifies a value indicating whether the ValidationSummary control updates itself using the client-side script
ForeColor	Obtains or specifies the foreground color of the control
HeaderText	Obtains or specifies the header text displayed at the top of the summary
ShowMessageBox	Obtains or specifies a value showing whether the validation summary is displayed in a message box
ShowSummary	Obtains or specifies a value showing whether the validation summary is displayed in line
ValidationGroup	Obtains or specifies the group of controls for which the ValidationSummary object displays validation messages

While using a ValidationSummary control in a Web application, if you want to display all the error messages on the same Web page, you must set the ShowSummary property of the ValidationSummary control to True. In case you want to display the error messages in a message box, set the ShowMessageBox property of the ValidationSummary control to True. By setting both these properties to True, you can display the error messages in both ways. You can also set the mode in which you want to display the error messages, by setting the DisplayMode property of the ValidationSummary control. The possible values for this property are List, BulletList, and SingleParagraph.

NOTE

You must add the following code snippet in the <configuration> tag in Web.config file of the application:
<appSettings>
<add key="ValidationSettings:UnobtrusiveValidationMode" value="None" />
</appSettings>

Immediate Solutions

Using the RequiredFieldValidator Control

To add a `RequiredFieldValidator` control on a Web page (Default.aspx), add the following code to the source code of the Web page:

```
<asp:RequiredFieldValidator ID="RequiredFieldValidator1" runat="server"
  ErrorMessage="RequiredFieldValidator"></asp:RequiredFieldValidator>
```

Now, let's create an application named RequiredFieldValidatorCS in C# and RequiredFieldValidatorVB in VB. You can add a `RequiredFieldValidator` control to a Web page either by dragging and dropping it from the Standard tab of the Toolbox or by double-clicking this control in the Toolbox.

NOTE

The applications in this chapter are created using the ASP.NET Empty Web Site template in the New Web Site dialog box. After creating the application, you need to add the Default.aspx page to the application.

In this example, we are adding two `RequiredFieldValidator` controls on a Web page for validating two `TextBox` controls. The `RequiredFieldValidator` controls ensure that the two `TextBox` controls are not kept empty by the user at runtime. Listing 6.1 shows the Default.aspx page for the `RequiredFieldValidator` control:

Listing 6.1: Showing the Code for the `Default.aspx` Page

In VB

```
<%@ Page Language="VB" AutoEventWireup="false" CodeFile="Default.aspx.vb"
  Inherits="_Default" %>
<!DOCTYPE html>
<html xmlns="http://www.w3.org/1999/xhtml">
<head runat="server">
    <title>RequiredFieldValidator Control Example</title>
</head>
<body>
   <form id="form1" runat="server">
   <div>
   <asp:Label ID="Label1" runat="server" Text="RequiredField Validator Control Example"
        Font-Bold="True" Font-Size="Medium" Font-Underline="True"></asp:Label>
        <br />
        <br />
        <asp:Label ID="Label2" runat="server" Font-Bold="True" Font-Size="Small"
              Text="User name:"></asp:Label>
        <asp:TextBox ID="TextBox1" runat="server" Height="22px"
              Width="175px"></asp:TextBox>
        <asp:RequiredFieldValidator ID="RequiredFieldValidator1" runat="server"
              ControlToValidate="TextBox1" ErrorMessage="User name can not be
              empty"></asp:RequiredFieldValidator>
        <br />
        <br />
        <asp:Label ID="Label3" runat="server" Font-Bold="True" Font-Size="Small"
              Text="Password:"></asp:Label>
        <asp:TextBox ID="TextBox2" runat="server" Height="22px" TextMode="Password"
              Width="175px"></asp:TextBox>
        <asp:RequiredFieldValidator ID="RequiredFieldValidator2" runat="server"
              ControlToValidate="TextBox2" ErrorMessage="Password can not be
              empty"></asp:RequiredFieldValidator>
        <br />
        <br />
```

```
        <br />
                    
                    
               
        <asp:Button ID="Button1" runat="server" BackColor="Black" Font-Bold="True"
               Font-Size="Medium" ForeColor="White" Text="Submit" />
    </div>
    </form>
</body>
</html>
```

In C#

```
<%@ Page Language="C#" AutoEventWireup="true" CodeFile="Default.aspx.cs"
  Inherits="_Default" %>
<!DOCTYPE html>
<html xmlns="http://www.w3.org/1999/xhtml">
<head runat="server">
    <title>RequiredFieldValidator Control Example</title>
</head>
<body>
    <form id="form1" runat="server">
    <div>
    <asp:Label ID="Label1" runat="server" Text="RequiredField Validator Control Example"
        Font-Bold="True" Font-Size="Medium" Font-Underline="True"></asp:Label>
        <br />
        <br />
        <asp:Label ID="Label2" runat="server" Font-Bold="True" Font-Size="Small"
               Text="User name:"></asp:Label>
          
        <asp:TextBox ID="TextBox1" runat="server" Height="22px"
               Width="175px"></asp:TextBox>
        <asp:RequiredFieldValidator ID="RequiredFieldValidator1" runat="server"
               ControlToValidate="TextBox1" ErrorMessage="User name can not be
               empty"></asp:RequiredFieldValidator>
        <br />
        <br />
        <asp:Label ID="Label3" runat="server" Font-Bold="True" Font-Size="Small"
               Text="Password:"></asp:Label>
            
        <asp:TextBox ID="TextBox2" runat="server" Height="22px" TextMode="Password"
               Width="175px"></asp:TextBox>
        <asp:RequiredFieldValidator ID="RequiredFieldValidator2" runat="server"
               ControlToValidate="TextBox2" ErrorMessage="Password can not be
               empty"></asp:RequiredFieldValidator>
        <br />
        <br />
        <br />
                     
                    
            
        <asp:Button ID="Button1" runat="server" BackColor="Black" Font-Bold="True"
        Font-Size="Medium" ForeColor="White" Text="Submit" />
    </div>
    </form>
</body>
</html>
```

Now, run the application by pressing the F5 key. If you click the Submit button without entering data in the two `TextBox` controls, both the `RequiredFieldValidator` controls display error messages, as shown in Figure 6.1:

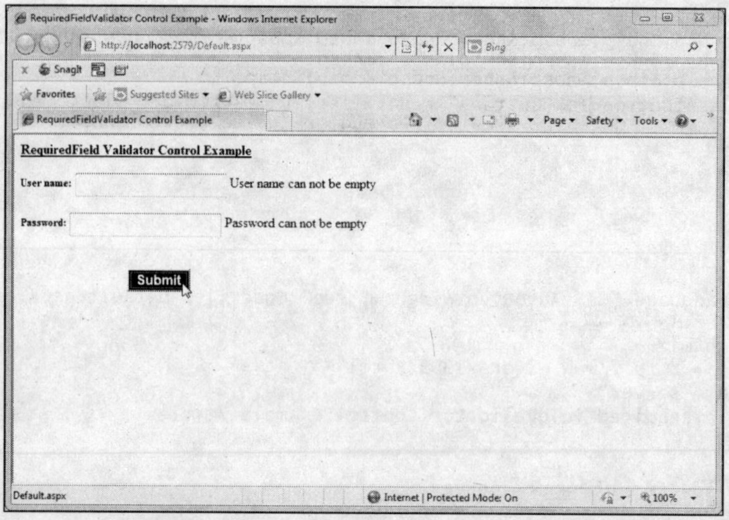

Figure 6.1: Two RequiredFieldValidator Controls on a Web Page Showing Error Messages

Using the RangeValidator Control

When you add a `RangeValidator` control on a Web page (Default.aspx), it adds the following code to the source code of the Web page:

```
<asp:RangeValidator ID="RangeValidator1" runat="server"
  ErrorMessage="RangeValidator"></asp:RangeValidator>
```

Now, let's create an application named RangeValidatorCS in C# and RangeValidatorVB in VB . In this example, we are adding two `RangeValidator` controls on a Web page for validating two `TextBox` controls. The first `RangeValidator` control ensures that the age entered in the first `TextBox` control is in the range 20-40 yrs. The second `RangeValidator` control ensures that the date of birth is in the range 1988/1/1 to 2028/1/1. Listing 6.2 shows the Default.aspx page for the `RangeValidator` control:

Listing 6.2: Showing the Code for the `Default.aspx` Page

In VB

```
<%@ Page Language="VB" AutoEventWireup="false" CodeFile="Default.aspx.vb"
  Inherits="_Default" %>
<!DOCTYPE html>
<html xmlns="http://www.w3.org/1999/xhtml">
<head runat="server">
    <title>RangeValidator Control Example</title>
</head>
<body>
    <form id="form1" runat="server">
    <div>
    <asp:Label ID="Label1" runat="server" Text="RangeValidator Control Example" Font-
         Bold="True" Font-Size="Medium" Font-Underline="True"></asp:Label>
         <br />
         <br />
         <br />
         <asp:Label ID="Label2" runat="server" Font-Bold="True" Font-Size="Small"
                Text="Your Age:"></asp:Label>
           
         <asp:TextBox ID="TextBox1" runat="server" Width="172px"></asp:TextBox>
         <asp:RangeValidator ID="RangeValidator1" runat="server"
                ControlToValidate="TextBox1" ErrorMessage="Invalid Age. Please enter
```

```
                the age between 20 to 40." MaximumValue="40" MinimumValue="20"
                Type="Integer"></asp:RangeValidator>
             <br />
            <asp:RequiredFieldValidator ID="RequiredFieldValidator1" runat="server"
                ControlToValidate="TextBox1" ErrorMessage="This field can not be
                blank."></asp:RequiredFieldValidator>
            <br />
            <br />
            <asp:Label ID="Label3" runat="server" Font-Bold="True" Font-Size="Small"
                Text="Date of Birth (YYYY/MM/DD format) :"></asp:Label>
               
            <asp:TextBox ID="TextBox2" runat="server" Width="172px"></asp:TextBox>
            <asp:RangeValidator ID="RangeValidator2" runat="server"
                ControlToValidate="TextBox2" ErrorMessage="Invalid DOB. It must be
                between 1988/1/1 to 2028/1/1." MaximumValue="2028/1/1"
                MinimumValue="1988/1/1" Type="Date"></asp:RangeValidator>
            <br />
            <asp:RequiredFieldValidator ID="RequiredFieldValidator2" runat="server"
                ControlToValidate="TextBox2" ErrorMessage="This field can not be
                blank."></asp:RequiredFieldValidator>
            <br />
            <br />
                        
                        
                       
            <asp:Button ID="Button1" runat="server" BackColor="Black" Font-Bold="True"
                Font-Size="Small" ForeColor="White" Text="Submit" />
        </div>
        </form>
    </body>
    </html>
```

In C#

```
<%@ Page Language="C#" AutoEventWireup="true" CodeFile="Default.aspx.cs"
  Inherits="_Default" %>
<!DOCTYPE html>
<html xmlns="http://www.w3.org/1999/xhtml">
<head runat="server">
    <title>RangeValidator Control Example</title>
</head>
<body>
    <form id="form1" runat="server">
    <div>
    <asp:Label ID="Label1" runat="server" Text="RangeValidator Control Example" Font-
        Bold="True" Font-Size="Medium" Font-Underline="True"></asp:Label>
        <br />
        <br />
        <br />
        <asp:Label ID="Label2" runat="server" Font-Bold="True" Font-Size="Small"
            Text="Your Age:"></asp:Label>
          
        <asp:TextBox ID="TextBox1" runat="server" Width="172px"></asp:TextBox>
        <asp:RangeValidator ID="RangeValidator1" runat="server"
            ControlToValidate="TextBox1" ErrorMessage="Invalid Age. Please enter
            the age between 20 to 40." MaximumValue="40" MinimumValue="20"
            Type="Integer"></asp:RangeValidator>
         <br />
        <asp:RequiredFieldValidator ID="RequiredFieldValidator1" runat="server"
            ControlToValidate="TextBox1" ErrorMessage="This field can not be
            blank."></asp:RequiredFieldValidator>
        <br />
        <br />
        <asp:Label ID="Label3" runat="server" Font-Bold="True" Font-Size="Small"
            Text="Date of Birth (YYYY/MM/DD format) :"></asp:Label>
```

```
               
            <asp:TextBox ID="TextBox2" runat="server" Width="172px"></asp:TextBox>
            <asp:RangeValidator ID="RangeValidator2" runat="server"
                    ControlToValidate="TextBox2" ErrorMessage="Invalid DOB. It must be
                    between 1988/1/1 to 2028/1/1." MaximumValue="2028/1/1"
                    MinimumValue="1988/1/1" Type="Date"></asp:RangeValidator>
            <br />
            <asp:RequiredFieldValidator ID="RequiredFieldValidator2" runat="server"
                    ControlToValidate="TextBox2" ErrorMessage="This field can not be
                    blank."></asp:RequiredFieldValidator>
            <br />
            <br />
                        
                        
                       
            <asp:Button ID="Button1" runat="server" BackColor="Black" Font-Bold="True"
            Font-Size="Small" ForeColor="White" Text="Submit" />
        </div>
        </form>
    </body>
    </html>
```

Now, execute the application by pressing the F5 key. Enter values in the text boxes and click the Submit button. If the values are outside the specified range in the `TextBox` controls the `RangeValidator` controls display error messages, as shown in Figure 6.2:

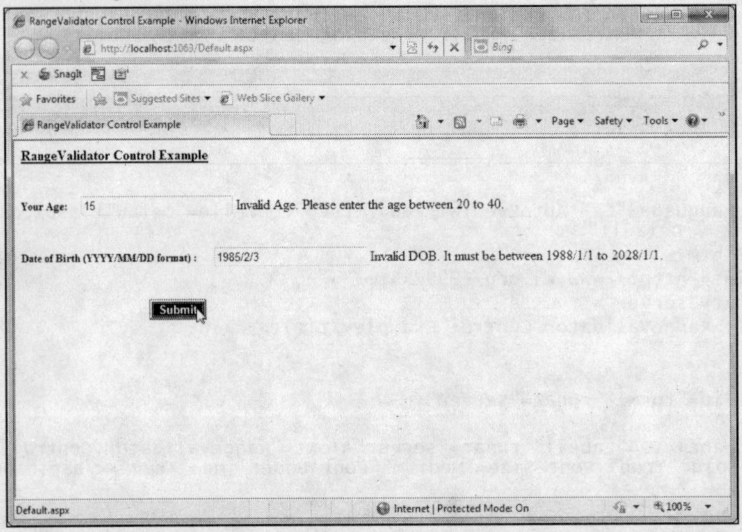

Figure 6.2: Two RangeValidator Controls on a Web Page Showing Error Messages

NOTE

It is mandatory to use a RequiredFieldValidator control with the RangeValidator, RegularExpressionValidator, CompareValidator, and CustomValidator controls because the latter do not work on blank input controls.

Using the RegularExpressionValidator Control

When you add a RegularExpressionValidator control on a Web page (Default.aspx), it adds the following code to the source code of the Web page:

```
<asp:RegularExpressionValidator ID="RegularExpressionValidator1" runat="server"
  ErrorMessage="RegularExpressionValidator"></asp:RegularExpressionValidator>
```

Now, let's create an application named RegularExpressionValidatorCS in C# and RegularExpressionValidatorVB in VB. In this example, we are taking two `RegularExpressionValidator` controls on a Web page for validating two `TextBox` controls. It ensures that the data (URL and email address) entered in both the `TextBox` controls is valid. Listing 6.3 shows the Default.aspx page for the RegularExpressionValidator control:

Listing 6.3: Showing the Code for the `Default.aspx` Page

In VB

```
<%@ Page Language="VB" AutoEventWireup="false" CodeFile="Default.aspx.vb"
  Inherits="_Default" %>
<!DOCTYPE html>
<html xmlns="http://www.w3.org/1999/xhtml">
<head runat="server">
    <title>RegularExpressionValidator Control Example</title>
</head>
<body>
    <form id="form1" runat="server">
    <div>
        <asp:Label ID="Label1" runat="server" Font-Bold="True" Font-Size="Medium" Font-
        Underline="True" Text="RegularExpressionValidator Control Example"></asp:Label>
        <br />
        <br />
        <br />
        <asp:Label ID="Label2" runat="server" Font-Bold="True" Font-Size="Small"
        Text="Enter URL:"></asp:Label>
                    
              
        <asp:TextBox ID="TextBox1" runat="server" Width="177px"></asp:TextBox>
        <asp:RegularExpressionValidator ID="RegularExpressionValidator1" runat="server"
        ControlToValidate="TextBox1" ErrorMessage="Not a Valid URL."
        ValidationExpression="http(s)?://([\w-]+\.)+[\w-]+(/[\w-
        ./?%&amp;=]*)?"></asp:RegularExpressionValidator>
        <br />
        <asp:RequiredFieldValidator ID="RequiredFieldValidator1" runat="server"
        ControlToValidate="TextBox1" ErrorMessage="This field can not be
        blank."></asp:RequiredFieldValidator>
        <br />
        <br />
        <asp:Label ID="Label3" runat="server" Font-Bold="True" Font-Size="Small"
        Text="Enter E-mail address:"></asp:Label>
          
        <asp:TextBox ID="TextBox2" runat="server" Width="177px"></asp:TextBox>
        <asp:RegularExpressionValidator ID="RegularExpressionValidator2" runat="server"
        ControlToValidate="TextBox2" ErrorMessage="Not a Valid E-mail address."
        ValidationExpression="\w+([-+.']\w+)*@\w+([-.]\w+)*\.\w+([-
        .]\w+)*"></asp:RegularExpressionValidator>
        <br />
        <asp:RequiredFieldValidator ID="RequiredFieldValidator2" runat="server"
        ControlToValidate="TextBox2" ErrorMessage="This field can not be
        blank."></asp:RequiredFieldValidator>
        <br />
        <br />
        <br />
                    
                     
                 
        <asp:Button ID="Button1" runat="server" BackColor="Black" Font-Bold="True"
        Font-Size="Small" ForeColor="White" Text="Submit" Width="60px" />
    </div>
    </form>
</body>
</html>
```

In C#

```
<%@ Page Language="C#" AutoEventWireup="true" CodeFile="Default.aspx.cs"
  Inherits="_Default" %>
<!DOCTYPE html>
<html xmlns="http://www.w3.org/1999/xhtml">
<head id="Head1" runat="server">
    <title>RegularExpressionValidator Control Example</title>
</head>
<body>
    <form id="form1" runat="server">
    <div>
        <asp:Label ID="Label1" runat="server" Font-Bold="True" Font-Size="Medium" Font-
        Underline="True" Text="RegularExpressionValidator Control Example"></asp:Label>
        <br />
        <br />
        <br />
        <asp:Label ID="Label2" runat="server" Font-Bold="True" Font-Size="Small"
        Text="Enter URL:"></asp:Label>
                   
              
        <asp:TextBox ID="TextBox1" runat="server" Width="177px"></asp:TextBox>
        <asp:RegularExpressionValidator ID="RegularExpressionValidator1" runat="server"
        ControlToValidate="TextBox1" ErrorMessage="Not a Valid URL."
        ValidationExpression="http(s)?://([\w-]+\.)+[\w-]+(/[\w-
        ./?%&amp;=]*)?"></asp:RegularExpressionValidator>
        <br />
        <asp:RequiredFieldValidator ID="RequiredFieldValidator1" runat="server"
        ControlToValidate="TextBox1" ErrorMessage="This field can not be
        blank."></asp:RequiredFieldValidator>
        <br />
        <br />
        <asp:Label ID="Label3" runat="server" Font-Bold="True" Font-Size="Small"
        Text="Enter E-mail address:"></asp:Label>
          
        <asp:TextBox ID="TextBox2" runat="server" Width="177px"></asp:TextBox>
        <asp:RegularExpressionValidator ID="RegularExpressionValidator2" runat="server"
        ControlToValidate="TextBox2" ErrorMessage="Not a Valid E-mail address."
        ValidationExpression="\w+([-+.']\w+)*@\w+([-.]\w+)*\.\w+([-
        .]\w+)*"></asp:RegularExpressionValidator>
        <br />
        <asp:RequiredFieldValidator ID="RequiredFieldValidator2" runat="server"
        ControlToValidate="TextBox2" ErrorMessage="This field can not be
        blank."></asp:RequiredFieldValidator>
        <br />
        <br />
        <br />
                    
                     
                 
        <asp:Button ID="Button1" runat="server" BackColor="Black" Font-Bold="True"
        Font-Size="Small" ForeColor="White" Text="Submit" Width="60px" />
    </div>
    </form>
</body>
</html>
```

Now, press the F5 key to execute the application and enter the values in the `TextBox` controls and click the Submit button. If the values are not in the specified format then the `RegularExpressionValidator` controls display error messages, as shown in Figure 6.3:

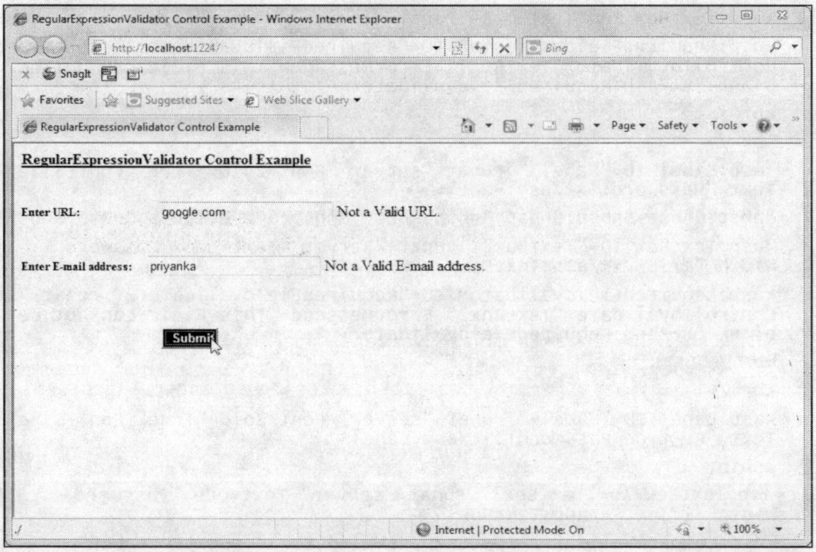

Figure 6.3: RegularExpressionValidator Controls Displaying Error Message on a Web Page

Using the CompareValidator Control

When you add a CompareValidator control on a Web page (Default.aspx), it adds the following code to the source code of the Web page:

```
<asp:CompareValidator ID="CompareValidator1" runat="server"
  ErrorMessage="CompareValidator"></asp:CompareValidator>
```

Now, let's create an application named CompareValidatorCS in C# and CompareValidatorVB in VB.

In this example, we take a `CompareValidator` control on a Web page, which validates the third `TextBox` control. It ensures that the data (password) entered in the third `TextBox` control is exactly the same as the data (`password`) entered in the second `TextBox` control. Listing 6.4 shows the Default.aspx page for the CompareValidator control:

Listing 6.4: Showing the Code for the `Default.aspx` Page

In VB

```
<%@ Page Language="VB" AutoEventWireup="false" CodeFile="Default.aspx.vb"
  Inherits="_Default" %>
<!DOCTYPE html>
<html xmlns="http://www.w3.org/1999/xhtml">
<head runat="server">
    <title>CompareValidator Control Example</title>
</head>
<body>
    <form id="form1" runat="server">
    <div>
    <asp:Label ID="Label1" runat="server" Font-Bold="True" Font-Size="Medium" Font-
  Underline="True" Text="CompareValidator Control Example"></asp:Label>
        <br />
        <br />
```

```
        <br />
        <asp:Label ID="Label2" runat="server" Font-Bold="True" Font-Size="Small"
        Text="User Name:"></asp:Label>
                  
        <asp:TextBox ID="TextBox1" runat="server" Width="173px"></asp:TextBox>
        <asp:RequiredFieldValidator ID="RequiredFieldValidator1" runat="server"
        ControlToValidate="TextBox1" ErrorMessage="This Field can not be
        blank."></asp:RequiredFieldValidator>
        <br />
        <br />
        <asp:Label ID="Label3" runat="server" Font-Bold="True" Font-Size="Small"
        Text="Password:"></asp:Label>
                    
        <asp:TextBox ID="TextBox2" runat="server" TextMode="Password"
        Width="173px"></asp:TextBox>
        <asp:RequiredFieldValidator ID="RequiredFieldValidator2" runat="server"
        ControlToValidate="TextBox2" ErrorMessage="This Field can not be
        blank."></asp:RequiredFieldValidator>
        <br />
        <br />
        <asp:Label ID="Label4" runat="server" Font-Bold="True" Font-Size="Small"
        Text="Re-type Password:"></asp:Label>
         
        <asp:TextBox ID="TextBox3" runat="server" TextMode="Password"
        Width="173px"></asp:TextBox>
        <asp:CompareValidator ID="CompareValidator1" runat="server"
        ControlToCompare="TextBox2" ControlToValidate="TextBox3" ErrorMessage="Password
        does not match."></asp:CompareValidator>
        <br />
        <br />
        <asp:RequiredFieldValidator ID="RequiredFieldValidator3" runat="server"
        ControlToValidate="TextBox3" ErrorMessage="This Field can not be
        blank."></asp:RequiredFieldValidator>
        <br />
        <br />
                   
                    
                  
        <asp:Button ID="Button1" runat="server" BackColor="Black" Font-Bold="True"
        Font-Size="Small" ForeColor="White" Text="Submit" />
    </div>
    </form>
</body>
</html>
```

In C#

```
<%@ Page Language="C#" AutoEventWireup="true" CodeFile="Default.aspx.cs"
  Inherits="_Default" %>
<!DOCTYPE html>
<html xmlns="http://www.w3.org/1999/xhtml">
<head id="Head1" runat="server">
    <title>CompareValidator Control Example</title>
</head>
<body>
    <form id="form1" runat="server">
    <div>
```

```
        <asp:Label ID="Label1" runat="server" Font-Bold="True" Font-Size="Medium" Font-
            Underline="True" Text="CompareValidator Control Example"></asp:Label>
            <br />
            <br />
            <br />
            <asp:Label ID="Label2" runat="server" Font-Bold="True" Font-Size="Small"
            Text="User Name:"></asp:Label>
                      
            <asp:TextBox ID="TextBox1" runat="server" Width="173px"></asp:TextBox>
            <asp:RequiredFieldValidator ID="RequiredFieldValidator1" runat="server"
            ControlToValidate="TextBox1" ErrorMessage="This Field can not be
            blank."></asp:RequiredFieldValidator>
            <br />
            <br />
            <asp:Label ID="Label3" runat="server" Font-Bold="True" Font-Size="Small"
            Text="Password:"></asp:Label>
                        
            <asp:TextBox ID="TextBox2" runat="server" TextMode="Password"
            Width="173px"></asp:TextBox>
            <asp:RequiredFieldValidator ID="RequiredFieldValidator2" runat="server"
            ControlToValidate="TextBox2" ErrorMessage="This Field can not be
            blank."></asp:RequiredFieldValidator>
            <br />
            <br />
            <asp:Label ID="Label4" runat="server" Font-Bold="True" Font-Size="Small"
            Text="Re-type Password:"></asp:Label>
             
           <asp:TextBox ID="TextBox3" runat="server" TextMode="Password"
            Width="173px"></asp:TextBox>
            <asp:CompareValidator ID="CompareValidator1" runat="server"
            ControlToCompare="TextBox2" ControlToValidate="TextBox3" ErrorMessage="Password
            does not match."></asp:CompareValidator>
            <br />
            <br />
            <asp:RequiredFieldValidator ID="RequiredFieldValidator3" runat="server"
            ControlToValidate="TextBox3" ErrorMessage="This Field can not be
            blank."></asp:RequiredFieldValidator>
            <br />
            <br />
                       
                        
                      
            <asp:Button ID="Button1" runat="server" BackColor="Black" Font-Bold="True"
            Font-Size="Small" ForeColor="White" Text="Submit" />
        </div>
        </form>
    </body>
    </html>
```

Now, run the application, and enter priyanka in the first `TextBox` control, password@12 in the second `TextBox` control, password in the third `TextBox` control, and then click the Submit button. The `CompareValidator` control displays an error message, as shown in Figure 6.4:

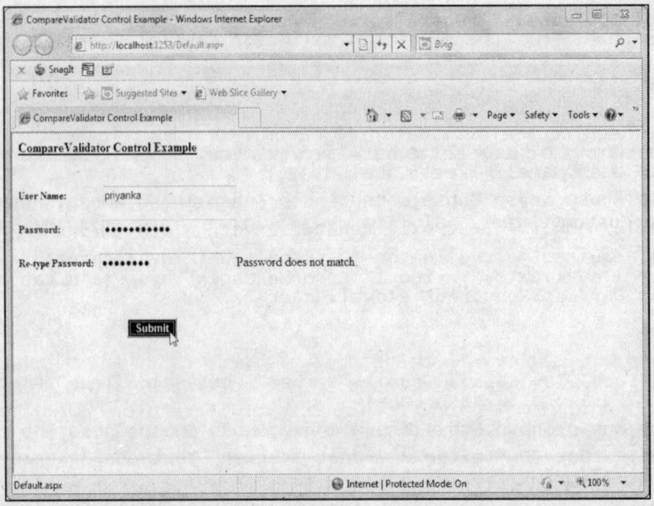

Figure 6.4: CompareValidator Control Displaying Error Message on a Web Page

Using the CustomValidator Control

When you add a CustomValidator control on a Web page (Default.aspx), it adds the following code to the source code of the Web page:

```
<asp:CustomValidator ID="CustomValidator1" runat="server"
  ErrorMessage="CustomValidator"></asp:CustomValidator>
```

Now, let's create an application named CustomValidatorCS in C# and CustomValidatorVB in VB. In this example, we are taking a `CustomValidator` control on a Web page, which validates the `TextBox` control and ensures that the user enters the correct data (username). Listing 6.5 shows the Default.aspx page for the CustomValidator control:

Listing 6.5: Showing the Code for the `Default.aspx` Page

In VB

```
<%@ Page Language="VB" AutoEventWireup="false" CodeFile="Default.aspx.vb"
  Inherits="_Default" %>
<!DOCTYPE html>
<html xmlns="http://www.w3.org/1999/xhtml">
<head runat="server">
    <title>CustomValidator Control Example</title>
</head>
<body>
    <form id="form1" runat="server">
    <script language="vbscript" type="text/vbscript">
        Sub Validate (source, arguments)
                If (arguments.Value = "testuser")Then
                        arguments.IsValid = True
                Else
                        arguments.IsValid = False
                End IF
        End Sub
        </script>
    <div>
    <asp:Label ID="Label1" runat="server" Font-Bold="True" Font-Size="Medium" Font-
        Underline="True" Text="CustomValidator Control Example"></asp:Label>
        <br />
        <br />
```

```
            <br />
            <asp:Label ID="Label2" runat="server" Font-Bold="True" Font-Size="Small"
            Text="Enter User Name:"></asp:Label>
              
            <asp:TextBox ID="TextBox1" runat="server" Width="179px"></asp:TextBox>
            <asp:RequiredFieldValidator ID="RequiredFieldValidator1" runat="server"
            ControlToValidate="TextBox1" ErrorMessage="This field can not be
            blank."></asp:RequiredFieldValidator>
            <br />
            <asp:CustomValidator ID="CustomValidator1" runat="server" ErrorMessage="Invalid
            entry. Correct username is 'testuser'." ClientValidationFunction="Validate"
            ControlToValidate="TextBox1"></asp:CustomValidator>
            <br />
            <br />
            <br />
                        
                        
            <asp:Button ID="Button1" runat="server" BackColor="Black" Font-Bold="True"
            Font-Size="Small" ForeColor="White" Text="Submit" />
           </div>
       </form>
   </body>
   </html>
```

In C#

```
<%@ Page Language="C#" AutoEventWireup="true" CodeFile="Default.aspx.cs"
  Inherits="_Default" %>
<!DOCTYPE html>
<html xmlns="http://www.w3.org/1999/xhtml">
<head id="Head1" runat="server">
    <title>CustomValidator Control Example</title>
</head>
<body>
    <form id="form1" runat="server">
    <script language="vbscript" type="text/vbscript">
         Sub Validate (source, arguments)
                 If (arguments.Value = "testuser")Then
                         arguments.IsValid = True
                 Else
                         arguments.IsValid = False
                 End IF
         End Sub
         </script>
    <div>
    <asp:Label ID="Label1" runat="server" Font-Bold="True" Font-Size="Medium" Font-
         Underline="True" Text="CustomValidator Control Example"></asp:Label>
         <br />
         <br />
         <br />
         <asp:Label ID="Label2" runat="server" Font-Bold="True" Font-Size="Small"
         Text="Enter User Name:"></asp:Label>
           
         <asp:TextBox ID="TextBox1" runat="server" Width="179px"></asp:TextBox>
         <asp:RequiredFieldValidator ID="RequiredFieldValidator1" runat="server"
         ControlToValidate="TextBox1" ErrorMessage="This field can not be
         blank."></asp:RequiredFieldValidator>
         <br />
         <asp:CustomValidator ID="CustomValidator1" runat="server" ErrorMessage="Invalid
         entry. Correct username is 'testuser'." ClientValidationFunction="Validate"
         ControlToValidate="TextBox1"></asp:CustomValidator>
         <br />
         <br />
```

```
            <br />
                        
                        
            <asp:Button ID="Button1" runat="server" BackColor="Black" Font-Bold="True"
            Font-Size="Small" ForeColor="White" Text="Submit" />
        </div>
    </form>
</body>
</html>
```

In the source file, `Default.aspx`, we have created a procedure named Validate in the `<script>` tag. The string that the user enters should be same to the string defined, testuser, in the script. Now, run the application and enter priyanka in the Enter user name text box and click the Sumit button. The `CustomValidator` control displays an error message, as shown in Figure 6.5:

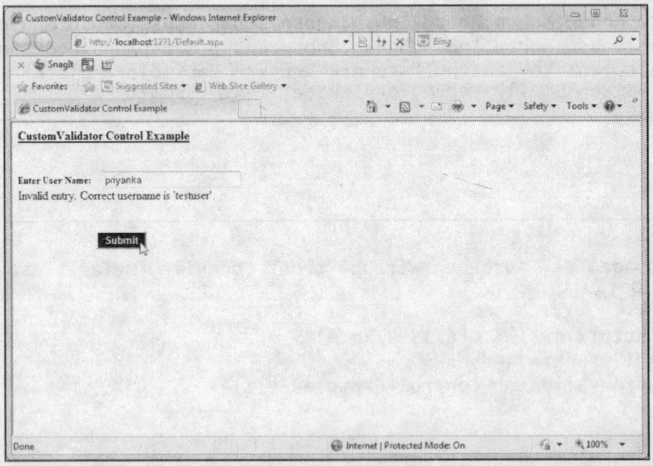

Figure 6.5: CustomValidator Control Displaying Error Message on a Web Page

Using the ValidationSummary Control

When you add a ValidationSummary control to a Web page (Default.aspx), it adds the following code to the source code of the Web page:

```
<asp:ValidationSummary ID="ValidationSummary1" runat="server" />
```

Now, let's create an application named ValidationSummaryCS in C# and ValidationSummaryVB in VB. In this example, we are taking two `RequiredFieldValidator` controls and one `ValidationSummary` control on a Web page. The `ValidationSummary` control displays a summary of the error messages from all the other Validation controls. Listing 6.6 shows the Default.aspx page for the ValidationSummary control:

Listing 6.6: Showing the Code for the `Default.aspx` Page

In VB

```
<%@ Page Language="VB" AutoEventWireup="false" CodeFile="Default.aspx.vb"
   Inherits="_Default" %>
<!DOCTYPE html>
<html xmlns="http://www.w3.org/1999/xhtml">
<head runat="server">
    <title>ValidationSummary Control Example</title>
</head>
<body>
    <form id="form1" runat="server">
    <div>
```

```
        <asp:Label ID="Label1" runat="server" Font-Bold="True" Font-Size="Medium" Font-
            Underline="True" Text="ValidationSummary Control Example"></asp:Label>
            <br />
            <br />
            <asp:Label ID="Label2" runat="server" Text="First Name:  "></asp:Label>
            <asp:TextBox ID="TextBox1" runat="server" Width="174px"></asp:TextBox>
            <asp:RequiredFieldValidator ID="RequiredFieldValidator1" runat="server"
            ControlToValidate="TextBox1" Display="None" ErrorMessage="First Name field can
            not be blank."></asp:RequiredFieldValidator>
            <br />
            <br />
            <asp:Label ID="Label3" runat="server" Text="Last Name:  "></asp:Label>
            <asp:TextBox ID="TextBox2" runat="server" Width="174px"></asp:TextBox>
            <asp:RequiredFieldValidator ID="RequiredFieldValidator2" runat="server"
            ControlToValidate="TextBox2" Display="None" ErrorMessage="Last Name field can
            not be blank."></asp:RequiredFieldValidator>
            <br />
            <br />
            <asp:ValidationSummary ID="ValidationSummary1" runat="server" Height="65px"
            Width="439px" />
            <br />
            <asp:Button ID="Button1" runat="server" BackColor="Black" Font-Bold="True"
            Font-Size="Small" ForeColor="White" Text="Submit" />
        </div>
        </form>
    </body>
    </html>
```

In C#

```
    <%@ Page Language="C#" AutoEventWireup="true" CodeFile="Default.aspx.cs"
      Inherits="_Default" %>
    <!DOCTYPE html>
    <html xmlns="http://www.w3.org/1999/xhtml">
    <head id="Head1" runat="server">
        <title>ValidationSummary Control Example</title>
    </head>
    <body>
        <form id="form1" runat="server">
        <div>
        <asp:Label ID="Label1" runat="server" Font-Bold="True" Font-Size="Medium" Font-
            Underline="True" Text="ValidationSummary Control Example"></asp:Label>
            <br />
            <br />
            <asp:Label ID="Label2" runat="server" Text="First Name:  "></asp:Label>
            <asp:TextBox ID="TextBox1" runat="server" Width="174px"></asp:TextBox>
            <asp:RequiredFieldValidator ID="RequiredFieldValidator1" runat="server"
            ControlToValidate="TextBox1" Display="None" ErrorMessage="First Name field can
            not be blank."></asp:RequiredFieldValidator>
            <br />
            <br />
            <asp:Label ID="Label3" runat="server" Text="Last Name:  "></asp:Label>
            <asp:TextBox ID="TextBox2" runat="server" Width="174px"></asp:TextBox>
            <asp:RequiredFieldValidator ID="RequiredFieldValidator2" runat="server"
            ControlToValidate="TextBox2" Display="None" ErrorMessage="Last Name field can
            not be blank."></asp:RequiredFieldValidator>
            <br />
            <br />
```

```
            <asp:ValidationSummary ID="ValidationSummary1" runat="server" Height="65px"
            Width="439px" />
            <br />
            <asp:Button ID="Button1" runat="server" BackColor="Black" Font-Bold="True"
            Font-Size="Small" ForeColor="White" Text="Submit" />
        </div>
        </form>
    </body>
    </html>
```

Now, run the application and click the Submit button without entering any value in both the TextBox controls. Notice that errors related to both the RequiredFieldValidator controls in the ValidationSummary control appears, as shown in Figure 6.6:

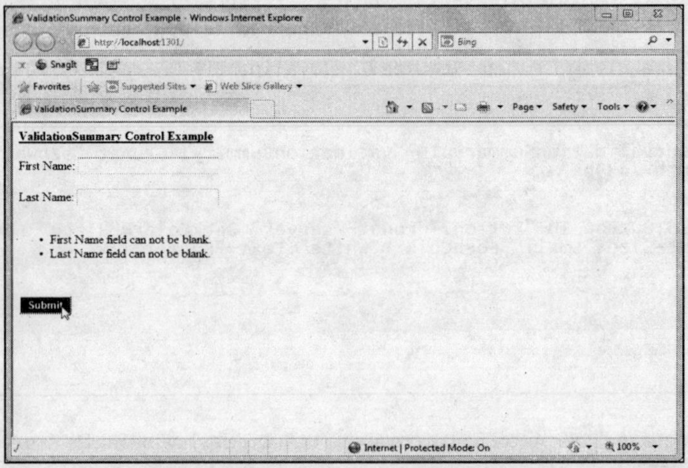

Figure 6.6: ValidationSummary Control on a Web Page Showing Error Messages

Summary

In this chapter, we have learned about the Validation controls, for example, RequiredFieldValidator, CustomValidator, and the rest. These controls are used to validate data entered by the user at the client-end. These Validation controls, in turn, helps in reducing the load on the server by eliminating the need to send every piece of data to the server for validation. The associated control property for each control needs to be set for its association with standard controls. At the time of designing a website, all the Validation controls require an expression property. This property helps validate the data entered by a user in the associated control.

In the next chapter, we describe the WebParts controls.

7

Introducing Web Parts Controls

In Depth

Web Parts controls in ASP.NET are set of controls that work together to enable you to create a Web page which an end user can modify by changing the appearance and behavior of the user interface. In other words, Web Parts controls enable you to build flexible websites that can be customized dynamically at run time. Web Parts are objects of a Web form on which users can perform multiple functions, such as open, close, minimize, or modify the content, behavior, or appearance of a Web Parts control, according to the requirements. Web pages with multiple Web Parts controls are created using `Portal` framework.

In this chapter, we focus on Web Parts controls and their classes that form an integral part of the Portal framework. This chapter also describes how to use Web Parts controls in Visual Studio 2012 to create customizable websites. In addition, you learn how to declare controls in Visual Basic and Visual C#. This chapter also covers the members (properties, methods, and events) of various Web Parts control classes. These members are essential to develop a customizable website.

This chapter mainly deals with the following Web Parts controls:

- WebPartManager
- ProxyWebPartManager
- WebPartZone
- CatalogZone
- DeclarativeCatalogPart
- PageCatalogPart
- ImportCatalogPart
- EditorZone
- LayoutEditorPart
- AppearanceEditorPart
- PropertyGridEditorPart
- BehaviorEditorPart
- ConnectionsZone

Now, let's discuss these controls one by one.

The WebPartManager Control

The `WebPartManager` control acts as a central point that manages all the other Web Parts controls, functionality and events on a Web page. This control coordinates the interaction between Web Parts controls and the events that occur on a Web page. The WebPartManager control manages the personalization states of Web Parts controls on a Web page. Personalization allows storing of user information and all the runtime customizations defined by the user storing of user-specific personalization settings on each page and displays the modes in which users can edit the appearance, properties, and behavior of controls. These customizations are loaded when the user visits the website next time. If you create a Web page that uses Web Parts control, ensure that the page contains a WebPartManager control. There must be only one WebPartManager control on each Web page that uses the Web Parts control, and it must be placed before other Web Parts controls are placed on the Web page. The WebPartManager control is an object of the WebPartManager class.

The `WebPartManager` control performs the following tasks to control the functionality of a Web page:

- Keeping track of different Web Parts controls on a Web page.
- Inserting and removing Web Parts controls on a Web page.

- Establishing, monitoring, and managing connections between various Web Parts controls.
- Enabling you to customize the appearance of a Web page by dragging various Web Parts controls to different locations on the page.
- Providing various views, which you can use to change and personalize the properties and behavior of Web Parts controls.
- Enabling you to toggle between different views of a Web page; thereby, simplifying certain tasks, such as modifying page layout and editing Web Parts controls.
- Enabling you to define and raise the lifecycle events associated with a Web Parts control. Lifecycle events keep track of the Web Parts control to determine when the control is inserted, moved, connected, or removed.

You can insert a `WebPartManager` control by dragging it from the Toolbox and dropping it on the Design view of any page such as Default.aspx page. Figure 7.1 shows the `WebPartManager` control in the Design view:

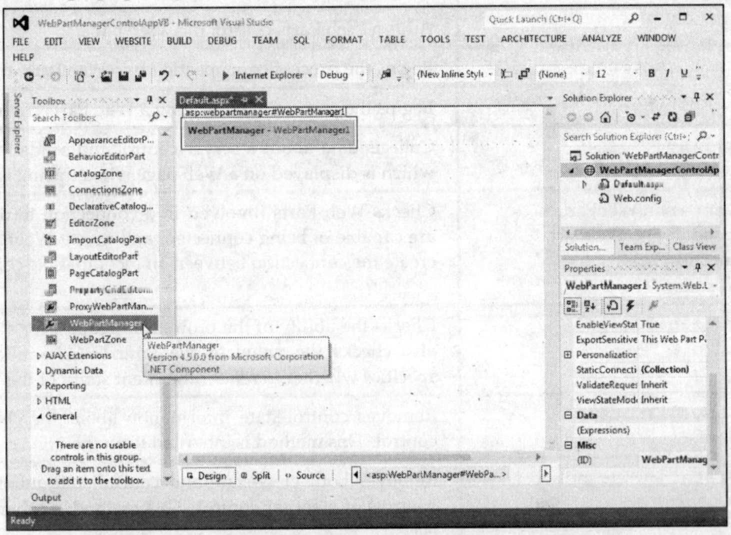

Figure 7.1: Displaying the WebPartManager Control

You can also add the `WebPartManager` control to an application by using the following code in the `<form>` element of the Default.aspx page:

```
<asp:WebPartManager ID="WebPartManager1" runat="server">
  </asp:WebPartManager>
```

NOTE

To use Web Parts controls on each page of a website, a separate WebPartManager control has to be used. However, if you want to use a single WebPartManager control on a multi-paged website containing Web Parts controls, place the WebPartManager control on the master page of the website.

The `WebPartManager` control is created by using the `WebPartManager` class of the .NET Framework class library. This class is available in the `System.Web.UI.WebControls.WebParts` namespace, which resides in the `System.Web` assembly. The inheritance hierarchy of the `WebPartManager` class is as follows:

```
System.Object
  System.Web.UI.Control
        System.Web.UI.WebControls.WebParts.WebPartManager
```

To use the `WebPartManager` control, you need to declare it in the source code of the Web page. The code to declare the source code of `WebPartManager` control in `VB` is:

```
Dim <object name> As WebPartManager
```

The `WebPartManager` class is declared in `VB` as follows:

```
Public Class WebPartManager
   Inherits Control
         Implements INamingContainer, IPersonalizable
```

A declaration for the `WebPartManager` control in `C#` is given as follows:

```
WebPartManager <object name>;
```

The `WebPartManager` class is declared in `C#` as follows:

```
public class WebPartManager : Control, INamingContainer, IPersonalizable
```

Noteworthy methods of the `WebPartManager` class are listed in Table 7.1:

Table 7.1: Noteworthy Methods of the WebPartManager Class

Method	Description
`ActivateConnections`	Activates all currently inactive connections on a Web page.
`AddWebPart`	Adds a Web Parts control to a Web page.
`BeginWebPartConnecting`	Begins the process of connecting two Web Parts control.
`BeginWebPartEditing`	Begins the process of modifying a Web Parts control.
`BuildProfileTree`	Collects data about a server control and sends it to the `Trace` property, which is displayed on a Web page when tracing is enabled for the page.
`CanConnectWebParts`(WebPart, ProviderConnectionPoint, WebPart, ConsumerConnectionPoint, WebPartTransformer)	Checks Web Parts involved in a connection to determine if the controls are capable of being connected. and uses a WebPartTransformer object to create the connection between an incompatible consumer and provider
`CheckRenderClientScript`	Checks the ability of the browser to request for a Web page. This method also checks the value of the `EnableClientScript` property, which specifies whether to render the client script of the Web page or not.
`ClearChildControlState`	Removes control-state information about the child controls of a server control. This method is inherited from the `Control` class.
`ClearChildState`	Removes both view-state and control-state information about the child controls of a server control. This method is inherited from the `Control` class.
`ClearChildViewState`	Removes view-state information about the child controls of a server control. This method is inherited from the `Control` class.
`CloseWebPart`	Closes a Web Parts control so that it is not rendered on a Web page, but can be reopened on the Web page.
`ConnectWebParts`(WebPart, ProviderConnectionPoint, WebPart, ConsumerConnectionPoint, WebPartTransformer)	Connects two Web Parts controls that exist in a `WebPartZoneBase` zone.
`CopyWebPart`	Creates a copy of a Web Parts or server control and inserts the control in a Web page. This method is used by a Web Parts control set. A Web Parts control set is a group of components, which enables users to modify the appearance and behavior of Web pages directly from the browser.
`CreateAvailableTransformers`	Creates a group of transformers specified in a configuration file of a website. These transformers are then added to a collection of transformers, which is referenced by the `AvailableTransformers` property. Transformers are used to create connections between Web Parts controls.

Table 7.1: Noteworthy Methods of the WebPartManager Class

Method	Description
`CreateChildControls`	Determines the server control to create child controls for posting back or rendering.
`CreateControlCollection`	Gets a collection of all the controls placed on a Web page that are managed by using the `WebPartManager` control.
`CreateDisplayModes`	Creates the set of display modes related to a website that has Web Parts controls.
`CreateDynamicConnectionID`	Returns a unique identification number for a dynamic connection.
`CreateDynamicWebPartID`	Creates a unique ID value for a dynamic Web Parts control.
`CreateErrorWebPart`	Creates and inserts a special control into a Web page. This control is displayed only when an error occurs while loading or creating a dynamic Web Parts control.
`CreatePersonalization`	Creates a personalization object that stores the personalization data of the user of a particular Web page.
`CreateWebPart`	Provides Web Parts control functionality to a server control that is not a Web Parts control.
`DeleteWebPart`	Deletes a dynamic instance of a Web Part control.
`DisconnectWebPart`	Deletes a Web Parts or server control, which has been closed or removed from the connections in which it is participating.
`DisconnectWebParts`	Starts the process of disconnecting two Web Part or server controls on a Web page.
`Dispose`	Disposes off a server control completely before releasing it from memory.
`EndWebPartConnecting`	Completes the process of connecting two or more Web Parts controls.
`EndWebPartEditing`	Completes the editing process of a Web Parts control.
`EnsureChildControls`	Identifies whether or not a server control contains child controls. This method also creates child controls for the server control if there are no child controls.
`EnsureID`	Creates an identifier for a Web Parts or server control if the control does not have an identifier assigned to it.
`Equals`	Determines whether a specified object is equal to the current object or not.
`ExportWebPart`	Creates the Extensible Markup Language (XML) file containing state and property information about a server control.
`Finalize`	Enables an object to free resources and perform cleanup operations before the object is retrieved for garbage collection.
`Focus`	Specifies and removes the focus to or from a WebPartManager control
`GetConsumerConnectionPoints`	Obtains a collection of `ConsumerConnectionPoint` objects, which act as connection points from a server control.
`GetCurrentWebPartManager`	Obtains the current instance of a `WebPartManager` control on a Web page.
`GetDesignModeState`	Retrieves design-time data related to a `WebPartManager` control.
`GetDisplayTitle`	Retrieves the string that contains the value for the `DisplayTitle` property of a Web Parts control.
`GetExportUrl`	Retrieves the relative virtual path and the query string when a user tries to export a Web Parts control.

Table 7.1: Noteworthy Methods of the WebPartManager Class

Method	Description
GetGenericWebPart	Obtains a reference to the instance of the GenericWebPart control, which contains a server control.
GetHashCode	Acts as a hash function for the object of the WebPartManager class. A hash function is used to encrypt and decrypt data to make it secure while transferring it over the Internet.
GetProviderConnectionPoints	Obtains a collection of ProviderConnectionPoint objects that serve as connection points from a server control that is acting as a provider within a Web Parts connection.
GetType	Returns a Type value for the current object.
HasControls	Verifies whether a server control contains child controls or not.
HasEvents	Obtains a value to specify whether events are registered for a Web Parts control or child controls.
ImportWebPart	Imports an XML description file containing the state and property data for a Web Parts control.
IsAuthorized	Specifies if a Web Parts or server control can be added to a Web page.
IsLiteralContent	Decides whether a server control stores only literal content. (Literal content is a content that is in plain text only, and not in the form of images or controls).
LoadControlState	Stores state data of a server control saved from a previous page request and return the data on a successive request.
LoadCustomPersonalizationState	Stores custom personalization data, which is passed by personalization objects to a WebPartManager control. Personalization data is used at the time of the initialization process. Personalization objects are used to personalize Web Parts controls.
LoadViewState	Returns view-state information requested by a previous page. The request is saved by the SaveViewState method.
MapPathSecure	Returns the physical path of a control, which is mapped by a virtual path that can be either absolute or relative.
MemberwiseClone	Constructs a copy of the current object source.
MoveWebPart	Changes the location of a server control from one WebPartZoneBase zone to another zone or to a new location within the same zone.
OnAuthorizeWebPart	Invokes the AuthorizeWebPart event and its handler.
OnBubbleEvent	Determines whether the event for a server control is passed up the user interface (UI) server control hierarchy of a Web page.
OnConnectionsActivated	Invokes the ConnectionActivated event to specify whether a Web page and its controls are loaded in the browser. It also indicates whether the connections on the Web page are activated to share data.
OnConnectionsActivating	Invokes the ConnectionActivating event to indicate that a Web page and its controls are loaded in the browser and the process of activating connections on the Web page can begin.
OnDataBinding	Invokes the DataBinding event.

Table 7.1: Noteworthy Methods of the WebPartManager Class	
Method	**Description**
OnDisplayModeChanged	Invokes the DisplayModeChanged event to specify that the process of changing the display mode on a Web page has been finished by the WebPartManager control.
OnDisplayModeChanging	Invokes the DisplayModeChanging event to specify that the WebPartManager control is in the process of changing the display mode on a Web page.
OnInit	Invokes the Init event. This is the first event in the lifecycle of the WebPartManager control.
OnLoad	Invokes the Load event.
OnPreRender	Generates the PreRender event before a WebPartManager control is rendered on a Web page. This method notifies the WebPartManager control to perform any necessary pre-rendering steps prior to saving view-state and rendering content.
OnSelectedWebPartChanged	Generates the SelectedWebPartChanged event after a Web Parts control is selected or its selection cleared.
OnSelectedWebPartChanging	Generates the SelectedWebPartChanging event while changing a selected WebPart control.
OnUnload	Generates the base Unload event to remove a WebPartManager instance from a Web page.
OnWebPartAdded	Generates the WebPartAdded event after a Web Parts control is added to a Web page.
OnWebPartAdding	Generates the WebPartAdding event when a Web Parts control is adding to a WebPartZoneBase zone.
OnWebPartClosed	Generates the WebPartClosed event to indicate the removal of a Web Parts control from a Web page.
OnWebPartClosing	Generates the WebPartClosing event when a Web Parts or server control is removing from a Web page.
OnWebPartDeleted	Generates the WebPartDeleted event after a Web Parts control is permanently deleted from a Web page.
OnWebPartDeleting	Raises the WebPartDeleting event, which indicates that a dynamic WebPart control (or server or user control that is contained in a WebPartZoneBase zone) is in the process of being deleted.
OnWebPartMoved	Generates the WebPartMoved event after a Web Parts control is moved to another location on a Web page.
OnWebPartMoving	Generates the WebPartMoving event to indicate that a Web Parts control in a WebPartZoneBase zone is in the process of being moved.
OnWebPartsConnected	Generates the WebPartsConnected event after a connection is established between Web Parts controls.
OnWebPartsConnecting	Generates the WebPartsConnecting event while establishing a connection between two Web Parts controls.
OnWebPartsDisconnected	Generates the WebPartsDisconnected event after a connection between Web Parts controls terminates.

Table 7.1: Noteworthy Methods of the WebPartManager Class

Method	Description
`OnWebPartsDisconnecting`	Generates the `WebPartsDisconnecting` event, which indicates that two Web Parts controls in a `WebPartZoneBase` zone are going to terminate a connection.
`OpenFile`	Retrieves a stream to read a file. The file path is specified as a parameter.
`RaiseBubbleEvent`	Provides the sources as well as information of the event of a child control to its parent control.
`RegisterClientScript`	Allows a `WebPartManager` control to provide client-side script used for personalization features, such as dragging Web Parts controls in a Web page.
`RemovedControl`	Allows a server control to be removed from the Controls collection of a Control object.
`Render`	Overrides the `Control.Render` (HtmlTextWriter) method so that the `WebPartManager` control is prevented from rendering any content.
`RenderChildren`	Provides the content of the child control of a server control to the `HtmlTextWriter` object, which writes the content to be rendered on the client.
`RenderControl`	Displays the content of a server control and stores information related to tracing, if tracing is enabled.
`ResolveAdapter`	Retrieves the control adapter that renders a specified control.
`ResolveClientUrl`	Obtains a URL used by the browser in which you want to run your website.
`ResolveUrl`	Converts a URL so that it is usable on the requesting client.
`SaveControlState`	Stores state-related data for a `WebPartManager` control. You can restore the data by requesting the Web page containing the `WebPartManager` control.
`SaveCustomPersonalizationState`	Stores custom personalization state data maintained by a `WebPartManager` control for a Web page, so that this data is reloaded whenever the Web page is reloaded.
`SaveViewState`	Stores the changes in a server control view-state. This method saves only those changes that occur when a Web page is posted back to the server.
`SetDesignModeState`	Specifies design-time data for a control.
`SetPersonalizationDirty`	Specifies a flag, which specifies whether the custom personalization data for a `WebPartManager` control has changed or not.
`SetRenderMethodDelegate`	Allocates an event handler delegate to provide the content of a server control to the parent control.
`SetSelectedWebPart`	Specifies the values for the `SelectedWebPart` property so that it is equal to the value of the currently selected Web Part control.
`ToString`	Returns a `String` value, which represents the current object.
`TrackViewState`	Enables tracking of the changes in the view-state data of a `WebPartManager` control. To enable tracking, the method calls the base Control.TrackViewState() method.

Noteworthy properties of the `WebPartManager` class are listed in Table 7.2:

Table 7.2: Noteworthy Properties of the WebPartManager Class

Property	Description
`Adapter`	Retrieves the browser-specific adapter for a `WebPartManager` control.
`AppRelativeTemplateSourceDirectory`	Retrieves or specifies the application-relative virtual directory of a Web page or object that contains a `WebPartManager` control.
`AvailableTransformers`	Retrieves a collection of `WebPartTransformer` objects available for creating Web Parts connections between server controls.
`BindingContainer`	Retrieves a server control containing a `WebPartManager` control's data-binding properties.
`ChildControlsCreated`	Retrieves a value that indicates whether or not the child controls of a server control are created.
`ClientID`	Enables you to use a server control identifier generated by ASP.NET.
`ClientIDSeparator`	Retrieves a character value that represents the separator character used in the `ClientID` property.
`CloseProviderWarning`	Retrieves and specifies a warning message displayed if a user closes a server control acting as a provider to the other server controls in a connection.
`Connections`	Retrieves a reference to a set of current connections on a Web page.
`Context`	Retrieves the `HttpContext` object for the current Web request. The `HttpContext` object encapsulates request information, such as the user and the machine accessing the website.
`Controls`	Retrieves a collection of all WebPart, server, or user controls contained in the `WebPartZoneBase` zones on a Web page.
`DeleteWarning`	Retrieves and specifies a custom warning message, displayed when a server control is deleted.
`DesignMode`	Retrieves a value that indicates if a server control is used on a design surface.
`DisplayMode`	Retrieves or specifies the display mode for a Web page containing Web Parts controls.
`DisplayModes`	Retrieves a set of display modes in the read-only mode associated with a `WebPartManager` control.
`DynamicConnections`	Retrieves a collection of dynamic connections that exist on a Web page.
`EnableClientScript`	Retrieves or specifies a value that specifies whether or not client-side scripting is enabled on a Web page containing `WebPartManager` control.
`EnableTheming`	Retrieves a value that determines whether or not a theme is enabled on a Web page.
`EnableViewState`	Retrieves or specifies a value to indicate whether a server control persists its view-state, and the view-state of any child controls it contains, to the requesting client.
`Events`	Retrieves a list of event handlers for a `WebPartManager` control.
`ExportSensitiveDataWarning`	Retrieves or specifies the text for a warning message, which is displayed when a user exports sensitive data from a WebPart control.
`HasChildViewState`	Retrieves a value that indicates whether or not the child controls of the current server control have saved view-state settings.
`ID`	Retrieves or specifies the identifier of a Web server control.

Table 7.2: Noteworthy Properties of the WebPartManager Class

Property	Description
IdSeparator	Retrieves the character used for separating control identifiers for the child controls of the WebPartManager control.
Internals	Retrieves a reference to the WebPartManagerInternals class, which is used to combine and separate a set of methods implemented in the WebPartManager class.
IsChildControlStateCleared	Retrieves a value indicating whether the child controls of the WebPartManager control possess control-state, which holds information specific to a control, which is essential to send to the server at the time of postback.
IsCustomPersonalizationState Dirty	Retrieves a value that indicates whether any personalization changes have been made that affect page-level personalization details of a WebPartManager control.
IsTrackingViewState	Retrieves a value indicating that a server control is saving the changes to its view-state.
IsViewStateEnabled	Retrieves a value that indicates whether the view-state is enabled for a WebPartManager control.
LoadViewStateByID	Retrieves a value that indicates whether the view-state of a WebPartManager control can be loaded by ID instead of index.
NamingContainer	Retrieves the reference to the naming container of the Web server control to create a unique namespace for every Web server control.
Page	Retrieves a reference to the Web page instance that contains a WebPartManager control.
Parent	Retrieves a reference to the parent control of a server control in the control hierarchy of a Web page.
Personalization	Retrieves a reference to the object containing the data needed to personalize a Web page.
SelectedWebPart	Returns a reference to the currently selected Web Parts or server control.
Site	Returns information about the container control, which stores the current control when it is modified in the Design view.
SkinID	Obtains or specifies an empty string to ensure that a user cannot apply any skin to a WebPartManager control.
StaticConnections	Returns a reference to the collection of all WebPartConnection objects that are defined as static connections on a Web page.
SupportedDisplayModes	Retrieves a set of all display modes available on a particular Web page. This is a read-only property.
TemplateControl	Obtains or specifies the reference to the template containing the current control.
TemplateSourceDirectory	Returns the virtual directory of the Web page containing the WebPartManager control. This property is inherited from the Control class.
UniqueID	Returns a unique identifier for a server control. This property is inherited from the Control class.

Table 7.2: Noteworthy Properties of the WebPartManager Class	
Property	**Description**
`ViewState`	Retrieves a dictionary of state information that allows users to save and restore the view-state of a server control across multiple requests for the same Web page.
`ViewStateIgnoresCase`	Gets a value that indicates whether the `StateBag` object is insensitive.
`Visible`	Retrieves a value to make the child controls of a `WebPartManager` control visible.
`WebParts`	Returns a reference to all WebPart controls on a Web page that are monitored by a `WebPartManager` control.
`Zones`	Returns a reference to a collection of all `WebPartZoneBase` zones included on a Web page.

Noteworthy events of the `WebPartManager` class are listed in Table 7.3:

Table 7.3: Noteworthy Events of the WebPartManager Class	
Event	**Description**
`AuthorizeWebPart`	Initiated when the `IsAuthorized` method is invoked. This event determines whether a WebPart or server control can be added to a Web page.
`ConnectionsActivated`	Initiated after all Web Parts connections specified on a Web page connect and start sharing data between consumer and provider controls. Consumer controls are those controls that receive data while provider controls are those that send data.
`ConnectionsActivating`	Initiated during the process of activating all established Web Parts connections on a Web page.
`DataBinding`	Initiated after a server control binds to a data source. This event is inherited from the `Control` class.
`DisplayModeChanged`	Initiated when the display mode of a Web page is changed.
`DisplayModeChanging`	Initiated after a user clicks a verb (a menu item displayed by a Web Part) on a Web page that begins the process of changing the display mode of Web page.
`Disposed`	Initiated when a server control of a Web page is released from memory, which is the last stage of the server control lifecycle when an ASP.NET page is requested.
`Init`	Initiated when a server control is initialized.
`Load`	Initiated when a server control is loaded into the Web page.
`PreRender`	Initiated when a server control is loaded but not yet rendered.
`SelectedWebPartChanged`	Initiated after moving or changing a selected WebPart or server control to another control.
`SelectedWebPartChanging`	Initiated during the process of changing the selected Web Parts or server control.
`Unload`	Initiated when a server control is unloaded from memory.
`WebPartAdded`	Initiated when a dynamic Web Parts or server control is added to a `WebPartZoneBase` zone. This event indicates that the control is added successfully.

Table 7.3: Noteworthy Events of the WebPartManager Class	
Event	**Description**
`WebPartAdding`	Occurs when a dynamic Web Parts or server control is added to a `WebPartZoneBase` zone at run time Successfully.
`WebPartClosed`	Initiated when a WebPart control is deleted from a Web page.
`WebPartClosing`	Initiated during the process of deleting a WebPart control from a Web page.
`WebPartDeleted`	Initiated after a Web Parts or server control is deleted from a `WebPartZoneBase` zone.
`WebPartDeleting`	Occurs when permanently deleting an instance of a dynamic WebPart control from a `WebPartZoneBase` zone.
`WebPartMoved`	Initiated when the location of a Web Parts or server control on a Web page has changed.
`WebPartMoving`	Initiated when a Web Parts or server control contained in the `WebPartZoneBase` zone is in the process of moving.
`WebPartsConnected`	Initiated after a connection between WebPart controls has been established.
`WebPartsConnecting`	Initiated during the process of establishing a connection between WebPart controls in a `WebPartZoneBase` zone.
`WebPartsDisconnected`	Initiated during the termination of the connection between two WebPart or server controls.
`WebPartsDisconnecting`	Initiated during the process of terminating the connection between WebPart or server controls.

The ProxyWebPartManager Control

As you know, a Web Parts application (an application using Web Parts controls) can contain a single `WebPartManager` control for each Web page, which manages all the Web Parts controls on that page. You also know that if the Web Parts application contains a master page and the `WebPartManager` control is placed in the master page, then all the content pages (Web pages inherited from the master page) use the `WebPartManager` control of the master page to manage their Web Parts controls. To do this, each content page declares a static link to connect to the `WebPartManager` control of the master page. To declare a static link in the content page, you need to add the `ProxyWebPartManager` control and the `<asp:WebPartConnection>` element in an ASP.NET application.

The `<asp:WebPartConnection>` element is derived from the `<staticconnections>` element, which is further derived from the `<asp:WebPartManager>` element. In this way, the `ProxyWebPartManager` control behave similar as the `WebPartManager` control of the master page in the content page. However, remember that because the `WebPartManager` control is already declared in the master page once, you cannot declare additional `WebPartManager` controls in the content pages. If you do want to declare more `WebPartManager` controls, you have to use the `ProxyWebPartManager` control. This is how a `ProxyWebPartManager` control imitates a `WebPartManager` control residing in a master page.

You can add a `ProxyWebPartManager` control to a Web page by dragging and dropping the control from the Toolbox to the Design view. Figure 7.2 shows the `ProxyWebPartManager` control in the Design view:

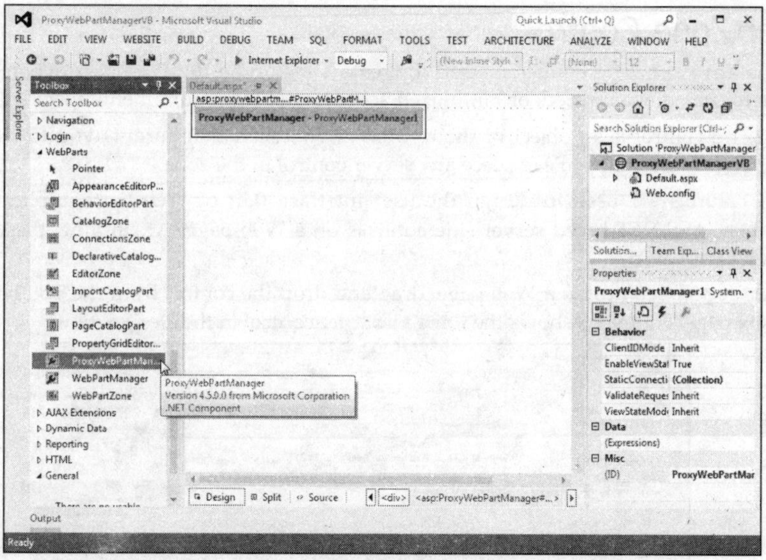

Figure 7.2: Displaying the ProxyWebPartManager Control

Although the `ProxyWebPartManager` control is used to replace the `WebPartManager` control for declaring static connections, the `ProxyWebPartManager` class is not derived from the `WebPartManager` class. Rather, it is derived from the `Control` class.

NOTE

A static connection is the connection that are always available to all users.

The `ProxyWebPartManager` control is an object of the `ProxyWebPartManager` class. You can also create the `ProxyWebPartManager` control by using the `ProxyWebPartManager` class, which belongs to the `System.Web.dll` assembly. The namespace hierarchy of the `ProxyWebPartManager` class is as follows:

```
System.Object
  System.Web.UI.Control
       System.Web.UI.WebControls.WebParts.ProxyWebPartManager
```

The `ProxyWebPartManager` class inherits various properties from the `Control` class, such as `EnableTheming` and `Visible`. This class uses these properties by overriding them. In addition to various inherited properties, the `ProxyWebPartManager` class also contains a non-inherited property, called `StaticConnections`. The `StaticConnections` property gets a collection of static connections declared within the `<asp:ProxyWebPartManager>` element on a content page. Similar to properties, the `ProxyWebPartManager` class also inherits various events and methods from the `Control` class.

The syntax to declare the `ProxyWebPartManager` control in `VB` is given as follows:

```
Dim <object name> As ProxyWebPartManager
```

The syntax for declaring the `ProxyWebPartManager` control using the `ProxyWebPartManager` class in `C#` is given as follows:

```
ProxyWebPartManager <object name>;
```

The `ProxyWebPartManager` class is declared in `VB` as follows:

```
Public Class ProxyWebPartManager
Inherits Control
```

The `ProxyWebPartManager` class is declared in `C#` as follows:

```
public class ProxyWebPartManager : Control
```

The WebPartZone Control

Technically, the `WebPartZone` control is used to create a region on the Web page where Web Parts or server controls can be relocated, maximized, or minimized according to the requirements specified by a user.

The `WebPartZone` control is an object of the `WebPartZone` class that permits you to create zones on a Web page. After the zone is created, you can place any server control in the zone.

`WebPartZone` controls are used to design the user interface (UI) of Web Parts applications. These controls enable you to host ASP.NET-based server-side controls on a Web page. At runtime, these server-side controls function as Web Parts controls.

To add a `WebPartZone` control to a Web page, drag and drop the control from the Toolbox to the Design view of a Default.aspx page. Figure 7.3 shows the `WebPartZone` control in the Design view:

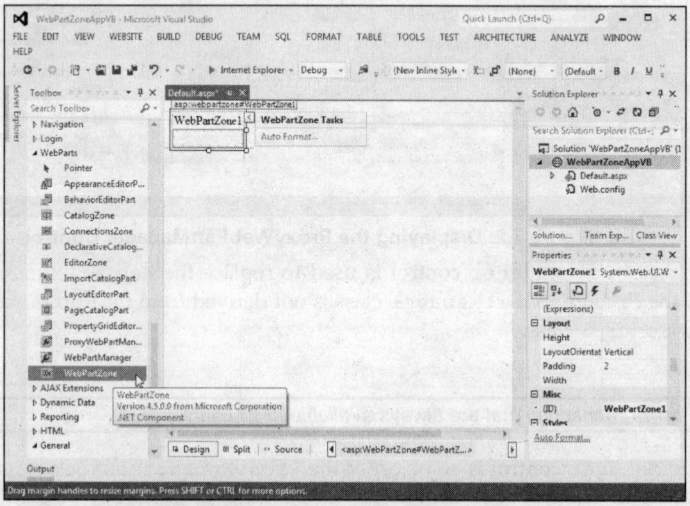

Figure 7.3: Displaying the WebPartZone Control

You can also add the `WebPartZone` control by inserting the following code in the `<form>` element of the `Default.aspx` page:

```
<asp:WebPartZone ID="WebPartZone1" runat="server">
  </asp:WebPartZone>
```

NOTE

The WebPartZone control also contains the <ZoneTemplate> element, which is used for storing other server controls, such as Label or Textbox.

The `WebPartZone` control is created by using the `WebPartZone` class of the .NET Framework class library. This class derives most of its functionalities from the base `WebZone` and `WebPartZoneBase` classes. The `WebPartZone` class is available in the `System.Web.UI.WebControls.WebParts` namespace. The namespace hierarchy of the `WebPartZone` class is as follows:

```
System.Object
   System.Web.UI.Control
           System.Web.UI.WebControls.WebControl
                     System.Web.UI.WebControls.CompositeControl
                               System.Web.UI.WebControls.WebParts.WebZone
                                         System.Web.UI.WebControls.WebParts.WebPartZoneBase
                                                   System.Web.UI.WebControls.WebParts.WebPartZone
```

You can use the various properties and methods of the `WebPartZone` class to use the `WebPartZone` control. The properties of the `WebPartZone` class allow you to set the appearance and behavior of the `WebPartZone` control on a Web page. The `WebPartZone` control is the primary control to add Web Parts controls on the Web page. You can add server controls in the `WebPartZone` control, which can be added to the Web page.

The syntax for creating a `WebPartZone` control in `VB` is given as follows:

```
Dim <object name> As WebPartZone
```

The syntax for creating a `WebPartZone` control in `C#` is given as follows:

```
WebPartZone <object name>;
```

Using the .NET Framework class library, the `WebPartZone` class is declared in `VB` as follows:

```
Public Class WebPartZone
   Inherits WebPartZoneBase
```

Using the .NET Framework class library, the `WebPartZone` class is declared in `C#` as follows:

```
public class WebPartZone : WebPartZoneBase
```

Noteworthy methods of the `WebPartZone` class are listed in Table 7.4:

Table 7.4: Noteworthy Methods of the WebPartZone Class

Method	Description
`CreateWebPartChrome`	Enables derived zones to substitute a custom `WebPartChrome` object to the appearance of Web Parts controls in a zone
`EditWebPart`	Initiates the process of editing a selected Web Parts control in a zone
`GetInitialWebParts`	Overrides the abstract base method and retrieves the initial set of values of static `WebPart` controls contained within a zone's template
`MinimizeWebPart`	Minimizes a selected Web Parts control in a zone
`OnCreateVerbs`	Raises the CreateVerbs event
`RenderDropCue`	Provides UI elements to indicate where a Web Parts control is dragged and dropped within a zone
`RestoreWebPart`	Restores a selected minimized Web Parts control to the normal state

Noteworthy properties of the `WebPartZone` class are listed in Table 7.5:

Table 7.5: Noteworthy Properties of the WebPartZone Class

Property	Description
`AllowLayoutChange`	Determines whether or not the layout of a Web Parts control can be modified. This property also allows you to specify a layout for the Web Parts control.
`DragDropEnabled`	Retrieves a value indicating whether or not Web Parts controls can be dragged and dropped into or out of a zone.
`EditVerb`	Obtains a reference to the `WebPartVerb` class object to change a Web Parts control into the `WebPartZone` control.
`ExportVerb`	Obtains a reference to the `WebPartVerb` class object to export an XML definition for a Web Parts control
`HelpVerb`	Obtains a reference to the `WebPartVerb` class object to access help content for using Web Parts controls in a `WebPartZone` control.
`LayoutOrientation`	Determines whether the controls in a `WebPartZone` control are aligned horizontally or vertically. This property also enables you to specify the alignment of the Web Parts controls in a `WebPartZone` control.
`MenuCheckImageStyle`	Determines the image style used as a check mark for a verbs menu of a Web Parts control in a `WebPartZone` control.

Table 7.5: Noteworthy Properties of the WebPartZone Class

Property	Description
`MenuCheckImageUrl`	Determines or specifies a URL for the image used as a check mark for the verbs menu of a Web Parts control in a `WebPartZone` control.
`MenuLabelHoverStyle`	Obtains or specifies the styles used to change the appearance of the label of a verbs menu when the mouse pointer is placed over it.
`MenuLabelStyle`	Obtains or specifies the style applied to the label of a verbs menu that is displayed in the title bar of a Web Parts control in a `WebPartZone` control.
`MenuLabelText`	Obtains or specifies the label for the verbs menu displayed in the title bar of a Web Parts control in a `WebPartZone` control.
`MenuPopupImageUrl`	Obtains or specifies the URL of the image that represents the verbs menu in the title bar of a Web Parts control in the `WebPartZone` control.
`MenuPopupStyle`	Obtains the style applied to the verbs menu of a Web Parts control in a `WebPartZone` control.
`MenuVerbHoverStyle`	Obtains the style applied to change the appearance of the verb displayed in a verbs menu when the mouse pointer is placed over the verb.
`MenuVerbStyle`	Obtains the style for the verb in a verbs menu of a Web Parts control in a `WebPartZone` control.
`MinimizeVerb`	Obtains a reference to the `WebPartVerb` class object to minimize a `Web Parts` control in a `WebPartZone` control.
`RestoreVerb`	Obtains a reference to the `WebPartVerb` class object to set the size of a `Web Parts` control in a `WebPartZone` control to normal.
`SelectedPartChromeStyle`	Obtains the style for a Web Parts control in a `WebPartZone` control.
`ShowTitleIcons`	Determines the icons displayed in the title bar of a Web Part control in the `WebPartZone` control.
`TitleBarVerbButtonType`	Determines the button type used for the verbs in the title bar of a Web Parts control.
`TitleBarVerbStyle`	Obtains the style for the verbs displayed in the title bar of a Web Parts control.
`VerbButtonType`	Retrieves or specifies the type of button associated with the verbs in the title bar of a Web Parts control.
`WebPartChrome`	Retrieves a reference to a `WebPartChrome` control that determines the peripheral rendering of a Web Parts control in a zone.
`WebParts`	Retrieves a collection of Web Parts controls within a zone.
`WebPartVerbRenderMode`	Retrieves or specifies a value indicating how the verbs should be rendered on Web Parts controls in a zone.
`ZoneTemplate`	Retrieves or specifies the template reference containing controls in a Web page.

Noteworthy event of the `WebPartZone` class is listed in Table 7.6:

Table 7.6: Noteworthy Event of the WebPartZone Class

Event	Description
`CreateVerbs`	Initiated when the verbs are created for a zone derived from the `WebPartZoneBase` class

The CatalogZone Control

You can personalize a website by adding the catalog functionality, which allows you to manage Web Parts controls efficiently. You can create a catalog-enabled Web page by adding a `CatalogZone` control to it.

A `CatalogZone` control helps to create a catalog of Web Parts controls. This allows a user to add or update the controls easily on a Web page. To add a `CatalogZone` control to a Web page, simply drag and drop the `CatalogZone` control from the Toolbox to the Design view of a Default.aspx page. Figure 7.4 shows the `CatalogZone` control in the Design view:

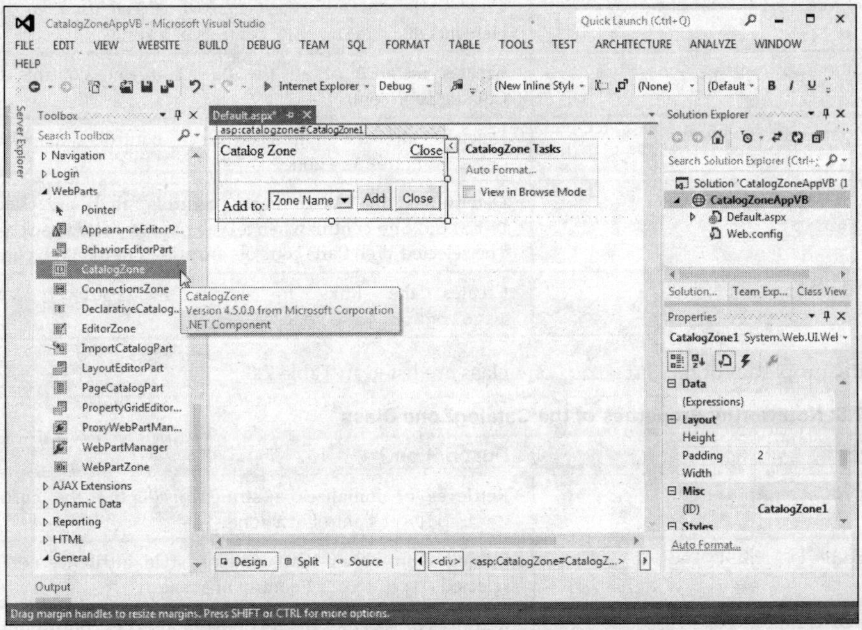

Figure 7.4: Displaying the CatalogZone Control

You can also add the `CatalogZone` control by inserting the following code in the `<form>` element of the `Default.aspx` page:

```
<asp:CatalogZone ID="CatalogZone1" runat="server">
  </asp:CatalogZone>
```

When you add a `CatalogZone` control to a Web page, a new mode, called the `Catalog` mode, appears in the Select mode list on the Web page. The `CatalogZone` control is displayed when the Web page is in the `Catalog` mode allowing users to add controls on the Web page contained in it and is also known as template control. Therefore, the control needs a template section, which is represented as the `<ZoneTemplate>` element inside the `CatalogZone control` section. Inside the template section, you can place several `CatalogPart` controls, where every `CatalogPart` control works as a container control for server controls, which can be added on a Web page. The `CatalogZone` control is an object of the `CatalogZone` class. Remember that you can view a `CatalogZone` control on a Web page only after changing the display mode of the control to the `CatalogDisplayMode` mode.

The `CatalogZone` control is created by using the `CatalogZone` class of the .NET Framework class library. This class is available in the `System.Web.UI.WebControls.WebParts` namespace.

The inheritance hierarchy of the `CatalogZone` class is as follows:

```
System.Object
  System.Web.UI.Control
     System.Web.UI.WebControls.WebControl
        System.Web.UI.WebControls.CompositeControl
```

```
System.Web.UI.WebControls.WebParts.WebZone
  System.Web.UI.WebControls.WebParts.ToolZone
    System.Web.UI.WebControls.WebParts.CatalogZoneBase
      System.Web.UI.WebControls.WebParts.CatalogZone
```

Noteworthy methods of the CatalogZone class are listed in Table 7.7:

Table 7.7: Noteworthy Methods of the CatalogZone Class

Method	Description
CreateCatalogPartChrome	Creates the CatalogPartChrome object used to render the UI elements of CatalogPart controls in a zone.
CreateCatalogParts	Creates instance of all the CatalogPart controls declared in a CatalogZone control.
InvalidateCatalogParts	Deletes all the CatalogPart controls associated with a CatalogZoneBase zone.
LoadPostData	Determines the Web Parts controls that are selected in the CatalogZone control when a Web page is posted back to a Web server. The selected Web Parts controls are added to the Web page.
RenderCatalogPartLinks	Creates the links to every CatalogPart control in a CatalogZoneBase zone.

Noteworthy properties of the CatalogZone class are listed in Table 7.8:

Table 7.8: Noteworthy Properties of the CatalogZone Class

Property	Description
SelectedCatalogPartID	Retrieves or initializes a string to identify the currently selected CatalogPart control in a zone.
SelectedPartLinkStyle	Retrieves an object that contains style attributes for the currently selected CatalogPart control in a zone.
SelectTargetZoneText	Retrieves or specifies the text next to a server control in the catalog UI. This allows a user to select the zone for adding selected controls.
ShowCatalogIcons	Retrieves or specifies a value to indicate whether server controls in a CatalogZone control display their associated icons or not.

The DeclarativeCatalogPart Control

The DeclarativeCatalogPart control is one of the three controls (the other controls are PageCatalogPart and ImportCatalogPart) used together with the CatalogZone control. This control is used to modify the functionality of a Web page. This control displays a list of Web Parts controls and other server controls, when the website is in the CatalogDisplayMode mode. A user can add controls from this catalog onto the Web page.

The DeclarativeCatalogPart control is an object of the DeclarativeCatalogPart class. You can add a DeclarativeCatalogPart control to a Default.aspx page by dragging and dropping the control from the Toolbox to the CatalogZone control in the Design view of a Default.aspx page. While adding a DeclarativeCatalogPart control to a Web page, ensure that the Web page contains the CatalogZone control.

Figure 7.5 shows the DeclarativeCatalogPart control inside the CatalogZone control in the Design view:

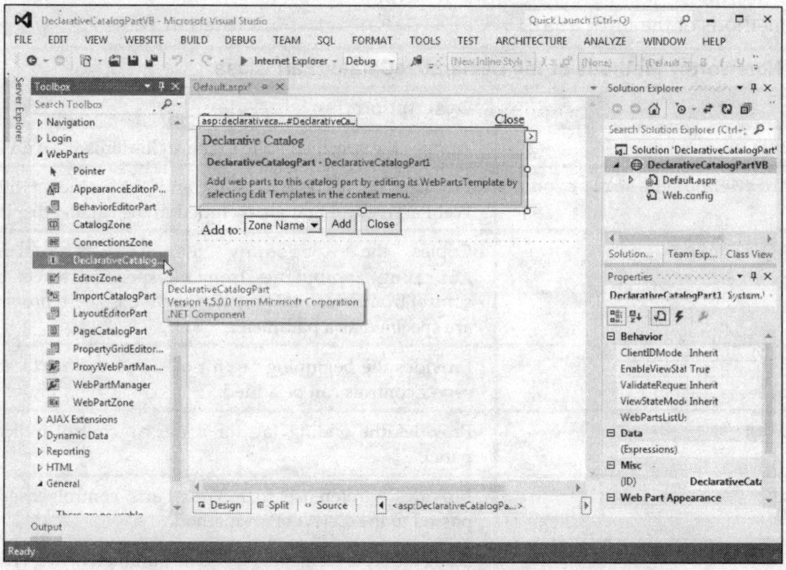

Figure 7.5: Displaying the DeclarativeCatalogPart Control

You can also add the `DeclarativeCatalogPart` control by using the following code in the `<form>` element of the `Default.aspx` page:

```
<asp:CatalogZone ID="CatalogZone1" runat="server">
   <ZoneTemplate>
   <asp:DeclarativeCatalogPart ID="DeclarativeCatalogPart1"
   runat="server">
   </asp:DeclarativeCatalogPart>
   </ZoneTemplate>
</asp:CatalogZone>
```

The `DeclarativeCatalogPart` control is created by using the `DeclarativeCatalogPart` class of the .NET Framework class library. This class is available in the `System.Web.UI.WebControls.WebParts` namespace.

The inheritance hierarchy of this class is as follows:

```
System.Object
   System.Web.UI.Control
       System.Web.UI.WebControls.WebControl
           System.Web.UI.WebControls.Panel
               System.Web.UI.WebControls.WebParts.Part
                   System.Web.UI.WebControls.WebParts.CatalogPart
                       System.Web.UI.WebControls.WebParts.DeclarativeCatalogPart
```

Now, let's identify the syntax for declaring the `DeclarativeCatalogPart` control by using the `DeclarativeCatalogPart` class.

The syntax for declaring the `DeclarativeCatalogPart` control in `VB` is given as follows:

```
Dim control  DeclarativeCatalogPart as DeclarativeCatalogPart
```

The syntax for declaring the `DeclarativeCatalogPart` control in `C#` is given as follows:

```
DeclarativeCatalogPart control_ DeclarativeCatalogPart;
```

You can create a user control made of one or more server controls and add it to the `DeclarativeCatalogPart` control. To do so, you have to set the `WebPartsListUserControlPath` property of the `DeclarativeCatalogPart` class to the path of the user control, which is preferred to adding server controls, because you can display the catalog of Web Parts controls on multiple pages of a website by using the same user control. When the Web Parts controls in a user control are modified, all the catalogs associated with the user control are updated automatically by the `DeclarativeCatalogPart` control.

Noteworthy methods of the `DeclarativeCatalogPart` class are listed in Table 7.9:

Table 7.9: Noteworthy Methods of the DeclarativeCatalogPart Class

Method	Description
`ApplyStyle`	Applies the specified style to the style elements of a WebPart control.
`GetAvailableWebpartDescriptions`	Provides details (such as ID and the value of other properties) of a WebPart control that are included in the catalog displayed on a Web page.
`CopyBaseAttributes`	Copies the `AccessKey`, `Enabled`, `ToolTip`, `TabIndex`, and `Attributes` properties from the specified server control to the server control from which this method is called. These properties and their values are specified as a parameter.
`RenderBeginTag`	Provides the beginning tag for a `Panel` control to add a panel on which server controls can be added.
`RenderEndTag`	Provides the ending tag for a `Panel` control indicating the end of the panel.
`GetWebPart`	Provides a reference to a Web Parts control based on the description passed to the GetWebPart method.
`MergeStyle`	Adds the style elements passed as parameters to a Web Parts control.

Noteworthy properties of the `DeclarativeCatalogPart` class are listed in Table 7.10:

Table 7.10: Noteworthy Properties of the DeclarativeCatalogPart Class

Property	Description
`AccessKey`	Represents a keyboard shortcut key with which you can access a DeclarativeCatalogPart control
`BackColor`	Specifies or determines the background color of a WebPart control
`ChromeType`	Determines or specifies the border of a WebPart control
`ChromeState`	Determines whether a WebPart control is in the minimized or normal state
`ControlStyle`	Determines the style of a WebPart control
`ControlStyleCreated`	Determines whether a style has been indicated for a WebPart control by using the `ControlStyle` property
`HasAttributes`	Determines whether a WebPart control has attributes set or not
`WebPartsListUserControlPath`	Determines or specifies the path of a user control that contains WebPart controls for a catalog
`WebPartsTemplate`	Specifies or determines a template reference for containing WebPart controls of a catalog
`BorderWidth`	Specifies or determines the width of the border of a WebPart control
`CssClass`	Specifies or determines the Cascading Style Sheet (`CSS`) class for a WebPart control
`Font`	Determines the font of a WebPart control
`ForeColor`	Specifies the foreground color of a WebPart control
`GroupingText`	Specifies a caption for the controls contained in a control
`Height`	Specifies the height of a WebPart control

Table 7.10: Noteworthy Properties of the DeclarativeCatalogPart Class

Property	Description
`HorizontalAlign`	Determines the horizontal alignment of the content in a `Panel` control
`ScrollBars`	Determines and specifies the setting for the scroll bars, such as their appearance and position
`TabIndex`	Determines the tab index of a WebPart control
`ToolTip`	Specifies the text that is displayed when the mouse pointer is placed on a WebPart control
`Width`	Specifies the width of a WebPart control
`Wrap`	Determines whether the text displayed in a control should wrap or not
`BackImageUrl`	Specifies the URL of the image displayed in a control

NOTE

These properties are not used by the Web Parts control set when rendering a DeclarativeCatalogPart control. The property is overridden only for the purpose of preventing it from appearing in Microsoft Visual Studio 2012 designer tools.

The PageCatalogPart Control

The `PageCatalogPart` control is used with the `CatalogZone` control to add a specific functionality to the catalog section of a Web page. This control allows users to restore previously deleted WebPart controls of a Web page. This is the only way users have to restore the deleted Web Parts controls. The `PageCatalogPart` control adds a list of check boxes to the catalog zone controls corresponding to each deleted Web Parts control. To restore these controls on the Web page, users simply need to select the required check box and a Web part zone where the Web Parts control is to be added, and click the Add button.

To add the `PageCatalogPart` control to the `CatalogZone` control, drag and drop the `PageCatalogPart` control from the Toolbox to the `CatalogZone` control in the Design view of a Default.aspx page. Figure 7.6 shows the `PageCatalogPart` control inside the `CatalogZone` control in the Design view:

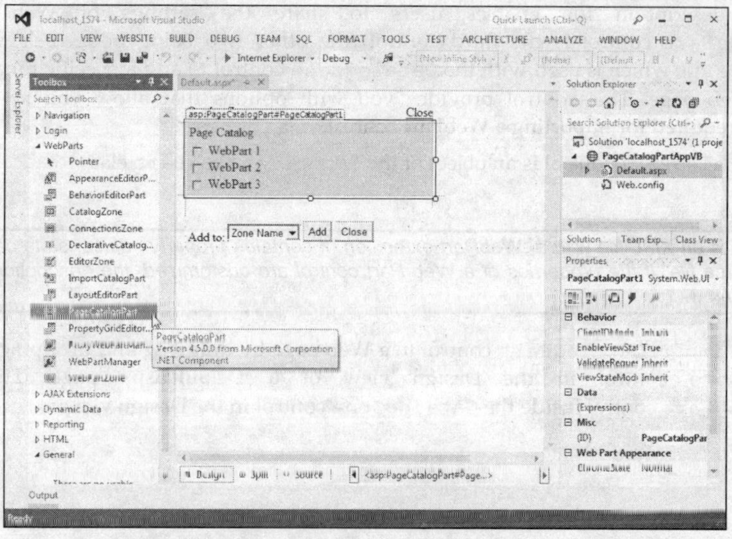

Figure 7.6: Displaying the PageCatalogPart Control

You can also add the PageCatalogPart control using the following code in the <form> element of the Default.aspx page:

```
<asp:CatalogZone ID="CatalogZone1" runat="server" Height="183px" Width="318px">
  <ZoneTemplate>
       <asp:PageCatalogPart ID="PageCatalogPart1" runat="server"
       Height="198px" />
  </ZoneTemplate>
</asp:CatalogZone>
```

The PageCatalogPart control is an object of the PageCatalogPart class. This control is associated to the PageCatalogPart class, which provides the same events, methods, and properties as those provided by the CatalogZone class.

The inheritance hierarchy of the PageCatalogPart control is given as follows:

```
System.Object
   System.Web.UI.Control
       System.Web.UI.WebControls.WebControl
           System.Web.UI.WebControls.Panel
               System.Web.UI.WebControls.WebParts.Part
                   System.Web.UI.WebControls.WebParts.CatalogPart
                        System.Web.UI.WebControls.WebParts.PageCatalogPart
```

You can declare the PageCatalogPart class in VB or C# programming language to add a PageCatalogPart control. The syntax to declare the PageCatalogPart class in VB is given as follows:

```
Dim pagecatalog1part as PageCatalogPart
```

The syntax to declare the PageCatalogPart class in C# is given as follows:

```
PageCatalogPart pagecatalog1part;
```

NOTE

To know more about the PageCatalogPart class, refer to the Immediate Solutions section of this chapter.

The ImportCatalogPart Control

The ImportCatalogPart control imports the description file of a Web Parts control or server control that is used as a Web Parts control. This enables the server control to be added to a Web page with pre-assigned settings. The description file enables users to share the settings of Web Parts controls. The ImportCatalogPart control is the third control (the other two being DeclarativeCatalogPart and PageCatalogPart), which is used with the CatalogZone control to add a specific functionality to the catalog section of a Web page. This control provides you with options that allow you to browse and upload a description file required for importing a WebPart control.

The ImportCatalogPart control is an object of the ImportCatalogPart class.

NOTE

A description file is an XML file with a .WebPart extension. It contains property values, state data, and reference to the assembly or source file. If the properties of a Web Part control are customized, the description file contains values for these properties as well.

You can add an ImportCatalogPart control to a Web page by dragging and dropping it from the Toolbox to the CatalogZone control in the Design view of a Default.aspx page. Figure 7.7 shows the ImportCatalogPart control inside the CatalogZone control in the Design view:

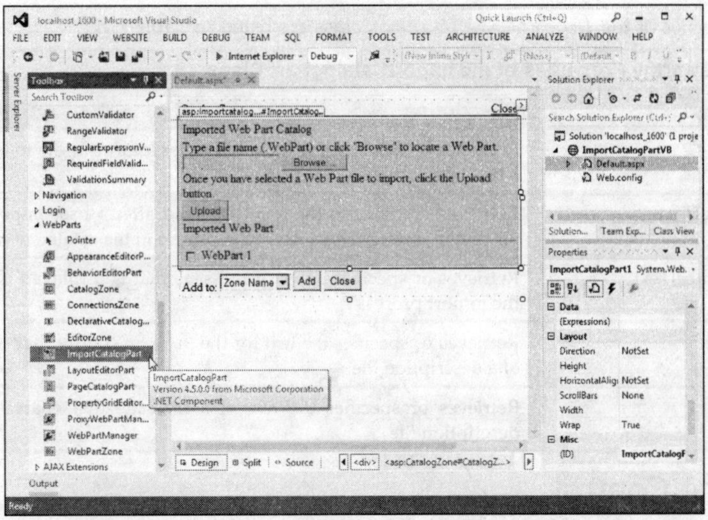

Figure 7.7: Displaying the ImportCatalogPart Control

You can also add the `ImportCatalogPart` control by using the following code in the `<form>` element of the `Default.aspx` page:

```
<asp:CatalogZone ID="CatalogZone1" runat="server">
   <ZoneTemplate>
         <asp:ImportCatalogPart ID="ImportCatalogPart1" runat="server" />
   </ZoneTemplate>
</asp:CatalogZone>
```

The `ImportCatalogPart` control is created by using the `ImportCatalogPart` class of the .NET Framework class library. This class is available in the `System.Web.UI.WebControls.WebParts` namespace.

The inheritance hierarchy of the `ImportCatalogPart` class is given as follows:

```
System.Object
   System.Web.UI.Control
      System.Web.UI.WebControls.WebControl
         System.Web.UI.WebControls.Panel
            System.Web.UI.WebControls.WebParts.Part
               System.Web.UI.WebControls.WebParts.CatalogPart
                  System.Web.UI.WebControls.WebParts.ImportCatalogPart
```

The syntax of the `ImportCatalogPart` control in `VB` is given as follows:

```
Dim ImportCatalogPart1 as new ImportCatalogPart
```

The syntax of the `ImportCatalogPart` control in `C#` is given as follows:

```
ImportCatalogPart ImportCatalogPart1;
```

You can use the various properties and methods of the `ImportCatalogPart` class to handle the `ImportCatalogPart` control. The properties of the `ImportCatalogPart` class allow you to specify the appearance and behavior of a zone on a Web page. The properties of the `ImportCatalogPart` control cannot be inherited by the derived classes of a base class. Noteworthy methods of the `ImportCatalogPart` class are listed in Table 7.11:

Table 7.11: Noteworthy Methods of the ImportCatalogPart Class

Method	Description
GetAvailableWebPartDescriptions	Retrieves a description of WebPart controls of a catalog
GetWebPart	Retrieves a WebPart control based on a description passed as a parameter

Noteworthy properties of the `ImportCatalogPart` class are listed in Table 7.12:

Table 7.12: Noteworthy Properties of the ImportCatalogPart Class

Property	Description
BrowseHelpText	Retrieves or specifies a text message that informs users to browse to the location of a description file
ImportedPartLabelText	Retrieves or specifies the text displayed after a user imports a description file to represent or describe an imported control in the catalog of imported controls
PartImportErrorLabelText	Retrieves or specifies an error message that is displayed if an error occurs during the import process
UploadButtonText	Retrieves or specifies the text for the `Button` control that starts the upload process of a description file
UploadHelpText	Retrieves or specifies the text of a message that enables the user to upload a description file

The EditorZone Control

Till now, you must have got some idea of important Web Parts controls. Now, suppose you want to change the appearance of a Web page. To do so, you have to go to the properties of the Web page to make the changes at design time. However, instead of this traditional approach, you can use a Web Parts control called `EditorZone`. The `EditorZone` control is one of the primary editing controls used to change the appearance, format, and structure of Web pages containing Web Parts controls at run time. In addition, you can use the `EditorZone` control to change the behavior and content of Web Parts controls. The `EditorZone` control is visible in the edit mode of the Web page. This control contains various `EditorPart` controls, such as `AppearanceEditorPart and BehaviorEditorPart`, which are used to customize the Web page. The `EditorZone` control is an object of the `EditorZone` class.

To add an `EditorZone` control to the Web page, drag and drop the `EditorZone` control from the Toolbox to the Design view of a `Default.aspx` page. Figure 7.8 shows the `EditorZone` control in the Design view:

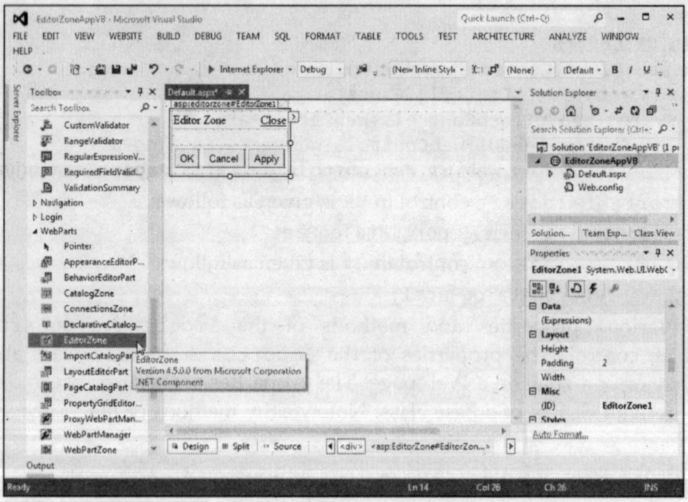

Figure 7.8: Displaying the EditorZone Control

You can also add an `EditorZone` control by using the following code in the `<form>` element of the Default.aspx page:

```
<asp:EditorZone ID="EditorZone1" runat="server">
</asp:EditorZone>
```

NOTE

You have to use the <ZoneTemplate> element inside the EditorZone control for the proper working of the EditorZone control.

The `EditorZone` control is created by using the `EditorZone` class of the .NET Framework class library. This class is available in the `System.Web.UI.WebControls.WebParts` namespace.

The inheritance hierarchy of the `EditorZone` class is given as follows:

```
System.Object
    System.Web.UI.Control
        System.Web.UI.WebControls.WebControl
            System.Web.UI.WebControls.CompositeControl
                System.Web.UI.WebControls.WebParts.WebZone
                    System.Web.UI.WebControls.WebParts.ToolZone
                        System.Web.UI.WebControls.WebParts.EditorZoneBase
                            System.Web.UI.WebControls.WebParts.EditorZone
```

The syntax to declare the `EditorZone` control in `VB` is given as follows:

```
Dim editorA as EditorZone
```

The syntax to declare the `EditorZone` control in `C#` is given as follows:

```
EditorZone editorA;
```

Noteworthy methods of the `EditorZone` class are listed in Table 7.13:

Table 7.13: Noteworthy Methods of the EditorZone Class

Method	Description
`AddAttributesToRender`	Adds Hyper Text Markup Language (HTML) attributes and styles provided to the specified `System.Web.UI.HtmlTextWriter` class
`CreateControlStyle`	Creates the style object, used by the `WebControl` class to execute all the properties related to the style
`CreateEditorPartChrome`	Retrieves a reference to an `EditorPartChrome` object, which provides the peripheral UI elements (such as a border, title, and icons) residing around an `EditorZoneBase` zone
`CreateEditorParts`	Creates all `EditorPart` controls specified in a zone template in page persistence format
`InvalidateEditorParts`	Removes all `EditorPart` controls associated with an `EditorZoneBase` zone
`RaisePostBackEvent`	Performs actions related to the verbs menu of an editor zone, or invokes an event that responds back to the server
`RenderBody`	Overrides the base method to Render the body area of a zone, which is obtained from the `EditorZoneBase` class
`RenderContents`	Provides the whole content of a zone control between the beginning and ending tags of the specified `HtmlTextWriter` class
`RenderFooter`	Specifies the verbs in the footer of a `ToolZone` control by overriding the base method
`RenderHeader`	Provides specialized rendering for the header area required by `ToolZone` controls, by overriding the base method
`Close`	Ends the process of modifying Web Parts controls and returns the browse mode of a Web page
`RenderVerb`	Provides a verb to a `ToolZone` control
`RenderVerbs`	Renders the verbs which apply at the zone level. (Inherited from EditorZoneBase.)

Noteworthy properties of the `EditorZone` class are listed in Table 7.14:

Table 7.14: Noteworthy Properties of the EditorZone Class

Property	Description
`ApplyVerb`	Retrieves a reference to a `WebPartVerb` object, which allows you to modify a Web Parts control in the edit mode
`AssociatedDisplayModes`	Retrieves the objects of the WebPartDisplayMode class activated when a `ToolZone` control is present on a Web page
`CancelVerb`	Retrieves a reference to a `WebPartVerb` object, which allows you to cancel the modification you made to a control in the edit mode
`EditorPartChrome`	Retrieves a reference to an instance of the `EditorPartChrome` class related to an `EditorZoneBase` zone
`EditorParts`	Retrieves all `EditorPart` controls contained in an `EditorZoneBase` zone
`EditUIStyle`	Retrieves the style attributes for the controls contained in a `ToolZone` control
`EmptyZoneText`	Specifies or retrieves a message text, which appears when a zone is empty and has no controls
`EmptyZoneTextStyle`	Retrieves the style attributes for text in an empty zone
`ErrorStyle`	Retrieves the style attributes of an `EditorZone` control for displaying an error message if the control is not loaded or created
`ErrorText`	Retrieves or specifies the text to display an error message in the editing UI
`FooterStyle`	Retrieves the style attributes for the footer area of a zone
`HeaderCloseVerb`	Retrieves a reference to a `WebPartVerb` object in the header of a `ToolZone` control to close the control
`HeaderStyle`	Retrieves the style attributes for the header area of a zone
`HeaderText`	Retrieves or specifies the text for the header area of a zone
`HeaderVerbStyle`	Retrieves the style attributes of all the header verbs displayed in a `ToolZone` control
`InstructionText`	Retrieves or specifies the text to instruct users how to use a `ToolZone` control
`InstructionTextStyle`	Retrieves the attributes for the text displayed at the top of a `ToolZone` control
`LabelStyle`	Retrieves the style attributes for the labels that appear in the editing controls of a `ToolZone` control
`OKVerb`	Retrieves a reference to a `WebPartVerb` object to apply editing changes to a control and hide the editing UI
`Padding`	Retrieves or specifies the attributes related to cell padding in a table containing Web Parts controls
`PartChromeStyle`	Retrieves the style attributes for the borders of Web Parts controls contained in a zone
`PartChromeType`	Retrieves or specifies the border type of Web Parts controls
`PartStyle`	Retrieves the style attributes for the border and content of Web Parts controls
`PartTitleStyle`	Retrieves the style attributes for the title bar of Web Parts controls
`VerbButtonType`	Retrieves or specifies the button to represent the verbs in a zone
`VerbStyle`	Retrieves style characteristics for the UI of verbs of Web Parts controls
`ZoneTemplate`	Provides a template to add child controls to an `EditorZone` control

The LayoutEditorPart Control

You can use the LayoutEditorPart control to create a full-fledged layout editor for Web Parts controls, which can have their respective LayoutEditorPart controls associated with them. To change the layout of a Web Parts control, simply make the required changes in the LayoutEditorPart control associated with the Web Parts control.

The LayoutEditorPart control is visible only when a Web page is in the edit mode. In this mode, you can select and change the properties of a Web Part control. The LayoutEditorPart control offers the following three options to modify a Web Parts control:

- **ChromeState**—Obtains or specifies the current state of a Web Parts control, which can be normal or minimized.
- **Zone**—Specifies the WebPartZoneBase zone, which consists of the Web Parts control you want to modify.
- **ZoneIndex**—Specifies the index position of Web Parts controls that reside in a WebPartZone control. This option allows you to determine the specific position of a Web Parts control within the WebPartZone control.

You must use the LayoutEditorPart control in page persistence format. This format enables the LayoutEditorPart control to retain its property values between browser sessions. To do this, you need to declare the <asp:LayoutEditorPart> element inside the <ZoneTemplate> element.

To add a LayoutEditorPart control to a Web page, drag and drop a LayoutEditorPart control from the Toolbox to the Design view of a Default.aspx page. Figure 7.9 shows the LayoutEditorPart control inside an EditorZone control in the Design view:

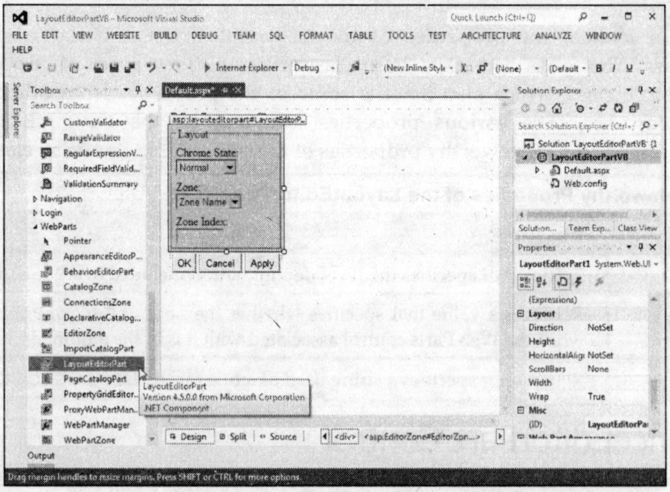

Figure 7.9: Displaying the LayoutEditorPart Control

You can also add the LayoutEditorPart control by using the following code in the <form> element of the Default.aspx page:

```
<asp:EditorZone ID="EditorZone1" runat="server">
  <ZoneTemplate>
       <asp:LayoutEditorPart ID="LayoutEditorPart1" runat="server" />
  </ZoneTemplate>
</asp:EditorZone>
```

The LayoutEditorPart control is an object of the LayoutEditorPart class.

NOTE

If you place LayoutEditorPart controls in any other zone except the EditorZone control, the designer generates an error.

The `LayoutEditorPart` control is created by using the `LayoutEditorPart` class of the .NET Framework class library. The `LayoutEditorPart` class allows you to modify the layout of the associated Web Parts control. This class is available in the `System.Web.UI.WebControls.WebParts` namespace. The inheritance hierarchy of the `LayoutEditorPart` class is given as follows:

```
System.Object
    System.Web.UI.Control
        System.Web.UI.WebControls.WebControl
            System.Web.UI.WebControls.Panel
                System.Web.UI.WebControls.WebParts.Part
                    System.Web.UI.WebControls.WebParts.EditorPart
                        System.Web.UI.WebControls.WebParts.LayoutEditorPart
```

The `LayoutEditorPart` control is associated with the `LayoutEditorPart` class. This class employs various methods to perform tasks, such as applying changes and style properties to a Web Parts control and determining if two object instances are equal. Noteworthy methods of the `LayoutEditorPart` class are listed in Table 7.15:

Table 7.15: Noteworthy Methods of the LayoutEditorPart Class

Method	Description
`ApplyChanges`	Updates the associated WebPart control properties with the changes made in a `LayoutEditorPart` control
`SyncChanges`	Obtains the property values from a WebPart control, which is then assigned to the associated `LayoutEditorPart` control

Now, let's take a look at the properties of the `LayoutEditorPart` class, which is inherited from the `EditorPart` class. This class acts as a base class that provides a set of properties and methods to the `LayoutEditorPart` class, which also inherits some of the properties from other classes, such as `Control`, `Part`, and `WebControl`. The various properties inherited by the `LayoutEditorPart` class are `Font`, `Enabled`, `Page`, and `Style`. Noteworthy properties of the `LayoutEditorPart` class are listed in Table 7.16:

Table 7.16: Noteworthy Properties of the LayoutEditorPart Class

Property	Description
DefaultButton	Retrieves or specifies the ID of default button included in a `Panel` control
Display	Retrieves a value that specifies whether the `LayoutEditorPart` control should be displayed when the Web Parts control associated with it is in the edit mode
Title	Retrieves or specifies a string used as a title for the `LayoutEditorPart` control

The AppearanceEditorPart Control

The `AppearanceEditorPart` control allows users to edit the properties associated with the appearance of a Web Parts control on the Web page. This control resides in an `EditorZone` zone and is visible only when a Web Parts control is selected for editing. The following options are displayed on the `AppearanceEditorPart` control:

- **Title**—Specifies a string value, which appears as a title of the AppearanceEditorPart control
- **Height**—Specifies the height of the AppearanceEditorPart control
- **Width**—Specifies the width of the AppearanceEditorPart control
- **ChromeType**—Selects the title and border type (dotted, single line, or double line) of the AppearanceEditorPart control by using the DropDownList control
- **Direction**—Selects the direction (horizontal or vertical) of content flow inside the AppearanceEditorPart control by using the DropDownList control
- **Hidden**—Hides or displays the AppearanceEditorPart control by using the CheckBox control

To add the AppearanceEditorPart control to the EditorZone control, drag and drop the control from the Toolbox to the EditorZone control in the Design view of a Default.aspx page. Figure 7.10 shows the AppearanceEditorPart control inside the EditorZone control in the Design view:

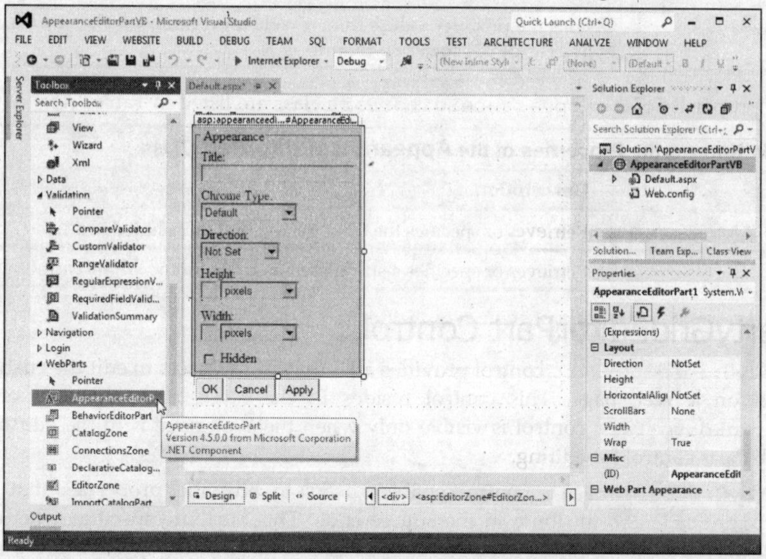

Figure 7.10: Displaying the AppearanceEditorPart Control

You can also add the AppearanceEditorPart control by using the following code in the <form> element of the Default.aspx page:

```
<asp:EditorZone ID="EditorZone1" runat="server">
   <ZoneTemplate>
         <asp:AppearanceEditorPart       ID="AppearanceEditorPart1"
         runat="server" />
   </ZoneTemplate>
</asp:EditorZone>
```

The AppearanceEditorPart control is created by using the AppearanceEditorPart class of the .NET Framework class library. The AppearanceEditorPart class provides an editor with control to modify the UI properties of the associated Web Parts control. This class is available in the System.Web.UI.WebControls.WebParts namespace. The inheritance hierarchy of the AppearanceEditorPart class is given as follows:

```
System.Object
   System.Web.UI.Control
      System.Web.UI.WebControls.WebControl
         System.Web.UI.WebControls.Panel
            System.Web.UI.WebControls.WebParts.Part
               System.Web.UI.WebControls.WebParts.EditorPart
                  System.Web.UI.WebControls.WebParts.AppearanceEditorPart
```

The AppearanceEditorPart class contains methods and properties that are used to work with the AppearanceEditorPart control at runtime. Noteworthy methods of the AppearanceEditorPart class are listed in Table 7.17:

Table 7.17: Noteworthy Methods of the AppearanceEditorPart Class

Method	Description
ApplyChanges	Updates the associated WebPart control properties with the changes made in the AppearanceEditorPart control

Table 7.17: Noteworthy Methods of the AppearanceEditorPart Class

Method	Description
SyncChanges	Obtains the property values from a WebPart control, which is then assigned to the associated AppearanceEditorPart control

Noteworthy properties of the `AppearanceEditorPart` class are listed in Table 7.18:

Table 7.18: Noteworthy Properties of the AppearanceEditorPart Class

Property	Description
DefaultButton	Retrieves or specifies the ID of default button included in a `Panel` control
Title	Retrieves or specifies a string used as a title for the `AppearanceEditorPart` control

The PropertyGridEditorPart Control

The `PropertyGridEditorPart` control provides a UI that allows users to edit the custom properties of a Web Parts control on a Web page. This control resides in the `EditorZone` control on the Web page. The `PropertyGridEditorPart` control is visible only when the Web page is in the edit mode or when the user selects a Web Parts control for editing.

The `PropertyGridEditorPart` control enables users to edit the properties that are marked with the `WebBrowsableAttribute` attribute in the source code. This attribute specifies whether or not the property should be displayed in the `PropertyGridEditorPart` control. After specifying the editable properties, the `PropertyGridEditorPart` control creates an editable UI based on the type of properties to be edited.

To add the `PropertyGridEditorPart` control to a Web page, first drag and drop an `EditorZone` control from the Toolbox to the Design view of a Default.aspx page, and then drag and drop the `PropertyGridEditorPart` control from the Toolbox to the `EditorZone` control in the Design view. Figure 7.11 shows the `PropertyGridEditorPart` control inside the `EditorZone` control in the Design view:

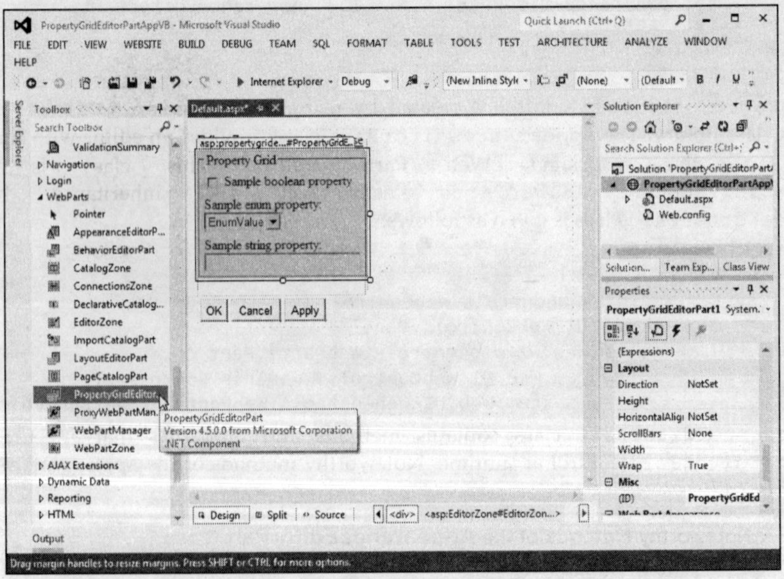

Figure 7.11: Displaying the PropertyGridEditorPart Control

You can also add the `PropertyGridEditorPart` control by using the following code in the `<form>` element of the Default.aspx page:

```
<asp:EditorZone ID="EditorZone1" runat="server">
   <ZoneTemplate>
         <asp:PropertyGridEditorPart ID="PropertyGridEditorPart1"
         runat="server" />
   </ZoneTemplate>
</asp:EditorZone>
```

The PropertyGridEditorPart control is an object of the PropertyGridEditorPart class. This control is created by using the PropertyGridEditorPart class of the .NET Framework class library. The PropertyGridEditorPart class enables users to modify the custom properties of the associated Web Parts or server control. This class is available in the System.Web.UI.WebControls.WebParts namespace. The inheritance hierarchy of the PropertyGridEditorPart class is given as follows:

```
System.Object
   System.Web.UI.Control
      System.Web.UI.WebControls.WebControl
         System.Web.UI.WebControls.Panel
            System.Web.UI.WebControls.WebParts.Part
               System.Web.UI.WebControls.WebParts.EditorPart
                  System.Web.UI.WebControls.WebParts.PropertyGridEditorPart
```

The syntax of the PropertyGridEditorPart control in VB is given as follows:

```
Dim propgridA as PropertyGridEditorPart
```

The syntax of the PropertyGridEditorPart control in C# is given as follows:

```
PropertyGridEditorPart propgridA;
```

The PropertyGridEditorPart class resides in the System.Web.UI.WebControls.WebParts namespace and cannot be inherited. This class consists of the Title and Display properties. The Title property is used to obtain or set a title text for a Web Parts control and the Display property is used to determine whether the control is displayed when the Web page is in the edit mode or not.

The two important methods in the PropertyGridEditorPart class are ApplyChanges and SyncChanges. The ApplyChanges method saves the value that a user sets on the PropertyGridEditorPart control to the corresponding properties of a Web Parts control. This method is called when the user clicks the OK or Apply button on the editing UI. It returns true if the values from the PropertyGridEditorPart control are saved to a WebPart control and returns false if the values are not saved in the WebPart control. The SyncChanges method updates the values of the PropertyGridEditorPart control so that the users can edit the values of these properties.

The BehaviorEditorPart Control

The BehaviorEditorPart control, as the name suggests, provides options that enable users to modify the behavior of Web Parts controls. This control usually remains hidden and is visible only when a Web page containing Web Parts controls is in the edit mode. Similar to other EditorPart controls, the BehaviorEditorPart control is also contained inside the EditorZone control.

The various options provided by the BehaviorEditorPart control are as follows:

- **Description** – Describes the functionality a Web Parts control in brief
- **TitleUrl** – Specifies the link for additional information about a Web Part control
- **TitleIconImageUrl** – Specifies an image, which appears in the title bar of a Web Part control
- **CatalogIconImageUrl** – Specifies an image, which appears as a representative of a Web Parts control in the catalog of controls
- **HelpUrl** – Specifies the link of the help file of a Web Parts control
- **HelpMode** – Specifies the type of UI to display the help content of a Web Part control
- **Hidden** – Hides or displays a Web Parts control
- **ImportErrorMessage** – Retrieves or specifies the error message, which appears when importing a Web Parts control

- **ExportMode** – Exports the properties of a Web Parts control
- **AuthorizationFilter** – Specifies a string value, which indicates whether you can add a Web Parts control to a Web page or not
- **AllowClose** – Specifies a value that allows a user to close a Web Parts control on a Web page
- **AllowEdit** – Specifies a value that allows a user to modify a Web Parts control on Web page
- **AllowHide** – Specifies a value that allows a user to hide a Web Parts control
- **AllowMinimize** – Specifies a value to minimize a Web Parts control
- **AllowZoneChange** – Specifies a value that indicates whether a Web Parts control can be moved from one zone to another

To add the `BehaviorEditorPart` control to a Web page, drag and drop the control from the Toolbox to the `EditorZone` control in the Design view of a Default.aspx page. Figure 7.12 shows the `BehaviorEditorPart` control inside the `EditorZone` control in the Design view:

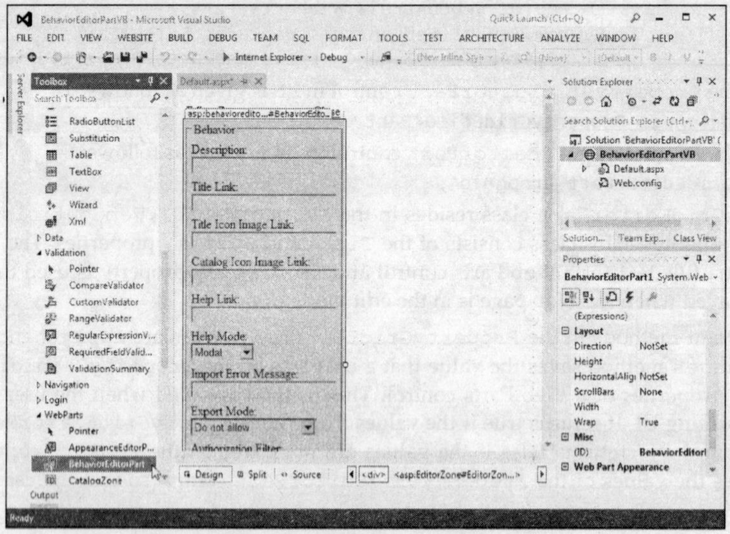

Figure 7.12: Displaying the BehaviorEditorPart Control

You can also add the `BehaviorEditorPart` control by using the following code in the `<zonetemplate>` element of the `EditorZone` control on the `Default.aspx` page:

```
<EditorZone>
<ZoneTemplate>
  <asp:BehaviorEditorPart ID="BehaviorEditorPart1" runat="server" />
</ZoneTemplate>
</EditorZone>
```

The `BehaviorEditorPart` control is an object of the `BehaviorEditorPart` class. The `BehaviorEditorPart` control is used for modifying UI properties, such as `Title`, `Link`, `Description` and `Help Link`, in a Web page. You can add the `BehaviorEditorPart` control by using the `BehaviorEditorPart` class, which belongs to the `System.Web.dll` assembly. The namespace hierarchy of the `BehaviorEditorPart` class is given as follows:

```
System.Object
    System.Web.UI.Control
        System.Web.UI.WebControls.WebControl
            System.Web.UI.WebControls.Panel
                System.Web.UI.WebControls.WebParts.Part
                    System.Web.UI.WebControls.WebParts.EditorPart
                        System.Web.UI.WebControls.WebParts.BehaviorEditorPart
```

The syntax of the `BehaviorEditorPart` control in VB is given as follows:

```
Dim behaviorA as BehaviorEditorPart
```

The syntax of the `BehaviorEditorPart` control in C# is given as follows:

```
BehaviorEditorPart behaviorA;
```

The `BehaviorEditorPart` class derives from the `EditorPart` class, which is used to modify the properties of the associated Web Parts control. The `BehaviorEditorPart` class inherits various methods, properties, and events from the `Control` class, such as `ApplyStyle`, `Title`, and `DataBinding`. Noteworthy properties of the `BehaviorEditorPart` class are listed in Table 7.19:

Table 7.19: Noteworthy Properties of the BehaviorEditorPart Class

Property	Description
`DefaultButton`	Retrieves or specifies the ID of default button included in a `Panel` control
`Display`	Retrieves a value that specifies whether the `BehaviorEditorPart` control should be displayed when the Web Parts control associated with it is in the edit mode
`Title`	Retrieves or specifies a string used as a title for the `BehaviorEditorPart` control

The ConnectionsZone Control

You can dynamically connect Web Parts controls with each other that reside in the `WebPartZoneBase` zone with the help of the `ConnectionsZone` control. However, to do this, the Web Parts controls must be enabled for such type of dynamic connection. When you add the `ConnectionsZone` control to a Web page, a new mode, the connection mode, appears in the Select mode list of the Web page. The `ConnectionsZone` control is an object of the `ConnectionsZone` class.

NOTE

While working with the ConnectionsZone control and the ConnectionsZone class, you must be aware of two terms, that is, Consumer and Provider. A Web Part control that receives data is called a Consumer and a Web Part control that sends data to other Web Part control(s) is called a Provider.

To add the `ConnectionsZone` control to the Web page, drag and drop the `ConnectionsZone` control from the Toolbox to the Design view of a Default.aspx page. The `ConnectionsZone` control in the Design view is shown in Figure 7.13:

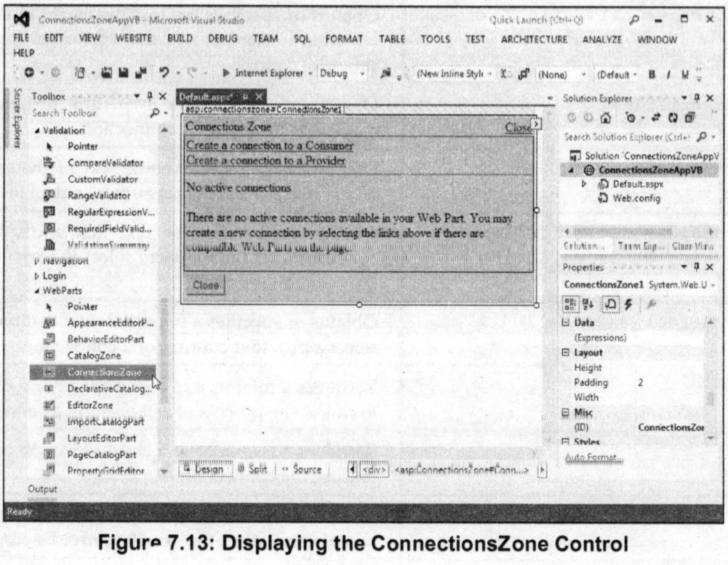

Figure 7.13: Displaying the ConnectionsZone Control

You can also add the `ConnectionsZone` control by using the following code in the `<form>` element of the `Default.aspx` page:

```
<asp:ConnectionsZone ID="ConnectionsZone1" runat="server">
</asp:ConnectionsZone>
```

The `ConnectionsZone` control is created by using the `ConnectionsZone` class of the .NET Framework class library. The `ConnectionsZone` control inherits from the `ToolZone` base class, which is available in the `System.Web.UI.WebControls.WebParts` namespace. The inheritance hierarchy of the `ConnectionsZone` class is given as follows:

```
System.Object
    System.Web.UI.Control
        System.Web.UI.WebControls.WebControl
            System.Web.UI.WebControls.CompositeControl
                System.Web.UI.WebControls.WebParts.WebZone
                    System.Web.UI.WebControls.WebParts.ToolZone
                        System.Web.UI.WebControls.WebParts.ConnectionsZone
```

The syntax of the `ConnectionsZone` control in `VB` is given as follows:

```
Dim ConnectionsZone1 as new ConnectionsZone
```

The syntax of the `ConnectionsZone` control in `C#` is given as follows:

```
ConnectionsZone ConnectionsZone1;
```

NOTE

To create a connection between Web Parts controls, a user needs to switch to the ConnectionDisplayMode and select the connection verb from the Web Part verb menu.

Noteworthy properties of the `ConnectionsZone` class are listed in Table 7.20:

Table 7.20: Noteworthy Properties of the ConnectionsZone Class

Property	Description
`ConfigureConnectionTitle`	Obtains or specifies the title text of a connection UI created by a `ConnectionsZone` control.
`ConfigureVerb`	Obtains a reference to a `WebPartVerb` object. You can use this reference to open the configuration view in a connection UI.
`ConnectToConsumerInstructionText`	Obtains or specifies the text displayed in the section of a connection UI where users select the consumer control to connect to the provider control.
`ConnectToConsumerText`	Obtains or specifies the hyperlink text that users click to select a consumer control for a connection.
`ConnectToConsumerTitle`	Obtains or specifies the title text of the section in a connection UI where users select the consumer control to connect with.
`ConnectToProviderInstructionText`	Obtains or specifies the text that is displayed in the section of a connection UI where users select the provider control to connect to the consumer control.
`ConnectToProviderText`	Obtains or specifies a hyperlink text that users click to open and then select a provider control for a connection.
`CancelVerb`	Retrieves a reference to a `WebPartVerb` object that enables the user to cancel the process of establishing a connection.
`CloseVerb`	Retrieves a reference to a `WebPartVerb` object that enables the user to close the connection UI.
`ConnectToProviderTitle`	Obtains or specifies the title text of the section in the connection UI where users select the specific provider control to connect with.

Table 7.20: Noteworthy Properties of the ConnectionsZone Class

Property	Description
`ConnectVerb`	Obtains a reference to a `WebPartVerb` object to allow two Web Parts controls to connect with each other.
`ConsumersInstructionText`	Obtains or specifies the instructional text contained in the consumers section of a connection UI, when a connection already exists.
`ConsumersTitle`	Obtains or specifies the title text of the consumers section present in a connection UI, when a connection already exists.
`DisconnectVerb`	Obtains a reference to a `WebPartVerb` object to enable the user to disconnect two connected WebPart controls.
`ExistingConnectionErrorMessage`	Obtains or specifies the message string that is displayed in a connection UI when an error occurs in an existing connection.
`GetFromText`	Obtains or specifies the text present before the name of provider in the connection UI. This provider is used by a consumer to retrieve data.
`GetText`	Obtains or specifies the text present before the name of consumer in the connection UI. This consumer retrieves the data from provider.
`InstructionTitle`	Obtains or specifies the description text for the action performed on a consumer or provider control in a connection UI to manage existing connections.
`NewConnectionErrorMessage`	Obtains or specifies a message string that is displayed in a connection UI when an error occurs while creating a new connection.
`NoExistingConnectionInstructionText`	Obtains or specifies the text contained in the body of a connection UI when there is no existing connection associated with a WebPart control.
`NoExistingConnectionTitle`	Obtains or specifies the title text of a connection UI when there is no existing connection associated with a WebPart control.
`ProvidersInstructionText`	Obtains or specifies the instructional text contained in the providers section of a connection UI, when a connection already exists.
`ProvidersTitle`	Obtains or specifies the title text above in the providers section of a connection UI, when a connection already exists.
`SendText`	Obtains or specifies the text present before the name of provider in the connection UI. This provider sends data to consumer.
`SendToText`	Obtains or specifies the text present in the connection UI before the name of the consumer to which a provider sends data.

NOTE

All Web Parts controls reside inside the <form> element of a Default.aspx page. However, there are some Web Parts Controls that cannot be used alone and require some specific control to work with. For example, the LayoutEditorPart or BehaviorEditorPart control cannot be used without the EditorZone control in the <form> element.

Immediate Solutions

Using the WebPartManager Class

The `WebPartManager` class allows users to toggle between various display modes. These display modes help the user to perform different actions on the Web page, such as changing the layout of a Web page or editing controls. The `WebPartManager` class has the following display modes:

- `BrowseDisplayMode`—Specifies the default display mode for pages that contain Web Parts controls.
- `CatalogDisplayMode`—Specifies the display mode in which a catalog of controls is visible. A user can add controls to a Web page from the catalog.
- `ConnectDisplayMode`—Represents the display mode in which the connection UI is visible and where users can manage the connections between the controls of a Web page.
- `DesignDisplayMode`—Represents the display mode in which the user can modify the layout of a Web page.
- `EditDisplayMode`—Specifies the display mode in which the user can change the appearance, properties, and behavior of server controls.

Creating the WebPartManager Control in Code

As discussed in the *In Depth* section of this chapter, you can create a `WebPartManager` control directly by using its class hierarchy. The `WebPartManager` control does not have any visual appearance in a Web page; therefore, the display mode property of the `WebPartManager` control is set to a Label control's Text property to see the corresponding default mode.

Let's create an application named `WebPartManagerControlAppCS` (`WebPartManagerControlAppCS` for C# and `WebPartManagerControlAppVB` for VB) to learn how to create the `WebPartManager` control through the control's class hierarchy.

NOTE

The applications in this chapter are created using the ASP.NET Empty Web Site template in the New Web Site dialog box. After creating the application, you need to add the Default.aspx page to the application.

Listing 7.1 shows the complete code for the `Default.aspx` page of the `WebPartManagerControlAppCS` website:

Listing 7.1: Showing the Code for the `Default.aspx` Page

In VB

```
<%@ Page Language="VB" AutoEventWireup="false" CodeFile="Default.aspx.vb"
   Inherits="_Default" %>
<!DOCTYPE html>
<html xmlns="http://www.w3.org/1999/xhtml">
<head runat="server">
    <title>WebPartManager Control Example</title>
</head>
<body>
    <form id="form1" runat="server">
    <div>
    <asp:Label ID="Label3" runat="server" Font-Bold="True" Font-Underline="True"
         ForeColor="#0000C0" Text="WebPart Manager:"></asp:Label>
         <br />
```

```
        <br />
        <asp:Panel ID="Panel1" runat="server" BackColor="#FFE0C0" BorderColor="#FFC080"
               BorderStyle="Double" Height="129px" Width="320px">
             <br />
            
       <asp:Label ID="Label1" runat="server" Font-Bold="True" ForeColor="Navy"
               Text="WEBPARTMANAGER CREATED!!!!" Visible="False"></asp:Label><br />
        <br />
        <asp:Button ID="Button1" runat="server" BackColor="#FFC080" Font-Bold="True"
               ForeColor="#0000C0" Text="DisplayMode" Width="213px" />
           
        <asp:Label ID="Label2" runat="server" Font-Bold="True" ForeColor="#0000C0"
               Visible="False"></asp:Label><br />
           
        </asp:Panel>
    </div>
    </form>
</body>
</html>
```

In C#

```
<%@ Page Language="C#" AutoEventWireup="true" CodeFile="Default.aspx.cs"
  Inherits="_Default" %>
<!DOCTYPE html>
<html xmlns="http://www.w3.org/1999/xhtml">
<head id="Head1" runat="server">
    <title>WebPartManager Control Example</title>
</head>
<body>
    <form id="form1" runat="server">
    <div>
    <asp:Label ID="Label3" runat="server" Font-Bold="True" Font-Underline="True"
         ForeColor="#0000C0" Text="WebPart Manager:"></asp:Label>
         <br />
         <br />
         <asp:Panel ID="Panel1" runat="server" BackColor="#FFE0C0" BorderColor="#FFC080"
         BorderStyle="Double" Height="129px" Width="320px">
              <br />
             
        <asp:Label ID="Label1" runat="server" Font-Bold="True" ForeColor="Navy"
         Text="WEBPARTMANAGER CREATED!!!!" Visible="False"></asp:Label><br />
         <br />
         <asp:Button ID="Button1" runat="server" BackColor="#FFC080" Font-Bold="True"
         ForeColor="#0000C0" Text="DisplayMode" Width="213px" OnClick="Button1_Click" />
            
         <asp:Label ID="Label2" runat="server" Font-Bold="True" ForeColor="#0000C0"
         Visible="False"></asp:Label><br />
            
         </asp:Panel>
    </div>
    </form>
</body>
</html>
```

Listing 7.2 shows the complete code for the CodeFile of the Default.aspx page of the `WebPartManagerControlAppCS` website:

Listing 7.2: Showing the Code for the CodeFile of the Default.aspx Page

In VB

```
Partial Class _Default
    Inherits System.Web.UI.Page
    Protected Sub Button1_Click(sender As Object, e As EventArgs) Handles Button2.Click
        Label2.Visible = True
        Button1.Visible = False
        Dim wpm As New WebPartManager
        Dim str As String
        str = wpm.DisplayMode.Name
        Label2.Text = str
        Label1.Visible = True
    End Sub
End Class
```

In C#

```
using System;
using System.Data;
using System.Configuration;
using System.Collections.Generic;
using System.Linq;
using System.Web;
using System.Web.Security;
using System.Web.UI;
using System.Web.UI.HtmlControls;
using System.Web.UI.WebControls;
using System.Web.UI.WebControls.WebParts;
using System.Xml.Linq;
public partial class _Default : System.Web.UI.Page
{
    protected void Page_Load(object sender, EventArgs e)
    {

    }
    protected void Button1_Click(object sender, EventArgs e)
    {
        Label2.Visible = true;
        Button1.Visible = false;
        WebPartManager wpm = new WebPartManager();
        string str;
        str = wpm.DisplayMode.Name;
        Label2.Text = str;
        Label1.Visible = true;
    }
}
```

Now, run the website and click the DisplayMode button; the output is as shown in Figure 7.14:

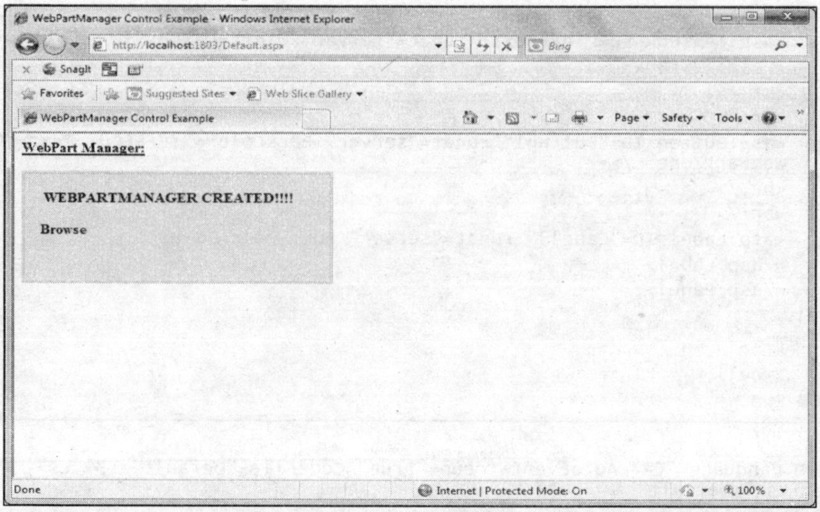

Figure 7.14: Displaying the Output of the WebPartManager Control Example

Creating the WebPartZone Control in Code

As learned earlier, the `WebPartZone` control is used to create a region where Web Parts or server controls can be relocated, maximized, or minimized by a user. Now, let's work with the `WebPartZone` control programmatically. After creating the various properties of a `WebPartZone` control, you can use the `WebPartZone` class to access and change these properties without using the UI.

Now, let's create a website named WebPartZoneAppCS (WebPartZoneAppCS for C# and WebPartZoneAppVB for VB) and learn how to use the `WebPartZone` control in the application. Listing 7.3 shows the complete code for the `Default.aspx` page of `the` WebPartZoneAppCS website:

Listing 7.3: Showing the Code for the `Default.aspx` Page

In VB

```
<%@ Page Language="VB" AutoEventWireup="false" CodeFile="Default.aspx.vb"
  Inherits="_Default" %>
<!DOCTYPE html>
<html xmlns="http://www.w3.org/1999/xhtml">
<head runat="server">
    <title>WebPartZone control Example</title>
</head>
<body>
    <form id="form1" runat="server">
    <div>
    <asp:Label ID="Label1" runat="server" Font-Bold="True" Font-Underline="True"
        ForeColor="Navy" Text="WebPart Zone:">
        </asp:Label>
        <br />
        <br />
        <asp:Panel ID="Panel1" runat="server" BackColor="#FFE0C0" BorderColor="#FF8000"
        BorderStyle="Double" Height="226px" Width="293px">
        <br />
        <asp:Label ID="Label2" runat="server" Font-Bold="True" Font-Underline="True"
        ForeColor="Navy" Text="Enter Header Text.">
        </asp:Label>
        <br />
        <br />
```

```
            <br />
            <asp:TextBox ID="TextBox1" runat="server" Width="230px">
            </asp:TextBox>
            <br />
            <br />
            <asp:Button ID="Button1" runat="server" BackColor="#FFFFC0" Text="Create
            WebPartZone" />
            <br />
            <br />
            <asp:Label ID="Label3" runat="server" Font-Bold="True">
            </asp:Label>
            </asp:Panel>
        </div>
        </form>
</body>
</html>
```

In C#

```
<%@ Page Language="C#" AutoEventWireup="true" CodeFile="Default.aspx.cs"
  Inherits="_Default" %>
<!DOCTYPE html>
<html xmlns="http://www.w3.org/1999/xhtml">
<head id="Head1" runat="server">
    <title>WebPartZone control Example</title>
</head>
<body>
    <form id="form1" runat="server">
    <div>
    <asp:Label ID="Label1" runat="server" Font-Bold="True" Font-Underline="True"
         ForeColor="Navy" Text="WebPart Zone:">
         </asp:Label>
         <br />
         <br />
         <asp:Panel ID="Panel1" runat="server" BackColor="#FFE0C0" BorderColor="#FF8000"
         BorderStyle="Double" Height="226px" Width="293px">
         <br />
         <asp:Label ID="Label2" runat="server" Font-Bold="True" Font-Underline="True"
         ForeColor="Navy" Text="Enter Header Text:">
         </asp:Label>
         <br />
         <br />
         <br />
         <asp:TextBox ID="TextBox1" runat="server" Width="230px">
         </asp:TextBox>
         <br />
         <br />
         <asp:Button ID="Button1" runat="server" BackColor="#FFFFC0" Text="Create
         WebPartZone" OnClick="Button1_Click" />
         <br />
         <br />
         <asp:Label ID="Label3" runat="server" Font-Bold="True">
         </asp:Label>
         </asp:Panel>
    </div>
    </form>
</body>
</html>
```

Listing 7.4 shows the complete code for the CodeFile of the Default.aspx page of the `WebPartZoneAppCS` website:

Listing 7.4: Showing the Code for the CodeFile of the Default.aspx Page

In VB

```
Partial Class _Default
    Inherits System.Web.UI.Page
    Protected Sub Button1_Click(sender As Object, e As EventArgs) Handles Button1.Click
        Dim wpm As New WebPartManager
        Dim wpz As New WebPartZone
        Dim str As String
        wpz.MenuLabelText = TextBox1.Text
        str = wpz.MenuLabelText
        Label3.Text = "Header text:" + str
    End Sub
End Class
```

In C#

```
using System;
using System.Data;
using System.Configuration;
using System.Collections.Generic;
using System.Linq;
using System.Web;
using System.Web.Security;
using System.Web.UI;
using System.Web.UI.HtmlControls;
using System.Web.UI.WebControls;
using System.Web.UI.WebControls.WebParts;
using System.Xml.Linq;
public partial class _Default : System.Web.UI.Page
{
    protected void Page_Load(object sender, EventArgs e)
    {

    }
    protected void Button1_Click(object sender, EventArgs e)
    {
        WebPartManager wpm = new WebPartManager();
        WebPartZone wpz = new WebPartZone();
        String str;
        wpz.MenuLabelText = TextBox1.Text;
        str = wpz.MenuLabelText;
        Label3.Text = "Header text:" + str;
    }
}
```

Now, run the application and enter Web Part Header in the Enter Header Text TextBox, and click the Create WebPartZone button. The output is as shown in Figure 7.15:

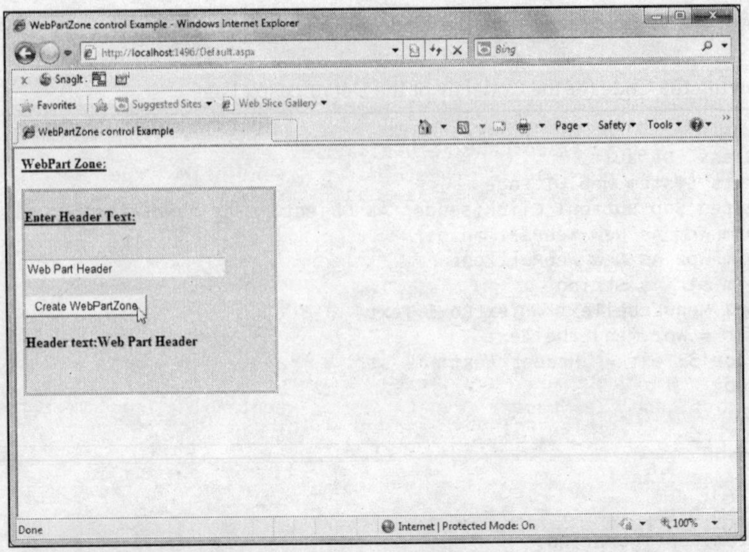

Figure 7.15: Displaying the Output of the WebPartZone Control Example

Creating the CatalogZone Control in Code

As discussed in the In Depth section of this chapter, the CatalogZone control is used to create a catalog of Web Parts controls. This control also allows the user to add or update the controls on a Web page. Similar to other Web Parts controls, you can also create the CatalogZone control by using classes. You can set most of the properties of the CatalogZone control by declaring the CatalogZone class.

To understand the use of the CatalogZone control, let's use it in an application. Let's create an application named CatalogZoneAppCS (CatalogZoneAppVB for VB and CatalogZoneAppCS for C#). In this application, we add seven Label controls and Button control. The Label controls are used to display the ZoneSelect, Mode, and EmptyZoneText controls on the Click event of the Button control. Listing 7.5 shows the complete code for the Default.aspx page of the application:

Listing 7.5: Showing the Code for the Default.aspx Page

In VB

```
<%@ Page Language="VB" AutoEventWireup="false" CodeFile="Default.aspx.vb"
  Inherits="_Default" %>
<!DOCTYPE html>
<html xmlns="http://www.w3.org/1999/xhtml">
<head runat="server">
    <title>CatalogZone Example</title>
</head>
<body>
    <form id="form1" runat="server">
    <div>
    <asp:Label ID="Label1" runat="server" Font-Bold="True" Font-Underline="True"
        ForeColor="Navy" Text="WebPart CatalogZone:"></asp:Label>
        <br />
        <br />
        <asp:Panel ID="Panel1" runat="server" BackColor="#FFE0C0" BorderColor="#FF8000"
                BorderStyle="Double" Height="150px" Width="367px">
        <br />
         
```

```
        <asp:Button ID="Button1" runat="server" BackColor="#FFE0C0" BorderStyle="None"
                Font-Bold="True" Font-Underline="True" ForeColor="Blue" Text="Property
                Settings :Custom" Width="174px" /><br />
        <br />
        <asp:Label ID="Label2" runat="server" Font-Bold="True" Font-Underline="True"
                ForeColor="Navy" Text="Selected CatalogPart
                ID:"></asp:Label>  
        <asp:Label ID="Label4" runat="server" Font-Bold="True" Text="Label"
                Visible="False"></asp:Label><br />
        <br />
        <asp:Label ID="Label5" runat="server" Font-Bold="True" Font-Underline="True"
                ForeColor="Navy" Text="EmptyZone Text:"></asp:Label> 
        <asp:Label ID="Label6" runat="server" Font-Bold="True" Text="Label"
                Visible="False"></asp:Label><br />
        <br />
        <asp:Label ID="Label7" runat="server" Font-Bold="True" Font-Underline="True"
                ForeColor="Navy" Text="Page Browse Mode:"></asp:Label> 
        <asp:Label ID="Label8" runat="server" Font-Bold="True" Text="Label"
                Visible="False"></asp:Label><br />
        <br />
        </asp:Panel>
    </div>
    </form>
</body>
</html>
```

In C#

```
<%@ Page Language="C#" AutoEventWireup="true" CodeFile="Default.aspx.cs"
  Inherits="_Default" %>
<!DOCTYPE html>
<html xmlns="http://www.w3.org/1999/xhtml">
<head id="Head1" runat="server">
     <title>CatalogZone Example</title>
</head>
<body>
    <form id="form1" runat="server">
    <div>
    <asp:Label ID="Label1" runat="server" Font-Bold="True" Font-Underline="True"
        ForeColor="Navy" Text="WebPart CatalogZone:"></asp:Label>
        <br />
        <br />
        <asp:Panel ID="Panel1" runat="server" BackColor="#FFE0C0" BorderColor="#FF8000"
                BorderStyle="Double" Height="150px" Width="367px">
        <br />
         
       <asp:Button ID="Button1" runat="server" BackColor="#FFE0C0" BorderStyle="None"
        Font-Bold="True" Font-Underline="True" ForeColor="Blue" Text="Property Settings
        :Custom" Width="174px" OnClick="Button1_Click" /><br />
        <br />
        <asp:Label ID="Label2" runat="server" Font-Bold="True" Font-Underline="True"
        ForeColor="Navy" Text="Selected CatalogPart ID:"></asp:Label>  
        <asp:Label ID="Label4" runat="server" Font-Bold="True" Text="Label"
        Visible="False"></asp:Label><br />
        <br />
        <asp:Label ID="Label5" runat="server" Font-Bold="True" Font-Underline="True"
                ForeColor="Navy" Text="EmptyZone Text:"></asp:Label> 
        <asp:Label ID="Label6" runat="server" Font-Bold="True" Text="Label"
                Visible="False"></asp:Label><br />
        <br />
        <asp:Label ID="Label7" runat="server" Font-Bold="True" Font-Underline="True"
                ForeColor="Navy" Text="Page Browse Mode:"></asp:Label> 
```

```
        <asp:Label ID="Label8" runat="server" Font-Bold="True" Text="Label"
                Visible="False"></asp:Label><br />
        <br />
        </asp:Panel>
    </div>
    </form>
</body>
</html>
```

Listing 7.6 shows the complete code for the CodeFile of the Default.aspx page of the `CatalogZoneAppCS` website:

Listing 7.6: Showing the Code for the CodeFile of the Default.aspx Page

In VB

```
Partial Class _Default
    Inherits System.Web.UI.Page
    Protected Sub Button1_Click(sender As Object, e As EventArgs) Handles Button1.Click
        Dim wpm As New WebPartManager
        Dim cz As New CatalogZone
        Dim str As String
        cz.EmptyZoneText = "no controls found!!!"
        Label4.Text = cz.EmptyZoneText
        cz.SelectedCatalogPartID = "selected zone.."
        Label6.Text = cz.SelectedCatalogPartID
        str = WebPartManager.CatalogDisplayMode.Name
        Label8.Text = str
        Label4.Visible = True
        Label6.Visible = True
        Label8.Visible = True
    End Sub
End Class
```

In C#

```
using System;
using System.Data;
using System.Configuration;
using System.Collections.Generic;
using System.Linq;
using System.Web;
using System.Web.Security;
using System.Web.UI;
using System.Web.UI.HtmlControls;
using System.Web.UI.WebControls;
using System.Web.UI.WebControls.WebParts;
using System.Xml.Linq;
public partial class _Default : System.Web.UI.Page
{
    protected void Page_Load(object sender, EventArgs e)
    {

    }
    protected void Button1_Click(object sender, EventArgs e)
    {
        WebPartManager wpm = new WebPartManager();
        CatalogZone cz = new CatalogZone();
        String str;
        cz.EmptyZoneText = "no controls found!!!";
        Label4.Text = cz.EmptyZoneText;
        cz.SelectedCatalogPartID = "selected zone..";
```

```
            Label6.Text = cz.SelectedCatalogPartID;
            str = WebPartManager.CatalogDisplayMode.Name;
            Label8.Text = str;
            Label4.Visible = true;
            Label6.Visible = true;
            Label8.Visible = true;
        }
    }
```

Now, run the application and click the Property Settings: Custom link. The output is as shown in Figure 7.16:

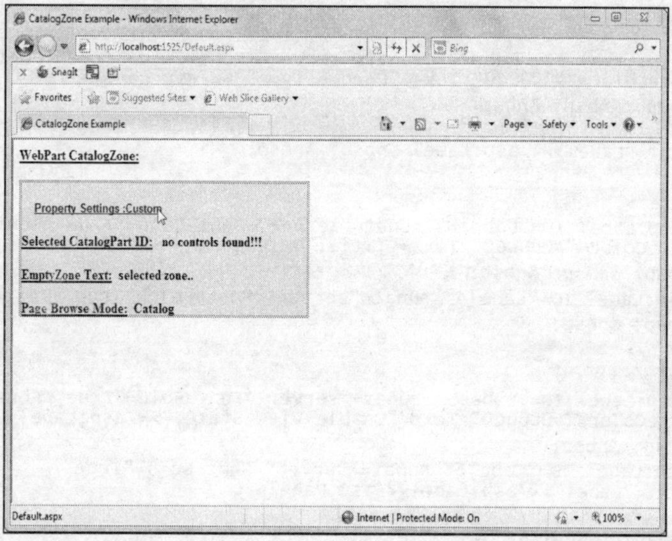

Figure 7.16: Displaying the Output of the CatalogZone Control Example

Creating the PageCatalogPart Control in Code

As learned earlier, the `PageCatalogPart` control is used to restore previously deleted Web Parts controls of a Web page. Now, let's learn how to create a `PageCatalogPart` control. For this, create an application named PageCatalogPartAppCS (`PageCatalogPartAppVB` for VB and `PageCatalogPartAppCS` for C#) and add nine Label controls and a Button control. The Label controls are used to display the `ChromeState`, `ChromeType`, `Title` and `View-State` properties of the `PageCatalogPart` class, when a user clicks the `Button` control.

Listing 7.7 shows the complete code for the `Default.aspx` page of the `PageCatalogPartAppCS` website:

Listing 7.7: Showing the Code for the `Default.aspx` Page

In VB

```
<%@ Page Language="VB" AutoEventWireup="false" CodeFile="Default.aspx.vb"
  Inherits="_Default" %>
<!DOCTYPE html>
<html xmlns="http://www.w3.org/1999/xhtml">
<head runat="server">
    <title>PageCatalogPart Control Example</title>
</head>
<body>
    <form id="form1" runat="server">
    <div>
    <asp:Label ID="Label1" runat="server" Font-Bold="True" Font-Underline="True"
        ForeColor="#0000C0" Text="Page Catalog Webpart"></asp:Label> <br />
```

```
        <br />
        <asp:Button ID="Button1" runat="server" BackColor="#FFE0C0"
        BorderColor="#FF8000" ForeColor="#0000C0" Text="Click" /><br />
        <asp:Panel ID="Panel1" runat="server" BackColor="#FFE0C0" BorderColor="#FF8000"
        BorderStyle="Double" Height="155px" Width="317px">
        <asp:Label ID="Label5" runat="server" Font-Bold="True" Font-Underline="True"
        ForeColor="#0000C0" Text="Chrome State:"></asp:Label>
            
       <asp:Label ID="Label2" runat="server" Font-Bold="True"
        Text="Label"></asp:Label>  
        <br />
        <br />
        <asp:Label ID="Label7" runat="server" Font-Bold="True" Font-Underline="True"
        ForeColor="#0000C0" Text="Chrome Type:"></asp:Label>
            
       <asp:Label ID="Label3" runat="server" Font-Bold="True"
        Text="Label"></asp:Label>   
        <br />
        <br />
        <asp:Label ID="Label8" runat="server" Font-Bold="True" Font-Underline="True"
        ForeColor="#0000C0" Text="Title:"></asp:Label>
            
       <asp:Label ID="Label4" runat="server" Font-Bold="True" Text="Label"></asp:Label>
          
        <br />
        <br />
        <asp:Label ID="Label9" runat="server" Font-Bold="True" Font-Underline="True"
        ForeColor="#0000C0" Text="Enable View State:"></asp:Label>
          
       <asp:Label ID="Label6" runat="server" Font-Bold="True"
        Text="Label"></asp:Label></asp:Panel>
        <br />
           <br />
        <br />
           <br />
           
        <br />
               <br />
        <br />
              
    </div>
    </form>
</body>
</html>
```

In C#

```
<%@ Page Language="C#" AutoEventWireup="true" CodeFile="Default.aspx.cs"
  Inherits="_Default" %>
<!DOCTYPE html>
<html xmlns="http://www.w3.org/1999/xhtml">
<head id="Head1" runat="server">
    <title>PageCatalogPart Control Example</title>
</head>
<body>
    <form id="form1" runat="server">
    <div>
    <asp:Label ID="Label1" runat="server" Font-Bold="True" Font-Underline="True"
         ForeColor="#0000C0" Text="Page Catalog Webpart"></asp:Label> <br />
         <br />
```

```
        <asp:Button ID="Button1" runat="server" BackColor="#FFE0C0"
                BorderColor="#FF8000" ForeColor="#0000C0" Text="Click"
                OnClick="Button1_Click" /><br />
        <asp:Panel ID="Panel1" runat="server" BackColor="#FFE0C0" BorderColor="#FF8000"
                BorderStyle="Double" Height="155px" Width="317px">
        <asp:Label ID="Label5" runat="server" Font-Bold="True" Font-Underline="True"
                ForeColor="#0000C0" Text="Chrome State:"></asp:Label>
             
        <asp:Label ID="Label2" runat="server" Font-Bold="True"
                Text="Label"></asp:Label>  
        <br />
        <br />
        <asp:Label ID="Label7" runat="server" Font-Bold="True" Font-Underline="True"
                ForeColor="#0000C0" Text="Chrome Type:"></asp:Label>
             
        <asp:Label ID="Label3" runat="server" Font-Bold="True"
                Text="Label"></asp:Label>   
        <br />
        <br />
        <asp:Label ID="Label8" runat="server" Font-Bold="True" Font-Underline="True"
                ForeColor="#0000C0" Text="Title:"></asp:Label>
             
        <asp:Label ID="Label4" runat="server" Font-Bold="True" Text="Label"></asp:Label>
           
        <br />
        <br />
        <asp:Label ID="Label9" runat="server" Font-Bold="True" Font-Underline="True"
                ForeColor="#0000C0" Text="Enable View State:"></asp:Label>
           
        <asp:Label ID="Label6" runat="server" Font-Bold="True"
                Text="Label"></asp:Label></asp:Panel>
        <br />
           <br />
        <br />
           <br />
           
        <br />
               <br />
        <br />
              
    </div>
    </form>
</body>
</html>
```

Listing 7.8 shows the complete code for the CodeFile of the Default.aspx page of the `PageCatalogPartAppCS` website:

Listing 7.8: Showing the Code for the CodeFile of the Default.aspx Page

In VB

```
Partial Class _Default
    Inherits System.Web.UI.Page
    Dim pcp As New PageCatalogPart
    Protected Sub Button1_Click(sender As Object, e As EventArgs) Handles Button1.Click
        Label2.Text = pcp.ChromeState.ToString
        Label3.Text = pcp.ChromeType.ToString
        Label4.Text = pcp.Title
        Label6.Text = pcp.EnableViewState
    End Sub
End Class
```

In C#

```
using System;
using System.Data;
using System.Configuration;
using System.Collections.Generic;
using System.Linq;
using System.Web;
using System.Web.Security;
using System.Web.UI;
using System.Web.UI.HtmlControls;
using System.Web.UI.WebControls;
using System.Web.UI.WebControls.WebParts;
using System.Xml.Linq;
public partial class _Default : System.Web.UI.Page
{
    PageCatalogPart pcp = new PageCatalogPart();
    protected void Page_Load(object sender, EventArgs e)
    {
    }
    protected void Button1_Click(object sender, EventArgs e)
    {
        Label2.Text = Convert.ToString(pcp.ChromeState);
        Label3.Text = Convert.ToString(pcp.ChromeType);
        Label4.Text = pcp.Title;
        Label6.Text = Convert.ToString(pcp.EnableViewState);
    }
}
```

Now, run the application and click the Click button. The output is as shown in Figure 7.17:

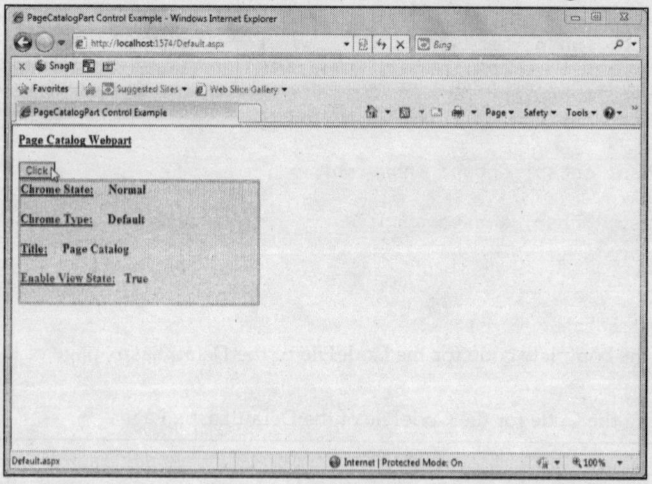

Figure 7.17: Displaying the Output of the PageCatalogPartAppCS Application

Creating the EditorZone Control in Code

As you know, the `EditorZone` control is used to change the appearance, format, and structure of Web pages containing Web Parts controls at runtime. The control can be created by simple drag and drop operations. In the following example, we show another way of creating this control, i.e., the class declaration method. For this, create an application named `EditorZoneAppCS (EditorZoneAppVB` for VB and `EditorZoneApppCS` for C#).

Listing 7.9 shows the complete code for the `Default.aspx` page of `the EditorZoneAppCS` website:

Listing 7.9: Showing the Code for the `Default.aspx` Page

In VB

```
<%@ Page Language="VB" AutoEventWireup="false" CodeFile="Default.aspx.vb"
  Inherits="_Default" %>
<!DOCTYPE html>
<html xmlns="http://www.w3.org/1999/xhtml">
<head runat="server">
    <title>EditorZone control Example</title>
</head>
<body>
    <form id="form1" runat="server">
    <div>
       
         <asp:Label ID="Label7" runat="server" Font-Bold="True" Font-Underline="True"
         ForeColor="#0000C0" Text="EditorZone Webpart"></asp:Label><br />
         <br />
         <asp:Panel ID="Panel1" runat="server" BackColor="#FFFFC0" BorderStyle="Outset"
                 Height="235px" Width="466px">
            
        <asp:Button ID="Button1" runat="server" BackColor="#FFC0C0" Font-Bold="True"
                 Text="Default Values" Width="221px" />
          <br />
            <br />
          
        <asp:Label ID="Label4" runat="server" Font-Bold="True" Font-Underline="True"
                 ForeColor="Navy" Text="Browse Mode:"></asp:Label>   
        <asp:Label ID="Label1" runat="server" Font-Bold="True"
                 Text="Label"></asp:Label><br />
         <br />
         <br />
         <asp:Label ID="Label5" runat="server" Font-Bold="True" Font-Underline="True"
         ForeColor="Navy" Text="Empty Zone Text:"></asp:Label>     
        <asp:Label ID="Label2" runat="server" Font-Bold="True"
         Text="Label"></asp:Label>   <br />
         <br />
            
         <br />
         <asp:Label ID="Label6" runat="server" Font-Bold="True" Font-Underline="True"
         ForeColor="Navy" Text="Header Text:"></asp:Label>   
        <asp:Label ID="Label3" runat="server" Font-Bold="True"
         Text="Label"></asp:Label><br />
            </asp:Panel>
    </div>
    </form>
</body>
</html>
```

In C#

```
<%@ Page Language="C#" AutoEventWireup="true" CodeFile="Default.aspx.cs"
  Inherits="_Default" %>
<!DOCTYPE html>
<html xmlns="http://www.w3.org/1999/xhtml">
<head id="Head1" runat="server">
    <title>EditorZone control Example</title>
</head>
<body>
    <form id="form1" runat="server">
    <div>
```

```
       
        <asp:Label ID="Label7" runat="server" Font-Bold="True" Font-Underline="True"
        ForeColor="#0000C0" Text="EditorZone Webpart"></asp:Label><br />
        <br />
        <asp:Panel ID="Panel1" runat="server" BackColor="#FFFFC0" BorderStyle="Outset"
        Height="235px" Width="466px">
           
        <asp:Button ID="Button1" runat="server" BackColor="#FFC0C0" Font-Bold="True"
        Text="Default Values" Width="221px" OnClick="Button1_Click" />
         <br />
           <br />
         
        <asp:Label ID="Label4" runat="server" Font-Bold="True" Font-Underline="True"
        ForeColor="Navy" Text="Browse Mode:"></asp:Label>   
        <asp:Label ID="Label1" runat="server" Font-Bold="True"
        Text="Label"></asp:Label><br />
        <br />
        <br />
        <asp:Label ID="Label5" runat="server" Font-Bold="True" Font-Underline="True"
        ForeColor="Navy" Text="Empty Zone Text:"></asp:Label>     
        <asp:Label ID="Label2" runat="server" Font-Bold="True"
        Text="Label"></asp:Label>   <br />
        <br />
           
        <br />
        <asp:Label ID="Label6" runat="server" Font-Bold="True" Font-Underline="True"
        ForeColor="Navy" Text="Header Text:"></asp:Label>   
        <asp:Label ID="Label3" runat="server" Font-Bold="True"
        Text="Label"></asp:Label><br />
           </asp:Panel>
    </div>
    </form>
</body>
</html>
```

Listing 7.10 shows the complete code for the CodeFile of the Default.aspx page of the `EditorZoneAppCS` website:

Listing 7.10: Showing the Code for the CodeFile of the Default.aspx Page

In VB

```
Partial Class _Default
    Inherits System.Web.UI.Page
    Dim ez As New EditorZone
    Protected Sub Button1_Click(sender As Object, e As EventArgs) Handles Button1.Click
        Dim str As String
        Dim str1 As String
        str = ez.EmptyZoneText
        Label2.Text = str
        str1 = ez.HeaderText
        Label3.Text = str1
    End Sub
    Protected Sub Page_Load(sender As Object, e As EventArgs) Handles Me.Load
        Label1.Text = WebPartManager.EditDisplayMode.Name
    End Sub
End Class
```

In C#

```
using System;
using System.Data;
using System.Configuration;
using System.Collections.Generic;
using System.Linq;
using System.Web;
using System.Web.Security;
using System.Web.UI;
using System.Web.UI.HtmlControls;
using System.Web.UI.WebControls;
using System.Web.UI.WebControls.WebParts;
using System.Xml.Linq;
public partial class _Default : System.Web.UI.Page
{
    EditorZone ez = new EditorZone();
    protected void Page_Load(object sender, EventArgs e)
    {
        Label1.Text = WebPartManager.EditDisplayMode.Name;
    }
    protected void Button1_Click(object sender, EventArgs e)
    {
        String str;
        String str1;
        str = ez.EmptyZoneText;
        Label2.Text - str;
        str1 = ez.HeaderText;
        Label3.Text = str1;
    }
}
```

Press F5 to execute the application.The output of the `EditorZoneAppCS` website after clicking the Default Values button is shown in Figure 7.18:

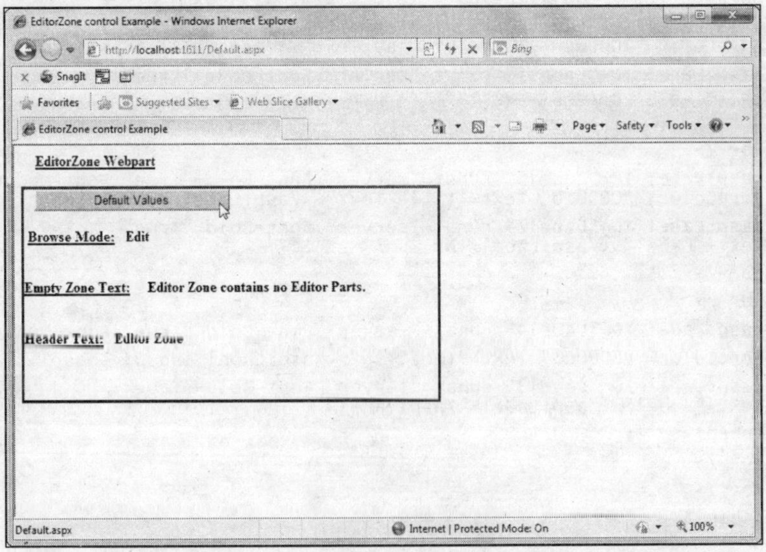

Figure 7.18: Displaying the Output of the EditorZone Control Example

Creating the PropertyGridEditorPart Control in Code

As discussed in the *In Depth* section of this chapter, the `PropertyGridEditorPart` control is used to edit the custom properties of a Web Parts control on a Web page. Now, let's learn how to create the `PropertyGridEditorPart` control. For this, we create an application named `PropertyGridEditorPartAppCS` (`PropertyGridEditorPartAppVB` for VB and `PropertyGridEditorPartAppCS` for C#). You can set the properties of the `PropertyGridEditorPart` control and use the methods of the `PropertyGridEditorPart` class after creating the control. Listing 7.11 shows the complete code for the `Default.aspx` page of the `PropertyGridEditorPartAppCS` website:

Listing 7.11: Showing the Code for the `Default.aspx` Page

In VB

```
<%@ Page Language="VB" AutoEventWireup="false" CodeFile="Default.aspx.vb"
  Inherits="_Default" %>
<!DOCTYPE html>
<html xmlns="http://www.w3.org/1999/xhtml">
<head runat="server">
    <title>PropertyGridEditorPart control Example</title>
</head>
<body>
    <form id="form1" runat="server">
    <div>
       <br />
        <asp:Label ID="Label7" runat="server" Font-Bold="True" Font-Underline="True"
        ForeColor="#0000C0" Text="Property Grid EditorPart"></asp:Label><br />
           <br />
        <asp:Button ID="Button1" runat="server" BackColor="#FFE0C0"
        BorderColor="#FF8000" Font-Bold="True" ForeColor="#0000C0" Text="CLICK" /><br />
           
       <asp:Panel ID="Panel1" runat="server" BackColor="#FFE0C0" BorderColor="#FF8000"
        BorderStyle="Double" Height="165px" Width="394px">
        <asp:Label ID="Label6" runat="server" Font-Bold="True" Font-Underline="True"
        ForeColor="#0000C0" Text="Display Text"></asp:Label>   
        <asp:Label ID="Label1" runat="server" Font-Bold="True"
        Text="Label"></asp:Label><br />
        <br />
        <br />
        <asp:Label ID="Label5" runat="server" Font-Bold="True" Font-Underline="True"
        ForeColor="#0000C0" Text="Title Text"></asp:Label>   
        <asp:Label ID="Label2" runat="server" Font-Bold="True"
        Text="Label"></asp:Label><br />
        <br />
        <br />
        <asp:Label ID="Label4" runat="server" Font-Bold="True" Font-Underline="True"
        ForeColor="#0000C0" Text="Tool Tip"></asp:Label>   
        <asp:Label ID="Label3" runat="server" Font-Bold="True"
        Text="Label"></asp:Label></asp:Panel>
         <br />
        <br />
        <br />
         
    </div>
    </form>
</body>
</html>
```

In C#

```
<%@ Page Language="C#" AutoEventWireup="true" CodeFile="Default.aspx.cs"
   Inherits="_Default" %>
<!DOCTYPE html>
<html xmlns="http://www.w3.org/1999/xhtml">
<head id="Head1" runat="server">
    <title>PropertyGridEditorPart control Example</title>
</head>
<body>
    <form id="form1" runat="server">
    <div>
       <br />
         <asp:Label ID="Label7" runat="server" Font-Bold="True" Font-Underline="True"
         ForeColor="#0000C0" Text="Property Grid EditorPart"></asp:Label><br />
            <br />
         <asp:Button ID="Button1" runat="server" BackColor="#FFE0C0"
         BorderColor="#FF8000" Font-Bold="True" ForeColor="#0000C0" Text="CLICK"
         OnClick="Button1_Click" /><br />
            
        <asp:Panel ID="Panel1" runat="server" BackColor="#FFE0C0" BorderColor="#FF8000"
         BorderStyle="Double" Height="165px" Width="394px">
         <asp:Label ID="Label6" runat="server" Font-Bold="True" Font-Underline="True"
         ForeColor="#0000C0" Text="Display Text"></asp:Label>   
         <asp:Label ID="Label1" runat="server" Font-Bold="True"
         Text="Label"></asp:Label><br />
         <br />
         <br />
         <asp:Label ID="Label5" runat="server" Font-Bold="True" Font-Underline="True"
         ForeColor="#0000C0" Text="Title Text"></asp:Label>   
         <asp:Label ID="Label2" runat="server" Font-Bold="True"
         Text="Label"></asp:Label><br />
         <br />
         <br />
         <asp:Label ID="Label4" runat="server" Font-Bold="True" Font-Underline="True"
         ForeColor="#0000C0" Text="Tool Tip"></asp:Label>   
         <asp:Label ID="Label3" runat="server" Font-Bold="True"
         Text="Label"></asp:Label></asp:Panel>
          <br />
         <br />
         <br />
          
    </div>
    </form>
</body>
</html>
```

Listing 7.12 shows the complete code for the CodeFile of the Default.aspx page of the `PropertyGridEditorPartAppCS` website:

Listing 7.12: Showing the Code for the CodeFile of the Default.aspx Page

In VB

```
Partial Class _Default
    Inherits System.Web.UI.Page
    Dim propgrid As New PropertyGridEditorPart
    Protected Sub Button1_Click(sender As Object, e As EventArgs) Handles Button1.Click
        Label1.Visible = True
```

```
            Label2.Visible = True
            Label3.Visible = True
            Label1.Text = propgrid.DisplayTitle
            propgrid.Title = "MY PROPERTY GRID EDITOR PART!!!"
            Label2.Text = propgrid.Title
            propgrid.ToolTip = "MY TOOLTIP"
            Label3.Text = propgrid.ToolTip
        End Sub
        Protected Sub Page_Load(sender As Object, e As EventArgs) Handles Me.Load
            Label1.Visible = False
            Label2.Visible = False
            Label3.Visible = False
        End Sub
    End Class
```

In C#

```
using System;
using System.Data;
using System.Configuration;
using System.Collections.Generic;
using System.Linq;
using System.Web;
using System.Web.Security;
using System.Web.UI;
using System.Web.UI.HtmlControls;
using System.Web.UI.WebControls;
using System.Web.UI.WebControls.WebParts;
using System.Xml.Linq;
public partial class _Default : System.Web.UI.Page
{
    PropertyGridEditorPart propgrid = new PropertyGridEditorPart();
    protected void Page_Load(object sender, EventArgs e)
    {
        Label1.Visible = false;
        Label2.Visible = false;
        Label3.Visible = false;
    }
    protected void Button1_Click(object sender, EventArgs e)
    {
        Label1.Visible = true;
        Label2.Visible = true;
        Label3.Visible = true;
        Label1.Text = propgrid.DisplayTitle;
        propgrid.Title = "MY PROPERTY GRID EDITOR PART!!!";
        Label2.Text = propgrid.Title;
        propgrid.ToolTip = "MY TOOLTIP";
        Label3.Text = propgrid.ToolTip;
    }
}
```

Now, run the application and click the CLICK button. The output is as shown in Figure 7.19:

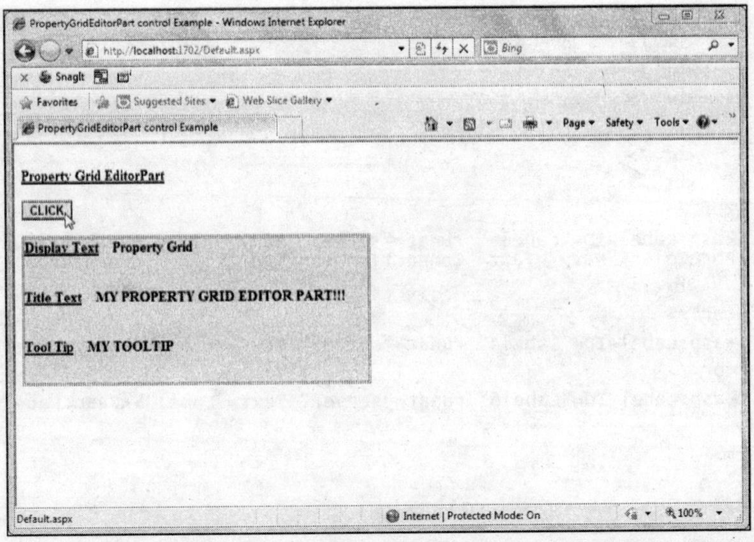

Figure 7.19: Displaying the Output of the PropertyGridEditorPart Control Example

Creating the ConnectionsZone Control in Code

We discussed the working of the `ConnectionsZone` control in the In Depth section of this chapter. We also discussed how to use the `ConnectionsZone` class to create the `ConnectionsZone` control. Now, let's create the `ConnectionsZone` control with the help of the `ConnectionsZone` class and specify the various properties of the control. For this, we create an application named `ConnectionsZoneAppCS` (`ConnectionsZoneAppVB` for VB and `ConnectionsZoneAppCS` for C#). Listing 7.13 shows the complete code for the `Default.aspx` page of the `ConnectionsZoneAppCS` website:

Listing 7.13: Showing the Code for the `Default.aspx` Page

In VB

```
<%@ Page Language="VB" AutoEventWireup="false" CodeFile="Default.aspx.vb"
   Inherits="_Default" %>
<!DOCTYPE html>
<html xmlns="http://www.w3.org/1999/xhtml">
<head runat="server">
     <title>ConnectionsZone control Example</title>
</head>
<body>
    <form id="form1" runat="server">
    <div>
    <asp:Label ID="Label2" runat="server" Font-Bold="True" Font-Underline="True"
   ForeColor="Navy" Text="ConnectionZone Webpart:"></asp:Label>
         <br />
        <br />
        <br />
         <asp:Panel ID="Panel1" runat="server" BackColor="#FFE0C0" BorderStyle="Ridge"
         Height="161px" Width="437px">
         <asp:Label ID="Label1" runat="server" Text="Connection Status:" Width="622px"
         Font-Bold="True" Font-Underline="True" ForeColor="Navy"></asp:Label><br />
         <br />
          <asp:Label ID="Label3" runat="server" Text="Label"></asp:Label>
         <br />
```

```
                <br />
                <br />
                <br />
                <br />
                <br />
                <br />
                <br />
            <br />
            <asp:Label ID="Label5" runat="server" Font-Bold="True" Font-Underline="True"
            ForeColor="Navy" Text="Connection Configuration:"></asp:Label>
                <br />
            <br />
            <asp:Label ID="Label4" runat="server" Text="Label"></asp:Label> 
            <br />
            <asp:Label ID="Label6" runat="server" Text="Label"></asp:Label></asp:Panel>
        </div>
        </form>
    </body>
    </html>
```

In C#

```
<%@ Page Language="C#" AutoEventWireup="true" CodeFile="Default.aspx.cs"
  Inherits="_Default" %>
<!DOCTYPE html>
<html xmlns="http://www.w3.org/1999/xhtml">
<head id="Head1" runat="server">
     <title>ConnectionsZone control Example</title>
</head>
<body>
    <form id="form1" runat="server">
    <div>
    <asp:Label ID="Label2" runat="server" Font-Bold="True" Font-Underline="True"
         ForeColor="Navy" Text="ConnectionZone Webpart:"></asp:Label>
         <br />
        <br />
        <br />
         <asp:Panel ID="Panel1" runat="server" BackColor="#FFE0C0" BorderStyle="Ridge"
         Height="161px" Width="437px">
         <asp:Label ID="Label1" runat="server" Text="Connection Status:" Width="622px"
         Font-Bold="True" Font-Underline="True" ForeColor="Navy"></asp:Label><br />
         <br />
          <asp:Label ID="Label3" runat="server" Text="Label"></asp:Label>
         <br />
             <br />
            <br />
            <br />
            <br />
            <br />
            <br />
            <br />
         <br />
         <asp:Label ID="Label5" runat="server" Font-Bold="True" Font-Underline="True"
         ForeColor="Navy" Text="Connection Configuration:"></asp:Label>
            <br />
         <br />
```

```
            <asp:Label ID="Label4" runat="server" Text="Label"></asp:Label> 
            <br />
            <asp:Label ID="Label6" runat="server" Text="Label"></asp:Label></asp:Panel>
        </div>
        </form>
    </body>
    </html>
```

Listing 7.14 shows the complete code for the CodeFile of the Default.aspx page of the `ConnectionsZoneAppCS` website:

Listing 7.14: Showing the Code for the CodeFile of the Default.aspx Page

In VB

```
Partial Class _Default
    Inherits System.Web.UI.Page
    Dim conn As New ConnectionsZone
    Protected Sub Page_Load(sender As Object, e As EventArgs) Handles Me.Load
        Dim value As String
        value = conn.NoExistingConnectionInstructionText
        conn.NoExistingConnectionInstructionText = value
        Label3.Text = conn.NoExistingConnectionInstructionText
        Label4.Text = "DEFAULT:" & conn.ConfigureConnectionTitle
        conn.ConfigureConnectionTitle = _
        "Configure a new connection"
        Label6.Text = "CUSTOM:" & conn.ConfigureConnectionTitle
    End Sub
End Class
```

In C#

```
using System;
using System.Data;
using System.Configuration;
using System.Collections.Generic;
using System.Linq;
using System.Web;
using System.Web.Security;
using System.Web.UI;
using System.Web.UI.HtmlControls;
using System.Web.UI.WebControls;
using System.Web.UI.WebControls.WebParts;
using System.Xml.Linq;
public partial class _Default : System.Web.UI.Page
{
    ConnectionsZone conn = new ConnectionsZone();
    protected void Page_Load(object sender, EventArgs e)
    {
        string value;
        value = conn.NoExistingConnectionInstructionText;
        conn.NoExistingConnectionInstructionText = value;
        Label3.Text = conn.NoExistingConnectionInstructionText;
        Label4.Text = "DEFAULT:" + conn.ConfigureConnectionTitle;
        conn.ConfigureConnectionTitle = "Configure a new connection";
        Label6.Text = "CUSTOM:" + conn.ConfigureConnectionTitle;
    }
}
```

Figure 7.20 shows the output of the `ConnectionsZoneAppCS` website:

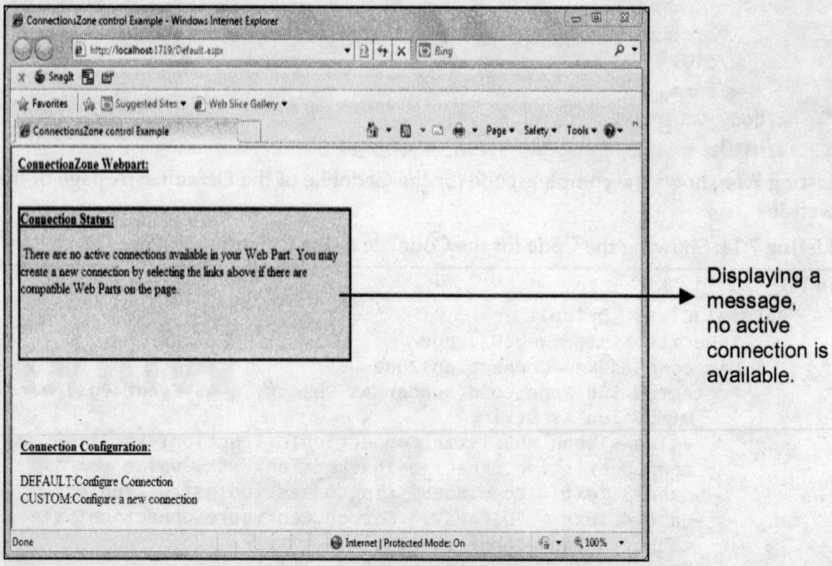

Figure 7.20: Displaying the ConnectionsZone Control in Action

Summary

This chapter has described the Web Parts controls available with Visual Studio 2012. These Web Parts controls enable you to create a website that can be personalized at runtime directly through the browser. In addition to a thorough discussion of the Web Parts controls, which includes a detailed description of their methods, properties, and events, this chapter also shows the use of these controls through sample Web applications.

In the next chapter, we discuss about Database Controls.

8

Working with Database Controls

In Depth

What is a database? Why do we need a database? How does a .NET application work with a database? We need to know the answers to these questions before we learn about working with database controls in ASP.NET.

A database is a collection of records or information that is stored in the form of tables in a systematic way so that a computer program can access the information easily whenever required. Structured Query Language (SQL) is used for retrieving, storing, deleting, and updating the records stored in a database. An application may need to use the databases for performing various functions, such as:

- Displaying data in a tabular format by retrieving the records from the database
- Displaying the data after processing the record retrieved from the database, such as calculating the service duration of each employee and then displaying the records
- Processing the retrieved data and updating them in the database
- Deleting the records from the database depending on the choice or condition specified by the user of the application

In this chapter, you learn about the use of various data sources and data bound controls supported by ASP.NET 4.5. The data bound controls are composite controls that are used with the data source controls to display and modify the data in a Web based application. Following is a list of data bound controls:

- The GridView Control
- The DataList Control
- The DetailsView Control
- The FormView Control
- The ListView Control
- The Repeater Control
- The DataPager Control
- The Chart Control
- The QueryExtender Control

Similarly, the data source controls allow you to work with different types of data sources, such as SQL server or an Extensible Markup Language (XML) file. Following is a list of data source controls:

- The SqlDataSource Control
- The AccessDataSource Control
- The LinqDataSource Control
- The ObjectDataSource Control
- The XmlDataSource Control
- The SiteMapDataSource Control
- The EntityDataSource Control

Now, let's start the discussion with the `GridView` control in detail.

The GridView Control

The `GridView` control is a data bound control that displays the values of a data source in the form of a table. In this table, each column represents a field and each row represents a record. The `GridView` control exists within the `System.Web.UI.WebControls` namespace. The inheritance hierarchy of the `GridView` control is as follows:

```
System.Object
   System.Web.UI.Control
       System.Web.UI.WebControls.WebControl
           System.Web.UI.WebControls.BaseDataBoundControl
              System.Web.UI.WebControls.DataBoundControl
                 System.Web.UI.WebControls.CompositeDataBoundControl
                   System.Web.UI.WebControls.GridView
```

When you drag and drop the GridView control on the designer page, the following syntax is added to the source view of the page:

```
<asp:GridView ID="GridView1" runat="server">  </asp:GridView>
```

The GridView data control has a built-in capability of sorting, paging, updating, and deleting data. You can also set the column fields through the AutoGenerateColumns property to indicate whether bound fields are automatically created for each field in the data source. Table 8.1 lists the different column field types of the GridView class:

Table 8.1: Column Field Types of the GridView Class

Field	Description
BoundField	Shows the value of a field in a data source. It is the default column type of the GridView control.
ButtonField	Shows a command button for each item in the GridView control. It allows us to create a column of custom button controls, such as the Add or the Remove button.
CheckBoxField	Shows a CheckBox control for each item in the GridView control. This column field type is commonly used to display fields with a Boolean value.
CommandField	Shows predefined command buttons to perform operations, such as select, edit, or delete.
HyperLinkField	Shows the value of a field in a data source as a hyperlink. This column field type allows you to bind a second field to the hyperlink's URL.
ImageField	Shows an image for each item in the GridView control.
TemplateField	Shows user-defined content for each item in the GridView control according to a specified template. This column field type enables us to create a custom column field.

You can also customize the appearance of the GridView control by setting the style properties. The different style properties are listed in Table 8.2:

Table 8.2: Style Properties of the GridView Class

Style Property	Description
EditRowStyle	Performs the style settings for the row that is edited in the GridView control
EmptyDataRowStyle	Performs the style settings for the empty data row displayed in the GridView control when the data source does not contain any records
FooterStyle	Performs the style settings for the footer row of the GridView control
HeaderStyle	Performs the style settings for the header row of the GridView control
PagerStyle	Performs the style settings for the pager row of the GridView control
SelectedRowStyle	Performs the style settings for the selected row in the GridView control

Noteworthy properties of the GridView class are listed in Table 8.3:

Table 8.3: Noteworthy Properties of the GridView Class

Property	Description
AllowPaging	Obtains or sets a value indicating whether the paging feature is enabled.
AllowCustomPaging	Obtains or specifies a value indicating whether custom paging is enabled or not
AllowSorting	Obtains or sets a value indicating whether the sorting feature is enabled.
AlternatingRowStyle	Obtains a reference to the TableItemStyle object that enables us to set the appearance of alternating data rows in a GridView control.
AutoGenerateColumns	Obtains or sets a value indicating whether bound fields are automatically created for each field in the data source.
AutoGenerateDeleteButton	Obtains or sets a value indicating whether a CommandField field column with a Delete button for each data row is automatically added to a GridView control.
AutoGenerateEditButton	Obtains or sets a value indicating whether a CommandField field column with an Edit button for each data row is automatically added to a GridView control.
AutoGenerateSelectButton	Obtains or sets a value indicating whether a CommandField field column with a Select button for each data row is automatically added to a GridView control.
BackImageUrl	Obtains or sets the URL to an image to display in the background of a GridView control.
BottomPagerRow	Obtains a GridViewRow object that represents the bottom pager row in a GridView control.
Caption	Obtains or sets the text to render in an HTML caption element in a GridView control. This property is provided to make the control more accessible to users of assistive technology devices.
CaptionAlign	Obtains or sets the horizontal or vertical position of the HTML caption element in a GridView control. This property is provided to make the control more accessible to users of assistive technology devices.
CellPadding	Obtains or sets the amount of space between the contents of a cell and the cell's border.
CellSpacing	Obtains or sets the amount of space between cells.
Columns	Obtains a collection of DataControlField objects that represent the column fields in a GridView control.
DataKeyNames	Obtains or sets an array that contains the names of the primary key fields for the items displayed in a GridView control.
DataKeys	Obtains a collection of DataKey objects that represent the data key value of each row in a GridView control.
EditIndex	Obtains or sets the index of the row to edit.
EditRowStyle	Obtains a reference to the TableItemStyle object that enables us to set the appearance of the row selected for editing in a GridView control.
EmptyDataRowStyle	Obtains a reference to the TableItemStyle object that enables us to set the appearance of the empty data row rendered when a GridView control is bound to a data source that does not contain any records.
EmptyDataTemplate	Obtains or sets the user-defined content for the empty data row rendered when a GridView control is bound to a data source that does not contain any records.

Table 8.3: Noteworthy Properties of the GridView Class

Property	Description
EmptyDataText	Obtains or sets the text to display in the empty data row rendered when a GridView control is bound to a data source that does not contain any records.
EnableSortingAndPagingCallbacks	Obtains or sets a value indicating whether client-side callbacks are used for sorting and paging operations.
FooterRow	Obtains a GridViewRow object that represents the footer row in a GridView control.
FooterStyle	Obtains a reference to the TableItemStyle object that enables us to set the appearance of the footer row in a GridView control.
GridLines	Obtains or sets the gridline style for a GridView control.
HeaderRow	Obtains a GridViewRow object that represents the header row in a GridView control.
HeaderStyle	Obtains a reference to the TableItemStyle object that enables us to set the appearance of the header row in a GridView control.
HorizontalAlign	Obtains or sets the horizontal alignment of a GridView control on the page.
PageCount	Obtains the number of pages required to display the records of the data source in a GridView control.
PageIndex	Obtains or sets the index of the currently displayed page.
PagerSettings	Obtains a reference to the PagerSettings object that enables us to set the properties of the pager buttons in a GridView control.
PagerStyle	Obtains a reference to the TableItemStyle object that enables us to set the appearance of the pager row in a GridView control.
PagerTemplate	Obtains or sets the custom content for the pager row in a GridView control.
PageSize	Obtains or sets the number of records to display on a page in a GridView control.
RowHeaderColumn	Obtains or sets the name of the column to use as the column header for the GridView control. This property is provided to make the control more accessible to users of assistive technology devices.
Rows	Obtains a collection of GridViewRow objects that represent the data rows in a GridView control.
RowStyle	Obtains a reference to the TableItemStyle object that enables us to set the appearance of the data rows in a GridView control.
SelectedDataKey	Obtains the DataKey object that contains the data key value for the selected row in a GridView control.
SelectedIndex	Obtains or sets the index of the selected row in a GridView control.
SelectedRow	Obtains a reference to a GridViewRow object that represents the selected row in the control.
SelectedRowStyle	Obtains a reference to the TableItemStyle object that enables us to set the appearance of the selected row in a GridView control.
SelectedValue	Obtains the data key value of the selected row in a GridView control.
ShowFooter	Obtains or sets a value showing whether the footer row is displayed in a GridView control.

Table 8.3: Noteworthy Properties of the GridView Class	
Property	**Description**
`ShowHeader`	Obtains or sets a value showing whether the header row is displayed in a `GridView` control.
`SortDirection`	Obtains the sort direction of the column being sorted.
`SortExpression`	Obtains the sort expression associated with the column or columns being sorted.
`TopPagerRow`	Obtains a `GridViewRow` object that represents the top pager row in a `GridView` control.
`UseAccessibleHeader`	Obtains or sets a value indicating whether a `GridView` control renders its header in an accessible format. This property makes the control more accessible to users of assistive technology devices.

Noteworthy methods of the `GridView` class are listed in Table 8.4:

Table 8.4: Noteworthy Methods of the GridView Class	
Method	**Description**
`DataBind`	Binds the data from the data source with the `GridView` control
`DeleteRow`	Deletes the record present at the specified location from the data source
`IsBindableType`	Determines whether the particular data type can bind to a Bound field in a `GridView` control
`Sort`	Sorts the `GridView` control according to the sort expression and direction specified
`UpdateRow`	Updates the of the row specified by index using the field values of that row

Noteworthy events of the `GridView` class are listed in Table 8.5:

Table 8.5: Noteworthy Events of the GridView Class	
Event	**Description**
`PageIndexChanged`	Invoked when one of the pager buttons is clicked, but after the `GridView` control handles the paging operation
`PageIndexChanging`	Invoked when one of the pager buttons is clicked, but before the `GridView` control handles the paging operation
`RowCancelingEdit`	Invoked when the Cancel button of a row in edit mode is clicked, but before the row exits the edit mode
`RowCommand`	Invoked when a button is clicked in a `GridView` control
`RowCreated`	Invoked when a row is created in a `GridView` control
`RowDataBound`	Invoked when a data row is bound to data in a `GridView` control
`RowDeleted`	Invoked when a row's Delete button is clicked, but after the `GridView` control deletes the row
`RowDeleting`	Invoked when a row's Delete button is clicked, but before the `GridView` control deletes the row
`RowEditing`	Invoked when a row's Edit button is clicked, but before the `GridView` control enters edit mode
`RowUpdated`	Invoked when a row's Update button is clicked, but after the `GridView` control updates the row

Table 8.5: Noteworthy Events of the GridView Class	
Event	**Description**
`RowUpdating`	Invoked when a row's Update button is clicked, but before the `GridView` control updates the row
`SelectedIndexChanged`	Invoked when a row's Select button is clicked, but after the `GridView` control handles the select operation
`SelectedIndexChanging`	Invoked when a row's Select button is clicked, but before the `GridView` control handles the select operation
`Sorted`	Invoked when the hyperlink to sort a column is clicked, but after the `GridView` control handles the sort operation
`Sorting`	Invoked when the hyperlink to sort a column is clicked, but before the `GridView` control handles the sort operation

Now, let's learn about the `DataList` control.

The DataList Control

The `DataList` control is a data bound control that displays data by using templates. These templates define controls and HTML elements that should be displayed for an item. The `DataList` control exists within the `System.Web.UI.WebControls` namespace. The inheritance hierarchy of the `DataList` control is as follows:

```
System.Object
    System.Web.UI.Control
        System.Web.UI.WebControls.WebControl
            System.Web.UI.WebControls.BaseDataList
                System.Web.UI.WebControls.DataList
```

You can change the content of the `DataList` control by using the templates described in Table 8.6:

Table 8.6: Templates of the DataList Class	
Template Name	**Description**
`AlternatingItemTemplate`	Provides the format and content for alternating cells in the `DataList` control.
`EditItemTemplate`	Provides the format and content for the items to be edited in the `DataList` control.
`FooterTemplate`	Provides the format and content for the footer section of the `DataList` control, when defined, else, the footer section does not appear.
`HeaderTemplate`	Provides the format and content for the header section of the `DataList` control, `else` the header section does not appear.
`ItemTemplate`	Provides the format and content for items in the `DataList` control. It is a mandatory template.
`SelectedItemTemplate`	Provides the format and content for the presently selected item in the `DataList` control.
`SeparatorTemplate`	Provides the format and content for the separator separating items in the `DataList` control else the separator does not appear.

We can also configure the `DataList` control to enable users to edit or delete a record in the table and it can render its items horizontally or vertically.

Noteworthy properties of the `DataList` class are listed in Table 8.7:

Table 8.7: Noteworthy Properties of the DataList Class

Property	Description
`AlternatingItemStyle`	Obtains the style properties for alternating items in the `DataList` control
`AlternatingItemTemplate`	Obtains or sets the template for alternating items in the `DataList control`
`EditItemIndex`	Obtains or sets the index number of the selected item in the `DataList` control to edit
`EditItemStyle`	Obtains the style properties for the item selected for editing in the `DataList` control
`EditItemTemplate`	Obtains or sets the template for the item selected for editing in the `DataList` control
`ExtractTemplateRows`	Obtains or sets a value that indicates whether the rows of a `Table` control, defined in each template of a `DataList` control, are extracted and displayed
`FooterStyle`	Obtains the style properties for the footer section of the `DataList` control
`FooterTemplate`	Obtains or sets the template for the footer section of the `DataList` control
`GridLines`	Obtains or sets the grid line style for the `DataList` control when the `RepeatLayout` property is set to `RepeatLayout.Table`
`HeaderStyle`	Obtains the style properties for the heading section of the `DataList` control
`HeaderTemplate`	Obtains or sets the template for the heading section of the `DataList` control
`Items`	Obtains a collection of `DataListItem` objects representing the individual items within the control
`ItemStyle`	Obtains the style properties, such as BackColor, for the items in the `DataList` control
`ItemTemplate`	Obtains or sets the template for the items in the `DataList` control
`RepeatColumns`	Obtains or sets the number of columns to display in the `DataList` control
`RepeatDirection`	Obtains or sets whether the `DataList` control displays vertically or horizontally
`RepeatLayout`	Obtains or sets whether the control is displayed in a table or flow layout
`SelectedIndex`	Obtains or sets the index of the selected item in the `DataList` control
`SelectedItem`	Obtains the selected item in the `DataList` control
`SelectedItemStyle`	Obtains the style properties for the selected item in the `DataList` control
`SelectedItemTemplate`	Obtains or sets the template for the selected item in the `DataList` control
`SelectedValue`	Obtains the value of the key field for the selected data list item
`SeparatorStyle`	Obtains the style properties of the separator between each item in the `DataList` control
`SeparatorTemplate`	Obtains or sets the template for the separator between the items of the `DataList` control
`ShowFooter`	Obtains or sets a value indicating whether the footer section is displayed in the `DataList` control
`ShowHeader`	Obtains or sets a value indicating whether the header section is displayed in the `DataList` control

Noteworthy events of `DataList` class are listed in Table 8.8:

Table 8.8: Noteworthy Events of the DataList Class

Event	Description
`CancelCommand`	Invoked when the `Cancel` button is clicked for an item in the `DataList` control
`DeleteCommand`	Invoked when the `Delete` button is clicked for an item in the `DataList` control
`EditCommand`	Invoked when the `Edit` button is clicked for an item in the `DataList` control
`ItemCommand`	Invoked when any button is clicked in the `DataList` control
`ItemCreated`	Invoked on the server when an item in the `DataList` control is created
`ItemDatabound`	Invoked when an item is data bound to the `DataList` control
`UpdateCommand`	Invoked when the `Update` button is clicked for an item in the `DataList` control

Now, let's learn about the `DetailsView` control.

The DetailsView Control

The `DetailsView` control is a data bound control that is used to display a single record from the associated data source in a table format, where each row of the table represents a field of the record. The `DetailsView` control uses the `DataSourceID` property to support two-way binding; consequently, it also supports insert, update, and delete operations.

The `DetailsView` control exists within the `System.Web.UI.WebControls namespace`. The inheritance hierarchy of the `DetailsView` control is:

```
System.Object
    System.Web.UI.Control
        System.Web.UI.WebControls. WebControl
            System.Web.UI.WebControls. BaseDataBoundControl
                System.Web.UI.WebControls. DataBoundControl
                    System.Web.UI.WebControls. CompositeDataBoundControl
                          System.Web.UI.WebControls.DetailsView
```

NOTE

Row fields, Row field types, and field types are the same as Fields in the DetailsView control.

Data rows of a `DetailsView` control are created by declaring a field control. Table 8.9 shows the different row fields:

Table 8.9: Row Field Types of the DetailsView Class

Field Type	Description
`BoundField`	Represents the value of a field present in a data base as text.
`ButtonField`	Represents a command button in the `DetailsView` control. Also, you can display a row with a custom button control, such as an Add or a Remove button.
`CheckBoxField`	Represents a check box in the `DetailsView` control. You can use it to display fields with a Boolean value.
`CommandField`	Represents built-in command buttons to perform operations such as edit, insert, or delete in the `DetailsView` control.
`HyperLinkField`	Represents the value of a field from the database as a hyperlink.
`ImageField`	Displays an image in the `DetailsView` control.
`TemplateField`	Represents the user-defined content for a row in the `DetailsView` control according to the defined template. You can also create a custom row field.

Noteworthy properties of the DetailsView class are listed in Table 8.10:

Table 8.10: Noteworthy Properties of the DetailsView Class

Property	Description
AllowPaging	Gets or sets a value indicating whether the paging feature is enabled.
AlternatingRowStyle	Obtains a reference to the TableItemStyle object that allows you to set the appearance of the alternating data rows in a DetailsView control.
AutoGenerateDeleteButton	Obtains or sets a value indicating whether the built-in controls, such as the GridView control, to delete the current record is displayed in a DetailsView control.
AutoGenerateEditButton	Obtains or sets a value indicating whether the built-in controls to edit the current record are displayed in a DetailsView control.
AutoGenerateInsertButton	Obtains or sets a value indicating whether the built-in controls to insert a new record are displayed in a DetailsView control.
AutoGenerateRows	Obtains or sets a value indicating whether the row fields for each field in the data source are automatically generated and displayed in a DetailsView control.
BackImageUrl	Obtains or sets the URL to an image to display in the background of a DetailsView control.
BottomPagerRow	Obtains a DetailsViewRow object that represents the bottom pager row in a DetailsView control.
Caption	Obtains or sets the text to render in an HTML caption element in a DetailsView control. This property is provided to make the control more accessible to users of assistive technology devices.
CaptionAlign	Obtains or sets the horizontal or vertical position of the HTML caption element in a DetailsView control. This property is provided to make the control more accessible to users of assistive technology devices.
CellPadding	Obtains or sets the amount of space between the contents of a cell and the cell's border.
CellSpacing	Gets or sets the amount of space between cells.
CommandRowStyle	Gets a reference to the TableItemStyle object that allows you to set the appearance of a command row in a DetailsView control.
CurrentMode	Obtains the current data-entry mode of the DetailsView control.
DataItem	Obtains the data item bound to the DetailsView control.
DataItemCount	Obtains the number of items in the underlying data source.
DataItemIndex	Obtains the index of the item displayed in a DetailsView control from the underlying data source.
DataKey	Obtains a DataKey object that represents the primary key of the displayed record.
DataKeyNames	Obtains or sets an array that contains the names of the key fields for the data source.
DefaultMode	Obtains or sets the default data-entry mode of the DetailsView control.
EditRowStyle	Obtains a reference to the TableItemStyle object that allows you to set the appearance of the data rows when a DetailsView control is in edit mode.

Property	Description
EmptyDataRowStyle	Obtains a reference to the TableItemStyle object that allows you to set the appearance of the empty data row displayed when the data source bound to a DetailsView control does not contain any records.
EmptyDataTemplate	Obtains or sets the user-defined content for the empty data row rendered when a DetailsView control is bound to a data source that does not contain any records.
EmptyDataText	Obtains or sets the text to display in the empty data row rendered when a DetailsView control is bound to a data source that does not contain any records.
EnablePagingCallbacks	Obtains or sets a value indicating whether client-side callback functions are used for paging operations in the DetailsView control.
FieldHeaderStyle	Obtains a reference to the TableItemStyle object that allows you to set the appearance of the header column in a DetailsView control.
Fields	Obtains a collection of DataControlField objects that represent the explicitly declared row fields in a DetailsView control.
FooterRow	Obtains a DetailsViewRow object that represents the footer row in a DetailsView control.
FooterStyle	Obtains a reference to the TableItemStyle object that allows you to set the appearance of the footer row in a DetailsView control.
FooterTemplate	Obtains or sets the user-defined content for the footer row in a DetailsView control.
FooterText	Obtains or sets the text to display in the footer row of a DetailsView control.
GridLines	Obtains or sets the gridline style for a DetailsView control.
HeaderRow	Obtains a DetailsViewRow object that represents the header row in a DetailsView control.
HeaderStyle	Obtains a reference to the TableItemStyle object that allows you to set the appearance of the header row in a DetailsView control.
HeaderTemplate	Obtains or sets the user-defined content for the header row in a DetailsView control.
HeaderText	Obtains or sets the text to display in the header row of a DetailsView control.
HorizontalAlign	Obtains or sets the horizontal alignment of a DetailsView control on the page.
InsertRowStyle	Obtains a reference to the TableItemStyle object that allows you to set the appearance of the data rows in a DetailsView control when the DetailsView control is in insert mode
PageCount	Obtains the number of the records in the data source.
PageIndex	Obtains or sets the index of the displayed record.
PagerSettings	Obtains a reference to the PagerSettings object that allows you to set the properties of the pager buttons in a DetailsView control.
PagerStyle	Obtains a reference to the TableItemStyle object that allows you to set the appearance of the pager row in a DetailsView control.
PagerTemplate	Obtains or sets the custom content for the pager row in a DetailsView control.

Table 8.10: Noteworthy Properties of the DetailsView Class

Table 8.10: Noteworthy Properties of the DetailsView Class	
Property	**Description**
Rows	Obtains a collection of DetailsViewRow objects that represent the data rows in a DetailsView control.
RowStyle	Obtains a reference to the TableItemStyle object that allows you to set the appearance of the data rows in a DetailsView control.
SelectedValue	Obtains the data key value of the current record in a DetailsView control.

NOTE

The AutoGenerateRows property of the DetailsView control is used to generate the row fields in the data source. The default value for the AutoGenerateRows property is true, which automatically generates the row fields. To explicitly declare the row fields, you need to set the AutoGenerateRows property to false.

Noteworthy methods of the DetailsView class are listed in Table 8.11:

Table 8.11: Noteworthy Methods of the DetailsView Class	
Method	**Description**
ChangeMode	Used to switch the DetailsView control to the specified mode
DataBind	Used to bind data from the data source to the control
DeleteItem	Used to delete the current record from the data source
InsertItem	Used to insert the current record in the data source
IsBindableType	Used to determine whether the specified data type can be bound to a field in the DetailsView control
UpdateItem	Used to update the current record in the data source

Noteworthy events of the DetailsView class are listed in Table 8.12:

Table 8.12: Noteworthy Events of the DetailsView Class	
Event	**Description**
ItemCommand	Invoked when a button within a DetailsView control is clicked
ItemCreated	Invoked when a record is created in a DetailsView control
ItemDeleted	Invoked when a Delete button within a DetailsView control is clicked, but after the delete operation
ItemDeleting	Invoked when a Delete button within a DetailsView control is clicked, but before the delete operation
ItemInserted	Invoked when an Insert button within a DetailsView control is clicked, but after the insert operation
ItemInserting	Invoked when an Insert button within a DetailsView control is clicked, but before the insert operation
ItemUpdated	Invoked when an Update button within a DetailsView control is clicked, but after the update operation
ItemUpdating	Invoked when an Update button within a DetailsView control is clicked, but before the update operation
ModeChanged	Invoked when a DetailsView control attempts to change between edit, insert, and read-only mode, but after the CurrentMode property is updated

Table 8.12: Noteworthy Events of the DetailsView Class	
Event	**Description**
`ModeChanging`	Invoked when a `DetailsView` control attempts to change between edit, insert, and read-only mode, but before the `CurrentMode` property is updated
`PageIndexChanged`	Invoked when the value of the `PageIndex` property changes after a paging operation
`PageIndexChanging`	Invoked when the value of the `PageIndex` property changes before a paging operation

Now, let's explore the `FormView` control.

The FormView Control

The `FormView` control displays a single record from the associated data source. Each row of the table displays each field of the record. For the FormView control to display content, you need to create templates for the different parts of the control. You must create a template for the mode in which the control is configured, even though most of the templates are optional. For example, a FormView control that supports inserting records must have an InsertItemTemplate defined. The `FormView` control exists within the `System.Web.UI.WebControls` namespace. The inheritance hierarchy of the `FormView` class is as follows:

```
System.Object
  System.Web.UI.Control
       System.Web.UI.WebControls. WebControl
          System.Web.UI.WebControls.BaseDataBoundControl
              System.Web.UI.WebControls.DataBoundControl
                 System.Web.UI.WebControls.CompositeDataBoundControl
                     System.Web.UI.WebControls.FormView
```

To display the content through the `FormView` control, you need to create templates for different parts of the control. The mode of the control and template should be same. For example, a `FormView` control that supports editing records must have an `EditItem` template. Table 8.13 lists the templates that are supported by the `FormView` control:

Table 8.13: Templates for the FormView Control	
Template Type	**Description**
`EditItemTemplate`	Describes the content for the data row when the `FormView` control is in edit mode. This template usually contains input controls and command buttons with which the user can edit an existing record.
`EmptyDataTemplate`	Describes the content for the empty data row displayed when the `FormView` control is bound to a data source that does not contain any records. This template usually contains content to alert the user that the data source does not contain any records.
`FooterTemplate`	Describes the content for the footer row. This template usually contains any additional content you would like to display in the footer row.
`HeaderTemplate`	Describes the content for the header row. This template usually contains any additional content you would like to display in the header row.
`ItemTemplate`	Describes the content for the data row when the `FormView` control is in read-only mode. This template usually contains content to display the values of an existing record.
`InsertItemTemplate`	Describes the content for the data row when the `FormView` control is in insert mode. This template usually contains input controls and command buttons with which the user can add a new record.

Table 8.13: Templates for the FormView Control	
Template Type	**Description**
`PagerTemplate`	Describes the content for the pager row displayed when the paging feature is enabled, that is, when the `AllowPaging` property is set to true. This template usually contains controls with the help of which the user can navigate to another record.

NOTE

We have to manually include command buttons to update, delete, or insert operations, because the FormView control does not provide a way to automatically generate command buttons.

Noteworthy properties of the `FormView` class are listed in Table 8.14:

Table 8.14: Noteworthy Properties of the FormView Class	
Property	**Description**
`AllowPaging`	Obtains or sets a value indicating whether the paging feature is enabled.
`BackImageUrl`	Obtains or sets the URL to an image to display in the background of a `FormView` control.
`BottomPagerRow`	Obtains the `FormViewRow` object that represents the pager row displayed at the bottom of the `FormView` control.
`Caption`	Obtains or sets the text to render in an HTML caption element in a `FormView` control. This property is provided to make the control more accessible to users of assistive technology devices.
`CaptionAlign`	Obtains or sets the horizontal or vertical position of the HTML caption element in a `FormView` control.
`CellPadding`	Obtains or sets the amount of space between the contents of a cell and the cell's border.
`CellSpacing`	Obtains or sets the amount of space between cells.
`CurrentMode`	Obtains the current data-entry mode of the `FormView` control.
`DataItem`	Obtains the data item bound to the `FormView` control.
`DataItemCount`	Obtains the number of data items in the data source.
`DataItemIndex`	Obtains the index of the data item bound to the `FormView` control from the data source.
`DataKey`	Obtains a `DataKey` object that represents the primary key of the displayed record.
`DataKeyNames`	Obtains or sets an array that contains the names of the key fields for the data source.
`DefaultMode`	Obtains or sets the data-entry mode to which the `FormView` control returns after an update, insert, or cancel operation.
`EditItemTemplate`	Obtains or sets the custom content for an item in edit mode.
`EditRowStyle`	Obtains a reference to the `TableItemStyle` object that allows you to set the appearance of the data row when a `FormView` control is in edit mode.
`EmptyDataRowStyle`	Obtains a reference to the `TableItemStyle` object that allows you to set the appearance of the empty data row displayed when the data source bound to a `FormView` control does not contain any records.
`EmptyDataTemplate`	Obtains or sets the user-defined content for the empty data row rendered when a `FormView` control is bound to a data source that does not contain any records.
`EmptyDataText`	Obtains or sets the text to display in the empty data row rendered when a `FormView` control is bound to a data source that does not contain any records.

Table 8.14: Noteworthy Properties of the FormView Class

Property	Description
EnableModelValidation	Obtains or sets a value that indicates whether a validator control will handle exceptions that occur during insert or update operations.
FooterRow	Obtains the FormViewRow object that represents the footer row in a FormView control.
FooterStyle	Obtains a reference to the TableItemStyle object that allows you to set the appearance of the footer row in a FormView control.
FooterTemplate	Obtains or sets the user-defined content for the footer row in a FormView control.
FooterText	Obtains or sets the text to display in the footer row of a FormView control.
GridLines	Obtains or sets the gridline style for a FormView control.
HeaderRow	Obtains the FormViewRow object that represents the header row in a FormView control.
HeaderStyle	Obtains a reference to the TableItemStyle object that allows you to set the appearance of the header row in a FormView control.
HeaderTemplate	Obtains or sets the user-defined content for the header row in a FormView control.
HeaderText	Obtains or sets the text to display in the header row of a FormView control.
HorizontalAlign	Obtains or sets the horizontal alignment of a FormView control on the page.
InsertItemTemplate	Obtains or sets the custom content for an item in insert mode.
InsertRowStyle	Obtains a reference to the TableItemStyle object that allows you to set the appearance of the data row in a FormView control when the control is in insert mode.
ItemTemplate	Obtains or sets the custom content for the data row in a FormView control when the control is in read-only mode.
PageCount	Obtains the total number of pages required to display every record in the data source.
PageIndex	Obtains or sets the index of the displayed page.
PagerSettings	Obtains a reference to the PagerSettings object that allows you to set the properties of the pager buttons in a FormView control.
PagerStyle	Obtains a reference to the TableItemStyle object that allows you to set the appearance of the pager row in a FormView control.
PagerTemplate	Obtains or sets the custom content for the pager row in a FormView control.
Row	Obtains the FormViewRow object that represents the data row in a FormView control.
RowStyle	Obtains a reference to the TableItemStyle object that allows you to set the appearance of the data row in a FormView control when the control is in read-only mode.
SelectedValue	Obtains the data key value of the current record in a FormView control.
TopPagerRow	Obtains the FormViewRow object that represents the pager row displayed at the top of a FormView control.

Noteworthy methods of the FormView class are listed in Table 8.15:

Table 8.15: Noteworthy Methods of the FormView Class

Method	Description
ChangeMode	Used to switch the DetailsView control to the specified mode
DataBind	Used to bind data from the data source to the control

Table 8.15: Noteworthy Methods of the FormView Class	
Method	**Description**
`DeleteItem`	Used to delete the current record from the data source
`InsertItem`	Used to insert the current record in the data source
`IsBindableType`	Used to determine whether the specified data type can be bound to a field in the `DetailsView` control
`UpdateItem`	Used to update the current record in the data source

Noteworthy events of the `FormView` class are listed in Table 8.16:

Table 8.16: Noteworthy Events of the FormView Class	
Event	**Description**
`ItemCommand`	Invokes when a button within a `FormView` control is clicked
`ItemCreated`	Invokes after all the rows are created in a `FormView` control
`ItemDeleted`	Invokes when a Delete button within a `FormView` control is clicked, but after the delete operation
`ItemDeleting`	Invokes when a Delete button within a `FormView` control is clicked, but before the delete operation
`ItemInserted`	Invokes when an Insert button within a `FormView` control is clicked, but after the insert operation
`ItemInserting`	Invokes when an Insert button within a `FormView` control is clicked, but before the insert operation
`ItemUpdated`	Invokes when an Update button within a `FormView` control is clicked, but after the update operation
`ItemUpdating`	Invokes when an Update button within a `FormView` control is clicked, but before the update operation.
`ModeChanged`	Invokes when the `FormView` control switches between edit, insert, and read-only mode, but after the mode has changed
`ModeChanging`	Invokes when the `FormView` control switches between edit, insert, and read-only mode, but before the mode changes
`PageIndexChanged`	Invokes when the value of the `PageIndex` property changes after a paging operation
`PageIndexChanging`	Invokes when the value of the `PageIndex` property changes before a paging operation

Now, let's learn about the `ListView` control.

The ListView Control

The `ListView` control is a data bound control used to display data from the associated data source. The `ListView` control enables a developer to display data in any format using templates and styles. This control provides excellent customization and extensibility features. It provides the developer with control on the rendered HTML output and provides support for adding new row, and sorting. When you drag the `ListView` control to the ASP.NET page, the following code appears in the Source view of the page:

```
<asp:ListView ID="ListView1" runat="server"> </asp:ListView>
```

The inheritance hierarchy of the ListView control is as follows:

```
System.Object
    System.Web.UI.Control
          System.Web.UI.WebControls.WebControl
               System.Web.UI.WebControls.BaseDataBoundControl
                     System.Web.UI.WebControls.DataBoundControl
                           System.Web.UI.WebControls.ListView
```

Noteworthy properties of the ListView class are listed in Table 8.17:

Table 8.17: Noteworthy Properties of the ListView Class

Property	Description
AccessKey	Overrides the WebControl.AccessKey property. Setting this property is not supported by the ListView control.
AlternatingItemTemplate	Obtains or sets the custom content for the alternating data item in a ListView control.
Controls	Obtains a ControlCollection object that represents the child controls of the ListView control.
ConvertEmptyStringToNull	Obtains or sets a value that indicates whether empty string values (" ") are automatically converted to null values when the data field is updated in the data source.
CssClass	Overrides the WebControl.CssClass property. Setting this property is not supported by the ListView control.
DataKeyNames	Obtains or sets an array that contains the names of the primary key fields for the items displayed in a ListView control.
DataKeys	Obtains a collection of DataKey objects that represent the data-key value for each item in a ListView control.
EditIndex	Obtains or sets the index of the item being edited.
EditItem	Obtains the item that is in edit mode in a ListView control.
EditItemTemplate	Obtains or sets the custom content for the item in edit mode.
EmptyDataTemplate	Obtains or sets the user-defined content for the empty template that is rendered when a ListView control is bound to a data source that does not contain any records.
EmptyItemTemplate	Obtains or sets the user-defined content for the empty item that is rendered in a ListView control when there are no more data items to display in the last row of the current data page.
Font	Overrides the WebControl.Font property. This property is not supported by the ListView control.
ForeColor	Overrides the WebControl.ForeColor property. Setting this property is not supported by the ListView control.
GroupItemCount	Obtains or sets the number of items to display per group in a ListView control.
GroupPlaceholderID	Obtains or sets the ID for the group placeholder in a ListView control.
GroupSeparatorTemplate	Obtains or sets the user-defined content for the separator between groups in a ListView control.
GroupTemplate	Obtains or sets the user-defined content for the group container in a ListView control.
Height	Overrides the WebControl.Height property. Setting this property is not supported by the ListView control.

Table 8.17: Noteworthy Properties of the ListView Class	
Property	**Description**
InsertItem	Obtains the insert item of a ListView control.
InsertItemPosition	Obtains or sets the location of the InsertItemTemplate template when it is rendered as part of the ListView control.
InsertItemTemplate	Obtains or sets the custom content for an insert item in the ListView control.
ItemPlaceholderID	Obtains or sets the ID for the item placeholder in a ListView control.
Items	Obtains a collection of ListViewDataItem objects that represent the data items of the current page of data in a ListView control.
ItemSeparatorTemplate	Obtains or sets the custom content for the separator between the items in a ListView control.
ItemTemplate	Obtains or sets the custom content for the data item in a ListView control.
LayoutTemplate	Obtains or sets the custom content for the root container in a ListView control.
SelectedDataKey	Obtains the data-key value for the selected item in a ListView control.
SelectedIndex	Obtains or sets the index of the selected item in a ListView control.
SelectedItemTemplate	Obtains or sets the custom content for the selected item in a ListView control.
SelectedValue	Obtains the data-key value of the selected item in a ListView control.
SortDirection	Obtains the sort direction of the field or fields that are being sorted.
SortExpression	Obtains the sort expression that is associated with the field or fields that are being sorted.

Noteworthy methods of the ListView class are listed in Table 8.18:

Table 8.18: Noteworthy Methods of the ListView Class	
Method	**Description**
DeleteItem	Removes the record at the specified index from the database
ExtractItemValues	Gets the values of each field that is defined in the specified item, and stores them in the specified IOrderedDictionary object
InsertNewItem	Inserts the new record in the database
Sort	Arranges the column in ascending or descending order in the ListView control, according to sort expression and direction
UpdateItem	Modifies the record at the specified index in the database

Noteworthy events of the ListView class are listed in Table 8.19:

Table 8.19: Noteworthy Events of the ListView Class	
Event	**Description**
ItemCanceling	Invoked when a cancel operation is requested, but before the ListView control cancels the insert or edit operation
ItemCommand	Invoked when a button in a ListView control is clicked
ItemCreated	Invoked when an item is created in a ListView control
ItemDataBound	Invoked when a data item is bound to the data in a ListView control

Table 8.19: Noteworthy Events of the ListView Class

Event	Description
`ItemDeleted`	Invoked when a delete operation is requested, after the `ListView` control deletes the item
`ItemDeleting`	Invoked when a delete operation is requested, before the `ListView` control deletes the item
`ItemEditing`	Invoked when an edit operation is requested, but before the `ListView` item is put in edit mode
`ItemInserted`	Invoked when an insert operation is requested, after the `ListView` control has inserted the item in the data source
`ItemInserting`	Invoked when an insert operation is requested, before the `ListView` control performs the insert operation
`ItemUpdated`	Invoked when an update operation is requested, after the `ListView` control updates the item
`ItemUpdating`	Invoked when an update operation is requested, before the `ListView` control updates the item
`LayoutCreated`	Invoked when the `LayoutTemplate` template is created in a `ListView` control
`PagePropertiesChanged`	Invoked when the page properties change, after the `ListView` control sets the new values
`PagePropertiesChanging`	Invoked when the page properties change, but before the `ListView` control sets the new values
`SelectedIndexChanged`	Invoked when an item's Select button is clicked, after the `ListView` control handles the select operation
`SelectedIndexChanging`	Invoked when an item's Select button is clicked, but before the ListView control handles the select operation
`Sorted`	Invoked when a sort operation is requested, after the `ListView` control handles the sort operation
`Sorting`	Invoked when a sort operation is requested, but before the `ListView` control handles the sort operation

Table 8.20 lists the templates supported by the `ListView` class:

Table 8.20: Types of Templates of the ListView Class

Template Type	Description
`LayoutTemplate`	Defines a container object, such as a table row (tr), div, or span element. These objects contain the content defined in the `ItemTemplate` or `GroupTemplate` template. It might also contain a `DataPager` object. It is used to define a Custom UI for the root container of the ListView control.
`ItemTemplate`	Describes the data bound content to display for individual items.
`ItemSeparatorTemplate`	Describes the content to render between individual items.
`GroupTemplate`	Describes a container object, such as a table cell (td), div, or span element that contains the content defined in the `ItemTemplate` and `EmptyItemTemplate` templates. The number of items that are displayed in a group is specified by the `GroupItemCount` property. It is used to create a tiled layout in the `ListView` control.
`GroupSeparatorTemplate`	Describes the content to render between groups of items.

Table 8.20: Types of Templates of the ListView Class	
Template Type	**Description**
`EmptyItemTemplate`	Describes the content to render for an empty item when a `GroupTemplate` template is used. For example, if the `GroupItemCount` property is set to 5, and the total number of items returned from the data source is 8, the last group of data displayed by the `ListView` control will contain three items as specified by the `ItemTemplate` template, and two items as specified by the `EmptyItemTemplate` template.
`EmptyDataTemplate`	Describes the content to render if the data source returns no data.
`SelectedItemTemplate`	Describes the content to render for the selected data item to differentiate the selected item from the other items.
`AlternatingItemTemplate`	Describes the content to render for alternating items to make it easier to distinguish between consecutive items.
`EditItemTemplate`	Describes the content to render when an item is being edited. The `EditItemTemplate` template is rendered in place of the `ItemTemplate` template for the data item that is edited.
`InsertItemTemplate`	Describes the content to render inserting an item. The `InsertItemTemplate` template is rendered in place of an `ItemTemplate` template at either the start or the end of the items that are displayed by the `ListView` control. You can specify where the `InsertItemTemplate` template is rendered using the `InsertItemPosition` property of the `ListView` control.

Now, let's explore the `Repeater` control.

The Repeater Control

The `Repeater` control is a data bound control that is used to display repeated list of items from the associated data source. It is a single Web control that allows splitting markup tags across the templates. The `Repeater` control does not provide support to in-built layout or styles. Therefore, while working with the `Repeater` control, you have to explicitly declare all layouts, formatting, and style. In other words, the `Repeater` control does not support built-in selection or editing features.

NOTE

The basic difference between the Repeater control and DataList control is that the latter explicitly places items in an HTML table but the former does not explicitly places items in an HTML table.

The `Repeater` control exists within the `System.Web.UI.WebControls` namespace. The inheritance hierarchy of the `Repeater` control is as follows:

```
System.Object
   System.Web.UI.Control
        System.Web.UI.WebControls.Repeater
```

Noteworthy properties of the `Repeater` class are listed in Table 8.21:

Table 8.21: Noteworthy Properties of the Repeater Class	
Property	**Description**
`AlternatingItemTemplate`	Obtains or sets the object implementing the `System.Web.UI.ITemplate` namespace that defines how alternating items in the control are displayed
`AppRelativeTemplateSourceDirectory`	Gets or sets the application-relative virtual directory of the Page or UserControl object that contains this control. (Inherited from Control.)
`BindingContainer`	Infrastructure. Gets the control that contains this control's data binding. (Inherited from Control.)

Table 8.21: Noteworthy Properties of the Repeater Class

Property	Description
`ChildControlsCreated`	Gets a value that indicates whether the server control's child controls have been created. (Inherited from Control.)
`ClientID`	Gets the server control identifier generated by ASP.NET. (Inherited from Control.)
`ClientIDSeparator`	Gets a character value representing the separator character used in the ClientID property. (Inherited from Control.)
`Context`	Gets the HttpContext object associated with the server control for the current Web request. (Inherited from Control.)
`Controls`	Obtains a `System.Web.UI.ControlCollection` namespace that contains the child controls of the `Repeater` control
`DataMember`	Obtains or sets the specific table in the `DataSource` to bind to the `Repeater` control
`DataSource`	Obtains or sets the data source that provides data for populating the list
`DataSourceID`	Obtains or sets the `ID` property of the data source control that the `Repeater` control should use to retrieve its data source
`DesignMode`	Gets a value indicating whether a control is being used on a design surface. (Inherited from Control.)
`EnableTheming`	Obtains or sets a value indicating whether the themes are applied to this control.
`EnableViewState`	Gets or sets a value indicating whether the server control persists its view state, and the view state of any child controls it contains, to the requesting client. (Inherited from Control.)
`Events`	Gets a list of event handler delegates for the control. This property is read-only. (Inherited from Control.)
`FooterTemplate`	Obtains or sets the `System.Web.UI.ITemplate` namespace that defines how the footer section of the Repeater control will be displayed
`HasChildViewState`	Gets a value indicating whether the current server control's child controls have any saved view-state settings. (Inherited from Control.)
`HeaderTemplate`	Obtains or sets the `System.Web.UI.ITemplate` that defines how the header section of the `Repeater` control will be displayed
`ID`	Gets or sets the programmatic identifier assigned to the server control. (Inherited from Control.)
`IdSeparator`	Gets the character used to separate control identifiers. (Inherited from Control.)
`Initialized`	Returns a value indicating whether the control has been initialized.
`IsBoundUsingDataSourceID`	Gets a value indicating whether the DataSourceID property is set.
`IsChildControlStateCleared`	Gets a value indicating whether controls contained within this control have control state. (Inherited from Control.)
`IsTrackingViewState`	Gets a value that indicates whether the server control is saving changes to its view state. (Inherited from Control.)

Table 8.21: Noteworthy Properties of the Repeater Class	
Property	**Description**
`IsViewStateEnabled`	Gets a value indicating whether view state is enabled for this control. (Inherited from Control.)
`Items`	Obtains a collection of the `RepeaterItem` objects in the `Repeater` control
`ItemTemplate`	Obtains or sets the `System.Web.UI_ITemplate` namespace that defines how items in the `Repeater` control will be displayed
`LoadViewStateByID`	Gets a value indicating whether the control participates in loading its view state by ID instead of index. (Inherited from Control.)
`Page`	Gets a reference to the Page instance that contains the server control. (Inherited from Control.)
`Parent`	Gets a reference to the server control's parent control in the page control hierarchy. (Inherited from Control.)
`RequiresDataBinding`	Gets or sets a value indicating whether the Repeater control needs to bind to its specified data source.
`SelectArguments`	Gets a DataSourceSelectArguments object that the Repeater control uses when retrieving data from a data source control.
`SeparatorTemplate`	Obtains or sets the `System.Web.UI.ITemplate` namespace that defines how the separator between the items is displayed

Noteworthy events of the `Repeater` class are listed in Table 8.22:

Table 8.22: Noteworthy Events of the Repeater Class	
Event	**Description**
`ItemCommand`	Invoked when a button is clicked in the `Repeater` control
`ItemCreated`	Invoked when an item is created in the `Repeater` control
`ItemDataBound`	Invoked after an item in the `Repeater` control is data bound but before it is rendered on the page

Now, let's learn about the `DataPager` control.

The DataPager Control

The `DataPager` control is used to provide paging functionality to the data bound controls, such as the `ListView` control. When you drag a `DataPager` control to the page, the following code appears in the Source view of the page:

```
<asp:DataPager ID="DataPager1" runat="server"> </asp:DataPager>
```

The inheritance hierarchy of the `DataPager` control is as follows:

```
System.Object
  System.Web.UI.Control
    System.Web.UI.WebControls.DataPager
```

Noteworthy properties of the `DataPager` class are listed in Table 8.23:

Table 8.23: Noteworthy Properties of the DataPager Class	
Property	**Description**
`Attributes`	Retrieves a list of customized attribute name/value pairs for the `DataPager` control.

Table 8.23: Noteworthy Properties of the DataPager Class

Property	Description
`BindingContainer`	Gets the control that contains this control's data binding. (Inherited from Control.)
`ChildControlsCreated`	Gets a value that indicates whether the server control's child controls have been created. (Inherited from Control.)
`ClientID`	Gets the server control identifier generated by ASP.NET. (Inherited from Control.)
`ClientIDSeparator`	Gets a character value representing the separator character used in the ClientID property. (Inherited from Control.)
`Context`	Gets the HttpContext object associated with the server control for the current Web request. (Inherited from Control.)
`Controls`	Obtains a `ControlCollection` object that represents the child controls for the `DataPager` control in the UI hierarchy.
`DesignMode`	Gets a value indicating whether a control is being used on a design surface. (Inherited from Control.)
`EnableTheming`	Gets or sets a value indicating whether themes apply to this control. (Inherited from Control.)
`EnableViewState`	Gets or sets a value indicating whether the server control persists its view state, and the view state of any child controls it contains, to the requesting client. (Inherited from Control.)
`Events`	Gets a list of event handler delegates for the control. This property is read-only. (Inherited from Control.)
`Fields`	Obtains a collection of `DataPagerField` objects that represent the pager fields that are specified in a `DataPager` control.
`HasChildViewState`	Gets a value indicating whether the current server control's child controls have any saved view-state settings. (Inherited from Control.)
`ID`	Gets or sets the programmatic identifier assigned to the server control. (Inherited from Control.)
`IdSeparator`	Infrastructure. Gets the character used to separate control identifiers. (Inherited from Control.)
`IsChildControlStateCleared`	Gets a value indicating whether controls contained within this control have control state. (Inherited from Control.)
`IsTrackingViewState`	Gets a value that indicates whether the server control is saving changes to its view state. (Inherited from Control.)
`IsViewStateEnabled`	Gets a value indicating whether view state is enabled for this control. (Inherited from Control.)
`LoadViewStateByID`	Gets a value indicating whether the control participates in loading its view state by ID instead of index. (Inherited from Control.)
`MaximumRows`	Obtains the maximum number of records that are displayed for each page of data.
`Page`	Gets a reference to the Page instance that contains the server control. (Inherited from Control.)
`PagedControlID`	Obtains or sets the ID of the control that contains the data that will be paged by the `DataPager` control.

Table 8.23: Noteworthy Properties of the DataPager Class

Property	Description
PageSize	Obtains or sets the number of records that are displayed for each page of data.
Parent	Gets a reference to the server control's parent control in the page control hierarchy. (Inherited from Control.)
QueryStringField	Obtains or sets the name of the query string field.
Site	Gets information about the container that hosts the current control when rendered on a design surface. (Inherited from Control.)
SkinID	Gets or sets the skin to apply to the control. (Inherited from Control.)
StartRowIndex	Obtains the index of the first record that is displayed on a page of data.
TagKey	Gets the HTML element that is used to render the DataPager control.
TemplateControl	Gets or sets a reference to the template that contains this control. (Inherited from Control.)
TemplateSourceDirectory	Gets the virtual directory of the Page or UserControl that contains the current server control. (Inherited from Control.)
TotalRowCount	Obtains the total number of records that are retrieved by the underlying data source object. This data source object is referenced by the associated data bound control.

Noteworthy methods of the `DataPager` class are listed in Table 8.24:

Table 8.24: Noteworthy Methods of the DataPager Class

Method	Description
DataBind	Used to bind a `DataPager` control and all its child controls to a data source
RenderBeginTag	Used to render the HTML opening tag of the `DataPager` control to the specified writer
SetPageProperties	Used to set the page-related properties in the `DataPager` control

The Chart Control

The Chart control enables you to present complex data in a simpler way.It helps you to analyse the data in a easier way with the help of charts. When you drag a Chart control to the page, the following code appears in the Source view of the page:

```
<asp:Chart ID="Chart1" runat="server">
        <Series>
                <asp:Series Name="Series1"></asp:Series>
        </Series>
        <ChartAreas>
                <asp:ChartArea Name="ChartArea1"></asp:ChartArea>
        </ChartAreas>
</asp:Chart>
```

The inheritance hierarchy of the Chart control is as follows:

```
System.Object
   System.Web.UI.Control
         System.Web.UI.WebControls.WebControl
              System.Web.UI.WebControls.BaseDataBoundControl
                   System.Web.UI.WebControls.DataBoundControl
                        System.Web.UI.DataVisualization.Charting.Chart
```

Noteworthy properties of the Chart class are listed in Table 8.25:

Table 8.25: Noteworthy Properties of the Chart Class

Property	Description
AlternateText	Displays the alternate text when the chart image is not shown
AccessKey	Stores the Keyboard shortcut(Inherited from the control)
BackImage	Gets or sets the background image path
BackImageAlignment	Gets or sets the alignment of the background image
ClientIDMode	Generates ClientID property for the control(Inherited from the control)
Compression	Stores the compression value
DataSourceID	Stores the ID of the data source control
ViewStateContent	Saves the chart content in the ViewState
ViewStateMode	Determines whether the view state is enabled for the chart control or not(Inherited from the control)
Visible	Decides whether the control should be visible or not

Noteworthy methods of the Chart class are listed in Table 8.26:

Table 8.26: Noteworthy Methods of the Chart Class

Method	Description
CopyBaseAttributes	Allows you to copy only those properties that are not encapsulated by the Style object from the defined Web server control to the Web server control that called this method.
MergeStyle	Allows you to copy non-blank elements of the defined style to the Web control and does not overwrite any existing elements of the control.
Paint	Allows you to draw the chart image in graphics.
RenderBeginTag	Writes the opening tag of the specified markup element to the output stream.
RenderEndtag	Writes the end tag of a markup element to the output stream (Inherited from the control).

Noteworthy events of the Chart class are listed in Table 8.27:

Table 8.27: Noteworthy Events of the Chart Class

Event	Description
Click	Invokes when the control is clicked
Customize	Invokes before the chart image is drawn
DataBound	Invokes when the control is DataBound(Inherited from the control)
Disposed	Invokes when the control is disposed
PostPaint	Invokes when the chart element is painted

The QueryExtender Control

The QueryExtender control is a data source control that helps in retrieving only those records from the database which meet the specific criteria or in other words,to filter the records.Filtering of records helps in displaying the records in various ways on the Web page without affecting the dataset. When you drag a `QueryExtender` control to the page, the following code appears in the Source view of the page:

```
<asp:QueryExtender ID="QueryExtender1" runat="server"> </asp:QueryExtender>
```

The inheritance hierarchy of the `QueryExtender` control is as follows:

```
System.Object
   System.Web.UI.Control
         System.Web.UI.WebControls.QueryExtender
```

Noteworthy properties of the QueryExtender class are listed in Table 8.28:

Table 8.28: Noteworthy Properties of the QueryExtender Class

Property	Description
`ClientIDMode`	Generates ClientID property for the control(Inherited from the control)
`EnableViewState`	Decides whether the control save its view state automatically or not (Inherited from the control)
`TargetControlID`	Saves the id of the target control
`ViewStateMode`	Determines whether the view state is enabled for the chart control or not
`Visible`	Decides whether the control should be visible or not

Noteworthy events of the QueryExtender class are listed in Table 8.29:

Table 8.29: Noteworthy Events of the QueryExtender Class

Event	Description
`Disposed`	Invokes when the control is disposed
`Init`	Invokes when the Web page is initialized
`Load`	Invokes when the Web page is loaded
`Unload`	Invokes when the Web page is unloaded

Noteworthy methods of the QueryExtender class are listed in Table 8.30:

Table 8.30: Noteworthy Methods of the QueryExtender Class

Method	Description
`ApplyStyleSheetSkin`	Applies the styles to the control defined in the style sheet
`DataBind`	Binds the data source control with the database
`Dispose`	Enables the control to complete the final steps before releasing from the memory
`FindControl`	Searches the server control with the help of the its id
`Focus`	Sets the focus on the control
`HasControls`	Determines the child server control in the parent server control

Noteworthy expressions of the QueryExtender class are listed in Table 8.31:

Table 8.31: Noteworthy Expressions of the QueryExtender Class

Expressions	Description
`SearchExpression`	Searches the string value and compare with the given string value
`RangeExpression`	Defines the range using the pair of values
`PropertyExpression`	Compares the value of a column in a table with the given string value
`OrderByExpression`	Sorts the data by a particular column
`CustomExpression`	Provides the LINQ expression that can be customized

Table 8.31: Noteworthy Expressions of the QueryExtender Class

Expressions	Description
`DynamicFilterExpression`	Filters the data dynamically in dynamic data Web site
`ControlFilterExpression`	Filters the control in dynamic data Web site

The SqlDataSource Control

The `SqlDataSource` control is a data source control that allows a server control, such as the `GridView` control, to access data located in a relational database, such as Microsoft SQL Server and Oracle. This control also generates a connection string to interact with the data in an ASP.NET page. These connection strings are generated through the `Configure Data Source` wizard. A connection string contains information about the server, database, and security you are working with in your application, for example:

```
Data Source=.\sqlexpress; Initial Catalog=Northwind; Integrated Security=True
```

NOTE

To learn more about the Configure Data Source Wizard in detail, refer to the Immediate Solutions section of this chapter.

The `SqlDataSource` control automatically opens a database connection, which is provided in the connection string, executes the SQL queries, and then closes the connection. When you add a `SqlDataSource` control to an ASP.NET page, the following code appears in the Source view of a page:

```
<asp:SqlDataSource ID="SqlDataSource1" runat="server"></asp:SqlDataSource>
```

The inheritance hierarchy of the `SqlDataSource` control is as follows:

```
System.Object
   System.Web.UI.Control
         System.Web.UI.DataSourceControl
                  System.Web.UI.WebControls.SqlDataSource
```

Noteworthy properties of the `SqlDataSource` class are listed in Table 8.32:

Table 8.32: Noteworthy Properties of the SqlDataSource Class

Property	Description
`CacheDuration`	Obtains or sets the length of time, in seconds, for which the data source control caches data that is retrieved by the `Select` method.
`CacheExpirationPolicy`	Obtains or sets the cache expiration behavior that, when combined with the duration, describes the behavior of the cache that the data source control uses.
`CacheKeyDependency`	Obtains or sets a user-defined key dependency that is linked to all data cache objects that are created by the data source control. All cache objects explicitly expire when the key expires.
`CancelSelectOnNullParameter`	Obtains or sets a value indicating whether a data retrieval operation is canceled when any parameter that is contained in the `SelectParameters` collection evaluates to null reference.
`ChildControlsCreated`	Gets a value that indicates whether the server control's child controls have been created. (Inherited from Control)
`ClientID`	Gets the server control identifier generated by ASP.NET. (Inherited from DataSourceControl)
`ClientIDSeparator`	Gets a character value representing the separator character used in the ClientID property. (Inherited from Control)

Table 8.32: Noteworthy Properties of the SqlDataSource Class

Property	Description
`ConflictDetection`	Obtains or sets the value indicating how the `SqlDataSource` control performs, updates, and deletes when data in a row in the underlying database changes during the time of the operation.
`ConnectionString`	Obtains or sets the ADO.NET provider-specific connection string that the `SqlDataSource` control uses to connect to an underlying database.
`Context`	Gets the HttpContext object associated with the server control for the current Web request. (Inherited from Control)
`Controls`	Gets a ControlCollection object that represents the child controls for a specified server control in the UI hierarchy. (Inherited from DataSourceControl)
`DataSourceMode`	Obtains or sets the data retrieval mode such as DataSet and DataReader that the `SqlDataSource` control uses to fetch data.
`DeleteCommand`	Obtains or sets the SQL string that the `SqlDataSource` control uses to delete the data from the underlying database.
`DeleteCommandType`	Obtains or sets a value indicating whether the text in the `DeleteCommand` property is an SQL statement or is the name of a stored procedure.
`DeleteParameters`	Obtains the parameters collection that contains the parameters that are used by the `DeleteCommand` property from the `SqlDataSourceView` object that is associated with the `SqlDataSource` control.
`DesignMode`	Gets a value indicating whether a control is being used on a design surface. (Inherited from Control)
`EnableCaching`	Obtains or sets a value indicating whether the `SqlDataSource` control has data caching enabled.
`EnableTheming`	Gets a value indicating whether this control supports themes. (Inherited from DataSourceControl)
`EnableViewState`	Gets or sets a value indicating whether the server control persists its view state, and the view state of any child controls it contains, to the requesting client. (Inherited from Control)
`Events`	Gets a list of event handler delegates for the control. This property is read-only. (Inherited from Control)
`FilterExpression`	Obtains or sets a filtering expression that is applied when the `Select` method of data source is called.
`FilterParameters`	Obtains a collection of parameters that are associated with any parameter placeholders that are in the `FilterExpression` string.
`HasChildViewState`	Gets a value indicating whether the current server control's child controls have any saved view-state settings. (Inherited from Control)
`ID`	Gets or sets the programmatic identifier assigned to the server control. (Inherited from Control)
`IdSeparator`	Gets the character used to separate control identifiers. (Inherited from Control)
`InsertCommand`	Obtains or sets the SQL string that the `SqlDataSource` control uses to insert data into the underlying database.
`InsertCommandType`	Obtains or sets a value indicating whether the text in the `InsertCommand` property is an SQL statement or the name of a stored procedure.

Table 8.32: Noteworthy Properties of the SqlDataSource Class

Property	Description
`InsertParameters`	Obtains the parameters collection that contains the parameters that are used by the `InsertCommand` property from the `SqlDataSourceView` object that is associated with the `SqlDataSource` control.
`IsChildControlStateCleared`	Gets a value indicating whether controls contained within this control have control state. (Inherited from Control)
`IsTrackingViewState`	Gets a value that indicates whether the server control is saving changes to its view state. (Inherited from Control)
`IsViewStateEnabled`	Gets a value indicating whether view state is enabled for this control. (Inherited from Control)
`LoadViewStateByID`	Gets a value indicating whether the control participates in loading its view state by ID instead of index. (Inherited from Control)
`OldValuesParameterFormatString`	Obtains or sets a format string to apply to the names of any parameters that are passed to the `Delete` or `Update` method.
`Page`	Allows you to get the reference to the Page instance that contains server control. (Inherited from Control)
`Parent`	Gets a reference to the server control's parent control in the page control hierarchy. (Inherited from Control)
`ProviderName`	Obtains or sets the name of the .NET Framework data provider that the `SqlDataSource` control uses to connect to an underlying data source.
`SelectCommand`	Obtains or sets the SQL string that the `SqlDataSource` control uses to retrieve data from the underlying database.
`SelectCommandType`	Obtains or sets a value indicating whether the text in the `SelectCommand` property is an SQL query or the name of a stored procedure.
`SelectParameters`	Obtains the parameters collection that contains the parameters that are used by the `SelectCommand` property from the `SqlDataSourceView` object that is associated with the `SqlDataSource` control.
`Site`	Gets information about the container that hosts the current control when rendered on a design surface. (Inherited from Control)
`SkinID`	Gets the skin to apply to the DataSourceControl control. (Inherited from DataSourceControl)
`SortParameterName`	Obtains or sets the name of a stored procedure parameter that is used to sort retrieved data when data retrieval is performed using a stored procedure.
`SqlCacheDependency`	Obtains or sets a semicolon-delimited string that indicates which databases and tables to use for the Microsoft SQL Server cache dependency.
`TemplateControl`	Gets or sets a reference to the template that contains this control. (Inherited from Control)
`TemplateSourceDirectory`	Gets the virtual directory of the Page or UserControl that contains the current server control. (Inherited from Control)
`UniqueID`	Gets the unique, hierarchically qualified identifier for the server control. (Inherited from Control)
`UpdateCommand`	Obtains or sets the SQL string that the SqlDataSource control uses to update data in the underlying database.

Table 8.32: Noteworthy Properties of the SqlDataSource Class	
Property	**Description**
`UpdateCommandType`	Obtains or sets a value indicating whether the text in the `UpdateCommand` property is an SQL statement or the name of a stored procedure.
`UpdateParameters`	Obtains the parameters' collection that contains the parameters that are used by the `UpdateCommand` property from the `SqlDataSourceView` control. The `SqlDataSourceView` control is associated with the `SqlDataSource` control.

Noteworthy methods of the `SqlDataSource` class are listed in the following Table 8.33:

Table 8.33: Noteworthy Methods of the SqlDataSource Class	
Method	**Description**
`Delete`	Deletes the data from the database by using the `DeleteCommand` SQL string and any parameters that are in the `DeleteParameters` collection
`Insert`	Inserts the data in the database by using the `InsertCommand` SQL string and any parameters that are in the `InsertParameters` collection
`Select`	Retrieves the data from the database by using the `SelectCommand` SQL string and any parameters that are in the `SelectParameters` collection
`Update`	Updates the data in the database by using the `UpdateCommand` SQL string and any parameters that are in the `UpdateParameters` collection

Now, let's learn about the `AccessDataSource` control.

The AccessDataSource Control

The `AccessDataSource` control is a data source control that allows a Web server control to access a Microsoft Access database. This control does not support connection strings, but the `DataFile` property of this control allows you to specify the Access file (`.mdb` file) that you want to use to access the data. When you add an `AccessDataSource` control to your ASP.NET page, the following line of code appears in the Source view of page:

```
<asp:AccessDataSource ID="AccessDataSource1" runat="server"></asp:AccessDataSource>
```

The `AccessDataSource` control does not allow you to provide username and password to access the data. If you need to use a password-protected Access database, select the `SqlDataSource` control to access the database. The inheritance hierarchy of the `AccessDataSource` control is as follows:

```
System.Object
   System.Web.UI.Control
      System.Web.UI.DataSourceControl
         System.Web.UI.WebControls.SqlDataSource
            System.Web.UI.WebControls.AccessDataSource
```

Noteworthy properties of the `AccessDataSource` class are listed in Table 8.34:

Table 8.34: Noteworthy Properties of the AccessDataSource Class	
Property	**Description**
`ConnectionString`	Obtains the connection string that is used to connect to the Microsoft Access database
`Context`	Gets the HttpContext object associated with the server control for the current Web request. (Inherited from Control)
`Controls`	Gets a ControlCollection object that represents the child controls for a specified server control in the UI hierarchy. (Inherited from DataSourceControl)

Table 8.34: Noteworthy Properties of the AccessDataSource Class

Property	Description
`DataFile`	Specifies the path of the Microsoft Access `.mdb` file
`DataSourceMode`	Gets or sets the data retrieval mode that the SqlDataSource control uses to fetch data. (Inherited from SqlDataSource)
`DeleteCommand`	Gets or sets the SQL string that the SqlDataSource control uses to delete data from the underlying database. (Inherited from SqlDataSource)
`DeleteCommandType`	Gets or sets a value indicating whether the text in the DeleteCommand property is an SQL statement or the name of a stored procedure. (Inherited from SqlDataSource)
`DeleteParameters`	Gets the parameters collection that contains the parameters that are used by the DeleteCommand property from the SqlDataSourceView object that is associated with the SqlDataSource control. (Inherited from SqlDataSource)
`DesignMode`	Gets a value indicating whether a control is being used on a design surface. (Inherited from Control)
`EnableCaching`	Gets or sets a value indicating whether the SqlDataSource control has data caching enabled. (Inherited from SqlDataSource)
`EnableTheming`	Gets a value indicating whether this control supports themes. (Inherited from DataSourceControl)
`EnableViewState`	Gets or sets a value indicating whether the server control persists its view state, and the view state of any child controls it contains, to the requesting client. (Inherited from Control)
`Events`	Gets a list of event handler delegates for the control. This property is read-only. (Inherited from Control)
`FilterExpression`	Gets or sets a filtering expression that is applied when the Select method is called. (Inherited from SqlDataSource)
`FilterParameters`	Gets a collection of parameters that are associated with any parameter placeholders that are in the FilterExpression string. (Inherited from SqlDataSource)
`HasChildViewState`	Gets a value indicating whether the current server control's child controls have any saved view-state settings. (Inherited from Control)
`ID`	Gets or sets the programmatic identifier assigned to the server control. (Inherited from Control)
`IdSeparator`	Infrastructure. Gets the character used to separate control identifiers. (Inherited from Control)
`InsertCommand`	Gets or sets the SQL string that the SqlDataSource control uses to insert data into the underlying database. (Inherited from SqlDataSource)
`InsertCommandType`	Gets or sets a value indicating whether the text in the InsertCommand property is an SQL statement or the name of a stored procedure. (Inherited from SqlDataSource)
`InsertParameters`	Gets the parameters collection that contains the parameters that are used by the InsertCommand property from the SqlDataSourceView object that is associated with the SqlDataSource control. (Inherited from SqlDataSource)
`IsChildControlStateCleared`	Gets a value indicating whether controls contained within this control have control state. (Inherited from Control)
`IsTrackingViewState`	Gets a value that indicates whether the server control is saving changes to its view state. (Inherited from Control)

Table 8.34: Noteworthy Properties of the AccessDataSource Class	
Property	**Description**
IsViewStateEnabled	Gets a value indicating whether view state is enabled for this control. (Inherited from Control)
LoadViewStateByID	Gets a value indicating whether the control participates in loading its view state by ID instead of index. (Inherited from Control)
OldValuesParameterFormatString	Gets or sets a format string to apply to the names of any parameters that are passed to the Delete or Update method. (Inherited from SqlDataSource)
Page	Gets a reference to the Page instance that contains the server control. (Inherited from Control)
Parent	Gets a reference to the server control's parent control in the page control hierarchy. (Inherited from Control)
ProviderName	Obtains the name of the .NET data provider that the AccessDataSource control uses to connect to a Microsoft Access database
SelectCommand	Gets or sets the SQL string that the SqlDataSource control uses to retrieve data from the underlying database. (Inherited from SqlDataSource)
SelectCommandType	Gets or sets a value indicating whether the text in the SelectCommand property is an SQL query or the name of a stored procedure. (Inherited from SqlDataSource)
SelectParameters	Gets the parameters collection that contains the parameters that are used by the SelectCommand property from the SqlDataSourceView object that is associated with the SqlDataSource control. (Inherited from SqlDataSource)
Site	Gets information about the container that hosts the current control when rendered on a design surface. (Inherited from Control)
SkinID	Gets the skin to apply to the DataSourceControl control. (Inherited from DataSourceControl)
SortParameterName	Gets or sets the name of a stored procedure parameter that is used to sort retrieved data when data retrieval is performed using a stored procedure. (Inherited from SqlDataSource)
SqlCacheDependency	Specifies a semicolon-delimited string that signifies which database and table to utilize for the Microsoft SQL Server cache dependency

Now, let's explore the LinqDataSource control.

The LinqDataSource Control

The LinqDataSource control is a data source control that allows a Web server control to access data located in the relational databases or in the memory data collection, such as an array and context objects. This control enables Web developers to use LINQ, which simplifies the interaction between object-oriented programming and relational data by applying the principles of object-oriented programming to relational data. The LinqDataSource control provides with the capability to connect to data from either a database or an in-memory collection, such as an array. This control enables a user to handle operations, such as insert and delete, without using SQL commands to perform these tasks.

The inheritance hierarchy of the LinqDataSource control is as follows:

```
System.Object
   System.Web.UI.Control
         System.Web.UI.DataSourceControl.QueryableDataSource
                System.Web.UI.WebControls.ContextDataSource
                            System.Web.UI.WebControls.LinqDataSource
```

Noteworthy properties of the `LinqDataSource` class are listed in Table 8.35:

Table 8.35: Noteworthy Properties of the LinqDataSource Class

Property	Description
`AutoGenerateOrderByClause`	Gets or sets a value that indicates whether the `LinqDataSource` control dynamically creates an Order By clause based on values in the `OrderByParameters` collection
`AutoGenerateWhereClause`	Obtains or sets a value that indicates whether the `LinqDataSource` control dynamically creates a Where clause based on values defined in the `WhereParameters` collection
`AutoPage`	Obtains or sets a value that indicates whether the `LinqDataSource` control supports navigation through sections of the data at run time
`AutoSort`	Obtains or sets a value that indicates whether the `LinqDataSource` control supports sorting of the data at run time
`BindingContainer`	Allows you to get the control that contains data binding of this control. (Inherited from Control)
`ChildControlsCreated`	Allows you to get a value that indicates whether the child controls have been created for a server control. (Inherited from Control)
`ClientID`	Allows you to get the server control identifier generated by ASP.NET. (Inherited from DataSourceControl)
`ClientIDSeparator`	Allows you to get a character value representing the separator character used in the ClientID property. (Inherited from Control)
`Context`	Allows you to get the HttpContext object associated with the server control for the current Web request. (Inherited from Control)
`ContextTypeName`	Obtains or sets the name of the type of data that contains the property whose value has the data that you want to retrieve
`Controls`	Gets a ControlCollection object that represents the child controls for a specified server control in the UI hierarchy. (Inherited from DataSourceControl)
`DeleteParameters`	Obtains the collection of parameters that are used during a delete operation
`DesignMode`	Gets a value indicating whether a control is being used on a design surface. (Inherited from Control)
`EnableDelete`	Obtains or sets a value that indicates whether data records can be deleted through the `LinqDataSource` control
`EnableInsert`	Obtains or sets a value that indicates whether data records can be inserted through the `LinqDataSource` control
`EnableTheming`	Gets a value indicating whether this control supports themes. (Inherited from DataSourceControl)
`EnableUpdate`	Obtains or sets a value that indicates whether data records can be updated through the `LinqDataSource` control
`EnableViewState`	Gets or sets a value indicating whether the server control persists its view state, and the view state of any child controls it contains, to the requesting client. (Inherited from Control)
`Events`	Gets a list of event handler delegates for the control. This property is read-only. (Inherited from Control)
`GroupBy`	Obtains or sets a value that specifies which properties are used for grouping the retrieved data

Table 8.35: Noteworthy Properties of the LinqDataSource Class

Property	Description
`GroupByParameters`	Obtains the collection of parameters that are used to create the Group By clause
`HasChildViewState`	Gets a value indicating whether the current server control's child controls have any saved view-state settings. (Inherited from Control)
`ID`	Gets or sets the programmatic identifier assigned to the server control. (Inherited from Control)
`IdSeparator`	Infrastructure. Gets the character used to separate control identifiers. (Inherited from Control)
`InsertParameters`	Obtains the collection of parameters that are used during an insert operation
`IsChildControlState Cleared`	Gets a value indicating whether controls contained within this control have control state. (Inherited from Control)
`IsTrackingViewState`	Gets a value that indicates whether the server control is saving changes to its view state. (Inherited from Control)
`IsViewStateEnabled`	Gets a value indicating whether view state is enabled for this control. (Inherited from Control)
`LoadViewStateByID`	Gets a value indicating whether the control participates in loading its view state by ID instead of index. (Inherited from Control)
`OrderBy`	Obtains or sets a value that specifies which fields are used for ordering the retrieved data
`OrderByParameters`	Obtains the collection of parameters that are used to create the Order By clause.
`Page`	Gets a reference to the Page instance that contains the server control. (Inherited from Control)
`Parent`	Gets a reference to the server control's parent control in the page control hierarchy. (Inherited from Control)
`Select`	Obtains or sets the properties and calculated values that are included in the retrieved data
`SelectParameters`	Obtains the collection of parameters that are used during a data-retrieval operation
`Site`	Gets information about the container that hosts the current control when rendered on a design surface. (Inherited from Control)
`SkinID`	Gets the skin to apply to the DataSourceControl control. (Inherited from DataSourceControl)
`StoreOriginalValuesInView State`	Obtains or sets a value that indicates whether the data from the data source should be stored in view state to make sure that the data has not been changed by another process before it is updated or deleted
`TableName`	Obtains or sets the name of the property or field in the data context object that represents a data collection
`TemplateControl`	Gets or sets a reference to the template that contains this control. (Inherited from Control)
`TemplateSourceDirectory`	Gets the virtual directory of the Page or UserControl that contains the current server control. (Inherited from Control)
`UniqueID`	Gets the unique, hierarchically qualified identifier for the server control. (Inherited from Control)

Table 8.35: Noteworthy Properties of the LinqDataSource Class	
Property	**Description**
UpdateParameters	Obtains the collection of parameters that are used during an update operation
ViewState	Gets a dictionary of state information that allows you to save and restore the view state of a server control across multiple requests for the same page. (Inherited from Control)
ViewStateIgnoresCase	Gets a value that indicates whether the StateBag object is case-insensitive. (Inherited from Control)
Visible	Gets or sets a value indicating whether the control is visually displayed. (Inherited from DataSourceControl)
Where	Obtains or sets a value that specifies what conditions must be true for a record to be included in the retrieved data
WhereParameters	Obtains the collection of parameters that is used to create the Where clause

Noteworthy methods of the `LinqDataSource` control are listed in Table 8.36:

Table 8.36: Noteworthy Methods of the LinqDataSource Class	
Method	**Description**
Delete	Deletes the data from the database
Insert	Inserts the data in the database
Update	Updates the data in the database

Noteworthy events of the `LinqDataSource` class are listed in Table 8.37:

Table 8.37: Noteworthy Events of the LinqDataSource Class	
Event	**Description**
ContextCreated	Invoked after an instance of the context type object is created
ContextCreating	Invoked before an instance of the context type object is created
ContextDisposing	Invoked before disposing the context type object
DataBinding	Occurs when the server control binds to a data source. (Inherited from Control)
Deleted	Invoked when a delete operation has finished
Deleting	Invoked before a delete operation starts
Disposed	Occurs when a server control is released from memory, which is the last stage of the server control lifecycle when an ASP.NET page is requested. (Inherited from Control)
Init	Occurs when the server control is initialized, which is the first step in its lifecycle. (Inherited from Control)
Inserted	Invoked when an insert operation has finished
Inserting	Invoked before an insert operation starts
Load	Occurs when the server control is loaded into the Page object. (Inherited from Control)
PreRender	Occurs after the Control object is loaded but prior to rendering. (Inherited from Control)
Selected	Invoked when a data retrieval operation has finished

Table 8.37: Noteworthy Events of the LinqDataSource Class	
Event	**Description**
`Selecting`	Invoked before a data-retrieval operation starts
`Unload`	Occurs when the server control is unloaded from memory. (Inherited from Control)
`Updated`	Invoked when an update operation has finished
`Updating`	Invoked before an update operation starts

Now, let's learn about the `ObjectDataSource` control.

The ObjectDataSource Control

The `ObjectDataSource` control represents the business objects and allows you to use the `ObjectDataSource` control in conjunction with a data-bound control to display, edit, and sort the data on a Web page with little or no code. This control is used to create Web applications that rely on the middle-tier objects to manage data. The inheritance hierarchy of the `ObjectDataSource` control is as follows:

```
System.Object
  System.Web.UI.Control
        System.Web.UI.DataSourceControl
               System.Web.UI.WebControls.ObjectDataSource
```

Noteworthy properties of the `ObjectDataSource` class are listed in Table 8.38:

Table 8.38: Noteworthy Properties of the ObjectDataSource Class	
Property	**Description**
`CacheDuration`	Obtains or sets the length of time, in seconds, for which the data source control caches data that is retrieved by the `SelectMethod` property.
`CacheExpirationPolicy`	Obtains or sets the cache expiration behavior that, when combined with the duration, describes the behavior of the cache that the data source control uses.
`CacheKeyDependency`	Obtains or sets a user-defined key dependency that is linked to all data cache objects that are created by the data source control.
`ChildControlsCreated`	Gets a value that indicates whether the server control's child controls have been created. (Inherited from Control)
`ClientID`	Gets the server control identifier generated by ASP.NET. (Inherited from DataSourceControl)
`ClientIDSeparator`	Gets a character value representing the separator character used in the ClientID property. (Inherited from Control)
`ConflictDetection`	Obtains or sets a value that determines whether or not just the new values are passed to the `Update` method or both the old and new values are passed to the `Update` method.
`Context`	Gets the HttpContext object associated with the server control for the current Web request. (Inherited from Control)
`Controls`	Gets a ControlCollection object that represents the child controls for a specified server control in the UI hierarchy. (Inherited from DataSourceControl)
`ConvertNullToDBNull`	Obtains or sets a value indicating whether the `Parameter` values that are passed to an update, insert, or delete operation are automatically converted from nullNothingnullptra null reference (`Nothing` in Visual Basic) to the `Value` value by the `ObjectDataSource` control.

Table 8.38: Noteworthy Properties of the ObjectDataSource Class	
Property	**Description**
`DataObjectTypeName`	Obtains or sets the name of a class that the `ObjectDataSource` control uses for a parameter in an update, insert, or delete data operation. It allows you to pass multiple values instead of passing individual values from the data-bound control.
`DeleteMethod`	Obtains or sets the name of the method or function that the `ObjectDataSource` control invokes to delete the data.
`DeleteParameters`	Obtains the parameters collection that contains the parameters that are used by the `DeleteMethod` method.
`DesignMode`	Gets a value indicating whether a control is being used on a design surface. (Inherited from Control)
`EnableCaching`	Obtains or sets a value indicating whether the `ObjectDataSource` control has data caching enabled.
`EnablePaging`	Obtains or sets a value that indicates whether the data source control supports paging through the set of data that it retrieves.
`EnableTheming`	Gets a value indicating whether this control supports themes. (Inherited from DataSourceControl)
`EnableViewState`	Gets or sets a value indicating whether the server control persists its view state, and the view state of any child controls it contains, to the requesting client. (Inherited from Control)
`Events`	Gets a list of event handler delegates for the control. This property is read-only. (Inherited from Control)
`FilterExpression`	Obtains or sets a filtering expression that is applied when the method that is specified by the `SelectMethod` property is called.
`FilterParameters`	Obtains a collection of parameters that are associated with any parameter placeholders in the `FilterExpression` string.
`HasChildViewState`	Gets a value indicating whether the current server control's child controls have any saved view-state settings. (Inherited from Control)
`ID`	Gets or sets the programmatic identifier assigned to the server control. (Inherited from Control)
`IdSeparator`	Infrastructure. Gets the character used to separate control identifiers. (Inherited from Control)
`InsertMethod`	Obtains or sets the name of the method or function that the `ObjectDataSource` control invokes to insert data.
`InsertParameters`	Obtains the parameters collection that contains the parameters that are used by the `InsertMethod` property.
`IsChildControlStateCleared`	Gets a value indicating whether controls contained within this control have control state. (Inherited from Control.)
`IsTrackingViewState`	Gets a value that indicates whether the server control is saving changes to its view state. (Inherited from Control)
`IsViewStateEnabled`	Gets a value indicating whether view state is enabled for this control. (Inherited from Control)
`LoadViewStateByID`	Gets a value indicating whether the control participates in loading its view state by ID instead of index. (Inherited from Control)

Table 8.38: Noteworthy Properties of the ObjectDataSource Class	
Property	**Description**
`MaximumRowsParameterName`	Obtains or sets the name of the business object data retrieval method parameter that is used to indicate the number of records to retrieve for data source paging support.
`OldValuesParameterFormatString`	Obtains or sets a format string to apply to the names of the parameters for original values that are passed to the `Delete` or `Update` methods.
`Page`	Gets a reference to the Page instance that contains the server control. (Inherited from Control)
`Parent`	Gets a reference to the server control's parent control in the page control hierarchy. (Inherited from Control)
`SelectCountMethod`	Obtains or sets the name of the method or function that the `ObjectDataSource` control invokes to retrieve a row count.
`SelectMethod`	Obtains or sets the name of the method or function that the `ObjectDataSource` control invokes to retrieve data.
`SelectParameters`	Obtains the parameters collection that contains the parameters that are used by the method specified by the `SelectMethod` property.
`Site`	Gets information about the container that hosts the current control when rendered on a design surface. (Inherited from Control)
`SkinID`	Gets the skin to apply to the DataSourceControl control. (Inherited from DataSourceControl)
`SortParameterName`	Obtains or sets the name of the business object that the `SelectMethod` parameter uses to specify a sort expression for data source sorting support.
`SqlCacheDependency`	Obtains or sets a semicolon-delimited string that indicates which databases and tables to use for the Microsoft SQL Server cache dependency.
`StartRowIndexParameterName`	Obtains or sets the name of the data retrieval method parameter that is used to indicate the value of the identifier of the first record to retrieve for data source paging support.
`TemplateControl`	Gets or sets a reference to the template that contains this control. (Inherited from Control)
`TemplateSourceDirectory`	Gets the virtual directory of the Page or UserControl that contains the current server control. (Inherited from Control.)
`TypeName`	Obtains or sets the name of the class that the `ObjectDataSource` object represents.
`UniqueID`	Allows the server control to get the unique, hierarchically qualified identifier. (Inherited from Control)
`UpdateMethod`	Obtains or sets the name of the method or function that the `ObjectDataSource` control invokes to update data.
`UpdateParameters`	Obtains the parameters collection that contains the parameters that are used by the method that is specified by the `UpdateMethod` property.

Noteworthy methods of the ObjectDataSource class are listed in Table 8.39:

Table 8.39: Noteworthy Methods of the ObjectDataSource Class

Method	Description
Delete	Deletes the data from the database by calling the method that is identified by the DeleteMethod property with any parameters that are in the DeleteParameters collection
Insert	Inserts the data in the database by calling the method that is identified by the InsertMethod property and any parameters in the InsertParameters collection
Select	Retrieves the data from the database by calling the method that is identified by the SelectMethod property with the parameters in the SelectParameters collection
Update	Updates the data in the database by calling the method that is identified by the UpdateMethod property and any parameters that are in the UpdateParameters collection

Noteworthy events of the ObjectDataSource class are listed in Table 8.40:

Table 8.40: Noteworthy Events of the ObjectDataSource Class

Event	Description
Deleted	Invokes when a Delete operation has been completed
Deleting	Invokes before a delete operation starts
Disposed	Occurs when a server control is released from memory, which is the last stage of the server control lifecycle when an ASP.NET page is requested. (Inherited from Control)
Filtering	Invokes before a filter operation starts
Init	Occurs when the server control is initialized, which is the first step in its lifecycle. (Inherited from Control.)
Inserted	Invokes when an Insert operation has been completed
Inserting	Invokes before an Insert operation starts.
Load	Occurs when the server control is loaded into the Page object. (Inherited from Control)
ObjectCreated	Invokes after the object that is identified by the TypeName property is created
ObjectCreating	Invokes before the object that is identified by the TypeName property is created
ObjectDisposing	Invokes before the object that is identified by the TypeName property is discarded
PreRender	Occurs after the Control object is loaded but prior to rendering. (Inherited from Control)
Selected	Invokes when a Select operation has completed
Selecting	Invokes before a Select operation starts
Unload	Occurs when the server control is unloaded from memory. (Inherited from Control)
Updated	Invokes when an Update operation has been completed
Updating	Invokes before an Update operation starts

Now, let's explore the `XmlDataSource` control.

The XmlDataSource Control

The XmlDataSource control allows a data bound control to bind the data from a XML document. This control also supports `XPath` expressions that allow you to return only certain nodes from the XML document.

The inheritance hierarchy of the `XmlDataSource` control is as follows:

```
System.Object
   System.Web.UI.Control
           System.Web.UI. HierarchicalDataSourceControl
                     System.Web.UI.WebControls.XmlDataSource
```

Noteworthy properties of the `XmlDataSource` class are listed in Table 8.41:

Table 8.41: Noteworthy Properties of the XmlDataSource Class

Property	Description
`CacheDuration`	Obtains or sets the length of time, in seconds, for which the data source control caches the data it has retrieved.
`CacheExpirationPolicy`	Obtains or sets the cache expiration policy that is combined with the cache duration to describe the caching behavior of the cache that the data source control uses.
`CacheKeyDependency`	Obtains or sets a user-defined key dependency that is linked to all data cache objects created by the data source control. All cache objects explicitly expire when the key expires.
`ChildControlsCreated`	Gets a value that indicates whether the server control's child controls have been created. (Inherited from Control)
`ClientID`	Gets the server control identifier generated by ASP.NET. (Inherited from HierarchicalDataSource Control)
`ClientIDSeparator`	Gets a character value representing the separator character used in the ClientID property. (Inherited from Control)
`Context`	Gets the HttpContext object associated with the server control for the current Web request. (Inherited from Control)
`Controls`	Gets a ControlCollection object that represents the child controls for a specified server control in the UI hierarchy. (Inherited from HierarchicalDataSource Control)
`Data`	Obtains or sets a block of XML data that the data source control binds to.
`DataFile`	Specifies the file name of an XML file that the data source binds to.
`DesignMode`	Gets a value indicating whether a control is being used on a design surface. (Inherited from Control)
`EnableCaching`	Obtains or sets a value indicating whether the `XmlDataSource` control has data caching enabled.
`EnableTheming`	Gets a value indicating whether this control supports themes. (Inherited from HierarchicalDataSourceControl)
`EnableViewState`	Gets or sets a value indicating whether the server control persists its view state, and the view state of any child controls it contains, to the requesting client. (Inherited from Control)
`Events`	Gets a list of event handler delegates for the control. This property is read-only. (Inherited from Control)
`HasChildViewState`	Gets a value indicating whether the current server control's child controls have any saved view-state settings. (Inherited from Control)

Table 8.41: Noteworthy Properties of the XmlDataSource Class

Property	Description
`ID`	Gets or sets the programmatic identifier assigned to the server control. (Inherited from Control)
`IdSeparator`	Gets the character used to separate control identifiers. (Inherited from Control)
`IsChildControlStateCleared`	Gets a value indicating whether controls contained within this control have control state. (Inherited from Control)
`IsTrackingViewState`	Gets a value that indicates whether the server control is saving changes to its view state. (Inherited from Control)
`IsViewStateEnabled`	Gets a value indicating whether view state is enabled for this control. (Inherited from Control)
`LoadViewStateByID`	Gets a value indicating whether the control participates in loading its view state by ID instead of index. (Inherited from Control)
`Page`	Gets a reference to the Page instance that contains the server control. (Inherited from Control)
`Parent`	Gets a reference to the server control's parent control in the page control hierarchy. (Inherited from Control)
`Site`	Gets information about the container that hosts the current control when rendered on a design surface. (Inherited from Control)
`SkinID`	Gets or sets the skin to apply to the HierarchicalDataSourceControl control. (Inherited from HierarchicalDataSourceControl)
`TemplateControl`	Gets or sets a reference to the template that contains this control. (Inherited from Control)
`TemplateSourceDirectory`	Gets the virtual directory of the Page or UserControl that contains the current server control. (Inherited from Control)
`Transform`	Obtains or sets a block of Extensible Stylesheet Language (XSL) data that defines an XSL transformation to be performed on the XML data, managed by the `XmlDataSource` control.
`TransformArgumentList`	Obtains a list of XSLT arguments that are used with the style sheet defined by the `Transform` or `TransformFile` properties to perform a transformation on the XML data.
`TransformFile`	Defines the file name of an XSL file (`.xsl`) that specifies the XSLT transformation for performing on the XML data; manages by the `XmlDataSource` control.
`UniqueID`	Gets the unique, hierarchically qualified identifier for the server control. (Inherited from Control)
`ViewState`	Gets a dictionary of state information that allows you to save and restore the view state of a server control across multiple requests for the same page. (Inherited from Control)
`ViewStateIgnoresCase`	Gets a value that indicates whether the StateBag object is case-insensitive. (Inherited from Control)
`Visible`	Gets or sets a value indicating whether the control is visually displayed. (Inherited from HierarchicalDataSourceControl)
`XPath`	Defines an XPath expression that can be applied on the XML data contained by the `Data` property or by the XML file specified by the `DataFile` property

Noteworthy methods of the XmlDataSource class are listed in Table 8.42:

Table 8.42: Noteworthy Methods of the XmlDataSource Class

Method	Description
GetXmlDocument	Copies the XML data into memory from the database directly or from the cache, and returns it as XmlDataDocument object
Save	Stores the XML data into memory by using the XmlDataSource control

Noteworthy event of the XmlDataSource class is listed in Table 8.43:

Table 8.43: Noteworthy Event of the XmlDataSource Class

Event	Description
Transforming	Invokes before the style sheet that is defined by the Transform property or identified by the TransformFile property is applied to XML data

Now, let's learn about the EntityDataSource control.

The EntityDataSource Control

The EntityDataSource control helps you to connect with ADO.NET Entity Data Model (EDM) to perform various database operations, such as create, insert, remove, and update. When you add an EntityDataSource control to your ASP.NET page, the following line of code appears in the Source view page:

```
<asp:EntityDataSource ID="EntityDataSource1" runat="server">   </asp:EntityDataSource>
```

The inheritance hierarchy of the EntityDataSource control is as follows:

```
System.Object
   System.Web.UI.Control
        System.Web.UI.DataSourceControl
               System.Web.UI.WebControls.EntityDataSource
```

Noteworthy properties of the EntityDataSource class are listed in Table 8.44:

Table 8.44: Noteworthy Properties of the EntityDataSource Class

Property	Description
AutoGenerateOrderByClause	Gets or sets a value that indicates whether the EntityDataSource control dynamically creates an Order By clause based on values in the OrderByParameters collection
AutoGenerateWhereClause	Obtains or sets a value that indicates whether the EntityDataSource control dynamically creates a Where clause based on values defined in the WhereParameters collection
AutoPage	Obtains or sets a value that indicates whether the EntityDataSource control supports navigation through sections of the data at run time
AutoSort	Obtains or sets a value that indicates whether the EntityDataSource control supports sorting of the data at run time
BindingContainer	Allows you to get the control that contains data binding for this control. (Inherited from Control)
ChildControlsCreated	Allows you to get a value that indicates whether the child controls have been created for a server control. (Inherited from Control)
ClientID	Allows you to get the server control identifier generated by ASP.NET. (Inherited from DataSourceControl)
ClientIDSeparator	Allows you to get a character value representing the separator character used in the ClientID property. (Inherited from Control)

Table 8.44: Noteworthy Properties of the EntityDataSource Class

Property	Description
`Context`	Allows you to get the HttpContext object linked with the server control for the current Web request. (Inherited from Control)
`ContextTypeName`	Obtains or sets the name of the type of data that contains the property whose value has the data that you want to retrieve
`Controls`	Gets a ControlCollection object that represents the child controls for a specified server control in the UI hierarchy. (Inherited from DataSourceControl)
`DesignMode`	Gets a value indicating whether a control is being used on a design surface. (Inherited from Control)
`EnableDelete`	Obtains or sets a value that indicates whether data records can be deleted through the `EntityDataSource` control
`EnableInsert`	Obtains or sets a value that indicates whether data records can be inserted through the `EntityDataSource` control
`EnableTheming`	Gets a value indicating whether this control supports themes. (Inherited from DataSourceControl)
`EnableUpdate`	Obtains or sets a value that indicates whether data records can be updated through the `EntityDataSource` control
`EnableViewState`	Gets or sets a value indicating whether the server control persists its view state, and the view state of any child controls it contains, to the requesting client. (Inherited from Control)
`Events`	Gets a list of event handler delegates for the control. This property is read-only. (Inherited from Control)
`GroupBy`	Obtains or sets a value that specifies which properties are used for grouping the retrieved data
`HasChildViewState`	Gets a value indicating whether the current server control's child controls have any saved view-state settings. (Inherited from Control)
`ID`	Gets or sets the programmatic identifier assigned to the server control. (Inherited from Control)
`IdSeparator`	Gets the character used to separate control identifiers. (Inherited from Control)
`InsertParameters`	Obtains the collection of parameters that are used during an insert operation
`IsChildControlStateCleared`	Gets a value indicating whether controls contained within this control have control state. (Inherited from Control)
`IsTrackingViewState`	Gets a value that indicates whether the server control is saving changes to its view state. (Inherited from Control)
`IsViewStateEnabled`	Gets a value indicating whether view state is enabled for this control. (Inherited from Control)
`LoadViewStateByID`	Gets a value indicating whether the control participates in loading its view state by ID instead of index. (Inherited from Control)
`OrderBy`	Obtains or sets a value that specifies which fields are used for ordering the retrieved data
`OrderByParameters`	Obtains the collection of parameters that are used to create the Order By clause
`Page`	Gets a reference to the Page instance that contains the server control. (Inherited from Control)

Table 8.44: Noteworthy Properties of the EntityDataSource Class

Property	Description
`Parent`	Gets a reference to the server control's parent control in the page control hierarchy. (Inherited from Control)
`Select`	Obtains or sets the properties and calculated values that are included in the retrieved data
`SelectParameters`	Obtains the collection of parameters that are used during a data-retrieval operation
`Site`	Gets information about the container that hosts the current control when rendered on a design surface. (Inherited from Control)
`SkinID`	Gets the skin to apply to the DataSourceControl control. (Inherited from DataSourceControl)
`StoreOriginalValuesInViewState`	Obtains or sets a value that indicates whether the data from the data source should be stored in view state to make sure that the data has not been changed by another process before it is updated or deleted
`TemplateControl`	Gets or sets a reference to the template that contains this control. (Inherited from Control)
`TemplateSourceDirectory`	Gets the virtual directory of the Page or UserControl that contains the current server control. (Inherited from Control)
`UniqueID`	Gets the unique, hierarchically qualified identifier for the server control. (Inherited from Control)
`UpdateParameters`	Obtains the collection of parameters that are used during an update operation
`ViewState`	Gets a dictionary of state information that allows you to save and restore the view state of a server control across multiple requests for the same page. (Inherited from Control)
`ViewStateIgnoresCase`	Gets a value that indicates whether the StateBag object is case-insensitive. (Inherited from Control)
`Visible`	Gets or sets a value indicating whether the control is visually displayed. (Inherited from DataSourceControl)
`Where`	Obtains or sets a value that specifies what conditions must be true for a record to be included in the retrieved data
`WhereParameters`	Obtains the collection of parameters that is used to create the Where clause

Noteworthy methods of the EntityDataSource class are listed in Table 8.45:

Table 8.45: Noteworthy Methods of the EntityDataSource Class

Method	Description
`DataBind`	Binds the data source control with the database
`Dispose`	Enables the control to complete the final steps before releasing from the memory

Noteworthy events of the Entity`DataSource` class are listed in Table 8.46:

Table 8.46: Noteworthy Events of the EntityDataSource Class

Event	Description
`ContextCreated`	Invokes after an instance of the context type object is created

Table 8.46: Noteworthy Events of the EntityDataSource Class

Event	Description
ContextCreating	Invokes before an instance of the context type object is created
ContextDisposing	Invokes before disposing the context type object
DataBinding	Occurs when the server control binds to a data source. (Inherited from Control.)
Deleted	Invokes when a delete operation has finished
Deleting	Invokes before a delete operation starts
Disposed	Occurs when a server control is released from memory, which is the last stage of the server control lifecycle when an ASP.NET page is requested. (Inherited from Control.)
Init	Occurs when the server control is initialized, which is the first step in its lifecycle. (Inherited from Control.)
Inserted	Invokes when an insert operation has finished
Inserting	Invokes before an insert operation starts
Load	Occurs when the server control is loaded into the Page object. (Inherited from Control.)
PreRender	Occurs after the Control object is loaded but prior to rendering. (Inherited from Control.)
Selected	Invokes when a data retrieval operation has finished
Selecting	Invokes before a data-retrieval operation starts
Unload	Occurs when the server control is unloaded from memory. (Inherited from Control.)
Updated	Invokes when an update operation has finished
Updating	Invokes before an update operation starts

Now, let's learn about the SiteMapDataSource control.

The SiteMapDataSource Control

The SiteMapDataSource control allows you to work with the data stored in the SiteMap configuration file. This control also provides with the capability to customize site navigation by using site map data with data server controls, irrespective of the fact that controls are not navigation controls. The inheritance hierarchy of the SiteMapDataSource control is as follows:

```
System.Object
   System.Web.UI.Control
        System.Web.UI.HierarchicalDataSourceControl
                  System.Web.UI.WebControls.SiteMapDataSource
```

Noteworthy properties of the SiteMapDataSource class are listed in Table 8.47:

Table 8.47: Noteworthy Properties of the SiteMapDataSource Class

Property	Description
ContainsListCollection	Obtains a value indicating whether the data source control contains a collection of data source view objects
Context	Gets the HttpContext object associated with the server control for the current Web request. (Inherited from Control.)

Table 8.47: Noteworthy Properties of the SiteMapDataSource Class

Property	Description
`Controls`	Gets a ControlCollection object that represents the child controls for a specified server control in the UI hierarchy. (Inherited from HierarchicalDataSourceControl.)
`DesignMode`	Gets a value indicating whether a control is being used on a design surface. (Inherited from Control.)
`EnableTheming`	Gets a value indicating whether this control supports themes. (Inherited from HierarchicalDataSourceControl.)
`EnableViewState`	Gets or sets a value indicating whether the server control persists its view state, and the view state of any child controls it contains, to the requesting client. (Inherited from Control.)
`Events`	Gets a list of event handler delegates for the control. This property is read-only. (Inherited from Control.)
`HasChildViewState`	Gets a value indicating whether the current server control's child controls have any saved view-state settings. (Inherited from Control.)
`ID`	Gets or sets the programmatic identifier assigned to the server control. (Inherited from Control.)
`IdSeparator`	Gets the character used to separate control identifiers. (Inherited from Control.)
`IsChildControlStateCleared`	Gets a value indicating whether controls contained within this control have control state. (Inherited from Control.)
`IsTrackingViewState`	Gets a value that indicates whether the server control is saving changes to its view state. (Inherited from Control.)
`IsViewStateEnabled`	Gets a value indicating whether view state is enabled for this control. (Inherited from Control.)
`LoadViewStateByID`	Gets a value indicating whether the control participates in loading its view state by ID instead of index. (Inherited from Control.)
`Page`	Gets a reference to the Page instance that contains the server control. (Inherited from Control.)
`Parent`	Gets a reference to the server control's parent control in the page control hierarchy. (Inherited from Control.)
`Provider`	Gets or sets a `SiteMapProvider` object that is associated with the data source control
`ShowStartingNode`	Obtains or sets a value indicating whether the starting node is retrieved and displayed
`Site`	Gets information about the container that hosts the current control when rendered on a design surface. (Inherited from Control.)
`SiteMapProvider`	Obtains or sets the name of the site map provider that the data source binds to
`SkinID`	Gets or sets the skin to apply to the HierarchicalDataSourceControl control. (Inherited from HierarchicalDataSourceControl.)
`StartFromCurrentNode`	Obtains or sets a value indicating whether or not the site map node tree is retrieved using the node that represents the current page

Table 8.47: Noteworthy Properties of the SiteMapDataSource Class	
Property	**Description**
`StartingNodeOffset`	Obtains or sets a positive or negative integer offset from the starting node that determines the root hierarchy that is exposed by the data source control
`StartingNodeUrl`	Obtains or sets a node in the site map that the data source then uses as a reference point to retrieve nodes from a hierarchical site map

Noteworthy methods of the `SiteMapDataSource` class are listed in Table 8.48:

Table 8.48: Noteworthy Methods of the SiteMapDataSource Class	
Method	**Description**
`GetList`	Get a list of data source controls that can be used as sources of lists of data
`GetView`	Get a named view on the site map data of the site map provider according to the starting node and other properties of the data source
`GetViewNames`	Get a collection of named views for the data source control

Immediate Solutions

Using the SqlDataSource Control

In this chapter, you have learned that you can display or customize data through data bound controls, such as the `GridView` control, using any data source controls, such as the `SqlDataSource` control. The selection of a data source control and data bound control depends on the requirement of an application.

NOTE

In this section, we will cover all the data source controls using the GridView control.

Now, let's understand the SqlDataSource control. Implement the following steps to display data in a `GridView` control by using the `SqlDataSource` control:

1. Create a Web application and save it as `SqlDataSourceCS`. You can find the code for this application under the `SqlDataSourceCS` (for C#) and `SqlDataSourceVB` (for VB) folders.

NOTE

The applications in this chapter are created using the ASP.NET Empty Web Site template in the New Web Site dialog box. After creating the application, you need to add the Default.aspx page to the application.

2. Drag and drop a `SqlDataSource` control on the Design view of the `Default.aspx` page. Now, click the Smart Tag, as shown in Figure 8.1:

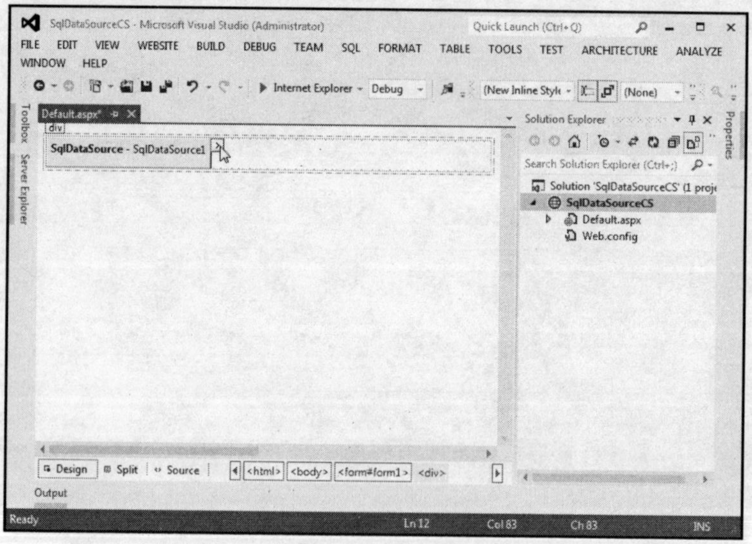

Figure 8.1: Adding a SqlDataSource Control to the Web Page

NOTE

The arrow symbol on the right of the SqlDataSource control in Figure 8.1 represents the Smart Tag.

3. Click the Configure Data Source option to configure a data source with the SqlDataSource control, as shown in Figure 8.2:

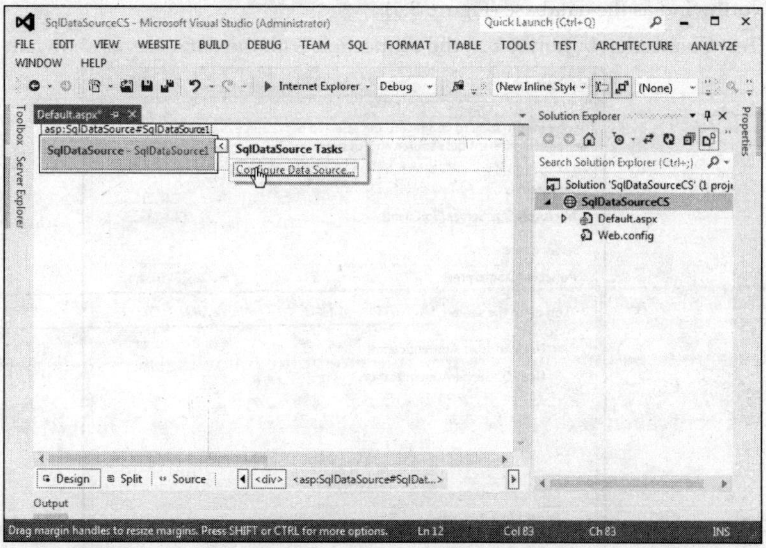

Figure 8.2: Configuring Data Source of the SqlDataSource Control

The Configure Data Source wizard appears (Figure 8.3).

4. Click the New Connection button, as shown in Figure 8.3:

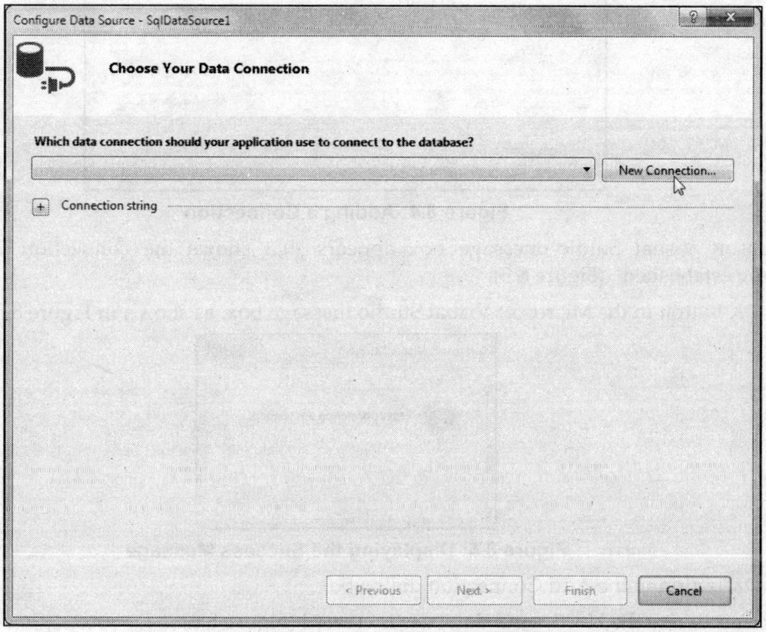

Figure 8.3: Clicking the New Connection Button

The Add Connection dialog box appears (Figure 8.4).

5. Select a server name from the Server name combo box and database name from the Select or enter a database name combo box, respectively in the Add Connection dialog box. In this example, we have selected Northwind as the database (Figure 8.4).
6. Click the Test Connection button to test the connection with the database, as shown in Figure 8.4:

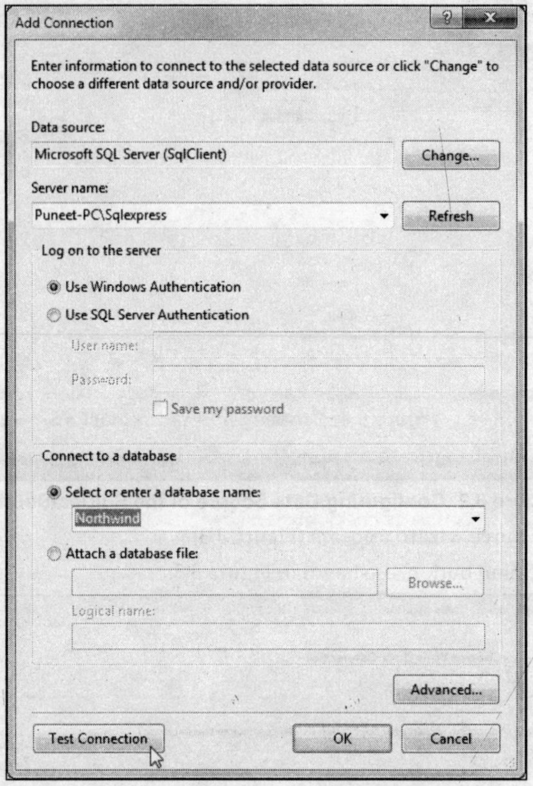

Figure 8.4: Adding a Connection

The Microsoft Visual Studio message box appears that shows the connection with the database is successfully established (Figure 8.5).

7. Click the OK button in the Microsoft Visual Studio message box, as shown in Figure 8.5:

Figure 8.5: Displaying the Success Message

8. Click the OK button in the Add Connection dialog box.

   Now, a connection to the Northwind database is created (Figure 8.6).
9. Click the Next button, as shown in Figure 8.6:

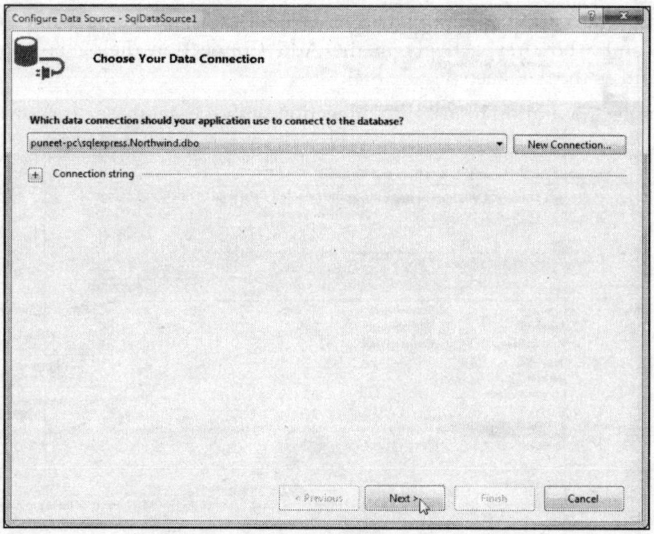

Figure 8.6: Creating a Data Connection

The Save the Connection String to the Application Configuration File page of the Configure Data Source wizard appears (Figure 8.7).

10. Select the Yes, save this connection as check box and click the Next button, as shown in Figure 8.7:

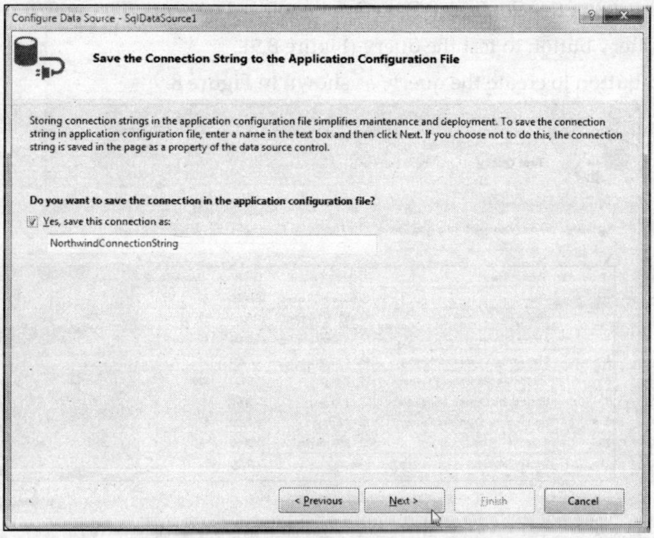

Figure 8.7: Saving the Data Connection

Now, the Configure the Select Statement page appears in the wizard (Figure 8.8).

11. Now, select Specify columns from a table or view radio button and select the columns of the table, which you want to display on the Web page. In this example, we have taken the Products table of the Northwind database and selected the ProductID, ProductName, QuantityPerUnit, UnitPrice, and UnitsInStock columns to display these columns on the Web page at runtime (Figure 8.8).

12. Click the Next button, as shown in Figure 8.8:

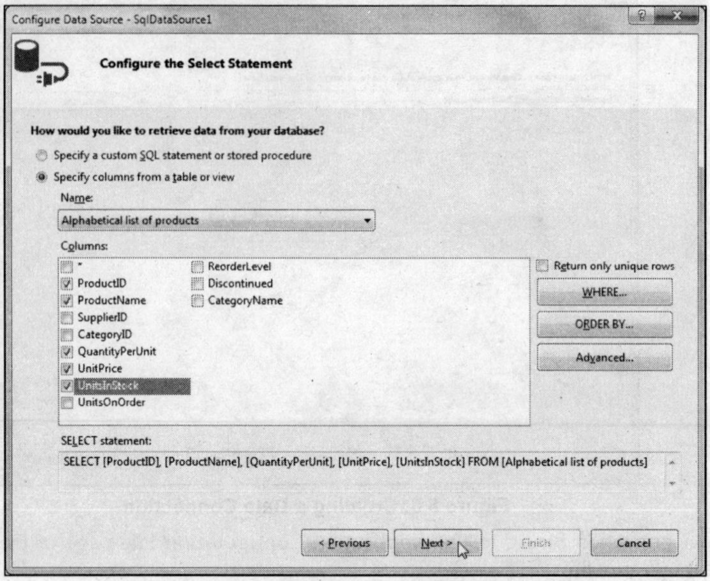

Figure 8.8: Configuring the Select Statement

The Test Query page of the Configure Data Source wizard appears (Figure 8.9).

13. Click the Test Query button to test the query (Figure 8.9).
14. Click the Finish button to create the query, as shown in Figure 8.9:

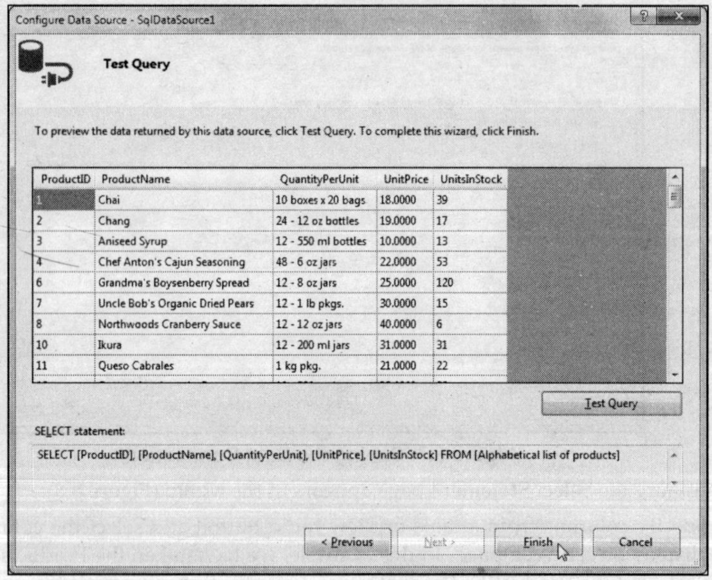

Figure 8.9: Finishing the Configure Data Source Wizard

15. Drag and drop a GridView control on the Design view of the Default.aspx page (Figure 8.10).

16. Select SqlDataSource1 option from the Choose Data Source drop-down list, as shown in Figure 8.10:

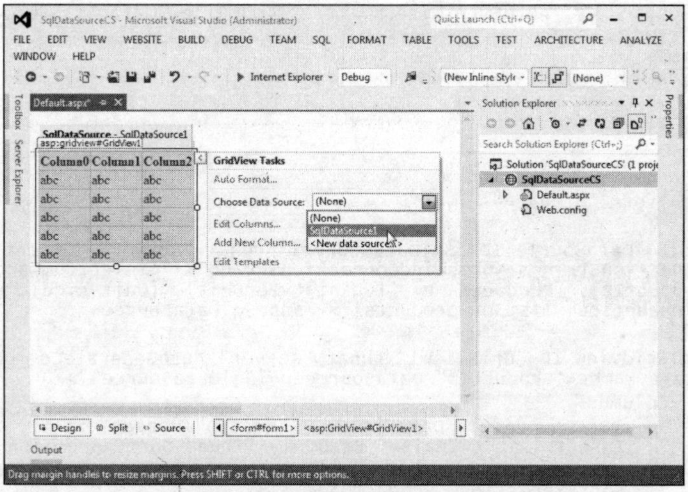

Figure 8.10: Selecting the Data Source

After configuring the data source, the `Default.aspx` page for the `SqlDataSourceCS` application is shown in Listing 8.1:

Listing 8.1: Showing the Code of the `Default.aspx` Page

In VB

```
<%@ Page Language="VB" AutoEventWireup="false" CodeFile="Default.aspx.vb"
  Inherits="_Default" %>
<!DOCTYPE html>
<html xmlns="http://www.w3.org/1999/xhtml">
<head runat="server">
    <title></title>
</head>
<body>
    <form id="form1" runat="server">
    <div>
        <asp:SqlDataSource ID="SqlDataSource1" runat="server" ConnectionString="<%$
        ConnectionStrings:NorthwindConnectionString %>" SelectCommand="SELECT
        [ProductID], [ProductName], [QuantityPerUnit], [UnitPrice], [UnitsInStock] FROM
        [Alphabetical list of products]"></asp:SqlDataSource>
        <asp:GridView ID="GridView1" runat="server" AutoGenerateColumns="False"
        DataKeyNames="ProductID" DataSourceID="SqlDataSource1">
            <Columns>
                <asp:BoundField DataField="ProductID" HeaderText="ProductID"
                InsertVisible="False" ReadOnly="True" SortExpression="ProductID" />
                <asp:BoundField DataField="ProductName" HeaderText="ProductName"
                SortExpression="ProductName" />
                <asp:BoundField DataField="QuantityPerUnit" HeaderText="QuantityPerUnit"
                SortExpression="QuantityPerUnit" />
                <asp:BoundField DataField="UnitPrice" HeaderText="UnitPrice"
                SortExpression="UnitPrice" />
                <asp:BoundField DataField="UnitsInStock" HeaderText="UnitsInStock"
                SortExpression="UnitsInStock" />
            </Columns>
        </asp:GridView>
    </div>
    </form>
</body>
</html>
```

In C#

```
<%@ Page Language="C#" AutoEventWireup="true" CodeFile="Default.aspx.cs"
  Inherits="_Default" %>
<!DOCTYPE html>
<html xmlns="http://www.w3.org/1999/xhtml">
<head runat="server">
    <title></title>
</head>
<body>
    <form id="form1" runat="server">
    <div>
        <asp:SqlDataSource ID="SqlDataSource1" runat="server" ConnectionString="<%$
         ConnectionStrings:NorthwindConnectionString %>" SelectCommand="SELECT
         [ProductID], [ProductName], [QuantityPerUnit], [UnitPrice], [UnitsInStock] FROM
         [Alphabetical list of products]"></asp:SqlDataSource>
    </div>
        <asp:GridView ID="GridView1" runat="server" AutoGenerateColumns="False"
         DataKeyNames="ProductID" DataSourceID="SqlDataSource1">
            <Columns>
                <asp:BoundField DataField="ProductID" HeaderText="ProductID"
                 InsertVisible="False" ReadOnly="True" SortExpression="ProductID" />
                <asp:BoundField DataField="ProductName" HeaderText="ProductName"
                 SortExpression="ProductName" />
                <asp:BoundField DataField="QuantityPerUnit" HeaderText="QuantityPerUnit"
                 SortExpression="QuantityPerUnit" />
                <asp:BoundField DataField="UnitPrice" HeaderText="UnitPrice"
                 SortExpression="UnitPrice" />
                <asp:BoundField DataField="UnitsInStock" HeaderText="UnitsInStock"
                 SortExpression="UnitsInStock" />
            </Columns>
        </asp:GridView>
    </form>
</body>
</html>
```

17. Press the F5 key on the keyboard to execute the application. The output is shown in Figure 8.11:

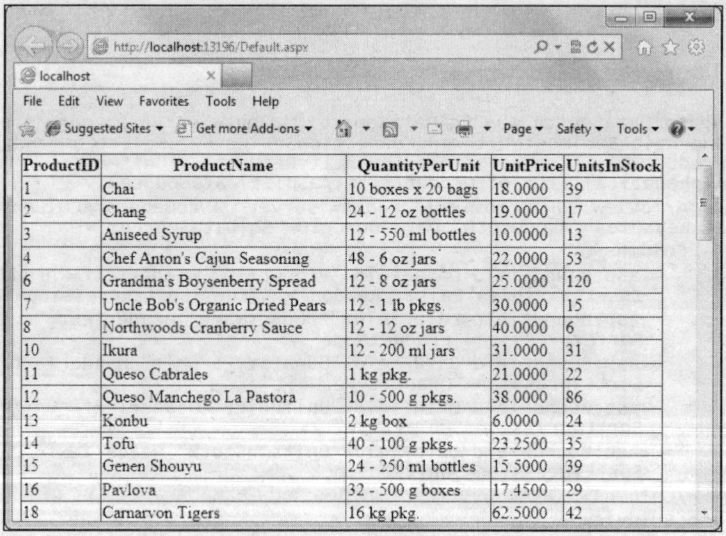

ProductID	ProductName	QuantityPerUnit	UnitPrice	UnitsInStock
1	Chai	10 boxes x 20 bags	18.0000	39
2	Chang	24 - 12 oz bottles	19.0000	17
3	Aniseed Syrup	12 - 550 ml bottles	10.0000	13
4	Chef Anton's Cajun Seasoning	48 - 6 oz jars	22.0000	53
6	Grandma's Boysenberry Spread	12 - 8 oz jars	25.0000	120
7	Uncle Bob's Organic Dried Pears	12 - 1 lb pkgs.	30.0000	15
8	Northwoods Cranberry Sauce	12 - 12 oz jars	40.0000	6
10	Ikura	12 - 200 ml jars	31.0000	31
11	Queso Cabrales	1 kg pkg.	21.0000	22
12	Queso Manchego La Pastora	10 - 500 g pkgs.	38.0000	86
13	Konbu	2 kg box	6.0000	24
14	Tofu	40 - 100 g pkgs.	23.2500	35
15	Genen Shouyu	24 - 250 ml bottles	15.5000	39
16	Pavlova	32 - 500 g boxes	17.4500	29
18	Carnarvon Tigers	16 kg pkg.	62.5000	42

Figure 8.11: Displaying the Output of the SqlDataSourceCS Application

Using the AccessDataSource Control

Let's understand how to use the `AccessDataSource` control in a Web site by performing the following steps:

1. Create a Web application and save it as `AccessDataSourceCS`. Now, add the Microsoft Access database in the application. The code for this application can be found under the `AccessDataSourceCS` (for C#) and `AccessDataSourceVB` (for VB) folders.
2. Add an AccessDataSource control on the Design view of the `Default.aspx` page (Figure 8.12).
3. Click the Smart Tag and select the Configure Data Source option, as shown in Figure 8.12:

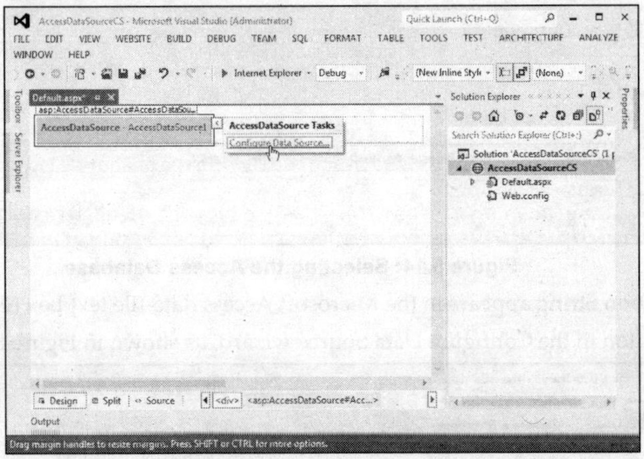

Figure 8.12: Adding an AccessDataSource Control

Now, the Configure Data Source wizard appears (Figure 8.13).

4. Click the Browse button in the wizard, as shown in Figure 8.13:

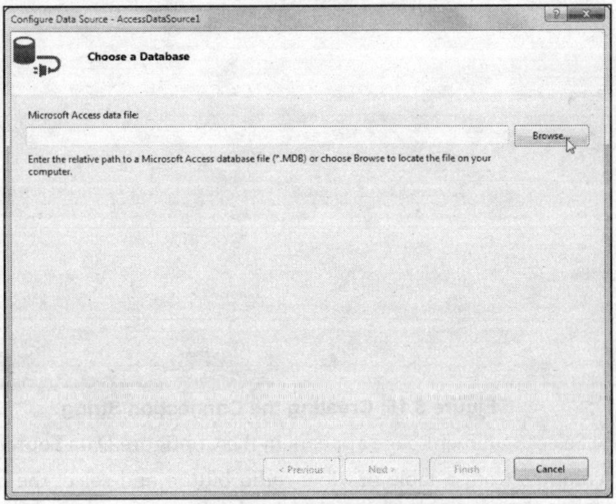

Figure 8.13: Choosing a Database

Now, the Select Microsoft Access Database dialog box appears (Figure 8.14).

5. Select the student.accdb Access database in the Contents of folder pane (Figure 8.14).
6. Click the OK button to save the selection in the Select Microsoft Access Database dialog box, as shown in Figure 8.14:

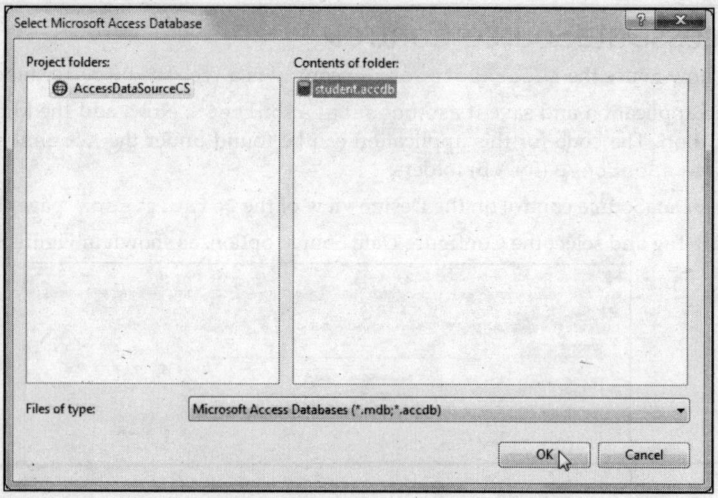

Figure 8.14: Selecting the Access Database

Now, the Connection String appears in the Microsoft Access data file text box (Figure 8.15).

7. Click the Next button in the Configure Data Source wizard, as shown in Figure 8.15:

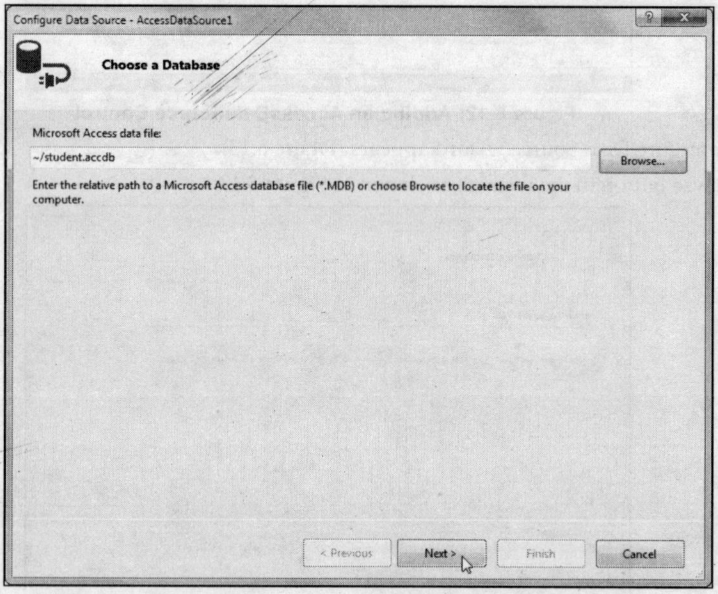

Figure 8.15: Creating the Connection String

Now, Configure the Select Statement page appears in the Configure Data Source wizard (Figure 8.16).

8. Select the Specify columns from a table or view radio button and select the columns of the table. In this example, we have taken the Studtable of the student database and selected the ID, Studname, Rollno, and Class columns to display these columns on the Web page at runtime (Figure 8.16).
9. Click the Next button to save the selection, as shown in Figure 8.16:

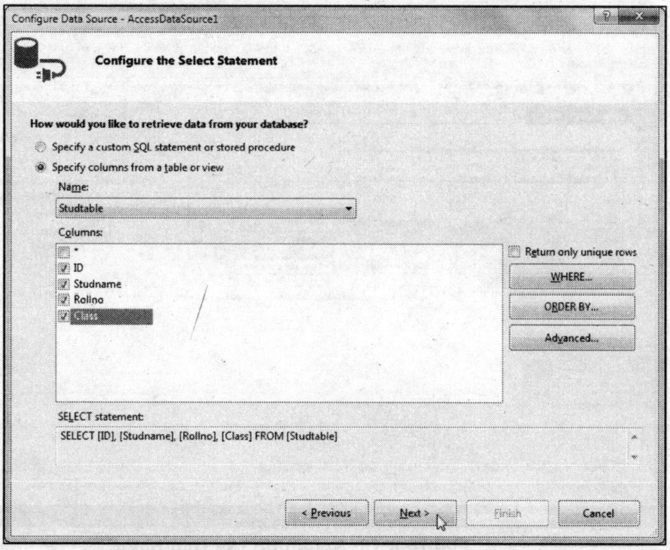

Figure 8.16: Selecting the Columns of the Table

Now, the Test Query page appears (Figure 8.17).

10. Click the Test Query button to preview the output (Figure 8.17).
11. Click the Finish button, as shown in Figure 8.17:

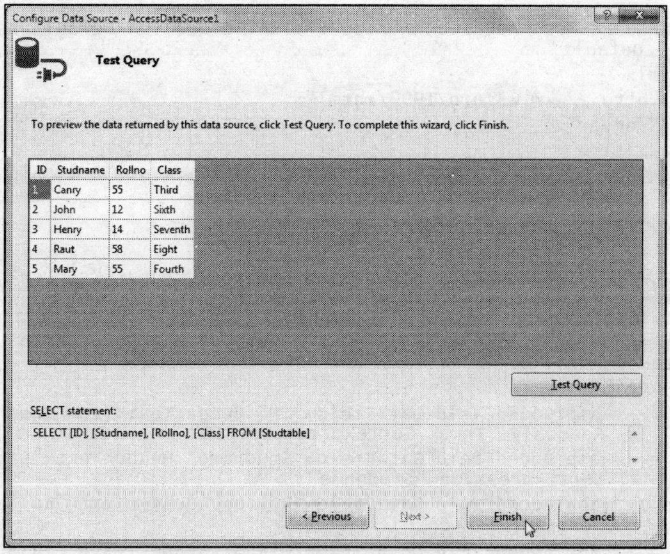

Figure 8.17: Testing the Query

12. Drag and drop a GridView control on the Design view of the Default.aspx page (Figure 8.18).
13. Select the AccessDataSource1 option from the Choose Data Source drop-down list, as shown in Figure 8.18:

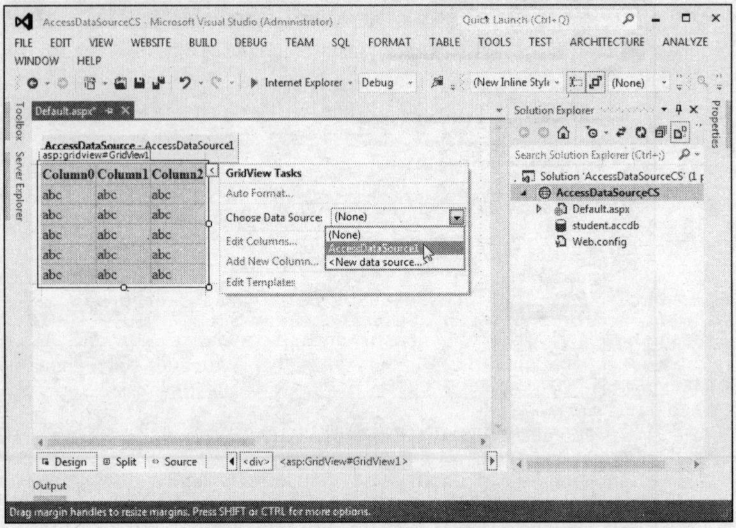

Figure 8.18: Selecting the Database

After configuring the data source, the `Default.aspx` page for the `AccessDataSourceCS` application is shown in Listing 8.2:

Listing 8.2: Showing the Code of the `Default.aspx` Page

In VB

```
<%@ Page Language="VB" AutoEventWireup="false" CodeFile="Default.aspx.vb"
 Inherits="_Default" %>
<!DOCTYPE html>
<html xmlns="http://www.w3.org/1999/xhtml">
<head runat="server">
    <title></title>
</head>
<body>
    <form id="form1" runat="server">
    <div>
        <asp:AccessDataSource ID="AccessDataSource1" runat="server"
         DataFile="~/student.accdb" SelectCommand="SELECT * FROM
         [Studtable]"></asp:AccessDataSource>
        <asp:GridView ID="GridView1" runat="server" AutoGenerateColumns="False"
         DataKeyNames="ID" DataSourceID="AccessDataSource1">
            <Columns>
                <asp:BoundField DataField="ID" HeaderText="ID" InsertVisible="False"
                 ReadOnly="True" SortExpression="ID" />
                <asp:BoundField DataField="Studname" HeaderText="Studname"
                 SortExpression="Studname" />
                <asp:BoundField DataField="Rollno" HeaderText="Rollno"
                 SortExpression="Rollno" />
                <asp:BoundField DataField="Class" HeaderText="Class"
                 SortExpression="Class" />
            </Columns>
        </asp:GridView>
    </div>
    </form>
</body>
</html>
```

In C#

```
<%@ Page Language="C#" AutoEventWireup="true" CodeFile="Default.aspx.cs"
  Inherits="_Default" %>
<!DOCTYPE html>
<html xmlns="http://www.w3.org/1999/xhtml">
<head runat="server">
    <title></title>
</head>
<body>
    <form id="form1" runat="server">
    <div>
    <asp:AccessDataSource ID="AccessDataSource1" runat="server"
        DataFile="~/student.accdb" SelectCommand="SELECT [ID], [Studname], [Rollno],
        [Class] FROM [Studtable]"></asp:AccessDataSource>
        <asp:GridView ID="GridView1" runat="server" AutoGenerateColumns="False"
        DataKeyNames="ID" DataSourceID="AccessDataSource1">
            <Columns>
                <asp:BoundField DataField="ID" HeaderText="ID" InsertVisible="False"
                ReadOnly="True" SortExpression="ID" />
                <asp:BoundField DataField="Studname" HeaderText="Studname"
                SortExpression="Studname" />
                <asp:BoundField DataField="Rollno" HeaderText="Rollno"
                SortExpression="Rollno" />
                <asp:BoundField DataField="Class" HeaderText="Class"
                SortExpression="Class" />
            </Columns>
        </asp:GridView>
    </div>
    </form>
</body>
</html>
```

14. Press the F5 key on the keyboard to execute the application.The output is shown in Figure 8.19:

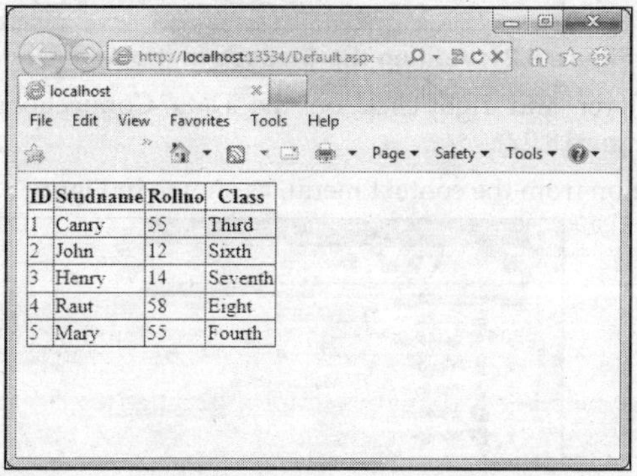

Figure 8.19: Displaying the Output of the AccessDataSourceCS Application

Using the LinqDataSource Control

Let's create a LinqDataSourceCS application to display data on the Web page by performing the following steps:

1. Create a Web application and save it as `LinqDataSourceControlCS`. You can find the code for this application under the `LinqDataSourceControlCS` (for C#) and `LinqDataSource`VB (for VB) folders.
2. Right-click the application name in the Solution Explorer and select the Add New Item option from the context menu.

   The Add New Item dialog box appears (Figure 8.20).

3. Add a LINQ to SQL Classes file (DataClasses.dbml) to the project, as shown in Figure 8.20:

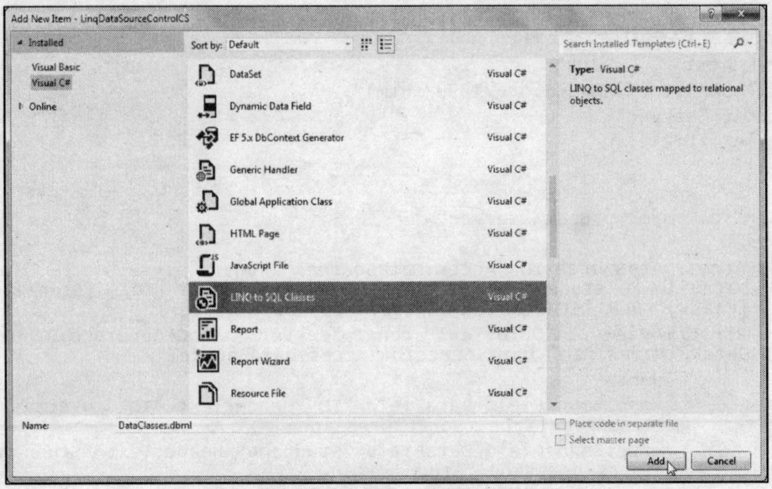

Figure 8.20: Adding LINQ to SQL Classes

Now, the Microsoft Visual Studio message box appears (Figure 8.21).

4. Click the Yes button to add the LINQ to SQL Classes in the App_Code folder, as shown in Figure 8.21:

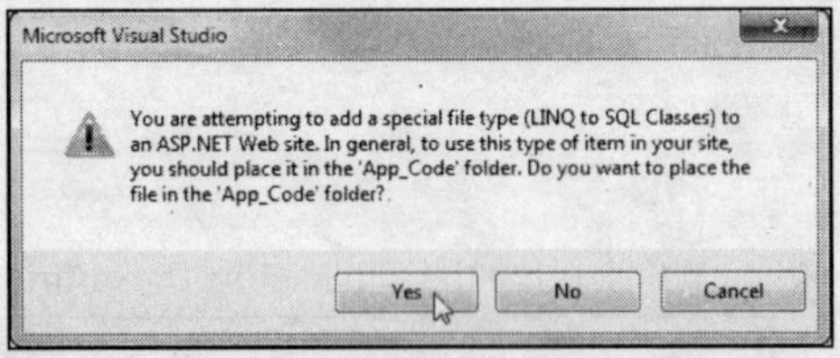

Figure 8.21: Adding the Classes in the App_Code Folder

5. Open the Server Explorer and right-click on the Data Connections to create a connection with the Northwind database (Figure 8.22).

6. Select the Add Connection from the context menu, as shown in Figure 8.22:

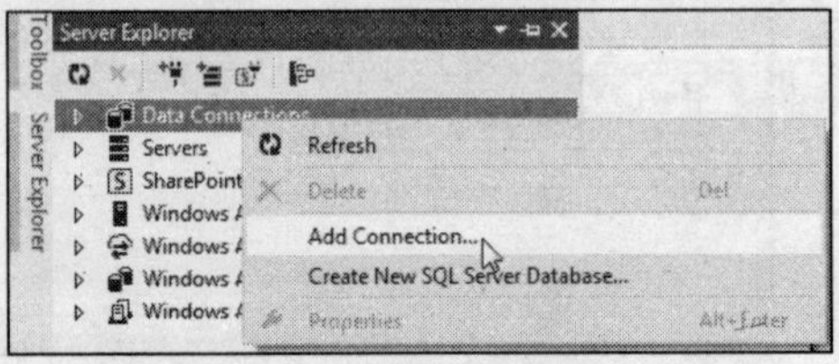

Figure 8.22: Creating the Connection

The Add Connection dialog box appears.

7. Create the connection by providing the server name and the database name as done in the SqlDataSourceCS application.

Now, the tables present in the Northwind database appear in the Tables node in the Server Explorer (Figure 8.23).

8. Drag and drop the Products table to the design surface of the DataClasses.`dbml` file. The output of DataClasses.`dbml` is shown in Figure 8.23:

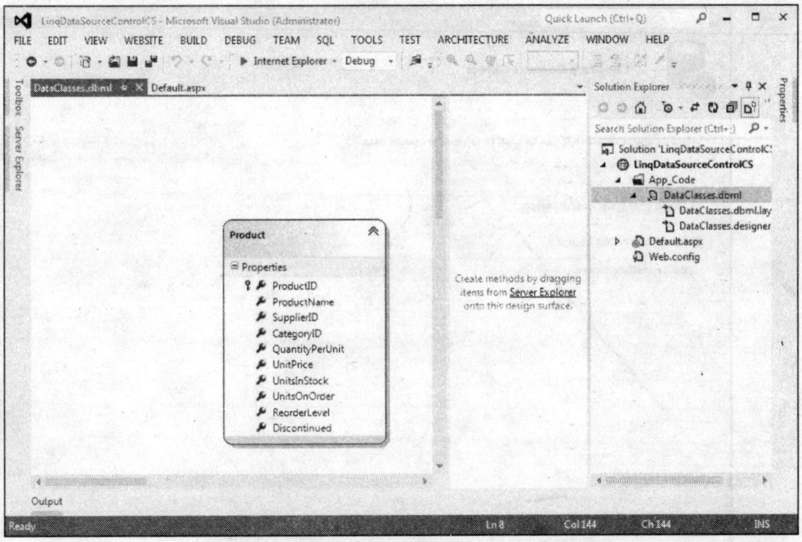

Figure 8.23: Selecting the Product Table

9. Drag and drop the LinqDataSource control on the Web page and click the Smart Tag to select the Configure Data Source option, as shown in Figure 8.24:

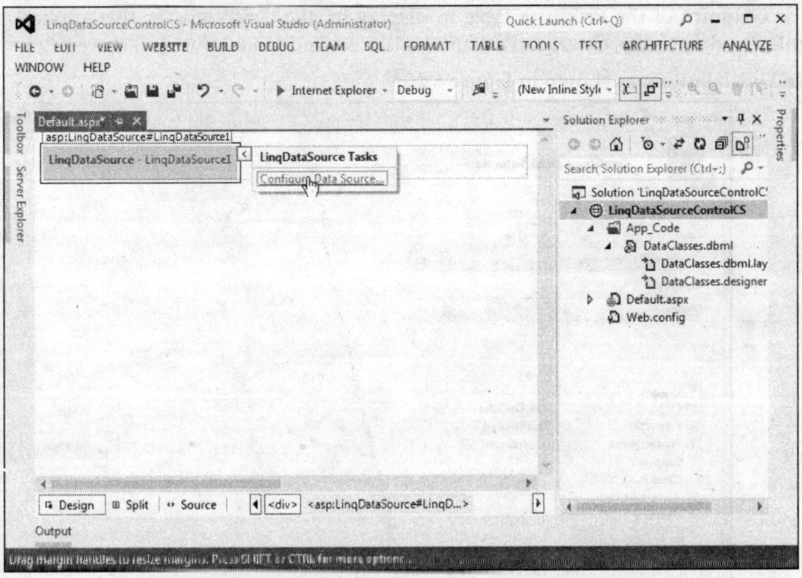

Figure 8.24: Adding the LinqDataSource Control

Now,the Configure Data Source wizard appears (Figure 8.25).

10. Click the Next button in the Choose a Context Object page in the Configure Data Source wizard, as shown in Figure 8.25:

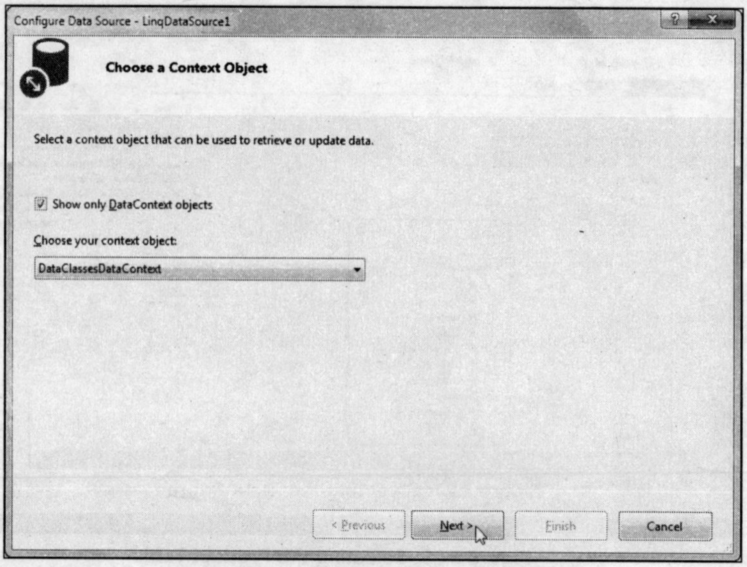

Figure 8.25: Selecting the Context Object

Now, the Configure Data Selection page appears in the wizard (Figure 8.26).

11. Select the Columns of the Products table to display in the GridView. In this application we have selected ProductID, ProductName, QuantityPerUnit, UnitPrice, and UnitsInStock (Figure 8.26).
12. Click the Finish button, as shown in Figure 8.26:

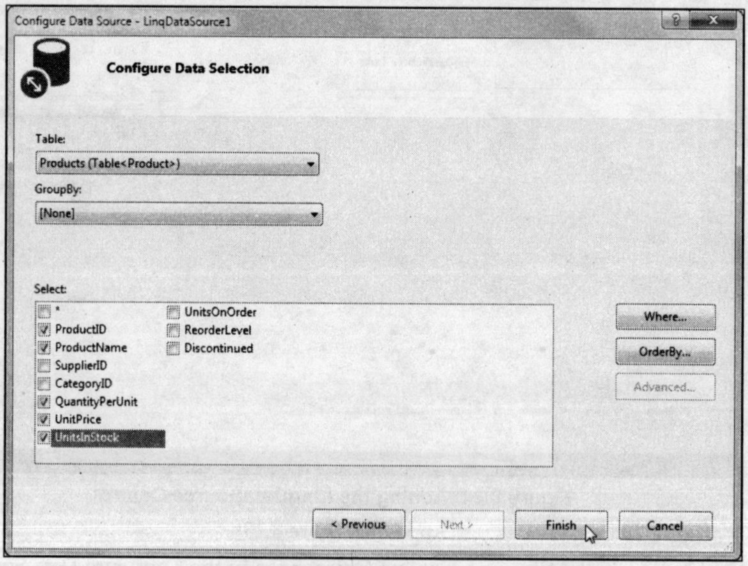

Figure 8.26: Selecting the Columns of the Table

13. Drag and drop the GridView control on the Design view of the Default.aspx page (Figure 8.27).
14. Select the LinqDataSource1 option from the Choose Data Source drop-down list in the GridView Tasks, as shown in Figure 8.27:

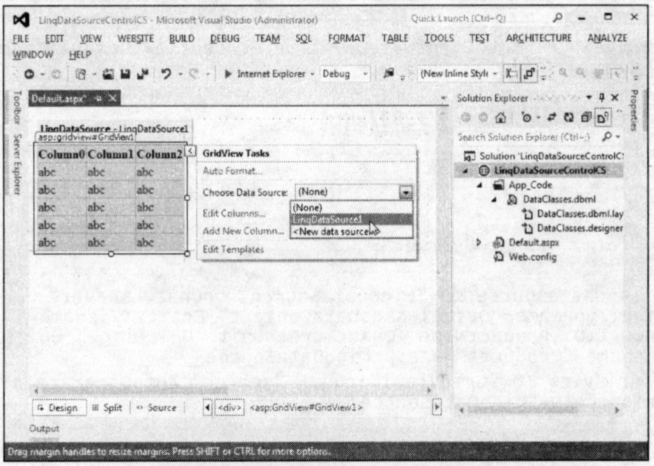

Figure 8.27: Selecting the Data Source

After configuring the data source, the `Default.aspx` page for the Linq`DataSourceCS` application is shown in Listing 8.3:

Listing 8.3: Showing the Code of the `Default.aspx` Page

In VB

```
<%@ Page Language="VB" AutoEventWireup="false" CodeFile="Default.aspx.vb"
  Inherits="_Default" %>
<!DOCTYPE html>
<html xmlns="http://www.w3.org/1999/xhtml">
<head runat="server">
    <title></title>
</head>
<body>
    <form id="form1" runat="server">
    <div>
        <asp:LinqDataSource ID="LinqDataSource1" runat="server"
         ContextTypeName="DataClassesDataContext" EntityTypeName="" Select="new
         (ProductID, ProductName, QuantityPerUnit, UnitPrice, UnitsInStock)"
         TableName="Products"></asp:LinqDataSource>
        <asp:GridView ID="GridView1" runat="server" AutoGenerateColumns="False"
         DataSourceID="LinqDataSource1">
            <Columns>
                <asp:BoundField DataField="ProductID" HeaderText="ProductID"
                 ReadOnly="True" SortExpression="ProductID" />
                <asp:BoundField DataField="ProductName" HeaderText="ProductName"
                 ReadOnly="True" SortExpression="ProductName" />
                <asp:BoundField DataField="QuantityPerUnit" HeaderText="QuantityPerUnit"
                 ReadOnly="True" SortExpression="QuantityPerUnit" />
                <asp:BoundField DataField="UnitPrice" HeaderText="UnitPrice"
                 ReadOnly="True" SortExpression="UnitPrice" />
                <asp:BoundField DataField="UnitsInStock" HeaderText="UnitsInStock"
                 ReadOnly="True" SortExpression="UnitsInStock" />
            </Columns>
        </asp:GridView>
    </div>
    </form>
</body>
</html>
```

In C#

```
<%@ Page Language="C#" AutoEventWireup="true" CodeFile="Default.aspx.cs"
   Inherits="_Default" %>
<!DOCTYPE html>
<html xmlns="http://www.w3.org/1999/xhtml">
<head runat="server">
    <title></title>
</head>
<body>
    <form id="form1" runat="server">
    <div>
        <asp:LinqDataSource ID="LinqDataSource1" runat="server"
         ContextTypeName="DataClassesDataContext" EntityTypeName="" Select="new
         (ProductID, ProductName, QuantityPerUnit, UnitPrice, UnitsInStock)"
         TableName="Products"></asp:LinqDataSource>
        <asp:GridView ID="GridView1" runat="server" AutoGenerateColumns="False"
         DataSourceID="LinqDataSource1">
            <Columns>
                <asp:BoundField DataField="ProductID" HeaderText="ProductID"
                 ReadOnly="True" SortExpression="ProductID" />
                <asp:BoundField DataField="ProductName" HeaderText="ProductName"
                 ReadOnly="True" SortExpression="ProductName" />
                <asp:BoundField DataField="QuantityPerUnit" HeaderText="QuantityPerUnit"
                 ReadOnly="True" SortExpression="QuantityPerUnit" />
                <asp:BoundField DataField="UnitPrice" HeaderText="UnitPrice"
                 ReadOnly="True" SortExpression="UnitPrice" />
                <asp:BoundField DataField="UnitsInStock" HeaderText="UnitsInStock"
                 ReadOnly="True" SortExpression="UnitsInStock" />
            </Columns>
        </asp:GridView>
    </div>
    </form>
</body>
</html>
```

15. Press the F5 key on the keyboard to run the application. The output is as shown in Figure 8.28:

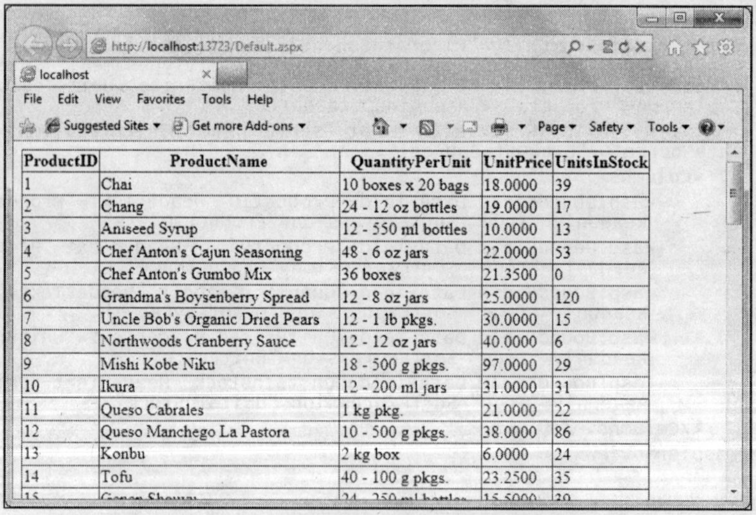

ProductID	ProductName	QuantityPerUnit	UnitPrice	UnitsInStock
1	Chai	10 boxes x 20 bags	18.0000	39
2	Chang	24 - 12 oz bottles	19.0000	17
3	Aniseed Syrup	12 - 550 ml bottles	10.0000	13
4	Chef Anton's Cajun Seasoning	48 - 6 oz jars	22.0000	53
5	Chef Anton's Gumbo Mix	36 boxes	21.3500	0
6	Grandma's Boysenberry Spread	12 - 8 oz jars	25.0000	120
7	Uncle Bob's Organic Dried Pears	12 - 1 lb pkgs.	30.0000	15
8	Northwoods Cranberry Sauce	12 - 12 oz jars	40.0000	6
9	Mishi Kobe Niku	18 - 500 g pkgs.	97.0000	29
10	Ikura	12 - 200 ml jars	31.0000	31
11	Queso Cabrales	1 kg pkg.	21.0000	22
12	Queso Manchego La Pastora	10 - 500 g pkgs.	38.0000	86
13	Konbu	2 kg box	6.0000	24
14	Tofu	40 - 100 g pkgs.	23.2500	35

Figure 8.28: Displaying the Output

Using the ObjectDataSource Control

Now, let's understand how to use the `ObjectDataSource` control by performing the following steps:

1. Create a Web application and save it as `ObjectDataSourceCS`. The code for this application can be found under the `ObjectDataSourceCS` (for C#) and `ObjectDataSourceVB` (for VB) folders.
2. Add a class file(with the name ClassProduct.cs) to the project and replace the code of the ClassProduct.`cs` (for C#) or ClassProduct.`vb` (for VB) file with the code shown in Listing 8.4:

Listing 8.4: Showing the Code for the Class File

In VB (ClassProduct.`vb`)

```
Imports Microsoft.VisualBasic
Imports System.Data
Imports System.Data.SqlClient
Public Class ClassProduct
    Public Function getinfo() As DataSet
        Dim con As New SqlConnection("Data Source=PUNEET-PC\SQLEXPRESS;Initial
         Catalog=Northwind;Integrated Security=True")
        Dim da As New SqlDataAdapter("Select * from Products", con)
        Dim ds As New DataSet()
        da.Fill(ds)
        Return ds
    End Function
End Class
```

In C# (ClassProduct.`cs`)

```
using System;
using System.Collections.Generic;
using System.Linq;
using System.Web;
using System.Data;
using System.Data.SqlClient;
/// <summary>
/// Summary description for ClassProduct
/// </summary>
public class ClassProduct
{
    public DataSet getinfo()
    {
        SqlConnection con = new SqlConnection ("Data Source=PUNEET-
         PC\\SQLEXPRESS;Initial
         Catalog=Northwind;Integrated Security=True");
        SqlDataAdapter da = new SqlDataAdapter ("Select * from Products", con);
        DataSet ds = new DataSet();
        da.Fill(ds);
        return ds;
    }
}
```

3. Drag and drop an `ObjectDataSource` control on the Design view of the `Default.aspx` page (Figure 8.29).
4. Click the Smart Tag and select the Configure Data Source option, as shown in Figure 8.29:

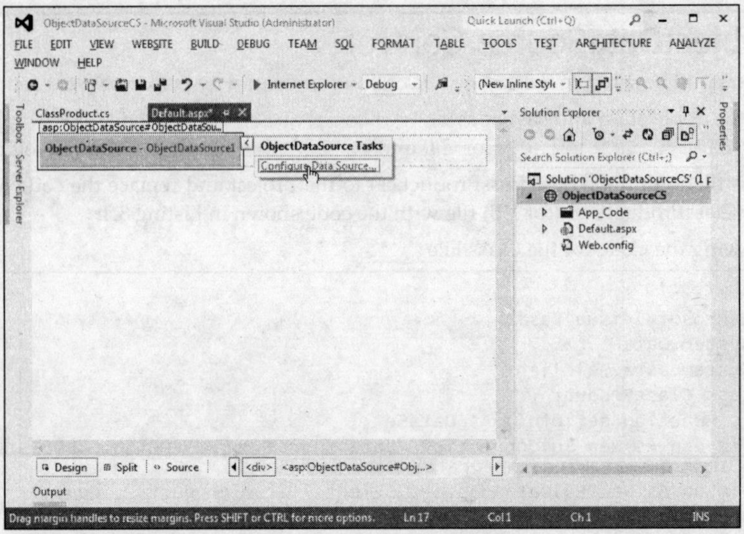

Figure 8.29: Configuring the ObjectDataSource Control

Now,the Configure Data Source wizard appears (Figure 8.30).

5. Select the class name from the Choose your business object drop-down list and click the Next button in the Configure Data Source wizard, as shown in Figure 8.30:

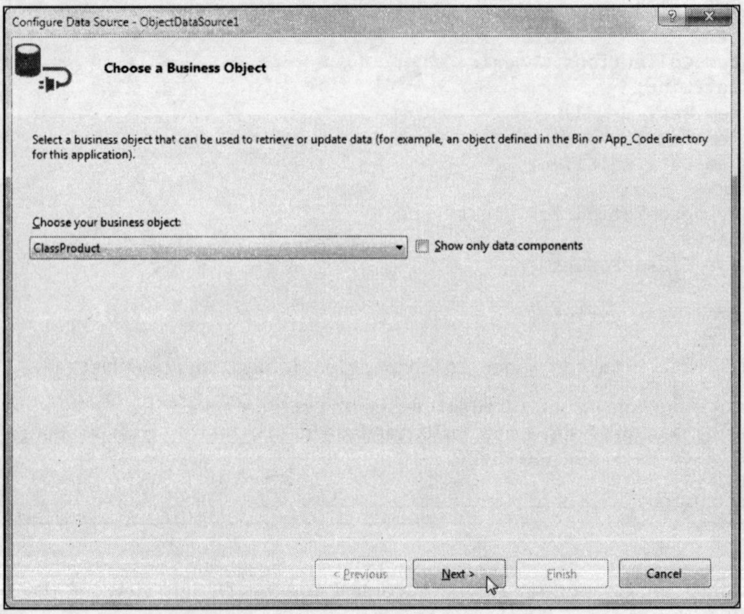

Figure 8.30: Selecting Class from the Drop-down List

Now,the Define Data Methods page appears in the Configure Data Source wizard (Figure 8.31).

6. Select the method name from the Choose a method drop-down list and click the Finish button, as shown in Figure 8.31:

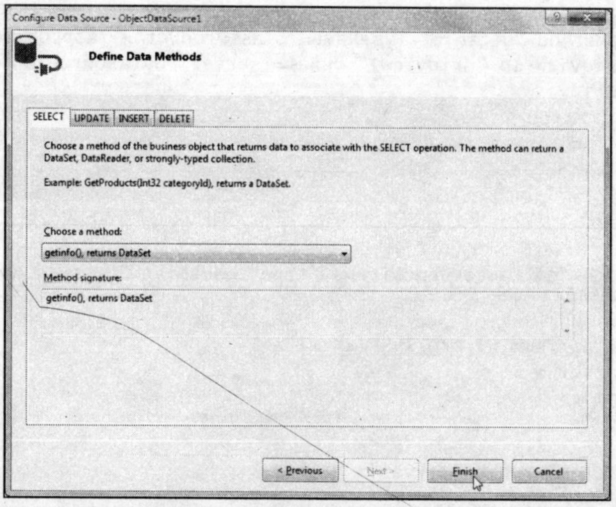

Figure 8.31: Selecting the Method

7. Drag and drop the GridView control on the Design view of the Default.aspx page (Figure 8.32).
8. Select the ObjectDataSource1 from the Choose Data Source drop-down list, as shown in Figure 8.32:

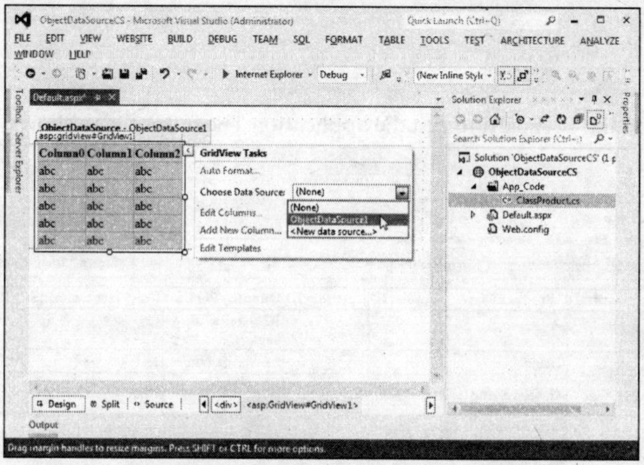

Figure 8.32: Selecting the Data Source

After configuring the data source, the `Default.aspx` page for the `ObjectDataSourceCS` application is shown in Listing 8.5:

Listing 8.5: Showing the Code of the `Default.aspx` Page

In VB

```
<%@ Page Language="VB" AutoEventWireup="false" CodeFile="Default.aspx.vb"
  Inherits="_Default" %>
<!DOCTYPE html>
<html xmlns="http://www.w3.org/1999/xhtml">
<head runat="server">
    <title></title>
</head>
<body>
    <form id="form1" runat="server">
    <div>
```

```
            <asp:ObjectDataSource ID="ObjectDataSource1" runat="server"
             SelectMethod="getinfo" TypeName="ClassProduct"></asp:ObjectDataSource>
            <asp:GridView ID="GridView1" runat="server" DataSourceID="ObjectDataSource1">
            </asp:GridView>
        </div>
        </form>
</body>
</html>
```

In C#

```
<%@ Page Language="C#" AutoEventWireup="true" CodeFile="Default.aspx.cs"
   Inherits="_Default" %>
<!DOCTYPE html>
<html xmlns="http://www.w3.org/1999/xhtml">
<head runat="server">
    <title></title>
</head>
<body>
    <form id="form1" runat="server">
    <div>
        <asp:ObjectDataSource ID="ObjectDataSource1" runat="server"
         SelectMethod="getinfo" TypeName="ClassProduct"></asp:ObjectDataSource>
        <asp:GridView ID="GridView1" runat="server" DataSourceID="ObjectDataSource1">
        </asp:GridView>
    </div>
    </form>
</body>
</html>
```

9. Press the F5 key on the keyboard to run the application.The output is as shown in Figure 8.33:

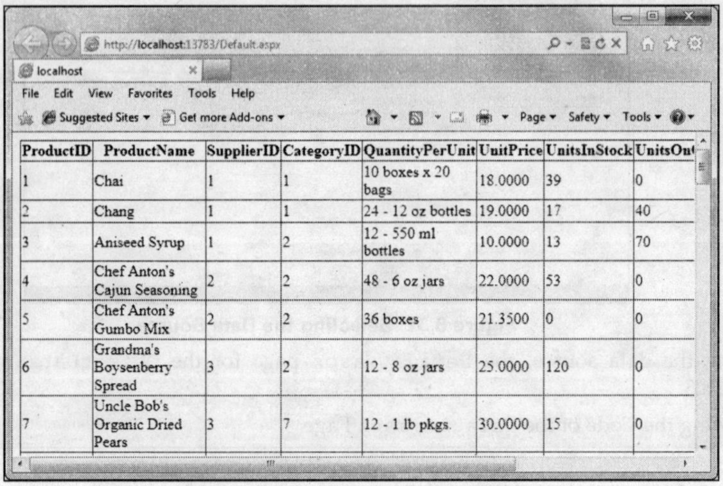

Figure 8.33: Displaying the Output

Using the XmlDataSource Control

Now, let's understand how to use the `XmlDataSource` control to bind the data with the `GridView` control by performing the following steps:

1. Create a Web application and save it as `XmlDataSourceCS`. You can find the code for this application under the `XmlDataSourceCS` (for C#) and `XmlDataSourceVB` (for VB) folders.
2. Add an XML file in the Solution Explorer. Add the code in the XMLFile`.xml` file with the following code:

```
<Student>
  <student Name="John" RollNo="A001" Standard="X"/>
  <student Name="David" RollNo="A002" Standard="XI"/>
  <student Name="Lisa" RollNo="A003" Standard="XII"/>
</Student>
```

3. Drag and drop the XmlDataSource control on the design view of Default.aspx page (Figure 8.34).
4. Click the Smart Tag and select the Configure Data Source option, as shown in Figure 8.34:

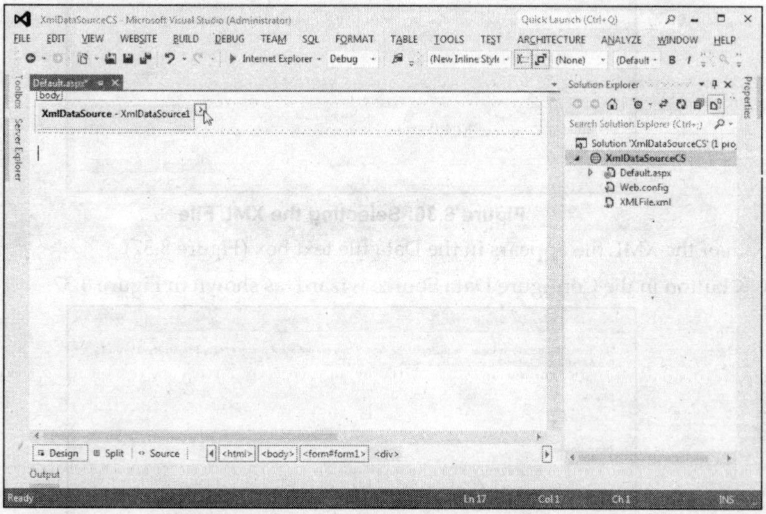

Figure 8.34: Configuring the Data Source

Now,the Configure Data Source wizard appears (Figure 8.35).

5. Click the Browse button to add the XML file , as shown in Figure 8.35:

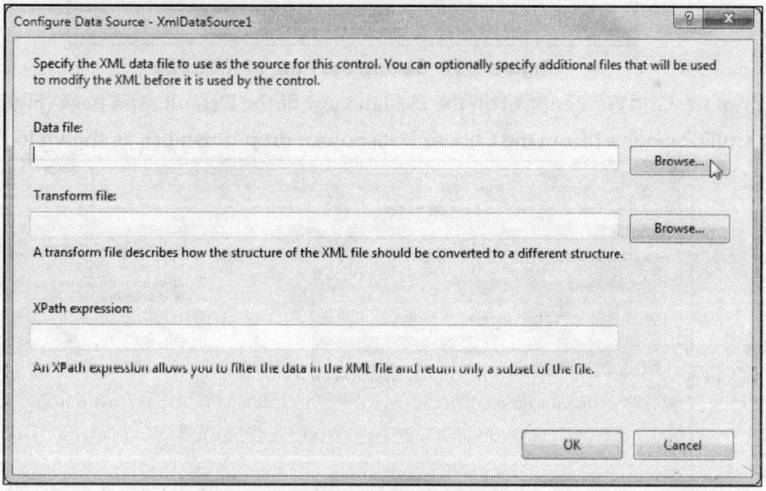

Figure 8.35: Browsing the Data Source

Now, the Select XML File dialog box appears (Figure 8.36).

6. Select the XMLFile.xml file from the Contents of folder pane and click the OK button, as shown in Figure 8.36:

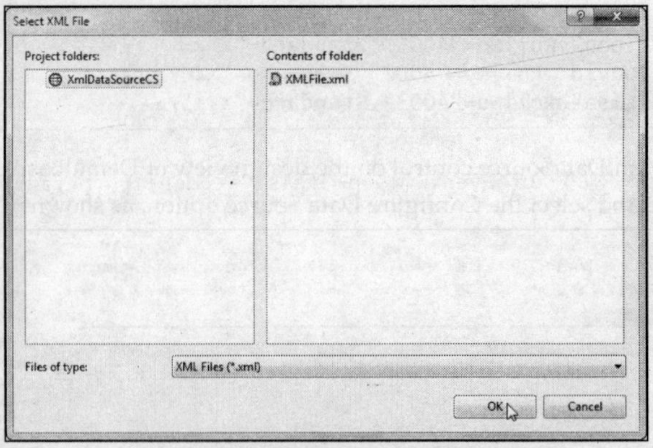

Figure 8.36: Selecting the XML File

Now,the path of the XML file appears in the Data file text box (Figure 8.37).

7. Click the OK button in the Configure Data Source wizard, as shown in Figure 8.37:

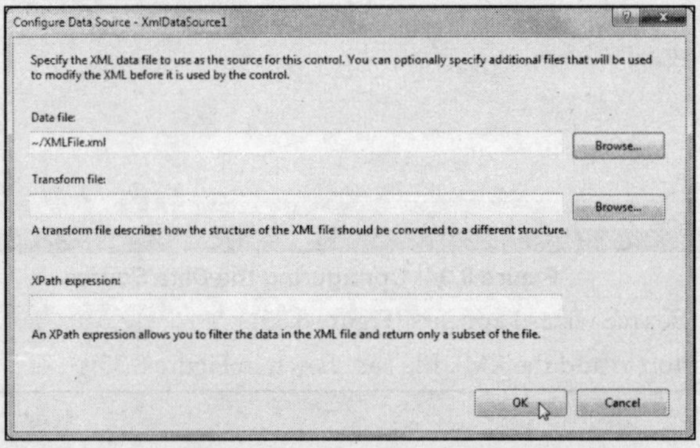

Figure 8.37: Saving the Path of XML File

8. Drag and drop the GridView control on the Design view of the Default.aspx page (Figure 8.38).
9. Select the XmlDataSource1 from the Choose Data Source drop-down list, as shown in Figure 8.38:

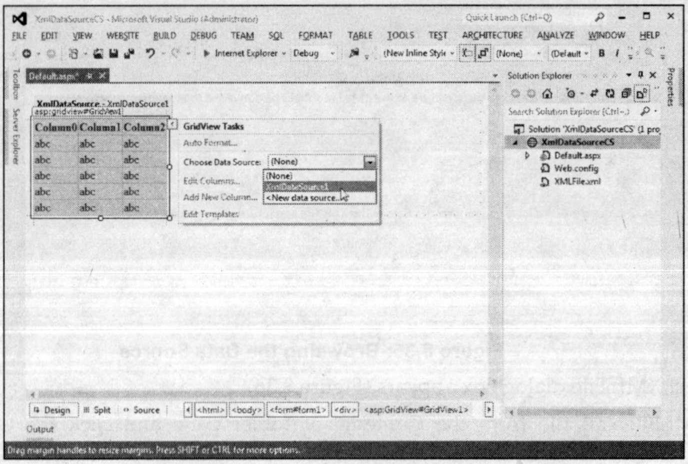

Figure 8.38: Selecting the XML Data Source

After configuring the data source, the `Default.aspx` page for the Xml`DataSourceCS` application is shown in Listing 8.6:

Listing 8.6: Showing the Code of the `Default.aspx` Page

In VB

```
<%@ Page Language="VB" AutoEventWireup="false" CodeFile="Default.aspx.vb"
  Inherits="_Default" %>
<!DOCTYPE html>
<html xmlns="http://www.w3.org/1999/xhtml">
<head runat="server">
    <title></title>
</head>
<body>
    <form id="form1" runat="server">
      <div>
        <asp:XmlDataSource ID="XmlDataSource1" runat="server"
        DataFile="~/XMLFile.xml"></asp:XmlDataSource>
    <asp:GridView ID="GridView1" runat="server" AutoGenerateColumns="False"
        DataSourceID="XmlDataSource1">
        <Columns>
            <asp:BoundField DataField="Name" HeaderText="Name" SortExpression="Name" />
            <asp:BoundField DataField="RollNo" HeaderText="RollNo"
                SortExpression="RollNo" />
            <asp:BoundField DataField="Standard" HeaderText="Standard"
                SortExpression="Standard" />
        </Columns>
    </asp:GridView>
    </div>
</form>
</body>
</html>
```

In C#

```
<%@ Page Language="C#" AutoEventWireup="true" CodeFile="Default.aspx.cs"
  Inherits="_Default" %>
<!DOCTYPE html>
<html xmlns="http://www.w3.org/1999/xhtml">
<head runat="server">
    <title></title>
</head>
<body>
    <form id="form1" runat="server">
    <div>
        <asp:XmlDataSource ID="XmlDataSource1" runat="server"
         DataFile="~/XMLFile.xml"></asp:XmlDataSource>
        <asp:GridView ID="GridView1" runat="server" AutoGenerateColumns="False"
         DataSourceID="XmlDataSource1">
            <Columns>
            <asp:BoundField DataField="Name" HeaderText="Name" SortExpression="Name" />
            <asp:BoundField DataField="RollNo" HeaderText="RollNo"
                SortExpression="RollNo" />
             <asp:BoundField DataField="Standard" HeaderText="Standard"
                SortExpression="Standard" />
            </Columns>
        </asp:GridView>
    </div>
    </form>
</body>
</html>
```

10. Press the F5 key on the keyboard to run the application .The output is shown in Figure 8.39:

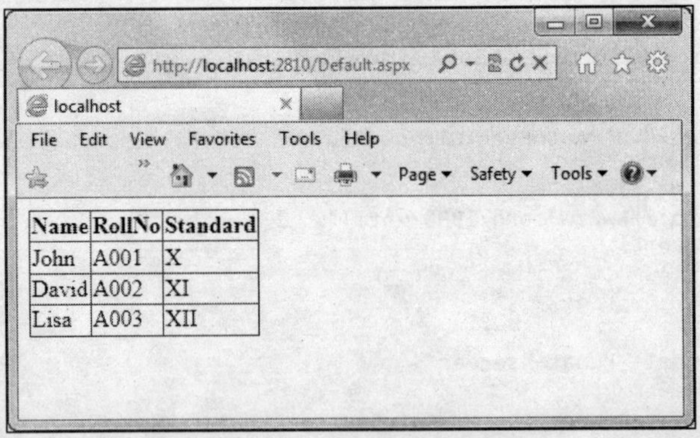

Figure 8.39: Displaying the Output of the XmlDataSourceCS Application

The EntityDataSource Control

Now, let's understand how to use the `EntityDataSource` control to bind the data with the `GridView` control by performing the following steps:

1. Create a Web application and save it as `EntityDataSourceCS`. You can find the code for this application under the `EntityDataSourceCS` (for C#) and `EntityDataSourceVB` (for VB) folders.
2. Right-click the App_Data in Solution Explorer and select Add→Add New Item option.
3. Add ADO.NET Entity Data Model (Model.edmx) in the App_Code folder in the Solution Explorer.

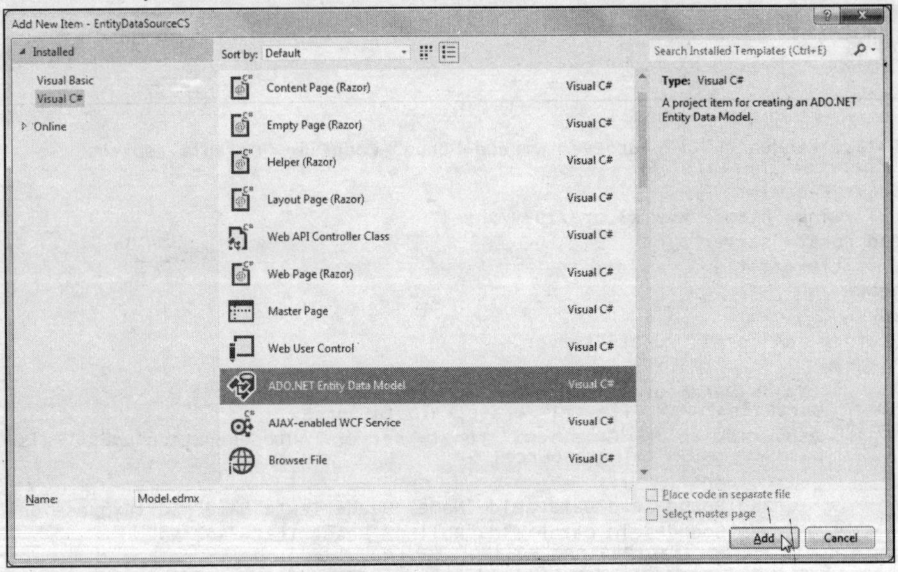

Figure 8.40: Selecting the Data Model

The Entity Data Model Wizard appears (Figure 8.41).

4. Select the Generate from database option in the wizard and click the Next button, as shown in Figure 8.41:

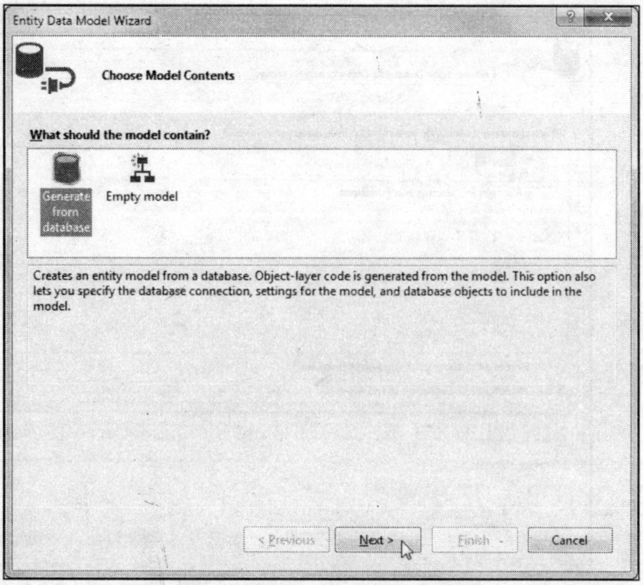

Figure 8.41: Selecting the Option

The Choose Your Data Connection page appears in the Entity Data Model Wizard after creating the connection with the database (Figure 8.42).

5. Click the Next button in the Choose Your Data Connection page in the Entity Data Model Wizard, as shown in Figure 8.42:

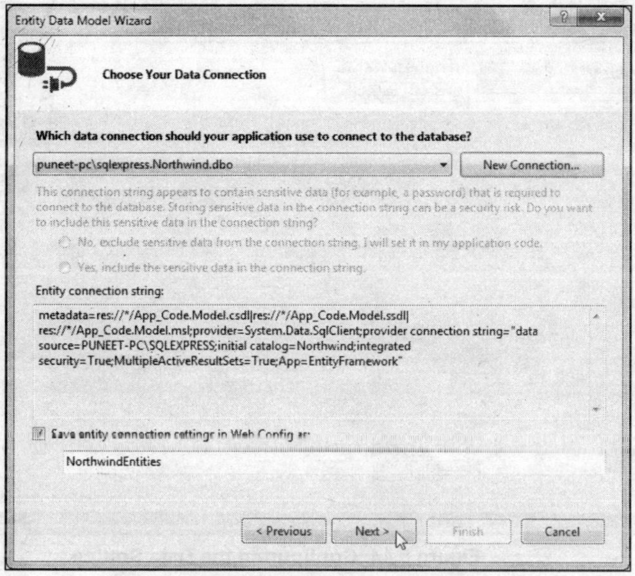

Figure 8.42: Selecting the Data Connection

The Choose Your Database Objects and Settings page appears in the Entity Data Model Wizard(Figure 8.43).

6. Select the Tables check box in the Which database objects do you want to include in your model pane in the Choose Your Database Objects and Settings page in the Entity Data Model Wizard and click the Finish button, as shown in Figure 8.43:

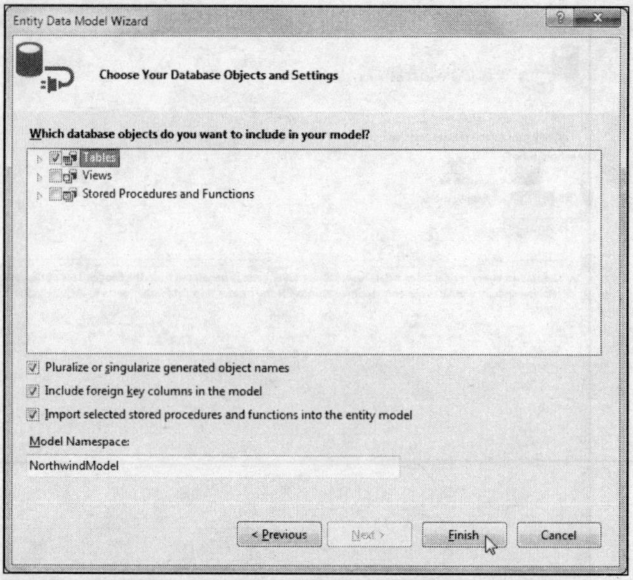

Figure 8.43: Selecting the Database Objects

7. Drag and drop the EntityDataSource control on the Design view of the Default.aspx page(Figure 8.44).
8. Select the Configure Data Source option using Smart Tag , as shown in Figure 8.44:

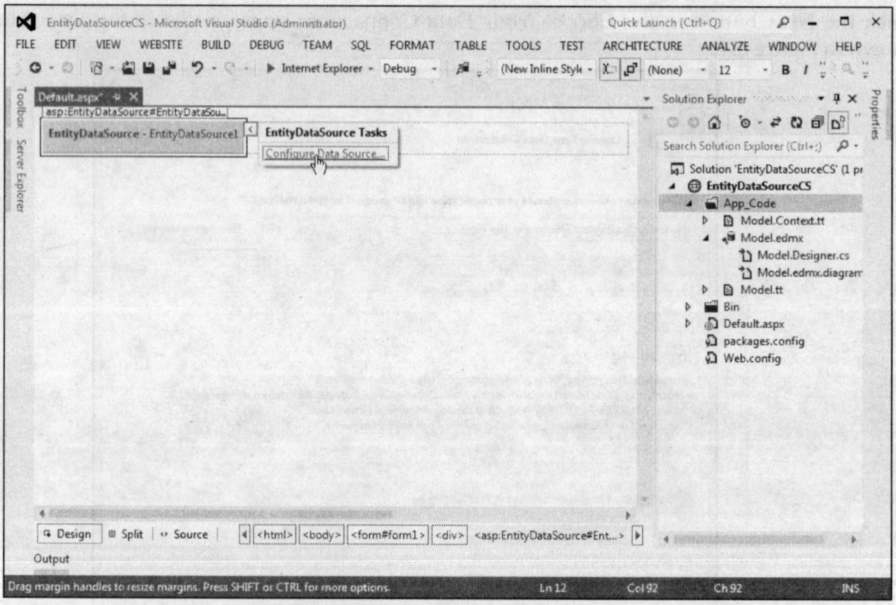

Figure 8.44: Configuring the Data Source

The Configure ObjectContext page appears in the Configure Data Source wizard (Figure 8.45).

9. Select the connection name in the Named Connection drop-down list and click the Next button, as shown in Figure 8.45:

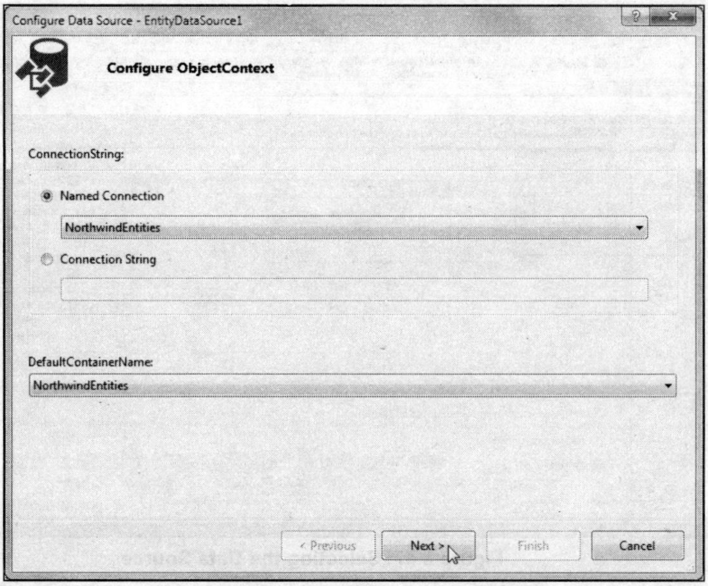

Figure 8.45: Selecting the Connection

The Configure Data Selection page appears in the Configure Data Source wizard (Figure 8.46).

10. Select the table name in the EntitySetName drop-down list and click the Finish button. In this application, we have selected the Products table in the EntitySetName, as shown in Figure 8.46:

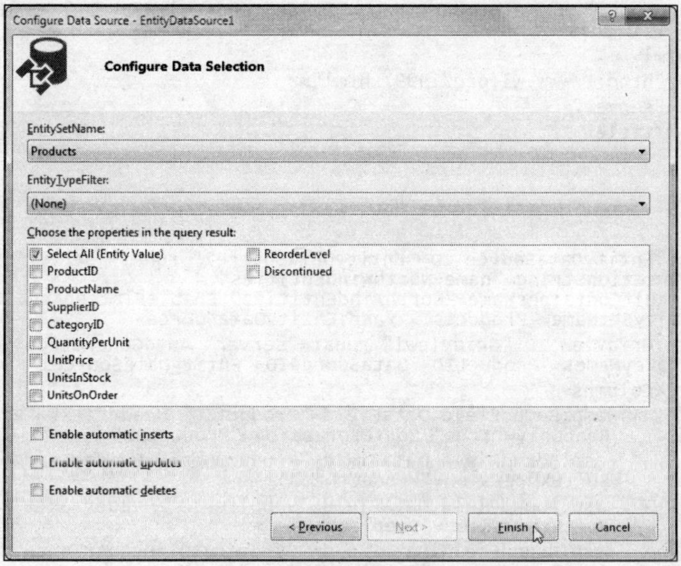

Figure 8.46: Selecting the Table

11. Drag and drop the GridView control on the Design view of the Default.aspx page and select the EntityDataSource1 from the Choose Data Source drop-down list, as shown in Figure 8.47:

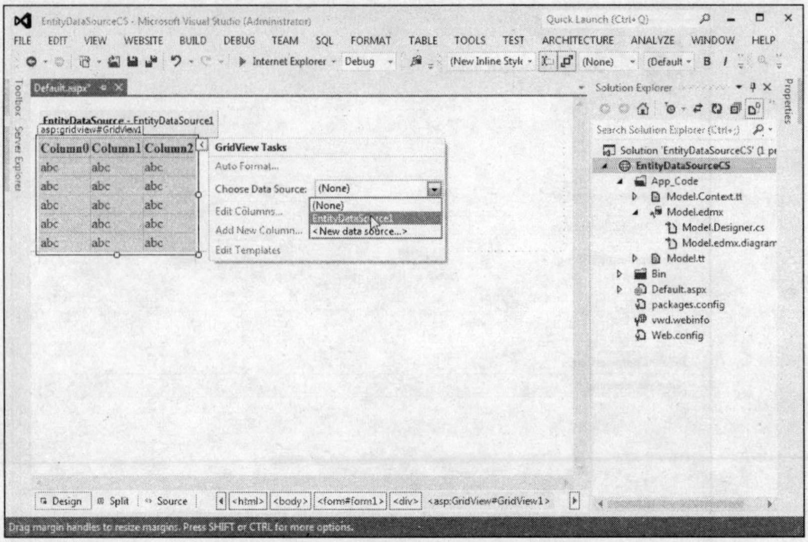

Figure 8.47: Selecting the Data Source

After configuring the data source, the `Default.aspx` page for the `EntityDataSourceCS` application is shown in Listing 8.7:

Listing 8.7: Showing the Code of the `Default.aspx` Page

In VB

```
<%@ Page Language="VB" AutoEventWireup="false" CodeFile="Default.aspx.vb"
  Inherits="_Default" %>
<!DOCTYPE html>
<html xmlns="http://www.w3.org/1999/xhtml">
<head runat="server">
    <title></title>
</head>
<body>
    <form id="form1" runat="server">
    <div>
        <asp:EntityDataSource ID="EntityDataSource1" runat="server"
         ConnectionString="name=NorthwindEntities"
         DefaultContainerName="NorthwindEntities" EnableFlattening="False"
         EntitySetName="Products"></asp:EntityDataSource>
        <asp:GridView ID="GridView1" runat="server" AutoGenerateColumns="False"
         DataKeyNames="ProductID" DataSourceID="EntityDataSource1">
            <Columns>
                <asp:BoundField DataField="ProductID" HeaderText="ProductID"
                 ReadOnly="True" SortExpression="ProductID" />
                <asp:BoundField DataField="ProductName" HeaderText="ProductName"
                 SortExpression="ProductName" />
                <asp:BoundField DataField="SupplierID" HeaderText="SupplierID"
                 SortExpression="SupplierID" />
                <asp:BoundField DataField="CategoryID" HeaderText="CategoryID"
                 SortExpression="CategoryID" />
                <asp:BoundField DataField="QuantityPerUnit" HeaderText="QuantityPerUnit"
                 SortExpression="QuantityPerUnit" />
                <asp:BoundField DataField="UnitPrice" HeaderText="UnitPrice"
                 SortExpression="UnitPrice" />
                <asp:BoundField DataField="UnitsInStock" HeaderText="UnitsInStock"
                 SortExpression="UnitsInStock" />
```

```
                <asp:BoundField DataField="UnitsOnOrder" HeaderText="UnitsOnOrder"
                 SortExpression="UnitsOnOrder" />
                <asp:BoundField DataField="ReorderLevel" HeaderText="ReorderLevel"
                 SortExpression="ReorderLevel" />
                <asp:CheckBoxField DataField="Discontinued" HeaderText="Discontinued"
                 SortExpression="Discontinued" />
            </Columns>
        </asp:GridView>
    </div>
    </form>
</body>
</html>
```

In C#

```
<%@ Page Language="C#" AutoEventWireup="true" CodeFile="Default.aspx.cs"
  Inherits="_Default" %>
<!DOCTYPE html>
<html xmlns="http://www.w3.org/1999/xhtml">
<head runat="server">
    <title></title>
</head>
<body>
    <form id="form1" runat="server">
    <div>
        <asp:EntityDataSource ID="EntityDataSource1" runat="server"
         ConnectionString="name=NorthwindEntities"
         DefaultContainerName="NorthwindEntities" EnableFlattening="False"
         EntitySetName="Products"></asp:EntityDataSource>
        <asp:GridView ID="GridView1" runat="server" AutoGenerateColumns="False"
         DataKeyNames="ProductID" DataSourceID="EntityDataSource1">
            <Columns>
                <asp:BoundField DataField="ProductID" HeaderText="ProductID"
                 ReadOnly="True" SortExpression="ProductID" />
                <asp:BoundField DataField="ProductName" HeaderText="ProductName"
                 SortExpression="ProductName" />
                <asp:BoundField DataField="SupplierID" HeaderText="SupplierID"
                 SortExpression="SupplierID" />
                <asp:BoundField DataField="CategoryID" HeaderText="CategoryID"
                 SortExpression="CategoryID" />
                <asp:BoundField DataField="QuantityPerUnit" HeaderText="QuantityPerUnit"
                 SortExpression="QuantityPerUnit" />
                <asp:BoundField DataField="UnitPrice" HeaderText="UnitPrice"
                 SortExpression="UnitPrice" />
                <asp:BoundField DataField="UnitsInStock" HeaderText="UnitsInStock"
                 SortExpression="UnitsInStock" />
                <asp:BoundField DataField="UnitsOnOrder" HeaderText="UnitsOnOrder"
                 SortExpression="UnitsOnOrder" />
                <asp:BoundField DataField="ReorderLevel" HeaderText="ReorderLevel"
                 SortExpression="ReorderLevel" />
                <asp:CheckBoxField DataField="Discontinued" HeaderText="Discontinued"
                 SortExpression="Discontinued" />
            </Columns>
        </asp:GridView>
    </div>
    </form>
</body>
</html>
```

12. Press the F5 key on the keyboard to run the application.The output of the application, as shown in Figure 8.48:

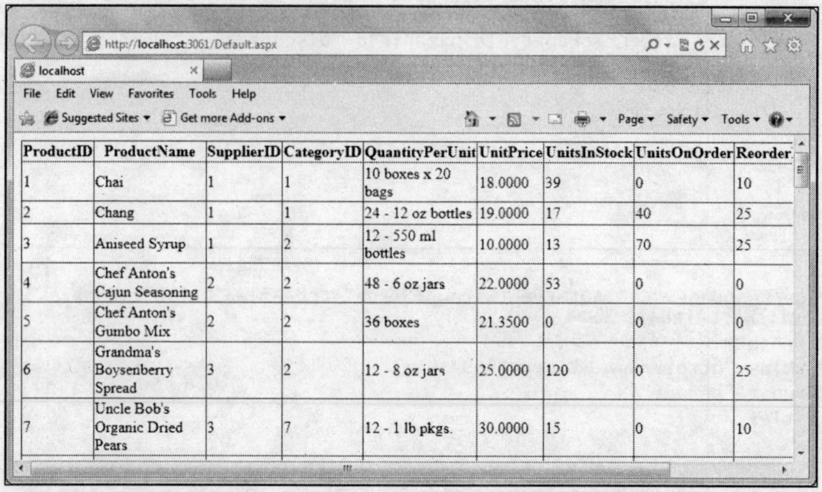

Figure 8.48: Displaying the Output of the EntityDataSourceCS Application

Using the GridView Control

Now, let's display data in the GridView control by performing the following steps:

1. Create a Web site and save it as `GridViewControlCS`. The code for this application can be found under the `GridViewControlCS` (for C#) and `GridViewControlVB` (for VB) folders.
2. Drag and drop the GridView control on the Design view of the Default.aspx page and select the New data source option from the Choose Data Source drop-down list, as shown in Figure 8.49:

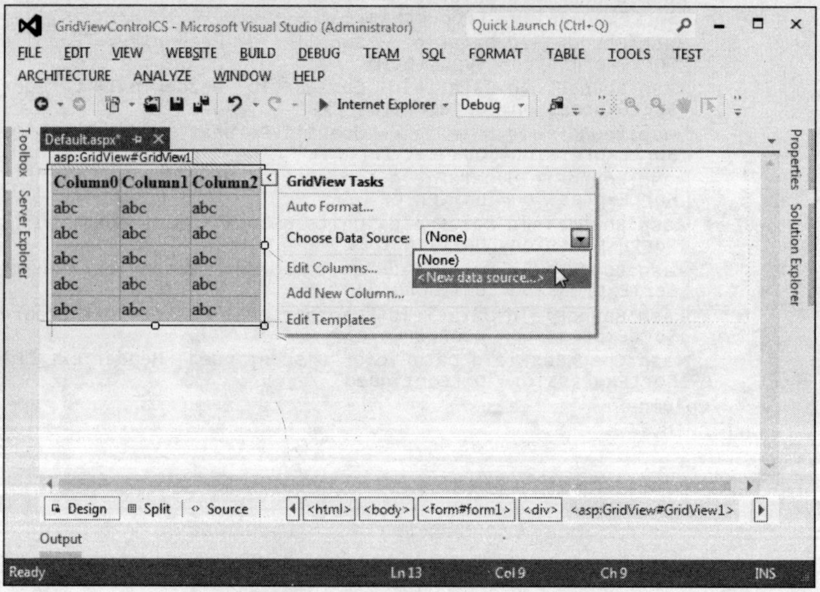

Figure 8.49: Selecting the New Data Source

The Data Source Configuration Wizard appears (Figure 8.50).

3. Select the SQL Database option in the Where will the application get data from pane in the Data Source Configuration Wizard and click the OK button, as shown in Figure 8.50:

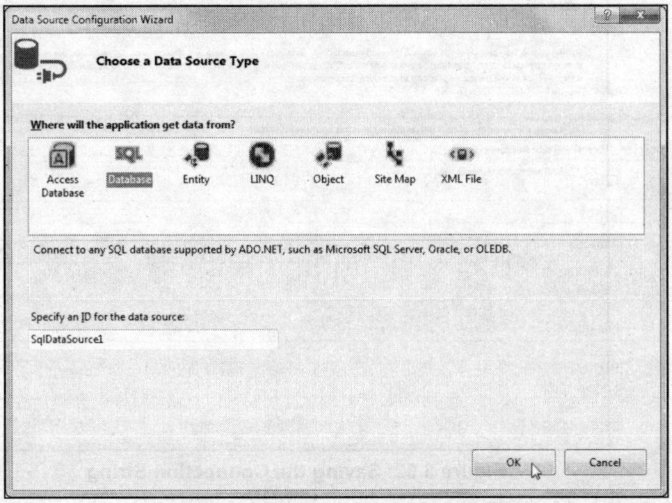

Figure 8.50: Selecting the Database

The Choose Your Data Connection page appears in the Configure Data Source wizard (Figure 8.51).

4. Click the New Connection button to create the connection with the database.

   The Add Connection dialog box appears.

5. Provide the server name and the database name in the Add Connection dialog box to create the connection.

6. Click the Next button in the Choose Your Data Connection page in the Configure Data Source wizard, as shown in Figure 8.51:

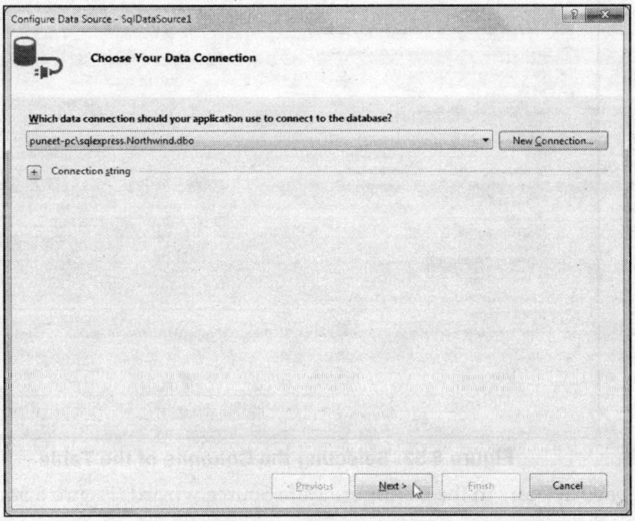

Figure 8.51: Selecting the Connection String

The Save the Connection String to the Application Configuration File page appears in the Configure Data Source (Figure 8.52).

7. Click the Next button to save the connection string, as shown in Figure 8.52:

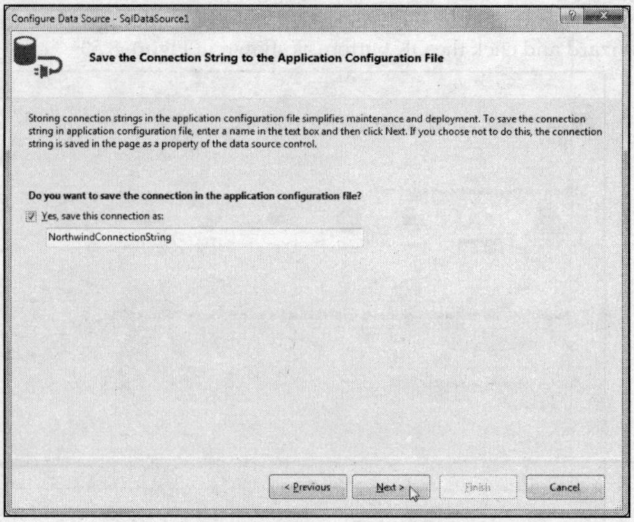

Figure 8.52: Saving the Connection String

The Configure the Select Statement page appears in the Configure Data Source wizard (Figure 8.53).

8. Select the Specify columns from a table or view radio button and select the table and then columns in the Columns pane that you want to display in the GridView control. In this application, we have selected ProductID, ProductName, QuantityPerUnit, UnitPrice, and UnitsInStock (Figure 8.53).
9. Click the Next button to save the selection, as shown in Figure 8.53:

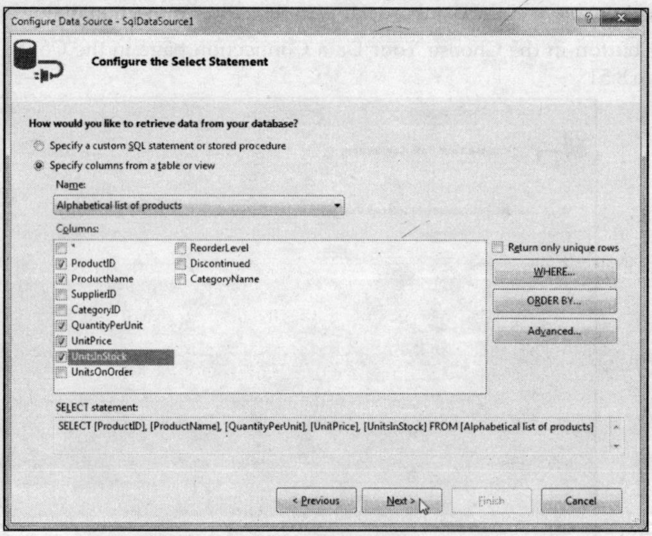

Figure 8.53: Selecting the Columns of the Table

The Test Query page appears in the Configure Data Source wizard (Figure 8.54).

10. Click the Test Query button to test the query and then click the Finish button to save the select statement, as shown in Figure 8.54:

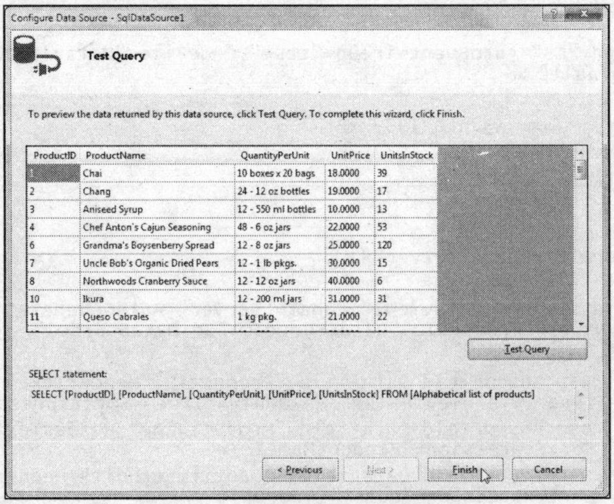

Figure 8.54: Completing the Wizard

After configuring the data source of the GridView control, the `Default.aspx` page for the GridViewControlCS application is shown in Listing 8.8:

Listing 8.8: Showing the Code of the `Default.aspx` Page

In VB

```
<%@ Page Language="VB" AutoEventWireup="false" CodeFile="Default.aspx.vb"
  Inherits="_Default" %>
<!DOCTYPE html>
<html xmlns="http://www.w3.org/1999/xhtml">
<head runat="server">
    <title></title>
</head>
<body>
    <form id="form1" runat="server">
    <div>
        <asp:GridView ID="GridView1" runat="server" AutoGenerateColumns="False"
         DataKeyNames="ProductID" DataSourceID="SqlDataSource1">
            <Columns>
                <asp:BoundField DataField="ProductID" HeaderText="ProductID"
                 InsertVisible="False" ReadOnly="True" SortExpression="ProductID" />
                <asp:BoundField DataField="ProductName" HeaderText="ProductName"
                 SortExpression="ProductName" />
                <asp:BoundField DataField="QuantityPerUnit" HeaderText="QuantityPerUnit"
                 SortExpression="QuantityPerUnit" />
                <asp:BoundField DataField="UnitPrice" HeaderText="UnitPrice"
                 SortExpression="UnitPrice" />
                <asp:BoundField DataField="UnitsInStock" HeaderText="UnitsInStock"
                 SortExpression="UnitsInStock" />
            </Columns>
        </asp:GridView>
        <asp:SqlDataSource ID="SqlDataSource1" runat="server" ConnectionString="<%$
         ConnectionStrings:NorthwindConnectionString %>" SelectCommand="SELECT
         [ProductID], [ProductName], [QuantityPerUnit], [UnitPrice], [UnitsInStock] FROM
         [Alphabetical list of products]"></asp:SqlDataSource>
    </div>
    </form>
</body>
</html>
```

In C#

```
<%@ Page Language="CS" AutoEventWireup="true" CodeFile="Default.aspx.cs"
  Inherits="_Default" %>
<!DOCTYPE html>
<html xmlns="http://www.w3.org/1999/xhtml">
<head runat="server">
    <title></title>
</head>
<body>
    <form id="form1" runat="server">
    <div>
        <asp:GridView ID="GridView1" runat="server" AutoGenerateColumns="False"
         DataKeyNames="ProductID" DataSourceID="SqlDataSource1">
            <Columns>
                <asp:BoundField DataField="ProductID" HeaderText="ProductID"
                 InsertVisible="False" ReadOnly="True" SortExpression="ProductID" />
                <asp:BoundField DataField="ProductName" HeaderText="ProductName"
                 SortExpression="ProductName" />
                <asp:BoundField DataField="QuantityPerUnit" HeaderText="QuantityPerUnit"
                 SortExpression="QuantityPerUnit" />
                <asp:BoundField DataField="UnitPrice" HeaderText="UnitPrice"
                 SortExpression="UnitPrice" />
                <asp:BoundField DataField="UnitsInStock" HeaderText="UnitsInStock"
                 SortExpression="UnitsInStock" />
            </Columns>
        </asp:GridView>
        <asp:SqlDataSource ID="SqlDataSource1" runat="server" ConnectionString="<%$
         ConnectionStrings:NorthwindConnectionString %>" SelectCommand="SELECT
         [ProductID], [ProductName], [QuantityPerUnit], [UnitPrice], [UnitsInStock] FROM
         [Alphabetical list of products]"></asp:SqlDataSource>
    </div>
    </form>
</body>
</html>
```

11. Press the F5 key on the keyboard to run the application. The output of the application is shown in Figure 8.55:

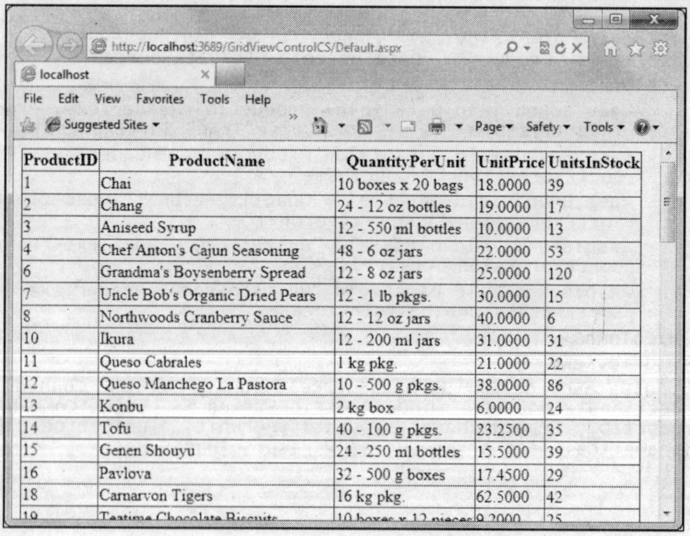

ProductID	ProductName	QuantityPerUnit	UnitPrice	UnitsInStock
1	Chai	10 boxes x 20 bags	18.0000	39
2	Chang	24 - 12 oz bottles	19.0000	17
3	Aniseed Syrup	12 - 550 ml bottles	10.0000	13
4	Chef Anton's Cajun Seasoning	48 - 6 oz jars	22.0000	53
6	Grandma's Boysenberry Spread	12 - 8 oz jars	25.0000	120
7	Uncle Bob's Organic Dried Pears	12 - 1 lb pkgs.	30.0000	15
8	Northwoods Cranberry Sauce	12 - 12 oz jars	40.0000	6
10	Ikura	12 - 200 ml jars	31.0000	31
11	Queso Cabrales	1 kg pkg.	21.0000	22
12	Queso Manchego La Pastora	10 - 500 g pkgs.	38.0000	86
13	Konbu	2 kg box	6.0000	24
14	Tofu	40 - 100 g pkgs.	23.2500	35
15	Genen Shouyu	24 - 250 ml bottles	15.5000	39
16	Pavlova	32 - 500 g boxes	17.4500	29
18	Carnarvon Tigers	16 kg pkg.	62.5000	42

Figure 8.55: Displaying the Output of the GridViewControlCS Application

Using the DataList Control

Now, let's use a `DataList` control to display data from a database by performing the following steps:

1. Create an application and save it as `DataListControlCS`. You can find the code for this application under the `DataListControlCS` (for C#) and `DataListControlVB` (for VB) folders.
2. Drag and drop the DataList control on the Design view of the Default.aspx page.
3. Select the New data source option from the Choose Data Source drop-down list to create the connection with the database, as shown in Figure 8.56:

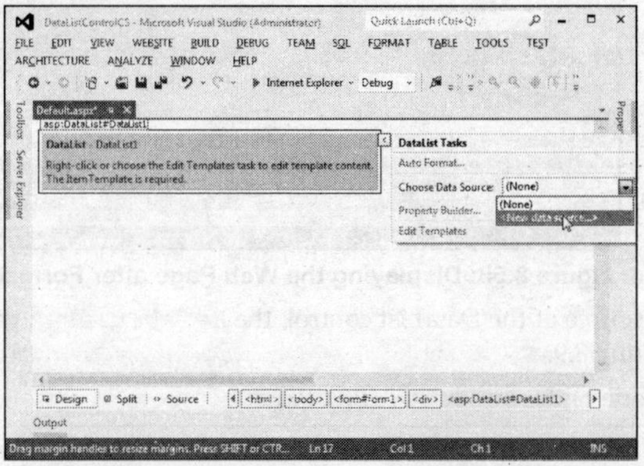

Figure 8.56: Creating Connection with the Data Source

The Configure Data Source wizard appears.

4. Create connection of the DataList control with the database. In this case, we are creating the connection with the Products table of the Northwind database.

NOTE

You can refer to the GridViewControlCS application for the steps of creating connection with the database.

5. Click the Smart Tag of the DataList control and select the Auto Format link. The AutoFormat dialog box appears in which you can apply colorful format on the DataList control (Figure 8.57).
6. Select the Colorful option from the Select a scheme pane and click the OK button, as shown in Figure 8.57:

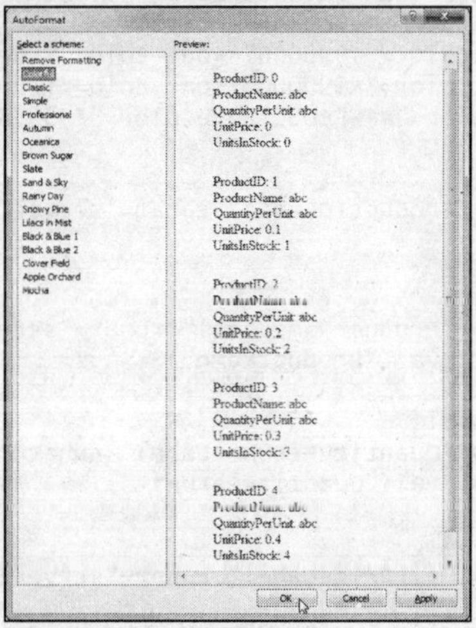

Figure 8.57: Selecting the Format

The DataList control after creating the connection and applying the formatting appears, as shown in Figure 8.58:

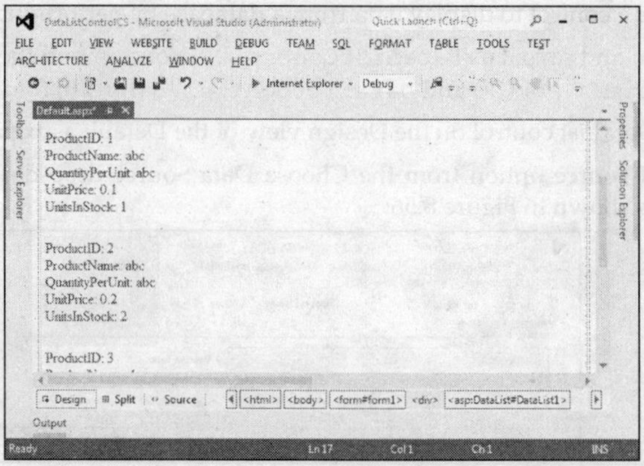

Figure 8.58: Displaying the Web Page after Formatting

After configuring the data source of the DataList control, the `Default.aspx` page for the DataListControlCS application is shown in Listing 8.9:

Listing 8.9: Showing the Code of the `Default.aspx` Page

In VB

```
<%@ Page Language="VB" AutoEventWireup="false" CodeFile="Default.aspx.vb"
  Inherits="_Default" %>
<!DOCTYPE html PUBLIC "-//W3C//DTD XHTML 1.0 Transitional//EN"
  "http://www.w3.org/TR/xhtml1/DTD/xhtml1-transitional.dtd">
<html xmlns="http://www.w3.org/1999/xhtml">
<head runat="server">
    <title></title>
</head>
<body>
    <form id="form1" runat="server">
    <div>
    </div>
    <asp:DataList ID="DataList1" runat="server" CellPadding="4"
        DataKeyField="ProductID" DataSourceID="SqlDataSource1" ForeColor="#333333">
        <AlternatingItemStyle BackColor="White" />
        <FooterStyle BackColor="#990000" Font-Bold="True" ForeColor="White" />
        <HeaderStyle BackColor="#990000" Font-Bold="True" ForeColor="White" />
        <ItemStyle BackColor="#FFFBD6" ForeColor="#333333" />
        <ItemTemplate>
           ProductID:
           <asp:Label ID="ProductIDLabel" runat="server" Text='<%# Eval("ProductID") %>'
                 />
            <br />
            ProductName:
            <asp:Label ID="ProductNameLabel" runat="server"
                Text='<%# Eval("ProductName") %>' />
            <br />
            QuantityPerUnit:
            <asp:Label ID="QuantityPerUnitLabel" runat="server"
                Text='<%# Eval("QuantityPerUnit") %>' />
            <br />
           UnitPrice:
           <asp:Label ID="UnitPriceLabel" runat="server" Text='<%# Eval("UnitPrice") %>'
                 />
            <br />
```

```
            UnitsInStock:
            <asp:Label ID="UnitsInStockLabel" runat="server"
                Text='<%# Eval("UnitsInStock") %>' />
            <br />
         <br />
        </ItemTemplate>
        <SelectedItemStyle BackColor="#FFCC66" Font-Bold="True" ForeColor="Navy" />
    </asp:DataList>
    <asp:SqlDataSource ID="SqlDataSource1" runat="server"
        ConnectionString="<%$ ConnectionStrings:NorthwindConnectionString %>"
        SelectCommand="SELECT [ProductID], [ProductName], [QuantityPerUnit],
         [UnitPrice],
         [UnitsInStock] FROM [Alphabetical list of products]">
    </asp:SqlDataSource>
    </form>
</body>
</html>
```

In C#

```
<%@ Page Language="C#" AutoEventWireup="true" CodeFile="Default.aspx.cs"
  Inherits="_Default" %>
<!DOCTYPE html>
<html xmlns="http://www.w3.org/1999/xhtml">
<head runat="server">
    <title></title>
</head>
<body>
    <form id="form1" runat="server">
    <div>
        <asp:DataList ID="DataList1" runat="server" CellPadding="4"
         DataKeyField="ProductID" DataSourceID="SqlDataSource1" ForeColor="#333333">
            <AlternatingItemStyle BackColor="White" />
            <FooterStyle BackColor="#990000" Font-Bold="True" ForeColor="White" />
            <HeaderStyle BackColor="#990000" Font-Bold="True" ForeColor="White" />
            <ItemStyle BackColor="#FFFBD6" ForeColor="#333333" />
            <ItemTemplate>
                ProductID:
                <asp:Label ID="ProductIDLabel" runat="server" Text='<%#
                 Eval("ProductID") %>' />
                <br />
                ProductName:
                <asp:Label ID="ProductNameLabel" runat="server" Text='<%#
                 Eval("ProductName") %>' />
                <br />
                QuantityPerUnit:
                <asp:Label ID="QuantityPerUnitLabel" runat="server" Text='<%#
                 Eval("QuantityPerUnit") %>' />
                <br />
                UnitPrice:
                <asp:Label ID="UnitPriceLabel" runat="server" Text='<%#
                 Eval("UnitPrice") %>' />
                <br />
                UnitsInStock:
                <asp:Label ID="UnitsInStockLabel" runat="server" Text='<%#
                 Eval("UnitsInStock") %>' />
                <br />
                 <br />
            </ItemTemplate>
            <SelectedItemStyle BackColor="#FFCC66" Font-Bold="True" ForeColor="Navy" />
        </asp:DataList>
        <asp:SqlDataSource ID="SqlDataSource1" runat="server" ConnectionString="<%$
         ConnectionStrings:NorthwindConnectionString %>" SelectCommand="SELECT
```

```
            [ProductID], [ProductName], [QuantityPerUnit], [UnitPrice], [UnitsInStock] FROM
            [Alphabetical list of products]"></asp:SqlDataSource>
        </div>
        </form>
    </body>
    </html>
```

7. Press the F5 key on the keyboard to execute the application. The output on the Web page is as shown in Figure 8.59:

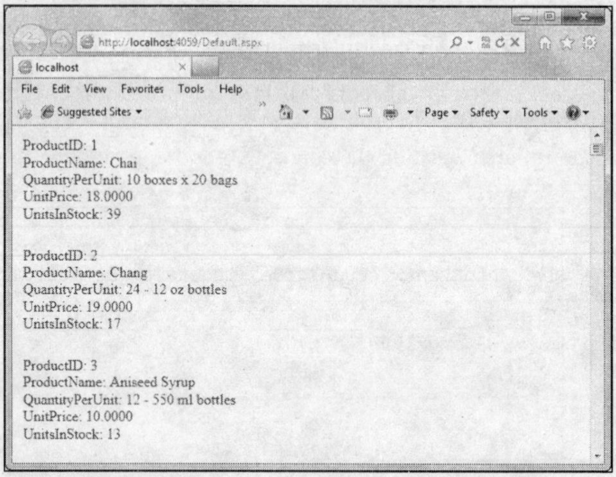

Figure 8.59: Displaying the Output of the DataListControlCS Application

Using the DetailsView Control

Now, let's use a `DetailsView` control to display the data from a database by performing the following steps:

1. Create an application and save it as `DetailsViewControlCS`. You can find the code for this application under the `DetailsViewControlCS` (for C#) and `DetailsViewControlVB` (for VB) folders.
2. Drag and drop `DetailsViewControlCS` on the Design view of the Default.aspx page and select the New data source option from the Choose Data Source drop-down list, as shown in Figure 8.60:

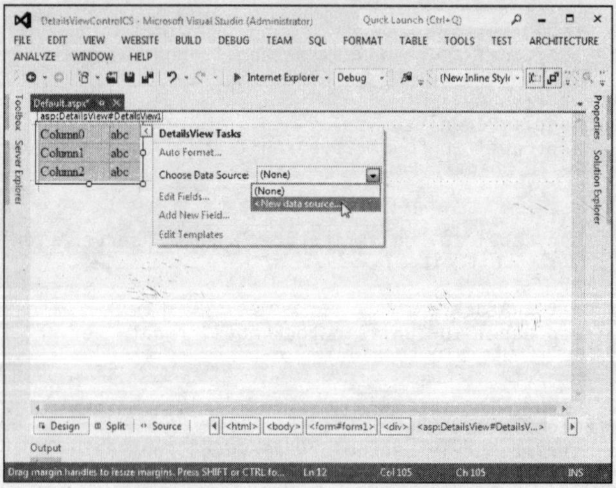

Figure 8.60: Selecting the Data Source

The Configure Data Source Wizard appears.

3. Create a connection of the DetailsView control with the database. In this case, we are creating the connection with the Products table of the Northwind database.

NOTE

You can refer to the GridViewControlCS application for the steps of creating connection with the database.

4. Click the Smart Tag of the DetailsView control and select the Auto Format link. The AutoFormat dialog box appears which can be used to apply colorful layout on the DetailsView control.
5. Select the Slate option from the Select a scheme pane and click the OK button.
6. Select the Enable Paging check box to provide paging in the control.

The DetailsView control after creating the connection and applying the formatting appears, as shown in Figure 8.61:

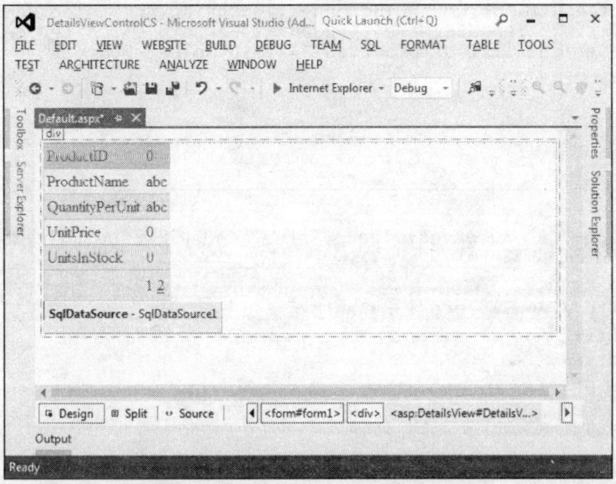

Figure 8.61: Displaying the Web Page

After configuring the data source of the DetailsView control, the `Default.aspx` page for the DetailsView ControlCS application is shown in Listing 8.10:

Listing 8.10: Showing the Code of the `Default.aspx` Page

In VB

```
<%@ Page Language="VB" AutoEventWireup="false" CodeFile="Default.aspx.vb"
  Inherits="_Default" %>
<!DOCTYPE html>
<html xmlns="http://www.w3.org/1999/xhtml">
<head runat="server">
    <title></title>
</head>
<body>
    <form id="form1" runat="server">
    <div>
        <asp:DetailsView ID="DetailsView1" runat="server" Height="50px" Width="125px"
        AllowPaging="True" AutoGenerateRows="False" BackColor="White"
        BorderColor="#E7E7FF" BorderStyle="None" BorderWidth="1px" CellPadding="3"
        DataKeyNames="ProductID" DataSourceID="SqlDataSource1" GridLines="Horizontal">
            <AlternatingRowStyle BackColor="#F7F7F7" />
            <EditRowStyle BackColor="#738A9C" Font-Bold="True" ForeColor="#F7F7F7" />
            <Fields>
```

```
                <asp:BoundField DataField="ProductID" HeaderText="ProductID"
                 InsertVisible="False" ReadOnly="True" SortExpression="ProductID" />
                <asp:BoundField DataField="ProductName" HeaderText="ProductName"
                 SortExpression="ProductName" />
                <asp:BoundField DataField="QuantityPerUnit" HeaderText="QuantityPerUnit"
                 SortExpression="QuantityPerUnit" />
                <asp:BoundField DataField="UnitPrice" HeaderText="UnitPrice"
                 SortExpression="UnitPrice" />
                <asp:BoundField DataField="UnitsInStock" HeaderText="UnitsInStock"
                 SortExpression="UnitsInStock" />
            </Fields>
          <FooterStyle BackColor="#B5C7DE" ForeColor="#4A3C8C" />
          <HeaderStyle BackColor="#4A3C8C" Font-Bold="True" ForeColor="#F7F7F7" />
          <PagerStyle BackColor="#E7E7FF" ForeColor="#4A3C8C" HorizontalAlign="Right" />
            <RowStyle BackColor="#E7E7FF" ForeColor="#4A3C8C" />
        </asp:DetailsView>
        <asp:SqlDataSource ID="SqlDataSource1" runat="server" ConnectionString="<%$
         ConnectionStrings:NorthwindConnectionString %>" SelectCommand="SELECT
         [ProductID], [ProductName], [QuantityPerUnit], [UnitPrice], [UnitsInStock] FROM
         [Alphabetical list of products]"></asp:SqlDataSource>
    </div>
    </form>
</body>
</html>
```

In C#

```
<%@ Page Language="C#" AutoEventWireup="true" CodeFile="Default.aspx.cs"
  Inherits="_Default" %>
<!DOCTYPE html>
<html xmlns="http://www.w3.org/1999/xhtml">
<head runat="server">
    <title></title>
</head>
<body>
    <form id="form1" runat="server">
    <div>
        <asp:DetailsView ID="DetailsView1" runat="server" Height="50px" Width="125px"
         AllowPaging="True" AutoGenerateRows="False" BackColor="White"
         BorderColor="#E7E7FF" BorderStyle="None" BorderWidth="1px" CellPadding="3"
         DataKeyNames="ProductID" DataSourceID="SqlDataSource1" GridLines="Horizontal">
            <AlternatingRowStyle BackColor="#F7F7F7" />
            <EditRowStyle BackColor="#738A9C" Font-Bold="True" ForeColor="#F7F7F7" />
            <Fields>
                <asp:BoundField DataField="ProductID" HeaderText="ProductID"
                 InsertVisible="False" ReadOnly="True" SortExpression="ProductID" />
                <asp:BoundField DataField="ProductName" HeaderText="ProductName"
                 SortExpression="ProductName" />
                <asp:BoundField DataField="QuantityPerUnit" HeaderText="QuantityPerUnit"
                 SortExpression="QuantityPerUnit" />
                <asp:BoundField DataField="UnitPrice" HeaderText="UnitPrice"
                 SortExpression="UnitPrice" />
                <asp:BoundField DataField="UnitsInStock" HeaderText="UnitsInStock"
                 SortExpression="UnitsInStock" />
          </Fields>
          <FooterStyle BackColor="#B5C7DE" ForeColor="#4A3C8C" />
          <HeaderStyle BackColor="#4A3C8C" Font-Bold="True" ForeColor="#F7F7F7" />
          <PagerStyle BackColor="#E7E7FF" ForeColor="#4A3C8C" HorizontalAlign="Right" />
            <RowStyle BackColor="#E7E7FF" ForeColor="#4A3C8C" />
        </asp:DetailsView>
        <asp:SqlDataSource ID="SqlDataSource1" runat="server" ConnectionString="<%$
         ConnectionStrings:NorthwindConnectionString %>" SelectCommand="SELECT
```

```
            [ProductID], [ProductName], [QuantityPerUnit], [UnitPrice], [UnitsInStock] FROM
            [Alphabetical list of products]"></asp:SqlDataSource>
        </div>
        </form>
    </body>
    </html>
```

7. Press the F5 key on the keyboard to execute the application.The output is shown in Figure 8.62:

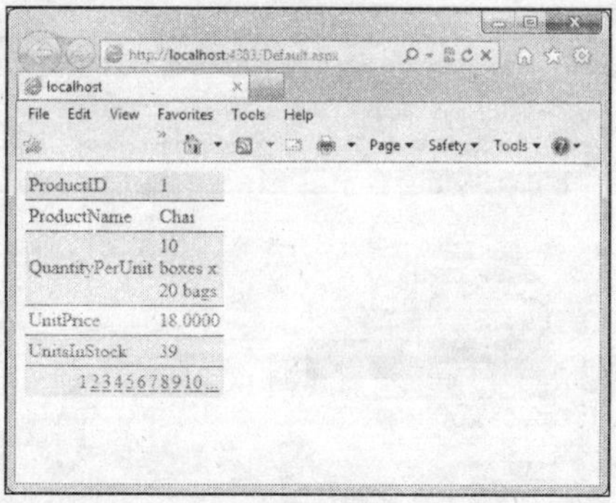

Figure 8.62: Displaying the Output of the DetailsViewControlCS Application

Using the FormView Control

Now, let's see how a `FormView` control is used to display data from a database, by performing the following steps:

1. Create a Web application and save it as `FormViewControlCS`. The code for this application can be found under the `FormViewControlCS` (for C#) and `FormViewControlVB` (for VB) folders.
2. Drag and drop the FormView control on the Design view of the Default.aspx page and select the New data source option from the Choose Data Source drop-down list, as shown in Figure 8.63:

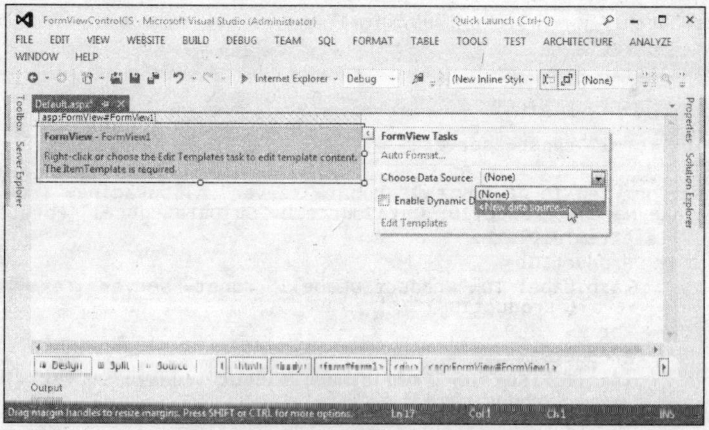

Figure 8.63: Selecting the Data Source

3. Create a connection of the FormView control with the database. In this case, we are creating the connection with the Products table of the Northwind database.

NOTE

You can refer to the GridViewControlCS application for the steps of creating connection with the database.

4. Click the Smart Tag of the FormView control and select the Auto Format link. The AutoFormat dialog box appears in which you can apply colorful layout on the FormView control.
5. Select the Classic option from the Select a scheme pane and click the OK button.
6. Select the Enable Paging check box to provide paging in the FormView control.

   The FormView control after creating the connection and applying the formatting appears, as shown in Figure 8.64:

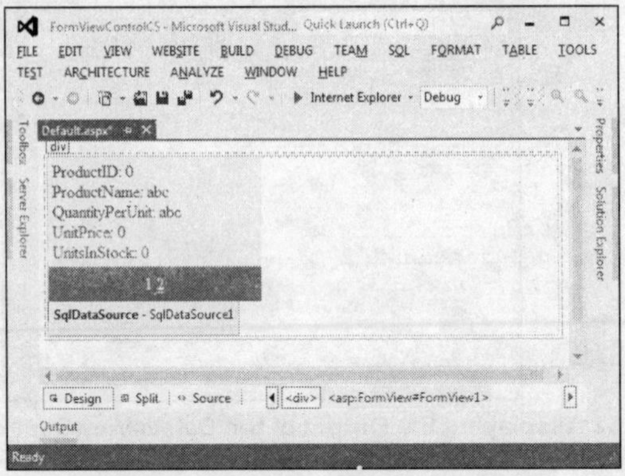

Figure 8.64: Displaying the Web Page

After configuring the data source of the FormView control, the `Default.aspx` page for the FormView ControlCS application is shown in Listing 8.11:

Listing 8.11: Showing the Code of the `Default.aspx` Page

In VB

```
<%@ Page Language="VB" AutoEventWireup="false" CodeFile="Default.aspx.vb"
  Inherits="_Default" %>
<!DOCTYPE html>
<html xmlns="http://www.w3.org/1999/xhtml">
<head runat="server">
    <title></title>
</head>
<body>
    <form id="form1" runat="server">
    <div>
        <asp:FormView ID="FormView1" runat="server" AllowPaging="True" CellPadding="4"
         DataKeyNames="ProductID" DataSourceID="SqlDataSource1" ForeColor="#333333">
            <EditItemTemplate>
                ProductID:
                <asp:Label ID="ProductIDLabel1" runat="server" Text='<%#
                 Eval("ProductID") %>' />
                <br />
                ProductName:
                <asp:TextBox ID="ProductNameTextBox" runat="server" Text='<%#
                 Bind("ProductName") %>' />
                <br />
                QuantityPerUnit:
                <asp:TextBox ID="QuantityPerUnitTextBox" runat="server" Text='<%#
                 Bind("QuantityPerUnit") %>' />
                <br />
                UnitPrice:
                <asp:TextBox ID="UnitPriceTextBox" runat="server" Text='<%#
                 Bind("UnitPrice") %>' />
                <br />
                UnitsInStock:
```

```
            <asp:TextBox ID="UnitsInStockTextBox" runat="server" Text='<%#
             Bind("UnitsInStock") %>' />
            <br />
            <asp:LinkButton ID="UpdateButton" runat="server" CausesValidation="True"
             CommandName="Update" Text="Update" />
             <asp:LinkButton ID="UpdateCancelButton" runat="server"
             CausesValidation="False" CommandName="Cancel" Text="Cancel" />
        </EditItemTemplate>
        <EditRowStyle BackColor="#2461BF" />
        <FooterStyle BackColor="#507CD1" Font-Bold="True" ForeColor="White" />
        <HeaderStyle BackColor="#507CD1" Font-Bold="True" ForeColor="White" />
        <InsertItemTemplate>
            ProductName:
            <asp:TextBox ID="ProductNameTextBox" runat="server" Text='<%#
             Bind("ProductName") %>' />
            <br />
            QuantityPerUnit:
            <asp:TextBox ID="QuantityPerUnitTextBox" runat="server" Text='<%#
             Bind("QuantityPerUnit") %>' />
            <br />
            UnitPrice:
            <asp:TextBox ID="UnitPriceTextBox" runat="server" Text='<%#
             Bind("UnitPrice") %>' />
            <br />
            UnitsInStock:
            <asp:TextBox ID="UnitsInStockTextBox" runat="server" Text='<%#
             Bind("UnitsInStock") %>' />
            <br />
            <asp:LinkButton ID="InsertButton" runat="server" CausesValidation="True"
             CommandName="Insert" Text="Insert" />
             <asp:LinkButton ID="InsertCancelButton" runat="server"
             CausesValidation="False" CommandName="Cancel" Text="Cancel" />
        </InsertItemTemplate>
        <ItemTemplate>
            ProductID:
            <asp:Label ID="ProductIDLabel" runat="server" Text='<%#
             Eval("ProductID") %>' />
            <br />
            ProductName:
            <asp:Label ID="ProductNameLabel" runat="server" Text='<%#
             Bind("ProductName") %>' />
            <br />
            QuantityPerUnit:
            <asp:Label ID="QuantityPerUnitLabel" runat="server" Text='<%#
             Bind("QuantityPerUnit") %>' />
            <br />
            UnitPrice:
            <asp:Label ID="UnitPriceLabel" runat="server" Text='<%#
             Bind("UnitPrice") %>' />
            <br />
            UnitsInStock:
            <asp:Label ID="UnitsInStockLabel" runat="server" Text='<%#
             Bind("UnitsInStock") %>' />
            <br />
        </ItemTemplate>
        <PagerStyle BackColor="#2461BF" ForeColor="White" HorizontalAlign="Center" />
        <RowStyle BackColor="#EFF3FB" />
    </asp:FormView>
    <asp:SqlDataSource ID="SqlDataSource1" runat="server" ConnectionString="<%$
     ConnectionStrings:NorthwindConnectionString %>" SelectCommand="SELECT
     [ProductID], [ProductName], [QuantityPerUnit], [UnitPrice], [UnitsInStock] FROM
     [Alphabetical list of products]"></asp:SqlDataSource>
</div>
```

```
        </form>
    </body>
    </html>
```

In C#

```
    <%@ Page Language="C#" AutoEventWireup="true" CodeFile="Default.aspx.cs"
      Inherits="_Default" %>
    <!DOCTYPE html>
    <html xmlns="http://www.w3.org/1999/xhtml">
    <head runat="server">
        <title></title>
    </head>
    <body>
        <form id="form1" runat="server">
        <div>
            <asp:FormView ID="FormView1" runat="server" AllowPaging="True" CellPadding="4"
             DataKeyNames="ProductID" DataSourceID="SqlDataSource1" ForeColor="#333333"
             Width="206px">
                <EditItemTemplate>
                    ProductID:
                    <asp:Label ID="ProductIDLabel1" runat="server" Text='<%#
                     Eval("ProductID") %>' />
                    <br />
                    ProductName:
                    <asp:TextBox ID="ProductNameTextBox" runat="server" Text='<%#
                     Bind("ProductName") %>' />
                    <br />
                    QuantityPerUnit:
                    <asp:TextBox ID="QuantityPerUnitTextBox" runat="server" Text='<%#
                     Bind("QuantityPerUnit") %>' />
                    <br />
                    UnitPrice:
                    <asp:TextBox ID="UnitPriceTextBox" runat="server" Text='<%#
                     Bind("UnitPrice") %>' />
                    <br />
                    UnitsInStock:
                    <asp:TextBox ID="UnitsInStockTextBox" runat="server" Text='<%#
                     Bind("UnitsInStock") %>' />
                    <br />
                    <asp:LinkButton ID="UpdateButton" runat="server" CausesValidation="True"
                     CommandName="Update" Text="Update" />
                     <asp:LinkButton ID="UpdateCancelButton" runat="server"
                     CausesValidation="False" CommandName="Cancel" Text="Cancel" />
                </EditItemTemplate>
                <EditRowStyle BackColor="#2461BF" />
                <FooterStyle BackColor="#507CD1" Font-Bold="True" ForeColor="White" />
                <HeaderStyle BackColor="#507CD1" Font-Bold="True" ForeColor="White" />
                <InsertItemTemplate>
                    ProductName:
                    <asp:TextBox ID="ProductNameTextBox" runat="server" Text='<%#
                     Bind("ProductName") %>' />
                    <br />
                    QuantityPerUnit:
                    <asp:TextBox ID="QuantityPerUnitTextBox" runat="server" Text='<%#
                     Bind("QuantityPerUnit") %>' />
                    <br />
                    UnitPrice:
                    <asp:TextBox ID="UnitPriceTextBox" runat="server" Text='<%#
                     Bind("UnitPrice") %>' />
                    <br />
                    UnitsInStock:
```

```
                <asp:TextBox ID="UnitsInStockTextBox" runat="server" Text='<%#
                 Bind("UnitsInStock") %>' />
                <br />
                <asp:LinkButton ID="InsertButton" runat="server" CausesValidation="True"
                 CommandName="Insert" Text="Insert" />
                 <asp:LinkButton ID="InsertCancelButton" runat="server"
                 CausesValidation="False" CommandName="Cancel" Text="Cancel" />
            </InsertItemTemplate>
            <ItemTemplate>
                ProductID:
                <asp:Label ID="ProductIDLabel" runat="server" Text='<%#
                 Eval("ProductID") %>' />
                <br />
                ProductName:
                <asp:Label ID="ProductNameLabel" runat="server" Text='<%#
                 Bind("ProductName") %>' />
                <br />
                QuantityPerUnit:
                <asp:Label ID="QuantityPerUnitLabel" runat="server" Text='<%#
                 Bind("QuantityPerUnit") %>' />
                <br />
                UnitPrice:
                <asp:Label ID="UnitPriceLabel" runat="server" Text='<%#
                 Bind("UnitPrice") %>' />
                <br />
                UnitsInStock:
                <asp:Label ID="UnitsInStockLabel" runat="server" Text='<%#
                 Bind("UnitsInStock") %>' />
                <br />
            </ItemTemplate>
           <PagerStyle BackColor="#2461BF" ForeColor="White" HorizontalAlign="Center" />
            <RowStyle BackColor="#EFF3FB" />
        </asp:FormView>
        <asp:SqlDataSource ID="SqlDataSource1" runat="server" ConnectionString="<%$
         ConnectionStrings:NorthwindConnectionString %>" SelectCommand="SELECT
         [ProductID], [ProductName], [QuantityPerUnit], [UnitPrice], [UnitsInStock] FROM
         [Alphabetical list of products]"></asp:SqlDataSource>
    </div>
    </form>
</body>
</html>
```

7. Press the F5 key on the keyboard to execute the application.The output of the application is shown in Figure 8.65:

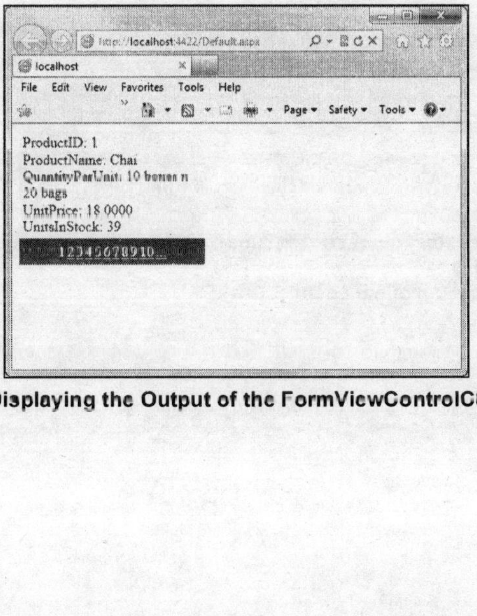

Figure 8.65: Displaying the Output of the FormViewControlCS Application

Using the Repeater Control

Now, let's use a `Repeater` control to display data from a database by performing the following steps:

1. Create a Web application and save it as `RepeaterControlCS`. You can find the code for this application under the `RepeaterControlCS` (for C#) and `RepeaterControlVB` (for VB) folders.
2. Drag and drop the Repeater control on the Design view of the Default.aspx Web page and select the New data source option from the Choose Data Source drop-down list, as shown in Figure 8.66:

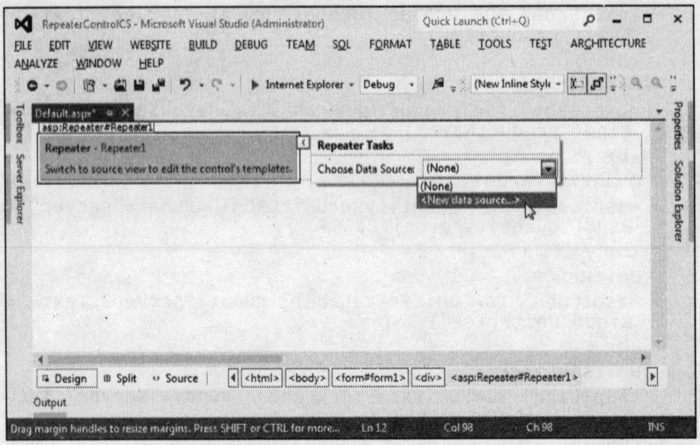

Figure 8.66: Selecting the Data Source

3. Create a connection of the Repeater control with the database. In this case, we are creating the connection with the Products table of the Northwind database.

NOTE

You can refer to the GridViewControlCS application for the steps of creating connection with the database.

4. Add the highlighted code in the Source view of the Default.aspx page, as shown in Listing 8.12:

Listing 8.12: Showing the Code of the `Default.aspx` Page

In VB

```
<%@ Page Language="VB" AutoEventWireup="false" CodeFile="Default.aspx.vb"
  Inherits="_Default" %>
<!DOCTYPE html>
<html xmlns="http://www.w3.org/1999/xhtml">
<head runat="server">
    <title></title>
</head>
<body>
    <form id="form1" runat="server">
    <div>
     <table>
        <asp:Repeater ID="Repeater1" runat="server" DataSourceID="SqlDataSource1">
         <HeaderTemplate>
         <tr style="background-color: Gray">
         <th>
         ProductId
         </th>
         <th>
         ProductName
         </th>
```

```
            <th>
            QuantityPerUnit
            </th>
            <th>
            UnitPrice
            </th>
            <th>
            UnitsInStock
            </th>
            </tr>
            </HeaderTemplate>
            <ItemTemplate>
            <tr>
            <td>
            <%#DataBinder.Eval(Container, "DataItem.ProductID")%>
            </td>
            <td>
            <%#DataBinder.Eval(Container, "DataItem.ProductName")%>
            </td>
            <td style="background-color: Gray">
            <%#DataBinder.Eval(Container, "DataItem.QuantityPerUnit")%>
            </td>
            <td>
            <%#DataBinder.Eval(Container, "DataItem.UnitPrice")%>
            </td>
            <td>
            <%#DataBinder.Eval(Container, "DataItem.UnitsInStock")%>
            </td>
            </tr>
            </ItemTemplate>
            <AlternatingItemTemplate>
            <tr>
            <td style="background-color: Gray">
            <%#DataBinder.Eval(Container, "DataItem.ProductID")%>
            </td>
            <td style="background-color: Gray">
            <%#DataBinder.Eval(Container, "DataItem.ProductName")%>
            </td>
            <td style="background-color: Gray">
            <%#DataBinder.Eval(Container, "DataItem.QuantityPerUnit")%>
            </td>
            <td style="background-color: Gray">
            <%#DataBinder.Eval(Container, "DataItem.UnitPrice")%>
            </td>
            <td style="background-color: Gray">
            <%#DataBinder.Eval(Container, "DataItem.UnitsInStock")%>
            </td>
            </tr>
            </AlternatingItemTemplate>
            </asp:Repeater>
            </table>
            <asp:SqlDataSource ID="SqlDataSource1" runat="server" ConnectionString="<%$
            ConnectionStrings:NorthwindConnectionString %>" SelectCommand="SELECT
            [ProductID], [ProductName], [QuantityPerUnit], [UnitPrice], [UnitsInStock] FROM
            [Alphabetical list of products]"></asp:SqlDataSource>
        </div>
        </form>
</body>
</html>
```

In C#

```
<%@ Page Language="C#" AutoEventWireup="true" CodeFile="Default.aspx.cs"
  Inherits="_Default" %>
<!DOCTYPE html>
<html xmlns="http://www.w3.org/1999/xhtml">
<head runat="server">
    <title></title>
</head>
<body>
    <form id="form1" runat="server">
    <div>
        <table>
        <asp:Repeater ID="Repeater1" runat="server" DataSourceID="SqlDataSource1">
         <HeaderTemplate>
         <tr style="background-color: Gray">
         <th>
         ProductId
         </th>
         <th>
         ProductName
         </th>
        <th>
         QuantityPerUnit
         </th>
         <th>
         UnitPrice
         </th>
         <th>
         UnitsInStock
         </th>
         </tr>
         </HeaderTemplate>
         <ItemTemplate>
         <tr>
         <td>
         <%#DataBinder.Eval(Container, "DataItem.ProductID")%>
         </td>
         <td>
         <%#DataBinder.Eval(Container, "DataItem.ProductName")%>
         </td>
        <td style="background-color: Gray">
         <%#DataBinder.Eval(Container, "DataItem.QuantityPerUnit")%>
         </td>
         <td>
         <%#DataBinder.Eval(Container, "DataItem.UnitPrice")%>
         </td>
         <td>
         <%#DataBinder.Eval(Container, "DataItem.UnitsInStock")%>
         </td>
         </tr>
         </ItemTemplate>
         <AlternatingItemTemplate>
         <tr>
         <td style="background-color: Gray">
         <%#DataBinder.Eval(Container, "DataItem.ProductID")%>
         </td>
         <td style="background-color: Gray">
         <%#DataBinder.Eval(Container, "DataItem.ProductName")%>
         </td>
```

```
<td style="background-color: Gray">
<%#DataBinder.Eval(Container, "DataItem.QuantityPerUnit")%>
</td>
<td style="background-color: Gray">
<%#DataBinder.Eval(Container, "DataItem.UnitPrice")%>
</td>
<td style="background-color: Gray">
<%#DataBinder.Eval(Container, "DataItem.UnitsInStock")%>
</td>
</tr>
</AlternatingItemTemplate>
</asp:Repeater>
</table>
<asp:SqlDataSource ID="SqlDataSource1" runat="server" ConnectionString="<%$
ConnectionStrings:NorthwindConnectionString %>" SelectCommand="SELECT
[ProductID], [ProductName], [QuantityPerUnit], [UnitPrice], [UnitsInStock] FROM
[Alphabetical list of products]"></asp:SqlDataSource>
    </div>
    </form>
</body>
</html>
```

The Web page appears after adding the code, as shown in Figure 8.67:

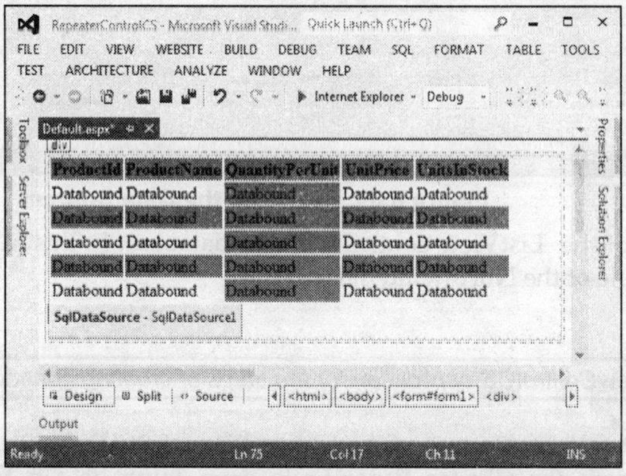

Figure 8.67: Displaying the Control after Adding the Code

5. Press the F5 key on the keyboard to execute the application, as shown in Figure 8.68:

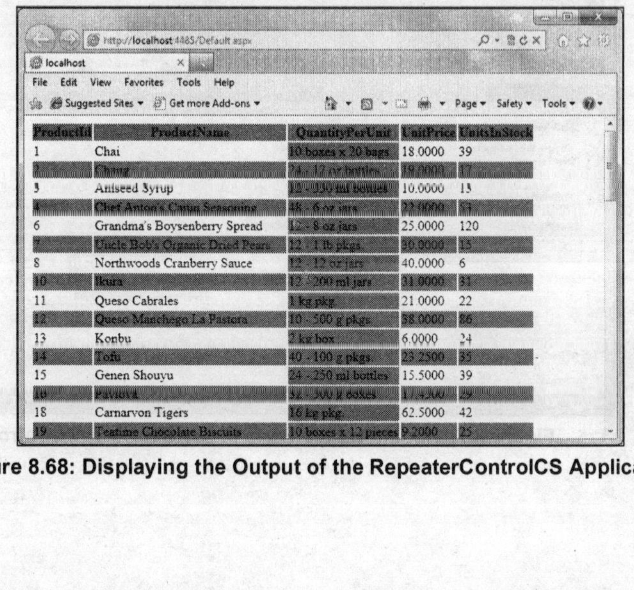

Figure 8.68: Displaying the Output of the RepeaterControlCS Application

Using the ListView and DataPager Controls

Let's learn how to use the `ListView` and `DataPager` controls to display paging of records, by performing the following steps:

1. Create an application and save it as `ListViewControlCS`. You can find the code for this application under the `ListViewControlCS` (for C#) and `ListViewControlVB` (for VB) folders.
2. Drag and drop ListView control from the Toolbox and select New data source option from the Choose Data Source drop-down list, as shown in Figure 8.69:

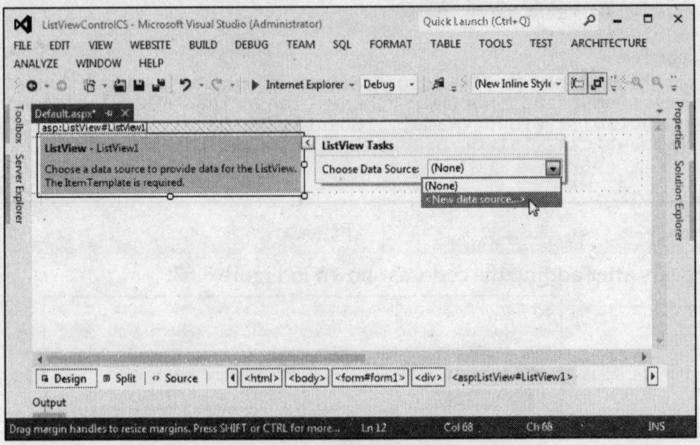

Figure 8.69: Selecting the Data Source

3. Create a connection of the ListView control with the database. In this case, we are creating the connection with the Products table of the Northwind database.

NOTE

You can refer to the GridViewControlCS application for the steps of creating connection with the database.

4. Drag and drop the DataPager control on the Design view of the Default.aspx page and select the style of the DataPager control from the Choose Pager Style drop-down list. In this application, we have selected Numeric Pager style from the Choose Pager Style drop-down list, as shown in Figure 8.70:

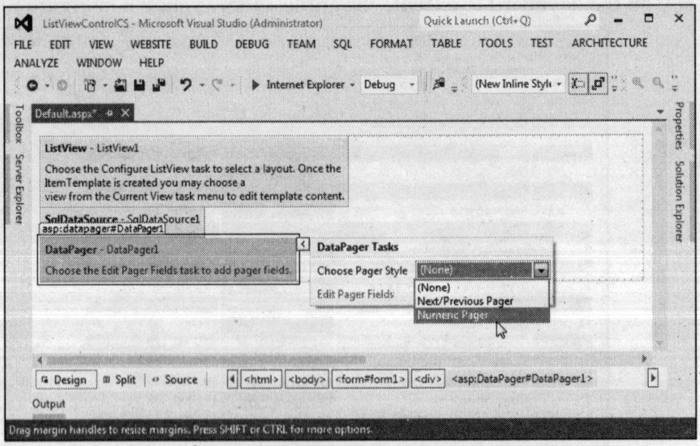

Figure 8.70: Selecting the Style of the DataPager Control

5. Open the Properties window of the DataPager and set the PagedControlID to ListView1, as shown in Figure 8.71:

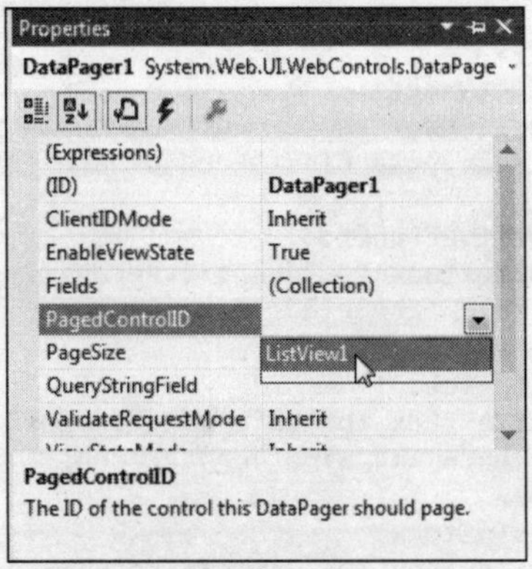

Figure 8.71: Setting the Property of the DataPager Control

6. Open the Source view of the Default.aspx and add the highlighted code, as shown in Listing 8.13:

Listing 8.13: Showing the Code of the `Default.aspx` Page

In VB

```
<%@ Page Language="VB" AutoEventWireup="false" CodeFile="Default.aspx.vb"
  Inherits="_Default" %>
<!DOCTYPE html>
<html xmlns="http://www.w3.org/1999/xhtml">
<head runat="server">
    <title></title>
</head>
<body>
    <form id="form1" runat="server">
    <div>
        <asp:ListView ID="ListView1" runat="server" DataSourceID="SqlDataSource1">
                <AlternatingItemTemplate>
                <li style="background-color: #FFFFFF;color: #284775;">ProductID:
                    <asp:Label ID="ProductIDLabel" runat="server" Text='<%#
                         Eval("ProductID") %>' />
                    <br />
                    ProductName:
                    <asp:Label ID="ProductNameLabel" runat="server"
                        Text='<%# Eval("ProductName") %>' />
                    <br />
                     QuantityPerUnit:
                    <asp:Label ID="QuantityPerUnitLabel" runat="server"
                        Text='<%# Eval("QuantityPerUnit") %>' />
                    <br />
                    UnitPrice:
                    <asp:Label ID="UnitPriceLabel" runat="server" Text='<%#
                         Eval("UnitPrice") %>' />
                    <br />
                    UnitsInStock:
                    <asp:Label ID="UnitsInStockLabel" runat="server"
                        Text='<%# Eval("UnitsInStock") %>' />
                    <br />
                </li>
            </AlternatingItemTemplate>
            <EditItemTemplate>
```

```
        <li style="background-color: #999999;">ProductID:
            <asp:Label ID="ProductIDLabel1" runat="server"
                Text='<%# Eval("ProductID") %>' />
            <br />
            ProductName:
            <asp:TextBox ID="ProductNameTextBox" runat="server"
                Text='<%# Bind("ProductName") %>' />
            <br />
            QuantityPerUnit:
            <asp:TextBox ID="QuantityPerUnitTextBox" runat="server"
                Text='<%# Bind("QuantityPerUnit") %>' />
            <br />
             UnitPrice:
            <asp:TextBox ID="UnitPriceTextBox" runat="server"
                Text='<%# Bind("UnitPrice") %>' />
            <br />
            UnitsInStock:
            <asp:TextBox ID="UnitsInStockTextBox" runat="server"
                Text='<%# Bind("UnitsInStock") %>' />
            <br />

            <asp:Button ID="UpdateButton" runat="server" CommandName="Update"
                Text="Update" />
            <asp:Button ID="CancelButton" runat="server" CommandName="Cancel"
                Text="Cancel" />
        </li>
    </EditItemTemplate>
    <EmptyDataTemplate>
        No data was returned.
    </EmptyDataTemplate>
    <InsertItemTemplate>
        <li style="">ProductName:
            <asp:TextBox ID="ProductNameTextBox" runat="server"
                Text='<%# Bind("ProductName") %>' />
            <br />
            QuantityPerUnit:
            <asp:TextBox ID="QuantityPerUnitTextBox" runat="server"
                Text='<%# Bind("QuantityPerUnit") %>' />
            <br />
            UnitPrice:
            <asp:TextBox ID="UnitPriceTextBox" runat="server"
                Text='<%# Bind("UnitPrice") %>' />
            <br />UnitsInStock:
            <asp:TextBox ID="UnitsInStockTextBox" runat="server"
                Text='<%# Bind("UnitsInStock") %>' />
            <br />
            <asp:Button ID="InsertButton" runat="server" CommandName="Insert"
                Text="Insert" />
            <asp:Button ID="CancelButton" runat="server" CommandName="Cancel"
                Text="Clear" />
        </li>
    </InsertItemTemplate>
    <ItemSeparatorTemplate>
         <br />
    </ItemSeparatorTemplate>
    <ItemTemplate>
        <li style="background-color: #E0FFFF;color: #333333;">ProductID:
            <asp:Label ID="ProductIDLabel" runat="server" Text='<%#
```

```
                Eval("ProductID") %>' />
                    <br />
                    ProductName:
                    <asp:Label ID="ProductNameLabel" runat="server"
                        Text='<%# Eval("ProductName") %>' />
                    <br />
                     QuantityPerUnit:
                    <asp:Label ID="QuantityPerUnitLabel" runat="server"
                        Text='<%# Eval("QuantityPerUnit") %>' />
                            <br />
                    UnitPrice:
                    <asp:Label ID="UnitPriceLabel" runat="server" Text='<%#
                Eval("UnitPrice") %>' />
                    <br />
                    UnitsInStock:
                    <asp:Label ID="UnitsInStockLabel" runat="server"
                        Text='<%# Eval("UnitsInStock") %>' />
                    <br />
                </li>
            </ItemTemplate>
            <LayoutTemplate>
                <ul ID="itemPlaceholderContainer" runat="server"
                    style="font-family: Verdana, Arial, Helvetica, sans-serif;">
                    <li runat="server" id="itemPlaceholder" />
                </ul>
                <div style="text-align: center;background-color: #5D7B9D;font-family:
                Verdana, Arial, Helvetica, sans serif;color: #FFFFFF;">
                </div>
            </LayoutTemplate>
            <SelectedItemTemplate>
                <li style="background-color: #E2DED6;font-weight: bold;color:
                #333333;">ProductID:
                    <asp:Label ID="ProductIDLabel" runat="server" Text='<%#
                        Eval("ProductID") %>' />
                    <br />
                    ProductName:
                    <asp:Label ID="ProductNameLabel" runat="server"
                        Text='<%# Eval("ProductName") %>' />
                    <br />
                     QuantityPerUnit:
                    <asp:Label ID="QuantityPerUnitLabel" runat="server"
                        Text='<%# Eval("QuantityPerUnit") %>' />
                    <br />
                    UnitPrice:
                    <asp:Label ID="UnitPriceLabel" runat="server" Text='<%#
                        Eval("UnitPrice") %>' />
                    <br />
                    UnitsInStock:
                    <asp:Label ID="UnitsInStockLabel" runat="server"
                        Text='<%# Eval("UnitsInStock") %>' />
                    <br />
                </li>
            </SelectedItemTemplate>
        </asp:ListView>
        <asp:SqlDataSource ID="SqlDataSource1" runat="server" ConnectionString="<%$
        ConnectionStrings:NorthwindConnectionString %>" SelectCommand="SELECT
        [ProductID], [ProductName], [QuantityPerUnit], [UnitPrice], [UnitsInStock] FROM
        [Alphabetical list of products]"></asp:SqlDataSource>
    </div>
```

```
            <asp:DataPager ID="DataPager1" runat="server" PagedControlID="ListView1">
                <Fields>
                    <asp:NextPreviousPagerField ButtonType="Button"
                     ShowFirstPageButton="True" ShowNextPageButton="False"
                     ShowPreviousPageButton="False" />
                    <asp:NumericPagerField />
                    <asp:NextPreviousPagerField ButtonType="Button"
                     ShowLastPageButton="True" ShowNextPageButton="False"
                     ShowPreviousPageButton="False" />
                </Fields>
            </asp:DataPager>
        </form>
    </body>
    </html>
```

In C#

```
    <%@ Page Language="C#" AutoEventWireup="true" CodeFile="Default.aspx.cs"
      Inherits="_Default" %>
    <!DOCTYPE html>
    <html xmlns="http://www.w3.org/1999/xhtml">
    <head runat="server">
        <title></title>
    </head>
    <body>
        <form id="form1" runat="server">
        <div>
            <asp:ListView ID="ListView1" runat="server" DataSourceID="SqlDataSource1">

                    <AlternatingItemTemplate>
                    <li style="background-color: #FFFFFF;color: #284775;">ProductID:
                        <asp:Label ID="ProductIDLabel" runat="server" Text='<%#
                             Eval("ProductID") %>' />
                        <br />
                        ProductName:
                        <asp:Label ID="ProductNameLabel" runat="server"
                            Text='<%# Eval("ProductName") %>' />
                        <br />
                         QuantityPerUnit:
                        <asp:Label ID="QuantityPerUnitLabel" runat="server"
                            Text='<%# Eval("QuantityPerUnit") %>' />
                        <br />
                        UnitPrice:
                        <asp:Label ID="UnitPriceLabel" runat="server" Text='<%#
                             Eval("UnitPrice") %>' />
                        <br />
                        UnitsInStock:
                        <asp:Label ID="UnitsInStockLabel" runat="server"
                            Text='<%# Eval("UnitsInStock") %>' />
                        <br />
                    </li>
                </AlternatingItemTemplate>
                <EditItemTemplate>
                    <li style="background-color: #999999;">ProductID:
                        <asp:Label ID="ProductIDLabel1" runat="server"
                            Text='<%# Eval("ProductID") %>' />
                        <br />
                        ProductName:
                        <asp:TextBox ID="ProductNameTextBox" runat="server"
                            Text='<%# Bind("ProductName") %>' />
```

```
                <br />
                QuantityPerUnit:
                <asp:TextBox ID="QuantityPerUnitTextBox" runat="server"
                    Text='<%# Bind("QuantityPerUnit") %>' />
                <br />
                 UnitPrice:
                <asp:TextBox ID="UnitPriceTextBox" runat="server"
                    Text='<%# Bind("UnitPrice") %>' />
                <br />
                UnitsInStock:
                <asp:TextBox ID="UnitsInStockTextBox" runat="server"
                    Text='<%# Bind("UnitsInStock") %>' />
                <br />
                <asp:Button ID="UpdateButton" runat="server" CommandName="Update"
                    Text="Update" />
                <asp:Button ID="CancelButton" runat="server" CommandName="Cancel"
                    Text="Cancel" />
            </li>
        </EditItemTemplate>
        <EmptyDataTemplate>
            No data was returned.
        </EmptyDataTemplate>
        <InsertItemTemplate>
            <li style="">ProductName:
                <asp:TextBox ID="ProductNameTextBox" runat="server"
                    Text='<%# Bind("ProductName") %>' />
                <br />
                QuantityPerUnit:
                <asp:TextBox ID="QuantityPerUnitTextBox" runat="server"
                    Text='<%# Bind("QuantityPerUnit") %>' />
                <br />
                UnitPrice:
                <asp:TextBox ID="UnitPriceTextBox" runat="server"
                    Text='<%# Bind("UnitPrice") %>' />
                <br />UnitsInStock:
                <asp:TextBox ID="UnitsInStockTextBox" runat="server"
                    Text='<%# Bind("UnitsInStock") %>' />
                <br />
                <asp:Button ID="InsertButton" runat="server" CommandName="Insert"
                    Text="Insert" />
                <asp:Button ID="CancelButton" runat="server" CommandName="Cancel"
                    Text="Clear" />
            </li>
        </InsertItemTemplate>
        <ItemSeparatorTemplate>
             <br />
        </ItemSeparatorTemplate>
        <ItemTemplate>
            <li style="background-color: #E0FFFF;color: #333333;">ProductID:
                <asp:Label ID="ProductIDLabel" runat="server" Text='<%#
             Eval("ProductID") %>' />
                <br />
                ProductName:
                <asp:Label ID="ProductNameLabel" runat="server"
                    Text='<%# Eval("ProductName") %>' />
                <br />
                 QuantityPerUnit:
                <asp:Label ID="QuantityPerUnitLabel" runat="server"
```

```
                Text='<%# Eval("QuantityPerUnit") %>' />
                   <br />
                UnitPrice:
                <asp:Label ID="UnitPriceLabel" runat="server" Text='<%#
             Eval("UnitPrice") %>' />
                <br />
                UnitsInStock:
                <asp:Label ID="UnitsInStockLabel" runat="server"
                    Text='<%# Eval("UnitsInStock") %>' />
                <br />
            </li>
        </ItemTemplate>
        <LayoutTemplate>
            <ul ID="itemPlaceholderContainer" runat="server"
                style="font-family: Verdana, Arial, Helvetica, sans-serif;">
                <li runat="server" id="itemPlaceholder" />
            </ul>
            <div style="text-align: center;background-color: #5D7B9D;font-family:
             Verdana, Arial, Helvetica, sans-serif;color: #FFFFFF;">
            </div>
        </LayoutTemplate>
        <SelectedItemTemplate>
            <li style="background-color: #E2DED6;font-weight: bold;color:
             #333333;">ProductID:
                <asp:Label ID="ProductIDLabel" runat="server" Text='<%#
                     Eval("ProductID") %>' />
                <br />
                ProductName:
                <asp:Label ID="ProductNameLabel" runat="server"
                    Text='<%# Eval("ProductName") %>' />
                <br />
                 QuantityPerUnit:
                <asp:Label ID="QuantityPerUnitLabel" runat="server"
                    Text='<%# Eval("QuantityPerUnit") %>' />
                <br />
                UnitPrice:
                <asp:Label ID="UnitPriceLabel" runat="server" Text='<%#
                     Eval("UnitPrice") %>' />
                <br />
                UnitsInStock:
                <asp:Label ID="UnitsInStockLabel" runat="server"
                    Text='<%# Eval("UnitsInStock") %>' />
                <br />
            </li>
        </SelectedItemTemplate>
    </asp:ListView>
     <asp:SqlDataSource ID="SqlDataSource1" runat="server" ConnectionString="<%$
     ConnectionStrings:NorthwindConnectionString %>" SelectCommand="SELECT
     [ProductID], [ProductName], [QuantityPerUnit], [UnitPrice], [UnitsInStock] FROM
     [Alphabetical list of products]"></asp:SqlDataSource>
     <asp:DataPager ID="DataPager1" runat="server" PagedControlID="ListView1">
         <Fields>
             <asp:NextPreviousPagerField ButtonType="Button"
              ShowFirstPageButton="True" ShowNextPageButton="False"
              ShowPreviousPageButton="False" />
             <asp:NumericPagerField />
             <asp:NextPreviousPagerField ButtonType="Button"
              ShowLastPageButton="True" ShowNextPageButton="False"
              ShowPreviousPageButton="False" />
```

```
                </Fields>
            </asp:DataPager>
        </div>
        </form>
    </body>
    </html>
```

7. The Web page appears after adding the code in the Source view of the Default.aspx page, as shown in Figure 8.72:

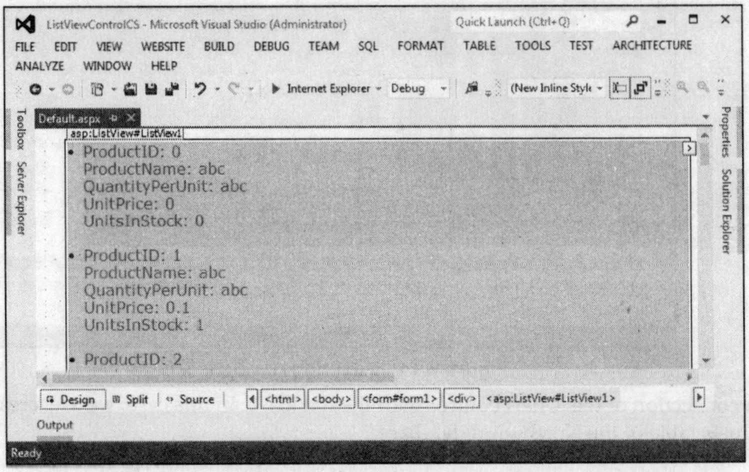

Figure 8.72: Showing the Web Page after Adding the Code

8. Press the F5 key on the keyboard to execute the application.The output appears, as shown in Figure 8.73:

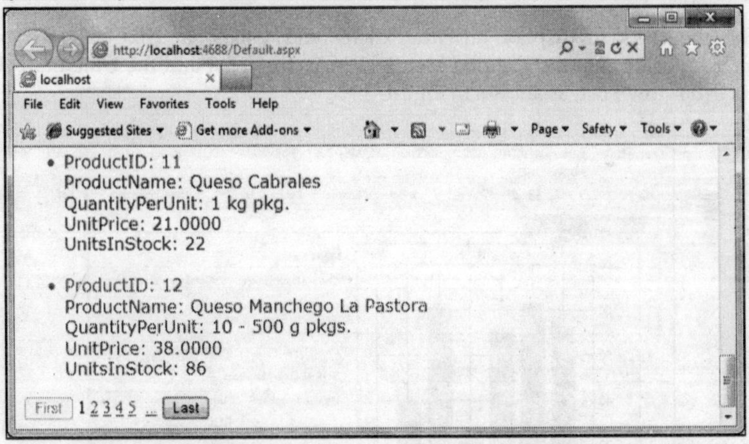

Figure 8.73: Displaying the Output of the ListViewControlCS Application

Using the Chart Control

Let's learn how to use the Chart control to display the records, by performing the following steps:

1. Create an application and save it as `ChartControlCS`. You can find the code for this application under the `ChartControlCS` (for C#) and `ChartControlVB` (for VB) folders.
2. Drag and drop the Chart control from the Toolbox and select the New data source option from the Choose Data Source drop-down list, as shown in Figure 8.74:

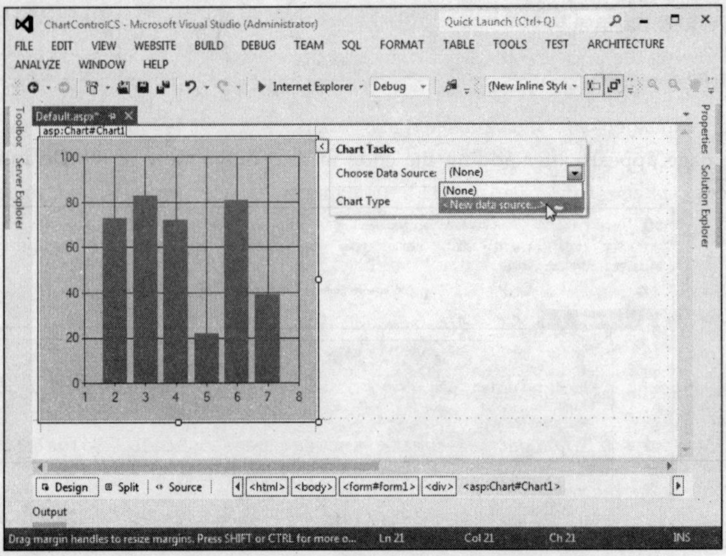

Figure 8.74: Selecting the Data Source

3. Create a connection of the Chart control with the database. In this case, we are creating the connection with the Products table of the Northwind database.

NOTE

You can refer to the GridViewControlCS application for the steps of creating connection with the database.

4. Select the members to display on the x-axis and y-axis. In this application, we have selected the UnitsOnOrder column in the X Value Member drop-down list and the UnitsInStock column in the Y Value Members drop-down list, as shown in Figure 8.75:

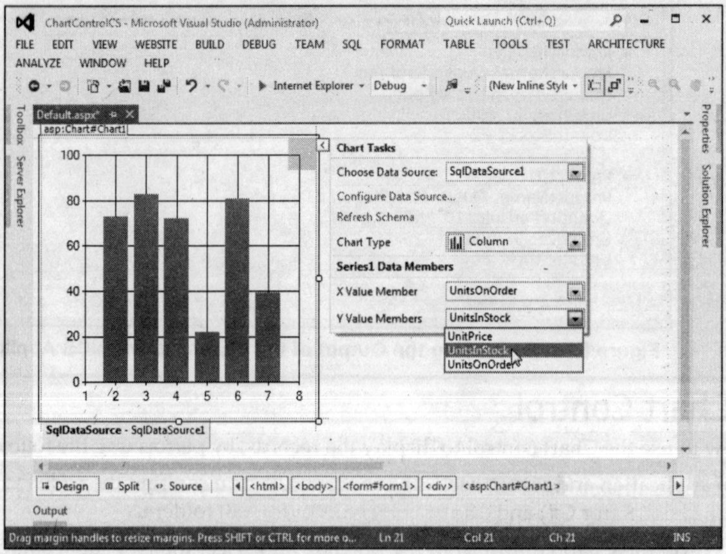

Figure 8.75: Selecting the Members to Display on the Axis

After setting the properties of the Chart control, the Source view of the Default.aspx is shown in Listing 8.14:

Listing 8.14: Showing the Code for the `Default.aspx` page

In VB

```
<%@ Page Language="VB" AutoEventWireup="false" CodeFile="Default.aspx.vb"
  Inherits="_Default" %>
<%@ Register Assembly="System.Web.DataVisualization, Version=4.0.0.0, Culture=neutral,
  PublicKeyToken=31bf3856ad364e35" Namespace="System.Web.UI.DataVisualization.Charting"
  TagPrefix="asp" %>
<!DOCTYPE html>
<html xmlns="http://www.w3.org/1999/xhtml">
<head runat="server">
    <title></title>
</head>
<body>
    <form id="form1" runat="server">
    <div>
        <asp:Chart ID="Chart1" runat="server" DataSourceID="SqlDataSource1"
         Width="458px">
            <Series>
                <asp:Series Name="Series1" XValueMember="UnitsOnOrder"
                 YValueMembers="UnitsInStock"></asp:Series>
            </Series>
            <ChartAreas>
                <asp:ChartArea Name="ChartArea1"></asp:ChartArea>
            </ChartAreas>
        </asp:Chart>
        <asp:SqlDataSource ID="SqlDataSource1" runat="server" ConnectionString="<%$
         ConnectionStrings:NorthwindConnectionString %>" SelectCommand="SELECT
         [UnitPrice], [UnitsInStock], [UnitsOnOrder] FROM [Alphabetical list of
         products]"></asp:SqlDataSource>
    </div>
    </form>
</body>
</html>
```

In C#

```
<%@ Page Language="C#" AutoEventWireup="true" CodeFile="Default.aspx.cs"
  Inherits="_Default" %>
<%@ Register Assembly="System.Web.DataVisualization, Version=4.0.0.0, Culture=neutral,
  PublicKeyToken=31bf3856ad364e35" Namespace="System.Web.UI.DataVisualization.Charting"
  TagPrefix="asp" %>
<!DOCTYPE html>
<html xmlns="http://www.w3.org/1999/xhtml">
<head runat="server">
    <title></title>
</head>
<body>
    <form id="form1" runat="server">
    <div>
        <asp:Chart ID="Chart1" runat="server" DataSourceID="SqlDataSource1"
         Width="503px">
            <Series>
                <asp:Series Name="Series1" XValueMember="UnitsOnOrder"
                 YValueMembers="UnitsInStock"></asp:Series>
            </Series>
            <ChartAreas>
                <asp:ChartArea Name="ChartArea1"></asp:ChartArea>
            </ChartAreas>
```

```
        </asp:Chart>
        <asp:SqlDataSource ID="SqlDataSource1" runat="server" ConnectionString="<%$
        ConnectionStrings:NorthwindConnectionString %>" SelectCommand="SELECT
        [UnitPrice], [UnitsInStock], [UnitsOnOrder] FROM [Alphabetical list of
        products]"></asp:SqlDataSource>
    </div>
    </form>
</body>
</html>
```

5. Press the F5 key on the keyboard to execute the application.The output is as shown in Figure 8.76:

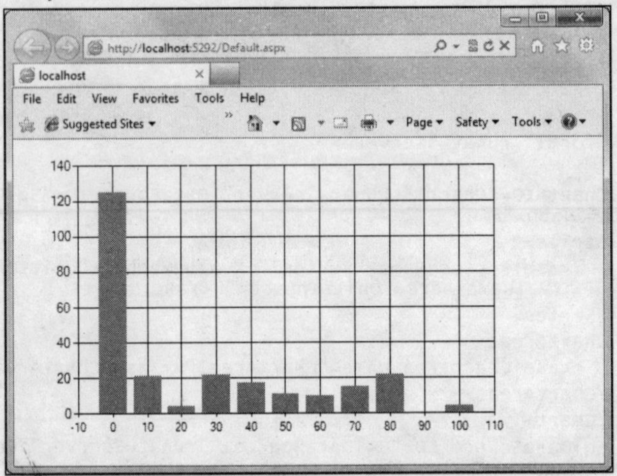

Figure 8.76: Displaying the Output of the Chart Control

Using the QueryExtender Control

Let's learn how to use the QueryExtender control to display a set of records, by performing the following steps:

1. Create an application and save it as `QueryExtenderControlCS`. You can find the code for this application under the `QueryExtenderControlCS` (for C#) and `QueryExtenderControlVB` (for VB) folders.
2. Drag and drop a TextBox and a Button control on the Design view of the Default.aspx page.
3. Set the text property of the Button control to Search.
4. Drag and drop the LinqDataSource control on the Design view and connect it with the database as done in the LinqDataSourceCS application.
5. Drag and drop the GridView control on the Design view of the page and select the data source name as LinqDataSource1 in the Choose Data Source drop-down list.
6. Drag and drop a QueryExtender control on the Design view of the Default.aspx and add the highlighted code in the Source view of the Default.aspx page, as shown in Listing 8.15:

Listing 8.15: Showing the Code of the `Default.aspx` Page

In VB

```
<%@ Page Language="VB" AutoEventWireup="false" CodeFile="Default.aspx.vb"
  Inherits="_Default" %>
<!DOCTYPE html>
<html xmlns="http://www.w3.org/1999/xhtml">
<head runat="server">
    <title></title>
</head>
<body>
```

```
    <form id="form1" runat="server">
        <div>
    Enter Product Name:<asp:TextBox ID="TextBox1" runat="server"></asp:TextBox>
    <asp:Button ID="Button1" runat="server" Text="Search" />
        <asp:LinqDataSource ID="LinqDataSource1" runat="server"
         ContextTypeName="DataClassesDataContext" EntityTypeName="" Select="new
         (ProductID, ProductName)" TableName="Products"></asp:LinqDataSource>
    <asp:GridView ID="GridView1" runat="server" AutoGenerateColumns="False"
        DataSourceID="LinqDataSource1">
        <Columns>
            <asp:BoundField DataField="ProductID" HeaderText="ProductID" ReadOnly="True"
                SortExpression="ProductID" />
            <asp:BoundField DataField="ProductName" HeaderText="ProductName"
                ReadOnly="True" SortExpression="ProductName" />
        </Columns>
    </asp:GridView>
    <asp:QueryExtender ID="QueryExtender1" runat="server"
  TargetControlID="LinqDataSource1">
    <asp:SearchExpression SearchType="StartsWith"  DataFields="ProductName">
  <asp:ControlParameter ControlID="TextBox1" />
</asp:SearchExpression>
    </asp:QueryExtender>
    </div>
    </form>
</body>
</html>
```

In C#

```
<%@ Page Language="C#" AutoEventWireup="true" CodeFile="Default.aspx.cs"
  Inherits="_Default" %>
<!DOCTYPE html>
<html xmlns="http://www.w3.org/1999/xhtml">
<head runat="server">
    <title></title>
</head>
<body>
    <form id="form1" runat="server">
    <div>
    <div>
    Enter Product Name:<asp:TextBox ID="TextBox1" runat="server"></asp:TextBox>
    <asp:Button ID="Button1" runat="server" Text="Search" />
        <asp:LinqDataSource ID="LinqDataSource1" runat="server"
         ContextTypeName="DataClassesDataContext" EntityTypeName="" Select="new
         (ProductID, ProductName)" TableName="Products"></asp:LinqDataSource>
    <asp:GridView ID="GridView1" runat="server" AutoGenerateColumns="False"
        DataSourceID="LinqDataSource1">
        <Columns>
            <asp:BoundField DataField="ProductID" HeaderText="ProductID" ReadOnly="True"
                SortExpression="ProductID" />
            <asp:BoundField DataField="ProductName" HeaderText="ProductName"
                ReadOnly="True" SortExpression="ProductName" />
        </Columns>
    </asp:GridView>
    <asp:QueryExtender ID="QueryExtender1" runat="server"
  TargetControlID="LinqDataSource1">
    <asp:SearchExpression SearchType="StartsWith"  DataFields="ProductName">
  <asp:ControlParameter ControlID="TextBox1" />
</asp:SearchExpression>
```

```
        </asp:QueryExtender>
        </div>
        </div>
        </form>
    </body>
    </html>
```

7. Press the F5 key on the keyboard to view the output of the QueryExtenderControlCS application (Figure 8.77).
8. Enter the product name in the text box and click the Search button, as shown in Figure 8.77:

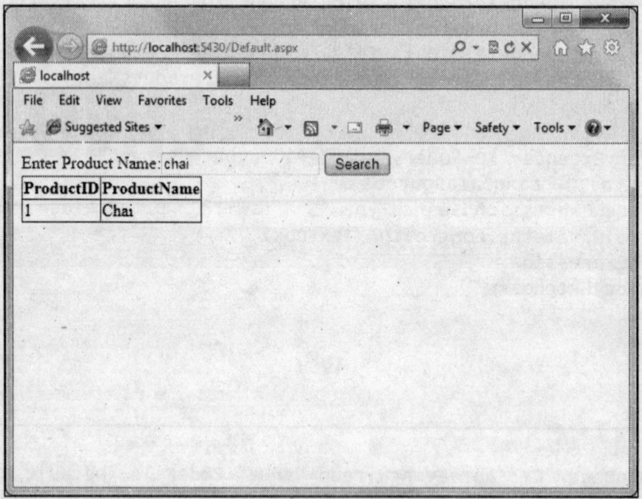

Figure 8.77: Displaying the Output of the QueryExtenderControlCS Application

Summary

In this chapter, you have learned about the use of the data bound controls, such as the `GridView`, `DataList`, `DetailsView`, `FormView`, and `Repeater` controls, to display database records. In this chapter, you have also been introduced to two new data bound controls, namely the `ListView` and `DataPager` controls. The chapter has also described data source controls, such as `SqlDataSource`, `AccessDataSource`, `LinqDataSource`, `EntityDataSource`, and `ObjectDataSource`, to access data. You also have learned how to filter data using the `QueryExtender control and display data using the Chart control.` You have also learned to change and modify various styles and layouts of a data bound control. In addition, you have learned about various data source controls used to configure data connections.

In the next chapter, you learn about LINQ queries and their implementation in ASP.NET 4.5.

9

LINQ Queries

In Depth

Language-Integrated Query (LINQ) was introduced as a new component of .NET Framework 3.0. The basic function of LINQ is to add native data querying capabilities to .NET Framework by using the syntax similar to Structured Query Language (SQL). LINQ allows you to define statements that query a data source to generate the requested result set.

LINQ is a programming model that is used to provide a consistent method to obtain and manipulate data. You can use LINQ directly within the ASP.NET 4.5 programming language entities called query expressions, which are used to query and transform data from a LINQ enabled data source. For example, a query expression can query and retrieve data from a SQL Server database and then display output as an XML data. These query expressions are based on numerous query operators, which are actually set of instructions about how a query is to be processed. The query operators are designed to work in a manner similar to that of SQL. LINQ defines the set of query operators, which are used to query and filter the data. The difference between LINQ and SQL is that unlike SQL, the query expressions in LINQ can be used to interact with numerous types of data, even the data that does not belong to a relational database.

.NET Framework 4.5, also includes a programming model for writing efficient and multithreaded queries, which is called Parallel LINQ (PLINQ). PLINQ is a parallel implementation of LINQ to Objects. This implies that PLINQ implements the standard query operators of LINQ as the extension methods and includes additional operators for implementing parallel operations. Therefore, PLINQ provides similar functionality with the use of declarative syntax.

In .NET 4.0, due to large internal implementation details queries running in parallel would actually run more slowly than running sequentially. These issues have been addressed in the .NET 4.5 Framework. The new version of .NET Framework runs queries parallel with efficient speed.

This chapter introduces you to the concept of LINQ. You also learn about the basic LINQ queries, and the query operators used to query data from a data source. You learn how to retrieve data from various data sources, such as LINQ to Object, LINQ to ADO.NET, and LINQ to XML. In addition, you also learn about the use of the LinqDataSource control, which is a separate data source control used in ASP.NET. You also learn about extension methods, anonymous methods, and lambda expressions used in LINQ. In addition to all these, you also learn about the concept of PLINQ.

Introducing LINQ Queries

A query is an expression that retrieves the requested data from a data source. A LINQ query specifies the information that you want to retrieve from a data source. LINQ queries can also perform additional functions, such as sorting and grouping the retrieved data. The LINQ queries are written in declarative query syntax. The various methods that you can use with the LINQ query are `From`, `Where`, `OrderBy`, and `Select`. They are the predefined methods that you can use for the execution of a LINQ query.

NOTE

You should note that the casing of methods of LINQ is different in case of C# and VB. For example, the where method is written as such in C#, but in VB it is written as the Where method.

The basic syntax of a LINQ query is that the LINQ query expressions must start with the `From` method and end with the `Select` or the `Group` method. In addition, you can use the `Where` and `OrderBy` methods to perform additional functions, such as retrieving the data.

The following are the three basic steps of a LINQ query execution:

1. Obtain the data source that can be either an SQL database or an XML file
2. Create the query

3. Execute the LINQ query

You need to be aware of the following basic concepts before you work with LINQ queries:

- Data Sources in LINQ Queries
- Deferred Query Execution and Immediate Execution
- LINQ and Generic Types

Let's explore these concepts one by one in detail.

Data Sources in LINQ Queries

The data source in a LINQ query can be a data structure, a Web service, a file system, or a database. LINQ query execution is simple because the syntax and the pattern of the query do not change with the change in the data source. The different ways in which you can use LINQ with different data sources are as follows:

- Implement the IEnumerable<T> (or IEnumerable (Of T) interface in case of VB) interface to enable the LINQ to Objects querying.
- Create the standard query operator methods, such as Where and Select, to enable custom LINQ queries.
- Create a provider for your data source that implements the IQueryable<T> (or IQueryable (Of T) interface in case of VB) interface to enable LINQ queries. A provider that implements this interface receives LINQ queries in the form of expression trees (which represent code in a tree structure, where each node of the tree is an expression).
- Create a provider that enables not only querying but also insert, update, and delete operations.

When you retrieve data in an ASP.NET application using LINQ, the source of data, such as an XML file or Access database, is not important. The execution of LINQ queries is independent of data types of data and structure of original data source.

LINQ previews the data source as an `IEnumerable<T>` or `IQueryable<T>` collection. For example, in LINQ to XML, the source data is made visible as an `IEnumerable<XElement>` collections element. In LINQ to DataSet, the source data is made visible as an `IEnumerable<DataRow>` collection.

Deferred Query Execution and Immediate Execution

The LINQ query variable only stores query commands. When you define a query in LINQ during runtime, the query does not run. The query actually runs when you request the data. Therefore, the actual execution of LINQ query is held back until the request for the data is made by you. This concept of holding back the actual execution is termed as deferred query execution. You can use the ForEach statement to retrieve the LINQ query results. For example, in a database that is updated continuously, you can create a LINQ query that retrieves the latest data, and you can also execute it repeatedly at different intervals to retrieve different results every time.

If the queries perform aggregation functions over a range of items, the query must first iterate over the range. This is called immediate execution. These functions must first iterate over the source elements and then display the result. The methods that perform such kind of forced execution are `Count`, `Max`, `Min`, and `Average`. Unlike deferred execution, immediate execution of queries does not require an explicit `ForEach` statement to return the result.

If you compare deferred to immediate query execution, deferred query execution has an edge over the immediate query execution. This is because in deferred query execution the query does not hold the result and you can execute it as often as you like. You can also update the data source on a regular basis by a separate application. You can retrieve the latest data in deferred query execution. This kind of functioning is not possible in immediate query execution.

LINQ and Generic Types

The LINQ queries are based on generic types and they were introduced with .NET Framework 2.0. The generic types are used to maximize code reuse, type safety, and performance. The most common use of generic types is to create collection classes. There are two basic concepts of the generic types used in LINQ:

- Create an instance of a generic collection class, such as List<T>, and then replace the T with the type of objects that the list holds in a LINQ query. For example, a list of strings is represented as List<String> and a list of Customer object is represented as List<Customer>. A generic list provides many benefits over the collections that store their elements as objects. For example, if you try to add a Customer to a List<String>, you get a compile-time error. In such cases, it is easy to use generic collections as you do not need to perform run-time type-casting.
- Use the IEnumerable<T> interface, which enables the generic collection classes to be enumerated by using the ForEach loop. For example, a LINQ query variable, which is typed as IEnumerable<Customer>, means that when the query is executed, it produces a sequence of zero or more Customer objects.

Let us now learn about the standard query operators.

Standard Query Operators

The standard query operators are the methods that form the LINQ pattern. These operators provide query capabilities including filtering, projection, aggregation, and sorting. The standard query operator in LINQ is an `Application Programming Interface (API)` that enables querying of any .NET array or collection. You can use these standard query operators to operate on the sequence of items.

The following are two set of standard query operators in LINQ:

- Operates on objects of the type IEnumerable<T>
- Operates on objects of the type IQueryable<T>

The standard query operators differ in the time that they take for their execution. The time depends on whether they have to return a single value or a sequence of values. The methods that return a single value execute immediately. The methods that return a sequence of values reschedule the query execution and return an enumerable object.

Table 9.1 lists all the standard query operators used in LINQ:

Table 9.1: Standard Query Operators

Operator	Description
Filtering Operators	Restricts the result set to contain those elements that satisfy a specific condition that are returned
Projection Operators	Transforms an object into a different type of new object
Sorting Operators	Changes the order of elements of sequence returned by the query
Join Operators	Combines collections
Grouping Operators	Puts the data into groups
Quantifier Operators	Checks whether an element of a sequence satisfies a condition
Partitioning Operators	Returns a subset of collection
Set Operators	Returns a result set which is in the form of a collection
Element Operators	Returns just one element
Aggregate Operators	Computes a single value from a collection
Conversion Operators	Converts the collection to an array
Generation Operators	Returns a new sequence of values

This was just a brief description of the standard query operators used in LINQ. Now, let's discuss these operators in detail.

Filtering Operators

Filtering, as the name suggests, refers to the operation of filtering the result set so that it contains only those elements that satisfy a specified given condition. The `where` method in C# or the Where method in VB is used as the Filtering operators in LINQ. The `where` method is used to filter a sequence based on a given condition. The syntax of using the `Where` method with LINQ is as follows:

In C#

```
public static IEnumerable<T> where<T>(
   this IEnumerable<T> source,
   Func<T, bool> predicate)
```

In VB

```
<ExtensionAttribute> _
Public Shared Function Count(Of TSource) ( _
   source As IEnumerable(Of TSource), _
   predicate As Func(Of TSource, Boolean) _
) As Integer
```

The Where method is used in a query expression to specify which elements from the data source is returned in the query expression. For example, you can use the Where method to filter numbers except those that are less than 5.

You can find the detailed example of using the `Where` method in the *Immediate Solutions* section of this chapter.

Projection Operators

The projection operators are used to transform an object into a new object of a different type. You can construct a new object of a different type that is built from each object by using the Projection operators. The `Select` and `SelectMany` methods are the Projection operators used in LINQ.

The `Select` method performs a projection over a sequence and projects the value that is based on a transform function. The function of the Select method is implemented using the select method in C# or Select method in VB. The `Select` method in LINQ performs function just as the `Select` statement in SQL and it specifies which elements are to be retrieved. For example, you can use the Select method to project the first letter from each string in a list of strings. The syntax of using the `Select` method is as follows:

In C#

```
public static IEnumerable<TResult> Select<TSource, TResult>(
   this IEnumerable<TSource> source,
   Func<TSource, int, TResult> selector
)
```

In VB

```
<ExtensionAttribute> _
Public Shared Function Select(Of TSource, TResult) ( _
   source As IEnumerable(Of TSource), _
   selector As Func(Of TSource, Integer, TResult) _
) As IE
```

The second type of Projection operators used in LINQ is the `SelectMany` method. It projects a sequence of values that are based on a transform function and then organize them into a sequence. The function of the SelectMany method is implemented using the from method in C# or the From method in VB. The syntax of using the `From` method is as follows:

In C#

```
public static IEnumerable<TResult> SelectMany<TSource, TResult>(
   this IEnumerable<TSource> source,
   Func<TSource, IEnumerable<TResult>> selector
)
```

In VB

```
<ExtensionAttribute> _
Public Shared Function SelectMany(Of TSource, TResult) ( _
   source As IEnumerable(Of TSource), _
   selector As Func(Of TSource, IEnumerable(Of TResult)) _
) As IEnumerable(Of TResult)
```

You must be wondering about the difference between the `Select` and `SelectMany` methods. Both the methods are used to produce a result value from a source of values. However, the difference lies in the result value. The `Select` method is used to produce one result value for every source value. The result value is a collection that has the same number of elements from the query.

In contrast, the `SelectMany` method produces a single result that contains a concatenated collection from the query.

You can find the detailed example of using the projection operators in the *Immediate Solutions* section of this chapter.

Sorting Operators

The sorting operators in LINQ arranges the elements of a sequence based on one or more attributes. This implies that for using the Sorting operators, first you need to specify a particular attribute and perform primary sorting on the elements. Then you need to specify the second sort criterion and sort the elements within the primary sorted group. The different Sorting operators are the OrderBy, OrderByDescending, ThenBy, ThenByDescending, and Reverse methods.

The sorting functionality is achieved using the `OrderBy` in C# or the `OrderBy` method in VB. Sorting can either be ascending or descending. The default behavior of the `orderby` method is to sort the data in the ascending order. If you want to order your data in the descending order, you need to use the `OrderByDescending` method in C# or the `OrderByDescending` in VB.

The syntax of using the `OrderBy` method is as follows:

In C#

```
public static IOrderedEnumerable<TSource> OrderBy<TSource, TKey>(
   this IEnumerable<TSource> source,
   Func<TSource, TKey> keySelector
)
```

In VB

```
<ExtensionAttribute> _
Public Shared Function OrderBy(Of TSource, TKey) ( _
   source As IEnumerable(Of TSource), _
   keySelector As Func(Of TSource, TKey) _
) As IOrderedEnumerable(Of TSource)
```

Similarly, you can use the `OrderByDescending` method to sort the string in a descending order, as shown in the following code:

In C#

```
public static IOrderedEnumerable<TSource> OrderByDescending<TSource, TKey>(
   this IEnumerable<TSource> source,
   Func<TSource, TKey> keySelector
)
```

In VB

```
<ExtensionAttribute> _
Public Shared Function OrderByDescending(Of TSource, TKey) ( _
   source As IEnumerable(Of TSource), _
   keySelector As Func(Of TSource, TKey) _
) As IOrderedEnumerable(Of TSource)
```

You can find the detailed example of using the Sorting operators in the *Immediate Solutions* section of this chapter.

Join Operators

The join operators in LINQ are used to join objects in one data source with objects that share a common attribute in another data source. The `Join` and `GroupJoin` methods act as the Join operators in LINQ. The `Join` method implements an inner join, which is the type of join in which only those objects that have a match in other data set are returned. The `GroupJoin` method joins two sequence based on a key selector functions and groups the results. The syntax of using the `Join` method is as follows:

In C#

```
public static IEnumerable<TResult> Join<TOuter, TInner, TKey, TResult>(
   this IEnumerable<TOuter> outer,
   IEnumerable<TInner> inner,
   Func<TOuter, TKey> outerKeySelector,
   Func<TInner, TKey> innerKeySelector,
   Func<TOuter, TInner, TResult> resultSelector
)
```

In VB

```
<ExtensionAttribute> _
Public Shared Function Join(Of TOuter, TInner, TKey, TResult) ( _
   outer As IEnumerable(Of TOuter), _
   inner As IEnumerable(Of TInner), _
   outerKeySelector As Func(Of TOuter, TKey), _
   innerKeySelector As Func(Of TInner, TKey), _
   resultSelector As Func(Of TOuter, TInner, TResult) _
) As IEnumerable(Of TResult)
```

You can find the practical implementation of the Join operators in the *Immediate Solutions* section of this chapter.

Grouping Operators

The grouping operators in LINQ is used to put data into groups so that the elements in each group share a common attribute. The `GroupBy` method in C# or the GroupBy in VB is the Grouping operators used in LINQ and it returns a sequence of `IGrouping<TKey, TElement>` objects that contain zero or more items that match the key value for the group.

The syntax of using the `GroupBy` method is as follows:

In C#

```
public static IEnumerable<IGrouping<TKey, TSource>> GroupBy<TSource, TKey>(
   this IEnumerable<TSource> source,
   Func<TSource, TKey> keySelector
)
```

In VB

```
<ExtensionAttribute> _
Public Shared Function GroupBy(Of TSource, TKey) ( _
   source As IEnumerable(Of TSource), _
   keySelector As Func(Of TSource, TKey) _
) As IEnumerable(Of IGrouping(Of TKey, TSource))
```

You can find the practical implementation of the GroupBy method in the *Immediate Solutions* section of this chapter.

Quantifier Operators

The quantifier operators return a Boolean value if the elements of the sequence satisfy a specific condition. The methods that are classified as the Quantifier operators are `Any`, `All`, and `Contains`. The `Any` method determines whether any element in a sequence satisfies a condition. This method enumerates the source sequence and returns `True` if any element satisfies the condition. The enumeration of the source sequence is terminated as soon as the result is known. The `ArgumentNullException` exception is thrown if the argument is null. The syntax of using the `Any` method is as follows:

In C#

```
public static bool Any<TSource>(
   this IEnumerable<TSource> source
)
```

In VB

```
<ExtensionAttribute> _
Public Shared Function Any(Of TSource) ( _
   source As IEnumerable(Of TSource) _
) As Boolean
```

The `All` method determines whether all the elements in the sequence satisfy the given condition. This method enumerates the source sequence and returns `True` if no element fails the test passed by the query. The `All` method returns a `True` value for an empty sequence. The `ArgumentNullException` exception is thrown if any argument is null.

The syntax of using the `All` method is as follows:

In C#

```
public static bool All<TSource>(
   this IEnumerable<TSource> source,
   Func<TSource, bool> predicate
)
```

In VB

```
<ExtensionAttribute> _
Public Shared Function All(Of TSource) ( _
   source As IEnumerable(Of TSource), _
   predicate As Func(Of TSource, Boolean) _
) As Boolean
```

The Contains method determines whether a sequence contains the specified element. The Contains method checks the source sequence to determine if it contains the specified element. When the matching element is found, the Contains method returns the result.

The syntax of the Contains method is as follows:

In C#

```
public static bool Contains<TSource>(
   this IEnumerable<TSource> source,
   TSource value
)
```

In VB

```
<ExtensionAttribute> _
Public Shared Function Contains(Of TSource) ( _
   source As IEnumerable(Of TSource), _
   value As TSource _
) As Boolean
```

Partitioning Operators

The partitioning operators in LINQ are used to divide an input sequence into two sections, without rearranging the elements, and then returning the result set with one of the sections that satisfies the given condition. The `Take`, `Skip`, `TakeWhile`, and `SkipWhile` methods are referred to as the Partitioning operators. The `Take` method takes the elements up to a specified position in a sequence. The `TakeWhile` method takes the elements based on the specified function until an element does not satisfy the given condition.

The syntax of the `Take` method is as follows:

In C#

```
public static IEnumerable<TSource> Take<TSource>(
  this IEnumerable<TSource> source,
  int count
)
```

In VB

```
<ExtensionAttribute> _
Public Shared Function Take(Of TSource) ( _
  source As IEnumerable(Of TSource), _
  count As Integer _
) As IEnumerable(Of TSource)
```

The `Skip` method skips elements up to the specified position in the sequence. The `SkipWhile` method skips the elements based on the given function until an element does not satisfy the given condition.

The syntax of the `Skip` method is as follows:

In C#

```
public static IEnumerable<TSource> Skip<TSource>(
  this IEnumerable<TSource> source,
  int count
)
```

In VB

```
<ExtensionAttribute> _
Public Shared Function Skip(Of TSource) ( _
  source As IEnumerable(Of TSource), _
  count As Integer _
) As IEnumerable(Of TSource)
```

You learn more about the Partitioning operators in the *Immediate Solutions* section of this chapter.

Set Operators

The set operators in LINQ refer to the query operations that produce a result set. The result is based on the presence or absence of the equivalent elements that are present within the same or separate collection. The `Distinct`, `Union`, `Intersect`, and `Except` method s are classified as the Set operators. The `Distinct` method removes duplicate values from a collection.

The syntax of the `Distinct` method is as follows:

In C#

```
public static IEnumerable<TSource> Distinct<TSource>(
  this IEnumerable<TSource> source
)
```

In VB

```
<ExtensionAttribute> _
Public Shared Function Distinct(Of TSource) ( _
  source As IEnumerable(Of TSource) _
) As IEnumerable(Of TSource)
```

The Union method returns the union of two sets. The result elements are the unique elements that are common in the two sets.

The syntax of the Union method is as follows:

In C#

```
public static IEnumerable<TSource> Union<TSource>(
   this IEnumerable<TSource> first,
   IEnumerable<TSource> second
)
```

In VB

```
<ExtensionAttribute> _
Public Shared Function Union(Of TSource) ( _
   first As IEnumerable(Of TSource), _
   second As IEnumerable(Of TSource) _
) As IEnumerable(Of TSource)
```

The Intersect method returns the set intersection and the elements appear in each of the two collections. The syntax of the Intersect method is as follows:

In C#

```
public static IEnumerable<TSource> Intersect<TSource>(
   this IEnumerable<TSource> first,
   IEnumerable<TSource> second
)
```

In VB

```
<ExtensionAttribute> _
Public Shared Function Intersect(Of TSource) ( _
   first As IEnumerable(Of TSource), _
   second As IEnumerable(Of TSource) _
) As IEnumerable(Of TSource)
```

The Except method returns the set difference. The result of the Except method returns the elements of one collection that do not appear in the second collection.

The syntax of the Except method is as follows:

In C#

```
public static IEnumerable<TSource> Except<TSource>(
   this IEnumerable<TSource> first,
   IEnumerable<TSource> second
)
```

In VB

```
<ExtensionAttribute> _
Public Shared Function Except(Of TSource) ( _
   first As IEnumerable(Of TSource), _
   second As IEnumerable(Of TSource) _
) As IEnumerable(Of TSource)
```

You learn more about the Set operators in the *Immediate Solutions* section of this chapter.

Element Operators

The element operators in LINQ return just one element. The ElementAt, ElementAtOrDefault, First, FirstOrDefault, Last, LastOrDefault, Single, and SingleOrDefault methods are termed as the Element operators. The ElementAt method returns the element at a specified index in a collection. The ElementAtOrDefault method returns the element at a specified index in a collection or the default value if the index is out of range. The First method returns the first element of the collection, or the first element that satisfies the given condition. It returns a default value if there is no such element. The FirstOrDefault method returns the first element of a collection or the first element that satisfies a given condition. It returns a default value if there is no such element. The `Last` method returns the last element of the collection, or the last element that satisfies a given condition. The `LastOrDefault` method returns the last element of the collection, or the last element that satisfies the given condition. It returns a default value if there is no matching element. The `Single` method returns the only element of the collection that satisfies the given condition. The `SingleOrDefault` method returns the only element of the collection that satisfies the condition.

The syntax of the `First` method is as follows:

In C#

```
public static TSource First<TSource>(
   this IEnumerable<TSource> source
)
```

In VB

```
<ExtensionAttribute> _
Public Shared Function First(Of TSource) ( _
   source As IEnumerable(Of TSource) _
) As TSource
```

An `ArgumentNullException` exception is thrown if any argument is null in the collection. An `InvalidOperationException` exception is thrown if no element matches the condition or the source sequence is empty.

The syntax of the `FirstOrDefault` method is as follows:

In C#

```
public static TSource FirstOrDefault<TSource>(
   this IEnumerable<TSource> source
)
```

In VB

```
<ExtensionAttribute> _
Public Shared Function FirstOrDefault(Of TSource) ( _
   source As IEnumerable(Of TSource) _
) As TSource
```

Aggregate Operators

The aggregate operators compute a single value from a collection. The different aggregate operators are `Aggregate`, `Average`, `Count`, `LongCount`, `Max`, `Min`, and `Sum`. The Aggregate method calculates a sum value of the values in the collection. The `Average` method calculates the average value of the collection of the values. The `Count` method counts the elements in the collection. The `LongCount` method counts the elements in a large collection. The `Max` method determines the maximum value in a collection. The `Min` method determines the minimum value of the collection. The `Sum` method calculates the sum of values in the collection.

The syntax of the `Count` method is as follows:

In C#

```
public static int Count<TSource>(
   this IEnumerable<TSource> source
)
```

In VB

```
<ExtensionAttribute> _
Public Shared Function Count(Of TSource) ( _
   source As IEnumerable(Of TSource) _
) As Integer
```

The `Count` method throws an `ArgumentNullException` exception, if any argument is null in the collection and an `OverflowException` exception is thrown if the count exceeds the maximum value.

The syntax of the `Sum` method is as follows:

In C#

```
public static decimal Sum(
  this IEnumerable<decimal> source
)
```

In VB

```
<ExtensionAttribute> _
Public Shared Function Sum ( _
  source As IEnumerable(Of Decimal) _
) As Decimal
```

The `Sum` method returns 0 for an empty sequence. The method does not include null values in its result.

The Aggregate method applies a function over a sequence. The syntax of the Aggregate method is as follows:

In C#

```
public static TSource Aggregate<TSource>(
  this IEnumerable<TSource> source,
  Func<TSource, TSource, TSource> func
)
```

In VB

```
<ExtensionAttribute> _
Public Shared Function Aggregate(Of TSource) ( _
  source As IEnumerable(Of TSource), _
  func As Func(Of TSource, TSource, TSource) _
) As TSource
```

The LongCount method counts the number of elements in the given sequence. The syntax of the LongCount method is as follows:

In C#

```
public static long LongCount<TSource>(
  this IEnumerable<TSource> source
)
```

In VB

```
<ExtensionAttribute> _
Public Shared Function LongCount(Of TSource) ( _
  source As IEnumerable(Of TSource) _
) As Long
```

The Min method finds the minimum value of the given sequence. The syntax of the Min method is as follows:

In C#

```
public static decimal Min(
  this IEnumerable<decimal> source
)
```

In VB

```
<ExtensionAttribute> _
Public Shared Function Min ( _
  source As IEnumerable(Of Decimal) _
) As Decimal
```

The Max method returns the maximum value of the given sequence. The syntax of the Max method is as follows:

In C#

```
public static decimal Max(
  this IEnumerable<decimal> source)
```

In VB

```
<ExtensionAttribute> _
Public Shared Function Max ( _
   source As IEnumerable(Of Decimal) _
) As Decimal
```

The Average method computes the average of the given sequence. The syntax of the Average method is as follows:

In C#

```
public static decimal Average(
   this IEnumerable<decimal> source)
```

In VB

```
<ExtensionAttribute> _
Public Shared Function Average ( _
   source As IEnumerable(Of Decimal) _
) As Decimal
```

You learn more about the aggregate operators in the *Immediate Solutions* section of this chapter.

Conversion Operators

The conversion operators convert a collection to an array. A Conversion operator changes the type of input objects. The different conversion operators are `ToSequence`, `ToArray`, `ToList`, `ToDictionary`, `ToLookup`, `OfType`, and `Cast`.

The `ToSequence` method simply returns the source argument by changing it to the `IEnumerable<T>` collection. The `ToArray` method enumerates the source sequence and returns an array containing the elements of the sequence. The `ToList` method enumerates the source sequence and returns a `List<T>` class containing the elements of the sequence. The `ToDictionary` method lists the source sequence and evaluates the `keySelector` and `elementSelector` functions for each element to produce the element key and value of the source sequence. The `ToLookup` method implements one-to-many dictionary that maps the key to the sequence of values. The `OfType` method allocates and returns an enumerable object that captures the source argument. The `Cast` method also allocates and returns an enumerable object that captures the source argument.

The syntax of the `ToList` method is as follows:

In C#

```
public static List<TSource> ToList<TSource>(
   this IEnumerable<TSource> source)
```

In VB

```
<ExtensionAttribute> _
Public Shared Function ToList(Of TSource) ( _
   source As IEnumerable(Of TSource) _
) As List(Of TSource)
```

You learn more about the conversion operators in the *Immediate Solutions* section of this chapter.

Generation Operators

The generation operators, which are `DefaultIfEmpty`, `Empty`, `Range`, and `Repeat`, help in creating a new sequence of values. The `DefaultIfEmpty` method replaces an empty collection with a default single collection. The `Empty` method refers to an empty collection. The `Range` method generates a collection that contains a sequence of numbers. The `Repeat` method generates a collection that contains at least one repeated value.

The syntax of the `Range` method is as follows:

In C#

```
public static IEnumerable<int> Range(
   int start,
   int count)
```

In VB

```
Public Shared Function Range ( _
   start As Integer, _
   count As Integer _
) As IEnumerable(Of Integer)
```

The `Range` method throws an `ArgumentOutOfRangeException` exception if the count of the collection is less than 0.

The syntax of the `Empty` method is as follows:

In C#

```
public static IEnumerable<TResult> Empty<TResult>()
```

In VB

```
Public Shared Function Empty(Of TResult) As IEnumerable(Of TResult)
```

The `Empty` method caches a single empty sequence of the given type.

You learn more about the generation operators in the *Immediate Solutions* section of this chapter.

Zip Operator

The zip operator helps in combining two collections into one. It uses the Zip method to merge the two sequences, which are identical in length, into one. The Zip method uses the order of elements to combine the elements from two given sequences. This implies that the Zip method takes an element from the first source and an element from the second source, which is at the same location, and returns a combined type.

The syntax of the `Zip` method is as follows:

In C#

```
public static IEnumerable<TResult> Zip<TFirst, TSecond, TResult>(
   this IEnumerable<TFirst> first,
   IEnumerable<TSecond> second,
   Func<TFirst, TSecond, TResult> resultSelector)
```

In VB

```
<ExtensionAttribute> _
Public Shared Function Zip(Of TFirst, TSecond, TResult) ( _
   first As IEnumerable(Of TFirst), _
   second As IEnumerable(Of TSecond), _
   resultSelector As Func(Of TFirst, TSecond, TResult) _
) As IEnumerable(Of TResult)
```

You learn more about the Zip operator in the *Immediate Solutions* section of this chapter.

Introducing LINQ to Objects

LINQ to Objects refer to the use of LINQ queries with any `IEnumerable` or `IEnumerable<T>` collection directly, without the use of any intermediate LINQ provider or interface. You can use LINQ to Objects for having an entirely new cast of characters in the form of classes that must be used to get benefit of LINQ. LINQ to Objects represents a new approach to collections. Earlier, you had to write complex `ForEach` loops that specified how to retrieve data from a collection. In such a scenario, you can easily use LINQ to Objects to write declarative code that describes what you want to retrieve. LINQ to Objects is more beneficial because of the following specific reasons:

```
                    style="margin-left: 157px; margin-top: 82px"
                    Width="225px"></asp:ListBox>
                    <br />
                    <br />
                    <br />
                    <asp:Button ID="Button1" runat="server" style="margin-left: 199px;
                    height: 26px;" Text="Ascending" Width="97px" />
                    <asp:Button ID="Button2" runat="server" style="margin-left: 35px;
                    margin-top: 0px" Text="Descending" />
                    </div>
                    <div id="footer">
                            <p class="left">
                            All content copyright &copy; Kogent Solutions Inc.</p>
                    </div>
            </div>
        </form>
</body>
</html>
```

In C#

```
<%@ Page Language="C#" AutoEventWireup="true" CodeFile="Default.aspx.cs"
  Inherits="_Default" %>
<!DOCTYPE html>
<html xmlns="http://www.w3.org/1999/xhtml">
<head id="Head1" runat="server">
    <title>Using Sorting Operator</title>
        <link href="StyleSheet.css" rel="stylesheet" type="text/css" />
        <style type="text/css">
        .itemContent {
                height: 398px;
                width: 581px;
        }
    </style>
</head>
<body>
    <form id="form1" runat="server">
        <div id="header">
                <h1>
                        ASP.NET 4.5 Black Book
                </h1>
        </div>
        <div id="sidebar">
                <div id="nav">
                         
                </div>
        </div>
        <div id="content">
                <div class ="itemContent">
                <asp:ListBox ID="ListBox1" runat="server" Height="126px"
                style="margin-left: 157px; margin-top: 82px"
                Width="225px"></asp:ListBox>
                <br />
                <br />
                <br />
                <asp:Button ID="Button1" runat="server" style="margin-left: 199px"
                Text="Ascending" Width="97px" OnClick="Button1_Click" />
                <asp:Button ID="Button2" runat="server" style="margin-left: 35px;
                margin-top: 0px" Text="Descending" OnClick="Button2_Click" />
                </div>
                <div id="footer">
```

```
                            <p class="left">
                            All content copyright &copy; Kogent Solutions Inc.</p>
                      </div>
                </div>
        </form>
      </body>
      </html>
```

After modifying the code in the source file, change the code in the code-behind file of the Default.aspx page, as shown in Listing 9.17:

Listing 9.17: Showing the Code for the Code-Behind File of the Default.aspx Page

In VB

```
Partial Class _Default
    Inherits System.Web.UI.Page
    Dim doubles() As Double = {500, 700, 100, 200, 400, 600, 900, 300, 800}
    Protected Sub Button1_Click(sender As Object, e As EventArgs) Handles Button1.Click
        ListBox1.Items.Clear()
        Dim sorting = From d In doubles _
                      Order By d _
         Select d
        For Each d In sorting
            ListBox1.Items.Add(d.ToString())
        Next d
    End Sub
    Protected Sub Button2_Click(sender As Object, e As EventArgs) Handles Button2.Click
        ListBox1.Items.Clear()
        Dim DescendingSorting = From d In doubles _
         Order By d Descending _
         Select d
        For Each d In DescendingSorting
            ListBox1.Items.Add(d.ToString())
        Next d
    End Sub
End Class
```

In C#

```
using System;
using System.Collections.Generic;
using System.Linq;
using System.Web;
using System.Web.UI;
using System.Web.UI.WebControls;
public partial class _Default : System.Web.UI.Page
{
    double[] doubles = { 500, 700, 100, 200, 400, 600, 900, 300, 800 };
    protected void Page_Load(object sender, EventArgs e)
    {

    }
    protected void Button1_Click(object sender, EventArgs e)
    {
        ListBox1.Items.Clear();
        var sorting = from d in doubles
                      orderby d
                      select d;
        foreach (var d in sorting)
        {
            ListBox1.Items.Add(d.ToString());
        }
```

```
        }
        protected void Button2_Click(object sender, EventArgs e)
        {
            ListBox1.Items.Clear();
            var DescendingSorting = from d in doubles
                                    orderby d descending
                                    select d;
            foreach (var d in DescendingSorting)
            {
                ListBox1.Items.Add(d.ToString());
            }
        }
    }
```

Now, let's run the application by pressing the F5 key on the keyboard. When you click the Ascending button, the list box displays the data in the ascending order by using the Sorting operators, as shown in Figure 9.12:

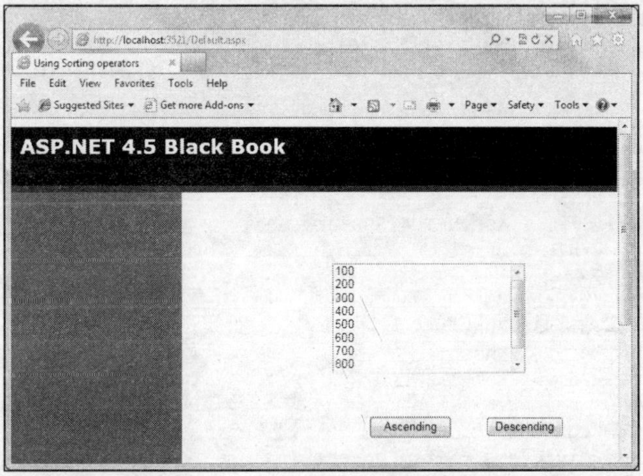

Figure 9.12: Displaying the Data in the Ascending Order

Similarly, when you click the Descending button, the listbox displays the data in the descending order, as shown in Figure 9.13:

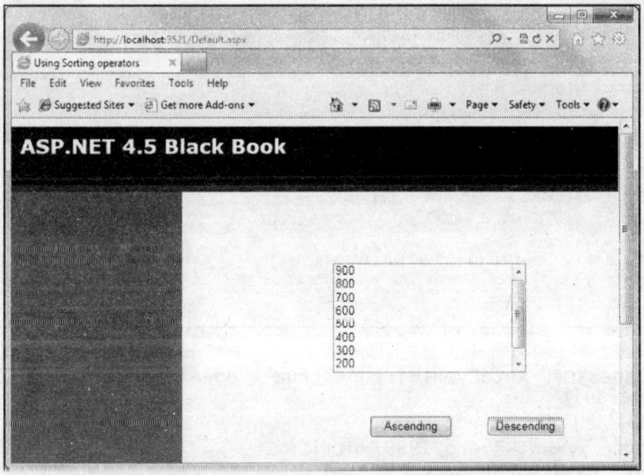

Figure 9.13: Displaying the Data in the Descending Order

Using the Join Method

You can use the Join method to combine two sources of data based on specific criteria. You should be having two lists of data that you need to join using the Join method in the Join operators. Now, let's create an application in which you can join two sources of data. Create a website and save it as JoinOperator. You can find the code for this application in the JoinOperatorCS (for C#) and JoinOperatorVB (for VB) folders. To add the required controls, you can find the code for the Default.aspx page in Listing 9.18:

Listing 9.18: Showing the Code for the Default.aspx Page

In VB

```
<%@ Page Language="VB" AutoEventWireup="false" CodeFile="Default.aspx.vb"
  Inherits="_Default" %>
<!DOCTYPE html>
<html xmlns="http://www.w3.org/1999/xhtml">
<head id="Head1" runat="server">
   <title>Join Operator Example</title>
        <link href="StyleSheet.css" rel="stylesheet" type="text/css" />
</head>
<body>
  <form id="form1" runat="server">
        <div id="header">
                <h1>
                        ASP.NET 4.5 Black Book
                </h1>
        </div>
        <div id="sidebar">
                <div id="nav">
                         
                </div>
        </div>
        <div id="content">
                <div class ="itemContent">
                        <asp:ListBox ID="ListBox1" runat="server" Height="135px"
                        style="margin-left: 189px; margin-top: 104px"
                        Width="229px"></asp:ListBox>
                        <br/>
                        <asp:Button ID="Button1" runat="server" Text="Button"
                        style="height: 26px; margin-left: 263px; margin-top: 38px"
                        Width="56px" />
                </div>
                <div id="footer">
                        <p class="left">
                        All content copyright &copy; Kogent Solutions Inc.</p>
                </div>
        </div>
  </form>
</body>
</html>
```

In C#

```
<%@ Page Language="C#" AutoEventWireup="true" CodeFile="Default.aspx.cs"
  Inherits="_Default" %>
<!DOCTYPE html>
<html xmlns="http://www.w3.org/1999/xhtml">
<head id="Head1" runat="server">
    <title>Join Operator Example</title>
        <link href="StyleSheet.css" rel="stylesheet" type="text/css" />
```

```
</head>
<body>
  <form id="form1" runat="server">
        <div id="header">
                <h1>
                        ASP.NET 4.5 Black Book
                </h1>
        </div>
        <div id="sidebar">
                <div id="nav">
                         
                </div>
        </div>
        <div id="content">
                <div class ="itemContent">
                        <asp:ListBox ID="ListBox1" runat="server" Height="135px"
                        style="margin-left: 189px; margin-top: 104px"
                        Width="229px"></asp:ListBox>
                        </br>
                        <asp:Button ID="Button1" runat="server" Text="Button"
                        style="height: 26px; margin-left: 263px; margin-top: 38px"
                        Width="56px" OnClick="Button1_Click" />
                </div>
                <div id="footer">
                        <p class="left">
                        All content copyright &copy; Kogent Solutions Inc.</p>
                </div>
        </div>
  </form>
</body>
</html>
```

After modifying the code in the source file, change the code in the code-behind file of the Default.aspx page, as shown in Listing 9.19:

Listing 9.19: Showing the Code for the Code-Behind File of the Default.aspx Page

In VB

```
Partial Class _Default
    Inherits System.Web.UI.Page
    Public Class Customer
         Public Key As Integer
        Public Name As String
    End Class
    Public Class Order
        Public Key As Integer
        Public OrderNumber As String
    End Class

    Protected Sub Button1_Click(sender As Object, e As EventArgs) Handles Button1.Click
        Dim customers = New List(Of Customer)(New Customer() {New Customer With {.Key =
         1, .Name = "Neha"}, New Customer With {.Key = 2, .Name = "Amar"}, New Customer
        With {.Key = 3, .Name = "Neeraj"}, New Customer With {.Key = 4, .Name =
        "Priya"}, New Customer With {.Key = 5, .Name = "Jyoti"}})
        Dim orders = New List(Of Order)(New Order() {New Order With {.Key = 1,
    .OrderNumber = "Number 1"}, New Order With {.Key = 2, .OrderNumber = "Number 2"},
    New Order With {.Key = 3, .OrderNumber = "Number 3"}, New Order With {.Key = 4,
    .OrderNumber = "Number 4"}, New Order With {.Key = 5, .OrderNumber = "Number 5"}})
        Dim q = From c In customers _
         Join o In orders On c.Key Equals o.Key _
         Select New With {Key c.Name, Key o.OrderNumber}
```

```
            For Each i In q
                ListBox1.Items.Add(i.OrderNumber.ToString() & " " & i.Name)
            Next i
        End Sub
    End Class
```

In C#

```
using System;
using System.Collections.Generic;
using System.Linq;
using System.Web;
using System.Web.UI;
using System.Web.UI.WebControls;
public partial class _Default : System.Web.UI.Page
{
    protected void Page_Load(object sender, EventArgs e)
    {

    }
    public class Customer
    {
        public int Key;
        public string Name;
    }
    public class Order
    {
        public int Key;
        public string OrderNumber;
    }
    protected void Button1_Click(object sender, EventArgs e)
    {
        var customers = new List<Customer>()
         {
                new Customer {Key = 1, Name = "Neha" },
                new Customer {Key = 2, Name = "Amar" },
                new Customer {Key = 3, Name = "Neeraj" },
                new Customer {Key = 4, Name = "Priya" },
                new Customer {Key = 5, Name = "Jyoti" }
         };
         var orders = new List<Order>()
         {
                new Order {Key = 1, OrderNumber = "Number 1" },
                new Order {Key = 2, OrderNumber = "Number 2" },
                new Order {Key = 3, OrderNumber = "Number 3" },
                new Order {Key = 4, OrderNumber = "Number 4" },
                new Order {Key = 5, OrderNumber = "Number 5" }
         };
        var q = from c in customers
               join o in orders on c.Key equals o.Key
               select new { c.Name, o.OrderNumber };
        foreach (var i in q)
        {
            ListBox1.Items.Add(i.OrderNumber.ToString() + " " + i.Name);
        }
    }
}
```

In Listing 9.19, the Customer data and the Order data are joined using the `Join` method. Now, let's run the application by pressing the F5 key on the keyboard. The output of the application after clicking the Button button is as shown in Figure 9.14:

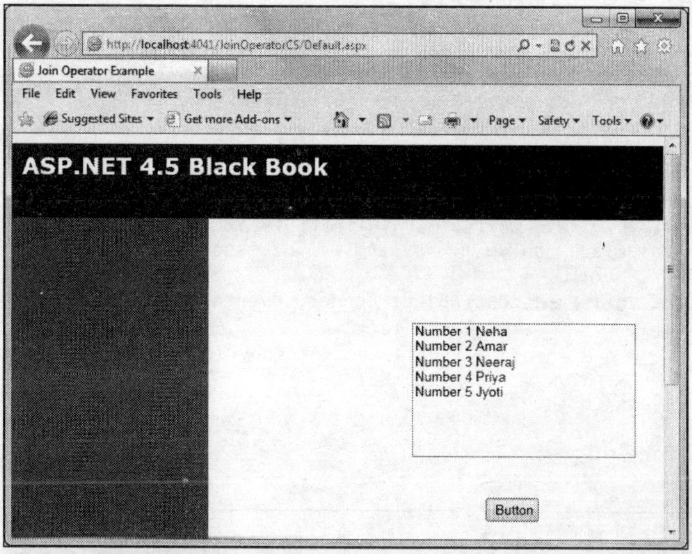

Figure 9.14: Displaying the Output of the JoinOperatorCS Application

Using the Grouping Operators

You can use the group query results based on some key value. The `GroupBy` method is used to group the query in LINQ based on a common key. Now, let's create an application in which you can group your query using the `GroupBy` method. Create a website and save it as `GroupOperator`. You can find the code for this application in the GroupOperatorCS (for C#) and GroupOperatorVB (for VB) folders.

To add the required controls, you can find the code for the Default.aspx page in Listing 9.20:

Listing 9.20: Showing the Code for the Default.aspx Page

In VB

```
<%@ Page Language="VB" AutoEventWireup="false" CodeFile="Default.aspx.vb"
  Inherits="_Default" %>
<!DOCTYPE html>
<html xmlns="http://www.w3.org/1999/xhtml">
<head id="Head1" runat="server">
    <title>Using GroupBy Method</title>
        <link href="StyleSheet.css" rel="stylesheet" type="text/css" />
</head>
<body>
  <form id="form1" runat="server">
        <div id="header">
                <h1>
                        ASP.NET 4.5 Black Book
                </h1>
        </div>
        <div id="sidebar">
                <div id="nav">
                         
                </div>
        </div>
```

```
        <div id="content">
                <div class ="itemContent">
                        <br />
                        <br />
                        Displays data by using GroupBy method<br />
                         <br />
                         <asp:ListBox ID="ListBox1" runat="server" Height="150px"
                        style="margin-left: 120px"
                        Width="295px"></asp:ListBox>
                        <br />
                        <br />
                        <asp:Button ID="Button1" runat="server"
                        style="margin-left: 152px" Text="Display" Width="105px" />
                        <br />
                </div>
                <div id="footer">
                        <p class="left">
                                All content copyright &copy; Kogent Solutions Inc.</p>
                </div>
        </div>
    </form>
</body>
</html>
```

In C#

```
<%@ Page Language="C#" AutoEventWireup="true" CodeFile="Default.aspx.cs"
  Inherits="_Default" %>
<!DOCTYPE html>
<html xmlns="http://www.w3.org/1999/xhtml">
<head id="Head1" runat="server">
    <title>Using GroupBy Method</title>
        <link href="StyleSheet.css" rel="stylesheet" type="text/css" />
</head>
<body>
  <form id="form1" runat="server">
        <div id="header">
                <h1>
                        ASP.NET 4.5 Black Book
                </h1>
        </div>
        <div id="sidebar">
                <div id="nav">
                         
                         
                </div>
        </div>
        <div id="content">
                <div class ="itemContent">
                        <br />
                        <br />
                        Displays data by using GroupBy method<br />
                         <br />
                         <asp:ListBox ID="ListBox1" runat="server" Height="150px"
                        style="margin-left: 120px" Width="295px"></asp:ListBox>
                        <br />
                        <br />
                        <asp:Button ID="Button1" runat="server" OnClick="Button1_Click"
                        style="margin-left: 152px" Text="Display" Width="105px" />
                        <br />
                </div>
```

```
                <div id="footer">
                        <p class="left">
                                All content copyright &copy; Kogent Solutions Inc. </p>
                </div>
        </div>
   </form>
</body>
</html>
```

After modifying the code in the source file, change the code in the code-behind file of the Default.aspx page, as shown in Listing 9.21:

Listing 9.21: Showing the Code for the Code-Behind File of the Default.aspx Page

In VB

```
Partial Class _Default
    Inherits System.Web.UI.Page
    Protected Sub Button1_Click(sender As Object, e As EventArgs) Handles Button1.Click
        Dim words() As String = {"apple", "banana", "pineapple", "apricot", "papaya",
         "blueberry", "abascus", "cheery", "parrot", "black"}
        Dim GroupWords = From w In words Group By w.First() Into Group
        For Each Group In GroupWords
            ListBox1.Items.Add("Words that starts from letter: " &
                 Group.First.ToString())
            For Each w In Group.Group
                ListBox1.Items.Add(w)
            Next w
        Next Group
    End Sub
End Class
```

In C#

```
using System;
using System.Collections.Generic;
using System.Linq;
using System.Web;
using System.Web.UI;
using System.Web.UI.WebControls;
public partial class _Default : System.Web.UI.Page
{
    protected void Page_Load(object sender, EventArgs e)
    {
    }
    protected void Button1_Click(object sender, EventArgs e)
    {
        string[] words = { "apple", "banana", "pineapple", "apricot", "papaya",
         "blueberry", "abascus", "cheery", "parrot", "black" };
        var GroupWords = from w in words
        group w by w[0] into g
        select new { FirstLetter = g.Key, Words = g };
        foreach (var g in GroupWords)
        {
                ListBox1.Items.Add("Words that starts from
                letter:"+g.FirstLetter.ToString());
                foreach (var w in g.Words)
                {
                        ListBox1.Items.Add(w);
                }
        }
    }
}
```

NOTE

In the preceding code for VB, Grouping is done by using the First() function, whereas in C# you are using index to group words on the basis of the first letter.

Now, let's run the application by pressing the F5 key on the keyboard. When you click the Display button, the output of the application is as shown in Figure 9.15:

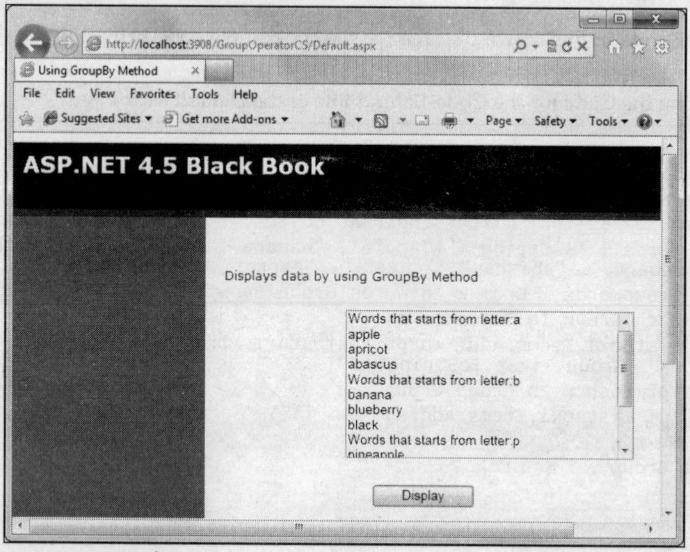

Figure 9.15: Displaying the Output of the GroupOperatorCS Application

Using the Partitioning Operators

The Partitioning operators are useful to navigate easily in the application through your query. The `Take` and `Skip` methods are the Partitioning operators used in LINQ. The Skip method skips the specified number of elements from the input sequence starting from the beginning of the sequence, and returns the rest of the sequence. The `Take` method returns the specified number of elements from the input sequence, from the beginning of the sequence. Let's create an application in which you can use the Partitioning operators. Create a website and save it as `PartioningOperator`. You can find the code for this application in the PartioningOperatorCS (for C#) and PartioningOperatorVB (for VB) folders. To add the required controls, you can find the code for the Default.aspx page in Listing 9.22:

Listing 9.22: Showing the Code for the Default.aspx Page

In VB

```
<%@ Page Language="VB" AutoEventWireup="false" CodeFile="Default.aspx.vb"
   Inherits="_Default" %>
<!DOCTYPE html>
<html xmlns="http://www.w3.org/1999/xhtml">
<head id="Head1" runat="server">
     <title>Using Partioning Operators</title>
   <link href="StyleSheet.css" rel="stylesheet" type="text/css" />
</head>
<body>
   <form id="form1" runat="server">
          <div id="header">
                 <h1>
                        ASP.NET 4.5 Black Book
                 </h1>
```

```
        </div>
        <div id="sidebar">
                <div id="nav">
                         
                </div>
        </div>
        <div id="content">
                <div class ="itemContent">
                Displays data in Listbox by using partioning operators<br/>
                <asp:ListBox ID="ListBox1" runat="server" Height="211px"
                style="margin-left: 199px; margin-top: 91px"
                Width="209px"></asp:ListBox>
                <br />
                <asp:Button ID="Button1" runat="server" style="margin-left: 211px"
                Text="Display" Width="108px"/>
                </div>
                <div id="footer">
                        <p class="left">
                                All content copyright &copy; Kogent Solutions Inc.</p>
                </div>
        </div>
   </form>
</body>
</html>
```

In C#

```
<%@ Page Language="C#" AutoEventWireup="true" CodeFile="Default.aspx.cs"
  Inherits="_Default" %>
<!DOCTYPE html>
<html xmlns="http://www.w3.org/1999/xhtml">
<head id="Head1" runat="server">
    <title>Using Partioning Operators</title>
  <link href="StyleSheet.css" rel="stylesheet" type="text/css" />
</head>
<body>
  <form id="form1" runat="server">
        <div id="header">
                <h1>
                        ASP.NET 4.5 Black Book
                </h1>
        </div>
        <div id="sidebar">
                <div id="nav">
                         
                </div>
        </div>
        <div id="content">
                <div class ="itemContent">
                Displays data in Listbox by using partioning operators
                <asp:ListBox ID="ListBox1" runat="server" Height="211px"
        style="margin-left: 199px; margin-top: 91px" Width="209px"></asp:ListBox>
                <br />
                <asp:Button ID="Button1" runat="server" style="margin-left: 211px"
                Text="Display" Width="108px" OnClick="Button1_Click"/>
                </div>
                <div id="footer">
                        <p class="left">
                                All content copyright &copy; Kogent Solutions Inc.</p>
                </div>
```

```
            </div>
        </form>
    </body>
    </html>
```

After modifying the code in the source file, change the code in the code-behind file of the Default.aspx page, as shown in Listing 9.23:

Listing 9.23: Showing the Code for the Code-Behind File of the Default.aspx Page

In VB

```
Partial Class _Default
    Inherits System.Web.UI.Page
    Protected Sub Button1_Click(sender As Object, e As EventArgs) Handles Button1.Click
        Dim presidents() As String = {"Adams", "Arthur", "Buchanan", "Bush", "Carter",
         "Cleveland", "Clinton", "Coolidge", "Eisenhower", "Fillmore", "Ford",
         "Grafiled", "Grant", "Harrison", "Hoover", "Lincoln", "Washington", "Wilson",
         "Tyler", "Polk", "Nixon", "Truman"}
        Dim PageSize As Integer = 5
        Dim numberPages As Integer = CInt(Fix(Math.Ceiling(presidents.Count() /
         CDbl(PageSize))))
        For page As Integer = 0 To numberPages - 1
            ListBox1.Items.Add("Page " & page & ":")
            Dim names = (From p In presidents _
             Order By p Descending _
             Select p).Skip(page * PageSize).Take(PageSize)
            For Each name In names
                ListBox1.Items.Add(name)
            Next name
        Next page
    End Sub
End Class
```

In C#

```
using System;
using System.Collections.Generic;
using System.Linq;
using System.Web;
using System.Web.UI;
using System.Web.UI.WebControls;
public partial class _Default : System.Web.UI.Page
{
    protected void Page_Load(object sender, EventArgs e)
    {

    }
    protected void Button1_Click(object sender, EventArgs e)
    {
        string[] presidents = {"Adams", "Arthur", "Buchanan", "Bush",
         "Carter","Cleveland", "Clinton", "Coolidge", "Eisenhower", "Fillmore",
         "Ford","Grafiled", "Grant", "Harrison", "Hoover", "Lincoln",
         "Washington","Wilson", "Tyler", "Polk", "Nixon", "Truman"};
        int PageSize = 5;
        int numberPages = (int)Math.Ceiling(presidents.Count() / (double)PageSize);
        for (int page = 0; page < numberPages; page++)
        {
            ListBox1.Items.Add("Page " + page + ":");
            var names = (from p in presidents
                         orderby p descending
                         select p).Skip(page * PageSize).Take(PageSize);
            foreach (var name in names)
```

```
                {
                    ListBox1.Items.Add(name);
                }
            }
        }
    }
```

Now, let's run the application by pressing the F5 key on the keyboard. When you click the Display button, the output of the application is as shown in Figure 9.16:

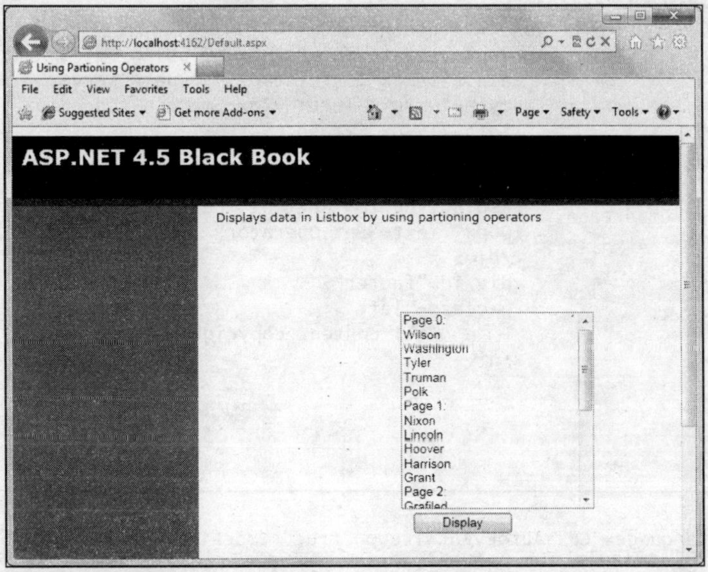

Figure 9.16: Displaying the Output of the PartioningOperatorCS Application

Using the Set Operators

The Set operators in LINQ are used to perform the mathematical set-type operations on the sequences. There are four different types of Set operators used in LINQ, Distinct, Union, Intersect, and Except. You have already learned about them in the *In Depth* section of the chapter. In this section, you learn about the `Intersect` method, which returns the set intersection of the two source sequences. Let's create an application in which you can use the Intersect method. Create a website and save it as SetOperator. You can find the code for this application in the SetOperatorCS (for C#) and SetOperatorVB (for VB) folders.

To add the required controls, you can find the code for the Default.aspx page in Listing 9.24:

Listing 9.24: Showing the Code for the Default.aspx Page

In VB

```
<%@ Page Language="VB" AutoEventWireup="false" CodeFile="Default.aspx.vb"
  Inherits="_Default" %>
<!DOCTYPE html>
<html xmlns="http://www.w3.org/1999/xhtml">
<head id="Head1" runat="server">
    <title>Using Set Operator</title>
        <link href="StyleSheet.css" rel="stylesheet" type="text/css" />
        </head>
<body>
  <form id="form1" runat="server">
        <div id="header">
              <h1>
```

```
                ASP.NET 4.5 Black Book
            </h1>
        </div>
        <div id="sidebar">
            <div id="nav">
                 
            </div>
        </div>
        <div id="content">
            <div class ="itemContent">
                Displays data in ListBox by using Set Operator <br/>
                <asp:ListBox ID="ListBox1" runat="server"
                style="margin-left: 97px; margin-top: 81px" Height="97px"
                Width="154px"></asp:ListBox>
                <br />
                <br />
                <asp:Button ID="Button1" runat="server" style="margin-left:
                100px" Text="Set Operator" />
                </div>
                <div id="footer">
                <p class="left">
                    All content copyright &copy; Kogent Solutions Inc.</p>
                </div>
            </div>
    </form>
</body>
</html>
```

In C#

```
<%@ Page Language="C#" AutoEventWireup="true" CodeFile="Default.aspx.cs"
  Inherits="_Default" %>
<!DOCTYPE html>
<html xmlns="http://www.w3.org/1999/xhtml">
<head id="Head1" runat="server">
    <title>Using Set Operator</title>
        <link href="StyleSheet.css" rel="stylesheet" type="text/css" />
</head>
<body>
  <form id="form1" runat="server">
        <div id="header">
            <h1>
                ASP.NET 4.5 Black Book
            </h1>
        </div>
        <div id="sidebar">
            <div id="nav">
                 
            </div>
        </div>
        <div id="content">
            <div class ="itemContent">
                Displays data in ListBox by using Set Operator <br />
                <asp:ListBox ID="ListBox1" runat="server"
                style="margin-left: 97px; margin-top: 81px" Height="97px"
                Width="154px"></asp:ListBox>
                <br />
                <br />
                <asp:Button ID="Button1" runat="server" style="margin-left:
                100px" Text="Set Operator" OnClick="Button1_Click"/>
                </div>
                <div id="footer">
                <p class="left">
```

```
                                        All content copyright &copy; Kogent Solutions Inc.</p>
                                </div>
                        </div>
                </form>
        </body>
        </html>
```

After modifying the code in the source file, change the code in the code-behind file of the Default.aspx page, as shown in Listing 9.25:

Listing 9.25: Showing the Code for the Code-Behind File of the Default.aspx Page

In VB

```
Partial Class _Default
    Inherits System.Web.UI.Page
    Protected Sub Button1_Click(sender As Object, e As EventArgs) Handles Button1.Click
        Dim fruits() As String = {"apple", "banana", "peach", "mango"}
        Dim words() As String = {"hello", "peach", "linq", "mango", "set"}
        Dim common = fruits.Intersect(words)
        ListBox1.Items.Add("Common in both arrays: ")
        For Each n In common
            ListBox1.Items.Add(n)
        Next n
    End Sub
End Class
```

In C#

```
using System;
using System.Collections.Generic;
using System.Linq;
using System.Web;
using System.Web.UI;
using System.Web.UI.WebControls;
public partial class _Default : System.Web.UI.Page
{
    protected void Page_Load(object sender, EventArgs e)
    {
    }
    protected void Button1_Click(object sender, EventArgs e)
    {
        string[] fruits = { "apple", "banana", "peach", "mango" };
        string[] words = { "hello", "peach", "linq", "mango", "set" };
        var common = fruits.Intersect(words);
        ListBox1.Items.Add("Common in both arrays: ");
        foreach (var n in common)
        {
            ListBox1.Items.Add(n);
        }
    }
}
```

Now, let's run the application by pressing the F5 key on the keyboard. When you click the Set Operator button, the output of the application is as shown in Figure 9.17:

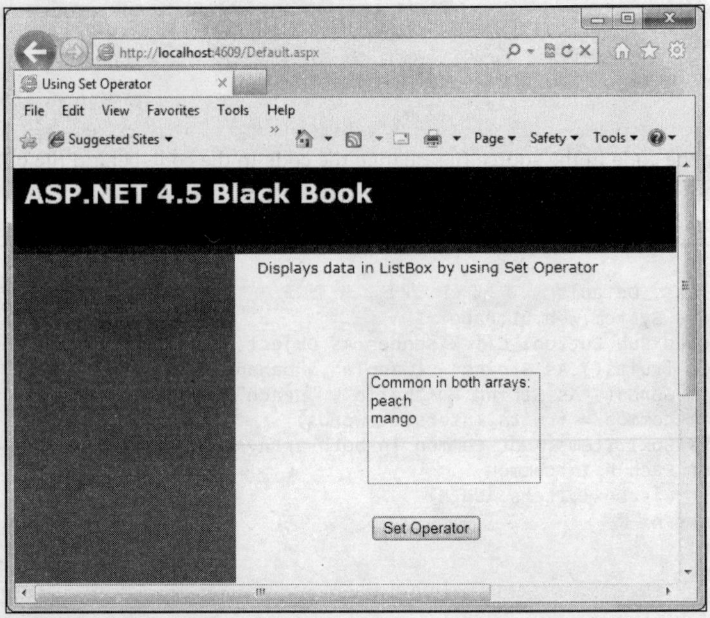

Figure 9.17: Displaying the Output of the SetOperatorCS Application

Using the Aggregate Operators

The Aggregate operators are used to calculate a value. The different Aggregate operators are `Count`, `Sum`, `Min`, `Max`, `Average`, and `Aggregate`. You have already learned about them in the *In Depth* section of this chapter. The `Aggregate` operators do not return a sequence. It returns only a single value. Now, let's create an application, `AggregateOperators`, in which you can use the Aggregate operators. You can find the code for this application in the AggregateOperatorsCS (for C#) and AggregateOperatorsVB (for VB) folders.

To add the required controls, you can find the code for the Default.aspx page in Listing 9.26:

Listing 9.26: Showing the Code for the Default.aspx Page

In VB

```
<%@ Page Language="VB" AutoEventWireup="false" CodeFile="Default.aspx.vb"
  Inherits="_Default" %>
<!DOCTYPE html>
<html xmlns="http://www.w3.org/1999/xhtml">
<head id="Head1" runat="server">
    <title>Using Aggregate operators</title>
         <link href="StyleSheet.css" rel="stylesheet" type="text/css" />
</head>
<body>
   <form id="form1" runat="server">
         <div id="header">
                 <h1>
                         ASP.NET 4.5 Black Book
                 </h1>
         </div>
         <div id="sidebar">
                 <div id="nav">
                          
                 </div>
         </div>
```

```
        <div id="content">
                <div class ="itemContent">
                        <asp:ListBox ID="ListBox1" runat="server" Font-Bold="True"
                        Font-Italic="True" ForeColor="Black" Height="179px"
                        style="margin-left: 142px; margin-top: 91px"
                        Width="333px"></asp:ListBox>
                        <br />
                        <br />
                        <asp:Button ID="Button1" runat="server"
                        style="margin-left: 189px" Text="Display" Width="124px" />
                </div>
                <div id="footer">
                        <p class="left">
                                All content copyright &copy; Kogent Solutions Inc.</p>
                </div>
        </div>
  </form>
</body>
</html>
```

In C#

```
<%@ Page Language="C#" AutoEventWireup="true" CodeFile="Default.aspx.cs"
  Inherits="_Default" %>
<!DOCTYPE html>
<html xmlns="http://www.w3.org/1999/xhtml">
<head id="Head1" runat="server">
    <title>Using Aggregate operators </title>
        <link href="StyleSheet.css" rel="stylesheet" type="text/css" />
</head>
<body>
  <form id="form1" runat="server">
        <div id="header">
                <h1>
                        ASP.NET 4.5 Black Book
                </h1>
        </div>
        <div id="sidebar">
                <div id="nav">
                         
                </div>
        </div>
        <div id="content">
                <div class ="itemContent">
                        <asp:ListBox ID="ListBox1" runat="server" Font-Bold="True"
                        Font-Italic="True" ForeColor="Black" Height="179px"
                        style="margin-left: 142px; margin-top: 91px"
                        Width="333px"></asp:ListBox>
                        <br />
                        <br />
                        <asp:Button ID="Button1" runat="server" OnClick="Button1_Click"
                        style="margin-left: 189px" Text="Display" Width="124px" />
                </div>
                <div id="footer">
                        <p class="left">
                                All content copyright &copy; Kogent Solutions Inc.</p>
                </div>
        </div>
  </form>
</body>
</html>
```

After modifying the code in the source file, change the code in the code-behind file of the Default.aspx page, as shown in Listing 9.27:

Listing 9.27: Showing the Code for the Code-Behind File of the Default.aspx Page

In VB

```
Partial Class _Default
    Inherits System.Web.UI.Page
    Protected Sub Button1_Click(sender As Object, e As EventArgs) Handles Button1.Click
     Dim numbers() As Integer = {5, 4, 1, 3, 9, 10, 35, 29, 20, 87, 100, 26, 42, 78, 91}
        Dim OddNumbers As Integer = numbers.Count(Function(n) n Mod 2 = 1)
        ListBox1.Items.Add("The Count of odd Numbers are: " & OddNumbers)
        Dim numSum As Double = numbers.Sum()
        ListBox1.Items.Add("The sum of numbers is :" & numSum)
        Dim minNum As Integer = numbers.Min()
        ListBox1.Items.Add("Minimum number is:" & minNum)
        Dim maxNum As Integer = numbers.Max()
        ListBox1.Items.Add("Maximum number is :" & maxNum)
        Dim avgNum As Double = numbers.Average()
        ListBox1.Items.Add("Average of numbers is : " & avgNum)
    End Sub
End Class
```

In C#

```
using System;
using System.Collections.Generic;
using System.Linq;
using System.Web;
using System.Web.UI;
using System.Web.UI.WebControls;
public partial class _Default : System.Web.UI.Page
{
    protected void Page_Load(object sender, EventArgs e)
    {

    }
    protected void Button1_Click(object sender, EventArgs e)
    {
        int[] numbers = { 5, 4, 1, 3, 9, 10, 35, 29, 20, 87, 100, 26, 42, 78, 91 };
        int OddNumbers = numbers.Count(n => n % 2 == 1);
        ListBox1.Items.Add("The Count of odd Numbers are: " + OddNumbers);
        double numSum = numbers.Sum();
        ListBox1.Items.Add("The sum of numbers is :" + numSum);
        int minNum = numbers.Min();
        ListBox1.Items.Add("Minimum number is:" + minNum);
        int maxNum = numbers.Max();
        ListBox1.Items.Add("Maximum number is :" + maxNum);
        double avgNum = numbers.Average();
        ListBox1.Items.Add("Average of numbers is : " + avgNum);
    }
}
```

Now, let's run the application by pressing the F5 key on the keyboard. The output of the application is as shown in Figure 9.18:

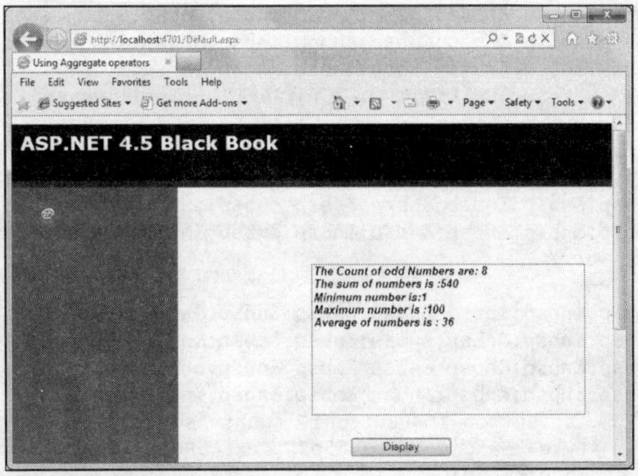

Figure 9.18: Displaying the Output of the AggregateOperatorsCS Application

Using the Conversion Operators

The Conversion operators are used to change the type of input objects. They provide a simple and convenient way for converting sequences to other collection types. You have already learned about the different Conversion operators in the In Depth section of this chapter. In this section, you learn about the `ToList` Conversion operators. Let's create an application in which you can use the `ToList` Conversion operators. Create a website and save it as `ConversionOperator`. You can find the code for this application in the ConversionOperatorCS (for C#) and ConversionOperatorVB (for VB) folders. You can find the code for the Default.aspx page to add the required controls in Listing 9.28:

Listing 9.28: Showing the Code for the Default.aspx Page

In VB

```
<%@ Page Language="VB" AutoEventWireup="false" CodeFile="Default.aspx.vb"
  Inherits="_Default" %>
<!DOCTYPE html>
<html xmlns="http://www.w3.org/1999/xhtml">
<head id="Head1" runat="server">
    <title>Using Conversion Operator</title>
         <link href="StyleSheet.css" rel="stylesheet" type="text/css" />
</head>
<body>
  <form id="form1" runat="server">
         <div id="header">
                <h1>
                       ASP.NET 4.5 Black Book
                </h1>
         </div>
         <div id="sidebar">
                <div id="nav">
                        
                </div>
         </div>
         <div id="content">
                <div class ="itemContent">
               <asp:Label ID="Label1" runat="server"
                   Text=" Display data by using the OfType Operator"></asp:Label>
                <br />
            
```

```
              
              
         
                    <asp:ListBox ID="ListBox1" runat="server"
                Height="144px"  Width="232px"></asp:ListBox>
             
              
              
           
                <br />
                <br />
              
              
              
          
                <asp:Button ID="Button1" runat="server"
                style="margin-left: 85px" Text="For String " Width="94px" />
                  
                <asp:Button ID="Button2" runat="server" Text="For Numeric"
                Width="111px" />
                </div>
                <div id="footer">
                        <p class="left">
                                All content copyright &copy; Kogent Solutions Inc.</p>
                </div>
        </div>
  </form>
</body>
</html>
```

In C#

```
<%@ Page Language="C#" AutoEventWireup="true" CodeFile="Default.aspx.cs"
  Inherits="_Default" %>
<!DOCTYPE html>
<html xmlns="http://www.w3.org/1999/xhtml">
<head id="Head1" runat="server">
    <title>Using Conversion Operator</title>
        <link href="StyleSheet.css" rel="stylesheet" type="text/css" />
</head>
<body>
  <form id="form1" runat="server">
        <div id="header">
                <h1>
                        ASP.NET 4.5 Black Book
                </h1>
        </div>
        <div id="sidebar">
                <div id="nav">
                         
                </div>
        </div>
        <div id="content">
        <div class ="itemContent">Displays data by using OfType operator <br/>
            <asp:ListBox ID="ListBox1" runat="server"
                Height="144px"
        style="margin-left: 314px; margin-top: 75px" Width="232px"></asp:ListBox><br />
                <br />
                <br />
```

```
             
              
              
              
                <asp:Button ID="Button1" runat="server" style="margin-left: 85px"
                Text="For String " Width="94px" OnClick="Button1_Click"/>
                <asp:Button ID="Button2" runat="server" style="margin-left: 40px;
                margin-top: 28px" Text="For Numeric" Width="111px"
                OnClick="Button2_Click" />
                </div>
                <div id="footer">
                        <p class="left">
                                All content copyright &copy; Kogent Solutions Inc.</p>
                </div>
        </div>
   </form>
</body>
</html>
```

After modifying the code in the source file, change the code in the code-behind file of the Default.aspx page, as shown in Listing 9.29:

Listing 9.29: Showing the Code for the Code-Behind File of the Default.aspx Page

In VB

```
Partial Class _Default
    Inherits System.Web.UI.Page
    Dim list() As Object = {"hello", 34, "mango", 90, "nice", "example", 7.3D, 8.0F,
   "linq"}
    Protected Sub Button1_Click(sender As Object, e As EventArgs) Handles Button1.Click
        ListBox1.Items.Clear()
        Dim str = List.OfType(Of String)()
        ListBox1.Items.Add("The String Characters are: ")
        For Each s In str
            ListBox1.Items.Add(s)
        Next s
    End Sub
    Protected Sub Button2_Click(sender As Object, e As EventArgs) Handles Button2.Click
        ListBox1.Items.Clear()
        Dim num = List.OfType(Of Integer)()
        ListBox1.Items.Add("The Numeric Characters are: ")
        For Each n In num
            ListBox1.Items.Add(n.ToString())
        Next n
    End Sub
End Class
```

In C#

```
using System;
using System.Collections.Generic;
using System.Linq;
using System.Web;
using System.Web.UI;
using System.Web.UI.WebControls;
public partial class _Default : System.Web.UI.Page
{
    object[] list = { "hello", 34, "mango", 90, "nice", "example", 7.3m, 8.0f, "linq" };
    protected void Page_Load(object sender, EventArgs e)
    {

    }
    protected void Button1_Click(object sender, EventArgs e)
    {
        ListBox1.Items.Clear();
```

```
            var str = list.OfType<string>();
            ListBox1.Items.Add("The String Characters are: ");
            foreach (var s in str)
            {
                ListBox1.Items.Add(s);
            }
        }
        protected void Button2_Click(object sender, EventArgs e)
        {
            ListBox1.Items.Clear();
            var num = list.OfType<int>();
            ListBox1.Items.Add("The Numeric Characters are: ");
            foreach (var n in num)
            {
                ListBox1.Items.Add(n.ToString());
            }
        }
    }
```

In the preceding code, different sets of characters are passed in the query. In the output, the string and the numeric characters are sorted by using the `OfType` method. Now, let's run the application by pressing the F5 key on the keyboard. The output of the application is as shown in Figure 9.19:

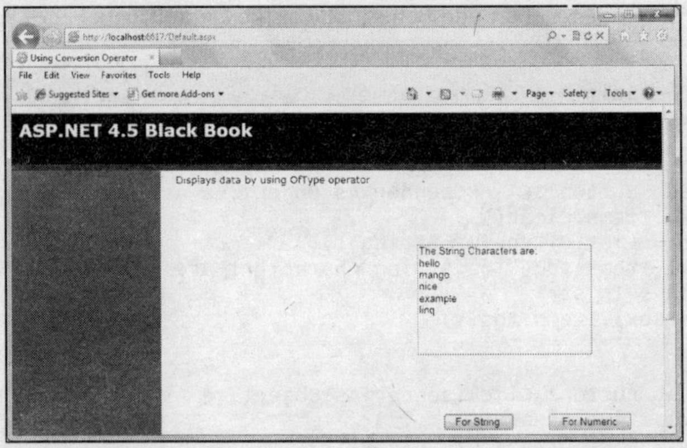

Figure 9.19: Displaying the String Data from the List

When you click the For String button, the list box displays the string data entered into the list by using the `ToList` operator. Similarly, when you click the For Numeric button, the listbox displays the numeric data entered into the list, as shown in Figure 9.20:

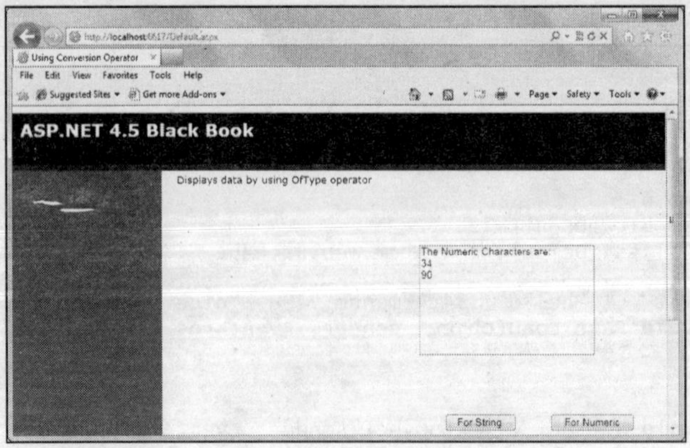

Figure 9.20: Displaying the Numeric Data from the List

Using the Generation Operators

The Generation operators enable you to generate sequence. The different Generation operators are `Range`, `Empty`, and `Repeat`. You have already learned about them in the *In Depth* section of this chapter. In this section, you learn about their practical implementation. Now, let's create an application, `GenerationOperators`, in which you can use the Generation operators. You can find the code for this application in the GenerationOperatorsCS (for C#) and GenerationOperatorsVB (for VB) folders. To add the required controls, you can find the code for the Default.aspx page in Listing 9.30:

Listing 9.30: Showing the Code for the Default.aspx Page

In VB

```
<%@ Page Language="VB" AutoEventWireup="false" CodeFile="Default.aspx.vb"
  Inherits="_Default" %>
<!DOCTYPE html>
<html xmlns="http://www.w3.org/1999/xhtml">
<head id="Head1" runat="server">
   <title>Using Generation Operators </title>
        <link href="StyleSheet.css" rel="stylesheet" type="text/css" />
</head>
<body>
  <form id="form1" runat="server">
        <div id="header">
                <h1>
                        ASP.NET 4.5 Black Book
                </h1>
        </div>
        <div id="sidebar">
                <div id="nav">
                         
                </div>
        </div>
        <div id="content">
                <div class ="itemContent">
                Displays data by using Generic Operators
                <br/>
                <asp:ListBox ID="ListBox1" runat="server" Height="290px"
                style="margin-left: 149px; margin-right: 85px; margin-top: 44px"
                Width="190px"></asp:ListBox>
                <br />
                <br />
                <asp:Button ID="Button1" runat="server"
                style="margin-left: 185px" Text="Display" Width="131px" />
                </div>
                <div id="footer">
                        <p class="left">
                        All content copyright &copy; Kogent Solutions Inc.</p>
                </div>
        </div>
  </form>
</body>
</html>
```

In C#

```
<%@ Page Language="C#" AutoEventWireup="true" CodeFile="Default.aspx.cs"
  Inherits="_Default" %>
<!DOCTYPE html>
<html xmlns="http://www.w3.org/1999/xhtml">
<head id="Head1" runat="server">
    <title>Using Generation Operators </title>
        <link href="StyleSheet.css" rel="stylesheet" type="text/css" />
</head>
<body>
  <form id="form1" runat="server">
        <div id="header">
                <h1>
                        ASP.NET 4.5 Black Book
                </h1>
        </div>
        <div id="sidebar">
                <div id="nav">
                         
                </div>
        </div>
        <div id="content">
                <div class ="itemContent">
                Displays data by using Generic Operators
                <br/>
                <asp:ListBox ID="ListBox1" runat="server" Height="290px"
                style="margin-left: 149px; margin-right: 85px; margin-top: 44px"
                Width="190px"></asp:ListBox>
                <br />
                <br />
                <asp:Button ID="Button1" runat="server" OnClick="Button1_Click"
                style="margin-left: 185px" Text="Display" Width="131px" />
                </div>
                <div id="footer">
                        <p class="left">
                        All content copyright &copy; Kogent Solutions Inc.</p>
                </div>
        </div>
  </form>
</body>
</html>
```

After modifying the code in the source file, let us now change the code in the code-behind file of the Default.aspx page, as shown in Listing 9.31:

Listing 9.31: Showing the Code for the Code-Behind File of the Default.aspx Page

In VB

```
Partial Class _Default
    Inherits System.Web.UI.Page
    Protected Sub Button1_Click(sender As Object, e As EventArgs) Handles Button1.Click
        Dim numbers = From n In Enumerable.Range(1, 50)
        Select New With {Key .Number = n, Key .OddEven = If(n Mod 2 = 1, "odd", "even")}
        For Each n In numbers
            ListBox1.Items.Add("The number is " & n.Number & n.OddEven)
        Next n
    End Sub
End Class
```

In C#

```
using System;
using System.Collections.Generic;
using System.Linq;
using System.Web;
using System.Web.UI;
using System.Web.UI.WebControls;
public partial class _Default : System.Web.UI.Page
{
    protected void Page_Load(object sender, EventArgs e)
    {
    }
    protected void Button1_Click(object sender, EventArgs e)
    {
            var numbers = from n in Enumerable.Range(1, 50)
                  select new { Number = n, OddEven = n % 2 == 1 ? "odd" : "even" };
        foreach (var n in numbers)
        {
            ListBox1.Items.Add("The number is " + n.Number + n.OddEven);
        }
    }
}
```

Now, let's run the application by pressing the F5 key on the keyboard. When you click the Display button, the output of the application is as shown in Figure 9.21:

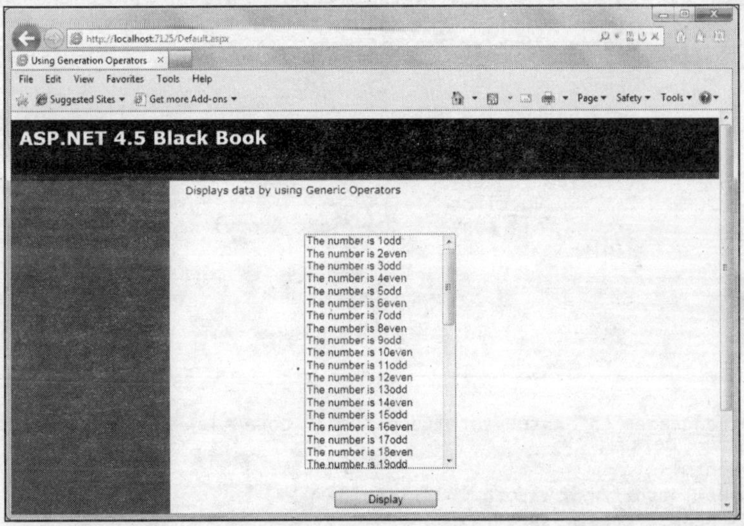

Figure 9.21: Displaying the Output of the GenerationOperatorsCS Application

Using the Zip Operator

The Zip operator parses the elements at the same index position in each sequence. When one of the sequences finishes reading its elements, the result is returned. You have already learned about them in the *In Depth* section of this chapter. In this section, you learn about their practical implementation. Now, let's create an application, `ZipOperators`, in which you can use the Zip operator. You can find the code for this application in the ZipOperatorsCS (for C#) and ZipOperatorsVB (for VB) folders. To add the required controls, you can find the code for the Default.aspx page in Listing 9.32:

Listing 9.32: Showing the Code for the Default.aspx Page

In VB

```
<%@ Page Language="VB" AutoEventWireup="false" CodeFile="Default.aspx.vb"
  Inherits="_Default" %>
<!DOCTYPE html>
<html xmlns="http://www.w3.org/1999/xhtml">
<head id="Head1" runat="server">
   <title>Using Zip Operator</title>
<link href="StyleSheet.css" rel="stylesheet" type="text/css" />
</head>
<body>
  <form id="form1" runat="server">
        <div id="header">
                <h1>
                        ASP.NET 4.5 Black Book
                </h1>
        </div>
        <div id="sidebar">
                <div id="nav">
                         
                </div>
        </div>
        <div id="content">
                <div class ="itemContent">
                Displays data by using Zip Operators
                <br/>
                <asp:ListBox ID="ListBox1" runat="server" Height="290px"
                style="margin-left: 149px; margin-right: 85px; margin-top: 44px"
                Width="479px"></asp:ListBox>
                <br />
                <br />
                <asp:Button ID="Button1" runat="server" OnClick="Button1_Click"
                style="margin-left: 185px" Text="Display" Width="131px" />
                </div>
                <div id="footer">
                        <p class="left">
                        All content copyright &copy; Kogent Solutions Inc.</p>
                </div>
        </div>
  </form>
</body>
</html>
```

In C#

```
<%@ Page Language="C#" AutoEventWireup="true" CodeFile="Default.aspx.cs"
  Inherits="_Default" %>
<!DOCTYPE html>
<html xmlns="http://www.w3.org/1999/xhtml">
<head id="Head1" runat="server">
    <title>Using Zip Operator</title>
<link href="StyleSheet.css" rel="stylesheet" type="text/css" />
</head>
<body>
  <form id="form1" runat="server">
        <div id="header">
                <h1>
                        ASP.NET 4.5 Black Book
                </h1>
        </div>
        <div id="sidebar">
                <div id="nav">
                         
```

```
                </div>
        </div>
        <div id="content">
                <div class ="itemContent">
                Displays data by using Zip Operators
                <br/>
                <asp:ListBox ID="ListBox1" runat="server" Height="290px"
                style="margin-left: 149px; margin-right: 85px; margin-top: 44px"
                Width="479px"></asp:ListBox>
                <br/>
                <br/>
                <asp:Button ID="Button1" runat="server"  OnClick="Button1_Click"
                style="margin-left: 185px" Text="Display" Width="131px" />
                </div>
                <div id="footer">
                        <p class="left">
                        All content copyright &copy; Kogent Solutions Inc.</p>
                </div>
        </div>
    </form>
</body>
</html>
```

After modifying the code in the source file, let us change the code in the code-behind file of the Default.aspx page, as shown in Listing 9.33:

Listing 9.33: Showing the Code for the Code-Behind File of the Default.aspx Page

In VB

```
Partial Class _Default
    Inherits System.Web.UI.Page
    Protected Sub Button1_Click(sender As Object, e As EventArgs) Handles Button1.Click
        Dim names As String() = New String() {"Ram", "Priya", "Puja", "Rita", "Jhonny",
         "Steve"}
        Dim position As String() = New String() {"Manager", "Team Leader", "Developer",
         "Writer", "Director"}
        Dim years As Integer() = New Integer() {1, 2, 4, 8, 9}
        Dim q = names.Zip(position, Function(a, b) a & " is the " & b & " of the
         company")
        Dim r = q.Zip(years, Function(c, d) c & " with " & d & " years of experience.")
        For Each result In r
            ListBox1.Items.Add(result)
        Next result
    End Sub
End Class
```

In C#

```
using System;
using System.Collections.Generic;
using System.Linq;
using System.Web;
using System.Web.UI;
using System.Web.UI.WebControls;
public partial class _Default : System.Web.UI.Page
{
    protected void Page_Load(object sender, EventArgs e)
    {
    }
    protected void Button1_Click(object sender, EventArgs e)
    {
```

```
        string[] names = new string[] { "Ram", "Priya", "Puja", "Rita", "Jhonny","Steve" };
           string[] position = new string[] { "Manager", "Team Leader",
            "Developer","Writer", "Director" };
           int[] years = new int[] { 1, 2, 4, 8, 9 };
           var q = names.Zip(position, (a, b) => a + " is the " + b + " of the company");
           var r = q.Zip(years, (c, d) => c + " with " + d + " years of experience.");
           foreach (var result in r)
           {
               ListBox1.Items.Add(result);
           }
       }
   }
```

Now, let's run the application by pressing the F5 key on the keyboard. When you click the Display button, the output of the application is as shown in Figure 9.22:

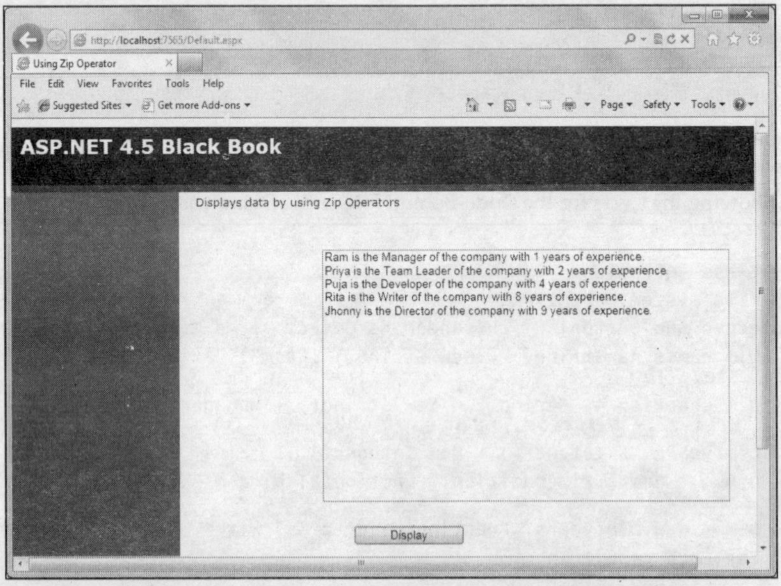

Figure 9.22: Displaying the Output of the ZipOperatorsCS Application

Creating a Simple PLINQ Query

A simple PLINQ query works on a large collection of data. This implies that on a small collection of data, the effect of a PLINQ is not visible. You have already learned about PLINQ in the *In Depth* section of this chapter. In this section, you learn about its practical implementation. Now, let's create an application in which you can use the PLINQ query. Create a website and save it as `PLINQQuery`. You can find the code for this application in the PLINQQueryCS (for C#) and PLINQQueryVB (for VB) folders. To add the required controls, you can find the code for the Default.aspx page in Listing 9.34:

Listing 9.34: Showing the Code for the Default.aspx Page

In VB

```
<%@ Page Language="VB" AutoEventWireup="false" CodeFile="Default.aspx.vb"
  Inherits="_Default" %>
<!DOCTYPE html>
<html xmlns="http://www.w3.org/1999/xhtml">
<head id="Head1" runat="server">
    <title>Using a Simple PLINQ Query</title>
<link href="StyleSheet.css" rel="stylesheet" type="text/css" />
```

```
    </head>
    <body>
       <form id="form1" runat="server">
            <div id="header">
                    <h1>
                            ASP.NET 4.5 Black Book
                    </h1>
            </div>
            <div id="sidebar">
                    <div id="nav">
                             
                    </div>
            </div>
            <div id="content">
                    <div class ="itemContent">
                            Displays data by using PLINQ Query
                            <br />
                   <br />
                            <asp:Label ID="Label1" runat="server" Text="Enter a
                            number"></asp:Label>
                 
                 
               
      <asp:TextBox ID="TextBox1" runat="server"> </asp:TextBox>
                   <br />
                   <br />
           <asp:Label ID="Label2" runat="server" Text="Enter another number">
    </asp:Label>           
                   
            
           <asp:TextBox ID="TextBox2" runat="server"></asp:TextBox>
                   <br />
                   <br />
           <asp:Label ID="Label3" runat="server" Text="Range divided by number">
    </asp:Label>           
                 
     
           <asp:TextBox ID="TextBox3" runat="server"></asp:TextBox><br />
                        
                   <br />
           <br />
                 
                 
                 
           <asp:Button ID="Button1" runat="server" Text="Click Me"
                       Width="130px" />
                   <br />
           <h3>List of numbers: </h3>
                 <asp:ListBox ID="ListBox1" runat="server" Height="199px"
                    Width="155px"></asp:ListBox>
                    </div>
                    <div id="footer">
                            <p class="left">
                            All content copyright &copy; Kogent Solutions Inc.</p>
                    </div>
            </div>
       </form>
    </body>
    </html>
```

In C#

```
    <%@ Page Language="C#" AutoEventWireup="true" CodeFile="Default.aspx.cs"
      Inherits="_Default" %>
    <!DOCTYPE html>
    <html xmlns="http://www.w3.org/1999/xhtml">
```

```
<head id="Head1" runat="server">
    <title>Using a Simple PLINQ Query</title>
<link href="StyleSheet.css" rel="stylesheet" type="text/css" />
</head>
<body>
  <form id="form1" runat="server">
        <div id="header">
                <h1>
                        ASP.NET 4.5 Black Book
                </h1>
        </div>
        <div id="sidebar">
                <div id="nav">
                         
                </div>
        </div>
        <div id="content">
                <div class ="itemContent">
                        Displays data by using PLINQ Query
                        <br />
                <br />
                        <asp:Label ID="Label1" runat="server" Text="Enter a
                                number"></asp:Label>
              
              
              
    <asp:TextBox ID="TextBox1" runat="server"> </asp:TextBox>
                <br />
                <br />
        <asp:Label ID="Label2" runat="server" Text="Enter another number">
  </asp:Label>           
               
        
        <asp:TextBox ID="TextBox2" runat="server"></asp:TextBox>
                <br />
                <br />
        <asp:Label ID="Label3" runat="server" Text="Range divided by number">
  </asp:Label>           
                
        <asp:TextBox ID="TextBox3" runat="server"></asp:TextBox><br />
                     
                <br />
        <br />
             
             
             
        <asp:Button ID="Button1" runat="server" Text="Click Me" OnClick="Button1_Click"
                    Width="130px" />
                <br />
        <h3>List of numbers: </h3>
             <asp:ListBox ID="ListBox1" runat="server" Height="199px"
                Width="155px"></asp:ListBox>
                </div>
                <div id="footer">
                        <p class="left">
                        All content copyright &copy; Kogent Solutions Inc.</p>
                </div>
        </div>
  </form>
</body>
</html>
```

After modifying the code in the source file, let us change the code in the code-behind file of the Default.aspx page, as shown in Listing 9.35:

Listing 9.35: Showing the Code for the CodeFile of the Default.aspx Page

In VB

```
Partial Class _Default
    Inherits System.Web.UI.Page
    Protected Sub Button1_Click(sender As Object, e As EventArgs)
         Handles Button1.Click
        Dim i, j, n As Integer
        i = Convert.ToInt32(TextBox1.Text)
        j = Convert.ToInt32(TextBox2.Text)
        n = Convert.ToInt32(TextBox3.Text)
        Dim source = Enumerable.Range(i, j)
        Dim parallelQuery = From num In source.AsParallel().AsOrdered()
         Where num Mod n = 0 Select num
        For Each v In parallelQuery
          If v<j Then
            ListBox1.Items.Add(v.ToString())
         Endif
        Next v
    End Sub
End Class
```

In C#

```
using System;
using System.Collections.Generic;
using System.Linq;
using System.Web;
using System.Web.UI;
using System.Web.UI.WebControls;
public partial class _Default : System.Web.UI.Page
{
    protected void Page_Load(object sender, EventArgs e)
    {

    }
    protected void Button1_Click(object sender, EventArgs e)
    {
        int i, j, n;
        i = Convert.ToInt32(TextBox1.Text);
        j = Convert.ToInt32(TextBox2.Text);
        n = Convert.ToInt32(TextBox3.Text);
        var source = Enumerable.Range(i, j);
        var parallelQuery = from num in source.AsParallel().AsOrdered()
                            where num % n == 0
                            select num;
        foreach (var v in parallelQuery)
        {
            if (v < j)
            {
                ListBox1.Items.Add(v.ToString());
            }
        }
    }
}
```

Now, let's run the application by pressing the F5 key on the keyboard. Enter a number in the Enter a number text box, which in this case is 23, and then enter a number in the Enter another number text box, which in this case is 54. Enter the number by which you want to divide the range of numbers specified in the first and the second text boxes in the Range divided by number text box, which in this case is 5. Now click the Click Me button, which displays only those numbers that are divisible by the number specified in the Range divided by number text box. The output of the application is as shown in Figure 9.23:

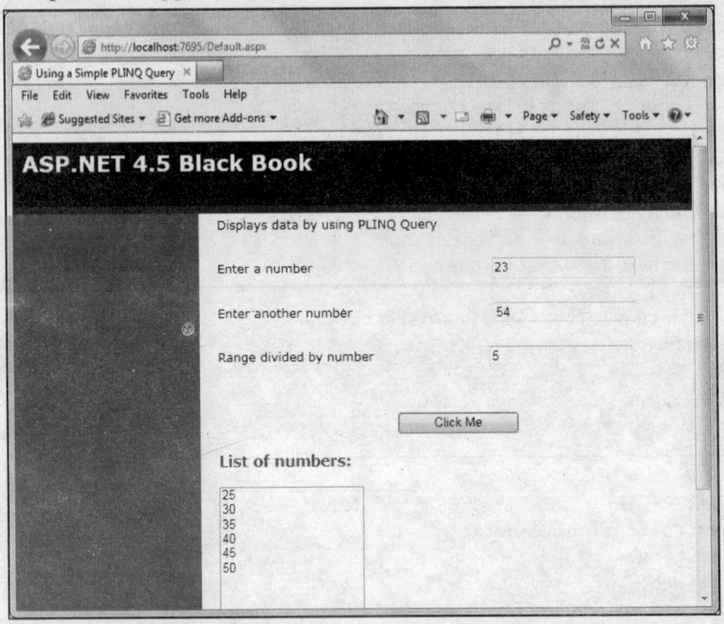

Figure 9.23: Displaying the Output of the PLINQQueryCS Application

Summary

In this chapter, you have learned about the different LINQ queries. You have also learned about the different Standard Query Operators used in LINQ. The LINQ to Objects, LINQ to ADO.NET, and LINQ to XML concepts are also discussed in the chapter. In addition, you have learned the concepts of extension methods, Anonymous methods, and Lambda Expressions. You have also learned about the new concept introduced in LINQ, PLINQ query.

In the next chapter, you learn about the ADO.NET Entity Framework. You also learn how to create and retrieve the data from the conceptual models in the ASP.NET websites.

10

ADO.NET Entity Framework

In Depth

Till now we have learned how to access data from databases in our applications through the concepts of ADO.NET and Language Integrated Query (LINQ). We also know that to develop any database for a project, first, a conceptual schema has to be designed based on which the logical schema or model is designed. Earlier, to develop a project, you first had to design a conceptual model on a paper or a whiteboard. This was a time-consuming and error-prone process, where the developer had to remember every detail of data on which the conceptual model was based. We could not even work with entities in our application in the executable form.

To overcome all these problems, ADO.NET introduced the concept of Entity Framework. ADO.NET Entity Framework enables users to visually design models and map databases, tables, and views by using Visual Studio 2012 and .NET Framework 4.5. ADO.NET Entity Framework also provides the users with the capability of programming a conceptual model. The ultimate goal of introducing Entity Framework in programming is to raise the level of abstraction for data programming and help developers to increase productivity.

ADO.NET Entity Framework enables a developer to show essential features of a logical schema of the data and presents its conceptual schema to the application. In a `logical schema`, the data is stored in the form of tables in a database. For example, details for a product can be stored in the `Products` table, orders corresponding to products can be stored in the `Orders` table, and contact details can be stored in the `Contacts` table. While creating an application that implements these tables, a developer should know about the database in which these tables reside. The disadvantage of using a logical schema is that very often an application has to use the JOIN clause to retrieve data from tables because it is not always necessary that a logical database always represents the required view of the data for an application. In such a case, if the logical schema is changed, the application is also affected and needs modification according to the changed schema.

Let's explain this with the help of an example. Suppose we need to create a query in an application that returns the names and results of all the students of batch 2012 in a school. For this, we can use the following query:

```
SELECT c.FirstName, s.Rollnumber
FROM Students s
INNER JOIN Contact c on s.StudentID = c.ContactID
Where admission date >='2012-01-01'
```

In the preceding query, the `JOIN` clause has been used for all the related tables to obtain the result. Based on the preceding syntax, the following are the problems that a developer faces while implementing such a query:

- The syntax is complicated, which unnecessarily consumes more effort and time. In this example, to retrieve the required information, the application has to deal with both the tables, that is, Students and Contacts tables.
- Sometimes, a logical schema of a database is not capable of using certain part of an application according to the requirement of a developer. In such scenario, the application has to deal with the entire logical schema, which unnecessarily puts additional load on the server.
- A logical schema is unable to understand business entities and their relationships among each other because models, such as a relational model, cannot render the conceptual domain knowledge of the application.
- If an application deals with a subset of data, the developers should be able to indicate the appropriate subset that is required in the application.

These problems are very common across data-centric applications. To solve such issues, ADO.NET has introduced the concept of `Entity Framework`, which is designed to solve the mismatch between the formats of data. The data is stored in a database in the form of tables and consumed through `object-oriented programming` languages. ADO.NET Entity Framework consists of data models and provides design-time and run-time services that allow the developers to describe the application data.

When we use a logical schema, the queries return certain values, which are not related to the source of data. It implies that there is no common relationship among the elements of a database throughout the application about the core application concepts. Entity Framework allows the developers to describe the application data and isolates the application from the underlying logical database schemas.

In this chapter, you learn about the ADO.NET Entity Framework and its features. Next, you learn about the Entity Data Model (EDM), which includes data modeling, conceptual schema dentition language, storage schema definition language, mapping specification language, the EDM types, type constraints, and data model tools. In addition to these, you also learn about object services, entity Structured Query Language (SQL) and its operators, the EntityClient provider, ADO.NET metadata, and the EDM generator tool.

Let's explore the concept of Entity Framework in more detail.

Exploring ADO.NET Entity Framework

ADO.NET Entity Framework does not support direct mapping of object-oriented classes and properties to relational tables and columns. It maps relational tables, columns, and foreign key constraints to entities and relationships in conceptual models. Now, let's understand the architecture of Entity Framework.

ADO.NET Entity Framework is designed to support data-centric applications and services, and provides a platform for programming, which raises the level of abstraction from the logical relational level to the conceptual level. ADO.NET Entity Framework supports code that is independent of any particular data storage, such as the SQL Server engine or a logical schema, by enabling the developers to work with data at a greater level of abstraction. Conceptual models are generally used as tools for capturing knowledge of data and explaining the requirements of an application that are usually discussed at early stages of a project. Entity Framework provides the capability to normalize the entities and relationships to tables with foreign key constraints. Therefore, it makes an application capable of avoiding hard-coded dependencies on a particular data engine or even a particular logical model. Figure 10.1 shows the architecture of Entity Framework:

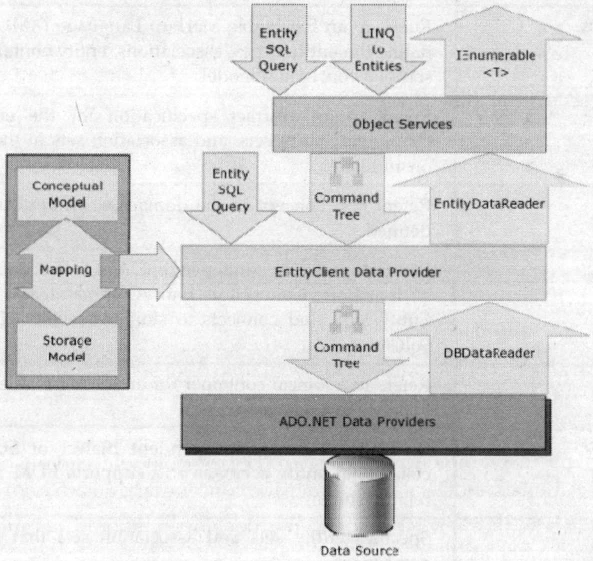

Figure 10.1: Displaying the ADO.NET Entity Framework Architecture

It can be seen in Figure 10.1 how various user-accessible programming interfaces are related with each other in the Entity Framework. A downward arrow indicates a query against the persistent store, and an upward arrow indicates returned data. Object Services generate a `command tree` that represents a LINQ to Entities or Entity SQL operation against the conceptual model. EntityClient Data Provider then transforms this canonical command tree that is generated from Object Services to a new canonical command tree. We cover these concepts in detail later in this chapter.

Entity Framework generates a set of classes and instances of classes that are populated with data. Any changes in the data are based on the mapping that is defined between the conceptual and storage models. Table 10.1 lists the noteworthy terminologies employed in Entity Framework:

Table 10.1: Noteworthy Entity Framework Terminologies

Term	Definition
association	Defines the relationship between entity types in a Framework.
association set	Refers to a logical container for instances of `associations` of the same type.
base type	Refers to a parent type or super type in the EDM from which the derived types inherit some of their properties.
command tree	Refers to a common programmatic representation of all Entity Framework queries that are composed of one or more expressions.
complex object	Refers to an instance of a complex type that exists within an object context.
constraint	Restricts the possible values of a property and makes sure that the values are valid.
container	Refers to a logical grouping of entity and association sets.
concurrency	Defines a process that allows multiple users to access and change shared data at the same time. Entity Framework implements an optimistic concurrency model.
direction	Refers to the asymmetrical nature of some associations. A direction is specified with the `FromRole` and `ToRole` attributes of a NavigationProperty or `ReferentialConstraint` element in a schema.
end	Refers to a participating entity in an association.
conceptual schema definition language (CSDL)	Refers to an Extensible Markup Language (XML)-based language that is used to define the entity types, associations, entity containers, entity sets, and association sets of a conceptual model.
conceptual model	Refers to an abstract specification for the entity types, associations, entity containers, entity sets, and association sets in the domain of an application built on an EDM.
entity	Refers to a concept in the domain of an application from which a data type is defined.
EntityClient	Refers to a storage-independent ADO.NET data provider that contains classes such as EntityConnection, EntityCommand, and EntityDataReader. It works with Entity SQL and connects to storage-specific ADO.NET data providers such as SqlClient.
entity set	Refers to a logical container for entities of a given type and its subtypes mapped to tables in a database.
Entity SQL	Refers to a storage-independent dialect of SQL, which works directly with conceptual entity schemas and supports EDM features such as inheritance and relationships.
entity container	Specifies entity sets and association sets that are implemented in a specified namespace.
EntityType	Refers to a specification for a data type that includes a named set of properties and represents a top-level item in a data model.
key	Refers to an attribute of an entity type that specifies which property or a set of properties is used to identify unique instances of the entity type.

Table 10.1: Noteworthy Entity Framework Terminologies

Term	Definition
mapping specification language (MSL)	Refers to an XML-based language that is used to map items defined in a conceptual model to items in a storage model.
query path	Represents a string of a path that specifies which related objects to return when a typed object query is executed. A query path is defined by calling the Include method on the ObjectQuery class.
object context	Represents the entity container defined in the conceptual schema. It contains a connection to the underlying data store and provides services such as change tracking.
object query	Represents a query executed against an EDM within an object context that returns data as objects.
Object Services	Refers to a service provided by Entity Framework that enables application code to operate on entities in terms of .NET Framework objects.
referential constraint	Defines an EDM, which indicates that an entity has a dependent relationship to another entity. This constraint means that an instance of a dependent entity cannot exist without a corresponding instance of the principal entity.
relationship	Represents a logical connection between entities.
role	Represents the name given to each End of an association. It helps to clarify the semantics of relationships.
scalar property	Represents a property of an entity that maps to a single field in the storage schema.
simple type	Defines a primitive type that is used for defining properties in the conceptual schema. The storage schema uses data types of the storage model.
storage schema definition language (SSDL)	Refers to an XML-based language that is used to define the entity types, associations, entity containers, entity sets, and association sets of a storage model often corresponding to a database schema.
table-per-hierarchy (TPH)	Refers to a method of modeling a type hierarchy in a database that includes the attributes of all the types in the hierarchy in one table.
table-per-type (TPT)	Refers to a method of modeling a type hierarchy in a database. The database consists of multiple tables with one-to-one relationships to model various types.
XML (simple type)	Contains well-formed XML or valid XML data. The different facets of this type specify the kind of XML data that can be contained in it.
complex type	Represents a complex property as defined in the conceptual model.

Next, let's learn about the features of Entity Framework.

Exploring the Features of Entity Framework

For developing an Entity Framework application, we need to create a conceptual model, a logical model, and a programmable object model in Visual Studio 2012. A conceptual model defines the entities and relationships in an application. A programmable object model is then generated from the conceptual model. A logical model represents a relational model and a mapping between the conceptual and relational models. Some of the features of Entity Framework that elevate the level of abstraction for data programming and help the developers to increase productivity are as follows:

- Enhances performance by improving the speed of object query execution and makes generation of SQL query simpler.

- Performs operations with disconnected components, which locally caches datasets and entity sets for using Entity Framework in an occasionally connected environment.
- Enhances extensibility and business logics by using partial methods in code generation for changes in property and property changed events.
- Constitutes many query improvements such as addition of canonical functions for LINQ to Entities and addition of more operations to work with a database.
- Expands the data model that describes data during the development process. EDM provides two data models, that is, conceptual data model and storage model, and a mapping that performs translation between these two models.

Let's learn about some more features of Entity Framework in the .NET Framework 4.5, which are as follows:

- The foreign keys allows the process of creating and modifying relationships between entity types is simplified. The developers had two views regarding the inclusion of foreign keys in conceptual and object models. Some felt that the inclusion of foreign keys is very advantageous, while some felt that the foreign keys pollutes their conceptual and object models. Therefore, in .NET Framework 4.5, a support for new type of association called FK association has been added. This association simplifies the process of generation of a conceptual model when the foreign keys are exposed as entity properties. When you generate a model from an existing database, the default nature of the Entity Designer tool is to create scalar properties on entity types that are corresponding to the respective foreign keys columns in the database.
- The Plain-Old Common Language Runtime Objects (POCO), allows the developers to create classes that are not only simple, but also can be included in the Entity Framework. In the previous versions of .NET Framework, the classes that derived from a model are inherited from the EntityObject class. This was a hindrance for the developers if they wanted to create simple classes that are not bound to a Framework. POCO helps the Entity Framework to use custom data classes along with the data model without making any changes to the data classes. In simpler langauge, if you have a class called Employee with name, address, and phone number, then the Entity Framework will not change the class while implementing it. This implies that the class will not include EntityKey or any other property, which requires you to implement any interface specific to Entity Framework while creating an application.
- The lazy loading feature is a common feature of many Object Relational Mapping (ORM) tools such as LINQ to SQL. The lazy loading feature, in simple terms, is a design pattern that helps in rescheduling the intialization of an object till the point in it is needed. This feature helps in improving the efficiency of the operation of a program. In Entity Framework, the lazy loading feature will load the related objects when they are accessed through a navigation property. This new feature can be implemented in Entity Framework by setting the LazyLoadingEnabled property to true (which by default is set to false). The LazyLoadingEnabled property is an instance of the ObjectContext class, which is the primary class for interacting with data as objects in Entity Framework.
- The support for the QueryExtender control and POCO for the EntityDataSource control. The EntityDataSource control is an ASP.NET data source control, which was a part of the earlier version of Entity Framework. However, with the new version, the EntityDataSource control has been improved to support the new feature introduced in ASP.NET, that is, the QueryExtender control, which helps in having more control over data retrival from a data source. The QueryExtender control is a very helpful control in developing Rapid Application Development (RAD) websites.
- Along with the support for the QueryExtender control, the EntityDataSource control now supports the POCO entities also, which helps the EntityDataSource control to use the generated classes for its functioning.
- The Entity Framework provides support to binary property types that are mapped as entity/foreign key (commonly known as binary keys).
- The ObjectMaterialized event in the Entity Framework, makes possible to write logic that can be exceuted immediately after the object has been materialized.

- The object services, that is, Application Programming Interface (API) improvements, to enable N-tier and self-tracking entities. This implies that now you can access the updated data to establish the original state of an entity by using the ObjectStateEntry.GetUpdatableOriginalValues method.
- The SQL statements when querying Entity Framework performs removal of joins and elimination of constants used for internal purposes.
- The navigation property management that would help the developers to delete and add navigation property, and also enables the creation of one-way associations.
- Provide support for Microsoft SQL Server Compact Edition(SQL CE). This will help in simplifying customization of database generation.
- Extensibility of APIs help in adding custom properties to any object in the model.
- The model first development technique, which implies that a developer can start from EDM and then generate the associated T-SQL and customized code from the model.
- The testing applications that use the Entity Framework, which includes an interface that helps in better testing of applications that use Entity Framework.
- The persistence ignorance helps the developers to use their own classes in an Entity Framework application, without introducing interfaces or elements that are specificto Entity Framework.

Let's now understand the entity data model.

Understanding the Entity Data Model

A data model is usually designed in the analysis or planning phase of a project. This is done since the relationships among data types, their attributes, and the constraints in the data must be organized conceptually before they can be implemented in the application code. `EDM` is used to extend models that application designers use to describe data during the development process. These models provide a specification to define data used by an application. An application based on EDM defines the entities and relationships in the domain of the application in the design schema used to generate programmable classes that are further used by the application code.

In EDM, mapping specification connects the `design schema` and `storage schema`. The storage structure that contains data for the application is represented in a storage schema. The storage schema is mapped to the design schema so that the mapping specification effectively connects programmable classes to storage structures. Now, let's understand the following concepts related to the design of EDM:

- Data modeling
- CSDL
- SSDL
- MSL
- The EDM types
- Type constraints
- Data model tools

Let's now learn about these concepts one by one in detail.

Data Modeling

Data modeling is a technique to structure and organize data that are needed to support an application. For example, an entity in an application must be represented by data, such as customers, orders, and products, whereas, a relationship specifies the logical connection among the entities. Defining entities and relationships can be a very complex process. It might require unexpected amount of detail, for example, an order might be a telephone order, a catalogue order, or an Internet order, which is quite confusing. To overcome this problem, EDM defines entities and uses data readers to read entities in a serialized form or as materialized objects.

An object model represents the classes that are programmable in Common Language Runtime (CLR) and can be built from the conceptual model defined in the design schema. An EDM conceptual model is a specification for entities and relationships in the domain of an application. Object model and storage metadata, which consist of logical description of database structure, are mapped to the conceptual layer.

Now, let's discuss about design and implementation of an EDM and its mapping to different platforms.

Design and Implementation

EDM types are designed in schemas to preserve the logical integrity of data and the constraints of business and technical applications. According to EDM specifications, the following three stages of development are required to implement the data model:

- Entities and relationships in the domain of an application are specified in an XML file
- Metadata that describes the structures of the database is also specified in an XML file
- Mapping of entities and relationships to corresponding databases is specified in the storage metadata file

EDM Mapping to CLR and Database Management Systems

EDM supports application scenarios across various storage models and maps to both the CLR and the database management system such as SQL Server. With the introduction of EDM, ADO.NET provides a comprehensive platform that connects application code to storage structures. It uses a store-independent view mechanism that takes advantage of the concepts of a Relational Database Management System (RDBMS) to implement mapping among schemas, programming languages, and database tables. The EDM data services are not dependent on any particular storage schema. Applications that require multiple data sources can maintain individual mappings for each data source.

Developing an application by using Entity Framework requires creating and mapping conceptual EDM and storage entity models. Entity Framework has made entity-relationship modeling executable through a combination of XML files such as `Conceptual schema definition language (.csdl)`, `Storage schema definition language (.ssdl)`, and `Mapping specification language (.msl)`.

Conceptual Schema Definition Language

`CSDL` contains a design schema that provides a design template for an object model. An application uses the object model based on CSDL. A schema is an XML text file that describes entity and relationship types. It also defines a container that contains instances of these types in a logically organized form. CSDL is an XML syntax used to describe both the EDM types, those that are provided when Entity Framework is installed and those that are designed by the developer. The following code snippet shows the overall structure of a CSDL file:

```
<? xml version="1.0" encoding="utf-8"?>
<Schema xmlns:cg="http://schemas.microsoft.com/ado/2006/04/codegeneration"
  xmlns="http://schemas.microsoft.com/ado/2006/04/edm"
  Namespace="Humanresource.SalarySchema" Alias="Self">
<Documentation>
  <Summary>Shows general Syntax of
  Conceptual schema (csdl) </Summary>
</Documentation>
<EntityType Name="Employee">
  <Key>
       <PropertyRef Name="EmployeeId" />
  </Key>
  <Property Name=" EmployeeId " Type="Guid" Nullable="false" />
       <!-- Other properties-->
</EntityType>
<Association Name="Monthly_Salary">
  <End Role="Employee" Type="Self.Employee" Multiplicity="0..1" />
</Association>
  <EntityContainer Name=" Humanresource.SalarySchema ">
       <EntitySet Name="Employee" EntityType="Self. Employee" />
```

```
        <AssociationSet Name="Monthly_Salary">
        Association="Self.Monthly_Salary">
        <End Role="Employee" EntitySet="Employees" />
        <!-- Other roles -->
        </AssociationSet>
   </EntityContainer>
</Schema>
```

Some elements and attributes used in the preceding code snippet are as follows:

- **Schema**—Refers to the root element of every XML schema. It indicates that the elements used in the schema have been extracted from `http://schemas.microsoft.com/ado/2006/04/edm`. This element consists of the following two attributes:
  - `Namespace`—Refers to the top-level node in a schema that assigns a namespace which should be unique. The types defined in a schema are logically organized under the `Humanresource.SalarySchema` namespace.
  - `Alias`—Refers to the attribute that can be used to shorten the name of a namespace in the rest of the schema, such as `Humanresource.SalarySchema`. For example, the Employee table can be shortened by using alias Self, which is declared for the namespace such as `Self.Employee`.
- `Using`—Refers to the element that is used to shorten the syntax while referring to types defined in a separate namespace. It consists of the following two attributes:
  - `Namespace`—Specifies the external namespace
  - `Alias`—Provides an alias for the namespace
- `Documentation`—Refers to the element in CSDL file of an EDM that provides information for using entities and associations declared in a schema. It has the following two subelements:
  - `Summary`—Provides a brief description of the type. This attribute is optional.
  - `LongDescription`—Includes a wide range of text information. This attribute is also optional.

NOTE

An empty Documentation element is also valid in the syntax of a CSDL file.

- `EntityType`—Refers to the element that is used by EDM in a CSDL schema to specify an object in the domain of the application designed. It consists of the following attributes:
  - `Key`—Specifies one or more properties of the entities as keys. It uniquely identifies instances of an `entity` for all operations and can be composed of more than one property.
  - `Name`—Identifies the type in the `Object Model` designed and the mapping specification.
  - `NavigationProperty`—Declares a shortcut that is used to navigate to and from entities related by the `Association type`.
  - `Property element`—Contains most of the information about entities used in an application.
  - `Type`—Refers to the attribute of a property element that is set to `Guid` to specify a unique value for a key
- `Association`—Refers to the element that specifies a logical relationship between entities in the EDM.
- `EntityContainer`—Refers to the element that is different from a `Schema` element even though the `EntityContainer` element is defined in a schema. The `EntityContainer` elements in a conceptual schema are mapped to the corresponding `EntityContainer` elements in the storage metadata. It also controls the scope of entities and associations in the object model that is defined.
- `AssociationSet`—Refers to the element that specifies an association in the class that is built from a conceptual schema. The object model, built from a conceptual schema, requires both programmable classes and storage structures to contain data for an application based on it. The attributes of the `AssociationSet` element are as follows:

- `AssociationSetMapping`—Connects the `AssociationSet` element defined in CSDL to the `AssociationSet` element in `SSDL` describing the storage structures
- `Name`—Specifies the name of a class in an object model built on the EDM
- `Extends`—Provide a means to add entities and associations to an existing schema

The subelements of the `AssociationSet` element are as follows:

- `EntitySet`—Specifies a type in the class that is built from the conceptual schema
- `ReferentialConstraint`—Specifies different roles of an association

NOTE

The syntax of CSDL is expressed in XML, but it is not XML Schema Definition (XSD) based.

Storage Schema Definition Language

The storage metadata schema is a formal description of the database that persist data for an application based on EDM. It is the basis for mapping entities and associations described in a conceptual schema to the corresponding entities and associations defined in the storage model. A declaration of entities in SSDL is not different from a declaration of entities in CSDL. A basic difference between these two schemas lies in data types used in the declaration of entities. EDM is capable of mapping these different data types used in a storage metadata schema and a conceptual schema. The third type of XML file is MSL.

Mapping Specification Language

MSL connects the data types declared in CSDL to the database metadata. This metadata preserves data for an application that uses the defined object model. The Namespace Name and EntityContainer Name tags declared in the CSDL schema identify entities and associations that are contained in the conceptual schema. The MSL syntax maps these entities and associations to store metadata in the SSDL file. Figure 10.2 shows the mapping of a conceptual model and a logical model:

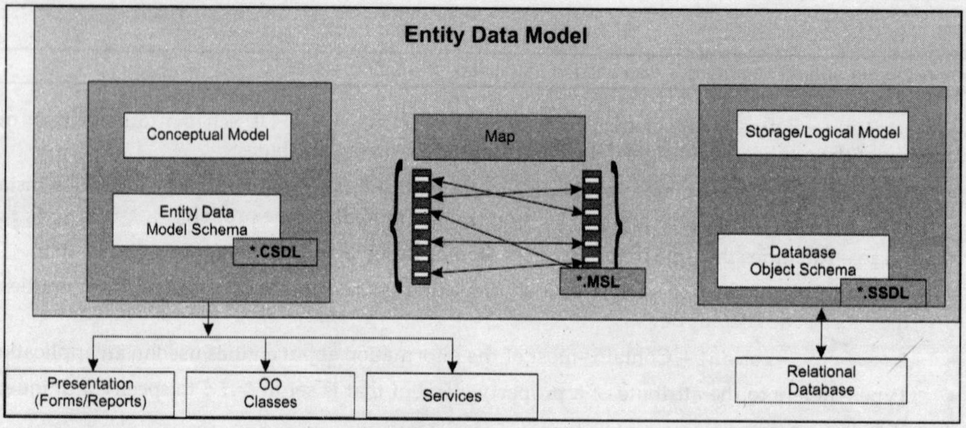

Figure 10.2 Mapping of a Conceptual Model and a Logical Model

The MSL file consists of the following elements:

- `Mapping element`—Specifies mapping between types defined by using CSDL and metadata in SSDL. The syntax of using a Mapping element is as follows:

```
<?xml version="1.0" encoding="utf-8"?>
<Mapping Space="C-S" >
```

- `EntityContainerMapping element`—Maps the EntityContainer element declared in a conceptual schema to the EntityContainer element declared in the storage metadata schema. In the conceptual schema, an EntityContainer element is the specification for a class in a programming object model. In the metadata schema, an EntityContainer element is the designation for the database structures used by applications that are based on object models.
- `EntitySetMapping element`—Connects an `EntitySet` defined in CSDL to an `EntitySet` defined in SSDL.

The EDM Types

EDM provides a basic structure to declare the schema of entities. The EDM EntityType is the basic type defined by the EDM for a top-level application concept such as e-commerce websites. The following points prove that EDM types are more based on structure than on behavior:

- EDM types cannot be encapsulated
- EDM types do not have associated methods
- EDM supports structural inheritance but not behavioral inheritance
- EDM types use simple as well as complex entity types

Now, let's discuss the following types of EDM:

- Simple types
- Entity types
- Complex types

Simple Types

In EDM, simple types are used in schemas to specify the content contained in the properties of entities. It supports attribute-constraining facets and interoperability across multiple systems. Data types can be customized according to application requirements through facets. Table 10.2 lists the simple types of EDM:

Table 10.2: Simple Types of EDM

Type	Description
`Binary (EDM)`	Represents fixed or variable-length binary data.
`Boolean (EDM)`	Represents the mathematical concept of two-value logics such as true or false, yes or no, and 0 or 1.
`DateTime (EDM)`	Represents date and time with values ranging from 12:00:00 midnight, January 1, 0001 A.D., to 11:59:59 P.M, December 31, 2999 A.D. The maximum precision is milliseconds.
`Decimal (EDM)`	Represents numeric values with fixed precision and scale. This type can describe a numeric value ranging from negative 10^38 + 1 to positive 10^38 –1.
`Float(EDM)`	Represents a floating point number with seven-digit precision that can represent values with approximate range of ± 1.18e –38 through ± 3.40e +38.
`Double (EDM)`	Represents a floating point number with 15-digit precision that can represent values with an approximate range of ± 2.23e –308 to ± 1.79e +308.
`Guid (EDM)`	Represents a 16-byte (128 bit) Globally Unique Identifier (GUID) value.
`SByte (EDM)`	Represents a signed 8-bit integer value.
`Int16 (EDM)`	Represents a signed 16-bit integer value.
`Int32 (EDM)`	Represents a signed 32-bit integer value.
`Int64 (EDM)`	Represents a signed 64-bit integer value.
`Byte (EDM)`	Represents an unsigned 8-bit integer value.

Table 10.2: Simple Types of EDM

Type	Description
`UInt16 (EDM)`	Represents an unsigned 16-bit integer value.
`UInt32 (EDM)`	Represents an unsigned 32-bit integer value.
`UInt64 (EDM)`	Represents an unsigned 64-bit integer value.
`Single (EDM)`	Represents a single-precision floating-point variable as 32-bit (4-byte) floating-point number, ranging in value from -3.402823E38 to -1.401298E-45 for negative values, and 1.401298E-45 to 3.402823E38 for positive values.
`String (EDM)`	Represents fixed or variable-length character data.

NOTE

The String data type does not specify the kind of Unicode to use. The designer must specify the appropriate kind of Unicode from the type system hosting EDM.

Entity Types

An entity type in EDM is the design template for a data type in the application domain. In a schema, the entity type has a name, properties, and a key that identifies the data type when instantiated by an application code. After it has been schematically defined, the entity type becomes an operational unit for application development, each possessing a unique identity.

Complex Types

The complex type in the EDM is a data type with internal structure, but does not contain the key property. It is used to implement a property that has internal properties of its own.

Sometimes, we need to put constraints to restrict certain properties of an entity. To do this, EDM provides Type constraints. Let's explore the type constraints next.

Type Constraints

In EDM, we can put certain constraints over the properties of entity types. Constraints restrict the possible values of a property and verify that the assigned value not only corrects the data types, but also checks that it is working according to the business requirement of the application. Some of the main constraints are as follows:

- `Nullable` **constraint**—Specifies whether the value of the property can be unassigned
- `MaxLength` **constraint**—Limits the length of string properties

`Entity Framework` also provides certain tools to help in working with models, which we describe next.

Data Model Tools

ADO.NET Entity Framework allows a user to bring data from efficient storage engines, such as SQL Server, to object-oriented programming. Many developers implement complicated data access codes to move data between applications and the database. ADO.NET Entity Framework provides the following tools that help us to develop applications with EDM:

- `ADO.NET Entity Data Model Item Template`—Refers to the template that is available for Visual Basic (VB) and C# projects, and ASP.NET website and Web application projects. It is basically used to launch Entity Data Model Wizard.
- `Entity Data Model Wizard`—Generates EDM from an existing database and also adds a connection string to the App.Config or Web.Config file, and configures a single file generator to run on the conceptual model contained in the .edmx file, which encapsulates generated EDM through the wizard. A conceptual model defined in an .edmx file helps to generate C# or VB code.

- The ADO.NET Entity Data Model Designer—Enables us to open an .edmx file in the designer, and creates entities and map entities to database tables and columns through some visual tools included with EDM Designer.
- EDMGen.exe—Refers to the command tool that can be used to generate models and perform other functions on EDM metadata files such as validating existing models.

All data types in EDM are supported by LINQ and Entity SQL. This is achieved through Object Services. Now, let's understand Object Services in detail.

Understanding Object Services

In Entity Framework, Object Services is a service that supports both LINQ and Entity SQL queries for all the types defined in EDM. Object Services return data as objects including any changes in the object back to the data store. The support of LINQ and Entity SQL queries makes the Object Services capable of performing the QUERY, INSERT, UPDATE, and DELETE data operations. This service is also capable of tracking changes, binding objects to controls, and handling concurrency.

Classes of Object Services

The concept of Object Services is implemented by classes in the System.Data.Objects and System.Data.Objects.DataClasses namespaces. Some classes that are used with Object Services are as follows:

- The ObjectContext Class – Represents a primary class for interacting with data in the form of objects that are instances of the entity types defined in EDM. The ObjectContext class encapsulates a connection between .NET Framework and the database. This class serves as a gateway for the CREATE, UPDATE, and DELETE operations. An instance of the ObjectContext class encapsulates the following:
    - An EntityConnection object, which specifies a connection to the database
    - A MetadataWorkspace object, which describes the model
    - An ObjectStateManager object, which manages objects present in the cache

The ObjectContext class uses the System.Data.Objects namespace and System.Data.Entity assembly (in system.data.entity.dll) for working with entity data as objects. The inheritance hierarchy of the System.Data.Objects.ObjectContext class is as follows:

```
System.Object
   System.Data.Objects.ObjectContext
```

The syntax to declare the ObjectContext class in VB is as follows:

```
Public Class ObjectContext
   Implements IDisposable
```

The syntax to declare the ObjectContext class in C# is as follows:

```
public class ObjectContext : IDisposable
```

- The EntityConnection **class**—Represents a connection to an underlying data store. This class cannot be inherited. You need to use the System.Data.EntityClient namespace and the System.Data.Entity assembly (in system.data.entity.dll) to use this class. The inheritance hierarchy of the System.Data.EntityClient.EntityConnection class is as follows:

```
System.Object
   System.MarshalByRefObject
         System.ComponentModel.Component
                 System.Data.Common.DbConnection
                         System.Data.EntityClient.EntityConnection
```

The syntax to declare the EntityConnection class in VB is as follows:

```
Public NotInheritable Class EntityConnection
   Inherits DbConnection
```

The syntax to declare the EntityConnection class in C# is as follows:

```
public sealed class EntityConnection : DbConnection
```

- The `MetadataWorkspace` **class**—Represents the ADO.NET metadata runtime service component that provides support for retrieving metadata from various sources. You need to use the `System.Data.Metadata.Edm` namespace and the System.Data.Entity assembly (in system.data.entity.dll) to use this class. The inheritance hierarchy of the `System.Data.Metadata.Edm.MetadataWorkspace` class is as follows:

```
System.Object
   System.Data.Metadata.Edm.MetadataWorkspace
```

The syntax to declare the `ObjectContext` class in VB is as follows:

```
Public Class ObjectContext
   Implements IDisposable
```

The syntax to use the `MetadataWorkspace` class in C# is as follows:

```
public sealed class MetadataWorkspace
```

- The `ObjectStateManager` **class**—Maintains the object state and identifies management for entity instances and relationship instances. You need to use the `System.Data.Objects` namespace and the `System.Data.Entity` assembly (in system.data.entity.dll) to use this class. The inheritance hierarchy of the `System.Data.Objects.ObjectStateManager` class is as follows:

```
System.Object
   System.Data.Objects.ObjectStateManager
```

The syntax to use the `ObjectStateManager` class in VB is as follows:

```
Public Class ObjectStateManager
```

The syntax to use the `ObjectStateManager` class in C# is as follows:

```
Public class ObjectStateManager
```

Entity Framework generates object layer code by using CSDL. The object layer code includes a class that represents the `EntityContainer` element for the model. Another class, which is inherited from the `EntityObject class`, of the object layer code represents entities. After generating the code, it works with entity data as objects and takes advantage of the Object Services features.

Features of Object Services

Object Services provides the following features for programming in Entity Framework:

- **Querying data as objects**—Allows you to use LINQ, Entity SQL, or query builder methods to execute queries for EDM and returns data as objects. Entity Framework contains the ObjectQuery generic class. It represents a query that returns a collection of zero or more typed entities. It is always related to the existing object context that provides the connection and metadata information.
- **Shaping query results**—Returns only those objects that are specifically requested in the query. We can specify whether or not a query returns related objects in case a relationship exists between the objects.
- **Adding, changing, and deleting objects**—Holds data objects in memory and enables us to add, modify, and delete objects within an object context.
- **Saving changes to the persisted data store**—Caches changes to objects in the object context. When we call a service explicitly, the changes are stored back to the data store.
- **Binding objects to controls**—Enables binding of objects to controls. These controls must support data bindings such as the DataGridView control.
- **Managing concurrency**—Tracks concurrency when the ConcurrencyMode attribute for one or more properties is set to fixed. Object Services raise specific exceptions when concurrency violations are detected in the application.
- **Attaching and detaching objects**—Refers to the fact that the ObjectContext instance should persist for the duration of application execution. For example, as long as the application executes, the objects should remain bound to Form controls. Objects can be detached to release the resources that are no longer required. It helps in increasing the context size of the object.

- **Serializing objects**—Supports both XML serialization and binary serialization. XML serialization serializes only the public fields and property values of an object into an XML stream, and binary serialization especially proves useful while using ViewState property to persist objects in an ASP.NET application.
- **Managing object identities and tracking changes**—Uses identity values that help to track changes of objects, handle conflicts, and decide when to retrieve data from the data store.
- **Managing connections**—Provide our own connection for the object context, and we can also explicitly manage the connection used by an object.
- **Managing transactions**—Supports .NET Framework transactions to coordinate operations against the data store and enlist distributed transactions. It also supports automatic enlisting of transactions.
- **Using custom objects with an EDM**—Enables you to manually define your own objects or use existing objects with an EDM.

Let's now learn about Entity SQL language in the next section.

Understanding Entity SQL Language

Entity SQL is a language similar to SQL, and is provided by ADO.NET Entity Framework to support EDM. Entity SQL supports EDM constructs that enable users to query the data represented by an entity model. Object Services and the `EntityClient provider` help return data, including scalar results, result sets, and object graphs. Both Object Services and the EntityClient provider enable us to use Entity SQL to execute queries against an EDM and return data as strongly typed CLR objects that are instances of entity types. To create `EntityCommand` objects, we can specify a stored procedure name or the text of a query by assigning an Entity SQL query string to its `System.Data.EntityClient.EntityCommand.CommandText` property. Now, let's discuss the features of Entity SQL in detail.

Features of Entity SQL

Due to the increasing popularity of e-commerce websites, business applications need to be more interactive while dealing with databases. The use of Entity SQL, provided by ADO.NET Entity Framework, solves many problems of developers in this context, such as performance and ease of handling databases. Some of the features of Entity SQL are as follows:

- `Inheritance and relationships support`—Specifies that the `OfType` operator in Entity SQL provides the capability of selecting instances of a `subtype` from a collection of supertype instances. Entity SQL supports EDM features such as inheritance and relationships.
- `Uniform treatment of subqueries`—Specifies that in traditional SQL, a subquery in the `FROM` clause is considered to be a multiset, but the same subquery used in the `SELECT` clause is considered to be a scalar subquery. A subquery used on the left-hand side of an `IN` operator is considered to be a scalar subquery, while that used on the right-hand side is expected to be a multiset subquery. Entity SQL considers all the subqueries to be multiset subqueries and provides the `anyelement` operator that operates on a collection, such as arrays.
- `Left correlation and aliasing`—Specifies that the Entity SQL generalizes left correlations in the `FROM` clause and treats them uniformly. In Entity SQL expressions using the `FROM` clause, we can refer to definitions in the same clause without the need for additional syntax. Entity SQL also imposes additional restrictions on queries involving group by clauses. We can use the following code in Transact-SQL, but it is invalid in Entity SQL:

```
select z.a + z.b from Z as z group by z.a + z.b
```

To perform the same query through Entity SQL, the following syntax is used:

```
select k from Z as z group by (z.a + z.b) as k
```

Expressions contained in the `SELECT` clause and `HAVING` clause of such queries may only refer to `GROUP BY` keys through aliases.

- `Referencing columns of tables`—Specifies that in Entity SQL, all column references must be qualified with the table alias. The following syntax is valid in Transact-SQL, but invalid in Entity-SQL:

```
select x from Z
```

In the preceding expression, we have assumed that x is a valid column of table Z.

The syntax to write the same query by using Entity SQL is as follows:

```
select Z.x as X from Z as z
```

Table aliases are optional in the FROM clause. The name of the table can be used as the implicit alias. The unqualified references in a query can cause certain errors; so, care should be taken during schema evolution.

- Support for Expressions—Specifies that for better support of collections and nested collections, Entity SQL treats each line of code as an expression. The following syntax is valid in Transact-SQL, but invalid in Entity-SQL:

```
sal > all (select salary from employees)
sal > any (select salary from employees)
```

Equivalent expressions can be written in Entity SQL as follows:

```
not exists(select 0 from employees as emp where salary > e.salaries)
exists(select 0 from employees as emp where salary > e.salaries)
```

The following are the valid Entity SQL queries:

```
1+2 *3
"abc"
row(1 as a, 2 as b)
{ 1, 3, 5}
e1 union all e2
set(e1)
```

- **Navigation through objects**—Specifies that Entity SQL uses a specific notation to support navigation through properties of an object. Suppose if emp is an expression of type employee, then the following is the Entity SQL syntax to refer to the address of the city in a table named as employee.

```
emp.Address.City
```

- Collection-based aggregates—Specifies that Entity SQL supports two kinds of aggregates, namely, SQL-style aggregates and collection-based aggregates. The syntax of the SQL-style aggregates is as follows:

```
select x, sum(z.y) from Z as z group by z.x as x
```

The collection-based aggregates operate on collections and produce the aggregated result. We can write it anywhere in the query and do not require a GROUP BY clause to obtain a result. The syntax of the collection-based aggregates is as follows:

```
select z.x as x, count({1,2,3}) as y from T as z
```

- No support for *—Specifies that Entity SQL does not support the * construct. The syntax * has been supported by Transact-SQL as an alias for the entire row. It also allows a special count (*) aggregate that includes nulls, and such constructs are able to handle inheritance. The following code is valid in Transact-SQL, but invalid in Entity SQL:

```
select * from E and select E1.* from E1, E2...
```

Equivalent expressions can be written in Entity SQL as follows:

```
select value e from E as e and select value e1 from E1 as e1, E2 as e2...
```

Entity SQL does not support the count(*) aggregate but the same result can be obtained by using the count(0) method instead.

- Changes to Group By—Specifies that Entity SQL supports aliasing of the GROUP BY clause. Expressions in the SELECT clause and HAVING clause must refer to the GROUP BY keys through the aliases as shown here. The following code is valid in Transact-SQL, but invalid in Entity SQL:

```
select b + c, count(*), sum(a)
from Z
group by b + c
```

In Entity SQL, the same expression can be expressed as follows:

```
select k1, count(z.a), sum(z.a)
from Z as z
group by z.b + z.c as k1
```

- `ORDER BY clause usage`—Specifies that Entity SQL provides the capability of using a nested `ORDER BY` expression. It can be placed anywhere in the query. According to the need of the application, the developer can use the `Order BY` clause in any order.

In Transact-SQL, we use the ORDER BY clause in the topmost block as follows:

```
SELECT e1.FirstName, e1.LastName
  FROM Company_details.employees as e1
  ORDER BY e1.LastName
```

The order of nested queries can be ignored in Entity SQL, as shown in the following syntax:

```
SELECT e2.FirstName, e2.LastName
  FROM (SELECT e1.FirstName, e1.LastName
        FROM Company_details.employees as e1
        ORDER BY e1.LastName) as e2
```

- `Transact-SQL functionality not available in Entity SQL`—Specifies that the transact functionalities are not supported in Entity SQL. The functionalities of SQL that are not supported in Entity SQL are as follows:
  - **Data Manipulation Language (DML)**—Entity SQL does not provide support for DML statements such as INSERT, UPDATE, and DELETE
  - **Data Definition Language (DDL)**—Entity SQL does not provide support for DDL statements such as CREATE, GRANT, and REVOKE
  - **Imperative programming**—Entity SQL supports functional programming languages rather than supporting imperative programming.
  - **Grouping functions**—Entity SQL does not provide support for grouping functions such as CUBE, ROLLUP, and GROUPING_SET.
  - **Analytic functions**—Entity SQL does not provide support for analytic functions.
- `Built-in functions and operators`—Specifies that Entity SQL provides support for subsets of Transact-SQL built-in functions and operators that are supported by database providers. Entity Framework also provides the capability of declaring built-in and user-defined existing database functions.
- `Paging`—Specifies that Entity SQL supports physical paging by using the `SKIP` and `LIMIT` subclauses in the `ORDER BY` clause. We cannot use the SKIP and LIMIT subclauses together.

By using SKIP, the result set includes rows that start from the next row immediately after the SKIP expression. Suppose a table has 10 rows. Now, if we use `SKIP 6` here, it returns the result from the seventh row.

The use of the LIMIT subclause restricts the resulting number of rows in a result set returned by the LIMIT expression. For example, `LIMIT 4` restricts the result set to four rows.

NOTE

Entity SQL does not support any mechanisms for query hints.

Now, let's take a look into the operators supported by Entity SQL.

Operators for Entity SQL

Entity SQL supports many operators to specify an action performed on one or more expressions. Table 10.3 lists the noteworthy operators for Entity SQL:

Table 10.3: Noteworthy Operators for Entity SQL

Type of Operators	Description
`Arithmetic Operators`	Describes the Entity SQL arithmetic operators. These perform mathematical operations on two expressions of one or more numeric data types, such as addition.
`Comparison Operators`	Describes the Entity SQL comparison operators. These test whether two expressions are the same, such as =.

Table 10.3: Noteworthy Operators for Entity SQL	
Type of Operators	**Description**
`Logical Operators`	Describes the Entity SQL logical operators such as AND.
`Member Access Operator`	Describes the Entity SQL member access operator such as the dot operator (.).
`String Concatenation Operator`	Describes the Entity SQL string concatenation operator such as plus (+).

Now, let's learn about the `EntityClient provider` in more detail.

Understanding the EntityClient Provider

The EntityClient provider is an ADO.NET-managed provider that supports retrieving data described in an EDM. Entities are combined together with other related entities that can have different types of relationships among them. The EntityClient provider allows a user to query data described in a conceptual model. It is capable of returning results such as scalar results, result sets, and object graphs. The EntityClient provider is located within the `System.Data.EntityClient` namespace. Table 10.4 lists the noteworthy classes of the `System.Data.EntityClient` namespace:

Table 10.4: Noteworthy Classes of the System.Data.EntityClient Namespace	
Class	**Description**
`EntityCommand`	Represents a command to be executed against an EDM.
`EntityConnection`	Represents a connection to an underlying data store. This class cannot be inherited.
`EntityConnectionStringBuilder`	Represents a simple way to create and manage the contents of connection strings used by the `EntityClient` class.
`EntityParameter`	Represents a parameter in an `EntityCommand` class. This class cannot be inherited.
`EntityParameterCollection`	Represents a collection of parameters associated with the `EntityCommand` class.
`EntityProviderFactory`	Represents a set of methods for creating instances of a provider's implementation of the data source classes.
`EntityTransaction`	Specifies the transaction for an `EntityCommand class`.

The `EntityClient` provider uses standard ADO.NET providers, such as `.NET Framework Data Provider` (SqlClient), to communicate with databases, such as SQL Server. Table 10.5 lists EDM type facets to corresponding provider type names in the table:

Table 10.5: EDM Type Facets to Corresponding Provider Type Names		
Provider Type Name	**EDM Type Name**	**EDM Type Facets**
bit: Supports the Equal Comparable and Order Comparable attributes when set to True	Boolean	Not applicable
tinyint: Supports the Equal Comparable and Order Comparable attributes when set to True	Byte	Not applicable

Table 10.5: EDM Type Facets to Corresponding Provider Type Names

Provider Type Name	EDM Type Name	EDM Type Facets		
smallint: Supports the Equal Comparable and Order Comparable attributes when set to True	Int16	Not applicable		
int: Supports the Equal Comparable and Order Comparable attributes when set to True	Int32	Not applicable		
float: Supports the Equal Comparable and Order Comparable attributes when set to True	Double	Not applicable		
real: Supports the Equal Comparable and Order Comparable attributes when set to True	Double	Not applicable		
decimal: Supports the Equal Comparable and Order Comparable attributes when set to True	Decimal	**Facet Name**	**Attribute Name**	**Value**
		Precision	Minimum	1
			Maximum	38
			Default	18
			Constant	False
		Scale	Minimum	0
			Maximum	38
			Default	0
			Constant	False
numeric: Supports the Equal Comparable and Order Comparable attributes when set to True	Decimal	**Facet Name**	**Attribute Name**	**Value**
		Precision	Minimum	1
			Maximum	38
			Default	18
			Constant	False
		Scale	Minimum	0
			Maximum	38
			Default	0
			Constant	False
smallmoney: Supports the Equal Comparable and Order Comparable attributes when set to True	Decimal	**Facet Name**	**Attribute Name**	**Value**
		Precision	Default	10
			Constant	True
		Scale	Default	4
			Constant	True

Table 10.5: EDM Type Facets to Corresponding Provider Type Names

Provider Type Name	EDM Type Name	EDM Type Facets		
		Facet Name	**Attribute Name**	**Value**
money: Supports the Equal Comparable and Order Comparable attributes when set to True	Decimal	Precision	Default	19
			Constant	True
		Scale	Default	4
			Constant	True
		Facet Name	**Attribute Name**	**Value**
binary: Supports the Equal Comparable and Order Comparable attributes when set to True	Binary	MaxLength	Minimum	1
			Maximum	8000
			Default	8000
			Constant	False
		FixedLength	Default	True
			Constant	True
		Facet Name	**Attribute Name**	**Value**
varbinary: Supports the Equal Comparable and Order Comparable attributes when set to True	Binary	MaxLength	Minimum	1
			Maximum	8000
			Default	8000
			Constant	False
		FixedLength	Default	False
			Constant	True
		Facet Name	**Attribute Name**	**Value**
varbinary(max): Supports the Equal Comparable and Order Comparable attributes when set to True	Binary	MaxLength	Default	214748364780
			Constant	True
		FixedLength	Default	False
			Constant	True
		Facet Name	**Attribute Name**	**Value**
image: Supports the Equal Comparable and Order Comparable attributes when set to False	Binary	MaxLength	Default	2147483647
			Constant	True
		FixedLength	Default	False
			Constant	True
		Facet Name	**Attribute Name**	**Value**
timestamp: Supports the Equal Comparable and Order Comparable attributes when set to True	Binary	MaxLength	Default	8
			Constant	True
		FixedLength	Default	True
			Constant	True

Provider Type Name	EDM Type Name	EDM Type Facets: Facet Name	Attribute Name	Value
rowversion: Supports the Equal Comparable and Order Comparable attributes when set to True	Binary	**Facet Name**	**Attribute Name**	**Value**
		MaxLength	Default	8
			Constant	True
		FixedLength	Default	True
			Constant	True
smalldatetime: Supports the Equal Comparable and Order Comparable attributes when set to True	DateTime	**Facet Name**	**Attribute Name**	**Value**
		PreserveSeconds	Default	False
			Constant	True
		DateTimeKind	Default	Unspecified
			Constant	True
datetime: Supports the Equal Comparable and Order Comparable attributes when set to True	DateTime	**Facet Name**	**Attribute Name**	**Value**
		PreserveSeconds	Default	True
			Constant	True
		DateTimeKind	Default	Unspecified
			Constant	True
nvarchar: Supports the Equal Comparable and Order Comparable attributes when set to True	String	**Facet Name**	**Attribute Name**	**Value**
		MaxLength	Minimum	1
			Maximum	4000
			Default	4000
			Constant	False
		Unicode	Default	True
			Constant	True
		FixedLength	Default	False
			Constant	True
varchar: Supports the Equal Comparable and Order Comparable attributes when set to True	String	**Facet Name**	**Attribute Name**	**Value**
		MaxLength	Minimum	1
			Maximum	8000
			Default	8000
			Constant	False
		Unicode	Default	False
			Constant	True
		FixedLength	Default	False
			Constant	True
char: Supports the Equal Comparable and Order Comparable attributes when set to True	String	**Facet Name**	**Attribute Name**	**Value**
		MaxLength	Minimum	1
			Maximum	8000
			Default	8000
			Constant	False

Table 10.5: EDM Type Facets to Corresponding Provider Type Names

Table 10.5: EDM Type Facets to Corresponding Provider Type Names

Provider Type Name	EDM Type Name	EDM Type Facets		
		Unicode	Default Constant	False True
		FixedLength	Default Constant	True True
nchar: Supports the Equal Comparable and Order Comparable attributes when set to True	String	**Facet Name**	**Attribute Name**	**Value**
		MaxLength	Minimum Maximum Default Constant	1 4000 4000 False
		Unicode	Default Constant	True True
		FixedLength	Default Constant	True True
varchar(max): Supports the Equal Comparable and Order Comparable attributes when set to True	String	**Facet Name**	**Attribute Name**	**Value**
		MaxLength	Default Constant	2147483647 True
		Unicode	Default Constant	False True
		FixedLength	Default Constant	False True
nvarchar(max): Supports the Equal Comparable and Order Comparable attributes when set to True	String	**Facet Name**	**Attribute Name**	**Value**
		MaxLength	Default Constant	1073741823 True
		Unicode	Default Constant	True True
		FixedLength	Default Constant	False True
ntext: Supports the Equal Comparable and Order Comparable attributes when set to False	String	**Facet Name**	**Attribute Name**	**Value**
		MaxLength	Default Constant	1073741823 True
		Unicode	Default Constant	False True
		FixedLength	Default Constant	False True
text: Supports the Equal Comparable and Order Comparable attributes when set to False	String	**Facet Name**	**Attribute Name**	**Value**
		MaxLength	Default Constant	2147483647 True

Table 10.5: EDM Type Facets to Corresponding Provider Type Names

Provider Type Name	EDM Type Name	EDM Type Facets		
		Unicode	Default Constant	False True
		FixedLength	Default Constant	False True
Unique identifier: Supports the Equal Comparable and Order Comparable attributes when set to True	Guid	n/a		
`XML`: Supports the Equal Comparable and Order Comparable attributes when set to False	String	**Facet Name**	**Attribute Name**	**Value**
		MaxLength	Default Constant	1073741823 True
		Unicode	Default Constant	True True
		FixedLength	Default Constant	False True

In the next section, let's learn about ADO.NET metadata.

ADO.NET Metadata

ADO.NET Entity Framework uses ADO.NET metadata that provides infrastructure and type hierarchy to exhibit the conceptual entities, fundamental tables, and CLR classes according to EDM. ADO.NET uses the `System.Data.Metadata.Edm` namespace to manage the metadata services for Entity Framework. Table 10.6 lists the noteworthy classes of the `System.Data.Metadata.Edm` namespace:

Table 10.6: Noteworthy Classes of the System.Data.Metadata.Edm Namespace

Class	Description
`AssociationEndMember`	Represents End of association in the EDM.
`AssociationSet`	Represents an association set in the EDM.
`AssociationSetEnd`	Represents End of the association set in the EDM.
`AssociationType`	Represents an association in the EDM.
`CollectionType`	Represents a collection of instances of a specific type. We cannot define a CollectionType property in the EDM schema explicitly.
`ComplexType`	Represents a complex type in the EDM.
`Documentation`	Represents the documentation associated with an EDM construct.
`EdmError`	Encapsulates the error information for a generic EDM error.
`EdmFunction`	Represents information about those functions that are invoked from the queries written by using Entity SQL.
`EdmMember`	Represents a member that can be declared in any StructuralTypeclass.
`EdmProperty`	Derives from the EdmMember class and provides the Default and the Nullable facets for the type of this EdmProperty class.
`EdmType`	Represents a base class for all the types in EDM.
`EntityContainer`	Represents an entity container in EDM. An EntityContainer class is a logical

Table 10.6: Noteworthy Classes of the System.Data.Metadata.Edm Namespace

Class	Description
	grouping of entity sets and association sets.
`EntitySet`	Represents an entity set in EDM. An EntitySet class for an EntityType contains instances of the EntityType or any of its subtypes. More than one EntitySet class can be defined by using the same EntityType.
`EntityType`	Represents a particular type of data, such as a customer entity or an order entity in the EDM.
`Facet`	Provides additional information about members. In the `ADO.NET metadata` type hierarchy, facets provide additional information about members through the declared type for the member.
`FacetDescription`	Specifies a description of the facet.
`FunctionParameter`	Describes the parameters of an EdmFunction class.
`GlobalItem`	Represents the base item class for all the EDM types and the entity containers.
`MetadataItem`	Represents the base item class for all the metadata in the ADO.NET metadata type hierarchy.
`MetadataProperty`	Represents a metadata attribute for an item in the ADO.NET metadata hierarchy.
`MetadataWorkspace`	Represents the ADO.NET metadata runtime service component that provides support for retrieving metadata from various sources.
`NavigationProperty`	Represents the navigation from one entity type to another entity type in EDM.
`ReadOnlyMetadataCollection`	Represents a collection of members in the ADO.NET metadata hierarchy by providing a read-only collection with advanced lookup capabilities. This class is derived from the ReadOnlyCollection class.
`PrimitiveType`	Describes the .NET Framework primitive types, EDM primitive types, and storage provider-specific primitive types.
`ReferentialConstraint`	Describes the referential constraints on the relationships in the EDM.
`RefType`	Provides the address of an entity for operations that use the entity. We cannot define RefType in the EDM schema explicitly.
`RelationshipSet`	Represents a relationship set in the EDM.
`RelationshipType`	Represents the base class for relationships in the EDM.
`RowType`	Describes a row, such as the result of a query. This class is derived from the StructuralType class. The structure of the row type depends on database columns projected in the query. We cannot define a RowType in the EDM schema explicitly.
`SimpleType`	Represents a base class that describes primitive types in the EDM.
`StructuralType`	Represents a base type for all the types in the EDM that have members.
`TypeUsage`	Describes a type and a set of facets for that type.

Table 10.7 lists the noteworthy enumerations of the `System.Data.Metadata.Edm` namespace:

Table 10.7: Noteworthy Enumerations of the System.Data.Metadata.Edm Namespace

Enumeration	Description
BuiltInTypeKind	Represents an enumeration that specifies the list of all built-in types in the EDM.
ConcurrencyMode	Represents the concurrency options for the properties in the EDM.

Table 10.7: Noteworthy Enumerations of the System.Data.Metadata.Edm Namespace	
Enumeration	**Description**
DataSpace	Represents the default names for the models in Entity Framework.
OperationAction	Represents the list of possible actions performed when the parent End of the RelationshipType property, which represents the base class for relationships in a conceptual model, is deleted.
ParameterMode	Represents the direction of a parameter.
ParameterTypeSemantics	Represents the type semantics that are used to resolve the function overloads. Each store provider must use these enumeration flags in the provider manifest file for every function definition.
PrimitiveTypeKind	Represents the kinds of all primitive types defined by the EDM.
PropertyKind	Represents the kinds of item attributes in the EDM.
RelationshipMultiplicity	Represents the multiplicity information about the End of a relationship type.
StoreGeneratedPattern	Represents an enumeration that checks whether the column in the SSDL needs a value during the insert and update operations.

Now, let's understand the EdmGen.exe tool in detail.

EDM Generator Tool

Entity Framework does not support compile-time validation of EDM files in ASP.NET website projects. ASP.NET website projects do not support pre-build events; validating entities in pre-build events can be a very time-consuming task. ADO.NET runtime validates the files when we run or debug the applications. The EdmGen.exe tool is installed in the .NET Framework directory, which is located in C:\Windows\Microsoft.NET\Framework\v4.0.30319. We can also access the EdmGen.exe tool from the Visual Studio command prompt by performing the following steps:

1. Click Start → All Programs→Microsoft Visual Studio 2012→Visual Studio Tools→ Developer Command Prompt for VS2012.

   The Developer Command Prompt for VS2012 opens with the default path on the screen. In our case, the default path is C:\Program Files\Microsoft Visual Studio 11.0>. The general syntax of the EDM Generator tool is as follows:

```
EdmGen /mode:choice [options]
```

2. Type EdmGen/help to see all the EdmGen options on Developer Command Prompt for VS2012. All the options available with the EDM Generator tool, as shown in Figure 10.3:

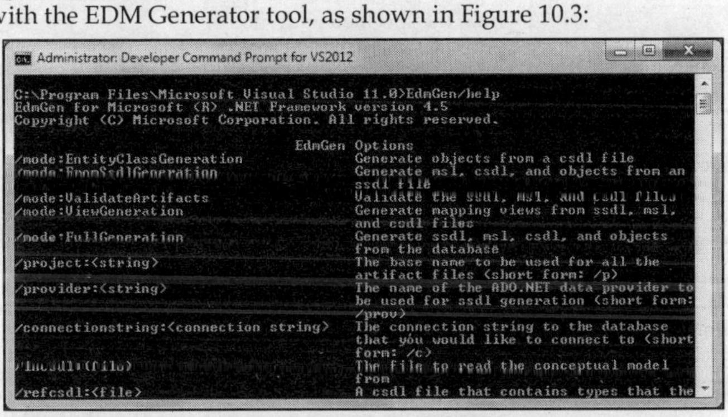

Figure 10.3: Using the EdmGen.exe Tool

3. Scroll down the screen to see all the EdmGen options (Figure 10.3). The Examples shown in Figure 10.4 (encircled by ellipse) shows how to use EdmGen.exe tool to generate and validate an EDM using the Northwind database:

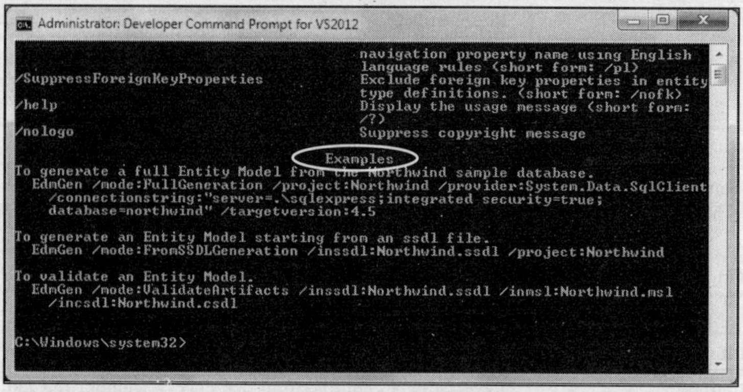

Figure 10.4: Displaying Options to Generate a Entity Model from Northwind Database

The syntax to validate an Entity Model is:

```
EdmGen /mode:ValidateArtifacts /incsdl:<filename> /inmsl:<filename> /inssdl:<filename>
```

The EDM Generator tool provides five modes to perform specific functions, as listed in Table 10.8:

Table 10.8: Modes of the EDM Generator Tool

Mode	Description
/mode:ValidateArtifacts	Requires at least one /inssdl or /incsdl argument. If /inmsl is specified, the /inssdl and /incsdl arguments are also required. You can specify this mode when you want to validate and display errors or warnings in the .csdl, .ssdl, and .msl files.
/mode:FullGeneration	Requires a /connectionstring argument and either a /project argument or /outssdl, /outcsdl, /outmsdl, /outobjectlayer, /outviews, /namespace, and /entitycontainer arguments. This mode generates the .csdl, .ssdl, .msl, object layer, and view files by using the database information specified in the /connectionstring option.
/mode:FromSSDLGeneration	Requires the /inssdl argument and either a /project argument or the /outcsdl, /outmsl, /outobjectlayer, /outviews, /namespace, and /entitycontainer arguments. This mode generates the .csdl and .msl files, source code, and views from the specified .ssdl file.
/mode:EntityClassGeneration	Requires the /incsdl argument and either a /project argument or the /outobjectlayer argument. The /language argument is optional. This mode creates a source code file that contains the classes generated from the .csdl file.
/mode:ViewGeneration	Requires the /inssdl, /incsdl, /inmsl, and either the /project or /outviews arguments. The /language argument is optional. This mode creates a source code file that contains the view generated from the .ssdl, .csdl, and .msl files.

Table 10.9 lists the noteworthy options of the EdmGen.exe tool:

Table 10.9: Options for the EdmGen.exe Tool

Option	Description
/p[roject]:<string>	Specifies the project name to be used with the EdmGen.exe tool. By default, a project name is used as a namespace. The project name is also used for the names of EDM files and the name of view generation source file.

Table 10.9: Options for the EdmGen.exe Tool	
Option	**Description**
/c[onnectionstring]:<connection string>	Specifies a connection string that is required to connect to the data source.
/incsdl:<file>	Specifies a directory that contains a .csdl file. We can use this argument multiple times if we want to specify more than one directory or .csdl files. It is mostly used in cases during entity class or views.
/refcsdl:<file>	Is required when we refer another .csdl file from the source .csdl file. This argument can be specified multiple times.
/inmsl:<file>	Specifies .msl or location of .msl files. We can use this argument multiple times if we want to specify more than one directory or .msl files. It is mostly used in cases during entity class or views. This is required in situations such as when the conceptual model is split.
/inssdl:<file>	Specifies the .ssdl file or a directory where the .ssdl file is located.
/outcsdl:<file>	Specifies the name of the .csdl file that will be created by the EdmGen.exe tool.
/outmsl:<file>	Specifies the name of the .msl file that will be created by the EdmGen.exe tool.
/outssdl:<file>	Specifies the name of the .ssdl file that will be created by the EdmGen.exe tool.
/outobjectlayer:<file>	Specifies the name of the source code file that contains the objects generated from the .csdl file.
/outviews:<file>	Specifies the name of the source code file that contains the views that were generated.
/language:[VB|CSharp]	Specifies the language for the generated source code files. By default, the language is C#.
/namespace:<string>	Specifies the namespace we want to use. The namespace is set in the .csdl file when running the /mode:FullGeneration or /mode:FromSSDLGeneration mode. The namespace is not used when running the /mode:EntityClassGeneration mode.
/entitycontainer:<string>	Specifies the name used to apply to <EntityContainer> element in the generated EDM files.

In the next section, we learn how to use various tools, templates, and wizards provided by Entity Framework

Immediate Solutions

After getting familiar with Entity Framework and its components, let's now move further and learn how to use this Framework in our applications.

Let's perform the following steps to learn to use Entity Framework in an ASP.NET 4.5 application:

1. Open Microsoft Visual Studio 2012.
2. Create an ASP.NET website and save it as EDMgenerationCS (EDMgenerationCS for C# and EDMgenerationVB for VB).
3. Right-click the EDMgenerationCS website in Solution Explorer and select the Add→Add New Item option. The Add New Item dialog box appears, as shown in Figure 10.5:

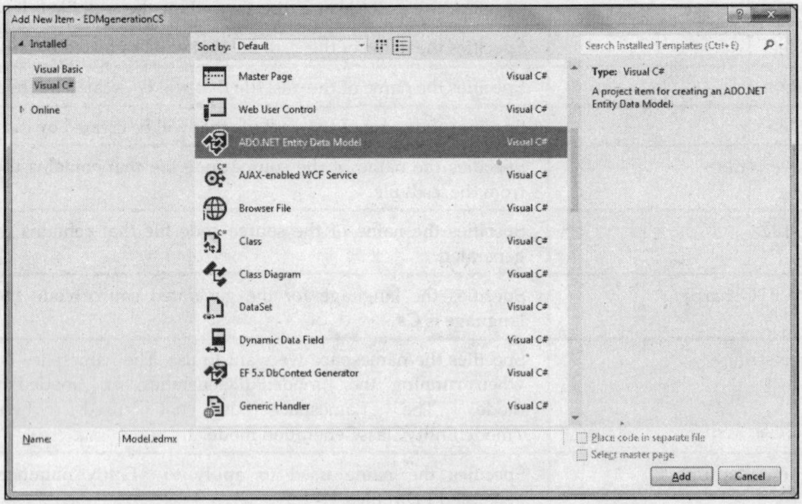

Figure 10.5: Displaying the Add New Item Dialog Box

NOTE

The applications in this chapter are created using the ASP.NET Empty Web Site template in the New Web Site dialog box. After creating the application, you need to add the Default.aspx page to the application.

Therefore, as shown in Figure 10.5, you can add the ADO.NET Entity Data Model template from the Add New Item dialog box in the similar way. In the In Depth section, we discussed that Entity Framework provides tools such as the Entity Data Model template and wizard. Now, let's discuss how to implement these tools in an application.

Creating an Entity Data Model

An EDM can be created by using the ADO.NET Entity Data Model template. We can also use this template to create VB and C# projects. This template can be added to the Console Application, Windows Application, Class Library, ASP.NET Web Application, or ASP.NET website projects. A single project can contain multiple Entity Data items, which might be generated from different databases or different tables within a database. Now, the following steps are performed to add an Entity Data Model template to the website:

1. Right-click the website name, namely, EDMgenerationCS, in Solution Explorer, as shown in Figure 10.6:

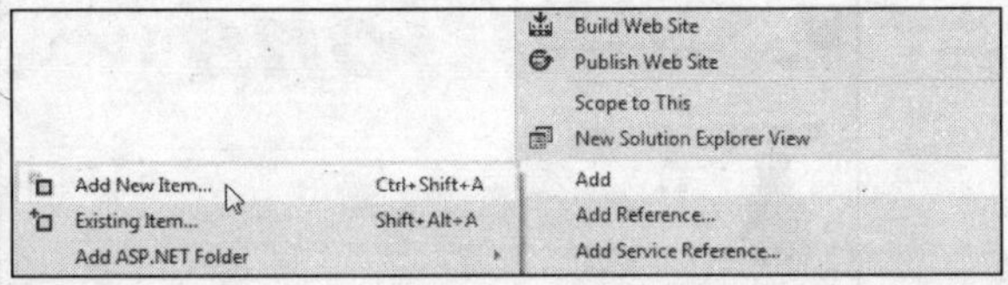

Figure 10.6: Adding a New Item in the EDMgeneration Website

2. Select the Add→`Add New Item` option. The Add New Item dialog box appears (Figure 10.7).
3. Select the ADO.NET Entity Data Model template and click the Add button to include the template in the `EDMgeneration` website, as shown in Figure 10.7:

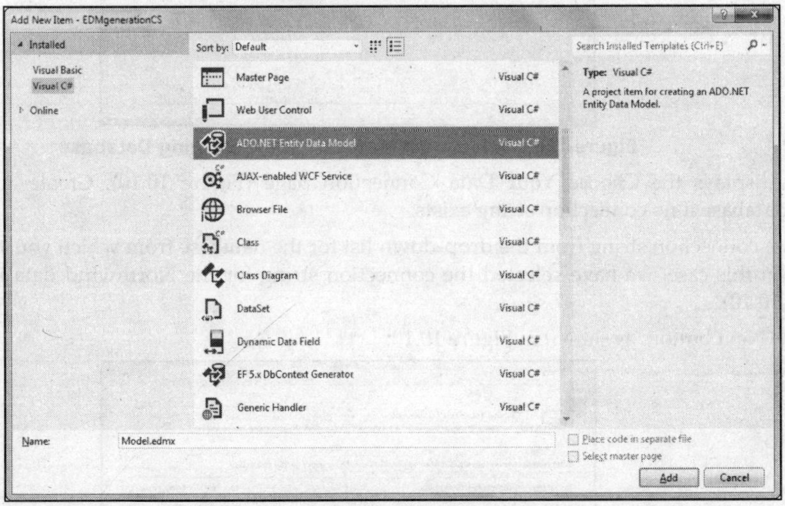

Figure 10.7: Adding the Entity Data Model Template in EDMgeneration Website

A message box prompting to place the ADO.NET Entity Data Model into a folder App_Code appears (Figure 10.8).

4. Click the Yes button, as shown in Figure 10.8:

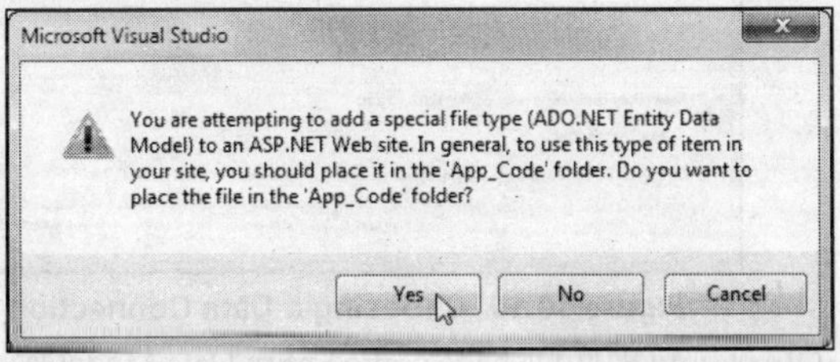

Figure 10.8: Locating the File in the App_Code Folder

A folder App_Code is created in the application. The Entity Data Model Wizard starts displaying two options to create a model, that is, Generate from database and Empty model (Figure 10.9).

5. Select the `Generate from database` option from the Choose Model Contents page and click the Next button to generate a model from the existing database, as shown in Figure 10.9:

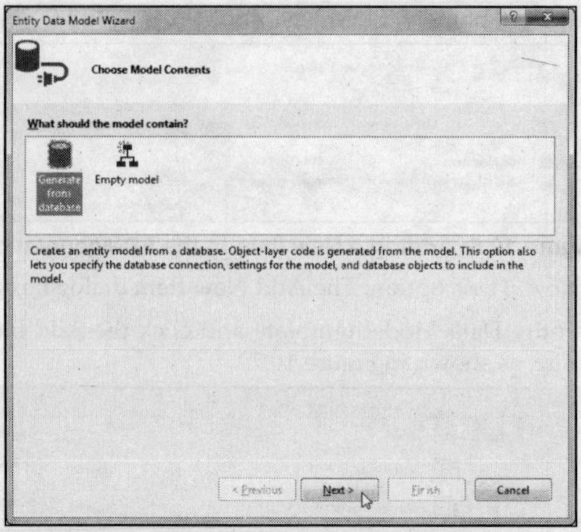

Figure 10.9: Selecting a Model from the Existing Database

The wizard displays the Choose Your Data Connection page (Figure 10.10). Create a connection with the Northwind database if no connection string exists.

6. Select the connection string from the drop-down list for the database from which you want to generate your model. In this case, we have selected the connection string for the Northwind database from SQL Server (Figure 10.10).
7. Click the Next button, as shown in Figure 10.10:

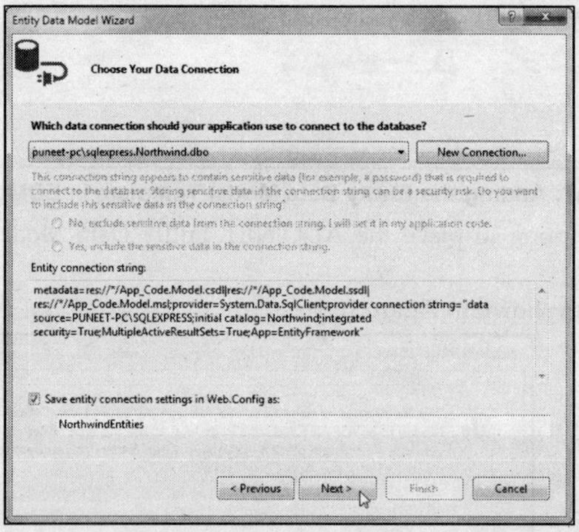

Figure 10.10: Choosing a Data Connection

The Choose Your Database Objects and Settings page of the Entity Data Model Wizard appears (Figure 10.11).

NOTE

When we work with EDM tools in an ASP.NET website, the entity connection string is saved in the Web.config file; however, in a Windows application, the entity connection string is saved in the App.config file. The location of the metadata files is specified as metadata=res://;. Therefore, ensure that the Save entity connection settings in Web.Config as check box is selected and the value is specified (Figure 10.10); otherwise, the connections settings will not be saved.*

8. Select the Tables, Views, and Stored Procedures and Functions check boxes, which you need to create an EDM from the database, and click the Finish button, as shown in Figure 10.11:

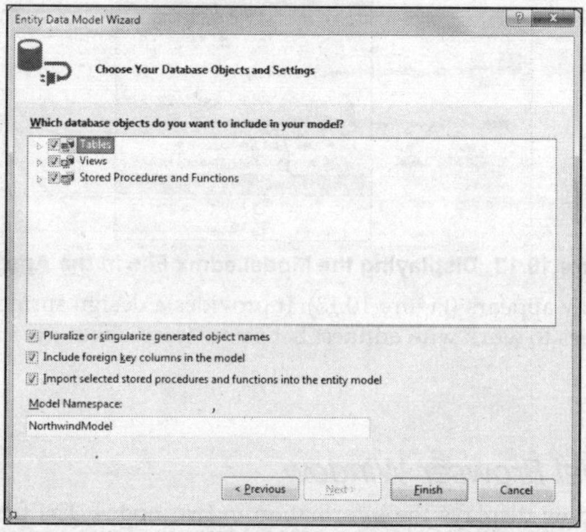

Figure 10.11: Selecting the Database Objects

The EDM that is created from the Northwind database is loaded in the website, as shown in Figure 10.12:

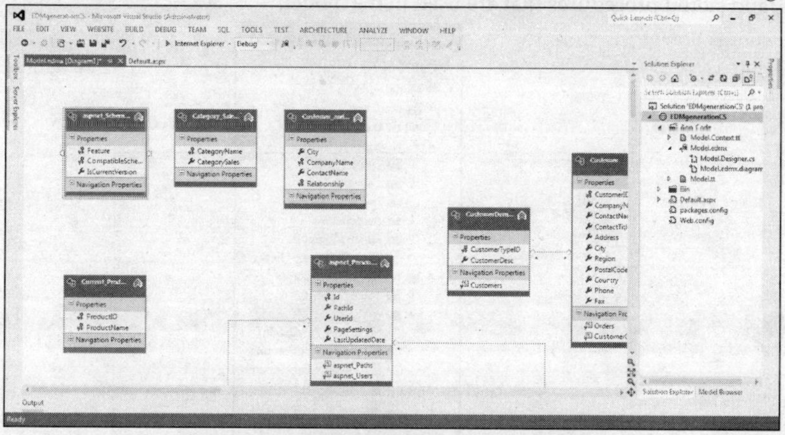

Figure 10.12: Showing the Output of EDM

NOTE

In Figure 10.11, the Model Namespace textbox contains NorthwindModel value. It causes the ADO.NET runtime to load the EDM metadata artifact files, such as .csdl files from resources in the assembly that is dynamically compiled by ASP.NET.

The EDM includes tables, views, and stored procedures that we have selected at the time of selecting database objects. The Model.edmx file created by the wizard must be added to the App_Code folder of the ASP.NET website project. If we select to relocate the .edmx file to another directory, then the model is not supported by the EDM build provider for ASP.NET. Now, let's understand how to work with ADO.NET Entity Data Model Designer.

Working with Entity Data Model Designer

ADO.NET Entity Data Model Designer works with an .edmx file that is an encapsulation of the CSDL, the SSDL, and the MSL files. This .edmx file is created and added to our project after the creation of EDM. We can make changes to the EDM through the .edmx file by using ADO.NET Entity Data Model Designer. To open the EDM designer, double-click the Model .edmx file in Solution Explorer, as shown in Figure 10.13:

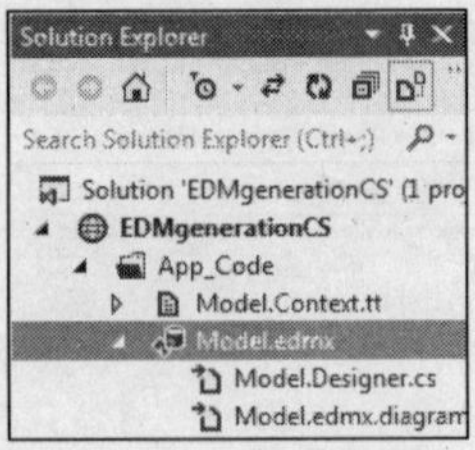

Figure 10.13: Displaying the Model.edmx File in the App_Code Folder

The EDM designer window appears (Figure 10.13). It provides a design surface for editing the conceptual model that provides functionalities to work with entities. Let's now learn about the following windows:

- Model Browser
- Mapping Details

Using the Entity Model Browser Window

The Model Browser window displays the information in two nodes. The first node displays the details of the conceptual model. We can expand the underlying nodes to view all entity types and associations included in the model. The second node displays the details of targeted database models. Figure 10.14 displays parts of database tables, views, and stored procedures that are used in the model:

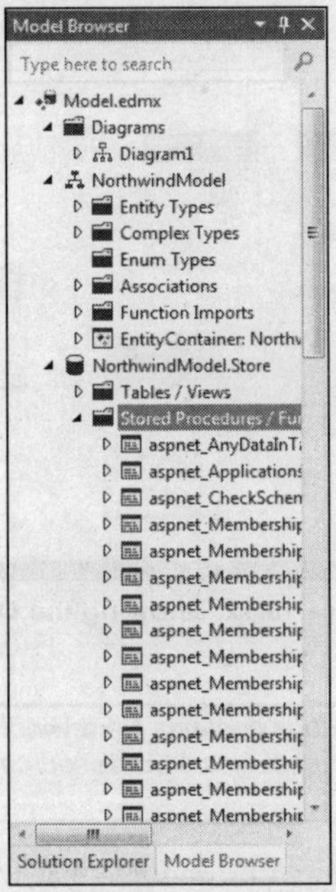

Figure 10.14: Viewing the Model.edmx File in Model Browser Window

NOTE

You can view the Model Browser window by double click the Model.edmx file and then open VIEW → Other Windows → Entity Data Model Browser option from the menu bar.

The Model Browser window also provides the capability of creating CSDL function import entries that are used to invoke the stored procedure, and specifies the return type for the function import. Now, let's see how to create a function import through the Model Browser window by following the succeeding steps:

1. Expand the Stored Procedures/Functions node in the Model Browser window (Figure 10.15).

A list of available stored procedures appears.

2. Right-click any stored procedure from the list and then select the Add Function Import option from the context menu, as shown in Figure 10.15:

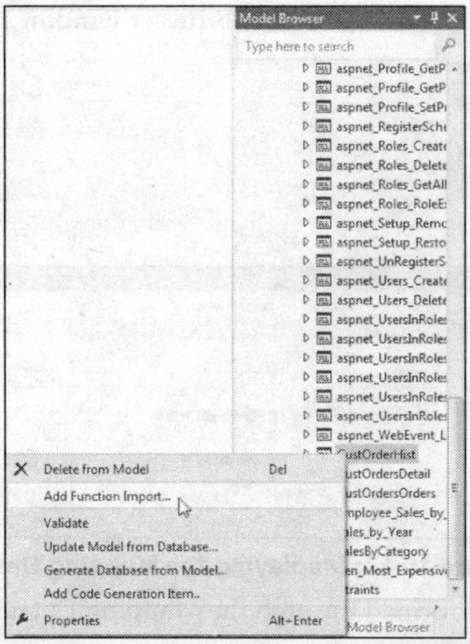

Figure 10.15: Creating Function Import for a Stored Procedure

The `Add Function Import` dialog box appears, as shown in Figure 10.16:

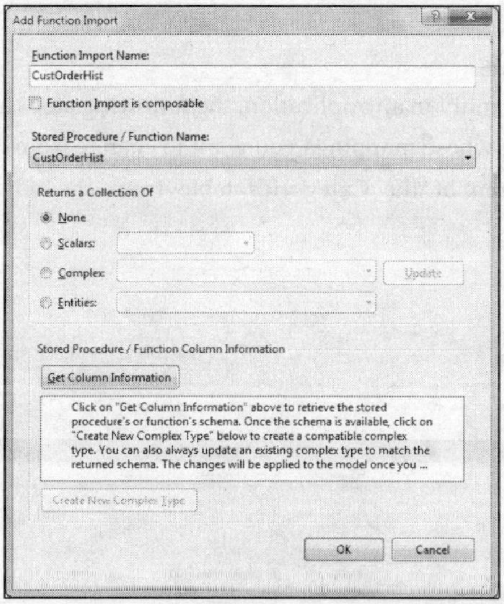

Figure 10.16: Specifying the Fields

The `Add Function Import` dialog box displays three fields— `Stored Procedure/Function Name`, `Function Import Name`, and `Returns a Collection Of`. The `Stored Procedure Name` field specifies the name of the database for which we are creating a function import. The `Function Import Name` field specifies the name of the function import. The `Return Type` field specifies the return type for function import.

By specifying the values for each of these fields, we can create a CSDL function import entry in a stored procedure. Now, let's see how to modify the mappings of database objects by using the `Mapping Details` window.

Using the Mapping Details Window

The Mapping Details window enables us to view and edit the mappings in the EDM. We can access this window by selecting the Entity Types option in the Model Browser window. The Mapping Details window shows the mappings of the selected entity objects in the Model Browser window, as shown in Figure 10.17:

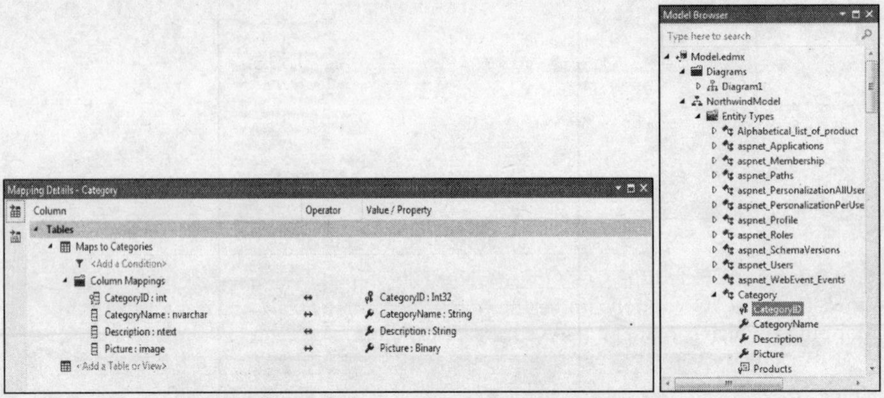

Figure 10.17: Displaying the Mapping Details Window

The following functions can be performed through the Mapping Details window:

- Modifying mappings of entities
- Adding a table or view
- Adding a condition

Modifying Mappings of Entities

To modify the mapping of an entity in an application, the following steps are performed:

1. Select the Category name whose mappings you want to change from the Column Mappings folder.
2. Select the desired column of the Categories table from the adjoining drop-down list, as shown in Figure 10.18:

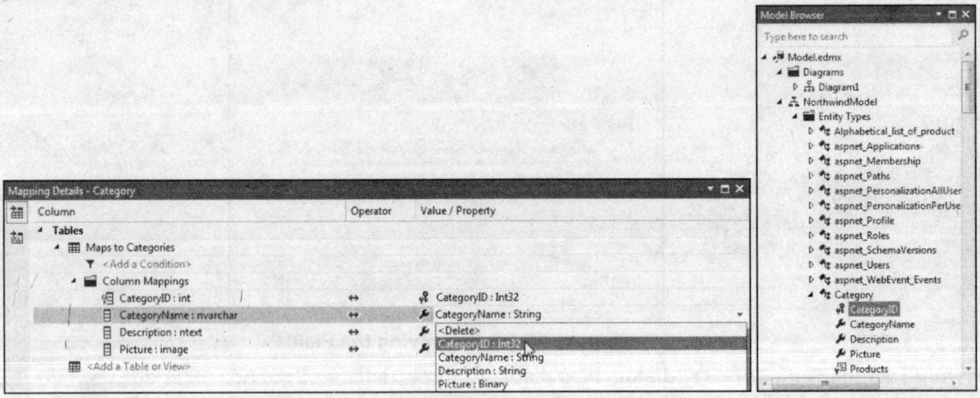

Figure 10.18: Modifying the Mapping of Entities

In Figure 10.18, we have changed the mapping of the CategoryName column.

Adding a Table or View

To add a table or view in an application, the following steps are performed:

1. Select the <Add a Table or View> option in the Mapping Details window.

A drop-down list appears, displaying a list of tables and views (Figure 10.19).

2. Select the desired table or view, as shown in Figure 10.19:

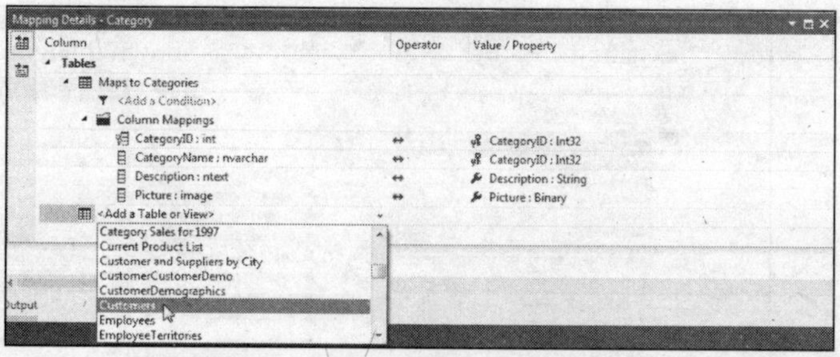

Figure 10.19: Adding a Table or View

In Figure 10.19, we have selected the Customers table. The Maps to Customers option is added to the Mapping Details window. There are two options under the Maps to Customers tab, one is <Add a Condition> and another is Column Mappings, which contain all the columns of the table, as shown in Figure 10.20:

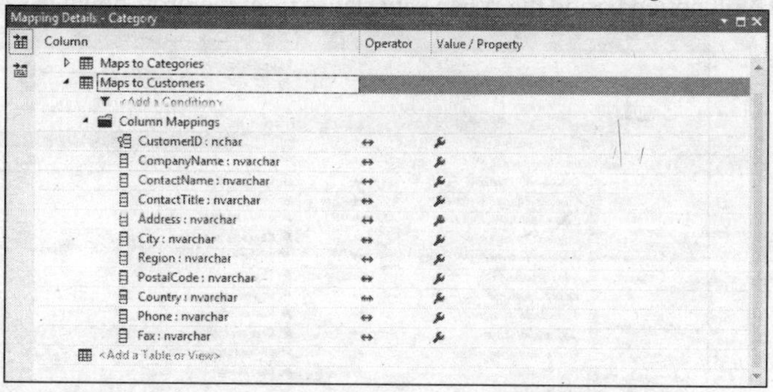

Figure 10.20: Displaying the Mapping Details Window

Adding a Condition to a Field

To add a condition to a field of a column, we first need to enable the <Add a Condition> option, which is done by performing the following steps:

1. Select the Customer table in the Model Browser window under the Entity Types folder, as shown in Figure 10.21:

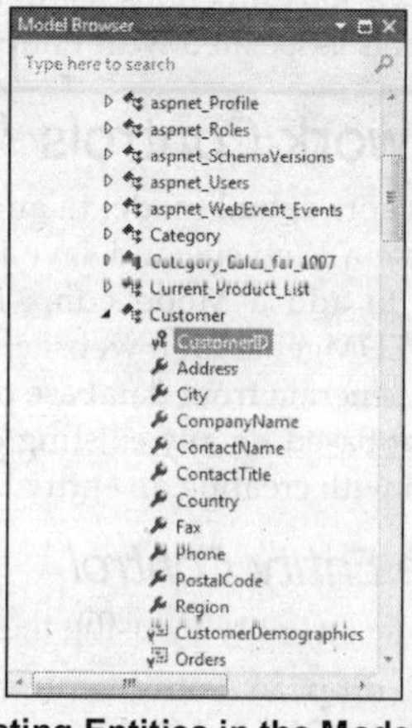

Figure 10.21: Selecting Entities in the Model Browser Window

2. Now, select a column, say, City, where we want to put a condition, by selecting the <Add a Condition> option as shown in Figure 10.22:

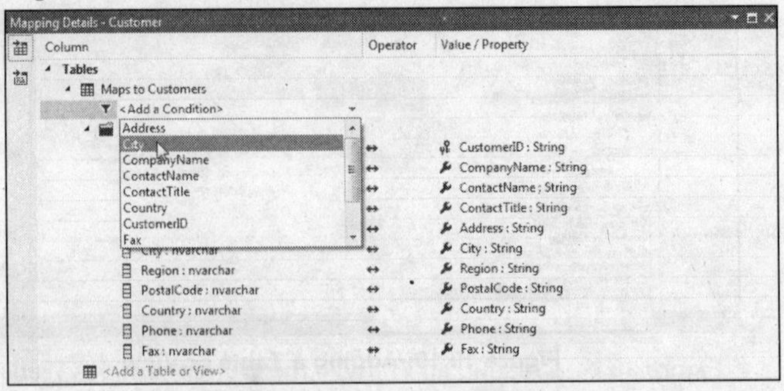

Figure 10.22: Adding a Condition

Now, the screen displays the condition associated with the City column (Figure 10.23).

3. Select the Not Null option beside the When City clause from the drop-down list, as shown in Figure 10.23:

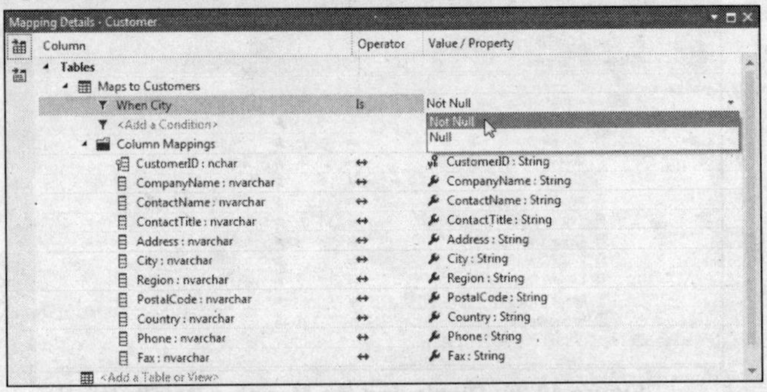

Figure 10.23: Selecting the Not Null Option

The desired condition, that is, Not Null, is added to the City column.

NOTE

The Mapping Details window allows a table to have more than one condition.

Here, we have learned how to perform various functions using the Entity Data Model Designer tool. Now, let's move ahead and understand some controls associated with Entity Framework.

Working with Entity Framework Controls

In this section, we learn how to create a conceptual model in an application by using the three controls—Entity, Association, and Inheritance. First, create a Web site and save it as WorkingEntities (WorkingEntitiesCS in C# and WorkingEntitiesVB in VB). Now, to add a Model.edmx file in the Web site, follow the same steps as followed while creating an EDM in the EDMgeneration website. The only difference is that in this case we select the Empty model option instead of the Generate from database option (Figure 10.9). After the Model.edmx file is added to the Web application that is not based on any existing database, the output of the application will be a blank designer surface. Now, let's begin with creating an entity by using Entity Control.

Creating an Entity by Using the Entity Control

Let's perform the following steps to create an entity by using the Entity control from the Toolbox:

1. To create a new entity, drag and drop an Entity control from the Toolbox on the designer surface of Model.edmx file, as shown in Figure 10.24:

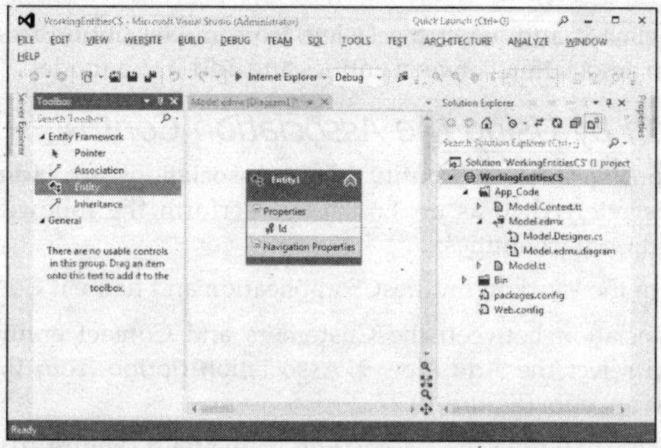

Figure 10.24: Creating an Entity in the WorkingEntities Website

2. Specify a Name for the entity, say, Customers, through the Properties window (Figure 10.25).
3. Select the None option beside the Base Type field (Figure 10.25).

   In the case of a derived entity, we need to set a base type for the new entity by choosing the desired base type from the available base types.
4. Set the Entity Set Name property to CustomersEntitySet, as shown in Figure 10.25:

Figure 10.25: Specifying the Properties of an Entity

In case of a derived entity, the `Entity Set Name` field is disabled.

NOTE

We can also create an entity through the designer surface (without using the Entity control from the Toolbox) by performing the following steps:

1. *Right-click anywhere on the designer window. A context menu opens.*
2. *Click the Add New→ Entity option from the context menu. The Add Entity dialog box appears (Figure 10.26).*
3. *Specify the properties of the entity through the Add Entity dialog box, as shown in Figure 10.26:*

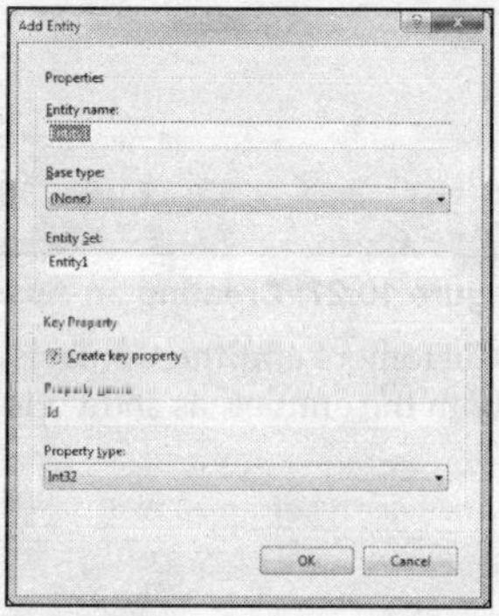

Figure 10.26: Displaying the Add Entity Dialog Box

A key property can be created only if the base type is selected as None, whereas in the case of derived entities, this option is disabled.

To delete an entity, right-click it and select the Delete from model option from the context menu. Now, let's understand how to form an association between entities and add it to a model.

Creating an Association by Using the Association Control

Associations define relationships between entity types. Associations are bidirectional and each participating entity in the association is referred to as an End. Let's perform the following steps to form an association between the Customers and Contact entities:

1. Create another entity in the WorkingEntitiesCS application and name it Contact.
2. Now, to form an association between the Customers and Contact entities, right-click anywhere on the designer window and select the Add New→ Association option from the context menu. The Add New Association dialog box appears (Figure 10.27).
3. Enter a name for the association in the Association Name field (Figure 10.27). In this case, we have named the association CustomersContact.
4. Select values for both entities from the Multiplicity drop-down lists (Figure 10.27). In this application, we create `One to Many` multiplicity between the Customers and Contact entities.
5. Enter the values in the Navigation Property field for both the entities (Figure 10.27).
6. Click the OK button, as shown in Figure 10.27:

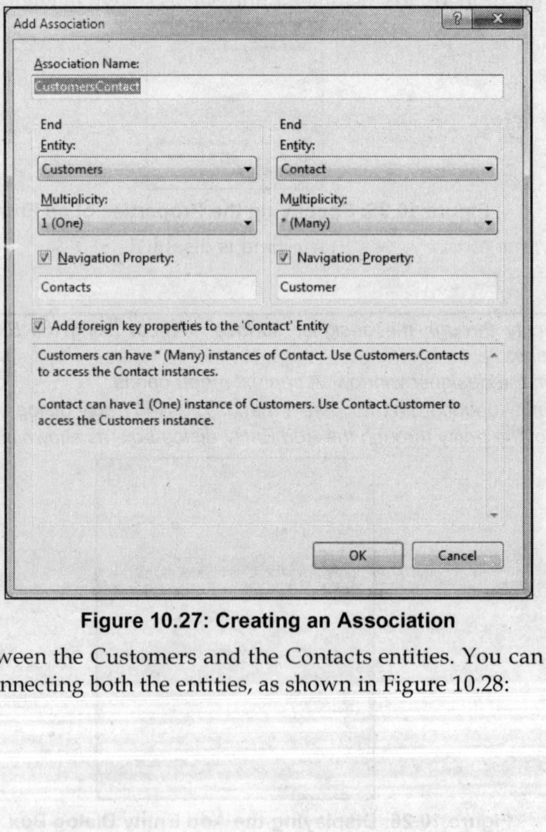

Figure 10.27: Creating an Association

An association is formed between the Customers and the Contacts entities. You can see the association as a line, that is, CustomersContact, connecting both the entities, as shown in Figure 10.28:

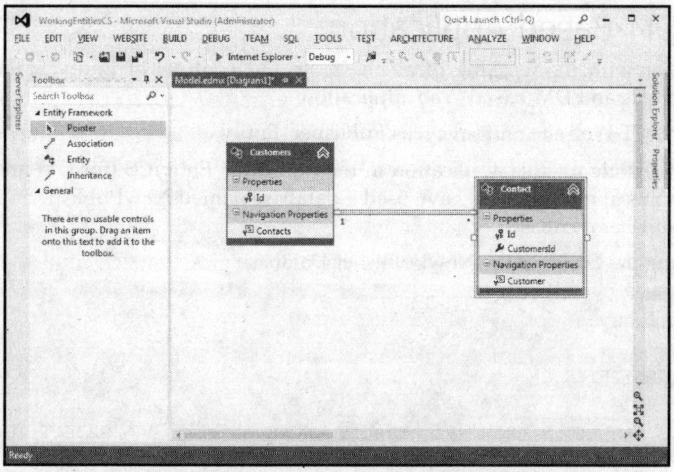

Figure 10.28: Displaying the Association of Two Entities

Entity Framework allows us to form more than one association between the same pair of entities. The second line, in Figure 10.28 shows that the Many to Many association is also formed along with the One to Many association between the Customers and the Contact entities. To delete an association, right-click it and select the Delete from model option from the context menu. Now, let's understand the Inheritance tool.

Creating an Inheritance by Using the Inheritance Control

The Inheritance tool permits one type to be derived from another type, but the source and target ends must be different. Suppose we have another entity named Vendor and we want both the Vendor and Customers entities should be inherited from the Contact entity. In this case, the Contact entity is the `Base type`, and the Vendor and Customers entities are called derived types. For this, set the Contact entity as base type for the Vendors and Customers entities in the Base Type field from their respective Properties windows.

The inheritance between the three entities is shown in Figure 10.29:

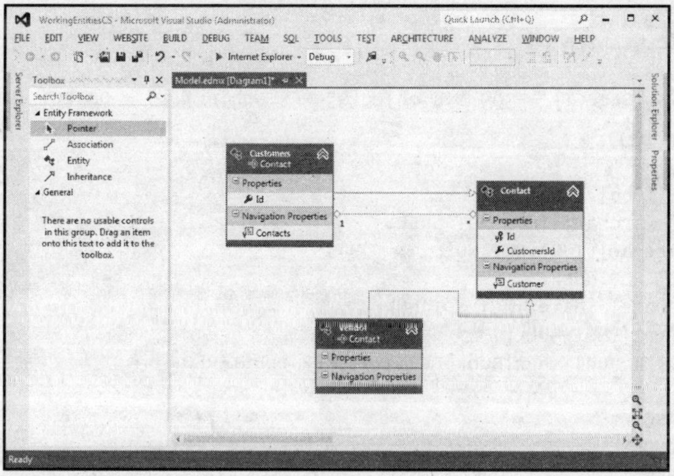

Figure 10.29: Displaying the Inheritance Relationships Among Entities

Here, we have learned how to create an entity, associate it with other entities, and define inheritance among different entities by using various controls from the Toolbox. Now, let's move ahead to create a Web application based on EDM.

Creating an EDM-Based Application

After getting familiar with the working of all the tools and controls of Entity Framework, let's perform the following steps to create an EDM-based Web application:

1. Create an ASP.NET Web site and save it as Publisher_Entity.

   You can find the code for this application in the Publisher_EntityCS (for C#) and Publisher_EntityVB (for VB) folders. In this application, we have used a database named NewPublisher. Listing 10.1 shows the code for the NewPublisher database:

Listing 10.1: Showing the Code for the NewPublisher Database

```
USE NEWPUBLISHER
SET ANSI_NULLS ON
GO
SET QUOTED_IDENTIFIER ON
GO
IF NOT EXISTS (SELECT * FROM sys.objects WHERE object_id = OBJECT_ID(N'[dbo].[Author]')
   AND type in (N'U'))
BEGIN
CREATE TABLE [dbo].[Author](
[AuthorID] [int] NOT NULL,
[LastName] [nvarchar](50) NOT NULL,
[FirstName] [nvarchar](50) NOT NULL,
[OnPanelDate] [datetime] NULL,
 CONSTRAINT [PK_Publisher.Author] PRIMARY KEY CLUSTERED
(
[AuthorID] ASC
)WITH (PAD_INDEX  = OFF, IGNORE_DUP_KEY = OFF) ON [PRIMARY]
) ON [PRIMARY]
END
GO
SET ANSI_NULLS ON
GO
SET QUOTED_IDENTIFIER ON
GO
IF NOT EXISTS (SELECT * FROM sys.objects WHERE object_id = OBJECT_ID(N'[dbo].[Book]')
   AND
   type in (N'U'))
BEGIN
CREATE TABLE [dbo].[Book](
[BookISBN] [nvarchar](100) NOT NULL,
[Title] [nvarchar](100) NOT NULL,
[Pages] [int] NOT NULL,
[Publishing_Date] [datetime] NOT NULL,
[AuthorID] [int] NOT NULL,
 CONSTRAINT [PK_Publisher.Book] PRIMARY KEY CLUSTERED
(
[BookISBN] ASC
)WITH (PAD_INDEX  = OFF, IGNORE_DUP_KEY = OFF) ON [PRIMARY]
) ON [PRIMARY]
END
GO
IF NOT EXISTS (SELECT * FROM sys.foreign_keys WHERE object_id =
   OBJECT_ID(N'[dbo].[FK_Author_Book]') AND parent_object_id =
   OBJECT_ID(N'[dbo].[Book]'))
```

```
ALTER TABLE [dbo].[Book]  WITH CHECK ADD  CONSTRAINT [FK_Author_Book] FOREIGN
  KEY([AuthorID])
REFERENCES [dbo].[Author] ([AuthorID])
GO
ALTER TABLE [dbo].[Book] CHECK CONSTRAINT [FK_Author_Book]
```

Now, we need to generate an EDM in our Publisher_Entity application based on the NewPublisher database by using the Entity Data Model Wizard.

3. Select the Generate from database option (refer to Figure 10.9) from the Entity Data Model Wizard while creating a Model.edmx file for the application.

The Model.edmx file is added to the application, as shown in Figure 10.30:

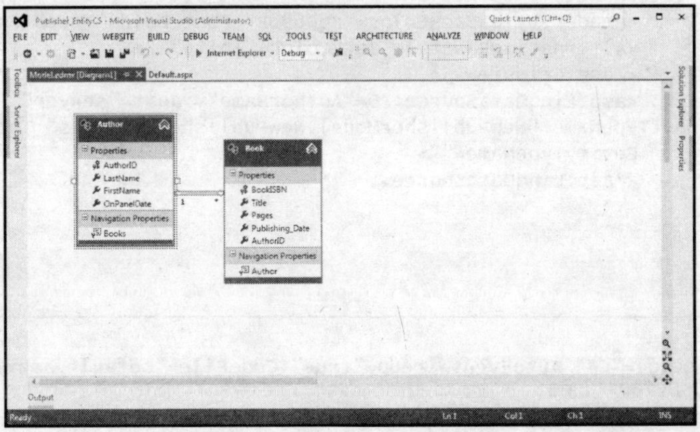

Figure 10.30: Displaying EDM of the Publisher Database

3. Replace the code for the Default.aspx page with that given in Listing 10.2 to add the controls required for the application. Listing 10.2 shows the code for the Default.aspx page:

Listing 10.2: Showing the Code for the Default.aspx Page

In VB

```
<%@ Page Language="VB" AutoEventWireup="false" CodeFile="Default.aspx.vb"
  Inherits="_Default" %>
<!DOCTYPE html>
<html xmlns="http://www.w3.org/1999/xhtml">
<head runat="server">
        <title>Entity Framework Application</title>
</head>
<body>
    <form id="form1" runat="server">
    <div>
   <br />
                Demo showing the use of Entity Framework in database application<br />
                <br />
         ------------------------------------------------------------------------
                <br />
                <i>Select the Author Name from the Drop - Down list to view the books
                asscociated with author<br />
        <br />
        </i><br />
                <i>Author Name</i>
                <asp:DropDownList ID="DropDownList1" runat="server"
                DataSourceID="AuthorName"
                DataTextField="FirstName" DataValueField="AuthorID" AutoPostBack="True"
          Height="20px" Width="80px"
```

```
            onselectedindexchanged="DropDownList1_SelectedIndexChanged">
                </asp:DropDownList>
                <br />
                <br />
                <span class="style1">Book Details of Author</span><asp:GridView
                ID="GridView1"
        runat="server" BackColor="White" BorderColor="#DEDFDE" BorderStyle="None"
        BorderWidth="1px" CellPadding="4" ForeColor="Black" GridLines="Vertical">
                <RowStyle BackColor="#F7F7DE" />
                <FooterStyle BackColor="#CCCC99" />
        <PagerStyle BackColor="#F7F7DE" ForeColor="Black" HorizontalAlign="Right" />
        <SelectedRowStyle BackColor="#CE5D5A" Font-Bold="True" ForeColor="White" />
                <HeaderStyle BackColor="#6B696B" Font-Bold="True" ForeColor="White" />
                <AlternatingRowStyle BackColor="White" />
                </asp:GridView>
                <asp:LinqDataSource ID="AuthorName" runat="server"
        ContextTypeName="NewPublisherModel.NewPublisherEntities" TableName="Authors"
                EntityTypeName="">
                </asp:LinqDataSource>
    </div>
    </form>
</body>
</html>
```

In C#

```
<%@ Page Language="C#" AutoEventWireup="true" CodeFile="Default.aspx.cs"
  Inherits="_Default" %>
<!DOCTYPE>
<html xmlns="http://www.w3.org/1999/xhtml">
<head runat="server">
       <title>Entity Framework Application</title>
</head>
<body>
    <form id="form1" runat="server">
    <div>
    <br />
                Demo showing the use of Entity Framework in database application<br />
                <br />
        ------------------------------------------------------------------------
                <br />
                <i>Select the Author Name from the Drop - Down list to view the books
                asscociated with author<br />
        <br />
        </i><br />
                <i>Author Name</i>
                <asp:DropDownList ID="DropDownList1" runat="server"
                DataSourceID="AuthorName"
                DataTextField="FirstName" DataValueField="AuthorID" AutoPostBack="True"
            Height="20px" Width="80px"
            onselectedindexchanged="DropDownList1_SelectedIndexChanged">
                </asp:DropDownList>
                <br />
                <br />
                <span class="style1">Book Details of Author</span><asp:GridView
                ID="GridView1"
        runat="server" BackColor="White" BorderColor="#DEDFDE" BorderStyle="None"
        BorderWidth="1px" CellPadding="4" ForeColor="Black" GridLines="Vertical">
                <RowStyle BackColor="#F7F7DE" />
```

```
                <FooterStyle BackColor="#CCCC99" />
            <PagerStyle BackColor="#F7F7DE" ForeColor="Black" HorizontalAlign="Right" />
            <SelectedRowStyle BackColor="#CE5D5A" Font-Bold="True" ForeColor="White" />
                <HeaderStyle BackColor="#6B696B" Font-Bold="True" ForeColor="White" />
                <AlternatingRowStyle BackColor="White" />
                </asp:GridView>
                <asp:LinqDataSource ID="AuthorName" runat="server"
            ContextTypeName="NewPublisherModel.NewPublisherEntities" TableName="Authors"
                EntityTypeName="">
                </asp:LinqDataSource>
        </div>
        </form>
    </body>
    </html>
```

4. Now, add the code as shown Listing 10.3 in the code-behind file of the Default.aspx page for creating an EDM-based application:

Listing 10.3: Showing the Code for the Code-Behind File for the Default.aspx Page

In VB

```
Imports NewPublisherModel
Partial Class _Default
    Inherits System.Web.UI.Page
    Private PublisherContext As NewPublisherEntities
    Protected Sub DropDownList1_SelectedIndexChanged(sender As Object, e As
  EventArgs) Handles DropDownList1.SelectedIndexChanged
        Dim AuthorID As Int32 = Convert.ToInt32(DropDownList1.SelectedValue)
        Dim BookDetails = From bookD In PublisherContext.Books
        Where bookD.Author.AuthorID = AuthorID _
        Select New With _
        { _
         .BookName = bookD.Title, _
         .Pages = bookD.Pages, _
         .ISBN = bookD.BookISBN _
        }
        GridView1.DataSource = BookDetails
        GridView1.DataBind()
    End Sub
    Protected Sub Page_Load(sender As Object, e As EventArgs) Handles
  Me.Load
        PublisherContext = New NewPublisherEntities()
    End Sub
End Class
```

In C#

```
using System;
using System.Collections.Generic;
using System.Linq;
using System.Web;
using System.Web.UI;
using System.Web.UI.WebControls;
using NewPublisherModel;
public partial class _Default : System.Web.UI.Page
{
    private NewPublisherEntities PublisherContext;
    protected void Page_Load(object sender, EventArgs e)
    {
        PublisherContext = new NewPublisherEntities();
    }
```

```
    protected void DropDownList1_SelectedIndexChanged(object sender, EventArgs e)
    {
        Int32 AuthorID = Convert.ToInt32(DropDownList1.SelectedValue);
        var BookDetails = from bookD in PublisherContext.Books
                          where bookD.Author.AuthorID == AuthorID
                          select new
                          {
                              BookName = bookD.Title,
                              Pages = bookD.Pages,
                              ISBN = bookD.BookISBN
                          };
        GridView1.DataSource = BookDetails;
        GridView1.DataBind();
    }
}
```

In the preceding code, the DropDownList1_SelectedIndexChanged event contains the code to bind the GridView1 control to the DropDownList1 control.

5. Press the F5 key to run the application.
6. Now, select an author name, say, Puneet, from the drop-down list beside the Author Name field. The book details associated with the author change in the GridView control accordingly, as shown in Figure 10.31:

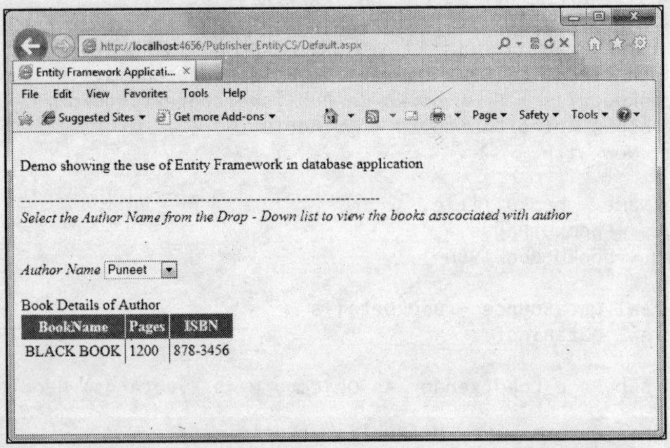

Figure 10.31: Displaying Book Details of Authors

Figure 10.31 shows that the details, such as BookName, Pages, and the ISBN number of the book authored by Puneet, are added to the GridView control.

Summary

This chapter provides an in depth coverage of ADO.NET Entity Framework. We have discussed about the benefits of developing Web applications by using Entity Framework. Then the various features and components supported by Entity Framework, such as EDM, Object Services, Entity SQL, Client provider, and mapping between conceptual and storage schemas, have been discussed. We have also discussed the implementation of various tools and controls associated with Entity Framework.

In the next chapter, we learn about files and streams in ASP.NET.

11

Working With Files and Streams

In Depth

We know that data can be retrieved from both databases as well as files. Generally, it is preferred to work with databases as they enable us to handle data in an efficient and secure manner. However, in certain conditions, we need to perform various operations in a file system, such as drives and directories. Till now, we have focused on how to store and retrieve data from a database, and in this chapter, we explore how to work with file systems.

A file is typically the principal means by which you can interact with a program. For example, a file can be a data set that you can read, create and modify or a stream of bytes that are generated by a program. In ASP.NET, you can easily manipulate files. .NET Framework provides the System.IO namespace to work with file systems; i.e., drives, directories, and files.

In this chapter, we learn how to work with file systems programmatically, such as storing and retrieving data from a file. Now, let's start with the overview of the System.IO namespace and its classes, which enable us to work with files and directories.

Introducing the System.IO Namespace

The System.IO namespace contains classes and enumerations that you can use to read and write data on data streams and files. Streams provide a way to read and write to a backing store, such as network, memory, and tape streams. Noteworthy classes of the System.IO namespace are listed in Table 11.1:

Table 11.1: Noteworthy Classes of the System.IO Namespace

Class	Description
BinaryReader	Allows you to read primitive data types the same as binary values in a particular encoding.
`BinaryWriter`	Allows you to write primitive data types in binary to a stream and allows writing strings.
`BufferedStream`	Allows you to include a buffering layer to read and write operations on other stream and cannot be inherited.
`Directory`	Provides the static methods for creating, moving, and enumerating through directories and subdirectories. You cannot inherit this class.
`DirectoryInfo`	Provides the instance methods for creating, moving, and enumerating through directories and subdirectories. You cannot inherit this class.
`DirectoryNotFoundException`	Throws an exception, when part of a file or directory cannot be found.
`DriveInfo`	Provides access to information available on a drive.
`DriveNotFoundException`	Throws an exception, when trying to access a drive or share that is not available.
`EndOfStreamException`	Throws an exception, when reading is attempted at the end of a stream.
`ErrorEventArgs`	Exposes data for the `Error event`.
`File`	Provides static methods that support creation, copying, moving, and opening of files, in the creation of `FileStream` objects.
`FileFormatException`	Throws an exception, when an input file or a data stream is distorted.
`FileInfo`	Provides instance methods that support the creation, deletion, moving, and opening of files in the creation of FileStream objects. This class cannot be inherited.

Table 11.1: Noteworthy Classes of the System.IO Namespace

Class	Description
`FileLoadException`	Throws an exception, when a managed assembly is found but cannot be loaded.
`FileNotFoundException`	Throws an exception, when an attempt to access a file that does not exist fails.
`FileStream`	Exposes a Stream around a file that supports both synchronous and asynchronous read and write operations.
`FileSystemEventArgs`	Provides data for the directory events, such as `Changed`, `Created`, and `Deleted`.
`FileSystemInfo`	Allows you to use the base class for both the `FileInfo` and `DirectoryInfo` objects.
`FileSystemWatcher`	Raises events when a directory or a file in a directory changes.
`InternalBufferOverflowException`	Throws an exception, when the internal buffer overflows.
`InvalidDataException`	Throws an exception, when a data stream is in an invalid format.
`IODescriptionAttribute`	Sets the description that visual designers can display, when referencing an event.
`IOException`	Throws an exception, when an I/O error occurs.
`MemoryStream`	Creates a stream that resides in memory.
`Path`	Performs operations on String instances that contain file or directory path information. These operations are performed in a cross-platform manner.
`PathTooLongException`	Specifies an exception that is thrown when a pathname or filename is longer than the system-defined maximum length.
`PipeException`	Throws an exception, when an error occurs within a named pipe.
`RenamedEventArgs`	Provides data for the event that is renamed.
`Stream`	Provides a generic view of a sequence of bytes.
`StreamReader`	Implements a `TextReader` that reads characters from a byte stream in a particular encoding.
`StreamWriter`	Provides a `TextWriter` for a stream in a particular encoding to write characters.
`StringReader`	Implements a `TextReader` that reads from a string.
`StringWriter`	Implements a `TextWriter` for writing information to a string. The information is stored in an underlying `StringBuilder`.
`TextReader`	Works with a reader that can read a sequential series of characters.
`TextWriter`	Represents a class that represents a writer. The writer is used to write sequential series of characters. This class is abstract.
`UnmanagedMemoryStream`	Provides access to unmanaged blocks of memory from managed code.
`UnmanagedMemoryAccessor`	Allows you to access to unmanaged blocks of memory from managed code randomly.

Noteworthy enumerations of the System.IO namespace are listed in Table 11.2:

Table 11.2: Noteworthy Enumerations of the System.IO Namespace

Enumeration	Description
`DriveType`	Provides constants for drive types that include `CDROM`, Fixed, Network, `NoRootDirectory`, RAM, Removable, and Unknown
`FileAccess`	Provides constants for read, write, or read/write access to a file
`FileAttributes`	Provides files and directories attributes.
`FileMode`	Describes how the operating system should open a file
`FileOptions`	Specifies additional options for declaring a `FileStream` object
`FileShare`	Defines constants for restricting the kind of access that the other `FileStream` objects can have as compare to the same file
`HandleInheritability`	Describes whether the mentioned handle is inheritable by child processes.
`NotifyFilters`	Defines modifications to look at for in a file or folder.
`SearchOption`	Describes whether to search the current directory, or the current directory and all subdirectories
`SeekOrigin`	Defines the fields that describes reference points in streams for looking data
`WatcherChangeTypes`	Writes changes that can happen to a file or a directory

Now, let's explore the classes that we use to work with drives, directories, and files in detail.

Working with Drives and Directories

We often need to interact with drives and directories located in our system. .NET Framework provides classes that help us in performing various tasks, such as reading and writing in a file, to interact with the file system. These classes are as follows:

- Directory
- DirectoryInfo
- DriveInfo

Now, let's discuss each of these classes in detail one by one.

Exploring the Directory Class

The Directory class provides static methods to create, move, and enumerate directories and subdirectories. This class is located under the System.IO namespace and is not inherited by any other class. Using the Directory class, we can accomplish a number of operations, such as moving a directory from one location to another and renaming a directory. We do not need to create objects of the Directory class because this class provides static methods. A drawback of the Directory class is that it takes longer time to execute, since every time we call a method, the Directory class performs a security check to verify the call.

The inheritance hierarchy of the Directory class is as follows:

```
System.Object
   System.IO.Directory
```

Noteworthy methods of the `Directory` class are listed in Table 11.3:

Table 11.3: Noteworthy Methods of the Directory Class

Method	Description
`CreateDirectory`	Builds all the directories that are described in a path.
`Delete`	Removes a specified directory.
`Exists`	Checks whether the given path refers to an existing directory on disk.
`GetCreationTime`	Retrieves the creation date and time of a directory.
`GetCurrentDirectory`	Retrieves the current working directory of the application.
`GetDirectories`	Retrieves the names of subdirectories in a specified directory.
`GetDirectoryRoot`	Returns the volume information, root information, or both for the specified path.
`GetFiles`	Returns the names of files in a specified directory.
`GetFileSystemEntries`	Returns the names of all files and subdirectories in a specified directory.
`GetAccessControl`	Returns the Windows access control list (ACL) for a directory.
`GetCreationTimeUtc`	Creates date and time, in Coordinated Universal Time (UTC) format, of a directory.
`GetLastAccessTimeUtc`	Returns the date and time, in UTC format. It specifies the time when a file or directory was last accessed.
`GetLastWriteTimeUtc`	Returns the date and time, in UTC format.
`GetLogicalDrives`	Retrieves the names of the logical drives on this computer in the form `"<drive letter>:\"`.
`GetParent`	Retrieves the parent directory of the specified path. It also includes both absolute and relative paths.
`Move`	Copies a file or a directory and its contents to a new location.
`SetAccessControl`	Applies ACL entries described by a **`DirectorySecurity`** object to the specified directory.
`SetCreationTime`	Assigns the date and time for the specified file or directory when created.
`SetCreationTimeUtc`	Creates date and time in UTC format, for the specified file or directory.
`SetLastAccessTime`	Assigns the date and time for a mentioned file or directory.
`SetLastAccessTimeUtc`	Assigns the date and time, in UTC format.
`SetLastWriteTime`	Assigns the date and time when a directory was last written.
`SetLastWriteTimeUtc`	Assigns the date and time in UTC format when the directory was last written.

When you use the Move method in the Directory class that moves a file or a directory and its contents to the new specified location, the exceptions occur. Noteworthy exceptions of the Directory class are listed in Table 11.4:

Table 11.4: Noteworthy Exceptions of the Directory Class

Exception Type	Condition
`ArgumentException`	Specifies that the specified *path* is a zero-length string and contains only white space. It might contain one or more implementation-specific invalid characters.
`ArgumentNullException`	Occurs when the path is null.
`DirectoryNotFoundException`	Occurs when the path was not found.

Table 11.4: Noteworthy Exceptions of the Directory Class

Exception Type	Condition
`IOException`	Specifies that the specified directory by *path* is read-only. The specified *path* is not an empty directory.
`UnauthorizedAccessException`	Occurs when the user does not have the necessary permissions.
`PathTooLongException`	Raises when the specified file name or path name or both exceed the maximum length defined in the system.

The DirectoryInfo Class

Most of the functions performed by the Directory class can also be performed by the DirectoryInfo class. The basic difference between the Directory and DirectoryInfo classes is that the former provides static methods, whereas to use the DirectoryInfo class, we have to create its instances. It is advisable to use the DirectoryInfo class if we want to perform multiple operations on a folder. The reason is that when we create an object to represent a folder by using the DirectoryInfo class, it contains all the necessary information about the folder, such as the time of creation and last access time. Another reason to use the DirectoryInfo class is that it consumes less time to execute an application because it performs security check only once.

The inheritance hierarchy of the DirectoryInfo class is as follows:

```
System.Object
  System.MarshalByRefObject
        System.IO.FileSystemInfo
               System.IO.DirectoryInfo
```

Noteworthy methods of the `DirectoryInfo` class are listed in Table 11.5:

Table 11.5: Noteworthy Methods of the DirectoryInfo Class

Method	Description
`Create`	Allows you to create a directory.
CreateSubdirectory	Allows you to create a subdirectory or subdirectories according to the specified path.
`Delete`	Allows you to delete a `DirectoryInfo` instance and its content from the specified path whether it is empty.
GetAccessControl	Gets the ACL entries for the current directory. The method can be overloaded.
`GetDirectories`	Returns the subdirectories of the current directory. The method can be overloaded.
`GetFiles`	Retrieves a file list from the current directory.
`GetFileSystemInfos`	Retrieves an array of strongly typed `FileSystemInfo` objects representing files and subdirectories of the current directory. It can be overloaded.
SetAccessControl	Applies ACL entries described by a `DirectorySecurity` object to the directory described by the current `DirectoryInfo` object.
`ToString`	Retrieves the original path passed by the user. The method is also used to override `Object.ToString()`.

Noteworthy properties of the `DirectoryInfo` class are listed in Table 11.6:

Table 11.6: Noteworthy Properties of the DirectoryInfo Class

Property	Description
`Exists`	Retrieves a value to indicate whether the directory exists or not. This property overrides FileSystemInfo.Exists property.
`Extension`	Retrieves the string describing the extension part of the file.

Property	Description
FullName	Retrieves the full path of the directory or file.
LastAccessTime	Retrieves or sets the time of the current file or directory when it was last accessed.
LastWriteTime	Assigns or Retrieves the time when the current file or directory was last written.
Name	Retrieves the name of this DirectoryInfo instance.
Parent	Retrieves the parent directory of the mentioned subdirectory.
Root	Retrieves the root portion of the specified path.

Table 11.6: Noteworthy Properties of the DirectoryInfo Class

The DriveInfo Class

The DriveInfo class provides access to information related to a drive, such as space available on a drive, total storage space of the drive, and drive name. The DriveInfo class can also be used to query the format of a drive, such as New Technology File System(NTFS) or File Allocation Table (FAT32), and type of the drive, such as fixed, CD-ROM, or removable. This class throws an exception if a drive is currently not ready. For example, if we want to get information of a CD-ROM that does not contain a CD in it, the DriveInfo class will throw an exception. We can avoid such exceptions by using the IsReady property of the DriveInfo class. If the DriveInfo property returns true, we can access the drive without an exception.

The inheritance hierarchy of the DriveInfo class is as follows:

```
System.Object
  System.IO.DriveInfo
```

Noteworthy methods of the `DriveInfo` class to access information of a drive are listed in Table 11.7:

Table 11.7: Noteworthy Methods of the DriveInfo Class

Method	Description
Equals	Recognizes whether the mentioned object is equal to the current object.
GetDrives	Retrieves the drive names of all the logical drives on a computer.
GetHashCode	Provides a hash function for a specific type.
GetType	Retrieves the Type of the current instance.

Noteworthy properties of the `DriveInfo` class to access information of a drive are listed in Table 11.8:

Table 11.8: Noteworthy Properties of the DriveInfo Class

Property	Description
AvailableFreeSpace	Indicates the amount of available free space on a drive
DriveFormat	Retrieves the name of the file system, such as NTFS or FAT32
DriveType	Retrieves the drive type
IsReady	Retrieves a value indicating whether a drive is ready
Name	Retrieves the name of a drive
RootDirectory	Retrieves the root directory of a drive
TotalFreeSpace	Retrieves the total amount of free space available on a drive
TotalSize	Retrieves the total size of storage space on a drive
VolumeLabel	Retrieves the volume label of a drive

Now, let's proceed further and explore how to work with files in a file system.

Working With Files

The .NET Framework 4.5 provides certain classes to work with files, such as the File and FileInfo classes. These classes enable a user to perform different operations on files programmatically. The File and FileInfo classes allow you to perform various functions, such as creating, deleting, moving, renaming, and appending files. The basic difference between these two classes is that the File class provides static methods, whereas the FileInfo class needs to create its instances. It is advisable to use the FileInfo class instead of the File class when we want to perform multiple operations on a file. We can use the File class if we want to perform a single operation on a file. Another difference between these two classes is that the File class takes longer time to execute an application as compared to the FileInfo class. This is due to the reason that whenever we call a method, the File class performs a security check that affects the performance of an application.

The inheritance hierarchy of the File class is as follows:

```
System.Object
    System.IO.File
```

Noteworthy methods of the File class are listed in Table 11.9:

Table 11.9: Noteworthy Methods of the File Class

Method	Description
AppendAllText	Appends the text in a file. It creates the file,if the file is not present.
AppendText	Appends UTF-8 encoded text to an existing file by creating StreamWriter.
Copy	Moves the contents of an existing file to a new file.
Create	Creates a file according to the specified path.
CreateText	Writes UTF-8 encoded text in a file
Decrypt	Decrypts an encrypted file by using the `Encrypt` method.
Delete	Deletes the file from the specified location.
Encrypt	Encrypts a file that can be decrypted only by the account used to encrypt the file.
Exists	Finds whether file exists at the specified location.
GetAccessControl	Retrieves a `FileSecurity` object for a specified file that encapsulates the ACL entries.
GetAttributes	Retrieves the `FileAttributes` enumerations of the file on the specified path.
GetCreationTime	Gives the creation date and time of the file or directory that is specified.
GetCreationTimeUtc	Gives the creation date and time, in UTC, of file or directory that is specified.
GetLastAccessTime	Gives the date and time of the specified file or directory that was last accessed.
GetLastAccessTimeUtc	Gives the date and time, in UTC, of the specified file or directory that was last accessed.
GetLastWriteTime	Gives the date and time of the specified file or directory when it was last modified.
GetLastWriteTimeUtc	Gives the date and time, in UTC, of the specified file or directory when it was last modified.
Move	Moves a particular file to a new specified location and using the option that specifies a new file name.
Open	Opens the object of the FileStream in the specified path. It can be overloaded.
OpenRead	Opens the specified file for reading the content.
OpenText	Opens the specified UTF-8 encoded text file for reading the content.
OpenWrite	Opens the file for writing if it exists.

Table 11.9: Noteworthy Methods of the File Class	
Method	**Description**
`ReadAllBytes`	Reads the contents of the file into a byte array, and then closes the file.
`ReadAllLines`	Reads all lines of the file and retrieves it into a string array, and then closes the file.
`ReadAllText`	Reads all lines of the file into a string, and then closes the file.
`Replace`	Creates a backup of the replaced file after replacing the content of a specified file with the content of another file and then deletes the original file.
`SetAccessControl`	Implements ACL entries to the specified file described by a `FileSecurity` object.
`SetAttributes`	Applies the specified `FileAttributes` object of the file on the mentioned path.
`SetCreationTime`	Assigns the date and time on which the specified file was created.
`SetCreationTimeUtc`	Assigns the date and time, in UTC, on which the specified file was created.
`SetLastAccessTime`	Sets the last accessed date and time of the specified file.
`SetLastAccessTimeUtc`	Set the last accessed date and time of the specified file, in UTC.
`SetLastWriteTime`	Sets the last modified date and time of the specified file.
`SetLastWriteTimeUtc`	Sets the last modified date and time, in UTC of the specified file.

Noteworthy methods of the FileInfo class are listed in Table 11.10:

Table 11.10: Noteworthy Methods of the FileInfo Class	
Method	**Description**
`AppendText`	Creates a `StreamWriter` object that appends text to the file represented by this instance of the `FileInfo` class.
`CopyTo`	Copies an existing file to a new file.
`Create`	Creates a file.
CreateText	Creates a `StreamWriter` that writes a new text file.
`Decrypt`	Decrypts a file that was encrypted by the current account using the `Encrypt` method.
`Delete`	Deletes a file permanently.
`Encrypt`	Encrypts a file in such a manner that only the account used to encrypt the file can decrypt it.
GetAccessControl	Gets a `FileSecurity` object that encapsulates the ACL entries for the file described by the current `FileInfo` object.
MoveTo	Moves a specified file to a new location, providing the option to specify a new file name.
`Open`	Opens a file with various read/write and sharing privileges. This method can be overloaded.
`OpenRead`	Creates a read-only `FileStream`.
`OpenText`	Creates a `StreamReader` with UTF-8 encoding that reads from an existing text file.
`OpenWrite`	Creates a write-only `FileStream`.
`Refresh`	Refreshes the state of the object.
`Replace`	Replaces the content of a specified file with the file described by the current `FileInfo`.
`SetAccessControl`	Applies ACL entries described by a `FileSecurity` object to the file described by the current `FileInfo` object.

Now, let's discuss how to access attributes and properties of a file through classes.

Working with File Properties and ACL

Every file contains certain attributes and properties used to retrieve information of a file. These attributes and properties help to retrieve data, such as date of creation and last modification.

You can view properties of a file by right-clicking the file. Perform the following steps to see the properties and ACL information of a file:

1. Create a file and save it as BlackBook.txt in the system.
2. Right-click the BlackBook.txt file and select the Properties option from the context menu. The Properties dialog box appears displaying all the properties and attributes of the file, as shown in Figure 11.1:

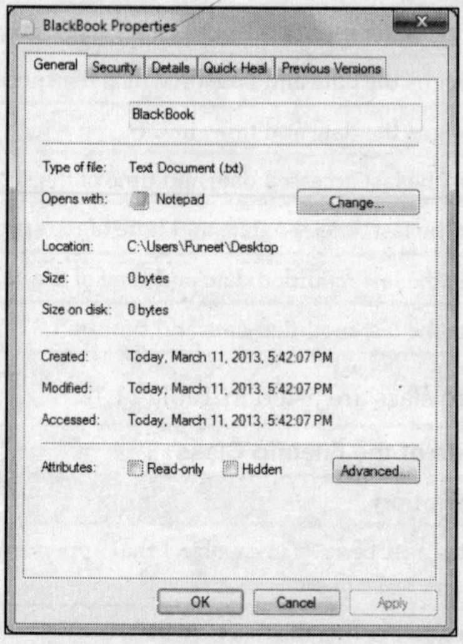

Figure 11.1: Displaying the Properties and Attributes of a File

We can also access attributes of a file programmatically by using the File and FileInfo classes.

Noteworthy attributes of a file are listed in Table 11.11:

Table 11.11: Noteworthy attributes of a File

Attributes	Description
`Archive`	Specifies the file's archive status.
`Compressed`	Specifies if the file is compressed.
`Encrypted`	Specifies whether the file or directory is encrypted or not.
`Hidden`	Specifies the file is hidden, and therefore it is not included in an ordinary directory listing.
`Normal`	Specifies the file is normal and has no other attributes set. This attribute is valid only if used alone.
`NotContentIndexed`	Specifies that the file will not be indexed by the operating system's content indexing service.
`ReadOnly`	Specifies that the file is read-only.
`ReparsePoint`	Specifies that the file contains a reparse point, which is a block of user-defined data associated with a file or a directory.
`SparseFile`	Specifies that the file is a sparse file. The Sparse files are typically large files that consist of null data.
`System`	Specifies that file is a system file. It means that the file is part of the operating system.

Table 11.11: Noteworthy attributes of a File	
Attributes	**Description**
`Temporary`	Specifies that the file is temporary. A temporary file should be deleted by the application as soon as it is no longer needed.
`Read`	Specifies about read access to the file. Data can be read from the file.
`ReadWrite`	Specifies about read and write access to the file. Data can be written to and read from the file.
`Write`	Specifies about write access to the file. Data can be written to the file.

A user is also able to make changes in the ACL of a file through the new System.Security.AccessControl namespace.

3. Click the Security tab in the BlackBook Properties dialog box, as shown in Figure 11.2. A list of usernames is displayed in the Group or user names pane in the dialog box, as shown in Figure 11.2:

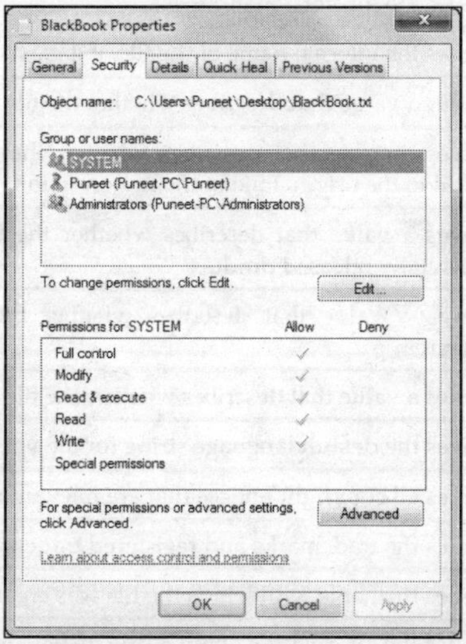

Figure 11.2: Displaying Access Control List of a File

You can query the file system by using the System.Security.AccessControl namespace for the ACL information of a computer and display it in a webpage of an application.

Further, we can also get version information of a file by using the FileVersionInfo class. Noteworthy methods of the FileVersionInfo class are listed in Table 11.12:

Table 11.12: Noteworthy Methods of the FileVersionInfo Class	
Method	**Description**
`Equals`	Compares whether the specified object `Object` is equal to the current object
`GetHashCode`	Gets a hash function for a particular type
`GetType`	Retrieves the Type of the current instance
`GetVersionInfo`	Gets a `FileVersionInfo` describing the version information associated with the particular file
ToString	Gets a partial list of properties in the `FileVersionInfo` class and their values

Noteworthy properties of the `FileVersionInfo` class are listed in Table 11.13:

Table 11.13: Noteworthy Properties of the FileVersionInfo Class

Property	Description
`Comments`	Retrieves the comments linked with the file
`CompanyName`	Retrieves the name of the company that created the file
`FileBuildPart`	Retrieves the build number of the file
`FileMajorPart`	Retrieves the major part of the version number
`FileMinorPart`	Retrieves the minor part of the version number of the file
`FileName`	Retrieves the name of the file that this described by the instance of `FileVersionInfo`
`FilePrivatePart`	Retrieves the file private part number
`FileVersion`	Retrieves the file version number
`InternalName`	Retrieves the internal name of the file, if it exists
`IsDebug`	Retrieves a value that describes whether the file contains debugging information
`IsPatched`	Retrieves a value that describes whether the file has been modified and should not be identical to the original file of the same version number.
`IsPreRelease`	Retrieves a value that describes whether the file is a development version, other than a commercially released product
`IsPrivateBuild`	Retrieves a value that describes whether the file was created using standard release procedures
`IsSpecialBuild`	Retrieves a value that describes whether the file is a special build
`Language`	Retrieves the default language string for the version info block
`LegalCopyright`	Retrieves all copyright notices that are relevant to the specified file
`LegalTrademarks`	Retrieves the trademarks and registered trademarks that are relevant to the file
`OriginalFilename`	Retrieves the name with which the file was created
`PrivateBuild`	Retrieves the information about a private version of the file
`ProductBuildPart`	Retrieves the build number of the product with which the file is associated
`ProductMajorPart`	Retrieves the major part of the version number for the product with which the file is associated
`ProductMinorPart`	Retrieves the minor part of the version number for the product with which the file is associated
`ProductName`	Retrieves the name of the product with which the file is distributed
`ProductPrivatePart`	Retrieves the private part number of the product with which the file is associated
`ProductVersion`	Retrieves the version of the product with which this file is distributed
`SpecialBuild`	Retrieves the special build information for the mentioned file

Understanding the System.IO.Stream Class

.NET Framework provides the Stream class that includes various classes to work with files. A stream represents a sequence of bytes to be stored in a storage medium or retrieved from a storage medium. You can use the Stream class to read, write, and query a file. The inheritance hierarchy of the Stream class is as follows:

```
System.Object
  System.MarshalByRefObject
        System.IO.Stream
```

The Stream class contains the FileStream class used to read from, write to, open, and close files on a file system. The inheritance hierarchy of the FileStream class is as follows:

```
System.Object
  System.MarshalByRefObject
        System.IO.Stream
               System.IO.FileStream
```

Noteworthy methods of the FileStream class are listed in Table 11.14:

Table 11.14: Noteworthy Methods of the FileStream Class

Method	Description
`BeginRead`	Starts asynchronous reading of the file.
`Close`	Releases the resources and closes the current stream.
EndRead	Allows you to wait for the awaiting asynchronous read to complete EndRead(IAsyncResult)
`EndWrite`	Stops an asynchronous write operation on a file, till the I/O operation has completed EndWrite(IAsyncResult)
`Equals`	Specifies whether the mentioned `Object` is equal to the current `Object`
`Finalize`	Assures that resources should be free and other cleanup operations should be performed when the garbage collector regain the FIleStream class
`Flush`	Cleans all buffers for this stream and allows the buffered data to be written to the file system
`GetAccessControl`	Retrieves a `FileSecurity` object that sum up the ACL entries for the file explained by the current `FileStream` object
Lock	Avoids other processes from modifying the `FileStream` object with read access permissions
`Read`	Reads the stream that consists of block of bytes and writes the data in the specified buffer.
`ReadByte`	Advances the read position by one byte after reading a byte from the file
`Seek`	Assigns the current position of this stream to the particular value
`SetAccessControl`	Implements ACL entries explained by a `FileSecurity` object to the file mentioned by the current `FileStream` object
`SetLength`	Assigns the size of this stream to the given value
`ToString`	Gets a `String` that describes the current `Object`
`Unlock`	Permits access of a file that was previously locked
`Write`	Writes a block of bytes by using data from a buffer to this stream
`WriteByte`	Writes a byte to the mentioned position in the file stream

Noteworthy properties of the `FileStream` class are listed in Table 11.15:

Table 11.15: Noteworthy Properties of the FileStream Class

Property	Description
`CanRead`	Gets a value indicating whether the current stream supports reading
`CanSeek`	Gets a value indicating whether the current stream supports seeking
`CanTimeout`	Gets a value that determines whether the current streams can time out
`CanWrite`	Gets a value indicating whether the current stream supports writing

Table 11.15: Noteworthy Properties of the FileStream Class

Property	Description
Handle	Gets the operating system file handle for the file that the current FileStream object encapsulates
IsAsync	Gets a value indicating whether the FileStream was opened asynchronously or synchronously
Length	Gets the value indicating the length of the FileStream
Name	Gets the name of the FileStream that was passed to the constructor
Position	Gets or sets the current position of this stream
ReadTimeout	Gets or set a value, in milliseconds that determines how long the stream will attempt to read before timing out
SafeFileHandle	Gets a SafeFileHandle object that represents the operating system file handle for the file that the current FileStream object encapsulates

A file can be compressed to use less disk space. Now, let's discuss how to compress a file programmatically.

Understanding File Compression

We can compress or decompress the data in a file by using the GZipStream or DeflateStream class. The GZipStream objects that are written to a file support the .gz extension. The GZipStream class does not support .zip archives. The inheritance hierarchy of the GZipStream class is as follows:

```
System.Object
   System.MarshalByRefObject
         System.IO.Stream
                System.IO.Compression.GZipStream
```

The DeflateStream class uses the gzip format of data and does not support .zip archives. The inheritance hierarchy of the DeflateStream class is as follows:

```
System.Object
   System.MarshalByRefObject
         System.IO.Stream
                System.IO.Compression.DeflateStream
```

Noteworthy methods of the DeflateStream class are listed in Table 11.16:

Table 11.16: Noteworthy Methods of the DeflateStream Class

Method	Description
BeginRead	Starts an asynchronous read operation
BeginWrite	Starts an asynchronous write operation
Close	Release the resources linked with the current stream and closes the current stream
CreateWaitHandle	Assigns a WaitHandle object
EndRead	Allows you to wait for the remaining asynchronous read to finish
EndWrite	Finishes an asynchronous write operation
Equals	Describes whether the specified Object is equal to the current Object (Inherited from Object)
Finalize	Calls an Object to free resources and to do other cleanup operations prior to the Object is removed by garbage collection
Flush	Flushes the data of the internal buffer of the present stream object to the principal stream
Read	Reads a collection of decompressed bytes into the mentioned byte array

Table 11.16: Noteworthy Methods of the DeflateStream Class	
Method	**Description**
`ReadByte`	Allows you to read a byte from the stream and moves the position within the stream by one byte and returns -1 when the pointer is at the end of the stream
`Write`	Allows you to write compressed bytes to the underlying stream from the particular byte array
`WriteByte`	Allows a byte to the current position and advances the position within the stream by a single byte

Noteworthy properties of the DeflateStream class are listed in Table 11.17:

Table 11.17: Noteworthy Properties of the DeflateStream Class	
Property	**Description**
`BaseStream`	Retrieves a reference to the described stream.
`CanRead`	Retrieves a value indicating whether the stream allows reading a file while decompressing it.
`CanSeek`	Retrieves a value indicating whether the stream supports seeking.
`CanTimeout`	Retrieves a value that determines whether the current stream can time out.
`CanWrite`	Retrieves a value indicating whether the stream supports writing.
`ReadTimeout`	Determines how long the stream will try to read before the time out (set in milliseconds).
`WriteTimeout`	Determines how long the stream will try to write before time out (set in milliseconds).

NOTE

The GZipStream and DeflateStream classes share common methods and properties

Working with Serial Ports

A serial port is a physical interface used for serial communication to transfer information between a computer and a peripheral device.

Serial ports transfer the data from the connected devices, such as USB modem, to a computer. The .NET Framework 4.5 supports the SerialPort component that we can add to the component designer of a Web page. The .NET Framework 4.5 provides the SerialPort class under the System.IO.Ports namespace. The SerialPort class is used to control the serial port file resources. For example, the SerialPort class allows two users to chat from two computers connected by a cable. The inheritance hierarchy of the SerialPort class is as follows:

```
System.Object
   System.MarshalByRefObject
           System.ComponentModel.Component
                     System.IO.Ports.SerialPort
```

Noteworthy methods of the SerialPort class are listed in Table 11.18:

Table 11.18: Noteworthy Methods of the SerialPort Class	
Method	**Description**
`Close`	Closes the port connection. It sets the `IsOpen` property to false.
`DiscardInBuffer`	Rejects data from the serial driver's receive buffer.
`DiscardOutBuffer`	Rejects data from the serial driver's transmit buffer.
`Dispose`	Releases the unmanaged resources used by the `SerialPort` object.
`Open`	Allows you to open a new serial port connection.

Table 11.18: Noteworthy Methods of the SerialPort Class

Method	Description
`Read`	Read from the `SerialPort` input buffer.
`ReadByte`	Reads synchronously one byte from the `SerialPort` input buffer.
`ReadChar`	Reads synchronously one character from the SerialPort input buffer.
`ReadExisting`	Reads all the existing bytes that are based on the encoding, present in the stream and the input buffer of the `SerialPort` object.
`ReadLine`	Allows you to read up to the newline value in the input buffer.
`ReadTo`	Allows you to read a string up to the specified value in the input buffer.
`ToString`	Gets a string having the name of the Component. This method cannot not be overridden.
`Write`	Writes data to the serial port output buffer.
`WriteLine`	Allows you to write the particular string and the NewLine value to the output buffer.

Noteworthy properties of the SerialPort class are listed in Table 11.19:

Table 11.19: Noteworthy Properties of the SerialPort Class

Property	Description
`BaseStream`	Gets the underlying `Stream` object for a `SerialPort` object
`BaudRate`	Gets or sets the serial baud rate
`BreakState`	Gets or sets the break signal state
`BytesToRead`	Gets the number of bytes of data in the receive buffer
`BytesToWrite`	Gets the number of bytes of data in the send buffer
`CanRaiseEvents`	Gets a value indicating whether the component can raise an event
`CDHolding`	Gets the state of the `Carrier Detect` line for the port
`DiscardNull`	Gets or sets a value that indicates whether null bytes are ignored when transmitted between the port and the receive buffer
`DsrHolding`	States the Data Set Ready (DSR) signal
`DtrEnable`	Gets or sets a value that enables the Data Terminal Ready (DTR) signal during serial communication
`Encoding`	Gets or sets the byte encoding for pre- and post-transmission conversion of text
`Handshake`	Gets or sets the handshaking protocol for serial port transmission of data
`IsOpen`	Gets a value indicating the open or closed status of the SerialPort object
`NewLine`	Gets or sets the value used to interpret the end of a call to the ReadLine and WriteLine methods
`Parity`	Gets or sets the parity-checking protocol
`ParityReplace`	Gets or sets the byte that replaces invalid bytes in a data stream when a parity error occurs
`PortName`	Gets or sets the port for communications
`ReadBufferSize`	Gets or sets the size of the SerialPort input buffer

Table 11.19: Noteworthy Properties of the SerialPort Class	
Property	**Description**
`ReadTimeout`	Gets or sets the number of milliseconds before a time-out occurs when a read operation does not finish
`ReceivedBytesThreshold`	Gets or sets the number of bytes in the internal input buffer before a `DataReceived` event occurs
`RtsEnable`	Gets or sets a value indicating whether the Request to Send (RTS) signal is enabled during serial communication
`StopBits`	Gets or sets the standard number of `stopbits` per byte
`WriteBufferSize`	Gets or sets the size of the serial port output buffer
`WriteTimeout`	Gets the number of milliseconds before a time-out occurs when a write operation does not finish

Immediate Solutions

Retrieving Drive Information

Now, let's discuss how to retrieve information related to a drive, such as the size of the drive. Perform the following steps to retrieve information related to a drive:

1. Create an ASP.NET Empty Web Site and add a Web page to it. You can save the Website as RetrieveDriveInfoVB. The code for this application is available in the RetrieveDriveInfoCS (for C#) and RetrieveDriveInfoVB (for VB) folders.
2. Drag and drop a Button control, a DropDownList control, and Four Label controls from the Toolbox on the Design view of the Default.aspx page.
3. Set the Text property of the Button control to Show Drives, ID property of the Button control to BtnShow and AutoPostBack property of the DropDownList control to True in the Properties window.

After setting the properties of the control, the code of the Default.aspx page appears, as shown in Listing 11.1:

Listing 11.1: Showing the Code of the Default.aspx Page

In VB

```
<%@ Page Language="VB" AutoEventWireup="false" CodeFile="Default.aspx.vb"
   Inherits="_Default" %>
<!DOCTYPE html>
<html xmlns="http://www.w3.org/1999/xhtml">
<head runat="server">
    <title></title>
</head>
<body>
    <form id="form1" runat="server">
    <div>
       <b> Displays list of Drives available on your system</b>
                 <br />
                 <br />
                 <br />
                 <asp:Button ID="BtnShow" runat="server" Text="Show Drives" />
                 <asp:DropDownList ID="DropDownList1" runat="server"
                         AutoPostBack="True">
                 </asp:DropDownList>
                         <br />
                         <br />
                         <br />
                         <asp:Label ID="Label1" runat="server" Font-Bold="True" Font-
                         Italic="True"></asp:Label>
                         <br />
                         <br />
                         <asp:Label ID="Label2" runat="server" Font-Bold="True" Font-
                         Italic="True" ></asp:Label>
                         <br />
                         <asp:Label ID="Label3" runat="server" Font-Bold="True" Font-
                         Italic="True" ></asp:Label><br/>
                         <asp:Label ID="Label4" runat="server" Font-Bold="True" Font-
                         Italic="True" ></asp:Label>
                         <br />
    </div>
    </form>
</body>
</html>
```

In C#

```
<%@ Page Language="C#" AutoEventWireup="true" CodeFile="Default.aspx.cs"
  Inherits="_Default" %>
<!DOCTYPE html>
<html xmlns="http://www.w3.org/1999/xhtml">
<head runat="server">
    <title></title>
</head>
<body>
    <form id="form1" runat="server">
    <div>
   <b> Displays list of Drives available on your system</b>
                <br />
                <br />
                <br />
        <asp:Button ID="BtnShow" runat="server" Text="Show Drives"
            OnClick="BtnShow_Click" />
        <asp:DropDownList ID="DropDownList1" runat="server" AutoPostBack="True"
           onselectedindexchanged="DropDownList1_SelectedIndexChanged">
       </asp:DropDownList>
                <br />
                <br />
                <br />
                <asp:Label ID="Label1" runat="server" Font-Bold="True" Font-
                  Italic="True"></asp:Label>
                <br />
                <br />
                <asp:Label ID="Label2" runat="server" Font-Bold="True" Font-
                   Italic="True" ></asp:Label>
                <br />
                <asp:Label ID="Label3" runat="server" Font-Bold="True" Font-
                  Italic="True" ></asp:Label><br/>
                <asp:Label ID="Label4" runat="server" Font-Bold="True" Font-
                  Italic="True" ></asp:Label>
                <br />
        </div>
  </form>
  </body>
</html>
```

NOTE

Imports System.IO namespace before creating any application

4. Double-click the Button control then add the following highlighted code in the Click event.

```
Dim str As String() = Directory.GetLogicalDrives()
For i As Integer = 0 To str.Length - 1
  DropDownList1.Items.Add(str(i))
Next
```

Similarly, add the following code in the SelectedIndexChanged event of the DropDownList control.

The code of the CodeFile file is shown in Listing 11.2:

Listing 11.2: Showing the Code of the CodeFile of the Default.aspx Page

In VB

```
Imports System.IO
Partial Class _Default
    Inherits System.Web.UI.Page
    Protected Sub DropDownList1_SelectedIndexChanged(sender As Object, e As
  EventArgs) Handles DropDownList1.SelectedIndexChanged
```

```
        Try
            Dim driv As String = DropDownList1.SelectedValue
            Label1.Text = "You Have Selected Drive " & driv
            Dim retrieve_drive_info As New System.IO.DriveInfo(driv)
            Label2.Text = "Drive Type : " & retrieve_drive_info.DriveType.ToString()
            Label4.Text = "Free Space on Drive: " &
                retrieve_drive_info.AvailableFreeSpace.ToString()
            Label3.Text = "Total Size : " & retrieve_drive_info.TotalSize.ToString()
        Catch ex As Exception
            Label2.Text = ex.Message
            Label4.Text = ""
            Label3.Text = ""
        End Try
    End Sub
    Protected Sub BtnShow _Click(sender As Object,e As EventArgs)
  Handles BtnShow.Click
        Dim str() As String = Directory.GetLogicalDrives()
        For i As Integer = 0 To str.Length - 1
            DropDownList1.Items.Add(str(i))
        Next i
    End Sub
End Class
```

In C#

```
using System;
using System.Collections.Generic;
using System.Linq;
using System.Web;
using System.Web.UI;
using System.Web.UI.WebControls;
using System.IO;
public partial class _Default : System.Web.UI.Page
{
    protected void Page_Load(object sender, EventArgs e)
    {
    }
    protected void BtnShow_Click(object sender, EventArgs e)
    {
        string[] str = Directory.GetLogicalDrives();
        for (int i = 0; i < str.Length; i++)
        {
            DropDownList1.Items.Add(str[i]);
        }
    }
    protected void DropDownList1_SelectedIndexChanged(object sender, EventArgs e)
    {
         try
         {
                string driv = DropDownList1.SelectedValue;
                Label1.Text = "You Have Selected Drive " + driv;
                System.IO.DriveInfo retrieve_drive_info = new
                System.IO.DriveInfo(driv);
                Label2.Text = "Drive Type : " +
                 retrieve_drive_info.DriveType.ToString();
                Label4.Text = "Free Space on Drive: " +
                  retrieve_drive_info.AvailableFreeSpace.ToString();
         Label3.Text = "Total Size : " + retrieve_drive_info.TotalSize.ToString();
         }
         catch (Exception ex)
```

```
            {
                    Label2.Text=ex.Message;
                Label4.Text = " ";
                Label3.Text = " ";
            }
        }
    }
```

5. Press the F5 key on the keyboard to execute the application. The output of the application appears (Figure 11.3).
6. Click the Show Drives button (Figure11.3).

The Drive names appear in the drop-down list.

7. Select the Drive from the drop-down list. The information of the selected drive appears on the Web page, as shown in Figure 11.3:

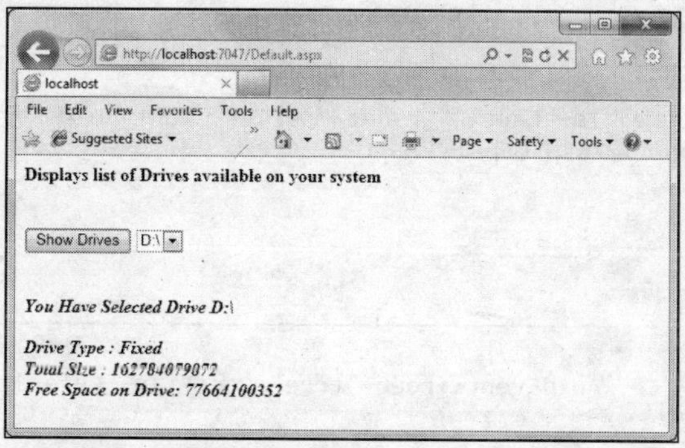

Figure 11.3: Displaying the Information of the Drive

Let's learn how to create the directory.

Creating a Directory

Now, let's discuss how to create a directory in the drive. Perform the following steps to create the directory in the drive:

1. Create an ASP.NET Empty Web Site and add a Web page to it. Now, save the Website as CreateDirectoryCS. You can find the code for this application in the CreateDirectoryCS (for C#) and CreateDirectoryVB (for VB) folders.
2. Drag and drop a Button control, a TextBox control, and two Label controls from the Toolbox on the Design view of the Default.aspx page.
3. Set the Text property of the Button control to CreateDirectory, ID property of the Button control to BtnCreate, and Text property of Label1 control to Enter the Path To Create a directory in the Properties window.

After setting the properties of the control, the code of the Default.aspx page appears, as shown in Listing 11.3.

Listing 11.3: Showing the Code of the Default.aspx Page

In VB

```
<%@ Page Language="VB" AutoEventWireup="false" CodeFile="Default.aspx.vb"
  Inherits="_Default" %>
<!DOCTYPE html>
<html xmlns="http://www.w3.org/1999/xhtml">
<head runat="server">
    <title></title>
</head>
<body>
```

```
        <form id="form1" runat="server">
        <div>
        <h4>This Application creates a directory at specified path in the textbox </h4>
            <h4>For example
               C:/ProgramFiles/DirectoryName</h4><br />
             <br />
             <br />
             <asp:Label ID="Label1" runat="server" Font-Bold="True" Font-Italic="True"
             Text="Enter the Path To Create a directory "></asp:Label>
             <asp:TextBox ID="TextBox1" runat="server" Width="323px"></asp:TextBox>
             <br />
             <br />
             <br />
             <asp:Button ID="BtnCreate" runat="server" Text="Create Directory"
                 Width="111px" />
                 <br />
            <br />
            <br />
                 <asp:Label ID="Label2" runat="server" Font-Bold="True" Font-Italic="True"
             Text="Label"></asp:Label>
        </div>
        </form>
    </body>
    </html>
```

In C#

```
    <%@ Page Language="C#" AutoEventWireup="true" CodeFile="Default.aspx.cs"
      Inherits="_Default" %>
    <!DOCTYPE html>
    <html xmlns="http://www.w3.org/1999/xhtml">
    <head runat="server">
        <title></title>
    </head>
    <body>
        <form id="form1" runat="server">
        <div>
         <h4>This Application creates a directory at specified path in the textbox </h4>
            <h4>For example
               C:/ProgramFiles/DirectoryName</h4><br />
             <br />
             <br />
             <asp:Label ID="Label1" runat="server" Font-Bold="True" Font-Italic="True"
             Text="Enter the Path To Create a directory "></asp:Label>
             <asp:TextBox ID="TextBox1" runat="server" Width="323px"></asp:TextBox>
             <br />
             <br />
             <br />
             <asp:Button ID="BtnCreate" runat="server" Text="Create Directory"
                 Width="111px" OnClick="BtnCreate_Click" />
                 <br />
            <br />
            <br />
                 <asp:Label
             ID="Label2" runat="server" Font-Bold="True" Font-Italic="True"
             Text="Label"></asp:Label>
        </div>
        </form>
    </body>
    </html>
```

4. Double -click the Button control (BtnCreate) and add the following highlighted code in the Click event.

The code of the CodeFile is shown in Listing 11.4:

Listing 11.4: Showing the Code of the CodeFile of the Default.aspx Page

In VB

```
Imports System.IO
Partial Class _Default
    Inherits System.Web.UI.Page
    Protected Sub BtnCreate_Click(sender As Object,e As EventArgs)
         Handles BtnCreate.Click
        Dim path As String = TextBox1.Text
        Label2.Text = ""
        Try
            If (Not Directory.Exists(path)) Then
                Directory.CreateDirectory(path)
                Label2.Text = "Directory is Created...." & path
            Else
                If Directory.Exists(path) Then
                    Label2.Text = " Directory Is already Created at " & path
                End If
            End If
        Catch ex As Exception
            Label2.Text = "Please Check The Path and Name of Directory, " &
               ex.Message
        End Try
    End Sub
End Class
```

In C#

```
using System;
using System.Collections.Generic;
using System.Linq;
using System.Web;
using System.Web.UI;
using System.Web.UI.WebControls;
using System.IO;
public partial class _Default : System.Web.UI.Page
{
    protected void Page_Load(object sender, EventArgs e)
    {
    }
    protected void BtnCreate_Click(object sender, EventArgs e)
    {
        string path = TextBox1.Text;
        Label2.Text = "";
        try
        {
                if (!Directory.Exists(path))
                {
                        Directory.CreateDirectory(path);
                        Label2.Text = "Directory is Created...."+path;
                }
                else
                {
                        if (Directory.Exists(path))
                        {
                        Label2.Text = " Directory Is already Created at " + path;
                        }
                }
```

```
            }
            catch (Exception ex)
            {
            Label2.Text = "Please Check The Path and Name of Directory, " + ex.Message;
            }
    }
}
```

5. Press the F5 key on the keyboard to execute the application. The output of the application appears (Figure 11.4).
6. Enter the path in the text box and click the Create Directory button to create the directory, as shown in Figure 11.4:

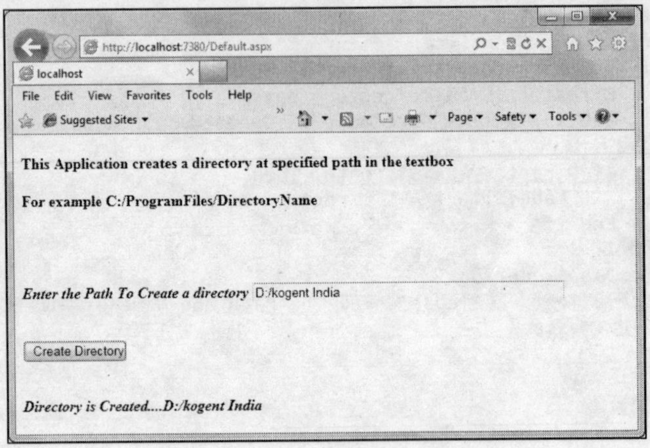

Figure 11.4: Creating the Directory

Let's now learn how to copy the Directory.

Copying a Directory

Now, let's discuss how to copy a directory. Perform the following steps to copy the directory:

1. Create an ASP.NET Empty Web Site and add a Web page to it. You can save the Website as CopyDirectoryCS. The code for this application is available in the CopyDirectoryCS (for C#) and CopyDirectoryVB (for VB) folders.
2. Drag and drop a Button control, two TextBox controls, and three Label controls from the Toolbox on the Design view of the Default.aspx page.
3. Set the Text property of the Button control to CopyDirectory, ID property of the Button control to BtnCopy, Text property of the Label1 control to Enter path and name of source directory, and Text property of the Label2 control to Enter path and name of destination directory in the Properties window.

After setting the properties of the control, the code of the Default.aspx page appears, as shown in Listing 11.5:

Listing 11.5: Showing the Code of the Default.aspx Page

In VB

```
<%@ Page Language="VB" AutoEventWireup="false" CodeFile="Default.aspx.vb"
  Inherits="_Default" %>
<!DOCTYPE html>
<html xmlns="http://www.w3.org/1999/xhtml">
<head runat="server">
    <title></title>
</head>
<body>
    <form id="form1" runat="server">
```

```
        <div>
        Copy a Directory and its content from one location to other<br />
            <br />
                     
            <asp:Label ID="Lblsource" runat="server" Font-Bold="True" Font-Italic="True"
            Text="Enter path and name of source directory"></asp:Label>
                      
            <asp:TextBox ID="TextBox1"  runat="server" style="margin-left: 0px"
                Width="231px"></asp:TextBox>
            <br />
            <br />
                      
            <asp:Label ID="Lbldestination" runat="server" Font-Bold="True" Font-
            Italic="True"
            Text="Enter path and name of destination directory "></asp:Label>
            <asp:TextBox ID="TextBox2" runat="server" Width="238px"></asp:TextBox>
            <br />
            <br />
            <br />
            <asp:Button ID="BtnCopy" runat="server"  Font-Bold="True" Font-Italic="False"
                Text="Copy Directory" Width="182px" />
            <br />
            <br />
            <br />
            <asp:Label ID="Label2" runat="server" Font-Bold="True" Font-
            Italic="True"></asp:Label>
        </div>
        </form>
    </body>
    </html>
```

In C#

```
    <%@ Page Language="C#" AutoEventWireup="true" CodeFile="Default.aspx.cs"
      Inherits="_Default" %>
    <!DOCTYPE html>
    <html xmlns="http://www.w3.org/1999/xhtml">
    <head runat="server">
        <title></title>
    </head>
    <body>
        <form id="form1" runat="server">
        <div>
        Copy a Directory and its content from one location to other<br />
            <br />
                     
            <asp:Label ID="Lblsource" runat="server" Font-Bold="True" Font-Italic="True"
            Text="Enter path and name of source directory"></asp:Label>
                      
            <asp:TextBox ID="TextBox1"  runat="server" style="margin-left: 0px"
                Width="231px"></asp:TextBox>
            <br />
            <br />
                      
            <asp:Label ID="Lbldestination" runat="server" Font-Bold="True" Font-
            Italic="True"
            Text="Enter path and name of destination directory "></asp:Label>
            <asp:TextBox ID="TextBox2" runat="server" Width="238px"></asp:TextBox>
            <br />
            <br />
            <br />
```

```
            <asp:Button ID="BtnCopy" runat="server"  Font-Bold="True" Font-Italic="False"
               Text="Copy Directory" Width="182px" OnClick="BtnCopy_Click" />
            <br />
            <br />
            <br />
            <asp:Label ID="Label2" runat="server" Font-Bold="True" Font-
            Italic="True"></asp:Label>
        </div>
        </form>
    </body>
    </html>
```

4. Double-click the Button control (BtnCopy) and add the following highlighted code in the Click event.

The code of the CodeFile is shown in Listing 11.6:

Listing 11.6: Showing the CodeFile of Default.aspx Page

In VB

```
Imports System.IO
Partial Class _Default
    Inherits System.Web.UI.Page
    Protected Sub BtnCopy_Click(sender As Object,e As EventArgs)
         Handles BtnCopy.Click
        Try
            Dim SDir As New DirectoryInfo(TextBox1.Text)
            Dim DDir As New DirectoryInfo(TextBox2.Text)
            CpyDir(SDir, DDir)
            Label2.Text = "Directory is copied "
        Catch ex As Exception
            Label2.Text = ex.Message
        End Try
    End Sub
    Shared Sub CpyDir(src As DirectoryInfo,destin As DirectoryInfo)
        If (Not destin.Exists) Then
            destin.Create()
            ' To Copy all files
            Dim files() As FileInfo = src.GetFiles()
            For Each file As FileInfo In files
                file.CopyTo(Path.Combine(destin.FullName, file.Name))
            Next file
            ' Process subdirectories.
            Dim dirs() As DirectoryInfo = src.GetDirectories()
            For Each dir As DirectoryInfo In dirs
                Dim destinationDir As String = Path.Combine(destin.FullName, dir.Name)
                CpyDir(dir, New DirectoryInfo(destinationDir))
            Next dir
        End If
    End Sub
End Class
```

In C#

```
using System;
using System.Collections.Generic;
using System.Linq;
using System.Web;
using System.Web.UI;
using System.Web.UI.WebControls;
using System.IO;
public partial class _Default : System.Web.UI.Page
{
```

```
        protected void Page_Load(object sender, EventArgs e)
        {

        }
        protected void BtnCopy_Click(object sender, EventArgs e)
        {
            try
            {
                DirectoryInfo SDir = new DirectoryInfo(TextBox1.Text);
                DirectoryInfo DDir = new DirectoryInfo(TextBox2.Text);
                CpyDir(SDir, DDir);
                Label2.Text = "Directory is copied ";
            }
            catch (Exception ex)
            {
                Label2.Text = ex.Message;
            }
        }
        static void CpyDir(DirectoryInfo src, DirectoryInfo destin)
        {
            if (!destin.Exists)
            {
                destin.Create();
                FileInfo[] files = src.GetFiles();
                foreach (FileInfo file in files)
                {
                    file.CopyTo(Path.Combine(destin.FullName, file.Name));
                }
                DirectoryInfo[] dirs = src.GetDirectories();
                foreach (DirectoryInfo dir in dirs)
                {
                    string destinationDir = Path.Combine(destin.FullName, dir.Name);
                    CpyDir(dir, new DirectoryInfo(destinationDir));
                }
            }
        }
    }
```

5. Press the F5 key on the keyboard to execute the application. The output of the application appears (Figure 11.5).
6. Enter the source and destination path in the respective text boxes and click the Copy Directory button, as shown in Figure 11.5:

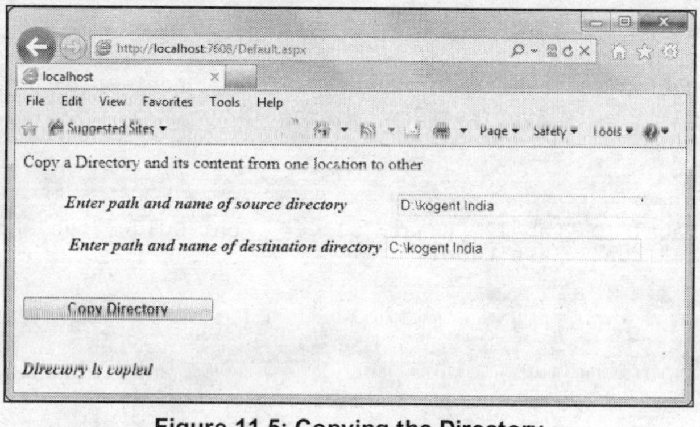

Figure 11.5: Copying the Directory

Let's now learn how to create the subdirectory.

Creating a Subdirectory

Now, let's discuss how to create a subdirectory. Perform the following steps to create the subdirectory:

1. Create an ASP.NET Empty Web Site and add a Web page to it. Now, save the Website as CreateSubdirectoryCS. You can find the code for this application in the CreateSubdirectoryCS (for C#) and CreateSubdirectoryVB (for VB) folders.
2. Drag and drop a Button control, two TextBox controls, and three Label controls from the Toolbox on the Design view of the Default.aspx page.
3. Set the Text property of the Button control to Create SubDirectory, ID property of the Button control to BtnCreate, Text property of the Label1 control to Enter path and name of source directory, and Text property of the Label2 control to Enter name of Subdirectory in the Properties window.

After setting the properties of the control, the code of the Default.aspx page appears, as shown in Listing 11.7:

Listing 11.7: Showing the Code of the Default.aspx Page

In VB

```
<%@ Page Language="VB" AutoEventWireup="false" CodeFile="Default.aspx.vb"
  Inherits="_Default" %>
<!DOCTYPE html>
<html xmlns="http://www.w3.org/1999/xhtml">
<head runat="server">
    <title></title>
</head>
<body>
    <form id="form1" runat="server">
    <div>
     Create a SubDirectory<br />
        <br />
                 
        <asp:Label ID="Lblsource" runat="server" Font-Bold="True" Font-Italic="True"
        Text="Enter path and name of source directory"></asp:Label>
                  
        <asp:TextBox ID="TextBox1"  runat="server" style="margin-left: 0px"
           Width="231px"></asp:TextBox>
        <br />
        <br />
                  
        <asp:Label ID="Lbldestination" runat="server" Font-Bold="True" Font-
        Italic="True" Text="Enter name of Subdirectory "></asp:Label>
        <asp:TextBox ID="TextBox2" runat="server" Width="238px"></asp:TextBox>
        <br />
        <br />
        <br />
        <asp:Button ID="BtnCreate" runat="server"  Font-Bold="True" Font-Italic="False"
           Text="Create SubDirectory" Width="182px"  />
        <br />
        <br />
        <br />
        <asp:Label ID="Label2" runat="server" Font-Bold="True" Font-
        Italic="True"></asp:Label>
    </div>
    </form>
</body>
</html>
```

In C#

```
<%@ Page Language="C#" AutoEventWireup="true" CodeFile="Default.aspx.cs"
  Inherits="_Default" %>
<!DOCTYPE html>
<html xmlns="http://www.w3.org/1999/xhtml">
<head runat="server">
    <title></title>
</head>
<body>
    <form id="form1" runat="server">
    <div>
        Create a SubDirectory<br />
        <br />
                 
        <asp:Label ID="Lblsource" runat="server" Font-Bold="True" Font-Italic="True"
        Text="Enter path and name of source directory"></asp:Label>
                  
        <asp:TextBox ID="TextBox1"  runat="server" style="margin-left: 0px"
           Width="231px"></asp:TextBox>
        <br />
        <br />
                  
        <asp:Label ID="Lbldestination" runat="server" Font-Bold="True" Font-
        Italic="True" Text="Enter name of Subdirectory "></asp:Label>
        <asp:TextBox ID="TextBox2" runat="server" Width="238px"></asp:TextBox>
        <br />
        <br />
        <br />
        <asp:Button ID="BtnCreate" runat="server"  Font-Bold="True" Font-Italic="False"
           Text="Create SubDirectory" Width="182px" OnClick="BtnCreate_Click"   />
        <br />
        <br />
        <br />
        <asp:Label ID="Label2" runat="server" Font-Bold="True" Font-
        Italic="True"></asp:Label>
    </div>
    </form>
</body>
</html>
```

4. Double-click the Button control (BtnCreate) and add the following highlighted code in the Click event.

The code of the CodeFile is shown in Listing 11.8:

Listing 11.8: Showing the Code of the CodeFile of the Default.aspx Page

In VB

```
Imports System.IO
Partial Class _Default
    Inherits System.Web.UI.Page
    Protected Sub BtnCreate_Click(sender As Object,e As EventArgs)
       Handles BtnCreate.Click
        Dim directorypath As String = TextBox1.Text
        Dim subdir As System.IO.DirectoryInfo = New DirectoryInfo(TextBox1.Text)
        Try
            Dim subname As String = TextBox2.Text
            subdir.CreateSubdirectory(subname)
            Label2.Text = "Subdirectory: " & subname & " is created at " & directorypath
        Catch ex As Exception
            Label2.Text = ex.Message
        End Try
    End Sub
End Class
```

In C#

```
using System;
using System.Collections.Generic;
using System.Linq;
using System.Web;
using System.Web.UI;
using System.Web.UI.WebControls;
using System.IO;
public partial class _Default : System.Web.UI.Page
{
    protected void Page_Load(object sender, EventArgs e)
    {
    }
    protected void BtnCreate_Click(object sender, EventArgs e)
    {
        string directorypath = TextBox1.Text;
        System.IO.DirectoryInfo subdir = new DirectoryInfo(TextBox1.Text);
        try
        {
                string subname = TextBox2.Text;
                {
                subdir.CreateSubdirectory(subname);
        Label2.Text = "Subdirectory: " + subname + "  is created at "+directorypath;
                }
        }
        catch(Exception ex)
        {
                Label2.Text = ex.Message;
        }
    }
}
```

5. Press the F5 key on the keyboard to execute the application. The output of the application appears (Figure 11.6).
6. Enter the location of the directory and name of the subdirectory in their respective text boxes (Figure 11.6).
7. Click the Create SubDirectory button to create the subdirectory in the source directory, as shown in Figure 11.6:

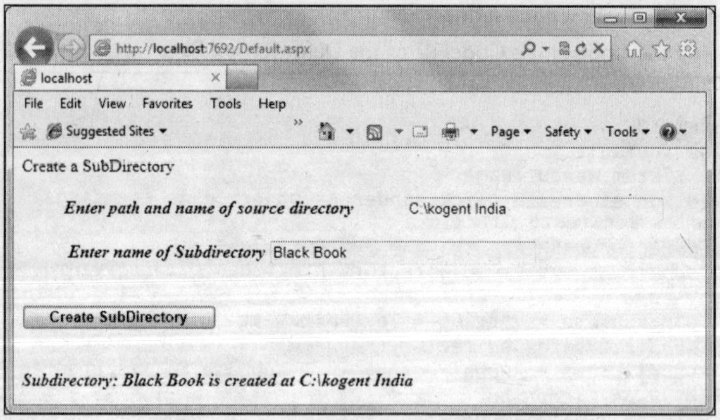

Figure11.6: Creating the Subdirectory

Let's create an application to view subdirectories of the directory.

Viewing Subdirectories of a Directory

Now, let's discuss how to view the subdirectories present in the directory. Perform the following steps to view the subdirectory:

1. Create an ASP.NET Empty Web Site and add a Web page to it. You can save the Website as ViewSubdirectoryCS. The code for this application is available in the ViewSubdirectoryCS (for C#) and ViewSubdirectoryVB (for VB) folders.
2. Drag and drop a Button control, one TextBox control, one ListBox control, and one Label control from the Toolbox on the Design view of the Default.aspx page.
3. Set the Text property of the Button control to Show SubDirectories, ID property of the Button control to Btnshow, and Text property of the Label1 control to Enter path and name of directory, in the Properties window.

After setting the properties of the controls, the code of the Default.aspx page appears, as shown in Listing 11.9:

Listing 11.9: Showing the Code of the Default.aspx Page

In VB

```
<%@ Page Language="VB" AutoEventWireup="false" CodeFile="Default.aspx.vb"
  Inherits="_Default" %>
<!DOCTYPE html>
<html xmlns="http://www.w3.org/1999/xhtml">
<head runat="server">
    <title></title>
</head>
<body>
    <form id="form1" runat="server">
    <div>
         Displays list of subdirectory for the directory mentioned in the text box.
         <br />
         <br />
         <br />
                     
         <asp:Label ID="Label1" runat="server" Font-Bold="True" Font-Italic="True"
         Text="Enter path and name of directory"></asp:Label>
         <asp:TextBox ID="TextBox1" runat="server"></asp:TextBox>
         <br />
          <br />
         <br />
         <asp:Button ID="Btnshow" runat="server" Text="Show SubDirectories" />
               
         <asp:ListBox ID="ListBox1" runat="server" Height="181px" Width="269px">
         </asp:ListBox>
    </div>
    </form>
</body>
</html>
```

In C#

```
<%@ Page Language="C#" AutoEventWireup="true" CodeFile="Default.aspx.cs"
  Inherits="_Default" %>
<!DOCTYPE html>
<html xmlns="http://www.w3.org/1999/xhtml">
<head runat="server">
    <title></title>
</head>
<body>
    <form id="form1" runat="server">
```

```
        <div>
            Displays list of subdirectory for the directory mentioned in the text box.
            <br />
            <br />
            <br />
                        
            <asp:Label ID="Label1" runat="server" Font-Bold="True" Font-Italic="True"
            Text="Enter path and name of directory"></asp:Label>
            <asp:TextBox ID="TextBox1" runat="server"></asp:TextBox>
            <br />
             <br />
            <br />
            <asp:Button ID="Btnshow" runat="server" OnClick="Btnshow_Click"
            Text="Show SubDirectories" />
                  
            <asp:ListBox ID="ListBox1" runat="server" Height="181px" Width="269px">
            </asp:ListBox>
        </div>
        </form>
    </body>
    </html>
```

4. Double-click the Button control and add the following highlighted code in the Click event.

The CodeFile of the Default.aspx page is shown in Listing 11.10:

Listing 11.10: Showing the Code of the CodeFile of the Default.aspx Page

In VB

```
Imports System.IO
Partial Class _Default
    Inherits System.Web.UI.Page
    Protected Sub Btnshow_Click(sender As Object, e As EventArgs)
  Handles Btnshow.Click
        Dim path As String = TextBox1.Text
        Dim maindir As New DirectoryInfo(path)
        If maindir.Exists Then
            Dim subdir() As DirectoryInfo = maindir.GetDirectories()
            For i As Integer = 0 To subdir.Length - 1
                ListBox1.Items.Add("Name : " & subdir(i).ToString)
            Next i
        Else
            ListBox1.Items.Add("Main Directory Does not exists")
        End If
    End Sub
End Class
```

In C#

```
using System;
using System.Collections.Generic;
using System.Linq;
using System.Web;
using System.Web.UI;
using System.Web.UI.WebControls;
using System.IO;
public partial class _Default : System.Web.UI.Page
{
    protected void Page_Load(object sender, EventArgs e)
    {

    }
    protected void Btnshow_Click(object sender, EventArgs e)
```

```
        {
            string path = TextBox1.Text;
            DirectoryInfo maindir = new DirectoryInfo(path);
            if (maindir.Exists)
            {
                DirectoryInfo[] subdir = maindir.GetDirectories();
                for (int i = 0; i < subdir.Length; i++)
                {
                    ListBox1.Items.Add("Name : " + subdir[i]);
                }
            }
            else
            {
                ListBox1.Items.Add("Main Directory Does not exists");
            }
        }
    }
```

5. Press the F5 key on the keyboard to execute the application. The output of the application appears (Figure 11.7).
6. Enter a directory in the text box and click the Show SubDirectories button to view the subdirectories in the list box, as shown in Figure 11.7:

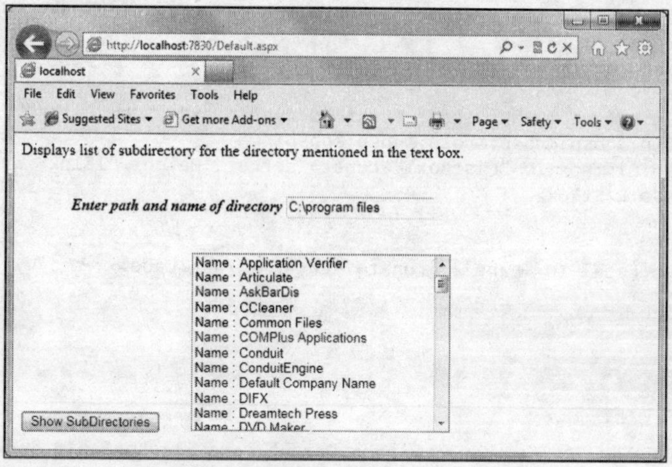

Figure 11.7: Showing the Subdirectories

Let's create an application to retrieve files from a directory.

Retrieving Files from a Directory

Now, let's discuss how to view the files present in the directory. Perform the following steps to view the files from the directory:

1. Create an ASP.NET Empty Web Site and add a Web page to it. You can save the Website as RetrieveDirectoryfilesCS. The code for this application is available in the RetrieveDirectoryfilesCS (for C#) and RetrieveDirectoryfilesVB (for VB) folders.
2. Drag and drop a Button control, one TextBox control, one ListBox control, and one Label control from the Toolbox on the Design view of the Default.aspx page.
3. Set the Text property of the Button1 control to Show Files, ID property of the Button1 control to Btnshow and Text property of the Label1 control to Enter path and name of directory, in the Properties window.

After setting the properties of the control, the code of the Default.aspx page appears, as shown in Listing 11.11:

Listing 11.11: Showing the Code of the Default.aspx Page

In VB

```
<%@ Page Language="VB" AutoEventWireup="false" CodeFile="Default.aspx.vb"
  Inherits="_Default" %>
<!DOCTYPE html>
<html xmlns="http://www.w3.org/1999/xhtml">
<head runat="server">
    <title></title>
</head>
<body>
    <form id="form1" runat="server">
    <div>
    Displays List of Files for the Directory Mentioned in the text box.
         <br />
         <br />
         <br />
                     
         <asp:Label ID="Label1" runat="server" Font-Bold="True" Font-Italic="True"
         Text="Enter path and name of directory"></asp:Label>
         <asp:TextBox ID="TextBox1" runat="server"></asp:TextBox>
         <br />
          <br />
         <br />
         <asp:Button ID="Btnshow" runat="server" Text="Show Files" />
               
         <asp:ListBox ID="ListBox1" runat="server" Height="181px" Width="269px">
         </asp:ListBox>
        <br />
        <br />
         <asp:Label ID="Label2" runat="server"></asp:Label>
    </div>
    </form>
</body>
</html>
```

In C#

```
<%@ Page Language="C#" AutoEventWireup="true" CodeFile="Default.aspx.cs"
  Inherits="_Default" %>
<!DOCTYPE>
<html xmlns="http://www.w3.org/1999/xhtml">
<head runat="server">
    <title></title>
</head>
<body>
    <form id="form1" runat="server">
    <div>
        Displays List of Files for the Directory Mentioned in the text box.
         <br />
         <br />
         <br />
                     
         <asp:Label ID="Label1" runat="server" Font-Bold="True" Font-Italic="True"
         Text="Enter path and name of directory"></asp:Label>
         <asp:TextBox ID="TextBox1" runat="server"></asp:TextBox>
         <br />
          <br />
```

```
            <br />
            <asp:Button ID="Btnshow" runat="server" OnClick="Btnshow_Click"
            Text="Show Files" />
                  
            <asp:ListBox ID="ListBox1" runat="server" Height="181px" Width="269px">
            </asp:ListBox>
           <br />
           <br />
           <asp:Label ID="Label2" runat="server"></asp:Label>
        </div>
        </form>
    </body>
    </html>
```

4. Double-click the Button control (Btnshow) and add the following highlighted code in the Click event.

The code of the CodeFile of Default.aspx page is shown in Listing 11.12:

Listing 11.12: Showing the Code of the CodeFile of the Default.aspx Page

In VB

```
    Imports System.IO
    Partial Class _Default
        Inherits System.Web.UI.Page
        Protected Sub Btnshow_Click(sender As Object, e As EventArgs)
      Handles Btnshow.Click
            Dim path As String = TextBox1.Text
            Dim dir As New DirectoryInfo(path)
            If dir.Exists Then
                Dim files() As FileInfo = dir.GetFiles("*")
                For Each file As FileInfo In files
                    ListBox1.Items.Add("Name " & file.Name & "  Size: " &
                       file.Length.ToString())
                Next file
                Label2.Text = "Directory Exists"
            Else
                Label2.Text = "Directory at " & path & "Does not exists"
            End If
        End Sub
    End Class
```

In C#

```
    using System;
    using System.Collections.Generic;
    using System.Linq;
    using System.Web;
    using System.Web.UI;
    using System.Web.UI.WebControls;
    using System.IO;
    public partial class _Default : System.Web.UI.Page
    {
        protected void Page_Load(object sender, EventArgs e)
        {

        }
        protected void Btnshow_Click(object sender, EventArgs e)
        {
            string path = TextBox1.Text;
            DirectoryInfo dir = new DirectoryInfo(path);
            if (dir.Exists)
```

```
        {
            FileInfo[] files = dir.GetFiles("*");
            foreach (FileInfo file in files)
            {
           ListBox1.Items.Add("Name " + file.Name + "  Size: " +
                file.Length.ToString());
            }
            Label2.Text="Directory Exists";
        }
        else
        {
            Label2.Text = "Directory at " + path + " Does not exists";
        }
    }
}
```

5. Press the F5 key on the keyboard to execute the application. The output of the application appears (Figure 11.8).
6. Enter any directory in the text box and click the Show Files button to view the files present in the directory, as shown in Figure 11.8:

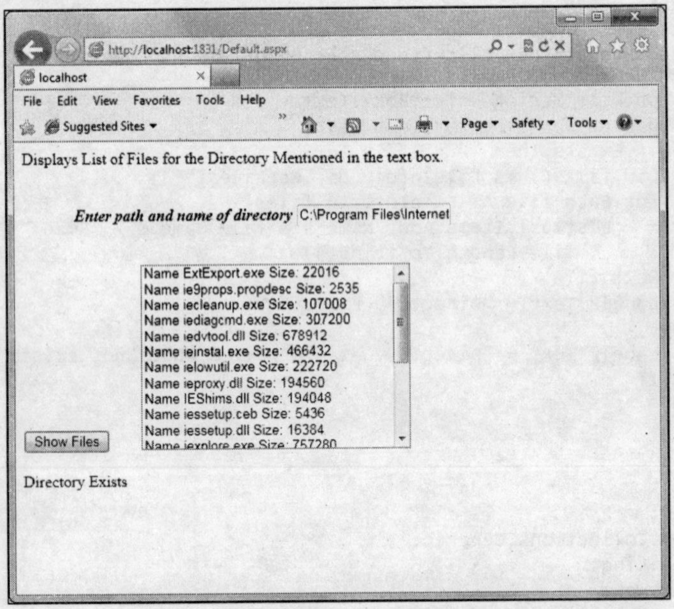

Figure 11.8: Displaying the List of Files

Creating a File

Now, let's discuss how to create a file in a directory. Perform the following steps to create the file:

1. Create an ASP.NET Empty Web Site and add a Web page to it. You can save the Website as CreatetextfileCS. The code for this application is available in the CreatetextfileCS (for C#) and CreatetextfileVB (for VB) folders.
2. Drag and drop a Button control, two TextBox controls, and two Label control from the Toolbox on the Design view of the Default.aspx page.
3. Set the Text property of the Button1 control to Create & Write to File, ID property of the Button1 control to BtnCreate, Text property of the Label1 control to Enter name and path of File, and TextMode property of the TextBox2 control to MultiLine in the Properties window.

After setting the properties of the control, the code of the Default.aspx page appears, as shown in Listing 11.13:

Listing 11.13: Showing the Code of the Default.aspx Page

In VB

```
<%@ Page Language="VB" AutoEventWireup="false" CodeFile="Default.aspx.vb"
  Inherits="_Default" %>
<!DOCTYPE html>
<html xmlns="http://www.w3.org/1999/xhtml">
<head runat="server">
    <title></title>
</head>
<body>
    <form id="form1" runat="server">
    <div>Creates a file and opens it to work with it.Mention the path and file name such
           as D:/directoryname/filename.doc<br />
         <br />
         <br />
                
         <asp:Label ID="Label1" runat="server" Font-Bold="True" Font-Italic="True"
         Text="Enter name and path of File "></asp:Label>

         <asp:TextBox ID="TextBox1" runat="server" Width="205px"></asp:TextBox>
          <br />
         <br />
         <br />
               Write the text into the multiline text
           box.   
         <br />
         <asp:TextBox ID="TextBox2" runat="server" Height="135px" TextMode="MultiLine"
         Width="405px"></asp:TextBox><br />
         <br />
        <asp:Button ID="BtnCreate" runat="server"  Text="Create & Write to File"
           Width="212px" Font-Bold="True"
         Font-Italic="True"/>
        <br />        <br />        <br />
    <asp:Label ID="Label2" runat="server" Text=""></asp:Label>
    </div>
    </form>
</body>
</html>
```

In C#

```
<%@ Page Language="C#" AutoEventWireup="true" CodeFile="Default.aspx.cs"
  Inherits="_Default" %>
<!DOCTYPE html>
<html xmlns="http://www.w3.org/1999/xhtml">
<head runat="server">
    <title></title>
</head>
<body>
    <form id="form1" runat="server">
    <div>
    Creates a file and opens it to work with it.Mention the path and file name such
           as D:/directoryname/filename.doc<br />
         <br />
         <br />
                
         <asp:Label ID="Label1" runat="server" Font-Bold="True" Font-Italic="True"
```

```
            Text="Enter name and path of File "></asp:Label>
            <asp:TextBox ID="TextBox1" runat="server" Width="205px"></asp:TextBox>
             <br />
            <br />
            <br />
                  Write the text into the multiline text
              box.   
            <br />
            <asp:TextBox ID="TextBox2" runat="server" Height="135px" TextMode="MultiLine"
            Width="405px"></asp:TextBox><br />
            <br />
           <asp:Button ID="BtnCreate" runat="server"  Text="Create & Write to File"
              Width="212px" Font-Bold="True"
            Font-Italic="True" OnClick="BtnCreate_Click"  />
          <asp:Label ID="Label2" runat="server" Text=""></asp:Label>
      </div>
      </form>
  </body>
  </html>
```

4. Double-click the Button control (BtnCreate) and add the following highlighted code in the Click event.

The code of the CodeFile of Default.aspx page is shown in Listing 11.14:

Listing 11.14: Showing the Code of the CodeFile of the Default.aspx Page

In VB

```
Imports System.IO
Partial Class _Default
    Inherits System.Web.UI.Page
    Protected Sub BtnCreate_Click(sender As Object, e As EventArgs)
  Handles BtnCreate.Click
        Dim path As String
        Dim sw As StreamWriter
        Try
            path = TextBox1.Text
            If (Not File.Exists(path)) Then
                sw = File.CreateText(path)
                sw.WriteLine(TextBox2.Text)
                sw.Close()
                Label2.Text = "File Created"
            Else
                Label1.Text = " The File already Exists at this location..Please change
                 the file name"
            End If
        Catch ex As Exception
            TextBox2.Text = ex.Message
        End Try
    End Sub
End Class
```

In C#

```
using System;
using System.Collections.Generic;
using System.Linq;
using System.Web;
using System.Web.UI;
using System.Web.UI.WebControls;
using System.IO;
public partial class _Default : System.Web.UI.Page
{
```

```
        protected void Page_Load(object sender, EventArgs e)
        {
        }
        protected void BtnCreate_Click(object sender, EventArgs e)
        {
            string path;
            StreamWriter sw;
            try
             {
                    path = TextBox1.Text;
                    if (!File.Exists(path))
                    {
                            sw = File.CreateText(path);
                            sw.WriteLine(TextBox2.Text);
                            sw.Close();
                            Label2.Text = "File Created";
                    }
                    else
                    {
                      Label1.Text = " The File already exists at this location. Please
                    change the file name";
                    }
             }
             catch (Exception ex)
             {
                    TextBox2.Text = ex.Message;
             }
       }
    }
```

5. Press the F5 key on the keyboard to execute the application.The output of the application appears (Figure 11.9).
6. Enter the name and path of file in the TextBox1 and the content in the TextBox2 (MultiLine) control (Figure 11.9).
7. Click the Create & Write to File button to create the file, as shown in Figure 11.9:

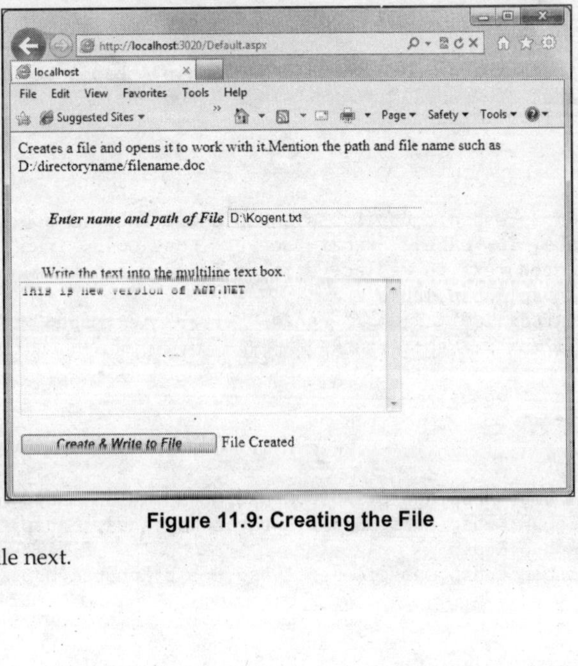

Figure 11.9: Creating the File

Let's learn how to open a file next.

Opening a File

Now, let's discuss how to open a file present in the directory. Perform the following steps to open the file:

1. Create an ASP.NET Empty Web Site and add a Web page to it. You can save the Website as OpenfileCS. The code for this application is available in the OpenfileCS (for C#) and OpenfileVB (for VB) folders.
2. Drag and drop one Button controls, two TextBox controls, and one Label control from the Toolbox on the Design view of the Default.aspx page.
3. Set the Text property of the Button1 control to Open File, Label1 control to Enter the path and name of a file, Label2 control to Enter text to replace data of file, TextMode property of the TextBox2 control to MultiLine, and ID property of the Button1 control to Btnfile in the Properties window.

After setting the properties of the control, the code of the Default.aspx page appears, as shown in Listing 11.15:

Listing 11.15: Showing the Code of the Default.aspx Page

In VB

```
<%@ Page Language="VB" AutoEventWireup="false" CodeFile="Default.aspx.vb"
  Inherits="_Default" %>
<!DOCTYPE html>
<html xmlns="http://www.w3.org/1999/xhtml">
<head runat="server">
    <title></title>
</head>
<body>
    <form id="form1" runat="server">
    <div>
         Open a existing file<span lang="en-us"> and writes into the file.</span><br />
         <br />
         <br />
               
         <asp:Label ID="Lblpath" runat="server" Font-Bold="True" Font-Italic="True"
         Text="Enter the path and name of a file"></asp:Label>
         <span lang="en-us">        
         <asp:TextBox ID="TextBox1" runat="server" Width="271px"></asp:TextBox>
         </span>
         <br />
         <br />
                    
         <asp:Label ID="Label1" runat="server" Font-Bold="True" Font-
         Italic="True"></asp:Label>
         <br />
         <br />
         <br />
                      
         <asp:Label ID="Label2" runat="server" Font-Bold="True" Font-Italic="True"
         Text="Enter text to replace data of file"></asp:Label>
             
         <asp:TextBox ID="TextBox2" runat="server" TextMode="MultiLine" Height="55px"
         Width="177px"></asp:TextBox>
         <br />
         <span lang="en-us">
         <br />
         </span>
         <br />
                  
                     
            
                     
```

```
                 
            <asp:Button ID="Btnfile" runat="server" Font-Bold="True" Font-Italic="True"
            Text="Open File" Width="134px" />
            <br />
            <br />
            <br />
                         
            <asp:Label ID="Lbldisplay" runat="server" Font-Bold="True" Font-
            Italic="True"></asp:Label>
        </div>
        </form>
</body>
</html>
```

In C#

```
<%@ Page Language="C#" AutoEventWireup="true" CodeFile="Default.aspx.cs"
  Inherits="_Default" %>
<!DOCTYPE html>
<html xmlns="http://www.w3.org/1999/xhtml">
<head runat="server">
    <title></title>
</head>
<body>
    <form id="form1" runat="server">
    <div>Open a existing file<span lang="en-us"> and writes into the file.</span><br />
        <br />
        <br />
              
        <asp:Label ID="Lblpath" runat="server" Font-Bold="True" Font-Italic="True"
        Text="Enter the path and name of a file"></asp:Label>
        <span lang="en-us">        
        <asp:TextBox ID="TextBox1" runat="server" Width="271px"></asp:TextBox>
        </span>
        <br />
        <br />
                   
        <asp:Label ID="Label1" runat="server" Font-Bold="True" Font-
        Italic="True"></asp:Label>
        <br />
        <br />
        <br />
                     
        <asp:Label ID="Label2" runat="server" Font-Bold="True" Font-Italic="True"
        Text="Enter text to replace data of file"></asp:Label>
            
        <asp:TextBox ID="TextBox2" runat="server" TextMode="MultiLine" Height="55px"
        Width="177px"> </asp:TextBox>
        <br />
        <br />
                 
                    
           
                    
             
        <asp:Button ID="Btnfile" runat="server" Font-Bold="True" Font-Italic="True"
        OnClick="Btnfile_Click" Text="Open File" Width="144px" />
        <br />
        <br />
        <br />
```

```
                     
        <asp:Label ID="Lbldisplay" runat="server" Font-Bold="True" Font-
        Italic="True"></asp:Label>
    </div>
    </form>
</body>
</html>
```

4. Double-click the Btnfile and add the following highlighted code in the Click event (Btnfile_Click).

The code of the CodeFile of Default.aspx page is shown in Listing 11.16:

Listing 11.16: Showing the Code of the CodeFile of the Default.aspx Page

In VB

```
Imports System.IO
Partial Class _Default
    Inherits System.Web.UI.Page
    Protected Sub Btnfile_Click(sender As Object,e As EventArgs)
  Handles Btnfile.Click
        Dim fs As FileStream
        Try
            fs = File.Open(TextBox1.Text, FileMode.Open)
            Dim sw As New StreamWriter(fs)
            If File.Exists(TextBox1.Text) Then
                Label1.Text = "File is opened"
                sw.WriteLine(TextBox2.Text)
                sw.Close()
        Lbldisplay.Text = "File is saved at" & TextBox1.Text & "  and data is replaced
        with the new data"
            End If
        Catch ex As Exception
            Lbldisplay.Text = ex.Message
        End Try
    End Sub
End Class
```

In C#

```
using System;
using System.Collections.Generic;
using System.Linq;
using System.Web;
using System.Web.UI;
using System.Web.UI.WebControls;
using System.IO;
public partial class _Default : System.Web.UI.Page {
    protected void Page_Load(object sender, EventArgs e) {
    }
    protected void Btnfile_Click(object sender, EventArgs e)
    {
        FileStream fs;
        try
        {
            fs = File.Open(TextBox1.Text, FileMode.Open);
            StreamWriter sw = new StreamWriter(fs);
            if (File.Exists(TextBox1.Text))
            {
                Label1.Text = "File is opened";
                sw.WriteLine(TextBox2.Text);
                sw.Close();
                 Lbldisplay.Text = "File is saved at" + TextBox1.Text + "  and data is
                 replaced with the new data";
            }
        }
        catch (Exception ex)
```

```
            {
                Lbldisplay.Text = ex.Message;
            }
        }
    }
```

5. Press the F5 key on the keyboard to execute the application.The output of the application appears.
6. Enter the path and name of a file in the TextBox1 control (Figure 11.10).
7. Enter text in the TextBox2 (MultiLine) control and click the Open File buton to replace the old content with the new content in the file, as shown in Figure 11.10:

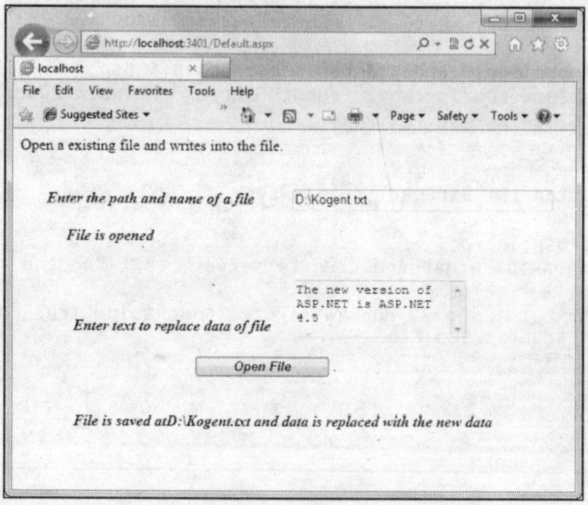

Figure 11.10: Opening an Existing File

Reading and Appending Text to a File

Now, let's discuss how to read the text from a file and append the text in it. Perform the following steps to read and append the file:

1. Create an ASP.NET Empty Web Site and add a Web page to it. You can save the Website as AppendreadfileCS. The code for this application is available in the AppendreadfileCS (for C#) and AppendreadfileVB (for VB) folders.
2. Drag and drop two Button controls, two TextBox controls, and two Label controls from the Toolbox on the Design view of the Default.aspx page.
3. Set the Text property of the Button1 control to Read, Button2 control to Append Text, ID property of the Button1 control to BtnRead, ID property of the Button2 control to BtnAppend, Text property of the Label1 control to Enter path and name of File, and TextMode property of the TextBox2 control to MultiLine in the Properties window.

After setting the properties of the controls, the code of the Default.aspx page appears, as shown in Listing 11.17:

Listing 11.17: Showing the Code of the Default.aspx Page

In VB

```
<%@ Page Language="VB" AutoEventWireup="false" CodeFile="Default.aspx.vb"
  Inherits="_Default" %>
<!DOCTYPE html>
<html xmlns="http://www.w3.org/1999/xhtml">
<head runat="server">
    <title></title>
</head>
```

```
<body>
    <form id="form1" runat="server">
    <div>
       Reading contents of a file on a screen
         <br />
        <br />
         <br />
   <asp:Label ID="Label1" runat="server" Font-Bold="True" Font-Italic="True"
         Text="Enter path and name of File"></asp:Label>
                     
                     
         <asp:TextBox ID="TextBox1" runat="server" Width="232px"></asp:TextBox>
         <br />
                 
         <asp:TextBox ID="TextBox2" runat="server" Height="206px" TextMode="MultiLine"
         Width="628px"></asp:TextBox>
         <br />
         <br />
         <asp:Button ID="BtnRead" runat="server" Text="Read "
         Width="89px" />
            
        <asp:Button ID="BtnAppend" runat="server" Text="Append Text" /><br />
        <br />
        <asp:Label ID="Label2" runat="server" Font-Bold="True" Font-
         Italic="True"></asp:Label>
    </div>
    </form>
</body>
</html>
```

In C#

```
<%@ Page Language="C#" AutoEventWireup="true" CodeFile="Default.aspx.cs"
  Inherits="_Default" %>
<!DOCTYPE html>
<html xmlns="http://www.w3.org/1999/xhtml">
<head runat="server">
    <title></title>
</head>
<body>
    <form id="form1" runat="server">
    <div>
    Reading contents of a file on a screen
         <br />
        <br />
         <br />
         <asp:Label ID="Label1" runat="server" Font-Bold="True" Font-Italic="True"
         Text="Enter path and name of File"></asp:Label>
                     
                     
         <asp:TextBox ID="TextBox1" runat="server" Width="232px"></asp:TextBox>
         <br />
                 
         <asp:TextBox ID="TextBox2" runat="server" Height="206px" TextMode="MultiLine"
         Width="628px"></asp:TextBox>
         <br />
         <br />
         <asp:Button ID="BtnRead" runat="server" Text="Read "
         Width="89px" OnClick="BtnRead_Click" />
               
         <asp:Button ID="BtnAppend" runat="server" OnClick="BtnAppend_Click"
         Text="Append Text" />
        <br />
        <br />
```

```
            <asp:Label ID="Label2" runat="server" Font-Bold="True" Font-
             Italic="True"></asp:Label>
        </div>
        </form>
    </body>
    </html>
```

4. Double-click the Button control(BtnRead) and add the following highlighted code in its Click event.

Similarly, Double-click the Button control(BtnAppend) and add the following highlighted code in its Click event. The code of the CodeFile of Default.aspx page is shown in Listing 11.18:

Listing 11.18: Showing the Code of the CodeFile of the Default.aspx Page

In VB

```
Imports System.IO
Partial Class _Default
    Inherits System.Web.UI.Page
    Protected Sub BtnRead_Click(sender As Object, e As EventArgs)
  Handles BtnRead.Click
        Try
            Dim filename As String = Server.MapPath(TextBox1.Text)
            Dim reader As StreamReader
            Dim str As String
            reader = File.OpenText(filename)
            str = reader.ReadToEnd()
            TextBox2.Text = str
            reader.Close()
            Label2.Text = "File Found and Read successfully!"
        Catch ex As Exception
            Label2.Text = ex.Message
        End Try
    End Sub
    Protected Sub BtnAppend_Click(sender As Object, e As EventArgs)
  Handles BtnAppend.Click
        Try
            Dim filename As String = Server.MapPath(TextBox1.Text)
            Dim sw As StreamWriter = File.AppendText(filename)
            sw.Write(TextBox2.Text)
            sw.Close()
            Label2.Text = "Text Appended successfully!"
        Catch ex As Exception
            Label2.Text = ex.Message
        End Try
    End Sub
End Class
```

In C#

```
using System;
using System.Collections.Generic;
using System.Linq;
using System.Web;
using System.Web.UI;
using System.Web.UI.WebControls;
using System.IO;
public partial class _Default : System.Web.UI.Page {
    protected void Page_Load(object sender, EventArgs e) {

    }
    protected void BtnRead_Click(object sender, EventArgs e)
    {
        try
        {
            String filename = Server.MapPath(TextBox1.Text);
            StreamReader reader;
            reader = File.OpenText(filename);
```

```
                String str = reader.ReadToEnd();
                TextBox2.Text = str;
                reader.Close();
                Label2.Text = "File Found and Read successfully!";
            }
            catch (Exception ex)
            {
                Label2.Text = ex.Message;
            }
        }
        protected void BtnAppend_Click(object sender, EventArgs e)
        {
            try
            {
                String filename = Server.MapPath(TextBox1.Text);
                StreamWriter sw = File.AppendText(filename);
                sw.WriteLine(TextBox2.Text);
                sw.Close();
                Label2.Text = "Text Appended successfully!";
            }
            catch (Exception ex)
            {
                Label2.Text = ex.Message;
            }
} }
```

5. Press the F5 key on the keyboard to execute the application.The output of the application appears (Figure 11.11).
6. Enter the path of file and click the Read button to read the content from the file, as shown in Figure 11.11:

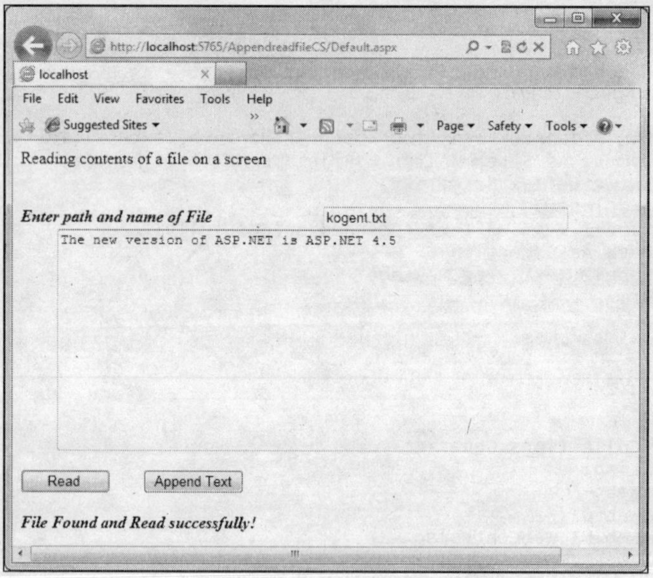

Figure 11.11: Reading the Text from the File

7. Enter some other text in the TextBox2 control and click the Append Text button to append the text in the file, as shown in Figure 11.12:

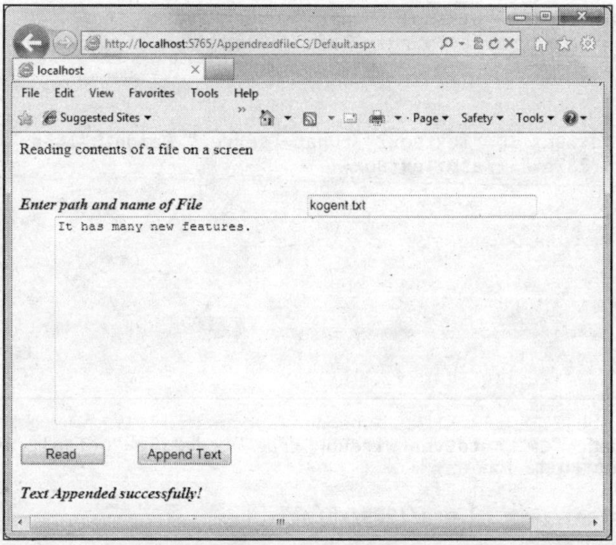

Figure 11.12: Appending the Text Successfully

Let's now discuss Retrieving the details of a file.

Retrieving Details of a File

Now, let's discuss how to retrieve the details of a file .Perform the following steps to retrieve the Details of the file:

1. Create an ASP.NET Empty Web Site and add a Web page to it. You can save the Website as RetrievedetailCS. The code for this application is available in the RetrievedetailCS (for C#) and RetrievedetailVB (for VB) folders.
2. Drag and drop one Button control, two TextBox controls, and one Label control from the Toolbox on the Design view of the Default.aspx page.
3. Set the Text property of the Button1 control to Show, ID property of the Button1 control to Btnshow, Text property of the Label1 control to Enter Name and path of File, and TextMode property of the TextBox2 control to MultiLine in the Properties window.

After setting the properties of the control, the code of the Default.aspx page appears, as shown in Listing 11.19:

Listing 11.19: Showing the Code of the Default.aspx Page

In VB

```
<%@ Page Language="VB" AutoEventWireup="false" CodeFile="Default.aspx.vb"
  Inherits="_Default" %>
<!DOCTYPE html>
<html xmlns="http://www.w3.org/1999/xhtml">
<head runat="server">
    <title></title>
</head>
<body>
    <form id="form1" runat="server">
    <div>
    <asp:Label ID="Label1" runat="server" Font-Bold="True" Font-Italic="True"
         Text="Enter Name and path of File "></asp:Label>
         <asp:TextBox ID="TextBox1" runat="server" Width="177px"></asp:TextBox>
         <br />
         <br />
              
```

```
            <asp:Button ID="Btnshow" runat="server" Text="Show"
            Width="78px" style="margin-left: 204px" />
            <br />
            <br />
            <br />
            <asp:TextBox ID="TextBox2" runat="server" Height="183px" TextMode="MultiLine"
            Width="287px"></asp:TextBox>
            <br />
            <br />
            <br />
            <br />
        </div>
        </form>
    </body>
    </html>
```

In C#

```
    <%@ Page Language="C#" AutoEventWireup="true" CodeFile="Default.aspx.cs"
      Inherits="_Default" %>
    <!DOCTYPE html>
    <html xmlns="http://www.w3.org/1999/xhtml">
    <head runat="server">
        <title></title>
    </head>
    <body>
        <form id="form1" runat="server">
        <div>
        <asp:Label ID="Label1" runat="server" Font-Bold="True" Font-Italic="True"
            Text="Enter Name and path of File "></asp:Label>
                    <asp:TextBox ID="TextBox1" runat="server" Width="177px"></asp:TextBox>
            <br />
            <br />
                 
            <asp:Button ID="Btnshow" runat="server" Text="Show"
            Width="78px" style="margin-left: 204px" OnClick="Btnshow_Click" />
            <br />
            <br />
            <br />
            <asp:TextBox ID="TextBox2" runat="server" Height="183px" TextMode="MultiLine"
            Width="287px"></asp:TextBox>
            <br />
            <br />
            <br />
            <br />
        </div>
        </form>
    </body>
    </html>
```

4. Double-click the Button control (Btnshow) and add the following highlighted code in the Click event respectively.

The code of the CodeFile of Default.aspx page is shown in Listing 11.20:

Listing 11.20: Showing the Code of the CodeFile of the Default.aspx Page

In VB

```
    Imports System.IO
    Partial Class _Default
        Inherits System.Web.UI.Page
        Protected Sub Btnshow_Click(sender As Object,e As EventArgs)
      Handles Btnshow.Click
```

```
            Dim str As String
            Dim l As String
            Dim attr As String = ""
            Try
                str = TextBox1.Text
                l = File.GetAttributes(str)
                If l = "32" Then
                    attr = "Archive"
                End If
                If l = "16" Then
                    attr = "Directory"
                End If
                     TextBox2.Text = " File Attributes :   " & attr & " Created at: " &
                     File.GetCreationTime(str).ToString() & " Last Accessed at :" &
                     File.GetLastAccessTime(str)
            Catch ex As Exception
                TextBox2.Text = ex.Message
            End Try
        End Sub
    End Class
```

In C#

```
using System;
using System.Collections.Generic;
using System.Linq;
using System.Web;
using System.Web.UI;
using System.Web.UI.WebControls;
using System.IO;
public partial class _Default : System.Web.UI.Page
{
    protected void Page_Load(object sender, EventArgs e)
    {
    }
    protected void Btnshow_Click(object sender, EventArgs e)
    {
        string str;
        try
        {
            str = TextBox1.Text;
            TextBox2.Text = " File Attributes :   " + File.GetAttributes(str)+"  Created
                at: " + File.GetCreationTime(str).ToString() +" Last Accessed at :" +
                File.GetLastAccessTime(str);
        }
        catch (Exception ex)
        {
            TextBox2.Text = ex.Message;
        }
    }
}
```

5. Press the F5 key on the keyboard to execute the application.The output of the application appears on the Web page (Figure 11.13).
6. Enter name and path of the file in the text box and click the Show button to view the details of the file, as shown in Figure 11.13:

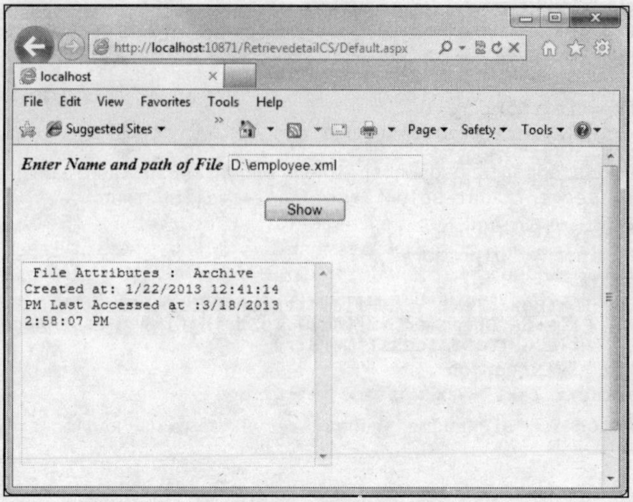

Figure 11.13: Showing the Details of the File

Let's discuss how to rename or move a file in the directory.

Renaming a File

Now, let's discuss how to rename or move a file in the directory. Perform the following steps to rename the file:

1. Create an ASP.NET Empty Web Site and add a Web page to it. You can save the Website as RenamingFileCS. The code for this application is available in the RenamingFileCS (for C#) and RenamingFileVB (for VB) folders.
2. Drag and drop one Button control, two TextBox controls, and three Label controls from the Toolbox on the Design view of the Default.aspx page.
3. Set the Text property of the Button1 control to Rename File, ID property of the Button1 control to BtnRename, Text property of the Label1 control to Enter path and name of file, and Text property of the Label2 control to Enter path and Rename the File in the Properties window.

After setting the properties of the controls, the code of the Default.aspx page appears, as shown in Listing 11.21:

Listing 11.21: Showing the Code of the Default.aspx Page

In VB

```
<%@ Page Language="VB" AutoEventWireup="false" CodeFile="Default.aspx.vb"
  Inherits="_Default" %>
<!DOCTYPE html>
<html xmlns="http://www.w3.org/1999/xhtml">
<head runat="server">
    <title></title>
</head>
<body>
    <form id="form1" runat="server">
    <div>
     Rename the File
    <br/>
    <br />
            <asp:Label ID="Label1"
  runat="server"
  Font-Bold="True" Font-Italic="True" Text="Enter path and name of file"></asp:Label>
```

```
              &n
bsp;             &nbs
p;    
        <asp:TextBox ID="TextBox1" runat="server" Height="23px"
        Width="198px"></asp:TextBox>
        <br />
        <br />
                <asp:Label ID="Label2"
          runat="server" Font-Bold="True" Font-Italic="True"
        Text="Enter path and Rename the File "></asp:Label>
                   
                    
        <asp:TextBox ID="TextBox2" runat="server" Height="26px"
          Width="192px"></asp:TextBox>
        <br />
        <br />
        <br />
        <asp:Button ID="BtnRename" runat="server"  Text="Rename File "/>
        <br />
        <br />
        <br />
        <asp:Label ID="Label3" runat="server" Font-Bold="True" Font-
        Italic="True"></asp:Label>
    </div>
    </form>
</body>
</html>
```

In C#

```
<%@ Page Language="C#" AutoEventWireup="true" CodeFile="Default.aspx.cs"
  Inherits="_Default" %>
<!DOCTYPE html>
<html xmlns="http://www.w3.org/1999/xhtml">
<head runat="server">
    <title></title>
</head>
<body>
    <form id="form1" runat="server">
    <div>
    Rename the File
    <br/>
    <br />
            <asp:Label ID="Label1"
  runat="server"
  Font-Bold="True" Font-Italic="True" Text="Enter path and name of file"></asp:Label>
                &n
  bsp;             &nbs
  p;    
        <asp:TextBox ID="TextBox1" runat="server" Height="23px"
        Width="198px"></asp:TextBox>
        <br />
        <br />
                <asp:Label ID="Label2"
          runat="server" Font-Bold="True" Font-Italic="True"
        Text="Enter path and Rename the File "></asp:Label>
                   
                    
        <asp:TextBox ID="TextBox2" runat="server" Height="26px"
          Width="192px"></asp:TextBox>
        <br />
```

```
            <br />
            <br />
            <asp:Button ID="BtnRename" runat="server"  Text="Rename File
            OnClick="BtnRename_Click" />
            <br />
            <br />
            <br />
            <asp:Label ID="Label3" runat="server" Font-Bold="True" Font-
            Italic="True"></asp:Label>
        </div>
        </form>
    </body>
    </html>
```

4. Double-click the Button control (BtnRename) and add the following highlighted code in the Click event respectively.

The code of CodeFile of Default.aspx page is shown in Listing 11.22:

Listing 11.22: Showing the CodeFile of Default.aspx Page

In VB

```
Imports System.IO
Partial Class _Default
    Inherits System.Web.UI.Page
    Protected Sub BtnRename_Click(sender As Object, e As EventArgs)
  Handles BtnRename.Click
        Dim strsorc As String = TextBox1.Text
        Dim strdest As String = TextBox2.Text
        Try
            Dim sourcefile As New FileInfo(strsorc)
            If sourcefile.Exists Then
                sourcefile.MoveTo(strdest)
                Label3.Text = " File is renamed"
            Else
                Label3.Text = "file not found"
            End If
        Catch ex As Exception
            Label3.Text = ex.Message
        End Try
    End Sub
End Class
```

In C#

```
using System;
using System.Collections.Generic;
using System.Linq;
using System.Web;
using System.Web.UI;
using System.Web.UI.WebControls;
using System.IO;
public partial class _Default : System.Web.UI.Page
{
    protected void Page_Load(object sender, EventArgs e)
    {

    }
    protected void BtnRename_Click(object sender, EventArgs e)
    {
        string strsorc = TextBox1.Text;
```

```
            string strdest = TextBox2.Text;
            try
            {
                FileInfo sourcefile = new FileInfo(strsorc);
                if (sourcefile.Exists)
                {
                    sourcefile.MoveTo(strdest);
                    Label3.Text = " File is renamed";
                }
                else
                {
                    Label3.Text = "file not found";
                }
            }
            catch (Exception ex)
            {
                Label3.Text = ex.Message;
            }
        }
    }
```

5. Press the F5 key on the keyboard to execute the application. The output of the application appears (Figure 11.14).
6. Enter the name of the file in the TextBox1, rename the file in the TextBox2, and click the Rename File button, as shown in Figure 11.14:

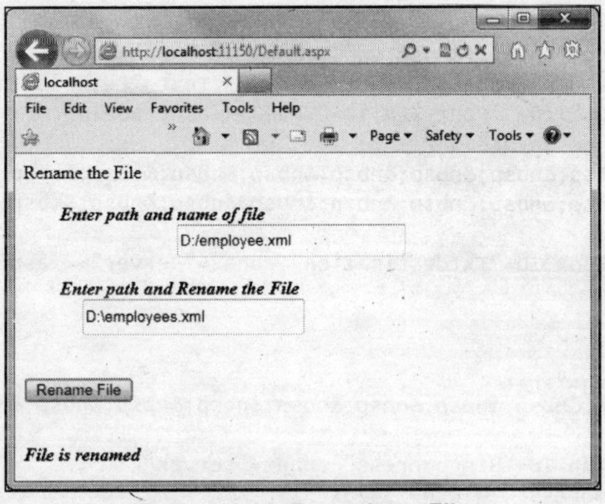

Figure 11.14: Renaming a File

Compressing a File

Now, let's discuss how to compress a file in the directory. Perform the following steps to compress the file.

1. Create an ASP.NET Empty Web Site and add a Web page to it. You can save the Website as CompressFileCS. The code for this application is available in the CompressFileCS (for C#) and CompressFileVB (for VB) folders.
2. Drag and drop one Button control, two TextBox controls, and three Label controls from the Toolbox on the Design view of the Default.aspx page.
3. Set the Text property of the Button1 control to Compress, ID property of the Button1 control to Btncompress, Text property of the Label1 control to Enter path and name of source file, and Text property of the Label2 control to Enter path and name of destination in the Properties window.

After setting the properties of the controls, the code of the Default.aspx page appears, as shown in Listing 11.23:

Listing 11.23: Showing the Code of the Default.aspx Page

In VB

```
<%@ Page Language="VB" AutoEventWireup="false" CodeFile="Default.aspx.vb"
  Inherits="_Default" %>
<!DOCTYPE html PUBLIC>
<html xmlns="http://www.w3.org/1999/xhtml">
<head runat="server">
    <title></title>
</head>
<body>
    <form id="form1" runat="server">
    <div>
    <asp:Label ID="Label1" runat="server" Font-Bold="True" Font-Italic="True"
         Text="Enter path and name of source file"></asp:Label>
         <span lang="en-us">
                     
                     
            
         </span>
         <asp:TextBox ID="Txtsrc" runat="server"></asp:TextBox>
          <br />
         <br />
         <br />
         <span lang="en-us">     </span>
         <asp:Label ID="Label2" runat="server" Text="Enter path and name of destination"
         Font-Bold="True" Font-Italic="True"></asp:Label>
         <span lang="en-us">
                     
                      
         </span>
         <asp:TextBox ID="Txtdestination" runat="server"></asp:TextBox>
         <br />
         <br />
         <br />
         <span lang="en-
         us">           
         </span>
         <asp:Button ID="Btncompress" runat="server"
         Text="Compress " Width="147px" />
         <br />
         <br />
         <br />
         <span lang="en-us">         
         </span>
         <asp:Label ID="lbldisplay" runat="server" Font-Bold="True" Font-
         Italic="True"></asp:Label>
    </div>
    </form>
</body>
</html>
```

In C#

```
<%@ Page Language="C#" AutoEventWireup="true" CodeFile="Default.aspx.cs"
  Inherits="_Default" %>
<!DOCTYPE html>
<html xmlns="http://www.w3.org/1999/xhtml">
<head runat="server">
    <title></title>
</head>
<body>
    <form id="form1" runat="server">
    <div>
    <asp:Label ID="Label1" runat="server" Font-Bold="True" Font-Italic="True"
         Text="Enter path and name of source file"></asp:Label>
         <span lang="en-us">
                     
                     
            
         </span>
         <asp:TextBox ID="Txtsrc" runat="server"></asp:TextBox>
          <br />
         <br />
         <br />
         <span lang="en-us">     </span>
         <asp:Label ID="Label2" runat="server" Text="Enter path and name of destination"
         Font-Bold="True" Font-Italic="True"></asp:Label>
         <span lang="en-us">
                     
                      
         </span>
         <asp:TextBox ID="Txtdestination" runat="server"></asp:TextBox>
         <br />
         <br />
         <br />
         <span lang="en-
         us">           
         </span>
         <asp:Button ID="Btncompress" runat="server"
         Text="Compress " Width="147px" OnClick="Btncompress_Click" />
         <br />
         <br />
         <br />
         <span lang="en-us">         
         </span>
         <asp:Label ID="lbldisplay" runat="server" Font-Bold="True" Font-
         Italic="True"></asp:Label>
    </div>
    </form>
</body>
</html>
```

4. Add the System.IO.Compression namespace in the application.
5. Double-click the Button control (Btncompress) and add the following highlighted code in the Click event respectively.

The code of CodeFile of Default.aspx page is shown in Listing 11.24:

Listing 11.24: Showing the CodeFile of the Default.aspx Page

In VB

```
Imports System.IO
Imports System.IO.Compression
Partial Class _Default
    Inherits System.Web.UI.Page
    Protected Sub Btncompress_Click(sender As Object, e As EventArgs)
         Handles Btncompress.Click
        Dim path As String = Txtsrc.Text
        Dim sourceFile As FileStream
        Dim destinationfile As FileStream
        Dim zip As GZipStream = Nothing
        Try
            sourceFile = File.OpenRead(path)
            destinationfile = File.Create(Txtdestination.Text & ".gzip")
            Dim buffer(sourceFile.Length - 1) As Byte
            sourceFile.Read(buffer, 0, buffer.Length)
            zip = New GZipStream(destinationfile, CompressionMode.Compress)
            zip.Write(buffer, 0, buffer.Length)
            zip.Close()
            sourceFile.Close()
            destinationfile.Close()
            lbldisplay.Text = "File is compressed and located at " & Txtdestination.Text
        Catch ex As Exception
            lbldisplay.Text = ex.Message
        End Try
    End Sub
End Class
```

In C#

```
using System;
using System.Collections.Generic;
using System.Linq;
using System.Web;
using System.Web.UI;
using System.Web.UI.WebControls;
using System.IO;
using System.IO.Compression;
public partial class _Default : System.Web.UI.Page
{
    protected void Page_Load(object sender, EventArgs e)
    {

    }
    protected void Btncompress_Click(object sender, EventArgs e)
    {
        string path = Txtsrc.Text;
        FileStream sourceFile;
        FileStream destinationfile;
        GZipStream zip = null;
        try
        {
            sourceFile = File.OpenRead(path);
            destinationfile = File.Create(Txtdestination.Text + ".gzip");
            byte[] buffer = new byte[sourceFile.Length];
            sourceFile.Read(buffer, 0, buffer.Length);
```

```
                zip = new GZipStream(destinationfile, CompressionMode.Compress);
                zip.Write(buffer, 0, buffer.Length);
                zip.Close();
                sourceFile.Close();
                destinationfile.Close();
                lbldisplay.Text = "File is compressed and located at " +
                    Txtdestination.Text;
            }
            catch (Exception ex)
            {
                lbldisplay.Text = ex.Message;
            }
        }
    }
```

6. Press the F5 key on the keyboard to execute the application. The output of the application appears (Figure 11.15).
7. Enter the name and path of the file in the TextBox1 and destination path in the TextBox2 (Figure 11.15).
8. Click the Compress button to compress the file, as shown in Figure 11.15:

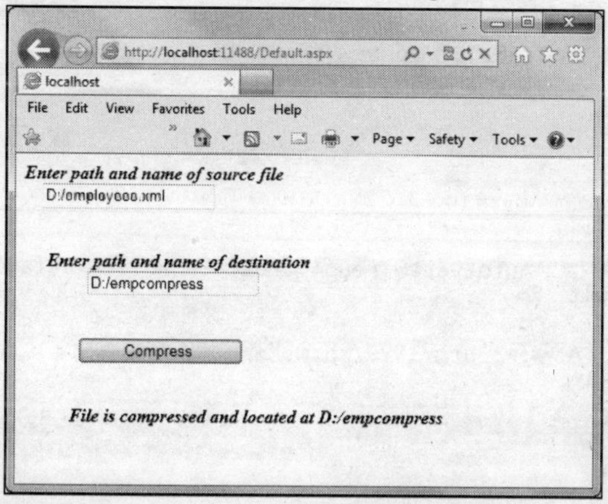

Figure 11.15: Compressing the File

Let's discuss the writing to serial ports.

Writing to Serial Ports

Now, let's discuss how to write data to serial ports. Perform the following steps to write data to serial ports:

1. Create an ASP.NET Empty Web Site and save it as WriteSerialportCS. You can find the code for this application in the WriteSerialportCS (for C#) and WriteSerialportVB (for VB) folders.
2. Drag and drop one Button control, one TextBox controls, and two Label controls from the Toolbox on the Design view of the Default.aspx page.
3. Set the Text property of the Button1 control to Send, ID property of the Button1 control to BtnSend, and Text property of the Label1 control to Enter text to send to serial port in the Properties window.

After setting the properties of the controls, the code of the Default.aspx page appears, as shown in Listing 11.25:

Listing 11.25: Showing the Code of the Default.aspx Page

In VB

```
<%@ Page Language="VB" AutoEventWireup="false" CodeFile="Default.aspx.vb"
   Inherits="_Default" %>
<!DOCTYPE html>
<html xmlns="http://www.w3.org/1999/xhtml">
```

```
<head runat="server">
    <title></title>
</head>
<body>
    <form id="form1" runat="server">
    <div>
    <asp:Label ID="Label1" runat="server" Font-Bold="True" Font-Italic="True"
         Text="Enter text to send to serial port"></asp:Label>
         <br />
         <br />
         <span lang="en-us">    
         </span>
         <asp:TextBox ID="TextBox1" runat="server" Height="64px" TextMode="MultiLine"
         style="margin-left: 163px"></asp:TextBox>
         <br />
         <br />
          <asp:Button ID="BtnSend" runat="server" Text="Send"
         Width="127px" style="margin-left: 153px" />
        <br />
        <br />
        <asp:Label ID="Label2" runat="server"></asp:Label>
    </div>
    </form>
</body>
</html>
```

In C#

```
<%@ Page Language="C#" AutoEventWireup="true" CodeFile="Default.aspx.cs"
   Inherits="_Default" %>
<!DOCTYPE html>
<html xmlns="http://www.w3.org/1999/xhtml">
<head runat="server">
    <title></title>
</head>
<body>
    <form id="form1" runat="server">
    <div>
         <asp:Label ID="Label1" runat="server" Font-Bold="True" Font-Italic="True"
         Text="Enter text to send to serial port"></asp:Label>
         <br />
         <br />
         <span lang="en-us">    
         </span>
         <asp:TextBox ID="TextBox1" runat="server" Height="64px" TextMode="MultiLine"
         style="margin-left: 163px"></asp:TextBox>
         <br />
         <br />
          <asp:Button ID="BtnSend" runat="server" Text="Send"
         Width="127px" style="margin-left: 153px" OnClick="BtnSend_Click" />
        <br />
        <br />
        <asp:Label ID="Label2" runat="server"></asp:Label>
    </div>
    </form>
</body>
</html>
```

4. Double-click the Button control (BtnSend) and add the following highlighted code in the Click event respectively.

The CodeFile of Default.aspx page is shown in Listing 11.26:

Listing 11.26: Showing the CodeFile of the Default.aspx Page

In VB

```
Imports System.IO.Ports
Partial Class _Default
    Inherits System.Web.UI.Page
    Protected Sub BtnSend_Click(sender As Object,e As EventArgs)
  Handles BtnSend.Click
        Try
            Dim senddata As New SerialPort()
            senddata.PortName = "COM1"
            senddata.Open()
            senddata.Write(TextBox1.Text & "!%")
            senddata.Close()
            Label2.Text = "Data is sent to the serial port"
        Catch ex As Exception
        End Try
    End Sub
End Class
```

In C#

```
using System;
using System.Collections.Generic;
using System.Linq;
using System.Web;
using System.Web.UI;
using System.Web.UI.WebControls;
using System.IO.Ports;
public partial class _Default : System.Web.UI.Page
{
    protected void Page_Load(object sender, EventArgs e)
    {

    }
    protected void BtnSend_Click(object sender, EventArgs e)
    {
        try
        {
            SerialPort senddata = new SerialPort();
            senddata.PortName = "COM1";
            senddata.Open();
            senddata.Write(TextBox1.Text + "!%");
            senddata.Close();
            Label2.Text = "Data is sent to the serial port";
        }
        catch (Exception ex)
        {
            Label2.Text = ex.Message;
        }
    }
}
```

5. Press the F5 key on the keyboard to execute the application. The output of the application appears (Figure 11.16).
6. Enter the text in the Textbox1 and click the Send button to send the text to serial port, as shown in Figure 11.16:

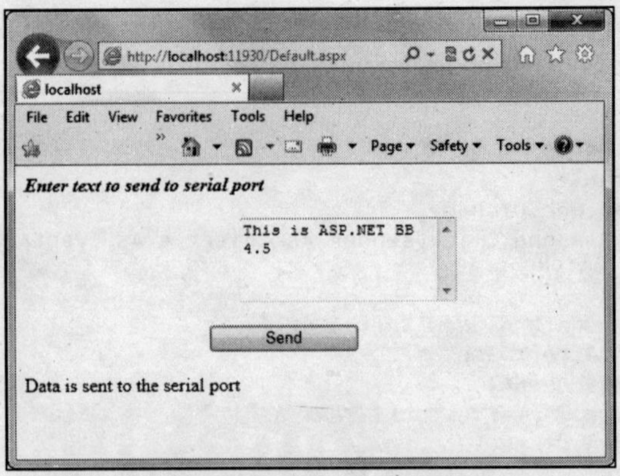

Figure 11.16: Sending the Text to Serial Port

Let's now summarize the contents of this chapter.

Summary

In this chapter, you have learned how to handle file systems programmatically. This chapter has also discussed various classes of the System.IO namespace, such as FileInfo, File, DirectoryInfo, Directory, and FileStream, to handle file system programmatically. It has also covered the implementation of various operations performed on the hard drive and files, such as retrieving drive information, creating a directory, copying a directory, viewing subdirectories of a directory, and retrieving files from directory.

In the next chapter, you learn about building dynamic data applications.

12

Building ASP.NET Dynamic Data Applications

If you need an Immediate Solution to:	See page:
Creating a Web Site Using ASP.NET Dynamic Data	597

In Depth

ASP.NET Dynamic Data is a framework that enables you to easily build data-driven Web applications based on the Entity Framework or LINQ to SQL data models. In addition to these two data models, ASP.NET Dynamic Data can also be used to make Web applications based on any other data model. The ASP.NET Dynamic Data also support multiple instances of data model provided they are of same type. A data model is used to represent information about the data in a database and depict the relation between the items of the database.

The ASP.NET Dynamic Data Framework manages basic database operations, relations, and display of User Interface (UI). This Framework helps you to develop application modeling, UI code, and validation logic. You can use Dynamic Data controls to create data-driven Web sites that require minimum code and that can use the capabilities of the Dynamic Data Framework. The Dynamic Data control controls the appearance and behavior of the data fields of the database at run time by its dynamic nature by performing automated validation. The Dynamic Data control enhances the functionality of the data-bound controls, such as DetailsView, GridView, FormView, and ListView controls.

In this chapter, we learn about the concepts related to ASP.NET Dynamic Data, including the data model, and dynamic data templates. We also learn about the other functionalities related to this Framework. In addition, we create a Web site by using ASP.NET Dynamic Data.

Overview of ASP.NET Dynamic Data

ASP.NET Dynamic Data is used to create data-driven Web applications with minimal coding. ASP.NET Dynamic Data have the advantage of using all the capabilities of the Dynamic Data Framework. You can also add specific capabilities of Dynamic Data to an existing Web application, such as:

- Web scaffolding, which is a mechanism to enhance the existing ASP.NET Page Framework by dynamically displaying Web pages based on the data model. Web scaffolding involves running a Web application by reading the underlying database schema. Dynamic Data Scaffolding can generate a standard user interface (UI) from the data model.
- Full access to data operations (such as create, update, remove, and display), relational operations, and data validation.
- Support for foreign-key relationships that allows Dynamic Data to detect the relationships among tables and create a UI that facilitates users to view data from related tables.
- Ability to customize the UI that is rendered to display and edit specific data fields of a specific table.
- Ability to customize data field validation. This allows you to hold the business logic in the data layer without involving the presentation layer.

There are three layers in the ASP.NET Dynamic Data Framework architecture, as shown in Figure 12.1:

- **Presentation layer**—Contains the elements that help in creating the UI for displaying and editing data entities
- **Data layer**—Contains the data model that represent the database entities as Common Language Runtime (CLR) types
- **Data source mapping layer**—Contains the elements that are basically a part of CLR but are used as dynamic data

The various presentation layer elements in the ASP.NET Dynamic Data Framework are as follows:

- **Page templates**—Refers to the Web pages that help in rendering data from any table in the database. This implies that when you create a Dynamic Data Web site, a DynamicData\PageTemplates folder is added to the application, which consists of the default page templates. The page templates help in viewing the data in different formats, such as List View (which is the default view), Details view, and Edit view. The default page templates are:
    - **Details.aspx**—Refers to the default template for select operations, which provides a detailed view of a single row in the database. This template uses the DetailsView control.
    - **Edit.aspx**—Refers to the default template for edit operations, which helps in editing a single row of the database. This template uses the DetailsView control.
    - **Insert.aspx**—Refers to the default template for insert operations, which helps in inserting a single row in the database. This template uses the DetailsView control.
    - **List.aspx**—Refers to the default template used for displaying a table. This template uses the GridView control to display the table and the DropDownList control to enable the user to filter the data.
    - **ListDetails.aspx**—Displays a list of rows from the database by using the GridView control. This template also includes the DetailsView control to let the user insert a new row in the database.
- **Entity templates**—Helps in creating custom UI and applying it to the default or custom page templates. When you create a Dynamic Data Web site, a DynamicData\EntityTemplates folder is added to the application, which contains the default entity templates. The main operation of entity templates is display, edit, and insert data. The entity template displays data in two columns, using a label to display the column name.
- **Field templates**—Refers to the user controls that provide the UI for individual data fields. For example, the Dynamic Data application uses Boolean field template to display Boolean data and Text field template to display textual data. The Dynamic Data application includes a DynamicData\FieldTemplates folder, which contains the default field templates. The default field templates are:
    - **Boolean.ascx**—Uses the CheckBox control to display the Boolean data. The CheckBox control is disabled by default.
    - **Boolean_Edit.ascx**—Helps the users to edit the Boolean value.
    - **Children.ascx**—Displays the fields that have one-to-many relationship. It helps in redirecting the user to the child page by using the HyperLink control.
    - **Children_Insert.ascx**—Disables navigation to the child page when a parent item is being created.
    - **DateTime.ascx**—Uses the Literal control to display the DateTime data.
    - **DateTime_Edit.ascx**—Uses the TextBox control so that the users can edit the DateTime data.
    - **Decimal_Edit.ascx**—Uses the TextBox control so that the users can edit the Decimal data.
    - **EmailAddress.ascx**-Uses the HyperLink control to display the EmailAddress data
    - **EmailAddress_Edit**-Uses the TextBox control so that the users can edit the EmailAddress data.
    - **Enumeration.ascx**—Uses the Literal control to display enumeration values.
    - **Enumeration_Edit.ascx**—Uses the DropDownList control to enable the users to select a list of enumeration values.
    - **ForeignKey.ascx**—Displays the fields that have many-to-one relationship. It helps in redirecting the user to the relationship page by using the HyperLink control.
    - **ForeignKey_Edit.ascx**—Uses the DropDownList control to modify the data fields that have many-to-one relationship.
    - **Interger_Edit.ascx** Uses the TextBox control so that the users can edit the Integer data.
    - **Multiline_Edit.ascx**—Helps in editing the database fields. This template uses the TextBox control whose TextMode property is set to MultiLine.

    - **Text.ascx**—Uses the Literal control to display String and Numeric data.
    - **Text_Edit.ascx**—Uses the TextBox control (whose TextMode property is set to SingleLine) to enable users to edit String data.
    - **Url.ascx**—Uses the HyperLink control to display URLs.
    - **Url_Edit.ascx**— Uses the TextBox control so that the users can edit the Url.
- **Filter templates**—Refers to the user controls that provide UI for data filtering. This implies that the user can select the table rows to be displayed on the Web page by using the filter templates. The Dynamic Data Web site includes a DynamicData\FilterTemplates folder, which contains the default filter templates. The default filter templates are:
    - **Boolean.ascx**—Uses the DropDownList control to display the Boolean data. The different values displayed in the DropDownList control are All, True, and False.
    - **Enumeration.ascx**—Uses the DropDownList control to display the enumeration values. The value displayed in the DropDownList control is All.
    - **ForeignKey.ascx**—Uses the DropDownList control to display the foreign keys. The values displayed in the DropDownList control are All and the values from the related table.

Figure 12.1 displays the architecture of the ASP.NET Dynamic Data Framework:

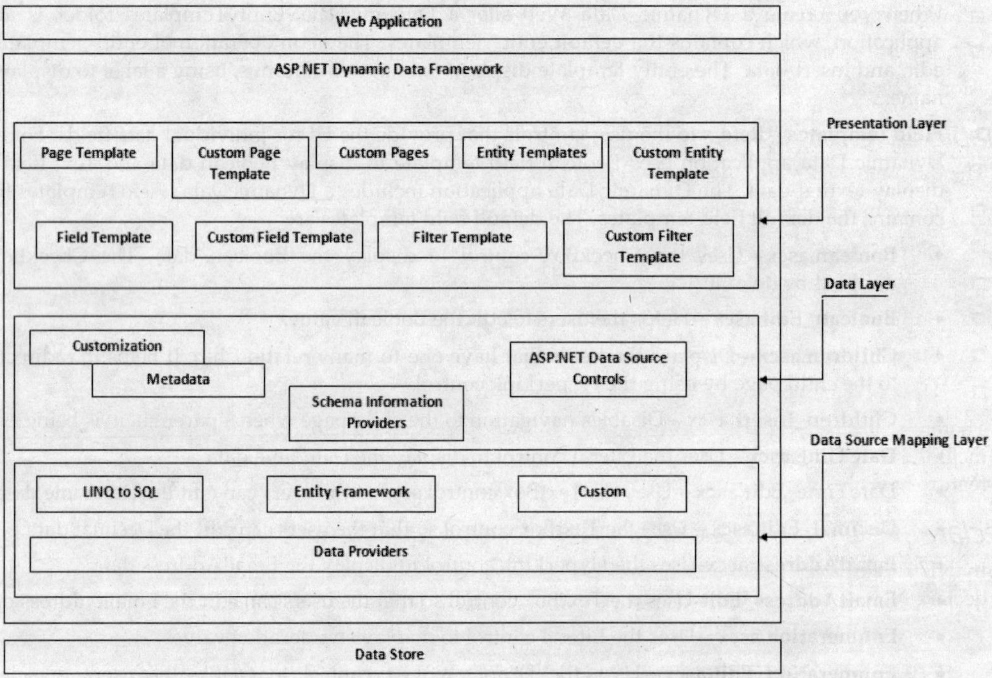

Figure 12.1: Displaying the Dynamic Data Framework Architecture

NOTE

The DynamicData folder therefore consists of the pre-generated ASP.NET application that helps you in working with the database through the Web browser.

Exploring Features of Dynamic Data

The ASP.NET Dynamic Data Framework supports multiple features. It controls the data access operations, such as create, update, remove, display, relational operations, and data validation. It also supports the foreign-key relationships automatically. It can detect relationships between tables, which contains data, and creates UI that makes users to view data from related tables easily. The Dynamic Data control customizes the UI that can display and edit specific data fields, and also the data field validation by keeping only the Business Logic Layer (BLL) in the Data Logic Layer (DLL) without including the Presentation layer or UI. It also generates standard UI from the data model using Dynamic Data scaffolding.

The scaffolding feature of the ASP.NET Dynamic Data Framework refers to the ability to generate Web pages for each table in a database and provide the CRUD (create, read, update, and delete) operations for each table. The various elements of the presentation layer have the scaffolding feature enabled. The advantages of the scaffolding feature are:

- Minimal or no code required for creating a data-driven Web application
- Automatic generation of functional pages
- Automatic Universal Resource Locator (URL) routing
- Built-in data validation
- Automatic creation of data filters for foreign keys
- Easy to change the appearance and behavior of data fields

Along with these, the following new features are included in the ASP.NET Dynamic Data Framework.

Enable Dynamic Data in Existing Projects

The dynamic data feature was introduced in .NET Framework 3.5 SP1, with the following features:

- Customizing the look of data controls by using field templates
- Specifying validation for common situations, such as range checking or type checking
- However, these features had the following requirements:
- Support for data access layer that is based on either Entity Framework or LINQ to SQL
- Support for all the data source controls other than EntityDataSource and LinqDataSource controls
- Use of Dynamic Data or Dynamic Data Entity template in a Web site

Therefore, to fulfill the pereceding requirements, support of dynamic data for any ASP.NET application has been included in .NET Framework 4.0. For example, while editing the data in a GridView control, the dynamic data feature helps in checking that the data has been entered in the proper format.

Declarative DynamicDataManager Control Syntax

In .NET Framework 4.0, the DynamicDataManager control has been enhanced so that you can easily configure it declaratively, instead of only in code. The markup of the DynamicDataManager control would be as follows:

```
<asp:DynamicDataManager ID="DynamicDataManager1"
  runat="server"> </asp:DynamicDataManager>
```

Entity Templates

The entity templates provide a new way to customize the layout of data. The DetailsView control, which was used in the earlier version of page templates of Dynamic Data applications, has been replaced by the FormView and DynamicEntity control. Hence, you are not required to create a custom page to view different types of data.

The entity templates now include different templates for performing displaying, editing, and inserting operations. You can also edit the default templates to change the way the site is displayed in the Web browser.

New Field Templates for URLs and E-mail Addresses

Two new field templates, EmailAddress.ascx and Url.ascx, are included in the dynamic data applications for the fields that have EmailAddress or URL as their DataType attribute. The fields that have EmailAddress as their DataType attribute are displayed as hyperlink, which when clicked, redirects to the user's e-mail client and creates an outline message. On the other hand, the fields that has URL as their DataType attribute are displayed as normal hyperlinks.

Create Links with the DynamicHyperLink Control

A new control, the DynamicHyperLink control, has been introduced, which helps in linking the pages in a Dynamic Data Web site. The following code snippet displays the use of the DynamicHyperLink control:

```
<asp:DynamicHyperLink ID="ListHyperLink" runat="server"
    Action="List" TableName="Products">
    Show all products
</asp:DynamicHyperLink>
```

In the preceding code snippet, a hyperlink is created which directs to the page, which contains the Products table.

Support for Inheritance in the Data Model

The data source mapping layer of the Dynamic Data architecture now supports both the Entity Framework and the LINQ to SQL. This helps the Dynamic Data applications to understand the concept of inherited objects and therefore support the scaffolding feature for the inherited objects. For example, a database might contain a Loan, HomeLoan, and CarLoan table. The HomeLoan and CarLoan tables have the same columns as the Loan table and some more columns as well. In that case, the Dynamic Data application would support inheritance in the data model and therefore would be able to differentiate between the tables.

New Attributes to Control Display and Support Enumerations

A new class, the DisplayAttribute class has been introduced in Dynamic Data Framework, which helps in specifying more options of how the fields are displayed on the Web page. For example, it helps in specifying the order in which the fields are displayed.

The EnumDataTypeAttribute class has been added that helps in mapping fields to enumerations. For this purpose, a new field template, Enumeration.ascx, has been introduced that maps the values from the database to the names in the enumeration.

Enhanced Support for Filters

In the previous version of Dynamic Data applications, the filters that were included did not specify the order in which the data is to be displayed..NET Framework 4.5 supports the DisplayAttribute attribute, which helps in specifying the order in which the data of a particular column is displayed on the Web page.

Exploring Dynamic Data Controls

The ASP.NET Dynamic Data Framework provides six controls that provide support for dynamic data. The System.Web.DynamicData namespace contains the classes that provide the functionality for the ASP.NET Dynamic Data controls. The controls are:

- The DynamicControl control
- The DynamicDataManager control
- The DynamicEntity control
- The DynamicFilter control
- The DynamicHyperLink control
- The DynamicValidator control

Let's discuss about each one of them in detail.

The DynamicControl Control

The DynamicControl control helps in displaying the content that is defined in the data-bound controls, such as the FormView or ListView control, by using the ASP.NET Dynamic Data features. The DynamicControl control is mainly used inside the templates and therefore it provides more flexibility in the manner the data is displayed on the Web page. The inheritence hierarch of the DynamicControl Control is as follows:

```
System.Object
   System.Web.UI.Control
      System.Web.DynamicData.DynamicControl
```

Table 12.1 lists the noteworthy public properties of the DynamicControl class:

Table 12.1: Noteworthy Public Properties of the DynamicControl Class

Property	Description
`ApplyFormatInEditMode`	Specifies whether the formatting string specified by the DataFormatString property is applied to the field value (when the field value is in the edit mode)
`AppRelativeTemplateSourceDirectory`	Specifies the virtual directory of the Page or UserControl class that contains the DynamicControl class (Inherited from Control class)
`ClientID`	Specifies the control ID for HTML markup (Inherited from Control class)
`Column`	Specifies the column object associated with the DynamicControl class
`ConvertEmptyStringToNull`	Specifies if the empty string values are automatically converted to null values when the data field is updated in the data source
`DataField`	Specifies the name of the data field to which the DynamicControl class is bound to
`DataFormatString`	Specifies the display format of the value of the field
`FieldTemplate`	Specifies the field template that is created for the DynamicControl class
`HtmlEncode`	Specifies the value that indicates if the data for the control is HTML-encoded before rendering
`Mode`	Specifies the rendering mode of the control
`NullDisplayText`	Specifies the caption that is displayed when the data field value is set to null (or Nothing in VB)
`Page`	Specifies the Page class instance that contains the control (Inherited from Control class)
`Table`	Specifies the table object that is associated with the control
`TemplateControl`	Specifies the reference to the template that contains the control (Inherited from Control class)

Table 12.2 lists the noteworthy public methods of the DynamicControl class:

Table 12.2: Noteworthy Public Methods of the DynamicControl Class

Method	Description
`ApplyStyleSheetSkin`	Sets the style properties to the control that are specified in the style sheet (Inherited from Control class)
`DataBind`	Binds the data source to the control and its child controls (Inherited from Control class)

Table 12.2: Noteworthy Public Methods of the DynamicControl Class

Method	Description
`Dispose`	Performs a final clean up before the control is released from the memory (Inherited from Control class)
`Equals(Object)`	Checks whether the specified object is equal to the current object (Inherited from Object class)
`FindControl`	Searches the container for the specified server control (Inherited from Control class)
`Focus`	Sets the input focus on the control (Inherited from Control class)
`GetAttribute`	Retrieves the attribute value by using a specified key
`GetRouteUrl`	Gets the URL that corresponds to a set of route parameters (Inherited from Control class)
`GetType`	Specifies the Type class of the control (Inherited from Object class)
`RenderControl`	Provides the server control content to the HtmlTextWriter class (Inherited from Control class)
`ResolveClientUrl`	Specifies the URL that can be used by the browser (Inherited from Control class)
`ResolveUrl`	Converts the URL so that it can be used by the requesting client (Inherited from Control class)
`SetAttribute`	Sets the specified attribute to the specified value

Table 12.3 lists the noteworthy public events of the DynamicControl class:

Table 12.3: Noteworthy Public Events of the DynamicControl Class

Event	Description
`DataBinding`	Occurs when the server control is binded to a data source (Inherited from Control class)
`Disposed`	Refers to the last stage of the life cycle of a server control in which a server control is released from memory (Inherited from Control class)
`Init`	Refers to the first stage of the life cycle of a server control in which the server control is initialized (Inherited from Control class)
`Load`	Specifies that the server control is loaded into the `Page` object (Inherited from Control class)
`PreRender`	Specifies that the server control is about to render to its containing `Page` object (Inherited from Control class)
`Unload`	Specifies that the server control is unloaded from memory (Inherited from Control class)

The DynamicDataManager Control

The DynamicDataManager control helps in enabling a dynamic behavior for the Web controls that support dynamic data. In other words, the DynamicDataManager control acts as a bond between the data bound, such as the GridView, DetailsView, or FormView control, and data source controls. The DynamicDataManager control is a necessary control on a Web page so that the data controls can use dynamic data support. The inheritence hierarch of the DynamicDataManager Control is as follows:

```
System.Object
   System.Web.UI.Control
     System.Web.DynamicData.DynamicDataManager
```

NOTE

You should note that the DynamicDataManager control cannot be placed inside the UpdatePanel control.

Table 12.4 lists the noteworthy public properties of the DynamicDataManager class:

Table 12.4: Noteworthy Public Properties of the DynamicDataManager Class

Property	Description
AutoLoadForeignKeys	Specifies a value that indicates if the foreign keys are automatically loaded for the LINQ to SQL data context
ClientID	Specifies the ClientID property for the control that is generated by ASP.NET
ClientIDMode	Retrieves the algorithm that is used to generate the value in the ClientID mode property
DataControls	Retrieves the list of data controls that are referenced in the DynamicDataManager control
Visible	Retrieves a value that specifies if the DynamicDataManager control is visible or not

Table 12.5 lists the noteworthy public methods of the DynamicDataManager class:

Table 12.5: Noteworthy Public Methods of the DynamicDataManager Class

Method	Description
DataBind	Binds the data source control to the server control and its child controls (Inherited from Control class)
FindControl	Helps in searching the container for the server control with the specified parameter (Inherited from Control class)
GetRouteUrl	Retrieves the URL that corresponds to a set of route parameters (Inherited from Control class)
RegisterControl	Registers the control with the DynamicDataManager control
RenderControl	Provides the server control content to the HtmlTextWriter class (Inherited from Control class)

NOTE

The events of the DynamicDataManager class are similar to the DynamicControl class and therefore are not listed separately.

The DynamicEntity Control

The DynamicEntity control represents an entity for use by the ASP.NET Dynamic Data applications. The inheritence hierarch of the DynamicEntity Control is as follows:

```
System.Object
   System.Web.UI.Control
      System.Web.DynamicData.DynamicEntity
```

Table 12.6 lists the noteworthy public properties of the DynamicEntity class:

Table 12.6: Noteworthy Public Properties of the DynamicEntity Class

Property	Description
Mode	Specifies the DataBoundControlMode value, which represents the different data-entry modes for a data-bound controls, for the control
UIHint	Specifies the UIHintAttribute attribute for the control
ValidationGroup	Specifies the validation group for the control

NOTE

The methods of the DynamicEntity class are similar to the DynamicDataManager class and therefore are not listed. The events of the DynamicEntity class are similar to the DynamicControl class and therefore are not listed separately.

The DynamicFilter Control

The DynamicFilter control provides a UI that helps in filtering table rows using a specified column. The DynamicFilter control, which is referenced by the DynamicFilterExpression instance, can be used with the QueryExtender control. The working of the DynamicFilter control inside the QueryExtender control to implement table row filtering is shown in Figure 12.2:

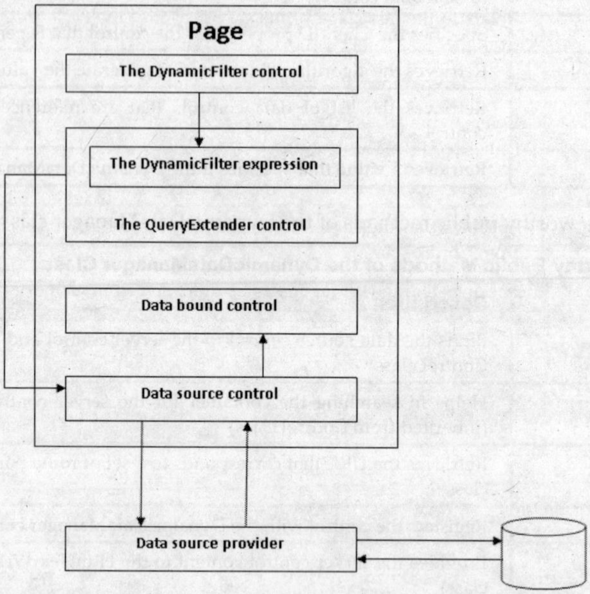

Figure 12.2: Displaying the Steps that Dynamic Data Performs

As shown in Figure 12.2, the DynamicFilter control passes the selected value to the QueryExtender control, which uses the value to create the query filtering information. This information is then passed to the data source control, which then passes the information to the data source provider. The data source provider passes the information to the database. The information is processed in the database and then the database returns the filtered table rows to the data source provider, which passes on the information to the data source control. Finally, the data source control passes the filtered tables rows to the data bound control for display. The inheritence hierarch of the DynamicFilter Control is as follows:

```
System.Object
   System.Web.UI.Control
     System.Web.DynamicData.DynamicFilter
```

Table 12.7 lists the noteworthy public properties of the DynamicFilter class:

Table 12.7: Noteworthy Public Properties of the DynamicFilter Class

Property	Description
`Column`	Specifies the table column to be used for filtering
`DataField`	Specifies the name of the column to be used for table row filtering
`FilterTemplate`	Specifies the filter template that is associated with the control
`FilterUIHint`	Specifies the name of the filter template that is used to create the UI

NOTE

The methods of the DynamicFilter class are similar to the DynamicDataManager class and therefore are not listed.

Table 12.8 lists the noteworthy public events of the DynamicFilter class:

Table 12.8: Noteworthy Public Events of the DynamicFilter Class

Event	Description
DataBinding	Occurs when the server control is binded to a data source (Inherited from Control class)
Disposed	Refers to the last stage of the server control life cycle in which a server control is released from memory (Inherited from Control class)
FilterChanged	Specifies that the user has selected a value for the foreign key
Init	Refers to the first step of the server control life cycle in which the server control is initialized (Inherited from Control class)
Load	Specifies that the server control is loaded into the Page object (Inherited from Control class)
PreRender	Specifies that the server control is about to render to its containing Page object (Inherited from Control class)
Unload	Specifies that the server control is unloaded from memory (Inherited from Control class)

The DynamicHyperLink Control

The DynamicHyperLink control helps in performing common tasks, such as edit, delete, and insert. The DynamicHyperLink control creates links that are based on table actions, which are defined in the Global.asax file. The various links that you can create using the DynamicHyperLink control are:

- Links to edit a row or view details of a row in a table
- Links to the MetaTable objects (represents the metadata that describes a table for use by the dynamic data pages) to perform specific actions, such as list and insert
- Links to create table outside a data-bound control

The inheritence hierarch of the DynamicHyperLink Control is as follows:

```
System.Object
   System.Web.UI.Control
     System.Web.DynamicData.DynamicHyperLink
```

Table 12.9 lists the noteworthy public properties of the DynamicHyperLink class:

Table 12.9: Noteworthy Public Properties of the DynamicHyperLink Class

Property	Description
Action	Specifies the action that is associated with the link
ContextTypeName	Specifies the data context for the data model that the link applies to
DataField	Specifies the display text of the link
TableName	Specifies the table for the link action

NOTE

The methods of the DynamicHyperLink class are similar to the DynamicDataManager class and therefore are not listed. The events of the DynamicHyperLink class are similar to the DynamicControl class and therefore are not listed separately.

The DynamicValidator Control

The DynamicValidator control, which can be used with data fields or data entities, helps in managing exception handling and the error display message for the exceptions that are thrown in a data model. This implies that the DynamicValidator control helps in catching the exceptions that are thrown in the LINQ-to-SQL classes or entity classes. Therefore, you can conclude that the DynamicValidator control is associated with the controls that accept user input, such as the TextBox control. The inheritence hierarch of the DynamicValidator Control is as follows:

```
System.Object
   System.Web.UI.Control
      System.Web.DynamicData.DynamicValidator
```

Table 12.10 lists the noteworthy public properties of the DynamicValidator class:

Table 12.10: Noteworthy Public Properties of the DynamicValidator Class

Property	Description
Column	Specifies the column to validate
ColumnName	Specifies the column name to validate

NOTE

The methods of the DynamicValidator class are similar to the DynamicDataManager class and therefore are not listed. The events of the DynamicValidator class are similar to the DynamicControl class and therefore are not listed separately.

Immediate Solutions

Creating a Web Site Using ASP.NET Dynamic Data

After discussing about the Dynamic Data Framework in ASP.NET 4.5 in the In Depth section of the chapter, lets' learn to create a simple ASP.NET Dynamic Data Web site. To do this, we are creating a Web site, DynamicDataCS in C# and DynamicDataVB in VB.

Perform the following steps to create a Dynamic Data Web site:

1. Open Visual Studio 2012.
2. Select FILE → New → Web Site option from the menu bar. The New Web Site dialog box opens.
3. Select the .NET Framework 4.0 option in dropdownlist in the New Web Site dialog box.
3. Select the ASP.NET Dynamic Data Linq to SQL Web Site template from the middle pane and click the OK button to create the DynamicDataCS in C# or DynamicDataVB in VB application.
4. Right-click the solution name in Solution Explorer and select the Add→ Add New Item option from the context menu. The Add New Item dialog box opens.
5. Select the LINQ to SQL Classes template from the middle pane, rename it to MyDataClass.dbml and click the Add button. A message box apperas for adding the MyDataClass.dbml file in the App_Code foder.
6. Click the Yes button. The Object Relational Designer window opens.
7. Drag and drop all the tables of the Northwind database from Server Explorer to the Object Relational Designer window.
8. Select BUILD → Build Web Site option from the menu bar.
9. Open the Global.asax file and replace the code given in Listing 12.1:

Listing 12.1: Showing the Code for the Global.asax Page

In VB

```
<%@ Application Language="VB" %>
<%@ Import Namespace="System.ComponentModel.DataAnnotations" %>
<%@ Import Namespace="System.Web.Routing" %>
<%@ Import Namespace="System.Web.DynamicData" %>
<script RunAt="server">
Private Shared s_defaultModel As New MetaModel
Public Shared ReadOnly Property DefaultModel() As MetaModel
    Get
        Return s_defaultModel
    End Get
End Property
Public Shared Sub RegisterRoutes(ByVal routes As RouteCollection)
    '                   IMPORTANT: DATA MODEL REGISTRATION
    ' Uncomment this line to register a LINQ to SQL model for ASP.NET Dynamic Data.
    ' Set ScaffoldAllTables = true only if you are sure that you want all tables in the
    ' data model to support a scaffold (i.e. templates) view. To control scaffolding for
    ' individual tables, create a partial class for the table and apply the
    ' <ScaffoldTable(true)> attribute to the partial class.
  ' Note: Make sure that you change "YourDataContextType" to the name of the data
 context
    ' class in your application.
        DefaultModel.RegisterContext(GetType(MyDataClassDataContext), New
 ContextConfiguration() With {.ScaffoldAllTables = True})
```

```
    ' The following statement supports separate-page mode, where the List, Detail,
  Insert, and
    ' Update tasks are performed by using separate pages. To enable this mode, uncomment
  the following
    ' route definition, and comment out the route definitions in the combined-page mode
  section that follows.
        'routes.Add(New DynamicDataRoute("{table}/{action}.aspx") With {
        '    .Constraints = New RouteValueDictionary(New With {.Action =
  "List|Details|Edit|Insert"}),
        '    .Model = DefaultModel})
    ' The following statements support combined-page mode, where the List, Detail,
  Insert, and
    ' Update tasks are performed by using the same page. To enable this mode, uncomment
  the
    ' following routes and comment out the route definition in the separate-page mode
  section above.
        routes.Add(New DynamicDataRoute("{table}/ListDetails.aspx") With {
            .Action = PageAction.List,
            .ViewName = "ListDetails",
            .Model = DefaultModel})

        'routes.Add(New DynamicDataRoute("{table}/ListDetails.aspx") With {
        '    .Action = PageAction.Details,
        '    .ViewName = "ListDetails",
        '    .Model = DefaultModel})
  End Sub
  Private Sub Application_Start(ByVal sender As Object, ByVal e As EventArgs)
      RegisterRoutes(RouteTable.Routes)
  End Sub
  </script>
```

In C#

```
  <%@ Application Language="C#" %>
  <%@ Import Namespace="System.ComponentModel.DataAnnotations" %>
  <%@ Import Namespace="System.Web.Routing" %>
  <%@ Import Namespace="System.Web.DynamicData" %>
  <script RunAt="server">
      private static MetaModel s_defaultModel = new MetaModel();
      public static MetaModel DefaultModel {
          get {
              return s_defaultModel;
          }
      }
      public static void RegisterRoutes(RouteCollection routes) {
       //                    IMPORTANT: DATA MODEL REGISTRATION
      // Uncomment this line to register a LINQ to SQL model for ASP.NET Dynamic Data.
      // Set ScaffoldAllTables = true only if you are sure that you want all tables in the
      // data model to support a scaffold (i.e. templates) view. To control scaffolding for
      // individual tables, create a partial class for the table and apply the
      // [ScaffoldTable(true)] attribute to the partial class.
      // Note: Make sure that you change "YourDataContextType" to the name of the data
   context
      // class in your application.
      DefaultModel.RegisterContext(typeof(MyDataClassDataContext), new
   ContextConfiguration() { ScaffoldAllTables = true });
      // The following statement supports separate-page mode, where the List, Detail,
   Insert, and
          // Update tasks are performed by using separate pages. To enable this mode,
           uncomment the following
```

```
        // route definition, and comment out the route definitions in the combined-page
    mode section that follows.
        //routes.Add(new DynamicDataRoute("{table}/{action}.aspx") {
        //    Constraints = new RouteValueDictionary(new { action =
"List|Details|Edit|Insert" }),
        //    Model = DefaultModel
        //});
        // The following statements support combined-page mode, where the List, Detail,
         Insert, and
        // Update tasks are performed by using the same page. To enable this mode,
         uncomment the
        // following routes and comment out the route definition in the separate-page
         mode section above.
        routes.Add(new DynamicDataRoute("{table}/ListDetails.aspx")
        {
            Action = PageAction.List,
            ViewName = "ListDetails",
            Model = DefaultModel
        });
        //routes.Add(new DynamicDataRoute("{table}/ListDetails.aspx") {
        //    Action = PageAction.Details,
        //    ViewName = "ListDetails",
        //    Model = DefaultModel
        //});
    }
    void Application_Start(object sender, EventArgs e) {
        RegisterRoutes(RouteTable.Routes);
    }
</script>
```

In Listing 12.1, you are registering the data model in the `Global.asax` file in the `RegisterRoutes` method.

10. Press the F5 key on the keyboard to run the application.

The output of the application is shown in Figure 12.3:

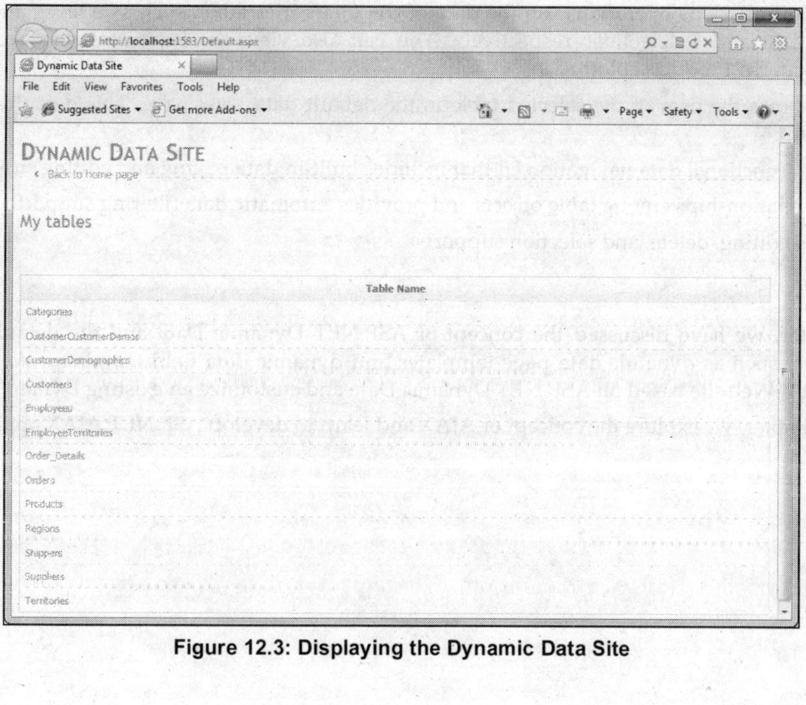

Figure 12.3: Displaying the Dynamic Data Site

As you can see in Figure 12.3, all the tables of the Northwind database are displayed on the Web page. This is because, we had added all the tables of the Northwind database in the Object Relational Designer window of the MyDataClass.dbml file. You can click on any of the table name, which are displayed as links, to view the data of the respective table. For example, when we click the Categories link, we are redirected to the Categories Web page, as shown in Figure 12.4:

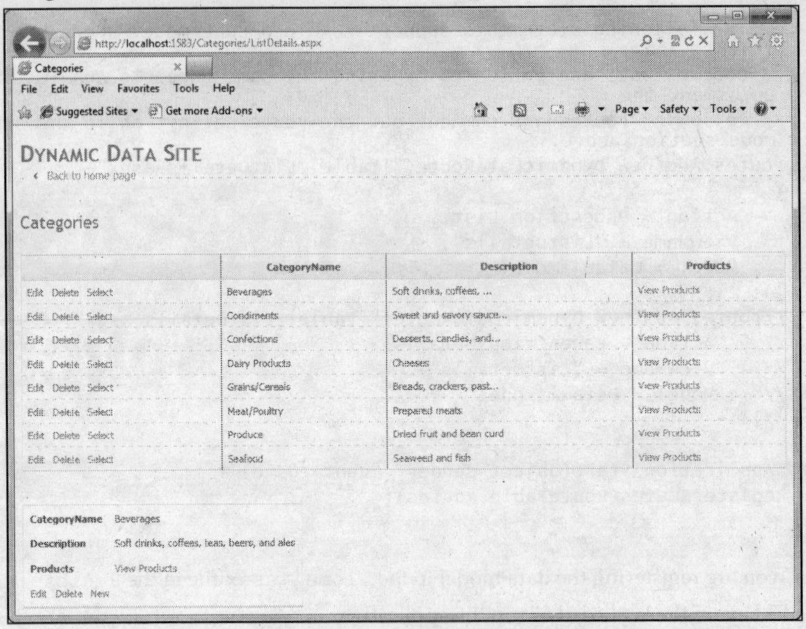

Figure 12.4: Displaying the Categories Page

You can perform various operations on the data of the Categories table, such as editing and deleting data by clicking the Edit and Delete links respectively. You can also view the Products table by clicking the View Products link in the Products column.

Figure 12.4 shows the data of the selected table in the default data view page. This default page performs the following tasks:

- Creates a functional data navigation UI that includes built-in data paging and editing support
- Depicts relationships among table objects and provides automatic data filtering support
- Provides editing, delete, and selection support

Summary

In this chapter, we have discussed the concept of ASP.NET Dynamic Data and the default templates of the dynamic data, such as dynamic data page templates and dynamic data field templates. We have also learned how to create a Web site based on ASP.NET Dynamic Data and customize an existing Dynamic Data Web site.

In the next chapter, we explore the concept of AJAX and learn to develop ASP.NET AJAX applications.

13

Developing ASP.NET AJAX Applications

In Depth

You are already familiar with the Web applications that use the postback model or method to refresh the content of a page. In the postback model, with every request made by you, the entire page is sent back to a server. The server then processes the request and performs modifications on the page, and sends the regenerated page to your browser to display the requested information.

The postback model has been in use since the beginning of the Internet. The advent of advance programming systems, such as ASP.NET, has tried to make your Web experience more responsive and interactive by providing the ability to perform complex tasks and update the Web pages quickly. However, as compared to Windows applications, Web applications were less interactive and responsive. Fortunately, today, there is no compulsion to use the postback model in the Web applications. Now, it is possible to program your Web applications in such a way that they can update the page information faster, without page flicker and without interrupting user interactions.

In the real world scenario, you can take an example of Google E-mail Service, that is. Gmail. In Gmail, when you need to attach a document with the text mail, you simply browse and attach the required document, while continuing to write the text message. The process of attaching the document is performed in the background. In other words, you need not wait to write the text message until the document is completely attached with the mail. The process of attaching the document in background is possible with a new technology called Asynchronous JavaScript and XML (AJAX). In AJAX, a call to the server for page refreshment takes place in the background and you does not even get a hint of when the request is sent to the server and new data is retrieved from the server. The call that takes place in the background is called asynchronous call. Another major feature of AJAX is partial updation, in which it updates only a particular portion of a Web page without modifying the rest of the page.

In this chapter, you learn about AJAX and how it is different from other technologies. Next, you learn about ASP.NET AJAX, its components, and ASP.NET technology that use the AJAX approach for Web development. You also learn about the extension controls and enhancements in AJAX delivered with Visual Studio 2012, and their use to implement AJAX functionality in your Web application.

Let's start the chapter by discussing AJAX in detail.

Exploring AJAX

AJAX is neither a new programming language nor a new platform for developing Web applications (or Web sites). You can call AJAX a new technique because it displays the refreshed content on a Web page by using the Partial Page Update approach rather than the Page Replacement approach, which was used in traditional Web applications. AJAX is built on existing technologies, such as Document Object Model (DOM), Cascading Style Sheet (CSS), and Extensible Hypertext Markup Language (XHTML). It is a collection of development components, tools, and techniques used to create highly interactive Web applications. AJAX uses client scripts to make asynchronous calls to a server and load only those parts of a Web page on the client machine that needs to be changed. The transfer of data from the server is carried out over the Extensible Markup Language/ Hypertext Transfer Protocol (XMLHTTP) protocol in the form of packets by using Extensible Markup Language (XML) and JavaScript Object Notation (JSON). AJAX is built using various technologies, which are as follows:

- JavaScript
- XHTML
- CSS
- DOM
- The `XMLHttpRequest` object

Let's learn about these technologies in detail, one by one.

Introducing JavaScript

JavaScript is a client-side dynamic scripting language. It has many capabilities that can be used to communicate with a server. There are many other client-side scripting languages but AJAX includes JavaScript, because JavaScript is the only client-side scripting environment supported by all the modern Web browsers. JavaScript is commonly hosted in a browser to add interactivity to Hyper Text Markup Language (HTML) pages. It is an interpreted language, and not a compiled language. It does not require static type checking as in C++ and C#. In JavaScript, you can declare a variable without specifying its type. This makes it easier to work with JavaScript.

Introducing XHTML

XHTML is a combination of HTML and XML. The objective behind XHTML is to combine features of XML and HTML. XHTML is quite similar to HTML and contains a set of pre-defined tags. However, by using XHTML, you can define your own tags and attributes when the existing set of tags does not meet your requirements.

XHTML is used with AJAX-enabled Web sites to ensure that the Web sites run consistently on all the browsers, including desktop browsers (Internet Explorer (IE), Mozilla Firefox, and Opera) and Wireless Application Protocol (WAP) browsers (NetFront and Opera Mobile) for hand-held device. XHTML is preferred over HTML because sometimes you come across Web pages containing inappropriate HTML tags, such as tags that do not have closing tags. The Web pages containing inappropriate HTML tags can run on desktop browsers, but not on the browsers of hand-held devices. XHTML resolves these issues by following XHTML specifications while running such Web pages; and thereby, ensures that the Web pages are compatible with all the browsers. The XHTML documents can be checked for validity with the W3C Markup Validation Service. In addition, XHTML is based on XML, which implies that it is a platform-independent language.

Introducing CSS

CSS is a file that defines the display pattern of a Web page. Using CSS, you can specify fonts, colors, styles, and size of controls. It is a text document that can be created by using any text editor and has the `.css` extension. After defining presentation styles in the CSS file, you need to attach the file with the Web form. The following code snippet shows how to define styles using CSS:

```
BODY
{
   font-family: Arial, Helvetica, sans-serif;
   color:            black;

   background-color: white;
}
```

You can manipulate the design of a Web form by changing the properties of each control on it. AJAX includes CSS as it provides the following advantages:

- Allows you to attach a reference of a single CSS file with more than one Web forms. This is beneficial as you do not need to define similar type of formatting styles again and again.
- Separates the working of form coding and designing, which in turn makes it easy for other developers to understand both the definition and design system of a Web form clearly.
- Helps in the processing of further requests on the same Web site quickly as CSS is cached in the browser memory in the first visit to the Web site.
- Enables you to represent same content in different ways by using different style sheets.

Exploring DOM

DOM represents a structured Web form in an object-oriented model. It is a platform and language-independent interface that allows programs and scripts to access and update the content of a Web form. DOM is recommended by World Wide Web Consortium (W3C) to manipulate the content of a Web form at runtime. It takes the path of a Web form as a parameter and represents the path in a tree structure (called document tree) by defining every element as a node in the tree structure's inner memory. It maintains relationship between the nodes of a document tree, such as parent and child nodes. This can be understood with the help of Figure 13.1:

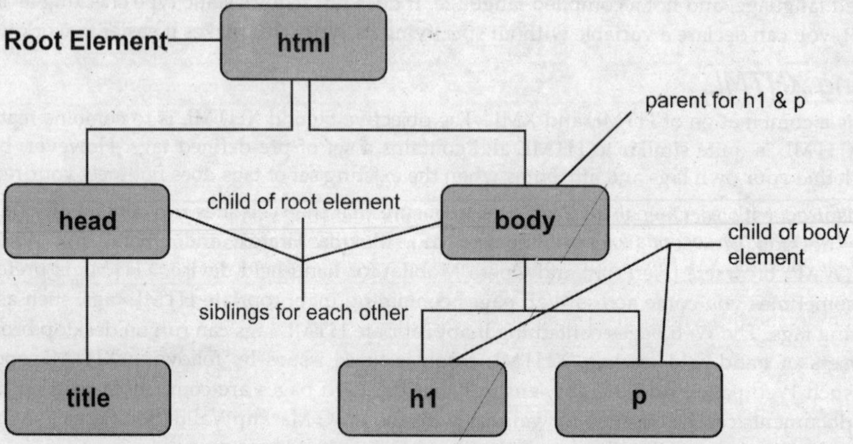

Figure 13.1: Displaying the Tree Representation of an HTML Document

Figure 13.1 shows various nodes of a HTML document and the relationship between the nodes. DOM has a rich set of methods, such as `insertBefore()`, `insertAfter()`, and `hasChildNodes()`, which are used to access and change the nodes and their corresponding values. The changes made to the nodes and their corresponding values are incorporated back to the Web form to reflect the updated content on the Web form. AJAX, which is also a platform and language-independent technology, uses DOM to update the content of a Web page, whenever required.

Introducing the XMLHttpRequest Object

The core of AJAX functionality is the `XMLHttpRequest` object, as it is responsible for making asynchronous requests to a server, updating the server response, and performing necessary changes in the current Web page. You can say that this object is the core of ASP.NET AJAX. The XMLHttpRequest object receives and sends data in the form of XML and contains various members in the form of properties, methods, and events.

Noteworthy properties of the `XMLHttpRequest` object are listed in Table 13.1:

Table 13.1: Noteworthy Properties of the XMLHttpRequest Object

Property	Description
`readyState`	Retrieves the current state of the request operation
`responseBody`	Retrieves the response body as an array of unsigned bytes
`responseText`	Retrieves the response body as a string
`responseXML`	Retrieves the response body as an XML DOM object
`status`	Retrieves the HTTP status code of a request
`statusText`	Retrieves the HTTP status of a request

Noteworthy methods of the `XMLHttpRequest` object are listed in Table 13.2:

Table 13.2: Methods of the XMLHttpRequest Object

Method	Description
`abort`	Aborts the current HTTP request
`getAllResponseHeaders`	Sends back the complete list of response headers
`getResponseHeader`	Sends back the specified response header
`open`	Allocates a method, destination URL, and other optional attributes of a pending request to the XMLHttpRequest object
`send`	Conveys an HTTP request to the server and retrieves a response
`setRequestHeader`	Inserts custom HTTP headers in a request

NOTE

The XMLHttpRequest object has an additional property named timeout, with IE 8. The timeout property obtains and sets the time out value in milliseconds for which client has to wait to receive response from a server. IE 8 provides an event named ontimeout to the XMLHttpRequest object to instruct a browser what to do when time-out period expires.

Let's now understand the need for AJAX.

Need for AJAX

AJAX has established a milestone in the history of Web development. Considering developers' perspective, AJAX has given them a new approach to design and implement functionality in their Web applications. They are not bound to follow the old and tedious request-response model. AJAX prevents the developers from designing more Web pages for displaying new information to the users. This is possible because AJAX reloads only the required section of a Web page, unlike other technologies. With the introduction of AJAX, the scalability of traditional applications has improved.

Considering users' perspective, AJAX has made their Web interaction faster, responsive, and more importantly stress-free. Using AJAX is money saving too, as users are not bound to buy new browsers to allow AJAX to enable the Web sites to run properly, because it is compatible with almost all the current browsers in use, such as IE 6, Firefox 1.0, and their advanced versions. AJAX-enabled Web sites can work easily even with slow connections, such as dial-up connection.

ASP.NET AJAX fulfills its aim of providing a comprehensive Web development environment that is rich in client-scripting features and supports ASP.NET server-side development. ASP.NET 4.5 has built-in AJAX's script libraries and server components to meet the complexity in developing AJAX-enabled Web sites.

Let's now discuss how AJAX is different from other technologies.

AJAX and Other Technologies

How does AJAX differ from other technologies, such as ASP.NET and Java Server Pages (JSP), which use the postback model? If this is not a new technology, as mentioned earlier, then what makes AJAX so popular? To answer these questions in an understanding manner, you first need to analyze how other technologies work. Let's understand the working of traditional Web applications with the help of Figure 13.2:

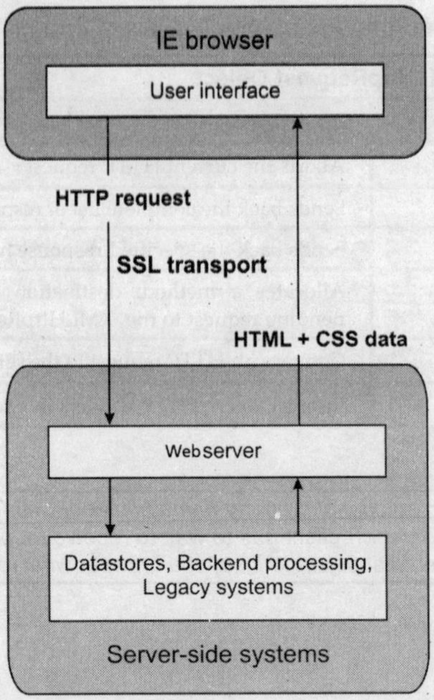

Figure 13.2: Displaying the Traditional Web Application Model

As shown in Figure 13.2, traditional Web applications are based on the request–response or postback model. For each client interaction with the User Interface (UI) of a traditional Web application, an HTTP request is sent to the server, which processes the request and sends the result back to the browser. At the time when this request-response process is in progress, seeing a blank screen can be quite frustrating at times. Considering today's modern scenario, when more and more transactions are taking place through the Internet from all over the world, this time-consuming process can be frustrating.

To remove this shortcoming, `AJAX`, which implements an entirely different approach to Web development, has been introduced. Figure 13.3 shows the `AJAX` Web application model:

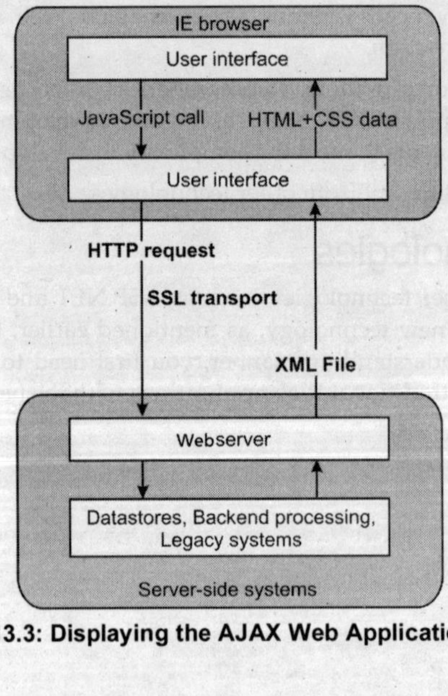

Figure 13.3: Displaying the AJAX Web Application Model

The AJAX Web application model handles the client-side activities, such as validations, without making a round trip to the server. The tasks that are required to be processed at the server end are handled by the AJAX engine. The AJAX engine makes asynchronous calls to the server without interrupting the user's interactions with the UI; therefore, it enhances the user-interactivity and performance, which makes AJAX different from other technologies.

Next, let's explore the new features of ASP.NET 4.5 AJAX.

Exploring Some Features of AJAX

The AJAX Framework has given foundation for building efficient Web sites after its inclusion in the ASP.NET. Therefore, Microsoft keeps enhancing the features of AJAX with every release of ASP.NET to provide more functionality to build rich Web applications. ASP.NET 4.5 AJAX includes the following features:

- Live data binding
- Client-side template rendering
- Declarative instantiation of client components
- Observer pattern for JavaScript objects and arrays
- Support for ADO.NET data services and data contexts
- Support for the `DataView` control

Let's discuss each of these features in detail.

Live Data Binding

Live data binding is a feature which ensures that data is bound with the server controls at runtime. ASP.NET 4.5 AJAX provides the support for live data binding with the help of an observer pattern, which is a software design pattern. This design pattern includes an object known as subject and maintains a list of its dependents known as observers. This design pattern is mainly used in distributed event handling systems.

The `Sys.Observer` interface is used to support live data binding. The live data binding can be used in different manners: one-way and two-way . In the one-way data binding, data is not updated automatically if there is any change in the data source. The code snippet for one-way data binding is as follows:

```
<h3>{{ ProducttName }}</h3>
```

On the other hand, in the two-way data binding, data is updated automatically if the data source changes. The code snippet for two-way data binding is as follows:

```
<input type="text" value="{binding ProductName}"/>
```

Client-Side Template Rendering

In the client-based development environment, templates are the efficient way of developing UI. Therefore, a new template engine is included in ASP.NET 4.5 AJAX that enables developers to execute applications at the client-side. The template engine includes the following features:

- **Performance**—States that the engine must be powerful enough to render a number of items by using an advance template before any interruption occurs while communicating with the application.
- **Simplicity**—States that the template syntax must be easy and used for the most common scenarios, such as for one-way binding.
- **Expression language**—States that the template must support an expression language to use simple syntax, preferably JavaScript syntax.
- **XHTML compliance**—States that the template should render XHTML-standard markup.
- **Components**—States that while using the template syntax, developers can trigger client side controls and behaviors that are bound to HTML elements.

In ASP.NET 4.5 AJAX, an HTML template is a `<div>` tag or any other container tag, declared with the `sys-template` class attribute, as shown in the following code snippet:

```
<div>
<ul id="MyTemplate" class="sys-template">
      <li>
        {{ Symbol }}, {{ Quote }}, {{ Change }}
      </li>
</ul>
</div>
```

The `sys-template` class attribute initially marks an element and its content invisible. It must be defined explicitly in the Master page or in every page of the application, as shown in the following code snippet:

```
<style type="text/css">
.sys-template { display:none; visibility:hidden; }
</style>
```

Declarative Instantiation of Client Components

ASP.NET 4.5 AJAX supports registration, instantiation, and configuration of client components using markup code, without writing any imperative JavaScript code. The declarative markup includes additional namespace attributes, such as xsi: schemaLocation and AccessAttribute (root), which are XHTML compliant. The declarative instantiation of controls works only when the declarative markup is present within an element that has been configured for this purpose only. To declaratively instantiate controls outside a template, you need to first configure a page to ensure that the `sys:attach` markup is present within an activated element. The following code snippet shows how to activate controls:

```
<body xmlns:sys="javascript:Sys" sys:activate="Button1,Button2">
```

In the preceding code snippet, we have activated the `Button` controls.

You can also activate every element in a document but it may cause a delay in the initialization of the document; therefore, this technique should not be used when a document contains a large amount of data. The following code snippet shows how to activate every element in a document:

```
<body xmlns:sys="javascript:Sys" sys:activate="*">
```

Observer Pattern for JavaScript Objects and Arrays

The observer pattern is used to implement functionality in which any modification to JavaScript objects raises notifications that can be handled in your code. The observer design pattern helps you to set observers on an object. The change in the state of an object is handled by the respective event handlers. The observer design pattern can also be used to establish live bindings between UI elements and objects or arrays, which might be provided by the JSON Web service. ASP.NET 4.5 AJAX uses the `Sys.Observer` class to support the observer design pattern.

In the preceding code snippet, we have defined a product object with three properties: pname, ID, and order. We have assigned this object to the callproduct variable and changed the order property to false with the help of the addPropertyChanged() method of the Sys.Observer class.

Support for ADO.NET Data Services and Data Contexts in ASP.NET 4.5

The data context object or data context enables you to bind a JavaScript array or object to a template. It can interact with JSON-based Web services. Two types of data contexts are provided by ASP.NET 4.5 AJAX: `Sys.Data.DataContext` and `Sys.Data.AdoNetDataContext`.

The data context recognizes all the changes in the data automatically by using a new `Sys.Observer` object. The AdoNetDataContext data context supports the enhanced features of ADO.NET data services, such as identity management, links, and association between entity sets. The following code snippet shows how to interact with Productlistservice ADO.NET data service:

```
var dataContext = new Sys.Data.AdoNetDataContext();
dataContext.set_serviceUri("Productlistservice.svc");
dataContext.initialize();
```

In the preceding code snippet, the `set_serviceUri()` method is used to interact with WCF service or ADO.NET data service. The `initialize()` method is used to initialize the data context.

Support for the DataView Control

The `DataView` control is used to display data in the tabular format. It is bound with live data, which can be defined as data at runtime. You can also use this control to develop a dynamic data-driven UI. The `DataView` control is defined in the `System.UI.DataView` namespace and contains two important properties: data and dataProvider. The data property is used to bind a JavaScript object with the data; whereas, the `data provider` property is used to connect to a WCF service. The following code snippet shows how to use the `DataView` control in ASP.NET 4.5 AJAX:

```
<body xmlns:sys="javascript:Sys"
    xmlns:dataview="javascript:Sys.UI.DataView"
    sys:activate="*">
    <ul sys:attach="dataview" class="sys-template"
        dataview:data="{{ dataArray }}">
        <li>          <h3>{{ProductName }}</h3> </li>
       <li>
            <div>{{ Price }}</div>
    </li>
       </ul>
</body>
```

In the preceding code snippet, we have used the data property of the DataView class to bind it with an JavaScript object. In our case, the JavaScript object is named dataArray.

Let's discuss the features that are included in the Microsoft AJAX Library.

Exploring Some Features in the Microsoft AJAX Library

The Microsoft AJAX library is a client-based JavaScript library that is compatible with all the modern browsers and offers a lot of functionality as compared to JavaScript. You can use the Microsoft AJAX library to build highly responsive and interactive database-driven Web applications that can run entirely within a Web browser. The Microsoft AJAX library can be used with both ASP.NET Web forms and ASP.NET MVC applications. Some features in the Microsoft AJAX library are as follows:

- Imperative syntax
- Clientscript loader
- Client data access
- The DataContext and AdoNetDataContext classes
- jQuery integration

Let's discuss these features in detail, one by one.

Imperative Syntax

The Microsoft AJAX library in ASP.NET 4.5 now supports simple imperative syntax that is used to create and manage controls. The following code snippet shows how to create and attach a watermark to an HTML element whose ID is `ProductName`:

```
Sys.create.watermark("#ProductName", {WatermarkText: "Add productname here..." } );
```

When an HTML document that contains the preceding code snippet is executed in a Web browser, a watermark is displayed.

Clientscript Loader

The Microsoft AJAX library in ASP.NET 4.5 includes a script loader, also known as Clientscript loader. The Clientscript loader retrieves all the scripts that are needed by one or more client components or controls automatically and executes the scripts in the order in which they are retrieved. The Clientscript loader provides the following advantages:

- Loads all the resources that are needed by a script automatically
- Ensures that each script is loaded only once
- Enhances the performance of an AJAX application by loading scripts in parallel and by combining scripts
- Loads the scripts only when they are needed, referred as lazy loading
- Loads third-party scripts, such as jQuery and user scripts

Client Data Access

The Microsoft AJAX library in ASP.NET 4.5 supports building of database-driven Web applications that can execute in a Web browser as well as allows you to access client data. The three features of Microsoft AJAX that are used to access client data are as follows:

- **Client data control**—Refers to a control that is used to display either a single database record or a set of records. You can display database records by using the `DataView` control, which is a type of client data control.
- **Client template**—Helps you display database records by using the `DataView` control.

Client DataContext and AdoNetDataContext Classes

The Microsoft AJAX library in ASP.NET 4.5 includes a client `DataContext` class that is related to the server-side LINQ to SQL `DataContext` or the Entity Framework `ObjectContext` class. The `DataContext` class provides the following advantages:

- Supports read and write permissions to data from a database
- Supports identity management and change tracking
- Supports complex links and associations between entities from multiple entity sets or tables

The Microsoft AJAX library now allows you to interact with ASP.NET or WCF services by providing a generic `DataContext` class. In addition, it also enables you to easily interact with an ADO.NET Data Services service with the help of the `AdoNetDataContext` class.

jQuery Integration

ASP.NET 4.5 AJAX supports jQuery integration. jQuery is an open-source JavaScript library that can be used with both ASP.NET Web forms and ASP.NET MVC. It is a fast, lightweight, and CSS compliant library that supports most of the browsers. The jQuery library can be easily used with CSS, AJAX, Events, and Animations. jQuery provides flexible plug-in using which you need not to code the same functionality in your applications again and again. You can use both jQuery plug-ins and Microsoft AJAX client controls within the same AJAX application. You can use jQuery in your Web page, as shown by the following code snippet:

```
<script src="Scripts/jquery-1.7.2.js" type="text/javascript"></script>
<script type="text/javascript">
  $("input").focus(function () { $(this).css("background-color", "green"); });
  $("input").ready(function () { alert("Welcome to the world of jquery"); });
  $('#Button1').click(function () { $(this).css('background-color', 'red').animate({
  width: '100px', height: '80px' }) });
  $('h2').css('font-size', '40px').fadeOut(5000);
</script>
```

Let's now learn about the ASP.NET AJAX architecture.

ASP.NET AJAX Architecture

Every technology has its working domain. This domain is defined by its architecture, which specifies how that specific technology works and what are the areas of its working. ASP.NET AJAX architecture comprises the client-side architecture and the server-side architecture. The ASP.NET AJAX client-side architecture is the client script that a Web application uses to call an application or a service on a server. On the other hand, the ASP.NET AJAX server-side architecture comprises ASP.NET Web services, ASP.NET server controls, and ASP.NET AJAX Extension controls.

Now, let's explore both the client-side architecture and the server-side architecture, one by one.

Client-Side Architecture

The ASP.NET AJAX client-side architecture comprises ASP.NET AJAX client script libraries, which contain a number of JavaScript files that support object-oriented development so that the client browser can request a server asynchronously. This asynchronous call support is quite new in a scripting environment and introduces a high level of modularity in client scripting. The client-side architecture contains non-visual components, controls, and behavior classes for cross-browser compatibility so that ASP.NET AJAX-enabled website can work with Web browsers, such as Internet Explorer, Mozilla Firefox, and Opera. Moreover, the client-side architecture shares data with Web servers mostly in the form of JSON and XML format, because both these formats are platform-independent. Figure 13.4 shows the client-side architecture:

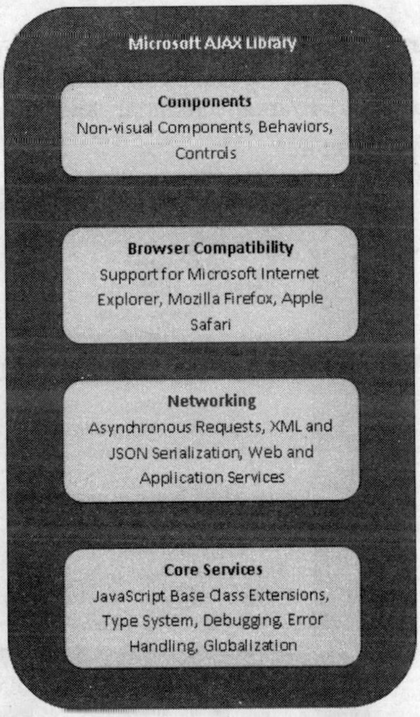

Figure 13.4: Displaying the Client-side Architecture

The client-side architecture comprises a number of layers, which are as follows:

- **Components**—Allow you to get robust functionalities without performing postbacks. The use of components varies as per the type of client behavior. Following three categories of components are available:
  - **Components**—Encapsulate the code to perform a task, but the task is not visible in a browser
  - **Behaviors**—Enhance the basic behavior of the existing DOM objects
  - **Controls**—Create new DOM objects having custom behaviors

- **Browser Compatibility**—Specifies that AJAX applications are compatible with almost all the browsers, such as IE, Mozilla Firefox, and Apple Safari. Therefore, a single script needs to be written for all the browsers instead of varied scripts for different browsers.
- **Networking**—Deals with the communication between the script in a browser, Web services, and applications. Moreover, it manages asynchronous remote method calls, which results in the usage of the networking layer automatically, without providing any code. It also supports accessing of server-based form authentication, role information, and profile information in the client script.
- **Core Services**—Support the object-oriented development. This results in a higher degree of consistency and modularity in client scripting. The AJAX client-side library offers the following core services:
  - Object-oriented extensions to JavaScript, such as classes, namespaces, and inheritance
  - A base class library that contains components, such as string builders
  - JavaScript libraries that are either embedded in an assembly or provided on the hard-disk drives
  - Globalization that enables the usage of a single code base to provide UI for multiple locales

The core services also provide the `Sys.Debug` class and error objects to support debugging and error handling. The `Sys.Debug` class provides methods to display objects in the readable form at the end of a Web page and show trace messages.

Server-Side Architecture

The ASP.NET AJAX server-side architecture contains a set of server controls and components to organize UI and maintain flow of application's execution. It also contains Web services to authenticate and define roles as well as manage user profiles. It also manages serialization, validation, and control extensibility.

Figure 13.5 shows the server-side architecture:

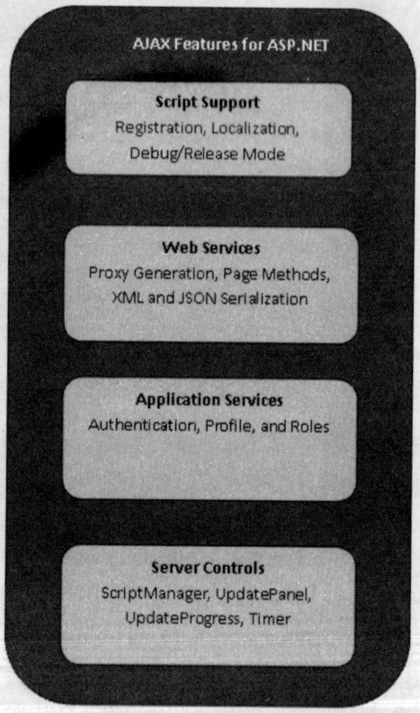

Figure 13.5: Displaying the Server-side Architecture

The various components of the server-side architecture are as follows:

- Script Support
- Web Services

- Application Services
- Server Controls

Now, let's discuss these components of the server-side architecture in detail, one by one.

Script Support

The server-side architecture of ASP.NET contains a rich set of JavaScript files that are used to implement AJAX functionality in ASP.NET applications. These files are sent by a Web server to a client browser. However, scripts forwarded by the server vary according to the functionality implemented in a Web application and support partial-page rendering. The Microsoft AJAX library, in the form of script, provides namespaces, inheritance, interfaces, and other related features to create a Web site. Sometimes while implementing AJAX functionality in the Web site, existing script files might be insufficient to accomplish a specific task. In such cases, you can create your own custom scripts. Such custom scripts can be saved as static JavaScript files or can be included as resources in an assembly. You need to register the custom scripts with Microsoft AJAX library to use them in your application. AJAX also supports localization; thereby, enabling you to create culture and language-specific applications. This localization support enables you to create your own script files for various languages and save them at a remote location. You can then selectively access these script files for a specific language and culture.

Web Services

A Web site that has AJAX functionality might need to call a Web service to implement certain functionality. For this purpose, you need to add the reference of certain script files from Microsoft Library in the Web page in which you need to call the Web service. Using the Visual studio IDE and AJAX server controls, the required script reference is automatically added to a Web page. In case you are not using the Visual Studio IDE and AJAX server controls for creating AJAX-enabled Web sites, you have to add the reference of the ASP.NET AJAX library and the required Web service in a Web page manually. After you have added the reference of script files, the required proxy classes are automatically created. These classes call the Web service from the client-side. The Web services are also capable of serializing objects so that the objects can travel over the network. This serialization occurs in the form of XML or JSON because XML and JSON are standards for cross-platform and cross-browser data transfer.

Application Services

The tasks of authenticating users, authorizing them specific roles, and preparing their profiles are performed through application services. These services are part of ASP.NET and can be used by any client script of an AJAX-enabled Web page. Various Web services that ASP.NET AJAX uses are as follows:

- **Profile**—Retains user information on a server
- **Membership**—Helps in authentication
- **Roles**—Implements role-based authorization for ASP.NET AJAX applications
- **Personalization**—Persists personalization data on a server
- **Globalization**—Incorporates culture-specific features in ASP.NET AJAX applications

Server controls

ASP.NET AJAX contains a set of built-in AJAX-enabled server controls, such as a `Button` control, which comprises code for implementing highly interactive client behavior. ASP.NET AJAX-specific server controls provide a more server-centric approach to the application development. Adding a server control ensures that the client script reference is added to the Web page automatically. The client script reference helps in executing sever controls.

AJAX Server or Extension Controls

Microsoft has introduced AJAX specific controls to ease the implementation of AJAX in a Web site. You can find these controls under the `AJAX Extensions` tab. When you add any of these controls to a Web form, the reference of corresponding script library is added automatically to the Web page. AJAX provides the following server controls:

- The ScriptManager control
- The ScriptManagerProxy control
- The Timer control
- The UpdatePanel control
- The UpdateProgress control

Let's discuss these controls in detail one by one.

The ScriptManager Control

The `ScriptManager` control helps in implementing the AJAX functionality in an ASP.NET Web site. You need to add this control on a Web page wherever AJAX functionality is required. In the absence of this control, no other AJAX server controls, such as `Timer`, `UpdatePanel`, and `UpdateProgress`, can be added to the Web page. The `ScriptManager` control is responsible for managing client scripts for AJAX-enabled Web site. This control uses a `ScriptManager` class to manage AJAX script libraries and script files. The inheritance hierarchy of the `ScriptManager` class is as follows:

```
System.Object
   System.Web.UI.Control
        System.Web.UI.ScriptManager
```

The `ScriptManager` control renders the AJAX library scripts to the browser and supports partial-page rendering, Web-service calls, and use of ASP.NET AJAX client library. You can add the `ScriptManager` control in a Web page by dragging the control from the Toolbox and dropping it on the Design view. The `ScriptManager` control is initialized using the following markup code snippet:

```
<asp:ScriptManager ID="ScriptManager1" runat="server">
</asp:ScriptManager>
```

Noteworthy properties of the `ScriptManager` class are listed in Table 13.3:

Table 13.3: Noteworthy Properties of ScriptManager Class

Property	Description
`AllowCustomErrorsRedirect`	Specifies a value to indicate whether to use the custom error section of the `Web.config` file when an error occurs during the asynchronous postback
`AsyncPostBackErrorMessage`	Specifies an error message that is returned to the client when an unhandled server exception occurs during an asynchronous postback
`AsyncPostBackSourceElementID`	Specifies the ID of the control that triggers the asynchronous postback
`AsyncPostBackTimeout`	Specifies a time value in seconds to timeout the asynchronous postback if the response is not received
`AuthenticationService`	Retrieves the `AuthenticationServiceManager` object that is associated with the current `ScriptManager` instance
`EnablePageMethods`	Specifies a value to indicate whether to call the page method in an ASP.NET page from the client script
`EnablePartialRendering`	Specifies a value to indicate whether to enable partial-page rendering

Table 13.3: Noteworthy Properties of ScriptManager Class

Property	Description
`EnableScriptGlobalization`	Specifies a value to indicate whether the `ScriptManager` control renders the script that supports parsing and formatting of different culture-specific information
`EnableScriptLocalization`	Specifies a value to indicate whether the `ScriptManager` control renders the localized versions of scripts
`IsDebuggingEnabled`	Specifies whether the `ScriptManager` control renders the debug versions of client script libraries
`IsInAsyncPostBack`	Specifies whether the `ScriptManager` control executes the current postback in a partial-page rendering
`LoadScriptsBeforeUI`	Specifies a value to indicate whether scripts are loaded before or after the page markup
`ProfileService`	Retrieves the `ProfileServiceManager` object that is associated with the current `ScriptManager` instance
`RoleService`	Retrieves the `RoleServiceManager` object that is associated with the current `ScriptManager` instance
`ScriptMode`	Specifies a value to indicate whether the `ScriptManager` control renders the debug or release versions of client script libraries
`ScriptPath`	Specifies the location of the root path that is used to build paths to ASP.NET AJAX and custom script files
`Scripts`	Retrieves a `ScriptReferenceCollection` object having multiple `ScriptReference` objects, each representing a script file rendered to a client
`Services`	Retrieves a `ServiceReferenceCollection` object that contains a `ServiceManager` object for each Web service that ASP.NET exposes on a client for AJAX functionality
`SupportsPartialRendering`	Specifies a value to indicate whether a client supports partial-page rendering

Noteworthy methods of the `ScriptManager` class are listed in Table 13.4:

Table 13.4: Noteworthy Methods of ScriptManager Class

Method	Description
`GetCurrent`	Obtains the `ScriptManager` instance for a given Web page object.
`GetRegisteredArrayDeclarations`	Obtains a read-only collection of `ECMAScript` (JavaScript) array declarations that were previously registered with the Web page object.
`GetRegisteredClientScriptBlocks`	Obtains a read-only collection of client script blocks that were previously registered with the `ScriptManager` control.
`GetRegisteredDisposeScripts`	Obtains a read-only collection of dispose scripts that were previously registered with the Web page object.
`GetRegisteredExpandoAttributes`	Obtains a read-only collection of custom attributes that were previously registered with the Web page object.
`GetRegisteredHiddenFields`	Obtains a read-only collection of hidden fields that were previously registered with the Web page object.

Table 13.4: Noteworthy Methods of ScriptManager Class

Method	Description
GetRegisteredOnSubmitStatements	Obtains a read-only collection of onsubmit statement that was previously registered with the Web page object.
GetRegisteredStartupScripts	Obtains a read-only collection of startup scripts that were previously registered with the Web page object.
RegisterArrayDeclaration	Registers an ECMAScript (JavaScript) array declaration with the ScriptManager control and adds the array to a Web page. It is an overloaded method.
RegisterAsyncPostBackControl	Registers a control as a trigger for asynchronous postbacks.
RegisterClientScriptBlock	Registers a client script block with the ScriptManager control and adds the script block to a Web page. It is an overloaded method.
RegisterClientScriptInclude	Registers a client script file with the ScriptManager control and adds the reference of the script file to a Web page. It is an overloaded method.
RegisterClientScriptResource	Registers a client script that is embedded in an assembly with the ScriptManager control. It is an overloaded method.
RegisterDataItem	Sends custom data to a control during partial-page rendering. It is an overloaded method.
RegisterDispose	Registers a dispose script for a control that is inside an UpdatePanel control.
RegisterExpandoAttribute	Registers a name/value pair with the ScriptManager control as a custom attribute of the specified control.
RegisterExtenderControl	Registers an extender control with the current ScriptManager instance.
RegisterHiddenField	Registers a hidden field with the ScriptManager control. It is an overloaded method.
RegisterOnSubmitStatement	Registers ECMAScript (JavaScript) code that is executed on submitting a Web Form. It is an overloaded method.
RegisterPostBackControl	Registers a control as a trigger for a postback.
RegisterScriptControl	Registers a script control with the current ScriptManager instance.
RegisterScriptDescriptors	Instructs the ScriptManager control to call back the ScriptControl or ExtenderControl classes to return scripts that support the client object. It is an overloaded method.
RegisterStartupScript	Registers a startup script block to the ScriptManager control and adds the script block to a Web page. It is an overloaded method.
SetFocus	Specifies the browser focus to the specified control. It is an overloaded method.

Noteworthy events of the ScriptManager class are listed in Table 13.5:

Table 13.5: Noteworthy Events of ScriptManager Class

Event	Description
AsyncPostBackError	Occurs when a page error is found during an asynchronous postback
ResolveScriptReference	Occurs when a member of the Scripts() collection is registered with the ScriptManager control

The ScriptManagerProxy Control

As you know, an AJAX-enabled website can contain only one `ScriptManager` control (on each Web page), which manages all the AJAX server controls on that page. Additionally, if the website contains a Master page and the `ScriptManager` control is added in the Master page, then all the content pages (Web pages inherited from the Master page) use the `ScriptManager` control of the Master Page to manage its AJAX server controls. For this purpose, each content page requires a link to connect to Master page's `ScriptManager` control. The content page uses the `ScriptManagerProxy` control to make a link with the Master page. The `ScriptManagerProxy` control of the content page works as a local object of the `ScriptManager` control of Master page. The objective of using the `ScriptManagerProxy` control in a content page is to override the configurations that have been set by the `ScriptManager` control of the Master page. For example, if the services and scripts added earlier in the `ScriptManager` control of the Master page are not useful for your current Web page, you can remove them by using the `ScriptManagerProxy` control. The `ScriptManagerProxy` control uses a `ScriptManagerProxy` class to override the configurations set by the `ScriptManager` control of the Master page. The inheritance hierarchy of the `ScriptManagerProxy` class is shown as follows:

```
System.Object
  System.Web.UI.Control
        System.Web.UI.ScriptManagerProxy
```

You can add the `ScriptManagerProxy` control in a Web page by dragging the control from the Toolbox and dropping it on the Design view. The `ScriptManagerProxy` control is initialized using the following mark up code snippet:

```
<asp:ScriptManagerProxy ID="ScriptManagerProxy1" runat="server">
</asp:ScriptManagerProxy>
```

The properties, methods, and events of the `ScriptManagerProxy` class are same as of the `ScriptManager` class.

The Timer Control

Sometimes, there can be a situation when you want to update the content of a page after a specific interval. Suppose a Web page shows the stock prices where the price of the stocks changes frequently. You are asked to update the stock prices after every minute. In this scenario, you need to use the `Timer` control. The `Timer` control contains the `Interval` property and the `Tick` event. The `Interval` property of the `Timer` control is used to specify the desired time limit in milliseconds; in our example, it is 1 minute, i.e. 60 seconds. When this time limit is over, it raises the `Tick` event. You can handle this `Tick` event to update the content of your Web page. A single AJAX-enabled Web page can contain more than one part; it is your choice whether to use single `Timer` control for all the parts of Web page or to use different `Timer` controls for every part of a Web page. Moreover, a single `Timer` control can refresh the content of more than one part of a Web page. Another useful property of the `Timer` control is the `Enabled` property. Using the Enabled property, you can turn the `Timer` control ON or OFF at runtime or at design time. The `Enabled` property controls the `Tick` event from firing. If the `Enabled` property is true, then the `Timer` control can fire the `Tick` event; otherwise, not. The `Timer` control is an instance of the `Timer` class. The inheritance hierarchy of the `Timer` class is as follows:

```
System.Object
  System.Web.UI.Control
        System.Web.UI.Timer
```

You can add the `Timer` control in a Web page by dragging the control from the Toolbox and dropping it on the Design view. The `Timer` control is initialized using the following markup code snippet:

```
<asp:Timer ID="Timer1" runat="server">
  </asp:Timer>
```

Noteworthy properties of the `Timer` class are listed in Table 13.6:

Table 13.6: Noteworthy Properties of Timer Class

Property	Description
`Enabled`	Specifies a value to indicate whether or not the `Timer` control initiates a `postback` when the interval time has elapsed
`Interval`	Specifies a time value in milliseconds to wait before the `Timer` control initiates a `postback`
`Visible`	Overrides the `Visible` property of the `Control` class

The UpdatePanel Control

The `UpdatePanel` control helps in dividing your Web page into parts, where each part can be updated independently. This control uses a synchronous `postback` to refresh the selected part of the page; but built-in client script transforms this `synchronous` request to an `asynchronous` request with the help of the `XMLHttpRequest` object, so that it can update the information without refreshing the page. A single Web page can contain multiple `UpdatePanel` controls where each control can create a separate part of your Web page. You need not to write any custom client script for partial-page rendering when you are using the `UpdatePanel` control. The `UpdatePanel` control uses the `UpdatePanel` class to support partial-page rendering. The inheritance hierarchy of the `UpdatePanel` class is as follows:

```
System.Object
   System.Web.UI.Control
        System.Web.UI.UpdatePanel
```

You can add the `UpdatePanel` control in a Web page by dragging the control from the Toolbox and dropping it on the Design view. The `UpdatePanel` control is initialized using the following mark up code snippet:

```
<asp:UpdatePanel ID="UpdatePanel1" runat="server">
</asp:UpdatePanel>
```

Noteworthy properties of the `UpdatePanel` class are listed in Table 13.7:

Table 13.7: Noteworthy Properties of the UpdatePanel Class

Property	Description
`ChildrenAsTriggers`	Specifies a value to indicate whether or not triggering the `postbacks` from immediate child controls of an `UpdatePanel` control updates the panel's content
`ContentTemplate`	Specifies a template to define the content of the `UpdatePanel` control
`ContentTemplateContainer`	Retrieves a control object to which you can programmatically add child controls
`Controls`	Retrieves the `ControlCollection` object having the child controls for the `UpdatePanel` control
`IsInPartialRendering`	Specifies a value to indicate whether or not to update the `UpdatePanel` control when a client triggers the asynchronous `postback`
`RenderMode`	Specifies a value to indicate whether or not the content of the `UpdatePanel` control is placed within the HTML `<div>` or `<span>` tags
`Triggers`	Retrieves an `UpdatePanelTriggerCollection` object having `AsyncPostBackTrigger` and `PostBackTrigger` objects that have been defined for the `UpdatePanel` control
`UpdateMode`	Specifies a value to indicate when the content of the `UpdatePanel` control is updated

An asynchronous `postback` is quite similar to the regular `postback` (where the resulting server page executes the entire page). However, the asynchronous `postback` executes the limited page regions that are enclosed within the `UpdatePanel` control. The `UpdatePanel` control with a code sample is discussed in the Immediate Solutions section of this chapter.

The UpdateProgress Control

While working with the `UpdatePanel` control, sometimes you need to show the status of the information requested by a user. In other words, you need to make the user aware of the progress status of the requested data to refresh the content of the `UpdatePanel` control. This task is accomplished with the help of the `UpdateProgress` control. As per your requirement, you can use image, text, or a progress bar to show the status of the requested data. This control is used in situations where your page contains more than one `UpdatePanel` control and the task of updating content is performed at different times. It is also useful when speed of updating content is slow. In this condition, the user gets an idea about how much information is processed and for how long he/she needs to wait. The UpdateProgress control is also used to show the status of partial-page updates. You can customize the content and layout of the UpdateProgress control according to your requirements. The `UpdateProgress` control uses the `UpdateProgress` class to support the properties involved in displaying the update progress. The inheritance hierarchy of the `UpdateProgress` class is as follows:

```
System.Object
   System.Web.UI.Control
         System.Web.UI.UpdateProgress
```

You can add the `UpdateProgress` control in a Web page by dragging the control from the Toolbox and dropping it on the Design view. The `UpdateProgress` control is initialized using the following mark up code snippet:

```
<asp:UpdateProgress ID="UpdateProgress1" runat="server">
</asp:UpdateProgress>
```

Noteworthy properties of the `UpdateProgress` class are listed in Table 13.8:

Table 13.8: Important Properties of the UpdateProgress Class

Property	Description
`AssociatedUpdatePanelID`	Specifies the ID of the `UpdatePanel` control for which the status has been displayed
`DisplayAfter`	Specifies a time value in milliseconds before which the `UpdateProgress` control is displayed
`DynamicLayout`	Specifies a value to indicate whether or not to render the progress template dynamically
`ProgressTemplate`	Specifies a template that defines the content of the `UpdateProgress` control

NOTE

To work with the UpdatePanel, UpdateProgress, and Timer controls, you need to add the ScriptManager control on a Web page, because the ScriptManager control contains a reference of the built-in script libraries to implement AJAX functionality.

Let's now move on to the Immediate Solutions section to learn the practical implementation of various concepts discussed in this chapter.

Immediate Solutions

Differentiating Between AJAX and Non-AJAX Applications

ASP.NET 4.5 provides AJAX-specific controls to create AJAX-enabled Web applications. Along with these controls, you can use other ASP.NET controls, such as Standard controls, Login controls, and Navigation controls. To understand AJAX better, you need to understand the difference in the functionalities of AJAX and non-AJAX applications. For this purpose, let's create two applications. We first create a simple ASP.NET Web application, and then extend it to implement the AJAX functionality in the application.

NOTE

Create an ASP.NET Empty Web application and add a Default.aspx page to it.

Creating a Simple Non-AJAX Application

You can create non-AJAX applications by simply using ASP.NET controls in them. Such applications are suitable for low traffic and static Web pages. Let's perform the following steps to create a simple ASP.NET Web application that displays current date and time on a button click:

1. Create an ASP.NET Web application and save it as `SimpleApplication`.
2. Drag and drop a `Button` control and two `Label` controls from the Toolbox to the Design view of the `Default.aspx` page.
3. Set the `Text` property of the `Label1` control to `Simple Application Without` AJAX, the Label2 control to Click the Button to Display Current Date and Time, the `Button1` control to `Display`, and the `ID` property of `Label1`, `Label2` and `Button1` to `lblHeading`, `lblTime`, and `Btndisplay`, respectively.

After setting the properties of the control, the code of the Default.aspx page appears, as shown in Listing 13.1:

Listing 13.1: Showing the Code for the Default.aspx Page

In VB

```
<%@ Page Language="VB" AutoEventWireup="false" CodeFile="Default.aspx.vb"
  Inherits="_Default" %>
<!DOCTYPE html>
<html xmlns="http://www.w3.org/1999/xhtml">
<head runat="server">
    <title></title>
</head>
<body>
    <form id="form1" runat="server">
    <div>
<h2>
     <asp:Label ID="lblHeading" runat="server" Text="Simple Application
              Without AJAX"></asp:Label>
</h2>
          <br />
         <br />
          <asp:Label ID="lblTime" runat="server" Text="Click the Button to Display
          Current Date and Time" ></asp:Label>
           
          <asp:Button ID="Btndisplay" runat="server" Text="Display"/>
    </div>
```

```
    </form>
</body>
</html>
```

In C#

```
<%@ Page Language="C#" AutoEventWireup="true" CodeFile="Default.aspx.cs"
  Inherits="_Default" %>
<!DOCTYPE html>
<html xmlns="http://www.w3.org/1999/xhtml">
<head runat="server">
    <title></title>
</head>
<body>
    <form id="form1" runat="server">
    <div>
<h2>
    <asp:Label ID="lblHeading" runat="server" Text="Simple Application
                Without AJAX"></asp:Label>
</h2>
         <br />
         <br />
         <asp:Label ID="lblTime" runat="server" Text="Click the Button to Display
         Current Date and Time" ></asp:Label>
          
         <asp:Button ID="Btndisplay" runat="server" Text="Display"
            OnClick="Btndisplay_Click" />
    </div>
    </form>
</body>
</html>
```

4. Double-click the Button control (Btndisplay) and add the highlighted code, shown in Listing 13.2, in the Click event:

Listing 13.2: Showing the CodeFile of Default.aspx Page

In VB

```
Partial Class _Default
    Inherits System.Web.UI.Page
    Protected Sub Btndisplay_Click(sender As Object, e As EventArgs)
    Handles Btndisplay.Click
        Dim myDateTime As String
        myDateTime = System.DateTime.Today.ToLongDateString() + " "
        myDateTime += System.DateTime.Now.ToLongTimeString()
        lblLabel.Text = myDateTime
    End Sub
End Class
```

In C#

```
using System;
using System.Collections.Generic;
using System.Linq;
using System.Web;
using System.Web.UI;
using System.Web.UI.WebControls;
public partial class _Default : System.Web.UI.Page
{
    protected void Page_Load(object sender, EventArgs e)
    {
    }
```

```
    protected void Btndisplay_Click(object sender, EventArgs e)
    {
        String myDateTime;
        myDateTime = System.DateTime.Today.ToLongDateString() + " ";
        myDateTime += System.DateTime.Now.ToLongTimeString();
        lblLabel.Text = myDateTime;
    }
}
```

5. Press the F5 key to execute the application. The output of the application appears (Figure 13.6).
6. Click the Display button to view the current time and date on the Web page, as shown in Figure 13.6:

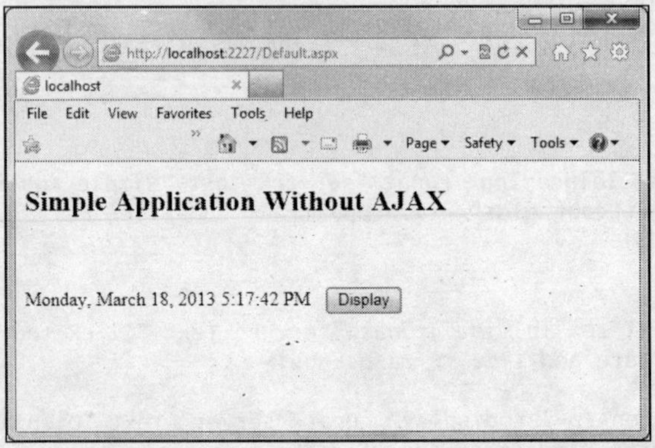

Figure 13.6: Displaying the Current Date and Time

Creating a Simple AJAX Application

Now, let's perform the following steps to create a simple AJAX ASP.NET website that displays current system date and time on a button click:

1. Create an ASP.NET website and save it as `SimpleAJAXapplication`. You can find the code for this application in the `SimpleAJAXapplication` (for C#) and `SimpleAJAXapplicationVB` (for VB) folder.
2. Add ScriptManager and UpdatePanel controls on the page.
3. Drag and drop a Button control and two Label controls from the Toolbox on the Design view of the Default.aspx page.
4. Set the Text property of the Label1 control to Simple Application With AJAX, the Button1 control to Display and ID property to Btndisplay.

After setting the properties of the control, the code of the Default.aspx page appears, as shown in Listing 13.3:

Listing 13.3: Showing the Code for the Default.aspx Page

In VB

```
<%@ Page Language="VB" AutoEventWireup="false" CodeFile="Default.aspx.vb"
  Inherits="_Default" %>
<!DOCTYPE html>
<html xmlns="http://www.w3.org/1999/xhtml">
<head runat="server">
    <title></title>
</head>
<body>
    <form id="form1" runat="server">
    <div>
    <asp:ScriptManager ID="ScriptManager1" runat="server">
                </asp:ScriptManager>
                <asp:UpdatePanel ID="UpdatePanel1" runat="server">
```

```
                <ContentTemplate>
                <h2>
                        <asp:Label ID="LabelHeading" runat="server" Text="Simple
                        Application With AJAX"></asp:Label>
                </h2>
                <asp:Label ID="TimeLabel" runat="server" Text="Click the Button to
                Display Current System Date and Time"></asp:Label>
                 
                <asp:Button ID="Btndisplay" runat="server" Text="Display" />
                </ContentTemplate>
                </asp:UpdatePanel>
    </div>
    </form>
</body>
</html>
```

In C#

```
<%@ Page Language="C#" AutoEventWireup="true" CodeFile="Default.aspx.cs"
  Inherits="_Default" %>
<!DOCTYPE html>
<html xmlns="http://www.w3.org/1999/xhtml">
<head runat="server">
    <title></title>
</head>
<body>
    <form id="form1" runat="server">
    <div>
    <asp:ScriptManager ID="ScriptManager1" runat="server">
                </asp:ScriptManager>
                <asp:UpdatePanel ID="UpdatePanel1" runat="server">
                <ContentTemplate>
                <h2>
                        <asp:Label ID="LabelHadding" runat="server" Text="Simple
                        Application With AJAX"></asp:Label>
                </h2>
                <asp:Label ID="TimeLabel" runat="server" Text="Click the Button to
                Display Current System Date and Time"></asp:Label>
                 
                <asp:Button ID="Btndisplay" runat="server" Text="Display"
                   OnClick="Btndisplay_Click" />
                </ContentTemplate>
                </asp:UpdatePanel>
    </div>
    </form>
</body>
</html>
```

5. Double-click the Button control (Btndisplay) and add the highlighted code, shown in Listing 13.4, in the Click event:

Listing 13.4: Showing the CodeFile of Default.aspx Page

In VB

```
Partial Class _Default
    Inherits System.Web.UI.Page
    Protected Sub Btndisplay_Click(sender As Object, e As EventArgs)
    Handles Btndisplay.Click
        Dim myDateTime As String
        myDateTime = System.DateTime.Today.ToLongDateString() + " "
        myDateTime += System.DateTime.Now.ToLongTimeString()
```

```
            TimeLabel.Text = myDateTime
        End Sub
    End Class
```

In C#

```
using System;
using System.Collections.Generic;
using System.Linq;
using System.Web;
using System.Web.UI;
using System.Web.UI.WebControls;
public partial class _Default : System.Web.UI.Page
{
    protected void Page_Load(object sender, EventArgs e)
    {
    }
    protected void Btndisplay_Click(object sender, EventArgs e)
    {
        String myDateTime;
        myDateTime = System.DateTime.Today.ToLongDateString() + " ";
        myDateTime += System.DateTime.Now.ToLongTimeString();
        TimeLabel.Text = myDateTime;
    }
}
```

6. Press the F5 key to execute the application. The output of the application appears (Figure 13.7).
7. Click the Display button to display the current date and time, as shown in Figure 13.7:

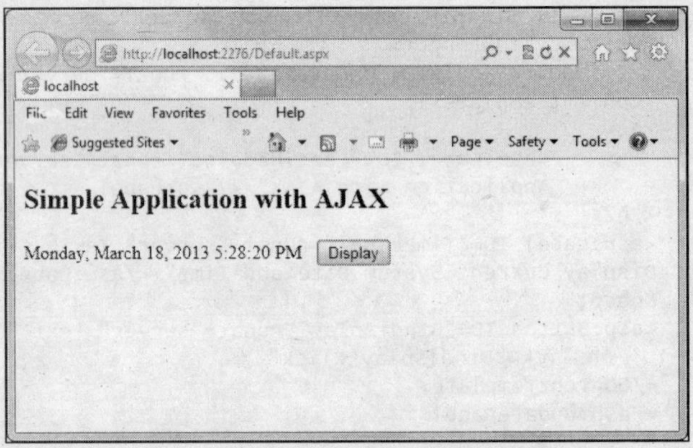

Figure 13.7: Displaying the Current Date and Time

Let's now learn how to use the AJAX server controls.

Using AJAX Server Controls

Now, you are familiar with a simple AJAX application and have understood the basic idea behind AJAX. In this section, you learn to use the following two AJAX Server controls:

- `Timer` control
- `UpdateProgress` control

Let's discuss these controls, one by one.

Timer Control

The `Timer` control is used to update content of the `UpdatePanel` control at predefined intervals. Single `Timer control` can refresh more than one `UpdatePanel` controls simultaneously. The `Timer control` has an `Interval` property that is used to define the time limit after which the content is refreshed. When this interval limit is over, the `Tick` event is raised. You can handle this event to update the content values defined in the `UpdatePanel` control. The `Timer` control can be used in the following two ways:

- Inside the `UpdatePanel` control
- Outside the `UpdatePanel` control

Let's discuss these ways in detail.

Using the Timer Control Inside the UpdatePanel Control

Now, let's perform the following steps to create a simple AJAX ASP.NET website that displays current system time using the Timer control inside the UpdatePanel control

1. Create an ASP.NET website and save it as Timercontrolinside. You can find the code for this application in the Timercontrolinside (for C#) and TimercontrolinsideVB (for VB) folder.
2. Drag and drop a ScriptManager control, UpdatePanel control, and two Label controls from the Toolbox on the Design view of the Default.aspx page. To use the `Timer` control inside the `UpdatePanel` Control, drag-and-drop the Timer control from the Toolbox as a sub-element of the `<ContentTemplate>` tag.
3. Set the Text property of the Label1 control to Application Using Timer control, Label2 control to Current System Time, ID property of the Label1 control to LabelHeading, ID property of the Label2 control to TimeLabel, ID property of the Timer control to TimeUpdater, and Interval property to 1000.

After setting the properties of the controls, the code of the Default.aspx page appears, as shown in Listing 13.5:

Listing 13.5: Showing the Code for the Default.aspx Page

In VB

```
<%@ Page Language="VB" AutoEventWireup="false" CodeFile="Default.aspx.vb"
  Inherits="_Default" %>
<!DOCTYPE html>
<html xmlns="http://www.w3.org/1999/xhtml">
<head runat="server">
    <title></title>
</head>
<body>
    <form id="form1" runat="server">
    <div>
    <asp:ScriptManager ID="ScriptManager1" runat="server">
        </asp:ScriptManager>
<h2>
        <asp:Label ID="LabelHadding" runat="server" Text="Application Using Timer
        Control"></asp:Label>
        </h2>
        <asp:UpdatePanel ID="UpdatePanel1" runat="server">
        <ContentTemplate>
        <asp:Timer ID="TimeUpdater" runat="server" Interval="1000" >
        </asp:Timer>
        <asp:Label ID="TimeLabel" runat="server" Text="Current System
        Time"></asp:Label>
         
        </ContentTemplate>
        </asp:UpdatePanel>
    </div>
    </form>
</body>
</html>
```

In C#

```
<%@ Page Language="C#" AutoEventWireup="true" CodeFile="Default.aspx.cs"
  Inherits="_Default" %>
<!DOCTYPE html>
<html xmlns="http://www.w3.org/1999/xhtml">
<head runat="server">
    <title></title>
</head>
<body>
    <form id="form1" runat="server">
    <div>
    <asp:ScriptManager ID="ScriptManager1" runat="server">
         </asp:ScriptManager>
  <h2>
         <asp:Label ID="LabelHeading" runat="server" Text="Application Using Timer
         Control"></asp:Label>
  </h2>
         <asp:UpdatePanel ID="UpdatePanel1" runat="server">
         <ContentTemplate>
         <asp:Timer ID="TimeUpdater" runat="server" Interval="1000"
         OnTick="TimeUpdater_Tick">
         </asp:Timer>
  <asp:Label ID="TimeLabel" runat="server" Text="Current System Time"></asp:Label>
          
         </ContentTemplate>
         </asp:UpdatePanel>
    </div>
    </form>
</body>
</html>
```

4. Double-click the `Timer` control (TimeUpdater) in the Design view and add the highlighted code, shown in Listing 13.6, in its `Tick` event:

Listing 13.6: Showing the CodeFile of Default.aspx Page

In VB

```
Partial Class _Default
    Inherits System.Web.UI.Page
    Protected Sub TimeUpdater_Tick(sender As Object, e As EventArgs)
     Handles TimeUpdater.Tick
        TimeLabel.Text = System.DateTime.Now.ToLongTimeString
    End Sub
End Class
```

In C#

```
using System;
using System.Collections.Generic;
using System.Linq;
using System.Web;
using System.Web.UI;
using System.Web.UI.WebControls;
public partial class _Default : System.Web.UI.Page
{
    protected void Page_Load(object sender, EventArgs e)
    {

    }
    protected void TimeUpdater_Tick(object sender, EventArgs e)
    {
```

```
            TimeLabel.Text = System.DateTime.Now.ToLongTimeString();
        }
    }
```

5. Press the F5 key to execute the application. The output of the application appears before the Tick event of the Timer control is fired, as shown in Figure 13.8:

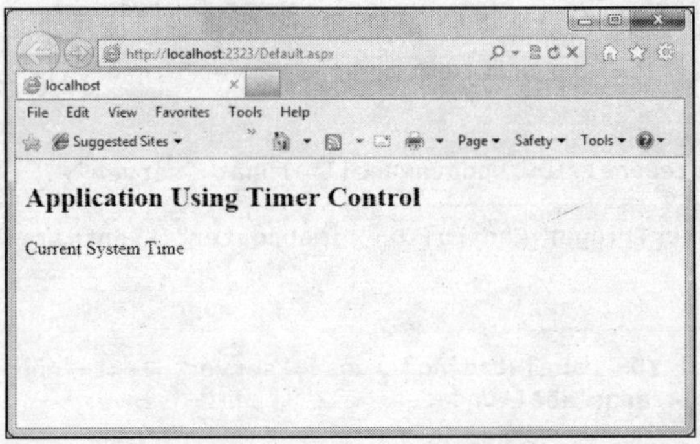

Figure 13.8: Displaying the Output of the Timer Control

After a second, the Tick event is fired and the current system time appear, as shown in Figure 13.9:

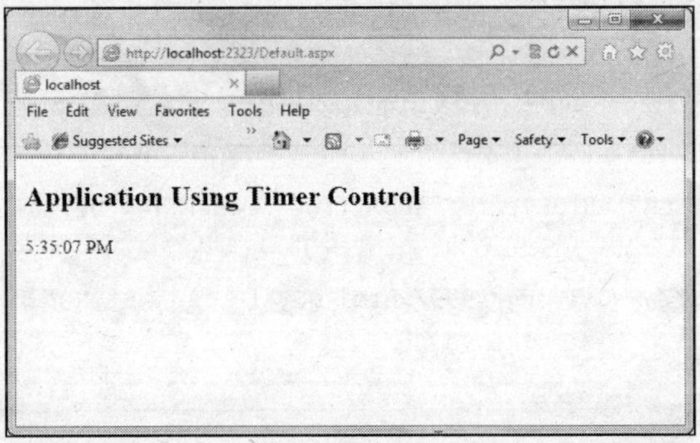

Figure 13.9: Displaying the Current System Time

Using the Timer Control Outside the UpdatePanel Control

Now, let's perform the following steps to create a simple AJAX ASP.NET website that displays current system time using the Timer control outside the UpdatePanel control:

1. Create an ASP.NET website and save it as Timercontroloutside. You can find the code for this application in the Timercontroloutside (for C#) and TimercontroloutsideVB (for VB) folder.
2. Drag and drop a ScriptManager control, UpdatePanel control, Timer control outside the UpdatePanel control and two Label controls from the Toolbox on the Design view of the Default.aspx page.
3. Set the Text property of the Label1 control to Application Using Timer Control, Label2 control to Current System Time, ID property of the Label1 control to LabelHeading, ID property of the Label2 control to TimeLabel, ID property of the Timer control to TimeUpdater, and Interval property to 1000.

After setting the properties of the controls, the code of the Default.aspx page appears, as shown in Listing 13.7:

Listing 13.7: Showing the Code for the Default.aspx Page

In VB

```
<%@ Page Language="VB" AutoEventWireup="false" CodeFile="Default.aspx.vb"
  Inherits="_Default" %>
<!DOCTYPE html>
<html xmlns="http://www.w3.org/1999/xhtml">
<head runat="server">
```

```
        <title></title>
    </head>
    <body>
        <form id="form1" runat="server">
        <div>
        <asp:ScriptManager ID="ScriptManager1" runat="server">
            </asp:ScriptManager>
            <asp:Timer ID="TimeUpdater" runat="server" Interval="1000"
            >
            </asp:Timer>
            <asp:UpdatePanel ID="UpdatePanel1" runat="server">
      <Triggers>
      <asp:AsyncPostBackTrigger ControlID="TimeUpdater" EventName="Tick" />
      </Triggers>
    <ContentTemplate>
    <h2>
            <asp:Label ID="LabelHeading" runat="server" Text="Application Using Timer
             Control"></asp:Label>
      </h2>
      <asp:Label ID="TimeLabel" runat="server" Text="Current System Time"></asp:Label>
    </ContentTemplate>
    </asp:UpdatePanel>    </div>
        </form>
    </body>
    </html>
```

In C#

```
    <%@ Page Language="C#" AutoEventWireup="true" CodeFile="Default.aspx.cs"
      Inherits="_Default" %>
    <!DOCTYPE html>
    <html xmlns="http://www.w3.org/1999/xhtml">
    <head runat="server">
        <title></title>
    </head>
    <body>
        <form id="form1" runat="server">
        <div>
        <asp:ScriptManager ID="ScriptManager1" runat="server">
            </asp:ScriptManager>
            <asp:Timer ID="TimeUpdater" runat="server" Interval="1000"
            OnTick="TimeUpdater_Tick">
            </asp:Timer>
            <asp:UpdatePanel ID="UpdatePanel1" runat="server">
      <Triggers>
      <asp:AsyncPostBackTrigger ControlID="TimeUpdater" EventName="Tick" />
      </Triggers>
    <ContentTemplate>
    <h2>
            <asp:Label ID="LabelHeading" runat="server" Text="Application Using Timer
             Control"></asp:Label>
      </h2>
      <asp:Label ID="TimeLabel" runat="server" Text="Current System Time"></asp:Label>
    </ContentTemplate>
    </asp:UpdatePanel>    </div>
        </form>
    </body>
    </html>
```

4. Now, double-click the `Timer` control (TimeUpdater) in the Design view and add the highlighted code, shown in Listing 13.8, in its `Tick` event:

Listing 13.8: Showing the CodeFile of Default.aspx Page

In VB

```
Partial Class _Default
    Inherits System.Web.UI.Page
    Protected Sub TimeUpdater_Tick(sender As Object, e As EventArgs)
   Handles TimerUpdater.Tick
        TimeLabel.Text = System.DateTime.Now.ToLongTimeString
    End Sub
End Class
```

In C#

```
using System;
using System.Collections.Generic;
using System.Linq;
using System.Web;
using System.Web.UI;
using System.Web.UI.WebControls;
public partial class _Default : System.Web.UI.Page
{
    protected void Page_Load(object sender, EventArgs e)
    {

    }
    protected void TimeUpdater_Tick(object sender, EventArgs e)
    {
        TimeLabel.Text = System.DateTime.Now.ToLongTimeString();
    }
}
```

5. Press the F5 key to execute the application. The output of the application appears before the Tick event of the Timer control is fired, as shown in Figure 13.10:

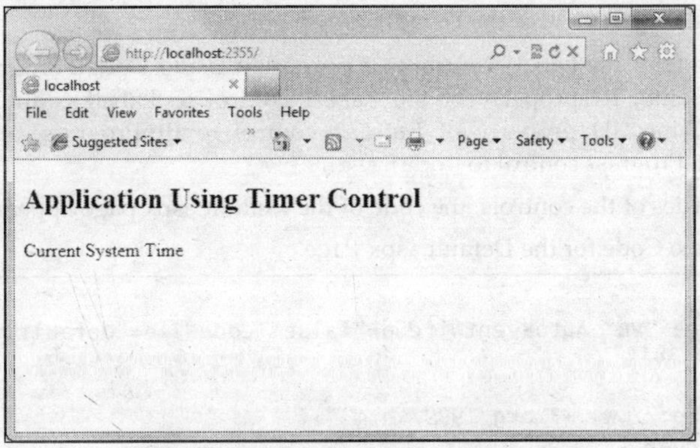

Figure 13.10: Displaying the Output

After a second, the Tick event is fired, the current system time appears, as shown in Figure 13.11:

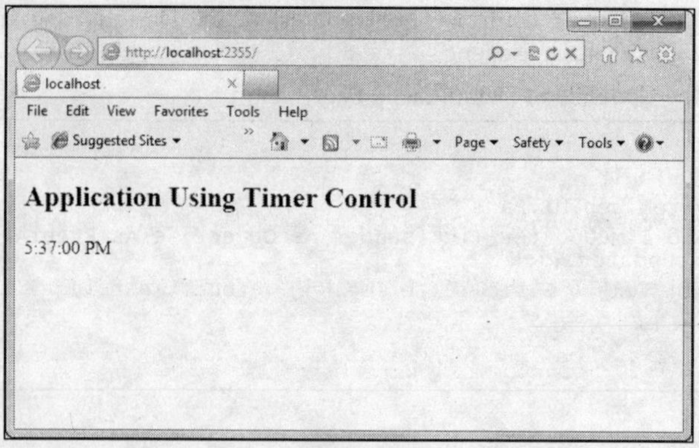

Figure 13.11: Displaying the Current Time

The UpdateProgress Control

One of the most important advantages of `AJAX` is that it updates the Web page content asynchronously. However, sometimes, this asynchronous updating creates a problem when the updating speed is very slow or data that needs to be updated is of large amount. In such a case, a user does not get any idea whether the request is being processed or not. To resolve this problem, you need to use the `UpdateProgress` control to show the status of request that is processed. You can use single `UpdateProgress` control either for single `UpdatePanel` control or for multiple `UpdatePanel` controls.

Using the UpdateProgress Control for Single UpdatePanel Control

Now, let's create an application named Updateprogress_single to use the `UpdateProgress` control for single `UpdatePanel` control. Perform the following steps to create the Updateprogress_single application:

1. Create an ASP.NET application and save it as Updateprogress_single. You can find the code for this application in the Updateprogress_single (for C#) and Updateprogress_singleVB(for VB) folder.
2. Drag and drop a ScriptManager control, updatePanel control, a Button control, and two Label controls from the Toolbox on the Design view of the Default.aspx page.
3. Set the Text property of the Label1 control to Application Using UpdateProgress Control, Label2 control to UpdateProgress Demo, ID property of the Label1 control to LabelHeading, ID property of the Label2 control to LabelDemo, ID property of Button1 control to BtnProgress, and AssociatedUpdatePanelID property of UpdateProgress control to `UpdatePanel1`.

After setting the properties of the controls, the code of the Default.aspx page appears, as shown in Listing 13.9:

Listing 13.9: Showing the Code for the Default.aspx Page

In VB

```
<%@ Page Language="VB" AutoEventWireup="false" CodeFile="Default.aspx.vb"
  Inherits="_Default" %>
<!DOCTYPE html>
<html xmlns="http://www.w3.org/1999/xhtml">
<head runat="server">
    <title></title>
</head>
<body>
    <form id="form1" runat="server">
    <div>
    <asp:ScriptManager ID="ScriptManager1" runat="server"></asp:ScriptManager>
        <asp:UpdatePanel ID="UpdatePanel1" runat="server">
        <ContentTemplate>
```

```
        <asp:UpdateProgress ID="UpdateProgress1" runat="server"
        AssociatedUpdatePanelID="UpdatePanel1">
                <ProgressTemplate>
                        <strong>
                                Updation is in progress
                        </strong>
                </ProgressTemplate>
        </asp:UpdateProgress>
        <h2>
        <asp:Label ID="LabelHeading" runat="server" Text="Application Using
        UpdateProgress Control"></asp:Label>
        </h2>
        <asp:Label ID="LabelDemo" runat="server" Text="UpdateProgress
        Demo"></asp:Label>
         
        <asp:Button ID="BtnProgress" runat="server" Text="Start Progress"
               />
        </ContentTemplate>
        </asp:UpdatePanel>
    </div>
    </form>
</body>
</html>
```

In C#

```
<%@ Page Language="C#" AutoEventWireup="true" CodeFile="Default.aspx.cs"
  Inherits="_Default" %>
<!DOCTYPE html>
<html xmlns="http://www.w3.org/1999/xhtml">
<head runat="server">
    <title></title>
</head>
<body>
    <form id="form1" runat="server">
    <div>
      <asp:ScriptManager ID="ScriptManager1" runat="server"></asp:ScriptManager>
        <asp:UpdatePanel ID="UpdatePanel1" runat="server">
        <ContentTemplate>
        <asp:UpdateProgress ID="UpdateProgress1" runat="server"
        AssociatedUpdatePanelID="UpdatePanel1">
                <ProgressTemplate>
                        <strong>
                                Updation is in progress
                        </strong>
                </ProgressTemplate>
        </asp:UpdateProgress>
        <h2>
        <asp:Label ID="LabelHeading" runat="server" Text="Application Using
        UpdateProgress Control"></asp:Label>
        </h2>
        <asp:Label ID="LabelDemo" runat="server" Text="UpdateProgress
        Demo"></asp:Label>
         
        <asp:Button ID="BtnProgress" runat="server" Text="Start Progress"
        OnClick="BtnProgress_Click" />
        </ContentTemplate>
        </asp:UpdatePanel>
```

```
      </div>
      </form>
    </body>
    </html>
```

4. Double-click the Button control(BtnProgress) and add the highlighted code, shown in Listing 13.10, in its Click event:

Listing 13.10: Showing the CodeFile of Default.aspx Page

In VB

```
Partial Class _Default
    Inherits System.Web.UI.Page
    Protected Sub BtnProgress_Click(sender As Object, e As EventArgs)
   Handles BtnProgress.Click
    System.Threading.Thread.Sleep(5000)
  LabelDemo.Text = "Demonstration on UpdateProgress Control taken place last time at " +
         System.DateTime.Now.ToLongTimeString
    End Sub
End Class
```

In C#

```
using System;
using System.Collections.Generic;
using System.Linq;
using System.Web;
using System.Web.UI;
using System.Web.UI.WebControls;
public partial class _Default : System.Web.UI.Page
{
    protected void Page_Load(object sender, EventArgs e)
    {
    }
    protected void BtnProgress_Click(object sender, EventArgs e)
    {
      System.Threading.Thread.Sleep(5000);
      LabelDemo.Text = "Demonstration on UpdateProgress control taken place last time at
         "+ System.DateTime.Now.ToLongTimeString();
    }
}
```

5. Press the F5 key to execute the application. The output of the application appears (Figure 13.12).
6. Click the Start Progress button (Figure 13.12).

The Updation is in progress message appears, as shown in Figure 13.12.

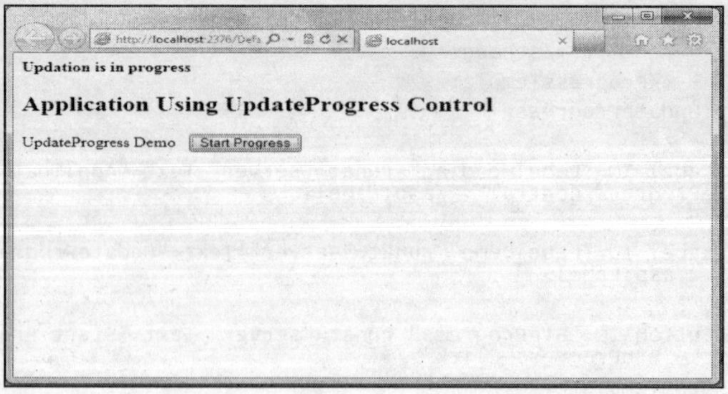

Figure 13.12: Displaying the Output of UpdateProgress Control

When the progress is finished, the system current date and time appears, as shown in Figure 13.13:

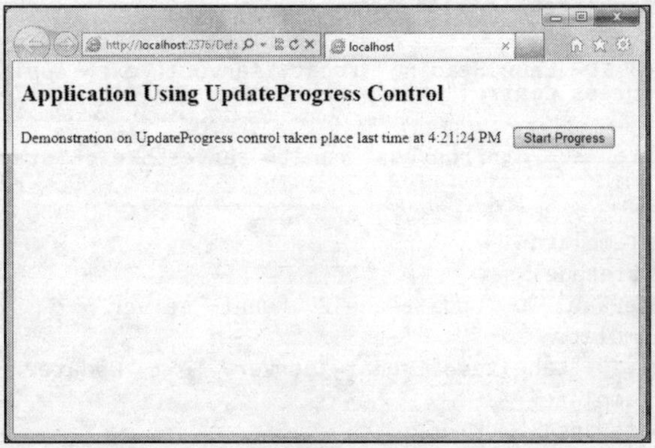

Figure 13.13: Displaying the Progress Finished Message

Using the UpdateProgress Control for Multiple UpdatePanel Controls

A single UpdateProgress control can also be used with multiple UpdatePanel controls. Now, let's create an application named Updateprogress_multiple to use the `UpdateProgress` control for multiple `UpdatePanel` controls. Perform the following steps to create the Updateprogress_multiple application:

1. Create an ASP.NET website and save it as Updateprogress_multiple. You can find the code for this application in the Updateprogress_multiple (for C#) and Updateprogress_multipleVB (for VB) folder.
2. Drag and drop a ScriptManager control, two UpdatePanel control, a Button control, and two Label controls from the Toolbox on the Design view of the Default.aspx page.
3. Set the Text property of the Label1 control to Application Using UpdateProgress Control, Label2 control to Label Demo, ID property of the Label1 control to LabelHeading, ID property of the Label2 control to LabelDemo, ID property of Button1 control to BtnProgress, Text property of Button1 control to Start Progress and AssociatedUpdatePanelID property of UpdateProgress control to `UpdatePanel1`.

After setting the properties of the controls, the code of the Default.aspx page appears, as shown in Listing 13.11:

Listing 13.11: Showing the Code for the Default.aspx Page

In VB

```
<%@ Page Language="VB" AutoEventWireup="false" CodeFile="Default.aspx.vb"
  Inherits="_Default" %>
<!DOCTYPE html>
<html xmlns="http://www.w3.org/1999/xhtml">
<head runat="server">
    <title></title>
</head>
<body>
    <form id="form1" runat="server">
    <div>
        <asp:ScriptManager ID="ScriptManager1" runat="server"></asp:ScriptManager>

        <asp:UpdateProgress ID="UpdateProgress1" runat="server"
        AssociatedUpdatePanelID="UpdatePanel1">
                <ProgressTemplate>
                        <strong>
                                Updation is in progress
                        </strong>
                </ProgressTemplate>
        </asp:UpdateProgress>
```

```
        <asp:UpdatePanel ID="UpdatePanel1" runat="server">
         <ContentTemplate>
        <h2>
         <asp:Label ID="LabelHeading" runat="server" Text="Application Using
         UpdateProgress Control"></asp:Label>
         </h2>
          <asp:Button ID="BtnProgress" runat="server" Text="Start Progress"
         />
          
         </ContentTemplate>
         </asp:UpdatePanel>
        <asp:UpdatePanel ID="UpdatePanel2" runat="server">
        <ContentTemplate>
        <asp:Label ID="LabelDemo" runat="server" Text="UpdateProgress Demo"></asp:Label>
        </ContentTemplate>
        </asp:UpdatePanel>
    </div>
    </form>
</body>
</html>
```

In C#

```
<%@ Page Language="C#" AutoEventWireup="true" CodeFile="Default.aspx.cs"
  Inherits="_Default" %>
<!DOCTYPE html>
<html xmlns="http://www.w3.org/1999/xhtml">
<head runat="server">
    <title></title>
</head>
<body>
    <form id="form1" runat="server">
    <div>
    <asp:ScriptManager ID="ScriptManager1" runat="server"></asp:ScriptManager>
         <asp:UpdateProgress ID="UpdateProgress1" runat="server"
         AssociatedUpdatePanelID="UpdatePanel1">
                <ProgressTemplate>
                        <strong>
                                Updation is in progress
                        </strong>
                </ProgressTemplate>
         </asp:UpdateProgress>
        <asp:UpdatePanel ID="UpdatePanel1" runat="server">
         <ContentTemplate>
        <h2>
         <asp:Label ID="LabelHeading" runat="server" Text="Application Using
         UpdateProgress Control"></asp:Label>
         </h2>
          <asp:Button ID="BtnProgress" runat="server" Text="Start Progress"
         onclick="BtnProgress_Click" />
          
         </ContentTemplate>
         </asp:UpdatePanel>
        <asp:UpdatePanel ID="UpdatePanel2" runat="server">
        <ContentTemplate>
        <asp:Label ID="LabelDemo" runat="server" Text="UpdateProgress Demo"></asp:Label>
        </ContentTemplate>
        </asp:UpdatePanel>
```

```
    </div>
    </form>
</body>
</html>
```

4. Double-click the Button control(BtnProgress) and add the highlighted code, shown in Listing 13.12, in its Click event:

Listing 13.12: Showing the CodeFile of Default.aspx Page

In VB

```
Partial Class _Default
    Inherits System.Web.UI.Page
    Protected Sub BtnProgress_Click(sender As Object, e As EventArgs)
   Handles BtnProgress.Click
      System.Threading.Thread.Sleep(5000)
      LabelDemo.Text = "Demonstration on UpdateProgress Control taken place last time at
         " + System.DateTime.Now.ToLongTimeString
    End Sub
End Class
```

In C#

```
using System;
using System.Collections.Generic;
using System.Linq;
using System.Web;
using System.Web.UI;
using System.Web.UI.WebControls;
public partial class _Default : System.Web.UI.Page
{
    protected void Page_Load(object sender, EventArgs e)
    {
    }
    protected void BtnProgress_Click(object sender, EventArgs e)
    {
      System.Threading.Thread.Sleep(5000);
      LabelDemo.Text = "Demonstration on UpdateProgress Control taken place last time at
         " + System.DateTime.Now.ToLongTimeString();
    }
}
```

5. Press the F5 key to execute the application. The output of the application appears (Figure 13.14).
6. Click the Start Progress button (Figure 13.14).The Updation is in progress message set in the UpdatePanel1 control appears, as shown in Figure 13.14:

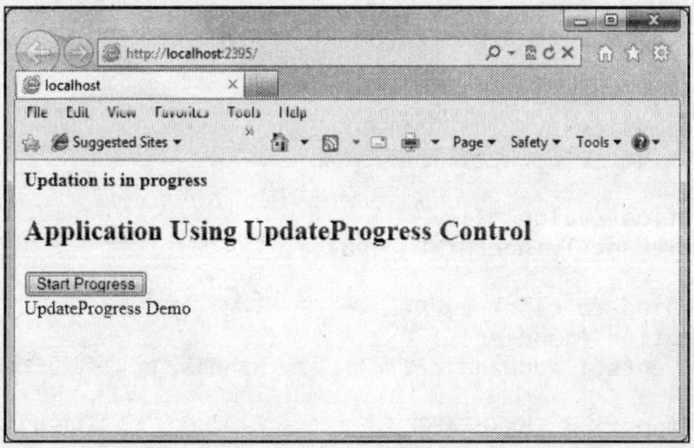

Figure 13.14: Displaying the Output of Multiple UpdatePanel Controls

When the progress is finished, the system current time appear, as shown in Figure 13.15:

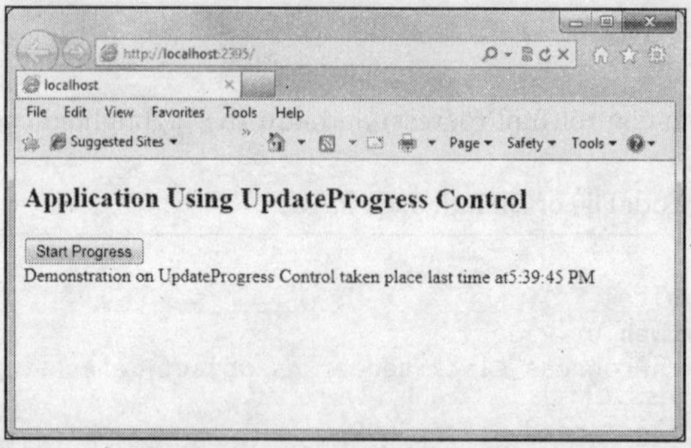

Figure 13.15: Displaying the Current Time of a System

Let's now learn how to customize AJAX controls.

Customizing AJAX Controls

As discussed, you can customize AJAX controls to add more functionality in your applications. Now, let's create an application named CustomizingAJAX to learn how to customize AJAX controls. Perform the following steps to create the CustomizingAJAX application:

1. Create an ASP.NET website and save it as CustomizingAJAX. You can find the code for this application in the CustomizingAJAX (for C#) and CustomizingAJAXVB(for VB) folder.
2. Add new `JavaScript` file to the website by right-clicking the website name in Solution Explorer and selecting the Add →New Item option. The Add New Item dialog box appears.
3. Select the `JavaScript` File (JScript.js) template from the Add New Item dialog box.
4. Click the Add button.
5. Add the code, shown in Listing 13.13, in the JavaScript file(JScript.js):

Listing 13.13: Showing the Code for the JScript.js File

In VB

```
Type.registerNamespace("CustomAJAXControl");
// Constructor
CustomAJAXControl.CustomButton = function (element) {
    CustomAJAXControl.CustomButton.initializeBase(this, [element]);
    this._clickDelegate = null;
    this._driftDelegate = null;
    this._undriftDelegate = null;
}
CustomAJAXControl.CustomButton.prototype =
{
    // text property accessors.
    get_text: function () {
        return this.get_element().innerHTML;
    },
    set_text: function (value) {
        this.get_element().innerHTML = value;
    },
    // Bind and unbind to click event.
    add_click: function (handler) {
        this.get_events().addHandler('click', handler);
    },
    remove_click: function (handler) {
        this.get_events().removeHandler('click', handler);
    },
```

```
    // Bind and unbind to drift event.
    add_drift: function (handler) {
        this.get_events().addHandler('drift', handler);
    },
    remove_drift: function (handler) {
        this.get_events().removeHandler('drift', handler);
    },
    // Bind and unbind to undrift event.
    add_undrift: function (handler) {
        this.get_events().addHandler('undrift', handler);
    },
    remove_undrift: function (handler) {
        this.get_events().removeHandler('undrift', handler);
    },
    // Release resources before control is disposed.
    dispose: function () {
        var element = this.get_element();
        if (this._clickDelegate) {
            Sys.UI.DomEvent.removeHandler(element, 'click', this._clickDelegate);
            delete this._clickDelegate;
        }
        if (this._driftDelegate) {
            Sys.UI.DomEvent.removeHandler(element, 'focus', this._driftDelegate);
            Sys.UI.DomEvent.removeHandler(element, 'mouseover', this._driftDelegate);
            delete this._driftDelegate;
        }
        if (this._undriftDelegate) {
            Sys.UI.DomEvent.removeHandler(element, 'blur', this._undriftDelegate);
            Sys.UI.DomEvent.removeHandler(element, 'mouseout',
                this._undriftDelegate);
            delete this._undriftDelegate;
        }
        CustomAJAXControl.CustomButton.callBaseMethod(this, 'dispose');
    },
    initialize: function () {
        var element = this.get_element();
        if (!element.tabIndex) element.tabIndex = 0;
        if (this._clickDelegate === null)
        {
            this._clickDelegate = Function.createDelegate(this, this._clickHandler);
        }
        Sys.UI.DomEvent.addHandler(element, 'click', this._clickDelegate);
        if (this._driftDelegate === null)
         {
            this._driftDelegate = Function.createDelegate(this, this._driftHandler);
        }
        Sys.UI.DomEvent.addHandler(element, 'mouseover', this._driftDelegate);
        Sys.UI.DomEvent.addHandler(element, 'focus', this._driftDelegate);
        if (this._undriftDelegate === null)
        {
            this._undriftDelegate = Function.createDelegate(this,
                this._undriftHandler);
        }
        Sys.UI.DomEvent.addHandler(element, 'mouseout', this._undriftDelegate);
        Sys.UI.DomEvent.addHandler(element, 'blur', this._undriftDelegate);
        CustomAJAXControl.CustomButton.callBaseMethod(this, 'initialize');
    },
    _clickHandler: function (event) {
        var h = this.get_events().getHandler('click');
        if (h) h(this, Sys.EventArgs.Empty);
    },
    _driftHandler: function (event) {
```

```
        var h = this.get_events().getHandler('drift');
        if (h) h(this, Sys.EventArgs.Empty);
    },
    _undriftHandler: function (event) {
        var h = this.get_events().getHandler('undrift');
        if (h) h(this, Sys.EventArgs.Empty);
    }
}
CustomAJAXControl.CustomButton.registerClass('CustomAJAXControl.CustomButton',Sys.UI.Con
  tr ol);
if (typeof (Sys) !== 'undefined') Sys.Application.notifyScriptLoaded();
```

In C#

```
Type.registerNamespace("CustomAJAXControl");
// Constructor
CustomAJAXControl.CustomButton = function (element) {
    CustomAJAXControl.CustomButton.initializeBase(this, [element]);
    this._clickDelegate = null;
    this._driftDelegate = null;
    this._undriftDelegate = null;
}
CustomAJAXControl.CustomButton.prototype =
{
    // text property accessors.
    get_text: function () {
        return this.get_element().innerHTML;
    },
    set_text: function (value) {
        this.get_element().innerHTML = value;
    },
    // Bind and unbind to click event.
    add_click: function (handler) {
        this.get_events().addHandler('click', handler);
    },
    remove_click: function (handler) {
        this.get_events().removeHandler('click', handler);
    },
    // Bind and unbind to drift event.
    add_drift: function (handler) {
        this.get_events().addHandler('drift', handler);
    },
    remove_drift: function (handler) {
        this.get_events().removeHandler('drift', handler);
    },
    // Bind and unbind to undrift event.
    add_undrift: function (handler) {
        this.get_events().addHandler('undrift', handler);
    },
    remove_undrift: function (handler) {
        this.get_events().removeHandler('undrift', handler);
    },
    // Release resources before control is disposed.
    dispose: function () {
        var element = this.get_element();
        if (this._clickDelegate) {
            Sys.UI.DomEvent.removeHandler(element, 'click', this._clickDelegate);
            delete this._clickDelegate;
        }
        if (this._driftDelegate) {
            Sys.UI.DomEvent.removeHandler(element, 'focus', this._driftDelegate);
            Sys.UI.DomEvent.removeHandler(element, 'mouseover', this._driftDelegate);
```

```
            delete this._driftDelegate;
        }
        if (this._undriftDelegate) {
            Sys.UI.DomEvent.removeHandler(element, 'blur', this._undriftDelegate);
            Sys.UI.DomEvent.removeHandler(element, 'mouseout',
                this._undriftDelegate);
            delete this._undriftDelegate;
        }
        CustomAJAXControl.CustomButton.callBaseMethod(this, 'dispose');
    },
    initialize: function () {
        var element = this.get_element();
        if (!element.tabIndex) element.tabIndex = 0;
        if (this._clickDelegate === null)
        {
            this._clickDelegate = Function.createDelegate(this, this._clickHandler);
        }
        Sys.UI.DomEvent.addHandler(element, 'click', this._clickDelegate);
        if (this._driftDelegate === null)
         {
            this._driftDelegate = Function.createDelegate(this, this._driftHandler);
        }
        Sys.UI.DomEvent.addHandler(element, 'mouseover', this._driftDelegate);
        Sys.UI.DomEvent.addHandler(element, 'focus', this._driftDelegate);
        if (this._undriftDelegate === null)
        {
            this._undriftDelegate = Function.createDelegate(this,
                this._undriftHandler);
        }
        Sys.UI.DomEvent.addHandler(element, 'mouseout', this._undriftDelegate);
        Sys.UI.DomEvent.addHandler(element, 'blur', this._undriftDelegate);
        CustomAJAXControl.CustomButton.callBaseMethod(this, 'initialize');
    },
    _clickHandler: function (event) {
        var h = this.get_events().getHandler('click');
        if (h) h(this, Sys.EventArgs.Empty);
    },
    _driftHandler: function (event) {
        var h = this.get_events().getHandler('drift');
        if (h) h(this, Sys.EventArgs.Empty);
    },
    _undriftHandler: function (event) {
        var h = this.get_events().getHandler('undrift');
        if (h) h(this, Sys.EventArgs.Empty);
    }
}
CustomAJAXControl.CustomButton.registerClass('CustomAJAXControl.CustomButton',Sys.UI.Con
  tr ol);
if (typeof (Sys) !== 'undefined') Sys.Application.notifyScriptLoaded();
```

5. Add the highlighted code, shown in Listing 13.14, in the Source view of the Default.aspx page:

Listing 13.14: Showing the Code for the Default.aspx Page

In VB

```
<%@ Page Language="VB" AutoEventWireup="false" CodeFile="Default.aspx.vb"
  Inherits="_Default" %>
<!DOCTYPE html>
<html xmlns="http://www.w3.org/1999/xhtml">
<head runat="server">
  <title></title>
</head>
<body>
```

```
        <form id="form1" runat="server">
        <div>
        <asp:ScriptManager runat="server" ID="ScriptManager01">
        <scripts>
              <asp:ScriptReference Path="~/JScript.js" />
        </scripts>
        </asp:ScriptManager>
              <br />
              <br />
              <br />
              <span style="text-decoration: underline">
                      <em>
                      <strong>
                      Click the button to see its working
                      <br />
                      </strong>
                      </em>
              </span>
              <br />
              <script type="text/javascript">
                  var app = Sys.Application;
                  app.add_load(apploadhand);
                  function apploadhand(send, argument) {
                  $create(CustomAJAXControl.CustomButton, { text: 'Custom
                      Controlfunction for movement of Mouse', element: { style: {
                      fontWeight: bold", borderWidth: "2px"
                      }
                      }
                      }, { click: start, drift: mousehovermovement, undrift:
                              mouseunhovermovement }, null, $get('Button1'));
                      }
                      function mousehovermovement(send, argument) {
                              messageonmousemovement = "State of Mouse is over the button"
                              $get('CustomLabel').innerHTML = messageonmousemovement;
                      }
                      function mouseunhovermovement(send, argument) {
                      $get('CustomLabel').innerHTML = "State of Mouse is out of the button";
                      }
                      function start(send, argument) {
                      $get('CustomLabel').innerHTML = "Handling the click event of the
                      Button";
                      }
              </script>
              <button type="button" id="Button1">
              </button>
               <br /><br /><br />
              <div id="CustomLabel">
              </div>
          </div>
          </form>
</body>
</html>
```

In C#

```
<%@ Page Language="C#" AutoEventWireup="true" CodeFile="Default.aspx.cs"
  Inherits="_Default" %>
<!DOCTYPE html>
<html xmlns="http://www.w3.org/1999/xhtml">
<head runat="server">
    <title></title>
</head>
<body>
```

```
<form id="form1" runat="server">
<div>
<asp:ScriptManager runat="server" ID="ScriptManager01">
                <scripts>
                        <asp:ScriptReference Path="~/JScript.js" />
                </scripts>
            </asp:ScriptManager>
            <br />
            <br />
            <br />
            <span style="text-decoration: underline">
            <em>
            <strong>
              Click the button to see its working
            <br />
            </strong>
            </em>
            </span>
            <br />
            <script type="text/javascript">
            var app = Sys.Application;
            app.add_load(apploadhand);
            function apploadhand(send, argument)
            {
            $create(CustomAJAXControl.CustomButton, {text: 'Custom
            Controlfunction for movement of Mouse',element: {style:{fontWeight:
            "bold", borderWidth: "2px"}}}, {click: start,drift:mousehovermovement,
            undrift: mouseunhovermovement},null,$get('Button1'));
            }
            function mousehovermovement(send,argument) {
                messageonmousemovement = "State of Mouse is over the button"
                $get('CustomLabel').innerHTML = messageonmousemovement;
                    }
            function mouseunhovermovement(send,argument) {
            $get('CustomLabel').innerHTML = "State of Mouse is out of the button";
            }
            function start(send, argument)
            {
             $get('CustomLabel').innerHTML ="Handling the click event of the
            Button";
            }
        </script>
        <button type="button" id="Button1">
        </button>
         <br /><br /><br />
        <div id="CustomLabel">
        </div>
    </div>
    </form>
</body>
</html>
```

6. Press the F5 key to execute the application.The output of the application appears (Figure 13.16).
7. Move the mouse over the Custom Controlfunction for movement of Mouse button, the message, State of Mouse is over the button, appears on the Web page, as shown in Figure 13.16:

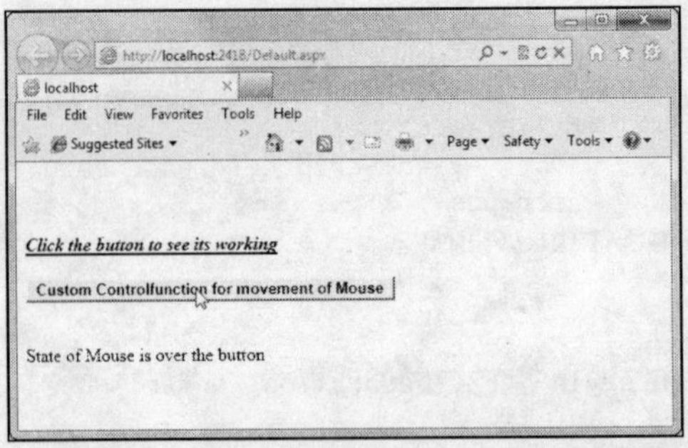

Figure 13.16:Displaying the Mouseover State

8. Click the Custom Controlfunction for movement of Mouse button (Figure 13.17).The message, Handling the click event of the Button, appears on the Web page, as shown in Figure 13.17:

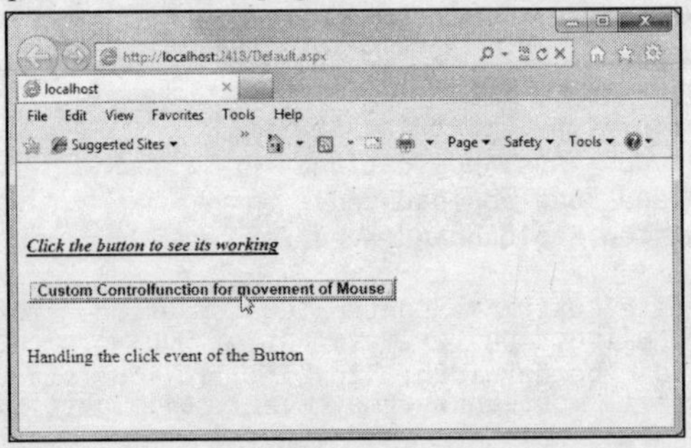

Figure 13.17:Handling the Click Event of the Mouse

9. Remove the mouse from the Custom Controlfunction for movement of Mouse button (Figure 13.18).The message, State of Mouse is out of the button, appears on the Web page, as shown in Figure 13.18:

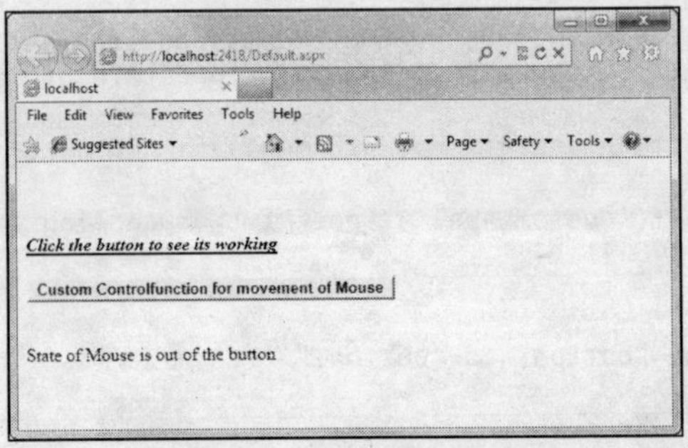

Figure 13.18: Displaying the Mouseout State

Summary

In this chapter, you have learned about `AJAX, which` calls a server asynchronously and updates a portion of your Web page without refreshing the entire page. The chapter has also discussed the need of implementing AJAX in your applications. You have understood the difference between AJAX and other technologies. Next, you have learned about the new features of AJAX and Microsoft AJAX library. You have also learned about the AJAX architecture, which is based on client-side and server-side architectures. Finally, you have learned about AJAX server controls.

In the next chapter, you learn about Inside Master Pages and Themes.

14

Inside Master Pages and Themes

In Depth

Earlier each page of a website had a different style applied to it, which made it difficult for the developers to provide a consistent look throughout the website. Therefore, the Web developers resorted to different techniques, such as a template driven solution, to provide a common style to all pages of a website. The developers also started using user controls and adding them in the Web pages to provide a user interface in a very standardized way. Implementing this technique made the developers to reuse the existing design and code. However, managing and updating a website was still an issue. In an attempt to provide a consistent layout to a website, the Web designers used to take a help of third party software solutions, such as Dreamweaver. However, it was not only very tedious but also time consuming task to use Dreamweaver to design Web pages.

Therefore, the concept of master pages and themes were introduced in ASP.NET 2.0 to remove the deficiencies of copying and pasting the same code in all the Web pages, which were being faced by the Web developers. In other words, a master page is not only used to incorporate visual inheritance in Web applications, but also to define the layout of a Web page. When you create a master page, what you actually do is create a sample layout, which in turn is derived by all the pages of a website. A master page provides a feature of standardized user interface which is common to all pages. Therefore, all pages in the Web application inherit the master page to maintain consistency in the Web application.

In addition to master pages, there is another concept included in ASP.NET, which is known as themes. A theme is a collection of property settings that defines the same appearance of controls and Web pages across the entire website. Themes are applied across all the pages in a Web application to maintain a consistent appearance.

In this chapter, you learn about the need of master pages and themes in a website. Next, you learn about the master pages and their types. In addition, you learn about ASP.NET AJAX master pages. Finally, you learn about themes in ASP.NET 4.5, which includes the types of themes and an attribute for applying a theme to every Web page.

Let's first learn about the need of master pages and themes in a website (or Web application).

Need for Master Pages and Themes

When you create a website, you need to define user interface of the website, which includes selecting a set of colors, layout, design, font, styles, menus, and images for the website. While creating a Web page that contains some common elements, such as buttons, text boxes, and labels, you need to customize the properties of different controls. You can design common layout and customize properties of different controls by using master pages and themes in your Web application.

In ASP.NET a master page defines a common structure and standardized layout of a website. It helps you in building a standard layout for all the Web pages. A master page contains markups and controls that you can share across different Web pages of your website. The functionality of master pages improves the maintainability of ASP.NET websites and avoids the duplication of code. Let's consider a scenario to understand the need of master pages. Suppose, you want to create a website in which you want to include header, footer, banners, and navigation menus. If you are not using ASP.NET master page, then you need to define the website layout as well as text and control elements in each and every page of the website. Along with this, you need to copy and paste the code for sharing the same layout in every page which obviously is a tedious and time consuming process. This might also affect the appearance of the Web page and also every page may require editing. Another drawback of not using master pages is that in case, you want to modify the banner or header of the site; you need to make the modifications in each page manually.

Therefore, to maintain consistency and manageability in your website, this is not the correct approach. However, if you are using a master page for your website, you only need to make the modifications in the master page and all the Web pages that inherit the content of master page are automatically modified. It means no overhead of copying and pasting the code in different pages is required.

In the same manner, themes can be used with master pages to define style of the website globally and implement the same style across the website. Themes are needed when you want to keep the style and layout information files separate from other website files. Themes can also include images and skin files that set the visual properties of ASP.NET controls.

Understanding Master Pages

Master pages enable the template-based development of a website. An ASP.NET master page defines the overall layout of a Web application and all the pages are derived from this master page. A master page can contain markups, controls, banners, navigation menus, and other elements that you want to include in all the pages of your website. It is an ASP.NET file, having .master as its extension. It includes standard and HyperText Markup Language (HTML) controls. You can define a master page by specifying the @ Master directive at the top of a Web page, as shown in the following code snippet:

In VB

```
<%@ Master Language="VB" CodeFile="MasterPage.master.vb" Inherits="MasterPage">
```

In C#

```
<%@ Master Language="C#" CodeFile="MasterPage.master.cs" Inherits="MasterPage">
```

The @ Master directive is similar to the @ Page directive in a Web form (.aspx). This directive states that it belongs to a master page file and its properties, such as banner, header, footer, and menus are inherited by the content pages. By default, a master page contains a single `ContentPlaceHolder` control which adds dynamic content to a Web page. However, you can add multiple ContentPlaceHolder controls in a master page. The syntax to add the `ContentPlaceHolder` control in a Web page is given as follows (common for VB and C#):

```
<asp: ContentPlaceHolder ID="head" runat="server">
```

As you see, the only difference between a simple Web page and a master page in terms of code is that the master page contains an empty `ContentPlaceHolder` control.

The `MasterPageFile` attribute of the @ `Page` directive helps in binding a master page file with the content page of a website, so that the content and elements of the master page are included in the content page. The syntax to refer a master page file is as follows:

```
<%@ Page Language="C#" MasterPageFile="~/MasterPage.master" Title="Content
   Page"%>
```

The following are the key functions of a master page:

- Defining common properties of a website, such as header, footer, banners, navigation menus, and other elements that can be accessed by the content pages
- Allowing single or multiple content pages to access single or multiple master pages
- Displaying the content of each content page in the content placeholder of the master pages

In other words, to create a master page for a website, you need to identify the controls that you want to display on all the pages and then add these controls to the master page. Next, you need to add the `ContentPlaceHolder` control for the master page to place the content of the Web pages. When you view the final Web page, the content page and the master page are combined.

In ASP.NET, master pages are of the following two types:

- Simple master page
- Nested master page

Let's discuss these in detail.

Simple Master Page

A simple master page lets you simplify your website design by creating master pages and the content pages. It helps in designing a website with no overhead of copying and pasting the code in different pages. The combination of simple master page and content page makes a final page. The functionality of simple master page is to define a common layout for all pages of a website and use it again and again. By creating a simple master page, you can preserve so many hours of time and easily maintain a website from a single place. The concept of simple master and content pages can be better visualized with the help of Figure 14.1:

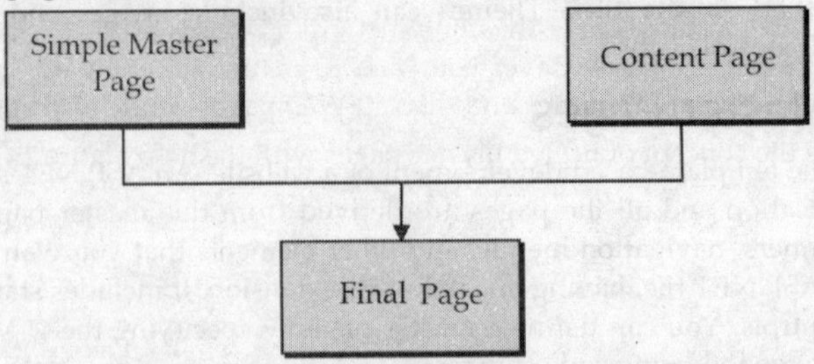

Figure 14.1: Displaying the Block Diagram of a Final Page

As you can see in Figure 14.1, the simple master and content pages are combined together to generate a single page that inherits properties from both the pages.

Nested Master Page

There can be instances when one master page references another master page, which is known as nested master page. In other words, a nested master page implies that a master page can be included inside another master page. The master page which contains a master page is known as parent master and the containing master page is known as child master. The concept of nested master page is very much similar to simple master page; therefore, a nested master page should be used when you want to create a hierarchy of templates for your Web application.

You can create a parent master by using the following syntax:

In VB

```
<%@ Master Language="VB" AutoEventWireup="true" CodeFile="Parent.master.vb"
    Inherits="Parent" %>
```

In C#

```
<%@ Master Language="C#" AutoEventWireup="true" CodeFile="Parent.master.cs"
    Inherits="Parent" %>
```

The syntax to create a child master is as follows:

In VB

```
<%@ Master Language="VB" MasterPageFile="~/Parent.master" AutoEventWireup="true"
    CodeFile="Child.master.vb" Inherits="Child" %>
```

In C#

```
<%@ Master Language="C#" MasterPageFile="~/Parent.master" AutoEventWireup="true"
    CodeFile="Child.master.cs" Inherits="Child" %>
```

Let's take an example to understand the concept of nested master pages. Consider a situation in which you have been asked to design a website for a company, which consists of three departments: Human Resource, Marketing, and Finance. The main page of the website consists of a header with the company logo and footer. When employees access the website, the home page appears. In the home page, the employees need to login to access the page of their particular department. You need to design a different interface for every department, which also includes the header and footer displayed on the main page.

In such situation, you can define a parent master and design a structure of main page including a header with company logo and footer. Furthermore, you can create three child master or sub master pages to lay down the different interface for each and every department. Each child master page would inherit the parent master structure (main page). Along with this, the sub master page also defines its own content in the `ContentPlaceHolder` control to display the content of its content pages. The content page of child master map with the parent master and finally makes a nested master page. Therefore, after creating the website, each department would get a different interface. An employee, after logging in, can observe the common parent master page combined with child master page for different departments.

In other words, a nested master page is the combination of a parent master page and child master page. The advantage of this technique is that whenever you want to change the company logo or design of header of your website, you need to modify parent master and then all Web pages would also get reflected with those changes.

You can best visualize the concept of nested master pages with the help Figure 14.2:

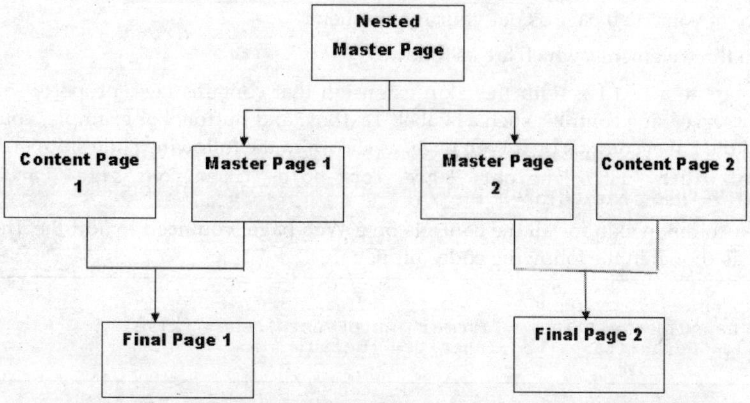

Figure 14.2: Displaying the Block Diagram of a Nested Master Page

An application can have a number of master pages depending on the level of hierarchy it incorporates.

In short, master pages help you in creating, maintaining, and modifying a website easily. If you further have a requirement of making changes, the changes can easily be done in a single master page, which make appropriate changes in the appearance of all the Web pages. You can also personalize your website by adding the features of a master page and theme.

Understanding ASP.NET AJAX Master Pages

In ASP.NET, you can use the AJAX technology, which improves a website's appeal and usability, to make your Web applications more interactive. The main functionality of AJAX-enabled Web page is that whenever a postback occurs, it enables partial rendering of a page. Otherwise, in normal ASP.NET Web pages, the whole page is refreshed.

If you want to create an AJAX-enabled website, you need to add the ScriptManager control on a Web page. This control is used to manage the ASP.NET AJAX script libraries and script files, partial-page rendering, and client proxy class generation for Web and application services. It enables you to build rich client applications quickly and easily.

NOTE

ASP.NET AJAX and its controls have already been discussed in Chapter 13: Developing ASP.NET AJAX Applications of the book.

You can implement the AJAX technology in your website by adding the ScriptManager control in the master page. The master page having the AJAX technology is known as AJAX master page. The controls in AJAX master page are added before the server side controls and `ContentPlaceHolder` control in a Web page.

Understanding Themes

As already discussed, master pages in ASP.NET allow you to build a standard layout and common structure for all the pages in your Web application. Themes, in ASP.NET, enable you to define the style properties and change the appearance of a Web page. They not only help in providing a user-friendly interface, but also help in providing a similar overall look to all the pages of a website. Therefore, themes can be defined as a collection of elements to define the style properties and provide a uniform and consistent look to your Web page.

- The key functions of themes are as follows:
- Providing flexibility to easily change the appearance of all Web pages just by making changes in few template files with minimum possible efforts
- Providing various options to customize a Web page. For example, in the Orkut website, you can change the appearance of your Web page as per your requirement.

Themes contain three elements, which are as follows:

- **Skin**— Refers to a text file with the .skin extension that contains tags, property settings, and formatting options for server side controls, such as Label, TextBox, and Button. For example, you can define a common skin for all the Label controls on a Web page, as shown in the following code snippet:

```
<asp:label width="350px" height="50px" font-bold="True" font-size="Large"
   forecolor="Red" backcolor="Blue"/>
```

After defining a common skin for all the controls on a Web page, you need to add the Theme attribute in the @ Page directive, as shown in the following code snippet:

In VB

```
<%@ Page Language="VB" Theme="Theme1" AutoEventWireup="false"
   CodeFile="Default.aspx.vb" Inherits="_Default" %>
```

In C#

```
<%@ Page Language="C#" Theme="Theme1" AutoEventWireup="true"
   CodeFile="Default.aspx.cs" Inherits="_Default" %>
```

Skins are divided into the following two groups:

- **Default**—Refers to the default skin that is applied automatically to all the controls of same type present on a Web page, when a theme is applied to the page. The SkinID attribute is used to determine whether the skin applied to a control on a Web page is a default skin or not. A skin is a default skin, if it does not have the SkinID attribute.
- **Named**—Refers to a customized skin that is applied to controls when a theme is applied to a Web page. The named skin has the SkinID property which allows you to set the different skins for the different controls contained in skin file.

NOTE

You can have multiple skins as a part of theme in a subfolder of the App_Themes folder in your website, about which you learn in the Immediate Solutions section of the chapter.

- **CSS**— Refers to the mechanism of adding fonts, colors, styles, and behavior to Web pages. Using CSS, you can apply formatting on different controls and create rich designs for HTML elements and Web server controls. It enables you to extend reusability and maintain consistency of a Web page. You can change the overall appearance of a website by making minor changes on the themes.

  CSS is used to provide the visual inheritance to all the Web pages in the website. It is an ASP.NET file with the .css extension and applies a style sheet as a part of theme in a Web page. You need to store the CSS file inside the subfolder of the App_Themes folder to use the CSS features, such as customizing and formatting the Standard as well as HTML controls.

NOTE

You can have multiple CSS as a part of theme in a subfolder of App_Themes folder in your website.

You can apply a CSS style sheet in your Web page by specifying the `link` attribute in the Web page, as shown in the following code snippet:

```
<link rel="stylesheet" type="text/css" href="Path of style sheet file">
```

- **Images** – Helps in making a Web page more interactive and user friendly.

Figure 14.3 displays the various elements included in themes:

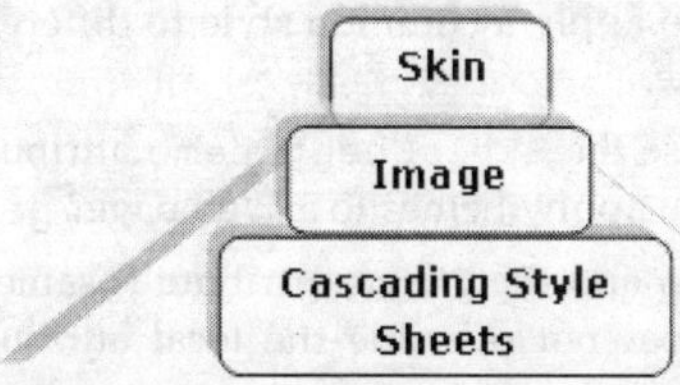

Figure 14.3: Exhibiting the Elements of ASP.NET 4.5 Themes

In addition to skins and CSS, themes can also include other resource files, such as script files or sound files, which can be used as style properties for the Web pages. These files are also placed inside the subfolder of the `App_Themes` folder in your website. If the resource file is stored outside the `App_Themes` folder, it can be accessed by using the tilde (~) symbol. For instance, to use the img1.jpg image which is saved in the Image folder located outside `App_Themes`, you need to use the following syntax:

```
<asp:Image ID="btn1" runat="server" ImageUrl=~/Image/img1.jpg />
```

Let's now learn about the types of themes in ASP.NET 4.5 and the StyleSheetTheme Attribute.

Exploring Types of Themes in ASP.NET 4.5

In ASP.NET 4.5, there are two types of themes, page and global. A page theme contains the control skins, style sheets, graphic files, and other resources stored inside the subfolder of the `App_Themes` folder. This theme is applied to a single page of a website. You need to create separate subfolders in the `App_Themes` folder for different themes. A page theme can be applied on a Web page by using the Theme attribute in the @ Page directive.

The syntax to apply a theme using the Theme attribute is as follows:

In VB

```
<%@ Page Language="VB" AutoEventWireup="false" CodeFile="Default.aspx.vb"
    Inherits="_Default" Theme="MyTheme" %>
```

In C#

```
<%@ Page Language="C#" AutoEventWireup="true" CodeFile="Default.aspx.cs"
    Inherits="_Default" Theme="MyTheme" %>
```

A global theme, on the other hand, is a theme that is applied to all the websites on a Web server and includes property settings, style sheets settings, and graphics. This theme allows you to maintain all the websites on the same Web server and define the same style for all the Web pages of all the websites. Similar to the page theme, it is also stored inside the subfolder of `App_Themes` and can be accessed anytime.

To apply themes throughout a website, you need to add the following code snippet in the <system.web> section of the Web.config file:

```
<configuration>
    <system.web>
        <pages theme ="MyTheme" />
  </system.web>
</configuration>
```

Or

```
<configuration>
    <system.web>
        <pages  styleSheetTheme ="MyTheme" />
  </system.web>
</configuration>
```

Understanding the StyleSheetTheme Attribute

The `StyleSheetTheme` attribute is an attribute of the @ Page directive that you can use to apply themes to a Web page. This attribute can be used to apply a common style to different pages of a website and maintain the consistency in appearance of the website.

Now, the question arises why do we use the `StyleSheetTheme` attribute instead of using the `Theme` attribute when the `Theme` attribute is also used to apply themes to a Web page?

The working of the `StyleSheetTheme` and the `Theme` attribute is same. However, the advantage of using the StyleSheetTheme attribute is that it does not override the local attributes of the controls with the attributes defined in a theme.

However, if you use both the attributes in a Web page, then they are used in the following order:

1. First, the properties of StyleSheetTheme attribute are applied to a Web page
2. Next, the properties of controls are applied, which implies that the Theme property overrides the StyleSheetTheme attributes
3. Finally, the Theme property is applied, which overrides both the Control properties and StyleSheetTheme properties. This means that the Theme attribute has higher precedence over the StyleSheetTheme attribute and Control properties.

Now, let's learn how to use master pages and themes in the *Immediate Solutions* section.

Immediate Solutions

Creating Master Pages

As already mentioned, the need for creating master pages arises when you want to incorporate a common look and feel across all the pages of a website. By creating a master page, you actually create a template that is applied to all the content pages of the Web application. A master page has a .master extension, while a content page has the .aspx extension.

Master pages in ASP.NET are of two types: simple and nested. In case of simple master pages, when a user requests for a Web page, the content page is displayed with the properties inherited from a simple master page. To create simple master pages, you need to create a master page and then a content page that inherits the properties of the master page. However, nested master pages are slightly different. They are created not only with a master page and content page(s), but also with child master pages. The child master page inherits properties of the master pages and content pages inherit properties of the child master pages. To create nested master pages, you need to create master pages, child master pages, and content pages that inherit the properties of both master and child master pages.

Creating Simple Master Pages

Now, let's create a Web application, MyOrganizationVB (MyOrganizationVB in VB and MyOrganizationCS in C#), which shows how to create a master page and a content page that inherits the created master page.

NOTE

The applications in this chapter are created by selecting the ASP.NET Empty Web Site template in the New Web Site dialog box. After creating the application, you need to add a Default.aspx file.

After creating the Web application, perform the following steps:

1. Right-click the Web application name in Solution Explorer and Select the Add→ Add New Item option from the context menu. The Add New item dialog box appears (Figure 14.4).
2. Select the Master Page template from the middle pane of the Add New Item dialog box and click the Add button, as shown in Figure 14.4:

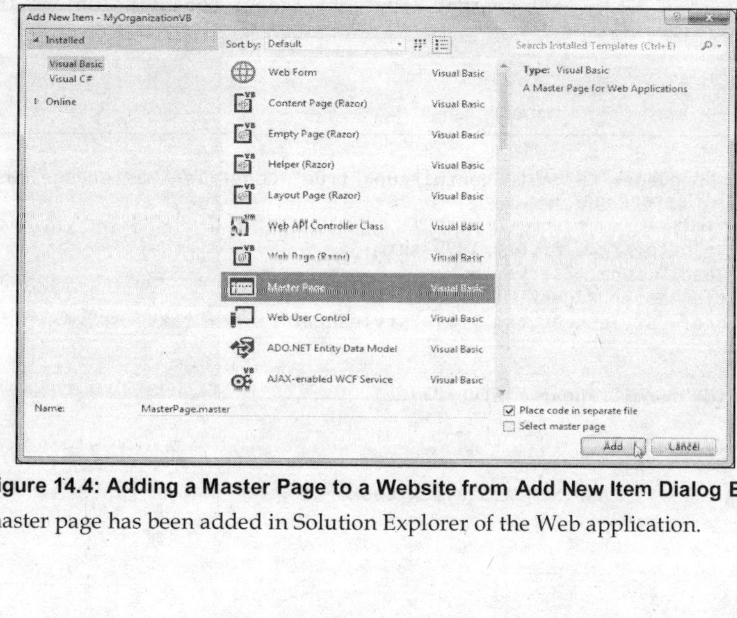

Figure 14.4: Adding a Master Page to a Website from Add New Item Dialog Box

The MasterPage.master page has been added in Solution Explorer of the Web application.

3. Add the code, shown in Listing 14.1, to the MasterPage.master page:

Listing 14.1: Showing the Code of the `MasterPage.master` Page

In VB

```
<%@ Master Language="VB" AutoEventWireup="false" CodeFile="MasterPage.master.vb"
  Inherits="MasterPage" %>
<!DOCTYPE html>
<html xmlns="http://www.w3.org/1999/xhtml">
<head runat="server">
      <title>Master Page</title>
    <link href="StyleSheet.css" rel="stylesheet" type="text/css" />
</head>
<body>
    <form id="form1" runat="server">
    <div>
    <div id="header">
                <h1>
                    ASP.NET 4.5 Black Book
                </h1>
            </div>
            <div id="sidebar">
                <div id="nav">
                     
                </div>
            </div>
            <div id="content">
                <div class ="itemContent">
                   <strong><em>My Organization Web Site<br />
                 <asp:Image ID="Image1" runat="server"
                 ImageUrl="~/images_organisation.jpg" />
                 <br />
                 </em></strong>
                 <br /></div>
        <asp:ContentPlaceHolder id="ContentPlaceHolder1" runat="server">
        </asp:ContentPlaceHolder>
        </div>
     <div id="footer">
                    <p class="left">
                        All content copyright &copy; Kogent Solutions Inc.</p>
    </div></div>
    </form>
</body>
</html>
```

In C#

```
<%@ Master Language="C#" AutoEventWireup="true" CodeFile="MasterPage.master.cs"
  Inherits="MasterPage" %>
<!DOCTYPE html>
<html xmlns="http://www.w3.org/1999/xhtml">
<head id="Head1" runat="server">
      <title>Master Page</title>
    <link href="StyleSheet.css" rel="stylesheet" type="text/css" />
</head>
<body>
    <form id="form1" runat="server">
    <div>
    <div id="header">
                <h1>
                    ASP.NET 4.5 Black Book
                </h1>
```

```
            </div>
            <div id="sidebar">
                <div id="nav">
                     
                </div>
            </div>
            <div id="content">
                <div class ="itemContent">
                   <strong><em>My Organization Web Site<br />
                 <asp:Image ID="Image1" runat="server"
                 ImageUrl="~/images_organisation.jpg" />
                 <br />
                 </em></strong>
                 <br /></div>
        <asp:ContentPlaceHolder id="ContentPlaceHolder1" runat="server">
        </asp:ContentPlaceHolder>
        </div>
     <div id="footer">
                     <p class="left">
                         All content copyright &copy; Kogent Solutions Inc.</p>
    </div></div>
    </form>
</body>
</html>
```

In Listing 14.1, the master page is designed as a template, which contains HTML elements, static text and images, for Web pages.

Listing 14.1 adds some text at the top and bottom of the master page and also inserts an image logo. It contains a `ContentPlaceHolder` control, which defines an area for the content pages to add their content. You can add multiple `ContentPlaceHolder` controls in a master page. You must also ensure that you add the logo image to the directory structure of the `MyOrganizationVB` application to add this image in the Web application. Figure 14.5 shows the master page in the Design view:

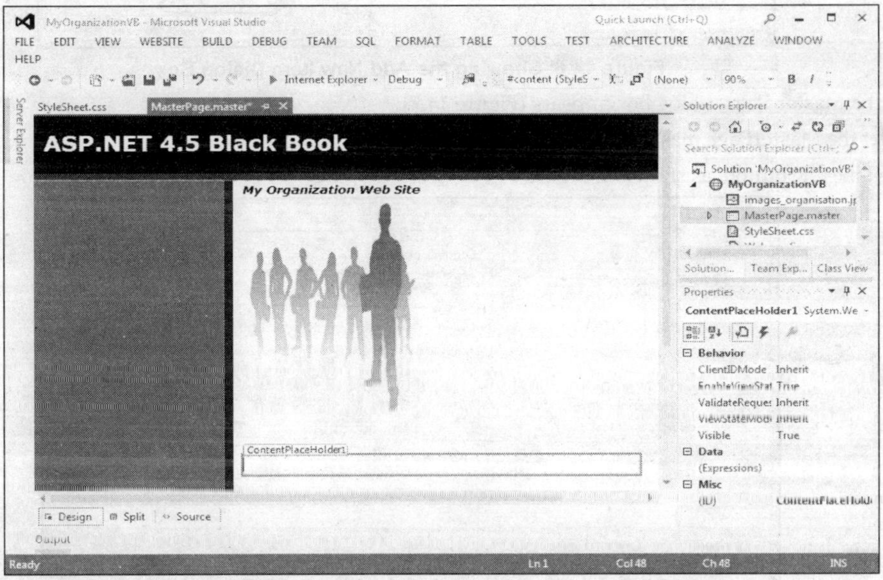

Figure 14.5: Showing the Design View of the Master Page

4. Add a Web form in the `MyOrganizationVB` application by selecting the Web Form option from the middle pane of the Add New Item dialog box (Figure 14.6).

NOTE

As shown in Figure 14.5, CSS has been applied in the application. In this chapter, we are using a common style sheet for all applications. You can refer Chapter 2: Introducing HTML Controls (online resource) to learn about style sheet and how to create a style sheet.

The content page (or the new Web form) inherits the properties of the master page. A content page is created in the same way as any other .aspx page, with a little difference in that you need to select the Select master page check box in the Add New Item dialog box while creating the content page.

5. Select the Select master page check box and click the Add button, as shown in Figure 14.6:

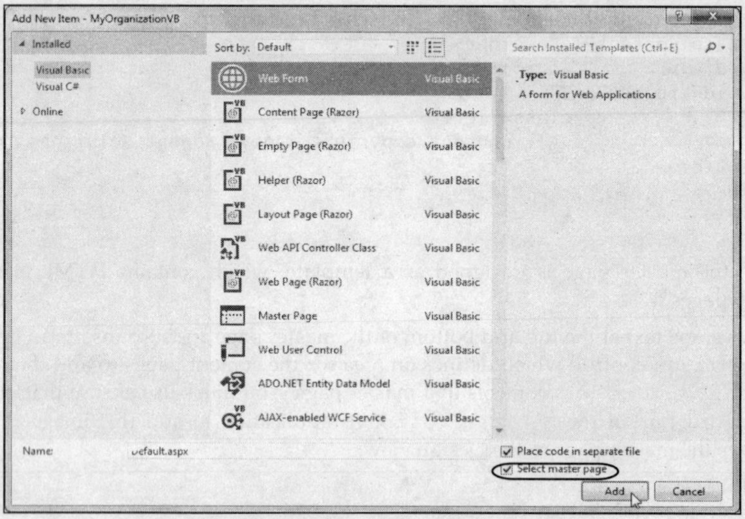

Figure 14.6: Showing the Add New Item Dialog Box

The Select a Master Page dialog box appears (Figure 14.7).

6. Select the MasterPage.master option from the Contents of folder pane.

7. Click the OK button, as shown in Figure 14.7:

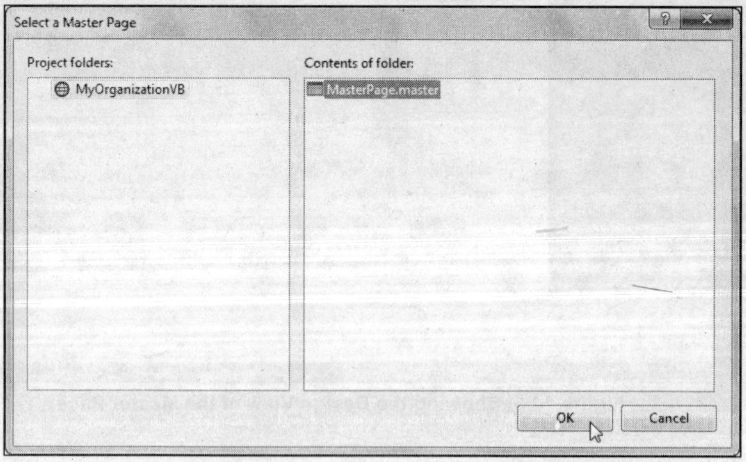

Figure 14.7: Showing the Select a Master Page Dialog Box

The `Default.aspx` page appears in Visual Studio 2012 IDE.

8. Add the code, shown in Listing 14.2, to the `Default.aspx` page:

Listing 14.2: Showing the Code for the `Default.aspx` Page

In VB

```
<%@ Page Title="" Language="VB" MasterPageFile="~/MasterPage.master"
  AutoEventWireup="false" CodeFile="Default.aspx.vb" Inherits="_Default" %>
<asp:Content ID="Content1" ContentPlaceHolderID="ContentPlaceHolder1" Runat="Server">
    Enter your name in the text box<br />
  <br />
  <asp:TextBox ID="TextBox1" runat="server"></asp:TextBox><br />
  <br />
  <asp:Button ID="Button1" runat="server" BackColor="Black" Font-Bold="True" Font-
  Size="Small" ForeColor="White" Text="Click to Submit" />
  <br /><br />
  <asp:Label ID="Label1" runat="server" CssClass="title" Text="Label" Visible="False"
  Width="132px"></asp:Label>
</asp:Content>
```

In C#

```
<%@ Page Title="" Language="C#" MasterPageFile="~/MasterPage.master"
  AutoEventWireup="true" CodeFile="Default.aspx.cs" Inherits="_Default" %>
<asp:Content ID="Content1" ContentPlaceHolderID="ContentPlaceHolder1" Runat="Server">
        Enter your name in the text box<br />
  <br />
  <asp:TextBox ID="TextBox1" runat="server"></asp:TextBox><br />
  <br />
  <asp:Button ID="Button1" runat="server" BackColor="Black" Font-Bold="True" Font-
  Size="Small" ForeColor="White" Text="Click to Submit" OnClick="Button1_Click" />
  <br /><br />
  <asp:Label ID="Label1" runat="server" CssClass="title" Text="Label" Visible="False"
  Width="132px"></asp:Label>
</asp:Content>
```

The code given in Listing 14.2 is similar to the code of the .aspx page, containing HTML elements and server controls. The difference is that this page contains a MasterPageFile attribute and file suffix with .master.

9. Add the code, shown in Listing 14.3, to the CodeFile of the `Default.aspx` page:

Listing 14.3: Showing the Code for the CodeFile of the `Default.aspx` Page

In VB

```
Partial Class _Default
    Inherits System.Web.UI.Page
    Protected Sub Button1_Click(sender As Object, e As EventArgs) Handles Button1.Click
        Label1.Text = "You have entered " & TextBox1.Text
        Label1.Visible = True
    End Sub
End Class
```

In C#

```
using System;
using System.Collections.Generic;
using System.Linq;
using System.Web;
using System.Web.UI;
using System.Web.UI.WebControls;
public partial class _Default : System.Web.UI.Page
{
    protected void Page_Load(object sender, EventArgs e)
```

```
    {
    }
    protected void Button1_Click(object sender, EventArgs e)
    {
        Label1.Text = "You have entered " + TextBox1.Text;
        Label1.Visible = true;
    }
}
```

10. Run the `MyOrganizationVB` Web application by pressing the F5 key. The ASP.NET engine combines both the content and master pages to generate a single final page. You can see the final output of the Web application in Figure 14.8:

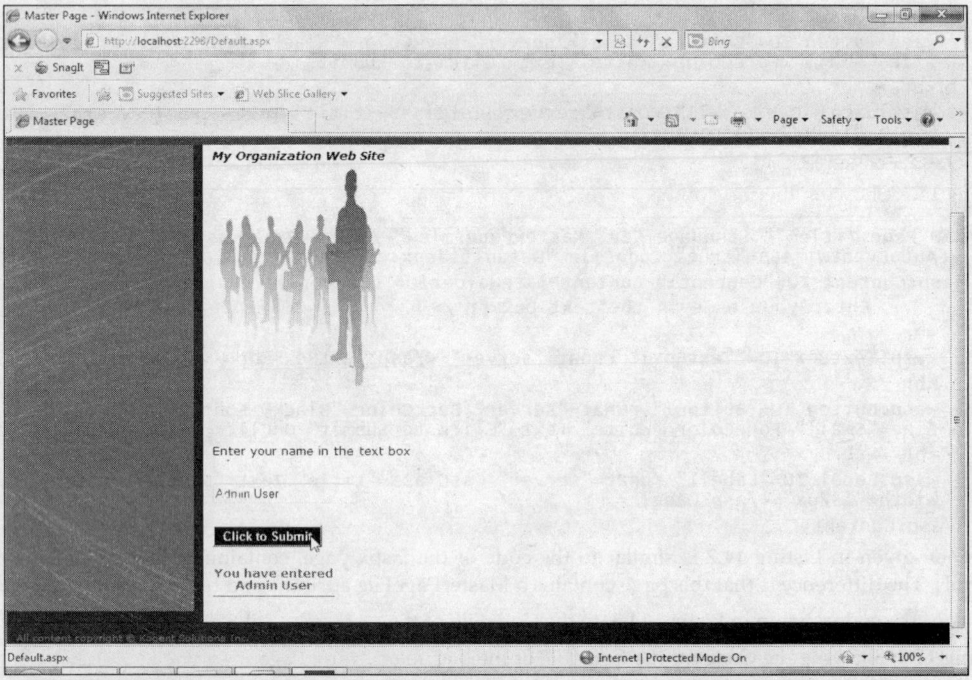

Figure 14.8: Displaying the Output of the MyOrganizationVB Web Application

Creating Nested Master Pages

In this section, we will add another master page to the `MyOrganizationVB` application created in the preceding section to understand the concept of nested master pages. You can find this modified application as `MyOrganizationNestedVB` in VB and `MyOrganizationNestedCS` in C#.

To create a new nested master page that inherits the properties of the main master page, you need to select the Select master page check box in the Add New Item dialog box. In our case, we have named this nested master page as `hrd.master`. Listing 14.4 shows the code of the `hrd.master` page:

Listing 14.4: Showing the Code for the `hrd.master` Page

In VB

```
<%@ Master Language="VB" MasterPageFile="~/MasterPage.master" AutoEventWireup="false"
  CodeFile="hrd.master.vb" Inherits="hrd" %>
<asp:Content ID="Content1" ContentPlaceHolderID="ContentPlaceHolder1" Runat="Server">
    <asp:Label ID="Label1" runat="server" BackColor="Aqua" BorderColor="Black"
  BorderWidth="2px" BorderStyle="Solid" Font-Size="Large" Text="Human Resource
  Department" Visible="true">
</asp:Label>
```

```
    <br />
    <br />
      <asp:ContentPlaceHolder ID="ContentPlaceHolder1" runat="server">
    </asp:ContentPlaceHolder>
</asp:Content>
```

In C#

```
<%@ Master Language="C#" MasterPageFile="~/MasterPage.master" autoeventwireup="true"
  CodeFile="hrd.master.cs" Inherits="hrd" %>
<asp:Content ID="Content2" ContentPlaceHolderID="ContentPlaceHolder1" Runat="Server">
    <asp:Label ID="Label1" runat="server" BackColor="Aqua" BorderColor="Black"
  BorderWidth="2px" BorderStyle="Solid" Font-Size="Large" Text="Human Resource
  Department" Visible="true">
</asp:Label>
<br />
<br />
<asp:ContentPlaceHolder ID="ContentPlaceHolder1" runat="server">
</asp:ContentPlaceHolder>
</asp:Content>
```

Listing 14.5: Showing the code of the `Default2.aspx` Page

In VB

```
<%@ Page Title="Nested Master Pages" Language="VB" MasterPageFile="~/hrd.master"
  autoeventwireup="true" CodeFile="Default2.aspx.vb" Inherits="Default2" %>
<asp:Content ID="Content1" ContentPlaceHolderID="ContentPlaceHolder1" Runat="Server">
    Enter your name in the text box<br />
  <br />
  <asp:TextBox ID="TextBox1" runat="server"></asp:TextBox><br />
  <br />
  <asp:Button ID="Button1" runat="server" BackColor="Black" Font-Bold="True" Font-
  Size="Small" ForeColor="White" Text="Click to Submit"/>
  <br /><br />
  <asp:Label ID="Label1" runat="server" CssClass="title" Text="Label" Visible="False"
  Width="132px"></asp:Label>
</asp:Content>
```

In C#

```
<%@ Page Language="C#" MasterPageFile="~/hrd.master" autoeventwireup="true"
  CodeFile="Default2.aspx.cs" Inherits="_Default2" Title="Nested Master Pages" %>
<asp:Content ID="Content1" ContentPlaceHolderID="ContentPlaceHolder1" runat="Server">
    Enter your name in the text box<br />
  <br />
  <asp:TextBox ID="TextBox1" runat="server"></asp:TextBox><br />
  <br />
  <asp:Button ID="Button1" runat="server" BackColor="Black" Font-Bold="True" Font-
  Size="Small" ForeColor="White" Text="Click to Submit" OnClick="Button1_Click"/>
  <br /><br />
  <asp:Label ID="Label1" runat="server" CssClass="title" Text="Label" Visible="False"
  Width="132px"></asp:Label>
</asp:Content>
```

Now, let's run the application and click the Click to Submit button to call the Click event of the button. Figure 14.9 shows the output after clicking the button on the Web page:

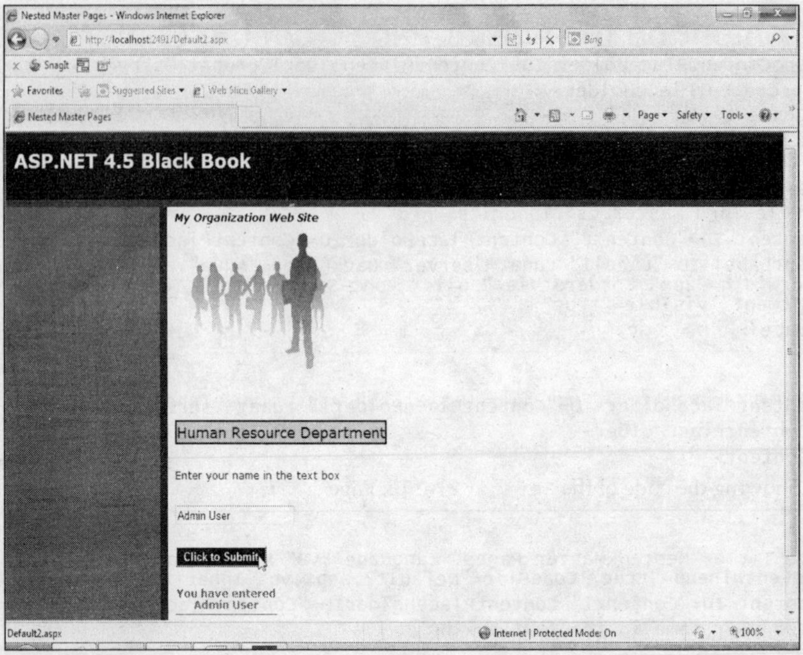

Figure 14.9: Displaying the Output of Nested Master Page

In Figure 14.9, the content and layout of the MasterPage, hrd, and Default2 pages are combined together to generate a single page.

Configuring Master Pages

You need to either specify the name of the master page in the content page by using the `@ Page` directive or specify the name of the master page in the Web application configuration file (Web.config), to associate a content page with a master page. Using configuration files to associate a content page with a master page helps you to easily maintain your website, because the configuration files provide a single location to change the master page associated with multiple content pages.

For example, to use the configuration file to associate the `MasterPage.master` page with the `Default.aspx` content page, open the `Web.config` file of your website and then add the following code snippet in the `<system.web>` section of the Web.config file (common for both VB and C#):

```
<pages masterPageFile="~/MasterPage.master" />
```

After adding the preceding code snippet in the web.config file, you are not required to exclusively set the `MasterPageFile` attribute in the @ Page directive of the `Default.aspx` page. However, the following points must be considered while configuring master pages:

- In case, a master page is included in the content page (Default.aspx) by using the `@ Page` directive, then it has higher precedence over specifying the name of the master page in the `web.config` file. This implies that if the master page is configured not only in the content page but also in the web.config file, then the master page path mentioned in the content page overrides the master page defined in the `web.config` file.
- If a website contains multiple `web.config` files located in different subfolders, each can be used to configure different master pages.

When you associate a master page with a content page, the content page automatically includes the Title attribute. You can change the title of the content page by modifying the `Title` attribute in the `@ Page` directive. If you want to use the title of a master page, you can remove the Title attribute from the @ Page directive given in the content page.

Modifying Content on the Master Page from the Content Page

You can update the content of the `master page` by selecting the control that needs to be modified on the master page from the content page. To demonstrate this, let's create an application named `CalendarUpdationCS` (`CalendarUpdationVB` in VB and `CalendarUpdationCS` in C#) and add a Calendar control on the master page. After creating the `CalendarUpdationCS` application, perform the following steps to modify the content of the master page:

1. Add a Master Page (`MasterPage.master`) in the `CalendarUpdationCS` application from the Add New Item dialog box.
2. Add the code, shown in Listing 14.6, to the `MasterPage.master` page:

Listing 14.6: Showing the Code for the `MasterPage.master` Page

In VB

```
<%@ Master Language="VB" CodeFile="MasterPage.master.vb" Inherits="MasterPage" %>
<!DOCTYPE html>
<html xmlns="http://www.w3.org/1999/xhtml">
<head runat="server">
     <title>Calendar Updation</title>
    <link href="StyleSheet.css" rel="stylesheet" type="text/css" />
</head>
<body>
    <form id="form1" runat="server">
    <div>
    <div id="header">
                <h1>
                    ASP.NET 4.5 Black Book
                </h1>
            </div>
            <div id="sidebar">
                <div id="nav">
                <br />
                <br />
                </div>
            </div>
            <div id="content">
                <div class ="itemContent">
                   <strong><em>Calendar<br />
                        <asp:Calendar ID="Calendar1" runat="server" BackColor="White"
                        BorderColor="Black" Font-Names="Verdana" Font-Size="9pt"
                        ForeColor="Black" Height="250px" NextPrevFormat="ShortMonth"
                        Width="220px" BorderStyle="Solid" CellSpacing="1">
                        <SelectedDayStyle BackColor="#333399" ForeColor="White" />
                        <TodayDayStyle BackColor="#999999" ForeColor="White" />
                        <DayStyle BackColor="#CCCCCC" />
                        <OtherMonthDayStyle ForeColor="#999999" />
                        <NextPrevStyle Font-Size="8pt" ForeColor="White" Font-
                        Bold="True" />
                        <DayHeaderStyle Font-Bold="True" Font-Size="8pt"
                        ForeColor="#333333" Height="7pt" />
                        <TitleStyle BackColor="#333399" Font-Bold="True" Font-
                     Size="12pt" ForeColor="White" Height="12pt" BorderStyle="Solid" />
                        </asp:Calendar>
                </em></strong>
                <br />
        <asp:ContentPlaceHolder id="ContentPlaceHolder1" runat="server">
        </asp:ContentPlaceHolder>
    </div></div>
```

```
        <div id="footer">
                    <p class="left">
                        All content copyright &copy; Kogent Solutions Inc.</p>
            </div></div>
        </form>
    </body>
    </html>
```

In C#

```
    <%@ Master Language="VB" CodeFile="MasterPage.master.vb" Inherits="MasterPage" %>
    <!DOCTYPE html>
    <html xmlns="http://www.w3.org/1999/xhtml">
    <head runat="server">
        <title>Calendar Updation</title>
        <link href="StyleSheet.css" rel="stylesheet" type="text/css" />
    </head>
    <body>
        <form id="form1" runat="server">
        <div>
        <div id="header">
                    <h1>
                        ASP.NET 4.5 Black Book
                    </h1>
                </div>
                <div id="sidebar">
                    <div id="nav">
                    <br />
                    <br />
                    </div>
                </div>
                <div id="content">
                    <div class ="itemContent">
                        <strong><em>Calendar<br />
                            <asp:Calendar ID="Calendar1" runat="server" BackColor="White"
                            BorderColor="Black" Font-Names="Verdana" Font-Size="9pt"
                            ForeColor="Black" Height="250px" NextPrevFormat="ShortMonth"
                            Width="220px" BorderStyle="Solid" CellSpacing="1">
                            <SelectedDayStyle BackColor="#333399" ForeColor="White" />
                            <TodayDayStyle BackColor="#999999" ForeColor="White" />
                            <DayStyle BackColor="#CCCCCC" />
                            <OtherMonthDayStyle ForeColor="#999999" />
                            <NextPrevStyle Font-Size="8pt" ForeColor="White" Font-
                            Bold="True" />
                            <DayHeaderStyle Font-Bold="True" Font-Size="8pt"
                            ForeColor="#333333" Height="7pt" />
                            <TitleStyle BackColor="#333399" Font-Bold="True" Font-
                         Size="12pt" ForeColor="White" Height="12pt" BorderStyle="Solid" />
                            </asp:Calendar>
                    </em></strong>
                    <br />
            <asp:ContentPlaceHolder id="ContentPlaceHolder1" runat="server">
            </asp:ContentPlaceHolder>
        </div></div>
         <div id="footer">
                    <p class="left">
                        All content copyright &copy; Kogent Solutions Inc.</p>
            </div></div>
        </form>
    </body>
    </html>
```

3. Add the code, shown in Listing 14.7, to the `Default.aspx` page:

Listing 14.7: Showing the Code for the `Default.aspx` Page

In VB

```
<%@ Page Title="" Language="VB" MasterPageFile="~/MasterPage.master"
  AutoEventWireup="false" CodeFile="Default.aspx.vb" Inherits="_Default" %>
<asp:Content ID="Content1" ContentPlaceHolderID="ContentPlaceHolder1" Runat="Server">
    Enter date(MM/DD/YY)in Textbox for updating Calendar control<br />
  <br />
  <asp:TextBox ID="TextBox1" runat="server"></asp:TextBox>   <asp:Label
  ID="Label1" runat="server" Text="Label"
  Visible="False"></asp:Label><br />
   <br />
  <asp:Button ID="Button1" runat="server" BackColor="Black" Font-Bold="True"
         Font-Size="Small" ForeColor="White" Text="Update Calendar"/>
</asp:Content>
```

In C#

```
<%@ Page Title="" Language="C#" MasterPageFile="~/MasterPage.master"
  AutoEventWireup="true" CodeFile="Default.aspx.cs" Inherits="_Default" %>
<asp:Content ID="Content1" ContentPlaceHolderID="ContentPlaceHolder1" Runat="Server">
        Enter date(MM/DD/YY)in Textbox for updating Calendar control<br />
  <br />
  <asp:TextBox ID="TextBox1" runat="server"></asp:TextBox>   <asp:Label
  ID="Label1" runat="server" Text="Label"
  Visible="False"></asp:Label><br />
   <br />
  <asp:Button ID="Button1" runat="server" BackColor="Black" Font-Bold="True"
         Font-Size="Small" ForeColor="White" Text="Update Calendar"
        OnClick="Button1_Click"/>
</asp:Content>
```

4. Add the code, shown in Listing 14.8, to the CodeFile of the `Default.aspx` page:

Listing 14.8: Showing the CodeFile

In VB

```
Partial Class _Default
    Inherits System.Web.UI.Page
    Protected Sub Button1_Click(sender As Object, e As EventArgs) Handles Button1.Click
        Try
            Dim cal As Calendar
            cal = CType(Master.FindControl("Calendar1"), Calendar)
            If Not cal Is Nothing Then
                cal.VisibleDate = TextBox1.Text
                cal.SelectedDate = TextBox1.Text
                Label1.Text = "You have entered " + TextBox1.Text
                Label1.Visible = True
            End If
        Catch
            Label1.Text = "Wrong Format Entered"
            Label1.Visible = True
        End Try
    End Sub
    Protected Sub Page_Load(sender As Object, e As EventArgs) Handles Me.Load
        Label1.Visible = False
    End Sub
End Class
```

In C#

```
using System;
using System.Collections.Generic;
using System.Linq;
using System.Web;
using System.Web.UI;
using System.Web.UI.WebControls;
public partial class _Default : System.Web.UI.Page
{
    protected void Page_Load(object sender, EventArgs e)
    {
        Label1.Visible = false;
    }
    protected void Button1_Click(object sender, EventArgs e)
    {
        try
        {
            Calendar cal;
            cal = (Calendar)Master.FindControl("Calendar1");
            if (cal != null)
            {
                cal.VisibleDate = Convert.ToDateTime(TextBox1.Text);
                cal.SelectedDate = Convert.ToDateTime(TextBox1.Text);
                Label1.Text = " You have entered " + TextBox1.Text;
                Label1.Visible = true;
            }
        }
        catch
        {
            Label1.Text = "Wrong Format Entered";
            Label1.Visible = true;
        }
    }
}
```

5. Run the application. Figure 14.10 shows the output of the CalendarUpdationCS application:

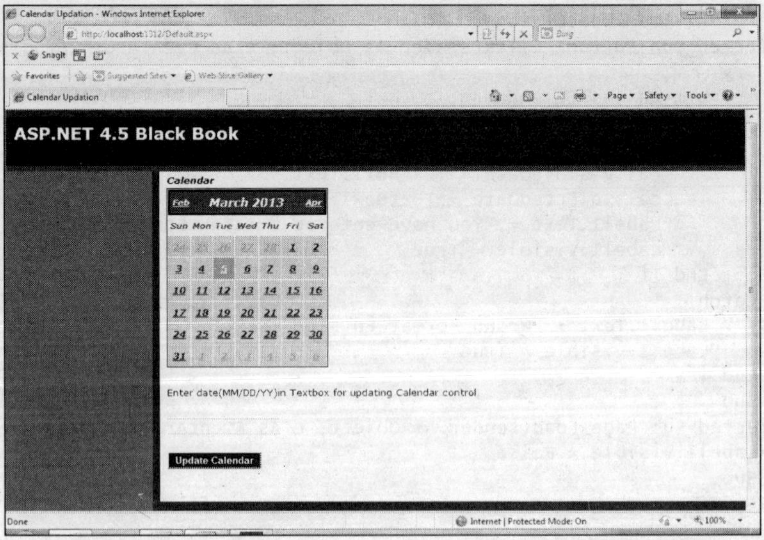

Figure 14.10: Displaying the Calendar Control on a Web Page

In Figure 14.10, the calendar displays 5th March 2013 as the selected date. You can modify the selected date by entering `10/25/2013` in a text box and clicking the Update Calendar button to update the calendar with the new date, as shown in Figure 14.11:

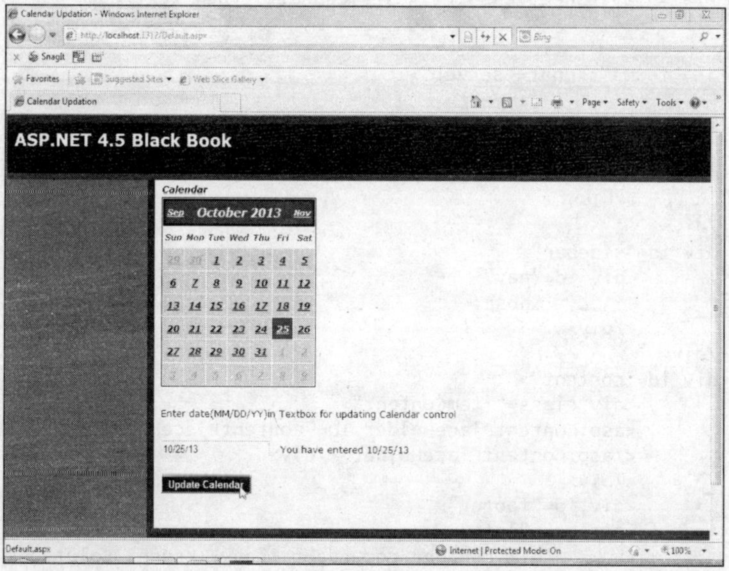

Figure 14.11: Modifying the Date in a Calendar

In Figure 14.11, the date displayed is in the MM/DD/YY format. In case, if you enter date as 25/10/13, the error message, Wrong Format Entered, appears.

Overriding Properties and Methods of a Master Page

You can override the properties and methods of a master page to increase the accessibility over the content of the master page. This is also called exposing properties and methods. By overriding properties, you can change the public properties of a master page. To understand this concept in detail, let's create a Web application, `DisplayingPropertiesCS` (`DisplayingPropertiesVB` in VB and `DisplayingPropertiesCS` in C#), and perform the following steps to override properties and methods of a master page:

1. Add a Master Page (`MasterPage.master`) in the `DisplayingPropertiesCS` application by selecting the Add New Item option from the context menu of Solution Explorer and add the code, shown in Listing 14.9, to the master page named `MasterPage.master`:

Listing 14.9: Showing the Code for the `MasterPage.master` Page

In VB

```
<%@ Master Language="VB" CodeFile="MasterPage.master.vb" Inherits="MasterPage" %>
<!DOCTYPE html>
<script runat="server">
  Private _header As String
  Public Property Header() As String
        Get
              Return _header
        End Get
        Set(value As String)
              _header = value
        End Set
  End Property
</script>
```

```
<html xmlns="http://www.w3.org/1999/xhtml">
<head runat="server">
     <title>Master Page</title>
   <link href="StyleSheet.css" rel="stylesheet" type="text/css" />
</head>
<body>
   <form id="form1" runat="server">
  <div>
        <div id="header">
              <h1>
                    ASP.NET 4.5 Black Book
              </h1>
        </div>
        <div id="sidebar">
              <div id="nav">
                     
              </div>
        </div>
        <div id="content">
              <div class="itemContent">
              <asp:ContentPlaceHolder ID="ContentPlaceHolder1" runat="server">
              </asp:ContentPlaceHolder></div>
              </div>
              <div id="footer">
              <p class="left">
                    All content copyright &copy; Kogent Solutions Inc.</p>
              </div>
       </div>
   </form>
</body>
</html>
```

In C#

```
<%@ Master Language="C#" AutoEventWireup="true" CodeFile="MasterPage.master.cs"
  Inherits="MasterPage" %>
<!DOCTYPE html>
<script runat="server">
   private string _header;
  public string Header
  {
       get
       {
             return _header;
       }
       set
       {
             _header = value;
       }
  }
</script>
<html xmlns="http://www.w3.org/1999/xhtml">
<head id="Head1" runat="server">
     <title>Master Page</title>
   <link href="StyleSheet.css" rel="stylesheet" type="text/css" />
</head>
<body>
   <form id="form1" runat="server">
  <div>
        <div id="header">
              <h1>
```

```
                    ASP.NET 4.5 Black Book
                </h1>
        </div>
        <div id="sidebar">
                <div id="nav">
                     
                </div>
        </div>
        <div id="content">
                <div class="itemContent">
                <asp:ContentPlaceHolder ID="ContentPlaceHolder1" runat="server">
                </asp:ContentPlaceHolder></div>
                </div>
                <div id="footer">
                <p class="left">
                    All content copyright &copy; Kogent Solutions Inc.</p>
                </div>
        </div>
    </form>
</body>
</html>
```

In Listing 14.9, the master page defines a property named Header. The content page passes the value of the header to the master page and displays the new header.

2. Add the content page (`Default.aspx`) to the Web application, and add the code, shown in Listing 14.10, to it:

Listing 14.10: Showing the Code for the Content Page

In VB

```
<%@ Page Title="" Language="VB" MasterPageFile="~/MasterPage.master"
  AutoEventWireup="false" CodeFile="Default.aspx.vb" Inherits="_Default" %>
<%@ MasterType VirtualPath="~/MasterPage.master" %>
<asp:Content ID="Content1" ContentPlaceHolderID="ContentPlaceHolder1" Runat="Server">
    Welcome to the Custom page Header
<br />
  <asp:Label ID="Label1" runat="server" Text="Label"></asp:Label>
</asp:Content>
```

In C#

```
<%@ Page Title="" Language="C#" MasterPageFile="~/MasterPage.master"
  AutoEventWireup="true" CodeFile="Default.aspx.cs" Inherits="_Default" %>
<%@ MasterType VirtualPath="~/MasterPage.master" %>
<asp:Content ID="Content1" ContentPlaceHolderID="ContentPlaceHolder1" Runat="Server">
    Welcome to the Custom page Header
<br />
  <asp:Label ID="Label1" runat="server" Text="Label"></asp:Label>
</asp:Content>
```

3. Add the code, shown in Listing 14.11, in the CodeFile of the `Default.aspx` page:

Listing 14.11: Showing the Code for the CodeFile

In VB

```
Partial Class _Default
    Inherits System.Web.UI.Page
    Protected Sub Page_Load(sender As Object, e As EventArgs) Handles Me.Load
        Master.Header = "Header"
        Master.Page.Title = "Content Page"
        Label1.Text = Master.Header
    End Sub
End Class
```

In C#

```
using System;
using System.Collections.Generic;
using System.Linq;
using System.Web;
using System.Web.UI;
using System.Web.UI.WebControls;
public partial class _Default : System.Web.UI.Page
{
    protected void Page_Load(object sender, EventArgs e)
    {
        Master.Header = "Header";
        Master.Page.Title = "Content Page";
        Label1.Text = Master.Header;
    }
}
```

4. Run the Web application. The Internet Explorer appears, displaying the content page, as shown in Figure 14.12:

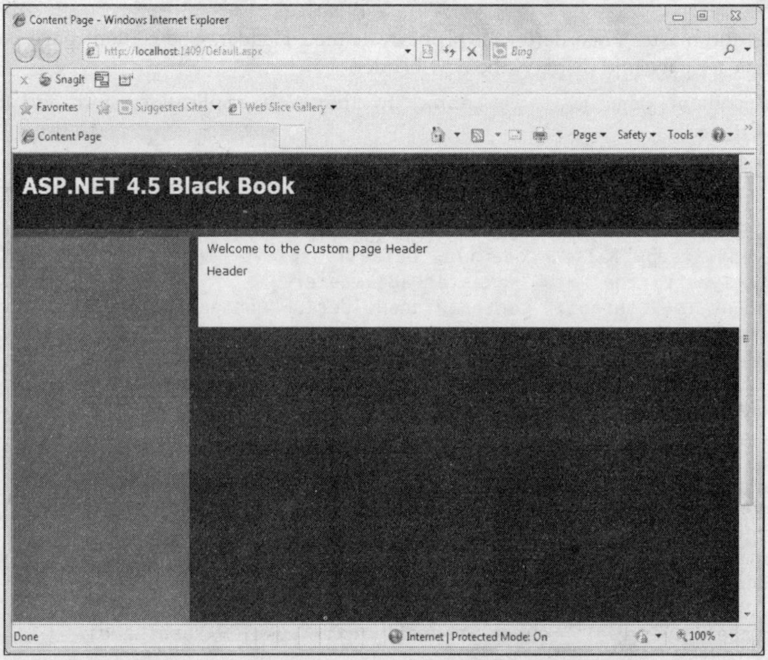

Figure 14.12: Displaying the header of the Content Page

In the Figure 14.12, we have created a title for master and content pages. As you run the application, the title specified in the master page gets overridden by the title given in the content page.

Loading Pages Dynamically

You can load the pages dynamically by providing a link of master pages on the content page. Dynamic loading of the master pages takes place during the `PreInit` event of a Web page and the `PreInit` event is coded in the content page. Now, let's create a Web application `DynamicMasterCS` (`DynamicMasterVB` in VB and `DynamicMasterCS` in C#) and perform the following steps to load the master page dynamically:

1. Add a master page (named `Master1.master`) to the `DynamicMasterCS` Web application and add the code, shown in Listing 14.12, to it:

Listing 14.12: Showing the Code for the `Master1.master` Page

In VB

```
<%@ Master Language="VB" CodeFile="Master1.master.vb" Inherits="Master1" %>
<!DOCTYPE html>
<script runat="server">
  Protected Sub LinkButton1_Click(sender As Object, e As EventArgs)
        Session("masterpage") = "Master2.master"
        Response.Redirect(Request.Url.ToString())
  End Sub
</script>
<html xmlns="http://www.w3.org/1999/xhtml">
<head runat="server">
     <title>Loading Pages Dynamically</title>
     <link href="StyleSheet.css" rel="stylesheet" type="text/css" />
</head>
<body>
    <form id="form1" runat="server">
    <div>
        <div id="header">
                <h1>
                        ASP.NET 4.5 Black Book
                </h1>
        </div>
        <div id="sidebar">
                <div id="nav">
                         
                </div>
        </div>
        <div id="content">
                <div class="itemContent">
                <h1>
                Master Page Without Color</h1>
                <asp:ContentPlaceHolder ID="ContentPlaceHolder1" runat="server">
                </asp:ContentPlaceHolder>
                <asp:LinkButton ID="LinkButton1" runat="server"
                OnClick="LinkButton1_Click">Page With Background Color
                </asp:LinkButton> </div>
        </div>
  </div>
  <div id="footer">
  <p class="left">
        All content copyright &copy; Kogent Solutions Inc.</p>
  </div>
    </form>
</body>
</html>
```

In C#

```
<%@ Master Language="C#" AutoEventWireup="true" CodeFile="Master1.master.cs"
  Inherits="Master1" %>
<!DOCTYPE html>
<script runat="server">
  void LinkButton1_Click(Object sender, EventArgs e)
  {
        Session["masterpage"] = "Master2.master";
        Response.Redirect(Request.Url.ToString());
  }
```

```
</script>
<html xmlns="http://www.w3.org/1999/xhtml">
<head runat="server">
     <title>Loading Pages Dynamically</title>
        <link href="StyleSheet.css" rel="stylesheet" type="text/css" />
</head>
<body>
    <form id="form1" runat="server">
    <div>
         <div id="header">
                 <h1>
                         ASP.NET 4.5 Black Book
                 </h1>
         </div>
         <div id="sidebar">
                 <div id="nav">
                          
                 </div>
         </div>
         <div id="content">
                 <div class="itemContent">
                 <h1>
                 Master Page Without Color</h1>
                 <asp:ContentPlaceHolder ID="ContentPlaceHolder1" runat="server">
                 </asp:ContentPlaceHolder>
                 <asp:LinkButton ID="LinkButton1" runat="server"
                 OnClick="LinkButton1_Click">Page With Background Color
                 </asp:LinkButton> </div>
         </div>
    </div>
    <div id="footer">
    <p class="left">
         All content copyright &copy; Kogent Solutions Inc.</p>
    </div>
      </form>
</body>
</html>
```

2. Create another master page (named `Master2.master`) for dynamic page loading and add the code, shown in Listing 14.13, to it:

Listing 14.13: Showing the Code for the `Master2.master` Page

In VB

```
<%@ Master Language="VB" CodeFile="Master2.master.vb" Inherits="Master2" %>
<!DOCTYPE html>
<script runat="server">

  Protected Sub LinkButton1_Click(sender As Object, e As EventArgs)
        Session("masterpage") = "Master1.master"
       Response.Redirect(Request.Url.ToString())
  End Sub
    </script>
<html xmlns="http://www.w3.org/1999/xhtml">
<head runat="server">
     <title>Loading Pages Dynamically</title>
   </head>
<body bgcolor="#99ccff">
  <form id="form1" runat="server">
  <div>
```

```
        <div id="header">
                <h1>
                ASP.NET 4.5 Black Book
                </h1>
        </div>
        <div id="sidebar">
                <div id="nav">
                         
                </div>
        </div>
        <div id="content">
                <div class="itemContent">
                <h1>
                Master Page With Color
                </h1>
                <asp:ContentPlaceHolder ID="ContentPlaceHolder1" runat="server">
                </asp:ContentPlaceHolder>
                <asp:LinkButton ID="LinkButton1" runat="server"
                OnClick="LinkButton1_Click">Page Without Background Color
                </asp:LinkButton></div>
        </div>
    </div>
                <div id="footer">
                <p class="left">
                All content copyright &copy; Kogent Solutions Inc.</p>
                </div>
    </form>
</body>
</html>
```

In C#

```
<%@ Master Language="C#" AutoEventWireup="true" CodeFile="Master2.master.cs"
   Inherits="Master2" %>
<!DOCTYPE html>
<script runat="server">
   void LinkButton1_Click(Object sender, EventArgs e)
   {
        Session["masterpage"] = "Master1.master";
        Response.Redirect(Request.Url.ToString());
   }
</script>
<html xmlns="http://www.w3.org/1999/xhtml">
<head runat="server">
     <title>Loading Pages Dynamically</title>
</head>
<body bgcolor="#99ccff">
   <form id="form1" runat="server">
   <div>
        <div id="header">
                <h1>
                ASP.NET 4.5 Black Book
                </h1>
        </div>
        <div id="sidebar">
                <div id="nav">
                         
                </div>
        </div>
```

```
            <div id="content">
                    <div class="itemContent">
                    <h1>
                    Master Page With Color
                    </h1>
                    <asp:ContentPlaceHolder ID="ContentPlaceHolder1" runat="server">
                    </asp:ContentPlaceHolder>
                    <asp:LinkButton ID="LinkButton1" runat="server"
                    OnClick="LinkButton1_Click">Page Without Background Color
                    </asp:LinkButton></div>
            </div>
    </div>
                    <div id="footer">
                    <p class="left">
                    All content copyright &copy; Kogent Solutions Inc.</p>
                    </div>
    </form>
  </body>
  </html>
```

The differences between the `Master1.master` and `Master2.master` pages are as follows:

- The Master1.master page does not contain a background color; whereas, the Master2.master page contains a background color.
- The heading (h1) on the Master1.master page is Master Page Without Color; whereas, the heading (h1) on the Master2.master page is Master Page With Color.
- The Text property of the LinkButton control is different in both the master pages.

To inherit the properties of master pages dynamically, you need a content page.

3. Create a content page (`Default.aspx`), and add the code, shown in Listing 14.14, to it:

Listing 14.14: Showing the Code for the `Default.aspx` Page

In VB

```
<%@ Page Title="" Language="VB" MasterPageFile="~/Master1.master"
  AutoEventWireup="false" CodeFile="Default.aspx.vb" Inherits="_Default" %>
<script runat="server" language="vb">
Sub Page_PreInit(sender As Object, e As EventArgs) _
        Handles Me.PreInit
        If Not Session("masterpage") Is Nothing Then
                Me.MasterPageFile = CType(Session("masterpage"), String)
        End If
  End Sub
  Protected Sub Button1_Click(sender As Object, e As EventArgs)
        label1.Text = "<b>Hello " & TextBox1.Text & "! Welcome to the WebSite.
          </b>"
  End Sub
</script>
<asp:Content ID="Content1" ContentPlaceHolderID="ContentPlaceHolder1" Runat="Server">
    <b>Enter Your Name: </b>
  <br />
  <asp:TextBox ID="TextBox1" runat="server" />
  <br />
  <br />
  <asp:Button ID="Button1" runat="server" Text="Enter" OnClick="Button1_Click" />
  <br />
  <asp:Label ID="label1" runat="server" />
</asp:Content>
```

In C#

```
<%@ Page Title="" Language="C#" MasterPageFile="~/Master1.master" AutoEventWireup="true"
  CodeFile="Default.aspx.cs" Inherits="_Default" %>
<script runat="server" language="cs">
  void Page_PreInit(Object sender, EventArgs e)
  {
        if (Session["masterpage"] != null)
        {
              this.MasterPageFile = (String)Session["masterpage"];
        }
  }
  protected void Button1_Click(Object sender, EventArgs e)
  {
        label1.Text = "<b>Hello " + TextBox1.Text + "! Welcome to the Web Site. </b>";
  }

</script>
<asp:Content ID="Content1" ContentPlaceHolderID="ContentPlaceHolder1" Runat="Server">
    <b>Enter Your Name: </b>
  <br />
  <asp:TextBox ID="TextBox1" runat="server" />
  <br />
  <br />
  <asp:Button ID="Button1" runat="server" Text="Enter" OnClick="Button1_Click" />
  <br />
  <asp:Label ID="label1" runat="server" />
</asp:Content>
```

4. Run the `DynamicMasterCS` Web application. The content page inherits properties from the Master1.master page, as shown in Figure 14.13:

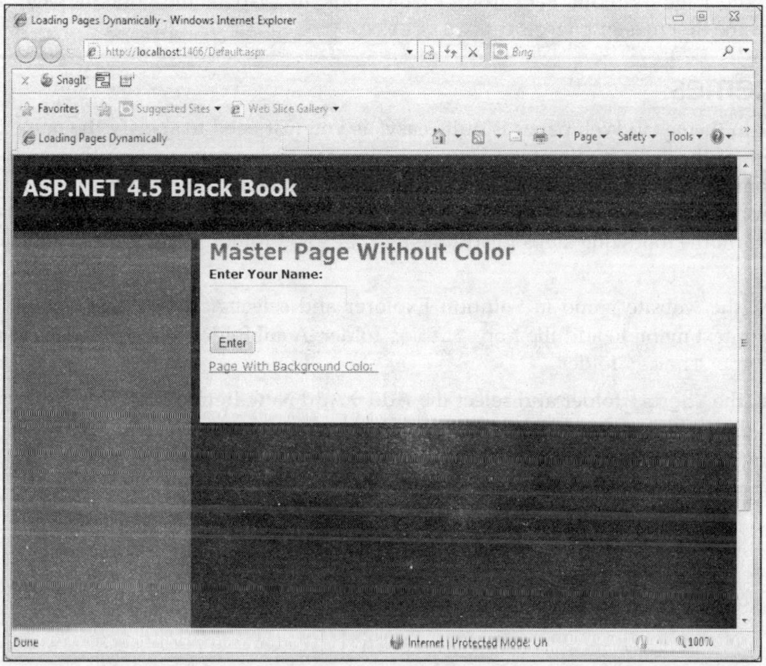

Figure 14.13: Showing the Properties of Master1.master Page at the Runtime

5. Click the Page With Background Color link. The content page inherits properties from the second master page, Master2.master, as shown in Figure 14.14:

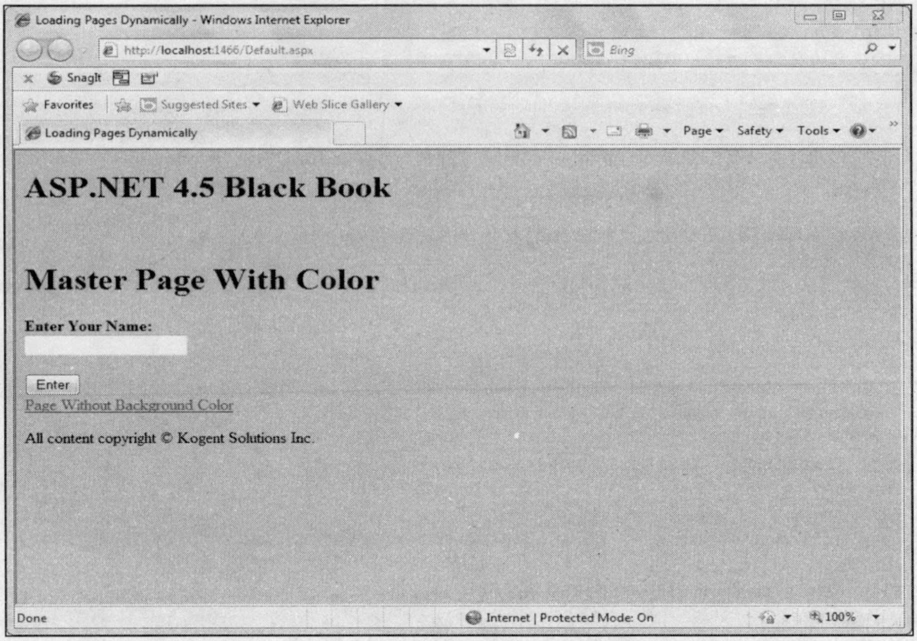

Figure 14.14: Showing the Properties of Master2.master Page at the Runtime

You can click the Page Without Background Color link to display the content page again, which inherits properties from the first master page, `Master1.master`.

Creating Themes

Applying built-in themes to Web pages is quite easy, as you just need to specify the name of the theme with the `Theme` attribute of the @ Page directive. However, you can also apply custom themes to Web pages. Prior to applying custom themes to Web pages, you first need to create a theme. To learn how to create themes, let's create a Web application named `CreatingThemesVB` (`CreatingThemesVB` in VB and `CreatingThemesCS` in C#). Now, perform the following steps to add the `App_Themes` folder in your application and create a theme for the website:

1. Right-click the website name in Solution Explorer and select `Add` → `Add ASP.NET Folder`→`Theme` from the context menu to add the `App_Themes` folder. A subfolder named `Theme1` is automatically created inside the `App_Themes` folder.
2. Right-click the `Theme1` folder and select the Add→Add New Item option from the context menu. The Add New Item dialog box appears (Figure 14.15).
3. Select the Skin File template option and specify the name of the skin as `Theme.skin`, and click the Add button, as shown in Figure 14.15:

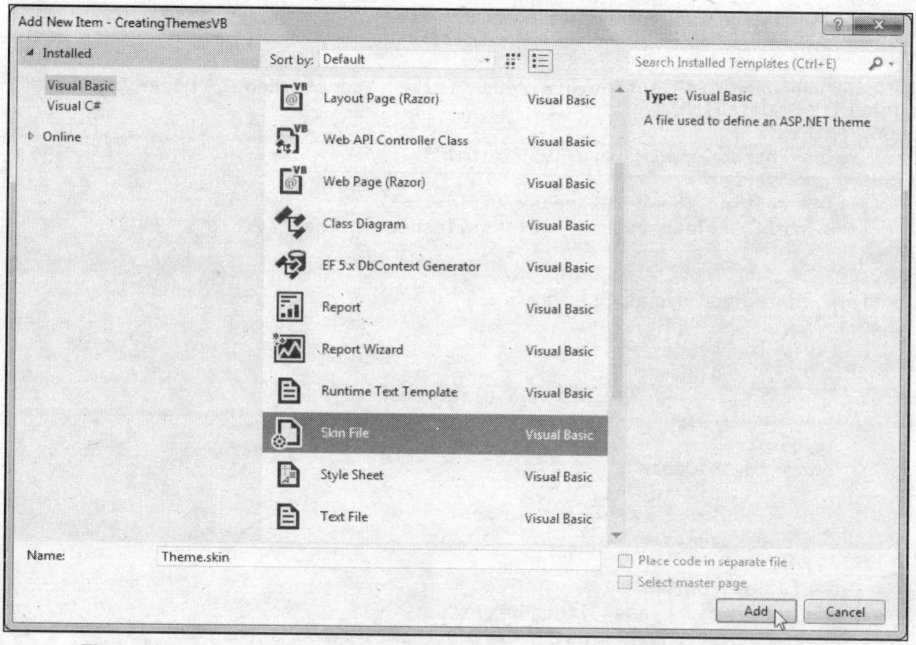

Figure 14.15: Adding the Theme.skin file from the Add New Item Dialog Box

The `Theme.skin` file is added to the `Theme1` folder in Solution Explorer, as shown in Figure 14.16:

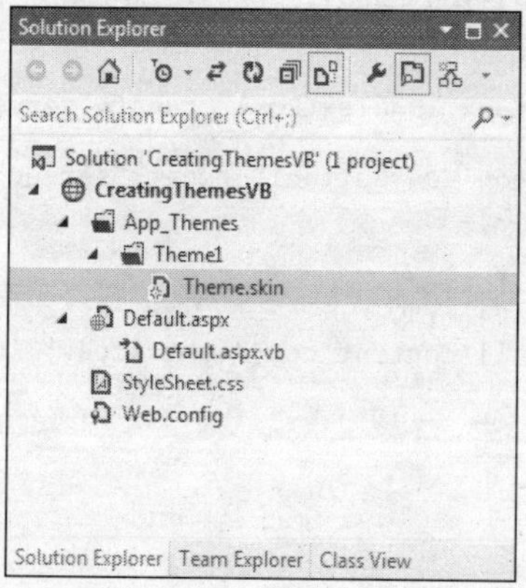

Figure 14.16: Showing the Theme.skin file in Solution Explorer

4. Add the code, shown in Listing 14.15, to the `Theme.skin` file to define its style properties:

Listing 14.15: Showing the Code for the `Theme.skin` File

In VB and C#

```
<asp:label runat="server" width="350px" height="50px" font-bold="True" font-size="Large"
  forecolor="Red" backcolor="Blue"/>
<asp:button runat="server" forecolor="Blue" backcolor="Silver"/>
<asp:textbox runat="server" font-bold="True" font-size="Medium" forecolor="Blue"
  backcolor="Silver" font-italic="True"/>
```

In Listing 14.15, we have defined style properties for three controls, Label, Button, and TextBox.

5. Add a Label control, a Button control, and a TextBox control in the `Default.aspx` page to test the skin, as shown in Listing 14.16:

Listing 14.16: Showing the Code for the `Default.aspx` Page

In VB

```
<%@ Page Language="VB" AutoEventWireup="false" Theme="Theme1" CodeFile="Default.aspx.vb"
  Inherits="_Default" %>
<!DOCTYPE html>
<html xmlns="http://www.w3.org/1999/xhtml">
<head runat="server">
    <title>Creating Themes Example</title>
    <link href="StyleSheet.css" rel="stylesheet" type="text/css" />
</head>
<body>
    <form id="form1" runat="server">
    <div>
        <div id="header">
                <h1>
                        ASP.NET 4.5 Black Book
                </h1>
        </div>
        <div id="sidebar">
                <div id="nav">
                         
                </div>
        </div>
        <div id="content">
                <div class="itemContent">
                <strong><em>Using Custom Themes</em></strong><br />
                <br />
                <br />
                <asp:Label ID="Label1" runat="server" Text="Enter Your Name in the Text
                Box"></asp:Label><br />
                <br />
                <asp:TextBox ID="TextBox1" runat="server"></asp:TextBox><br />
                <br />
                <asp:Button ID="Button1" runat="server" Text="Click To Submit" /></div>
            </div>
   </div>
                <div id="footer">
                <p class="left">
                        All content copyright &copy; Kogent Solutions Inc.</p>
                </div>
    </form>
</body>
</html>
```

In C#

```
<%@ Page Language="C#" AutoEventWireup="true" theme="Theme1" CodeFile="Default.aspx.cs"
  Inherits="_Default" %>
<!DOCTYPE html>
<html xmlns="http://www.w3.org/1999/xhtml">
<head runat="server">
    <title>Creating Themes Example</title>
    <link href="StyleSheet.css" rel="stylesheet" type="text/css" />
</head>
<body>
    <form id="form1" runat="server">
    <div>
        <div id="header">
                <h1>
                        ASP.NET 4.5 Black Book
                </h1>
```

```
        </div>
        <div id="sidebar">
                <div id="nav">
                         
                </div>
        </div>
        <div id="content">
                <div class="itemContent">
                <strong><em>Using Custom Themes</em></strong><br />
                <br />
                <br />
                <asp:Label ID="Label1" runat="server" Text="Enter Your Name in the Text
                Box"></asp:Label><br />
                <br />
                <asp:TextBox ID="TextBox1" runat="server"></asp:TextBox><br />
                <br />
                <asp:Button ID="Button1" runat="server" Text="Click To Submit" /></div>
          </div>
    </div>
                <div id="footer">
                <p class="left">
                        All content copyright &copy; Kogent Solutions Inc.</p>
                </div>
    </form>
</body>
</html>
```

In Listing 14.16, we have set the value of `Theme` attribute in the @ Page directive to `Theme1` to apply the theme specified in the `Theme.skin` file to all the controls on the `Default.aspx` page.

6. Run the application. Figure 14.17 shows the output of the `CreatingThemesVB` Web application:

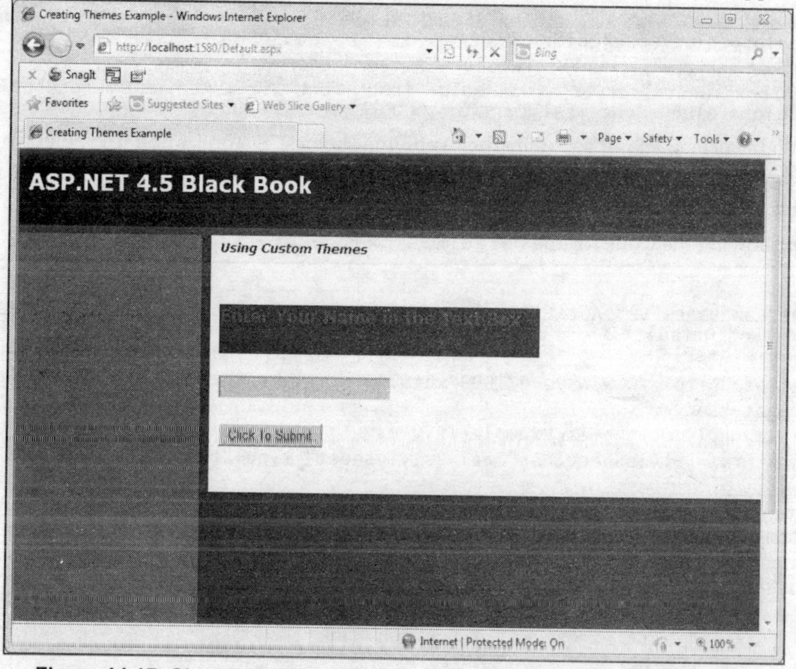

Figure 14.17: Showing the Output of the CreatingThemesVB Application

After creating themes in a Web application, let's learn how to apply the themes at control and runtime levels.

Applying Themes and Runtime Levels

In the previous section, we have created a theme and applied it to the entire page. You can also apply a theme at control level, that is, only to specific controls by using the `EnableTheming` and `Theme` properties, which are basically used to inherit the properties defined in the specified theme. You can set these properties to apply a theme on an individual control, as shown in the code snippet:

```
<asp:TextBox ID="TextBox1" runat="server" EnableTheming="true" Theme="Summer" />
```

To demonstrate how to apply themes at control and runtime levels, let's create a Web application, `ApplyingThemesCS` (`ApplyingThemesVB` in VB and `ApplyingThemesCS` in C#) and perform the following steps:

1. Create two folders, `Theme1` and `Theme2`, in Solution Explorer.
2. Create two themes, `Simple.skin` and `Inverse.skin`, and add them in the `Theme1` and `Theme2` folders, respectively.
3. Add the code, shown in Listing 14.17, to the `Simple.skin` file:

Listing 14.17: Showing the Code for the `Simple.skin` File

In VB and C#

```
<asp:label runat="server" width="350px" height="50px" font-bold="True" font-size="Large"
  forecolor="Red" backcolor="Blue"/>
<asp:button runat="server" forecolor="Blue" backcolor="Silver"/>
<asp:textbox runat="server" font-bold="True" font-size="Medium" forecolor="Blue"
  backcolor="Silver" font-italic="True"/>
```

4. Add the code, shown in Listing 14.18, to the `Inverse.skin` file:

Listing 14.18: Showing the Code for the `Inverse.skin` File

In VB and C#

```
<asp:label runat="server" width="350px" height="50px" font-bold="True" font-size="Large"
  forecolor="Blue" backcolor="Red"/>
<asp:button runat="server" forecolor="Silver" backcolor="Blue"/>
<asp:textbox runat="server" font-bold="True" font-size="Medium" forecolor="Silver"
  backcolor="Blue" font-italic="True"/>
```

5. Add a Web Form (Default.aspx) in the ApplyingThemesCS application by selecting the Web Form option from the middle pane of the Add New Item dialog box and then add the code, shown in Listing 14.19, to the `Default.aspx` page:

Listing 14.19: Showing the Code for the `Default.aspx` Page

In VB

```
<%@ Page Language="VB" AutoEventWireup="false" Theme="Theme1" CodeFile="Default.aspx.vb"
  Inherits="_Default" %>
<!DOCTYPE html>
<html xmlns="http://www.w3.org/1999/xhtml">
<head runat="server">
    <title>Applying themes Example</title>
    <link href="StyleSheet.css" rel="stylesheet" type="text/css" />
</head>
<body>
    <form id="form1" runat="server">
    <div>
        <div id="header">
            <h1>
                ASP.NET 4.5 Black Book
            </h1>
        </div>
        <div id="sidebar">
            <div id="nav">
```

```
                     
                </div>
            </div>
        <div id="content">
                <div class="itemContent">
                <div style="text-align: left">
                    <strong><em>Applying Themes at Runtime<br />
                </em></strong>
                <br />
                <asp:Image ID="Image1" runat="server"
                ImageUrl="~/Nested_Organisation.jpg" /><br />
                <br />
                <asp:Label ID="Label1" runat="server" Text="Enter your name in the text
                        box"></asp:Label>
                <br />
                <asp:TextBox ID="TextBox1" runat="server"></asp:TextBox><br />
                <br />
                <asp:Button ID="Button1" runat="server" BackColor="Black" Font-
                Bold="True" Font-Size="Small" ForeColor="White" Text="Click to Submit"
                /><br />
                <br />
                <asp:Button ID="Button3" BackColor="Black" Font-Bold="True" Font-
                Size="Small" ForeColor="White" runat="server" Text="Button" />
                <br />
                Select Theme   <a href="Default.aspx?Theme=Theme1">Simple</a>
                <a href="Default.aspx?Theme=Theme2">Inverse</a>
                <br />
                </div>  </div>
            </div>
                <div id="footer">
                        <p class="left">
                                All content copyright &copy; Kogent Solutions Inc.</p>
                </div>
                </div>
        </form>
    </body>
    </html>
```

In C#

```
<%@ Page Language="C#" autoeventwireup="true" Theme="Theme1" CodeFile="Default.aspx.cs"
  Inherits="_Default" %>
<!DOCTYPE html>
<html xmlns="http://www.w3.org/1999/xhtml">
<head runat="server">
    <title>Applying themes Example</title>
    <link href="StyleSheet.css" rel="stylesheet" type="text/css" />
</head>
<body>
    <form id="form1" runat="server">
    <div>
        <div id="header">
                <h1>
                        ASP.NET 4.5 Black Book
                </h1>
        </div>
        <div id="sidebar">
                <div id="nav">
                         
                </div>
```

```
        </div>
    <div id="content">
                <div class="itemContent">
                <div style="text-align: left">
                    <strong><em>Applying Themes at Runtime<br />
                </em></strong>
                <br />
                <asp:Image ID="Image1" runat="server"
                ImageUrl="~/Nested_Organisation.jpg" /><br />
                <br />
                <asp:Label ID="Label1" runat="server" Text="Enter your name in the text
                box"></asp:Label>
                <br />
                <asp:TextBox ID="TextBox1" runat="server"></asp:TextBox><br />
                <br />
                <asp:Button ID="Button1" runat="server" BackColor="Black" Font-
                Bold="True" Font-Size="Small" ForeColor="White" Text="Click to Submit"
                /><br />
                <br />
                <asp:Button ID="Button3" BackColor="Black" Font-Bold="True" Font-
                Size="Small" ForeColor="White" runat="server" Text="Button" />
                <br />
                Select Theme   <a href="Default.aspx?Theme=Theme1">Simple</a>
                <a href="Default.aspx?Theme=Theme2">Inverse</a>
                <br />
        </div>  </div>
    </div>
                <div id="footer">
                    <p class="left">
                        All content copyright &copy; Kogent Solutions Inc.</p>
                </div>
                </div>
    </form>
</body>
</html>
```

6. Add the code, shown in Listing 14.20, to the CodeFile of the `Default.aspx` page:

Listing 14.20: Showing the Code for the CodeFile

In VB

```
Partial Class _Default
    Inherits System.Web.UI.Page
    Protected Sub Page_PreInit(sender As Object, e As EventArgs) Handles
        Me.PreInit
        Page.Theme = Server.HtmlEncode(Request.QueryString("Theme"))
    End Sub
End Class
```

In C#

```
using System;
using System.Collections.Generic;
using System.Linq;
using System.Web;
using System.Web.UI;
using System.Web.UI.WebControls;
public partial class _Default : System.Web.UI.Page
{
    protected void Page_Load(object sender, EventArgs e)
    {
    }
```

```
    protected void Page_PreInit(object sender, EventArgs e)
    {
        Page.Theme = Server.HtmlEncode(Request.QueryString["Theme"]);
    }
}
```

7. Run the `ApplyingThemesCS` Web application. Figure 14.18 shows the output of this application:

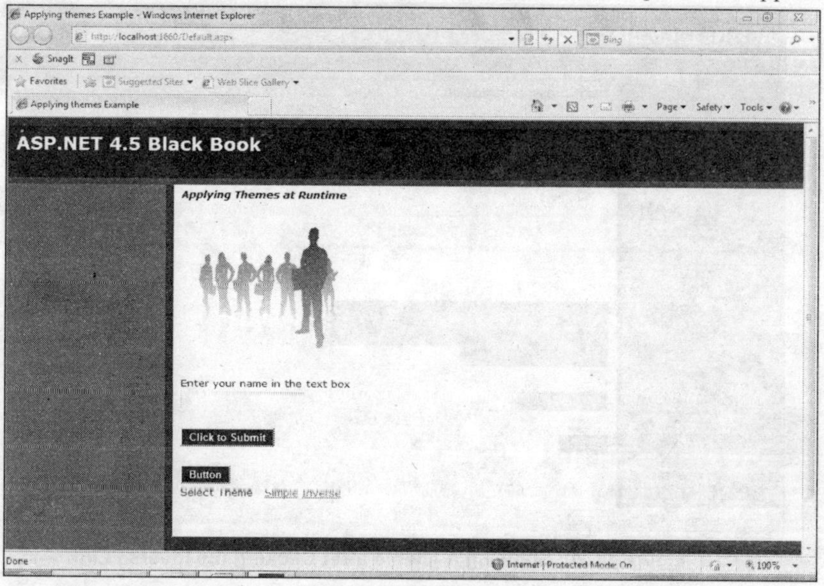

Figure 14.18: Displaying the Output of ApplyingThemesCs Application

Now, click the Simple link to change the theme at runtime. Figure 14.19 shows the output after clicking the Simple link:

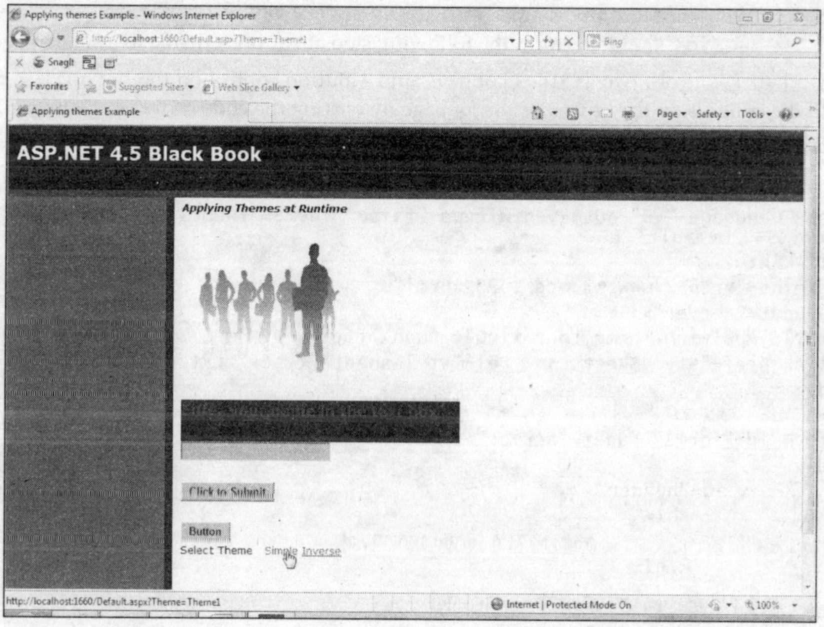

Figure 14.19: Showing a Theme after Clicking the Simple Link

Figure 14.20 displays the output of ApplyingThemesCS Web application after clicking the Inverse link:

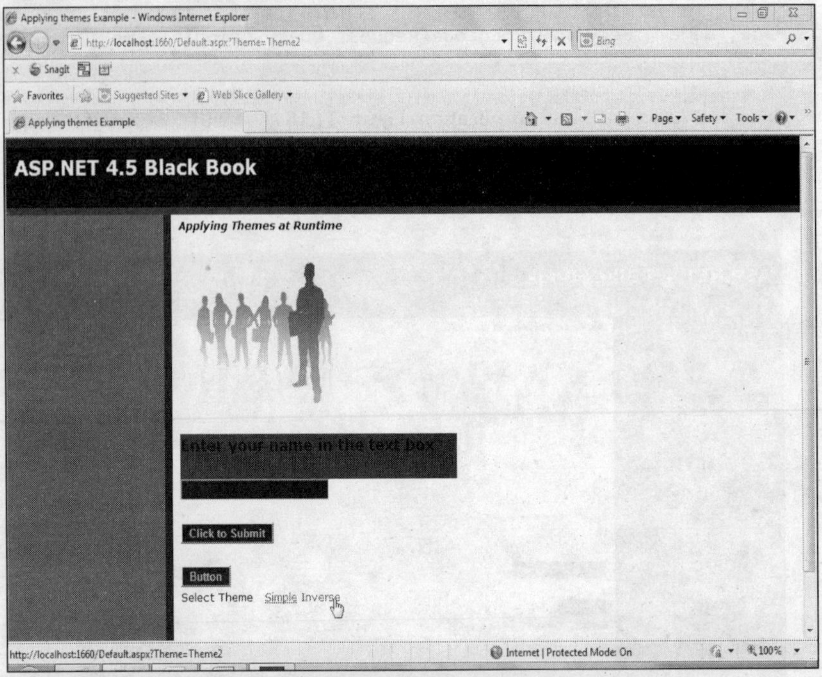

Figure 14.20: Showing a Theme after Clicking the Inverse Link

Now, let's how learn how to apply themes to a single page.

Applying Themes to a Single Page

Let's create a Web application named `SinglePageThemeVB` (`SinglePageThemeVB` in VB and `SinglePageThemeCS` in C#) and perform the following steps to apply a theme to a single page:

1. Drag two Label controls, two TextBox controls, and a Button control on the `Default.aspx` page. You can also add the controls on the `Default.aspx` page by writing the code shown in Listing 14.21:

Listing 14.21: Showing the Code for the `Default.aspx` Page

In VB

```
<%@ Page Language="VB" AutoEventWireup="false" Theme="Theme1" CodeFile="Default.aspx.vb"
  Inherits="_Default" %>
<!DOCTYPE html>
<html xmlns="http://www.w3.org/1999/xhtml">
<head runat="server">
    <title>Applying Theme to a Single Page</title>
    <link href="StyleSheet.css" rel="stylesheet" type="text/css" />
</head>
<body>
    <form id="form1" runat="server">
    <div>
         <div id="header">
                <h1>
                       ASP.NET 4.5 Black Book
                </h1>
         </div>
         <div id="sidebar">
```

```
                <div id="nav">
                         
    </div>
            </div>
            <asp:Label ID="Label1" runat="server" Text="Label"></asp:Label>
                
            <asp:TextBox ID="TextBox1" runat="server"></asp:TextBox>
            <br />
            <asp:Label ID="Label2" runat="server" Text="Label"></asp:Label>
                
            <asp:TextBox ID="TextBox2" runat="server" SkinID="TextBox"></asp:TextBox>
            <br /><br />
            <asp:Button ID="Button1" BackColor="Black" Font-Bold="True" Font-Size="Small"
            ForeColor="White" runat="server" Text="Button" />
            <div id="footer">
                <p class="left">
                        All content copyright &copy; Kogent Solutions Inc.</p>
            </div>
      </div>
        </form>
    </body>
    </html>
```

In C#

```
<%@ Page Language="C#" AutoEventWireup="true" Theme="Theme1" CodeFile="Default.aspx.cs"
  Inherits="_Default" %>
<!DOCTYPE html>
<html xmlns="http://www.w3.org/1999/xhtml">
<head runat="server">
    <title>Applying Theme to a Single Page</title>
    <link href="StyleSheet.css" rel="stylesheet" type="text/css" />
</head>
<body>
    <form id="form1" runat="server">
    <div>
        <div id="header">
            <h1>
                ASP.NET 4.5 Black Book
            </h1>
        </div>
        <div id="sidebar">
            <div id="nav">
                 
</div>
        </div>
        <asp:Label ID="Label1" runat="server" Text="Label"></asp:Label>
            
        <asp:TextBox ID="TextBox1" runat="server"></asp:TextBox>
        <br />
        <asp:Label ID="Label2" runat="server" Text="Label"></asp:Label>
            
        <asp:TextBox ID="TextBox2" runat="server" SkinID="TextBox"></asp:TextBox>
        <br /><br />
        <asp:Button ID="Button1" BackColor="Black" Font-Bold="True" Font-Size="Small"
        ForeColor="White" runat="server" Text="Button" />
        <div id="footer">
            <p class="left">
                All content copyright &copy; Kogent Solutions Inc.</p>
        </div>
```

```
        </div>
    </form>
</body>
</html>
```

2. Create a theme to apply it on the `Default.aspx` page. To create a theme, right-click the name of the application and select the Add → `Add ASP.NET Folder→Theme` option from the context menu. A subfolder named `Theme1` is automatically created inside the `App_Themes` folder.
3. Right-click the Theme1 folder and select the Add→Add New Item option from the context menu. The Add New Item dialog box appears (Figure 14.21).
4. Select the Skin File template and click the Add button. A file named `SkinFile.skin` is created in the `Theme1` folder, as shown in Figure 14.21:

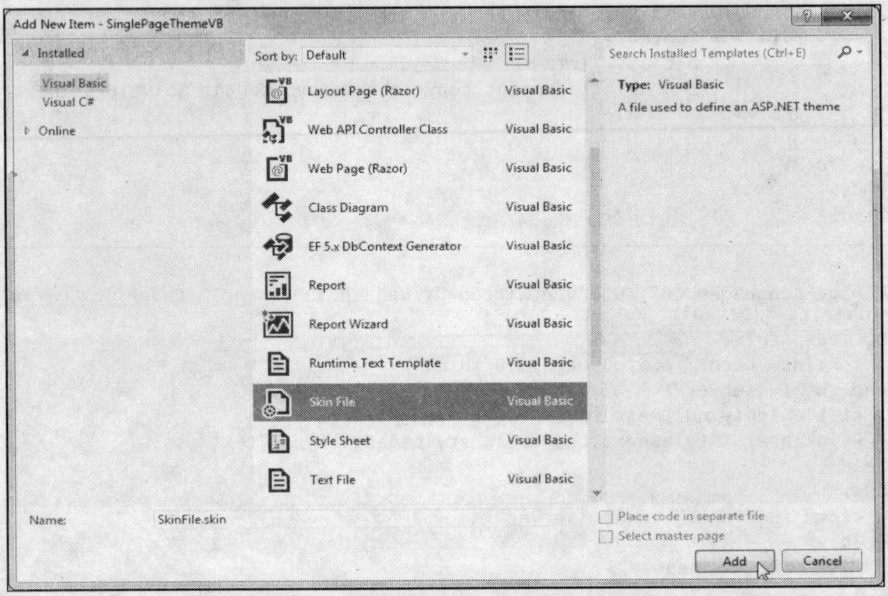

Figure 14.21: Selecting the Skin File Template

5. Add the code, shown in Listing 14.22, to the `SkinFile.skin` file:

Listing 14.22: Showing the Code for the `SkinFile.skin` File

In VB and C#

```
<asp:label runat="server" font-size="Large" forecolor="HotPink" backcolor="LightBlue"
   font-italic="True"/>
<asp:button runat="server" font-bold="True" width="200px" height="50px"
   forecolor="IndianRed" backcolor="Blue"/>
<asp:textbox runat="server" font-bold="True" font-size="Medium" forecolor="Red"
   backcolor="Yellow" />
<asp:textbox SkinID="TextBox" runat="server" font-italic="True" font-size="Medium"
   forecolor="Yellow" backcolor="Red" />
```

In Listing 14.22, we have used the `SkinID` property for a `TextBox` control. You can apply this theme only on the TextBox control, which is referred to with the `SkinID` property.

6. Run the application. The output appears in a Web browser, as shown in Figure 14.22:

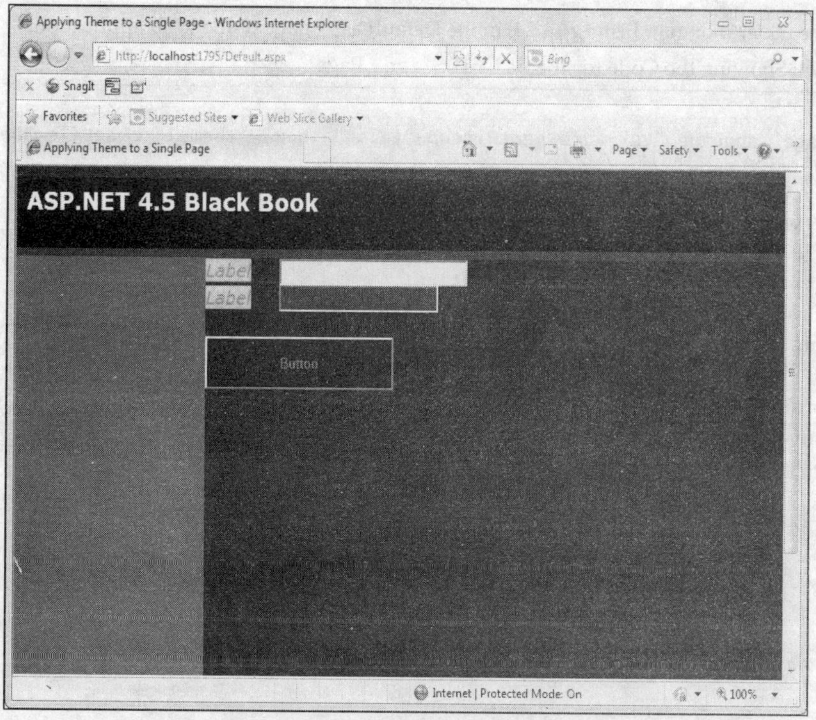

Figure 14.22: Applying a theme to a Single Page

In Figure 14.22, you can see that the color of the second `TextBox` control is not the same as the first `TextBox` control. The theme set with the SkinID property is only applied to the control referred to with the `SkinID` property.

Instead of using the `Theme` attribute in the @ Page directive, you can use the `StyleSheetTheme` attribute to apply the themes to a Web page. Now, let's learn about the `StyleSheetTheme` attribute.

Using the StyleSheetTheme Attribute

In the previous sections, we have used the Theme attribute to apply a theme to a Web page. Now, we use the `StyleSheetTheme` attribute for the same task. Let's create a new Web application in the Visual Studio 2012, and name it `StyleSheetThemeCS` (`StyleSheetThemeVB` in VB and `StyleSheetThemeCS` in C#). After creating the application, perform the following steps to use the `StyleSheetTheme` attribute:

1. Create a `SkinFile.skin` file in the `Theme1` folder.
2. Add the code, shown in Listing 14.23, to the `SkinFile.skin` file:

Listing 14.23: Showing the Code for the `SkinFile.skin` File

In VB and C#

```
<asp:label runat="server" width="350px" height="50px" font-bold="True" font-size="Large"
  forecolor="Red" backcolor="Blue"/>
<asp:button runat="server" forecolor="Blue" backcolor="Silver"/>
<asp:textbox runat="server" font-bold="True" font-size="Medium" forecolor="Blue"
  backcolor="Silver" font-italic="True"/>
```

In Listing 14.23, we have set the background and foreground colors of the controls that can be used in a Web page.

3. Add the code, shown in Listing 14.24, in the Default.aspx page of the Web application:

Listing 14.24: Showing the Code for the `Default.aspx` Page

In VB

```
<%@ Page Language="VB" AutoEventWireup="false" Theme="Theme1" CodeFile="Default.aspx.vb"
  Inherits="_Default" %>
<!DOCTYPE html>
<html xmlns="http://www.w3.org/1999/xhtml">
<head runat="server">
    <title>StyleSheetTheme Page</title>
    <link href="StyleSheet.css" rel="stylesheet" type="text/css" />
</head>
<body>
    <form id="form1" runat="server">
    <div>
         <div id="header">
                <h1>
                        ASP.NET 4.5 Black Book
                </h1>
         </div>
         <div id="sidebar">
                <div id="nav">
                         
                </div>
         </div>
         <div id="content">
                <div class="itemContent">
                <div style="text-align: left">
                <asp:Label ID="Label1" runat="server" Text="Label"></asp:Label>
                <br />
                <br />
                <asp:TextBox ID="TextBox1" runat="server"></asp:TextBox>
                <br />
                <br />
                <asp:Button ID="Button1" runat="server" Text="Button" ForeColor="Aqua"
                BackColor="DarkViolet" />
                </div></div>
   </div>
                <div id="footer">
                <p class="left">
                        All content copyright &copy; Kogent Solutions Inc.</p>
                </div>
    </form>
  </body>
  </html>
```

In C#

```
<%@ Page Language="C#" AutoEventWireup="true" Theme="Theme1" CodeFile="Default.aspx.cs"
   Inherits="_Default" %>
<!DOCTYPE html>
<html xmlns="http://www.w3.org/1999/xhtml">
<head runat="server">
    <title>StyleSheetTheme Page</title>
    <link href="StyleSheet.css" rel="stylesheet" type="text/css" />
</head>
<body>
    <form id="form1" runat="server">
    <div>
         <div id="header">
                <h1>
                       ASP.NET 4.5 Black Book
                </h1>
         </div>
         <div id="sidebar">
                <div id="nav">
                        
                </div>
         </div>
         <div id="content">
                <div class="itemContent">
                <div style="text-align: left">

                <asp:Label ID="Label1" runat="server" Text="Label"></asp:Label>
                <br />
                <br />
                <asp:TextBox ID="TextBox1" runat="server"></asp:TextBox>
                <br />
                <br />
                <asp:Button ID="Button1" runat="server" Text="Button" ForeColor="Aqua"
                BackColor="DarkViolet" />
         </div></div>
  </div>
                <div id="footer">
                <p class="left">
                       All content copyright &copy; Kogent Solutions Inc.</p>
                </div>
                </div>
    </form>
</body>
</html>
```

In Listing 14.24, we have added three controls, `Label`, `TextBox`, and `Button`, in the `Default.aspx` page. We have specified the `foreground` and `background colors` locally for the Button control. We have also added the `StyleSheetTheme` attribute in the @ Page directive of the `Default.aspx` page.

4. Run the Web application. The output appears, as shown in Figure 14.23:

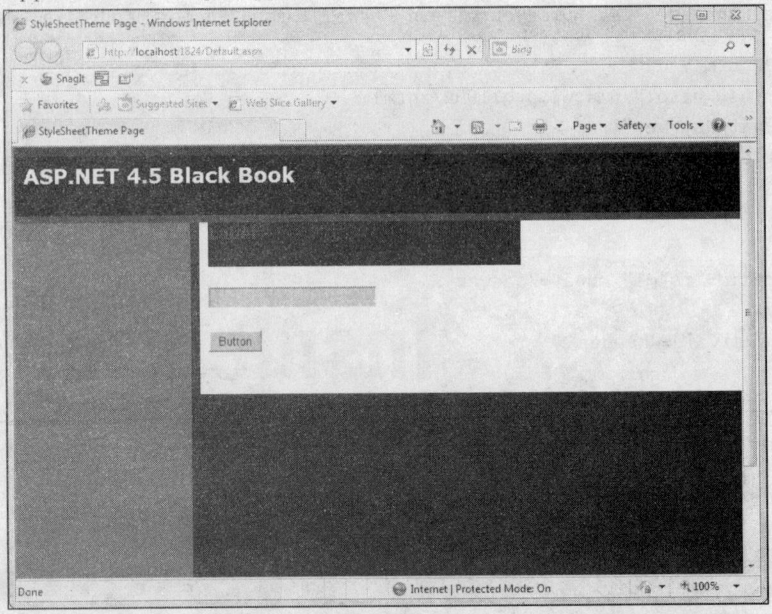

Figure 14.23: Displaying the Output of the StyleSheetThemeCS Application

The foreground and background colors of the `Button` control (Figure 14.23) are specified locally in the `Default.aspx` page. As discussed earlier in the *In Depth* section, the colors of the `Button` control are not overridden by the colors we have specified in the theme (`SkinFile.skin`) file. This is done by using the `StyleSheetTheme` attribute. On the other hand, if the `Theme` attribute is used, then it would display those colors of the `Button` control that we have specified in the `SkinFile.skin` file.

Summary

In this chapter, you have learned about the need of master pages and themes, and also learned how to create and apply master pages and themes on Web pages. You have also discussed about the ASP.NET AJAX master pages and the `StyleSheetTheme` attribute.

In the next chapter, you learn about Web Parts Framework, its need, and how to use various Web part controls.

15

Inside Web Parts Framework

In Depth

Web Parts Framework provides you with the means to create websites that are customizable as per the requirement of users. This feature helps users to focus only on the information relevant to them, while neglecting the irrelevant part. The information regarding the customization carried out on websites created by users is saved permanently, and this information is used to customize websites (according to the customization carried out) every time respective users visit the websites. ASP.NET 4.5 Web Parts Framework enables users to directly customize a Web page from a Web browser. It facilitates users to add, move, or delete the modular components, called Web Parts, on a Web page. Consequently, Web Parts Framework ensures that users gain significant control over the content and layout of the Web page. In addition to the primary objective of manipulating modular Web page components, there are some other features of Web Parts, such as:

- Helps in customization and personalization of Web Parts in a Web page
- Helps in exporting and importing of Web Parts
- Helps in exchanging data between Web Parts

In this chapter, you learn the concept and requirements of the ASP.NET 4.5 Web Parts Framework. You also learn about the other features of Web Parts Framework using Web Parts controls, such as personalizing Web Parts and exporting and importing of Web Parts. Now, let's take a quick look at the requirements for Web Parts Framework.

Requirements for Web Parts Framework

Why do we need a Web Parts Framework? There are many answers to this question, considering the enormous amount of built-in functionalities that the Framework supports. To sum up all the answers in one line, we can say that the Web Parts Framework provides an environment to create Web pages that can be customized according to the user's requirements.

Now-a-days, websites have become quite comprehensive as they incorporate a plethora of functionalities for the users. In such a scenario, there arises a need for a Framework that provides the users with the functionality to display and work with only the required Parts of a Web page. For example, if a user visits a Web page regularly to catch up with the local weather report, then it is quite cumbersome for the user to click three to four hyperlinks to display the required information, every time the user visits the website. Instead, if the Web page supports some sort of personalized mechanism that enables the user to permanently display the local weather report on the home page, it will be more convenient for the users to look for the required information.

You can take a real life scenario of the www.igoogle.com website. When you visit this website, you can observe the Create your own home page in under 30 seconds window prompted, containing options to select gadgets and themes. When you select the options, given in the Select Interests group, then the selected options are added to the Web Part zones of the Web page. It displays the Web Parts, which are being selected, and are added accordingly within the sections.

On the Web page (Figure 15.1), different Web Parts or gadgets such as weather forecasting, date and time with analog watch, Gmail, YouTube, and CNN news are displayed. It allows users to modify the Google page according to their requirements. In this website, Web Parts provide the functionality to allow users to customize this website by adding, deleting, and moving the controls around the Web page based on WebPartZones. Every Web Parts control is tagged with a drop-down list, which is known as a Verb Menu, and provides the following actions:

- **Edit settings**—Refers to the customization of gadget
- **Delete this Gadget**—Refers to remove the gadget from the Web page based on WebPartZones
- **Minimize this Gadget**—Refers to minimize the gadget

- **Share this Gadget**—Refers to the communication between Web Parts, exporting gadget to other zone
- **About this Gadget**—Refers to the description of the gadget

It also provides a placeholder placed on the title bar to move a gadget from one zone to another. You can easily migrate the gadget placing from one Web Part zone to another Web Part zone in a Web page, as shown in Figure 15.1:

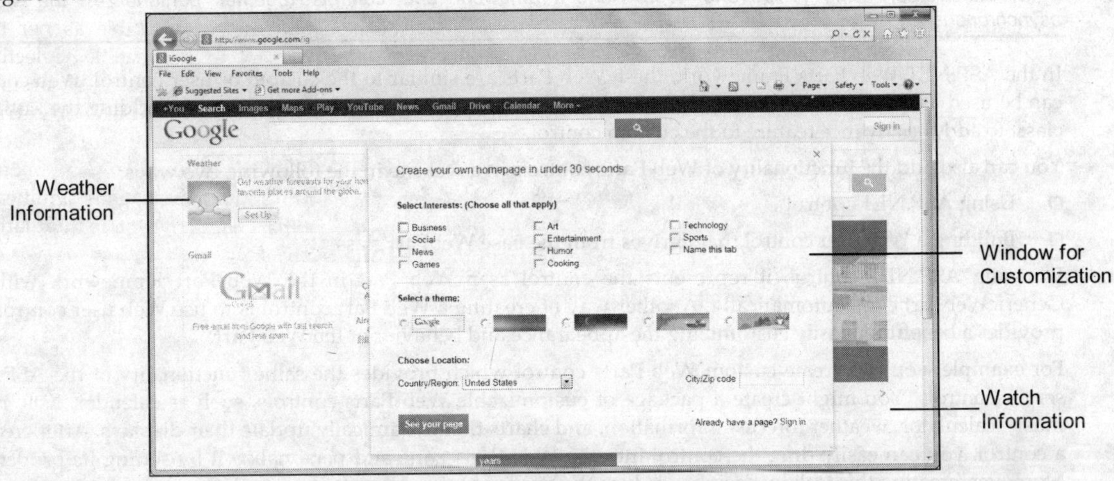

Figure 15.1: Displaying the Use of Web Parts in the iGoogle website

NOTE

WebPartZone is a Web Parts control that defines a zone of a page to place Web Parts or server controls. In the preceding example, the figure shows different zones placed at the page, such as Weather Zone and Date & Time Zone. For more information on Web Parts controls, refer to Chapter 7, Introducing Web Parts Controls.

Earlier, developers used to build a personalized website by creating a personalized Framework from scratch. As a result, it required the developers to write an extensive amount of code, which was obviously quite tedious and error-prone process. Microsoft realized this problem and shipped the much-required Web Parts Framework with ASP.NET 4.5. The developer community witnessed the ready-implementation of Web Parts Framework in the Windows SharePoint Services website, as shown in Figure 15.2:

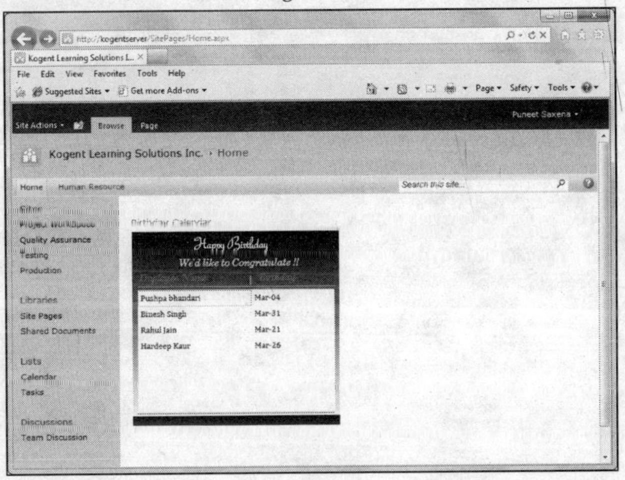

Figure 15.2: Showing the Windows SharePoint Services Website

Web Parts Framework provides a complete set of `WebParts` controls to create personalized websites. This set of Web Parts controls includes controls, such as `WebPartManager`, `WebPartZone`, and `CatalogZone`.

NOTE

You can also use Web Parts Framework controls with AJAX, so that any modifications made do not require a postback. In simple words, using AJAX and Web Parts Framework and controls together personalizes the website asynchronously.

In the ASP.NET Web Parts Framework, these Web Parts are similar to the custom or user control. Web controls can be used as a Web Part. You can also create Web Parts by using the custom controls by adding the `WebPart` class, to add the advance feature to the custom control.

You can also add the functionality of Web Parts controls in a website in the following two ways:

- Using ASP.NET control
- Building a Web user control that derives from the base WebPart class

By using ASP.NET control, it represents the control as a Web Part in the Web Part Framework with the GenericWebPart class automatically. Another way of creating a Web Part control is to use Web user control that provides a benefit for easily customizing the appearance and behavior of the Web Part.

For example, you can create custom Web Parts control which provides the same functionality of the ASP.NET server controls. You might create a package of customizable Web Parts controls, such as calendar, lists, news, music, calculator, weather forecast information, and charts that dynamically update their displays. After creating a control, you can easily drag the control into the Web Parts zone and personalize it by setting its properties.. Moreover, creating this task by designer reduce the burden of developer to do mundane programming.

Immediate Solutions

Personalizing Web Parts

Personalizing the Web Parts involves creating a modular, dynamic, and customizable website, which identifies the users, stores their modified settings, and provides them with a personalized environment whenever the users revisit the Web page. In other words, through personalization of Web Parts, users are provided with the controlled access to modify the Web Parts as per their preferences. These modifications are stored and later retrieved from the ASPNETDB.MDF database to display a Web page as configured by the user.

NOTE

ASPNETDB.MDF is the default database integrated with the Visual Studio 2012 and located inside the App_Data folder of the website. It is used for creating ASP.NET Application Services, such as profiles, roles, and membership. This database is automatically created when you create a user or a role using Web Site Administration Tool. In VS 2012 IDE, to open this tool, select the WEBSITE→ASP.NET Configuration option from the menu bar. We have implemented this concept of using the ASPNETDB.MDF file in the following application given in the Immediate Solutions of this chapter.

You should also note that the applications created in this chapter have Stylesheet included with. The applications are created using the ASP.NET Empty Website template from the Add New Item dialog box and the Default.aspx page is added to the application.

To understand the whole concept of personalizing the Web Parts, let's first create personalized websites, `WebPartsDemoAppCS` for C# and `WebPartsDemoAppVB` for VB. After creating the websites, add the code given in Listing 15.1 to the Default.aspx page:

Listing 15.1: Showing the Code for the `Default.aspx` Page

In VB

```
<%@ Page Language="VB" AutoEventWireup="false" CodeFile="Default.aspx.vb"
  Inherits="_Default" %>
<!DOCTYPE html>
<html xmlns="http://www.w3.org/1999/xhtml">
<head runat="server">
    <title>WebPartsDemo</title>
    <link href="StyleSheet.css" rel="stylesheet" type="text/css" />
</head>
<body>
  <form id="form1" runat="server">
        <div>
                <div id="header">
                        <h1>
                                ASP.NET 4.5 Black Book
                        </h1>
                </div>
                <div id="sidebar">
                        <div id="nav">
                                 
                        </div>
                </div>
                <div id="content">
                        <div class="itemContent">
                        <asp:WebPartManager ID="WebPartManager1" runat="server"
                        Personalization-Enabled="true">
                        </asp:WebPartManager>
```

```
     
<asp:LoginStatus ID="LoginStatus1" runat="server"
LogoutAction="RedirectToLoginPage" />
<br />
<br />
<br />
<asp:LinkButton ID="LinkButton2" runat="server">
Browse
</asp:LinkButton>
 
<asp:LinkButton ID="LinkButton3" runat="server">
Edit
</asp:LinkButton>
 
<asp:LinkButton ID="LinkButton4" runat="server">
Catalog
</asp:LinkButton>
 
<asp:LinkButton ID="LinkButton5" runat="server">
Design
</asp:LinkButton>
<table>
<tr>
<td valign="top" align="left">
<asp:WebPartZone ID="WebPartZone1" runat="server"
Height="166px" Width="273px" BorderColor="#CCCCCC"
Font-Names="Verdana" Padding="6"
LayoutOrientation="Horizontal">
<ZoneTemplate>
<asp:Calendar ID="Calendar1" runat="server" Title="My
Calendar"></asp:Calendar>
</ZoneTemplate>
<PartChromeStyle BackColor="#F7F6F3" BorderColor="#E2DED6"
Font-Names="Verdana" ForeColor="White" />
<MenuLabelHoverStyle ForeColor="#E2DED6" />
<EmptyZoneTextStyle Font-Size="0.8em" />
<MenuLabelStyle ForeColor="White" />
<MenuVerbHoverStyle BackColor="#F7F6F3" BorderColor="#CCCCCC"
BorderStyle="Solid"
BorderWidth="1px" ForeColor="#333333" />
<HeaderStyle Font-Size="0.7em" ForeColor="#CCCCCC"
HorizontalAlign="Center" />
<MenuVerbStyle BorderColor="#5D7B9D" BorderStyle="Solid"
BorderWidth="1px" ForeColor="White" />
<PartStyle Font-Size="0.8em" ForeColor="#333333" />
<TitleBarVerbStyle Font-Size="0.6em" Font-Underline="False"
ForeColor="White" />
<MenuPopupStyle BackColor="#5D7B9D" BorderColor="#CCCCCC"
BorderWidth="1px" Font-Names="Verdana"
Font-Size="0.6em" />
<PartTitleStyle BackColor="#5D7B9D" Font-Bold="True" Font-
Size="0.8em" ForeColor="White" />
</asp:WebPartZone>
</td>
<td valign="top" align="center">
<asp:WebPartZone ID="WebPartZone3" runat="server" Height="87px"
Width="87px" BorderColor="#CCCCCC"
Font-Names="Verdana" Padding="6">
<ZoneTemplate>
```

```
<asp:Image ID="Image1" runat="server" AlternateText="Error
Displaying Image" Height="50px"
ImageUrl="~/organisation.jpg" Width="100px" Title="My Logo" />
</ZoneTemplate>
<PartChromeStyle BackColor="#F7F6F3" BorderColor="#E2DED6"
Font-Names="Verdana" ForeColor="White" />
<MenuLabelHoverStyle ForeColor="#E2DED6" />
<EmptyZoneTextStyle Font-Size="0.8em" />
<MenuLabelStyle ForeColor="White" />
<MenuVerbHoverStyle BackColor="#F7F6F3" BorderColor="#CCCCCC"
BorderStyle="Solid"
BorderWidth="1px" ForeColor="#333333" />
<HeaderStyle Font-Size="0.7em" ForeColor="#CCCCCC"
HorizontalAlign="Center" />
<MenuVerbStyle BorderColor="#5D7B9D" BorderStyle="Solid"
BorderWidth="1px" ForeColor="White" />
<PartStyle Font-Size="0.8em" ForeColor="#333333" />
<TitleBarVerbStyle Font-Size="0.6em" Font-Underline="False"
ForeColor="White" />
<MenuPopupStyle BackColor="#5D7B9D" BorderColor="#CCCCCC"
BorderWidth="1px" Font-Names="Verdana"
Font-Size="0.6em" />
<PartTitleStyle BackColor="#5D7B9D" Font-Bold="True" Font-
Size="0.8em" ForeColor="White" />
</asp:WebPartZone>
<asp:WebPartZone ID="WebPartZone2" runat="server" Width="87px"
Height="67px" BorderColor="#CCCCCC"
Font-Names="Verdana" Padding="6">
<ZoneTemplate>
<asp:Label ID="Label1" runat="server" Text="City Name: New
York" Width="50px" Title="My City">
</asp:Label>
</ZoneTemplate>
<PartChromeStyle BackColor="#F7F6F3" BorderColor="#E2DED6"
Font-Names="Verdana" ForeColor="White" />
<MenuLabelHoverStyle ForeColor="#E2DED6" />
<EmptyZoneTextStyle Font-Size="0.8em" />
<MenuLabelStyle ForeColor="White" />
<MenuVerbHoverStyle BackColor="#F7F6F3" BorderColor="#CCCCCC"
BorderStyle="Solid"
BorderWidth="1px" ForeColor="#333333" />
<HeaderStyle Font-Size="0.7em" ForeColor="#CCCCCC"
HorizontalAlign="Center" />
<MenuVerbStyle BorderColor="#5D7B9D" BorderStyle="Solid"
BorderWidth="1px" ForeColor="White" />
<PartStyle Font-Size="0.8em" ForeColor="#333333" />
<TitleBarVerbStyle Font-Size="0.6em" Font-Underline="False"
ForeColor="White" />
<MenuPopupStyle BackColor="#5D7B9D" BorderColor="#CCCCCC"
BorderWidth="1px" Font-Names="Verdana"
Font-Size="0.6em" />
<PartTitleStyle BackColor="#5D7B9D" Font-Bold="True" Font-
Size="0.8em" ForeColor="White" />
</asp:WebPartZone>
</td>
<td valign="top" align="right">
<asp:EditorZone ID="EditorZone1" runat="server"
BackColor="#F7F6F3" BorderColor="#CCCCCC"
BorderWidth="1px" Font-Names="Verdana" Padding="6">
```

```
<ZoneTemplate>
<asp:AppearanceEditorPart ID="Appearanceeditorpart1"
runat="server" />
<asp:LayoutEditorPart ID="Layouteditorpart1" runat="server" />
<asp:PropertyGridEditorPart ID="Propertygrideditorpart1"
runat="server" />
</ZoneTemplate>
<LabelStyle Font-Size="0.8em" ForeColor="#333333" />
<HeaderStyle BackColor="#E2DED6" Font-Bold="True" Font-
Size="0.8em" ForeColor="#333333" />
<HeaderVerbStyle Font-Bold="False" Font-Size="0.8em" Font-
Underline="False" ForeColor="#333333" />
<PartChromeStyle BorderColor="#E2DED6" BorderStyle="Solid"
BorderWidth="1px" />
<PartStyle BorderColor="#F7F6F3" BorderWidth="5px" />
<FooterStyle BackColor="#E2DED6" HorizontalAlign="Right" />
<EditUIStyle Font-Names="Verdana" Font-Size="0.8em"
ForeColor="#333333" />
<InstructionTextStyle Font-Size="0.8em" ForeColor="#333333" />
<ErrorStyle Font-Size="0.8em" />
<VerbStyle Font-Names="Verdana" Font-Size="0.8em"
ForeColor="#333333" />
<EmptyZoneTextStyle Font-Size="0.8em" ForeColor="#333333" />
<PartTitleStyle Font-Bold="True" Font-Size="0.8em"
ForeColor="#333333" />
</asp:EditorZone>
</td>
<td valign="top" align="right" style="width: 312px">
<asp:CatalogZone ID="CatalogZone1" runat="server"
Height="122px" BackColor="#F7F6F3"
BorderColor="#CCCCCC" BorderWidth="1px" Font-Names="Verdana"
Padding="6">
<ZoneTemplate>
<asp:PageCatalogPart ID="PageCatalogPart1" runat="server" />
<asp:DeclarativeCatalogPart ID="DeclarativeCatalogPart1"
runat="server">
</asp:DeclarativeCatalogPart>
</ZoneTemplate>
<HeaderVerbStyle Font-Bold="False" Font-Size="0.8em" Font-
Underline="False" ForeColor="#333333" />
<PartTitleStyle BackColor="#5D7B9D" Font-Bold="True" Font-
Size="0.8em" ForeColor="White" />
<FooterStyle BackColor="#E2DED6" HorizontalAlign="Right" />
<PartChromeStyle BorderColor="#E2DED6" BorderStyle="Solid"
BorderWidth="1px" />
<InstructionTextStyle Font-Size="0.8em" ForeColor="#333333" />
<LabelStyle Font-Size="0.8em" ForeColor="#333333" />
<PartLinkStyle Font-Size="0.8em" />
<SelectedPartLinkStyle Font-Size="0.8em" />
<VerbStyle Font-Names="Verdana" Font-Size="0.8em"
ForeColor="#333333" />
<HeaderStyle BackColor="#E2DED6" Font-Bold="True" Font-
Size="0.8em" ForeColor="#333333" />
<EmptyZoneTextStyle Font-Size="0.8em" ForeColor="#333333" />
<EditUIStyle Font-Names="Verdana" Font-Size="0.8em"
ForeColor="#333333" />
<PartStyle BorderColor="#F7F6F3" BorderWidth="5px" />
</asp:CatalogZone>
</td>
```

```
                    </tr>
                    </table>
            </div></div>
            <div id="footer">
                    <p class="left">
                            All content copyright &copy; Kogent Solutions Inc.
                    </p>
        </div>
    </div>
      </form>
</body>
</html>
```

In C#

```
<%@ Page Language="C#" AutoEventWireup="true" CodeFile="Default.aspx.cs"
   Inherits="_Default" %>
<!DOCTYPE html>
<html xmlns="http://www.w3.org/1999/xhtml">
<head runat="server">
    <title>WebPartsDemo</title>
</head>
<link href="StyleSheet.css" rel="stylesheet" type="text/css" />
<body>
   <form id="form1" runat="server">
        <div>
            <div id="header">
                    <h1>
                            ASP.NET 4.5 Black Book
                    </h1>
            </div>
            <div id="sidebar">
                    <div id="nav">
                             
                    </div>
            </div>
            <div id="content">
                    <div class="itemContent">
                    <asp:WebPartManager ID="WebPartManager1" runat="server"
                    Personalization-Enabled="true">
                    </asp:WebPartManager>
                         
                    <asp:LoginStatus ID="LoginStatus1" runat="server"
                    LogoutAction="RedirectToLoginPage" />
                    <br />
                    <br />
                    <br />
                    <asp:LinkButton ID="LinkButton2" runat="server"
                    onclick="LinkButton2_Click">
                    Browse
                    </asp:LinkButton>
                     
                    <asp:LinkButton ID="LinkButton3" runat="server"
                    onclick="LinkButton3_Click">
                    Edit
                    </asp:LinkButton>
                     
                   <asp:LinkButton ID="LinkButton4" runat="server"
                    onclick="LinkButton4_Click">
                    Catalog
```

```
</asp:LinkButton>
 
<asp:LinkButton ID="LinkButton5" runat="server"
onclick="LinkButton5_Click">
Design
</asp:LinkButton>
<table>
<tr>
<td valign="top" align="left">
<asp:WebPartZone ID="WebPartZone1" runat="server"
Height="166px" Width="273px" BorderColor="#CCCCCC"
Font-Names="Verdana" Padding="6"
LayoutOrientation="Horizontal">
<ZoneTemplate>
<asp:Calendar ID="Calendar1" runat="server" Title="My
Calendar"></asp:Calendar>
</ZoneTemplate>
<PartChromeStyle BackColor="#F7F6F3" BorderColor="#E2DED6"
Font-Names="Verdana" ForeColor="White" />
<MenuLabelHoverStyle ForeColor="#E2DED6" />
<EmptyZoneTextStyle Font-Size="0.8em" />
<MenuLabelStyle ForeColor="White" />
<MenuVerbHoverStyle BackColor="#F7F6F3" BorderColor="#CCCCCC"
BorderStyle="Solid"
BorderWidth="1px" ForeColor="#333333" />
<HeaderStyle Font-Size="0.7em" ForeColor="#CCCCCC"
HorizontalAlign="Center" />
<MenuVerbStyle BorderColor="#5D7B9D" BorderStyle="Solid"
BorderWidth="1px" ForeColor="White" />
<PartStyle Font-Size="0.8em" ForeColor="#333333" />
<TitleBarVerbStyle Font-Size="0.6em" Font-Underline="False"
ForeColor="White" />
<MenuPopupStyle BackColor="#5D7B9D" BorderColor="#CCCCCC"
BorderWidth="1px" Font-Names="Verdana"
Font-Size="0.6em" />
<PartTitleStyle BackColor="#5D7B9D" Font-Bold="True" Font-
Size="0.8em" ForeColor="White" />
</asp:WebPartZone>
</td>
<td valign="top" align="center">
<asp:WebPartZone ID="WebPartZone3" runat="server" Height="87px"
Width="87px" BorderColor="#CCCCCC"
Font-Names="Verdana" Padding="6">
<ZoneTemplate>
<asp:Image ID="Image1" runat="server" AlternateText="Error
Displaying Image" Height="50px"
ImageUrl="~/organisation.jpg" Width="100px" Title="My Logo" />
</ZoneTemplate>
<PartChromeStyle BackColor="#F7F6F3" BorderColor="#E2DED6"
Font-Names="Verdana" ForeColor="White" />
<MenuLabelHoverStyle ForeColor="#E2DED6" />
<EmptyZoneTextStyle Font-Size="0.8em" />
<MenuLabelStyle ForeColor="White" />
<MenuVerbHoverStyle BackColor="#F7F6F3" BorderColor="#CCCCCC"
BorderStyle="Solid"
BorderWidth="1px" ForeColor="#333333" />
<HeaderStyle Font-Size="0.7em" ForeColor="#CCCCCC"
HorizontalAlign="Center" />
<MenuVerbStyle BorderColor="#5D7B9D" BorderStyle="Solid"
```

```
BorderWidth="1px" ForeColor="White" />
<PartStyle Font-Size="0.8em" ForeColor="#333333" />
<TitleBarVerbStyle Font-Size="0.6em" Font-Underline="False"
ForeColor="White" />
<MenuPopupStyle BackColor="#5D7B9D" BorderColor="#CCCCCC"
BorderWidth="1px" Font-Names="Verdana"
Font-Size="0.6em" />
<PartTitleStyle BackColor="#5D7B9D" Font-Bold="True" Font-
Size="0.8em" ForeColor="White" />
</asp:WebPartZone>
<asp:WebPartZone ID="WebPartZone2" runat="server" Width="87px"
Height="67px" BorderColor="#CCCCCC"
Font-Names="Verdana" Padding="6">
<ZoneTemplate>
<asp:Label ID="Label1" runat="server" Text="City Name: New
York" Width="50px" Title="My City">
</asp:Label>
</ZoneTemplate>
<PartChromeStyle BackColor="#F7F6F3" BorderColor="#E2DED6"
Font-Names="Verdana" ForeColor="White" />
<MenuLabelHoverStyle ForeColor="#E2DED6" />
<EmptyZoneTextStyle Font-Size="0.8em" />
<MenuLabelStyle ForeColor="White" />
<MenuVerbHoverStyle BackColor="#F7F6F3" BorderColor="#CCCCCC"
BorderStyle="Solid"
BorderWidth="1px" ForeColor="#333333" />
<HeaderStyle Font-Size="0.7em" ForeColor="#CCCCCC"
HorizontalAlign="Center" />
<MenuVerbStyle BorderColor="#5D7B9D" BorderStyle="Solid"
BorderWidth="1px" ForeColor="White" />
<PartStyle Font-Size="0.8em" ForeColor="#333333" />
<TitleBarVerbStyle Font-Size="0.6em" Font-Underline="False"
ForeColor="White" />
<MenuPopupStyle BackColor="#5D7B9D" BorderColor="#CCCCCC"
BorderWidth="1px" Font-Names="Verdana"
Font-Size="0.6em" />
<PartTitleStyle BackColor="#5D7B9D" Font-Bold="True" Font-
Size="0.8em" ForeColor="White" />
</asp:WebPartZone>
</td>
<td valign="top" align="right">
<asp:EditorZone ID="Editorzone1" runat="server"
BackColor="#F7F6F3" BorderColor="#CCCCCC"
BorderWidth="1px" Font-Names="Verdana" Padding="6">
<ZoneTemplate>
<asp:AppearanceEditorPart ID="Appearanceeditorpart1"
runat="server" />
<asp:LayoutEditorPart ID="Layouteditorpart1" runat="server" />
<asp:PropertyGridEditorPart ID="Propertygrideditorpart1"
runat="server" />
</ZoneTemplate>
<LabelStyle Font-Size="0.8em" ForeColor="#333333" />
<HeaderStyle BackColor="#E2DED6" Font-Bold="True" Font-
Size="0.8em" ForeColor="#333333" />
<HeaderVerbStyle Font-Bold="False" Font-Size="0.8em" Font-
Underline="False" ForeColor="#333333" />
<PartChromeStyle BorderColor="#E2DED6" BorderStyle="Solid"
BorderWidth="1px" />
<PartStyle BorderColor="#F7F6F3" BorderWidth="5px" />
```

```
                    <FooterStyle BackColor="#E2DED6" HorizontalAlign="Right" />
                    <EditUIStyle Font-Names="Verdana" Font-Size="0.8em"
                    ForeColor="#333333" />
                    <InstructionTextStyle Font-Size="0.8em" ForeColor="#333333" />
                    <ErrorStyle Font-Size="0.8em" />
                    <VerbStyle Font-Names="Verdana" Font-Size="0.8em"
                    ForeColor="#333333" />
                    <EmptyZoneTextStyle Font-Size="0.8em" ForeColor="#333333" />
                    <PartTitleStyle Font-Bold="True" Font-Size="0.8em"
                    ForeColor="#333333" />
                    </asp:EditorZone>
                    </td>
                    <td valign="top" align="right" style="width: 312px">
                    <asp:CatalogZone ID="CatalogZone1" runat="server"
                    Height="122px" BackColor="#F7F6F3"
                    BorderColor="#CCCCCC" BorderWidth="1px" Font-Names="Verdana"
                    Padding="6">
                    <ZoneTemplate>
                    <asp:PageCatalogPart ID="PageCatalogPart1" runat="server" />
                    <asp:DeclarativeCatalogPart ID="DeclarativeCatalogPart1"
                    runat="server">
                    </asp:DeclarativeCatalogPart>
                    </ZoneTemplate>
                    <HeaderVerbStyle Font-Bold="False" Font-Size="0.8em" Font-
                    Underline="False" ForeColor="#333333" />
                    <PartTitleStyle BackColor="#5D7B9D" Font-Bold="True" Font-
                    Size="0.8em" ForeColor="White" />
                    <FooterStyle BackColor="#E2DED6" HorizontalAlign="Right" />
                    <PartChromeStyle BorderColor="#E2DED6" BorderStyle="Solid"
                    BorderWidth="1px" />
                    <InstructionTextStyle Font-Size="0.8em" ForeColor="#333333" />
                    <LabelStyle Font-Size="0.8em" ForeColor="#333333" />
                    <PartLinkStyle Font-Size="0.8em" />
                    <SelectedPartLinkStyle Font-Size="0.8em" />
                    <VerbStyle Font-Names="Verdana" Font-Size="0.8em"
                    ForeColor="#333333" />
                    <HeaderStyle BackColor="#E2DED6" Font-Bold="True" Font-
                    Size="0.8em" ForeColor="#333333" />
                    <EmptyZoneTextStyle Font-Size="0.8em" ForeColor="#333333" />
                    <EditUIStyle Font-Names="Verdana" Font-Size="0.8em"
                    ForeColor="#333333" />
                    <PartStyle BorderColor="#F7F6F3" BorderWidth="5px" />
                    </asp:CatalogZone>
                    </td>
                    </tr>
                    </table>
            </div></div>
            <div id="footer">
                    <p class="left">
                            All content copyright &copy; Kogent Solutions Inc.
                    </p>
            </div>
    </div>
    </form>
</body>
</html>
```

In the preceding listing, the image tag inserts an image in the WebPartZone3. Therefore, you also need to add the corresponding image in the Solution Explorer. You can do that by using the `Add Existing Item` dialog box. Listing 15.2 shows the code for the CodeFile of the Default.aspx page:

Listing 15.2: Showing the Code for the CodeFile of the `Default.aspx` Page

In VB

```
Partial Class _Default
    Inherits System.Web.UI.Page
    Protected Sub LinkButton2_Click(sender As Object, e As EventArgs)
     Handles LinkButton2.Click
        WebPartManager1.DisplayMode = WebPartManager.BrowseDisplayMode
    End Sub
    Protected Sub LinkButton3_Click(sender As Object, e As EventArgs)
     Handles LinkButton3.Click
        WebPartManager1.DisplayMode = WebPartManager.EditDisplayMode
    End Sub
    Protected Sub LinkButton4_Click(sender As Object, e As EventArgs)
     Handles LinkButton4.Click
        WebPartManager1.DisplayMode = WebPartManager.CatalogDisplayMode
    End Sub
    Protected Sub LinkButton5_Click(sender As Object, e As EventArgs)
     Handles LinkButton5.Click
        WebPartManager1.DisplayMode = WebPartManager.DesignDisplayMode
    End Sub
End Class
```

In C#

```
using System;
using System.Collections.Generic;
using System.Linq;
using System.Web;
using System.Web.UI;
using System.Web.UI.WebControls;
using System.Web.UI.WebControls.WebParts;
public partial class _Default : System.Web.UI.Page
{
    protected void Page_Load(object sender, EventArgs e)
    {

    }
    protected void LinkButton2_Click(object sender, EventArgs e)
    {
        WebPartManager1.DisplayMode = WebPartManager.BrowseDisplayMode;
    }
    protected void LinkButton3_Click(object sender, EventArgs e)
    {
        WebPartManager1.DisplayMode = WebPartManager.EditDisplayMode;
    }
    protected void LinkButton4_Click(object sender, EventArgs e)
    {
        WebPartManager1.DisplayMode = WebPartManager.CatalogDisplayMode;
    }
    protected void LinkButton5_Click(object sender, EventArgs e)
    {
        WebPartManager1.DisplayMode = WebPartManager.DesignDisplayMode;
    }
}
```

We have now created our personalized websites. To do this, you need to create a `Login` page `(login.aspx)` that validates the user credentials before allowing them to explore the website.

NOTE

You can create new user accounts for your application by clicking the Create user link option on the Security tab of the ASP.NET Web Site Administration Tool.

Listing 15.3 shows the code for the `login.aspx` page of the website:

Listing 15.3: Showing the Code for the `login.aspx` Page

In VB

```
<%@ Page Language="VB" AutoEventWireup="false" CodeFile="login.aspx.vb" Inherits="login"
  %>
<!DOCTYPE html>
<html xmlns="http://www.w3.org/1999/xhtml">
<head id="Head1" runat="server">
   <title>Login Page</title>
   <link href="StyleSheet.css" rel="stylesheet" type="text/css" />
</head>
<body>
   <form id="form1" runat="server">
   <div>
        <div id="header">
               <h1>
                      ASP.NET 4.5 Black Book
               </h1>
        </div>
        <div id="sidebar">
               <div id="nav">
                       
               </div>
        </div>
        <div id="content">
               <div class="itemContent"><br />
               <table width="520px">

               <tr>
               <td style="width: 100px">
               </td>
               <td style="width: 100px">
               <asp:Login ID="Login1" runat="server" style="text-align: left">
               <LayoutTemplate>
               <table border="0" width="500px" cellpadding="1" style="border-right:
               blue thin groove;
               border-top: blue thin groove; border-left: blue thin groove; border-
               bottom: blue thin groove">
               <tr>
               <td style="width: 364px">
               <table border="0" cellpadding="0">
               <tr>
                   <td align="center" colspan="2">
                  <strong><span style="text-decoration: underline">User
               Login</span></strong></td>
               </tr>
               <tr>
               <td align="right" style="width: 109px; text-align: center;">
                   <asp:Label ID="UserNameLabel" runat="server"
               AssociatedControlID="UserName"
                  style="text-align: left" Width="56px">User Name:</asp:Label>
```

```
</td>
 <td style="width: 261px">
 <asp:TextBox ID="UserName" runat="server" Width="202px"></asp:TextBox>
 <asp:RequiredFieldValidator ID="UserNameRequired" runat="server"
 ControlToValidate="UserName"
 ErrorMessage="User Name is required." ToolTip="User Name is required."
 ValidationGroup="Login1">*</asp:RequiredFieldValidator>
 </td>
 </tr>
 <tr>
 <td align="right" style="width:109px; text-align: center;">
     <asp:Label ID="PasswordLabel" runat="server"
 AssociatedControlID="Password"
    style="text-align: center">Password:</asp:Label>
</td>
 <td style="width: 261px">
 <asp:TextBox ID="Password" runat="server" TextMode="Password"
 Width="201px"></asp:TextBox>
 <asp:RequiredFieldValidator ID="PasswordRequired" runat="server"
 ControlToValidate="Password"
 ErrorMessage="Password is required." ToolTip="Password is required."
 ValidationGroup="Login1">*</asp:RequiredFieldValidator>
 </td>
 </tr>
 <tr>
     <td colspan="2">
    <asp:CheckBox ID="RememberMe" runat="server" Text="Remember me next
 time." />
</td>
 </tr>
 <tr>
     <td align="center" colspan="2" style="color: red">
    <asp:Literal ID="FailureText" runat="server"
 EnableViewState="False"></asp:Literal>
</td>
 </tr>
 <tr>
     <td align="right" colspan="2">
    <asp:Button ID="LoginButton" runat="server" CommandName="Login"
 Text="OK"
         ValidationGroup="Login1" />
</td>
 </tr>
     <tr>
    <td align="right" colspan="2">
          </td>
</tr>
 </table>
 </td>
 </tr>
 </table>
 </LayoutTemplate>
 </asp:Login>
 </td>
 <td style="width: 100px">
 </td>
 </tr>
 <tr>
 <td style="width: 100px">
 </td>
```

```
                <td style="width: 100px">
                </td>
                <td style="width: 100px">
                </td>
                </tr>
                </table>
        </div></div>
        <div id="footer">
                <p class="left">
                        All content copyright &copy; Kogent Solutions Inc. </p>
        </div>
        </div>
    </form>
</body>
</html>
```

In C#

```
<%@ Page Language="C#" AutoEventWireup="true" CodeFile="login.aspx.cs" Inherits="login" %>
<!DOCTYPE html>
<html xmlns="http://www.w3.org/1999/xhtml">
<head runat="server">
    <title>Login Page</title>
    <link href="StyleSheet.css" rel="stylesheet" type="text/css" />
</head>
<body>
    <form id="form1" runat="server">
    <div>
        <div id="header">
                <h1>
                        ASP.NET 4.5 Black Book
                </h1>
        </div>
        <div id="sidebar">
                <div id="nav">
                         
                </div>
        </div>
  <div id="content">
                <div class="itemContent">
            <br />
                <table width="520px">

                <tr>
                <td style="width: 100px">
                </td>
                <td style="width: 100px">
                <asp:Login ID="Login1" runat="server" style="text-align: center">
                <LayoutTemplate>
                <table border="0" width="500px" cellpadding="1" style="border-right:
                blue thin groove;
                border-top: blue thin groove; border-left: blue thin groove; border-
                bottom: blue thin groove">
                <tr>
                <td style="width: 364px">
                <table border="0" cellpadding="0">
                <tr>
                    <td align="center" colspan="2">
                   <strong><span style="text-decoration: underline">User
                Login</span></strong></td>
                </tr>
```

```
<tr>
    <td align="right" style="width: 109px; text-align: center;">
   <asp:Label ID="UserNameLabel" runat="server"
AssociatedControlID="UserName"
       Width="56px">User Name:</asp:Label>
</td>
<td style="width: 261px">
<asp:TextBox ID="UserName" runat="server" Width="202px"></asp:TextBox>
<asp:RequiredFieldValidator ID="UserNameRequired" runat="server"
ControlToValidate="UserName"
ErrorMessage="User Name is required." ToolTip="User Name is required."
ValidationGroup="Login1">*</asp:RequiredFieldValidator>
</td>
</tr>
<tr>
<td align="right" style="width:109px; text-align: center;">
<asp:Label ID="PasswordLabel" runat="server"
AssociatedControlID="Password">Password:</asp:Label>
</td>
<td style="width: 261px">
<asp:TextBox ID="Password" runat="server" TextMode="Password"
Width="201px"></asp:TextBox>
<asp:RequiredFieldValidator ID="PasswordRequired" runat="server"
ControlToValidate="Password"
ErrorMessage="Password is required." ToolTip="Password is required."
ValidationGroup="Login1">*</asp:RequiredFieldValidator>
</td>
</tr>
<tr>
 <td colspan="2">
<asp:CheckBox ID="RememberMe" runat="server" Text="Remember me next
time." />
</td>
</tr>
<tr>
    <td align="center" colspan="2" style="color: red">
   <asp:Literal ID="FailureText" runat="server"
  EnableViewState="False"></asp:Literal>
</td>
</tr>
<tr>
    <td align="right" colspan="2">
   <asp:Button ID="LoginButton" runat="server" CommandName="Login"
       Text="OK"
      ValidationGroup="Login1" />
   <br /><br />
</td>
</tr>
</table>
</td>
</tr>
</table>
</LayoutTemplate>
</asp:Login>
</td>
<td style="width: 100px">
</td>
</tr>
<tr>
<td style="width: 100px">
</td>
```

```
                    <td style="width: 100px">
                    </td>
                    <td style="width: 100px">
                    </td>
                    </tr>
                    </table>
                    </div></div>
                    <div id="footer">
                            <p class="left">
                                    All content copyright &copy; Kogent Solutions Inc.</p>
                    </div>
            </div>
        </form>
    </body>
    </html>
```

You must ensure that you set the `login.aspx` page as the start page. You also need to add the following code inside the `<configuration>` section of the `Web.config` file, as shown in Listing 15.4:

Listing 15.4: Showing the Code for the `Web.config` File

In VB and C#

```
<?xml version="1.0"?>
<!--
  For more information on how to configure your ASP.NET application, please visit
  http://go.microsoft.com/fwlink/?LinkId=169433
  -->
<configuration>
<appSettings>
    <add key="ValidationSettings:UnobtrusiveValidationMode" value="None"></add>
  </appSettings>
    <system.web>
         <authentication mode="Forms" />
      <compilation debug="true" strict="false" explicit="true"  targetFramework="4.5" />
      <httpRuntime targetFramework="4.5" />
    </system.web>
</configuration>
```

Now, let's run the website. Figure 15.3 shows the login.aspx page of the website:

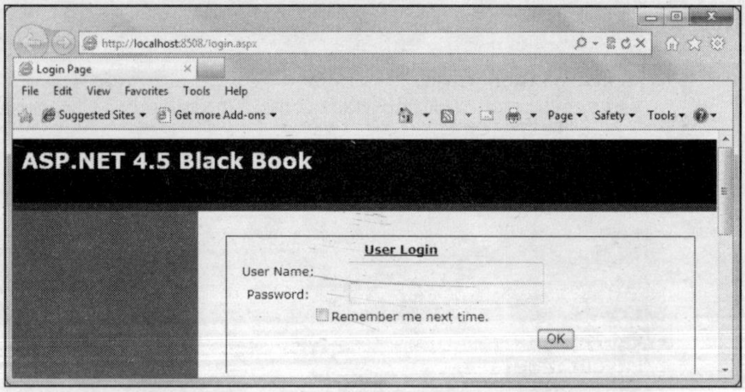

Figure 15.3: Demonstrating the Login Page of the Website

As soon as the `Login` page (`login.aspx`) is displayed, perform the following steps to personalize the website:

1. Enter the user name and password in the `User Name` and `Password` text boxes, respectively. In our case, user name is testuser and password is abc@123.

2. Click the `OK` button to log on to the website. After logging in successfully, the `Default.aspx` page is displayed, as shown in Figure 15.4:

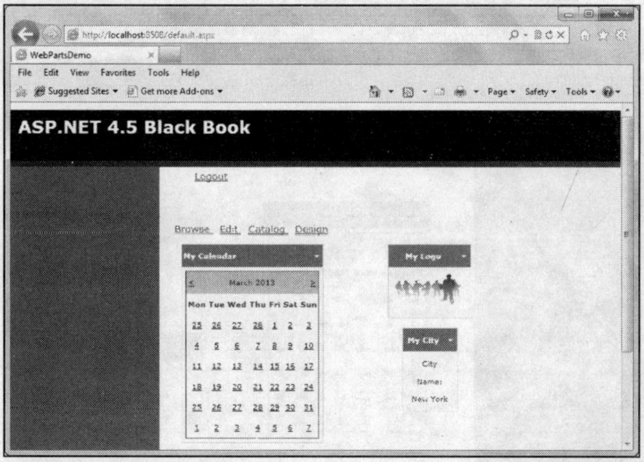

Figure 15.4: Showing the Default.aspx Page of the Website

As shown in Figure 15.4, the generated page contains three Web Parts and some link buttons. Using these link buttons, users can change the mode of the Web page. Various modes of the Web page are as follows:

- `Browse`—Allows users to browse the Web page. It is the normal view of a Web page in which the users cannot make any changes to the content and layout of the Web page.
- `Edit`—Allows users to edit a Web Parts control. This includes changing the Web Part's title, color, appearance, layout, and behavior.
- `Catalog`—Allows users to restore the closed Web Parts to their respective zones, or add entirely new Web Parts.
- `Design`—Allows users to rearrange the components within a Web zone or outside the zone.

After finishing the personalization of Web Parts, the changes can be seen in the Browse mode. In addition, if the user closes the Web page, the user is presented with the personalized Web page the next time the website is visited. To see how this happens, let's start with the manipulation of the Web page.

3. Click the `Design` link to change the mode to Design, as shown in Figure 15.5:

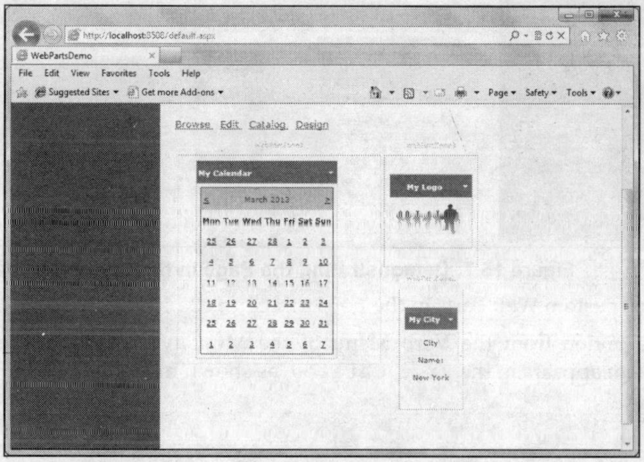

Figure 15.5: Viewing the Default.aspx Page in the Design Mode

Now, you can clearly see the various Web zones present on the Web page.

4. Move the Web Part present in the `WebPartZone2` to the `WebPartZone3`, as shown in Figure 15.6:

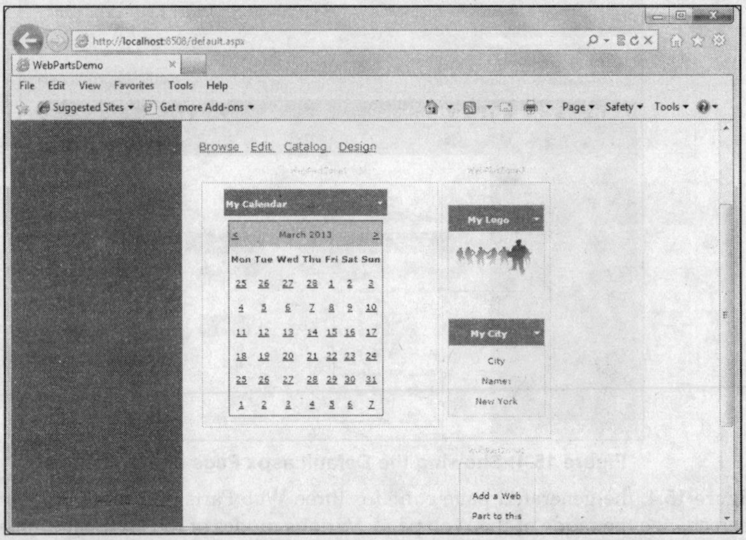

Figure 15.6: Displaying the Moved Web Part on the Page

Now, we obtain an empty Web zone with its Web Part moved to the `WebPartZone3`.

5. Switch to the `Catalog` mode by clicking the `Catalog` link. Figure 15.7 shows the Default.aspx page in the Catalog mode:

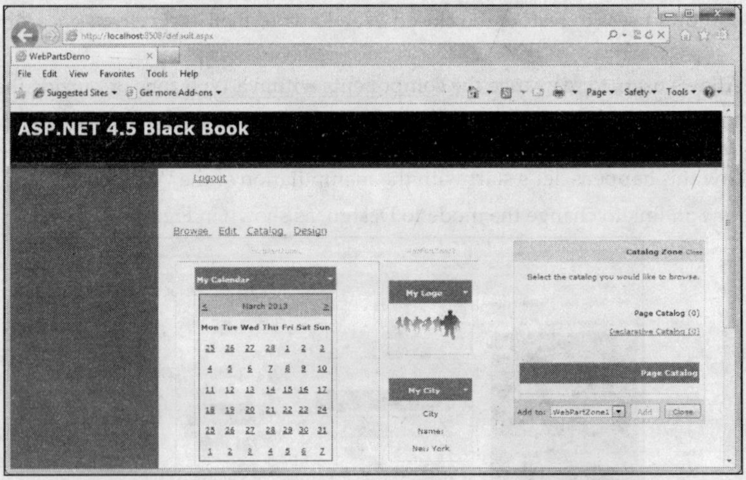

Figure 15.7: Demonstrating the Page in the Catalog Mode

Currently, there are no custom Web Parts in the `Declarative Catalog`, so we test the `Page Catalog` link.

6. Select the Close option from the Verb Menu of the My City Web Part. The Web Part is closed and a corresponding item appears in the `Page Catalog`, as shown in Figure 15.8:

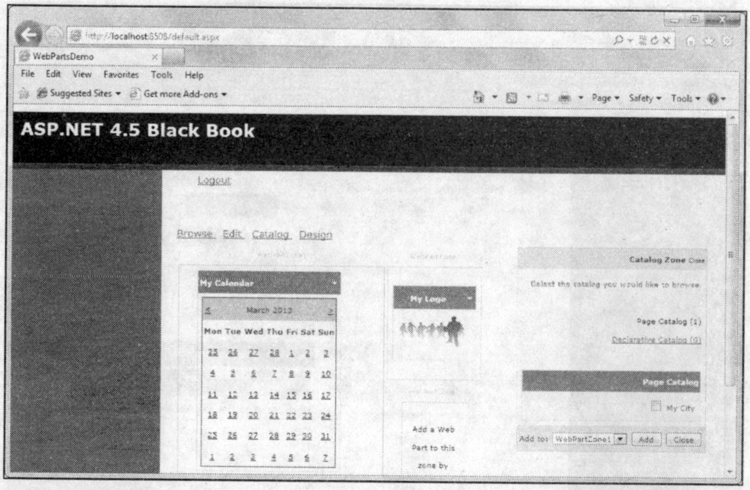

Figure 15.8: Showing the Default.aspx Page with My City Web Part Deleted

The closed Web Part can be restored to its original zone or to another zone by selecting the corresponding item in the Page Catalog and selecting the target Web zone from the Add to list of the Catalog zone.

After closing and moving the `WebParts`, let's switch our page to the next and most powerful mode, that is, the `Edit` mode.

7. Click the Edit link to switch to the Edit mode. As soon as you click the Edit link, a new option, Edit, appears in the Verb Menu of each Web Part.
8. Select the Edit option of My Calendar Web Part to see how the Editor Zone group appears, as shown in Figure 15.9:

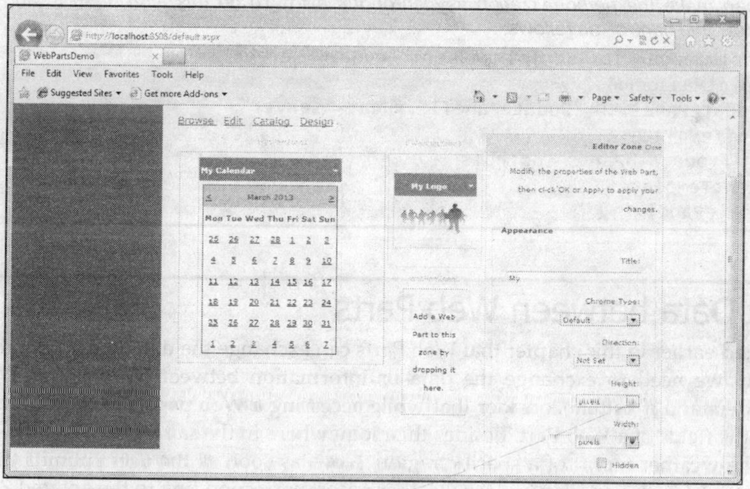

Figure 15.9: Using the Editor Zone Group

In Figure 15.9, you observe that the Editor Zone group contains two sections, Appearance and Layout. In the Editor Zone group, you can set the title, zone, properties, and many other things related to a Web Part.

9. Now, change the title of the My Calendar Web Part to My Personal Calendar, and the zone to `WebPartZone2`.
10. Click the Apply and OK buttons to apply the changes and close the Editor Zone group, respectively. Figure 15.10 shows the modified page in the Browse mode:

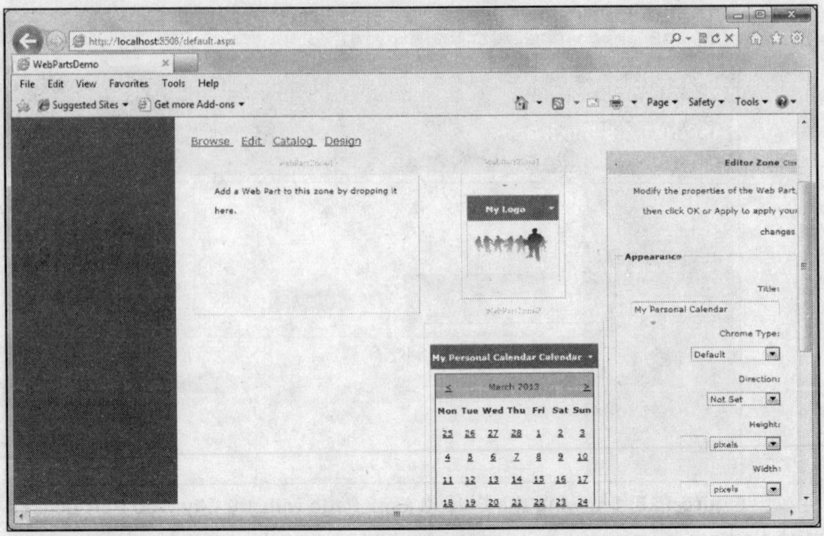

Figure 15.10: Displaying Modified Web Page

All these changes have taken place only for the current user. If another user visits the same Web page, then the default view of the Web page is presented (shown in Figure 15.4). In addition, when the current user revisits the Web page, the Web Parts appear as they had been modified on the previous visit. Therefore, each user gets the personalized version of the Web page.

NOTE

While personalizing the website, you see the page-flicker with every action, because of the synchronous postback. However, you can make the personalization asynchronous also. To do this, you need to add the WebParts controls inside the UpdatePanel control, as follows:

```
<asp:ScriptManager ID="ScriptManager1" runat="server">
</asp:ScriptManager>
   <asp:UpdatePanel ID="UpdatePanel1" runat="server">
   <ContentTemplate>
        //Your WebParts controls
   </ContentTemplate>
</asp:UpdatePanel>
```

Exchanging Data between Web Parts

You have learned earlier in this chapter that Web Parts can exchange the data with each other. Now, the question arises that why we need to exchange the data or information between Web Parts? We have given a short example to understand it better. Consider that while accessing a Web page, a user is prompted to enter the ZIP code in one of the fields of a Web Part. Besides this, somewhere in the same Web page, there is another Web Part that displays the weather report of a specific region. Now, as soon as the user submits the ZIP code in the first Web Part, the second Web Part displays the weather report corresponding to the entered ZIP code. This amazing functionality indicates the presence of some underlying mechanism that connects the two Web Parts together and exchanges data. During this exchange of data, one of the Web Parts acts as a Provider while the other acts as a Consumer.

To demonstrate how to connect two Web Parts and how to exchange data between them, let's create a new website, `ConnectionZoneAppCS`. You can find the code of this website as `ConnectionZoneAppVB` (for VB) and `ConnectionZoneAppCS` (for C#). First of all, we declare an interface, `IDataTransmit`, which contains the

RetrieveData function to fetch the data from another Web Part. This interface declaration is added in a class file, which you can add to your application from the Add New Item dialog box. When you add the `class` file to your application, you are prompted to add the `class` file in a separate `App_Code` folder that contains all the code files for your application. Listing 15.5 shows the code for the `IDataTransmit` interface of the `ConnectionZoneAppCS` website:

Listing 15.5: Showing the Code for the `IDataTransmit` Interface

In VB

```
Imports Microsoft.VisualBasic
Public Interface IDataTransmit
  Function RetriveData() As String
End Interface
```

In C#

```
using System;
using System.Collections.Generic;
using System.Linq;
using System.Web;
public interface IDataTransmit
{
  String  RetriveData();
}
```

Add two .ascx files(Web User Control) in the `ConnectionZoneAppCS`, Provider.ascx and Consumer.ascx, which contains two custom controls. Code for the `Consumer` Web Part page is contained in the `Consumer.ascx` file. Listing 15.6 shows the code for the `Consumer.ascx` file of the `ConnectionZone` website:

Listing 15.6: Showing the Code for the `Consumer.ascx` Page

In VB

```
<%@ Control Language="VB" AutoEventWireup="false" CodeFile="Consumer.ascx.vb"
  Inherits="Consumer" %>
<table width="360px" cellpadding="4" cellspacing="0"
  style=" height:88pt;
  border-right: silver thin groove; border-top: silver thin groove;
  border-left: silver thin groove; border-bottom: silver thin groove;
  background-color: #ececec; height:88pt;">
<tr>
  <td align="left" valign="top" style=" border-style: solid;
  border-color: #ffff99; text-align:center; height: 25px;">
   
  <span style="color: #003399; text-decoration: underline">
       <strong>
             Consumer WebPart
       </strong>
  </span>
  </td>
</tr>
<tr>
<td style="height: 46px; background-color: #ffffff;">
    
  <asp:Label ID="Label1" runat="server"
  Text="Retrived Data" Width="90px" BackColor="SeaShell" BorderColor="Red"
  BorderStyle="None">
  </asp:Label>
   
   
```

```
        <asp:Label ID="Label2" runat="Server" Text="Label" Width="170px">
        </asp:Label>
    </td>
    </tr>
    </table>
```

In C#

```
    <%@ Control Language="C#" AutoEventWireup="true" CodeFile="Consumer.ascx.cs"
      Inherits="Consumer" %>
    <table width="360px" cellpadding="4" cellspacing="0" style="border-right: silver thin
      groove;
      border-top: silver thin groove; border-left: silver thin groove;
      border-bottom: silver thin groove; background-color: #ececec; height:88pt;">
    <tr>
    <td align="left" valign="top" style="border-color: #ffff99;
      text-align:center; height: 25px;">
             
            <span style="color: #003399; text-decoration:underline">
            <strong>
            Consumer WebPart
            </strong>
            </span>
      </td>
    </tr>
    <tr>
    <td style="height: 46px">
        
      <asp:Label ID="Label1" runat="server" Text="Retrived Data" Width="90px"
      BackColor="SeaShell"
      BorderColor="Red" BorderStyle="None">
      </asp:Label>
       
       
      <asp:Label ID="Label2" runat="server" Text="Label" Width="170px">
      </asp:Label>
    </td>
    </tr>
    </table>
```

Listing 15.7 shows the code for the CodeFile of `Consumer` Web Part page:

Listing 15.7: Showing the Code of CodeFile of the `Consumer` Web Part page

In VB

```
Partial Class Consumer
    Inherits System.Web.UI.UserControl
    <WebControls.WebParts.ConnectionConsumer("Text", "TextConsumer")> _
    Public Sub RetriveDataInterface(ByVal sender As IDataTransmit)
        Label2.Text = sender.RetriveData()
    End Sub
End Class
```

In C#

```
using System;
using System.Collections.Generic;
using System.Linq;
using System.Web;
using System.Web.UI;
using System.Web.UI.WebControls;
```

```
using System.Web.UI.WebControls.WebParts;
public partial class Consumer : System.Web.UI.UserControl
{
    [ConnectionConsumer("Text", "TextConsumer")]
    public void RetriveDataInterface(IDataTransmit sender)
    {
        Label2.Text = sender.RetriveData();
    }

}
```

The code for the Provider Web Part page is contained in the `Provider.ascx` page. Listing 15.8 shows the code for the `Provider.ascx` page of the `ConnectionZoneAppCS` website:

Listing 15.8: Showing the Code for the `Provider.ascx` Page

In VB

```
<%@ Control Language="VB" AutoEventWireup="false" CodeFile="Provider.ascx.vb"
   Inherits="Provider" %>
<table width="360px" cellpadding="4" cellspacing="0" bgcolor="#ececec" style="border-
   right: silver thin groove; border-top: silver thin groove; border-left: silver thin
   groove; border-bottom: silver thin groove; background-color:
   #ececec;" title="Provider">
   <tr>
         <td align="left" style="width: 495px; text-align: center" valign="top">
         <strong><span style="color: #000099; text-decoration:
         underline">Provider WebPart</span></strong></td>
   </tr>
<tr>
<td align="left" valign="top" style="width: 495px">
This WebPart is acting as <span style="color: #cc0066">Provider Webpart</span>
for sending data to <span style="color: #cc0066">Consumer WebPart</span>
</td>
</tr>
<tr>
<td style="height: 33px; width: 495px;">
<span style="color: #000099"> </span><strong><span style="color:
   #3300cc"><span
   style="color: #000099; text-decoration: underline">Enter
   Data:</span> </span></strong>
    <asp:TextBox ID="TextBox1" runat="server" Width="173px"></asp:TextBox>
<asp:Button ID="Button1" Text="SEND" Runat="server" BorderStyle="Groove" />
</td>
</tr>
</table>
```

In C#

```
<%@ Control Language="C#" AutoEventWireup="true" CodeFile="Provider.ascx.cs"
   Inherits="Provider" %>
<table width="360px" cellpadding="4" cellspacing="0" bgcolor="#ececec" style="border-
   right: silver thin groove; border-top: silver thin groove; border-left: silver thin
   groove; border-bottom: silver thin groove; background-color:
#ececec;" title="Provider">
   <tr>
         <td align="left" style="width: 495px; text-align: center" valign="top">
         <strong><span style="color: #000099; text-decoration:underline">Provider
         WebPart</span></strong></td>
   </tr>
<tr>
<td align="left" valign="top" style="width: 495px">
This WebPart is acting as <span style="color: #cc0066">Provider Webpart</span>
for sending data to <span style="color: #cc0066">Consumer WebPart</span>
```

```
</td>
</tr>
<tr>
<td style="height: 33px; width: 495px;">
<span style="color: #000099"> </span><strong><span style="color:#3300cc"><span
   style="color: #000099; text-decoration: underline">Enter Data:</span> </span></strong>
    <asp:TextBox ID="TextBox1" runat="server" Width="173px"></asp:TextBox>
<asp:Button ID="Button1" Text="SEND" Runat="server" BorderStyle="Groove" />
</td>
</tr>
</table>
```

Listing 15.9 shows the code for the CodeFile of the `Provider` Web Part page:

Listing 15.9: Showing the Code for the CodeFile of the `Provider` Web Part page

In VB

```
Partial Class Provider
   Inherits System.Web.UI.UserControl
   Implements IDataTransmit
   <WebControls.WebParts.ConnectionProvider("Text", "TextProvider")> _
Public Function RetriveDataInterface() As IDataTransmit
   Return CType(Me, IDataTransmit)
End Function
Public Function RetriveData() As String Implements IDataTransmit.RetriveData
   Return textbox1.text
   End Function
End Class
```

In C#

```
using System;
using System.Collections.Generic;
using System.Linq;
using System.Web;
using System.Web.UI;
using System.Web.UI.WebControls;
using System.Web.UI.WebControls.WebParts;
public partial class Provider : System.Web.UI.UserControl, IDataTransmit
{
     [ConnectionProvider("Text", "TextProvider")]
     public IDataTransmit RetriveDataInterface()
     {
          return (IDataTransmit)this;
     }
     public string RetriveData()
     {
          return TextBox1.Text;
     }
}
```

In Listings 15.6, 15.7, 15.8, and 15.9, we have created two custom Web Parts (Consumer and Provider) that exchange the data with each other at runtime. However, for any two Web Parts to exchange data with each other, the `ConnectionsZone` control is a must. Therefore, let's add the `ConnectionsZone` control and also use the Consumer and Provider custom controls on the `WebParts zone` of the `Default.aspx` page. Listing 15.10 shows the code for the `Default.aspx` page of the `ConnectionZoneAppCS` website:

Listing 15.10: Showing the Code for the `Default.aspx` Page

In VB

```
<%@ Page Language="VB" AutoEventWireup="false" CodeFile="Default.aspx.vb"
  Inherits="_Default" %>
<%@ Register Src="Consumer.ascx" TagName="Consumer" TagPrefix="cc" %>
<%@ Register Src="Provider.ascx" TagName="Provider" TagPrefix="pp" %>
<!DOCTYPE html>
<html xmlns="http://www.w3.org/1799/xhtml">
<head runat="server">
    <title>Connection zone Example</title>
    <link href="StyleSheet.css" rel="stylesheet" type="text/css" />
</head>
<body>
    <form id="form1" runat="server">
    <div>
         <div id="header">
                <h1>
                        ASP.NET 4.5 Black Book
                </h1>
         </div>
         <div id="sidebar">
                <div id="nav">
                         
                </div>
         </div>

         <div id="content">
                <div class="itemContent">
                <asp:WebPartManager ID="WebPartManager1" runat="server"
                Personalization-Enabled="true">
                </asp:WebPartManager>
                <br />
                <asp:LinkButton ID="LinkButton1"
                runat="server">Connections</asp:LinkButton>  
                   <asp:LinkButton ID="LinkButton3"
                runat="server">Browse</asp:LinkButton>  <br />
                <asp:WebPartZone ID="WebPartZone1" runat="server" BorderColor="#CCCCCC"
                Font-Names="Verdana" Padding="6">
                <ZoneTemplate>
                <pp:Provider ID="ProviderWebPart1" runat="server" />
                </ZoneTemplate>
                <PartChromeStyle BackColor="#F7F6F3" BorderColor="#E2DED6" Font-
                Names="Verdana" ForeColor="White" />
                <MenuLabelHoverStyle ForeColor="#E2DED6" />
                <EmptyZoneTextStyle Font-Size="0.8em" />
                <MenuLabelStyle ForeColor="White" />
                <MenuVerbHoverStyle BackColor="#F7F6F3" BorderColor="#CCCCCC"
                BorderStyle="Solid"
                BorderWidth="1px" ForeColor="#333333" />
                <HeaderStyle Font-Size="0.7em" ForeColor="#CCCCCC"
                HorizontalAlign="Center" />
                <MenuVerbStyle BorderColor="#5D7B9D" BorderStyle="Solid"
                BorderWidth="1px" ForeColor="White" />
                <PartStyle Font-Size="0.8em" ForeColor="#333333" />
                <TitleBarVerbStyle Font-Size="0.6em" Font-Underline="False"
                ForeColor="White" />
                <MenuPopupStyle BackColor="#5D7B9D" BorderColor="#CCCCCC"
                BorderWidth="1px" Font-Names="Verdana"
                Font-Size="0.6em" />
```

```
                <PartTitleStyle BackColor="#5D7B9D" Font-Bold="True" Font-Size="0.8em"
                ForeColor="White" />
                </asp:WebPartZone>
                 <br />
                <asp:WebPartZone ID="WebPartZone2" runat="server">
                <ZoneTemplate>
                <cc:Consumer ID="ConsumerWebPart1" runat="server" />
                </ZoneTemplate>
                </asp:WebPartZone>
                     <br />
                <asp:ConnectionsZone ID="ConnectionsZone1" runat="server">
                <EditUIStyle BorderStyle="Solid" />
                </asp:ConnectionsZone>
                <br />
        </div>
    </div>
    </div>
    <div id="footer">
        <p class="left">
        All content copyright &copy; Kogent Solutions Inc.</p>
    </div>
     </form>
</body>
</html>
```

In C#

```
<%@ Page Language="C#" AutoEventWireup="true" CodeFile="Default.aspx.cs"
  Inherits="_Default" %>
<%@ Register Src="Consumer.ascx" TagName="Consumer" TagPrefix="cc" %>
<%@ Register Src="Provider.ascx" TagName="Provider" TagPrefix="pp" %>
<!DOCTYPE html PUBLIC "-//W3C//DTD XHTML 1.0 Transitional//EN"
  "http://www.w3.org/TR/xhtml1/DTD/xhtml1-transitional.dtd">
<html xmlns="http://www.w3.org/1999/xhtml">
<head runat="server">
    <title>Connection zone Example</title>
    <link href="StyleSheet.css" rel="stylesheet" type="text/css" />
</head>
<body>
    <form id="form1" runat="server">
    <div>
        <div id="header">
                <h1>
                        ASP.NET 4.5 Black Book
                </h1>
        </div>
        <div id="sidebar">
                <div id="nav">
                         
                </div>
        </div>
        <div id="content">
                <div class="itemContent">
                <asp:WebPartManager ID="WebPartManager1" runat="server"
                Personalization-Enabled="true">
                </asp:WebPartManager>
                <br />
                <asp:LinkButton ID="LinkButton1" runat="server"
                onclick="LinkButton1_Click">Connections</asp:LinkButton>  
```

```
                   <asp:LinkButton ID="LinkButton3"
                runat="server">Browse</asp:LinkButton>  <br />
                <asp:WebPartZone ID="WebPartZone1" runat="server" BorderColor="#CCCCCC"
                Font-Names="Verdana" Padding="6">
                <ZoneTemplate>
                <pp:Provider ID="ProviderWebPart1" runat="server" />
                </ZoneTemplate>
                <PartChromeStyle BackColor="#F7F6F3" BorderColor="#E2DED6" Font-
                Names="Verdana" ForeColor="White" />
                <MenuLabelHoverStyle ForeColor="#E2DED6" />
                <EmptyZoneTextStyle Font-Size="0.8em" />
                <MenuLabelStyle ForeColor="White" />
                <MenuVerbHoverStyle BackColor="#F7F6F3" BorderColor="#CCCCCC"
                BorderStyle="Solid"
                BorderWidth="1px" ForeColor="#333333" />
                <HeaderStyle Font-Size="0.7em" ForeColor="#CCCCCC"
                HorizontalAlign="Center" />
                <MenuVerbStyle BorderColor="#5D7B9D" BorderStyle="Solid"
                BorderWidth="1px" ForeColor="White" />
                <PartStyle Font-Size="0.8em" ForeColor="#333333" />
                <TitleBarVerbStyle Font-Size="0.6em" Font-Underline="False"
                ForeColor="White" />
                <MenuPopupStyle BackColor="#5D7B9D" BorderColor="#CCCCCC"
                BorderWidth="1px" Font-Names="Verdana"
                Font-Size="0.6em" />
                <PartTitleStyle BackColor="#5D7B9D" Font-Bold="True" Font-Size="0.8em"
                ForeColor="White" />
                </asp:WebPartZone>
                 <br />
                <asp:WebPartZone ID="WebPartZone2" runat="server">
                <ZoneTemplate>
                <cc:Consumer ID="ConsumerWebPart1" runat="server" />
                </ZoneTemplate>
                </asp:WebPartZone>
                     <br />
                <asp:ConnectionsZone ID="ConnectionsZone1" runat="server">
                <EditUIStyle BorderStyle="Solid" />
                </asp:ConnectionsZone>
                <br />
            </div>
        </div>
        </div>
        <div id="footer">
            <p class="left">
            All content copyright &copy; Kogent Solutions Inc.</p>
        </div>
        </form>
    </body>
    </html>
```

Listing 15.11 shows the code for the CodeFile of the Default.aspx page of the `ConnectionZoneAppCS` website:

Listing 15.11: Showing the Code for the CodeFile of the Default.aspx Page

In VB

```
Partial Class _Default
    Inherits System.Web.UI.Page
    Protected Sub LinkButton1_Click(sender As Object, e As EventArgs)
        Handles LinkButton1.Click
        Me.WebPartManager1.DisplayMode = WebPartManager.ConnectDisplayMode
    End Sub
```

```
        Protected Sub LinkButton3_Click(sender As Object, e As EventArgs)
            Handles LinkButton3.Click
            Me.WebPartManager1.DisplayMode = WebPartManager.BrowseDisplayMode
        End Sub
    End Class
```

In C#

```
using System;
using System.Collections.Generic;
using System.Linq;
using System.Web;
using System.Web.UI;
using System.Web.UI.WebControls;
using System.Web.UI.WebControls.WebParts;
public partial class _Default : System.Web.UI.Page
{
    protected void LinkButton1_Click(object sender, EventArgs e)
    {
        WebPartManager1.DisplayMode = WebPartManager.ConnectDisplayMode;
    }
    protected void LinkButton3_Click(object sender, EventArgs e)
    {
        WebPartManager1.DisplayMode = WebPartManager.BrowseDisplayMode;
    }
}
```

Now, let's run the `ConnectionZoneAppCS` website. The output of the website is shown in Figure 15.11:

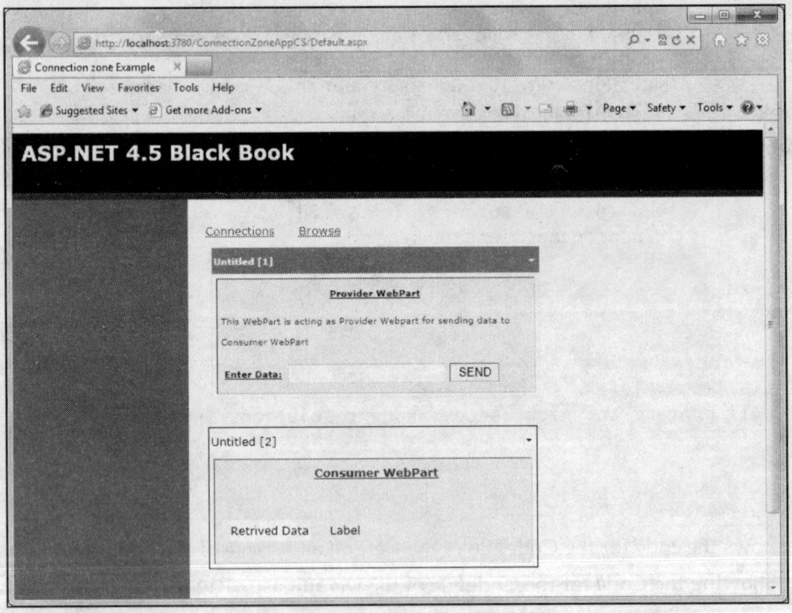

Figure 15.11: Showing the Consumer and Provider WebPart of the ConnectionZoneAppCS Website

In Figure 15.11, you observe that there are two Web Parts, Provider and Consumer. The Provider Web Part provides data to the Consumer Web Part. To exchange the data between the Web Parts, let's perform the following steps:

1. Click the Connections link to add the Connect option in the Verb Menu of both the Web Parts.

2. Now, click the Connect option from the Verb Menu of the Consumer WebPart to display the `Connections Zone` on the Web page.
3. Click the `Create a connection to a Provider` link in the `Connections Zone` to display various options for connecting to a Web Part, as shown in Figure 15.12:

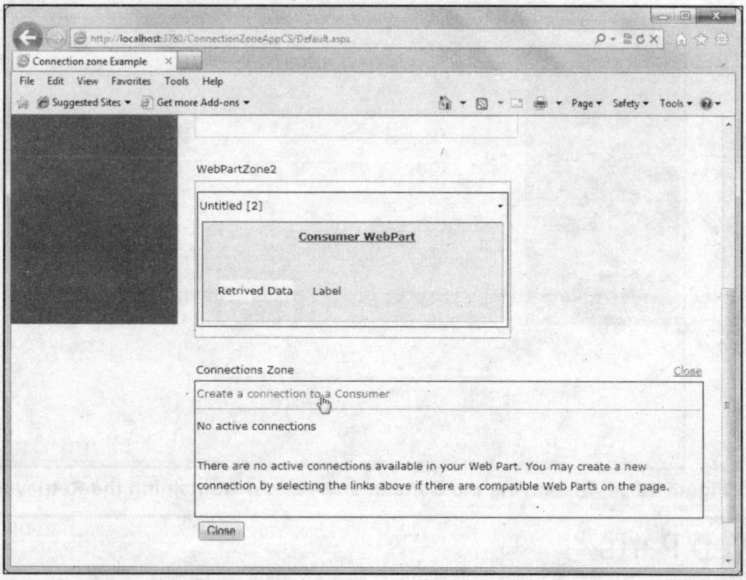

Figure 15.12: Connecting Web Parts using the Link Displayed in the Website

4. Select the name of the Provider Web Part from the `From drop-down list`, and click the `Connect` button to connect the two Web Parts together, as shown in Figure 15.13:

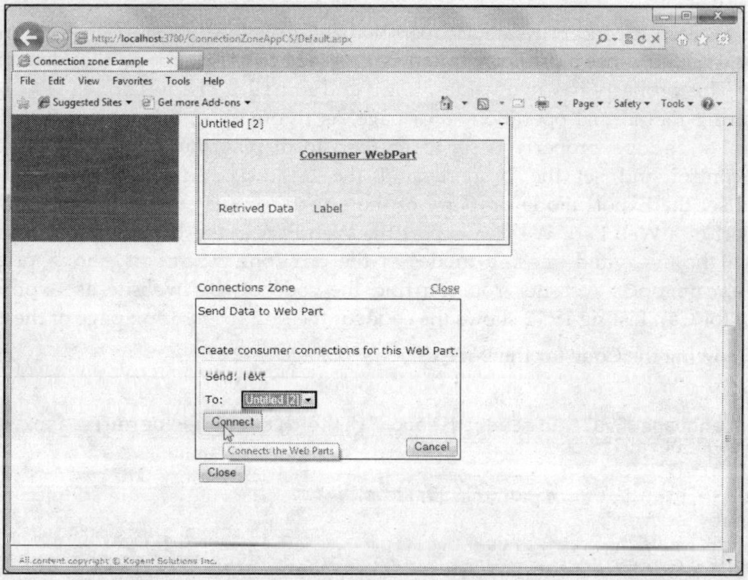

Figure 15.13: Connecting the Consumer Web Part to the Provider Web Part

5. Type any text in the Enter Data field of the Provider Web Part.

6. Now, click the Connect button. The text that you entered in the Provider Web Part now appears next to the Retrieved Data field of the Consumer Web Part, as shown in Figure 15.14:

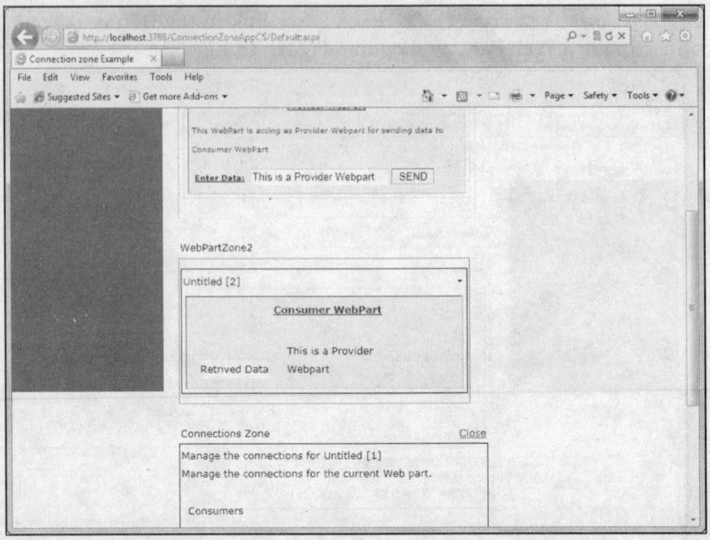

Figure 15.14: Displaying the Consumer Web Part Containing the Retrieved Data

Exporting Web Parts

Using Web Parts Framework, you can enable users to export a Web Part and later import them in another Web page. However, both the source and target Web pages must be capable of the export and import functionality. To demonstrate how to expcr: a Web Part, let's create an application called `Export` that exports a sample Web Part.

It is important to learn a concept related to personalization before we start creating the Export website. The `WebPartManager` control has a property called `personalization.scope` that determines the current scope of a Web page. This property has two values, `user` and `shared`. The `personalization.scope` property is set to `user` during the normal operations of a page, as in our case, to export a Web Part. Alternatively, the `personalization.scope` property is set to `shared` to display the `BehaviorEditorPart` control on the `EditorZone` control and set the properties of the `BehaviorEditorPart control`. In the `Export` application, we set the Export mode property of the `BehaviorEditorPart` control to `Export all data` to enable the export of a Web Part. We then export the Web Part in the Browse mode. Therefore, the application toggles between the `user` and `shared` modes of the `personalization.scope` property. Now, let's start creating the `ExportAppCS` website. You can find the code of this website as `ExportAppVB` (for VB) and `ExportAppCS` (for C#). Listing 15.12 shows the code for the `Default.aspx` page of the `Export` website:

Listing 15.12: Showing the Code for the `Default.aspx` Page

In VB

```
<%@ Page Language="VB" AutoEventWireup="false" CodeFile="Default.aspx.vb"
  Inherits="_Default" %>
<!DOCTYPE html>
<html xmlns="http://www.w3.org/1999/xhtml">
<head runat="server">
    <title>Exporting Web Parts</title>
    <link href="StyleSheet.css" rel="stylesheet" type="text/css" />
</head>
<body>
    <form id="form1" runat="server">
```

```
        <div>
            <div id="header">
                <h1>
                    ASP.NET 4.5 Black Book
                </h1>
            </div>
            <div id="sidebar">
                <div id="nav">
                     
                </div>
            </div>
            <div id="content">
                <div class="itemContent">
                <asp:WebPartManager ID="WebPartManager1" runat="server"
                Personalization-Enabled="true">
                </asp:WebPartManager>
                <br />
                <asp:Button ID="Button1" runat="server" Text="Reset All" />
                <br />
                <strong>
                <span style="color: #000099">
                Site For Exporting Web Parts
                <br />
                </span>
                </strong>
                </div>
                <asp:WebPartZone ID="WebPartZone1" runat="server" BorderColor="#CCCCCC"
                Font-Names="Verdana" Padding="6">
                <ZoneTemplate>
                <asp:TextBox ID="TextBox1" runat="server" title="Sample Web
                Part"></asp:TextBox>
                </ZoneTemplate>
                <PartChromeStyle BackColor="#F7F6F3" BorderColor="#E2DED6" Font-
                Names="Verdana" ForeColor="White" />
                <MenuLabelHoverStyle ForeColor="#E2DED6" />
                <EmptyZoneTextStyle Font-Size="0.8em" />
                <MenuLabelStyle ForeColor="White" />
                <MenuVerbHoverStyle BackColor="#F7F6F3" BorderColor="#CCCCCC"
                BorderStyle="Solid" BorderWidth="1px" ForeColor="#333333" />
                <HeaderStyle Font-Size="0.7em" ForeColor="#CCCCCC"
                HorizontalAlign="Center" />
                <MenuVerbStyle BorderColor="#5D7B9D" BorderStyle="Solid"
                BorderWidth="1px" ForeColor="White" />
                <PartStyle Font-Size="0.8em" ForeColor="#333333" />
                <TitleBarVerbStyle Font-Size="0.6em" Font-Underline="False"
                ForeColor="White" />
                <MenuPopupStyle BackColor="#5D7B9D" BorderColor="#CCCCCC"
                BorderWidth="1px" Font-Names="Verdana" Font-Size="0.6em" />
                <PartTitleStyle BackColor="#5D7B9D" Font-Bold="True" Font-Size="0.8em"
                ForeColor="White" />
                </asp:WebPartZone>
                <asp:RadioButton ID="RadioButton1" runat="server" AutoPostBack="True"
                Text="user" />
                <asp:RadioButton ID="RadioButton2" runat="server" AutoPostBack="True"
                Text="shared" /><br />
                <asp:LinkButton ID="LinkButton1" runat="server">Edit
                Mode</asp:LinkButton> 
                   <asp:LinkButton ID="LinkButton2"
                runat="server">Browse</asp:LinkButton> 
                 
                <asp:EditorZone
                ID="EditorZone1" runat="server">
```

```
                <ZoneTemplate>
                <asp:BehaviorEditorPart ID="BehaviorEditorPart1" runat="server"/>
                </ZoneTemplate>
                </asp:EditorZone>
                </div>
                <div id="footer">
                        <p class="left">
                                All content copyright &copy; Kogent Solutions Inc.</p>
                </div>
        </div>
    </form>
</body>
</html>
```

In C#

```
<%@ Page Language="C#" AutoEventWireup="true" CodeFile="Default.aspx.cs"
  Inherits="_Default" %>
<!DOCTYPE html>
<html xmlns="http://www.w3.org/1999/xhtml">
<head runat="server">
    <title>Exporting Web Parts</title>
    <link href="StyleSheet.css" rel="stylesheet" type="text/css" />
</head>
<body>
    <form id="form1" runat="server">
    <div>
        <div id="header">
                <h1>
                        ASP.NET 4.5 Black Book
                </h1>
        </div>
        <div id="sidebar">
                <div id="nav">
                         
                </div>
        </div>
        <div id="content">
                <div class="itemContent">
                <asp:WebPartManager ID="WebPartManager1" runat="server"
                Personalization-Enabled="true">
                </asp:WebPartManager>
                <br />
                <asp:Button ID="Button1" runat="server" Text="Reset All"
                onclick="Button1_Click" />
                <br />
                <strong>
                <span style="color: #000099">
                Site For Exporting Web Parts
                <br />
                </span>
                </strong>
                </div>
                <asp:WebPartZone ID="WebPartZone1" runat="server" BorderColor="#CCCCCC"
                Font-Names="Verdana" Padding="6">
                <ZoneTemplate>
                <asp:TextBox ID="TextBox1" runat="server" title="Sample Web
                Part"></asp:TextBox>
                </ZoneTemplate>
                <PartChromeStyle BackColor="#F7F6F3" BorderColor="#E2DED6" Font-
                Names="Verdana" ForeColor="White" />
                <MenuLabelHoverStyle ForeColor="#E2DED6" />
```

```
                <EmptyZoneTextStyle Font-Size="0.8em" />
                <MenuLabelStyle ForeColor="White" />
                <MenuVerbHoverStyle BackColor="#F7F6F3" BorderColor="#CCCCCC"
                BorderStyle="Solid" BorderWidth="1px" ForeColor="#333333" />
                <HeaderStyle Font-Size="0.7em" ForeColor="#CCCCCC"
                HorizontalAlign="Center" />
                <MenuVerbStyle BorderColor="#5D7B9D" BorderStyle="Solid"
                BorderWidth="1px" ForeColor="White" />
                <PartStyle Font-Size="0.8em" ForeColor="#333333" />
                <TitleBarVerbStyle Font-Size="0.6em" Font-Underline="False"
                ForeColor="White" />
                <MenuPopupStyle BackColor="#5D7B9D" BorderColor="#CCCCCC"
                BorderWidth="1px" Font-Names="Verdana" Font-Size="0.6em" />
                <PartTitleStyle BackColor="#5D7B9D" Font-Bold="True" Font-Size="0.8em"
                ForeColor="White" />
                </asp:WebPartZone>
                <asp:RadioButton ID="RadioButton1" runat="server" AutoPostBack="True"
               Text="user" oncheckedchanged="RadioButton1_CheckedChanged" />
                <asp:RadioButton ID="RadioButton2" runat="server" AutoPostBack="True"
               Text="shared" oncheckedchanged="RadioButton2_CheckedChanged" /><br />
                <asp:LinkButton ID="LinkButton1" runat="server"
                onclick="LinkButton1_Click">Edit Mode</asp:LinkButton> 
                   <asp:LinkButton ID="LinkButton2" runat="server"
               onclick="LinkButton2_Click">Browse</asp:LinkButton> 
                 
                <asp:EditorZone
                ID="EditorZone1" runat="server">
                <ZoneTemplate>
                <asp:BehaviorEditorPart ID="BehaviorEditorPart1" runat="server"
                  />
                </ZoneTemplate>
                </asp:EditorZone>
                </div>
                <div id="footer">
                        <p class="left">
                                All content copyright &copy; Kogent Solutions Inc.</p>
                </div>
        </div>
    </form>
</body>
</html>
```

Listing 15.13 shows the code for the CodeFile of the `Default.aspx` page of the `Export` website:

Listing 15.13: Showing the Code for the CodeFile of the Default.aspx Page

In VB

```
Partial Class _Default
    Inherits System.Web.UI.Page
    Protected Sub Page_InitComplete(sender As Object, e As EventArgs)
     Handles Me.InitComplete
        If WebPartManager1.Personalization.CanEnterSharedScope Then
            If WebPartManager1.Personalization.Scope = PersonalizationScope.User Then
                RadioButton1.Checked = True
            Else
                RadioButton2.Checked = True
            End If
        End If
    End Sub
    Sub Page_Init(sender As Object,e As EventArgs)
        AddHandler Page.InitComplete, AddressOf Page_InitComplete
    End Sub
```

```
    Protected Sub LinkButton2_Click(sender As Object,e As EventArgs)
    Handles LinkButton2.Click
        WebPartManager1.DisplayMode = WebPartManager.BrowseDisplayMode
    End Sub
    Protected Sub LinkButton1_Click(sender As Object, e As EventArgs)
    Handles LinkButton1.Click
        WebPartManager1.DisplayMode = WebPartManager.EditDisplayMode
    End Sub
    Protected Sub Button1_Click(sender As Object,e As EventArgs)
    Handles Button1.Click
        WebPartManager1.Personalization.ResetPersonalizationState()
    End Sub
    Protected Sub RadioButton1_CheckedChanged(sender As Object,e As
    EventArgs) Handles RadioButton1.CheckedChanged
        If WebPartManager1.Personalization.Scope = PersonalizationScope.Shared Then
            WebPartManager1.Personalization.ToggleScope()
        End If
    End Sub
    Protected Sub RadioButton2_CheckedChanged(sender As Object,e As
    EventArgs) Handles RadioButton2.CheckedChanged
        If WebPartManager1.Personalization.CanEnterSharedScope AndAlso _
         WebPartManager1.Personalization.Scope = PersonalizationScope.User Then
            WebPartManager1.Personalization.ToggleScope()
        End If
    End Sub
End Class
```

In C#

```
using System;
using System.Collections.Generic;
using System.Linq;
using System.Web;
using System.Web.UI;
using System.Web.UI.WebControls;
using System.Web.UI.WebControls.WebParts;
public partial class _Default : System.Web.UI.Page
{
    protected void Page_Init(object sender, EventArgs e)
    {
        Page.InitComplete += new EventHandler(Page_InitComplete);
    }
    protected void Page_InitComplete(object sender, EventArgs e)
    {
        if (WebPartManager1.Personalization.CanEnterSharedScope)
        {
            if (WebPartManager1.Personalization.Scope == PersonalizationScope.User)
                RadioButton1.Checked = true;
            else
                RadioButton2.Checked = true;
        }
    }
    protected void Button1_Click(object sender, EventArgs e)
    {
        WebPartManager1.Personalization.ResetPersonalizationState();
    }
    protected void LinkButton1_Click(object sender, EventArgs e)
    {
        WebPartManager1.DisplayMode = WebPartManager.EditDisplayMode;
    }
    protected void LinkButton2_Click(object sender, EventArgs e)
```

```
        {
            WebPartManager1.DisplayMode = WebPartManager.BrowseDisplayMode;
        }
        protected void RadioButton1_CheckedChanged(object sender, EventArgs e)
        {
            if (WebPartManager1.Personalization.Scope == PersonalizationScope.Shared)
                WebPartManager1.Personalization.ToggleScope();
        }
        protected void RadioButton2_CheckedChanged(object sender, EventArgs e)
        {
            if (WebPartManager1.Personalization.CanEnterSharedScope &&
                WebPartManager1.Personalization.Scope == PersonalizationScope.User)
                WebPartManager1.Personalization.ToggleScope();
        }
    }
```

Finally, add the following code inside the `<system.web>` section of the `Web.config` file. Listing 15.14 shows the code to be added inside the `<system.web>` section of the `Web.config` file:

Listing 15.14: Showing the Code to be Added Inside the `<system.web>` Section of the `Web.config` File

In VB and C#

```
<?xml version="1.0"?>
<!--
  For more information on how to configure your ASP.NET application, please visit
  http://go.microsoft.com/fwlink/?LinkId=169433
  -->
<configuration>
  <system.web>
        <compilation debug="true" targetFramework="4.5"/>
        <authentication mode="Windows"/>
        <webParts enableExport="true">
                <personalization>
                        <authorization>
                                <allow users="*" verbs="enterSharedScope"/>
                        </authorization>
                </personalization>
        </webParts>
  </system.web>
</configuration>
```

Now, run the ExportAppCS website and the output is as shown in Figure 15.15:

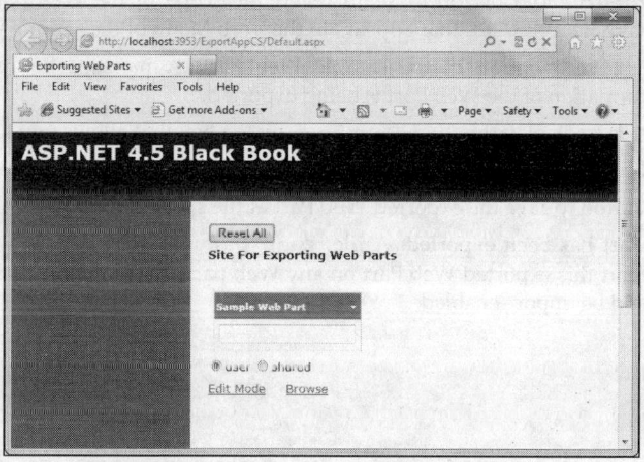

Figure 15.15: Exporting Web Parts of the Website

In the preceding figure, there are two radio buttons to toggle the scope of the Web page from `user` to `shared`. To export the sample Web Part, follow these steps:

1. Click the `shared` radio button to toggle the scope of the Web page from `user` to `shared`.
2. Click the `Edit Mode` link button to add the `Edit` option in the Verb Menu of the sample Web Part.
3. Select the `Edit` option from the `Verb` Menu of the sample Web Part to display the Editor Zone group.
4. Set the Export mode property of the `BehaviorEditorPart` control to Export all data, as shown in Figure 15.16:

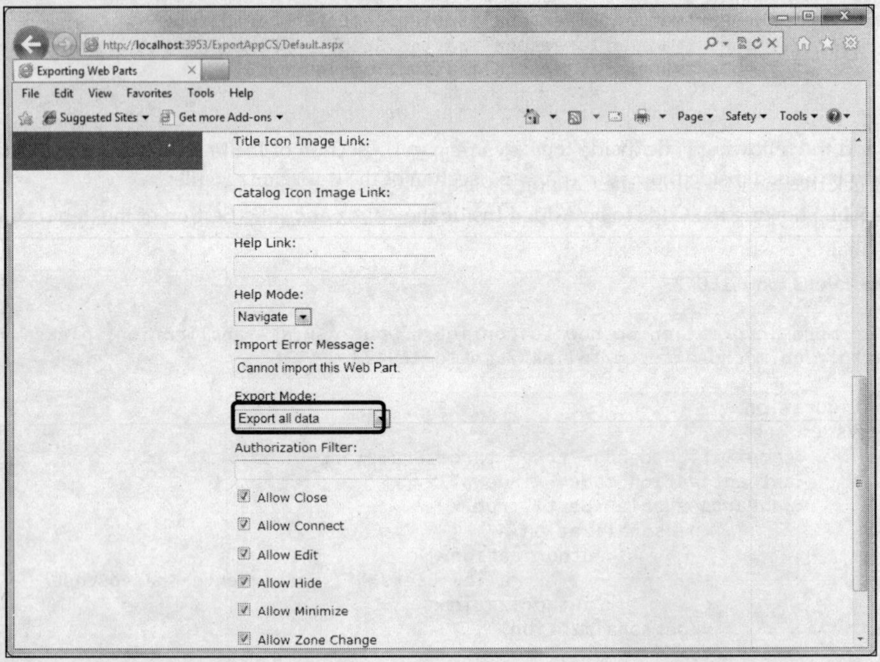

Figure 15.16: Setting the Export Mode Property of the BehaviorEditorPart Control

5. Click the Apply and OK buttons to close the Editor Zone group.
6. Now, select the `user` radio button to again revert the scope of the Web page back to the `user` mode. Observe a new verb item `Export` that appears in the Verb Menu of the sample Web Part.
7. Click the `Export` verb option of the sample Web Part. A message box appears indicating that the personalized information of the Web Part is being exported.
8. Click the `OK` button to display the `File Download` dialog box that allows you to export the Web Part.
9. Click the `Save` button and specify the name and location of the Web Part in the `Save As` dialog box.
10. Click the `Save` button to save the exported Web Part at the specified location.

With this, the Web Part has been exported. A file, `<wep_part_name>.WebPart,` is created at the specified location. You can import this exported Web Part on any Web page of your choice—the only condition is that the target Web page should be import-enabled.

Importing Web Parts

After exporting the sample Web Part, importing it on another Web page is very easy. The target Web page should be import-capable to import a Web Part and, for that, you need to insert the `ImportCatalogPart` control in the Catalog Zone. Now, extend the `WebPartsDemoAppVB` (for VB) and `WebPartsDemoAppCS` (for C#) applications to import the exported Web Part in another Web zone. To do this, you need to add the following additional code in the `<ZoneTemplate>` section of the `CatalogZone` control, contained in the `Default.aspx` page of the website:

```
<asp:ImportCatalogPart ID="ImportCatalogPart1" runat="server" />
```

This customized website is available as `WebPartsDemoAppVB_Again` (for VB) and `WebPartsDemoAppCS_Again` (for C#).

Now, let's import the sample Web Part by performing the following steps:

1. Configure the settings to import Web Part in the website by performing the steps given as follows:
   i. Click the `Catalog` link. The Catalog Zone appears on the Web page.
   ii. Click the `Imported Web Part Catalog` link from the Catalog Zone to display the Imported Web Part Catalog, as shown in Figure 15.17:

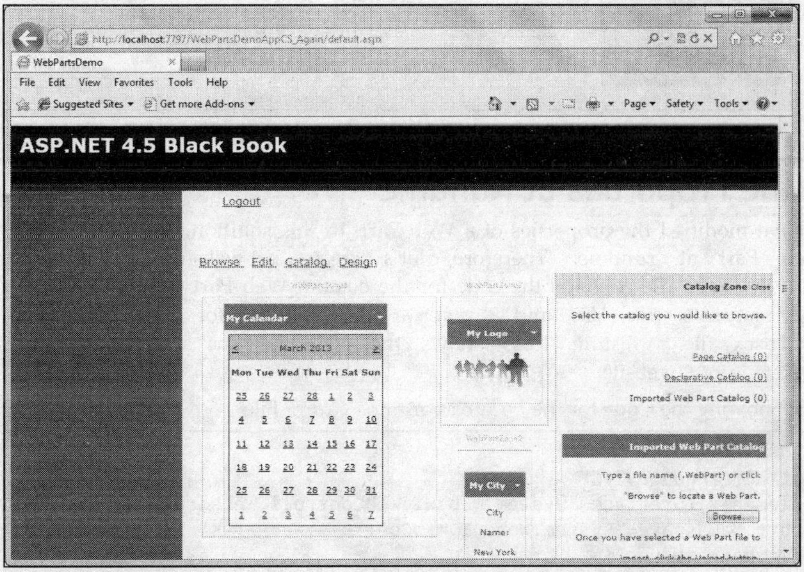

Figure 15.17: Using Imported Web Part Catalog

2. Click the Browse button on the `Imported Web Part Catalog` to display the `Choose File` dialog box.
3. Select your exported sample Web Part file from the `Choose File` dialog box and click the `Open` button.
4. Click the Upload button on the `Catalog zone`. The `Sample Web Part check box` appears in the `Catalog Zone`.
5. Select the Sample Web Part check box on the `Page Catalog` and also select the `WebPartZone1` option from the `Add to` drop-down list.
6. Now, click the `Add` button to import the sample Web Part into `WebPartZone1`.

You can see that `Sample Web Part` is added to `WebPartZone1`. Figure 15.18 shows the final output:

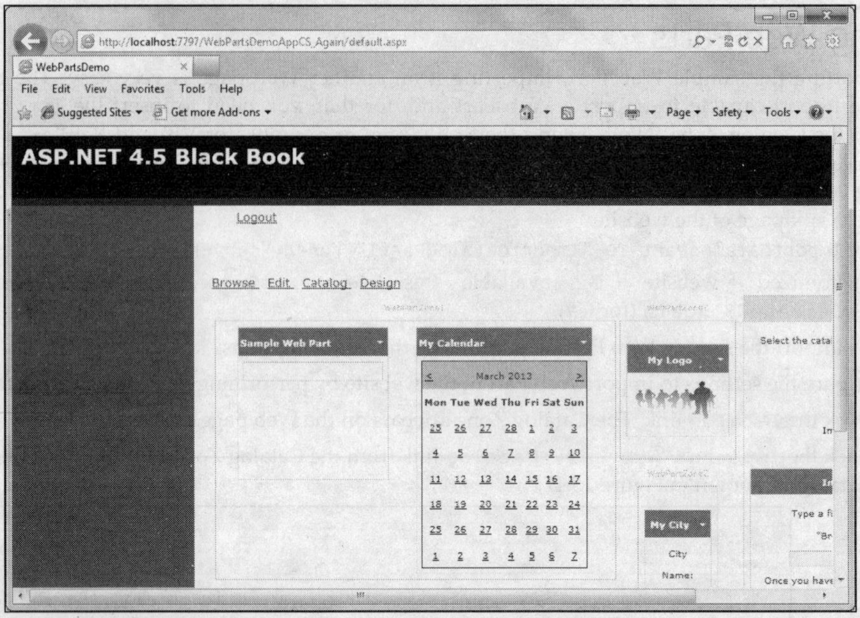

Figure 15.18: Exhibiting the Imported Web Part Appears in WebPartZone1

Modifying the Properties at Runtime

Earlier, we have modified the properties of a Web Part. In this solution, we try to modify the properties of a custom Web Part at runtime. Therefore, let's create a website, `CustomWebPartAppCS`, whose `customcontrol.ascx` file contains the code for the custom Web Part control. You can find this website as `CustomWebPartAppVB` (for VB) and `CustomWebPartAppCS` (for C#). Add .ascx file name it as customcontrol.ascx file. Listing 15.15 shows the code for the `customcontrol.ascx` file of the `CustomWebPartAppCS` website:

Listing 15.15: Showing the Code for the `customcontrol.ascx` File

In VB

```
<%@ Control Language="VB"%>
<%@ Implements Interface="System.Web.UI.WebControls.WebParts.IWebPart" %>
<%@ Import Namespace="System.Web.UI.WebControls.WebParts" %>
<script runat="server">
  Private image As String = String.Empty
  Private desc As String = String.Empty
  Private mySubtitle As String = "[0]"
  Private mytitle As String = "Custom Control "
    Public Property CatalogIconImageUrl() As String Implements
  IWebPart.CatalogIconImageUrl
        Get
            Return image
        End Get
        Set(ByVal value As String)
            image = value
        End Set
    End Property
  Public Property Description() As String Implements IWebPart.Description
        Get
                Return desc
```

```
            End Get
            Set(ByVal value As String)
                    desc = value
            End Set
      End Property
      Public ReadOnly Property Subtitle() As String Implements IWebPart.Subtitle
            Get
                    Return String.Empty
            End Get
      End Property
      Public Property Title() As String Implements IWebPart.Title
            Get
                    Return mytitle
            End Get
            Set(ByVal title As String)
            End Set
      End Property
        Public Property TitleIconImageUrl() As String Implements IWebPart.TitleIconImageUrl
           Get
                Return String.Empty
           End Get
           Set(ByVal mytitle As String)
           End Set
        End Property
      Public Property TitleUrl() As String Implements IWebPart.TitleUrl
            Get
                    Return String.Empty
            End Get
            Set(ByVal mytitle As String)
            End Set
      End Property
   </script>
   <asp:Label ID="Label1" Text="User Text Here: " Runat="server" />
   <asp:TextBox ID="TextBox1" Runat="server" />
   <br />
   <asp:Button ID="Button1" Text="OK" Runat="server" />
```

In C#

```
   <%@ Control Language="C#"%>
   <%@ Implements Interface="System.Web.UI.WebControls.WebParts.IWebPart" %>
   <%@ Import Namespace="System.Web.UI.WebControls.WebParts" %>
   <script runat="server">
      private String image = string.Empty;
      private String desc= string.Empty;
      private String mySubtitle = "[0]";
      private String mytitle = "Custom Control ";
      public String CatalogIconImageUrl
      {
            get { return image; }
            set { image = value; }
      }
      public String Description
      {
            get { return desc; }
            set { desc = value; }
      }
      public String Subtitle
      {
```

```
            get {return string.Empty; }
            set { ; }
    }
    public String Title
    {
            get { return mytitle; }
            set { mytitle = value; }
    }
    public String TitleIconImageUrl
    {
            get { return string.Empty; }
            set { ; }
    }
    public String TitleUrl
    {
            get { return string.Empty; }
            set { ; }
    }
</script>
<asp:Label ID="Label1" Text="Enter Text: " Runat="server"/>
<asp:TextBox ID="TextBox1" Runat="server"/>
<br />
<asp:Button ID="Button1" Text="OK" Runat="server" />
```

After creating the `customcontrol.ascx` file, add the code in the `Default.aspx` page of the `CustomWebPartAppCS` website. Listing 15.16 shows the code for the `Default.aspx` page of the `CustomWebPartAppCS` website:

Listing 15.16: Showing the Code for the `Default.aspx` Page

In VB

```
<%@ Page Language="VB" AutoEventWireup="false" CodeFile="Default.aspx.vb"
   Inherits="_Default" %>
<%@ Register  TagPrefix="cc1" TagName="customcontrol" Src="~/customcontrol.ascx" %>
<!DOCTYPE html>
<script runat="server">
    Protected Sub Page_Load(sender As Object, e As EventArgs) Handles
   Me.Load
         If WebPartManager1.Personalization.CanEnterSharedScope AndAlso _
          WebPartManager1.Personalization.Scope = PersonalizationScope.User Then
             WebPartManager1.Personalization.ToggleScope()
         End If
     End Sub
     Protected Sub LinkButton1_Click(sender As Object, e As EventArgs)
         WebPartManager1.DisplayMode = WebPartManager.EditDisplayMode
     End Sub
     Protected Sub LinkButton2_Click(sender As Object, e As EventArgs)
         WebPartManager1.DisplayMode = WebPartManager.BrowseDisplayMode
     End Sub
</script>
<html xmlns="http://www.w3.org/1999/xhtml">
<head runat="server">
     <title>custom control</title>
     <link href="StyleSheet.css" rel="stylesheet" type="text/css" />
</head>
<body>
     <form id="form1" runat="server">
     <div>
          <div id="header">
                <h1>
```

```
                ASP.NET 4.5 Black Book
            </h1>
        </div>
        <div id="sidebar">
            <div id="nav">
                 
            </div>
        </div>
        <div id="content">
            <div class="itemContent">
            <asp:WebPartManager ID="WebPartManager1" runat="server"
            Personalization-Enabled="true" />
            Custom WebPart  <br />
            <asp:LinkButton ID="LinkButton1" runat="server"
            OnClick="LinkButton1_Click">Edit Mode</asp:LinkButton>
            <asp:LinkButton ID="LinkButton2" runat="server"
            OnClick="LinkButton2_Click">Browse Mode</asp:LinkButton><br
            />
            <br />
            <asp:WebPartZone ID="WebPartZone2" runat="server">
            <ZoneTemplate>
            <cc1:customcontrol ID="customcontrol1"
            runat="server"></cc1:customcontrol>
            </ZoneTemplate>
            </asp:WebPartZone>
            <asp:EditorZone ID="EditorZone1" runat="server" BackColor="#F7F6F3"
            BorderColor="#CCCCCC"
            BorderWidth="1px" Font-Names="Verdana" Padding="6">
            <LabelStyle Font-Size="0.8em" ForeColor="#333333" />
            <HeaderStyle BackColor="#E2DED6" Font-Bold="True" Font-Size="0.8em"
            ForeColor="#333333" />
            <ZoneTemplate>
            <asp:BehaviorEditorPart ID="BehaviorEditorPart1" runat="server" />
            <asp:LayoutEditorPart ID="LayoutEditorPart1" runat="server" />
            </ZoneTemplate>
            <HeaderVerbStyle Font-Bold="False" Font-Size="0.8em" Font-
            Underline="False" ForeColor="#333333" />
            <PartChromeStyle BorderColor="#E2DED6" BorderStyle="Solid"
            BorderWidth="1px" />
            <PartStyle BorderColor="#F7F6F3" BorderWidth="5px" />
            <FooterStyle BackColor="#E2DED6" HorizontalAlign="Right" />
         <EditUIStyle Font-Names="Verdana" Font-Size="0.8em" ForeColor="#333333" />
            <InstructionTextStyle Font-Size="0.8em" ForeColor="#333333" />
            <ErrorStyle Font-Size="0.8em" />
          <VerbStyle Font-Names="Verdana" Font-Size="0.8em" ForeColor="#333333" />
            <EmptyZoneTextStyle Font-Size="0.8em" ForeColor="#333333"/>
          <PartTitleStyle Font-Bold="True" Font-Size="0.8em" ForeColor="#333333" />
            </asp:EditorZone>
            <br />
            <br />
            <br />
            </div></div>
            <div id="footer">
                <p class="left">
                    All content copyright &copy; Kogent Solutions Inc.</p>
            </div>
        </div>
    </form>
</body>
</html>
```

In C#

```
<%@ Page Language="C#" AutoEventWireup="true" CodeFile="Default.aspx.cs"
  Inherits="_Default" %>
<%@ Register TagName="customcontrol" TagPrefix="cc1" Src="~/customcontrol.ascx" %>
<!DOCTYPE html>
<script runat="server">
protected void Page_Load(object sender, EventArgs e)
{
  if (WebPartManager1.Personalization.CanEnterSharedScope &&
    WebPartManager1.Personalization.Scope == PersonalizationScope.User)
  {
        WebPartManager1.Personalization.ToggleScope();
  }
}
protected void LinkButton1_Click(object sender, EventArgs e)
{
  WebPartManager1.DisplayMode = WebPartManager.EditDisplayMode;
}
protected void LinkButton2_Click(object sender, EventArgs e)
{
  WebPartManager1.DisplayMode = WebPartManager.BrowseDisplayMode;
}
</script>
<html xmlns="http://www.w3.org/1999/xhtml">
<head runat="server">
    <title>custom control</title>
    <link href="StyleSheet.css" rel="stylesheet" type="text/css" />
</head>
<body>
    <form id="form1" runat="server">
    <div>
         <div id="header">
                <h1>
                       ASP.NET 4.5 Black Book
                </h1>
         </div>
         <div id="sidebar">
                <div id="nav">
                        
                </div>
         </div>
         <div id="content">
                <div class="itemContent">
                <asp:WebPartManager ID="WebPartManager1" runat="server"
                Personalization-Enabled="true" />
                Custom WebPart  <br />
                <asp:LinkButton ID="LinkButton1" runat="server"
                OnClick="LinkButton1_Click">Edit Mode</asp:LinkButton>
                <asp:LinkButton ID="LinkButton2" runat="server"
                OnClick="LinkButton2_Click">Browse Mode</asp:LinkButton><br/>
                <br />
                <asp:WebPartZone ID="WebPartZone2" runat="server">
                <ZoneTemplate>
                <cc1:customcontrol runat="server" id="customcontrol1"
                ></cc1:customcontrol>
                </ZoneTemplate>
                </asp:WebPartZone>
                <asp:EditorZone ID="EditorZone1" runat="server" BackColor="#F7F6F3"
                BorderColor="#CCCCCC" BorderWidth="1px" Font-Names="Verdana" Padding="6">
```

```
                <LabelStyle Font-Size="0.8em" ForeColor="#333333" />
                <HeaderStyle BackColor="#E2DED6" Font-Bold="True" Font-Size="0.8em"
                ForeColor="#333333" />
                <ZoneTemplate>
                <asp:BehaviorEditorPart ID="BehaviorEditorPart1" runat="server" />
                <asp:LayoutEditorPart ID="LayoutEditorPart1" runat="server" />
                </ZoneTemplate>
                <HeaderVerbStyle Font-Bold="False" Font-Size="0.8em" Font-
                Underline="False" ForeColor="#333333" />
                <PartChromeStyle BorderColor="#E2DED6" BorderStyle="Solid"
                BorderWidth="1px" />
                <PartStyle BorderColor="#F7F6F3" BorderWidth="5px" />
                <FooterStyle BackColor="#E2DED6" HorizontalAlign="Right" />
                <EditUIStyle Font-Names="Verdana" Font-Size="0.8em"
                ForeColor="#333333" />
                <InstructionTextStyle Font-Size="0.8em" ForeColor="#333333"/>
                <ErrorStyle Font-Size="0.8em" />
               <VerbStyle Font-Names="Verdana" Font-Size="0.8em" ForeColor="#333333" />
                <EmptyZoneTextStyle Font-Size="0.8em" ForeColor="#333333" />
               <PartTitleStyle Font-Bold="True" Font-Size="0.8em" ForeColor="#333333" />
                </asp:EditorZone>
                <br />
                <br />
                <br />
                </div>
                <div id="footer">
                        <p class="left">
                                All content copyright &copy; Kogent Solutions Inc.</p>
                </div>
         </div>
   </div>
    </form>
  </body>
  </html>
```

Finally, add the following code inside the <system.web> section of the Web.config file, as shown in Listing 15.17:

Listing 15.17: Showing the Code to be Added Inside the <system.web> Section of the Web.config File

In VB and C#

```
  <?xml version="1.0"?>
  <configuration>
    <system.web>
        <compilation debug="true" strict="false" explicit="true" targetFramework="4.5"/>
          <webParts>
          <personalization>
                <authorization>
                        <allow users="*" verbs="enterSharedScope"/>
                </authorization>
          </personalization>
          </webParts>
    </system.web>
  </configuration>
```

Now, run the website; the output appears as shown in Figure 15.19:

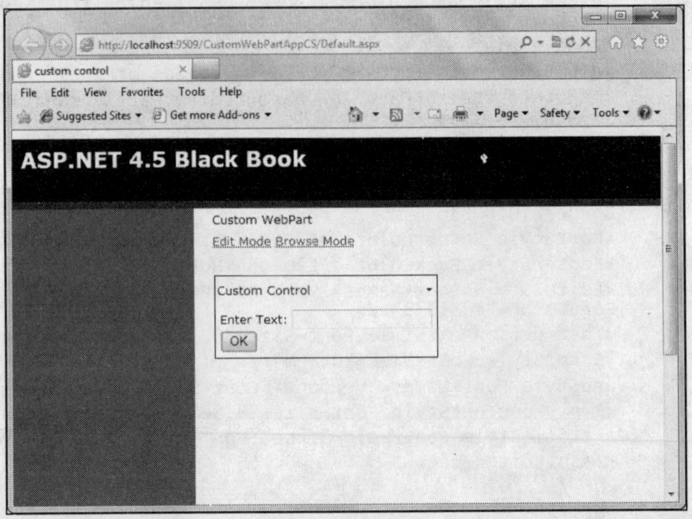

Figure 15.19: Showing the Output of the CustomWebPartAppCS Website

As shown in Figure 15.19, the `Custom Control` dialog box appears on the `Default.aspx` page. Perform the following steps to change the properties of this Custom Control dialog box:

1. Click the `Edit Mode` link to switch to the edit mode.
2. Now, click the Edit option from the Verb Menu to display the Editor Zone group on the Web page, as shown in Figure 15.20:

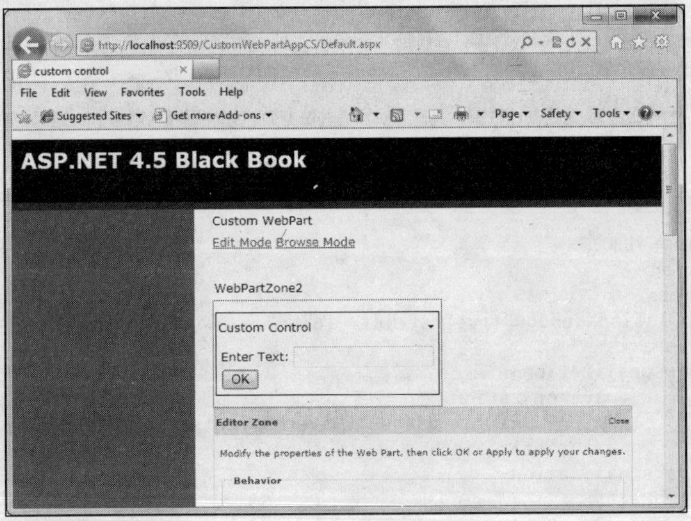

Figure 15.20: Editing Properties at Runtime in the Editor Zone Group

As shown in Figure 15.20, the Editor Zone group contains the `Behavior` and `Layout` parts that allow you to modify the behavior and layout of the custom Web Part. Modify the custom Web Part's properties as per your requirement by selecting appropriate options from the Editor Zone group. In this example, we have specified the Help link.

3. Now, click the Apply button and then click the OK button to apply the changes to the custom Web Part. In our case, the Help link appears in the Verb Menu. Figure 15.21 shows the modified custom Web Part:

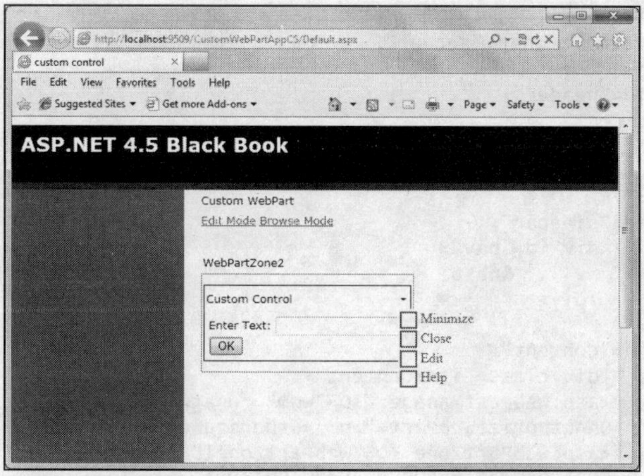

Figure 15.21: Displaying the Modified Custom Web Part

Figure 15.21 shows how we have modified the properties of the custom Web Part to minimize it and added a new Verb Menu item named Help.

Authorizing Web Parts

Web Parts are modular components residing in a single Web page. Using different modes of a Web page, we allow the users the liberty to modify the Web page. However, security is also a primary concern. There could be a scenario where you may require a bunch of users (having a specific role) and each Web Part can be viewed by the users of specific role, and Web Parts assigned to other roles are not available to these users.

In such a scenario, there arises a need for authorizing Web Parts, which is quite simple. To do so, we use the `AuthorizationFilter` property and assign a specific role to a Web Part. After assigning this property, only the authorized users would be able to see the Web Parts at runtime. Let's create a new website, `AuthorizingWebPartsAppCS, to put this concept into working`. You can find the code of this website as `AuthorizingWebPartsAppVB` (for VB) and `AuthorizingWebPartsAppCS` (for C#). Listing 15.18 shows the code for the `Default.aspx` page of the `AuthorizingWebPartsAppCS` website:

Listing 15.18: Showing the Code for the `Default.aspx` Page

In VB

```
<%@ Page Language="VB" AutoEventWireup="false" CodeFile="Default.aspx.vb"
  Inherits="_Default" %>
<!DOCTYPE html>
<script runat="server">
  Protected Sub wpm_AuthorizeWebPart(sender As Object,e As
  WebPartAuthorizationEventArgs)
        If Not String.IsNullOrEmpty(e.AuthorizationFilter) Then
              If e.AuthorizationFilter = "admin" Then
                    e.IsAuthorized = True
              Else
                    e.IsAuthorized = False
              End If
        End If
  End Sub
</script>
<html xmlns="http://www.w3.org/1999/xhtml">
<head runat="server">
    <title>Authorizing Web Parts Example</title>
    <link href="StyleSheet.css" rel="stylesheet" type="text/css" />
</head>
```

```
<body>
    <form id="form1" runat="server">
   <div>
        <div id="header">
              <h1>
                     ASP.NET 4.5 Black Book
              </h1>
        </div>
        <div id="sidebar">
              <div id="nav">
                      
              </div>
        </div>
        <div id="content">
              <div class="itemContent">
              <asp:WebPartManager ID="wpm" runat="server"
              OnAuthorizeWebPart="wpm_AuthorizeWebPart" />
              <asp:WebPartZone ID="WebPartZone1" runat="server" BorderColor="#CCCCCC"
              Font-Names="Verdana" Padding="6">
              <ZoneTemplate>
              <asp:HyperLink ID="HyperLink1" runat="server" Title="Allowed control"
              AuthorizationFilter="admin" NavigateUrl="~/Default.aspx">my
              link</asp:HyperLink>
              <asp:Label ID="Label1" runat="server" Text="My label" Title="Allowed
              control" AuthorizationFilter="admin" />
              <asp:TextBox ID="TextBox1" runat="server" Title="restricted control:"
              AuthorizationFilter="admins" />
              </ZoneTemplate>
              <PartChromeStyle BackColor="#F7F6F3" BorderColor="#E2DED6" Font-
              Names="Verdana" ForeColor="White" />
              <MenuLabelHoverStyle ForeColor="#E2DED6" />
              <EmptyZoneTextStyle Font-Size="0.8em" />
              <MenuLabelStyle ForeColor="White" />
              <MenuVerbHoverStyle BackColor="#F7F6F3" BorderColor="#CCCCCC"
              BorderStyle="Solid" BorderWidth="1px" ForeColor="#333333" />
              <HeaderStyle Font-Size="0.7em" ForeColor="#CCCCCC"
              HorizontalAlign="Center" />
              <MenuVerbStyle BorderColor="#5D7B9D" BorderStyle="Solid"
              BorderWidth="1px" ForeColor="White" />
              <PartStyle Font-Size="0.8em" ForeColor="#333333" />
              <TitleBarVerbStyle Font-Size="0.6em" Font-Underline="False"
              ForeColor="White" />
              <MenuPopupStyle BackColor="#5D7B9D" BorderColor="#CCCCCC"
              BorderWidth="1px" Font-Names="Verdana"  Font-Size="0.6em" />
              <PartTitleStyle BackColor="#5D7B9D" Font-Bold="True" Font-Size="0.8em"
              ForeColor="White" />
              </asp:WebPartZone>
              </div></div>
          <div id="footer">
                     <p class="left">
                            All content copyright &copy; Kogent Solutions Inc.</p>
              </div>
        </div>
    </form>
</body>
</html>
```

In C#

```
<%@ Page Language="C#" AutoEventWireup="true" CodeFile="Default.aspx.cs"
  Inherits="_Default" %>
<!DOCTYPE html>
<script runat="server">
```

```
protected void wpm_AuthorizeWebPart(object sender,
WebPartAuthorizationEventArgs e)
{
   if (!String.IsNullOrEmpty(e.AuthorizationFilter))
   {
          if (e.AuthorizationFilter == "admin")
                 e.IsAuthorized = true;
          else
                 e.IsAuthorized = false;
   }
}
</script>
<html xmlns="http://www.w3.org/1999/xhtml">
<head runat="server">
    <title>Authorizing Web Parts Example</title>
    <link href="StyleSheet.css" rel="stylesheet" type="text/css" />
</head>
<body>
    <form id="form1" runat="server">
    <div>
         <div id="header">
                <h1>
                       ASP.NET 4.5 Black Book
                </h1>
         </div>
         <div id="sidebar">
                <div id="nav">
                        
                </div>
         </div>
         <div id="content">
                <div class="itemContent">
                <asp:WebPartManager ID="wpm" runat="server"
                OnAuthorizeWebPart="wpm_AuthorizeWebPart" />
                <asp:WebPartZone ID="WebPartZone1" runat="server" BorderColor="#CCCCCC"
                Font-Names="Verdana" Padding="6">
                <ZoneTemplate>
                <asp:HyperLink ID="HyperLink1" runat="server" Title="Allowed control"
                AuthorizationFilter="admin" NavigateUrl="~/Default.aspx">my
                link</asp:HyperLink>
                <asp:Label ID="Label1" runat="server" Text="My label"
                Title="Allowed control" AuthorizationFilter="admin" />
                <asp:TextBox ID="TextBox1" runat="server" Title="restricted control:"
                AuthorizationFilter="admins" />
                </ZoneTemplate>
                <PartChromeStyle BackColor="#F7F6F3" BorderColor="#E2DED6" Font-
                Names="Verdana" ForeColor="White" />
                <MenuLabelHoverStyle ForeColor="#E2DED6" />
                <EmptyZoneTextStyle Font-Size="0.8em" />
                <MenuLabelStyle ForeColor="White" />
                <MenuVerbHoverStyle BackColor="#F7F6F3" BorderColor="#CCCCCC"
                BorderStyle="Solid" BorderWidth="1px" ForeColor="#333333" />
                <HeaderStyle Font-Size="0.7em" ForeColor="#CCCCCC"
                HorizontalAlign="Center" />
                <MenuVerbStyle BorderColor="#5D7B9D" BorderStyle="Solid"
                BorderWidth="1px" ForeColor="White" />
                <PartStyle Font-Size="0.8em" ForeColor="#333333" />
                <TitleBarVerbStyle Font-Size="0.6em" Font-Underline="False"
                ForeColor="White" />
                <MenuPopupStyle BackColor="#5D7B9D" BorderColor="#CCCCCC"
                BorderWidth="1px" Font-Names="Verdana"  Font-Size="0.6em" />
```

```
                    <PartTitleStyle BackColor="#5D7B9D" Font-Bold="True" Font-Size="0.8em"
                    ForeColor="White" />
                    </asp:WebPartZone>
                    </div>  </div>
                    <div id="footer">
                            <p class="left">
                                    All content copyright &copy; Kogent Solutions Inc.</p>
                    </div>
            </div>
        </form>
    </body>
    </html>
```

In addition, add the following code inside the <configuration> section of the Web.config file, as shown in Listing 15.19:

Listing 15.19: Showing the Code to be Added Inside the <configuration> Section of the Web.config File

In VB and C#

```
    <system.web>
      <compilation debug="true" strict="false" explicit="true" targetFramework="4.5"/>
            <authentication mode="Forms"/>
            <roleManager enabled="true"/>
    </system.web>
```

In Listing 15.18, there are three Web Parts used—two of which have been allotted the admin group through the AuthorizationFilter property, while one Web Part has been assigned the admins group.

Now, we can see the page, as shown in Figure 15.22:

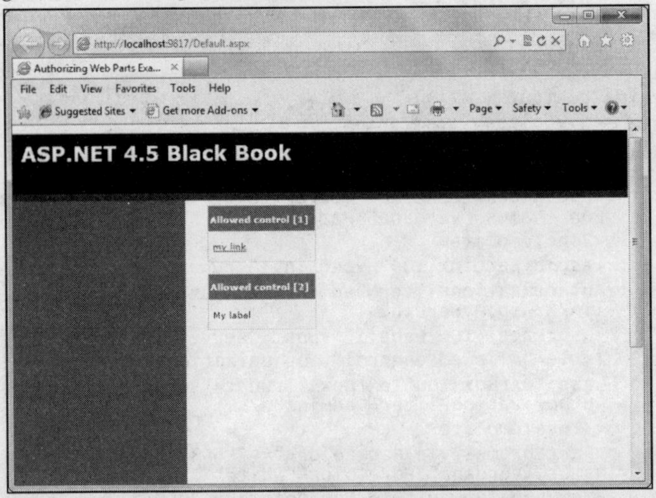

Figure 15.22: Filtering the Default.aspx Page of the AuthorizingWebPartsAppCS Website

In Figure 15.22, only those Web Parts have been displayed that are filtered with the admin group. If you change the AuthorizationFilter property value of the third Web Part from admins to admin, then it is also displayed on the Web page.

Summary

In this chapter, you have learned about the concept of Web Parts Framework and its use in Web application. You have also learned about personalizing and exchanging data between Web Parts, exporting and importing of Web Parts, modifying its properties, and authorizing the Web Parts.

In the next chapter, you learn about caching in Visual Studio 2012.

16

Caching in ASP.NET 4.5

In Depth

Caching, as the name suggests, is used to store data temporarily either on a Web server or on the client-side. It is useful in situations where several programs continually access the same set of data. This data can be easily stored in a cache and used in future. Accessing a database in an ASP.NET page is generally a slow and time-consuming process that involves connecting to the database and retrieving data from it. Caching is the best way to improve the performance of your Web application, as it allows you to access data from the cache itself, which is quicker than retrieving the data from the database on each request. Therefore, caching not only reduces the processing time of a Web application, but also reduces network traffic; thereby, improving the performance of your Web application and enhancing user experience.

In this chapter, you learn about caching techniques in ASP.NET, such as output caching, partial-page caching, the post-cache substitution, SQL cache notification and SQL cache invalidation, cache dependencies, and cache profiles, to improve the performance of Web applications.

Caching in ASP.NET

The execution of applications written in ASP.NET is faster than the applications written in Active Server Pages (ASP), in terms of retrieving data from a database. In ASP, caching is the main technique that developers use to improve the processing time of a Web application. You can cache data in application-level or session-level variables to speed up its retrieval. However, data retrival at both these levels is insufficient for large-scale Web applications. With ASP.NET, caching has improved dramatically. There are a number of classes in .NET Framework, specifically provided to deal with issues related to caching of data. However, before delving into the various intricacies of caching, let's discuss the concept of caching and then move on to discuss its implementation in ASP.NET.

As discussed earlier, cache is a place where data is stored temporarily. Let's take an example to understand how the concept of caching is used in Web applications. Suppose your application needs to query a database that contains one million records, every four seconds, for the same kind of result. Your database is updated in a time interval of, say, an hour.

Considering the given scenario, the data retrieved from the database remains the same for approximately 60 minutes, as the database is updated only after one hour. However, querying the database after every four seconds increases network traffic and the load on the database server or Web server (if the database is also hosted on the same server), which in turn has an adverse effect on the performance of the application.

Now, let's use caching to store the query results. We cache the data for a fixed period of time, say, 60 minutes, and when the first query is executed, the results are stored in cache. In the next 60 minutes, the same type of requests access the data from the cache itself without running the query again on the one million records of the database. This simple concept reduces the load on the database server as well as reduces the time users have to wait to access the specific data.

After exploring the concept of caching, let's leran about the features in caching in ASP.NET 4.5:

- **Ouput caching**—Enables you to store the page output and Hypertext Transfer Protocol (HTTP) responses in an in-memory cache, which stores the cache data in Random Access Memory (RAM) of the computer. This feature helps in generating the content faster by not regenerating the ouput from scratch. It was introduced with ASP.NET 1.0. However, in ASP.NET 4.0, the output caching feature has been extended as it now enables you to configure more than one custom output-cache provider. A new System.Web.Caching.OutputCacheProvider class has been introduced to enable you to create custom output-cache provider, which can then be registered within the Web.config file of an application by using the new <providers> subsection of the <outputCache> element.

- **HttpBrowserCapabilities object**—Determines the capabilities of the browser that a user is using to browse a site. This implies that the HttpBrowserCapabilities object determines whether or not the browser supports a particular version of JavaScript.
- **Object caching**—Helps in making caching available for all applications by introducing the new System.Runtime.Caching.dll assembly, which contains the new System.Runtime.Caching namespace. This assembly come under ObjectCache class

There are the following two set of classes in this namespace:

- Abstract types which provide the base for implementing custom cache
- The MemoryCache class

Now, let's learn about the various caching techniques available in ASP.NET that are used to cache a completely rendered Web page.

Output Caching

Output caching, also known as page level caching, is the simplest technique of caching in ASP.NET. In output caching, the complete HyperText Markup Language (HTML) output of a rendered ASP.NET page is stored in cache and subsequent requests for the page are sent from the cache itself. The cache engine, also known as cache server, checks the existing requests for the page. This engine acts as a server that stores Web pages and other Internet content locally. If it finds a request for the page, the cached HTML output is sent to the client. If no request is found, it renders the page again and saves a copy of the HTML output in cache.

Output caching is also very useful when you have static pages (pages whose content do not change), as the cache engine stores the data that is rendered on the page. For subsequent requests, the engine sends the cached HTML output from the cache itself; thereby, reducing the load on the Web server, as the processor does not get busy in rendering the page every time a request is made.

You can easily implement output caching by adding the `@ OutputCache` directive at the top of a Web page, as shown in the following code snippet:

```
<%@ OutputCache Duration="10" VaryByParam="None" %>
```

You can also define the location, such as client-side, server-side, or proxy server, to cache the data by including the `Location` attribute in the `@ OutputCache` directive, as shown in the following code snippet:

```
<%@ OutputCache Duration="90" Location="Any | Client | Downstream | Server |ServerAndClimt
        None" VaryByParam="None" %>
```

The `@ OutputCache` directive contains various attruibutes, which are described in Table 16.1:

Table 16.1: Attributes Supported by the @ OutputCache Directive

Attribute	Description
`CacheProfile`	Contains the setting of the cache to associate with a Web page. This is an optional attribute and by default it contains an empty string.
`Duration`	Defines the time duration in seconds for the Web page to be cached. This attribute is always required in the `@ OutputCache` directive.
`Location`	Defines the location where the cache is created. The possible values are Any, Client, Downstream, Server, ServerAndClient, and None.
`NoStore`	Contains a `Boolean` value that determines whether or not to prevent secondary storage of sensitive information.
`SqlDependency`	Contains a string value that identifies a set of database and table name pairs on which the output cache of a control or Web page depends.

Table 16.1: Attributes Supported by the @ OutputCache Directive

Attribute	Description
VaryByControl	Contains a semicolon-separated list of strings. These strings represent ID property values of ASP.NET server controls declared in the user control (a group of one or more server controls). If you are working with user controls, this attribute is necessary unless you are using the VaryByParam attribute. This attribute is not supported by ASP.NET Web pages.
VaryByCustom	Defines custom strings for custom output caching requirements.
VaryByHeader	Defines a semicolon-separated list of HTTP headers.
VaryByParam	Defines a semicolon-separated list of strings, which the output cache uses to identify the cache entry.

Now, let's discuss some of these attributes in more detail.

The Location Attribute

The `Location` attribute is used to define the location where the data is to be cached. It can be on the server-side, client-side, or even a proxy server. This attribute uses the `OutputCacheLocation` enumeration to specify the location. Table 16.2 lists the possible values of the `OutputCacheLocation` enumeration:

Table 16.2: Possible Values for the OutputCacheLocation Enumeration

Values	Description
Any	Specifies that the output cache can be located anywhere, such as on the client's browser, the proxy server, or the server itself
Client	Specifies that the output cache is only located on the client browser
Downstream	Specifies that the output cache is stored in any HTTP 1.1 cache-capable devices, other than the originating server including the proxy server and the requested client
None	Disables the output cache of the requested page
Server	Specifies that the output cache is only located on the processing Web server
ServerAndClient	Specifies that the output cache is stored on the Web server and on the client browser

NOTE

The Location attribute does not support @ OutputCache directives included in user controls (.ascx files). Therefore, this attribute can be used only for Web pages.

The VaryByCustom Attribute

The `VaryByCustom` attribute is used to define custom strings according to the requirements of a user. For example, if `browser` value is specified in this attribute, the cache engine saves multiple copies of the data, depending on the types of browsers. This is very useful when you want to cache different types of content for different browsers, such as images for Internet Explorer 7 (IE7), text for Opera, and videos for Mozilla Firefox.

You can also implement a custom logic to keep different copies of the data based on the conditions defined in the custom logic. If you implement a custom logic, then you must override the `HttpApplication.GetVaryByCustomString` method in your Web application's `Global.asax` file.

The following code snippet shows how to define the `GetVaryByCustomString` method in the `Global.asax` file:

In VB

```
<script>
Public Overrides Function GetVaryByCustomString(context As HttpContext, arg As_
   String) As String
   'your own custom logic
End Function
</script>
```

In C#

```
[script]
public override string GetVaryByCustomString(HttpContext context, string arg)
{
   'your own custom logic;
   //INSTANT C# NOTE: Inserted the following 'return' since all code paths must return a
     value in C#:
   return null;
}
[/script]
```

The VaryByParam Attribute

The `VaryByParam` attribute is used to cache different copies of a Web page when the Web page is generated dynamically, based on the parameters received in the form of `HTTP POST` or `HTTP GET`.

Let's consider an example to understand the `VaryByParam` attribute. Suppose that you have an ASP.NET Web page that generates the personal records of an employee based on a parameter named `EmployeeID` received through a query string. Now, imagine a situation where a user requests for the personal records of an employee with the `EmployeeID` parameter, 14, and the `VaryByParam` attribute set to its default value, `None`. In this case, the Web page will be rendered and its output will be cached. However, suppose that another user requests for the records of the employee with the `EmployeeID` parameter, 25. In this case, the cache engine, unable to differentiate between the two requests, sends the cached output for `EmployeeID` 14 to the user.

To overcome this problem, you can use the `VaryByParam` attribute and specify that the cache engine should vary its cache on the `EmployeeID` parameter by setting the `VaryByParam` attribute as `EmployeeID` at the top of the Web page. You can define more than one parameter name in the `VaryByParam` attribute. The cache engine then checks and keeps different copies of the Web page for each parameter defined in the `VaryByParam` attribute.

You can also set the value of the `VaryByParam` attribute to `*`, which directs the cache engine to check any `POST` parameter associated with the requests. An example to illustrate this has been given in the Immediate Solutions section of this chapter.

NOTE

*If you are unsure about the number of parameters passed through the VaryByParam attribute, which may increase or decrease later, then using the * value is the safest option.*

Partial-Page Caching

Caching of a complete Web page is not always required. Sometimes, you need to implement caching on specific parts of a Web page. This can be achived by partial or fragment caching. In this caching, specific parts of a Web page are cached, and the remaining content of the Web page is refreshed each time the page is requested. The steps to apply partial caching are as follows:

1. Identify the parts of the Web page that require more resource and processing than the other parts, while rendering.
2. Create a single or more user controls and decide the caching policies for them. Cache policies ensure the validity of the cached data on each user request.

You can cache the content of a user control by using the `@ OutputCache` directive or the `PartialCachingAttribute` class. The following code snippet shows how to cache a control in the output cache for 500 seconds:

```
<%@ OutputCache Duration="500" VaryByParam="None" %>
```

NOTE

A parser error occurs, if you do not include the VaryByParam attribute while using the @ OutputCache directive. If you do not want to use the functionality of VaryByParam attribute, set its value to None, as shown in the preceding code snippet.

You can also use the code-behind technique to define the content of a user control. In this case, you need to add the following code snippet in the metadata of your class declaration:

```
<PartialCaching(500)>
```

Now, when you request for the Web page where this user control is used, the cache engine stores the control for 500 seconds in its output cache and serves the control from the cache for subsequent requests. The remaining content of the Web page accesses the server on every request.

Let's take another scenario and suppose that the user control is cached for 200 seconds and nested in a Web page that has its output cache enabled for only 100 seconds. In such a situation, the user control is cached for 200 seconds, even though the cache for the page is re-generated after 100 seconds. The control is retrieved from the cache only after 200 seconds.

Let's now reverse the case, assuming that the page expires in 200 seconds, and the control expires in 100 seconds. In this situation, the complete page will be present in the cache for 200 seconds. You will see the practical implementation for both the situations in the Immediate Solutions section of this chapter.

Post-Cache Substitution and Substitution Control

The post-cache substitution feature of ASP.NET allows caching by substituting some of the content in a Web page dynamically. Caching is important because it improves the performance of Web applications. In some cases; however, you may want to cache a page, but at the same time you may want some of its content to be dynamically available as well. In such a situation, you can use the post-cache substitution feature.

Let's consider an example to understand how post-cache substitution works. Suppose a Web page contains information on automobiles. This information, being static, can be easily cached. However, if this page contains an AdRotator that changes on each page request, making this part of the page dynamic, you can use the post-cache substitution feature to cache the page that contains the static information on automobiles, while leaving the dynamic part containing the AdRotator. You can implement post-cache substitution by performing any of the following three tasks:

- Using the `Substitution` control to specify the part of the page that needs to be made dynamic, or is exempted from caching
- Using the `Substitution` control Application Programming Interface (API) to programmatically create that part of the page that needs to be made dynamic
- Using the `AdRotator` control (implicitly) to internally provide support for post-cache substitution

The `Substitution` control can be used to specify the part of a cached page that is exempted from caching. You can drag the `Substitution` control from the Toolbox and drop it on the page having the dynamic content.

The `MethodName` property of the `Substitution` control can be used to specify the method that the `Substitution` control calls at runtime. This method, specified by using the `MethodName` property, returns a `String` value that replaces the content of the `Substitution` control. When you use the `Substitution` control, the Web page is cached on the server instead of the client. This allows the method to retrieve the updated content of the `Substitution` control whenever the request for that Web page is made in future.

Programmatically, you can create dynamic content for a cached page by calling the `WriteSubstitution` method of the `Substitution` control API in the page code. The `WriteSubstitution` method takes the name of the method defined for performing the task of creating dynamic content as a parameter. This method for creating dynamic content takes an `HttpContext` parameter and returns a string, which is the content that is substituted at the specified location. The advantage of using the `WriteSubstitution` method instead of the `Substitution` control is that you can call a method of any arbitrary object through the `WriteSubstitution` method rather than a static method of the `Page` object.

The `AdRotator` server control can be used to provide post-cache substitution on a page internally. With this server control, you can render advertisments on every request regardless of whether the page is cached or not. A page that contains an `AdRotator` control is only cached on the server.

Data Caching

Data caching is one of the most powerful features in ASP.NET. So far, we have seen declarative ways of enabling caching in ASP.NET applications; whereas, data caching implements caching programmatically. Data caching is very useful when you need to cache custom data into cache memory. For example, if you need to cache a dataset to use it later in a Web application, you can use the data caching feature.

In ASP.NET, caching is implemented using two mechanisms, application caching and page out caching. Application caching allows you to cache data you generate, such as a dataset or custom report. Page out caching saves the output of a Web page and reuses it in future. It supports the following basic types of dependency models:

- **File dependency**—Allows you to validate a cached item with external file(s), such as Extensible Markup Language (XML) and Access database (.mdb). If there is any change in the external files, the cached item becomes obsolete and is removed from the cache.
- **Key dependency**—Allows you to manage the relationship among cached items, which depends on each other. This means that if one cached item is updated or removed, the dependent cache item is also updated or removed from the cache.
- **SQL dependency**—Allows you to validate a cached item with the SQL database. If there is any change in the SQL database, the cached item becomes obsolete and is removed from the cache.
- **Aggregate dependency**—Allows you to validate a cached item to multiple resources, such as the SQL database and external file(s). In other words, aggregate-based dependency validates the cached item on more than one resource.
- **Time dependency**—Allows you to define the expiration time of a particular item of a database.
- **Custom dependency**—Allows you to build and use your own dependencies instead of using the built-in dependencies.

Data caching in .NET is implemented by the `Cache` class or the `System.Web.Caching` namespace. Using the `Cache` class to store data in cache is easy if you are dealing with simple data. The `Cache` class offers a simple mechanism to store and access data by using the `Key/Value` format, as shown in following code snippet:

In VB

```
Cache("myvalue") = "value"
```

In C#

```
Cache["myvalue"] = "value"
```

Using data caching, you can perform the following three main tasks:

- Add items in cache
- Retrieve data from cache
- Delete items from cache

Let's discuss these tasks in detail.

Adding Items in Cache

To add items in cache, you can use a number of available techniques, from simple to complex, depending on the requirements. The following code snippet shows how to add an item in cache:

In VB

```
Cache("myvalue") = "value"
```

In C#

```
Cache["myvalue"] = "value"
```

The `Cache` class offers the `Cache.Add` and `Cache.Insert` methods to add items in the cache. Both these methods are useful when you need to manage different aspects of caching, such as expiration and dependency.

The following code snippet shows how to add an item in cache by using the `Cache.Insert` method:

In VB

```
Cache.Insert("myvalue", "value")
```

In C#

```
Cache.Insert("myvalue", "value");
```

Using the `Cache.Insert` method is similar to using the method with the `Cache("myvalue") = value` code.

Caching a complete XML document without associating the dependency feature may create a problem. Suppose a user accesses the XML document that has no dependency specified to it. In that case, any modification made in the server cannot be seen by the user until the cache expires and is re-generated. In this situation, you can use the dependency feature with the `Cache.Insert` method. The following code snippet shows how to specify the dependency of an item:

In VB

```
Cache.Insert("MyData", "data", New CacheDependency(Server.MapPath("data.xml")))
```

In C#

```
Cache.Insert("MyData", "data", new CacheDependency(Server.MapPath("data.xml")));
```

As discussed, the expiration time for an item needs to be specified while storing it in cache. While using the `Cache.Insert` method, you can specify absolute expiration and sliding expiration policies by using time-based dependency. Absolute expiration sets an absolute time for a cache item to expire and sliding expiration resets the expiration time of a Web page each time the page is requested. The following code snippet shows how to use the `Cache.Insert` method to add an item to cache with the absolute expiration time of five minutes:

In VB

```
Cache.Insert("Myvalue", "value", Nothing, DateTime.Now.AddMinutes(5),   TimeSpan.Zero)
```

In C#

```
Cache.Insert("Myvalue", "value", null, DateTime.Now.AddMinutes(5),
    System.Web.Caching.Cache.NoSlidingExpiration);
```

In the preceding code snippet, we have set `TimeSpan.Zero`, as we do not want to specify sliding time expiration for an item. The following code snippet uses the sliding time expiration policy:

In VB

```
Cache.Insert("Myvalue", "value", Nothing, DateTime.MaxValue,
    TimeSpan.FromSeconds(20))
```

In C#

```
Cache.Insert("Myvalue", "value", null, DateTime.MaxValue,
    TimeSpan.FromSeconds(20));
```

The preceding code snippet inserts the item in cache for 20 seconds with the sliding time expiration policy.

When you use the sliding time expiration policy, the value of absolute expiration does not matter, as this value varies according to the sliding time expiration. You can also disable the absolute expiration time by using the `DateTime.MaxValue` parameter. For example, if you specify the sliding time as 20 seconds and the item is accessed in the 18th second, then the whole time is calculated again for 20 seconds more and the item is available in cache for another 20 seconds. This means 18 seconds + 20 seconds = 38 seconds is the time for which the item will exist in the cache before the cache is destroyed, if it is not accessed in the last 20 seconds.

You can also define the importance of an item at the time of caching it by specifying a value from the `CacheItemPriority` enumeration. This priority setting informs the Web server about the importance of the item. While removing items from the cache, the Web server deletes the low-priority items before deleting the high-priority ones. The possible values for the `CacheItemPriority` enumeration are listed in Table 16.3:

Table 16.3: Possible Values for the CacheItemPriority Enumeration

Values	Description
`AboveNormal`	Specifies that the cache items with this value are not deleted frequently when the server frees system memory.
`BelowNormal`	Specifies that the cache items with this value are deleted frequently when the server frees system memory.
`Default`	Specifies that the default value for a cached item is `Normal`.
`High`	Specifies that the cache items with this value are least likely to be deleted when the server frees system memory.
`Low`	Specifies that the cache items with this value are most likely to be deleted when the server frees system memory.
`Normal`	Specifies that the cache items with this value are deleted after the deletion of the items of the `Low` and `BelowNormal` priorities. This is the default value for all cached items.
`NotRemovable`	Specifies that the cache items with this level are not deleted automatically.

You can define the `CacheItemPriority` enumeration while inserting an item in cache, as shown in the following code snippet:

In VB

```
Cache.Insert("Myvalue", "value", Nothing, DateTime.MaxValue, TimeSpan.FromSeconds(20),
   CacheItemPriority.High, null)
```

In C#

```
Cache.Insert("Myvalue", "value", Nothing, DateTime.MaxValue, TimeSpan.FromSeconds(20),
   CacheItemPriority.High, null);
```

The preceding code snippet adds the items into the cache by using the `Cache.Insert` method. However, you can also use the `Cache.Add` method for the same task. Therefore, it is important to keep the differences between both the methods in mind before using the `Cache.Add` method.

When you call the `Cache.Add` method, it always returns an object; whereas, in the case of the `Cache.Insert` method, no object is returned. Moreover, if you call the `Cache.Insert` method to add an item that already exists in the cache, the existing item is replaced by the new item. However, doing the same with the `Cache.Add` method will neither replace the existing item nor raise any exception.

Retrieving Data from Cache

Retrieving data from cache is one of the easiest tasks in ASP.NET. You can retrieve data from cache by specifying the key and value that represent the data. The following code snippet shows how to retrieve data from cache:

In VB

```
value=Cache("Myvalue")
```

In C#

```
value=Cache["Myvalue"];
```

It is important to note that before retrieving data from cache, you must check whether the data exists or not, as shown in the following code snippet:

In VB

```
value = Cache("Myvalue")
If value is Nothing then
   ' Do something here
Else
   ' Do something here
End If
```

In C#

```
value = Cache["Myvalue"];
if (value == null)
{
   // Do something here;
}
else
{
   // Do something here;
}
```

Deleting Items from Cache

The data is automatically deleted from cache on the basis of its expiration policy. However, there are times when you need to delete data from the cache manually. You can use the `Cache.Remove` method to delete data from the cache manually. The following code snippet shows how to delete the data from cache:

In VB

```
Cache.Remove("myvalue")
```

In C#

```
Cache.Remove["myvalue"];
```

SQL Cache Notification and SQL Cache Invalidation

SQL cache notification allows you to configure SQL Server to provide notification when any changes occur in the database on which the cache data is dependent. In ASP.NET you need to enable SQL cache notification. Perform the following steps to enable SQL cache notification:

1. Open the Command Prompt window and type the following command:

   ```
   cd %windir%\Microsoft .Net\Framework\v4.0.50727
   ```

   In the preceding command, `%windir%` represents the root directory, `C:\`.

2. Type the following command in the Command Prompt window to enable SQL cache notification:

   ```
   aspnet_regsql.exe -S <server> -U <username> -P <password> -ed -d <databasename>_       -
      et -t <tablename>
   ```

In the preceding command, the following notations have been used:

- `<server>`—Represents the server on which the SQL Server instance, which contains the database with dependent data, is installed
- `<username>`—Represents the username, such as `sa` (the default username of SQL Server), for the account that is used for SQL authentication

- <password>—Represents the password for the account that is used for SQL authentication
- <databasename>—Represents the name of the database that contains the data on which cache data is dependent
- <tablename>—Represents the name of the table that contains the data on which cache data is dependent

SQL cache invalidation makes cache data dependent on the data stored in an SQL Server database. If any modification is made on the data on which cache data is dependent, then the cached data is removed from the database and no validation is performed. This is done with the help of the SQL cache invalidation feature of ASP.NET.

Cache Dependencies

Cache dependencies allow a cache item to be validated based on an external file or another cache item. If a cache dependency, such as an external file or another cache item, is modified, the cache item is not validated and is removed from cache.

To understand how cache dependency works, consider a scenario in which an application reads financial data from an XML file that is periodically updated. After reading the data, the application processes the data and creates a graph to represent it in a format that can be used by other applications. The application also caches the data and inserts a cache dependency in the XML file. If any modification is made in the XML file, the data stored in cache is removed and the application reads the data from the XML file and caches its updated copy.

ASP.NET provides the `CacheDependency` class to develop custom cache dependencies. When you develop your own cache dependency, you have the advantage of using the cache invalidation method to keep the cache content updated with the data contained in an external file or another cache item. ASP.NET also provides two built-in classes of cache dependencies, `AggregateCacheDependency` and `SqlCacheDependency`. The `AggregateCacheDependency` class allows multiple dependencies to be aggregated for content, which depends on more than one resource. The `SqlCacheDependency` class allows a cache data to be dependent on a database. In SQL cache dependency, data is removed from cache only if changes have taken place in the database.

Cache Profiles and Configuration

Cache profiles allow you to define cache settings in the `Web.config` file of an application and refer these settings on individual pages included in the application. By using cache profiles in an application, you can apply cache settings to multiple pages simultaneously. For example, you can create a cache profile, `CacheHourly`, which sets the cache duration for a page to an hour, after which the cache is reloaded. You can apply this cache profile to individual pages of the application. If you change the `CacheHourly` cache profile to allow non-caching, then the pages of the application are not cached.

Besides cache profiles, ASP.NET allows you to configure resource allocation for the cache, by including the following three sections in the `<caching>` section of the `web.config` file:

- `Cache`—Contains application settings related to the cache, including features, such as limiting the use of memory and disabling memory
- `OutputCache`—Contains application settings related to the output cache, including features, such as disabling the output and fragmenting caching
- `OutputCacheSettings`—Contains cache settings that can be used by individual pages included in an application

The Cache Class

The `Cache` class is used to implement caching for a Web application in ASP.NET. This class cannot be inherited. The noteworthy properties of the `System.Web.Caching.Cache` class are listed in Table 16.4:

Table 16.4: Noteworthy Properties of the Cache Class

Property	Description
`Count`	Retrives the number of items stored in cache
`EffectivePercentagePhysicalMemoryLimit`	Obtains the percentage of the physical memory that can be consumed by a Web application before ASP.NET starts removing items from cache
`EffectivePrivateBytesLimit`	Obtains the number of bytes available for cache
`Item`	Obtains a cache item on pressing the specified key

The noteworthy methods of the `Cache` class are listed in Table 16.5:

Table 16.5: Noteworthy Methods of the Cache Class

Method	Description
`Add`	Adds a specified item to the `Cache` object
`Get`	Retrieves the specified item from the `Cache` object
`GetEnumerator`	Retrieves a dictionary enumerator to iterate through the key settings and their values contained in the cache
`Insert`	Inserts an item into the `Cache` object
`Remove`	Removes the specified item from the `Cache` object of an application

Let's now move to the Immedaite Solutions section of the chapter to have a better understanding of caching in ASP.NET 4.5.

Immediate Solutions

Using Output Caching

As discussed in the *In Depth* section, output caching is the simplest method of caching available in ASP.NET.

NOTE

The applications in this chapter have been created using the ASP.NET Empty Web Site template from the New Web Site dialog box. After the application is created, the Default.aspx page is added to the application.

To show the use of output caching, let's create a ASP.NET application named `OutputCache` (`OutputCacheVB` in VB and `OutputCacheCS` in C#) and perform the following steps:

1. Add the following code snippet in the `Default.aspx` page of the `OutputCache` application:

```
<%@ OutputCache Duration="10" VaryByParam="None" %>
```

2. Add three Label controls on the `Default.aspx` page of the `OutputCache` application by dragging the controls from the Toolbox to the page or by adding the code shown in Listing 16.1:

Listing 16.1: Showing the Code for the `Default`.aspx Page

In VB

```
<%@ Page Language="VB" AutoEventWireup="false" CodeFile="Default.aspx.vb"
  Inherits="_Default" %>
<%@ OutputCache Duration="10" VaryByParam="None" %>
<!DOCTYPE html>
<html xmlns="http://www.w3.org/1999/xhtml">
<head runat="server">
  <title>OutPut Cache Page</title>
</head>
<body>
  <form id="form1" runat="server">
  <div>
  <asp:Label ID="Label1" Style="z-index: 101; left: 232px; position: absolute; top:
  95px" runat="server" Font-Bold="True" Font-Names="Tahoma" Font-Size="Large"
  Height="15px" Width="284px">Output Cache example</asp:Label>
  <asp:Label ID="Label2" Style="z-index: 102; left: 358px; position: absolute; top:
  153px; width: 160px;" runat="server">Label</asp:Label>
  <asp:Label ID="Label3" Style="z-index: 103; left: 231px; position: absolute; top:
  263px" runat="server" Font-Bold="True" Font-Names="Tahoma" Width="440px">The above
  displayed time was cached for 10 seconds. Keep Refereshing the page to see the
  changes.</asp:Label>
  </div>
  </form>
</body>
</html>
```

In C#

```
<%@ Page Language="C#" AutoEventWireup="true" CodeFile="Default.aspx.cs"
  Inherits="_Default" %>
<%@ OutputCache Duration="10" VaryByParam="None" %>
<!DOCTYPE html>
<html xmlns="http://www.w3.org/1999/xhtml">
<head runat="server">
```

```
    <title>OutPut Cache Page</title>
</head>
<body>
    <form id="form1" runat="server">
    <div>
    <asp:Label ID="Label1" Style="z-index: 101; left: 232px; position: absolute; top:
    95px" runat="server" Font-Bold="True" Font-Names="Tahoma" Font-Size="Large"
    Height="15px" Width="284px">Output Cache example</asp:Label>
    <asp:Label ID="Label2" Style="z-index: 102; left: 358px; position: absolute; top:
    153px; width: 160px;" runat="server">Label</asp:Label>
    <asp:Label ID="Label3" Style="z-index: 103; left: 231px; position: absolute; top:
    263px" runat="server" Font-Bold="True" Font-Names="Tahoma" Width="440px">The above
    displayed time was cached for 10 seconds. Keep Refereshing the page to see the
    changes.</asp:Label>
    </div>
    </form>
</body>
</html>
```

3. Add the code, shown in Listing 16.2, in the code-behind file of the `Default.aspx` page to display the date and time on a Label control:

Listing 16.2: Showing the Code for the Code-behind File

In VB

```
Partial Class _Default
    Inherits System.Web.UI.Page
    Protected Sub Page_Load(sender As Object, e As EventArgs) Handles Me.Load
        Label2.Text = DateTime.Now.ToString()
    End Sub
End Class
```

In C#

```
using System;
using System.Collections.Generic;
using System.Linq;
using System.Web;
using System.Web.UI;
using System.Web.UI.WebControls;
public partial class _Default : System.Web.UI.Page
{
    protected void Page_Load(object sender, EventArgs e)
    {
        Label2.Text = DateTime.Now.ToString();
    }
}
```

4. Run the `OutputCache Web` application. The output appears, as shown in Figure 16.1:

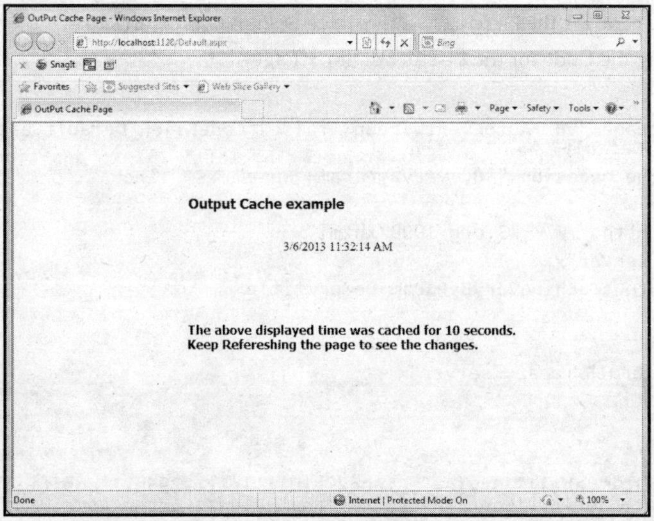

Figure 16.1: Displaying the Output of OutputCache Application

Using Output Caching with the VaryByParam Attribute

As described earlier, the `VaryByParam` attribute is used to cache different copies of the same Web page when the Web page is generated dynamically based on the received parameters. To demonstrate this, let's create a ASP.NET application named `OutPutCachingVaryByParam` (`OutPutCachingVaryByParamVB` in VB and `OutPutCachingVaryByParamCS` in C#). After creating the `OutPutCachingVaryByParam` application, perform these steps to use the `VaryByParam` attribute:

1. Drop three Label controls, a Textbox control, and a Button control on the `Default.aspx` page of the `OutPutCachingVaryByParam` Web application, as shown in Figure 16.2:

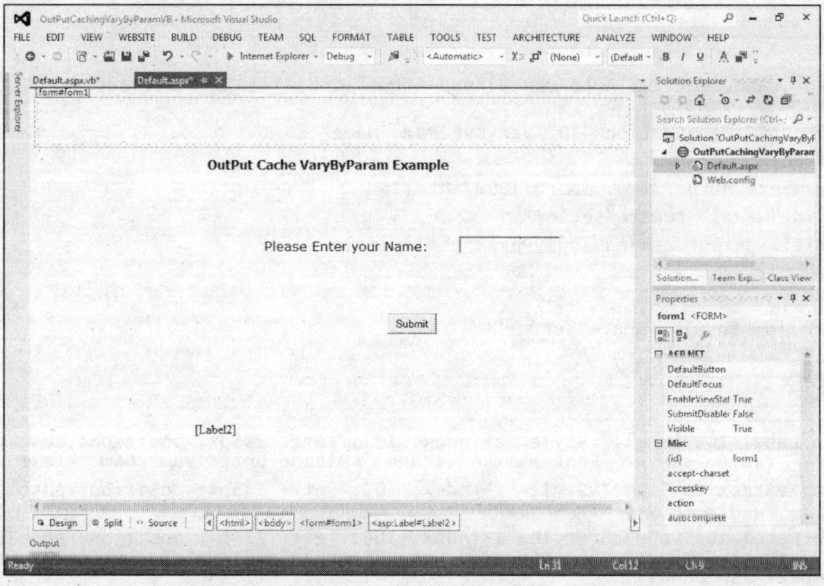

Figure 16.2: Showing the Default.aspx Page of the OutPutCachingVaryByParam Web Application

The complete source code for the `Default.aspx` page is shown in Listing 16.3:

Listing 16.3: Showing the Code for the `Default.aspx` Page

In VB

```
<%@ Page Language="VB" AutoEventWireup="false" CodeFile="Default.aspx.vb"
  Inherits="_Default" %>
<%@ OutputCache Duration="30" VaryByParam="Name" %>
<!DOCTYPE html>
<html xmlns="http://www.w3.org/1999/xhtml">
<head runat="server">
    <title>OutputCachingVaryByParam Demo</title>
</head>
<body>
  <form id="form1" runat="server">
  <div>
  <br />
  <br />
  <asp:Label ID="Label1" Style="z-index: 101; left: 295px; position: absolute; top:
  193px" runat="server" Font-Names="Verdana">Please Enter your Name:</asp:Label>
  <asp:TextBox ID="Name" Style="z-index: 103; left: 538px; position: absolute; top:
  189px" runat="server"></asp:TextBox>
  <asp:Label ID="Label3" Style="z-index: 104; left: 224px; position: absolute; top:
  88px" runat="server" Font-Names="tahoma" Font-Bold="True">OutPut Cache VaryByParam
  Example</asp:Label>
  <asp:Button ID="Button1" Style="z-index: 105; left: 449px; right: 288px; position:
  absolute; top: 288px" runat="server" Text="Submit"></asp:Button>
  </div>
  <asp:Label ID="Label2" Style="z-index: 102; left: 208px; position: absolute; top:
  427px" runat="server"></asp:Label>
  </form>
</body>
</html>
```

In C#

```
<%@ Page Language="C#" AutoEventWireup="true" CodeFile="Default.aspx.cs"
  Inherits="_Default" %>
<%@ OutputCache Duration="30" VaryByParam="Name" %>
<!DOCTYPE html>
<html xmlns="http://www.w3.org/1999/xhtml">
<head id="Head1" runat="server">
    <title>OutputCachingVaryByParam Demo</title>
</head>
<body>
  <form id="form1" runat="server">
  <div>
  <br />
  <br />
  <asp:Label ID="Label1" Style="z-index: 101; left: 295px; position: absolute; top:
  193px" runat="server" Font-Names="Verdana">Please Enter your Name:</asp:Label>
  <asp:TextBox ID="Name" Style="z-index: 103; left: 538px; position: absolute; top:
  189px" runat="server"></asp:TextBox>
  <asp:Label ID="Label3" Style="z-index: 104; left: 224px; position: absolute; top:
  88px" runat="server" Font-Names="tahoma" Font-Bold="True">OutPut Cache VaryByParam
  Example</asp:Label>
  <asp:Button ID="Button1" Style="z-index: 105; left: 449px; right: 288px; position:
  absolute; top: 288px" runat="server" Text="Submit"></asp:Button>
```

```
    </div>
    <asp:Label ID="Label2" Style="z-index: 102; left: 208px; position: absolute; top:
    427px" runat="server"></asp:Label>
    </form>
</body>
</html>
```

2. Add the code, shown in Listing 16.4, in the code-behind file of the `Default.aspx` page:

Listing 16.4: Showing the Code-behind File of the `Default.aspx` Page

In VB

```
Partial Class _Default
    Inherits System.Web.UI.Page
    Protected Sub Page_Load(sender As Object, e As EventArgs) Handles Me.Load
        If IsPostBack Then
            Name.Visible = False
            Label1.Visible = False
            Button1.Visible = False
            Label2.Visible = True
            Label2.Text = "This Output of this page was cached for " & Name.Text & ".
  The Current time Is " & DateTime.Now.ToString()
        End If
    End Sub
End Class
```

In C#

```
using System;
using System.Collections.Generic;
using System.Linq;
using System.Web;
using System.Web.UI;
using System.Web.UI.WebControls;
public partial class _Default : System.Web.UI.Page
{
    protected void Page_Load(object sender, EventArgs e)
    {
        if (IsPostBack)
        {
            Name.Visible = false;
            Label1.Visible = false;
            Button1.Visible = false;
            Label2.Visible = true;
            Label2.Text = "This Output of this page was cached for " + Name.Text + ".
                 The Current time is " + DateTime.Now.ToString();
        }
    }
}
```

In Listing 16.4, we have passed Name as a parameter to the server and then cache the different versions of the `Default.aspx` page, based on this parameter, for 30 seconds. You can test this by entering different names. The output will be the same for 30 seconds for each name.

3. Run the `OutPutCachingVaryByParam` application. The output appears, as shown in Figure 16.3:

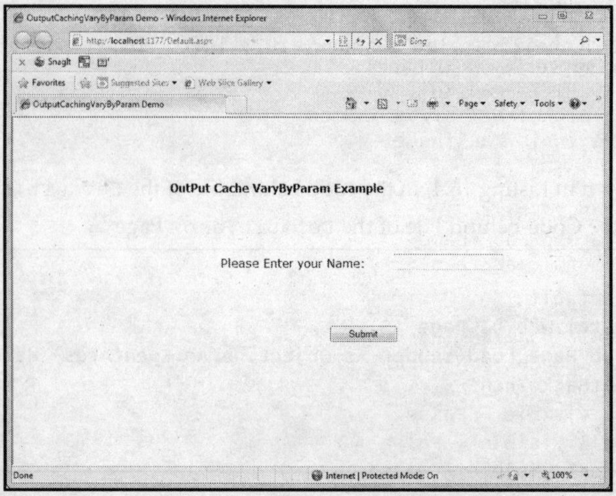

Figure 16.3: Showing the Output of the OutPutCachingVaryByParam Application

4. Enter your name in the textbox and click the Submit button. The output of the page will be cached, as shown in Figure 16.4:

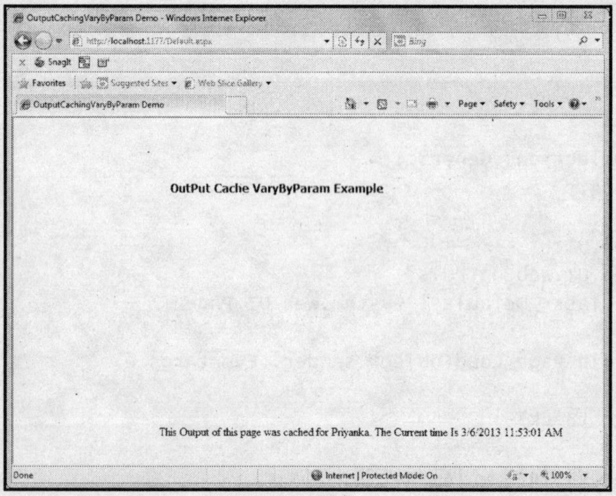

Figure 16.4: Displaying the Output after Page Caching

Using Data Caching

Data caching is used to store custom data in cache. To demonstrate data caching, let's create a ASP.NET empty Web application named `DataCachingExample` (`DataCachingExampleVB` in VB and `DataCachingExampleCS` in C#). In this application, we populate a dataset from an XML file named `Authors.xml` and store this dataset in cache by using the file dependency feature. Doing this ensures that the cached dataset is repopulated every time there is a change in the original XML file. In our case, the `Authors.xml` file contains the code shown in Listing 16.5:

Listing 16.5: Showing the Code of the `Authors.xml` File

```
<?xml version="1.0" encoding="utf-8" ?>
<authorslist>
  <authors>
    <au_id>409-56-7008</au_id>
    <au_lname>Tom</au_lname>
```

```
    <au_fname>Abraham</au_fname>
  </authors>
  <authors>
    <au_id>648-92-1872</au_id>
    <au_lname>Blotchet-Halls</au_lname>
    <au_fname>Reginald</au_fname>
  </authors>
  <authors>
    <au_id>238-95-7766</au_id>
    <au_lname>Carson</au_lname>
    <au_fname>Cheryl</au_fname>
  </authors>
  <authors>
    <au_id>722-51-5454</au_id>
    <au_lname>DeFrance</au_lname>
    <au_fname>Michel</au_fname>
  </authors>
  <authors>
    <au_id>712-45-1867</au_id>
    <au_lname>del Castillo</au_lname>
    <au_fname>Innes</au_fname>
  </authors>
  <authors>
    <au_id>427-17-2319</au_id>
    <au_lname>Dull</au_lname>
    <au_fname>Ann</au_fname>
  </authors>
  <authors>
    <au_id>213-46-8915</au_id>
    <au_lname>Green</au_lname>
    <au_fname>Marjorie</au_fname>
  </authors>
  <authors>
    <au_id>527-72-3246</au_id>
    <au_lname>Greene</au_lname>
    <au_fname>Morningstar</au_fname>
  </authors>
  <authors>
    <au_id>472-27-2349</au_id>
    <au_lname>Gringlesby</au_lname>
    <au_fname>Burt</au_fname>
  </authors>
  <authors>
    <au_id>846-92-7186</au_id>
    <au_lname>Hunter</au_lname>
    <au_fname>Sheryl</au_fname>
  </authors>
  <authors>
    <au_id>756-30-7391</au_id>
    <au_lname>Karsen</au_lname>
    <au_fname>Livia</au_fname>
  </authors>
  <authors>
    <au_id>486-29-1786</au_id>
    <au_lname>Locksley</au_lname>
    <au_fname>Charlene</au_fname>
  </authors>
  <authors>
    <au_id>724-80-9391</au_id>
    <au_lname>MacFeather</au_lname>
    <au_fname>Stearns</au_fname>
  </authors>
```

```
    <authors>
      <au_id>893-72-1158</au_id>
      <au_lname>McBadden</au_lname>
      <au_fname>Heather</au_fname>
    </authors>
    <authors>
      <au_id>267-41-2394</au_id>
      <au_lname>O'Leary</au_lname>
      <au_fname>Michael</au_fname>
    </authors>
    <authors>
      <au_id>807-91-6654</au_id>
      <au_lname>Panteley</au_lname>
      <au_fname>Sylvia</au_fname>
    </authors>
    <authors>
      <au_id>998-72-3567</au_id>
      <au_lname>Ringer</au_lname>
      <au_fname>Albert</au_fname>
    </authors>
    <authors>
      <au_id>899-46-2035</au_id>
      <au_lname>Ringer</au_lname>
      <au_fname>Anne</au_fname>
    </authors>
    <authors>
      <au_id>341-22-1782</au_id>
      <au_lname>Smith</au_lname>
      <au_fname>Meander</au_fname>
    </authors>
    <authors>
      <au_id>274-80-9391</au_id>
      <au_lname>Straight</au_lname>
      <au_fname>Dean</au_fname>
    </authors>
    <authors>
      <au_id>724-08-9931</au_id>
      <au_lname>Stringer</au_lname>
      <au_fname>Dirk</au_fname>
    </authors>
    <authors>
      <au_id>172-32-1176</au_id>
      <au_lname>White</au_lname>
      <au_fname>Johnson</au_fname>
    </authors>
    <authors>
      <au_id>672-71-3249</au_id>
      <au_lname>Yokomoto</au_lname>
      <au_fname>Akiko</au_fname>
    </authors>
</authorslist>
```

Now, let's perform the following steps to cahce data using data caching:

1. Add the code, shown in Listing 16.6, in the `Default.aspx` page:

Listing 16.6: Showing the Code for the `Default.aspx` Page

In VB

```
<%@ Page Language="VB" AutoEventWireup="false" CodeFile="Default.aspx.vb"
  Inherits="_Default" %>
<!DOCTYPE html>
<html xmlns="http://www.w3.org/1999/xhtml">
```

```
<head runat="server">
   <title>Data Caching Example</title>
</head>
<body>
   <form id="form1" runat="server">
   <div>
         <br />
         <br />
         <asp:DataGrid ID="DataGrid1" Style="z-index: 101; left: 216px; position:
   absolute; top: 123px" runat="server" BorderColor="Tan" BorderWidth="1px"
   BackColor="LightGoldenrodYellow" CellPadding="2" Width="664px" ForeColor="Black"
   GridLines="None">
         <FooterStyle BackColor="Tan"></FooterStyle>
         <SelectedItemStyle ForeColor="GhostWhite"
   BackColor="DarkSlateBlue"></SelectedItemStyle>
         <HeaderStyle Font-Bold="True" BackColor="Tan"></HeaderStyle>
         <PagerStyle HorizontalAlign="Center" ForeColor="DarkSlateBlue"
   BackColor="PaleGoldenrod"> </PagerStyle>
         <AlternatingItemStyle BackColor="PaleGoldenrod" />
         </asp:DataGrid>
         <asp:Label ID="Label1" Style="z-index: 102; left: 477px; position: absolute;
   top: 83px" runat="server" Font-Bold="True" Font-Names="Tahoma" Font-Size="Large">Data
   Caching Example</asp:Label>
         <asp:Label ID="Label2" Style="z-index: 104; left: 225px; position: absolute;
   top: 81px" runat="server">Label</asp:Label>
   </div>
   </form>
</body>
</html>
```

In C#

```
<%@ Page Language="C#" AutoEventWireup="true" CodeFile="Default.aspx.cs"
   Inherits="_Default" %>
<!DOCTYPE html>
<html xmlns="http://www.w3.org/1999/xhtml">
<head runat="server">
   <title>Data Caching Example</title>
</head>
<body>
   <form id="form1" runat="server">
   <div>
         <br />
         <br />
         <asp:DataGrid ID="DataGrid1" Style="z-index: 101; left: 216px; position:
         absolute; top: 123px" runat="server" BorderColor="Tan" BorderWidth="1px"
         BackColor="LightGoldenrodYellow" CellPadding="2" Width="664px"
         ForeColor="Black" GridLines="None">
         <FooterStyle BackColor="Tan"></FooterStyle>
         <SelectedItemStyle ForeColor="GhostWhite"
         BackColor="DarkSlateBlue"></SelectedItemStyle>
         <HeaderStyle Font-Bold="True" BackColor="Tan"></HeaderStyle>
         <PagerStyle HorizontalAlign="Center" ForeColor="DarkSlateBlue"
         BackColor="PaleGoldenrod"> </PagerStyle>
         <AlternatingItemStyle BackColor="PaleGoldenrod" />
         </asp:DataGrid>
         <asp:Label ID="Label1" Style="z-index: 102; left: 477px; position: absolute;
         top: 83px" runat="server" Font-Bold="True" Font-Names="Tahoma" Font-
         Size="Large">Data Caching Example</asp:Label>
         <asp:Label ID="Label2" Style="z-index: 104; left: 225px; position: absolute;
   top: 81px" runat="server">Label</asp:Label>
   </div>
   </form>
</body>
</html>
```

2. Add the code, shown in Listing 16.7, in the code-behind file of the `Default.aspx` page:

Listing 16.7: Showing the Code for the Code-behind File of the `Default.aspx` Page

In VB

```
Partial Class _Default
    Inherits System.Web.UI.Page
    Dim DataSet1 As New Data.DataSet
    Protected Sub Page_Load(sender As Object, e As EventArgs) Handles Me.Load
        If Cache("MyCacheDataset") Is Nothing Then
            DataSet1.ReadXml(Server.MapPath("Authors.xml"))
         Cache.Insert("MyCacheDataset", DataSet1, New
  CacheDependency(Server.MapPath("Authors.xml")))
            Label2.Text = "Cache Generated"
        Else
            Label2.Text = "Using pre-generated Cache"
        End If
        DataGrid1.DataSource = Cache("MyCacheDataset")
        DataGrid1.DataBind()
    End Sub
End Class
```

In C#

```
using System;
using System.Collections.Generic;
using System.Configuration;
using System.Data;
using System.Linq;
using System.Web;
using System.Web.Security;
using System.Web.UI;
using System.Web.UI.HtmlControls;
using System.Web.UI.WebControls;
using System.Web.UI.WebControls.WebParts;
using System.Xml.Linq;
public partial class _Default : System.Web.UI.Page
{
    DataSet DataSet1 = new DataSet();
    protected void Page_Load(object sender, EventArgs e)
    {
        if (Cache["MyCacheDataset"] == null)
        {
            DataSet1.ReadXml(Server.MapPath("Authors.xml"));
            Cache.Insert("MyCacheDataset", DataSet1, new
                System.Web.Caching.CacheDependency(Server.MapPath("Authors.xml")));
            Label2.Text = "Cache Generated";
        }
        else
        {
            Label2.Text = "Using pre-generated Cache";
        }
        DataGrid1.DataSource = Cache["MyCacheDataset"];
        DataGrid1.DataBind();
    }
}
```

Listing 16.7 first checks for the existence of a cache. If the cache exists, it simply binds the `GridView` control with the cached object. In addition, we have used file dependency in Listing 16.7. Therefore, after loading the page, its content cannot be changed until the original XML file is modified. If you modify the XML file, the cache expires immediately and then the dataset and cache will need to be populated again.

3. Run the `DataCachingExample` Web application. The first page of the Web application appears, as shown in Figure 16.5:

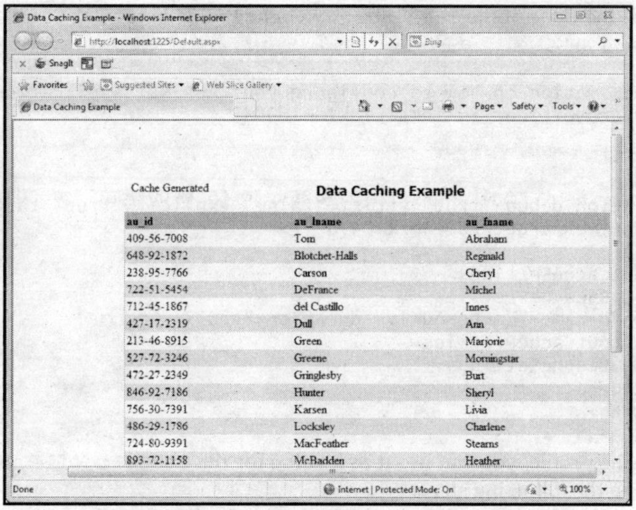

Figure 16.5: Generating Cache

When you refresh the `DataCachingExample` Web application, the Web page displays a pre-generated cache, as shown in Figure 16.6:

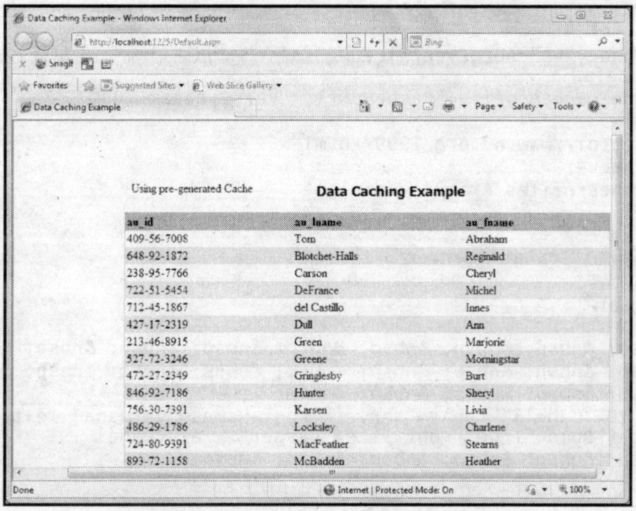

Figure 16.6: Using a Pre-generated Cache

To regenerate cache, you need to make modifications in the `Authors.xml` database file.

Using Cache Profiles

Cache profiles are used to describe specific cache settings that you can apply to pages, page items, and content types of your website. The setting of a cache profile includes time duration of the item to be stored in the cache, security of the cache, and user rights and permissions to access the cache. To use cache profiles for caching a page of a Web application, you need to first create a cache profile in the `Web.config` file of the Web application First, create a new ASP.NET application named `CacheProfiles` (`CacheProfilesVB` in VB and `CacheProfilesCS` in C#) and then create a cache profile named `CacheHourly` in the `Web.config` file, as shown in Listing 16.8:

Listing 16.8: Showing the Code of the `CacheHourly` Cache Profile in the `Web.config` File

```
<?xml version="1.0"?>
<!--
  For more information on how to configure your ASP.NET application, please visit
  http://go.microsoft.com/fwlink/?LinkId=169433
  -->
<configuration>
    <system.web>
      <compilation debug="true" strict="false" explicit="true" targetFramework="4.5" />
      <httpRuntime targetFramework="4.5" />
      <caching>
        <outputCacheSettings>
          <outputCacheProfiles>
            <add name="CacheHourly" duration="120"/>
          </outputCacheProfiles>
        </outputCacheSettings>
      </caching>
    </system.web>
</configuration>
```

After creating the cache profile, you can use it as a value for the `CacheProfile` attribute of the `OutputCache` element by performing the following steps:

1. Add the code, shown in Listing 16.9, in the `Default.aspx` page to use the `CacheHourly` cache profile in the `CacheProfiles` Web application:

Listing 16.9: Showing the Code for the `Default.aspx` Page

In VB

```
<%@ Page Language="VB" AutoEventWireup="false" CodeFile="Default.aspx.vb"
  Inherits="_Default" %>
<%@ OutputCache CacheProfile="CacheHourly" VaryByParam="name" %>
<!DOCTYPE html>
<html xmlns="http://www.w3.org/1999/xhtml">
<head runat="server">
    <title>CacheProfiles Example</title>
</head>
<body>
  <form id="form1" runat="server">
  <div>
  <br />
  <br />
                       
                       
             
  <asp:Label ID="Label3" runat="server" Font-Names="Verdana" Text="Cache Profiles
  Example" Font-Bold="True" Font-Size="Larger"></asp:Label>
               
  <br />
  <br />
  <br />
  <asp:Label ID="Label1" runat="server" Font-Names="Verdana" Text="Please Enter a
  Name"></asp:Label>
                        
  <asp:TextBox ID="Name" runat="server"></asp:TextBox>
   <br />
  <br />
                         
                     
  <asp:Button ID="Button1" runat="server" Text="Submit" /><br />
  <br />
  <asp:Label ID="Label2" runat="server" Font-Names="Verdana" Text="Label2"></asp:Label>
  </div>
  </form>
</body>
</html>
```

In C#

```
<%@ Page Language="C#" AutoEventWireup="true" CodeFile="Default.aspx.cs"
  Inherits="_Default" %>
<%@ OutputCache CacheProfile="CacheHourly" VaryByParam="name" %>
<!DOCTYPE html>
<html xmlns="http://www.w3.org/1999/xhtml">
<head id="Head1" runat="server">
    <title>CacheProfiles Example</title>
</head>
<body>
  <form id="form1" runat="server">
  <div>
  <br />
  <br />
                       
                       
             
  <asp:Label ID="Label3" runat="server" Font-Names="Verdana" Text="Cache Profiles
  Example" Font-Bold="True" Font-Size="Larger"></asp:Label>
               
  <br />
  <br />
  <br />
  <asp:Label ID="Label1" runat="server" Font-Names="Verdana" Text="Please Enter a
  Name"></asp:Label>
                        
  <asp:TextBox ID="Name" runat="server"></asp:TextBox>
   <br />
  <br />
                         
                     
  <asp:Button ID="Button1" runat="server" Text="Submit" /><br />
  <br />
  <asp:Label ID="Label2" runat="server" Font-Names="Verdana" Text="Label2"></asp:Label>
  </div>
  </form>
</body>
</html>
```

2. Add the code, shown in Listing 16.10, in the code-behind file of the `Default.aspx` page:

Listing 16.10: Showing the Code for the Code-behind File

In VB

```
Partial Class _Default
    Inherits System.Web.UI.Page
    Protected Sub Page_Load(sender As Object, e As EventArgs) Handles Me.Load
        If IsPostBack Then
            Name.Visible = False
            Label1.Visible = False
            Button1.Visible = False
            Label2.Visible = True
            Label2.Text = "The output of this page was cached for " & Name.Text & ". The
  Current time is" & DateTime.Now.ToString()
        End If
    End Sub
End Class
```

In C#

```
using System;
using System.Collections.Generic;
using System.Linq;
using System.Web;
using System.Web.UI;
using System.Web.UI.WebControls;
```

```
public partial class _Default : System.Web.UI.Page
{
    protected void Page_Load(object sender, EventArgs e)
    {
        if (IsPostBack)
        {
                Name.Visible = false;
                Label1.Visible = false;
                Button1.Visible = false;
                Label2.Visible = true;
                Label2.Text = "The output of this page was cached for " + Name.Text +
  ". The Current time is " + DateTime.Now.ToString();
        }
    }
}
```

3. Run the `CacheProfiles` Web application. The output appears, as shown in Figure 16.7:

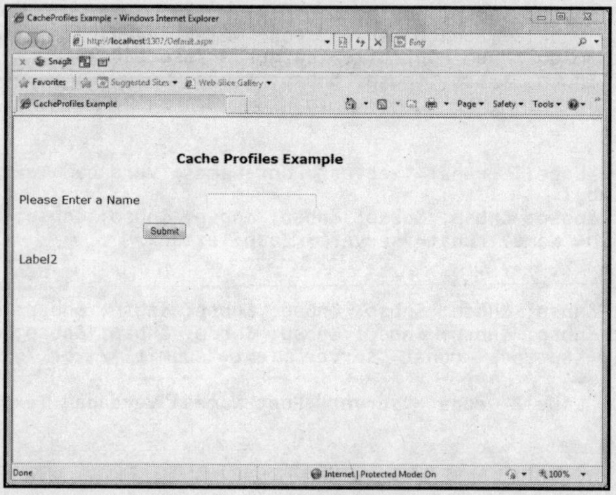

Figure 16.7: Displaying the Output of the CacheProfile Application

4. Enter your name in the Please Enter a Name text box and click the Submit button to cache the page. Figure 16.8 shows the output of the cached page:

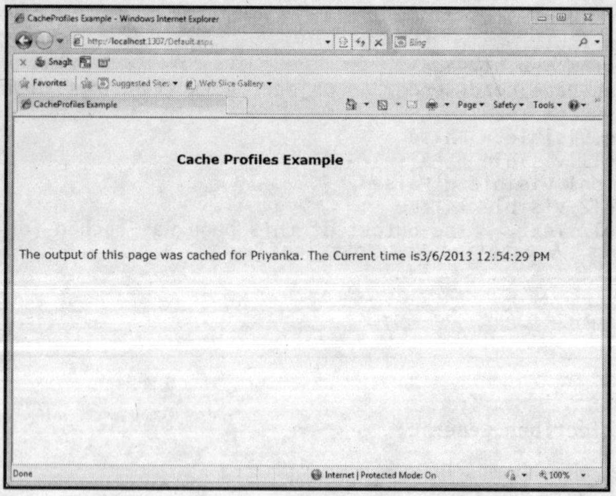

Figure 16.8: Displaying the Output of the CacheProfiles Application

Using the Substitution Control

As discussed in the In Depth section of this chapter, the Substitution control can be used in situations where you do not want to cache a part of a Web page. Now, let's create a ASP.NET application named `SubstitutionControl` (`SubstitutionControlVB` in VB and `SubstitutionControlCS` in C#), to see the functioning of the `Substitution` control. After creating the Web application, you need to add the code, shown in Listing 16.11, in the `Default.aspx` page of the Web application:

Listing 16.11: Showing the Code for the `Default.aspx` Page

In VB

```
<%@ Page Language="VB" AutoEventWireup="false" CodeFile="Default.aspx.vb"
   Inherits="_Default" %>
<%@ OutputCache Duration="10" VaryByParam="none" %>
<!DOCTYPE html>
<script runat="server">
    Shared Function GetTime(ByVal context As HttpContext) As String
        Return DateTime.Now.ToString("T")
    End Function
</script>
<html xmlns="http://www.w3.org/1999/xhtml">
<head runat="server">
    <title>Substitution control</title>
</head>
<body>
    <form id="form1" runat="server">
    <div>
    <h2>
        Using Substitution Control</h2>
        <div class="itemContent" style="font-family: 'Book Antiqua'; font-size: large">
        The Cached time is:<br />
        <%=DateTime.Now.ToString("T")%>
        <hr />
        The Substitution time is:
        <br />
        <asp:Substitution ID="Substitution1" MethodName="GetTime" runat="server" />
    </div>
    </form>
</body>
</html>
```

In C#

```
<%@ Page Language="C#" AutoEventWireup="true" CodeFile="Default.aspx.cs"
   Inherits="_Default" %>
<%@ OutputCache Duration="10" VaryByParam="none" %>
<!DOCTYPE html>
<script runat="server">
   static string GetTime(HttpContext context)
   {
        return DateTime.Now.ToString("T");
   }
</script>
<html xmlns="http://www.w3.org/1999/xhtml">
<head id="Head1" runat="server">
    <title>Substitution control</title>
</head>
<body>
    <form id="form1" runat="server">
    <div>
    <h2>
        Using Substitution Control</h2>
        <div class="itemContent" style="font-family: 'Book Antiqua'; font-size: large">
        The Cached time is:<br />
```

```
            <%=DateTime.Now.ToString("T")%>
            <hr />
            The Substitution time is:
            <br />
            <asp:Substitution ID="Substitution1" MethodName="GetTime" runat="server" />
        </div>
        </form>
    </body>
    </html>
```

After adding the preceding code in the `Default.aspx` file of the application, run the `SubstitutionControl` Web application. The output is shown in Figure 16.9:

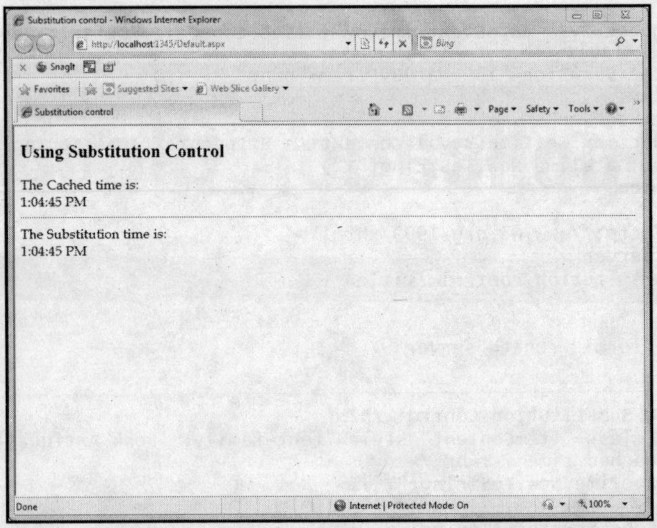

Figure 16.9: Displaying the Output of the SubstitutionControl Application

In Figure 16.9, you can see that only the substitution time changes every time you refresh the page. The cached time changes only after the expiry of the time period specified in the code.

Summary

In this chapter, you have learned about the concept of caching, which is used to improve the performance of a Web application. The chapter also described the various caching techniques, including output caching, partial-page caching, and data caching. You have also learned about SQL cache notification and SQL cache invalidation. Further, you have learned about cache dependencies, cache profiles and configuration, and the Cache class. In addition, the chapter demonstrated, through examples, how these techniques can be used in Web applications.

In the next chapter, you learn about application globalization, which is used to customize and display the content of a Web application based on different languages and cultures.

17

Application Globalization

In Depth

As Internet is making its global presence in almost all walks of life, it becomes quite imperative to move away from the traditional approach of application development to a more advanced one. The more advanced approach specifies that the content of a Web page is not restricted to a few international languages, so that a Web page is understandable to masses from all over the world. In ASP.NET, the concept of application globalization in application development facilitates displaying the content of an application according to different cultures from all over the world. Displaying the date and time according to the local culture of a region is an example of application globalization. It provides a culture-specific Web experience to the Internet users.

ASP.NET 4.5 provides built-in mechanisms to globalize Web applications that can adapt to different languages. However, it is the built-in mechanism of ASP.NET 4.5 that reconfigures the output of a Web application, so that the content, such as date and time objects, is presented in the appropriate culture-specific format. Basically, application globalization involves two sub-processes, internationalization and localization. Internationalization is the process of internationalizing application code as per some specific standards, and localization is the process of rendering the output of an application according to a specific language and culture.

In this chapter, you learn about the process of application globalization, which includes internationalization and localization. You then explore how to generate local and global resources to create globalization-enabled Web applications. You also learn to perform implicit and explicit localization and localize the script files. The chapter also describes how to perform localization of HyperText Markup Language (HTML) elements and static content.

Introducing Globalization

Globalization of Web application is the process of designing and developing Web applications that can display Web page contents in different languages and cultures. The process of globalizing an ASP.NET Web application involves separating the resources of the Web application that are culture-specific and need to be modified for different cultures. The next step is to customize the Web application for specific cultures.

The following two namespaces are used to globalize Web applications in .NET Framework:

- `System.Globalization`—Contains the classes defining information related to culture, such as language, country, format, and pattern for date, currency, and numbers
- `System.Resources`—Contains the classes and interfaces that you can use to create, store, and manage culture-specific resources used in a Web application

Table 17.1 lists the classes contained in the `System.Globalization` namespace:

Table 17.1: Classes in the System.Globalization Namespace

Class	Description
`Calendar`	Represents time in different parts, such as weeks, months, and years.
`CharUnicodeInfo`	Obtains information related to the Unicode character.
`ChineseLunisolarCalendar`	Represents time in different parts, such as months, days, and years. Days and months are calculated with a lunisolar calendar; whereas, years are calculated using a Chinese calendar.
`CompareInfo`	Provides methods to perform culture-specific string comparisons.
`CultureAndRegionInfoBuilder`	Specifies a customized culture that is new or based on another culture and country/region.
`CultureInfo`	Represents culture-specific information, such as name, region, and language.
`DateTimeFormatInfo`	Represents the formats for the culture-specific date and time.
`DaylightTime`	Represents the daylight-saving time period.

Table 17.1: Classes in the System.Globalization Namespace

Class	Description
`EastAsianLunisolarCalendar`	Represents division of time into months, days, years, and eras. Their dates are based on the cycles of the sun and the moon.
`GregorianCalendar`	Represents the Gregorian calendar.
`HebrewCalendar`	Represents the Hebrew calendar.
`HijriCalendar`	Represents the Hijri calendar.
`JapaneseCalendar`	Represents the Japanese calendar.
`JapaneseLunisolarCalendar`	Represents time in different parts, such as months, days, and years. Days and months are calculated with a lunisolar calendar; whereas, years are calculated using a Japanese calendar.
`JulianCalendar`	Represents the Julian calendar.
`KoreanCalendar`	Represents the Korean calendar.
`KoreanLunisolarCalendar`	Represents time in different parts, such as months, days, and years. Days and months are calculated with a lunisolar calendar; whereas, years are calculated using a Gregorian calendar.
`NumberFormatInfo`	Defines the manner in which culture-specific numeric information is formatted and parsed.
`PersianCalendar`	Represents the `Persian` calendar.
`RegionInfo`	Represents information about a country or region.
`SortKey`	Represents the mapping results obtained after mapping a string with its sort key.
`StringInfo`	Provides different string manipulation methods using which you can split a string into separate text elements and then iterate through those elements.
`TaiwanCalendar`	Represents the Taiwan calendar.
`TaiwanLunisolarCalendar`	Represents a Taiwan lunisolar calendar in which days and months are calculated with a lunisolar calendar; whereas, years are calculated using a Gregorian calendar.
`TextElementEnumerator`	Enumerates the text elements of a string.
`TextInfo`	Defines the properties and behavior of a writing system.
`ThaiBuddhistCalendar`	Represents the Thai Buddhist calendar.
`UmAlQuraCalendar`	Represents the Saudi Hijri (Um Al Qura) calendar.

Table 17.2 lists the classes contained in the `System.Resources` namespace:

Table 17.2: Classes in the System.Resources Namespace

Class	Description
`MissingManifestResourceException`	Represents the exception that is thrown when the main assembly does not contain neutral culture resources
`MissingSatelliteAssemblyException`	Represents the exception that is thrown when the satellite assembly for the neutral culture resources is not present

Table 17.2: Classes in the System.Resources Namespace

Class	Description
`NeutralResourcesLanguageAttribute`	Communicates to the `ResourceManager` class about the language used to write the neutral culture resources
`ResourceManager`	Provides dynamic access to the resources of a specific culture
`ResourceReader`	Allows you to read the resource names and the resource value pairs from the `.resources` files
`ResourceSet`	Stores the set of all localized resources corresponding to a specific culture, while neglecting resources of other cultures
`ResourceWriter`	Writes resources to an output stream or file in system's default format
`ResXDataNode`	Represents an element or data types in a resource file
`ResXFileRef`	Includes references of an external resource (`.resx`) file
`ResXFileRef.Converter`	Converts a `ResXFileRef` reference link to a string and vice versa
`ResXResourceReader`	Allows you to read the resource names and the resource value pairs from the `.resx` files
`ResXResourceSet`	Collects all items to create a single object of the `.resx` file
`ResXResourceWriter`	Writes resources in the `.resx` file or an output stream
`SatelliteContractVersionAttribute`	Ensures that the `ResourceManager` class retrieves the required version of a satellite assembly to simplify the updating process of the main assembly

Globalization of a Web application uses resources for user interface (UI) and static content of a Web application. As a result, different functional experts are required to build a globalized Web application. The different functional roles that are required to build a Web application are as follows:

- **Web designer**—Determines the Graphical User Interface (GUI) of a Web application. The Web designers decide how the content and controls are grouped on each Web page.
- **Developers**—Develop ASP.NET pages for the content and controls designed by Web designers. The developers also perform tasks, such as determining the structure for content storage, designing databases, and handling access to the content at runtime.
- **Translators**—Translate the content of the Web application to other languages. Translators are also required to work with Resource editors and XML editors to modify database content.
- **Stakeholders**—Coordinates between Web designers, developers, and translators. In addition, the role requires storing the content of a Web application such that the translators can access and modify the content. The stakeholders also ensure that the Web application supports new cultures without modifying the GUI of the Web application or database structure and other components of a Web application.

Globalization of Web application is related to the following two processes:

- Internationalization
- Localization

Now, let's discuss these in detail.

Internationalization

The process of Internationalization involves identifying different contents for different locales, such as date and time formats. To serve the purpose, you need to write the source code for the Web application such that the code is dynamically formatted to present the content of the Web application in the desired locale. The process of Internationalization ensures that the source code of a Web application is not modified when the application needs to be customized for specific culture or regions.

The goals of the process of Internationalization are as follows:

- Presenting the content in a single UI.
- Placing the content at a location so that it can be easily translated to another language. The location should also be programmatically accessible so that the content can be added to the UI of the Web application.
- Storing the content and user input as per the required culture.

Localization

Localization refers to the process of making changes in a Web application to meet the language and cultural requirements of users from a specific geographical location. The localization process involves configuring a Web application for a given culture. This implies translating and formatting content, such as time and date, according to the culture for which the Web application is to be localized. The elements, such as numeric data, date formats, and currency, are customized for a given culture in Web applications.

Prior to the introduction of ASP.NET 2.0, it was difficult to localize a Web application. As previously, the resource files and the `ResourceManager` class were used, which required considerable amount of effort and code. However, ASP.NET 2.0 simplifies the localization process by introducing following new features:

- Auto-detection of preferred culture of the client browser
- Accessing resources programmatically
- Compilation of files with the `.resx` or `.resource` extension
- Supporting the creation of resources at design-time
- Declarative resource expressions (implicit and explicit) to bind the controls or the properties of the controls to the resources

While building a multilingual Web application, it is beneficial to maintain the source code for the entire application in a single page, as it is easier to maintain a single page in comparison to maintaining separate sites for different languages. ASP.NET enables localization of a Web application into different languages without any changes to the source code through resource expressions. Resource expressions are the subfeatures of the overall expressions, such as the data-binding expressions feature of earlier versions of ASP.NET.

An amazing feature of ASP.NET 4.5 is that it supports the usage of different resource files in a Web application. These resource files follow a unique naming convention and have the `.resx` file extension. All the resource files related to a Web application are stored in a separate folder, which enables us to add more resource files to a Web application without performing the compilation process. Further, you learn about the samples executed for en-US (English-US), fr (French), and de (German) language. You can also use other languages in a Web application after creating resource files for that language and setting the language as a preferred language in your browser.

Now, you will learn how to deploy all the resources used in Globalization.

Introducing Resources

Resources, such as images and strings, are used in various elements, such as the toolbar and menu icons of a Web application to display different sets of information to the user. If you want to make changes in the strings or image resources used in a Web application, you need to search the entire source code of the Web application for the resource to be modified. To simplify the process of making changes to the resources used in a Web application, you can place the source code for strings and images used in the Web application in a separate file. You can then modify the code in the file to change the used resources. Such a file that contains source code for the various resources used in a Web application is called the resource file.

In the earlier versions of ASP.NET, the resources were deployed using the hub and spoke model. The hub refers to the main assembly that contains the non-localizable executable code and the resources for a default culture. Each spoke connects to a satellite assembly that contains the resources for a single culture, but does not include any code.

However, ASP.NET 2.0 supports site pre-compilation. This implies that the Web pages and the local resources are compiled into deployable assemblies. ASP.NET also supports dynamic runtime compilation. In dynamic runtime compilation, the source code, local and global resources are deployed in source format. The runtime compiler then parses the Web pages and generates assemblies for deployment.

A hybrid of site pre-compilation and dynamic runtime compilation is also possible in ASP.NET 4.5. This implies that ASP.NET 4.5 provides with the ability to deploy Web pages and resources as source and compile all these source files into binary assemblies. Compiling files into binary assemblies enables you to edit the Web page layout and resource content. You do not need to dynamically recompile the assemblies of unaffected applications.

Now let's consider a practical scenario on different concepts of Globalization in the *Immediate Solutions* section.

Immediate Solutions

Listing the Available Cultures

ASP.NET Framework provides the `CultureInfo` class residing in the `System.Globalization` namespace. The `CultureInfo` class contains culture-specific information, such as the language, country, and cultural conventions that are associated with a specific culture. The `CultureInfo` class also provides information required for performing culture-specific operations, such as formatting dates and numbers, casing, and comparing strings. In addition, you also need to use the `System.Resources` and `System.Threading` namespaces to set culture-specific information of a Web application.

You can use the `CultureInfo.GetCultures` method in the `CultureInfo` class to view the complete list of all the culture options according to which you can customize a Web application.

To use the `CultureInfo.GetCultures` method, follow these steps:

1. Create a console application in Visual Studio 2012 (VS 2012) and name it `Culture` (`CultureVB` for VB and `CultureCS` for C#).
2. Open the class file from the Solution Explorer (`Module1.vb` in VB or `Program.cs` in C#), and add the code shown in Listing 17.1:

Listing 17.1: Code for the Class File

In VB (Module1.vb)

```
Imports System.Globalization
Module Module1
    Sub Main()
        Dim cultinfo As CultureInfo
        For Each cultinfo In _
        CultureInfo.GetCultures(CultureTypes.AllCultures)
            Console.WriteLine(cultinfo)
        Next cultinfo
        Console.ReadLine()
    End Sub
End Module
```

In C# (Program.cs)

```
using System;
using System.Collections.Generic;
using System.Linq;
using System.Text;
using System.Threading.Tasks;
using System.Globalization;
namespace CultureCS
{
    class Program
    {
        static void Main(string[] args)
        {
            foreach (CultureInfo cultinfo in
            CultureInfo.GetCultures(CultureTypes.AllCultures))
            {
                Console.WriteLine(cultinfo);
            }
            Console.ReadLine();

        }
    }
}
```

3. Run the `Culture` application. The output of the application is shown in Figure 17.1:

Figure 17.1: Showing the List of Cultures

A Web page in a Web application consists of two culture values, `Culture` and `UICulture`. The `Culture` value determines the functions, such as date and currency. These `Culture` values are used to format data and numbers in a Web page. The `UICulture` value determines the resources that are loaded on a Web page of a Web application. Resources in a Web application represent data, such as strings or images, displayed in the UI of the Web application.

You can set the `Culture` and `UICulture` values in a Web application by using any one of the following methods:

- Through the `web.config` file
- In the code-inline page
- In the code-behind (CB) page

NOTE

To translate the content of a Web application from one language to another, you need to place the string value in a resource file.

The `Culture` value for a Web application is specified by the preceding methods so that the UI of the Web application is appropriate for the culture for which it is created. You can set the `Culture` and `UICulture` values in a Web application to override the user settings or operating system settings.

To set the `Culture` and `UICulture` values through the `web.config` file, write the following code in the Globalization section of the `web.config` file:

```
culture="en-US"
uiCulture="de-DE"
```

In the preceding code, the combination of the language and culture values for the Web application is set to US English (en-US). The `UICulture` value is set to German language (de).

To set the `Culture` and `UICulture` values in the source code of the Web page, you need to include the following values to the Page directive:

```
<%@ Page UICulture="de-DE" Culture="en-US"...%>
```

In the code-behind file, you can set the default culture for a Web application. ASP.NET provides the `CurrentCulture` and `CurrentUICulture` properties to set the default values for the `Culture` and `UICulture` attributes in the code-behind file. For this, you need to include the following code in the code-behind file to set the default culture to German.

The code to be added to the code-behind page in VB:

```
Imports System.Globalization
Imports System.Threading
Thread.CurrentThread.CurrentCulture = CultureInfo.CreateSpecificCulture ("de-DE")
Thread.CurrentThread.CurrentUICulture=new CultureInfo("de-DE")
```

The code to be added to the code-behind page in C#:

```
using System.Globalization;
using System.Threading;
Thread.CurrentThread.CurrentCulture = CultureInfo.CreateSpecificCulture ("de-DE");
Thread.CurrentThread.CurrentUICulture=new CultureInfo("de-DE");
```

ASP.NET also provides an autoculture-handling feature that enables you to easily localize a Web application. You need to include the `Culture="auto"` and `UICulture ="auto"` attributes in the Page directive of each Web page of the Web application to enable the auto-culture handling feature.

Working with Resources

To create resource files, first you need to identify the sections specific to a culture in a Web application. You then need to make different resource files for the cultures for which you need to develop a Web application. Based on the culture settings made by a user in the browser, the resource files are loaded in the Web application. For example, consider that you need to display the content of a Web application in French language. For this, you need to create resource file for the French language. You can create the resource file in either the `App_LocalResources` folder or the `App_GlobalResources` folder of a Web application. The language settings of the browser that are used to view the output of a Web application are then changed to load the resource file in the Web application.

In ASP.NET Framework, you can create global resources as well as local resources. The global resources are accessible from all the Web pages of an ASP.NET Web application, while the local resources are accessible from a single Web page of the ASP.NET Web application. Now, let's discuss these resources in detail.

Local Resources

The local resources for a specific Web page in the Web application are created in the `App_LocalResources` folder. Unlike the `App_GlobalResources` folder that resides in the root directory, the `App_LocalResources` folder can exist in any directory in the ASP.NET Web application. You can make a local resource file accessible to a Web page by using the name of the resource file. The naming convention of the resource file should match the base name of the Web page that accesses the resource file. The base name should be followed by the language name and the culture name for which the resource file is created. The name of the resource file should end with the extension `.resx`. For example, to associate a resource file for German language to the `Default.aspx` page, the naming convention for the resource file is given as follows:

```
Default.aspx.de.resx
```

In the preceding name for the resource file, the base name, `Default.aspx`, matches the name of the Web page. The `de` is the International Organization for Standardization (ISO) language code of the German language. The name of the resource file ends with the `.resx` extension.

To add local resources to a website, follow these steps:

1. Select the `FILE→New→Web Site` option from the menu bar to create a new website. This opens the New Web Site dialog box, as shown in Figure 17.2.

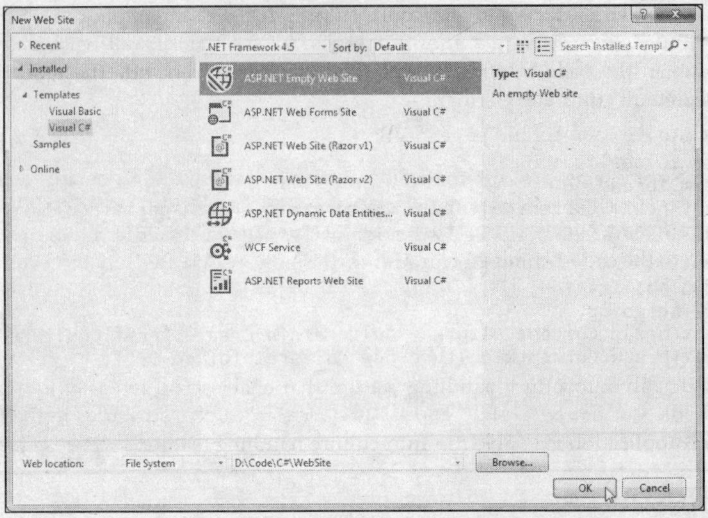

Figure 17.2: Displaying the New Web Site Dialog Box

2. Select the ASP.NET Empty Web Site template, enter the location and name of the website beside the Location field, and click the OK button.

This creates the website and adds the default files in the Solution Explorer, as shown in Figure 17.3:

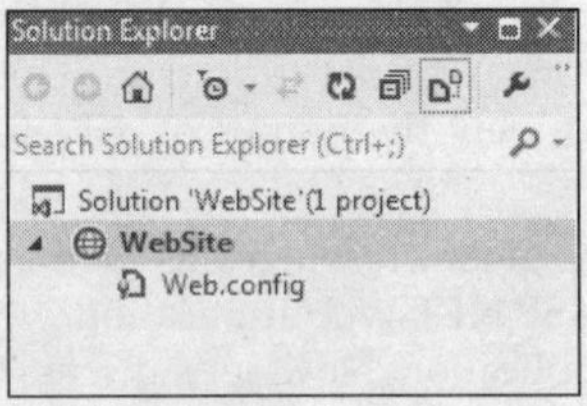

Figure 17.3: Showing the Default Files in the Solution Explorer

3. Right-click the name of the website (`Website`) and select the Add→ASP.NET `Folder`→`App_LocalResources` option from the context menu to add the `App_LocalResources` folder to the website.

Global Resources

Unlike local resources that are generated automatically, you need to add the global resources to a Web application. To add global resources, you can create a resource file with the `.resx` extension in the `App_GlobalResources` folder. The `App_GlobalResources` folder resides in the root directory of an ASP.NET Web application and contains the global resources for the Web application. In addition, the `App_GlobalResources` folder also provides a simple way to programmatically access global resources in a Web application.

The process of adding the global resources in a website is similar to the process of adding the local resources. The only difference is that you need to select the Add→ASP.NET `Folder`→`App_GlobalResources` option from the context menu to add the `App_GlobalResources` folder.

Using Localization Expression

The localization expressions are added for controls, such as labels and buttons, on the Web page of a Web application. The localization expressions enable you to access the local and global resources of the control programmatically to generate the localized content. When the localization expressions are added to a Web application, it results in modification of the control declaration on the Web page. The declarative statement meta:resourcekey, which is added to the control declaration, indicates that the ASP.NET parser should generate code to retrieve property values from either the local or the global resources that are created. The localization expressions generated for resources are either implicit localization expressions or explicit localization expressions.

Implicit Expression

Implicit localization expressions are automatically generated when resources are generated using implicit localization. While using implicit localization, the properties of the controls created on a Web page are read from a resource file. You create a resource file that contains localized values for properties, such as text, of the controls. At runtime, ASP.NET Framework examines the controls created on the Web page to verify if the controls are using implicit localization. The values of the controls that are using implicit localization are then substituted in the resource files.

To perform implicit localization, you need to create controls on a Web page and then generate a resource file for customizing the application for different languages.

To create controls on a Web page, create a new ASP.NET WebSite, named ImplicitLocalization (ImplicitLocalizationVB for VB and ImplicitLocalizationCS for C#), in Visual Studio 2012, and follow these steps:

1. Double-click the Default.aspx page in the Solution Explorer to open the page.
2. Switch to the Design view of the Default.aspx page and drop three Label controls (Label1, Label2 and Label3) and a Calendar control (Calendar1) from the Toolbox onto the Design view of the file to create a UI of the Web application. You can also write the code, as shown in Listing 17.2, in the Default.aspx page to add controls:

Listing 17.2: Code for the Default.aspx Page

In VB

```
<%@ Page Title="Home Page" Language="VB" MasterPageFile="~/Site.Master"
  AutoEventWireup="false" CodeFile="Default.aspx.vb" Inherits="_Default" culture="auto"
  meta:resourcekey="PageResource1" uiculture="auto"%>
<asp:Content runat="server" ID="FeaturedContent" ContentPlaceHolderID="FeaturedContent">
</asp:Content>
<asp:Content runat="server" ID="BodyContent" ContentPlaceHolderID="MainContent">
        <title>Implicit Localization</title>
    <h2>
        asp.net 4.5 black book</h2>
    <p>
         
        <div>
        <asp:Calendar ID="Calendar1" runat="server" BackColor="White"
                BorderColor="White"
                BorderWidth="1px" Font-Names="Verdana" Font-Size="9pt"
                ForeColor="Black" Height="190px"
                NextPrevFormat="FullMonth" Width="254px"
                meta:resourcekey="Calendar1Resource1">
                <SelectedDayStyle BackColor="#333399" ForeColor="White" />
                <TodayDayStyle BackColor="#CCCCCC" />
                <OtherMonthDayStyle ForeColor="#999999" />
                <NextPrevStyle Font-Bold="True" Font-Size="8pt" ForeColor="#333333"
                  VerticalAlign="Bottom" />
                <DayHeaderStyle Font-Bold="True" Font-Size="8pt" />
                <TitleStyle BackColor="White" BorderColor="Black" BorderWidth="4px"
                Font-Bold="True"
                Font-Size="12pt" ForeColor="#333399" />
                </asp:Calendar>
            </div>
            <div>
            <br />
                <br />
                                   
                      
```

```
                <table style="width: 383px; height: 193px; background-color: #99ffff">
                <tr>
                        <td colspan="2" style="width: 100px; background-color: white">
                                         
                             
                           <span style="text-decoration:
                          underline"><strong>I<span>mplicitLocalization</span>
                        </strong></span>
                        </td>
                </tr>
                <tr>
                        <td style="width: 75px; height: 18px; background-color: white">
                                  <strong>English</strong>
                        </td>
                        <td style="width: 100px; height: 18px; background-color:
                        white">
                                     
                        <asp:Label ID="Label1" runat="server" Font-Bold="True"
                          meta:resourcekey="Label1Resource1"
                        Text="English"></asp:Label>
                        </td>
                </tr>
                <tr>
                        <td style="width: 75px; background-color: white">
                        <span style="background-color:
                          White"><strong>French</strong>  </span>
                        </td>
                        <td style="width: 100px; background-color: White">
                        <strong>             
                                </strong><asp:Label
                        ID="Label2" runat="server" Font-Bold="True"
                          meta:resourcekey="Label2Resource1"
                        Text="French"></asp:Label>
                        </td>
                </tr>
                <tr>
                        <td style="width: 75px; background-color: white">
                                 <strong>German</strong>
                        </td>
                        <td style="width: 100px; background-color: white">
                                     
                        <asp:Label ID="Label3" runat="server" Font-Bold="True"
                          meta:resourcekey="Label3Resource1"
                        Text="German"></asp:Label>
                        </td>
                </tr>
                </table>
            </div>
        </p>
</asp:Content>
```

In C#

```
<%@ Page Title="Home Page" Language="C#" MasterPageFile="~/Site.Master"
  AutoEventWireup="true" CodeFile="Default.aspx.cs" Inherits="_Default" Culture="auto"
  UICulture="auto"%>
<asp:Content runat="server" ID="FeaturedContent" ContentPlaceHolderID="FeaturedContent">
</asp:Content>
<asp:Content runat="server" ID="BodyContent" ContentPlaceHolderID="MainContent">
    <title>Implicit Localization</title>
    <h2>
        asp.net 4.5 black book</h2>
    <p>
         
        <div>
```

```
        <asp:Calendar ID="Calendar1" runat="server" BackColor="White"
                BorderColor="White"
                BorderWidth="1px" Font-Names="Verdana" Font-Size="9pt"
                ForeColor="Black" Height="190px"
                NextPrevFormat="FullMonth" Width="254px">
                <SelectedDayStyle BackColor="#333399" ForeColor="White" />
                <TodayDayStyle BackColor="#CCCCCC" />
                <OtherMonthDayStyle ForeColor="#999999" />
                <NextPrevStyle Font-Bold="True" Font-Size="8pt" ForeColor="#333333"
                  VerticalAlign="Bottom" />
                <DayHeaderStyle Font-Bold="True" Font-Size="8pt" />
                <TitleStyle BackColor="White" BorderColor="Black" BorderWidth="4px"
                Font-Bold="True"
                Font-Size="12pt" ForeColor="#333399" />
                </asp:Calendar>
            </div>
            <div>
            <br />
                <br />
                                   
                      
                <table style="width: 383px; height: 193px; background-color: #99ffff">
                <tr>
                        <td colspan="2" style="width: 100px; background-color: white">
                                         
                             
                           <span style="text-decoration:
                          underline"><strong>I<span>mplicitLocalization</span>
                        </strong></span>
                        </td>
                </tr>
                <tr>
                        <td style="width: 75px; height: 18px; background-color: white">
                                  <strong>English</strong>
                        </td>
                        <td style="width: 100px; height: 18px; background-color:
                        white">
                                     
                        <asp:Label ID="Label1" runat="server" Font-Bold="True"
                          meta:resourcekey="Label1Resource1"
                        Text="English"></asp:Label>
                        </td>
                </tr>
                <tr>
                        <td style="width: 75px; background-color: white">
                        <span style="background-color:
                          White"><strong>French</strong>  </span>
                        </td>
                        <td style="width: 100px; background-color: White">
                        <strong>             
                                </strong><asp:Label
                        ID="Label2" runat="server" Font-Bold="True"
                          meta:resourcekey="Label2Resource1"
                        Text="French"></asp:Label>
                        </td>
                </tr>
                <tr>
                        <td style="width: 75px; background-color: white">
                                 <strong>German</strong>
                        </td>
                        <td style="width: 100px; background-color: white">
                                     
                        <asp:Label ID="Label3" runat="server" Font-Bold="True"
                          meta:resourcekey="Label3Resource1"
                        Text="German"></asp:Label>
```

```
                    </td>
                </tr>
                </table>
            </div>
        </p>
</asp:Content>
```

3. Generate a local resource file for the `Default.aspx` page. To do so, click the Design view of the `Default.aspx` page. Then, select the `Tools`→`Generate Local Resource` option from the menu bar.

   A new folder `App_LocalResources` is created in the Solution Explorer. Within the `App_LocalResources` folder, a file named `Default.aspx.resx` is created. In addition, a new `meta:resourcekey` attribute is added to all the control declarations and in the Page directive of the source code of the `Default.aspx` page. After creating the resource file, you need to use the Resource editor to place the localized text within the resource file.
4. Double-click the `Default.aspx.resx` resource file to open the Resource editor for the file. The Resource editor consists of the Name, Value, and Comment columns.
5. Change the property in the Value column as English, French, and German for the `Label1Resource1.Text`, `Label2Resource1.Text`, and `Label3Resource1.Text` fields, respectively, as shown in Figure 17.4:

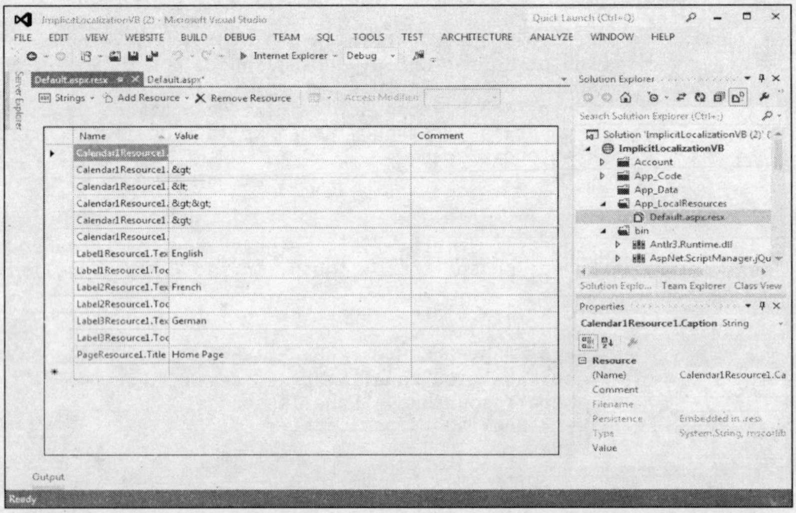

Figure 17.4: Displaying the Resource Editor of the Default.aspx.resx File

6. Press the `F5` key to run the Web application. The names of the labels in the Web application are displayed as edited in the `Default.aspx.resx` file.

   You need to create a unique resource file for each combination of culture and language that you need to include in a Web application.
7. Right-click the `Default.aspx.resx` resource file in the Solution Explorer and select the Copy option from the context menu to copy the resource file, to create a French language resource file for the Web application.
8. Right-click the `App_LocalResources` folder and select the Paste option from the context menu to paste the file in the `App_LocalResources` folder. A resource file named `Copy of Default.aspx.resx` file is created in the `App_LocalResources` folder.
9. Right-click the `copy of Default.aspx.resx` resource file and select the Rename option to rename the resource file as `Default.aspx.fr.resx`.

10. Double-click the `Default.aspx.fr.resx` resource file to open it, and then set the text property in the Value column as Anglais, Français, and Allemand for the `Label1Resource1.Text`, `Label2Resource1.Text` and `Label3Resource1.Text` controls respectively, as shown in Figure 17.5:

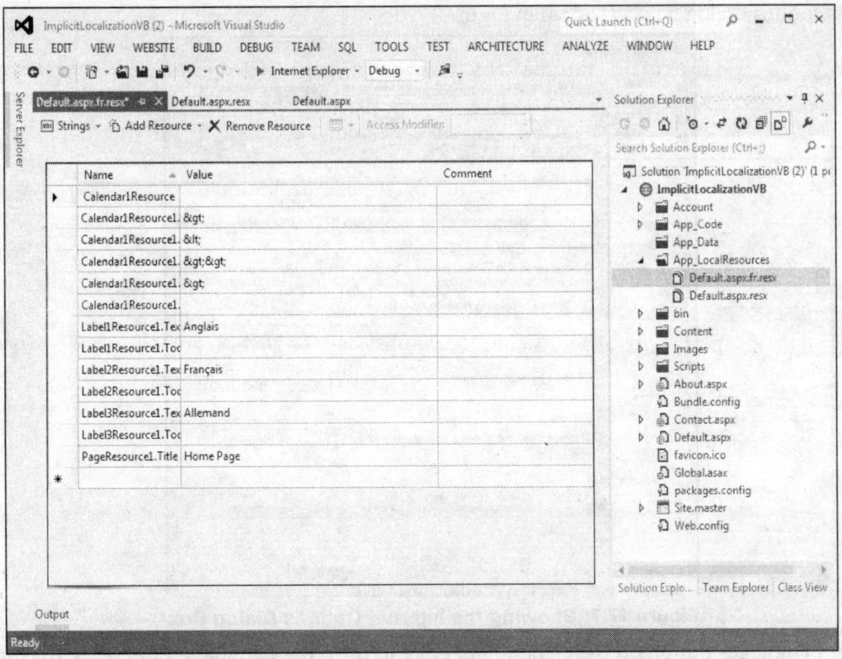

Figure 17.5: Displaying the Resource Editor for the Default.aspx.fr.resx File

11. Create and add a German language resource file (`Default.aspx.de.resx`) to the Web application. Figure 17.6 shows the Resource editor for German language:

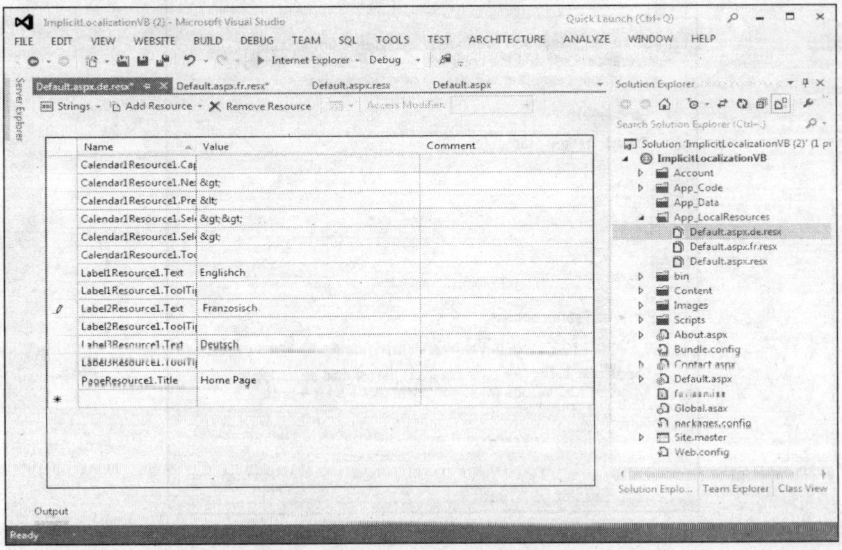

Figure 17.6: Displaying the Resource Editor for the Default.aspx.de.resx File

12. Alter the browser settings so that ASP.NET uses the resource file and includes the language and culture specified in the browser settings in the Web application. To change the language settings of the Microsoft Internet Explorer (IE) browser, select `Tools→Internet Options` on the menu bar of IE to open the Internet Options dialog box, as shown in Figure 17.7:

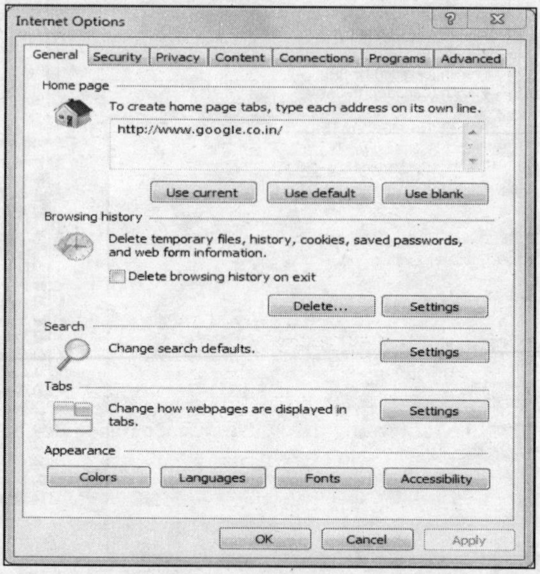

Figure 17.7: Showing the Internet Options Dialog Box

13. Click the Languages button on the General tab page to open the Language Preference dialog box, as shown in Figure 17.8:

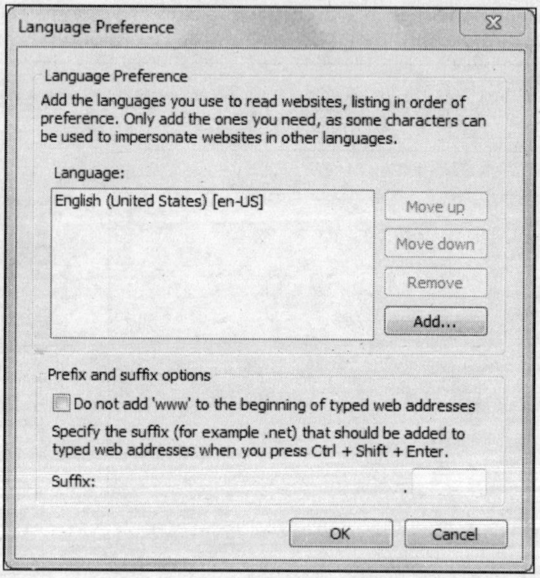

Figure 17.8: Showing the Language Preference Dialog Box

14. Click the Add button on the dialog box to open the Add Language dialog box. Select the `French (France) [fr-FR]` option in the Language list box, as shown in Figure 17.9:

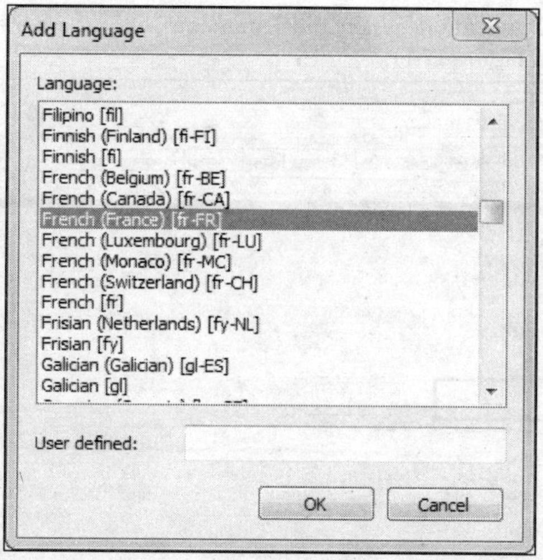

Figure 17.9: Showing the Add Language Dialog Box

15. Click the OK button to close the Add Language dialog box. Similarly, you can select `German (Germany)[de-DE]` language from the Add Language dialog box to add the German language. Select the `French [France][fr-FR]` option from the Language box of the Language Preference dialog box.
16. Click the Move Up button to move the selected language up in the order. The `French [France][fr-FR]` option is moved up in the Language box, as shown in Figure 17.10:

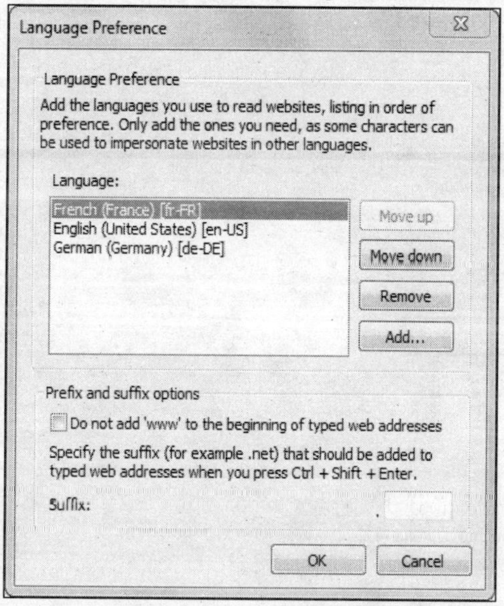

Figure 17.10: Showing the Language Preference Dialog Box

17. Click the OK button to close the Language Preference dialog box, and then close and apply the changes made in the Internet Options dialog box.
18. Run the Web application by pressing the F5 key to display the culture settings in the application by using implicit localization.

The output of the preceding application, when the Language settings in the browser indicate the preferred language as French, is shown in Figure 17.11:

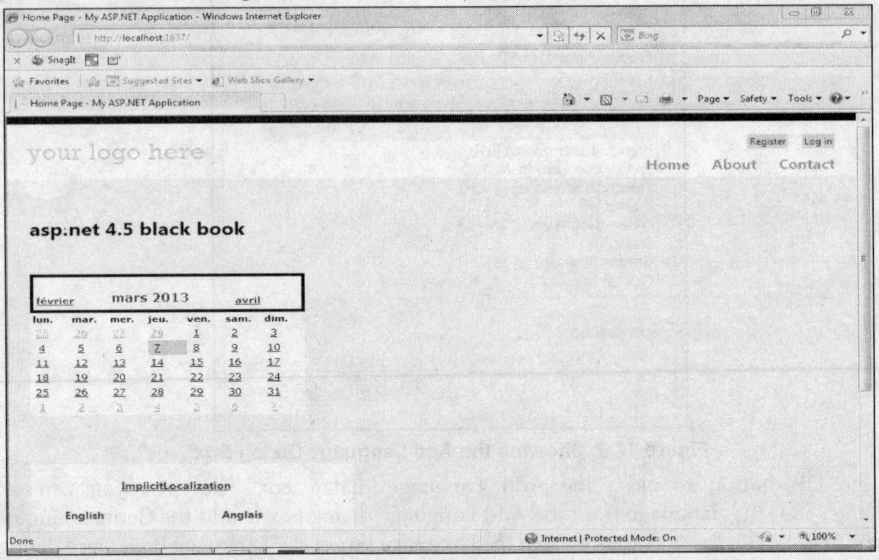

Figure 17.11: Displaying the Output of the Web Application with French as the Preferred Language

The output of the preceding application, when the Language settings in the browser indicate the preferred language as German, is shown in Figure 17.12:

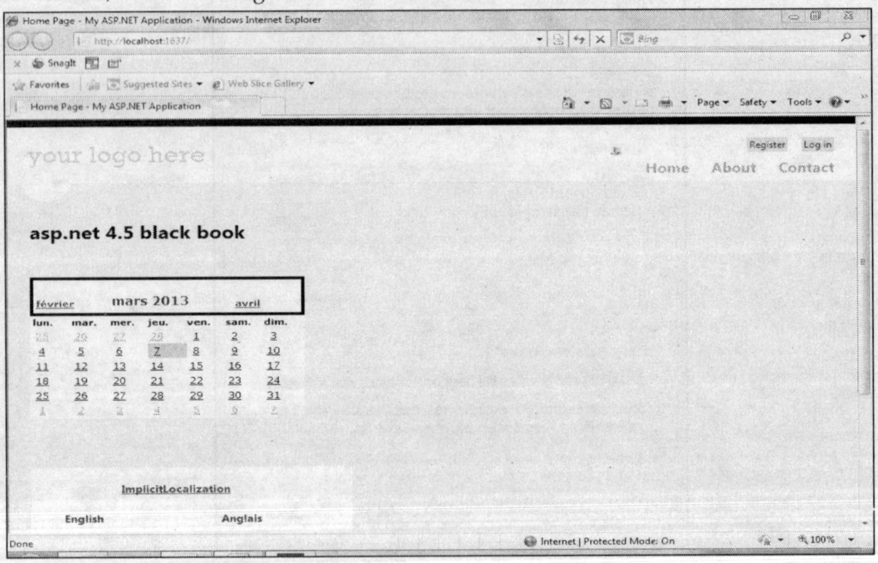

Figure 17.12: Displaying the Output of the Web Application with German as the Preferred Language

The output of the preceding application, when the Language settings in the browser indicate the preferred language as English, is shown in Figure 17.13:

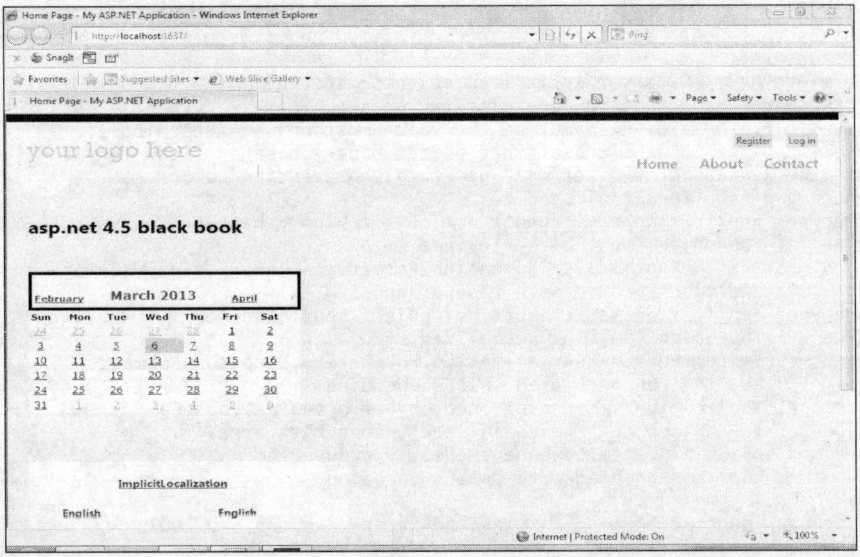

Figure 17.13: Displaying the Output of the Web Application with English as the Preferred Language

You can view the code of the resource files in XML(Text) Editor , by right-clicking the name of the file in the Solution Explorer, selecting the `Open With` option. The complete code of the resource file (`Default.aspx.resx`) is shown in Listing 17.3:

Listing 17.3: Complete Code for the `Default.aspx.resx` File

```
<?xml version="1.0" encoding="utf-8"?>
<root>
  <!--
    Microsoft ResX Schema
    Version 2.0
    The primary goals of this format is to allow a simple XML format
    that is mostly human readable. The generation and parsing of the
    various data types are done through the TypeConverter classes
    associated with the data types.
    Example:
    ... ado.net/XML headers & schema ...
    <resheader name="resmimetype">text/microsoft-resx</resheader>
    <resheader name="version">2.0</resheader>
    <resheader name="reader">System.Resources.ResXResourceReader, System.Windows.Forms,
  ...</resheader>
    <resheader name="writer">System.Resources.ResXResourceWriter, System.Windows.Forms,
  ...</resheader>
    <data name="Name1"><value>this is my long string</value><comment>this is a
  comment</comment></data>
    <data name="Color1" type="System.Drawing.Color, System.Drawing">Blue</data>
    <data name="Bitmap1" mimetype="application/x-microsoft.net.object.binary.base64">
        <value>[base64 mime encoded serialized .NET Framework object]</value>
    </data>
    <data name="Icon1" type="System.Drawing.Icon, System.Drawing"
         mimetype="application/x-microsoft.net.object.bytearray.base64">
        <value>[base64 mime encoded string representing a byte array form of the .NET
         Framework object]</value>
        <comment>This is a comment</comment>
    </data>
    There are any number of "resheader" rows that contain simple
```

```
    name/value pairs.
    Each data row contains a name, and value. The row also contains a
    type or mimetype. Type corresponds to a .NET class that support
    text/value conversion through the TypeConverter architecture.
    Classes that don't support this are serialized and stored with the
    mimetype set.
    The mimetype is used for serialized objects, and tells the
    ResXResourceReader how to depersist the object. This is currently not
    extensible. For a given mimetype the value must be set accordingly:
    Note - application/x-microsoft.net.object.binary.base64 is the format
    that the ResXResourceWriter will generate, however the reader can
    read any of the formats listed below.
    mimetype: application/x-microsoft.net.object.binary.base64
    value   : The object must be serialized with
            : System.Runtime.Serialization.Formatters.Binary.BinaryFormatter
            : and then encoded with base64 encoding.
    mimetype: application/x-microsoft.net.object.soap.base64
    value   : The object must be serialized with
            : System.Runtime.Serialization.Formatters.Soap.SoapFormatter
            : and then encoded with base64 encoding.
    mimetype: application/x-microsoft.net.object.bytearray.base64
    value   : The object must be serialized into a byte array
            : using a System.ComponentModel.TypeConverter
            : and then encoded with base64 encoding.
    -->
  <xsd:schema id="root" xmlns="" xmlns:xsd="http://www.w3.org/2001/XMLSchema"
  xmlns:msdata="urn:schemas-microsoft-com:xml-msdata">
    <xsd:import namespace="http://www.w3.org/XML/1998/namespace" />
    <xsd:element name="root" msdata:IsDataSet="true">
      <xsd:complexType>
        <xsd:choice maxOccurs="unbounded">
          <xsd:element name="metadata">
            <xsd:complexType>
              <xsd:sequence>
                <xsd:element name="value" type="xsd:string" minOccurs="0" />
              </xsd:sequence>
              <xsd:attribute name="name" use="required" type="xsd:string" />
              <xsd:attribute name="type" type="xsd:string" />
              <xsd:attribute name="mimetype" type="xsd:string" />
              <xsd:attribute ref="xml:space" />
            </xsd:complexType>
          </xsd:element>
          <xsd:element name="assembly">
            <xsd:complexType>
              <xsd:attribute name="alias" type="xsd:string" />
              <xsd:attribute name="name" type="xsd:string" />
            </xsd:complexType>
          </xsd:element>
          <xsd:element name="data">
            <xsd:complexType>
              <xsd:sequence>
      <xsd:element name="value" type="xsd:string" minOccurs="0" msdata:Ordinal="1" />
      <xsd:element name="comment" type="xsd:string" minOccurs="0" msdata:Ordinal="2" />
      </xsd:sequence>
      <xsd:attribute name="name" type="xsd:string" use="required" msdata:Ordinal="1" />
              <xsd:attribute name="type" type="xsd:string" msdata:Ordinal="3" />
              <xsd:attribute name="mimetype" type="xsd:string" msdata:Ordinal="4" />
              <xsd:attribute ref="xml:space" />
            </xsd:complexType>
          </xsd:element>
          <xsd:element name="resheader">
            <xsd:complexType>
              <xsd:sequence>
```

```
        <xsd:element name="value" type="xsd:string" minOccurs="0" msdata:Ordinal="1" />
              </xsd:sequence>
              <xsd:attribute name="name" type="xsd:string" use="required" />
            </xsd:complexType>
          </xsd:element>
        </xsd:choice>
      </xsd:complexType>
    </xsd:element>
  </xsd:schema>
  <resheader name="resmimetype">
    <value>text/microsoft-resx</value>
  </resheader>
  <resheader name="version">
    <value>2.0</value>
  </resheader>
  <resheader name="reader">
    <value>System.Resources.ResXResourceReader, System.Windows.Forms, Version=4.0.0.0,
  Culture=neutral, PublicKeyToken=b77a5c561934e089</value>
  </resheader>
  <resheader name="writer">
    <value>System.Resources.ResXResourceWriter, System.Windows.Forms, Version=4.0.0.0,
  Culture=neutral, PublicKeyToken=b77a5c561934e089</value>
  </resheader>
  <data name="Calendar1Resource1.Caption" xml:space="preserve">
    <value />
  </data>
  <data name="Calendar1Resource1.NextMonthText" xml:space="preserve">
    <value>&amp;gt;</value>
  </data>
  <data name="Calendar1Resource1.PrevMonthText" xml:space="preserve">
    <value>&amp;lt;</value>
  </data>
  <data name="Calendar1Resource1.SelectMonthText" xml:space="preserve">
    <value>&amp;gt;&amp;gt;</value>
  </data>
  <data name="Calendar1Resource1.SelectWeekText" xml:space="preserve">
    <value>&amp;gt;</value>
  </data>
  <data name="Calendar1Resource1.ToolTip" xml:space="preserve">
    <value />
  </data>
  <data name="Label1Resource1.Text" xml:space="preserve">
    <value>English</value>
  </data>
  <data name="Label1Resource1.ToolTip" xml:space="preserve">
    <value />
  </data>
  <data name="Label2Resource1.Text" xml:space="preserve">
    <value>French</value>
  </data>
  <data name="Label2Resource1.ToolTip" xml:space="preserve">
    <value />
  </data>
  <data name="Label3Resource1.Text" xml:space="preserve">
    <value>German</value>
  </data>
  <data name="Label3Resource1.ToolTip" xml:space="preserve">
    <value />
  </data>
  <data name="PageResource1.Title" xml:space="preserve">
    <value>Home Page</value>
  </data>
</root>
```

The complete code of another resource file (`Default.aspx.fr.resx`) is shown in Listing 17.4:

Listing 17.4: Complete Code for the `Default.aspx.fr.resx` File

```
<?xml version="1.0" encoding="utf-8"?>
<root>
  <!--
    Microsoft ResX Schema

    Version 2.0

    The primary goals of this format is to allow a simple XML format
    that is mostly human readable. The generation and parsing of the
    various data types are done through the TypeConverter classes
    associated with the data types.

    Example:

    ... ado.net/XML headers & schema ...
    <resheader name="resmimetype">text/microsoft-resx</resheader>
    <resheader name="version">2.0</resheader>
    <resheader name="reader">System.Resources.ResXResourceReader, System.Windows.Forms,
         ...</resheader>
    <resheader name="writer">System.Resources.ResXResourceWriter, System.Windows.Forms,
         ...</resheader>
    <data name="Name1"><value>this is my long string</value><comment>this is a
         comment</comment></data>
    <data name="Color1" type="System.Drawing.Color, System.Drawing">Blue</data>
    <data name="Bitmap1" mimetype="application/x-microsoft.net.object.binary.base64">
        <value>[base64 mime encoded serialized .NET Framework object]</value>
    </data>
    <data name="Icon1" type="System.Drawing.Icon, System.Drawing"
         mimetype="application/x-microsoft.net.object.bytearray.base64">
        <value>[base64 mime encoded string representing a byte array form of the .NET
         Framework object]</value>
        <comment>This is a comment</comment>
    </data>

    There are any number of "resheader" rows that contain simple
    name/value pairs.

    Each data row contains a name, and value. The row also contains a
    type or mimetype. Type corresponds to a .NET class that support
    text/value conversion through the TypeConverter architecture.
    Classes that don't support this are serialized and stored with the
    mimetype set.

    The mimetype is used for serialized objects, and tells the
    ResXResourceReader how to depersist the object. This is currently not
    extensible. For a given mimetype the value must be set accordingly:

    Note - application/x-microsoft.net.object.binary.base64 is the format
    that the ResXResourceWriter will generate, however the reader can
    read any of the formats listed below.

    mimetype: application/x-microsoft.net.object.binary.base64
    value   : The object must be serialized with
            : System.Runtime.Serialization.Formatters.Binary.BinaryFormatter
            : and then encoded with base64 encoding.

    mimetype: application/x-microsoft.net.object.soap.base64
    value   : The object must be serialized with
            : System.Runtime.Serialization.Formatters.Soap.SoapFormatter
            : and then encoded with base64 encoding.

    mimetype: application/x-microsoft.net.object.bytearray.base64
```

```
  value   : The object must be serialized into a byte array
          : using a System.ComponentModel.TypeConverter
          : and then encoded with base64 encoding.
  -->
<xsd:schema id="root" xmlns="" xmlns:xsd="http://www.w3.org/2001/XMLSchema"
xmlns:msdata="urn:schemas-microsoft-com:xml-msdata">
  <xsd:import namespace="http://www.w3.org/XML/1998/namespace" />
  <xsd:element name="root" msdata:IsDataSet="true">
    <xsd:complexType>
      <xsd:choice maxOccurs="unbounded">
        <xsd:element name="metadata">
          <xsd:complexType>
            <xsd:sequence>
              <xsd:element name="value" type="xsd:string" minOccurs="0" />
            </xsd:sequence>
            <xsd:attribute name="name" use="required" type="xsd:string" />
            <xsd:attribute name="type" type="xsd:string" />
            <xsd:attribute name="mimetype" type="xsd:string" />
            <xsd:attribute ref="xml:space" />
          </xsd:complexType>
        </xsd:element>
        <xsd:element name="assembly">
          <xsd:complexType>
            <xsd:attribute name="alias" type="xsd:string" />
            <xsd:attribute name="name" type="xsd:string" />
          </xsd:complexType>
        </xsd:element>
        <xsd:element name="data">
          <xsd:complexType>
            <xsd:sequence>
              <xsd:element name="value" type="xsd:string" minOccurs="0"
              msdata:Ordinal="1" />
              <xsd:element name="comment" type="xsd:string" minOccurs="0"
              msdata:Ordinal="2" />
            </xsd:sequence>
            <xsd:attribute name="name" type="xsd:string" use="required"
             msdata:Ordinal="1" />
            <xsd:attribute name="type" type="xsd:string" msdata:Ordinal="3" />
            <xsd:attribute name="mimetype" type="xsd:string" msdata:Ordinal="4" />
            <xsd:attribute ref="xml:space" />
          </xsd:complexType>
        </xsd:element>
        <xsd:element name="resheader">
          <xsd:complexType>
            <xsd:sequence>
              <xsd:element name="value" type="xsd:string" minOccurs="0"
              msdata:Ordinal="1" />
            </xsd:sequence>
            <xsd:attribute name="name" type="xsd:string" use="required" />
          </xsd:complexType>
        </xsd:element>
      </xsd:choice>
    </xsd:complexType>
  </xsd:element>
</xsd:schema>
<resheader name="resmimetype">
  <value>text/microsoft-resx</value>
</resheader>
<resheader name="version">
  <value>2.0</value>
</resheader>
<resheader name="reader">
  <value>System.Resources.ResXResourceReader, System.Windows.Forms, Version=4.0.0.0,
       Culture=neutral, PublicKeyToken=b77a5c561934e089</value>
</resheader>
```

```
  <resheader name="writer">
    <value>System.Resources.ResXResourceWriter, System.Windows.Forms, Version=4.0.0.0,
  Culture=neutral, PublicKeyToken=b77a5c561934e089</value>
  </resheader>
  <data name="Calendar1Resource1.Caption" xml:space="preserve">
    <value />
  </data>
  <data name="Calendar1Resource1.NextMonthText" xml:space="preserve">
    <value>&amp;gt;</value>
  </data>
  <data name="Calendar1Resource1.PrevMonthText" xml:space="preserve">
    <value>&amp;lt;</value>
  </data>
  <data name="Calendar1Resource1.SelectMonthText" xml:space="preserve">
    <value>&amp;gt;&amp;gt;</value>
  </data>
  <data name="Calendar1Resource1.SelectWeekText" xml:space="preserve">
    <value>&amp;gt;</value>
  </data>
  <data name="Calendar1Resource1.ToolTip" xml:space="preserve">
    <value />
  </data>
  <data name="Label1Resource1.Text" xml:space="preserve">
    <value>Anglais</value>
  </data>
  <data name="Label1Resource1.ToolTip" xml:space="preserve">
    <value />
  </data>
  <data name="Label2Resource1.Text" xml:space="preserve">
    <value>Français</value>
  </data>
  <data name="Label2Resource1.ToolTip" xml:space="preserve">
    <value />
  </data>
  <data name="Label3Resource1.Text" xml:space="preserve">
    <value>Allemand</value>
  </data>
  <data name="Label3Resource1.ToolTip" xml:space="preserve">
    <value />
  </data>
  <data name="PageResource1.Title" xml:space="preserve">
    <value>Home Page</value>
  </data>
</root>
```

The complete code of another resource file (`Default.aspx.de.resx`) is shown in Listing 17.5:

Listing 17.5: Complete Code for the `Default.aspx.de.resx` File

```
<?xml version="1.0" encoding="utf-8"?>
<root>
  <!--
    Microsoft ResX Schema

    Version 2.0

    The primary goals of this format is to allow a simple XML format
    that is mostly human readable. The generation and parsing of the
    various data types are done through the TypeConverter classes
    associated with the data types.

    Example:

    ... ado.net/XML headers & schema ...
    <resheader name="resmimetype">text/microsoft-resx</resheader>
    <resheader name="version">2.0</resheader>
```

```
    <resheader name="reader">System.Resources.ResXResourceReader, System.Windows.Forms,
         ...</resheader>
    <resheader name="writer">System.Resources.ResXResourceWriter, System.Windows.Forms,
         ...</resheader>
    <data name="Name1"><value>this is my long string</value><comment>this is a
         comment</comment></data>
    <data name="Color1" type="System.Drawing.Color, System.Drawing">Blue</data>
    <data name="Bitmap1" mimetype="application/x-microsoft.net.object.binary.base64">
        <value>[base64 mime encoded serialized .NET Framework object]</value>
    </data>
    <data name="Icon1" type="System.Drawing.Icon, System.Drawing"
         mimetype="application/x-microsoft.net.object.bytearray.base64">
        <value>[base64 mime encoded string representing a byte array form of the .NET
         Framework object]</value>
        <comment>This is a comment</comment>
    </data>
    There are any number of "resheader" rows that contain simple
    name/value pairs.

    Each data row contains a name, and value. The row also contains a
    type or mimetype. Type corresponds to a .NET class that support
    text/value conversion through the TypeConverter architecture.
    Classes that don't support this are serialized and stored with the
    mimetype set.
    The mimetype is used for serialized objects, and tells the
    ResXResourceReader how to depersist the object. This is currently not
    extensible. For a given mimetype the value must be set accordingly:

    Note - application/x-microsoft.net.object.binary.base64 is the format
    that the ResXResourceWriter will generate, however the reader can
    read any of the formats listed below.

    mimetype: application/x-microsoft.net.object.binary.base64
    value   : The object must be serialized with
            : System.Runtime.Serialization.Formatters.Binary.BinaryFormatter
            : and then encoded with base64 encoding.

    mimetype: application/x-microsoft.net.object.soap.base64
    value   : The object must be serialized with
            : System.Runtime.Serialization.Formatters.Soap.SoapFormatter
            : and then encoded with base64 encoding.

    mimetype: application/x-microsoft.net.object.bytearray.base64
    value   : The object must be serialized into a byte array
            : using a System.ComponentModel.TypeConverter
            : and then encoded with base64 encoding.
    -->
  <xsd:schema id="root" xmlns="" xmlns:xsd="http://www.w3.org/2001/XMLSchema"
  xmlns:msdata="urn:schemas-microsoft-com:xml-msdata">
    <xsd:import namespace="http://www.w3.org/XML/1998/namespace" />
    <xsd:element name="root" msdata:IsDataSet="true">
      <xsd:complexType>
        <xsd:choice maxOccurs="unbounded">
          <xsd:element name="metadata">
            <xsd:complexType>
              <xsd:sequence>
                <xsd:element name="value" type="xsd:string" minOccurs="0" />
              </xsd:sequence>
              <xsd:attribute name="name" use="required" type="xsd:string" />
              <xsd:attribute name="type" type="xsd:string" />
              <xsd:attribute name="mimetype" type="xsd:string" />
              <xsd:attribute ref="xml:space" />
            </xsd:complexType>
          </xsd:element>
          <xsd:element name="assembly">
            <xsd:complexType>
              <xsd:attribute name="alias" type="xsd:string" />
              <xsd:attribute name="name" type="xsd:string" />
            </xsd:complexType>
```

```
          </xsd:element>
          <xsd:element name="data">
            <xsd:complexType>
              <xsd:sequence>
                <xsd:element name="value" type="xsd:string" minOccurs="0"
                 msdata:Ordinal="1" />
                <xsd:element name="comment" type="xsd:string" minOccurs="0"
                 msdata:Ordinal="2" />
              </xsd:sequence>
              <xsd:attribute name="name" type="xsd:string" use="required"
                msdata:Ordinal="1" />
              <xsd:attribute name="type" type="xsd:string" msdata:Ordinal="3" />
              <xsd:attribute name="mimetype" type="xsd:string" msdata:Ordinal="4" />
              <xsd:attribute ref="xml:space" />
            </xsd:complexType>
          </xsd:element>
          <xsd:element name="resheader">
            <xsd:complexType>
              <xsd:sequence>
                <xsd:element name="value" type="xsd:string" minOccurs="0"
                 msdata:Ordinal="1" />
              </xsd:sequence>
              <xsd:attribute name="name" type="xsd:string" use="required" />
            </xsd:complexType>
          </xsd:element>
        </xsd:choice>
      </xsd:complexType>
    </xsd:element>
  </xsd:schema>
  <resheader name="resmimetype">
    <value>text/microsoft-resx</value>
  </resheader>
  <resheader name="version">
    <value>2.0</value>
  </resheader>
  <resheader name="reader">
    <value>System.Resources.ResXResourceReader, System.Windows.Forms, Version=4.0.0.0,
  Culture=neutral, PublicKeyToken=b77a5c561934e089</value>
  </resheader>
  <resheader name="writer">
    <value>System.Resources.ResXResourceWriter, System.Windows.Forms, Version=4.0.0.0,
        Culture=neutral, PublicKeyToken=b77a5c561934e089</value>
  </resheader>
  <data name="Calendar1Resource1.Caption" xml:space="preserve">
    <value />
  </data>
  <data name="Calendar1Resource1.NextMonthText" xml:space="preserve">
    <value>&amp;gt;</value>
  </data>
  <data name="Calendar1Resource1.PrevMonthText" xml:space="preserve">
    <value>&amp;lt;</value>
  </data>
  <data name="Calendar1Resource1.SelectMonthText" xml:space="preserve">
    <value>&amp;gt;&amp;gt;</value>
  </data>
  <data name="Calendar1Resource1.SelectWeekText" xml:space="preserve">
    <value>&amp;gt;</value>
  </data>
  <data name="Calendar1Resource1.ToolTip" xml:space="preserve">
    <value />
  </data>
  <data name="Label1Resource1.Text" xml:space="preserve">
    <value>Englishch</value>
  </data>
  <data name="Label1Resource1.ToolTip" xml:space="preserve">
    <value />
  </data>
  <data name="Label2Resource1.Text" xml:space="preserve">
    <value>Franzosisch</value>
```

```
    </data>
    <data name="Label2Resource1.ToolTip" xml:space="preserve">
      <value />
    </data>
    <data name="Label3Resource1.Text" xml:space="preserve">
      <value>Deutsch</value>
    </data>
    <data name="Label3Resource1.ToolTip" xml:space="preserve">
      <value />
    </data>
    <data name="PageResource1.Title" xml:space="preserve">
      <value>Home Page</value>
    </data>
  </root>
```

Listings 17.3, 17.4, and 17.5 contain the complete code of all the resource files of the `ImplicitLocalization` application, which can be used in both VB and C# languages.

Explicit Expression

Explicit localization expressions are automatically generated when resources are created using explicit localization. You need to use explicit localization in the ASP.NET Web pages to localize large text messages, in addition to the controls and labels that are localized.

Let's create a ASP.NET Empty Website for explicit localization, named `ExplicitLocalization` (`ExplicitLocalizationVB` for VB and `ExplicitLocalizationCS` for C#). After creating the application, follow these steps:

1. Right-click the root directory of the Web application in the Solution Explorer and select the `Add→ASP.NET Folder→App_GlobalResources` option from the context menu to add the `App_GlobalResources` folder in the Solution Explorer.
2. Right-click the `App_GlobalResources` folder and select the Add New Item option from the context menu to open the Add New Item dialog box, as shown in Figure 17.14:

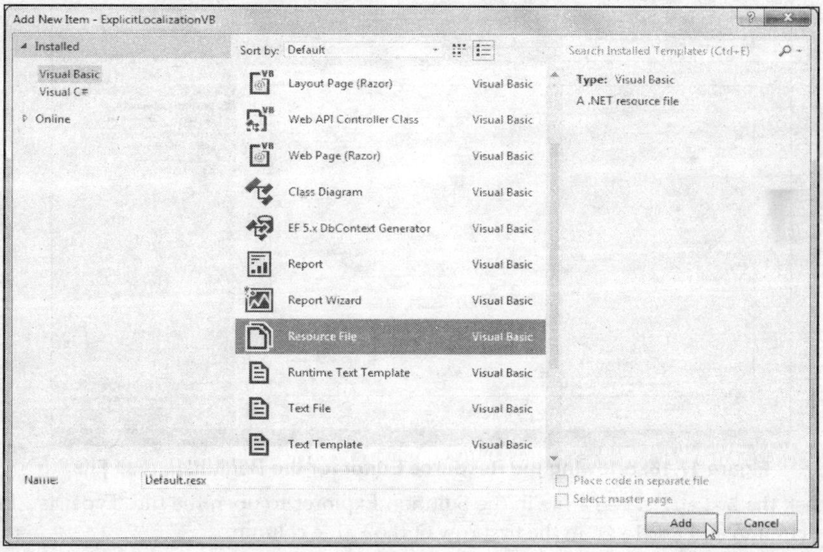

Figure 17.14: Adding a Resource File

3. Select Resource File in the Templates pane and type `Default.resx` in the Name field. Then, click the Add button to add the resource file in the `App_GlobalResources` folder.
4. Create two other resource files in the `App_GlobalResources` folder to include the resource files for the French and German languages. Name the resource files as `Default.fr.resx` and `Default.de.resx`.

5. Double-click the `Default.fr.resx` file in the Solution Explorer to open it. Type `msg` in the Name column and `Français` in the Value column, as shown in Figure 17.15:

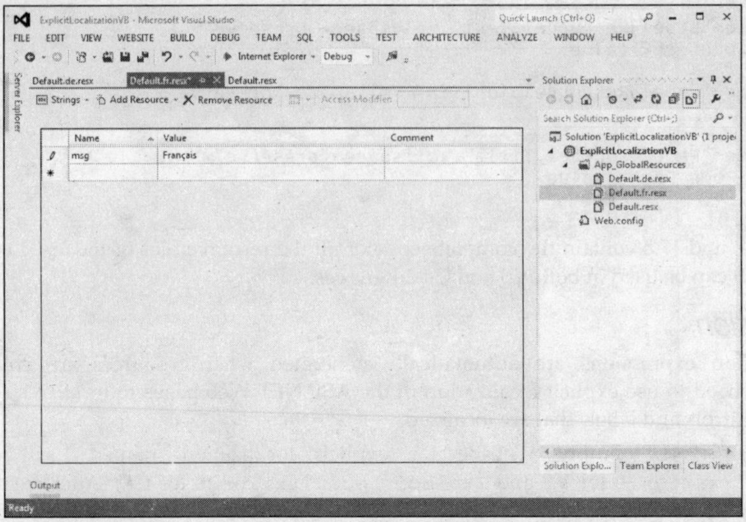

Figure 17.15: Showing the Resource Editor for the Default.fr.resx File

6. Double-click the `Default.de.resx` file in the Solution Explorer to open the file. Type `msg` in the first row of the Name column and `Deutsch` in the first row of the Value column, as shown in Figure 17.16:

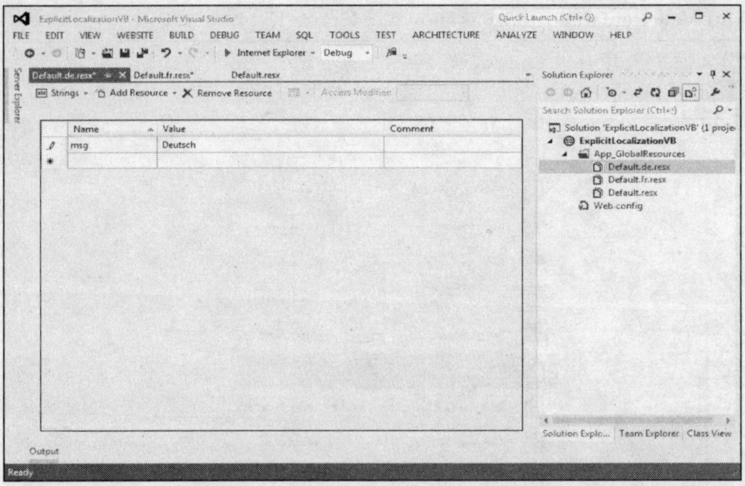

Figure 17.16: Showing the Resource Editor for the Default.de.resx File

7. Double-click the `Default.resx` file in the Solution Explorer to open the file. Type `msg` in the first row of the Name column and `English` in the first row of the Value column.

8. Add a `Label` control on the `Default.aspx` page to display the text of the language, whose resource file is loaded in the application.

9. Open the properties of the Label control and click the ellipsis button in the Expressions property in the Properties window, which displays the Label1 Expressions dialog box (the name of this dialog box may vary on the basis of the name control). The Text option is selected by default in the Bindable properties section of the Label1 Expressions dialog box.

10. Select Resources from the drop-down list in the Expression type section. Set `ClassKey` to Default and `ResourceKey` to `msg` in the `ClassKey` and `ResourceKey` Expression properties, respectively, as shown in Figure 17.17:

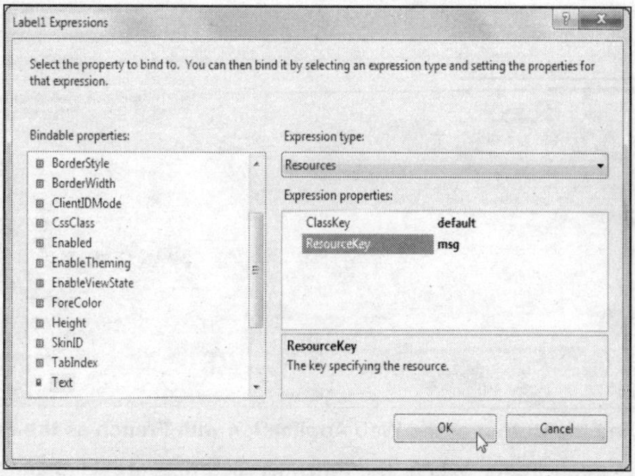

Figure 17.17: Specifying Values in the Label1 Expressions Dialog Box

11. Click the OK button to close the Label1 Expressions dialog box.
12. Add the Culture and UICulture attributes in the Page directive of the Default.aspx page and set their values to auto, as shown in the following code snippet:

```
<%@ Page Title="Explicit Localization " Language="C#" AutoEventWireup="true"
   CodeFile="Default.aspx.cs" Inherits="_Default" Culture="auto" UICulture="auto" %>
```

The Web page can automatically detect the preferred language specified in the browser by setting the Culture and UICulture attributes to auto.

After creating the UI for a Web application using explicit localization, you need to change the browser settings. The browser settings are changed so that the desired language is displayed when the Web application is executed. The output of the Web application, when the browser settings are changed to English, is shown in Figure 17.18:

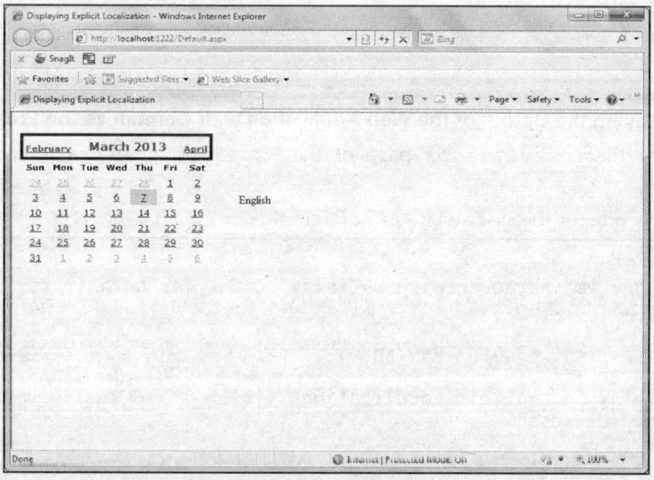

Figure 17.18: Displaying the Output of the Web Application with English as the Preferred Language

The output of the Web application, when the browser settings are changed to French, is shown in Figure 17.19:

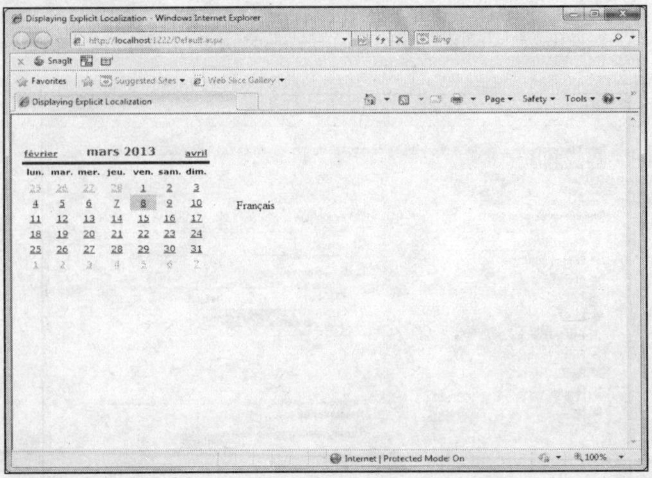

Figure 17.19: Displaying the Output of the Web Application with French as the Preferred Language

The output of the Web application, when the browser settings are changed to German, is shown in Figure 17.20:

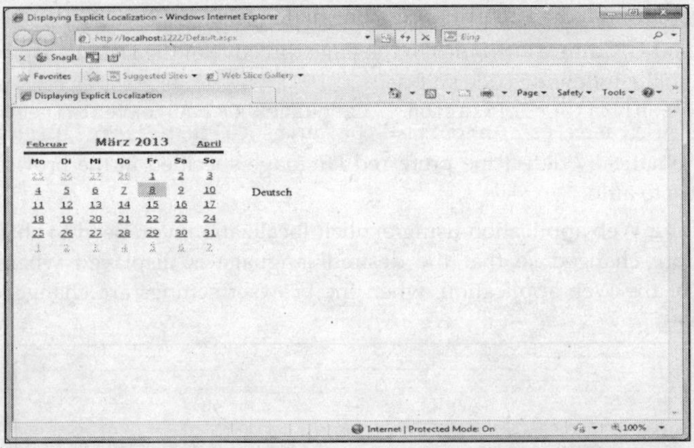

Figure 17.20: Displaying the Output of the Web Application with German as the Preferred Language

The complete code for the `Default.aspx` page of the `ExplicitLocalization` application is shown in Listing 17.6:

Listing 17.6: Complete Code for the `Default.aspx` Page

In VB

```
<%@ Page Language="VB" AutoEventWireup="false" CodeFile="Default.aspx.vb"
  Inherits="_Default" %>
<!DOCTYPE html>
<html xmlns="http://www.w3.org/1999/xhtml">
<head runat="server">
    <title>Displaying Explicit Localization</title>
   <style type="text/css">
        .style1
        {
            width: 100%;
            height: 191px;
        }
        .style2
        {
```

```
            width: 285px;
        }
    </style>

</head>
<body>
    <form id="form1" runat="server">
    <div>
          <br />
        <table class="style1">
            <tr>
                <td class="style2">
                 <asp:Calendar ID="Calendar1" runat="server" BackColor="White"
                 BorderColor="White" BorderWidth="1px" Font-Names="Verdana" Font-
                 Size="9pt" ForeColor="Black" Height="190px" NextPrevFormat="FullMonth"
                 Width="254px">
                 <SelectedDayStyle BackColor="#333399" ForeColor="White" />
                 <TodayDayStyle BackColor="#CCCCCC" />
                 <OtherMonthDayStyle ForeColor="#999999" />
                 <NextPrevStyle Font-Bold="True" Font-Size="8pt" ForeColor="#333333"
                 VerticalAlign="Bottom" />
                 <DayHeaderStyle Font-Bold="True" Font-Size="8pt" />
                 <TitleStyle BackColor="White" BorderColor="Black" BorderWidth="4px"
                 Font-Bold="True" Font-Size="12pt" ForeColor="#333399" />
                 </asp:Calendar>
                </td>
                <td>
               <asp:Label ID="Label1" runat="server" Text="<%$ Resources:Default, msg
                 %>"></asp:Label>
                </td>
            </tr>
            <tr>
                <td class="style2">
                     </td>
                <td>
                     </td>
            </tr>
        </table>
        <br />
        <br />
    </div>
    </form>
</body>
</html>
```

In C#

```
<%@ Page Language="C#" AutoEventWireup="true" CodeFile="Default.aspx.cs"
  Inherits="_Default" %>
<!DOCTYPE html>
<html xmlns="http://www.w3.org/1999/xhtml">
<head runat="server">
    <title>Displaying Explicit Localization</title>
    <style type="text/css">
        .style1
        {
            width: 100%;
            height: 191px;
        }
        .style2
        {
            width: 285px;
        }
    </style>
</head>
<body>
```

```
    <form id="form1" runat="server">
    <div>
        <br />
        <table class="style1">
            <tr>
                <td class="style2">
                   <asp:Calendar ID="Calendar1" runat="server" BackColor="White"
                 BorderColor="White" BorderWidth="1px" Font-Names="Verdana" Font-
                 Size="9pt" ForeColor="Black" Height="190px" NextPrevFormat="FullMonth"
                 Width="254px">
                 <SelectedDayStyle BackColor="#333399" ForeColor="White" />
                 <TodayDayStyle BackColor="#CCCCCC" />
                 <OtherMonthDayStyle ForeColor="#999999" />
                 <NextPrevStyle Font-Bold="True" Font-Size="8pt" ForeColor="#333333"
                 VerticalAlign="Bottom" />
                 <DayHeaderStyle Font-Bold="True" Font-Size="8pt" />
                 <TitleStyle BackColor="White" BorderColor="Black" BorderWidth="4px"
                 Font-Bold="True" Font-Size="12pt" ForeColor="#333399" />
                 </asp:Calendar>
                </td>
                <td>
                 <asp:Label ID="Label1" runat="server" Text="<%$ Resources:Default, msg
                 %>"></asp:Label>
                </td>
            </tr>
            <tr>
                <td class="style2">
                     </td>
                <td>
                     </td>
            </tr>
        </table>
        <br />
        <br />
    </div>
    </form>
</body>
</html>
```

The complete code of the resource file (`Default.de.resx`) is shown in Listing 17.7:

Listing 17.7: Complete Code for the `Default.de.resx` File

```
<?xml version="1.0" encoding="utf-8"?>
<root>
  <!--
    Microsoft ResX Schema
    Version 2.0
    The primary goals of this format is to allow a simple XML format
    that is mostly human readable. The generation and parsing of the
    various data types are done through the TypeConverter classes
    associated with the data types.

    Example:
    ... ado.net/XML headers & schema ...
    <resheader name="resmimetype">text/microsoft-resx</resheader>
    <resheader name="version">2.0</resheader>
    <resheader name="reader">System.Resources.ResXResourceReader, System.Windows.Forms,
  ...</resheader>
    <resheader name="writer">System.Resources.ResXResourceWriter, System.Windows.Forms,
  ...</resheader>
    <data name="Name1"><value>this is my long string</value><comment>this is a
        comment</comment></data>
    <data name="Color1" type="System.Drawing.Color, System.Drawing">Blue</data>
    <data name="Bitmap1" mimetype="application/x-microsoft.net.object.binary.base64">
        <value>[base64 mime encoded serialized .NET Framework object]</value>
    </data>
```

```
    <data name="Icon1" type="System.Drawing.Icon, System.Drawing"
        mimetype="application/x-microsoft.net.object.bytearray.base64">
        <value>[base64 mime encoded string representing a byte array form of the .NET
         Framework object]</value>
        <comment>This is a comment</comment>
    </data>

    There are any number of "resheader" rows that contain simple
    name/value pairs.

    Each data row contains a name, and value. The row also contains a
    type or mimetype. Type corresponds to a .NET class that support
    text/value conversion through the TypeConverter architecture.
    Classes that don't support this are serialized and stored with the
    mimetype set.

    The mimetype is used for serialized objects, and tells the
    ResXResourceReader how to depersist the object. This is currently not
    extensible. For a given mimetype the value must be set accordingly:

    Note - application/x-microsoft.net.object.binary.base64 is the format
    that the ResXResourceWriter will generate, however the reader can
    read any of the formats listed below.

    mimetype: application/x-microsoft.net.object.binary.base64
    value   : The object must be serialized with
            : System.Runtime.Serialization.Formatters.Binary.BinaryFormatter
            : and then encoded with base64 encoding.

    mimetype: application/x-microsoft.net.object.soap.base64
    value   : The object must be serialized with
            : System.Runtime.Serialization.Formatters.Soap.SoapFormatter
            : and then encoded with base64 encoding.

    mimetype: application/x-microsoft.net.object.bytearray.base64
    value   : The object must be serialized into a byte array
            : using a System.ComponentModel.TypeConverter
            : and then encoded with base64 encoding.
    -->
  <xsd:schema id="root" xmlns="" xmlns:xsd="http://www.w3.org/2001/XMLSchema"
  xmlns:msdata="urn:schemas-microsoft-com:xml-msdata">
    <xsd:import namespace="http://www.w3.org/XML/1998/namespace" />
    <xsd:element name="root" msdata:IsDataSet="true">
      <xsd:complexType>
        <xsd:choice maxOccurs="unbounded">
          <xsd:element name="metadata">
            <xsd:complexType>
              <xsd:sequence>
                <xsd:element name="value" type="xsd:string" minOccurs="0" />
              </xsd:sequence>
              <xsd:attribute name="name" use="required" type="xsd:string" />
              <xsd:attribute name="type" type="xsd:string" />
              <xsd:attribute name="mimetype" type="xsd:string" />
              <xsd:attribute ref="xml:space" />
            </xsd:complexType>
          </xsd:element>
          <xsd:element name="assembly">
            <xsd:complexType>
              <xsd:attribute name="alias" type="xsd:string" />
              <xsd:attribute name="name" type="xsd:string" />
            </xsd:complexType>
          </xsd:element>
          <xsd:element name="data">
            <xsd:complexType>
              <xsd:sequence>
```

```
                <xsd:element name="value" type="xsd:string" minOccurs="0"
                 msdata:Ordinal="1" />
                <xsd:element name="comment" type="xsd:string" minOccurs="0"
                 msdata:Ordinal="2" />
              </xsd:sequence>
              <xsd:attribute name="name" type="xsd:string" use="required"
                 msdata:Ordinal="1" />
              <xsd:attribute name="type" type="xsd:string" msdata:Ordinal="3" />
              <xsd:attribute name="mimetype" type="xsd:string" msdata:Ordinal="4" />
              <xsd:attribute ref="xml:space" />
            </xsd:complexType>
          </xsd:element>
          <xsd:element name="resheader">
            <xsd:complexType>
              <xsd:sequence>
                <xsd:element name="value" type="xsd:string" minOccurs="0"
                 msdata:Ordinal="1" />
              </xsd:sequence>
              <xsd:attribute name="name" type="xsd:string" use="required" />
            </xsd:complexType>
          </xsd:element>
        </xsd:choice>
      </xsd:complexType>
    </xsd:element>
  </xsd:schema>
  <resheader name="resmimetype">
    <value>text/microsoft-resx</value>
  </resheader>
  <resheader name="version">
    <value>2.0</value>
  </resheader>
  <resheader name="reader">
    <value>System.Resources.ResXResourceReader, System.Windows.Forms, Version=4.0.0.0,
  Culture=neutral, PublicKeyToken=b77a5c561934e089</value>
  </resheader>
  <resheader name="writer">
    <value>System.Resources.ResXResourceWriter, System.Windows.Forms, Version=4.0.0.0,
  Culture=neutral, PublicKeyToken=b77a5c561934e089</value>
  </resheader>
  <data name="msg" xml:space="preserve">
    <value>Deutsch</value>
  </data>
</root>
```

The complete code of another resource file (`Default.fr.resx`) is shown in Listing 17.8:

Listing 17.8: Complete Code for the `Default.fr.resx` File

```
<?xml version="1.0" encoding="utf-8"?>
<root>
  <!--
    Microsoft ResX Schema
    Version 2.0

    The primary goals of this format is to allow a simple XML format
    that is mostly human readable. The generation and parsing of the
    various data types are done through the TypeConverter classes
    associated with the data types.

    Example:

    ... ado.net/XML headers & schema ...
    <resheader name="resmimetype">text/microsoft-resx</resheader>
    <resheader name="version">2.0</resheader>
    <resheader name="reader">System.Resources.ResXResourceReader, System.Windows.Forms,
  ...</resheader>
```

```
    <resheader name="writer">System.Resources.ResXResourceWriter, System.Windows.Forms,
   ...</resheader>
    <data name="Name1"><value>this is my long string</value><comment>this is a
         comment</comment></data>
    <data name="Color1" type="System.Drawing.Color, System.Drawing">Blue</data>
    <data name="Bitmap1" mimetype="application/x-microsoft.net.object.binary.base64">
        <value>[base64 mime encoded serialized .NET Framework object]</value>
    </data>
    <data name="Icon1" type="System.Drawing.Icon, System.Drawing"
         mimetype="application/x-microsoft.net.object.bytearray.base64">
        <value>[base64 mime encoded string representing a byte array form of the .NET
         Framework object]</value>
        <comment>This is a comment</comment>
    </data>

    There are any number of "resheader" rows that contain simple
    name/value pairs.

    Each data row contains a name, and value. The row also contains a
    type or mimetype. Type corresponds to a .NET class that support
    text/value conversion through the TypeConverter architecture.
    Classes that don't support this are serialized and stored with the
    mimetype set.

    The mimetype is used for serialized objects, and tells the
    ResXResourceReader how to depersist the object. This is currently not
    extensible. For a given mimetype the value must be set accordingly:

    Note - application/x-microsoft.net.object.binary.base64 is the format
    that the ResXResourceWriter will generate, however the reader can
    read any of the formats listed below.

    mimetype: application/x-microsoft.net.object.binary.base64
    value   : The object must be serialized with
            : System.Runtime.Serialization.Formatters.Binary.BinaryFormatter
            : and then encoded with base64 encoding.

    mimetype: application/x-microsoft.net.object.soap.base64
    value   : The object must be serialized with
            : System.Runtime.Serialization.Formatters.Soap.SoapFormatter
            : and then encoded with base64 encoding.

    mimetype: application/x-microsoft.net.object.bytearray.base64
    value   : The object must be serialized into a byte array
            : using a System.ComponentModel.TypeConverter
            : and then encoded with base64 encoding.
    -->
  <xsd:schema id="root" xmlns="" xmlns:xsd="http://www.w3.org/2001/XMLSchema"
  xmlns:msdata="urn:schemas-microsoft-com:xml-msdata">
    <xsd:import namespace="http://www.w3.org/XML/1998/namespace" />
    <xsd:element name="root" msdata:IsDataSet="true">
      <xsd:complexType>
        <xsd:choice maxOccurs="unbounded">
          <xsd:element name="metadata">
            <xsd:complexType>
              <xsd:sequence>
                <xsd:element name="value" type="xsd:string" minOccurs="0" />
              </xsd:sequence>
              <xsd:attribute name="name" use="required" type="xsd:string" />
              <xsd:attribute name="type" type="xsd:string" />
              <xsd:attribute name="mimetype" type="xsd:string" />
              <xsd:attribute ref="xml:space" />
            </xsd:complexType>
          </xsd:element>
          <xsd:element name="assembly">
```

```
          <xsd:complexType>
            <xsd:attribute name="alias" type="xsd:string" />
            <xsd:attribute name="name" type="xsd:string" />
          </xsd:complexType>
        </xsd:element>
        <xsd:element name="data">
          <xsd:complexType>
            <xsd:sequence>
              <xsd:element name="value" type="xsd:string" minOccurs="0"
               msdata:Ordinal="1" />
              <xsd:element name="comment" type="xsd:string" minOccurs="0"
               msdata:Ordinal="2" />
            </xsd:sequence>
            <xsd:attribute name="name" type="xsd:string" use="required"
               msdata:Ordinal="1" />
            <xsd:attribute name="type" type="xsd:string" msdata:Ordinal="3" />
            <xsd:attribute name="mimetype" type="xsd:string" msdata:Ordinal="4" />
            <xsd:attribute ref="xml:space" />
          </xsd:complexType>
        </xsd:element>
        <xsd:element name="resheader">
          <xsd:complexType>
            <xsd:sequence>
              <xsd:element name="value" type="xsd:string" minOccurs="0"
               msdata:Ordinal="1" />
            </xsd:sequence>
            <xsd:attribute name="name" type="xsd:string" use="required" />
          </xsd:complexType>
        </xsd:element>
      </xsd:choice>
    </xsd:complexType>
  </xsd:element>
</xsd:schema>
<resheader name="resmimetype">
  <value>text/microsoft-resx</value>
</resheader>
<resheader name="version">
  <value>2.0</value>
</resheader>
<resheader name="reader">
  <value>System.Resources.ResXResourceReader, System.Windows.Forms, Version=4.0.0.0,
Culture=neutral, PublicKeyToken=b77a5c561934e089</value>
</resheader>
<resheader name="writer">
  <value>System.Resources.ResXResourceWriter, System.Windows.Forms, Version=4.0.0.0,
Culture=neutral, PublicKeyToken=b77a5c561934e089</value>
</resheader>
<data name="msg" xml:space="preserve">
  <value>Français</value>
</data>
</root>
```

The complete code of another resource file (`Default.resx`) is shown in Listing 17.9:

Listing 17.9: Complete Code for the `Default.resx` File

```
<?xml version="1.0" encoding="utf-8"?>
<root>
  <!--
    Microsoft ResX Schema

    Version 2.0

    The primary goals of this format is to allow a simple XML format
    that is mostly human readable. The generation and parsing of the
    various data types are done through the TypeConverter classes
    associated with the data types.
```

```
    Example:

    ... ado.net/XML headers & schema ...
    <resheader name="resmimetype">text/microsoft-resx</resheader>
    <resheader name="version">2.0</resheader>
    <resheader name="reader">System.Resources.ResXResourceReader, System.Windows.Forms,
        ...</resheader>
    <resheader name="writer">System.Resources.ResXResourceWriter, System.Windows.Forms,
        ...</resheader>
    <data name="Name1"><value>this is my long string</value><comment>this is a
        comment</comment></data>
    <data name="Color1" type="System.Drawing.Color, System.Drawing">Blue</data>
    <data name="Bitmap1" mimetype="application/x-microsoft.net.object.binary.base64">
        <value>[base64 mime encoded serialized .NET Framework object]</value>
    </data>
    <data name="Icon1" type="System.Drawing.Icon, System.Drawing"
        mimetype="application/x-microsoft.net.object.bytearray.base64">
        <value>[base64 mime encoded string representing a byte array form of the .NET
        Framework object]</value>
        <comment>This is a comment</comment>
    </data>

    There are any number of "resheader" rows that contain simple
    name/value pairs.

    Each data row contains a name, and value. The row also contains a
    type or mimetype. Type corresponds to a .NET class that support
    text/value conversion through the TypeConverter architecture.
    Classes that don't support this are serialized and stored with the
    mimetype set.

    The mimetype is used for serialized objects, and tells the
    ResXResourceReader how to depersist the object. This is currently not
    extensible. For a given mimetype the value must be set accordingly:

    Note - application/x-microsoft.net.object.binary.base64 is the format
    that the ResXResourceWriter will generate, however the reader can
    read any of the formats listed below.

    mimetype: application/x-microsoft.net.object.binary.base64
    value   : The object must be serialized with
            : System.Runtime.Serialization.Formatters.Binary.BinaryFormatter
            : and then encoded with base64 encoding.

    mimetype: application/x-microsoft.net.object.soap.base64
    value   : The object must be serialized with
            : System.Runtime.Serialization.Formatters.Soap.SoapFormatter
            : and then encoded with base64 encoding.

    mimetype: application/x-microsoft.net.object.bytearray.base64
    value   : The object must be serialized into a byte array
            : using a System.ComponentModel.TypeConverter
            : and then encoded with base64 encoding.
    -->
  <xsd:schema id="root" xmlns="" xmlns:xsd="http://www.w3.org/2001/XMLSchema"
  xmlns:msdata="urn:schemas-microsoft-com:xml-msdata">
    <xsd:import namespace="http://www.w3.org/XML/1998/namespace" />
    <xsd:element name="root" msdata:IsDataSet="true">
      <xsd:complexType>
        <xsd:choice maxOccurs="unbounded">
          <xsd:element name="metadata">
            <xsd:complexType>
              <xsd:sequence>
                <xsd:element name="value" type="xsd:string" minOccurs="0" />
              </xsd:sequence>
```

```
              <xsd:attribute name="name" use="required" type="xsd:string" />
              <xsd:attribute name="type" type="xsd:string" />
              <xsd:attribute name="mimetype" type="xsd:string" />
              <xsd:attribute ref="xml:space" />
            </xsd:complexType>
          </xsd:element>
          <xsd:element name="assembly">
            <xsd:complexType>
              <xsd:attribute name="alias" type="xsd:string" />
              <xsd:attribute name="name" type="xsd:string" />
            </xsd:complexType>
          </xsd:element>
          <xsd:element name="data">
            <xsd:complexType>
              <xsd:sequence>
                <xsd:element name="value" type="xsd:string" minOccurs="0"
                 msdata:Ordinal="1" />
                <xsd:element name="comment" type="xsd:string" minOccurs="0"
                 msdata:Ordinal="2" />
              </xsd:sequence>
              <xsd:attribute name="name" type="xsd:string" use="required"
                 msdata:Ordinal="1" />
              <xsd:attribute name="type" type="xsd:string" msdata:Ordinal="3" />
              <xsd:attribute name="mimetype" type="xsd:string" msdata:Ordinal="4" />
              <xsd:attribute ref="xml:space" />
            </xsd:complexType>
          </xsd:element>
          <xsd:element name="resheader">
            <xsd:complexType>
              <xsd:sequence>
                <xsd:element name="value" type="xsd:string" minOccurs="0"
                 msdata:Ordinal="1" />
              </xsd:sequence>
              <xsd:attribute name="name" type="xsd:string" use="required" />
            </xsd:complexType>
          </xsd:element>
        </xsd:choice>
      </xsd:complexType>
    </xsd:element>
  </xsd:schema>
  <resheader name="resmimetype">
    <value>text/microsoft-resx</value>
  </resheader>
  <resheader name="version">
    <value>2.0</value>
  </resheader>
  <resheader name="reader">
    <value>System.Resources.ResXResourceReader, System.Windows.Forms, Version=4.0.0.0,
  Culture=neutral, PublicKeyToken=b77a5c561934e089</value>
  </resheader>
  <resheader name="writer">
    <value>System.Resources.ResXResourceWriter, System.Windows.Forms, Version=4.0.0.0,
  Culture=neutral, PublicKeyToken=b77a5c561934e089</value>
  </resheader>
  <data name="msg" xml:space="preserve">
    <value>English</value>
  </data>
</root>
```

Listings 17.7, 17.8, and 17.9 contain the complete code of all the resource files, namely Default.de.resx, Default.fr.resx, and Default.resx, respectively, of the `ExplicitLocalization` application, which can be used in both VB and C# languages.

Implementing Localization

You can generate resources for Server control properties by using implicit and explicit localization expressions. The localization expressions to the @ Page directive and other sections of HTML can be applied to identify the areas that need to be localized before generating the resources.

To implement localization in a Web Application, you need to localize the following elements:

- HTML controls
- Static content

HTML Controls

HTML controls cannot be localized using implicit or explicit expressions, unless they are running on the server. To run the HTML controls on the server, you need to include the `runat="server"` attribute in the `@ Page` directive. After the HTML controls are marked as Server controls, local resources are automatically generated for the localizable properties, such as the Text and ToolTip properties of the controls. HTML Server controls can also be bound to implicit or explicit expressions; the latter is generated by using the Expressions dialog box as described earlier in the explicit localization section. You can also bind the HTML elements, such as page titles and style sheet links of the page directive, to the resources.

Static Content

You can use the localization expressions to localize the properties of controls used on a Web page. However, sometimes the Web application also includes static content, such as copyright information or disclaimer information. ASP.NET Framework allows you to localize the static content. To localize a static content in a Web application, the `<Localize runat="server">` tag is used.

For example, consider that you need to add the disclaimer information in a Web application. The following code snippet displays the code to be added in the `Default.aspx` page of the Web application to localize static content:

```
<asp:Localize runat="server" meta:resourcekey="Information"> Disclaimer: This
   sample application is not intended to provide accurate or
up-to-date information.</asp:Localize>
```

In the preceding code snippet, a local resource value is generated for the `Text` property of the `Localize` control. You can also set the text direction for the static content used in a Web application for a specific local culture of a region, where the content is read from right to left or vice versa. To do so, create a new Web application in Visual Studio 2012 named `StaticContentCulture` (`StaticContentCultureVB` for VB and `StaticContentCultureCS` for C#), and follow these steps:

1. Add the `App_GlobalResources` folder in the `StaticContentCulture` Web application.
2. Add a new item `Default.resx` in the `App_GlobalResources` folder of the Solution Explorer and set the Name field as msg and TextDirection and their corresponding value in the Value field as You can change the direction of the static content and (Left-to-Right) LTR respectively, as shown in Figure 17.21:

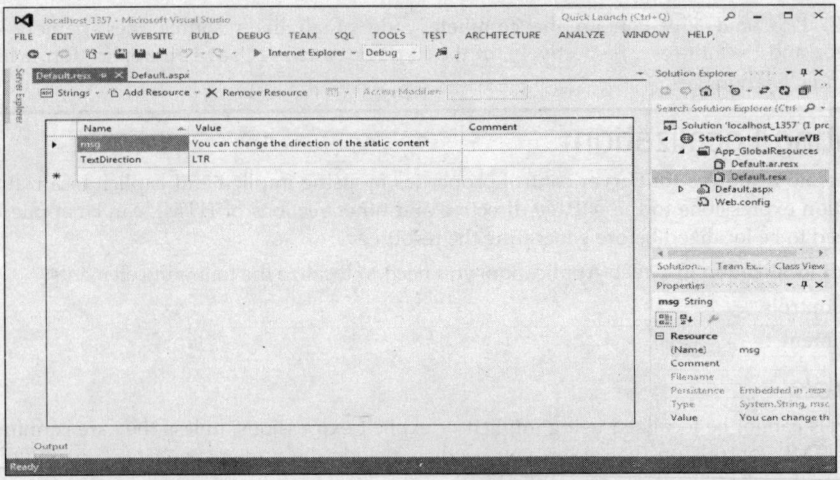

Figure 17.21: Displaying the Resource Editor for the Default.resx File

3. Add another new item `Default.ar.resx` for the Arabic language and set the values for the Name and Value fields in the Resource editor, as shown in Figure 17.22:

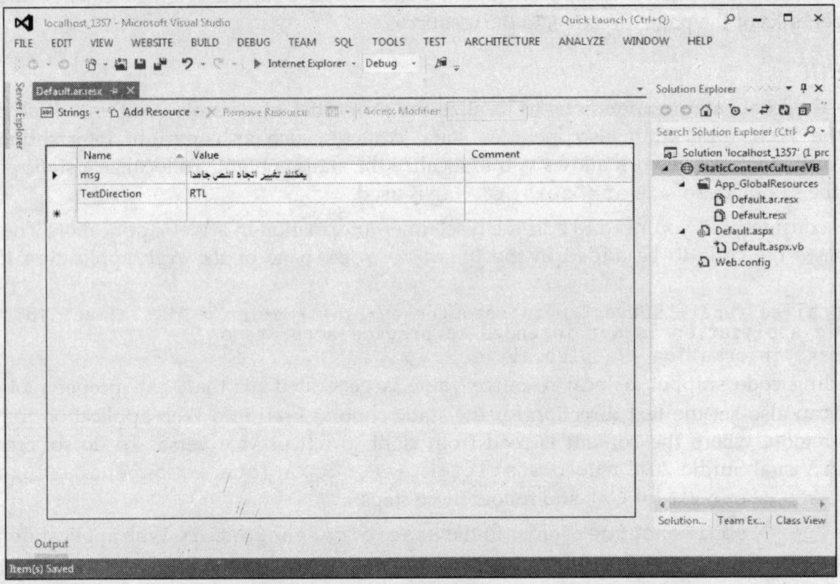

Figure 17.22: Displaying the Resource Editor for the Default.ar.resx File

4. Add a Label control in the Design view of the `Default.aspx` file and add the code, as shown in Listing 17.10, in the `Default.aspx` page of the Web application to set the direction property of the static content:

Listing 17.10: Code for the `Default.aspx` Page

In VB

```
<%@ Page Language="VB" AutoEventWireup="false" CodeFile="Default.aspx.vb"
   Inherits="_Default" Culture="auto" UICulture="auto"%>
<!DOCTYPE html>
<html id="Html1" runat="server" dir="<%$ Resources:default,TextDirection %>"
   xmlns="http://www.w3.org/1999/xhtml">
<head runat="server">
```

```
    <title>StaticContentCulture Example</title>
</head>
<body id="Body1" runat="server" dir="<%$ Resources:default,TextDirection %>">
    <form id="form1" runat="server">    <div>
        <strong>ASP.NET 4.5 BLACK BOOK</strong><br />
        <br />
    <asp:Label ID="Label1" runat="server" Text="<%$ Resources:default, msg
  %>"></asp:Label>
    </div>
    </form>
</body>
</html>
```

In C#

```
<%@ Page Language="VB" AutoEventWireup="false" CodeFile="Default.aspx.vb"
  Inherits="_Default" Culture="auto" UICulture="auto" %>
<!DOCTYPE html>
<html id="Html1" runat="server" dir="<%$ Resources:default,TextDirection %>"
  xmlns="http://www.w3.org/1999/xhtml">
<head runat="server">
    <title>StaticContentCulture Example</title>
</head>
<body id="Body1" runat="server" dir="<%$ Resources:default,TextDirection %>">
    <form id="form1" runat="server">
    <div>
    <strong>ASP.NET 4.5 BLACK BOOK</strong><br />
        <br />
    <asp:Label ID="Label1" runat="server" Text="<%$ Resources:default, msg
        %>"></asp:Label>
    </div>
    </form>
</body>
</html>
```

The complete code for the resource file, `Default.ar.resx`, is shown in Listing 17.11:

Listing 17.11: Code for the `Default.ar.resx` File

```
<?xml version="1.0" encoding="utf-8"?>
<root>
  <!--
    Microsoft ResX Schema

    Version 2.0

    The primary goals of this format is to allow a simple XML format
    that is mostly human readable. The generation and parsing of the
    various data types are done through the TypeConverter classes
    associated with the data types.

    Example:
    ... ado.net/XML headers & schema ...
    <resheader name="resmimetype">text/microsoft-resx</resheader>
    <resheader name="version">2.0</resheader>
    <resheader name="reader">System.Resources.ResXResourceReader, System.Windows.Forms,
        ...</resheader>
    <resheader name="writer">System.Resources.ResXResourceWriter, System.Windows.Forms,
        ...</resheader>
    <data name="Name1"><value>this is my long string</value><comment>this is a
        comment</comment></data>
    <data name="Color1" type="System.Drawing.Color, System.Drawing">Blue</data>
    <data name="Bitmap1" mimetype="application/x-microsoft.net.object.binary.base64">
        <value>[base64 mime encoded serialized .NET Framework object]</value>
```

```
    </data>
    <data name="Icon1" type="System.Drawing.Icon, System.Drawing"
        mimetype="application/x-microsoft.net.object.bytearray.base64">
        <value>[base64 mime encoded string representing a byte array form of the .NET
        Framework object]</value>
        <comment>This is a comment</comment>
    </data>

    There are any number of "resheader" rows that contain simple
    name/value pairs.

    Each data row contains a name, and value. The row also contains a
    type or mimetype. Type corresponds to a .NET class that support
    text/value conversion through the TypeConverter architecture.
    Classes that don't support this are serialized and stored with the
    mimetype set.

    The mimetype is used for serialized objects, and tells the
    ResXResourceReader how to depersist the object. This is currently not
    extensible. For a given mimetype the value must be set accordingly:

    Note - application/x-microsoft.net.object.binary.base64 is the format
    that the ResXResourceWriter will generate, however the reader can
    read any of the formats listed below.

    mimetype: application/x-microsoft.net.object.binary.base64
    value   : The object must be serialized with
            : System.Runtime.Serialization.Formatters.Binary.BinaryFormatter
            : and then encoded with base64 encoding.

    mimetype: application/x-microsoft.net.object.soap.base64
    value   : The object must be serialized with
            : System.Runtime.Serialization.Formatters.Soap.SoapFormatter
            : and then encoded with base64 encoding.

    mimetype: application/x-microsoft.net.object.bytearray.base64
    value   : The object must be serialized into a byte array
            : using a System.ComponentModel.TypeConverter
            : and then encoded with base64 encoding.
    -->
  <xsd:schema id="root" xmlns="" xmlns:xsd="http://www.w3.org/2001/XMLSchema"
  xmlns:msdata="urn:schemas-microsoft-com:xml-msdata">
    <xsd:import namespace="http://www.w3.org/XML/1998/namespace" />
    <xsd:element name="root" msdata:IsDataSet="true">
      <xsd:complexType>
        <xsd:choice maxOccurs="unbounded">
          <xsd:element name="metadata">
            <xsd:complexType>
              <xsd:sequence>
                <xsd:element name="value" type="xsd:string" minOccurs="0" />
              </xsd:sequence>
              <xsd:attribute name="name" use="required" type="xsd:string" />
              <xsd:attribute name="type" type="xsd:string" />
              <xsd:attribute name="mimetype" type="xsd:string" />
              <xsd:attribute ref="xml:space" />
            </xsd:complexType>
          </xsd:element>
          <xsd:element name="assembly">
            <xsd:complexType>
              <xsd:attribute name="alias" type="xsd:string" />
```

```
            <xsd:attribute name="name" type="xsd:string" />
          </xsd:complexType>
        </xsd:element>
        <xsd:element name="data">
          <xsd:complexType>
            <xsd:sequence>
              <xsd:element name="value" type="xsd:string" minOccurs="0"
               msdata:Ordinal="1" />
              <xsd:element name="comment" type="xsd:string" minOccurs="0"
               msdata:Ordinal="2" />
            </xsd:sequence>
            <xsd:attribute name="name" type="xsd:string" use="required"
              msdata:Ordinal="1" />
            <xsd:attribute name="type" type="xsd:string" msdata:Ordinal="3" />
            <xsd:attribute name="mimetype" type="xsd:string" msdata:Ordinal="4" />
            <xsd:attribute ref="xml:space" />
          </xsd:complexType>
        </xsd:element>
        <xsd:element name="resheader">
          <xsd:complexType>
            <xsd:sequence>
              <xsd:element name="value" type="xsd:string" minOccurs="0"
               msdata:Ordinal="1" />
            </xsd:sequence>
            <xsd:attribute name="name" type="xsd:string" use="required" />
          </xsd:complexType>
        </xsd:element>
      </xsd:choice>
    </xsd:complexType>
  </xsd:element>
</xsd:schema>
<resheader name="resmimetype">
  <value>text/microsoft-resx</value>
</resheader>
<resheader name="version">
  <value>2.0</value>
</resheader>
<resheader name="reader">
  <value>System.Resources.ResXResourceReader, System.Windows.Forms, Version=4.0.0.0,
Culture=neutral, PublicKeyToken=b77a5c561934e089</value>
</resheader>
<resheader name="writer">
  <value>System.Resources.ResXResourceWriter, System.Windows.Forms, Version=4.0.0.0,
Culture=neutral, PublicKeyToken=b77a5c561934e089</value>
</resheader>
<data name="msg" xml:space="preserve">
  <value>يمكنك تغيير اتجاه النص جامدا</value>
</data>
<data name="TextDirection" xml:space="preserve">
  <value>RTL</value>
</data>
</root>
```

The complete code for the resource file, `Default.resx`, is shown in Listing 17.12:

Listing 17.12: Code for the `Default.resx` File

```
<?xml version="1.0" encoding="utf-8"?>
<root>
  <!--
    Microsoft ResX Schema

    Version 2.0
```

```
    The primary goals of this format is to allow a simple XML format
    that is mostly human readable. The generation and parsing of the
    various data types are done through the TypeConverter classes
    associated with the data types.

    Example:

    ... ado.net/XML headers & schema ...
    <resheader name="resmimetype">text/microsoft-resx</resheader>
    <resheader name="version">2.0</resheader>
    <resheader name="reader">System.Resources.ResXResourceReader, System.Windows.Forms,
         ...</resheader>
    <resheader name="writer">System.Resources.ResXResourceWriter, System.Windows.Forms,
         ...</resheader>
    <data name="Name1"><value>this is my long string</value><comment>this is a
         comment</comment></data>
    <data name="Color1" type="System.Drawing.Color, System.Drawing">Blue</data>
    <data name="Bitmap1" mimetype="application/x-microsoft.net.object.binary.base64">
        <value>[base64 mime encoded serialized .NET Framework object]</value>
    </data>
    <data name="Icon1" type="System.Drawing.Icon, System.Drawing"
         mimetype="application/x-microsoft.net.object.bytearray.base64">
        <value>[base64 mime encoded string representing a byte array form of the .NET
         Framework object]</value>
        <comment>This is a comment</comment>
    </data>

    There are any number of "resheader" rows that contain simple
    name/value pairs.

    Each data row contains a name, and value. The row also contains a
    type or mimetype. Type corresponds to a .NET class that support
    text/value conversion through the TypeConverter architecture.
    Classes that don't support this are serialized and stored with the
    mimetype set.
    The mimetype is used for serialized objects, and tells the
    ResXResourceReader how to depersist the object. This is currently not
    extensible. For a given mimetype the value must be set accordingly:

    Note - application/x-microsoft.net.object.binary.base64 is the format
    that the ResXResourceWriter will generate, however the reader can
    read any of the formats listed below.

    mimetype: application/x-microsoft.net.object.binary.base64
    value   : The object must be serialized with
            : System.Runtime.Serialization.Formatters.Binary.BinaryFormatter
            : and then encoded with base64 encoding.

    mimetype: application/x-microsoft.net.object.soap.base64
    value   : The object must be serialized with
            : System.Runtime.Serialization.Formatters.Soap.SoapFormatter
            : and then encoded with base64 encoding.
    mimetype: application/x-microsoft.net.object.bytearray.base64
    value   : The object must be serialized into a byte array
            : using a System.ComponentModel.TypeConverter
            : and then encoded with base64 encoding.
    -->
  <xsd:schema id="root" xmlns="" xmlns:xsd="http://www.w3.org/2001/XMLSchema"
  xmlns:msdata="urn:schemas-microsoft-com:xml-msdata">
    <xsd:import namespace="http://www.w3.org/XML/1998/namespace" />
```

```
    <xsd:element name="root" msdata:IsDataSet="true">
      <xsd:complexType>
        <xsd:choice maxOccurs="unbounded">
          <xsd:element name="metadata">
            <xsd:complexType>
              <xsd:sequence>
                <xsd:element name="value" type="xsd:string" minOccurs="0" />
              </xsd:sequence>
              <xsd:attribute name="name" use="required" type="xsd:string" />
              <xsd:attribute name="type" type="xsd:string" />
              <xsd:attribute name="mimetype" type="xsd:string" />
              <xsd:attribute ref="xml:space" />
            </xsd:complexType>
          </xsd:element>
          <xsd:element name="assembly">
            <xsd:complexType>
              <xsd:attribute name="alias" type="xsd:string" />
              <xsd:attribute name="name" type="xsd:string" />
            </xsd:complexType>
          </xsd:element>
          <xsd:element name="data">
            <xsd:complexType>
              <xsd:sequence>
                <xsd:element name="value" type="xsd:string" minOccurs="0"
                 msdata:Ordinal="1" />
                <xsd:element name="comment" type="xsd:string" minOccurs="0"
                 msdata:Ordinal="2" />
              </xsd:sequence>
              <xsd:attribute name="name" type="xsd:string" use="required"
                 msdata:Ordinal="1" />
              <xsd:attribute name="type" type="xsd:string" msdata:Ordinal="3" />
              <xsd:attribute name="mimetype" type="xsd:string" msdata:Ordinal="4" />
              <xsd:attribute ref="xml:space" />
            </xsd:complexType>
          </xsd:element>
          <xsd:element name="resheader">
            <xsd:complexType>
              <xsd:sequence>
                <xsd:element name="value" type="xsd:string" minOccurs="0"
                 msdata:Ordinal="1" />
              </xsd:sequence>
              <xsd:attribute name="name" type="xsd:string" use="required" />
            </xsd:complexType>
          </xsd:element>
        </xsd:choice>
      </xsd:complexType>
    </xsd:element>
  </xsd:schema>
  <resheader name="resmimetype">
    <value>text/microsoft-resx</value>
  </resheader>
  <resheader name="version">
    <value>2.0</value>
  </resheader>
  <resheader name="reader">
    <value>System.Resources.ResXResourceReader, System.Windows.Forms, Version=4.0.0.0,
  Culture=neutral, PublicKeyToken=b77a5c561934e089</value>
  </resheader>
  <resheader name="writer">
    <value>System.Resources.ResXResourceWriter, System.Windows.Forms, Version=4.0.0.0,
  Culture=neutral, PublicKeyToken=b77a5c561934e089</value>
```

```
    </resheader>
    <data name="msg" xml:space="preserve">
      <value>You can change the direction of the static content</value>
    </data>
    <data name="TextDirection" xml:space="preserve">
      <value>LTR</value>
    </data>
</root>
```

5. Run the Web application by pressing the F5 key. The output of the `StaticContent` Web application, when the preferred language in the browser settings is changed to English, is shown in Figure 17.23:

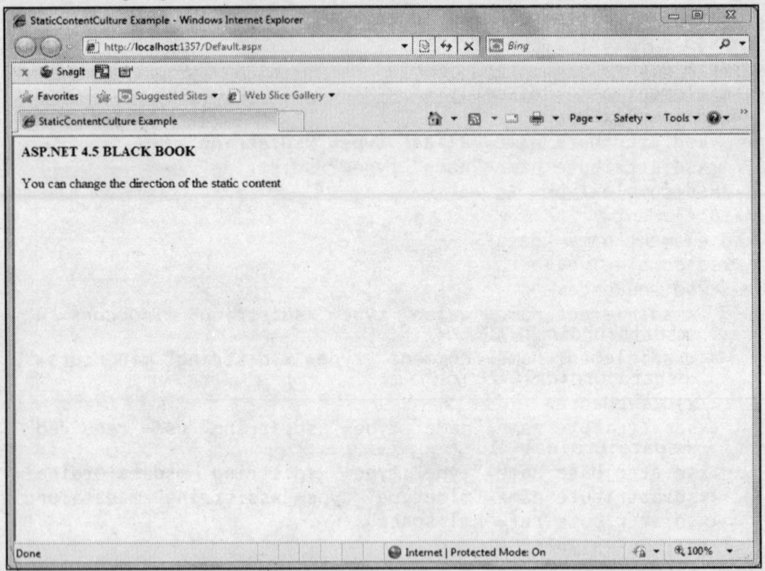

Figure 17.23: Showing the Output in English Language

The output of the Web application, when the preferred language in browser settings is changed to Arabic, is shown in Figure 17.24:

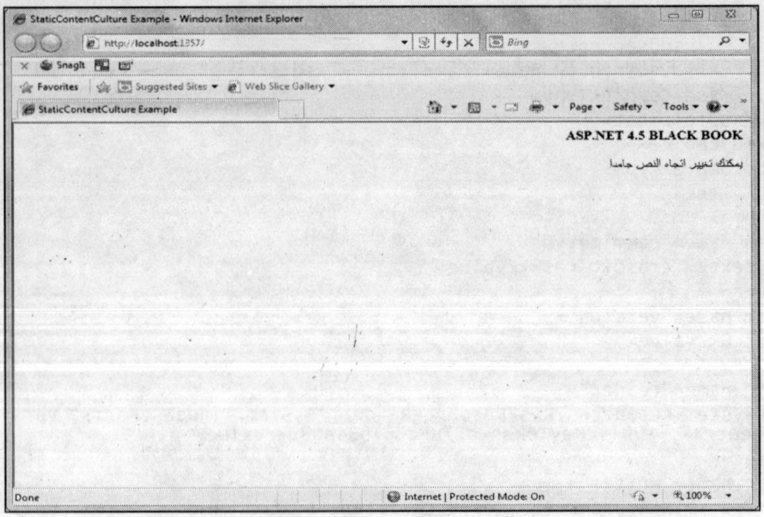

Figure 17.24: Showing the Output in Arabic Language

Localizing Script Files

You can localize your script files with the help of the `ScriptManager` control. The `ScriptManager` control enables certain automatic behaviors for localized applications, which include the following:

- Automatically locating script files based on settings and naming conventions
- Enabling the definition of cultures, including custom cultures.
- Caching scripts to efficiently manage many requests.

Now, let's create a Web application named `ScriptLocalization` (`ScriptLocalizationVB` for VB and `ScriptLocalizationCS` for C#), and follow these steps to localize the script files:

1. Add a Class Library project named `LocalizingResources` by right-clicking the name of the Solution in the Solution Explorer, and select `Add→New Project`, as shown in Figure 17.25:

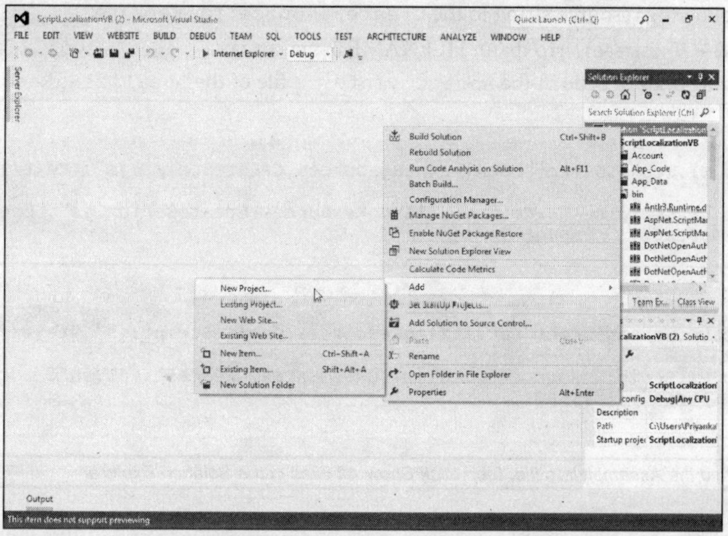

Figure 17.25: Adding New Project in the ScriptLocalization Application

The New Project option opens the Add New Project dialog box (Figure 17.26).

2. Select the Class Library template and change the name of the Class Library project as `LocalizingResources`, as shown in Figure 17.26:

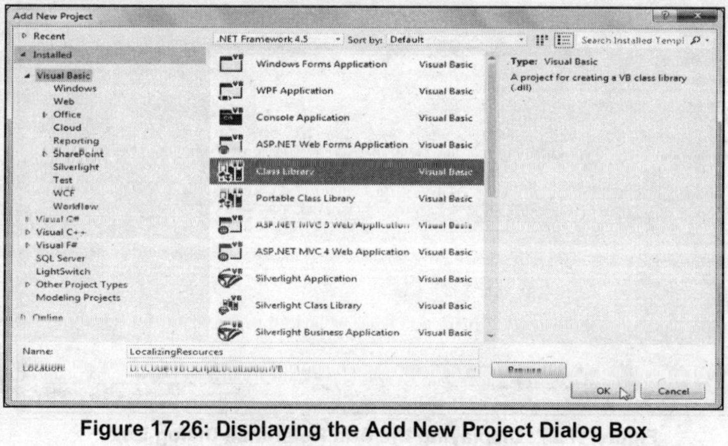

Figure 17.26: Displaying the Add New Project Dialog Box

3. Click the OK button. It adds the `LocalizingResources` application to the Solution Explorer.
4. Add the JavaScript file named `CreateScript.js` and change the value of the `Build Action` property of the script file to `Embedded Resource`.
5. Add the following code in the `CreateScript.js` file:

```
function CreateScript(fileName)
{
  alert (Message.FileCreated.replace(/FILENAME/, fileName));
}
```

6. Add two resource files in the `LocalizingResources` application as `CreateResource.resx` for English language and `CreateResource.ru.resx` for Russian language and add the following resource string to the `CreateResource.resx` file:
   - **FileCreated** – Indicates that the file FILENAME has been created

   Also add the following resource string to the `CreateResource.ru.resx` file:
   - **FileCreated** – Указывает, что файл FILENAME была создана
7. Add the following lines of code in the `AssemblyInfo.cs` file of the `LocalizingResources` application:

In VB

```
<Assembly:
  System.Web.UI.WebResource("LocalizingResources.CreateScript.js","text/javascript")>
<Assembly:
  System.Web.UI.ScriptResource("LocalizingResources.CreateScript.js","LocalizingResource
  s.CreateResource", "Message")>
```

In C#

```
[assembly:
  System.Web.UI.WebResource("LocalizingResources.CreateScript.js","text/javascript")]
[assembly:
  System.Web.UI.ScriptResource("LocalizingResources.CreateScript.js","LocalizingResource
  s.CreateResource", "Message")]
```

NOTE

If you are not able to find the AssemblyInfo file, then click Show All Files in the Solution Explorer.

8. Add references of the `System.Web` and `System.Web.Extensions` assemblies in the `LocalizingResources` project. You also need to add the reference of the `LocalizingResources` project in the `ScriptLocalization` project. You can see the `LocalizingResources` project in the Projects tab under Solution node of the Add Reference dialog box, as shown in Figure 17.27:

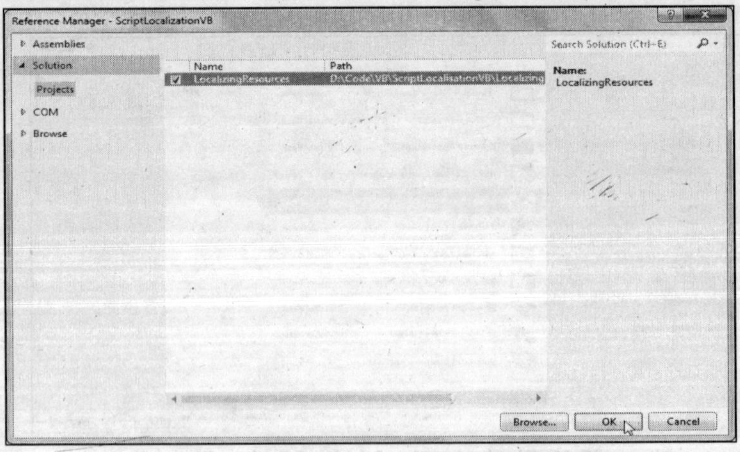

Figure 17.27: Displaying the Add Reference Dialog Box

9. Open the `Default.aspx` page of the `ScriptLocalization` application and add the code shown in Listing 17.13:

Listing 17.13: Code for the `Default.aspx` Page

In VB

```
<%@ Page Title="Home Page" Language="VB" MasterPageFile="~/Site.Master"
  AutoEventWireup="false" CodeFile="Default.aspx.vb" Inherits="_Default" Culture="auto"
  UICulture="auto"%>
<asp:Content runat="server" ID="FeaturedContent" ContentPlaceHolderID="FeaturedContent">
</asp:Content>
<asp:Content runat="server" ID="BodyContent" ContentPlaceHolderID="MainContent">
        <h2>
        ASP.NET 4.5 black book
    </h2>
     <br />
    <%--<asp:ScriptManager ID= "SM1" runat="server" EnableScriptLocalization="true">
    <Scripts>
    <asp:ScriptReference Assembly="LocalizingResources"
        Name="LocalizingResources.CreateScript.js" />
    </Scripts>
    </asp:ScriptManager>--%>
    <br />
    <br />
    <asp:Button ID="button" runat="server" OnClientClick="CreateScript('Hello
  World.txt');" Text="Create" Width="92px"/>
</asp:Content>
```

In C#

```
<%@ Page Title="Home Page" Language="C#" MasterPageFile="~/Site.Master"
  AutoEventWireup="true" CodeFile="Default.aspx.cs"
  Inherits="_Default"Culture="auto"UICulture="auto"%>
<asp:Content runat="server" ID="FeaturedContent" ContentPlaceHolderID="FeaturedContent">
  </asp:Content>
<asp:Content runat="server" ID="BodyContent" ContentPlaceHolderID="MainContent">
          <h2>
        ASP.NET 4.5 black book
    </h2>
     <br />
    <br />
    <br />
    <asp:Button ID="button" runat="server" OnClientClick="CreateScript('Hello
  World.txt');" Text="Create" Width="92px"/>
</asp:Content>
```

10. Open the `Site.master` page of the `ScriptLocalization` application and add the code shown in Listing 17.14:

Listing 17.14: Code for the `Site.master` Page

In VB

```
<%@ Master Language="VB" AutoEventWireup="true" CodeFile="Site.master.vb"
  Inherits="SiteMaster" %>

<!DOCTYPE html>
<html lang="en">
<head runat="server">
    <meta charset="utf-8" />
    <title><%: Page.Title %> - My ASP.NET Application</title>
    <asp:PlaceHolder runat="server">
        <%: Scripts.Render("~/bundles/modernizr") %>
    </asp:PlaceHolder>
    <webopt:BundleReference runat="server" Path="~/Content/css" />
    <link href="~/favicon.ico" rel="shortcut icon" type="image/x-icon" />
    <meta name="viewport" content="width=device-width" />
    <asp:ContentPlaceHolder runat="server" ID="HeadContent" />
```

```
</head>
<body>
    <form runat="server">
    <asp:ScriptManager runat="server" ID= "SM1" EnableScriptLocalization="true">
        <Scripts >
            <%--Framework scripts--%>
            <asp:ScriptReference Name="MsAjaxBundle" />
            <asp:ScriptReference Name="jquery" />
            <asp:ScriptReference Name="jquery.ui.combined" />
            <asp:ScriptReference Name="WebForms.js" Assembly="System.Web"
                Path="~/Scripts/WebForms/WebForms.js" />
            <asp:ScriptReference Name="WebUIValidation.js" Assembly="System.Web"
                Path="~/Scripts/WebForms/WebUIValidation.js" />
            <asp:ScriptReference Name="MenuStandards.js" Assembly="System.Web"
                Path="~/Scripts/WebForms/MenuStandards.js" />
            <asp:ScriptReference Name="GridView.js" Assembly="System.Web"
                Path="~/Scripts/WebForms/GridView.js" />
            <asp:ScriptReference Name="DetailsView.js" Assembly="System.Web"
                Path="~/Scripts/WebForms/DetailsView.js" />
            <asp:ScriptReference Name="TreeView.js" Assembly="System.Web"
                Path="~/Scripts/WebForms/TreeView.js" />
            <asp:ScriptReference Name="WebParts.js" Assembly="System.Web"
                Path="~/Scripts/WebForms/WebParts.js" />
            <asp:ScriptReference Name="Focus.js" Assembly="System.Web"
                Path="~/Scripts/WebForms/Focus.js" />
            <asp:ScriptReference Name="WebFormsBundle" />
            <asp:ScriptReference Assembly="LocalizingResources"
                Name="LocalizingResources.CreateScript.js" />
            <%--Site scripts--%>
        </Scripts>
    </asp:ScriptManager>
    <header>
        <div class="content-wrapper">
            <div class="float-left">
                <p class="site-title">
                    <a runat="server" href="~/">your logo here</a></p>
            </div>
            <div class="float-right">
                <section id="login">
                    <asp:LoginView runat="server" ViewStateMode="Disabled">
                       <AnonymousTemplate>
                       <ul>
                       <li><a id="registerLink" runat="server"
                         href="~/Account/Register.aspx">Register</a></li>
                         <li><a id="loginLink" runat="server"
                         href="~/Account/Login.aspx">Log in</a></li>
                         </ul>
                        </AnonymousTemplate>
                        <LoggedInTemplate>
                        <p>
                        Hello, <a runat="server" class="username"
                         href="~/Account/Manage.aspx" title="Manage your account">
                         <asp:LoginName runat="server" CssClass="username" />
                         </a>!
                         <asp:LoginStatus runat="server" LogoutAction="Redirect"
                         LogoutText="Log off" LogoutPageUrl="~/" />
                             </p>
                        </LoggedInTemplate>
                    </asp:LoginView>
                </section>
                <nav>
                    <ul id="menu">
                        <li><a runat="server" href="~/">Home</a></li>
                        <li><a runat="server" href="~/About.aspx">About</a></li>
                        <li><a runat="server" href="~/Contact.aspx">Contact</a></li>
                    </ul>
```

```
                </nav>
            </div>
        </div>
    </header>
    <div id="body">
        <asp:ContentPlaceHolder runat="server" ID="FeaturedContent" />
        <section class="content-wrapper main-content clear-fix">
            <asp:ContentPlaceHolder runat="server" ID="MainContent" />
        </section>
    </div>
    <footer>
        <div class="content-wrapper">
            <div class="float-left">
                <p>&copy; <%: DateTime.Now.Year %> - My ASP.NET Application
                </p>
            </div>
        </div>
    </footer>
    </form>
</body>
</html>
```

In C#

```
<%@ Master Language="C#" AutoEventWireup="true" CodeFile="Site.master.cs"
  Inherits="SiteMaster" %>
<!DOCTYPE html>
<html lang="en">
<head runat="server">
    <meta charset="utf-8" />
    <title><%: Page.Title %> - My ASP.NET Application</title>
    <asp:PlaceHolder runat="server">
        <%: Scripts.Render("~/bundles/modernizr") %>
    </asp:PlaceHolder>
    <webopt:BundleReference runat="server" Path="~/Content/css" />
    <link href="~/favicon.ico" rel="shortcut icon" type="image/x-icon" />
    <meta name="viewport" content="width=device-width" />
    <asp:ContentPlaceHolder runat="server" ID="HeadContent" />
</head>
<body>
    <form runat="server">
        <asp:ScriptManager runat="server" ID= "SM1" EnableScriptLocalization="true">
        <Scripts>
            <%--Framework scripts--%>
            <asp:ScriptReference Name="MsAjaxBundle" />
            <asp:ScriptReference Name="jquery" />
            <asp:ScriptReference Name="jquery.ui.combined" />
            <asp:ScriptReference Name="WebForms.js" Assembly="System.Web"
                Path="~/Scripts/WebForms/WebForms.js" />
            <asp:ScriptReference Name="WebUIValidation.js" Assembly="System.Web"
                Path="~/Scripts/WebForms/WebUIValidation.js" />
            <asp:ScriptReference Name="MenuStandards.js" Assembly="System.Web"
                Path="~/Scripts/WebForms/MenuStandards.js" />
            <asp:ScriptReference Name="GridView.js" Assembly="System.Web"
                Path="~/Scripts/WebForms/GridView.js" />
            <asp:ScriptReference Name="DetailsView.js" Assembly="System.Web"
                Path="~/Scripts/WebForms/DetailsView.js" />
            <asp:ScriptReference Name="TreeView.js" Assembly="System.Web"
                Path="~/Scripts/WebForms/TreeView.js" />
            <asp:ScriptReference Name="WebParts.js" Assembly="System.Web"
                Path="~/Scripts/WebForms/WebParts.js" />
            <asp:ScriptReference Name="Focus.js" Assembly="System.Web"
                Path="~/Scripts/WebForms/Focus.js" />
            <asp:ScriptReference Name="WebFormsBundle" />
            <asp:ScriptReference Assembly="LocalizingResources"
                Name="LocalizingResources.CreateScript.js" />
```

```
                <%--Site scripts--%>
            </Scripts>
        </asp:ScriptManager>
        <header>
            <div class="content-wrapper">
                <div class="float-left">
                    <p class="site-title">
                        <a runat="server" href="~/">your logo here</a></p>
                </div>
                <div class="float-right">
                    <section id="login">
                    <asp:LoginView runat="server" ViewStateMode="Disabled">
                    <AnonymousTemplate>
                    <ul>
                    <li><a id="registerLink" runat="server"
                     href="~/Account/Register.aspx">Register</a></li>
                     <li><a id="loginLink" runat="server" href="~/Account/Login.aspx">Log
                     in</a></li>
                     </ul>
                     </AnonymousTemplate>
                     <LoggedInTemplate>
                     <p>
                     Hello, <a runat="server" class="username" href="~/Account/Manage.aspx"
                     title="Manage your account">
                     <asp:LoginName runat="server" CssClass="username" />
                     </a>!
                     <asp:LoginStatus runat="server" LogoutAction="Redirect" LogoutText="Log
                     off" LogoutPageUrl="~/" />
                     </p>
                             </LoggedInTemplate>
                        </asp:LoginView>
                    </section>
                    <nav>
                        <ul id="menu">
                            <li><a runat="server" href="~/">Home</a></li>
                            <li><a runat="server" href="~/About.aspx">About</a></li>
                            <li><a runat="server" href="~/Contact.aspx">Contact</a></li>
                        </ul>
                    </nav>
                </div>
            </div>
        </header>
        <div id="body">
            <asp:ContentPlaceHolder runat="server" ID="FeaturedContent" />
            <section class="content-wrapper main-content clear-fix">
                <asp:ContentPlaceHolder runat="server" ID="MainContent" />
            </section>
        </div>
        <footer>
            <div class="content-wrapper">
                <div class="float-left">
                    <p>
                        &copy; <%: DateTime.Now.Year %> - My ASP.NET Application
                    </p>
                </div>
            </div>
        </footer>
        </form>
    </body>
    </html>
```

11. Press the F5 key to run the Web application. Notice that the Create button is displayed in the browser (Figure 17.28).

12. Click the Create button. A message box appears, as shown in Figure 17.28:

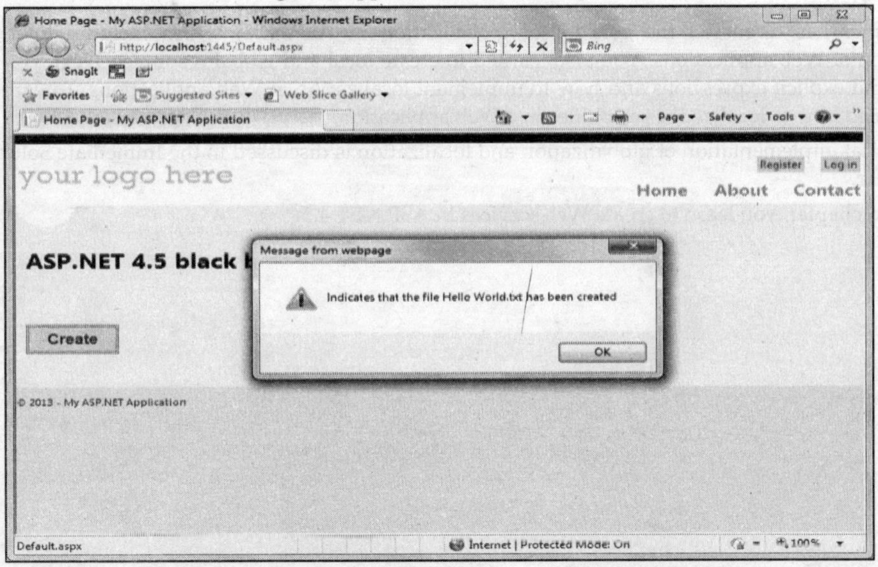

Figure 17.28: Displaying the Confirmation Message Box

In Figure 17.28, the preferred language is English.

13. Change the preferred language to Russian. The output of the `ScriptLocalization` application after changing the preferred language is shown in Figure 17.29:

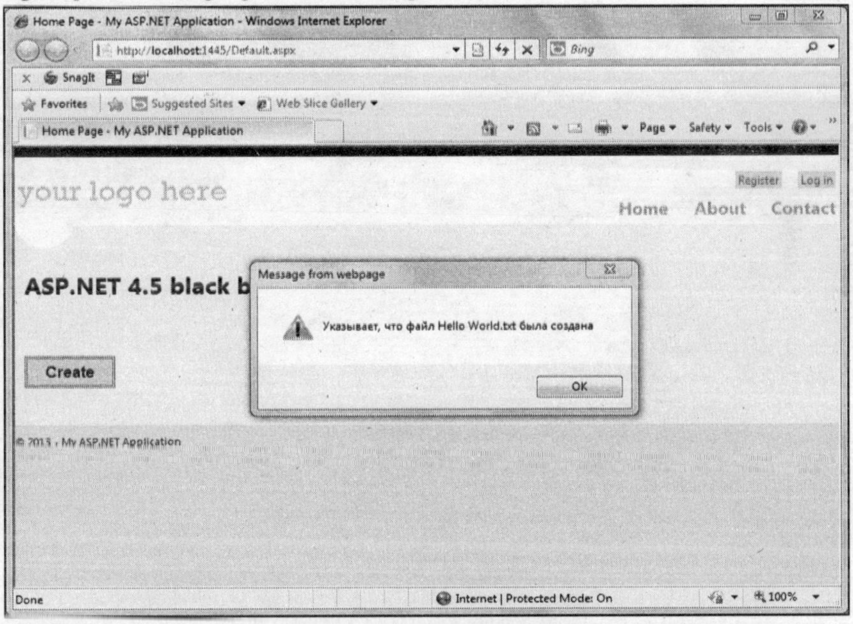

Figure 17.29: Displaying the Confirmation Message Box after Selecting Russian as the Preferred Language

Figure 17.29 displays a message box with a message in Russian language.

Summary

This chapter has discussed the concept of globalization in ASP.NET, which includes internalization and localization of Web applications. You also learned to create local and global resources. Next, you learned about implicit and explicit expressions and how to implement localization in Web applications. Towards the end, you have learned how to localize the script files in a Web application.

The practical implementation of globalization and localization is discussed in the Immediate Solutions section of this chapter.

In the next chapter, you learn to create Web services in ASP.NET 4.5.

18

ASP.NET Web Services

In Depth

A Web service may be defined as an independent and self-sustained unit of a software application hosted on the Internet. A Web service implements specific functionalities to execute the business logic of the application. A Web service can be used to implement various functionalities, such as preparing the pay slips for the employees of a company, calculating the income tax, broadcasting weather reports, and providing updated news. In .NET Framework, you can create Web services. A Web service created in ASP.NET is known as ASP.NET Web service and consists of an infrastructure that contains various components used to implement basic functionalities to a Web service, such as locating a Web service, calling a Web service, and so on. You can also use the code model and properties of an ASP.NET Web service while creating Web services. You can also create Web services that use the ASP.NET AJAX functionality. In addition, security measures to check unauthorized access to Web services also need to be incorporated in the Web services created.

In this chapter, you learn about Web services, infrastructure of ASP.NET Web services, code model of ASP.Net Web services, Web service properties, securing Web services, and the use of ASP.NET AJAX with Web services. You also learn how to create an ASP.NET Web service, how to use an ASP.NET Web service, how to share data across Web services, how to do communication between Web services asynchronously, how to work with ASP.NET AJAX-enabled Web services, and how to use an `UpdatePanel` control with a Web service.

Introducing Web Services

A Web service is an entity that you can program to provide a particular functionality to applications over the Internet. Suppose you want to host a website on the Internet that calculates the simple interest, compound interest, and income tax of an individual. To do this, you can use a Web service to calculate the simple interest, compound interest, and another Web service to calculate the income tax. In this scenario, a Web service is advantageous in the sense that you do not need to write the code in the Web site for calculating the simple interest, compound interest, and income tax. Instead, all you have to do is to use the Web services that provide these functionalities. You need to subscribe to the Web service before using a Web service in your website.

A Web service allows a website to communicate with other websites irrespective of the programming languages in which they are created. In addition, a Web service can be accessed by any application, regardless of the software and hardware platforms on which the application is running, because the Web service complies with common industry standards, such as Simple Object Access Protocol (SOAP) and Web Services Description Language (WSDL). A Web service does not have any user interface; it only contains the logic for providing specific services to its consumers. A Web service provides an abstraction between the consumer (client) and the provider of the Web service. The Web service only need information about input, output, and location of the client and Web service provider. Before the introduction of Web services, developers employed technologies, such as Component Object Model (COM) and Distributed Component Object Model (DCOM), to use the functionality of one application in another application. These technologies allowed a developer to create code components once and bundle the components so that they could be shared across multiple applications by multiple developers. However, there were some fundamental difficulties in using these components. One such difficulty was that these components needed to be physically distributed and explicitly registered on each client machine. Web services overcome these difficulties as they can be shared among multiple websites without the need to install them on each individual client machines.

Web services have become popular because of the added functionalities they provide over component-based technologies. The advantages of Web services over COM and DCOM are as follows:

- Web services are simple to use; and consequently, they can be implemented on varied platforms
- Web services are loosely coupled; as a result, their interfaces and methods can be extended
- Web services do not carry any state information with them so that multiple requests can be processed simultaneously

Web services are most appropriate while communicating across platforms or enforcing trusted connections between the server and the client. In addition, it is a good practice to use Web services under the following circumstances:

- Using caching features of ASP.NET
- Using Secure Socket Layer (SSL) security or Windows authentication
- Integrating ASP.NET Web applications with third-party systems

Infrastructure of ASP.NET Web Services

The infrastructure of ASP.NET Web services provides a simple Application Programming Interface(API) for Web services to create and understand SOAP messages that in turn help to invoke remote methods. Web services must not be dependent on the selection of the operating system, object model, and programming language. As with other Web-based technologies, Web services should be loosely coupled, should be able to communicate when needed, and have a universal data format to transfer data between the services and its users. The mechanisms included in the infrastructure of a Web service are as follows:

- Consists of a directory that provides a central location for Web service providers
- Consists of a discovery mechanism to locate Web services
- Consists of a service description to know how to use those Web services
- Consists of standard wire formats (protocols) to transmit data between Web services and its users

Figure 18.1 shows the main components in the infrastructure of ASP.NET Web services:

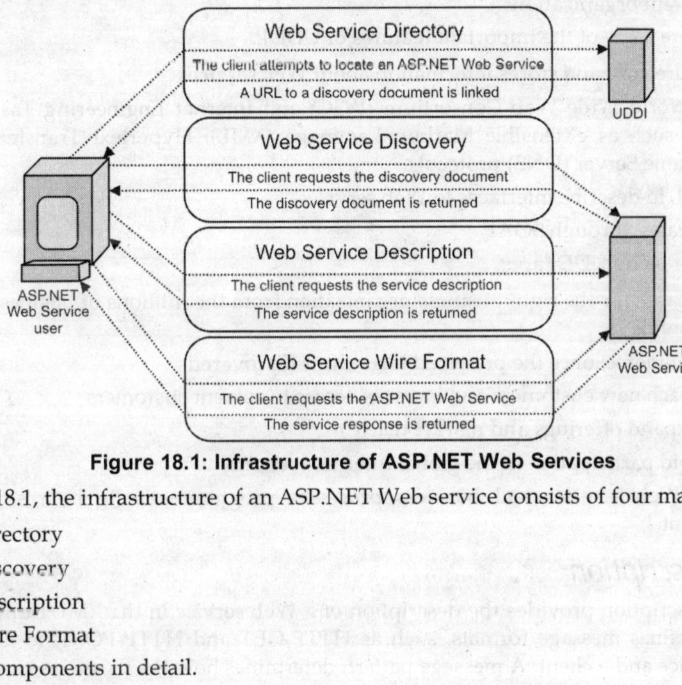

Figure 18.1: Infrastructure of ASP.NET Web Services

As shown in Figure 18.1, the infrastructure of an ASP.NET Web service consists of four main components:

- Web Service Directory
- Web Service Discovery
- Web Service Description
- Web Service Wire Format

Let's explore these components in detail.

Web Services Directory

The Web service directory provides a central location for Web service providers. In other words, it is a place where Web service users (consumers) can easily locate services offered by other companies and organizations. It is difficult to search a Web service without using any resource. Web service directories provide those centralized locations where you can publish information about your Web service. A Web service can be a directory for other Web services and can provide the result of the query to the Web service client. You need Web service directories to know about Web services provided by either multiple organizations or a particular organization. The Web service can be published and discovered by using the specification called Universal Description, Discovery, and Integration (UDDI). The schema associated with UDDI defines four types of information for Web services: business, Web service, binding, and specifications. These information types enable a developer to use a published Web service.

Web Services Discovery

The Web service discovery provides the capability to locate Web services. This component locates documents that describe a particular Web service, through WSDL. If you want to use a Web service in your website, you first need to know where the Web service is located. On the other hand, if you want other people to use your Web service, they also need to know where your Web service is located. In such a case, there must be a searching (discovery) mechanism, which can locate the required Web service. The following two methods are used to search the Uniform Resource Locator (URL) of a Web service:

- **The Web services discovery tool (Disco.exe)**—Used for publishing and discovering Web services. This tool discovers URLs of all the Web services located on a Web server and creates a list of them in a file called the DISCO file (a file with the .disco extension). An organization can publish its own DISCO files on its Web server. This file can be accessed by clients to know about the kind of Web services an organization provides.
- **UDDI**—Centralized directory where Web services offered by different organizations are published. It is a platform-independent method that is built into the .NET platform. A UDDI directory has an advantage over a DISCO file in that the directory provides a single location where clients can search the Web services offered by different organizations.

  The following are some of the important features of UDDI:

  - Acts as a directory and stores information about Web services
  - Uses the World Wide Web Consortium (W3C) and Internet Engineering Task Force (IETF) Internet standards, such as eXtensible Markup Language (XML), Hypertext Transfer Protocol (HTTP), and Domain Name Server (DNS) protocols
  - Uses WSDL to describe interfaces to Web services
  - Communicates through SOAP

  Some benefits of using UDDI are:

  - Helps to search for the right business organization from the millions of business organizations that are currently online
  - Enables commerce, once the preferred business is discovered
  - Helps to reach new customers and increase access to current customers
  - Helps to expand offerings and market reach
  - Allows rapid participation in the global Internet economy
  - Describes Web services and business processes programmatically in a single, open, and secure environment

Web Services Description

The Web service description provides the description of a Web service in the XML format, known as WSDL. A WSDL document defines message formats, such as HTTP-GET and HTTP-POST, to facilitate communication between a Web service and a client. A message pattern determines how the messages can be exchanged between a client and a service. A Web service defines and supports some message patterns, such as request/reply, one-way, or duplex. The behavior of a Web service depends on these message patterns, which theoretically state the requirements of a Web service user when a message is submitted to it. You learn more about message patterns in Chapter 19, *WCF Services*. Now, Let's discuss WSDL in more detail.

WSDL is an XML-based language that defines Web services. Every Web service consists of a corresponding WSDL document that specifies the location of the Web service and lists all the services that the Web service can perform.

A WSDL document is a simple XML document containing different XML elements to define a Web service. The main elements of a WSDL document are listed in Table 18.1:

Table 18.1: Elements of a WSDL Document

Element name	Description
types	Describes all data types that are used by a Web service
message	Describes messages that are used to communicate from one point to another when data is passed by the Web service
portType	Describes a set of abstract operations where each operation links to an input message and output message
binding	Describes the communication protocols that are used by the Web service
port	Describes an address for a binding, and therefore defining a communication endpoint
service	Describes a set of related endpoints, where an endpoint is defined as a collection of a binding and an address (URL)

Now, let's take a look at the structure of a WSDL document. Listing 18.1 shows the list of elements in the structure of a WSDL document:

Listing 18.1: Structure of a WSDL Document

```
<definitions>
<types>
<!-- This section contains definition of types-->
</types>
<message>
<!--This section contains definition of a message-->
</message>
<portType>
<!--This section contains definition of a port-->
</portType>
<binding>
<!--This section contains definition of a binding-->
</binding>
<port>
<!--This section contains definition of address for a binding -->
</port>
<service>
<!--This section contains definition of services-->
</service>
</definitions>
```

A WSDL document also contains other elements, for example, a service element, to combine the definitions of several Web services into a single WSDL document. Listing 18.2 shows a complete WSDL syntax, as described by W3C:

Listing 18.2: Syntax of a WSDL Document

```
<wsdl:definitions name="nmtoken"? targetNamespace="uri"?>
  <import namespace="uri" location="uri"/>*
  <wsdl:documentation .... /> ?
  <wsdl:types> ?
        <wsdl:documentation .... />?
        <xsd:schema .... />*
        <-- extensibility element --> *
  </wsdl:types>
  <wsdl:message name="nmtoken"> *
        <wsdl:documentation .... />?
```

```
            <part name="nmtoken" element="qname"? type="qname"?/> *
      </wsdl:message>
      <wsdl:portType name="nmtoken">*
            <wsdl:documentation .... />?
            <wsdl:operation name="nmtoken">*
            <wsdl:documentation .... /> ?
            <wsdl:input name="nmtoken"? message="qname">?
            <wsdl:documentation .... /> ?
            </wsdl:input>
            <wsdl:output name="nmtoken"? message="qname">?
            <wsdl:documentation .... /> ?
            </wsdl:output>
            <wsdl:fault name="nmtoken" message="qname"> *
            <wsdl:documentation .... /> ?
            </wsdl:fault>
            </wsdl:operation>
      </wsdl:portType>
      <wsdl:binding name="nmtoken" type="qname">*
            <wsdl:documentation .... />?
            <-- extensibility element --> *
            <wsdl:operation name="nmtoken">*
            <wsdl:documentation .... /> ?
            <-- extensibility element --> *
            <wsdl:input> ?
                  <wsdl:documentation .... /> ?
                  <-- extensibility element -->
            </wsdl:input>
            <wsdl:output> ?
                  <wsdl:documentation .... /> ?
                  <-- extensibility element --> *
            </wsdl:output>
            <wsdl:fault name="nmtoken"> *
                  <wsdl:documentation .... /> ?
                  <-- extensibility element --> *
            </wsdl:fault>
      </wsdl:operation>
      </wsdl:binding>
      <wsdl:service name="nmtoken"> *
            <wsdl:documentation .... />?
            <wsdl:port name="nmtoken" binding="qname"> *
            <wsdl:documentation .... /> ?
                  <-- extensibility element -->
            </wsdl:port>
            <-- extensibility element -->
      </wsdl:service>
      <-- extensibility element --> *
   </wsdl:definitions>
```

Web Services Wire Format

The Web service wire format provides an interface to transmit data between a Web service and its users through protocols, such as HTTP-GET and HTTP-POST. A Web service can use any Remote Procedure Call (RPC) protocol, such as DCOM or Common Object Request Broker Architecture (CORBA), to transmit data. However, these types of protocols are not recommended for creating universally available Web services. Therefore, you need to work with frequently used protocols, such as Hypertext Transfer Protocol (HTTP) and SOAP, to transfer data between a Web service and its users.

Table 18.2 lists the common protocols that Web services use to transmit data:

Table 18.2: Web Service Protocols Used for Data Transmission

Protocol Name	Description
HTTP-GET	Creates a query string of the name/value pair, such as name=joe, city=Chicago, and appends it to the Uniform Resource Locator (URL) of the requesting script on the server
HTTP-POST	Passes the name/value pair in the body of the HTTP request message
SOAP	Exchanges information in a decentralized, distributed environment
Multipurpose Internet Mail Extensions (MIME)	Defines the standard representation for complex message bodies, such as messages with embedded graphics or audio clips

The protocols listed in Table 18.2 are used to invoke Web methods of the Web service. The selection of a Web service protocol determines the types of parameters for a method and its return type.

Let's now explore some important protocols in detail.

HTTP-GET and HTTP-POST

Although you may know about HTTP-GET and HTTP-POST protocols used by the Web services to transmit data over the network, you must be aware of the fact that these methods of transportation of data are not rich enough to represent complex structures or classes. When you work with Web methods, you can use the HTTP-GET and HTTP-POST methods only with the data types listed in Table 18.3:

Table 18.3: Data Types Supported by HTTP-GET and HTTP-POST Protocols

Data Types	Description
Enumerations	Supports the transmission of .NET `System.Enum` types, provided they are represented as a static constant string.
Arrays	Creates arrays as a primitive type.
Strings	Refers to the string representation of Common Language Runtime (CLR) primitives, such as Int16, Int32, Int64, Boolean, Single, Double, and Decimal. HTTP-Get and HTTP-POST transmit all numerical data as a string token.

By default, HTTP-GET and HTTP-POST bindings are not enabled for remote Web service invocation. However, HTTP-POST is enabled to allow a machine to invoke a local Web service. These settings are established in the `machine.config` file using the `<protocol>` element. Listing 18.3 shows the partial code of the `machine.config` file:

Listing 18.3: Partial Code for the `machine.config` File

```
<!--In the machine.config file!-->
<webServices>
<protocols>
<add name="HttpSoap1.2"/>
<add name="HttpSoap"/>
<add name="Documentation"/>
<!--Http GET and POST are disabled!-->
<!--<add name="HttpPost"/>-->
<!--<add name="HttpGet"/>-->
<!-Used by the web service test page-->
<add name="HttpPostLocalhost"/>
</protocols>
</webServices>
```

You can enable the HTTP-GET and HTTP-POST protocols for a Web service, by adding the `HttpPost` and `HttpGet` names within the local `web.config` file, as shown in Listing 18.4:

Listing 18.4: Adding the `HttpPost` and `HttpGet` Names within the Local `web.config` File

```
<configuration>
   <system.web>
         <webServices>
               <protocols>
                     <add name="HttpPost"/>
                     <add name="HttpGet"/>
               </protocols>
         </webServices>
   </system.web>
</configuration>
```

When you use the HTTP-GET and HTTP-POST protocols, you cannot build Web methods that take complex types as parameters or return values, such as ADO.NET DataSet or structure type. For simple Web services, this limitation may be acceptable. However, if you want to build much more elaborate Web services, you can use SOAP bindings.

Simple Object Access Protocol

SOAP, one of the key elements in a Web service, is a protocol used for messaging. It is completely XML-based. SOAP specifications are standardized by W3C and are used by most companies that develop Web services.

SOAP provides a complete set of rules for messages, called SOAP envelopes, as well as the rules for issues, such as data encoding, message handling, and message binding, to other protocols, such as HTTP. One of the great advantages of using a SOAP message is that it is not restricted to any particular protocol. However, the HTTP protocol is most commonly used since it is not restricted to any one operating system.

A SOAP message is a simple XML document, which always contains the mandatory envelope and body elements and can contain a few optional elements, such as `<Header>` and `<Fault>`. Listing 18.5 shows the syntax of a SOAP message:

Listing 18.5: Syntax of a SOAP Message

```
<?xml version="1.0"?>
<soap:Envelope
xmlns:soap="http://www.w3.org/2001/12/soap-envelope"
soap:encodingStyle="http://www.w3.org/2001/12/soap-encoding">
   <soap:Header>
         ...
         ...
   </soap:Header>
   <soap:Body>
         ...
         ...
         <soap:Fault>
               ...
               ...
         </soap:Fault>
   </soap:Body>
</soap:Envelope>
```

As already mentioned, the envelope and body elements are always required in any SOAP message. The following is the syntax of both these elements:

```
<?xml version="1.0"?>
<soap:Envelope
xmlns:soap="http://www.w3.org/2001/12/soap-envelope"
soap:encodingStyle="http://www.w3.org/2001/12/soap-encoding">
   ...
```

Message information goes in the <body> element, as shown in Listing 18.6:

Listing 18.6: Message Information Inside the <body> Element

```
...
</soap:Envelope>
<?xml version="1.0"?>
<soap:Envelope
xmlns:soap="http://www.w3.org/2001/12/soap-envelope"
soap:encodingStyle="http://www.w3.org/2001/12/soap-encoding">
  <soap:Body>
        <m:GetName xmlns:m="http://www.mydomain.com/NamesData">
              <m:record>1</m:record>
        </m:GetName>
  </soap:Body>
</soap:Envelope>
```

After knowing about the infrastructure of ASP.NET Web services, let's move on to the code model of the ASP.NET Web services.

The Code Model of ASP.NET Web Services

A Web service contains two parts, the entry point for a Web service and the code that is used to implement the functionality of a Web service. In ASP.NET, the entry point for any Web service is a text file with the `.asmx` extension. This file references the code in precompiled assemblies, in a code-behind file or in the file with the `.asmx` extension itself.

The `WebService` directive determines the entry point for the implementation of a Web service, which is at the top of the `.asmx` file. When you create a Web service through the ASP.NET Web Service template, you will find a code-behind file, such as `Service.cs`, to write the code for the Web service.

The code model of ASP.NET Web services consists of the following two parts:

- The `WebService` directive
- The code-behind file

Now, let's discuss these two parts in detail.

The WebService Directive

The WebService directive defines Web service-specific attributes, such as Namespace and Description attributes, used by the ASP.NET compilers and parsers. The attributes of the `WebService` directive are as follows:

- **Language**—Notifies the ASP.NET compiler of the programming language in which the class has been written, such as `C#`, `VB`, or `JS`.
- **Class**—Notifies the ASP.NET compiler of the class name to expose as a Web service. A Web service application can contain multiple classes and it is not necessary that all the classes belong to the Web service; therefore, you must inform the ASP.NET compiler of the classes to expose.

For example,

In VB

```
<%@ WebService Language="VB" Class="MyFirstWebservice" %>
```

In C#

```
<%@ WebService Language="C#" Class="MyFirstWebservice" %>
```

In the preceding example, the programming languages used for the Web service are `VB` and `C#`, and the class is `MyFirstWebservice`.

The Code-Behind File

In the code-behind approach for programming Web services, the `WebService` directive is separated from the supporting source code. The `WebService` directive is placed on the file with the `.asmx` extension, and the supporting source code is placed on the file with the WebService`.cs` extension in C#, and with the WebService.vb extension in VB. Before using the Web service, the file with the source code must be compiled into an assembly and placed in the `\bin` directory of the particular Web service, which is automatically done when your project is built or compiled.

When a request is sent to a Web service for the first time, ASP.NET accesses the `.asmx` file and reads the `WebService` directive to get the name of the class file that contains the supporting logic. ASP.NET then searches for the compiled class in an assembly in the `\bin` directory of the Web service project, such as `MyFirstWebservice`. If there is more than one assembly in the `\bin` folder of Web service project, then ASP.NET examines each assembly until it finds the appropriate class.

The main advantage of storing the compiled source code in the code-behind file is that a malicious user is not able to gain access to the code, since the code is not stored in the Web server. The syntax of declaring a code-behind attribute is:

In VB

```
<%@ WebService Language="vb"
   CodeBehind=" CodeBehind="~/App_Code/ MyFirstWebService.vb"
   Class=" MyFirstWebservice " %>
```

In C#

```
<%@ WebService Language="c#"
   CodeBehind=" CodeBehind="~/App_Code/ MyFirstWebService.cs"
   Class="MyFirstWebservice " %>
```

Let's discuss the various attributes of the code-behind file.

The WebService Attribute

The `WebService` attribute is a member of the `System.Web.Services` namespace, and conveys information about a Web service, such as the name, description, and namespace of the Web service. The `WebService` attribute consists of the following three properties:

- **Name**—Defines a class name of the Web service used within the WSDL document. When a proxy uses the WSDL document and builds a proxy class, the name of the class generated corresponds to the name value of the Web service. This property allows overriding the default value.
- **Description**—Provides a brief description about the functions performed by a class, such as `MyFirstWebservice`, of the Web service.
- **Namespace**—Sets the XML namespace for the Web service, which is generally a URL. The reason for using a URL for setting the XML namespace of a Web service is that a URL is always unique.

For example,

In VB

```
<WebService(Name:="CalculateInterest",Description:="This class contains methods for
   calculating Simple Interest as well as Compound Interest  and population of DataSet
   with the calculated Amount.", Namespace:=http://www.InterestRate.com/")>
```

In C#

```
[WebService(Name="CalculateInterest",Description="This class contains methods for
   calculating Simple Interest as well as Compound Interest  and population of DataSet
   with the calculated Amount.", Namespace=http://www.InterestRate.com/")]
```

In the preceding example, the value of the `Name` property is defined as follows:

```
Name="CalculateInterest"
```

The value of the `Description` property is defined as follows:

```
Description="This class contains methods for calculating Simple Interest as well as
  Compound Interest  and population of DataSet with the calculated Amount."
```

The value of the `Namespace` property is defined as follows:

```
Namespace=http://www.InterestRate.com/"
```

The System.Web.Services.WebService Class

A Web service is inherited from the `System.Web.Services.WebService` class. The `WebService` class defines some common ASP.NET objects, such as `Application`, `User`, `Session`, and `Context`, so that you can use them directly in your Web service without redefining them.

The inheritance hierarchy for the `WebService` class is as follows:

```
System.Object
  System.ComponentModel.MarshalByValueComponent
       System.Web.Services.WebService
```

The WebMethod Attribute

A Web service class can include one or more `WebMethod` attributes, which are accessible across the HTTP protocol. The `WebMethod` attribute consists of the following six properties:

- **CacheDuration**—Specifies the time (in seconds) for the response of the request sent by a client. It should be held in the cache of the system. Caching is disabled by default. The performance of the Web service can be improved by putting the response of the service in cache. For example,

```
[WebMethod(CacheDuration=30)]
```

In the preceding example, the value of the `CacheDuration` property of the `[WebMethod]` attribute is set to `30`.

- **BufferResponse**—Allows the server to store the response produced by a Web service. After the whole response is stored, the response is transmitted to the clients, all at once. By default, the `BufferResponse` property is set to True. If the `BufferResponse` property is set to False, the response is transmitted to the client, as the response is constructed on the server.
- **Description**—Provides a brief description of the `[WebMethod]` attribute and this description becomes a part of the WSDL document.
- **EnableSession**—Enables the session state for a Web method. By default, this property is set to `False`.
- **MessageName**—Identifies the polymorphic methods within a class when working with overloaded Web methods.
- **TransactionOption**—Enables a Web method to act as a root object in the transaction. This means that the Web method can call other transaction-enabled objects, but it cannot be called by another object as a part of the transaction. This limitation exists because the HTTP protocol is stateless.

Till now, you have learned about the infrastructure of ASP.NET Web services and the code model of ASP.NET Web services. Now, let's discuss the properties of a Web service.

Web Service Properties

A Web service consists of many properties, which are defined in the `WebService` class. This class does not have any public method or event, which is non-inherited. Table 18.4 lists the public properties of the `WebService` class:

Table 18.4: Public Properties of the WebService Class

Property	Description
Application	Obtains the application object for the current HTTP request.
Context	Obtains the `HttpContext` object for the current request, which encapsulates all HTTP-specific context used by the HTTP server to process Web requests.

Table 18.4: Public Properties of the WebService Class

Property	Description
Server	Obtains the `HttpServerUtility` object for the current request.
Session	Obtains the `HttpSessionState` object for the current request.
SoapVersion	Obtains the version of the SOAP protocol used to make the SOAP request to a Web service.
User	Obtains the server User object. This property can be used to authenticate whether a user is authorized to execute the request.

After learning about the public properties of the `WebService` class, let's discuss the following properties in detail:

- Application
- Context
- Server
- Session

Application Property

The `Application` property of the `WebService` class is used to obtain the application object for the current HTTP request. The syntax of this property is:

In VB

```
<BrowsableAttribute(False)> _
Public ReadOnly Property Application As HttpApplicationState
```

In C#

```
[BrowsableAttribute(false)]
public HttpApplicationState Application
{
   get;
}
```

Now, let's take an example to show how the `Application` property obtains the application object for the current HTTP request. In this example, we show that the value of the `Visit_Counter` variable in the `Application` property obtains the application object and is incremented by `1` each time the browser calls a Web service. Listing 18.7 shows an example of the `Application` property:

Listing 18.7: Example of the `Application` Property

In VB

```
<%@ WebService Language="VB" Class="Util"%>
Imports System.Web.Services
Public Class Util
   Inherits WebService
   <WebMethod(Description := "Number of Visits", _
   EnableSession := False)> _
   Public Function Visit_Counter() As Integer
         If Application("Visit_Counter ") Is Nothing Then
               Application("Visit_Counter ") = 1
         Else
               Application("Visit_Counter ") = CInt(Application("Visit_Counter ")) + 1
         End If
         Return CInt(Application("Visit_Counter "))
   End Function
End Class
```

In C#

```
<%@ WebService Language="C#" Class="Util"%>
 using System.Web.Services;
public class Util: WebService
{
  [ WebMethod(Description="Number of Visits",EnableSession=false)]
  public int Visit_Counter () {
        if (Application["Visit_Counter"] == null)
        {
              Application["Visit_Counter"] = 1;
        }
        else
        {
          Application["Visit_Counter"] = ((int) Application["Visit_Counter"]) + 1;
        }
        return ((int) Application["Visit_Counter"]);
}  }
```

You can use both the application state and the session state in your Web service. The application state is enabled throughout the session during which a Web service is accessed, whereas in the preceding listing, the session state is disabled for a Web method by setting the `EnableSession` property of the `[WebMethod]` attribute to `False`.

Context Property

The `Context` property of the `WebService` class is used to obtain the `HttpContext` class for the current request that encapsulates all the HTTP-specific contexts, which the HTTP server uses to process Web requests. The syntax of this property is:

In VB

```
<BrowsableAttribute(False)> _
Public ReadOnly Property Context As HttpContext
```

In C#

```
[BrowsableAttribute(false)]
public HttpContext Context
{
  get;
}
```

Listing 18.8 demonstrates how to get the request time on the server by using the Context property:

Listing 18.8: Example of the `Context` Property

In VB

```
<%@ WebService Language="VB" Class="Util" %>
Imports System
Imports System.Web.Services
Public Class Util
  Inherits WebService
  <WebMethod(Description:="Get the Request Time on the Server", _
  EnableSession := False)> _
  Public Function GetTime() As String
        Return Context.Timestamp.TimeOfDay.ToString()
  End Function
End Class
```

In C#

```
<%@ WebService Language="C#" Class="Util" %>
   using System;
   using System.Web.Services;
   public class Util: WebService
   {
           [ WebMethod(Description="Get the Request Time on the
           Server",EnableSession=false)]
           public string GetTime()
           {
                   return Context.Timestamp.TimeOfDay.ToString();
   }
}
```

The preceding example returns the time of the request on the server by using the `Context` property.

Server Property

The `Server` property of the `WebService` class is used to obtain the `HttpServerUtility` class for the current request. The syntax of this property is:

In VB

```
<BrowsableAttribute(False)> _
Public ReadOnly Property Server As HttpServerUtility
```

In C#

```
[BrowsableAttribute(false)]
public HttpServerUtility Server
{
   get;
}
```

Listing 18.9 demonstrates how to get the name of the Web server by using the Server property:

Listing 18.9: Example of the `Server` Property

In VB

```
<%@ WebService Language="VB" Class="Util" %>
Imports System.Web.Services
Public Class Util
   Inherits WebService
   <WebMethod(Description := " Get The Computer Name of the Web  server ", _
   EnableSession := False)> _
   Public Function GetComputerName() As String
   Return Server.MachineName
   End Function
End Class
```

In C#

```
<%@ WebService Language="C#" Class="Util" %>
   using System.Web.Services;
   public class Util: WebService
   {
           [ WebMethod(Description="Get The Computer Name of the Web
           server",EnableSession=false)]
           public string GetComputerName()
           {
                   return Server.MachineName;
   }
}
```

Session Property

The `Session` property of the `WebService` class is used to obtain the `HttpSessionState` instance for the current request. The syntax of this property is:

In VB

```
<BrowsableAttribute(False)> _
Public ReadOnly Property Session As HttpSessionState
```

In C#

```
[BrowsableAttribute(false)]
public HttpSessionState Session
{
  get;
}
```

Listing 18.10 demonstrates how to count the number of times the `NumberOfSessions` method of a Web service has been accessed by a particular session by using the `Session` property:

Listing 18.10: Example of the `Session` Property

In VB

```
<%@ WebService Language="VB" Class="Util" %>
Imports System.Web.Services
Public Class Util
   Inherits WebService
   <WebMethod(Description := "Number of Sessions", _
   EnableSession := True)>
   Public Function NumberOfSessions() As Integer
           If Session("SessionNumber") Is Nothing Then
                   Session("SessionNumber") = 1
           Else
                   Session("SessionNumber") = CInt(Session("SessionNumber")) + 1

           End If
           Return CInt(Session("SessionNumber"))
   End Function
End Class
```

In C#

```
<%@ WebService Language="C#" Class="Util" %>
   using System.Web.Services;
   public class Util: WebService
   {
           [ WebMethod(Description="Number of Sessions",EnableSession=true)]
           public int NumberOfSessions()
           {
                   if (Session["SessionNumber"] == null) {
                           Session["SessionNumber"] = 1;
                   }
                   else {
                   Session["SessionNumber"] = ((int) Session["SessionNumber"]) + 1;
                   }
                   return ((int) Session["SessionNumber"]);
           }
   }
```

Next, let's find out how to use ASP.NET AJAX with Web services.

ASP.NET AJAX and Web Services

You can use ASP.NET AJAX to create ASP.NET AJAX enabled Web services. These Web services can be accessed through a client-side scripting language, such as JavaScript. The Web service communication layer enables Web pages to transport data to and from the server. This layer uses AJAX technology to call a Web service. The exchange of data between the client and the server happens in asynchronous mode in the JavaScript Object Notation (JSON) format.

The ASP.NET AJAX Web services architecture is categorized as follows:

- ASP.NET AJAX client architecture for Web services
- ASP.NET AJAX server architectuie for Web services

Now, let's describe them one by one.

ASP.NET AJAX Client Architecture for Web Services

The browser uses proxy classes to call a Web service method. A proxy class is a script generated when a Web page is loaded. The client's object of the proxy class represents the exposed messages of a Web service. When a user calls a Web service, the client script calls the related Web methods of the proxy class. These calls are made asynchronously through the `XMLHTTP` object. You have to enable proxy classes to make a call to a Web service through the library script types contained in the Web service communication layer present in the ASP.NET AJAX client architecture for Web services. The following two approaches are used to call a Web service:

- **Using the HTTP-POST Protocol**—Consists of a body containing the data that the client's browser sends to the server. There is restriction on the amount of data to be transmitted. Therefore, whenever the transmitted data exceeds the size limit of the `GET` request, you can use the `POST` request. The transmission of data starts from the client's browser, when the client serializes the request into the JSON format and sends it as `POST` data to the server. When the server gets the request, it first de-serializes the data in the JSON format into the .NET Framework compatible type and then makes the actual call to the Web service. In response, the server serializes the return values and passes them back to the client, and the client de-serializes these values into JavaScript objects for processing.
- **Using the HTTP-GET Protocol**—Consists of a query string to send the request parameters to the server. The `GET` request uses the `ScriptMethodAttribute` attribute to call a configured method of a Web service. The size of the data to be transmitted is restricted to the length of the URL allowed by the client's browser.

Figure 18.2 shows the ASP.NET AJAX client architecture for Web services:

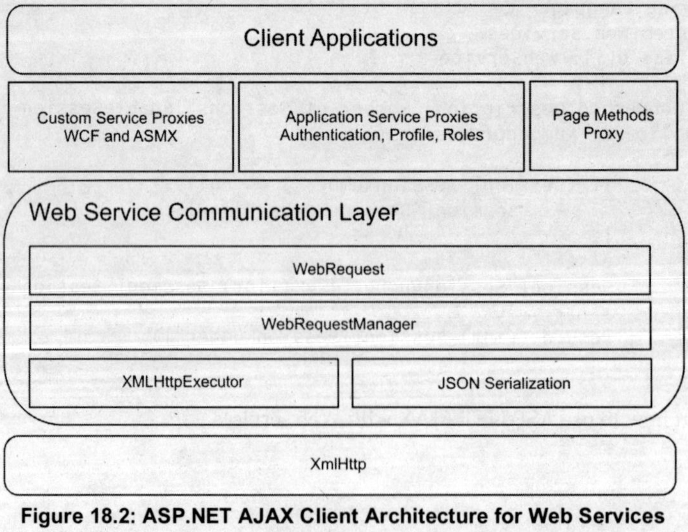

Figure 18.2: ASP.NET AJAX Client Architecture for Web Services

As shown in Figure 18.2, the elements of the ASP.NET AJAX client architecture are as follows:

- **Custom Service Proxies WCF and ASMX**—Contains the client script that the server automatically generates and downloads to the client's browser.
- **Application Service Proxies Authentication, Profile, Roles**—Enables you to log on or log off the Web browser using the JavaScript language without making a round trip to the server. The server authentication application service generates the `AuthenticationService` proxy class. The Role proxy class enables you to make a group of the users of Web services and treat each group as a single user through the JavaScript language, without making round trips to the server. The server roles application service generates the `RoleService` proxy class. This approach can be useful to grant or deny the access rights of resources on the server. The Profile proxy class enables clients to get information about the current user's profile through the JavaScript language without making round trips to the server. The server profile application service generates the `ProfileService` class.
- **Page Methods Proxy**—Provides scripting infrastructure for the client script, which enables you to call static methods as if they are the methods of a Web service.
- **Web Service Communication Layer**—Enables clients to communicate with Web services on the `server`. This element is a library of `client script` types. The Web service communication layer consists of the following elements:
  - **WebRequest**—Provides the functionality to the client script to make a Web request
  - **WebRequestManager**—Manages the flow of requests when the WebRequest object issues two or more requests for Web services
  - **XmlHttpExecutor**—Uses the browser's XMLHTTP support to make asynchronous network requests
  - **JSON Serialization**—Provides the serialization of JavaScript objects into the JSON format
  - **XMLHttp**-Used to send HTTP request to the server and load the response

ASP.NET AJAX Server Architecture for Web Services

The ASP.NET AJAX server consists of ASP.NET Web server controls and components that manage the user interface and execution flow of an application. It also manages serialization, validation, and control extensibility. There are also ASP.NET Web services that enable you to access ASP.NET application services for forms authentication, roles, and user profiles.

Figure 18.3 shows the ASP.NET AJAX server architecture of a Web service in which the elements that enable communication with client applications are included:

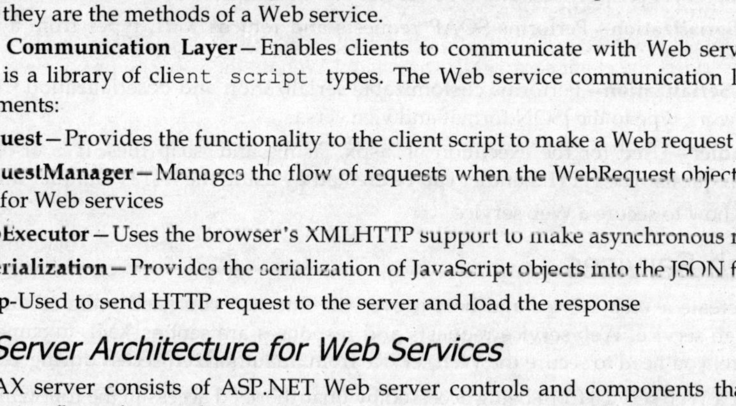

Figure 18.3: ASP.NET AJAX Server Architecture for Web Services

As shown in Figure 18.3, the elements of the ASP.NET AJAX server architecture are as follows:

- **Custom Services WCF and ASMX**—Provides the functionality to a Web service and returns suitable response to the client.
- **Application Service Authentication, Profile, Roles**—Enables you to log on or log off through the client JavaScript. The authentication service generates the Authentication proxy class. There is no need to instantiate the authentication service as it is always available to the user of the Web service. The Role service generates the roles information of the currently authenticated user accessed by the client's JavaScript of the role proxy class. The Profile service generates a profile proxy class to get and set the profile properties of the user associated with the current request.
- **Page Methods**—Enables a method in an ASP.NET page to be called as if it is a Web service method. This element must be defined in the page that performs the page method call.
- **Web Service Communication Layer**—Enables a server to communicate with the Web services. This element is a library of server script types. The Web service communication layer consists of the following elements:
  - **XML Serialization**—Performs SOAP requests and returns XML types from a JSON request in Web services.
  - **JSON Serialization**—Performs customizable serialization and deserialization from the common .NET Framework type to the JSON format and vice versa.
- **HTTP Handler**—Used for the execution of .aspx, .asmx, and .soap files. It is also used by ASP.NET to handle the requests. The HTTP handler can be created by using the IHTTPHandler interface.

Now, let's learn how to secure a Web service.

Securing Web Services

If you want to create a Web service and host it over the Internet, you need to be able to control and regulate access to the Web service. Web service requests and responses are sent as XML documents, which are in text format. Therefore, you need to secure the Web service from unauthorized access during such transmission.

You can prevent a Web service from being accessed by unauthorized access in the following two ways:

- Using encryption and message-based security
- Using authentication and access controls for the Web service

Now, let's learn about these methods in detail.

Encryption and Message-Based Security

Encryption is the process of scrambling the text that your Web service contains so that only the intended user is able to decrypt (convert encrypted data back into its original form) it with the help of a key.

Message-based security allows you to send encrypted messages to anyone, without worrying about the decryption of the messages by a malicious user. You can detect any modification made by someone in the message straightaway because the signature (private key) attached to the message becomes invalid, and you can then safely throw the message. This type of security works by encrypting the message at both the request and the response levels.

Authentication and Access Controls for the Web Service

Authentication is a process of validating a user against the user credentials provided by the user. One way to secure a Web service is to make it mandatory for the users, who want to use the Web service, to provide their credentials in the form of a user ID and password. If they fail to do that, they are refused access to the Web service.

Immediate Solutions

Creating a Web Service

Before looking at the tasks that we need to perform to create a Web service, let's look at the points to be considered while creating a Web service. The following list enumerates a few noteworthy points:

- Ensure that the communication between a Web application that requests a Web service and a Web server that provides the Web service is asynchronous. In asynchronous communication, the Web application does not need to stop its processes until the Web server responds to its request.
- Minimize the number of requests that a Web application needs to send to a Web server to obtain a Web service. You can do this by combining similar tasks of the Web service in a single method. For example, suppose you want to create a Web service that provides information about sports items. Instead of creating separate methods for providing information about the name, price, and manufacturer of each item, you can create a method that provides complete information about the items in a single request. The efficiency of the network over which the information is transmitted increases with the decrease in the number of requests required to obtain the Web service. This is because large amount of information, instead of small chunks, is transmitted at once.
- Ensure that the Web service is created by using the concepts of object-oriented programming. You can ensure this by abstracting the implementation details of the Web service from the Web application accessing the Web service and by using inheritance and polymorphism to create the Web service. Object-oriented programming concepts allow you to reuse code to create a Web service and simplify the design of the Web service.
- Minimize the time a Web server takes to respond to the request of a Web application. You can minimize the response time of the Web server by creating a cache to store the output of the request sent by a Web application to a Web server, for a specific period of time. Now, when a Web application requests a Web service, its request can be fulfilled from the cache. This reduces the time and amount of processing required to obtain the result of the request from the Web server.

Now, let's move on to the tasks that we need to perform while creating a Web service in ASP.NET. These include the following:

1. Creating a Web service project
2. Declaring the Web service
3. Setting the `WebService` attribute
4. Declaring methods for a Web service

Creating a Web Service Project

You can create a Web service project with the help of the Web Service template found in the middle template available in the Add New Item dialog box.

Figure 18.4 shows the Web Service template in the Add New Item dialog box:

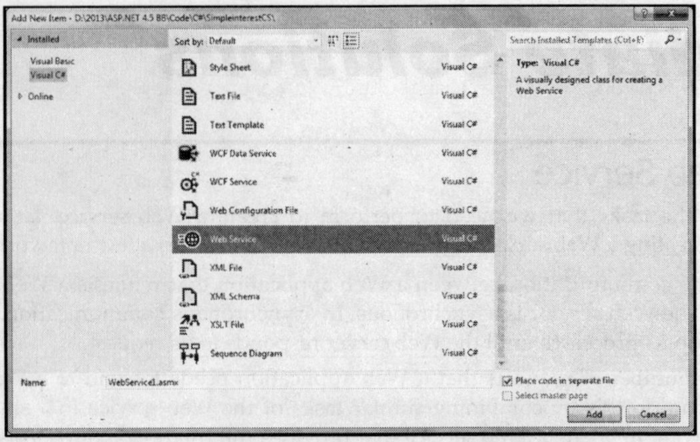

Figure 18.4: Displaying the Web Service Template

Select the Web Service template from the Add New Item dialog box to create a Web service. Next, select the required language for the Web service, enter the name of the Web service in the Name text box, and click the Add button.

When you create the Web service project, notice that it already contains a Web service, the functionality of which is defined in the `HelloWorld` function in the code-behind file. You can view the Web`Service` file by right-clicking the Web`Service.asmx` file and selecting the View Code option from the context menu. Another way of viewing the Web`Service` file is by expanding the `App_Code` node in the Solution Explorer window. You can modify the Web`Service.asmx` and Web`Service` file to create a new Web service according to your requirements.

Declaring the Web Service

The next step after creating the Web service project is to declare the Web service in a WebService.`asmx` file.

A Web service is declared using the `@ WebService` directive that provides information required by the compilers and parsers of ASP.NET to compile and run the Web service. This includes information on the following attributes of Web services:

- `Class`—Specifies the name of the class that implements the Web service.
- `CodeBehind`—Specifies the file name that contains the implementation of the Web service. This attribute is used when neither the file containing the `@ WebService` directive nor the file in the `Bin` folder contains the class that implements the Web service.
- `Debug`—Specifies whether to debug the Web service during compilation. The Web service is debugged during compilation if the value of the `Debug` attribute is set to `True`.
- `Language`—Specifies the language in which the Web service is compiled. You can set the `Language` attribute to any language supported by .NET, such as VB, C#, or jscript .

The syntax of the `@ WebService` directive is:

In VB and C#

```
<%@ WebService attribute="value"…] %>
```

Before declaring a Web service using these attributes, you need to determine whether the class containing the implementation of the Web service is present in the same assembly that contains the `@WebService` directive or in a separate assembly in the `Bin` folder. You need to determine this because the declaration of the Web service differs in both the cases.

If the class resides in the same assembly as the `@WebService` directive, you just need to specify the name of the class in the `Class` attribute. However, if the class resides in a separate assembly, you need to specify the name of the assembly in which the class resides, in addition to the class name, in the `Class` attribute. Now, let's consider an example to understand this concept better.

Suppose the name of the class that implements your Web service is `Webserv` and it resides in the same assembly that contains the `@WebService` directive.

You can declare this Web service in Visual Studio 2012 by writing the following single-line code in the `Service.aspx` page:

In VB

```
<%@ WebService Language="VB" Class="Webserv" %>
```

In C#

```
<%@ WebService Language="C#" Class="Webserv" %>
```

However, if the `Webserv` Web service resides in a separate assembly, `Webserv_assembly`, then you need to write the following single-line code in the `Service.aspx` page to declare the Web service in Visual Studio 2012:

In VB

```
<%@ WebService Language="VB" Class="Webserv,WebServ_assembly " %>
```

In C#

```
<%@ WebService Language="C#" Class=" WebServ,WebServ_assembly" %>
```

NOTE

You only need to change the Language attribute to C#, to declare the Web service in C#.

Till now, we have learned how to use the `@ WebService` directive to declare a Web service. Now, we look at one more directive, `@Assembly`. We need to understand this directive because in some situations we need to use it as well while declaring a Web service. We first look at such situations and then explore the attributes of this directive.

Suppose you want your Web service to use some assemblies that contain pre-defined interfaces and classes. These interfaces and classes can be user-defined as well as system-defined. If these assemblies reside in the same assembly as the `@ WebService` directive or in the `Bin` folder of the Web application containing your website, then they are linked to your Web service automatically. However, this may not always be the case. Therefore, in such situations, you need to use the `@ Assembly` directive to explicitly link these assemblies to the Web service.

The `@ Assembly` directive associates an assembly with a Web service when the Web service is compiled. This allows the Web service to use the classes and interfaces defined in that assembly. You need to specify the name of the assembly in its `Name` attribute to use the `@ Assembly` directive to associate an assembly with a Web service. You do not need to specify the extension of the assembly while setting the `Name` attribute. The syntax for setting the `Name` attribute is:

In VB and C#

```
<%@ Assembly Name="assemblyname" %>
```

The `@ Assembly` directive also allows you to include a code file other than the assembly in a Web service. For example, you can include a Visual Basic or C# code file in a Web service by using the `@ Assembly` directive. You can do so by specifying the path of the file in the `Src` attribute of the `@ Assembly` directive. The syntax for using the `Src` attribute is:

In VB and C#

```
<%@ Assembly Src="pathname" %>
```

Setting the WebService Attribute

The `WebService` attribute is used to provide additional information about a Web service, such as the functionality of the Web service. However, it is not mandatory to use the `WebService` attribute in a Web service.

You can also use the `WebService` attribute to set a default namespace, `http://tempuri.org`, for a Web service. However, to differentiate your Web service from other Web services available on the Internet, you should change the default namespace, while publishing the Web service. This allows users to uniquely identify their Web service. You need to apply it to the class that implements the Web service to set the `WebService` attribute. The syntax for using the `WebService` attribute is:

In VB

```
<WebService(Namespace:=" http://tempuri.org/")> _
Public Class classname
```

In C#

```
[WebService(Namespace="http://tempuri.org/")]
public class classname
```

Declaring Methods for a Web Service

You need to declare the methods that define the functionality of the Web service to implement a Web service. The methods of a Web service should be able to send and receive data to and from the Web applications over the Internet, so that the Web service can be accessed by the Web applications. You can enable Web service methods to communicate with the Web applications by declaring the methods `Public` and by applying the `WebMethod` attribute to the methods.

The `WebMethod` attribute enables a Web service method to communicate with a Web application located at a local or remote location. The syntax for using the `WebMethod` attribute with a Web service method is:

In VB

```
< WebMethod()> _
 Public Function functioname() As returntype
```

In C#

```
[ WebMethod]
public returntype functionname()
```

Till now, we have learned the procedure involved in creating a Web service. Now, let's take an example in which we implement this procedure to create a Web service.

NOTE

We have used ASP.NET Empty Web Site template for creating the application.

Suppose you want to create a Web service that can be used by other applications to calculate simple interest. To do this, create an ASP.NET Web service application named `SimpleInterestCS` (`SimpleinterestVB` in VB and `SimpleinterestCS` in C#). Now, follow these steps:

1. Create method for implementing the Web service, namely, WebService.asmx. Add the code to create the method, shown in Listing 18.11, in the code-behind file of the `WebService.asmx` file:

Listing 18.11: Code for the Code-Behind File of the `WebService.asmx` File

In VB

```
Imports System.Web
Imports System.Web.Services
Imports System.Web.Services.Protocols
' To allow this Web Service to be called from script, using ASP.NET AJAX, uncomment the
  following line.
' <System.Web.Script.Services.ScriptService()> _
<WebService(Namespace:="http://tempuri.org/")> _
<WebServiceBinding(ConformsTo:=WsiProfiles.BasicProfile1_1)> _
<Global.Microsoft.VisualBasic.CompilerServices.DesignerGenerated()> _
Public Class WebService
    Inherits System.Web.Services.WebService
   <WebMethod()> _
   Public Function HelloWorld() As String
```

```
        Return "Hello World"
    End Function
        <WebMethod()> _
    Public Function CalculateSimpleInterest(ByVal principal As Double, ByVal rate As
         Double, ByVal duration As Integer) As Double
        Dim SI As Double
        SI = principal * rate * duration / 100
        Return SI
    End Function
End Class
```

In C#

```
using System;
using System.Collections.Generic;
using System.Linq;
using System.Web;
using System.Web.Services;
/// <summary>
/// Summary description for WebService
/// </summary>
[WebService(Namespace = "http://tempuri.org/")]
[WebServiceBinding(ConformsTo = WsiProfiles.BasicProfile1_1)]
// To allow this Web Service to be called from script, using ASP.NET AJAX, uncomment the
  following line.
// [System.Web.Script.Services.ScriptService]
public class WebService : System.Web.Services.WebService {
    public WebService () {
        //Uncomment the following line if using designed components
        //InitializeComponent();
    }
    [WebMethod]
    public string HelloWorld() {
        return "Hello World";
    }
    [WebMethod]
    public double CalculateSimpleInterest(double principal, double rate, int duration)
    {
        double SI;
        SI = principal * rate * duration / 100;
        return SI;
    }
}
```

2. Press the F5 key on the keyboard to execute the Web service. The output is shown in Figure 18.5.
3. Click the CalculateSimpleInterest link, as shown in Figure 18.5:

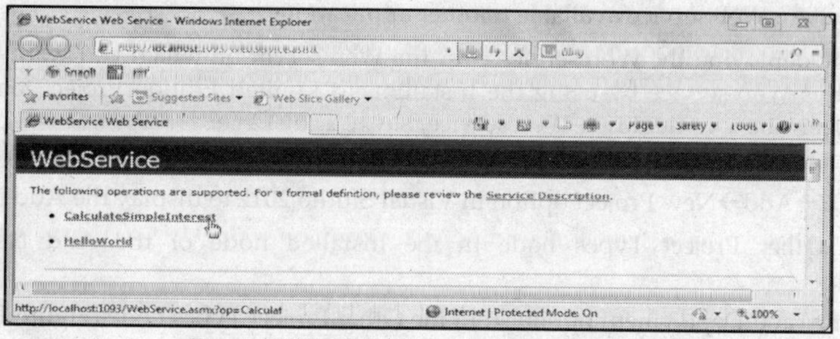

Figure 18.5: Selecting the Web Service

4. Enter the principal as 20000, rate as 5 and duration as 5 in the text boxes (Figure 18.6).
5. Click the Invoke button, as shown in Figure 18.6:

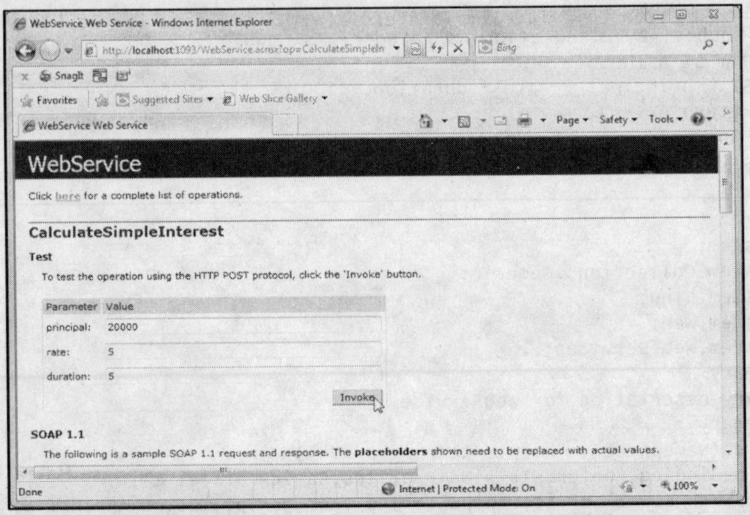

Figure 18.6: Entering Data to Calculate the Simple Interest

A new Internet Explorer window appears, displaying the resultant simple interest, as shown in Figure 18.7:

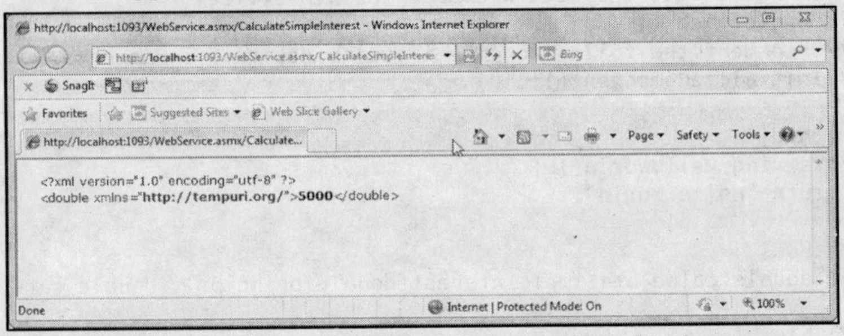

Figure 18.7:Displaying the Result of the Web Service

Now, let's know how to deploy this Web service so that it can be accessed by other Web applications.

Deploying a Web Service

After creating a Web service, the next step is to make the Web service available to other Web applications over the Internet. You need to transfer the Web service from the development environment to the production environment to make a Web service available to other applications.

You can do this by deploying the Web service over the Web server on which you want to run the Web service. You can deploy this Web service by using the InstallShield Limited Edition Project template of Visual Studio 2012. Now, let's learn how to deploy a Web service, say, `CalculateSimpleInterest`, created earlier. To do this, open the `CalculateSimpleInterest` Web service in Visual Studio 2012 and follow these steps:

1. Click the FILE→Add→New Project option in Visual Studio 2012 to display the Add New Project dialog box.
2. Expand the Other Project Types node in the Installed node of the Add New Project dialog box (Figure 18.8).
3. Select the Setup and Deployment option from the Other Project Types node (Figure 18.8).
4. Select the InstallShield Limited Edition Project from the middle pane (Figure 18.8).

5. Change the name Setup with SimpleInterestSetUp(SimpleInterestSetUpCS in C# and SimpleInterestSetUpVB in VB) in the Name text box and browse the location to save the project(Figure 18.8).
6. Click the OK button to add the SimpleInterestSetUpCS project in the Solution Explorer, as shown in Figure 18.8:

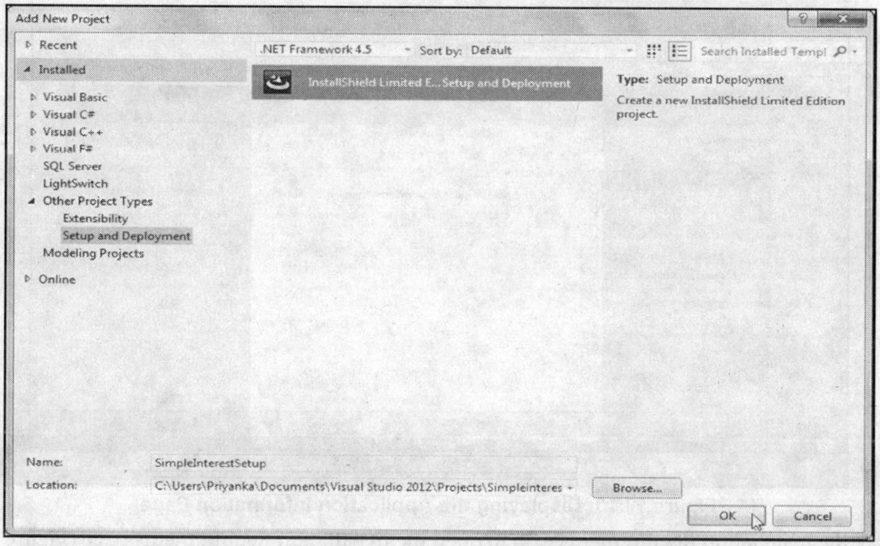

Figure 18.8: Creating Setup of the Web Service

The home page of the InstallShield Limited Edition Project software appears, as shown in Figure 18.9:

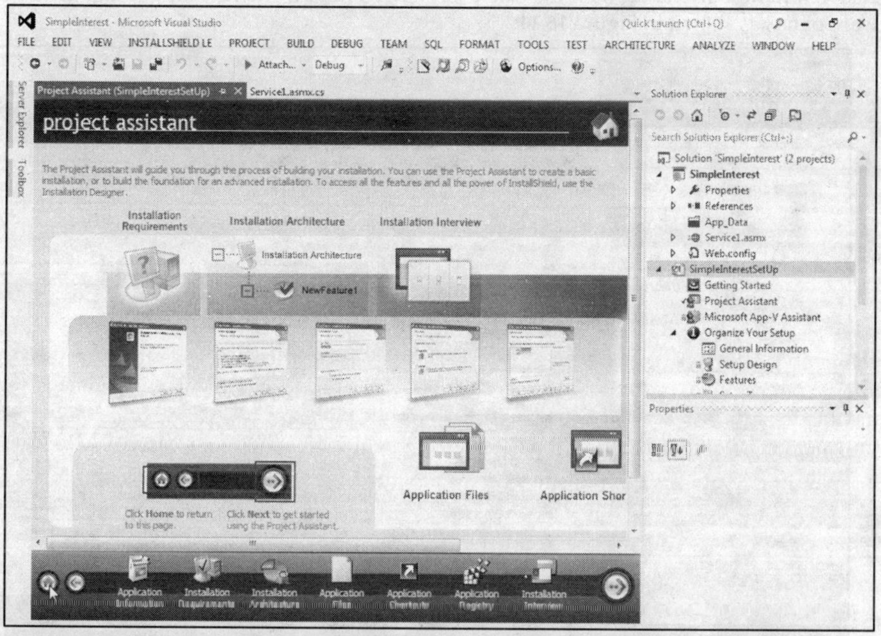

Figure 18.9: Displaying the Home Page of InstallShield Limited Edition Project

7. Click the Application Information icon to open the Application Information page (Figure 18.10).

8. Specify the general information about SimpleInterestSetUp, such as company name, version, and application name, as shown in Figure 18.10:

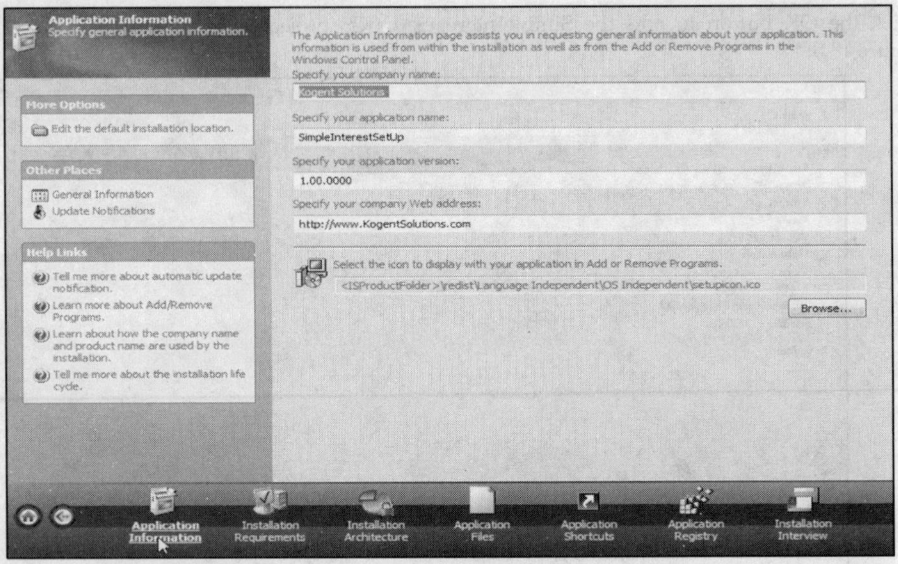

Figure 18.10: Displaying the Application Information Page

9. Click the Installation Requirements icon to open the Installation Requirements page (Figure 18.11).

10. Select any specific operating system or software required to run SimpleInterestSetUp. In our case, we have selected Yes radio button and then the Microsoft .NET Framework 4.5 Full package check box in Required Software pane , as shown in Figure 18.11:

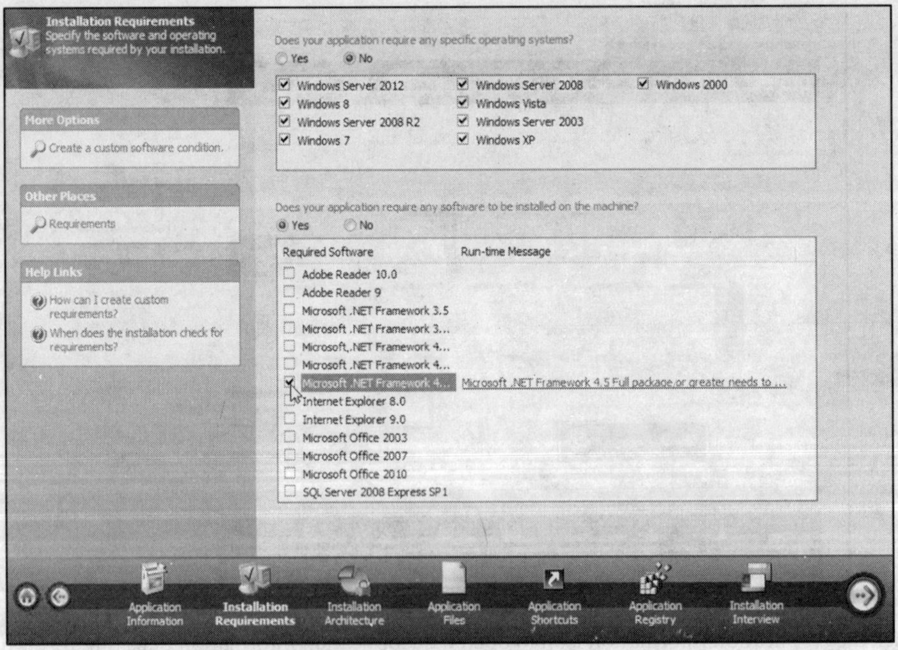

Figure 18.11: Showing the Installation Requirements Page

11. Click the Application Files icon to open the Application Files page, as shown in Figure 18.12:

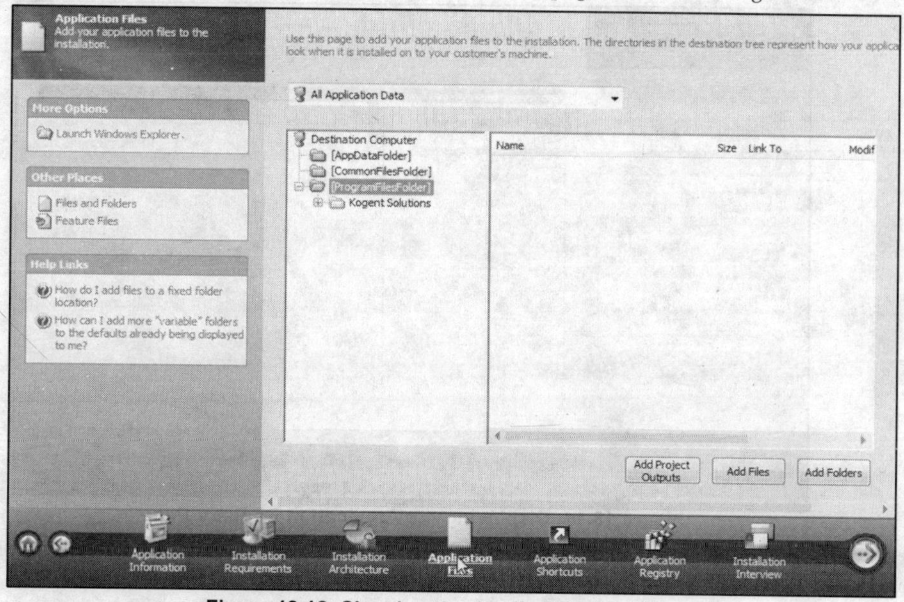

Figure 18.12: Showing the Application Files Page

12. Click the Add Project Outputs button. The Visual Studio Output Selector dialog box appears with a list of files in SimpleInterestSetUp (Figure 18.13).
13. Select the required files from the Visual Studio Output Selector dialog box (Figure 18.13).
14. Click the OK button, as shown in Figure 18.13:

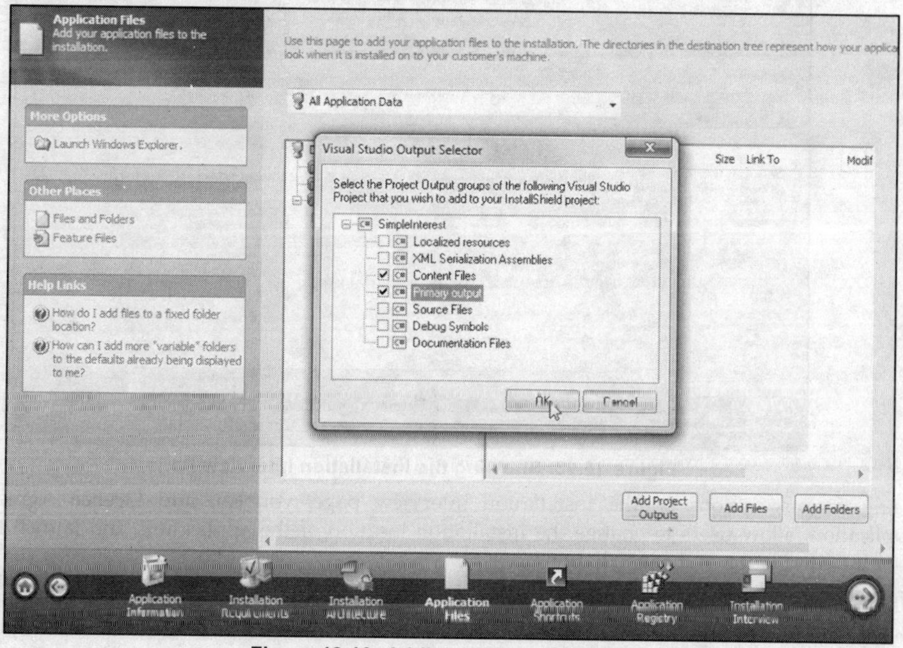

Figure 18.13: Adding the Required Files

15. Click the Application Registry icon to open the Application Registry page, as shown in Figure 18.14:

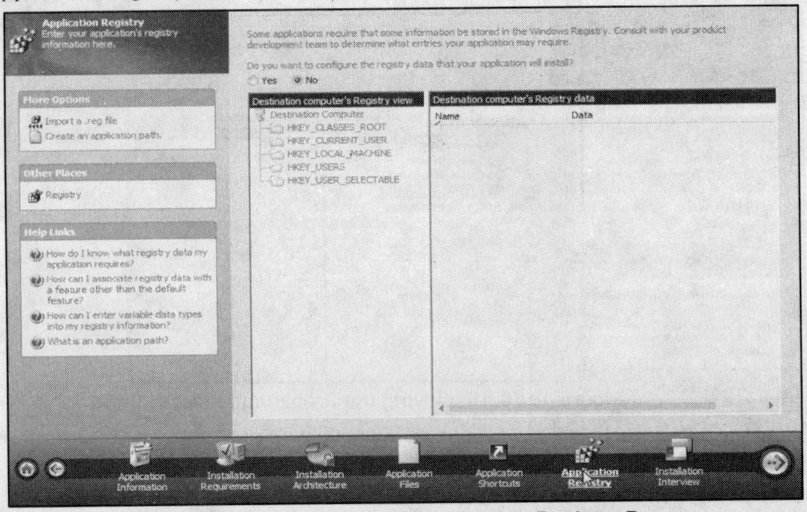

Figure 18.14: Displaying the Application Registry Page

You can add various registry keys to your application using the folders given under the Destination computer's Registry view.

16. Click the Installation Interview icon to open the Installation Interview page, as shown in Figure 18.15:

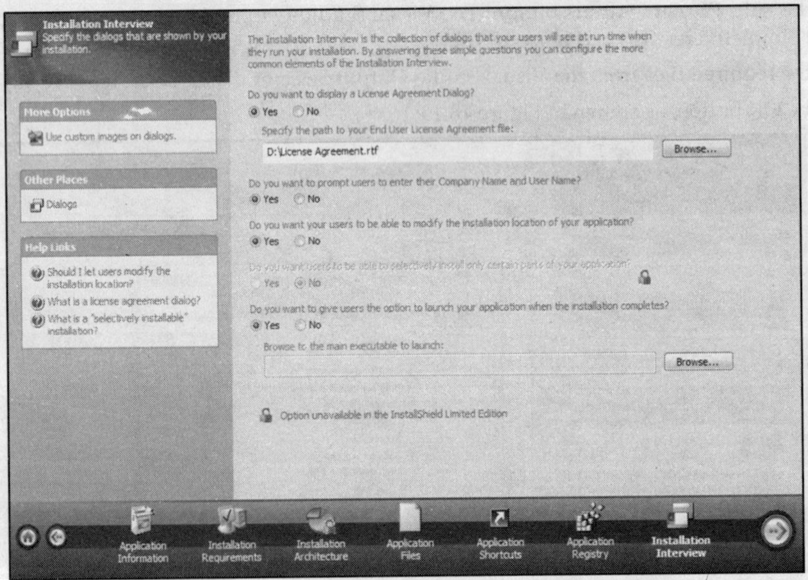

Figure 18.15: Showing the Installation Interview Page

Using various options on the Installation Interview page, you can add Licence Agreement to your application, allow users to change the installation location of the application, and launch the application after the completion of the installation.

17. Right-click the SimpleInterestSetUp project in Solution Explorer to open the context menu.
18. Select the Build option from the context menu to build the project. An .exe file of the SimpleInterestSetUp project is created at the same location of the project.

19. Browse the location of the .exe file of the project and double-click it to start the installation. InstallShield Wizard with the Preparing to Install page appears, as shown in Figure 18.16:

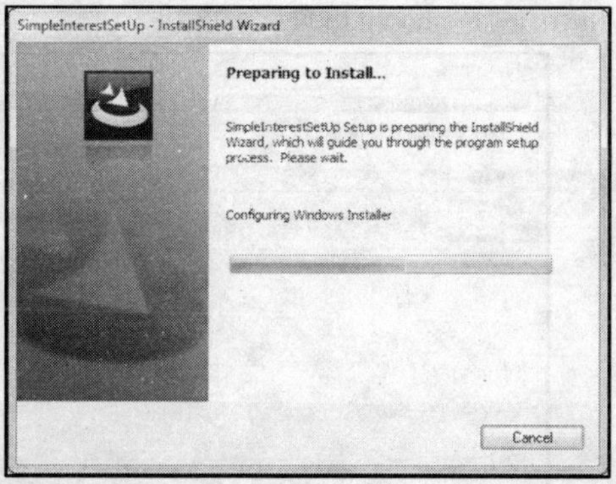

Figure 18.16: Displaying the Preparing to Install Page

The Welcome to the InstallShield Wizard for SimpleInterestSetUp page appears (Figure 18.17).

20. Click the Next button in the page to continue the installation, as shown in Figure 18.17:

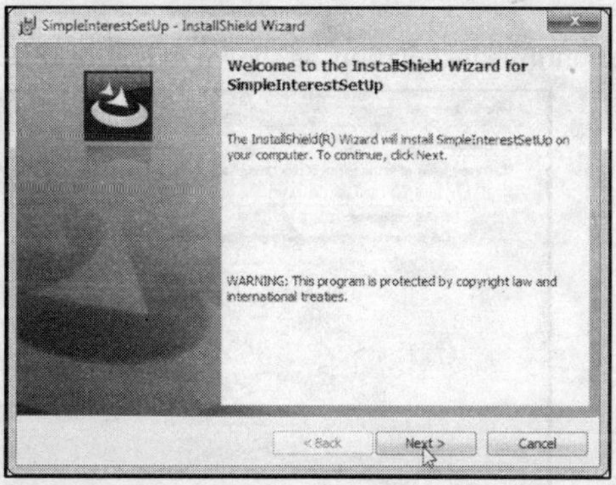

Figure 18.17: Displaying the Welcome to the InstallShield Wizard for SimpleInterestSetUp Page

The License Agreement page appears with the terms and conditions that you have written in the licence agreement file while creating the setup (Figure 18.18).

21. Select the I accept the terms in the license agreement radio button and then click the Next button to continue the installation, as shown in Figure 18.18:

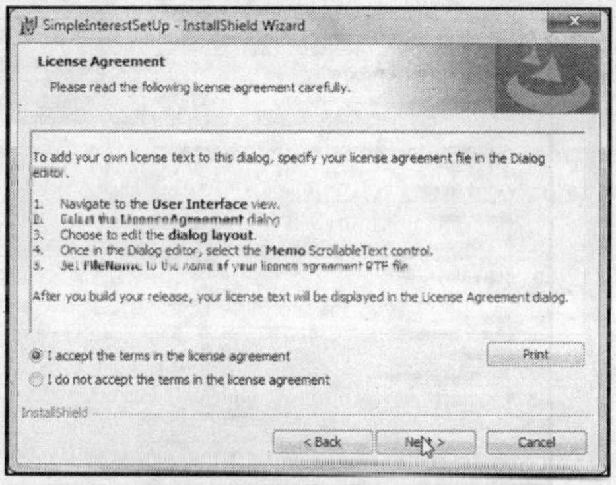

Figure 18.18: Displaying the License Agreement Page

The Customer Information page appears (Figure 18.19).

22. Specify the user name and organization name in the User Name and Organization text boxes, respectively (Figure 18.19).
23. Click the Next button in the page, as shown in Figure 18.19:

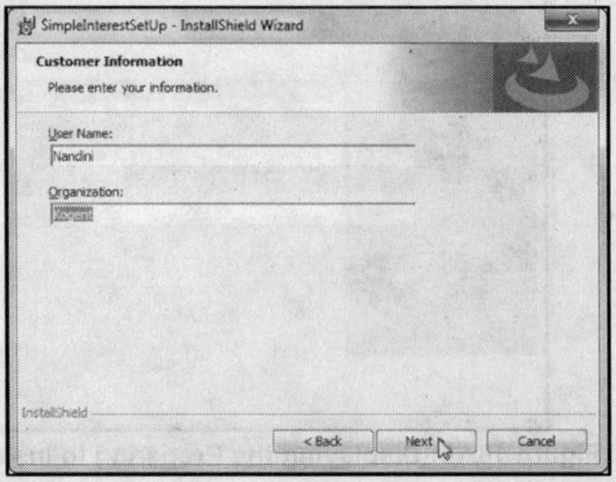

Figure 18.19: Displaying the Customer Information Page

The Destination Folder page appears showing the installation path of the SimpleInterestSetUp Web service (Figure 18.20).

24. Click the Next button to continue installation, as shown in Figure 18.20:

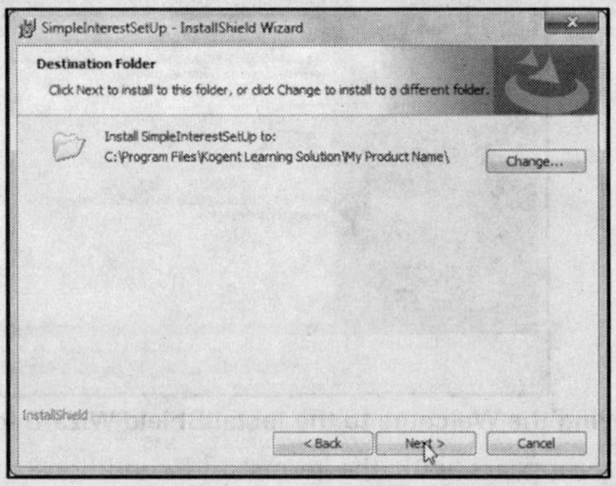

Figure 18.20: Displaying the Destination Folder Page

The Ready to Install the Program page appears to confirm the installation process (Figure 18.21).

25. Click the Install button to install the SimpleInterestSetUp Web service, as shown in Figure 18.21:

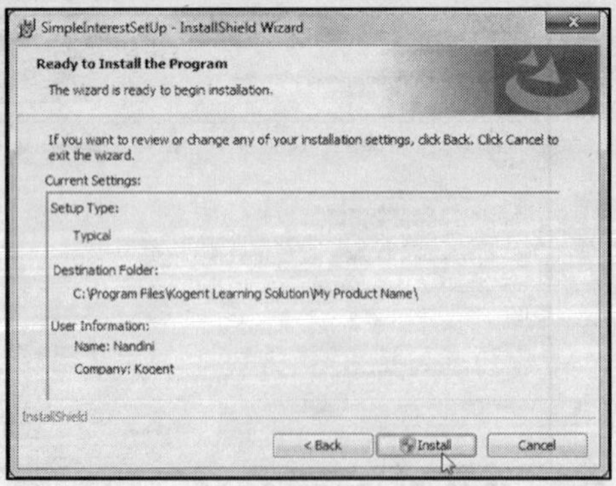

Figure 18.21: Displaying the Ready to Install the Program Page

26. The Installing SimpleInterestSetUp page appears displaying the installation status of SimpleInterestSetUp, as shown in Figure 18.22:

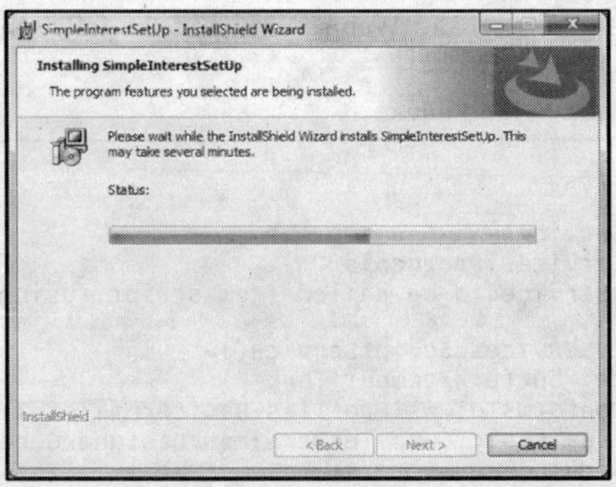

Figure 18.22: Displaying the Installation Process of SimpleInterestSetUp

The installation process can take few minutes. After the completion of installation process, the InstallShield Wizard Completed page appears (Figure 18.23).

27. Click the Finish button to exit the wizard, as shown in Figure 18.23:

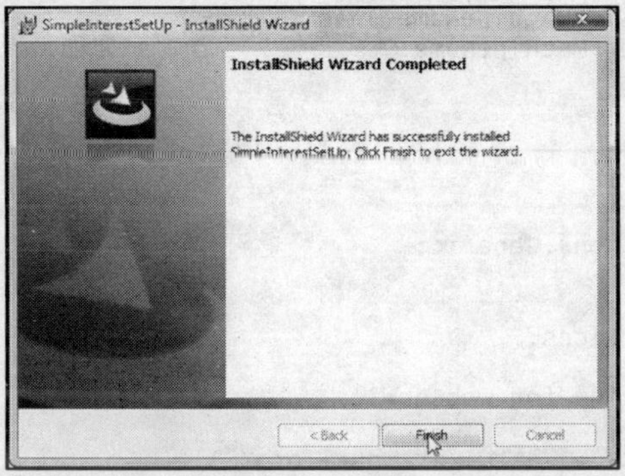

Figure 18.23: Displaying the InstallShield Wizard Completed Page

After the SimpleInterestSetUp Web service is installed, it is available to be accessed over the Internet.

Now, let's learn how to use the WebService class.

Using the WebService Class

Suppose you want to use common ASP.NET objects, such as Application, User, Session, and Context, in your Web service. What will you do in such a situation? Will you define these objects in your Web service and then use them? A better way to use these objects in your Web service is to inherit the class that implements the Web service from the `WebService` class.

The `WebService` class allows a Web service to access all the common ASP.NET objects as if they are the members of the class implementing the Web service. The `WebService` class resides in the `System.Web.Services` namespace and the `System.Web.Services` assembly. Now, let's create a Web service that uses the `WebService` class.

Suppose you want your Web service to determine the name of the server on which the Web service is running. You can determine the name of the server by using the `Server` object which is a member of the `WebService` class. Therefore, you should create your Web service by deriving the class that implements the Web service from the `WebService` class.

Now, create a Web service application, named `WebServiceClassCS` (`WebServiceClassVB` in VB and `WebServiceClassCS` in C#), and follow these steps:

1. After creating the `WebServiceClass` Web service, add the following code in the code-behind file of the Web service, as shown in Listing 18.12:

Listing 18.12: Code for the Code-Behind File

In VB

```
Imports System.Web
Imports System.Web.Services
Imports System.Web.Services.Protocols
' To allow this Web Service to be called from script, using ASP.NET AJAX, uncomment the
  following line.
' <System.Web.Script.Services.ScriptService()> _
<WebService(Namespace:="http://tempuri.org/")> _
<WebServiceBinding(ConformsTo:=WsiProfiles.BasicProfile1_1)> _
<Global.Microsoft.VisualBasic.CompilerServices.DesignerGenerated()> _
Public Class WebService
     Inherits System.Web.Services.WebService
    ' <WebMethod()> _
    ' Public Function HelloWorld() As String
    '   Return "Hello World"
    ' End Function
    <WebMethod()> _
    Public Function GetMachineName() As String
        Return Server.MachineName
    End Function
End Class
```

In C#

```
using System;
using System.Collections.Generic;
using System.Linq;
using System.Web;
using System.Web.Services;
/// <summary>
/// Summary description for WebService
/// </summary>
[WebService(Namespace = "http://tempuri.org/")]
[WebServiceBinding(ConformsTo = WsiProfiles.BasicProfile1_1)]
// To allow this Web Service to be called from script, using ASP.NET AJAX, uncomment the
  following line.
// [System.Web.Script.Services.ScriptService]
public class WebService : System.Web.Services.WebService {
    public WebService () {
        //Uncomment the following line if using designed components
        //InitializeComponent();
    }
   // [WebMethod]
   // public string HelloWorld() {
   //     return "Hello World";
   // }
    [WebMethod]
    public string GetMachineName()
    {
        return Server.MachineName;
    }
}
```

2. Run the Web service. The output is as shown in Figure 18.24.
3. Click the GetMachineName Web service, as shown Figure 18.24:

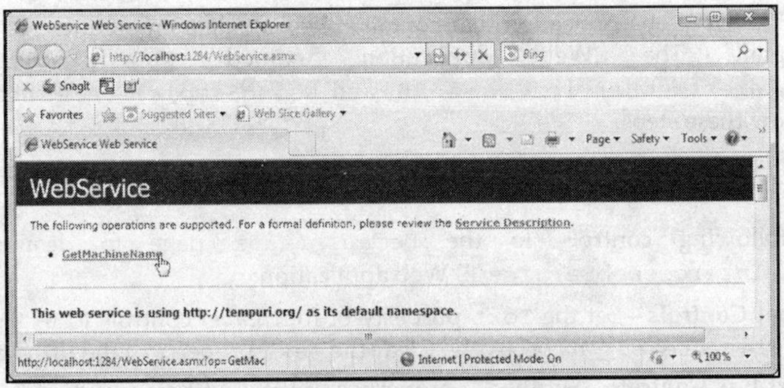

Figure 18.24: Executing the Web Service

4. Click the Invoke button to view the output of the Web service, as shown in Figure 18.25:

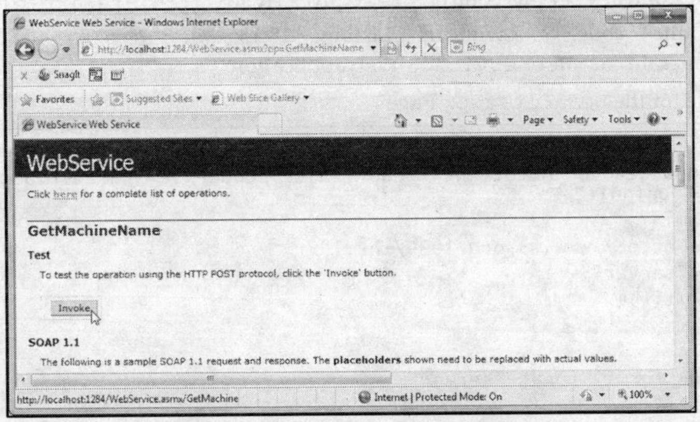

Figure 18.25: Invoking the Web Service

The output of the Web service now appears, as shown in Figure 18.26:

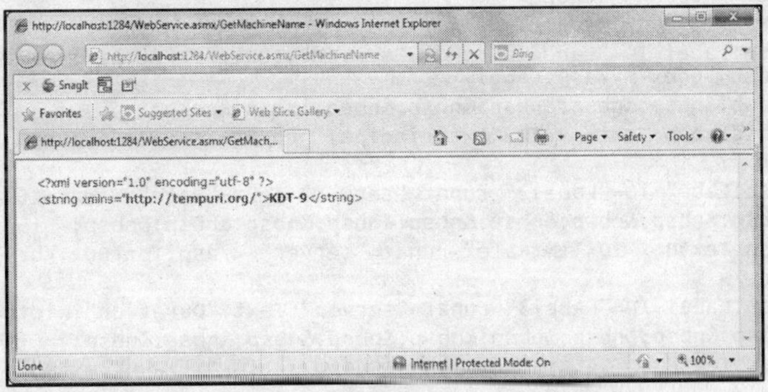

Figure 18.26: Displaying the Output of the Web Service

In Figure 18.18, the Web service displays the name of the server as KDT-9.

Using the Web Service

You need to create an ASP.NET Web application that accesses the Web service to use the Web service. You need to generate a proxy class for the Web service to allow a Web application to access the Web service. A proxy class is a local copy of the class that represents a Web service. You can generate a proxy class for a Web service by adding a Web reference to the website.

Let's create an ASP.NET Web application that contains the CalculateSimpleInterest Web service created earlier in this chapter. The Web application, named `UsingSimpleInterestWebServiceCS` (`UsingSimpleInterestWebServiceVB in VB` and `UsingSimpleInterestWebServiceCS in C#`) is created. Now, follow these steps:

1. Open the Design view of the `Default.aspx` page of the `UsingSimpleInterestWebServiceCS` Web application.
2. Add the following controls to the `Default.aspx` page to design the interface of the `UsingSimpleInterestWebServiceCS` Web application:
   - **Five Label Controls**—Set the `Text` property of four Label controls to `Principal`, `Rate`, `Duration`, and `Simple Interest`, respectively. Clear the `Text` property of the fifth Label control.
   - **Four Text Box Controls**—Set the `ID` properties of the Text Box controls to `txtPrincipal`, `txtRate`, `txtDuration`, and `txtSimpleInterest`, respectively.
   - **A Button Control**—Set this control's `Text` property to `CalculateSimpleInterest`.
3. Now add the code, shown in Listing 18.13, in the `Default.aspx` page of the `UsingSimpleInterestWebServiceCS` Web application:

Listing 18.13: Code for the `Default.aspx` Page

In VB

```
<%@ Page Language="VB" AutoEventWireup="false" CodeFile="Default.aspx.vb"
  Inherits="_Default" %>
<!DOCTYPE html>
<html xmlns="http://www.w3.org/1999/xhtml">
<head runat="server">
    <title></title>
</head>
<body>
    <form id="form1" runat="server">
    <div>
    <strong><span style="text-decoration: underline"><em>Calculate Simple Interest using
         the Web Service<br />
         </em></span></strong>
         <br />
         <asp:Label ID="Label1" runat="server" Text="Principal"
         Width="66px"></asp:Label>
                 
          <asp:TextBox ID="txtPrincipal" runat="server"></asp:TextBox><br />
         <br />
         <asp:Label ID="Label2" runat="server" Text="Rate" Width="63px"></asp:Label>
                  
         <asp:TextBox ID="txtRate" runat="server"></asp:TextBox><br />
         <br />
         <asp:Label ID="Label3" runat="server" Text="Duration" Width="63px"></asp:Label>
                  
         <asp:TextBox ID="txtDuration" runat="server"></asp:TextBox>
         <br />
         <br />
         <asp:Label ID="Label4" runat="server" Text="Simple Interest"
         Width="105px"></asp:Label>
         <asp:TextBox ID="txtSimpleInterest" runat="server"></asp:TextBox><br />
         <br />
         <asp:Label ID="Label5" runat="server" Width="66px"></asp:Label>
                  
         <asp:Button ID="Button1" runat="server" Text="Calculate Simple Interest"
         Width="220px"/>
    </div>
```

```
        </form>
    </body>
    </html>
```

In C#

```
    <%@ Page Language="C#" AutoEventWireup="true" CodeFile="Default.aspx.cs"
      Inherits="_Default" %>
    <!DOCTYPE html>
    <html xmlns="http://www.w3.org/1999/xhtml">
    <head runat="server"><title></title>
    </head>
    <body>
    <form id="form1" runat="server">
    <div>
    <strong><span style="text-decoration: underline"><em>Calculate Simple Interest using
            the Web Service<br />
            </em></span></strong>
            <br />
            <asp:Label ID="Label1" runat="server" Text="Principal"
            Width="66px"></asp:Label>
                    
             <asp:TextBox ID="txtPrincipal" runat="server"></asp:TextBox><br />
            <br />
            <asp:Label ID="Label2" runat="server" Text="Rate" Width="63px"></asp:Label>
                     
            <asp:TextBox ID="txtRate" runat="server"></asp:TextBox><br />
            <br />
            <asp:Label ID="Label3" runat="server" Text="Duration" Width="63px"></asp:Label>
                     
            <asp:TextBox ID="txtDuration" runat="server"></asp:TextBox>
            <br />
            <br />
            <asp:Label ID="Label4" runat="server" Text="Simple Interest"
            Width="105px"></asp:Label>
                
            <asp:TextBox ID="txtSimpleInterest" runat="server"></asp:TextBox><br />
            <br />
            <asp:Label ID="Label5" runat="server" Width="66px"></asp:Label>
                     
            <asp:Button ID="Button1" runat="server" Text="Calculate Simple Interest"
            Width="220px" OnClick="Button1_Click" />
    </div>
    </form>
    </body>
    </html>
```

4. Right-click the `UsingSimpleInterestWebServiceCS` Web application in the Solution Explorer window and select the Add Service Reference option from the context menu to display the Add Service Reference dialog box (Figure 18.27).
5. The Add Service Reference dialog box appears. Click the Advanced Button as shown in figure 18.27:

Figure 18.27: Add Service Reference Dialog Box

6. The Service Reference Settings dialog box appears. Click Add Web Reference dialog box as shown in Figure 18.28:

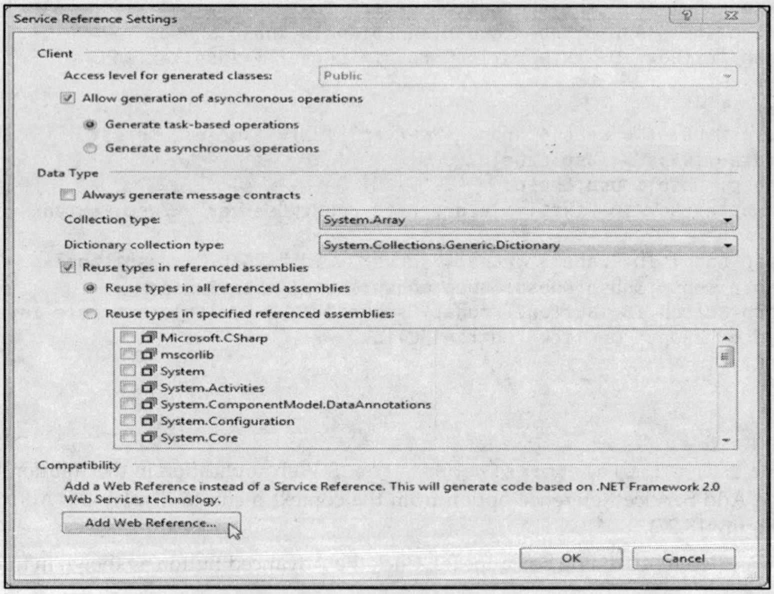

Figure 18.28: Service Reference Settings dialog box

You can locate the Web service either by specifying the location in the URL text box or by selecting the appropriate link in the `Browse to` pane. For example, select the Web services in this solution if the Web service resides in the application. As our Web service is present in the Web application, we click the corresponding hyperlink, as shown in Figure 18.29:

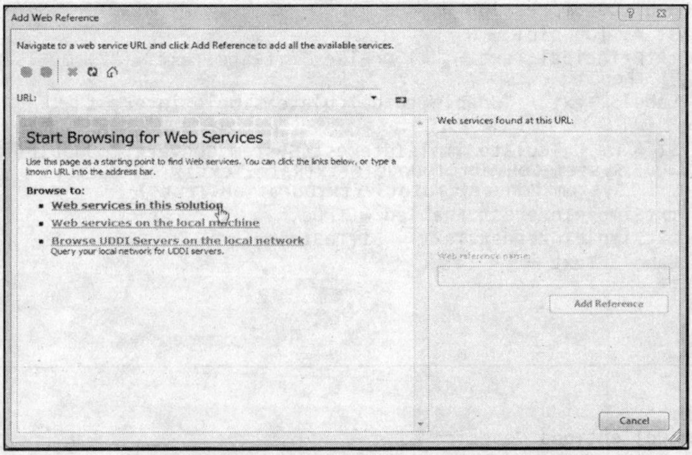

Figure 18.29: Browsing the Web Service

7. Select the WebService link from the Services column in the Web Services in this Solution pane

NOTE

The Add Reference button gets enabled only when you locate the Web service successfully.

8. Click the Add Reference button to add the reference in the Solution Explorer window, as shown in Figure 18.30:

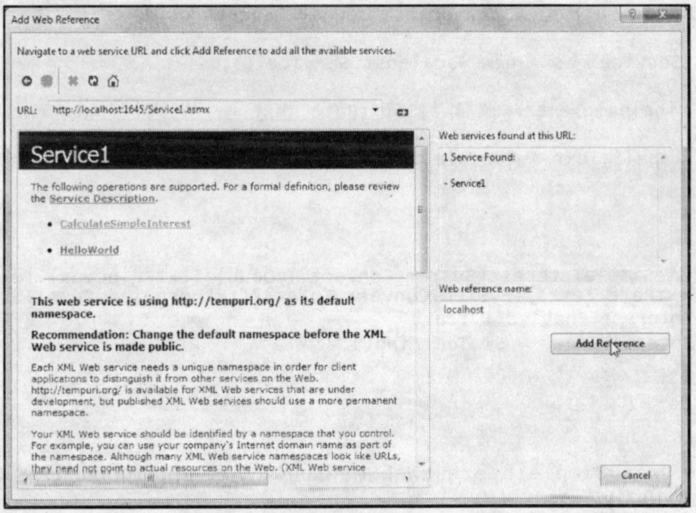

Figure 18.30: Adding the Reference

9. Add the code in the code behind file of the Default.aspx page in the Web application to create an instance of the Web reference, as shown in Listing 18.14:

Listing 18.14: Code of the `Default.aspx` File to Access the Web Method of the Web Service

In VB

```
Partial Class _Default
    Inherits System.Web.UI.Page
    Protected Sub Button1_Click(sender As Object, e As EventArgs) Handles Button1.Click
        Dim ws As New localhost.Service1()
```

```
        ws.EnableDecompression = True
        Dim SI As [Double] = 0
        If (txtPrincipal.Text = "") OrElse (txtRate.Text = "") OrElse (txtDuration.Text
         = "") Then
            Label5.Text = "Unable to calculate simple interest"
        Else
            SI = ws.CalculateSimpleInterest(System.Convert.ToDouble(txtPrincipal.Text),
                 System.Convert.ToDouble(txtRate.Text),
                 System.Convert.ToInt32(txtDuration.Text))
            txtSimpleInterest.Enabled = True
            txtSimpleInterest.Text = SI.ToString()
            Label5.Text = ""
        End If
    End Sub
End Class
```

In C#

```
using System;
using System.Collections.Generic;
using System.Linq;
using System.Web;
using System.Web.UI;
using System.Web.UI.WebControls;
public partial class _Default : System.Web.UI.Page
{
  protected void Page_Load(object sender, EventArgs e)
  {

  }
  protected void Button1_Click(object sender, EventArgs e)
  {
  localhost.Service1 ws = new localhost.Service1();
  Double SI=0;
  if ((txtPrincipal.Text == "") || (txtRate.Text == "") || (txtDuration.Text == ""))
  {
            Label5.Text = "Unable to calculate simple interest";
  }
  else
  {
  SI =
  ws.CalculateSimpleInterest(System.Convert.ToDouble(txtPrincipal.Text),System.Convert.T
  o Double(txtRate.Text), System.Convert.ToInt32(txtDuration.Text));
  txtSimpleInterest.Enabled = true;
  txtSimpleInterest.Text = SI.ToString();
  Label5.Text = "";
  }
  }
}
```

8. Now, run the `UsingSimpleInterestWebServiceCS` Web application. The output of the application appears (Figure 18.31).

NOTE

You should note that the Default.aspx page of the application is set the startup page of the project.

9. Enter the appropriate figures in the Principal, Rate, and Duration fields and click the Calculate Simple Interest button to calculate the simple interest, as shown in Figure 18.31:

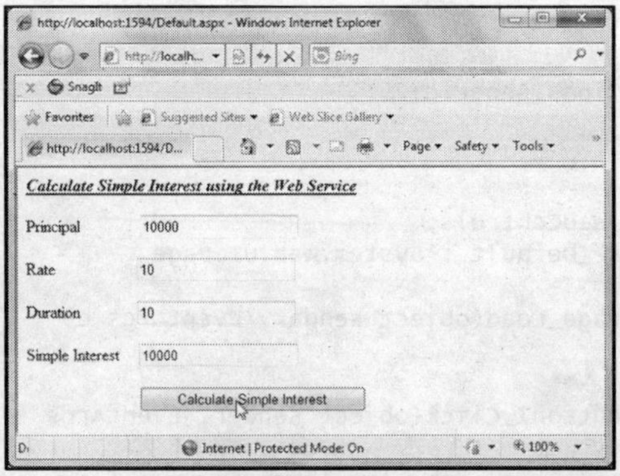

Figure 18.31: Displaying the Result Using Web Service

Now, Lets learn how to use the EnableDecompression property.

Using the EnableDecompression Property

Suppose that the Web server from which a Web service client requests for a Web service, supports compression (a technique used to minimize the size of data [or a file] by applying encoding). As the Web server supports compression, the Web service client receives a response to the request in the form of compressed data. Therefore, to understand the response of the Web server, the Web service client has to decompress (a technique used to convert the compressed data [or file] to its original form by decoding) the response.

This can be done with the `EnableDecompression` property, which, if set to True, enables the Web service client to decompress the data.

Likewise, decompression is disabled by setting the `EnableDecompression` property to False. This allows the Web service client to receive the response from the Web server in the original format.

You need to invoke the property on the instance of the Web reference to set the `EnableDecompression` property. Now, let's learn how to implement the `EnableDecompression` property in the `UsingSimpleInterestWebServiceCS` Web application created earlier. Add the following code, shown in Listing 18.15, in the code-behind file of the `UsingSimpleInterestWebServiceCS` Web application:

Listing 18.15: Code for Invoking the `EnableDecompression` Property

In VB

```
Partial Class _Default
    Inherits System.Web.UI.Page
    Protected Sub Button1_Click(ByVal sender As Object, ByVal e As System.EventArgs)
      Handles Button1.Click
        Dim ws As New localhost.Service1()
        Dim SI As Double
         ws.EnableDecompression = True
        If txtPrincipal.Text = Nothing Or txtRate.Text = Nothing Or txtDuration.Text =
         Nothing Then
            Label5.Text = "Unable to calculate simple interest"
        Else
            SI = ws.CalculateSimpleInterest(CDbl(txtPrincipal.Text),
             CDbl(txtRate.Text), CInt(txtDuration.Text))
            txtSimpleInterest.Enabled = True
            txtSimpleInterest.Text = SI.ToString()
            Label5.Text = ""
        End If
    End Sub
End Class
```

In C#

```
using System;
using System.Collections.Generic;
using System.Linq;
using System.Web;
using System.Web.UI;
using System.Web.UI.WebControls;
public partial class _Default : System.Web.UI.Page
{
    protected void Page_Load(object sender, EventArgs e)
    {
    }
    protected void Button1_Click(object sender, EventArgs e)
    {
      localhost.Service1 ws = new localhost.Service1();
      ws.EnableDecompression=true;
        Double SI=0;
        if ((txtPrincipal.Text == "") || (txtRate.Text == "") || (txtDuration.Text ==
        ""))
        {
            Label5.Text = "Unable to calculate simple interest";
        }
        else
        {
            SI =
  ws.CalculateSimpleInterest(System.Convert.ToDouble(txtPrincipal.Text),System.Convert.T
  o Double(txtRate.Text), System.Convert.ToInt32(txtDuration.Text));
  txtSimpleInterest.Enabled = true;
  txtSimpleInterest.Text = SI.ToString();
  Label5.Text = "";
  }
    }
}
```

Now, Lets learn how to share data across Web services.

Sharing Data Across Web Services

Suppose you want to create a Web application that needs to access two Web services, `TypeSharingWebService1` and `TypeSharingWebService2`, to execute the business logic. The `TypeSharingWebService1` Web service obtains the first name, middle name, and last name of an employee who uses the Web application, and the `TypeSharingWebService2` Web service retrieves and updates employee details by adding the employee ID and designation, and displays it on the Web application. As the operations of the `TypeSharingWebService2` Web service depend on the input of the `TypeSharingWebService1` Web service, both the Web services need to share data of similar data type.

Let's create the two Web services, named `TypeSharingWebService1` and `TypeSharingWebService2`, to understand how data can be shared among Web services. We also create a Web application that can access both the Web services to perform its tasks. Now, follow these steps to complete the data-sharing process between `TypeSharingWebService1` and `TypeSharingWebService2` using the `DataSharingWebServiceCS` Web application (DataSharingWebServiceCS for C# and DataSharingWebServiceVB for VB):

1. Write the code, shown in Listing 18.16, in the code-behind file of the `TypeSharingWebService1` Web service:

Listing 18.16: Code for the Code-Behind File of the `TypeSharingWebService1` Web Service

In VB

```
Imports System.Web
Imports System.Web.Services
Imports System.Web.Services.Protocols
' To allow this Web Service to be called from script, using ASP.NET AJAX, uncomment the
  following line.
' <System.Web.Script.Services.ScriptService()> _
<WebService(Namespace:="http://tempuri.org/")> _
<WebServiceBinding(ConformsTo:=WsiProfiles.BasicProfile1_1)> _
<Global.Microsoft.VisualBasic.CompilerServices.DesignerGenerated()> _
Public Class TypeSharingWebService1
     Inherits System.Web.Services.WebService
    Public Class EmpDetails
        Public EmpFirstName As String
        Public EmpMiddleName As String
        Public EmpLastName As String
        Public EmpID As String
        Public EmpDesignation As String
    End Class
    <WebMethod()> _
    Public Function ObtainEmpDetail(ByVal FName As String, ByVal MName As String, ByVal
         LName As String) As EmpDetails
        Dim EmpDetail As New EmpDetails()
        EmpDetail.EmpFirstName = FName
        EmpDetail.EmpMiddleName = MName
        EmpDetail.EmpLastName = LName
        Return EmpDetail
    End Function
    '<WebMethod()> _
    'Public Function HelloWorld() As String
    '   Return "Hello World"
    ' End Function
End Class
```

In C#

```
using System;
using System.Collections.Generic;
using System.Linq;
using System.Web;
using System.Web.Services;
/// <summary>
/// Summary description for TypeSharingWebService1
/// </summary>
[WebService(Namespace = "http://tempuri.org/")]
[WebServiceBinding(ConformsTo = WsiProfiles.BasicProfile1_1)]
// To allow this Web Service to be called from script, using ASP.NET AJAX, uncomment the
  following line.
// [System.Web.Script.Services.ScriptService]
public class TypeSharingWebService1 : System.Web.Services.WebService {
    public TypeSharingWebService1 () {
        //Uncomment the following line if using designed components
        //InitializeComponent();
    }
    public class EmpDetails
    {
        public string EmpFirstName;
        public string EmpMiddleName;
```

```
        public string EmpLastName;
        public string EmpID;
        public string EmpDesignation;
    }
    [WebMethod]
    public EmpDetails ObtainEmpDetail(string FName, string MName, string LName)
    {
        EmpDetails name = new EmpDetails();
        name.EmpFirstName = FName;
        name.EmpMiddleName = MName;
        name.EmpLastName = LName;
        return name;
    }
    //[WebMethod]
    //public string HelloWorld() {
    //    return "Hello World";
    //}
}
```

2. After adding the preceding listing to obtain the name of the employee, add the code, shown in Listing 18.17, to obtain the employee's ID and designation in the code-behind file of the `TypeSharingWebService2` Web service:

Listing 18.17: Code for the Code-Behind File of the `TypeSharingWebService2` Web Service

In VB

```
Imports System.Web
Imports System.Web.Services
Imports System.Web.Services.Protocols
' To allow this Web Service to be called from script, using ASP.NET AJAX, uncomment the
   following line.
' <System.Web.Script.Services.ScriptService()> _
<WebService(Namespace:="http://tempuri.org/")> _
<WebServiceBinding(ConformsTo:=WsiProfiles.BasicProfile1_1)> _
<Global.Microsoft.VisualBasic.CompilerServices.DesignerGenerated()> _
Public Class TypeSharingWebService2
     Inherits System.Web.Services.WebService
    ' <WebMethod()> _
    ' Public Function HelloWorld() As String
    '    Return "Hello World"
    'End Function
    Public Class EmpDetails
        Public EmpFirstName As String
        Public EmpMiddleName As String
        Public EmpLastName As String
        Public EmpID As String
        Public EmpDesignation As String
    End Class
    <WebMethod()> _
    Public Function UpdateEmpDetail(ByVal EmpDetail As EmpDetails, ByVal EmpID As
         String, ByVal EmpDesignation As String) As EmpDetails
        EmpDetail.EmpID = EmpID
        EmpDetail.EmpDesignation = EmpDesignation
        Return EmpDetail
    End Function
End Class
```

In C#

```
using System;
using System.Collections.Generic;
using System.Linq;
using System.Web;
using System.Web.Services;
/// <summary>
/// Summary description for TypeSharingWebService2
/// </summary>
[WebService(Namespace = "http://tempuri.org/")]
[WebServiceBinding(ConformsTo = WsiProfiles.BasicProfile1_1)]
// To allow this Web Service to be called from script, using ASP.NET AJAX, uncomment the
   following line.
// [System.Web.Script.Services.ScriptService]
public class TypeSharingWebService2 : System.Web.Services.WebService {
    public TypeSharingWebService2 () {
        //Uncomment the following line if using designed components
        //InitializeComponent();
    }
    public class EmpDetails
    {
        public string EmpFirstName;
        public string EmpMiddleName;
        public string EmpLastName;
        public string EmpID;
        public string EmpDesignation;
    }
    [WebMethod]
    public EmpDetails UpdateEmpDetail(EmpDetails name, string FID, string FDesignation)
    {
        //EmpDetails name = new EmpDetails();
        name.EmpID = FID;
        name.EmpDesignation = FDesignation;
        return name;
    }
   // [WebMethod]
   // public string HelloWorld() {
   //     return "Hello World";
   // }
}
```

3. In the DataSharingWebServiceCS Web application, add the Web references of both the Web services one by one in the Web application. After adding the Web references, the Solution Explorer window displays both the Web services, as shown in Figure 18.32:

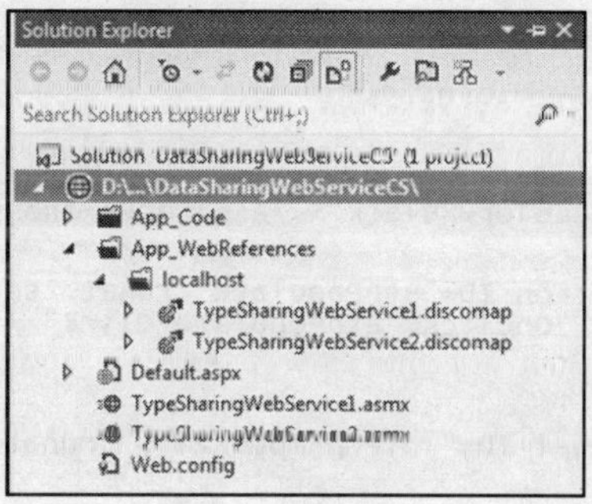

Figure 18.32: Displaying the Web Services

4. Now, add four Label controls and two Button controls in the `DataSharingWebService` Web application by dragging the controls from the Toolbox to the `Default.aspx` page or by adding the code in the `Default.aspx` page of the Web application, as shown in Listing 18.18:

Listing 18.18: Code for the `Default.aspx` Page

In VB

```
<%@ Page Language="VB" AutoEventWireup="false" CodeFile="Default.aspx.vb"
  Inherits="_Default" %>
<!DOCTYPE html>
<html xmlns="http://www.w3.org/1999/xhtml">
<head runat="server">
    <title></title>
</head>
<body>
       <form id="form1" runat="server">
    <div>
       <asp:Label ID="Label1" runat="server" Text="Use of Type Sharing Webservice" Font-
         Bold="True" ForeColor="Black"></asp:Label> <br />
                <br />
                <asp:Button ID="BtnPopulate" runat="server" Text="Populate Employee
                Details" OnClick="BtnPopulate_Click" />
                <br />
                <br />
                <asp:Label ID="lblPopEmpDetails" runat="server"></asp:Label>
                <br />
                <br />
                <asp:Button ID="BtnUpdateDetails" runat="server" Text="Update Details"
                OnClick="BtnUpdateDetails_Click" /><br />
                <br />
                <asp:Label ID="EmpDetailsLabel" runat="server"></asp:Label><br />
                <br />
                <asp:Label ID="ErrEmpDetails" runat="server"
                ForeColor="#C00000"></asp:Label>
    </div>
    </form>
</body>
</html>
```

In C#

```
<%@ Page Language="C#" AutoEventWireup="true" CodeFile="Default.aspx.cs"
  Inherits="_Default" %>
<!DOCTYPE html>
<html xmlns="http://www.w3.org/1999/xhtml">
<head runat="server">
    <title></title>
</head>
<body>
    <form id="form1" runat="server">
    <div>
       <asp:Label ID="Label1" runat="server" Text="Use of Type Sharing Webservice" Font-
         Bold="True" ForeColor="Black"></asp:Label> <br />
                <br />
                <asp:Button ID="BtnPopulate" runat="server" Text="Populate Employee
                Details" OnClick="BtnPopulate_Click" />
                <br />
                <br />
                <asp:Label ID="lblPopEmpDetails" runat="server"></asp:Label>
                <br />
                <br />
```

```
                <asp:Button ID="BtnUpdateDetails" runat="server" Text="Update Details"
                OnClick="BtnUpdateDetails_Click" /><br />
                <br />
                <asp:Label ID="EmpDetailsLabel" runat="server"></asp:Label><br />
                <br />
                <asp:Label ID="ErrEmpDetails" runat="server"
                ForeColor="#C00000"></asp:Label>
    </div>
    </form>
</body>
</html>
```

5. Now, write the code, shown in Listing 18.19, in the code-behind file of the `Default.aspx` page of the `DataSharingWebServiceCS` Web application:

Listing 18.19: Code for the Code-Behind File of the `DataSharingWebServiceCS` Web Application

In VB

```
Partial Class _Default
    Inherits System.Web.UI.Page
    Protected Sub BtnPopulate_Click(sender As Object, e As EventArgs) Handles
        BtnPopulate.Click
        Dim service1 As New localhost.TypeSharingWebService1()
        'Change this URL if the location of the Web service changes
        service1.Url - "http://localhost:1347/TypeSharingWebService1.asmx"
        Dim EmpDetail As localhost.EmpDetails = service1.ObtainEmpDetail("James",
         "Rojer","Frank")
        lblPopEmpDetails.Text = "Success!  You have Populated Employee Details."
        'Save the EmpDetails instance so that it can later be shared
        Session("EmpDetails") = EmpDetail
    End Sub
    Protected Sub BtnUpdateDetails_Click(sender As Object, e As EventArgs) Handles
        BtnUpdateDetails.Click
        If Session("EmpDetails") Is Nothing Then
            ErrEmpDetails.Text = "Error. You must first Populated Employee Details."
            Return
        End If
        Dim service2 As New localhost.TypeSharingWebService2()
        'Change this URL if the location of the Web service changes
        service2.Url = "http://localhost:1347/TypeSharingWebService2.asmx"
        'Retrieve the EmpDetails instance and pass it to the second service
        Dim EmpDetail As localhost.EmpDetails = CType(Session("EmpDetails"),
         localhost.EmpDetails)
        Dim updatedIEmpDetails As localhost.EmpDetails
         =service2.UpdateEmpDetail(EmpDetail, "EMP005", "Manager")
        'Print out the details from the updated updatedIEmpDetails
        Dim UpdatedEmpDetail As String = "Employee Details are : "
        UpdatedEmpDetail = UpdatedEmpDetail & "<br>First Name :" +
         updatedIEmpDetails.EmpFirstName
        UpdatedEmpDetail - UpdatedEmpDetail & "<br>Middle Name :"
         +updatedIEmpDetails.EmpMiddleName
        UpdatedEmpDetail = UpdatedEmpDetail & "<br>Last Name :" +
         updatedIEmpDetails.EmpLastName
        UpdatedEmpDetail = UpdatedEmpDetail & "<br>ID :" + updatedIEmpDetails.EmpID
        UpdatedEmpDetail = UpdatedEmpDetail & "<br>Designation :"
         +updatedIEmpDetails.EmpDesignation
        EmpDetailsLabel.Text = UpdatedEmpDetail
        'Save the updated EmpDetails instance
        Session("EmpDetails") = updatedIEmpDetails
    End Sub
End Class
```

In C#

```
using System;
using System.Collections.Generic;
using System.Linq;
using System.Web;
using System.Web.UI;
using System.Web.UI.WebControls;
public partial class _Default : System.Web.UI.Page
{
    protected void Page_Load(object sender, EventArgs e)
    {

    }
    protected void BtnPopulate_Click(object sender, EventArgs e)
    {
        localhost.TypeSharingWebService1 service1 = new
         localhost.TypeSharingWebService1();
        //'Change this URL if the location of the Web service changes
        service1.Url = "http://localhost:1546/TypeSharingWebService1.asmx";
        localhost.EmpDetails EmpDetail = service1.ObtainEmpDetail("James","Rojer",
         "Frank");
        lblPopEmpDetails.Text = "Success!  You have Populated Employee Details.";
        //Save the EmpDetails instance so that it can later be shared
        Session["EmpDetails"] = EmpDetail;
    }
    protected void BtnUpdateDetails_Click(object sender, EventArgs e)
    {
        if (Session["EmpDetails"] == null)
        {
            ErrEmpDetails.Text = "Error. You must first Populate Employee Details.";
            return;
        }
        localhost.TypeSharingWebService2 service2 = new
         localhost.TypeSharingWebService2();
        //Change this URL if the location of the Web service changes
        service2.Url = "http://localhost:1546/TypeSharingWebService2.asmx";
        //Retrieve the EmpDetails instance and pass it to the second service
        localhost.EmpDetails EmpDetail = (localhost.EmpDetails)Session["EmpDetails"];
        localhost.EmpDetails updatedIEmpDetails =
        service2.UpdateEmpDetail(EmpDetail, "EMP005", "Manager");
        //Print out the details from the updated updatedIEmpDetails
        string UpdatedEmpDetail = "Employee Details are : ";
        UpdatedEmpDetail = UpdatedEmpDetail + "<br>First Name :"
         +updatedIEmpDetails.EmpFirstName;
        UpdatedEmpDetail = UpdatedEmpDetail + "<br>Middle Name :"
         +updatedIEmpDetails.EmpMiddleName;
        UpdatedEmpDetail = UpdatedEmpDetail + "<br>Last Name :"
         +updatedIEmpDetails.EmpLastName;
        UpdatedEmpDetail = UpdatedEmpDetail + "<br>ID :" + updatedIEmpDetails.EmpID;
        UpdatedEmpDetail = UpdatedEmpDetail + "<br>Designation :"
         +updatedIEmpDetails.EmpDesignation;
        EmpDetailsLabel.Text = UpdatedEmpDetail;
        //Save the updated EmpDetails instance
        Session["EmpDetails"] = updatedIEmpDetails;
    }
}
```

NOTE

Change the URL of the Web services according to the location of your Web service. Also,build the website using the Build Menu.

6. Run the `DataSharingWebServiceCS` Web application. The output is shown in Figure 18.33:

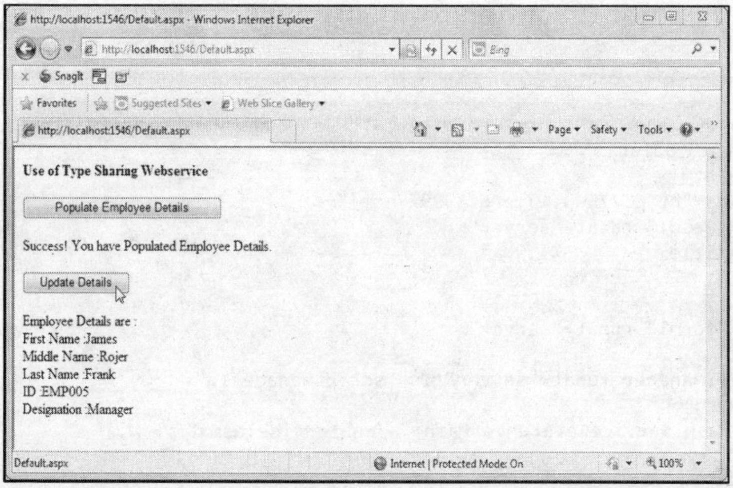

Figure 18.33: Sharing the Data using the Web Services

Now, let's learn how to call a Web service from the Client.

Calling a Web Service from the Client

We can also call a Web service with the help of script files from client-side. Perform the following steps to do so:

1. Open Visual Studio 2012 and create a Web application named `CallingWebServiceCS` (`CallingWebServiceVB in VB` and `CallingWebServiceCS in C#`).
2. After creating the Web application, add the code, shown in Listing 18.20, in the Default.aspx page of the CallingWebService Web application:

Listing 18.20: Code for the Default.aspx Page

In VB

```
<%@ Page Language="VB" AutoEventWireup="false" CodeFile="Default.aspx.vb"
  Inherits="_Default" %>
<!DOCTYPE html>
<html xmlns="http://www.w3.org/1999/xhtml">
<head runat="server">
    <title></title>
</head>
<body>
    <form id="form1" runat="server">
    <div>
    <asp:ScriptManager runat="server" ID="scriptManagerId">
  <Services>
        <asp:ServiceReference Path="~/WebService.asmx" />
  </Services>
<Scripts>
  <asp:ScriptReference Path="~/CallingWebService.js" />
</Scripts>
</asp:ScriptManager>
  <button id="BtnMultiply"  onclick="Multiplication(2, 5); return
  false;">Mutiply</button>
  <br />
  <br />
  <asp:Label ID="LblResult" runat="server" Text="Result"></asp:Label>
```

```
    </div>
    </form>
</body>
</html>
```

In C#

```
<%@ Page Language="C#" AutoEventWireup="true" CodeFile="Default.aspx.cs"
  Inherits="_Default" %>
<!DOCTYPE html>
<html xmlns="http://www.w3.org/1999/xhtml">
<head id="Head1" runat="server">
<title></title>
</head>
<body>
<form id="form1" runat="server">
<div>
<asp:ScriptManager runat="server" ID="scriptManagerId">
  <Services>
        <asp:ServiceReference Path="~/WebService.asmx" />
  </Services>
<Scripts>
  <asp:ScriptReference Path="~/CallingWebService.js" />
</Scripts>
</asp:ScriptManager>
  <button id="BtnMultiply"  onclick="Multiplication(2, 5); return
  false;">Mutiply</button>
  <br />
  <br />
  <asp:Label ID="LblResult" runat="server" Text="Result"></asp:Label>
</div>
</form>
</body>
</html>
```

3. Create a Web service by right-clicking the name of the Web application in the Solution Explorer window and selecting the Add→Add New Item option from the context menu to display the Add New Item dialog box.
4. Select the Web Service template in the Add New Item dialog box and click the Add button. Doing this adds a Web service named `WebService` in the `CallingWebServiceCS` Web application.
5. Add the code, shown in Listing 18.21, in the code-behind file of the `WebService` Web service:

Listing 18.21: Code for the Code-Behind File of the `WebService` Web Service

In VB

```
Imports System.Web
Imports System.Web.Services
Imports System.Web.Services.Protocols
' To allow this Web Service to be called from script, using ASP.NET AJAX, uncomment the
  following line.
' <System.Web.Script.Services.ScriptService()> _
<WebService(Namespace:="MyWebService")> _
<WebServiceBinding(ConformsTo:=WsiProfiles.BasicProfile1_1)> _
<Global.Microsoft.VisualBasic.CompilerServices.DesignerGenerated()> _
Public Class MyWebService
    Inherits System.Web.Services.WebService
    <WebMethod()> _
    Public Function HelloWorld() As String
        Return "Hello World"
    End Function
```

```
    <WebMethod> _
    Public Function Multiply(num1 As Integer, num2 As Integer) As String
       Dim multiplyVal As Integer = num1 * num2
        Dim result As String = [String].Format("The Multiplication result is {0}.",
         multiplyVal.ToString())
        Return result
    End Function
End Class
```

In C#

```
using System;
using System.Collections.Generic;
using System.Linq;
using System.Web;
using System.Web.Services;
///<summary>
/// Summary description for WebService
///</summary>
[WebService(Namespace = "WebService")]
[WebServiceBinding(ConformsTo = WsiProfiles.BasicProfile1_1)]
// To allow this Web Service to be called from script, using ASP.NET AJAX, uncomment the
   following line.
 [System.Web.Script.Services.ScriptService]
public class WebService : System.Web.Services.WebService {
public WebService () {
//Uncomment the following line if using designed components
//InitializeComponent();
    }
//[WebMethod]
//public string HelloWorld() {
//    return "Hello World";
//}
    [WebMethod]
public string Multiply(int num1, int num2)
    {
int multiplyVal = num1 * num2;
string result = String.Format("The Multiplication result is
   {0}.",multiplyVal.ToString());
return result;
    }
}
```

In Listing 18.21, we have declared a function `Multiply.` that accepts two parameters, `num1` and `num2`, in the `WebService` Web service.

6. Now, create a script file to call the `WebService` Web service, which we created in the `CallingWebServiceCS` Web application. Right-click the name of the Web application, and select the Add > Add New Item option from the context menu. In the Add New Item dialog box, select the JavaScript file template and change the name in the Name field to `CallingWebService.js`, as shown in Figure 18.34:

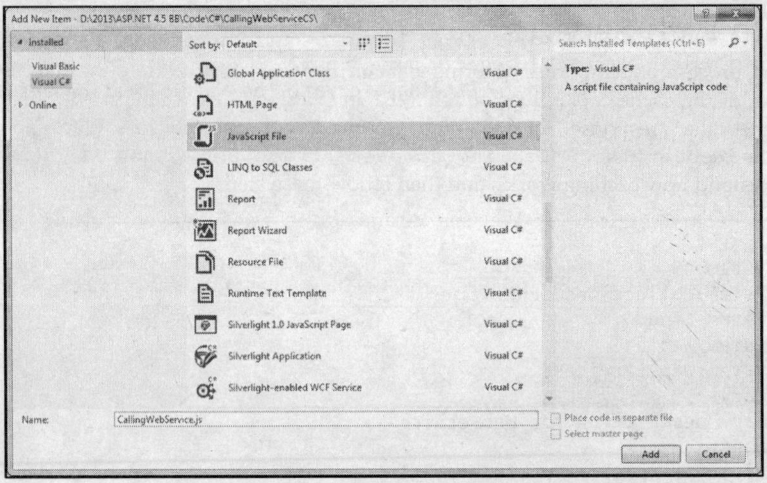

Figure 18.34:Adding the JavaScript File

7. Click the Add button to add the script file in the `CallingWebServiceCS` Web application and add the code, shown in Listing 18.22, in the `CallingWebService.js` file:

Listing 18.22: Code for the `CallingWebService.js` File

In VB and C#

```
function Multiplication(num1, num2) {
    WebService.Multiply(num1, num2, Succeeded);
}
function Succeeded(result, eventArgs) {
var Res = document.getElementById("LblResult");
    Res.innerHTML = result;
}
```

NOTE

The code for the CallingWebService.js file is the same in the VB and C# languages.

8. Press the F5 key on the keyboard to execute the `CallingWebServiceCS` Web application. The output after clicking the Multiply button is shown in Figure 18.35:

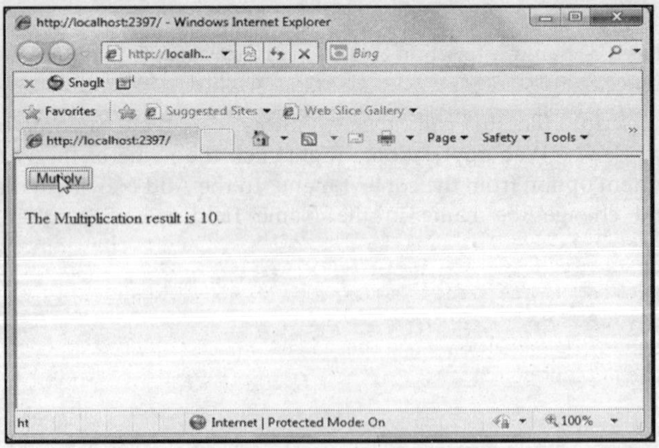

Figure 18.35:Executing the Web Service

Let's discuss caching feature in the Web Service.

Caching with Web Services

Caching is the process of temporarily storing data in memory, till the time the data is requested. We have discussed most of the cache capabilities of ASP.NET in Chapter 16, Caching in ASP.NET 4.5, ASP.NET allows you to cache the response of a Web service. Let's create a Web application named as `CallingCachedWebServiceCS` (`CallingCacheWebServiceVB` in VB and `CallingCacheWebServiceCS` in C#) to understand how caching works, and then follow these steps:

1. Create the `CachedWebService` Web service and add the code, shown in Listing 18.23, in the code-behind file:

Listing 18.23: Code for the Code-Behind File of the CachedWebService Web Service

In VB

```
Imports System.Web
Imports System.Web.Services
Imports System.Web.Services.Protocols
' To allow this Web Service to be called from script, using ASP.NET AJAX, uncomment the
  following line.
' <System.Web.Script.Services.ScriptService()> _
<WebService(Namespace:="http://tempuri.org/")> _
<WebServiceBinding(ConformsTo:=WsiProfiles.BasicProfile1_1)> _
<Global.Microsoft.VisualBasic.CompilerServices.DesignerGenerated()> _
Public Class CachedWebService
     Inherits System.Web.Services.WebService
    '<WebMethod()> _
    'Public Function HelloWorld() As String
    '    Return "Hello World"
    'End Function
    <WebMethod(CacheDuration:=60)> _
    Public Function GetCacheResult(ByVal num1 As Integer, ByVal num2 As Integer) As
  String
  Return "The result is " & (num1 + num2).ToString() & ", and the cached time is "
  &System.DateTime.Now.ToString()
    End Function
End Class
```

In C#

```
using System;
using System.Collections.Generic;
using System.Linq;
using System.Web;
using System.Web.Services;
/// <summary>
/// Summary description for CachedWebService
/// </summary>
[WebService(Namespace = "http://tempuri.org/")]
[WebServiceBinding(ConformsTo = WsiProfiles.BasicProfile1_1)]
// To allow this Web Service to be called from script, using ASP.NET AJAX, uncomment the
  following line.
// [System.Web.Script.Services.ScriptService]
public class CachedWebService : System.Web.Services.WebService {
    public CachedWebService () {
        //Uncomment the following line if using designed components
        //InitializeComponent();
    }
   // [WebMethod]
   // public string HelloWorld() {
   //     return "Hello World";
```

```
    // }
     [WebMethod(CacheDuration = 60)]
     public string GetCacheResult(int num1, int num2)
     {
         return "The result is " + (num1 + num2).ToString() + ", and the cached time is "
          +System.DateTime.Now.ToString();
     }
}
```

2. Now, add the code, shown in Listing 18.24, on the `Default.aspx` page of the `CallingCachedWebServiceCS` Web application:

Listing 18.24: Code for the Default.aspx page

In VB

```
<%@ Page Language="VB" AutoEventWireup="false" CodeFile="Default.aspx.vb"
  Inherits="_Default" %>
<!DOCTYPE html>
<html xmlns="http://www.w3.org/1999/xhtml">
<head runat="server">
    <title></title>
</head>
<body>
    <form id="form1" runat="server">
    <div>
    Enter the First Number
                
        <asp:TextBox ID="TextBox1" runat="server"></asp:TextBox>
                <br />
                Enter the Second Number
                   
                <asp:TextBox ID="TextBox2" runat="server"></asp:TextBox>
                <br />
                <br />
                <asp:Button ID="Button1" runat="server" Text="Display Result"
                OnClick="Button1_Click" />
                <br />
                <br />
         <asp:Label ID="Label1" runat="server" Text="Cached Result"></asp:Label>
    </div>
    </form>
</body>
</html>
```

In C#

```
<%@ Page Language="C#" AutoEventWireup="true" CodeFile="Default.aspx.cs"
  Inherits="_Default" %>
<!DOCTYPE html>
<html xmlns="http://www.w3.org/1999/xhtml">
<head runat="server">
    <title></title>
</head>
<body>
    <form id="form1" runat="server">
    <div>
    Enter the First Number
                
        <asp:TextBox ID="TextBox1" runat="server"></asp:TextBox>
                <br />
                Enter the Second Number
           
```

```
                    <asp:TextBox ID="TextBox2" runat="server"></asp:TextBox>
                    <br />
                    <br />
                    <asp:Button ID="Button1" runat="server" Text="Display Result"
                    OnClick="Button1_Click" />
                    <br />
                    <br />
            <asp:Label ID="Label1" runat="server" Text="Cached Result"></asp:Label>
    </div>
    </form>
</body>
</html>
```

3. Open the code-behind file of the `Default.aspx` page and add the code in the Click event of the Button1 control , as shown in Listing 18.25:

Listing 18.25: Code for the Code-Behind File of the Default.aspx Page

In VB

```
Partial Class _Default
    Inherits System.Web.UI.Page
    Protected Sub Button1_Click(sender As Object, e As EventArgs) Handles Button1.Click
        Dim service As New localhost.CachedWebService()
        Dim num1 As Integer = Convert.ToInt16(TextBox1.Text)
        Dim num2 As Integer = Convert.ToInt16(TextBox2.Text)
        Label1.Text = service.GetCacheResult(num1, num2)
    End Sub
End Class
```

In C#

```
using System;
using System.Collections.Generic;
using System.Linq;
using System.Web;
using System.Web.UI;
using System.Web.UI.WebControls;
public partial class _Default : System.Web.UI.Page
{
    protected void Page_Load(object sender, EventArgs e)
    {

    }
    protected void Button1_Click(object sender, EventArgs e)
    {
        localhost.CachedWebService service = new localhost.CachedWebService();
        int num1 = Convert.ToInt16(TextBox1.Text);
        int num2 = Convert.ToInt16(TextBox2.Text);
        Label1.Text = service.GetCacheResult(num1, num2);
    }
}
```

4. Add a reference to the `CachedWebService` Web service in the `CallingCachedWebServiceCS` Web application and run the Web application. The output of the application appears (Figure 18.36).
5. Enter the numbers in the text boxes and click the Display Result button, as shown in Figure 18.36:

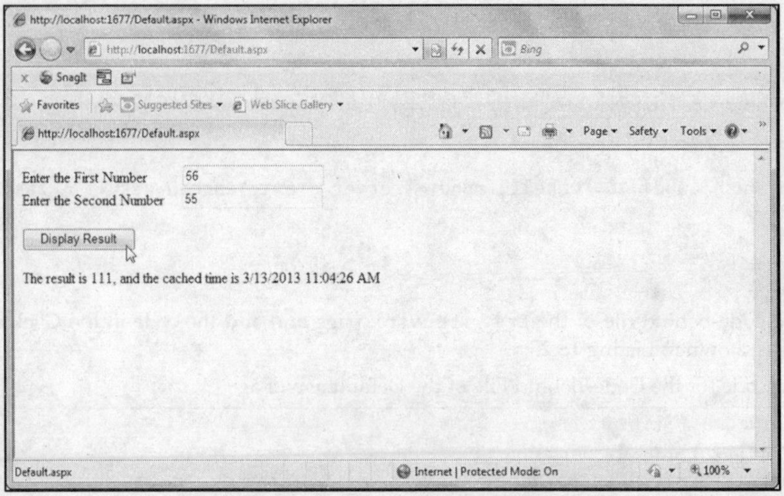

Figure 18.36:Displaying the Cached Result

Now, let's learn how to work with ASP.NET AJAX Enabled Web service.

Working with ASP.NET AJAX Enabled Web Services

As you know, a Web service is a collection of one or more server-side methods, which a client can call and use in applications at any remote location. The client first sends a request to the server using the HTTP protocol to call a Web service. The process is quite similar to that followed when a Web page processes the `postback` event, except that the body of the HTTP protocol request consists of those arguments that are passed to the methods of the Web service. An instance of the Web service is then created and the code inside the Web method is executed, which returns the result; the instance is destroyed afterwards. The Web services that are not AJAX-enabled use the SOAP protocol to send a request to the server and get a response, but AJAX-enabled Web services use the JSON format for this purpose.

Perform the following tasks to work with ASP.NET AJAX-enabled Web services:

- Creating the ASP.NET AJAX-enabled Web service
- Calling the ASP.NET AJAX enabled Web service from script

Creating the ASP.NET AJAX-Enabled Web Service

In ASP.NET AJAX, Web services are defined in the same way as a Web service without the AJAX functionality. As with any other ASP.NET Web service, the ASP.NET AJAX enabled Web service consists of two parts, an `.asmx` file, which acts a Web service endpoint and a `.cs` file, which contains the code for the Web service. Let's perform the following steps to create an ASP.NET AJAX enabled Web service:

1. Open Microsoft Visual Studio 2012 and select the FILE→New→ Web Site option from the menu bar and name the application `WebServiceCallAppCS(available as WebServiceCallAppCS in C# and WebServiceCallAppVB in VB).`
2. Select the Add→Add New Item option after right clicking on the application. The Add New Item dialog box opens. Next, select the Web Service template from the middle template of Visual Studio 2012 and name the Web service `TimeService` and click the Add button. A code-behind file, `TimeService`, and a Web service file, `TimeService.asmx`, are added to your Web application. When you open the `TimeService.asmx` file, you find the following single-line code there:

In VB

```
<%@ WebService Language="VB" CodeBehind="~/App_Code/TimeService.vb" Class="TimeService"
   %>
```

In C#

```
<%@ WebService Language="C#" CodeBehind="~/App_Code/TimeService.cs" Class="TimeService"
  %>
```

The code-behind class defines a class named `TimeService`, as shown in the following code:

In VB

```
<System.Web.Script.Services.ScriptService()> _
<WebService(Namespace:="http://tempuri.org/")> _
<WebServiceBinding(ConformsTo:=WsiProfiles.BasicProfile1_1)> _
<Global.Microsoft.VisualBasic.CompilerServices.DesignerGenerated()> _
Public Class TimeService
     Inherits System.Web.Services.WebService
```

In C#

```
[WebService(Namespace = "http://tempuri.org/")]
[WebServiceBinding(ConformsTo = WsiProfiles.BasicProfile1_1)]
// To allow this Web Service to be called from script, using ASP.NET AJAX, uncomment the
   following line.
// [System.Web.Script.Services.ScriptService]
public class TimeService : System.Web.Services.WebService {
public TimeService () {
        //Uncomment the following line if using designed components
        //InitializeComponent();
    }
```

Notice that the Web service class declaration consists of three attributes. The first is `WebService` (which sets an XML namespace for the Web service) and the second is `WebServiceBinding` (which indicates the level of the standards of conformity that the Web service can maintain). These two attributes are applied only when you are calling a Web service using SOAP, and are not relevant in the case of ASP.NET AJAX. However, the third attribute `ScriptService` is much more important. This attribute allows your Web service to be called from a client-side scripting language, such as JavaScript, by using the JSON format. In the absence of this attribute, you will not be able to use ASP.NET AJAX enabled Web service.

NOTE

By default, the ScriptService attribute is commented and you need to uncomment this attribute to create an ASP.NET AJAX enabled Web service.

3. Now, open the code-behind file of the `TimeService` Web Service placed in the `App_Code` folder and replace its existing code with the code shown in Listing 18.26:

Listing 18.26: Code of the Code-Behind File

In VB

```
Imports System.Web
Imports System.Web.Services
Imports System.Web.Services.Protocols
' To allow this Web Service to be called from script, using ASP.NET AJAX, uncomment the
  following line.
' <System.Web.Script.Services.ScriptService()> _
<WebService(Namespace:="http://tempuri.org/")> _
<WebServiceBinding(ConformsTo:=WsiProfiles.BasicProfile1_1)> _
<Global.Microsoft.VisualBasic.CompilerServices.DesignerGenerated()> _
Public Class TimeService
     Inherits System.Web.Services.WebService
    '<WebMethod()> _
    'Public Function HelloWorld() As String
```

```
        '   Return "Hello World"
        'End Function
        <WebMethod()> _
        Public Function ServerTime(ByVal myName As String) As String
            If myName = "" Then
                Throw New Exception("Please Enter Your Name")
            End If
            Return String.Format("Hello {0}, the time on the server is:  {1}",
             myName,DateTime.Now.ToString())
        End Function
    End Class
```

In C#

```
    using System;
    using System.Collections.Generic;
    using System.Linq;
    using System.Web;
    using System.Web.Services;
    /// <summary>
    /// Summary description for TimeService
    /// </summary>
    [WebService(Namespace = "http://tempuri.org/")]
    [WebServiceBinding(ConformsTo = WsiProfiles.BasicProfile1_1)]
    // To allow this Web Service to be called from script, using ASP.NET AJAX, uncomment the
      following line.
    // [System.Web.Script.Services.ScriptService]
    public class TimeService : System.Web.Services.WebService {
        public TimeService () {
            //Uncomment the following line if using designed components
            //InitializeComponent();
        }
       // [WebMethod]
        //public string HelloWorld() {
       //     return "Hello World";
       // }
        [WebMethod]
        public string ServerTime(string myName)
        {
            if (myName == "")
                throw new Exception("Please Enter Your Name");
            return string.Format("Hello {0}, the time on the server is:  {1}", myName,
             DateTime.Now.ToString());
        }
    }
```

Now, your ASP.NET AJAX enabled Web service is ready to run.

Now, Press the F5 key on the keyboard to execute the Web application. The output is displayed (Figure 18.37):

4. Click the ServerTime WebService as shown in the Figure 18.37.

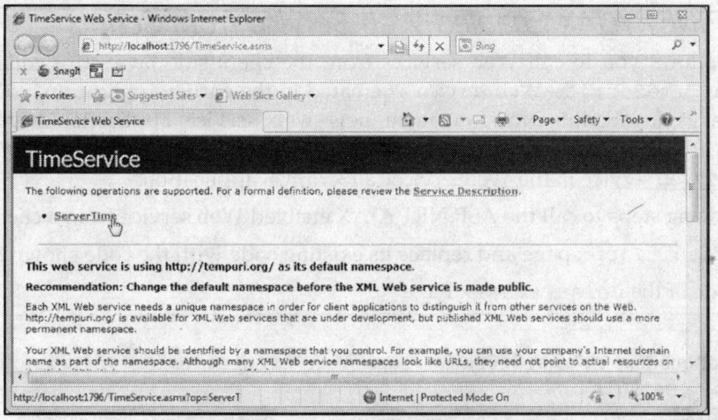

Figure 18.37: Selecting the Web Service

5. Enter the name and click the Invoke button, as shown in Figure 18.38:

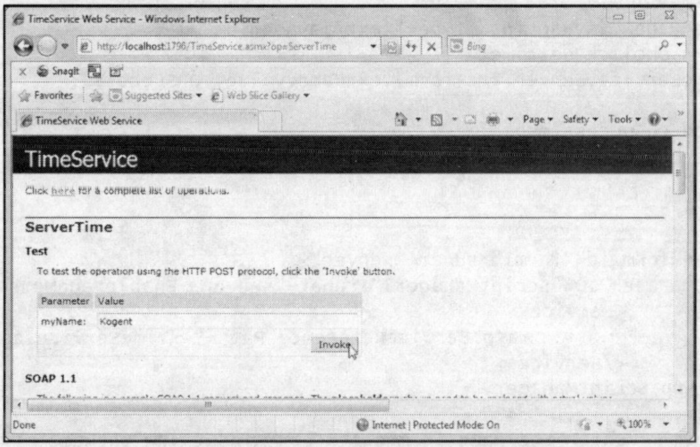

Figure 18.38: Invoking the Web Service

The Output displaying the server time appears, as shown in Figure 18.39:

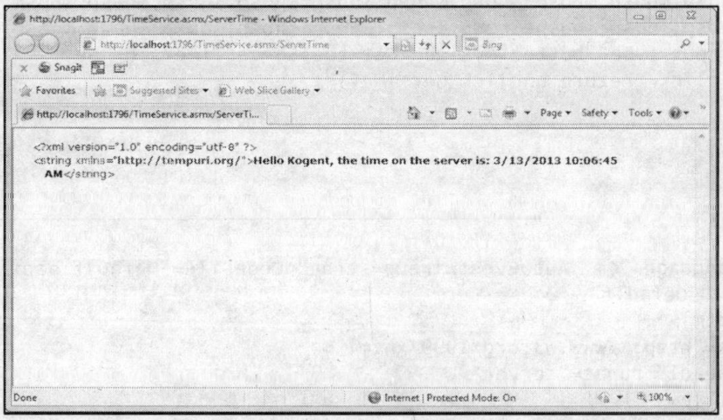

Figure 18.39: Displaying the Server Time using AJAX

Now, let's learn how to call the ASP.NET AJAX Enabled Web service from Script.

Calling the ASP.NET AJAX Enabled Web Service from Script

ASP.NET AJAX allows you to call Web services from the client-side JavaScript code using the JSON format. After creating the `TimeService` Web service as created in the earlier application, you can call it from a client-side script, such as JavaScript. Now, create a new web service application `WebServiceCallScriptCS` (`WebServiceCallScriptVB in VB` and `WebServiceCallScriptCS in C#)`. Add the reference of TimeService.asmx web service in the WebServiceCallScriptCS application.

Perform the following steps to call the ASP.NET AJAX enabled Web service from a client-side script:

1. Open the `Default.aspx` page and replace its existing code with the code shown in Listing 18.27:

Listing 18.27: Code of the `Default.aspx` Page

In VB

```
<%@ Page Language="VB" AutoEventWireup="true" CodeFile="Default.aspx.vb"
  Inherits="_Default"  %>
<!DOCTYPE html>
<html xmlns="http://www.w3.org/1999/xhtml">
<head id="Head1" runat="server">
<title></title>
<script language="javascript" type="text/javascript" >
    function onclick_GetTime() {
        TimeService.ServerTime(form1.txtName.value, OnSuccess);
    }
    function OnSuccess(msg) {
        alert(msg);
    }
</script>
</head>
 <body><form id="form1" runat="server">
<asp:ScriptManager ID="ScriptManager1" runat="server" EnablePageMethods="False">
                <Services>
                        <asp:ServiceReference Path="~/TimeService.asmx" />
                </Services>
        </asp:ScriptManager>
        <div>
                Enter the name in the textbox <input id="txtName" type="text" />
        <br />
        <br />
                     
                  
        <input type="button" value="Get the ServerTime" id="GetTime"
        onclick="return onclick_GetTime()" />
</div>
</form>
</body>
</html>
```

In C#

```
<%@ Page Language="C#" AutoEventWireup="true" CodeFile="Default.aspx.cs"
  Inherits="_Default"  %>
<!DOCTYPE html>
<html xmlns="http://www.w3.org/1999/xhtml">
<head id="Head1" runat="server">
<title></title>
<script language="javascript" type="text/javascript" >
    function onclick_GetTime() {
        TimeService.ServerTime(form1. TextBox1.value, OnSuccess);
    }
```

```
        function OnSuccess(msg) {
            alert(msg);
        }
    </script>
    </head>
    <body>
    <form id="form1" runat="server">
    <asp:ScriptManager ID="ScriptManager1" runat="server" EnablePageMethods="False">
                    <Services>
                            <asp:ServiceReference Path="~/TimeService.asmx" />
                    </Services>
            </asp:ScriptManager>
            <div>
                    Enter the name in the textbox: <asp:TextBox ID="TextBox1"
                    runat="server"></asp:TextBox>
    <br />
    <br />
                         
                      
            <input type="button" value="Get the ServerTime" id="GetTime"
            onclick="return onclick_GetTime()" />
    </div>
    </form>
    </body>
    </html>
```

2. Press the F5 key on the keyboard to execute the Web application. The output of the application appears (Figure 18.40).
3. Enter your name in the given text box and click the `Get the ServerTime` button. A message box is displayed, showing the server time along with your name, as shown in Figure 18.40:

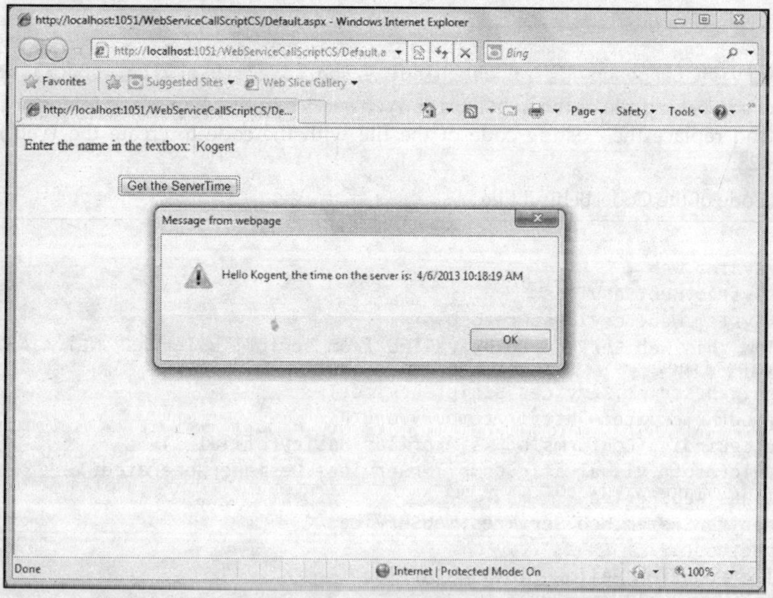

Figure 18.40: Displaying the Message from the Web Page

Now, let's learn how to use the `UpdatePanel` control with a Web service, which is used to refresh the specified part of a Web page instead of refreshing the whole Web page.

Using the UpdatePanel Control with a Web Service

The `UpdatePanel` control in ASP.NET enables you to make rich, client-centric ASP.NET AJAX enabled Web services. If you want your Web page to refresh certain selected parts without refreshing the whole page with a postback, you can use the `UpdatePanel` control. This type of page updating, where a small part of the Web page is updated instead of the whole page, is known as a partial page update. The `UpdatePanel` control is placed inside a `ScriptManager` control. You can have one or more `UpdatePanel` controls inside a `ScriptManager` control.

The `UpdatePanel` control is used to make the Web page more interactive. When you write a code to partially update a page, you require a thorough knowledge of JavaScript, but with the use of the `UpdatePanel` control, you can partially update a Web page without using any client-side script.

Perform the following steps to use the `UpdatePanel` control:

1. Open Visual Studio 2012, and then select the FILE→New→Web Site option and name the application `UsingUpdatePanelControlCS` (`UsingUpdatePanelControlVB` in VB and `UsingUpdatePanelControlCS` in C#).
2. Right-click the `UsingUpdatePanelControlCS` application in the Solution Explorer window and select the Add→Add New Item option. The Add New Item dialog box opens.
3. Select the Web Service template from the Visual Studio installed templates, name the Web service `WebService`, and click the Add button.

A code-behind file and a Web service file, WebService.cs and `WebService.asmx respectively`, are added to the `UsingUpdatePanelControlCS` application. When you open the `WebService.asmx` file, you find the following single-line code there:

In VB

```
<%@ WebService Language="VB" CodeBehind="~/App_Code/TimeService.vb" Class=" WebService "
  %>
```

In C#

```
<%@ WebService Language="C#" CodeBehind="~/App_Code/WebService.cs" Class="WebService" %>
```

4. Open the code-behind file of the `WebService` Web service in the App_Code folder of the Solution Explorer window and replace the existing code of the file with the code to create the Web service, as shown in Listing 18.28:

Listing 18.28: Code of the Code-Behind File

In VB

```
Imports System.Web
Imports System.Web.Services
Imports System.Web.Services.Protocols
' To allow this Web Service to be called from script, using ASP.NET AJAX, uncomment the
  following line.
' <System.Web.Script.Services.ScriptService()> _
<WebService(Namespace:="http://tempuri.org/")> _
<WebServiceBinding(ConformsTo:=WsiProfiles.BasicProfile1_1)> _
<Global.Microsoft.VisualBasic.CompilerServices.DesignerGenerated()> _
Public Class WebService
     Inherits System.Web.Services.WebService
    <WebMethod()> _
    Public Function HelloWorld() As String
        Return "Hello World"
    End Function
    <WebMethod()> _
    Public Function GetServerTime() As String
        Dim Time As String = DateTime.Today.ToLongDateString() + " " +
```

```
        DateTime.Now.ToLongTimeString()
        Return Time
    End Function
End Class
```

In C#

```
using System;
using System.Collections.Generic;
using System.Linq;
using System.Web;
using System.Web.Services;
/// <summary>
/// Summary description for WebService
/// </summary>
[WebService(Namespace = "http://tempuri.org/")]
[WebServiceBinding(ConformsTo = WsiProfiles.BasicProfile1_1)]
// To allow this Web Service to be called from script, using ASP.NET AJAX, uncomment the
  following line.
// [System.Web.Script.Services.ScriptService]
public class WebService : System.Web.Services.WebService {
    public WebService () {
        //Uncomment the following line if using designed components
        //InitializeComponent();
    }
    //[WebMethod]
    //public string HelloWorld() {
    //    return "Hello World";
   // }
    public string GetServerTime()
    {
        string Time = DateTime.Today.ToLongDateString() + " " +
        DateTime.Now.ToLongTimeString();
        return Time;
    }
}
```

5. Open the `Default.aspx` page and replace its existing code with the code shown in Listing 18.29:

Listing 18.29: Code of the `Default.aspx` Page

In VB

```
<%@ Page Language="VB" AutoEventWireup="false" CodeFile="Default.aspx.vb"
  Inherits="_Default" %>
<!DOCTYPE html>
<html xmlns="http://www.w3.org/1999/xhtml">
<head runat="server">
    <title></title>
</head>
<body>
    <form id="form1" runat="server">
    <asp:ScriptManager ID="ScriptManager1" runat="server">
         <Services>
                 <asp:ServiceReference Path="~/WebService.asmx" />
         </Services>
  </asp:ScriptManager>
  <div style="border-style: double; background-color: Gray; font-size: large; width:
  350px;">
  <asp:Label ID="Label1" runat="server"></asp:Label>
         <div>
```

```
                <asp:UpdatePanel ID="UpdatePanel1" runat="server">
                <ContentTemplate>
                <div style="border-style: dotted; background-color: Silver; font-size:
                larger; width: 300px;">
                <asp:Label ID="Label2" runat="server"></asp:Label>
                <asp:Button ID="Button1" runat="server" Text="Partial Update" />
        </div>
        <br />
        </ContentTemplate>
        </asp:UpdatePanel>
        <asp:Button ID="Button2" runat="server" Text="Full Update" />
        </div>
    </div>
    </form>
</body>
</html>
```

In C#

```
<%@ Page Language="C#" AutoEventWireup="true" CodeFile="Default.aspx.cs"
  Inherits="_Default" %>
<!DOCTYPE html>
<html xmlns="http://www.w3.org/1999/xhtml">
<head runat="server">
    <title></title>
</head>
<body>
    <form id="form1" runat="server">
   <asp:ScriptManager ID="ScriptManager1" runat="server">
        <Services>
                <asp:ServiceReference Path="~/WebService.asmx" />
        </Services>
   </asp:ScriptManager>
   <div style="border-style: double; background-color: Gray; font-size: large;
   width:350px;">
   <asp:Label ID="Label1" runat="server"></asp:Label>
        <div>
                <asp:UpdatePanel ID="UpdatePanel1" runat="server">
                <ContentTemplate>
                <div style="border-style: dotted; background-color: Silver; font-size:
                larger; width: 300px;">
                <asp:Label ID="Label2" runat="server"></asp:Label>
                <asp:Button ID="Button1" runat="server" Text="Partial Update" />
        </div>
        <br />
        </ContentTemplate>
        </asp:UpdatePanel>
        <asp:Button ID="Button2" runat="server" Text="Full Update" />
        </div>
    </div>
    </form>
</body>
</html>
```

6. Open the code-behind file of the `Default.aspx` page and replace its existing code with the code shown in Listing 18.30:

Listing 18.30: Code of the Code-Behind File of the `Default.aspx` Page

In VB

```
Partial Class _Default
    Inherits System.Web.UI.Page
    Protected Sub Page_Load(sender As Object, e As EventArgs) Handles Me.Load
        Dim ts As New WebService
        Label1.Text = ts.GetServerTime().ToString()
        Label2.Text = ts.GetServerTime().ToString()
    End Sub
End Class
```

In C#

```
using System;
using System.Collections.Generic;
using System.Linq;
using System.Web;
using System.Web.UI;
using System.Web.UI.WebControls;
public partial class _Default : System.Web.UI.Page
{
    protected void Page_Load(object sender, EventArgs e)
    {
        WebService ts = new WebService();
        Label1.Text = ts.GetServerTime().ToString();
        Label2.Text = ts.GetServerTime().ToString();
    }
}
```

In Listing 18.30, you can see that we have created an object of the `WebService` Web service with the name `ts`. Through the `ts` object, we are able to access the `GetServerTime` method of the `WebService` Web service.

7. Now, make the `Default.aspx` page your start-up page, right-click the `Default.aspx` page, and select the Set As Start Page option from the context menu.
8. Press the F5 key on the keyboard to execute the application. The output of the Web application appears (Figure 18.41).
9. Click the `Full Update` button; the whole page is refreshed, as shown in Figure 18.41:

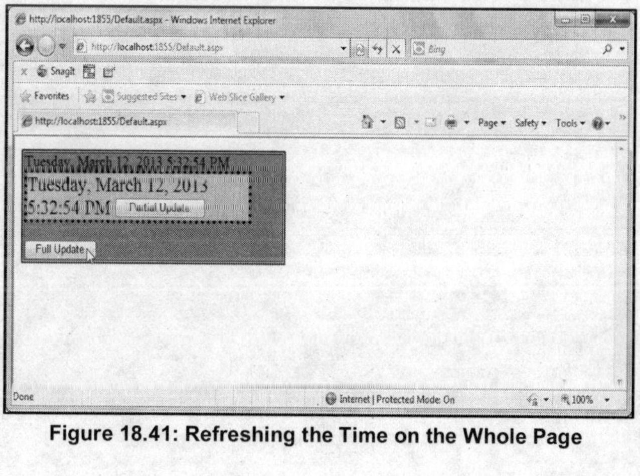

Figure 18.41: Refreshing the Time on the Whole Page

10. Click the `Partial Update` button, only the content inside the `UpdatePanel` control is refreshed, as shown in Figure 18.42:

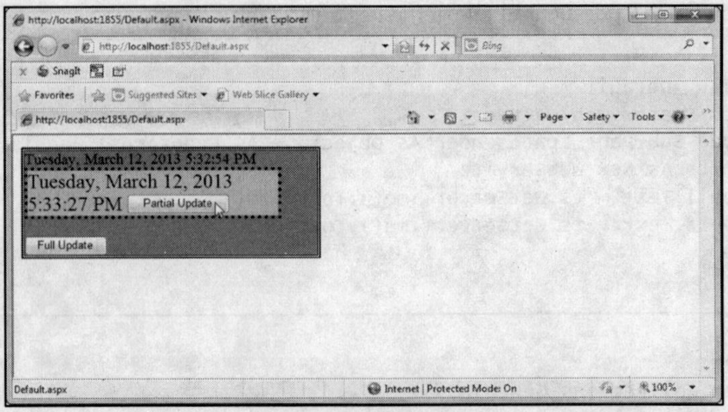

Figure 18.42: Refreshing the Time on the Partial Page

Let's now summarize the contents of the chapter.

Summary

In this chapter, you have learned about various aspects of Web services in ASP.NET. This includes a discussion on the infrastructure and properties of an ASP.NET Web service, as well as the code model used in the ASP.NET Web services.

This chapter also discusses various features, such as sharing data across Web services, calling a Web Service from the client, caching with Web services, working with ASP.NET AJAX enabled Web services, and using the `UpdatePanel` control with a Web service.

In the next chapter, you'll learn about Windows Communication Foundation (WCF) Services.

19

WCF Services

In Depth

In the previous versions of .NET Framework, such as 1.0, it was difficult to build applications for facilitating communication between a client and server. Though a number of technologies, such as ASP.NET Web service (which has .asmx as file extension), Web Service Enhancements (WSE), and .NET Remoting and the Microsoft Message Queuing (MSMQ) protocol have been provided by Microsoft to perform this task, it is confusing for the developers to select from these technologies as each of them is used to perform a different task. As different technologies offer different functionalities; therefore, to develop a distributed application, a developer has to master each of these technologies. Considering the difficulty of mastering each technology, Microsoft introduced the Windows Communication Foundation (WCF) technology. WCF brings together the functionalities of all these technologies under a unified programming model; thereby, simplifying the process of developing a distributed application.

WCF is a set of .NET technologies that is used for creation and consumption of data services in a website. It helps the developers to build secure and reliable websites. It provides a common platform for building service-oriented applications. The advantage of WCF over the previous technologies is that it provides a common runtime environment for the services; thereby, providing interoperability between services.

In this chapter, you learn about the architecture of WCF, which includes the contracts, service runtime, messaging, and activation and hosting layers. Next, you learn about the features of WCF, such as the endpoint support and enhanced transport layer. You also learn about the WCF clients. In addition, you learn about the different WCF tools, such as Svcutil.exe and FindPrivateKey.exe. Finally, you learn about the WCF Data Services, which was formerly known as ADO.NET Data Services.

Let's start by learning about the architecture of WCF.

Architecture of WCF

The WCF architecture consists of various layers that help in developing distributed applications. Figure 19.1 displays the layered architecture of WCF:

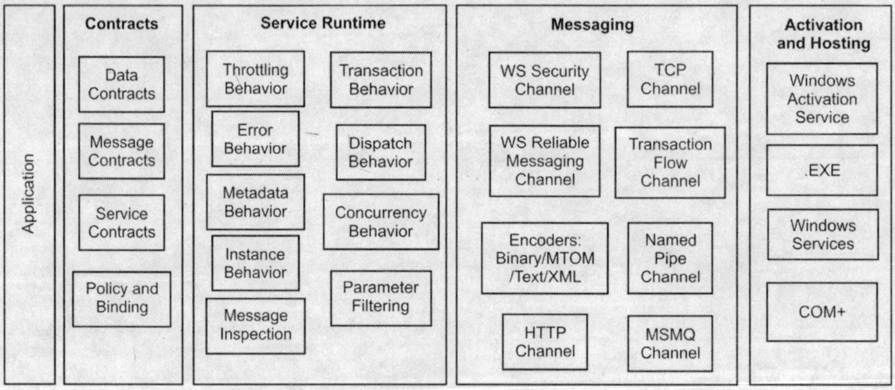

Figure 19.1: Displaying the Architecture of WCF

As shown in Figure 19.1, the WCF architecture contains the following layers:

- Contracts layer
- Service Runtime layer
- Messaging layer
- Activation and Hosting layer

Now, let's discuss all the layers in detail one by one.

The Contracts Layer

In the real world, a contract is a sort of agreement between two or more parties specifying the supply of goods and services. Contracts contain the details, such as what task is to be done and how it is to be done. A WCF contracts layer performs the same functions as that of a contract in real world and also contains very similar information. It is a binding between two or more machines that defines the terms and conditions for the messages to be exchanged. The contracts layer consists of the following components:

- Data contract
- Message contract
- Service contract
- Policy and binding

Let's discuss these in detail.

Data Contract

A data contract is a formal agreement made between a service and a client specifying the data that has to be exchanged between them. It defines the parameters and data structures that are used by the services to interact with clients. It also serializes and de-serializes data after mapping the Common Language Runtime (CLR) types with XML Schema Definitions (XSDs).

Message Contract

A message contract provides control over the Simple Object Access Protocol (SOAP) messages that are produced and consumed by WCF. It also provides direct access to the SOAP headers and bodies to change the SOAP message as per your requirements. However, majority of the time, the control over SOAP messages can be achieved by using data contract and defining the message schema.

The most important feature of SOAP messages is interoperability. A message contract provides the level of interoperability you need while communicating with clients or other systems.

Service Contract

A service contract is a contract that defines the operations or methods available at endpoints. It also defines the message exchange pattern, such as whether the behavior of the messages is one-way, duplex, or request/reply. A service contract exposes specific information to a client, which enables the client to understand what the service offers. This information includes the data types in the message, the protocol information and serialization format to ensure proper and successful communication, and message exchange patterns (MEPs).

NOTE

You learn about endpoints later in the chapter.

Policy and Binding

The policy and binding component of the contract layer specifies important information, such as security and protocol of a WCF service. Policy includes security requirements and other conditions that must be met to communicate with a service. Binding is a process used to enable communication between services and clients. It defines a transport protocol, such as Hypertext Transfer Protocol (HTTP), Transmission Control Protocol (TCP), and MSMQ, which is necessary to communicate with the endpoint of a service.

The Service Runtime Layer

The service runtime layer specifies and manages different behaviors of a service that occur during its operation, such as consuming or hosting the services. Service behaviors are objects that modify and control the runtime characteristics of WCF. These objects only control the behavior of the services; they do not have any control over endpoint or message behaviors. The following is a list of behaviors managed by the service runtime layer:

- **Throttling behavior**—Determines the number of processed messages. The number of processed messages varies according to the demand of services.

- **Error behavior**—Specifies the action to be taken if any of the messages gives error during service runtime.
- **Metadata behavior**—Specifies whether or not the metadata is available across the network.
- **Instance behavior**—Specifies the number of service instances that are available to process a message.
- **Message inspection**—Inspects all or a part of a message during service runtime.
- **Transaction behavior**—Enables the transacted operation for a service, which means that if any process fails during service runtime, the transaction rollbacks.
- **Dispatch behavior**—Determines how a message is handled and processed by the WCF infrastructure.
- **Concurrency behavior**—Specifies whether the messages are processed sequentially or concurrently by the services.
- **Parameter filtering**—Filters the message headers and executes preset actions.

The Messaging Layer

The messaging layer specifies the pattern of exchanging data between channels that are used during service communication. This layer consists of channels, which help in processing a message. There are two types of channels: transport and protocol. The transport channel reads and writes messages to the network or the Internet. Some of the transport channels use encoders to convert messages in the format that can be used by the network. Some examples of transport channels are HTTP, NamedPipe, TCP, and MSMQ.

Protocol channels implement message processing protocols in a WCF service, often by reading or writing additional headers in a message. Examples of such protocols are WS-Security and WS-Reliability.

The following channels are part of the messaging layer:

- **WS Security channel**—Enables you to secure the messages by implementing the WS-Security specification in the messaging layer of a service
- **WS Reliable Messaging channel**—Guarantees delivery of messages
- **Encoders**—Provides the number of encoders for messages, such as Extensible Markup Language (XML), binary, and Message Transmission Optimization Mechanism (MTOM)
- **HTTP channel**—Specifies that HTTP is used for delivering messages
- **TCP channel**—Specifies that TCP is used for delivering messages
- **Transaction Flow channel**—Governs the pattern in which a message is transacted
- **NamedPipe channel**—Enables Inter-Process Communication (IPC)
- **MSMQ channel**—Enables services to interoperate with MSMQ applications

The Activation and Hosting Layer

The activation and hosting layer renders various options for the services in which they can be activated as well as hosted. Services can be hosted in two ways, self-hosted and hosted on external agents, such as Internet Information Services (IIS) or Windows Activation Services (WAS). The hosting and activation options provided by this layer are as follows:

- **Windows Activation Service**—Enables WCF applications to automatically activate when deployed on a computer that is running WAS
- **.EXE**—Enables you to run WCF services as executable (.exe) files
- **Windows Services**—Enables you to run WCF services as Windows services
- **COM +**—Enables you to run WCF services as a COM + application

After learning about the architecture of WCF, let's learn about the features of WCF.

Features of WCF

Apart from inheriting a lot of features from the existing distributed stack, WCF also extends the existing features, which are as follows:

- Endpoint support
- Enhanced transport layer
- Queuing support
- Improved transactional process
- Improved security
- Support for hosting a WCF service on various servers
- AJAX integration and JavaScript Object Notation (JSON) support

Let's discuss these features in detail, one by one.

Endpoint Support

An endpoint is a resource on a network through which messages can be sent. Endpoints of the services in WCF are responsible for enabling communication between the client and service. In WCF, endpoints include various elements, which are as follows:

- Addresses to locate the services where they are running
- Bindings to communicate with services
- Contracts to specify the tasks to be performed while communicating with services
- A set of behaviors that specify local implementation of details of the endpoint

The Addresses, Bindings, and Contracts elements of the endpoints are also known as ABCs of WCF.

Addresses

Every endpoint is linked with addresses that are used to find and identify services. To send a message to a service, you need to have its address. An address in WCF consists of Uniform Resource Locator (URL) that determines the protocols used by a service, the host on which it is running, and the path of the service. For example, the http://www.microsoft.com:119/mathservice.svc/EndpointAddress address has the following parts:

- URL- http:
- Host- www.microsoft.com
- Path- /mathservice.svc/EndpointAddress

The port number, which is 119 in the preceding example, depends on the protocols used by the services and is mandatory in URLs. The specifications of an address are as follows:

- **Scheme** – Defines the transport protocol, such as HTTP and TCP, of a service.
- **Machine** – Defines the full domain name of the host machine.
- **Port** – Defines the port number where a WCF service is running. It is an optional field in the address specification. The default port for the HTTP addresses is 80.
- **Path** – Defines the path of the services. The name of the directories and sub-directories in the path can be separated by a forward slash.

The format of the address of a service is as follows:

```
scheme://domain_name:port/path1/path2
```

In the preceding format,

- **schema** – Refers to a protocol used to transfer services from servers to clients
- **domain_name** – Refers to the name of the server where the service is running

- **port**—Refers to the port number where the service is listening
- **path**—Contains the name of the directories and their subdirectories

An example of address is shown in the following URL:

```
http://localhost:8080/dir/sub-dir
```

In the preceding URL, scheme is the `http:` protocol, `localhost` is the domain name (`localhost` is the default name of the local machine. If the service is running on a remote server, then the name can be `www.MyService.com`), `:8080` is the port number, and `/dir/sub-dir` is the path of the services.

WCF supports several protocols and every protocol has its own addressing format. The services are based on the SOAP protocol that defines the basic message simple (remote) object access. In SOAP messages, endpoints are stated as WS-Addressing endpoints, which are used to add specific headers in the SOAP messages and also define the addresses for the replies of the messages. The different types of addressing formats are as follows:

- HTTP address
- TCP address
- MSMQ address
- Named Pipe address
- IIS address
- Base address

Let's discuss these addressing formats in detail.

HTTP Address

Services using HTTP can either be self-hosted or hosted on IIS. The following format is used while addressing the self-hosted HTTP service:

```
http://localhost:8080/services/MyServices
```

If the HTTP service is hosted on IIS, the Secure Socket Layer (SSL) protocol is required, for which you need to replace the http service with the https service. In the WCF configuration, you can define the HTTP address, as shown in the following code snippet:

```
<endpoint
  address = "http://localhost:8080/services/MyServices"
  bindingSectionName = "HTTPBinding"
  contracts = "IExchange" />
```

It is recommended that you run your service on a port other than 80 to avoid any conflict with IIS on that port. When hosting the services on IIS, you need to obtain the certificate from a valid certificate authority, such as VeriSign or Thawte.

TCP Address

The TCP address uses the same addressing rules as used by the HTTP address, excluding the scheme. The scheme used by the TCP address is `net`.tcp. The format of the TCP address is as follows:

```
net.tcp://localhost:8080/services/MyServices
```

In the WCF configuration, you can define the TCP address, as shown in the following code snippet:

```
<endpoint
  address = "net.tcp://localhost:8080/services/MyServices"
  bindingSectionName = "TCPBinding"
  contracts = "IExchange" />
```

MSMQ Address

The MSMQ address contains two types of messaging patterns to transport asynchronous one-way and duplex type of patterns. MSMQ also contains two types of queues, public and private. Public queues are the active queues that can be accessed by any remote system; whereas, private queues are the local queues that can only be accessible from a local machine. MSMQ addresses use the net.msmq scheme to transport messages from the server to the client. Instead of the port number, the MSMQ address uses the queue type.

NOTE

A duplex type of pattern refers to the ability of both the service and client to send messages to each other independently. In other words, it forms a two-way communication for services that must communicate directly with the client.

An example of an MSMQ address is as follows:

```
net.msmq://localhost/private/MyServices
```

The format of defining the MSMQ address in the WCF configuration is shown in the following code snippet:

```
<endpoint
  address = "net.msmq://localhost/private/MyServices"
  bindingSectionName = "MSMQBinding"
  contracts = "IExchange" />
```

Named Pipe Address

The services using Named pipe address can only accept calls from the same machine. This address can be used for single (one-way) or duplex communication between processes on a single computer. It should be used when communication from another machine is to be prevented and communication between WCF applications on the same machine is required. The format of a Named pipe address is as follows:

```
net.pipe://localhost/services/MyServices
```

The format of defining the Named pipe address in the WCF configuration is shown in the following code snippet:

```
<endpoint
  address = "net.pipe://localhost/services/MyServices"
  bindingSectionName = "NamedPipesBinding"
  contracts = "IExchange" />
```

IIS Address

An IIS address contains scheme, domain name, port number, name of the virtual directory, and the service (.svc) file name. The format of an IIS address is as follows:

```
http://domain_name:8080/virtualdirectory [.svc filename]
```

In the IIS address, `.svc` is the extension of the service file.

Base Address

A WCF service itself has an address known as base address (which serves as a reference point for other addresses). It can have multiple base addresses, but only one per Uniform Resource Identifier (URI) scheme. An example of defining multiple endpoints in the same base address is shown in the following code snippet:

```
<host>
  <baseAddress>
        <add baseAddress = "http://localhost:8080/services/MyService"/>
        <add baseAddress = "net.tcp://localhost:8080/services/MyService"/>
  </baseAddress>
</host>
//This allows you to define following endpoints
<endpoint
  name = "HTTPBinding"
  address = "Exchange"
  bindingsSectionName = "HTTPBinding"
  contract = "IExchange" />
<endpoint
  name = "TCPBinding"
  address = "Exchange"
  bindingsSectionName = "TCPBinding"
  contract = "IExchange" />
```

When you host a service on IIS, the base address of the service is the virtual directory in which the service (.svc) file resides. In the preceding code snippet, the `MyService.svc` file resides in `http://localhost:8080/services`, which is also the base address for the service.

Bindings

Binding is a process that facilitates communication between a client and server. It specifies the details of transport, encoding, and protocols required by servers and clients to communicate with each other. In other words, binding specifies the communication protocols that are to be used to access the services. The following are the predefined bindings that you can use to facilitate communication:

- basicHttpBinding
- wsHttpBinding
- wsDualHttpBinding
- wsFederationHttpBinding
- netTcpBinding
- netNamedPipeBinding
- netMsmqBinding
- msmqIntegrationBinding
- netPeerTcpBinding

Now, let's discuss each binding in detail.

*The **basicHttpBinding** Binding*

The basicHttpBinding binding is used by the WCF services to configure and expose those endpoints that are able to communicate with ASMX-based Web services and clients. While working with `basicHttpBinding`, you should know the issues present in this type of binding. First, its security is disabled by default. If you want security in this binding, you need to change the value `of BasicHttpSecurityMode` enumeration from None to either of the following values:

- **Transport**—Refers to the security that is provided by using HTTPS
- **Message**—Refers to the security provided by using a SOAP message
- **TransportWithMessageCredential**—Refers to the service that must be configured with a certificate
- **TransportCredentialOnly**—Refers to the value that provides only HTTP-based client authentication

You should not select the None value because it disables the security. Noteworthy attributes of the `basicHttpBinding` binding are listed in Table 19.1:

Table 19.1: Attributes of the basicHttpBinding Binding

Attributes	Description
`allowCookies`	Uses a Boolean value that specifies whether a client allows cookies or accept them in future. Its default value is False. This attribute can be used in case of the ASMX Web service. Using this attribute, it is confirmed that the cookies returned from the server are automatically copied to all future client requests for that service.
`bypassProxyOnLocal`	Uses a Boolean value that specifies whether or not to bypass the proxy server on a local machine. Its default value is False.
`closeTimeout`	Uses integer values in the time format (hh:mm:ss), which specify the time interval provided to the connection to close an operation. The value must be more than zero; by default, the value is 00:01:00 (1 minute).
`hostnameComparisonMode`	Uses Exact, StrongWildcard, and WeakWildcard values, which indicate how the hostname is used to send a message to a service endpoint. Its default value is StrongWildcard.
`maxBufferPoolSize`	Uses an integer value, which specifies the maximum size of memory allocated for use by the manager of the message buffer that receives the messages from a channel. Its default value is 524288 (0x80000) bytes.

Table 19.1: Attributes of the basicHttpBinding Binding

Attributes	Description
`maxBufferSize`	Uses integer values, which specify the maximum size of a buffer (in bytes) that receives messages from a channel. Its default value is 65536 bytes.
`maxReceivedMessageSize`	Uses integer values, which specify the maximum size of the message that is to be received on a channel configured with this binding. Its default value is 65536 bytes.
`messageEncoding`	Uses the Text and Mtom values, which specify the type of encoding used to encode the SOAP messages. Text uses the text message encoder and Mtom uses the Message Transmission Organization Mechanism 1.0 encoder. The default value is Text.
`messageVersion`	Uses integer values that specify the version of the messages used by the clients and services configured with the binding.
`Name`	Uses string values that specify the configuration name of the binding. The name of the binding should be unique because it is used as identification for the binding.
`openTimeout`	Uses integer values in the time format (hh:mm:ss), which specify the time interval provided for a connection to open before an exception is raised. This value should be greater than or equal to 0. Its default value is 1 minute (00:01:00).
`proxyAddress`	Contains a URI that gives the address of the HTTP proxy. It is used in conjunction with the useDefaultWebProxy attribute. If the useDefaultWebProxy attribute is set to True, this attribute must be null. Its default value is null.
`receiveTimeout`	Uses integer values in the time format (hh:mm:ss) that specify the time interval in which the connection can remain inactive. Its default value is 10 minutes (00:10:00).
`sendTimeout`	Uses integer values in the time format (hh:mm:ss) that specify the time interval in which the send operation has to complete. Its default value is 1 minute (00:01:00).
`textEncoding`	Uses BigEndianUnicode, Unicode (16-bit encoding), and UTF8 (8-bit encoding) values, which specify the character encoding set to be used for emitting messages on the binding. Its default value is UTF8.
`transferMode`	Uses the Buffered and Streamed values, which specify whether the messages to be sent as a request or response are in the buffered mode or the streamed mode. Its default value is Buffered.
`useDefaultWebProxy`	Uses a Boolean value that specifies whether or not the system auto-configured HTTP proxy should be used if one exists. Its default value is True.

Now, let's configure the `basicHttpBinding` host for the services. The following code snippet shows how to configure the host of the `basicHttpBinding` binding:

```
<?xml version="1.0" encoding="utf-8" ?>
<configuration>
   <System.serviceModel>
        <services>
                <service name="WCF.MyService">
                        <host>
                        <baseAddress>
                        <add baseAddress="http://localhost:8080/MyService"/>
                        </baseAddress>
                        </host>
                        <endpoint address=""
                        binding="basicHttpBinding"
                        contract="WCF.MyService" />
                </service>
        </services>
   </System.serviceModel>
</configuration>
```

You can also define or configure the clients of the basicHttpBinding binding to consume the services. The following code snippet shows how to configure the basicHttpBinding binding client:

```
<?xml version="1.0" encoding="utf-8" ?>
<configuration>
  <System.serviceModel>
        <client>
              <endpoint address="http://localhost:8080/MyService"
                    binding="basicHttpBinding"
                    contract="WCF.MyService">
              </endpoint>
        </client>
  </System.serviceModel>
</configuration>
```

The *wsHttpBinding* Binding

The wsHttpBinding binding supports the WS-(Reliable Messaging for reliability, and WS-Security for message security and authentication) functionality and distributed transactions with reliable and secure sessions using the SOAP security. It uses HTTP and HTTPS transport protocols for communication. Noteworthy attributes of the wsHttpBinding binding are listed in Table 19.2:

Table 19.2: Attributes of the wsHttpBinding Binding

Attributes	Description
allowCookies	Uses a Boolean value that specifies whether or not a client allows cookies or accepts them in future. Its default value is False. This attribute can be used in case of the ASMX Web service. Using this attribute, the cookies returned from the server are automatically copied to all future client requests for that service.
bypassProxyOnLocal	Uses a Boolean value that specifies whether or not to bypass the proxy server on a local machine. Its default value is False.
closeTimeout	Uses integer values in the time format (hh:mm:ss), which specify the time interval provided to the connection to close an operation. The value must be more than zero; by default, the value is 00:01:00 (1 minute).
hostnameComparisonMode	Uses Exact, StrongWildcard, and WeakWildcard values, which indicate how the hostname is used for sending a message to a service endpoint. Its default value is StrongWildcard.
maxBufferPoolSize	Uses an integer value, which specifies the maximum size of memory allocated for use by the manager of the message buffer that receives the messages from a channel. Its default value is 524288 bytes (512 * 1024).
maxReceivedMessageSize	Uses integer values, which specify the maximum size of the message that is to be received for the channel configured with this binding. Its default value is 65536 bytes.
messageEncoding	Uses the Text and Mtom values, which specify the type of encoding used to encode the messages. Text uses the text message encoder and Mtom uses the Message Transmission Organization Mechanism 1.0 encoder. Its default value is Text.
messageVersion	Specifies the version of the messages used by the clients and services configured with the binding.
name	Uses string values that specify the configuration name of the binding. The name of the binding should be unique because it is used as identification for the binding.
openTimeout	Uses integer values in the time format (hh:mm:ss), which specify the time interval provided for an open operation to complete. This value should be greater than or equal to 0. Its default value is 1 minute (00:01:00).

Table 19.2: Attributes of the wsHttpBinding Binding	
Attributes	**Description**
`proxyAddress`	Contains a URI that gives the address of the HTTP proxy. It is used in conjunction with the useSystemWebProxy attribute. If the useSystemWebProxy attribute is set to True, this value must be null. Its default value is null.
`receiveTimeout`	Uses integer values in the time format (hh:mm:ss) that specify the time interval in which the receive operation has to complete. Its default value is 1 minute(00:10:00).
`sendTimeout`	Uses integer values in the time format (hh:mm:ss) that specify the time interval in which the send operation has to complete. Its default value is 1 minute (00:01:00).
`textEncoding`	Allows you to specify the character set encoding to be used for emitting messages on the binding. The valid values are UnicodeFffeTextEncoding: Unicode BigEndian encoding, Utf16TextEncoding: 16-bit encoding, and Utf8TextEncoding: 8-bit encoding. The default is Utf8TextEncoding. This attribute is of type Encoding.
`transactionFlow`	Uses a Boolean value, which specifies whether or not the binding supports the WS-Transaction specification. Its default value is False.
`useDefaultWebProxy`	Uses a Boolean value that specifies whether or not the system auto-configured HTTP proxy should be used. Its default value is True.

Now, let's configure the `wsHttpBinding` host for the services. The following code snippet shows how to configure the host:

```
<?xml version="1.0" encoding="utf-8" ?>
<configuration>
  <System.serviceModel>
        <services>
              <service name="WCF.MyService">
                    <host>
                    <baseAddress>
                    <add baseAddress="http://localhost:8080/MyService"/>
                    </baseAddress>
                    </host>
                    <endpoint address=""
                          binding="wsHttpBinding" contract="WCF.MyService" />
              </service>
        </services>
  </System.serviceModel>
</configuration>
```

You can also define or configure the clients of the `wsHttpBinding` binding to consume services. The following code snippet shows how to configure the `wsHttpBinding` binding client:

```
<?xml version="1.0" encoding="utf-8" ?>
<configuration>
  <System.serviceModel>
        <client>
              <endpoint address="http://localhost:8080/MyService"
                    binding="wsHttpBinding" contract="WCF.MyService">
              </endpoint>
        </client>
  </System.serviceModel>
</configuration>
```

*The **wsDualHttpBinding** Binding*

The `wsDualHttpBinding` binding is almost identical to the `wsHttpBinding` binding. The only difference is that the `wsDualHttpBinding` binding supports the duplex communication pattern. It is designed for use with duplex service contracts that allow both the hosts and the clients to transport messages. Noteworthy attributes of the `wsDualHttpBinding` binding are listed in Table 19.3:

Table 19.3: Attributes of the wsDualHttpBinding Binding

Attributes	Description
bypassProxyOnLocal	Uses a Boolean value that specifies whether or not to bypass the proxy server on a local machine. Its default value is False.
clientBaseAddress	Uses string values that specify the base address of a client.
closeTimeout	Uses integer values in the time format (hh:mm:ss), which specify the time interval provided to the connection to close an operation. The value must be more than zero, by default it is 00:01:00 (1 minute).
hostnameComparisonMode	Uses the Exact, StrongWildcard, and WeakWildcard values, which indicate how the hostname is used for sending a message to a service endpoint. Its default value is StrongWildcard.
maxBufferPoolSize	Uses an integer value, which specifies the maximum size of memory allocated for use by the manager of the message buffer that receives the messages from a channel. Its default value is 524288 bytes (512 * 1024).
maxReceivedMessageSize	Uses integer values, which specify the maximum size of the message that is to be received for the channel configured with this binding. Its default value is 65536 bytes.
messageEncoding	Uses the Text and Mtom values, which specify the type of encoding used to encode the messages. The Text value uses the text message encoder and the Mtom value uses the Message Transmission Organization Mechanism 1.0 encoder. The default value is Text.
messageVersion	Uses integer values, which specify the version of the messages used by the clients and services configured with the binding.
name	Uses string values, which specify the configuration name of the binding. The name of the binding should be unique because it is used as identification for the binding.
openTimeout	Uses integer values in the time format (hh:mm:ss), which specify the time interval provided for an open operation to complete. This value should be greater than or equal to 0. Its default value is 1 minute (00:01:00).
proxyAddress	Contains a URI that gives the address of the HTTP proxy. It is used in conjunction with the useDefaultWebProxy attribute. If the useDefaultWebProxy attribute is set to True, this value must be null. Its default value is null.
receiveTimeout	Uses integer values in the time format (hh:mm:ss) that specify the time interval in which the receive operation has to complete. Its default value is 1 minute (00:10:00).
sendTimeout	Uses integer values in the time format (hh:mm:ss) that specify the time interval in which the send operation has to complete. Its default value is 1 minute (00:01:00).
textEncoding	Uses the BigEndianUnicode, Unicode (16-bit encoding), and UTF8 (8-bit encoding) values, which specify the character encoding set used to encode the message text. Its default value is UTF8.
transactionFlow	Uses a Boolean value, which specifies whether or not the binding supports the WS-Transaction specification. Its default value is False.
useDefaultWebProxy	Uses a Boolean value, which specifies whether or not the system auto-configured HTTP proxy should be used. Its default value is True.

Now, let's define or configure the `wsDualHttpBinding` host for the services. The following code snippet shows how to configure the host:

```
<?xml version="1.0" encoding="utf-8" ?>
<configuration>
    <System.serviceModel>
```

```
        <services>
                <service name="WCF.MyDuplexService">
                        <host>
                        <baseAddress>
                        <add baseAddress= "http://localhost:8080/MyDuplexService"/>
                        </baseAddress>
                        </host>
                        <endpoint address=""
                        binding="wsDualHttpBinding" contract="WCF.MyDuplexService" />
                </service>
        </services>
    </System.serviceModel>
</configuration>
```

You can also define or configure the clients of the wsDualHttpBinding binding to consume the services. The following code snippet shows how to configure the wsDualHttpBinding binding client:

```
<?xml version="1.0" encoding="utf-8" ?>
<configuration>
   <System.serviceModel>
        <client>
                <endpoint address="http://localhost:8080/MyDuplexService"
                        binding="wsDualHttpBinding" contract="WCF.MyDuplexService">
                </endpoint>
        </client>
   </System.serviceModel>
</configuration>
```

*The **wsFederationHttpBinding** Binding*

The wsFederationHttpBinding binding offers security and interoperability that supports the WS-Federation protocol. Federated HTTP supports SOAP security as well as mixed-mode security, but it does not support transport security. Noteworthy attributes of the wsFederationHttpBinding binding are listed in Table 19.4:

Table 19.4: Attributes of the wsFederationHttpBinding Binding

Attributes	Description
bypassProxyOnLocal	Uses a Boolean value that specifies whether or not to bypass the proxy server on a local machine. Its default value is False.
closeTimeout	Uses integer values in the time format (hh:mm:ss), which specify the time interval provided to the connection to close an operation. The value must be more than 0, by default the value is 00:01:00 (1 minute).
hostnameComparisonMode	Uses the Exact, StrongWildcard, and WeakWildcard values, which indicate how the hostname is used to send a message to a service endpoint. Its default value is StrongWildcard.
maxBufferPoolSize	Uses an integer value, which specifies the maximum size of memory allocated for use by the manager of the message buffer that receives the messages from a channel. Its default value is 524288 bytes (512 * 1024)
maxReceivedMessageSize	Uses integer values, which specify the maximum size of the message that is to be received for the channel configured with this binding. Its default value is 65536 bytes.
messageEncoding	Uses the Text and Mtom values, which specify the type of encoding used to encode the messages. The Text value uses the text message encoder and the Mtom value uses the Message Transmission Organization Mechanism 1.0 encoder. The default value is Text.
messageVersion	Uses integer values, which specify the version of the messages used by the clients and services configured with the binding.

Table 19.4: Attributes of the wsFederationHttpBinding Binding

Attributes	Description
`name`	Uses string values that specify the configuration name of the binding. The name of the binding should be unique because it is used as identification for the binding.
`openTimeout`	Uses integer values in the time format (hh:mm:ss), which specify the time interval provided for an open operation to complete. This value should be greater than or equal to 0. Its default value is 1 minute (00:01:00).
`privacyNoticeAt`	Uses string values that specify the URI where the privacy notice (or the copyright) is located.
`privacyNoticeVersion`	Uses integer values that specify the version of the current privacy notice for the binding.
`proxyAddress`	Contains a URI that gives the address of the HTTP proxy. It is used in conjunction with the `useDefaultWebProxy` attribute. If the `useDefaultWebProxy` attribute is set to True, this value must be null. Its default value is null.
`receiveTimeout`	Uses integer values in the time format (hh:mm:ss) that specify the time interval in which the receive operation has to complete. Its default value is 10 minutes (00:10:00).
`reliableSession`	Specifies whether or not a reliable session is established between channel endpoints.
`sendTimeout`	Uses integer values in the time format (hh:mm:ss) that specify the time interval in which the send operation has to complete. Its default value is 1 minute (00:01:00).
`textEncoding`	Uses the BigEndianUnicode, Unicode (16-bit encoding), and UTF8 (8-bit encoding) values, which specify the character encoding sets used to encode the emitting message text. Its default value is UTF8.
`transactionFlow`	Uses a Boolean value, which specifies whether the binding supports the WS-Transaction specification. Its default value is False.
`useDefaultWebProxy`	Uses a Boolean value that specifies whether the system auto-configured HTTP proxy should be used. Its default value is True.

Now, let's define or configure the `wsFederationHttpBinding` host for the services. The following code snippet shows how to configure the host:

```
<?xml version="1.0" encoding="utf-8" ?>
<configuration>
  <System.serviceModel>
        <services>
              <service name="WCF.MyService">
                    <host>
                    <baseAddress>
                    <add baseAddress= "http://localhost:8080/MyService"/>
                    </baseAddress>
                    </host>
                    <endpoint address=""
                    binding="wsFederationHttpBinding" contract="WCF.MyService" />
              </service>
        </services>
  </System.serviceModel>
</configuration>
```

In the same way, you can also define or configure the clients of the `wsFederationHttpBinding` binding to consume services. The following code snippet shows how to configure the `wsFederationHttpBinding` binding client:

```
<?xml version="1.0" encoding="utf-8" ?>
<configuration>
  <System.serviceModel>
        <client>
```

```
                <endpoint address="http://localhost:8080/MyService"
                     binding="wsFederationHttpBinding"
                     contract="WCF.MyService">
                </endpoint>
            </client>
        </system.serviceModel>
    </configuration>
```

The **netTcpBinding** Binding

The netTcpBinding binding is a secure and reliable binding when .NET-to-.NET cross-machine communication is required. In other words, this binding is designed to support communication between .NET applications that are deployed on different machines across the network. When both the applications are built on .NET, interoperability is not required. This makes the communication across the network more flexible and enhances performance. This binding supports SOAP security, transactions, and reliability and uses the TCP protocol for message security. Noteworthy attributes of the netTcpBinding binding are listed in Table 19.5:

Table 19.5: Attributes of the netTcpBinding Binding

Attributes	Description
closeTimeout	Uses integer values in the time format (hh:mm:ss), which specify the time interval provided to the connection to close an operation. The value must be more than zero, by default the value is 00:01:00 (1 minute).
hostnameComparisonMode	Uses the Exact, StrongWildcard, and WeakWildcard values, which indicate whether the hostname is used to send a message to a service endpoint. Its default value is StrongWildcard.
listenBacklog	Uses integer values, which specify the maximum number of queued connection requests that are pending. Its default value is 10. The connections that exceed the specified value are queued.
maxBufferPoolSize	Uses an integer value, which specifies the maximum size of memory allocated for use by the manager of the message buffer that receives the messages from a channel. Its default value is 524288 bytes (512 * 1024).
maxBufferSize	Uses integer values, which specify the maximum size of a buffer (in bytes) that receives messages from a channel. Its default value is 65536 bytes.
maxConnections	Uses integer values, which specify the maximum number of connection (inbound or outbound) that the service will create or accept. Its default value is 10.
maxReceivedMessageSize	Uses integer values, which specify the maximum size of the message that is to be received for the channel configured with this binding. Its default value is 65536 bytes.
name	Uses string values, which specify the configuration name of the binding. The name of the binding should be unique because it is used as identification for the binding.
openTimeout	Uses integer values in the time format (hh:mm:ss), which specify the time interval provided for an open operation to complete. This value should be greater than or equal to 0. Its default value is 1 minute (00:01:00).
portSharingEnabled	Uses a Boolean value that specifies whether the TCP port sharing is enabled for a connection. Its default value is False, which means the TCP port sharing is disabled and each binding uses its own exclusive port.
receiveTimeout	Uses integer values in the time format (hh:mm:ss) that specify the time interval in which the receive operation has to complete. Its default value is 10 minutes (00:10:00)
sendTimeout	Uses integer values in the time format (hh:mm:ss) that specify the time interval in which the send operation has to complete. Its default value is 1 minute (00:01:00).

Table 19.5: Attributes of the netTcpBinding Binding	
Attributes	**Description**
transactionFlow	Uses a Boolean value, which specifies whether or not the binding supports the WS-Transaction specification. Its default value is False.
transactionProtocol	Uses the OleTransactions or WSAtomicTransactionOctober2004 values, which specify the type of transaction protocol used by the services to flow transactions. Its default value is OleTransactions.
transferMode	Uses the Buffered and Streamed values, which specify whether to send the messages in buffered mode or in streamed mode on a request or response. Its default value is Buffered.

Now, let's define or configure the `netTcpBinding` host for the services. The following code snippet shows how to configure the host:

```
<?xml version="1.0" encoding="utf-8" ?>
<configuration>
  <System.serviceModel>
        <services>
                <service name="WCF.MyService">
                        <host>
                        <baseAddress>
                        <add baseAddress= "net.tcp://localhost:808/MyService"/>
                        </baseAddress>
                        </host>
                        <endpoint address="" binding="netTcpBinding"
                                contract="WCF.MyService" />
                </service>
        </services>
  </System.serviceModel>
</configuration>
```

In the same way, you can also define or configure the clients of the `netTcpBinding` binding to consume services. The following code snippet shows how to configure the `netTcpBinding` binding client:

```
<?xml version="1.0" encoding="utf-8" ?>
<configuration>
  <System.serviceModel>
        <client>
                <endpoint address="net.tcp://localhost:808/MyService"
                        binding="netTcpBinding"      contract="WCF.MyService">
                </endpoint>
        </client>
  </System.serviceModel>
</configuration>
```

*The **netPeerTcpBinding** Binding*

The `netPeerTcpBinding` binding is used for peer-to-peer (P2P) communication with WCF. This binding allows multiparty communication over the network. It uses TCP as the default transport protocol and binary as default message encoder. Noteworthy attributes of the `netPeerTcpBinding` binding are listed in Table 19.6:

Table 19.6: Attributes of the netPeerTcpBinding Binding	
Attributes	**Description**
closeTimeout	Uses integer values in the time format (hh:mm:ss), which specify the time interval provided to the connection to close an operation. The value must be more than zero; by default, the value is 00:01:00 (1 minute).

Table 19.6: Attributes of the netPeerTcpBinding Binding	
Attributes	**Description**
`listenIPAddress`	Uses string values, which specify the Internet Protocol (IP) address used for listening TCP messages.
`maxBufferPoolSize`	Uses integer values, which specify the maximum size of memory allocated for use by the manager of the message buffer that receives the messages from a channel. Its default value is 524288 bytes (512 * 1024).
`maxReceivedMessageSize`	Uses integer values, which specify the maximum size of the message that is to be received for the channel configured with this binding. Its default value is 65536 bytes.
`name`	Uses string values that specify the configuration name of the binding. The name of the binding should be unique because it is used as identification for the binding.
`openTimeout`	Uses integer values in the time format (hh:mm:ss), which specify the time interval provided for an open operation to complete. This value should be greater than or equal to 0. Its default value is 1 minute (00:01:00).
`Port`	Uses integer values that specify a listener port. Its default value is 0.
`receiveTimeout`	Uses integer values in the time format (hh:mm:ss) that specify the time interval in which the receive operation has to complete. Its default value is 10 minutes (00:10:00).
`sendTimeout`	Uses integer values in the time format (hh:mm:ss) that specify the time interval in which the send operation has to complete. Its default value is 1 minute (00:01:00).

Now, let's define or configure the `netPeerTcpBinding` host for the services. The following code snippet shows how to configure the host:

```
<?xml version="1.0" encoding="utf-8" ?>
<configuration>
  <System.serviceModel>
        <services>
              <service name="WCF.MyService">
                    <host>
                    <baseAddress>
                    <add baseAddress= "net.peer://localhost:0/MyService"/>
                    </baseAddress>
                    </host>
                    <endpoint address=""
                    binding="netPeerTcpBinding" contract="WCF.MyService" />
              </service>
        </services>
  </System.serviceModel>
</configuration>
```

In the same way, you can also define or configure the clients of the `netPeerTcpBinding` binding to consume services. The following code snippet shows how to configure the `netPeerTcpBinding` binding client:

```
<?xml version="1.0" encoding="utf 8" ?>
<configuration>
  <System.serviceModel>
        <client>
              <endpoint address="net.peer://localhost:0/MyService"
              binding="netPeerTcpBinding" contract="WCF.MyService">
              </endpoint>
        </client>
  </System.serviceModel>
</configuration>
```

The **netNamedPipeBinding** Binding

The `netNamedPipeBinding` binding is almost similar to the `netTcpBinding` binding. The only difference is that the `netNamedPipeBinding` binding is used for the IPC. You can use the namedpipes to communicate across the network, but WCF restricts the use of the namedpipes to local machine communication. Noteworthy attributes of the `netNamedPipeBinding` binding are listed in Table 19.7:

Table 19.7: Attributes of the netNamedPipeBinding Binding

Attributes	Description
`closeTimeout`	Uses integer values in the time format (hh:mm:ss), which specify the time interval provided to the connection to close an operation. The value must be more than zero; by default, it is 00:01:00 (1 minute).
`hostnameComparisonMode`	Uses the Exact, StrongWildcard, and WeakWildcard values, which indicate whether the hostname is used to send a message to a service endpoint. Its default value is StrongWildcard.
`maxBufferPoolSize`	Uses an integer value, which specifies the maximum size of memory allocated for use by the manager of the message buffer that receives the messages from a channel. Its default value is 524288 bytes (512 * 1024).
`maxBufferSize`	Uses integer values, which specify the maximum size of a buffer (in bytes) that receives messages from a channel. Its default value is 65536 bytes.
`maxConnections`	Uses integer values, which specify the maximum number of connection (inbound or outbound) that the service will accept or create. Its default value is 10.
`maxReceivedMessageSize`	Uses integer values, which specify the maximum size of the message that is to be received for the channel configured with this binding. Its default value is 65536 bytes.
`name`	Uses string values, which specify the configuration name of the binding. The name of the binding should be unique because it is used as identification for the binding.
`openTimeout`	Uses integer values in the time format (hh:mm:ss), which specify the time interval provided for an open operation to complete. This value should be greater than or equal to 0. Its default value is 1 minute (00:01:00).
`receiveTimeout`	Uses integer values in the time format (hh:mm:ss) that specify the time interval in which the receive operation has to complete. Its default value is 10 minutes (00:10:00).
`sendTimeout`	Uses integer values in the time format (hh:mm:ss) that specify the time interval in which the send operation has to complete. Its default value is 1 minute (00:01:00).
`transactionFlow`	Uses a Boolean value, which specifies whether or not the binding supports the WS-Transaction specification. Its default value is False.
`transactionProtocol`	Uses OleTransactions or WSAtomicTransactionOctober2004 values, which specify the type of transaction protocol used by services. Its default value is OleTransactions.
`transferMode`	Uses the Buffered and Streamed values, which specify whether to send messages in buffered mode or in streamed mode on a request or response. Its default value is Buffered.

Now, let's define or configure the `netNamedPipeBinding` host for the services. The following code snippet shows how to configure the host:

```
<?xml version="1.0" encoding="utf-8" ?>
<configuration>
   <System.serviceModel>
        <services>
```

```
                <service name="WCF.MyService">
                        <host>
                        <baseAddress>
                        <add baseAddress= "net.pipe://localhost/MyService"/>
                        </baseAddress>
                        </host>
                        <endpoint address=""
                        binding="netNamedPipeBinding" contract="WCF.MyService" />
                </service>
        </services>
    </System.serviceModel>
</configuration>
```

In the same way, you can also define or configure the clients of the netNamedPipeBinding binding to consume services. The following code snippet shows how to configure the netNamedPipeBinding binding client:

```
<?xml version="1.0" encoding="utf-8" ?>
<configuration>
    <System.serviceModel>
        <client>
                <endpoint address="net.pipe://localhost/MyService"
                        binding="netNamedPipeBinding"
                        contract="WCF.MyService">
                </endpoint>
        </client>
    </System.serviceModel>
</configuration>
```

*The **netMsmqBinding** Binding*

WCF supports queuing of messages by using MSMQ as a transport protocol, which enables support for disconnected operations, failure isolation, and load leveling. In the disconnected operations, it is not required by the clients and the services to be online at the same time. The clients can perform their transactions and disconnect. The service can accept the transaction and start working on it even if the client remains disconnected. In the failure isolation, if the message sent by the client fails, it does not affect the processing of other messages. The client can continue sending messages even if any of the messages failed to be received by services. All the messages are received by the messages queue. When the service starts running again, it starts pulling messages from the bottom of the queue. This process guarantees message reliability and system stability.

Noteworthy attributes of the `netMsmqBinding` binding are listed in Table 19.8:

Table 19.8: Attributes of the netMsmqBinding Binding

Attributes	Description
`closeTimeout`	Uses integer values in the time format (hh:mm:ss), which specify the time interval provided to the connection to close an operation. The value must be more than zero; by default, the value is 00:01:00 (1 minute).
`customDeadLetterQueue`	Uses string values that specify the URI of the location where the queue of the dead letters is stored. Dead letters refer to the failed or expired letters.
`deadLetterQueue`	Uses the values which specify the type of the dead letter queue to be used. Its default value is null.
`durable`	Uses a Boolean value that specifies whether the messages in the queue are durable or volatile. Its default value is True.
`exactlyOnce`	Uses a Boolean value that specifies whether the message is delivered only once. Its default value is True, which means that the message is delivered only once.

Table 19.8: Attributes of the netMsmqBinding Binding

Attributes	Description
`maxBufferPoolSize`	Uses an integer value, which specifies the maximum size of memory allocated for use by the manager of the message buffer that receives the messages from a channel. Its default value is 8.
`maxReceivedMessageSize`	Uses integer values, which specify the maximum size of the message that is to be received for the channel configured with this binding. Its default value is 65536 bytes.
`maxRetryCycles`	Uses integer values, which specify the maximum number of retry attempts, before a message is considered as poisoned. A message becomes poisoned when it is not delivered in any of the attempts made. Its default value is 3.
`name`	Uses string values that specify the configuration name of the binding. The name of the binding should be unique because it is used as identification for the binding.
`openTimeout`	Uses integer values in the time format (hh:mm:ss), which specify the time interval provided for an open operation to complete. This value should be greater than or equal to 0. Its default value is 1 minute (00:01:00).
`QueueTransferProtocol`	Uses the Native, Srmp (Soap Reliable Messaging Protocol), and SrmpSecure values, which specify the type of the queue transfer protocol used by this binding. Its default value is Native.
`receiveErrorHandling`	Uses the Drop, Fault, Move, and Reject values, which handle the poisoned messages (the messages that exceed the maximum number of delivery attempts to an application). Its default value is Fault.
`receiveRetryCount`	Uses integer values, which specify the maximum number of attempts to be made to send a message.
`receiveTimeout`	Uses integer values in the time format (hh:mm:ss) that specify the time interval in which the receive operation has to complete. Its default value is 10 minutes (00:10:00).
`retryCycleDelay`	Uses integer values in the time format (hh:mm:ss), which specify the time interval between the retry cycle of the failed message delivery. Its default value is 10 minutes (00:10:00).
`sendTimeout`	Uses integer values in the time format (hh:mm:ss) that specify the time interval in which the send operation has to complete. Its default value is 1 minute (00:01:00).
`timeToLive`	Uses integer values in the time format (hh:mm:ss) that specify a time period in which a message is considered as valid. After the specified time period is over, the message expires and is sent to the dead letter queue. Its default value is 1 day (1.00:00:00).
`usingActiveDirectory`	Uses a Boolean value that specifies whether or not the queue address should be converted into a direct format name using Active Directory (AD).
`useMsmqTracing`	Uses a Boolean value that specifies whether to use the MSMQ tracing of the messages processed by this binding. Its default value is False.
`useSourceJournal`	Uses a Boolean value that specifies whether or not the copy of messages should be stored in a source journal queue. Its default value is False.

Now, let's define or configure the `netMsmqBinding` host for the services. The following code snippet shows how to configure the host:

```
<?xml version="1.0" encoding="utf-8" ?>
<configuration>
  <System.serviceModel>
```

```
        <services>
            <service name="WCF.MyService">
                <host>
                <baseAddress>
                <add baseAddress="net.msmq://localhost/private/MyService"/>
                </baseAddress>
                </host>
                <endpoint address=""
                binding="netMsmqBinding" contract="WCF.MyService" />
            </service>
        </services>
    </System.serviceModel>
</configuration>
```

In the same way, you can also define or configure the clients of the `netMsmqBinding` binding to consume services. The following code snippet shows how to configure the `netMsmqBinding` binding client:

```
<?xml version="1.0" encoding="utf-8" ?>
<configuration>
    <System.serviceModel>
        <client>
            <endpoint address="net.msmq://localhost/private/MyService"
            binding="netMsmqBinding" contract="WCF.MyService">
            </endpoint>
        </client>
    </System.serviceModel>
</configuration>
```

The *msmqIntegrationBinding* Binding

The `msmqIntegrationBinding` binding enables WCF to directly communicate with MSMQ. You should use the `msmqIntegrationBinding` binding only when a WCF application communicates with a non-WCF application. Noteworthy attributes of the `netMsmqBinding` binding are listed in Table 19.9:

Table 19.9: Attributes of the msmqIntegrationBinding Binding

Attributes	Description
`closeTimeout`	Uses integer values in the time format (hh:mm:ss), which specify the time interval provided to the connection to close an operation. The value must be more than zero; by default, it is 00:01:00 (1 minute).
`customDeadLetterQueue`	Uses string values that specify the URI of the location where the queue of the dead letters is stored.
`deadLetterQueue`	Uses the None, System or Custom values that specify the type of the dead letter. Its default value is None.
`durable`	Uses a Boolean value that specifies whether the messages in the queue are durable or volatile. Its default value is True.
`exactlyOnce`	Uses a Boolean value that specifies whether a message is delivered only once. Its default value is True, which means that the message is delivered exactly once.
`maxReceivedMessageSize`	Uses integer values, which specify the maximum size of the message that is to be received for the channel configured with this binding. Its default value is 65536 bytes.
`maxRetryCycles`	Uses integer values, which specify the maximum number of retry attempts, before a message is considered poisoned. A message becomes poisoned when it fails all delivery attempts of all cycles. Its default value is 2.
`name`	Uses string values that specify the configuration name of the binding. The name of the binding should be unique because it is used as identification for the binding.

Table 19.9: Attributes of the msmqIntegrationBinding Binding	
Attributes	**Description**
`openTimeout`	Uses integer values in the time format (hh:mm:ss), which specify the time interval provided for an open operation to complete. This value should be greater than or equal to 0. Its default value is 1 minute (00:01:00).
`receiveErrorHandling`	Uses the Drop, Fault, Move, and Reject values, which handle the poisoned messages. Its default value is Fault.
`receiveRetryCount`	Uses integer values, which specify the maximum number of attempts to be made to send a message. Its default value is 5.
`receiveTimeout`	Uses integer values in the time format (hh:mm:ss) that specify the time interval in which the receive operation has to complete. Its default value is 10 minutes (00:10:00).
`retryCycleDelay`	Uses integer values in the time format (hh:mm:ss), which specify the time interval between the retry cycle of the failed message delivery. Its default value is 30 minutes (00:30:00).
`sendTimeout`	Uses integer values in the time format (hh:mm:ss) that specify the time interval in which the send operation has to complete. Its default value is 1 minute (00:01:00).
`serializationFormat`	Uses the XML, Binary, ActiveX, ByteArray, and Stream values that specify the serialized format of the message body. Its default value is XML.
`timeToLive`	Uses integer values in the time format (hh:mm:ss) that specify a time period in which a message is considered as valid. After the specified time period is over, the message expires and is sent to the dead letter queue. Its default value is 1 day (1.00:00:00).
`useMsmqTracing`	Uses a Boolean value, which specifies whether to use the MSMQ tracing of the messages processed by this binding. Its default value is False.
`useSourceJournal`	Uses a Boolean value, which specifies whether or not the copy of messages should be stored in a source journal queue. Its default value is False.

Now, let's define or configure the `msmqIntegrationBinding` host for the services. The following code snippet shows how to configure the host:

```
<?xml version="1.0" encoding="utf-8" ?>
<configuration>
  <System.serviceModel>
        <services>
                <service name="WCF.MyService">
                <host>
                <baseAddress>
                <add baseAddress="msmq.fromatname:Direct=OS:.\private$\MyService" />
                </baseAddress>
                </host>
                <endpoint address=""
                binding="msmqIntegrationBinding" contract="WCF.MyService" />
                </service>
        </services>
  </System.serviceModel>
</configuration>
```

In the same way, you can also define or configure the clients of the `msmqIntegrationBinding` binding to consume services. The following code snippet shows how to configure the `msmqIntegrationBinding` binding client:

```
<?xml version="1.0" encoding="utf-8" ?>
<configuration>
  <System.serviceModel>
      <client>
            <endpoint address="msmq.formatname:Direct=OS:.\private$\MyService"
                  binding="msmqIntegrationBinding" contract="WCF.MyService">
            </endpoint>
      </client>
  </System.serviceModel>
</configuration>
```

Contracts

Contracts in WCF are the agreements between the services and their clients. The contracts of the services contain the information regarding the agreement, such as providing the interoperability that the service needs to communicate with the client. It is through contracts that clients and services agree to the types of operations and structures they will use during the period they communicate with each other. Without contracts, no work is accomplished. The following are three basic contracts used to define a WCF service:

- **Service contract**—Defines the methods of a service. In other words, the service contract informs the client about the services, such as the message data type and operation locations.
- **Data contract**—Defines the data types used by the available service methods.
- **Message contract**—Provides the ability to control the message headers during the creation of a message.

Endpoint Behavior

Endpoint behaviors are used to customize the runtime behavior of the service endpoint by participating in the process of building a WCF runtime. The `ListenUri` property is an example of the endpoint behavior. This property allows you to specify a different listening address than the SOAP or Web Services Description Language (WSDL) address.

Enhanced Transport Layer

The transport layer is at the lowest level of the channel stack as it includes four levels–Security, Interoperability, Message Patterns, and Transport. A channel stack is used by the WCF endpoints to communicate with other Web applications or services over the Internet. The main transport protocols used in WCF are HTTP, HTTPS, TCP, and Named Pipe. HTTP works as a request/response protocol between clients and servers. The most common application consists of Web browser clients that communicate with a Web server. The client sends a request to a server. After receiving the request, the server gives response to the client, which contains the status of the request. The HTTP protocol does not maintain state after sending the response. To know more about states, refer Chapter 3, *Applications Structure and State*.

NOTE

A channel stack is a layered communication stack, which is constructed with one or more channels, such as transport channels and protocol channels that process messages. The channel stack constructed with TCP transport and transaction protocol channels enables sending and receiving messages across a network using the TCP protocol.

Unlike the HTTP protocol, the TCP protocol is connection-based, which means that a communication session between the client and the server is maintained before exchanging messages. The TCP protocol helps in performing the following tasks:

- Notifying the sender about packet delivery
- Guaranteeing that the order in which the packets are delivered is the same as they are sent
- Ensuring the non-duplication of packets
- Retransmitting lost or undelivered packets

The Named Pipe protocol is used when communication is required between different WCF applications on the same machine and you do not want to communicate with another machine. The Named pipe protocol has a name and can be used for one-way or duplex communication on the same machine.

Queuing Support

WCF supports queuing that allows messages to be safely stored in a queue and provides a consistent state of communication. Queuing collects, stores, and forwards sent messages to the receiving application. This provides a safe and reliable message delivery mechanism. WCF enables queuing by providing support for the MSMQ transport.

Improved Transactional Process

A transaction is a unit of work that either fully succeeds or completely fails. For instance, if a transaction needs to perform four actions on a database and the third action fails to execute. Now, the two actions that take place before the third action will be roll backed to their original state. This implies that the transaction commits only when all the four actions are completed successfully.

WCF incorporates the Atomicity, Consistency, Isolation, and Durability (ACID) features of a transaction into communication between clients and services. At the enterprise level, this feature allows you to execute transactions across different platforms.

Improved Security

In WCF, the messages to clients and servers are authenticated. WCF also ensures that during transit, messages should remain in the order in which they are sent. In WCF, when you create a secure distributed application with existing technologies, such as using HTTPS protocol or user name and password for authentication, WCF integrates the application into an existing security infrastructure for exchanging secure messages and also extends the distributed security outside the Windows-only environment.

Support for Hosting a WCF Service on Various Servers

WCF hosting allows services to be hosted in different environments, such as Windows NT Services, Windows Forms, Console applications, IIS, and Windows Process Activation Services (WAS). Hosting a service in IIS allows the service to take advantages of many of the native IIS features. For example, IIS can control starting and stopping of the service automatically.

Hosting in IIS

IIS helps in hosting a WCF service because it provides automatic processing activation, which means that you are not responsible for starting and stopping the service. This implies that when a message is received for a service in IIS, the service automatically starts. IIS is an excellent base for hosting services due to its scalability, reliability, and security.

IIS also provides the facility of monitoring the health of services. It recycles the process of sending messages that are determined as unhealthy processes (the processes that do not respond to the requests or take longer time to execute).

Hosting in Windows Process Activation Service

WAS is an infrastructure to host WCF services. The WAS process model allows HTTP and non-HTTP protocols to be used in a hosting environment by removing the dependency on HTTP. WAS also provides a mechanism in which hosted applications can be more flexible, easily manageable, and use resources much more efficiently.

AJAX Integration and JSON Support

WCF supports ASP.NET AJAX and JSON data format, which allows WCF services to expose operations to AJAX clients. JSON is an effective data format used to quickly exchange small amount of data between the AJAX-enabled Web services and their clients. The `Sys.Net.WebServiceProxy` class of the Microsoft AJAX library contains proxy classes for using AJAX integration and JSON support in WCF.

Enhanced Features of WCF

The new version of WCF, that is, WCF 4.5, is introduced with the .NET Framework 4.5. Major enhancements have been done in WCF 4.5 to ease the development and maintenance of WCF services. These enhancements are as follows:

- **Task-based Async Support**—The Add Service Reference option generates Task-returning async service operation methods for both synchronous and asynchronous methods. This enables you to invoke the service operations asynchronously with the help of new Task based async programming model. When you invoke the generated proxy method, WCF creates a Task object to denote the asynchronous operation and returns that Task to you. While using an async operation you can use it as a task-based async operation. The Task completes with the operation.
- **Configuration Files**—In Visual Studio Integrated Development Environment (IDE), when a developer adds a WCF service reference or uses SvcUtil.exe, a configuration file is automatically generated. In the previous versions of WCF, configuration files are used to contain every binding property even if it holds the default value. Following is an example of the configuration file that is generated in WCF 3.0:

```
<?xml version="1.0"?>
<configuration>
  <!--
      Note: As an alternative to hand editing this file you can use the
      web admin tool to configure settings for your application. Use
      the Website->Asp.Net Configuration option in Visual Studio.
      A full list of settings and comments can be found in
      machine.config.comments usually located in
      \Windows\Microsoft.Net\Framework\vx.x\Config
  -->
  <appSettings/>
  <connectionStrings/>
  <system.web>
    <!--
        Set compilation debug="true" to insert debugging
        symbols into the compiled page. Because this
        affects performance, set this value to true only
        during development.
    -->
    <compilation debug="false">
    </compilation>
    <!--
        The <authentication> section enables configuration
        of the security authentication mode used by
        ASP.NET to identify an incoming user.
    -->
    <authentication mode="Windows" />
    <!--
        The <customErrors> section enables configuration
        of what to do if/when an unhandled error occurs
        during the execution of a request. Specifically,
        it enables developers to configure html error pages
        to be displayed in place of a error stack trace.

        <customErrors mode="RemoteOnly" defaultRedirect="GenericErrorPage.htm">
         <error statusCode="403" redirect="NoAccess.htm" />
         <error statusCode="404" redirect="FileNotFound.htm" />
        </customErrors>
    -->
  </system.web>
  <system.webServer>
```

```
      <!--
          To browse web app root directory during debugging, set the value below to true.
          Set to false before deployment to avoid disclosing web app folder information.
        -->
      <directoryBrowse enabled="true"/>
    </system.webServer>
    <system.serviceModel>
      <services>
        <service name="Service" behaviorConfiguration="ServiceBehavior">
          <!-- Service Endpoints -->
          <endpoint address="" binding="basicHttpBinding" contract="IService">
            <!--
                Upon deployment, the following identity element should be removed or
                   replaced to reflect the
                identity under which the deployed service runs.  If removed, WCF will
                   infer an appropriate identity
                automatically.
            -->
            <identity>
              <dns value="localhost"/>
            </identity>
          </endpoint>
          <endpoint address="max" binding="maxHttpBinding" contract="IMetadataExchange"/>
        </service>
      </services>
      <behaviors>
        <serviceBehaviors>
          <behavior name="ServiceBehavior">
            <!-- To avoid disclosing metadata information, set the value below to false
                 before deployment -->
            <serviceMetadata httpGetEnabled="true"/>
            <!-- To receive exception details in faults for debugging purposes, set the
           value below to true.  Set to false before deployment to avoid disclosing
           exception information -->
            <serviceDebug includeExceptionDetailInFaults="false"/>
          </behavior>
        </serviceBehaviors>
      </behaviors>
    </system.serviceModel>
  </configuration>
```

However, with the release of WCF 4.5, configuration files have been simplified. In WCF 4.5, configuration files contain only those binding properties that have non-default values. Following is an example of the configuration file that is generated in WCF 4.5:

```
<?xml version="1.0"?>
<configuration>
  <appSettings>
    <add key="aspnet:UseTaskFriendlySynchronizationContext" value="true"/>
  </appSettings>
  <system.web>
    <compilation debug="true" targetFramework="4.5"/>
    <httpRuntime targetFramework="4.5"/>
  </system.web>
  <system.serviceModel>
    <behaviors>
      <serviceBehaviors>
        <behavior>
          <!-- To avoid disclosing metadata information, set the values below to false
         before deployment -->
          <serviceMetadata httpGetEnabled="true" httpsGetEnabled="true"/>
```

```
        <!-- To receive exception details in faults for debugging purposes, set the
             value below to true.  Set to false before deployment to avoid
             disclosing exception information -->
        <serviceDebug includeExceptionDetailInFaults="false"/>
      </behavior>
    </serviceBehaviors>
  </behaviors>
  <protocolMapping>
    <add binding="basicHttpsBinding" scheme="https"/>
  </protocolMapping>
  <serviceHostingEnvironment aspNetCompatibilityEnabled="true"
      multipleSiteBindingsEnabled="true"/>
 </system.serviceModel>
 <system.webServer>
  <modules runAllManagedModulesForAllRequests="true"/>
  <!--
      To browse web app root directory during debugging, set the value below to true.
      Set to false before deployment to avoid disclosing web app folder information.
    -->
  <directoryBrowse enabled="true"/>
 </system.webServer>
</configuration>
```

- **Contract-First Development**—The WCF 4.5 supports contract-first development with the help of the svcutil.exe tool. This tool has a /serviceContract switch that allows developers to create service and data contract files from a WSDL document.
- **Add Service Reference from a Portable Subset Project**—In WCF 4.5, portable subset projects allow developers to maintain single source code and build applications for various .NET platforms, such as Desktop, Silverlight, Windows Phone, and XBOX. Portable subset projects only reference the .NET portable libraries and can be easily used by any .NET platform application. Adding a portable subset project is similar to adding a service reference within any WCF client application.
- **ASP.NET Compatibility Model Default Changed**—Developers can use the ASP.NET compatibility mode by setting the AspNetCompatibilityEnabled attribute to true in the <serviceHostingEnvironment> section of the web.config file. WCF 4.5 allows developers to use powerful features, such as request processing, content redirection, and filtering of ASP.NET HTTP pipeline, while developing WCF services. To use the ASP.NET pipeline features, services running under the default appDomain need to have the RequirementsMode property on AspNetCompatibilityRequirementsAttribute set to Allowed or Required. By default, the AspNetCompatibilityRequirementsAttribute attribute is set to Allowed and the AspNetCompatibilityEnabled attribute is set to true for WCF 4.5 applications.
- **Streaming Improvements**—The limitations of message buffering for IIS-hosted WCF services are removed with the following improvements in WCF 4.5:
  a. **Asynchronous Streaming**—WCF 4.5 supports asynchronous streaming to enhance the scalability of services while sending the streamed messages to multiple clients, which are reading the messages slowly. Moreover, WCF 4.5 does not block one thread per client and frees up the thread to service another client.
  b. **Buffering Limitation**—In the previous versions of WCF, while receiving the messages for an IIS-hosted service using streaming message transfer, ASP.NET would buffer the entire message before passing it to a WCF service. This results in the use of large amount of memory. Therefore, in .NET 4.5, this buffering limitation has been removed. Now, IIS-hosted WCF services start processing the incoming stream before the entire message has been received from a client. It improves the performance and allows WCF IIS-hosted services to respond more quickly.
- **WCF Configuration Validation**—In WCF 4.5, configuration files are validated during the build process. Visual Studio shows the validation errors and warnings in case the validation fails.

- **XML Editor Tooltips**—The XML editor in Visual Studio 2012 provides tooltips for each configuration element and its properties. This helps developers to easily configure WCF services.
- **Multiple Authentication Support**—In WCF 4.5, a single WCF endpoint can response to multiple authentication modes at a time.
- **BasicHttpBindings**—This enables IIS to control WCF security settings.
- **New transport default values**—A number of transport property default values have changed to simplify configuration. Table 19.10 describes the settings that have changed:

Table 19.10: Property and their values

Property	On	New Default
channelInitializationTimeout	NetTcpBinding	30 seconds
listenBacklog	NetTcpBinding	12 * number of processors
maxPendingAccepts	ConnectionOrientedTransportBinding Element SMSvcHost.exe	2 * number of processors for transport 4 * number of processors for SMSvcHost.exe
maxPendingConnections	ConnectionOrientedTransportBinding Element	12 * number of processors
receiveTimeout	SMSvcHost.exe	30 seconds

- **XmlDictionaryReaderQuotas**—It comprises configurable quota values for XML dictionary readers which limit the size of memory used by an encoder to create a message. While these quotas are configurable, the default values are modified to reduce the effort of a developer to set them explicitly.
- **Simplifying Exposing an Endpoint Over HTTPS with IIS**—An HTTPS protocol mapping has been added to simplify exposing an endpoint over this protocol. Before enabling an HTTPS endpoint for the virtual directory that hosts the service, make sure that your website has a configured HTTPS binding and SSL certificate. If metadata is already enabled for the service, then it will also be exposed over HTTPS.
- **Generating a Single WSDL Document**—WCF enables you to display all the WSDL information that is returned in a single document. Earlier, some third-party WSDL processing stacks were not capable to process WSDL documents that were dependent on other documents through a xsd:import.
- **WebSocket Support**—WebSockets is a technology that allows true bidirectional communication over ports 80 and 443 with performance characteristics similar to TCP. Two new bindings are added to support communication over a WebSocket transport. These bindings are NetHttpBinding and NetHttpsBinding.
- **Configuring WCF Services in Code**—WCF allows you to configure services using configuration files or code. Configuration files are beneficial when a service requires to be configured after deployment. While using configuration files, you only need to update the configuration file and no recompilation is required. However, configuration files are complex and difficult to maintain because you cannot debug them. Moreover, configuration elements are called by names that makes writing configuration files error-prone and difficult.
- **ChannelFactory Caching**—The ChannelFactory class is used to create a communication channel with a WCF service. However, creating ChannelFactory instances have some overheads as they perform the following operations:
  1. Constructing the ContractDescription tree
  2. Reflecting all the required CLR types
  3. Constructing the channel stack
  4. Disposing of resources

WCF can cache channel factories while using a WCF client proxy to minimize this overhead.

- **Compression and the Binary Encoder**—In WCF 4.5, the WCF binary encoder adds support for compression that is configured with the help of the CompressionFormat property. Both the client and the service must configure the CompressionFormat property. Compression only works for HTTP, HTTPS, and TCP protocols.
- **UDP**—UDP adds support for a UDP transport that allows developers to write services to use "fire and forget" messaging. A client sends a message to a service and expects no response from the service.
- **IDN Support**—This support is added in WCF 4.5 to use WCF services with Internationalized Domain Names.
- **HttpClient**—This class is added to make working with HTTP requests much easier.
- **Configuration Intellisense**—Attribute values in configuration files for custom attributes defined in the project now support Intellisense to enable working with configurations quickly and accurately.
- **Configuration tooltips**—WCF elements and attributes now display tooltips in the XML editor to identify the purpose of the element or attribute easily and accurately.
- **Paste Data as Classes**—In a WCF project, data types defined in XML can be pasted directly into a code page. The XML type will be pasted as a CLR type.
- **WebServiceHost and default endpoints**—In WCF 4.5, WebServiceHost will only create a default endpoint if no endpoints are explicitly added. If your client is expecting the default endpoint, you can explicity add an endpoint and direct the client to it.
- **IHttpCookieContainerManager**—The IHttpCookieContainerManager interface, exposed by HttpChannelFactory, makes working with cookies on the client side much easier. This interface enables you to verify a user with a service and use the authentication cookie returned by that service to verify with other services.

Now, let's discuss about the WCF clients.

WCF Clients

A WCF client, also known as a WCF consumer, consists of a proxy that enables an application to communicate with a WCF service. The `App.config` file at the client-side generates the proxy and also includes information regarding the type and the methods exposed by the services. The information includes the address of the service, type of binding used by the service, and the service contract. If any service exposes multiple endpoints to the client, the client selects the endpoint as per the requirement.

There are various types of communication patterns used by the WCF consumers to communicate with the services. These communication patterns are as follows:

- **One-way**—Communicates in a single direction that flows from a client to service without any reply from the service. In this type of communication pattern, the errors that occur during the execution of messages are not communicated back to the client. The client has no idea about the success or failure of the messages.
- **Request-Reply**—Communicates in two-way (request-reply) directions. When a client sends a message to a service, it awaits for the response from the service. The client cannot make further execution until it receives the reply from the service.
- **Duplex**—Communicates in bi-directional. In this communication pattern, both a client and a service can communicate as well as respond to the incoming messages. Unlike the request-replay pattern, the client can make further execution after sending a request to the service without waiting for the reply.
- **Asynchronous**—Refers to the type of communication pattern in which applications can continue processing other tasks after calling a method asynchronously. For example, a client sends a request to a server and starts another process without waiting for the response of that request.

Let's now learn about the WCF tools.

WCF Tools

WCF tools are designed to enable you to easily create, deploy, and manage WCF applications. Table 19.10 lists the WCF tools:

Table 19.10: Tools of WCF

Tools	Description
`ServiceModel Metadata Utility Tool (Svcutil.exe)`	Generates the service model code from metadata documents including client `config` file and also uses the service model to generate metadata documents.
`Find Private Key Tool (FindPrivateKey.exe)`	Finds the name and the location of the private key from a specified certificate store. The two options that are used with this tool are `storeName` for the name of the certificate store and `storeLocation` for the location of the certificate store.
`ServiceModel Registration Tool (ServiceModelReg.exe)`	Registers the service model with IIS. The service model is used to host the WCF service in IIS. Even if IIS is already installed on a machine, the service model is registered automatically with it. In addition to registering service model, this can also be used for unregistering, re-registering, listing, and verifying all the registered components.
`COM+ Service Model Configuration Tool (ComSvcConfig.exe)`	Configures the COM + interfaces to be exposed as Web services.
`Configuration Editor Tool (SvcConfigEditor.exe)`	Creates and modifies the configuration settings for WCF services using Graphical User Interface (GUI).
`Service Trace Viewer Tool (SvcTraceViewer.exe)`	Views, groups, and filters the traces generated by WCF so that you can diagnose, repair, and verify the WCF service issues.
`WS-AtomicTransaction Configuration Utility (wsatConfig.exe)`	Configures basic WS-AtomicTransaction support setting by using the command line tool.
`WS-AtomicTransaction Configuration MMC Snap-in`	Configures a part or basic WS-AtomicTransaction setting on both local and remote machines by using Microsoft Management Console (MMC) Snap-in.
`WorkFlow Service Registration Tool (WFServicesReg.exe)`	Adds, removes, or repairs the configuration elements for Windows Workflow Foundation (WF) services. This tool performs the following tasks: • Inspects the `web.config` file and registers .NET Framework 4.5 reference assemblies, a build provider for `.xoml` files, and HTTP handlers for `.xoml` and `.rules` files, in the web.config file • Inspects the Machine.config file and registers behaviorExtension, bidingElementExtensions, and bindingExtensions extensions in the Machine.config file • Registers the `policyImporters` and `wsdlImporters` client metadata importers in the configuration file • Registers the `.xoml` and `.rules` scriptmaps and handlers in the IIS metabase, which acts as a repository for IIS configuration values
`WCF Service Host (WcfSvcHost.exe)`	Hosts the WCF services contained in .dll files.
`WCF Test Client (WcfTestClient.exe)`	Allows you to enter the test parameters and submit the parameters to the services. It is a Graphical User Interface (GUI) tool.

Let's now learn about concepts of WCF Data Services.

WCF Data Services

WCF Data Services is a Microsoft technology used to create and consume data services, which makes it easy to separate the presentation layer from the data layers while working with them. This service provides facilities to query the data in the address bar of a Web browser. Data services are naturally integrated with Web and enable you to add a query string in the address bar of a Web browser to retrieve data. To make it easier to work with Data Services, Microsoft integrated the concept of WCF Data Services with VS 2012 and .NET Framework 4.5. The advantages of WCF Data Services are as follows:

- Creating and accessing data services for not only the Internet but also the Intranet by exposing data as resources that are addressed by URIs
- Using the entity-relationship conventions to use Entity Data Model (EDM)
- Using Internet standards to address and update resources
- Including a set of client libraries: one for the general .NET Framework client applications and the other for Silverlight applications

WCF Data Services introduced with .NET Framework 4.5 supports the new Open Data Protocol (OData) version 2.0 functionality. The following features were supported by the ADO.NET in 3.5 and now supported by the OData in 4.5:

- The $count path segment can receive only the total number of resources returned by a URI and the new $inlinecount query option enables you to receive the same total resource count together with the resource data in a single response
- The query results can be modified to include a subset of properties by using the new $select query option.
- The data service can now return a partial list of the entities requested by a URI, together with a URI that is used to obtain the next set of entities in the result. The new $skiptoken query option is used to request the next page of results.
- The data service can now be configured to return requested resources as a set of paged responses.
- The new DataServiceCollection class helps you to provide simplified binding of data service data to Windows Presentation Framework (WPF) controls.
- The entity can be described as media link entry, with a reference link to an associated media resource. This helps you to retrieve and save binary large object data independent of the entity to which it belongs. You can create a data service that returns binary property data as a stream instead of first loading the entire entity, including binary data, into memory.
- The implementation of new set of data service provider interfaces; you can use various types of data with a data service, even when the data model changes during execution.

Architecture of WCF Data Services Framework

WCF Data Services Framework processes the data by accepting an HTTP request for a resource identified by a URI. After identifying the request, the data service deserializes it and then passes its information to the data access provider, which executes the request based on the underlying data store. The architecture of WCF Data Services Framework is shown in Figure 19.2:

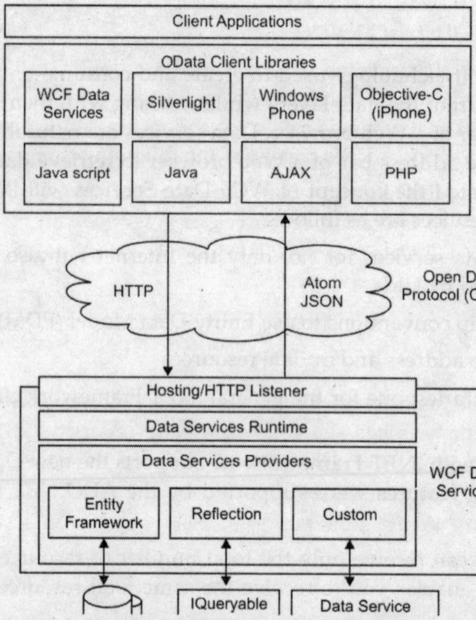

Figure 19.2: Showing the WCF Data Services Framework Architecture

In Figure 19.2, you can see that the data access layer consists of Entity Framework and custom LINQ provider. This data access layer is capable of working with both relational and non-relational data. It organizes the data and its associations in the form of entities. To work with relational data, data services use Entity Framework to create the EDM model. Data services use LINQ to SQL, which is a database-access technology, for other data sources or non-relational data. This technology provides a mechanism to enable any data source and its associations to be modeled as entities. In Figure 19.2, IQueryable `[+ Updatable]` (also known as `IQueryable + "extensions for update"`) is an interface that includes semantics for the updates of data services implementation. This interface enables WCF Data Services to expose any data source by using the Representational State Transfer (REST) protocol. Now, let's understand the features of WCF Data Services.

Features of WCF Data Services Framework

WCF Data Services provide the capability of creating flexible data services that are naturally integrated with Web. Certain features provided by WCF Data Services are as follows:

- Supports more than one format to represent data, which helps to broaden the scope of its usage. The default format is `Atom`, but a client can select the `JSON` format also. The ATOM format represents the data in the form of XML with some added semantics; whereas, the JSON format is more compatible with JavaScript-based applications.
- Allows uniform patterns, which are created by clear semantics from the data model. It also helps in building reusable components that provide abstraction for developers.
- Accommodates other aspects, such as well-established HTTP caching infrastructure.
- Eliminates the need of using the syntax of SQL Server for accessing the data by using addressing schemes based on URI.
- Separates the WCF Data Services protocol, which consists of URI, payload formats, and interaction model, from the data source. This separation of protocol enables data services to expose data irrespective of data source. It represents data at the level of abstraction presented to it by the provider that might be different from the schema of the underlying store.

After discussing the features of WCF Data Services, let's discuss the addressing schemes of data services.

The Data Services Addressing Scheme

WCF Data Services use an addressing scheme, which is based on URIs, to locate data. The methods to access resources may be different but data services are not confined to any specific method to identify a resource. Data services implement such a process that whenever new identifiers are defined or introduced, they do not interfere with the existing identifiers. Data services URIs consist of the following three parts:

- `Service root`—Specifies the location of the root of WCF Data Services. All `EntitySet`, `AssociationSet`, and service operation resources of a service can be described through the resources associated with the root of WCF Data Services. The following code snippet shows a valid URI that includes only the schema and service root elements:

```
http://servername
```

- Resource path—Specifies how resource set, resource type, resource navigation property, resource navigation link, resource property, resource complex type, and service operation names can be combined together to create a URI. The resource path element of the URI allows filtering and traversing through the graph of resources in a data service. The following code snippet shows a valid URI that includes the schema, service root, and resource path elements:

```
http://localhost/myservice.svc/Products
```

- Query options—Enables you to mention multiple query options in a single URI query string. A query option contains case-sensitive names and values. The sequence of query options within a query is insignificant and can be presented in any order in a query string. A specific query option can appear only once in a query string of a request URI.

Table 19.11 lists noteworthy data services terminologies:

Table 19.11: Noteworthy Terminologies of Data Services

Term	Definition
`Conceptual Schema Definition Language (CSDL)`	Defines the entity types, associations, entity containers, entity sets, and association sets of a conceptual model. CSDL is a file that is based on an XML format.
`EDM`	Defines specification for the data used by applications built on Entity Framework.
`Hypertext Transfer Protocol (HTTP)`	Specifies an application-level protocol for distributed, collaborative, and hypermedia information systems. It is a generic and stateless protocol.
`Query string`	Refers to the component of a URI that contains non-hierarchical data. The query component is indicated by the question mark (?) character and terminated by a number sign (#) character or by the end of the URI.
`Query options, System query options`	Refers to the name/value pairs within a query string. For example, in the `http://Publisher.svc?Name=Peter` URI, Name is a query string option. Query string options that start with the ($) character are known as System Query Options and denote actions supported by WCF Data Services.
`Representational State Transfer (REST)`	Refers to the style of software architecture for distributed hypermedia systems, such as the World Wide Web. REST refers to a collection of network architecture principles that outline how resources are defined and addressed. This term is often used to describe any simple interface that transmits domain-specific data in HTTP without an additional messaging layer, such as SOAP or session tracking.
`Entity container`	Contains definition of all entity sets within the scope of an entity container. The entity container contains the description of entity sets that may use types defined in one or more namespaces. In EDM terms, an entity container is equivalent to an EntityContainer class.
`Entity set`	Represents a logical group of entity types.

Table 19.11: Noteworthy Terminologies of Data Services

Term	Definition
`Entity type`	Represents an instance of an entity type. An entity has a unique identity, independent existence, and forms the operational unit of consistency.
`Entity key`	Contains one or more properties of the entity type. Any set of non-nullable, immutable, and SimpleType properties can serve as the entity key. It must uniquely identify an entity-type instance within an entity set.
`Property`	Describes an aspect of an EntityType data or a ComplexType data by associating a unique name and type with it.
`Complex type`	Represents a set of related information in a single property item. Similar to an entity type, a complex type contains one or more properties of a primitive or complex type, but complex types are not associated with any key.
`Navigation property`	Refers to navigation paths of entities that describe the ends of a relationship. Standard properties describe a value associated with an entity, but navigation properties describe a relationship.
`Navigation link`	Refers to a navigation path that describes a one-way association between entity types. The direction of the association is from the declaring entity type to the target entity type. The multiplicity of such associations may be one-to-one or one-to-many.
`Link`	Refers to a one-way association from a source object to a target object.
`Simple Object Access Protocol (SOAP)`	Refers to a lightweight XML-based messaging protocol commonly used to encode the information in Web service request and response messages before sending it over a network. SOAP messages are independent of any operating system or protocol and may be transported using a variety of Internet protocols.
`Service operation`	Allows WCF Data Services to deploy a method on a server, which is identified by a URI similar to all other WCF Data Services resources.
`URI`	Refers to a compact sequence of characters that identifies an abstract or physical resource.

Data Services Resource Path

WCF Data Services consist of specific resource path semantics and rules. The following rules need to be considered while constructing a resource path:

- If the default resource container does not contain a resource set, the address must be organized by using the `/ServiceName/<ResourceContainer>/<ResourceSet>` syntax.
- You need to follow the same order of key values in a compound key as they are listed in CSDL description of a data service.
- A resource navigation property can be replaced by a resource link property as per the requirement.
- A service operation can be replaced by the first occurrence of a resource set in a path segment as per the requirement.

Now, let's see how the preceding rules are used in WCF Data Services URIs:

- **URI: serviceName/<entity set>**—Represents all instances of resource types in a specified resource set. A resource set can consist of one or more than one resource instance types. For example, the URI to retrieve all products from the Products resource set is as follows:

```
http://localhost/dataservice.svc/Products
```

An equivalent LINQ syntax to perform the same operation as the preceding URI is as follows:

```
from p in Products
select p
```

- **URI: serviceName/<entity set> (keyPredicate)**—Represents the resource-type instance whose key is equal to the key predicate in the specified resource set. For example, the URI to retrieve all the products identified by the Books key is as follows :

```
http://localhost/dataservice.svc/Products('Books')
```

An equivalent LINQ syntax to perform the same operation as the preceding URI is as follows:

```
(from p in Products
where p.keyProperty == "Books"
select p).First()
```

- **URI: serviceName/<entity set>(keyPredicate)/<Complex Type>**—Shows the complex-type instance on the specified resource type whose key is equal to the key predicate and within the specified resource set. For example, the URI to retrieve suppliers of the products identified by the Books key in the Products resource set is as follows:

```
http://localhost/dataservice.svc/Products('Books')/Supplier
```

An equivalent LINQ syntax to perform the same operation as the preceding URI is as follows:

```
(from p in Products
where p.keyProperty == "Books"
select p.ResourceComplexType).First()
```

- **URI: ServiceName/<entity set>(KeyPredicate)/< Complex Type>/<Property>**—Represents the resource property associated with a complex type within the resource-type instance whose key is equal to the key predicate and within the specified resource set. You can append a `/$value` segment at the URI end in a resource property. The `$value` segment acts as a dereference operator. It points to the fact that only value of the property should be returned without additional metadata or surrounding syntax. For example, the URI to retrieve the name of all the suppliers by the Books key in the Products resource set is as follows:

```
http://localhost/dataservice.svc/Products ('Books')/Supplier/Name/$value
```

In the preceding URI, `/$value` represents the value of the property that is free of any surrounding metadata. An equivalent LINQ syntax to perform the same operation is as follows:

```
(from p in Products
where p.keyProperty == "Books"
select p.ResourceComplexType.ResourceProperty).First()
```

- **URI: serviceName/<entity set>(KeyPredicate)/<NavigationProperty>**—Shows a resource set that contains a collection of zero to many instances of a resource type. The resource set only contains instances that are associated with the resource type instance. For example, the URI to retrieve values of orders for the customers identified by the Books key is as follows:

```
http://localhost/dataservice.svc/Products ('Books')/Orders
```

The preceding URI represents a resource set that contains a collection of zero to many instances of a resource type. The resource set only contains instances that are associated with the resource-type instance in the prior path segment. An equivalent LINQ syntax to perform the same operation is as follows:

```
from p in Products
from p2 in p.RelatedResourceSet
where p.keyProperty == "Books"
select p2
```

An alternative LINQ syntax for the preceding expression is as follows:

```
Db.Products.Where(p => k.keyProperty.Equals("Books")).SelectMany(p =>
  p.RelatedResourceSet);
```

Now, let's understand various query options used for querying data in data services.

Data Services Query Options

A query option is a segment of the URI that specifies system query options and service operations parameters. Let's, discuss the query options that are supported and not supported by each type of URI syntax. The URI syntaxes are as follows:

- URI – serviceName/<EntitySet>
- URI – serviceName/<ResourceSet>(KeyPredicate)
- URI – serviceName/<ResourceSet>(KeyPredicate)/<ResourceComplexType>/<ResourceProperty>
- URI – serviceName/<ResourceSet>(KeyPredicate)/<ResourceProperty>
- URI – serviceName/<Resource Set>(KeyPredicate)/<ResourceNavigationProperty>

Table 19.12 lists the query options for the `URI: serviceName/<EntitySet>` syntax:

Table 19.12: Supported Query Options for the URI: serviceName/<EntitySet> Syntax

Option	Supported	Notes
$expand	Yes	Returns an entity set
$filter	Yes	Returns an entity set
$orderby	Yes	Returns an entity set
$skip	Yes	Returns an entity set
$top	Yes	Returns an entity set

Table 19.13 lists the query options for the `URI: serviceName/<ResourceSet>(KeyPredicate)` syntax:

Table 19.13: Supported Query Options for the URI: serviceName/<ResourceSet>(KeyPredicate) Syntax

Option	Supported	Notes
$expand	Yes	Ensures that the complex types are always expanded even if the $expand option is not present in URI
$filter	Yes	Returns a complex type instance if the filter condition is True; otherwise, a 404 Resource Not Found error is returned
$orderby	No	
$skip	No	
$top	No	

Table 19.14 lists the query options for the URI serviceName/<ResourceSet>(KeyPredicate)/<ResourceComplexType>/<ResourceProperty> syntax:

Table 19.14: Supported Query Options for the URI serviceName/<ResourceSet>(KeyPredicate)/<ResourceComplexType>/<ResourceProperty> Syntax

Option	Supported	Notes
$expand	Yes	Ensures that complex types are always expanded even if the $expand option is not present in URI. The resource property has no properties of its own that can be expanded if it is not a complex type.
$filter	No	
$orderby	No	
$skip	No	
$top	No	

Table 19.15 lists the query options for the URI serviceName/<ResourceSet>(KeyPredicate)/ <ResourceProperty> syntax:

Table 19.15: Supported Query Options for the URI serviceName/<ResourceSet>(KeyPredicate)/<ResourceProperty> Syntax

Option	Supported	Notes
$expand	Yes	Ensures that complex types are always expanded even if `$expand` is not present in URI. The resource property has no properties of its own that can be expanded if it is not a complex type.
$filter	No	
$orderby	No	
$skip	No	
$top	No	

Table 19.16 lists the query options if the navigation property in the URI `serviceName/<Resource Set>(KeyPredicate)/<ResourceNavigationProperty>` syntax represents a one-to-one or many-to-one relationship:

Table 19.16: Supported Query Options for the URI serviceName/<Resource Set>(KeyPredicate)/<ResourceNavigationProperty> Syntax

Option	Supported	Notes
$expand	Yes	Returns an entity-type instance
$filter	Yes	Returns an entity-type instance
$orderby	No	
$skip	No	
$top	No	

However, in case the navigation property in the same syntax represents a one-to-many or many-to-many relationship, the query options are as listed in Table 19.17:

Table 19.17: Supported Query Options

Option	Supported	Notes
$expand	Yes	Returns an entity set
$filter	Yes	Returns an entity set
$orderby	Yes	Returns an entity set
$skip	Yes	Returns an entity set
$top	Yes	Returns an entity set

Let's now understand the practical implementation of WCF services in ASP.NET 4.5 in the *Immediate Solutions* section of the chapter.

Immediate Solutions

Creating WCF Services

Creating a WCF service becomes easy in Visual Studio 2012 because it has built-in support for WCF services. In earlier versions (earlier than 3.5) of Visual Studio, you need to first install the components of WCF to create WCF services. Now, let's perform the following steps to create a WCF service using a template provided in Visual Studio 2012:

1. Open Visual Studio 2012 and select `FILE→New→Web Site`. The New Web Site dialog box appears (Figure 19.3).
2. Select the language in which you want to develop your project from the Installed→ Templates node and click the OK button (Figure 19.3).
2. Select the WCF Service template in the New Web Site dialog box (Figure 19.3).
3. Enter the location and specify the name as `WCFService (WCFServiceVB` in VB and `WCFServiceCS` in C#) in the text box beside the Browse button, as shown in Figure 19.3:

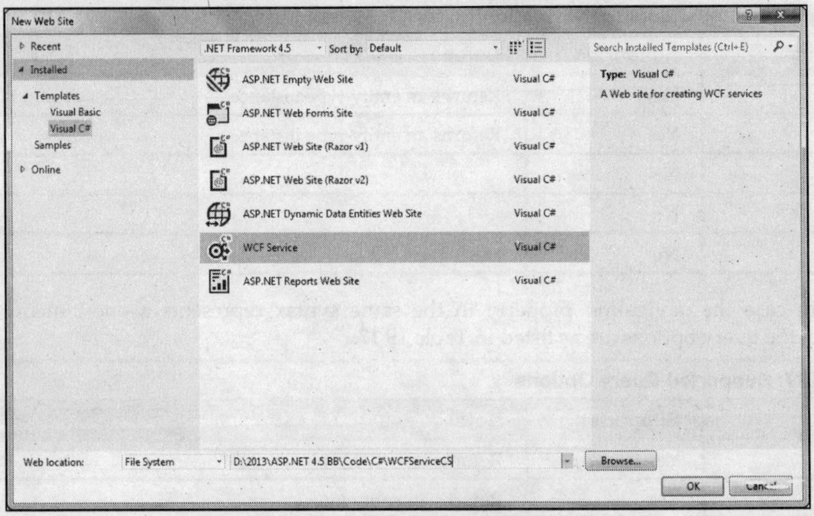

Figure 19.3: Showing the New Web Site Dialog Box

The files are displayed in the Solution Explorer in the App_Code folder, as shown in Figure 19.4:

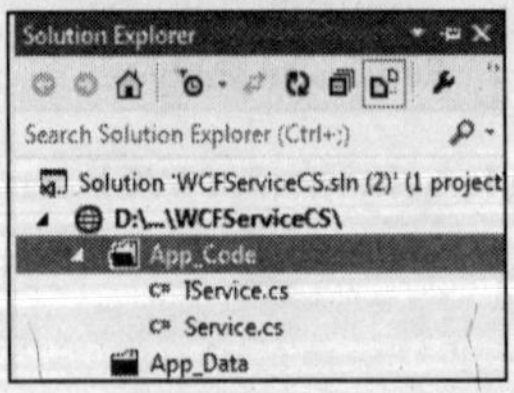

Figure 19.4: Showing the System Generated Files in the Solution Explorer

To build a service, you must perform two main steps. First, you need to create a service contract. Second, you must create a data contract. You need to add the code, shown in Listing 19.1, in the code-behind file (Service.cs or Service.vb) of the `WCFService` service, to create service and data contracts:

Listing 19.1: Showing the Code for the Code-Behind File

In VB

```
Imports System.ServiceModel
Imports System.Runtime.Serialization
' NOTE: If you change the class name "Service" here, you must also update the reference
  to "Service" in Web.config and in the associated .svc file.
<ServiceContract()> _
Public Interface IMyService
    <OperationContract()> _
    Function MyTask1(ByVal MyValue As String) As String
    <OperationContract()> _
    Function MyTask2(ByVal dcValue As DataContract1) As String
End Interface
Public Class Service
    Implements IMyService
    Public Function MyTask1(ByVal Myvalue As String) As String Implements
  IMyService.MyTask1
        Return "Hello: " & Myvalue
    End Function
    Public Function MyTask2(ByVal dcValue As DataContract1) As String Implements
  IMyService.MyTask2
        Return "Hello: " & dcValue.FirstName
    End Function
End Class
<DataContract()> _
Public Class DataContract1
    Private firstName_Renamed As String
    Private lastName_Renamed As String
    <DataMember()> _
    Public Property FirstName() As String
        Get
            Return firstName_Renamed
        End Get
        Set(ByVal value As String)
            firstName_Renamed = value
        End Set
    End Property
    <DataMember()> _
    Public Property LastName() As String
        Get
            Return lastName_Renamed
        End Get
        Set(ByVal value As String)
            lastName_Renamed = value
        End Set
    End Property
End Class
```

In C#

```
using System;
using System.Collections.Generic;
using System.Linq;
using System.Runtime.Serialization;
using System.ServiceModel.Web;
using System.Text;
[ServiceContract()]
public interface IMyService
{
  [OperationContract]
```

```
    string MyTask1(string MyValue);
    [OperationContract]
    string MyTask2(DataContract1 dcValue);
}
// NOTE: If you change the class name "Service" here, you must also update the reference
    to "Service" in Web.config and in the associated .svc file.
public class Service : IMyService
{
    public string MyTask1(string Myvalue)
    {
          return "Hello: "+Myvalue;
    }
    public string MyTask2(DataContract1 dcValue)
    {
          return "Hello: " + dcValue.FirstName;
    }
}
[DataContract]
public class DataContract1
{
    string firstName;
    string lastName;
    [DataMember]
    public string FirstName
    {
          get { return firstName; }
          set { firstName = value; }
    }
    [DataMember]
    public string LastName
    {
          get { return lastName; }
          set { lastName = value; }
    }
}
```

Let's now learn how to configure a WCF service.

Configuring a WCF Service

After creating a service, the next step is to configure the service. Configuring WCF services includes defining the ABC for the services. Now, perform the following steps to configure the WCF service, `WCFService` service, created in the preceding section:

1. Open the `Web.config` file by double-clicking it in the Solution Explorer and add the code, shown in Listing 19.2, for defining the endpoints:

Listing 19.2: Showing the Code for the `Web.config` File

In VB

```
<?xml version="1.0"?>
<configuration>
  <system.web>
        <compilation debug="true" strict="false" explicit="true"
        targetFramework="4.5"/>
        <pages>
              <namespaces>
                    <add namespace="System.Runtime.Serialization"/>
                    <add namespace="System.ServiceModel"/>
                    <add namespace="System.ServiceModel.Web"/>
              </namespaces>
        </pages>
```

```
    </system.web>
    <system.serviceModel>
          <services>
                <service name="Service" behaviorConfiguration="ServiceBehavior">
                      <!--Service Endpoints-->
                      <endpoint address="" binding="wsHttpBinding"
                      contract="IMyService">
                            <!-- Upon deployment, the following identity element
                      should be removed or
                replaced to reflect the
                identity under which the deployed service runs.  If removed, WCF will
                infer an appropriate identity
                automatically.-->
                            <identity>
                                  <dns value="localhost"/>
                            </identity>
                      </endpoint>
                      <endpoint address="mex" binding="mexHttpBinding"
                      contract="IMetadataExchange"/>
                </service>
          </services>
          <behaviors>
                <serviceBehaviors>
                      <behavior name="ServiceBehavior">
                      <!-- To avoid disclosing metadata information, set the
                      value below to false and remove the metadata endpoint above
                      before deployment -->
                      <serviceMetadata httpGetEnabled="true"/>
                      <!-- To receive exception details in faults for debugging
                      purposes, set the value below to true.  Set to false before
                      deployment to avoid disclosing exception information -->
                      <serviceDebug includeExceptionDetailInFaults="false"/>
                      </behavior>
                </serviceBehaviors>
          </behaviors>
          <serviceHostingEnvironment multipleSiteBindingsEnabled="true"/>
    </system.serviceModel>
    <system.webServer>
          <modules runAllManagedModulesForAllRequests="true"/>
    </system.webServer>
  </configuration>
```

In C#

```
  <?xml version="1.0"?>
  <configuration>
    <system.web>
          <compilation debug="true" targetFramework="4.5"/>
    </system.web>
    <system.serviceModel>
          <services>
                <service name="Service" behaviorConfiguration="ServiceBehavior">
                <!--Service Endpoints-->
                <endpoint address="" binding="wsHttpBinding" contract="IMyService">
                <!-- Upon deployment, the following identity element should be removed
                or
                replaced to reflect the
                identity under which the deployed service runs.  If removed, WCF will
                infer an appropriate identity
                automatically.-->
                <identity>
                <dns value="localhost"/>
```

```
                    </identity>
                    </endpoint>
                    <endpoint address="mex" binding="mexHttpBinding"
                    contract="IMetadataExchange"/>
                    </service>
            </services>
            <behaviors>
                    <serviceBehaviors>
                            <behavior name="ServiceBehavior">
                            <!-- To avoid disclosing metadata information, set the value
                            below to false and remove the metadata endpoint above before
                            deployment -->
                            <serviceMetadata httpGetEnabled="true"/>
                            <!-- To receive exception details in faults for debugging
                            purposes, set the value below to true.  Set to false before
                            deployment to avoid disclosing exception information -->
                            <serviceDebug includeExceptionDetailInFaults="false"/>
                            </behavior>
                    </serviceBehaviors>
            </behaviors>
            <serviceHostingEnvironment multipleSiteBindingsEnabled="true"/>
    </system.serviceModel>
    <system.webServer>
            <modules runAllManagedModulesForAllRequests="true"/>
    </system.webServer>
</configuration>
```

2. Press the F5 key to run the project. The output is shown in Figure 19.5:

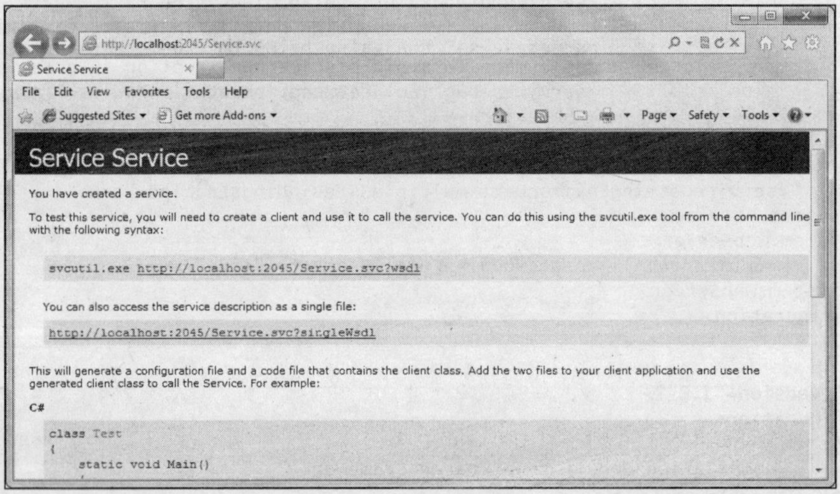

Figure 19.5: Showing the Output after Running the WCF Service

3. Create a client using the `svcutil.exe` tool from the command line, to test this service, as shown in the following syntax:

```
svcutil.exe http://localhost:2045/Service.svc?wsdl
```

NOTE

The port number, which is 2045 in the preceding command line, may vary according to your system.

4. Open the Developer Command Prompt for VS2012 and run the preceding command where the application exists. The output is shown in Figure 19.6:

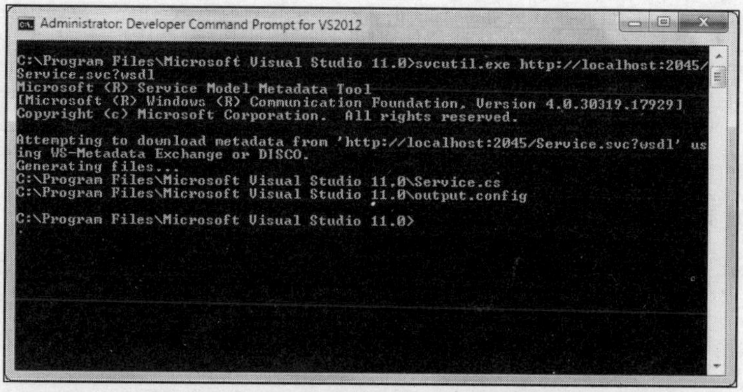

Figure 19.6: Displaying the Developer Command Prompt for VS2012

The preceding command generates a configuration file and a code file that contain the client class.

5. Add the generated files (`Service.vb` in VB or `Service.cs` in C#), which are the code files, and `output.config`, which is the configuration file) to your client application and use them to call the service. Listing 19.3 shows the code of the generated code file:

Listing 19.3: Showing the Code of the Generated Code Service.cs File

```
//------------------------------------------------------------------------------
// <auto-generated>
//     This code was generated by a tool.
//     Runtime Version:4.0.30319.17929
//
//     Changes to this file may cause incorrect behavior and will be lost if
//     the code is regenerated.
// </auto-generated>
//------------------------------------------------------------------------------
using System.Runtime.Serialization;
[System.Diagnostics.DebuggerStepThroughAttribute()]
[System.CodeDom.Compiler.GeneratedCodeAttribute("System.Runtime.Serialization",
  "4.0.0.0")]
[System.Runtime.Serialization.DataContractAttribute(Name="DataContract1",
  Namespace="http://schemas.datacontract.org/2004/07/")]
public partial class DataContract1 : object,
  System.Runtime.Serialization.IExtensibleDataObject
{
    private System.Runtime.Serialization.ExtensionDataObject extensionDataField;
    private string FirstNameField;
    private string LastNameField;
    public System.Runtime.Serialization.ExtensionDataObject ExtensionData
    {
        get
        {
            return this.extensionDataField;
        }
        set
        {
            this.extensionDataField = value;
        }
    }
    [System.Runtime.Serialization.DataMemberAttribute()]
    public string FirstName
    {
        get
        {
```

```
            return this.FirstNameField;
        }
        set
        {
            this.FirstNameField = value;
        }
    }
    [System.Runtime.Serialization.DataMemberAttribute()]
    public string LastName
    {
        get
        {
            return this.LastNameField;
        }
        set
        {
            this.LastNameField = value;
        }
    }
}
[System.CodeDom.Compiler.GeneratedCodeAttribute("System.ServiceModel", "4.0.0.0")]
[System.ServiceModel.ServiceContractAttribute(ConfigurationName="IMyService")]
public interface IMyService
{

  [System.ServiceModel.OperationContractAttribute(Action="http://tempuri.org/IMyService/
  MyTask1", ReplyAction="http://tempuri.org/IMyService/MyTask1Response")]
    string MyTask1(string MyValue);

  [System.ServiceModel.OperationContractAttribute(Action="http://tempuri.org/IMyService/
  MyTask1", ReplyAction="http://tempuri.org/IMyService/MyTask1Response")]
    System.Threading.Tasks.Task<string> MyTask1Async(string MyValue);

  [System.ServiceModel.OperationContractAttribute(Action="http://tempuri.org/IMyService/
  MyTask2", ReplyAction="http://tempuri.org/IMyService/MyTask2Response")]
    string MyTask2(DataContract1 dcValue);

  [System.ServiceModel.OperationContractAttribute(Action="http://tempuri.org/IMyService/
  MyTask2", ReplyAction="http://tempuri.org/IMyService/MyTask2Response")]
    System.Threading.Tasks.Task<string> MyTask2Async(DataContract1 dcValue);
}
[System.CodeDom.Compiler.GeneratedCodeAttribute("System.ServiceModel", "4.0.0.0")]
public interface IMyServiceChannel : IMyService, System.ServiceModel.IClientChannel
{
}
[System.Diagnostics.DebuggerStepThroughAttribute()]
[System.CodeDom.Compiler.GeneratedCodeAttribute("System.ServiceModel", "4.0.0.0")]
public partial class MyServiceClient : System.ServiceModel.ClientBase<IMyService>,
  IMyService
{
    public MyServiceClient()
    {
    }
    public MyServiceClient(string endpointConfigurationName) :
            base(endpointConfigurationName)
    {
    }
    public MyServiceClient(string endpointConfigurationName, string remoteAddress) :
            base(endpointConfigurationName, remoteAddress)
    {
    }
```

```
        public MyServiceClient(string endpointConfigurationName,
      System.ServiceModel.EndpointAddress remoteAddress) :
              base(endpointConfigurationName, remoteAddress)
        {
        }
      public MyServiceClient(System.ServiceModel.Channels.Binding binding,
      System.ServiceModel.EndpointAddress remoteAddress) :
              base(binding, remoteAddress)
        {
        }
        public string MyTask1(string MyValue)
        {
            return base.Channel.MyTask1(MyValue);
        }
        public System.Threading.Tasks.Task<string> MyTask1Async(string MyValue)
        {
            return base.Channel.MyTask1Async(MyValue);
        }
        public string MyTask2(DataContract1 dcValue)
        {
            return base.Channel.MyTask2(dcValue);
        }
        public System.Threading.Tasks.Task<string> MyTask2Async(DataContract1 dcValue)
        {
            return base.Channel.MyTask2Async(dcValue);
        }
    }
```

NOTE

The code shown in Listing 19.4 is same for both the VB and C# languages.

The code of the generated configuration file (`output.config`) is shown in Listing 19.4:

Listing 19.4: Showing the Code of the `output.config` File

In VB and In C#

```
    <?xml version="1.0" encoding="utf-8"?>
    <configuration>
        <system.serviceModel>
            <bindings>
                <wsHttpBinding>
                    <binding name="WSHttpBinding_IMyService" />
                </wsHttpBinding>
            </bindings>
            <client>
                <endpoint address="http://localhost:2045/Service.svc"
                     binding="wsHttpBinding"
                    bindingConfiguration="WSHttpBinding_IMyService" contract="IMyService"
                    name="WSHttpBinding_IMyService">
                    <identity>
                        <dns value="localhost" />
                    </identity>
                </endpoint>
            </client>
        </system.serviceModel>
    </configuration>
```

Let's now learn how to deploy a WCF service.

Deploying WCF Services

After configuring a WCF service, the next step is to make the Web service available to other Web applications over the Internet. To make a WCF service available to other applications, you need to transfer the WCF service from the development environment to the production environment.

You can deploy the WCF service on the Web server on which you want to run it by using Web Setup Project. Perform the following steps to deploy a WCF service:

1. Open the WCFServiceCS application in Microsoft Visual Studio 2012.
2. Click `FILE`→`New`→`Project`. The New Project dialog box appears.
3. Expand the Installed→Other Project Types→Setup and Deployment node in the middle Templates pane of the New Project dialog box.
4. Select the InstallShield Limited Edition Project template from the middle pane (Figure 19.7).
5. Specify the name of setup project as `WCFServiceSetupCS` in the Name text box (Figure 19.7). You can find this WCF Services setup as `WCFServiceSetupVB` and `WCFServiceSetupCS`.
6. Select the Add to solution option from the Solution drop-down list and click the OK button, as shown in Figure 19.7:

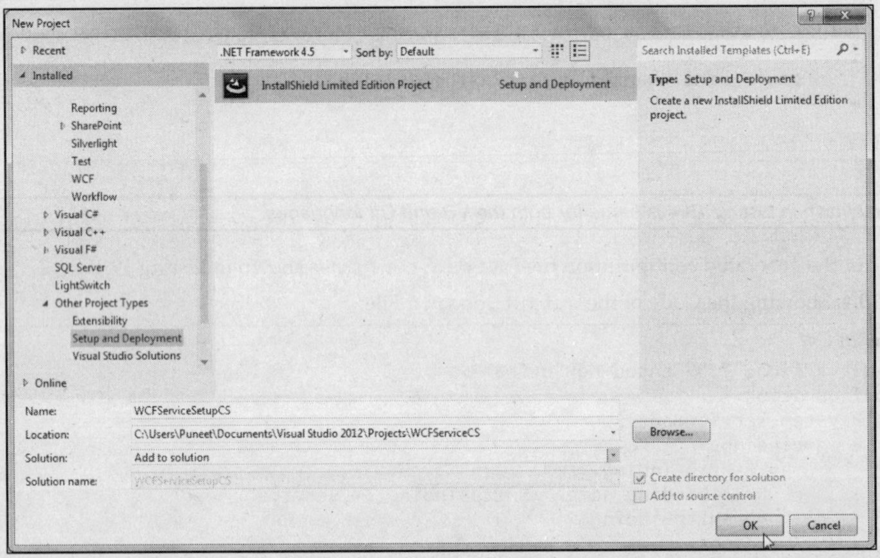

Figure 19.7: Showing the New Project Dialog Box

NOTE

You need to install InstallShield Limited Edition Project for creating setup.

The Project Assistant Window appears (Figure 19.8).

7. Click the Application Information icon to open the Application Information page (Figure 19.8).
8. Enter your organization name and click the Installation Requirements icon as shown in Figure 19.8:

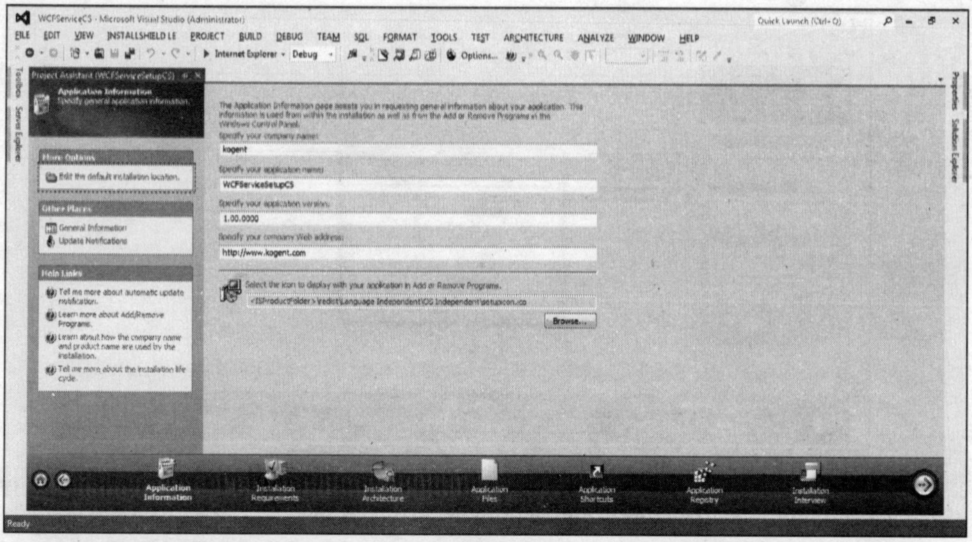

Figure 19.8: Showing the Solution Explorer Containing the WCFServiceSetup Project

9. Select the Yes radio button and then select the Microsoft .NET Framework 4.5 Full package check box (Figure 19.9).
10. Click the Application Files icon, as shown in Figure 19.9:

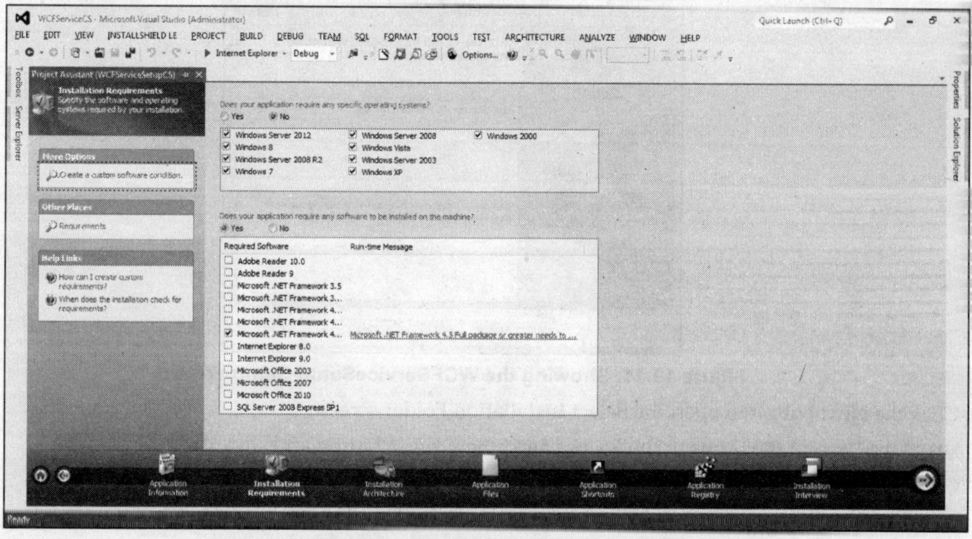

Figure 19.9: Entering the Installation Requirements

The Application Files page appears (Figure 19.10)

11. Click the Add Project Outputs button to open the Visual Studio Output Selector dialog box (Figure 19.10).
12. Click the Content Files check box and click the OK button, as shown in Figure 19.10:

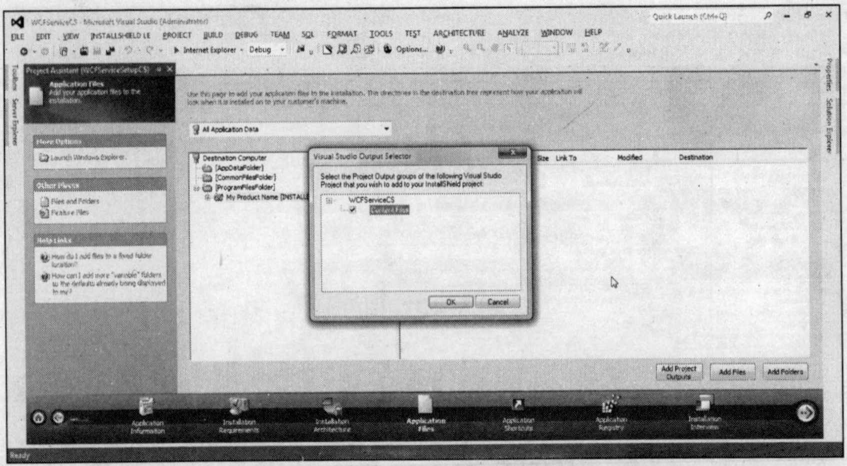

Figure 19.10: Showing the Visual Studio Output Selector Dialog Box

14. Select the Build WCFServiceSetupCS option from the BUILD menu.

    When you build the `WCFServiceSetup` project, the setup file can be located at the specified location. In our case, it is located at C:\Users\Puneet\Documents\Visual Studio 2012\Projects\WCFServiceSetupCS \WCFServiceSetupCS\ WCFServiceSetupCS\Express\DVD-5\DiskImages\DISK1.

15. Double-click the WCFServiceSetupCS installer file. The WCFServiceSetupCS-InstallShield Wizard appears

Figure 19.11: Showing the WCFServiceSetup Setup Wizard

13. Click the Next button to open the Select Installation Folder screen.
14. Select the I accept the terms in the license agreement radio button and click the next button.
15. Click the Next button again to continue with the installation and finally, click the Install button.
16. Click the Finish button in the Installation complete screen to close the wizard.

Let's now learn to build a WCF client.

Building WCF Clients

After creating the WCF service, you can consume or use the WCF service in a Web application. To use a WCF service, you need to build a WCF client. Let's perform the following steps to build a WCF client:

1. Open Visual Studio 2012 and select the `FILE→New→Web Site` option from the menu bar. The New Web Site dialog box appears (Figure 19.12).
2. Select the ASP.NET Empty Web Site template from the middle pane in the New Web Site dialog box.

3. Enter the location and the name of the application such as WCFClientCS and click the OK button, as shown in Figure 19.12:

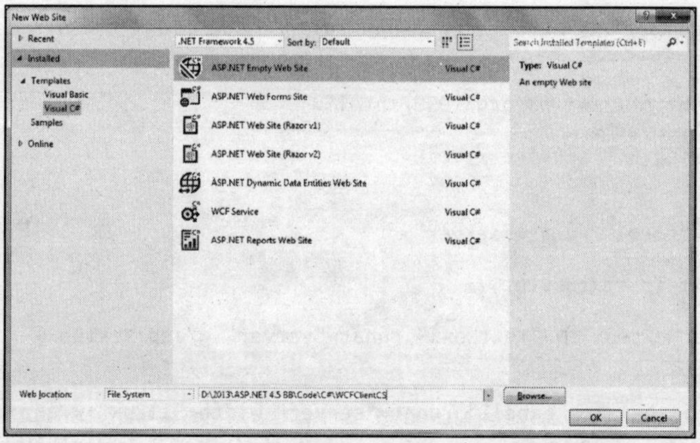

Figure 19.12: Selecting the ASP.NET Empty Web Site Template

4. Add a new Web Form to the project.
5. Add the reference of the WCF service to the project by right-clicking the name of the project in the Solution Explorer and selecting the Add Service Reference option from the context menu, as shown in Figure 19.13:

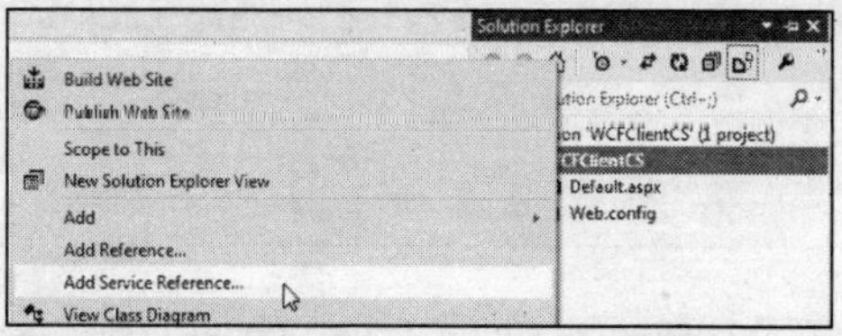

Figure 19.13: Selecting the Add Service Reference Option

5. Enter the address of the service and click the GO button in the Add Service Reference dialog box. It will not attach if the service is in execution mode. A list of services appears under the Services pane, as shown in Figure 19.14:

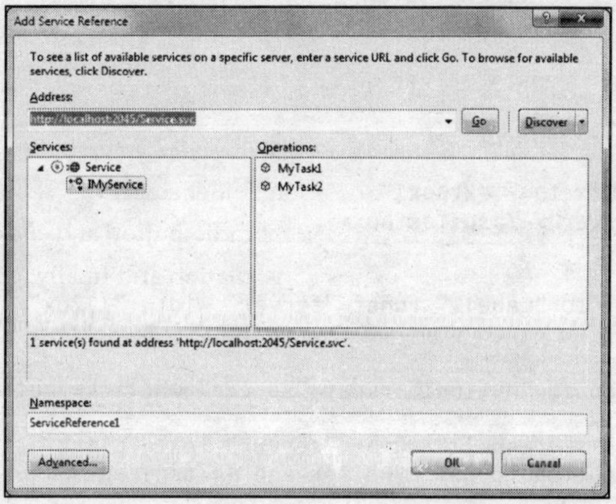

Figure 19.14: Showing the Add Service Reference Dialog Box

6. Enter the name of namespace in the Namespace text box, which in this case is ServiceReference1, and click the OK button. The reference of the service is added in the project. Now, add the code, shown in Listing 19.5, in the Default.`aspx` page.

Listing 19.5: Showing the Code for the `Default.aspx` Page

In VB

```
<%@ Page Language="VB" AutoEventWireup="false" CodeFile=" Default.aspx.vb"
  Inherits="_ Default" %>
<!DOCTYPE html>
<html xmlns="http://www.w3.org/1999/xhtml">
<head runat="server">
    <title>Using WCF service</title>
</head>
<body>
    <form id="form1" runat="server">
    <div>
    Enter text in textbox<br />
         <br />
         <asp:TextBox ID="TextBox1" runat="server"></asp:TextBox>
         <br />
         <br />
         <asp:Label ID="Label1" runat="server" Width="112px"></asp:Label>
         <br />
         <br />
         <asp:Button ID="Button1" runat="server" OnClick="Button1_Click"
         Text="CALL" />
         <br />
         <asp:Label ID="Label2" runat="server" Text="Click
         the CALL button to call the service"></asp:Label>
    </div>
    </form>
</body>
</html>
```

In C#

```
<%@ Page Language="C#" AutoEventWireup="true" CodeFile=" Default.aspx.cs"
  Inherits="_ Default" %>
<!DOCTYPE html>
<html xmlns="http://www.w3.org/1999/xhtml">
<head runat="server">
    <title>Using WCF service</title>
</head>
<body>
    <form id="form1" runat="server">
    <div>
    Enter text in textbox<br />
         <br />
         <asp:TextBox ID="TextBox1"
         runat="server"></asp:TextBox>
         <br />
         <br />
         <asp:Label ID="Label1" runat="server" Width="112px"></asp:Label>
         <br />
         <br />
         <asp:Button ID="Button1" runat="server" OnClick="Button1_Click" Text="CALL" />
         <br />
         <asp:Label ID="Label2" runat="server" Text="Click
         the CALL button to call the service"></asp:Label>
    </div>
    </form>
</body>
</html>
```

In Listing 19.5, we have added a `Textbox` control for the input, a `Label` control for the output, and a `Button` control to call the service.

7. Create a folder, `App_Code`, in the Solution Explorer window and add the `Service.cs` file in VB and `Service.cs` file in C# to the folder.
8. Replace the `Web.config` file with the `output.config` file and rename it as Web.config.
9. Add the code, shown in Listing 19.6, on the click event of the `Button` control in the CodeFile of the `Default.aspx` page:

Listing 19.6: Showing the Code for the Code-Behind File

In VB

```
Partial Class _ Default
    Inherits System.Web.UI.Page
    Protected Sub Button1_Click(sender As Object, e As EventArgs)
  Handles Button1.Click
        Dim Client As New MyServiceClient()
        Label1.Text = Client.MyTask1(TextBox1.Text)
        Client.Close()
    End Sub
End Class
```

In C#

```
using System;
using System.Collections.Generic;
//using System.Linq;
using System.Web;
using System.Web.UI;
using System.Web.UI.WebControls;
public partial class _ Default: System.Web.UI.Page
{
    protected void Page_Load(object sender, EventArgs e)
    {
    }
    protected void Button1_Click(object sender, EventArgs e)
    {
        MyServiceClient Client = new MyServiceClient();
        Label1.Text = Client.MyTask1(TextBox1.Text);
        Client.Close();
    }
}
```

10. Run the project. Enter some text in the text box and click the CALL button on the form. The output is shown in Figure 19.15:

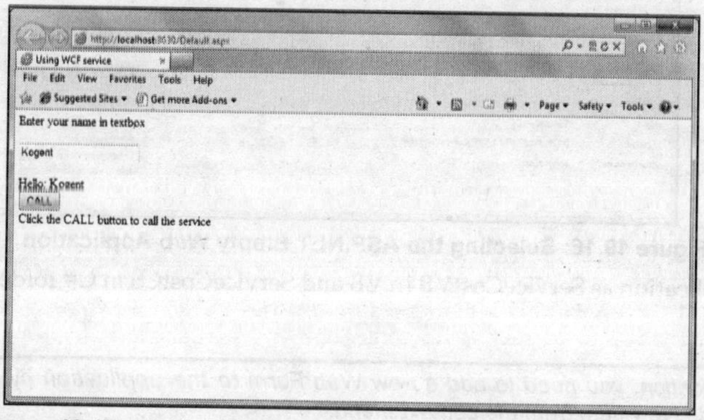

Figure 19.15: Displaying the Output after Calling the WCF Service

You can find this WCF service application's code as `WCFClientVB` and `WCFClientCS`.

Using WCF Services with ASP.NET AJAX

WCF also supports the ASP.NET AJAX and JSON data formats. The WCF supported data format allows the WCF service to expose operations to AJAX clients (Web pages running the JavaScript code). You can use the WCF services with an ASP.NET AJAX application by performing the following steps:

- Exposing the WCF service to an ASP.NET AJAX application
- Calling the WCF service from client-side

Let's perform these steps, one by one.

Exposing the WCF Services to an ASP.NET AJAX Web Application

Prior to exposing the WCF services to an ASP.NET AJAX Web application, you need to create a Web application considering the following requirements:

- A Web application containing the `.svc` file extension, which contains the `@ Service, Host` directive, must host a WCF service.
- To call the WCF service from the script, you need to configure a Web application.

You should also ensure that the WCF service must be a class that implements an interface marked with the `ServiceContractAttribute` attribute. Individual service operations (methods) to be called from the script must be qualified with the `OperationContractAttribute` attribute.

After discussing the requirements for an AJAX-enabled WCF service, let's perform the following steps to create a WCF service that satisfies all the requirements:

1. Open Visual Studio 2012 and select `FILE→New→Project`. The New Project dialog box appears (Figure 19.16).
2. Select the ASP.NET Empty Web Application template from the middle pane.
3. Enter `ServiceCostCS` as the name of the application beside the Name field and click the OK button, as shown in Figure 19.16:

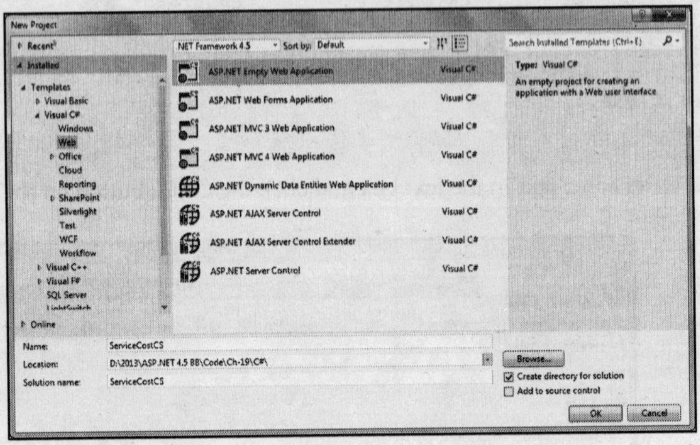

Figure 19.16: Selecting the ASP.NET Empty Web Application Template

You can find this application as ServiceCostVB in VB and ServiceCostCS in C# folder.

NOTE

After creating an application, you need to add a new Web Form to the application by right-clicking the Project name and selecting Add→Add New Item from the context menu.

4. Right-click the project name and select `Add→Add New Item` from the context menu in the Solution Explorer window. The Add New Item dialog box appears, as shown in Figure 19.17:

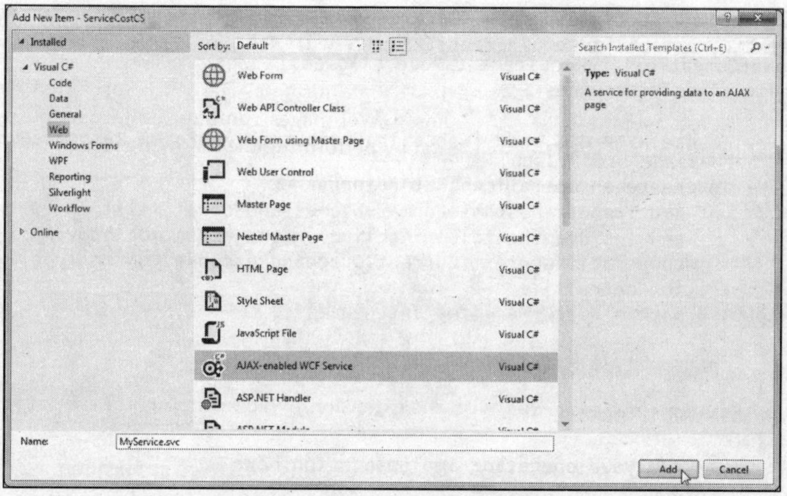

Figure 19.17: Adding the AJAX-Enabled WCF Service

5. Select the AJAX-enabled WCF Service template. Enter the name, MyService.svc, in the Name field (Figure 19.17), and click the Add button.

This adds a `MyService.svc` file and its code-behind file in the Server Explorer. Open the code-behind file(`MyService.svc.cs`) and add the code, shown in Listing 19.7, to it:

Listing 19.7: Showing the Code for the Code-Behind File

In VB

```
Imports System.ServiceModel
Imports System.ServiceModel.Activation
Imports System.ServiceModel.Web
<ServiceContract(Namespace:="ServiceCostVB")> _
<AspNetCompatibilityRequirements(RequirementsMode:=AspNetCompatibilityRequirementsMode.A
  ll
  owed)> _
Public Class MyService
  ' Add <WebGet()> attribute to use HTTP GET
  <OperationContract()> _
  Public Function CostOfServices(ByVal quantity As Integer) As Double
        Return 1.25 * quantity
  End Function
  Public Sub DoWork()
        ' Add your operation implementation here
  End Sub
  ' Add more operations here and mark them with <OperationContract()>
End Class
```

In C#

```
using System;
using System.Collections.Generic;
using System.Linq;
using System.Runtime.Serialization;
using System.ServiceModel;
using System.ServiceModel.Activation;
using System.ServiceModel.Web;
using System.Text;
namespace ServiceCostCS
{
```

```
    [ServiceContract(Namespace = "ServiceCostCS")]
    [AspNetCompatibilityRequirements(RequirementsMode =
    AspNetCompatibilityRequirementsMode.Allowed)]
    public class MyService
    {
        // To use HTTP GET, add [WebGet] attribute. (WebForm1 ResponseFormat is
         WebMessageFormat.Json)
        // To create an operation that returns XML,
        //     add [WebGet(ResponseFormat=WebMessageFormat.Xml)],
        //     and include the following line in the operation body:
        //    WebOperationContext.Current.OutgoingResponse.ContentType = "text/xml";
        [OperationContract]
        public double CostOfServices(int quantity)
        {
            return 1.25 * quantity;
        }
        public void DoWork()
        {
            // Add your operation implementation here
            return;
        }
        // Add more operations here and mark them with [OperationContract]
    }
}
```

In Listing 19.7, we have specified the namespace, ServiceCost, in the ServiceContract attribute. In the `CostOfServices` method, 1.25 is the cost of the service that multiplies with the quantity, and returns the total cost of the services.

6. Run the application. The output appears, as shown in Figure 19.18:

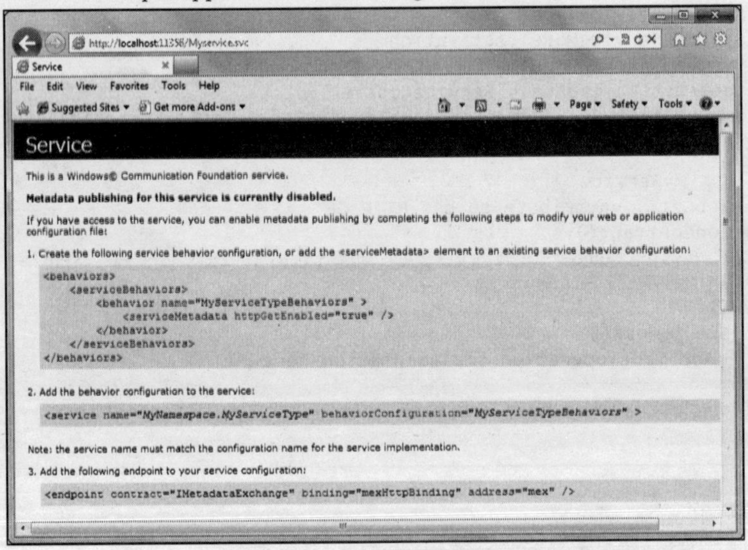

Figure 19.18: Showing the Output of the WCF Service

Calling WCF Services from Client-Side Script

After creating the AJAX-enabled WCF service, you need a client to use that service. Now, let's learn how to call the `MyService` WCF service from the client-side script by performing the following steps:

1. Open the Design view of the `WebForm1.aspx` page of the ServiceCost application and add the `ScriptManager` control from the AJAX Extensions tab of the Toolbox on the `WebForm1.aspx` page.

2. Open the properties of the `ScriptManager` control and expand the Services property to open the ServiceReference Collection Editor dialog box (Figure 19.19).
3. Click the Add button to add the service reference to the application. Enter MyService.svc as the path reference in the Path property, and click the OK button, as shown in Figure 19.19:

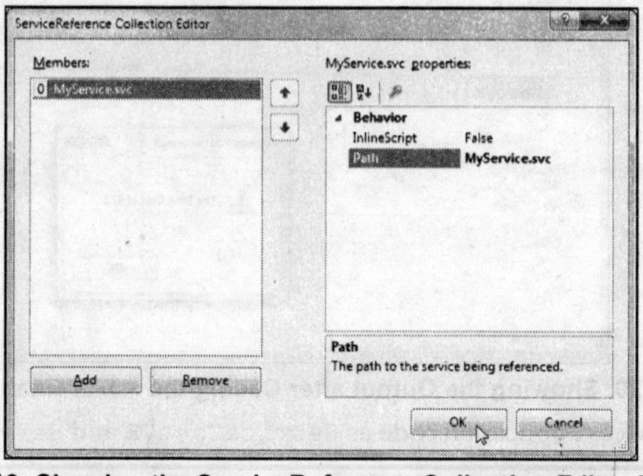

Figure 19.19: Showing the ServiceReference Collection Editor Dialog Box

4. Add the Input (Text) and the Input (Button) controls on the `WebForm1.aspx` page from the HTML tab of the Toolbar.
5. Change the Value property of the Input (Button) control to Show Total in the Properties window.
6. Double-click the Input (Button) control to access the JavaScript code and add the JavaScript code, shown in Listing 19.8, within the <script> element:

Listing 19.8: Showing the JavaScript Code of the `WebForm1.aspx` Page

In VB

```
function Button1_onclick() {
   var service = new ServiceCostVB.MyService();
   service.CostOfServices(document.getElementbyId("Text1").value, onSucess, onerror,
   null, null);
}
function onSucess(result) {
   alert("The Total Cost is: " + result);
}
function onerror(a) {
   alert("Error" + a);
}
```

In C#

```
function Button1_onclick() {
   var service = new ServiceCostCS.MyService();
   service.CostOfServices(document.getElementbyId("Text1").value, onSucess, onerror,
   null, null);
}
function onSucess(result)
{
     alert("The Total Cost is: " + result);
}
function onerror(a) {
     alert("Error" + a);
}
```

7. Run this application to call the WCF service from client-side scripts.
8. Enter a number in the text box and click the Show Total button. The total will be displayed in a message box after multiplying the number entered in the text box with the cost of service 1.25 (specified in the `MyService.svc.cs` file). Figure 19.20 shows the output of the AJAX-enabled WCF service:

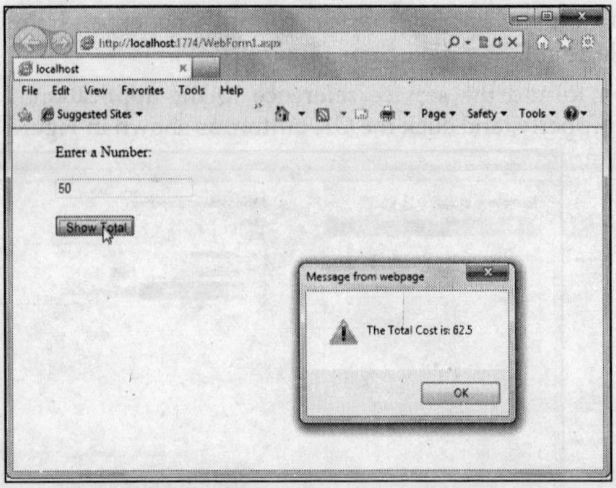

Figure 19.20: Showing the Output after Calling the AJAX-Enabled WCF Service

You can find this WCF Services application code as `ServiceCostVB` and `ServiceCostCS`.

Creating WCF Data Services

To understand how to create a data service and consume it through a client, perform the following steps:

1. Create a new empty website by selecting Visual Studio 2012→New→Web Site and name it as `WCFDataServiceCS`. You can find the code for the WCFDataService website as `WCFDataServiceCS` (for C#) and `WCFDataServiceVB` (for VB).
2. Add the Default.aspx page to the `WCFDataServiceCS` website.
3. Select an ADO.NET Entity Data Model template to create an Entity Data Model (EDM), as shown in Figure 19.21:

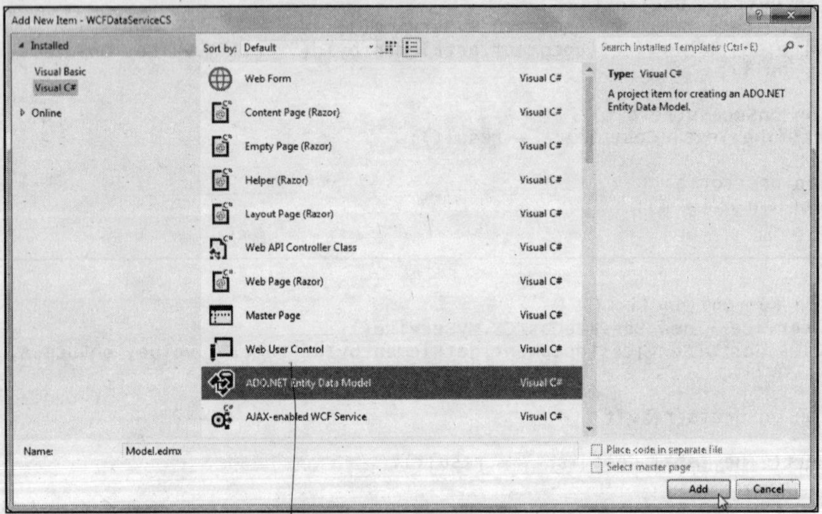

Figure 19.21: Selecting the ADO.NET Entity Data Model Template

NOTE

In this application, we are creating EDM by using the Northwind database.

The `Model.edmx` file is added to the WCFDataService application after an EDM is created and the `Model.edmx` page opens, as shown in Figure 19.22:

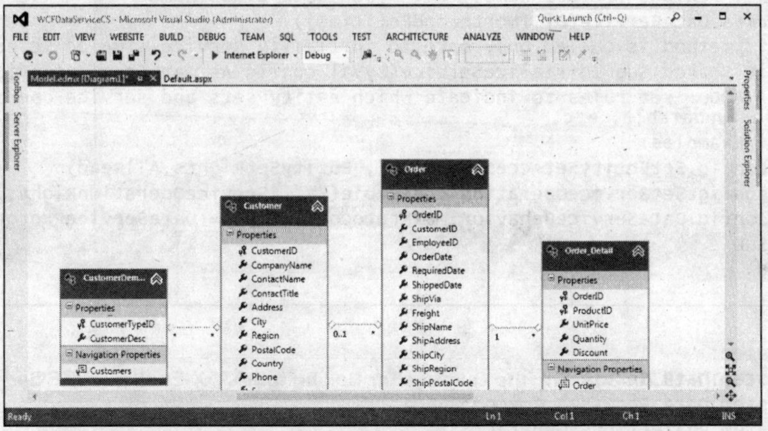

Figure 19.22: Showing EDM of the Northwind Database

In the Model.edmx page, you can see that EDM of the Northwind database consists of entities and associations between the entities, which describe the relationship between the tables.

4. Add the WCF Data Services template required to create a data service to the application, as shown in Figure 19.23:

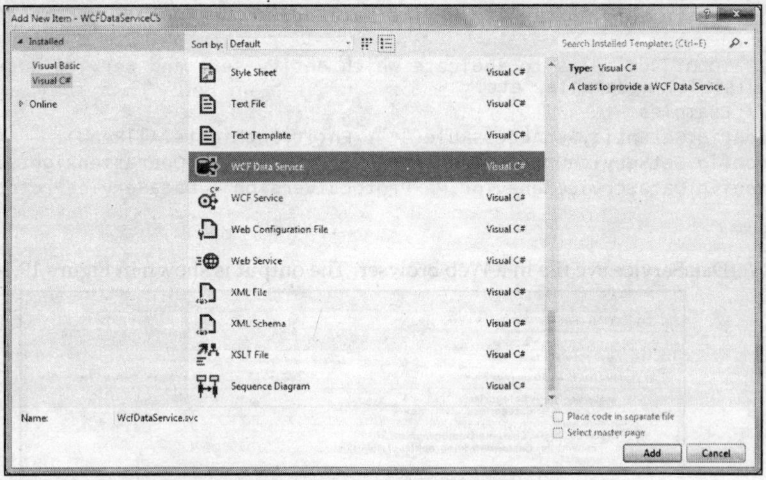

Figure 19.23: Adding WCF Data Service Template

After adding the WCF Data Service template, two files, `WcfDataService.cs` or WcfDataService and `WcfDataService.svc`, are added to the application.

5. Modify the WcfDataService.cs file to provide data source to the data service. Listing 19.9 shows the code for the WcfDataService.cs file:

Listing 19.9: Showing the Code for the WcfDataService.cs File

In VB:

```
Imports System.Data.Services
Imports System.Data.Services.Common
Imports System.Linq
Imports System.ServiceModel.Web
```

```
Imports System.Web
Public Class WcfDataService
    ' TODO: replace [[class name]] with your data class name
    Inherits DataService(Of [NorthwindEntities])
    ' This method is called only once to initialize service-wide policies.
    Public Shared Sub InitializeService(ByVal config As DataServiceConfiguration)
        ' TODO: set rules to indicate which entity sets and service operations are
  visible, updatable, etc.
        ' Examples:
        config.SetEntitySetAccessRule("*", EntitySetRights.AllRead)
        config.SetServiceOperationAccessRule("*", ServiceOperationRights.All)
        config.DataServiceBehavior.MaxProtocolVersion = DataServiceProtocolVersion.V2
    End Sub
End Class
```

In C#:

```
using System;
using System.Data.Services;
using System.Data.Services.Common;
using System.Collections.Generic;
using System.Linq;
using System.ServiceModel.Web;
using System.Web;
public class WcfDataService : DataService< NorthwindEntities >
{
    // This method is called only once to initialize service-wide policies.
    public static void InitializeService(DataServiceConfiguration config)
    {
        // TODO: set rules to indicate which entity sets and service operations are
         visible, updatable, etc.
        // Examples:
        config.SetEntitySetAccessRule("*", EntitySetRights.AllRead);
        config.SetServiceOperationAccessRule("*", ServiceOperationRights.All);
        config.DataServiceBehavior.MaxProtocolVersion = DataServiceProtocolVersion.V2;
    }
}
```

6. View the WcfDataService.svc file in a Web browser. The output is shown in Figure 19.24:

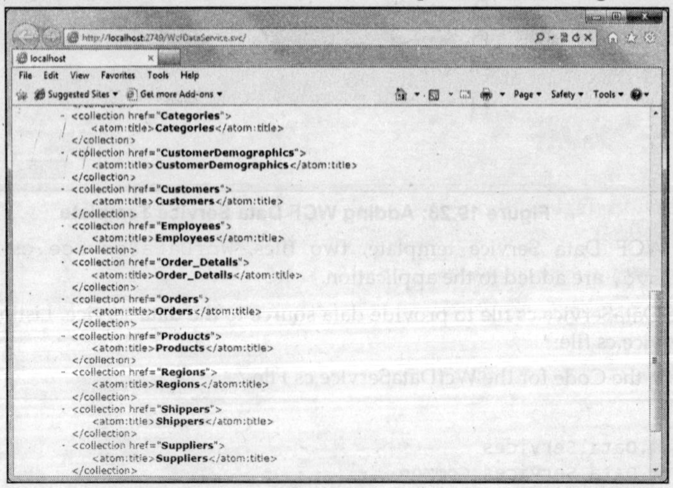

Figure 19.24: Displaying WcfDataService.svc on Internet Explorer

7. Add the Products query string in the URL of WebDataService.svc to query the data in the address itself, as shown in Figure 19.25:

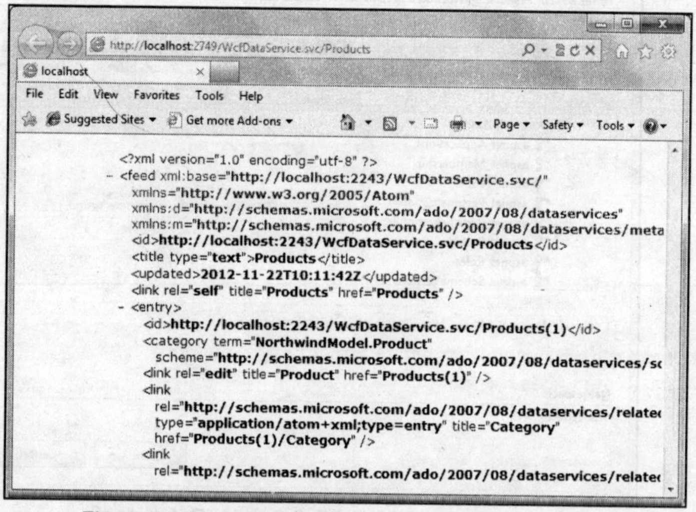

Figure 19.25: Displaying Data after Adding the Query

NOTE

You can read the data in a table by specifying the particular entity set in URL. This implies that you can read the Products table in the Northwind database by typing the following query in the address bar: http://localhost:2749/WcfDataService.svc/Products.

You can read a specific item of a table by specifying the ID of the item in URL. For example, you can view the 4th product in the Products table of the Northwind database by typing the following query in the address bar: http://localhost:2749/WcfDataService.svc/Products

You can also the read a specific item by specifying the value in one of the columns of a table in URL. For example, if you want to view the 1st entry in the Customers table, you can specify the following query in the address bar, instead of specifying the ID of the item: http://localhost:2749/WcfDataService.svc/Customers('ALFKI')

After creating the WCF Data Service, you need to add the service reference in the WCFDataService application.

8. Right-click the solution name and select the Add Service Reference option from the context menu. The Add Service Reference dialog box opens (Figure 19.26).
9. Click the Discover button (Figure 19.26). A list of available WCF service references is displayed in the Address text box when the application is in running mode and port number is system specific. (Figure 19.26).
10. Click the Go button (Figure 19.26). The NorthwindEntities service reference is displayed in the Address text box (Figure 19.26).
11. Provide a name for the service reference in the Namespace text box, which in this case is ServiceReference1 (Figure 19.26).
12. Click the OK button to add the service reference to the application, as shown in Figure 19.26:

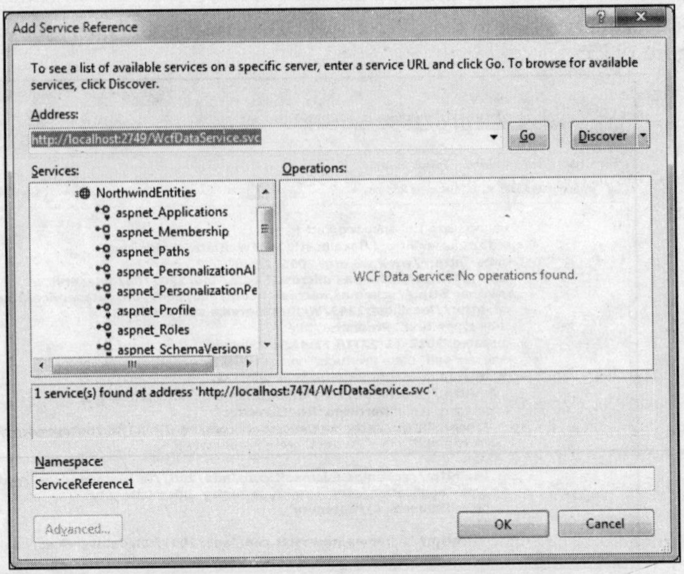

Figure 19.26: Adding Service Reference

To create a client to consume data services, you need to add some controls in the application.

13. Modify the code of Default.aspx with the code shown in Listing 19.10 to create a client for the data service:

Listing 19.10: Showing the Code for the Default.aspx Page

In VB

```
<%@ Page Language="VB" AutoEventWireup="false" CodeFile=" Default.aspx.vb"
  Inherits="_ Default " %>
<!DOCTYPE html>
<html xmlns="http://www.w3.org/1999/xhtml">
<head runat="server">
    <title>Consuming Data Services</title>
</head>
<body>
    <form id="form1" runat="server">
    <div>
  <asp:GridView ID="GridView1" runat="server" BackColor="White" BorderColor="#CC9966"
          BorderStyle="None" BorderWidth="1px" CellPadding="4">
        <FooterStyle BackColor="#FFFFCC" ForeColor="#330099" />
        <HeaderStyle BackColor="#990000" Font-Bold="True" ForeColor="#FFFFCC" />
        <PagerStyle BackColor="#FFFFCC" ForeColor="#330099" HorizontalAlign="Center" />
        <RowStyle BackColor="White" ForeColor="#330099" />
        <SelectedRowStyle BackColor="#FFCC66" Font-Bold="True" ForeColor="#663399" />
        <SortedAscendingCellStyle BackColor="#FEFCEB" />
        <SortedAscendingHeaderStyle BackColor="#AF0101" />
        <SortedDescendingCellStyle BackColor="#F6F0C0" />
        <SortedDescendingHeaderStyle BackColor="#7E0000" />
                        </asp:GridView>
    </div>
    </form>
</body>
</html>
```

In C#

```
<%@ Page Language="C#" AutoEventWireup="true" CodeFile=" Default.aspx.cs"
  Inherits="_ Default " %>
<!DOCTYPE html>
<html xmlns="http://www.w3.org/1999/xhtml">
<head runat="server">
    <title>Consuming Data Services</title>
</head>
<body>
    <form id="form1" runat="server">
    <div>
    <asp:GridView ID="GridView1" runat="server" BackColor="White" BorderColor="#CC9966"
            BorderStyle="None" BorderWidth="1px" CellPadding="4">
        <FooterStyle BackColor="#FFFFCC" ForeColor="#330099" />
        <HeaderStyle BackColor="#990000" Font-Bold="True" ForeColor="#FFFFCC" />
        <PagerStyle BackColor="#FFFFCC" ForeColor="#330099" HorizontalAlign="Center" />
        <RowStyle BackColor="White" ForeColor="#330099" />
        <SelectedRowStyle BackColor="#FFCC66" Font-Bold="True" ForeColor="#663399" />
        <SortedAscendingCellStyle BackColor="#FEFCEB" />
        <SortedAscendingHeaderStyle BackColor="#AF0101" />
        <SortedDescendingCellStyle BackColor="#F6F0C0" />
        <SortedDescendingHeaderStyle BackColor="#7E0000" />
                        </asp:GridView>
    </div>
    </form>
</body>
</html>
```

14. Modify the code of code-behind files of the Default.aspx file. Listing 19.11 shows the code for the code-behind file of Default.aspx page:

Listing 19.11: Showing the Code for the Code-Behind File of the Default.aspx Page

In VB

```
Imports ServiceReference1
Imports System.Data.Services
Imports System.Data.Services.Client
Partial Class _ Default
    Inherits System.Web.UI.Page
    Protected Sub Page_Load(sender As Object, e As EventArgs) Handles
  Me.Load
        Dim svc As New NorthwindEntities()
        GridView1.DataSource = svc.Customers
        GridView1.DataBind()
    End Sub
End Class
```

In C#

```
using System;
using System.Collections.Generic;
using System.Linq;
using System.Web;
using System.Web.UI;
using System.Web.UI.WebControls;
using System.Data.Services.Client;
```

```
    using System.Data.Services;
    public partial class _ Default: System.Web.UI.Page
    {
        protected void Page_Load(object sender, EventArgs e)
        {
            NorthwindEntities svc = new NorthwindEntities();
            GridView1.DataSource = svc.Customers;
            GridView1.DataBind();
        }
    }
```

15. Run the application. The output is shown in Figure 19.27:

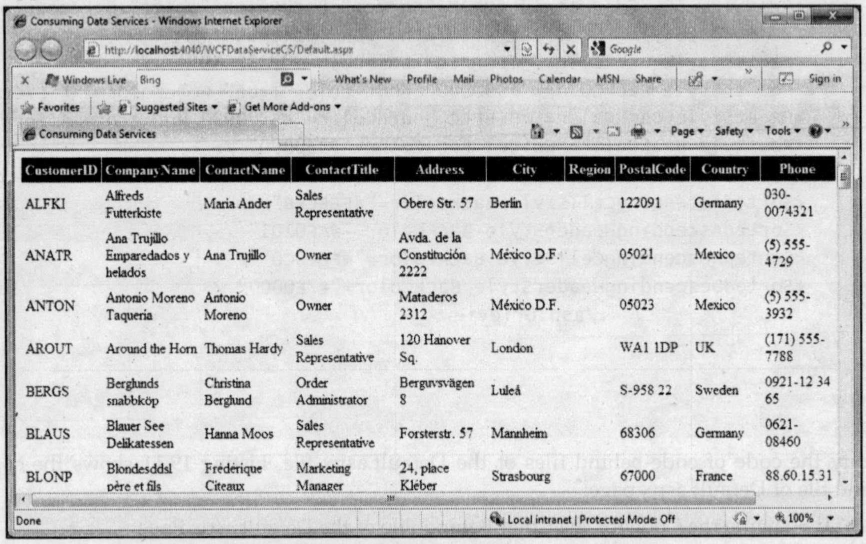

Figure 19.27: Displaying the Output of Data Services

Figure 19.27 displays the data of the Northwind database in the GridView control, which is bound to the URL of the WcfDataService.cs or WcfDataService.vb data service.

Summary

In this chapter, you have learned about WCF, its architecture, and features. You have also learned about creating, configuring, and deploying the WCF services in Visual Studio 2012 with .NET Framework 4.5. In addition, you have learned to create the clients applications which use or consume these services. You have also learned to use the WCF service with ASP.NET AJAX and call the services from the client-side JavaScript. In addition, you have learned about the new WCF Data Services features and its usage.

The next chapter explores ASP.NET Model-View-Controller (MVC) Framework, its features, and the MVC model.

20

ASP.NET MVC Framework

If you need an Immediate Solution to: See page:

In Depth

An application usually provides different sets of information to its users, which is presented to users on different pages in different formats. For example, a user may want to view the static information of a website on a different page, while another user may want to view the same information along with some other dynamic content. There are also instances when different users may require multiple types of interfaces, such as Hypertext Markup Language (HTML) for Web customer, a Wireless Markup Language (WML) for wireless customers, Java or .NET for administrators, and XML-based Web service for suppliers. Therefore, in an application, we may need to create multiple views for a single model.

When developing a small application, it sounds logical to interweave data access, business logic, presentation logic, and control together. However, for a large enterprise-level application, interweaving makes code files more complex; therefore, it will be difficult to manage while implementing changes in future. This results in the duplication of data access and business logic code in the application at various points. As a result, the implementation, testing, and maintenance efforts are also duplicated. It is always a good idea to reduce duplication by separating presentation logic, business logic, and control logic as different components, which can easily be reused. The solution to these problems comes in the form of a Model-View-Controller (MVC) design pattern, which separates data access, business logic, and presentation logic and enables creation of a number of views accessing the same enterprise application model.

In this chapter, we discuss MVC architecture, and ASP.NET MVC framework and its features. We will also understand the concept of the Controller class and Uniform Resource Locator (URL) Routing. Now, let's start with MVC architecture.

Model-View-Controller Architecture

Nowadays, a Web application requires interaction with different types of clients with different types of user interfaces. A Web application may require presenting an `HTML` View to a Web user, a `WML` View to a wireless user, and a `Form` View to the administrator, as shown in Figure 20.1:

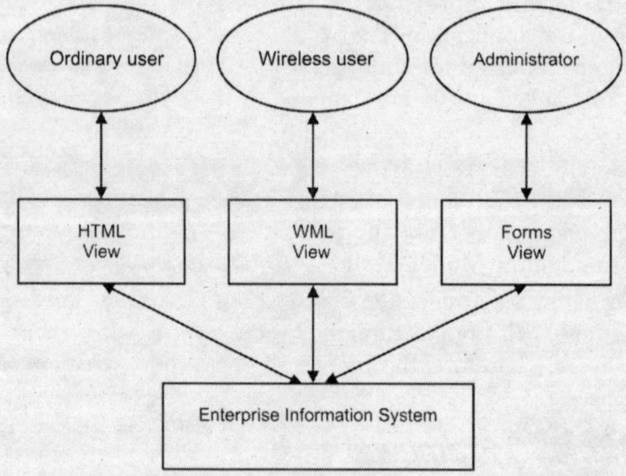

Figure 20.1: Interacting with Different Types of Clients

When there is requirement to support only one type of client with one type of interface, it is always a good idea to combine client-specific data and business logic with the interface-specific logic. If Web applications require interaction with multiple types of clients, different applications are required to support each type of client. This leads to the repetition of non-interface specific code in each interface-specific code, which further leads to increased effort in designing, debugging, and maintenance.

The solution of this problem is the use of MVC architecture while designing an application. The idea behind the MVC architecture is to separate the core business model functionality of the Web application from the presentation and control logic of the interface-specific application. With this sort of arrangement, it is possible to see multiple views of the same data model of the Web application. Under this architecture, data (`Model`) and user interface (`View`) are separated from each other so that any change in the user interfaces does not affect the data in the database and vice versa. The three components of MVC—the `Model`, the `View`, and the `Controller`--must communicate with each other if the application needs to manage a coherent interaction with the user. Although, the `View` and the `Controller` communicates with each other directly because these two components are specifically designed to work together. However, the `Model` communicates whenever it is required by the Controller.

Microsoft provides built-in support for developing Web applications by using an MVC-based architecture in ASP.NET. Now, let's know about the MVC framework associated with ASP.NET.

ASP.NET MVC Framework

The ASP.NET MVC framework is not a substitute for the ASP.NET Web Forms pattern. It just provides an alternative choice to the developer while designing and developing a Web application. It enables you to achieve and maintain a clear separation of presentation layer (UI), logic, and data access. It also facilitates test-driven development (TDD) environment, where you implement automated unit tests, which define and verify the requirements of new code before you actually write the code itself.

It is a lightweight, extremely testable presentation framework that is appended to existing ASP.NET features, such as `master pages` and `membership-based` authentication. The MVC framework resides inside the `System.Web.Mvc` namespace. This namespace is an elementary supported part of the `System.Web` namespace, which forms the basis of any Web application. MVC framework consists of the following components:

- Model
- View
- Controller

Now, let's start our discussion with Model in MVC framework.

Understanding Model in MVC Framework

The Model in the MVC framework represents the data and the business logic of the application, and is not related to the presentation of the application. The Model components focus on keeping track of the state of your application. The business logic required for your application is maintained here. The Model component contains the data that needs to be displayed but is not exposed to the information about the view and the manner in which data is to be displayed. It also does not know about view actions used to manipulate the data. However, the data is accessed and manipulated through methods that are independent of the view.

A Model can be considered as the foundation of the MVC architecture. Its core is composed of the business logic and data access code. For example, if an application has to find out the gross salary of employees, the computation part is performed in the Model layer.

It is the Model that defines what the application exactly does. The View and Controller interact with the Model for performing any task. In the MVC architecture, the Model layer is self-contained and functions independent of the View and Controller layers. Therefore, the core application code, which is based on the Model, can be used with multiple user interfaces.

Understanding View in MVC Framework

The `View` provides the User Interface (`UI`) for the `Model`. The user interacts with the application through a `View`. It represents the information based on the `Model` and allows the user to alter the data. Typically, this `UI` is created from the Model data. The main responsibilities of a View are as follows:

- **Rendering the content of the** `Model`—The `View` is responsible for representing the information in a form which is understandable to the user.
- **Requesting the updates from the** `Model`—In case of any change in the `Model`, the `View` requests the `Model` to provide the changed-state information. For example, the `Model` manages the database, whose content can be changed frequently. Any change in the database must be represented to the user as soon as possible.

- **Sending user inputs to the** Controller—If the user wants to modify the content of the Model, in such a case, user does not communicate with the Model directly. The user communicates through the View, which further communicates with the Controller about the user input. The Controller then makes changes in the Model according to the users' requirements and notifies all the other associated Views.
- **Allowing the** Controller **to select the** View—Data might have different Views for different users. View allows the Controller to determine which View is suitable for which user and provides them accordingly.

Understanding Controller in MVC Framework

Controllers are the components that handle all the Views associated to a Model, and then select a View to display UI. When the user interacts with the View and tries to update the Model, the Controller invokes methods to update the Model. The Controller controls the data flow and transformation between the Model and the View. Its main responsibilities are as follows:

- **Mapping the user actions into** Model **updates**—Input from the user is not fed directly to the Model. Instead, the Controller first provides this input to the Model, which further updates the Model.
- **Selecting the** View **for responses**—Application provides multiple Views of an application. The Controller selects the most appropriate View and delivers it to the user.

Figure 20.2 shows the interaction between the three components of MVC architecture—Model, View, and Controller:

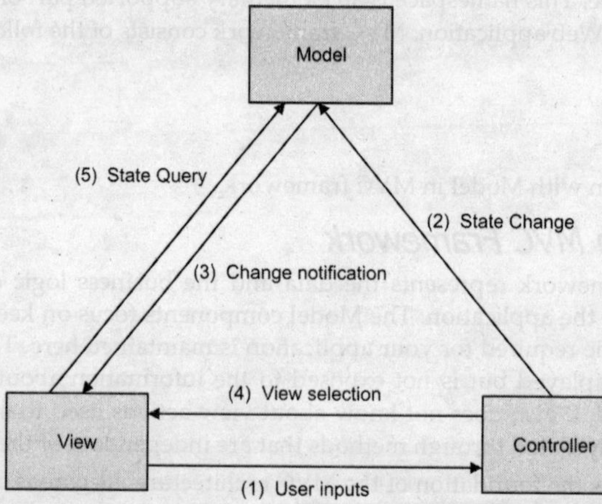

Figure 20.2: Interaction Between the MVC Architecture Components

Each user may get different views displaying required information customized for the value and layout according to that particular user. The application updates all the View as soon as any change in the data takes place. If the user wishes to change the data, it sends a request to the Controller, which further consults the Model to update all the View. It is to be noted that the View does not communicate directly with the Model. Rather this communication takes place through the Controller. The control flow can be broken down into the following steps:

1. The user sends a request through a UI provided by the View, which further passes this request to the Controller.
2. The Controller receives the input request coming from the user through the interface provided by the View and processes the request according to the Controller logic. If access to the Model is not required, Controller moves to step 4; otherwise, the Model is accessed, and its state is changed.
3. If the Model is accessed and modified, all the associated Views are notified of the changes.
4. The Controller then selects the new View to be displayed.
5. The View presents a UI according to the Model. The View data is also contained within the Model. View queries about the state of the Model to show the current data.

The `View` remains idle after the current interaction and waits for the next interaction to begin. The entire algorithm is repeated when a new request is serviced, in the same way as followed for other requests. Now, let's discuss about the ASP.NET MVC 4 framework and its new features.

ASP.NET MVC 4 Framework

The ASP.NET MVC framework was first included with ASP.NET 3.5 SP1. Now, ASP.NET 4.5 contains new features and capabilities in the framework and included it as the ASP.NET MVC 4 framework. The new MVC framework includes enhancements, changes, and features that emphasize on increasing productivity. Basically, MVC 4 framework is an extension of MVC 3 framework. The MVC 4 framework can be installed on the same computer along with the MVC 3 framework and therefore, provides the facility to the developers to upgrade their Web applications.

Before, discussing about the new features, let's discuss some changes that are introduced in the ASP.NET MVC 4 framework:

- Change in property validation behavior for classes that implement IDataErrorInfo interface
- IIS script-mapping script is no longer available in the MVC installer
- The Html.Substitute helper method in MVC is removed
- The IValueProvider interface replaces all the uses of IDictionary<string,ValueProviderResult>
- The new CSS classes are added in the Site.css file
- The HTML helpers can now return an MVCHtmlString object
- The JsonResult class in MVC responds only to the HTTP POST requests
- The ModelMetadata property is added to the ModelBindingContext class
- The Custom Controller factories require new signatures due to changes in the DefaultControllerFactory class
- Area is now a reserved route-value key and cannot be used with route URL

Now, let's discuss the new features of MVC 4 framework and Application Programming Interface (API) improvements.

Introducing New Features in MVC 4

ASP.NET MVC 4 is the latest version of MVC and is included in ASP.NET 4.5 Framework. The new features included in ASP.NET MVC 4 are as follows:

- **Improvements in Web API**—Includes new features such as modern HTTP programming model, full support for routing, content negotiation, model binding and validation, filters, query composition, improved testability, code-based configuration, improved support for IoC containers, Self-host, creation of custom help and test pages, monitoring and diagnostics, link generation, new Web API project template, and Scaffolding of Web API controller on the basis of Entity Framework and model type.
- **Enhancements in Default Project templates**—Specifies the enhancement of previous project templates to modern-looking templates.
- **Adaptive rendering**—Specifies the technique due to which a template appears good in both desktop browsers and mobile browsers without requiring any customization.
- **Mobile Application project template**—Specifies the inclusion of Mobile Application project template that is used for creating applications for mobile devices and tablet browsers.
- **Display Modes feature**—Allows an application to select views depending upon the browser that is sending the request.
- **jQuery Mobile library** —Allows you to develop applications that can run on mobile devices and tablet browsers.
- **Task support for asynchronous controllers**—Allows you to create asynchronous action methods as single methods that return an object of type Task.

- **Support for Azure Software Development Kit (SDK)**—Specifies that ASP.NET MVC 4 supports 1.6 and latest version of Windows Azure SDK.
- **Support database migrations**—Specifies that ASP.NET MVC 4 include Entity Framework 5 for supporting database migrations. This feature allows you to easily develop a database schema using a code-focused migration without modifying data in the database.
- **Empty project template**—Specifies that ASP.NET MVC 4 include Empty project template so that you can develop your application from scratch.
- **Add Controller to any project folder**—Specifies the inclusion of Controller from any project folder in your MVC project.
- **Bundling and Minification**—Allows you to decrease the number of HTTP requests that a Web page requires to make by integrating individual files into a single, that is, bundling of files for combining scripts and CSS. On the other hand, minifying includes activities such as eliminating whitespace to shorten names of variables and collapsing of CSS selectors on the basis of their semantics.
- **Enabling Logins from Facebook and other sites**—Specifies the support for OAuth and OpenID login by the default templates in ASP.NET MVC 4 Internet Project template using the DotNetOpenAuth library.

Let's now learn about the Controller class.

Understanding the Controller Class

In the ASP.NET applications that do not use MVC framework, user interaction is structured in the sequence of Web pages, and handles the events from those pages. On the contrary, user interaction with ASP.NET MVC applications is structured around Controllers and action methods. The Action methods usually have a one-to-one mapping with user interactions. For example, user interactions include entering a URL into the browser, clicking a link, and the rest. Each of these user interactions results in a request being sent to the server. In every case, the requested URL includes information that MVC framework needs to raise an action method.

`The Controller classes` are the classes that are mapped by the ASP.NET MVC framework URLs. The Controller classes process the incoming requests, tackle the user input and interactions, and finally execute appropriate application logic. A Controller class typically calls a separate View component to generate the HTML markup for any incoming request. The base class for all the Controllers is the `Controller` class, which performs general `MVC handling`. The `Controller` class implements the `IController`, `IActionFilter`, and `IDisposable` interfaces. Classes derived from the `Controller` class are responsible for the following processing stages:

- Locating the appropriate action method to call and validate
- Getting the values to use as the action method's arguments
- Handling all errors that might occur during the execution of the action method
- Providing with the default `WebFormViewFactory` class for rendering ASP.NET page types

NOTE

All the Controller classes must be named by using the Controller suffix.

The following example shows a sample Controller class, MyHomeController, which contains action methods and provides methods for rendering View pages:

The sample code in VB is as follows:

```
Public Class MyHomeController
    Inherits System.Web.Mvc.Controller
    Function Index()
        ViewData("Title") = "Home Page"
        ViewData("Message") = "Welcome to MVC World!"
        Return View()
    End Function
    Function About()
        ViewData("Title") = "About Page"
```

```
        Return View()
    End Function
End Class
```

The sample code in C# is as follows:

```
public class MyHomeController : Controller
{
    public ActionResult Index()
    {
          ViewData["Title"] = "Home Page";
          ViewData["Message"] = " Welcome to MVC World!";
          return View();
    }
    public ActionResult About()
    {
          ViewData["Title"] = "About Page";
          return View();
    }
}
```

ASP.NET MVC framework uses routing to map URLs to Controller classes and actions. Now, let's discuss URL Routing.

Understanding the URL Routing

ASP.NET MVC framework works on the concept of routing to map URLs to Controller classes and actions defined in the Controller. Routing validates variables used in the `URL` definition according to a pattern mentioned in it, and also automatically passes them as parameter arguments to a Controller action after validation.

ASP.NET applications, not using routing, specifically maps the URL-based incoming request to physical files, such as .aspx on the disk. To understand this process, let's take an example of the following URL based request: http://server/application/Customers.aspx?id=3.

In this request, the URL is mapped to a file named Customer.aspx that uses id=3 for displaying the content, which is beyond the capacity of a user to understand. However, if routing is enabled for this Web application, then URL displays results on the basis of pattern defined in the routing. Similar to the example of the URL http://server/application/Customers/show/category, the routing validator takes Customers, show, and category as variables for passing the values to the request, which can be understood by the user.

In the Visual Studio project templates, there are preconfigured `URL routes` for ASP.NET MVC framework. These routes are defined in the ASP.NET Application class inside the `Global.asax` file. The preconfigured routes allow you to start an ASP.NET MVC application without explicitly configuring routes for the most common scenarios.

The following syntax shows the default routes in VB that are included in an MVC application:

```
Shared Sub RegisterRoutes(routes As RouteCollection)
  ' Note: Change the URL to "{controller}.mvc/{action}/{id}" to enable
  '       automatic support in IIS 6.0 and in IIS 7.0 classic mode.
  ' Handler to stop URL routing for Web resources.
  routes.IgnoreRoute("{resource}.axd/{*pathInfo}")
  ' MapRoute takes the following parameters, in order:
  ' (1) Route name
  ' (2) URL with parameters
  ' (3) Parameter defaults
  ' (4) Parameter constraints
  routes.MapRoute( _
        "Default", _
        "{controller}/{action}/{id}", _
        New With {.controller = "Home", .action = "Index", .id = ""} _
  )
End Sub
```

The following syntax shows the default routes in C# that are included in an MVC application:

```
public static void RegisterRoutes(RouteCollection routes)
{
   // Note: Change the URL to "{controller}.mvc/{action}/{id}" to enable
   //       automatic support in IIS 6.0 and in IIS 7.0 classic mode.
   // Handler to stop URL routing for Web resources.
   routes.IgnoreRoute("{resource}.axd/{*pathInfo}");
   routes.MapRoute(
         "Default",                                          // Route name
         "{controller}/{action}/{id}",                       // URL with parameters
         new { controller = "Home", action = "Index", id = "" }  // Parameter defaults
   );
}
```

In the preceding code, the `MapRoute` and `IgnoreRoute` methods are added to the routes. These methods are used as extension methods of the `RouteCollection` class. The `MapRoute` method makes use of the Route object property and creates an instance of Route, while the `IgnoreRoute` method works with the `StopRoutingHandler` class. This class blocks the additional processing request by routing.

NOTE

You can also use the Add method of the RouteCollection class for adding routes.

The route following the pattern, `{resource}.axd/{*pathInfo}`, is used to prevent requests for the Web resource, such as `WebResource.axd` or `ScriptResource.axd`, from getting passed to a `Controller`.

Now, you are familiar with MVC framework. Now, let's discuss its working in the Immediate Solutions section

Immediate Solutions

Creating an ASP.NET MVC Application

Let's create an application named BookDetailMVCAppCS in C# and BookDetailMVCAppVB in VB folders. In this application, we create our own View by using the self-created class, ClassBook. In this View, we display the name of the Book and its details on the Web page in the MVC 4 framework. Now, let's create an application by following the given steps:

1. Open Visual Studio 2012 and select the New→ Project option from the FILE menu to open the New Project dialog box (Figure 20.3).
2. Select Web ASP.NET MVC 4 Web Application and then enter the appropriate name such as BookDetailMVCAppCS and location of the application in the dialog box (Figure 20.3).
3. Click the OK button to save the name and location of the application, as shown in Figure 20.3:

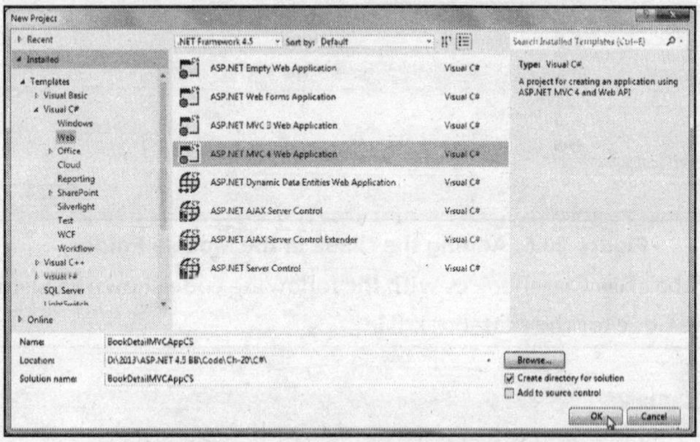

Figure 20.3: Creating the MVC 4 Application

The New ASP.NET MVC 4 Project dialog box appears (Figure 20.4).

4. Select Internet Application template and click the OK button, as shown in Figure 20.4:

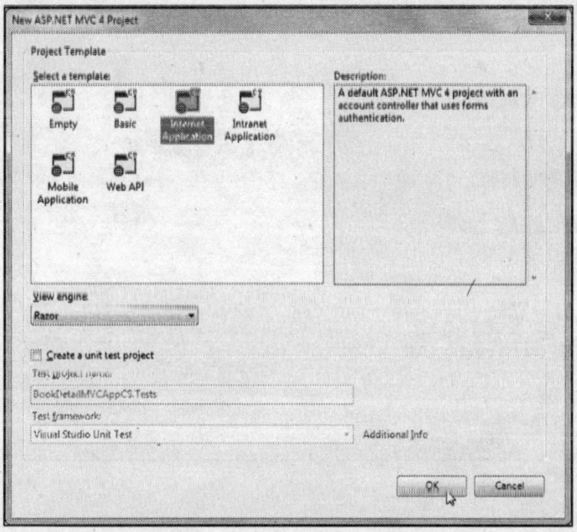

Figure 20.4: Displaying New ASP.NET MVC 4 Project Dialog Box

5. Right-click the Models folder in the Solution Explorer window and select Add→Class option from the context menu (Figure 20.5).

6. Select Installed→Visual C#→ Web→Class template and name it as ClassBook.cs in the Name textbox in the Add New Item dialog box (Figure 20.5).
7. Click the Add button in the Add New Item dialog box to add the ClassBook in the Models folder, as shown in Figure 20.5:

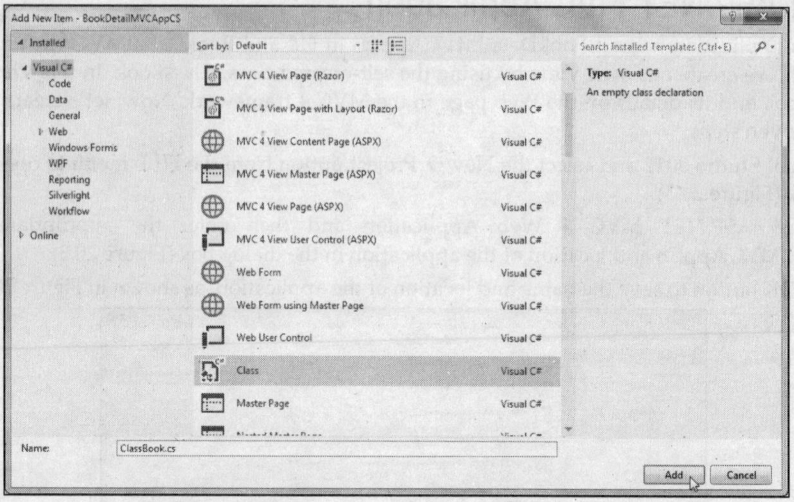

Figure 20.5: Adding the Class in the Models Folder

8. Replace the code of the class ClassBook.cs with the following code shown in Listing 20.1:

Listing 20.1: Showing the Code for the ClassBook File

In VB

```
Public Class ClassBook
#Region "properties"
    Public Property BName() As String
        Get
            Return m_BName
        End Get
        Set(ByVal value As String)
            m_BName = value
        End Set
    End Property
    Private m_BName As String
    Public Property BPrice() As String
        Get
            Return m_BPrice
        End Get
        Set(ByVal value As String)
            m_BPrice = value
        End Set
    End Property
    Private m_BPrice As String
    Public Property BEdition() As String
        Get
            Return m_BEdition
        End Get
        Set(ByVal value As String)
            m_BEdition = value
        End Set
    End Property
    Private m_BEdition As String
    Public Property BISBN() As String
        Get
```

```
            Return m_BISBN
        End Get
        Set(ByVal value As String)
            m_BISBN = value
        End Set
    End Property
    Private m_BISBN As String
    Public Property publisher() As String
        Get
            Return m_publisher
        End Get
        Set(ByVal value As String)
            m_publisher = value
        End Set
    End Property
    Private m_publisher As String
#End Region
End Class
```

In C#

```
using System;
using System.Collections.Generic;
using System.Linq;
using System.Web;
namespace BookDetailMVCAppCS.Models
{
    public class ClassBook
    {
        #region properties
        public string BName { get; set; }
        public string BPrice { get; set; }
        public string BEdition { get; set; }
        public string BISBN { get; set; }
        public string publisher { get; set; }
        #endregion
    }
}
```

9. Right-click the Controllers folder and select Add→Controller from the context menu to open the Add Controller dialog box (Figure 20.6).
10. Enter the name in the Controller name text box as BookController and click the Add button to add the class in the Controllers folder, as shown in Figure 20.6:

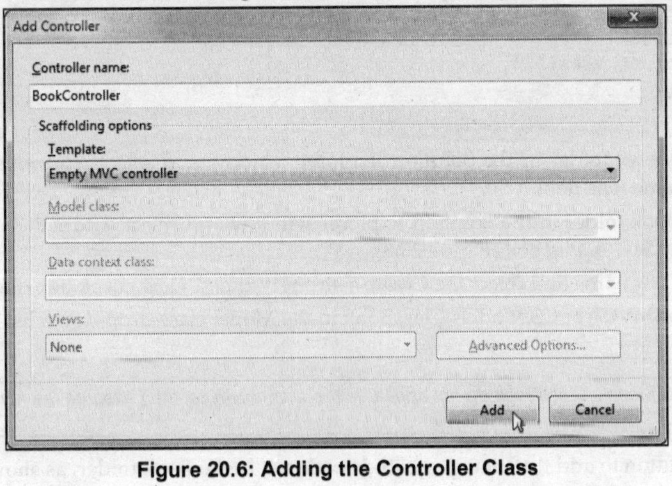

Figure 20.6: Adding the Controller Class

11. Replace the Index function with the following code, as shown in Listing 20.2:

Listing 20.2: Showing the Code for the BookController File

In VB

```
Imports System.Web.Mvc
Namespace BookDetailMVCAppVB
    Public Class BookController
        Inherits System.Web.Mvc.Controller

        '
        ' GET: /Book
        Function Index() As ActionResult
            Dim bs As New ClassBook()
            bs.BName = "Black Book ASP.NET 4.5"
            bs.BEdition = "2012"
            bs.BPrice = "800"
            bs.BISBN = "111-2222"
            bs.publisher = "Kogent Learning Solutions"
            Return View(bs)
        End Function
    End Class
End Namespace
```

In C#

```
using System;
using System.Collections.Generic;
using System.Linq;
using System.Web;
using System.Web.Mvc;
namespace BookDetailMVCApp.Controllers
{
    public class BookController : Controller
    {
        //
        // GET: /Book/
        public ActionResult Index()
        {
            BookDetailMVCAppCS.Models.ClassBook bs = new
             BookDetailMVCAppCS.Models.ClassBook();
            bs.BName = "Black Book ASP.NET 4.5";
            bs.BEdition = "2012";
            bs.BPrice = "800";
            bs.BISBN = "111-2222";
            bs.publisher = "Kogent Learning Solutions";
            return View(bs);
        }
    }
}
```

12. Right-click the Views folder in the Solution Explorer window and select Add→New Folder option in the context menu, name it as Book.
13. Right-click the Book folder in the Solution Explorer window and select Add→View from the context menu to open the Add View dialog box (Figure 20.8).
14. Enter Index as View name and select the Create a strongly-typed view check box (Figure 20.8).
15. Select BookDetailMVCAppCS.Models.ClassBook in the Model class drop-down list (Figure 20.8).

NOTE

If BookDetailMVCAppCS.Models.ClassBook do not appear in the drop-down list then execute the application before adding the View.

16. Click the Add button to add the View page (Index.cshtml) in the Book folder, as shown in Figure 20.8:

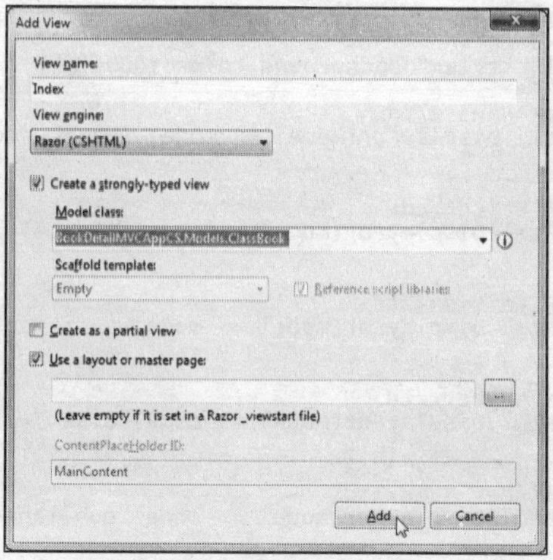

Figure 20.8: Adding the View Page

17. Replace the code in the Index.cshtml page with the following code listed in Listing 20.3:

Listing 20.3: Showing the Code for the Index.cshtml Page

In VB

```
@ModelType BookDetailMVCAppVB.ClassBook
@Code
    ViewData("Title") = "Index"
End Code
    <h2>ASP.NET 4.5 BB</h2>
<fieldset>
    <legend>ClassBook</legend>
   <div class="display-data">
      <table border="2">
    <tr>
    <td align="center" style="background-color:Silver">BookName</td>
    <td>@Html.DisplayFor(Function(model) model.BName)</td>
    </tr>
    <tr>
    <td align="center" style="background-color:Silver">Edition</td>
    <td>@Html.DisplayFor(Function(model) model.BEdition)</td>
    </tr>
     <tr>
    <td align="center" style="background-color:Silver">Price</td>
    <td>@Html.DisplayFor(Function(model) model.BPrice)</td>
    </tr>
<tr>
    <td align="center" style="background-color:Silver">ISBN number</td>
    <td>@Html.DisplayFor(Function(model) model.BISBN)</td>
    </tr>
<tr>
    <td align="center" style="background-color:Silver">PublisherName</td>
    <td>@Html.DisplayFor(Function(model) model.publisher)</td>
    </tr>
           </table>
    </div>
</fieldset>
<p>
</p>
```

In C#

```
@model BookDetailMVCAppCS.Models.ClassBook
@{
    ViewBag.Title = "Index";
}
<h2>ASP.NET 4.5 BB</h2>
<fieldset>
```

```
        <legend>ClassBook</legend>
        <div class="display-data">
            <table border="1" style=" background-color:#0094ff">
                <tr>
                    <td> Book Name </td>
                    <td> @Html.DisplayFor(model => model.BName)</td>
                </tr>
                <tr>
                    <td>Book Price</td>
                    <td>  @Html.DisplayFor(model => model.BPrice)</td>
                </tr>
                <tr>
                    <td>Book Edition</td>
                    <td>  @Html.DisplayFor(model => model.BEdition)</td>
                </tr>
                <tr>
                    <td>ISBN Number</td>
                    <td>  @Html.DisplayFor(model => model.BISBN)</td>
                </tr>
                <tr>
                    <td>Publisher Name</td>
                    <td>  @Html.DisplayFor(model => model.publisher)</td>
                </tr>
            </table>
        </div>
    </fieldset>
    <p>
        @Html.ActionLink("Edit", "Edit", new { /* id=Model.PrimaryKey */ }) |
        @Html.ActionLink("Back to List", "Index")
    </p>
```

20. Press the F5 key on the keyboard to execute the application. The output of the application appears after replacing the URL as http://localhost:12275/Book is shown in Figure 20.9:

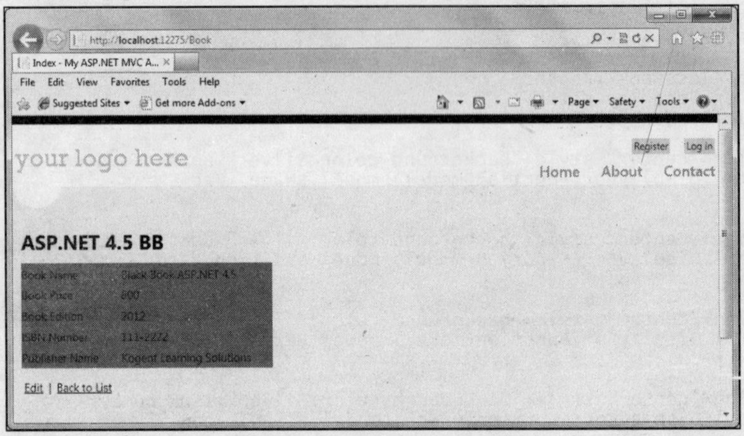

Figure 20.9: Displaying the Output

NOTE

This URL http://localhost:12275/Book is system specific

Summary

In this chapter, we have learned about ASP.NET MVC framework, and its architecture. This chapter also focuses on the features of the MVC 4 framework, Controller class, URL routing, and MVC templates. In addition, we have also learned to create an application in MVC 4 framework.

In the next chapter, we learn how to develop websites compliant with Web standards.

21

Developing Websites Compliant with Web Standards

In Depth

We all know that websites can be accessed through the Internet from any place in the world. However, people with visual or physical disability might have problems accessing websites. While designing a website, you must ensure that it is a valid website and is easily accessible to the underprivileged users. Now, the question that arises is what makes a website a valid website? What are the standards that one needs to follow while developing a website to make it valid? The answer is Web standards developed by the World Wide Web Consortium (W3C). The W3C, established by Tim Berners-Lee, co-founder of the Internet, is an international organization that creates, monitors, and modifies the Web standards and techniques to be followed. The Web standards are recommendations given by W3C that define the guidelines and best practices for designing a website. The adherence to these Web standards helps the Web developers to develop a more accessible, usable, and search engine friendly website. A website that follows the Web standards is accessible through any user agent, such as a desktop graphical browser, voice browser, text browser, mobile phone, or multimedia player.

ASP.NET 4.5 provides support to create a website that conforms to the various Web standards, such as `Extensible Hypertext Markup Language` (XHTML) and Accessibility. This makes the website accessible in the form of Sound or Braille text, so that a person with physical or visual disability can also access the website.

This chapter familiarizes you with the two widely used Web standards, XHTML and Accessibility. You learn about various tags and attributes provided by ASP.NET 4.5 for developing websites compliant to these Web standards. This chapter also explains how to ensure that your website conforms to a particular version of the XHTML standard. In addition, you learn to build Web pages that can be accessed by a broad category of users. Finally, you learn to validate your Web pages to verify that Web pages comply with the Web standards.

Introducing to Web Standards

Web standards are a set of rules that enable you to create accessible, dynamic, and best-quality websites. Web standards ensure that the website should meet the needs of its viewer, unknowingly whether they are normal people or physically or visually challenged. In other words, Web standards ensure that a website is accessible to the widest possible audience. Moreover, these Web standards enable you to design a website that can be displayed in every browser, such as Internet Explorer, Netscape Navigator, or Opera, in exactly the same manner. If Web standards are followed while making a website, it will be more consistent and user friendly.

ASP.NET 4.5 provides a Framework for building websites that adhere to the Web standards. ASP.NET 4.5 also provides various controls that have been extensively tested to support these Web standards. It also supports new tools that help to validate Web pages against both XHTML and Accessibility Standards. In short, we can say that ASP.NET 4.5 helps us to develop a valid website. Now, let's discuss the two most important Web standards, XHTML and Accessibility, in detail.

Understanding XHTML

`XHTML` has been introduced as the replacement for Hypertext Markup Language (HTML). XHTML came into existence with the following major objectives:

- Separating the structure of a document from its presentation.
- Bringing the positive aspects of both HTML (used to display data) and XML (used to define data).
- Ensuring that a Web page is structured properly. This implies that every start tag must have an end tag or every empty tag must have a forward slash (/) in it.
- Ensuring that a Web page is rendered consistently by all modern Web browsers.
- Making the Web page easy to read and modify at runtime.

The first objective emphasizes the use of style sheets to specify how a Web page is displayed in the Web browser. XHTML uses markups to describe the contents of a Web page and not for specifying the appearance of the Web page. Earlier, using the markup tags to define the layout of a Web page reduced its portability and tied the functionality of a Web page to some specific browsers and platforms only. To remove this rift, XHTML specifies all the formatting elements, which describe the look and feel of a Web page, separately in style sheets.

The second objective defines XHTML as the XML vocabulary. XHTML forces the developers to work according to the stringent rules of XML. The target is to assess the benefits provided by XML, such as cross-browser, cross-device, and cross-operating system compatibility for developing websites.

The three versions of XHTML 1.0 available, corresponding to HTML 4.01, are as follows:

- **XHTML 1.0 Transitional**—Includes all the tags and elements found in HTML 4.01 Transitional. This version is backward compatible with old browsers and enables the designers to slowly adapt to XHTML, while working with the existing HTML Web pages.
- **XHTML 1.0 Strict**—Does not include any of the HTML 4.01 tags and attributes that are explicitly designed to specify the appearance of a page in a Web browser. This standard strictly emphasizes on the use of Cascading Style Sheets to specify the presentation of the Web pages and on the use of markup to describe the structure and data of these Web pages.
- **XHTML 1.0 Frameset**—Includes the HTML 4.01 elements in addition to XHTML 1.0 Frameset, which uses the <frameset> tag to divide a Web browser into multiple frames. This standard is used only when the website needs to present the information using frames. The <frameset> tag is not available in XHTML 1.0 Transitional and XHTML 1.0 Strict.

The basic rules required to create valid XHTML Web pages are as follows:

- The XHTML document must include the DOCTYPE declaration at the beginning of the document to specify the Document Type Definition (DTD) that it uses. DTD identifies the elements, attributes, and entities that are used to create and validate an XHTML document. The four standard XHTML DOCTYPE declarations for different versions of XHTML are as follows:
  - XHTML 1.0 Transitional

```
<!DOCTYPE html
  PUBLIC "-//W3C//DTD XHTML 1.0 Transitional//EN"
         "http://www.w3.org/TR/xhtml1/DTD/xhtml1-transitional.dtd">
```

  - XHTML 1.0 Strict

```
<!DOCTYPE html
  PUBLIC "-//W3C//DTD XHTML 1.0 Strict//EN"
         "http://www.w3.org/TR/xhtml1/DTD/xhtml1-strict.dtd">
```

  - XHTML 1.0 Frameset

```
<!DOCTYPE html
  PUBLIC "-//W3C//DTD XHTML 1.0 Frameset//EN"
                "http://www.w3.org/TR/xhtml1/DTD/xhtml1-frameset.dtd">
```

  - XHTML 1.1

```
<!DOCTYPE html
  PUBLIC "-//W3C//DTD XHTML 1.1//EN"
         "http://www.w3.org/TR/xhtml11/DTD/xhtml11.dtd">
```

- The root element of the XHTML document must refer to the XHTML namespace. The root element is `html` and is placed immediately after the DOCTYPE declaration in a XHTML document. For example, the start tag of the html element for XHTML 1.0 Transitional is:

```
<html xmlns="http://www.w3.org/1999/xhtml" xml:lang="en" lang="en">
```

  The names of the elements and attributes used by the XHTML document must be in lowercase. This is because, similar to XML, XHTML is also case-sensitive. For example, the tag <b> is different from tag <B>, because XHTML supports tags only in lowercase; the tag <B> is not recognizable.
- The attribute values of the XHTML tags must be quoted by using either single or double quotation marks.
- Every non-empty element that has an opening tag must have a corresponding closing tag. For example, if an opening <p> tag is included in the XHTML document to indicate the beginning of a paragraph, and then you should also include the closing </p> tag to indicate the end of the paragraph. However, it supports the empty tags. The tags that do not contain any data or content within them are called empty tags, such as the line break tag <br />. Such empty tags must contain a slash in them preceded by a space, as you can see in the case of the `line break` tag.

- The overlapped tags cannot be used in the valid XHTML document. However, you can nest tags. The following is an instance of invalid XHTML containing the overlapped tags:

```
<b><i>The XHTML document</b></i>
```

  Valid XHTML for the preceding example is:

```
<b><i>The XHTML document</i></b>
```

- The attributes of the XHTML tags must have a specific value. For example, the following XHTML is invalid because a value for the `checked` attribute has not been specified here:

```
<input type ="checkbox" checked/>
```

  The following is the correct XHTML, where the `checked` attribute has been assigned a value:

```
<input type ="checkbox" checked="checked"/>
```

- In XHTML, the `id` attribute is used instead of the `name` attribute (also used in HTML). In HTML, the `name` attribute is used to identify elements, such as `<a>`, `<applet>`, and `<form>`; however, in XHTML, these elements are identified using the `id` attribute.

Understanding Accessibility Standards

Accessibility standards are a set of rules used to create websites that can also be accessed by physically challenged or sensory impaired users. Creating websites that comply with the accessibility standards ensures that the people with disabilities can perceive, understand, navigate, and interact with the website and they can even contribute to the website. The Accessibility standards are also beneficial for old age people, who have disabilities due to aging, such as loss in vision, hearing, dexterity, and memory. Accessibility standards provide equal access and opportunity to physically challenged people and make them able to actively participate in society.

There are many standards and laws (refer http://www.w3.org/WAI) already available for building websites that can be easily used by physically challenged users. Accessibility standards are generally derived from W3C Web Content Accessibility Guidelines 1.0 (WCAG). The WCAG standard consists of 14 guidelines mentioned in W3C that are further defined by checkpoints. Checkpoints specify the way to apply the guidelines to a particular feature of the Web page. Each checkpoint is assigned a priority range from 1 to 3. A checkpoint assigned with Priority 1 implies that website content must satisfy this checkpoint. However, a checkpoint assigned with priority 2 or 3 are not mandatory for being satisfied by the website content. Websites can have different conformance levels depending on the WCAG guidelines to which a website conforms. These conformance levels are:

- **Conformance Level A**—Specifies that the website meets all the checkpoints of the WCAG guidelines with priority 1
- **Conformance Level Double-A**—Specifies that the website meets all the checkpoints of the WCAG guidelines with priority 1 and 2
- **Conformance Level Triple-A**—Specifies that the website meets all the checkpoints of the WCAG guidelines

Section 508 of the US Rehabilitation Act of 1973 (amended in 1998) contains a set of guidelines (refer this section on W3C) that have been derived from the WCAG guidelines. These guidelines are used by the Federal sectors of the United States to ensure compatibility with the technologies that are used by individuals with disabilities to access websites.

ASP.NET 4.5 allows you to develop a website that is compatible with the WCAG priority 1 and priority 2 checkpoints and meet all the guidelines given under Section 508 of W3C.

Immediate Solutions

Using the xhtmlConformance Tag to Specify the Level of XHTML Conformance

By default, ASP.NET 4.5 and Visual Studio 2012 use the XHTML 1.0 Transitional standard. The reason is that it is the only standard that gives developers enough flexibility to work with the existing HTML pages of a website.

However, there can be situations when this standard becomes a restriction for website developers. For example, a developer may want to create a website using XHTML 1.0 Strict in ASP.NET 4.5 Framework. Now, there are certain tags and attributes that are allowed according to the XHTML 1.0 Transitional standards but not according to the XHTML 1.0 Strict standards. As ASP.NET 4.5 targets XHTML 1.0 Transitional, certain attributes that do not conform to XHTML 1.0 Strict standards may also be rendered. Consequently, conformance to XHTML 1.0 Strict standards is not achieved by a website.

Finally, what should a designer or a developer of a website do to develop a website that conforms to the XHTML 1.0 Strict standards? ASP.NET 4.5 provides a simple solution to overcome such problems. ASP.NET 4.5 provides the `xhtmlConformance` tag that helps to specify the XHTML standards that you need to conform to. In other words, the `xhtmlConformance` tag specifies the level of XHTML conformance for your website.

The `xhtmlConformance` tag is defined in the configuration file, `Web.config`, of your website. You just need to change the `mode` attribute value of this tag to specify the level of XHTML conformance.

The `xhtmlConformance` tag used in the `Web.config` file is as follows:

```
<configuration>
   <system.web>
         <!--
                     <xhtmlConformance mode = "transitional" [transitional | legacy |
                     strict] />
         -->
         <xhtmlConformance mode=" Transitional" />
   </system.web>
</configuration>
```

By default, the value of the `mode` attribute of the `xhtmlConformance` tag is set to transitional. You can change this value to either strict or legacy according to your requirement.

Using the alt Attribute for Accessibility

An individual, suffering from vision impairment uses the assistive technologies, such as screen reader and Braille display, to access the content of a Web page. A screen reader is a voice output technology that uses a synthetic voice to read the content of a Web page aloud to the user. A Braille display translates the textual information on a Web page to Braille representation.

If your website contains any non-textual information, such as graphics and animation, you need to provide the textual equivalent of such information to make it accessible to the users with visual impairment. The textual equivalent is used by the assistive technologies to convey the meaning of an image in words. This allows a visually impaired user to understand the image in a manner similar to a user who can view the image.

When you include an image in a Web page using the `<img>` tag, you can use the `alt` attribute to specify the textual equivalent of this image. The following is the syntax to use the `alt` attribute in the `img` tag:

```
<img src=" Url of the image " alt="Equivalent Text " />
```

Now, let's understand the use of the `alt` attribute with an example. Suppose a shopping website contains a Web page that displays the images of the items available for sale to its customers. To make this website accessible to every user, the website needs to specify the text to describe the images by using the `alt` attribute. This specified text will be read by the screen reader to help the visually impaired users to visualize items, which otherwise are not visible to them. You can do so by creating an application as `altExpAppVB` for VB and `altExpAppCS` for C#. You can find the code for the `Default.aspx` page in Listing 21.1:

Listing 21.1: Showing the Code for the `Default.aspx` Page

In VB

```
<%@ Page Language="VB" AutoEventWireup="false" CodeFile="Default.aspx.vb"
  Inherits="_Default" %>
<!DOCTYPE html>
<html xmlns="http://www.w3.org/1999/xhtml">
<head runat="server">
    <title>Alt Example</title>
</head>
<body>
    <form id="form1" runat="server">
    <div>
    <br />
         Items available for sale are:  <br />
         <br />
         <img src="Images/prod1.jpg"  alt="Item1: Camera"/> <br />
         <br />
         <br />
         <img src="Images/prod2.jpg"  alt="Item2: IPod"/>
    </div>
    </form>
</body>
</html>
```

In C#

```
<%@ Page Language="C#" AutoEventWireup="true" CodeFile="Default.aspx.cs"
  Inherits="_Default" %>
<!DOCTYPE html>
<html xmlns="http://www.w3.org/1999/xhtml">
<head runat="server">
    <title>Alt Example</title>
</head>
<body>
    <form id="form1" runat="server">
    <div>
    <br />
         Items available for sale are:  <br />
         <br />
         <img src="Images/prod1.jpg"  alt="Item1: Camera"/> <br />
         <br />
         <br />
         <img src="Images/prod2.jpg"  alt="Item2: IPod"/>
    </div>
    </form>
</body>
</html>
```

Now, press the F5 key on the keyboard to run the application. The output is as shown in Figure 21.1:

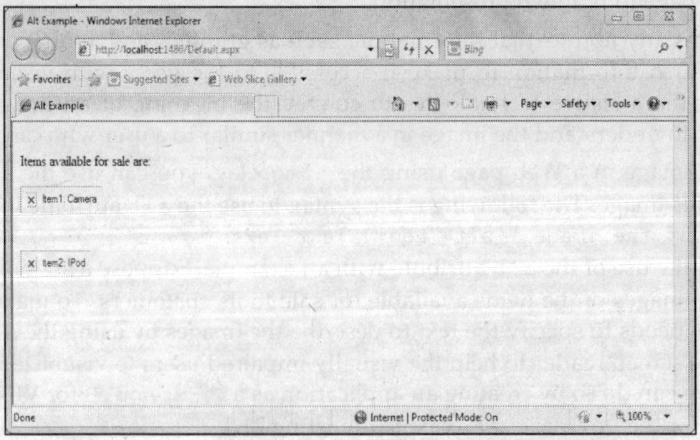

Figure 21.1: Web Page Created using the alt Attribute

In this Web page, the screen reader reads the text associated with each item one by one to convey the list of available items to the visually impaired individuals. In this way, the images in the Web page can be made accessible to users using the `alt` attribute.

Using the <label> Tag for Accessibility

The `<label>` tag is used to increase the accessibility of Web forms to the users with diminished vision. These users access the Web form using a screen reader. Web forms are one of the common and simple ways to receive information from a user and submit it to a website. However, a person who accesses the Web form using a screen reader finds it difficult to link a Web form element, such as text box, radio button, and check box, to its corresponding label. The label refers to the text that is used to specify the purpose of the Web form element. For example, the label Name may be used for a text box, which accepts the name of the user as input.

In most cases, a Web form uses tables to control the layout of the form elements. Though using a table enhances the visual appearance of the Web form, it can reduce its accessibility. This can be understood through an example. Now, create an application `LabelExpAppCS` (`LabelExpAppVB` for VB and `LabelExpAppCS` for C#). You can find the code for the `Default.aspx` page in Listing 21.2:

Listing 21.2: Showing the Code for the `Default.aspx` Page

In VB

```
<%@ Page Language="VB" AutoEventWireup="false" CodeFile="Default.aspx.vb"
  Inherits="_Default" %>
<!DOCTYPE html>
<html xmlns="http://www.w3.org/1999/xhtml">
<head runat="server">
    <title>Need of Label Tag</title>
</head>
<body>
    <form id="form1" runat="server">
    <div>
    <strong><span style="text-decoration: underline"><em>
                Enter Student Information </em>
                </span></strong>
                <table style="width: 616px; height: 82px">
                <tr>
                <td bgcolor="#ffccff" style="width: 127px; text-align: center">
                Student Name
                </td>
                <td bgcolor="#ffccff" style="width: 185px; text-align: center">
                Age</td>
                <td bgcolor="#ffccff" style="width: 180px; text-align: center">
                City</td>
                </tr>
                <tr>
                <td style="width: 127px">
                    <br />
                <input id="Text1" type="text" style="width: 179px" /> 
                </td>
                <td style="width: 185px">
                <input id="Text3" style="width: 180px" type="text" /></td>
                <td style="width: 180px">
                <input id="Text4" style="width: 240px" type="text" /></td>
                </tr>
                </table>
    </div>
    </form>
</body>
</html>
```

In C#

```
<%@ Page Language="C#" AutoEventWireup="true" CodeFile="Default.aspx.cs"
  Inherits="_Default" %>
<!DOCTYPE html>
<html xmlns="http://www.w3.org/1999/xhtml">
<head runat="server">
    <title>Need of Label Tag</title>
</head>
<body>
    <form id="form1" runat="server">
    <div>
    <strong><span style="text-decoration: underline"><em>
                Enter Student Information </em>
                </span></strong>
                <table style="width: 616px; height: 82px">
                <tr>
                <td bgcolor="#ffccff" style="width: 127px; text-align: center">
                Student Name
                </td>
                <td bgcolor="#ffccff" style="width: 185px; text-align: center">
                Age</td>
                <td bgcolor="#ffccff" style="width: 180px; text-align: center">
                City</td>
                </tr>
                <tr>
                <td style="width: 127px">
                    <br />
                <input id="Text1" type="text" style="width: 179px" /> 
                </td>
                <td style="width: 185px">
                <input id="Text3" style="width: 183px" type="text" /></td>
                <td style="width: 180px">
                <input id="Text4" style="width: 240px" type="text" /></td>
                </tr>
                </table>
    </div>
    </form>
</body>
</html>
```

Now, press the F5 key on the keyboard to run the application. The output is as shown in Figure 21.2:

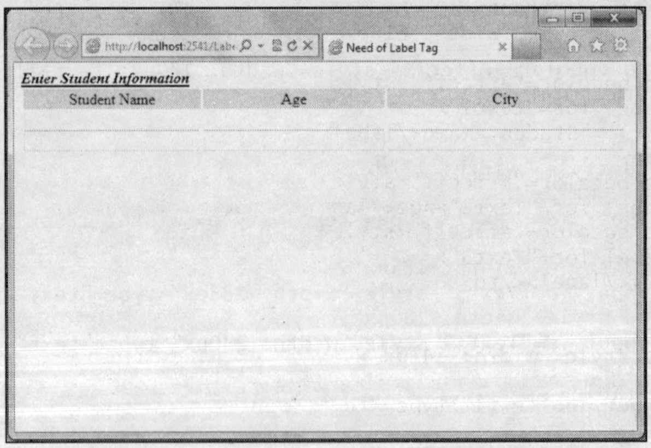

Figure 21.2: Web Page Created Using a Table

While translating the preceding Web form to speech, the screen reader reads the content of the cells of the Web form linearly one by one. It means that the table is read row by row (left to right) from top to bottom. For example, the screen reader will read the preceding Web page as:

```
Student Name. Age. City. Edit. Edit. Edit.
```

This information will confuse the user as where to actually enter the information or where to edit it. Therefore, the screen reader may garble the information presented in a table.

To ensure that such a Web form is accessed and interpreted correctly by a user using the screen reader, you need to enable the user to properly associate the form element to its label. To ensure this, you can use the `<label>` tag that associates a label to a form element. Before using the `<label>` tag, the label is positioned adjacent to the form element, which implies that the label should be placed to the left of the input boxes, text areas, and drop-down boxes and be placed to the right of checkboxes and radio boxes. The correct positioning makes it easier for a user to hear the Web form contents using the screen reader to understand it.

To use the `<label>` tag to make a Web form accessible, the `<for>` attribute of this tag should have the same value as the `<id>` attribute of the input `<form>` element. For example, the code to associate a text box to its corresponding label is:

```
<label for="text1">Student Name</label>
<input id="text1" type="text" />
```

In the preceding code, the values of the `id` attribute of the input text box element and `for` attribute of the label element are the same `text1`.

While using tables to present the content of a Web page, you should place the `<label>` tag and the input `<form>` element in the adjacent cells. For this, specify the `<label>` tag between the pair of the `<td>` and `</td>` tags that appear before the pair of the `<td>` and `</td>` tags containing the input `<form>` element. To understand it better, let's create an example. Create an application `LabelExp2AppCS (LabelExp2AppVB` for VB and `LabelExp2AppCS` for C#). You can find the code for the `Default.aspx` page in Listing 21.3:

Listing 21.3: Showing the Code for the `Default.aspx` Page

In VB

```
<%@ Page Language="VB" AutoEventWireup="false" CodeFile="Default.aspx.vb"
  Inherits="_Default" %>
<!DOCTYPE html>
<html xmlns="http://www.w3.org/1999/xhtml">
<head runat="server">
    <title>Need of Label Tag</title>
</head>
<body>
    <form id="form1" runat="server">
    <div>
    <strong><span style="text-decoration: underline"><em>
                Enter Student Information </em>
                </span></strong>
                <table style="width: 616px; height: 82px">
                <tr>
                <td bgcolor="#ffccff" style="width: 141px; text-align: center">
                <label for="text1">
                        Student Name</label>
                </td>
                <td bgcolor="#ffccff" style="width: 185px; text-align: center">
                <label for="Text2">Age</label></td>
                <td bgcolor="#ffccff" style="width: 180px; text-align: center">
                <label for="Text3">
                City</label></td>
                </tr>
                <tr>
                <td style="width: 141px">
                    <br />
                <input id="Text1" type="text" style="width: 179px" /> 
                </td>
                <td style="width: 185px">
                <label for="Text3">
                </label>
                <input id="Text3" style="width: 183px" type="text" /></td>
                <td style="width: 180px">
                <input id="Text4" style="width: 240px" type="text" /></td>
```

```
                </tr>
                </table>
        </div>
    </form></body></html>
```

In C#

```
<%@ Page Language="C#" AutoEventWireup="true" CodeFile="Default.aspx.cs"
  Inherits="_Default" %>
<!DOCTYPE html>
<html xmlns="http://www.w3.org/1999/xhtml">
<head runat="server">
    <title>Need of Label Tag</title>
</head>
<body>
    <form id="form1" runat="server">
    <div>
    <strong><span style="text-decoration: underline"><em>
                Enter Student Information </em>
                </span></strong>
                <table style="width: 616px; height: 82px">
                <tr>
                <td bgcolor="#ffccff" style="width: 141px; text-align: center">
                <label for="text1">
                        Student Name</label>
                </td>
                <td bgcolor="#ffccff" style="width: 185px; text-align: center">
                <label for="Text2">Age</label></td>
                <td bgcolor="#ffccff" style="width: 180px; text-align: center">
                <label for="Text3">
                City</label></td>
                </tr>
                <tr>
                <td style="width: 141px">
                    <br />
                <input id="Text1" type="text" style="width: 179px" /> 
                </td>
                <td style="width: 185px">
                <label for="Text3">
                </label>
                <input id="Text3" style="width: 183px" type="text" /></td>
                <td style="width: 180px">
                <input id="Text4" style="width: 240px" type="text" /></td>
                </tr>
                </table>
    </div>
</form></body></html>
```

Now, press the F5 key on the keyboard to run the application. The output is as shown in Figure 21.3:

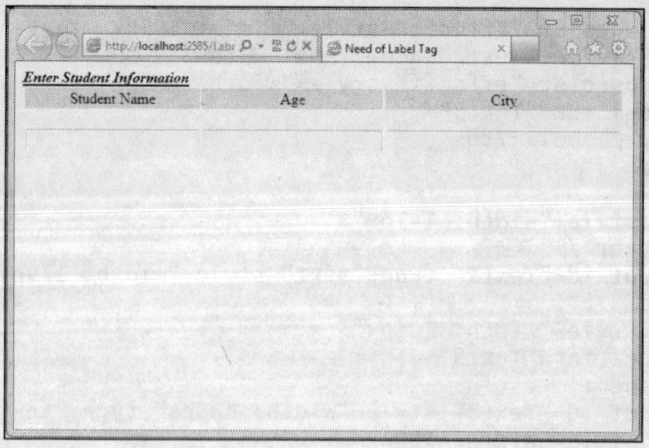

Figure 21.3: Using the <label> Tag with the for Attribute

The screen reader will read this Web form as:

```
Student Name. Edit. Age. Edit. City. Edit.
```

Using the preceding method, the user, using the screen reader, can also easily relate a label to its input field and can correctly fill the Web form.

There is one more advantage of using the `<label>` tag in the Web forms. It increases the area that can be clicked for accessing the form control. This is useful especially for the users who have low eyesight, but can still use mouse to fill the Web form. For the `text input` element, click anywhere on the label and the text input element will place the cursor within the `textbox`. Similarly, a `radio button` or `checkbox` can be selected by clicking either the `label` or the `radio button` or `checkbox`.

Using the <fieldset> Tag for Accessibility

The Web pages with large Web forms may also cause problems for the users, who use screen reader to access the Web page content. While listening to these Web forms with the help of a screen reader, the user may lose track of the section of the Web form that the user is listening to.

Therefore, the `<fieldset>` tag helps increase the readability of large Web forms by enabling you to divide the form into multiple blocks. This tag results in a well-organized Web form where the related information is grouped together in a single block. The `<fieldset>` tag is used with the `<legend>` tag, which specifies the name or the purpose of a block.

Now, let's see how the `<fieldset>` tag is used to create a Web form for the Student Registration System. In this system, the student-related information can be divided into various blocks, such as personal and academic. You can create a website to use the `<fieldset>` tag. Now, create an application `FieldSetAppCS` (`FieldSetAppVB` for VB and `FieldSetAppCS` for C#). You can find the code for the `Default.aspx` page in Listing 21.4:

Listing 21.4: Showing the Code for the `Default.aspx` Page

In VB

```
<%@ Page Language="VB" AutoEventWireup="false" CodeFile="Default.aspx.vb"
  Inherits="_Default" %>
<!DOCTYPE html>
<html xmlns="http://www.w3.org/1999/xhtml">
<head runat="server">
      <title>College Registration System</title>
</head>
<body>
    <form id="form1" runat="server">
    <div>
    <fieldset>
                <legend>Personal Information of Student</legend>
                <br />
                <table width="50%" border="0" cellspacing="0" cellpadding="4">
                <tr>
                <td style="width: 195px">
                <p align="right">
                <label for="name">
                        Name of Student
                </label>
                </p>
                </td>
                <td style="width: 226px">
                <input id="name" type="text" name="text1" size="12"/>
                </td>
                </tr>
                <tr>
                <td style="width: 195px">
                <p align="right">
                <label for="father">
                        Name of Father</label></p>
```

```
                    </td>
                    <td style="width: 226px">
                    <input id="father" type="text" name="text2" size="12"/>
                    </td>
                    </tr>
                    <tr>
                    <td style="width: 195px">
                    <p align="right">
                    <label for="add">
                    Address</label></p>
                    </td>
                    <td style="width: 226px">
                     <input id="ass" type="text" name="text3" style="width: 95px"/>
                    </td>
                    </tr>
                    <tr>
                            <td style="width: 195px">
                            <p align="right">
                                    <label for="city">
                                    City</label></p>
                            </td>
                            <td style="width: 226px">
                                    <input id="city" type="text" name="text4" size="12"/>
                            </td>
                    </tr>
                    </table>
                    </fieldset>
                    <fieldset>
                    <legend>Academic background</legend>
                    <br />
                    <fieldset>
                    <legend>Last Qualifying Exam Passed</legend>
                    <br />
                    <input id="BSc" type="radio" name="radio1" value="radiobutton"/>
                    <label for="BSc">
                    Bachelor of Computer Science (BSc)</label><br/>
                    <input id="BCom" type="radio" name="radio1" value="radiobutton"/>
                    <label for="BCom">
                    Bachelor of Commerce (BCom)</label><br/>
                    <input id="BA" type="radio" name="radio1" value="radiobutton"/>
                    <label for="BA">
                    Bachelor of Arts (BA)</label><br />
                    <br />
                    </fieldset>
                    <fieldset>
                    <legend>Percentage Obtained in Qualifying Exam</legend>
                    <br />
                    <br />
                    <input id="belw60" type="radio" name="radio2" value="radiobutton"/>
                    <label for="belw60">
                    Below 60</label><br/>
                    <input id="bw" type="radio" name="radio2" value="radiobutton"/>
                    <label for="bw">
                    Between 60 and 80</label><br/>
                    <input id="abv80" type="radio" name="radio2" value="radiobutton"/>
                    <label for="abv80">
                    Above 80</label><br/>
                    </fieldset>
                    </fieldset>
        </div>
        </form>
    </body>
    </html>
```

In C#

```
<%@ Page Language="C#" AutoEventWireup="true" CodeFile="Default.aspx.cs"
  Inherits="_Default" %>
<!DOCTYPE html>
<html xmlns="http://www.w3.org/1999/xhtml">
<head id="Head1" runat="server">
     <title>College Registration System</title>
</head>
<body>
    <form id="form1" runat="server">
    <div>
    <fieldset>
                <legend>Personal Information of Student</legend>
                <br />
                <table width="50%" border="0" cellspacing="0" cellpadding="4">
                <tr>
                <td style="width: 195px">
                <p align="right">
                <label for="name">
                        Name of Student
                </label>
                </p>
                </td>
                <td style="width: 226px">
                <input id="name" type="text" name="text1" size="12"/>
                </td>
                </tr>
                <tr>
                <td style="width: 195px">
                <p align="right">
                <label for="father">
                        Name of Father</label></p>
                </td>
                <td style="width: 226px">
                <input id="father" type="text" name="text2" size="12"/>
                </td>
                </tr>
                <tr>
                <td style="width: 195px">
                <p align="right">
                <label for="add">
                Address</label></p>
                </td>
                <td style="width: 226px">
                 <input id="ass" type="text" name="text3" style="width: 95px"/>
                </td>
                </tr>
                <tr>
                        <td style="width: 195px">
                        <p align="right">
                                <label for="city">
                                City</label></p>
                        </td>
                        <td style="width: 226px">
                                <input id="city" type="text" name="text4" size="12"/>
                        </td>
                </tr>
                </table>
                </fieldset>
                <fieldset>
                <legend>Academic background</legend>
                <br />
                <fieldset>
                <legend>Last Qualifying Exam Passed</legend>
                <br />
                <input id="BSc" type="radio" name="radio1" value="radiobutton"/>
```

```
                    <label for="BSc">
                    Bachelor of Computer Science (BSc)</label><br/>
                    <input id="BCom" type="radio" name="radio1" value="radiobutton"/>
                    <label for="BCom">
                    Bachelor of Commerce (BCom)</label><br/>
                    <input id="BA" type="radio" name="radio1" value="radiobutton"/>
                    <label for="BA">
                    Bachelor of Arts (BA)</label><br />
                    <br />
                    </fieldset>
                    <fieldset>
                    <legend>Percentage Obtained in Qualifying Exam</legend>
                    <br />
                    <br />
                    <input id="belw60" type="radio" name="radio2" value="radiobutton"/>
                    <label for="belw60">
                    Below 60</label><br/>
                    <input id="bw" type="radio" name="radio2" value="radiobutton"/>
                    <label for="bw">
                    Between 60 and 80</label><br/>
                    <input id="abv80" type="radio" name="radio2" value="radiobutton"/>
                    <label for="abv80">
                    Above 80</label><br/>
                    </fieldset>
                    </fieldset>
        </div>
    </form></body></html>
```

Now, press the F5 key on the keyboard to run the application. The output is as shown in Figure 21.4:

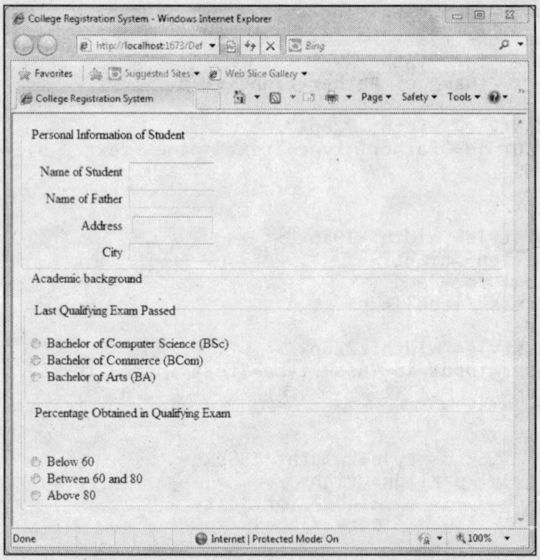

Figure 21.4: Web Form Created using the <fieldset> Tag

In the Web form, the fields, such as Name of Student and City, related to personal details of a student, are grouped under one block by using the `<fieldset>` tag. The block containing the personal information has been marked with the name Personal Information of Student by using the `<legend>` tag. Similarly, the fields to retrieve the academic details of a student have been specified in a separate block.

NOTE

By default, the <fieldset> tag is visually displayed using a border. You can modify the appearance of the border or can even remove it with the help of cascading style sheets.

Using the accesskey and tabindex Attributes

The users with reduced motor coordination find it difficult to interact with large Web forms. Such users interact with the Web forms using the keyboard or an assistive device, which works similar to a keyboard. Using these devices enables users to navigate through Web forms by pressing the tab or accessing the keys. Therefore, you need to make your Web form keyboard accessible to ensure its usability by all the users.

You can use the `<accesskey>` and `<tabindex>` attributes to make your Web form keyboard accessible. The `<tabindex>` attribute defines the tabbing order of the form elements. The tabbing order specifies the sequence in which the elements on Web forms are focused when navigated by a user through keyboard. The `<accesskey>` attribute allows the user to access an input field by pressing the ALT and the specified alphabet key together on the keyboard while using Internet Explorer and Firefox, and `SHIFT+ESC+access key on the keyboard`, while using the `Opera` Web browser. Now, let's create an example `tabindexAppCS` (`tabindexAppVB` for VB and `tabindexAppCS` for C#) to understand it better. You can find the code for the `Default.aspx` page in Listing 21.5:

Listing 21.5: Showing the Code for the `Default.aspx` Page

In VB

```
<%@ Page Language="VB" AutoEventWireup="false" CodeFile="Default.aspx.vb"
  Inherits="_Default" %>
<!DOCTYPE html>
<html xmlns="http://www.w3.org/1999/xhtml">
<head runat="server">
    <title>Using accesskey and tabindex</title>
</head>
<body>
    <form id="form1" runat="server">
    <div>
    <strong><span style="text-decoration: underline"><em>Enter Student Information </em>
                </span></strong>
                <table style="width: 616px; height: 82px">
                <tr>
                <td style="width: 123px; text-align: left; background-color: #ffccff;">
                           
                        <label for="Text1" accesskey="S">
                                <u style="text-decoration: underline">S</u>tudent Name
                        </label>
                </td>
                <td style="width: 127px">
                <input id="Text1" type="text" tabindex="1" style="width: 179px"/>
                         
                </td>
                </tr>
                <tr>
                <td style="width: 123px; text-align: left; background-color: #ffccff;">
                        <label for="Text2" accesskey="A">
                            <u style="text-decoration: underline">A</u>ge
                        </label>
                </td>
                <td style="width: 127px">
                <input id="Text2" type="text" tabindex="2" style="width: 179px" /> 
                </td>
                </tr>
                <tr>
                <td style="width: 123px; text-align: left; background-color: #ffccff;">
                           
                        <label for="Text3" accesskey="C" >
                        <u style="text decoration:underline">C</u>ity
                        </label>
                </td>
                <td style="width: 127px">
                <input id="Text3" type="text" tabindex="3" style="width: 179px" /> 
```

```
                    </td>
                    </tr>
                    </table>
        </div>
        </form>
    </body>
    </html>
```

In C#

```
    <%@ Page Language="C#" AutoEventWireup="true" CodeFile="Default.aspx.cs"
      Inherits="_Default" %>
    <!DOCTYPE html>
    <html xmlns="http://www.w3.org/1999/xhtml">
    <head id="Head1" runat="server">
        <title>Using accesskey and tabindex</title>
    </head>
    <body>
        <form id="form1" runat="server">
        <div>
        <strong><span style="text-decoration: underline"><em>Enter Student Information </em>
                    </span></strong>
                    <table style="width: 616px; height: 82px">
                    <tr>
                    <td style="width: 123px; text-align: left; background-color: #ffccff;">
                               
                            <label for="Text1" accesskey="S">
                                    <u style="text-decoration: underline">S</u>tudent Name
                            </label>
                    </td>
                    <td style="width: 127px">
                    <input id="Text1" type="text" tabindex="1" style="width: 179px"/>
                             
                    </td>
                    </tr>
                    <tr>
                    <td style="width: 123px; text-align: left; background-color: #ffccff;">
                            <label for="Text2" accesskey="A">
                                <u style="text-decoration: underline">A</u>ge
                            </label>
                    </td>
                    <td style="width: 127px">
                    <input id="Text2" type="text" tabindex="2" style="width: 179px" /> 
                    </td>
                    </tr>
                    <tr>
                    <td style="width: 123px; text-align: left; background-color: #ffccff;">
                               
                            <label for="Text3" accesskey="C" >
                            <u style="text-decoration:underline">C</u>ity
                            </label>
                    </td>
                    <td style="width: 127px">
                    <input id="Text3" type="text" tabindex="3" style="width: 179px" /> 
                    </td>
                    </tr>
                    </table>
        </div>
        </form>
    </body>
    </html>
```

Now, press the F5 key on the keyboard to run the application. The output is as shown in Figure 21.5:

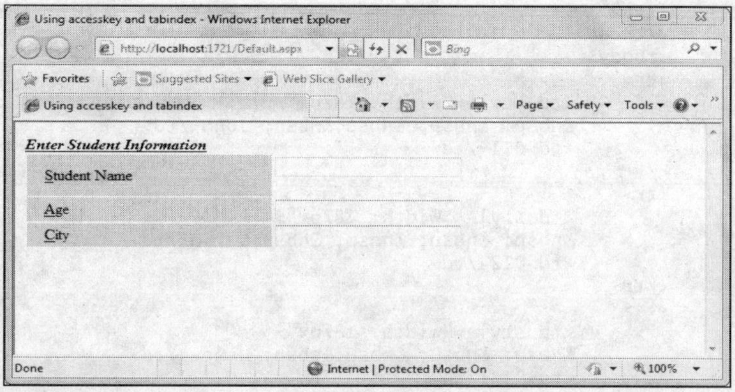

Figure 21.5: Making Web Form Keyboard Accessible using the <accesskey> Attribute

The fields in the output of the Web form can be navigated by using the tab key in the order specified by using the `<tabindex>` attribute. You can also move the focus to a field by pressing the specified access key. For example, you can move the focus to an input field corresponding to `Student Name` by pressing the ALT and S keys together on the keyboard.

Setting Headers for Accessibility

ASP.NET 4.5 uses a variety of controls, such as `GridView`, `DetailsView`, and `DataList`, for displaying data stored in database(s) associated with a Web application. By default, the `GridView`, `DetailsView`, and `DataList` controls use HTML tables to display the information stored in a database. Using the HTML tables for displaying data often results in problems related to accessibility as it becomes difficult to keep track of the current position in the table while reading HTML tables aloud. For instance, consider the case of an HTML table that is used to display the inventory information of a variety of products. While reading the table content using the screen reader, it may be difficult to identify whether a particular cell in the HTML table denotes the name, quantity, or price of a product. Users without any disability can easily interpret the meaning of a cell just by looking at either the column or row heading of the cell in the HTML table. The table can also be made accessible to users who are using screen readers by putting a little effort. All you need to do is to specifically mark the table headers and then link the headers with each cell in the table. You can mark the table headers by using the `<th>` tag. Now, let's create an example `HeaderAppCS` (`HeaderAppVB` for VB and `HeaderAppCS` for C#) to understand it better. You can find the code for the `Default.aspx` page in Listing 21.6:

Listing 21.6: Showing the Code for the `Default.aspx` Page

In VB

```
<%@ Page Language="VB" AutoEventWireup="false" CodeFile="Default.aspx.vb"
  Inherits="_Default" %>
<!DOCTYPE html>
<html xmlns="http://www.w3.org/1999/xhtml">
<head runat="server">
    <title>Student Information System</title>
</head>
<body>
    <form id="form1" runat="server">
    <div>
    <em><strong><span style="text-decoration:underline">Student Information
                <br />
                <br />
                </span></strong></em>
                <table>
                <thead>
                <tr>
                        <th style="width: 187px">Student Name</th>
                        <th>Roll Number</th>
```

```
                    </tr>
                    </thead>
                    <tbody>
                    <tr>
                            <td style="width: 187px">
                                   John</td>
                            <td>011</td>
                    </tr>
                    <tr>
                            <td style="width: 187px">
                                   David</td>
                            <td>012</td>
                    </tr>
                    <tr>
                            <td style="width: 187px">
                                   Henry</td>
                            <td>013</td>
                    </tr>
                    </tbody>
                    </table>
        </div>
        </form>
    </body>
    </html>
```

In C#

```
    <%@ Page Language="C#" AutoEventWireup="true" CodeFile="Default.aspx.cs"
      Inherits="_Default" %>
    <!DOCTYPE html>
    <html xmlns="http://www.w3.org/1999/xhtml">
    <head id="Head1" runat="server">
        <title>Student Information System</title>
    </head>
    <body>
        <form id="form1" runat="server">
        <div>
        <em><strong><span style="text-decoration:underline">Student Information
                    <br />
                    <br />
                    </span></strong></em>
                    <table>
                    <thead>
                    <tr>
                            <th style="width: 187px">Student Name</th>
                            <th>Roll Number</th>
                    </tr>
                    </thead>
                    <tbody>
                    <tr>
                            <td style="width: 187px">
                                   John</td>
                            <td>011</td>
                    </tr>
                    <tr>
                            <td style="width: 187px">
                                   David</td>
                            <td>012</td>
                    </tr>
                    <tr>
                            <td style="width: 187px">
                                   Henry</td>
                            <td>013</td>
                    </tr>
                    </tbody>
                    </table>
```

```
        </div>
        </form>
    </body>
    </html>
```

In Listing 21.6, the `<th>` tag has been used to set the headers of two columns, Student Name and Roll Number. By default, the text enclosed in the `<th>` tag is `centered` and `bold-faced`. Now, press the F5 key on the keyboard to run the application. The output is as shown in Figure 21.6:

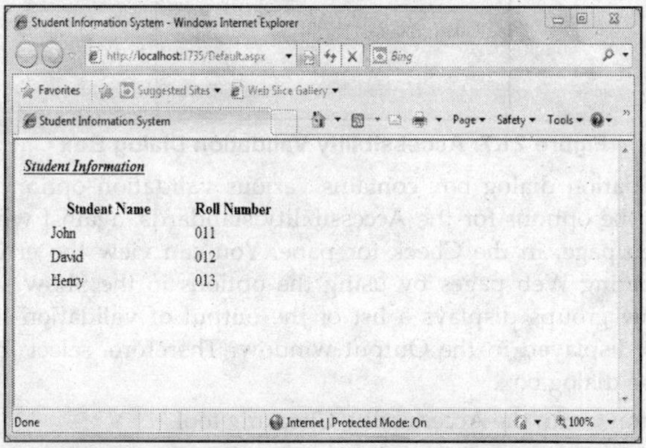

Figure 21.6: Using the <th> Tag for Setting Headers

Validating Pages for Web Standards Compliance

You can ensure that the Web pages created using Visual Studio 2012 are accessible by all possible target audience by verifying the Web page against Web standards, such as XHTML.

By default, Visual Studio 2012 validates Web pages against the schema of Internet Explorer 6.0 and later. When you create pages in Visual Studio, the pages are automatically validated for errors and warnings in the source view. The content that contains validation errors, such as a missing closing tag, and the rest, is marked using the red squiggles. Similarly, the content corresponding to any validation warning, such as deprecated tags, is marked using the green squiggles.

Visual Studio enables you to alter the default validation behavior to validate the pages against a specific Web standard. You can specify the XHTML standard, such as XHTML 1.0 Transitional and XHTML 1.0 Strict, against which you want to validate the Web pages by using the Validation option. To use this option, you need to select `Tools→Options` from the menu bar. Then, expanding the `Text Editor` tab, you will find the `HTML` tab, and on expanding the HTML tab select the `Validation` option. A list of the XHTML standards gets displayed, from which you can select the desired XHTML schema for validation.

You can also validate your Web pages for accessibility to check how much your Web pages conform to the accessibility standards. However, unlike XHTML, there is no automated validation software for accessibility. The available accessibility validation tools are limited in functionality and only provide a checklist of accessibility issues for which you can manually check Web pages. The functionality of these tools is limited because these cannot emulate the human thinking process that is required to judge the accessibility of a Web page. For example, it is difficult for a tool to determine whether or not the `alt` attribute of `<img>` element is used to provide text equivalent to defining an image.

Visual Studio simplifies your task of validating Web page's accessibility to some extent by providing the Accessibility Checker tool. This tool helps to verify the conformance of HTML markup of a Web page to the WCAG Priority 1 checkpoints, WCAG Priority 2 checkpoints, and Access Board Section 508. Perform the following steps to run the Accessibility checker tool to validate Web pages:

1. Open Visual Studio 2012 IDE to open any website on which you want to check for accessibility
2. Select `Tools→Check Accessibility` from the menu bar. The Accessibility Validation dialog box appears, as shown in Figure 21.7:

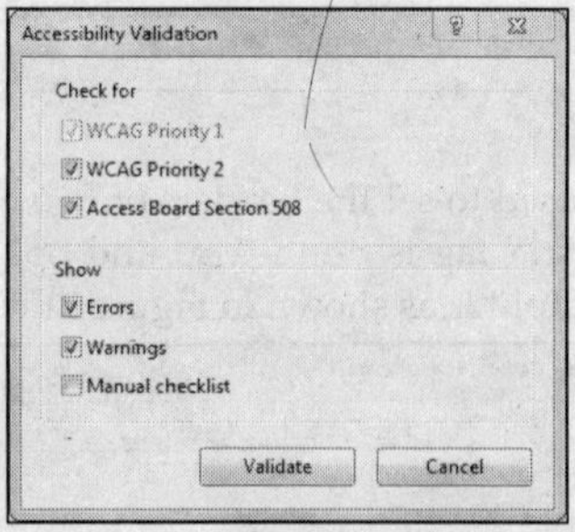

Figure 21.7: Accessibility Validation Dialog Box

The Accessibility Validation dialog box contains various validation options in the Check for and Show panes. You can select the options for the Accessibility standards, against which you want to validate the conformance of a Web page, in the Check for pane. You can view the errors and warnings, which are generated while validating Web pages by using the options in the Show section. The Manual checklist option under the Show groups displays a list of the output of validation in the Error List window. By default, the output is displayed in the Output window. Therefore, select the required options from the Accessibility Validation dialog box.

3. Click the Validate button to run the Accessibility Checking tool.
4. Select `View→Error List` to view the output. The Error List window appears, as shown in Figure 21.8:

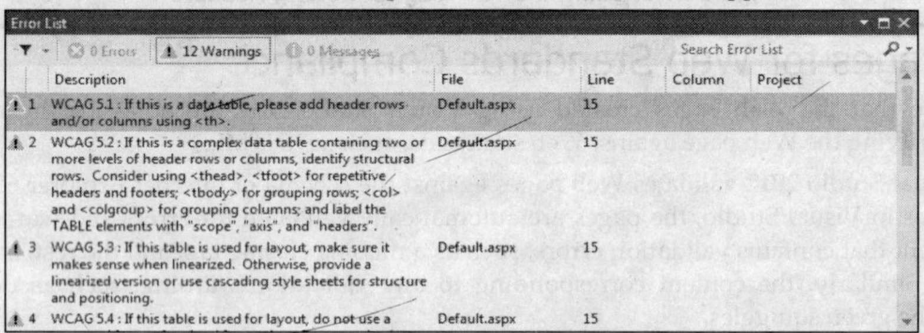

Figure 21.8: The Error List Window

The Error List window displays a list of accessibility issues, which are not automatically validated by the Accessibility Checking tool. You can manually evaluate your Web page to verify that the page conforms to the issues specified in the list.

As an alternative to the built-in features, Validation option and the Accessibility Checking, Visual Studio supports the existing validation software for validating Web pages. The existing validation software, such as Bobby and WAVE, are the third-party software that can check the conformance of a Web page to the XHTML and Accessibility standards. You need to either supply the Universal Resource Locator (URL) or upload the source code of the Web page to be verified to the existing validation software. The Web page will be verified and the results will be displayed, similar to the output of the Accessibility Checker tool.

Summary

In this chapter, you have learned about the Web standards introduced by W3C, such as XHTML and Accessibility Standards. You have also learned how to develop a website according to XHTML and Accessibility Web standards. In addtion, you learned how to use Accessibility tags, such as the `alt` attribute, `label` tag, and `th` tag for tables.

In the next chapter, you learn how to administer your applications by creating Event Logs, custom errors, and using performance counters. You also learn to debug your application and handle exceptions using the `Page_Error` and `Application_Error` methods.

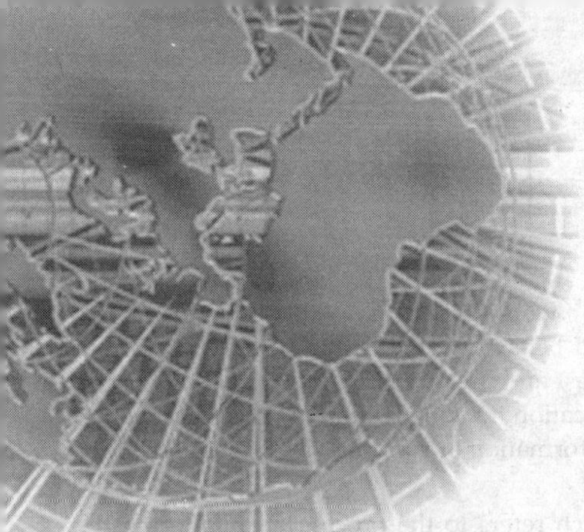

22

Application Tracking

In Depth

In spite of implementing all the controls and functionalities in your website, you may still sometimes come across situations wherein your website does not exhibit the required behavior. That is, the website is still not robust and user-friendly. What can you do to make your website robust and user-friendly, one that is essentially error-free? In this chapter, we try to answer such questions. The application tracking feature in ASP.NET enables you to follow the execution of a Web page, display the diagnostic information at run time, and debug the Web page.

In this chapter, you learn how to perform application tracking, which refers to the process of monitoring the health of a Web application or website to ensure effective working of the website. This chapter also includes detailed discussion on the various features used in application tracking, such as performance counters, which, as the name suggests, monitor the performance of the website; Web events, which can be used to check whether the website is working efficiently; debugging the website to identify errors in it; error or exception handling; and tracing a website to diagnose its problems. Now, let's discuss application monitoring and the features related to it.

Application Monitoring

Application monitoring involves monitoring a website to detect and handle various problems or errors that prevent a website from functioning efficiently. These problems usually crop up in the process of developing the website, and need to be resolved before the website is successfully hosted and made available to the users. Out of the various mechanisms provided by ASP.NET, some are meant to resolve debugging problems that occur while developing the website, while others help to monitor the performance of the website after its deployment. ASP.NET provides various classes and methods to debug the errors that occur while developing and executing a website.

As already stated, ASP.NET also provides various features to investigate and diagnose the problems related to websites. Now, let's discuss these features one by one.

Performance Counters

Performance counters are used to monitor the performance of a website. Performance, for a user, implies the response time of the website, where a lower response time implies higher performance. For an administrator, performance is the measure of the resources of a server, utilized by various programs. ASP.NET provides a wide list of performance counters, which can be categorized as application performance counters and system performance counters. When monitoring the performance of ASP.NET websites, you can track the performance counters related to different performance objects, as listed in Table 22.1:

Table 22.1: Performance Objects and Related Performance Counters

Performance Object	Performance Counter
ASP.NET	Application Restarts
ASP.NET	Requests Queued
ASP.NET	Worker Process Restarts
ASP.NET Applications	Errors Total
ASP.NET Applications	Requests/Sec
Processor	Percentage of CPU Utilization

ASP.NET also supports ASP.NET system performance counters and application performance counters. The ASP.NET system performance counters are listed in Table 22.2:

Table 22.2: ASP.NET System Performance Counters

Counter Name	Description
`Application Restarts`	Tracks the number of times a Web application has been restarted during the Web server's lifetime. The value of this counter is incremented every time the `Application_OnEnd` event is raised. A Web application restart can occur due to changes in the Web.config file, changes to the assemblies stored in the Web application's Bin directory, or when it is necessary to recompile the Web application due to numerous changes in its pages. Unnecessary increments in this counter reflect the problems in the Web application that need to be solved immediately.
`Application Running`	Tracks the number of applications running concurrently on the server.
`Requests Disconnected`	Tracks the number of requests that have been disconnected because of communication failure.
`Requests Queued`	Tracks the number of requests in queue waiting for service. When this number starts to increase linearly with increased client load, it means that the server has reached the limit of concurrent requests that it can process. The default maximum for this counter is 5,000, which can be changed in the machine.config file.
`Requests Rejected`	Tracks the number of failed requests due to the absence of required server resources to process them. In other words, this counter represents the number of requests that return a 503 HTTP status code, indicating that the server is too busy.
`Request Wait Time`	Tracks the number of milliseconds that the most recent request spent waiting in the queue for processing.
`Session State Server Connections Total`	Tracks the total number of session-state connections made to the computer on which the out-of-process session-state data is stored. Out-of-process session-state data is stored in a persistent data store, typically a SQL server database.
`Session SQL Server Connections Total`	Tracks the total number of session-state connections made to the Microsoft SQL Server database in which session-state data is stored.
`State Server Sessions Abandoned`	Tracks the number of user sessions that have been explicitly abandoned by specific user actions, such as closing the browser or navigating to another site. This counter is available only on the computer where the `aspnet_state` service is running.
`State Server Sessions Active`	Tracks the number of currently active user sessions. You can find this counter only on the computer where the `aspnet_state` state server service is running.
`State Server Sessions Timed Out`	Tracks the number of user sessions that have become inactive through user inaction. You can find this counter only on the computer where the `aspnet_state` state server service is running.
`State Server Sessions Total`	Tracks the number of sessions created during the lifetime of the process running on the server. This counter takes the total value of the `State Server Sessions Active`, `State Server Sessions Abandoned`, and `State Server Sessions Timed Out` performance counters.
`Worker Process Restarts`	Tracks the number of times a worker process is restarted on the server. A worker process is a process in which multiple application domains are hosted and ensures that each application works in its own application domain. A worker process automatically restarts when it fails unexpectedly or it is intentionally restarted. An unexpected increase in this counter should be investigated immediately.
`Worker Process Running`	Tracks the number of worker processes running on the server.

Various application performance counters supported by ASP.NET are listed in Table 22.3:

Table 22.3: ASP.NET Application Performance Counters

Counter Name	Description
`Anonymous Requests`	Tracks the number of requests that users have made using anonymous authentication.
`Anonymous Requests/Sec`	Tracks the number of requests per second that users have made using anonymous authentication.
`Cache Total Entries`	Tracks the total entries in cache made by an ASP.NET application through cache APIs and ASP.NET Page Framework.
`Cache Total Hits`	Tracks the total hits from a cache made by an ASP.NET application through cache APIs and ASP.NET Page Framework.
`Cache Total Misses`	Tracks total number of failed cache requests made by ASP.NET Page Framework and ASP.NET application through cache APIs.
`Cache Total Hit Ratio`	Tracks the ratio of total to missed cache requests. This counter is available for both the ASP.NET Page Framework cache and application cache.
`Cache Total Turnover Rate`	Tracks additions to and removals from the cache per second. A high turnover rate means that the cache is not used effectively and vice versa.
`Cache API Entries`	Tracks the total number of entries in the application cache.
`Cache API Hits`	Tracks the total hits from the cache when accessed by external cache APIs only.
`Cache API Misses`	Tracks the total number of failed requests to the cache when accessed by external cache APIs only.
`Cache API Hit Ratio`	Tracks the ratio of hit-to-miss for cache requests made by external cache APIs only.
`Cache API Turnover Rate`	Tracks the additions to and removals from the cache per second through external cache APIs only. A high turnover rate means that the cache is not being used effectively, and vice versa.
`Compilations Total`	Tracks the sum of compilations that have taken place during the lifetime of the current Web server process. Compilation takes place when a file is compiled dynamically on the server. A file can be of `.aspx`, `.asmx`, `.ascx`, or `.ashx` type or a CodeFile source file.
`Debugging Requests`	Tracks the number of requests that occur while debugging is enabled.
`Errors During Preprocessing`	Tracks the total number of parsing errors. This counter does not include runtime and compilation errors.
`Errors During Compilation`	Tracks the total number of dynamic compilation errors. This counter does not include runtime and parsing errors.
`Errors During Execution`	Tracks the total number of errors that occur during the execution of an HTTP request. This counter does not include compilation and parsing errors.
`Errors Unhandled During Execution`	Tracks the total number of unhandled errors that may occur during the execution of HTTP requests. This counter not tracks the error when: • Custom errors are enabled, or an error page is defined, or both. • The code contained the `Page_Error` event and the error is either cleared (using the `ClearError` method) or user is redirected to another location.
`Errors Unhandled During Execution/Sec`	Tracks the number of unhandled exceptions that occur per second during the execution of HTTP requests.
`Errors Total`	Tracks the total number of errors that occur during the execution of HTTP requests, which includes parser, compilation, or runtime errors. This counter is the sum of the Errors During Compilation, Errors During Preprocessing, and Errors During Execution counters. Before testing the performance of your application, you should identify and fix the bugs, as a well-functioning application should not generate errors.

Table 22.3: ASP.NET Application Performance Counters

Counter Name	Description
Errors Total/Sec	Tracks the total number of errors that occur per second during the execution of an HTTP request, including compilation, runtime, and parsing errors.
Output Cache Entries	Tracks total number of entries in the output cache.
Output Cache Hits	Tracks total number of requests serviced from the output cache.
Output Cache Misses	Tracks the number of failed output cache requests for each application.
Output Cache Hit Ratio	Tracks the percentage of total requests serviced from the output cache.
Output Cache Turnover Rate	Tracks the additions to or removals from the output cache per second. A high turnover rate means that the cache is not used effectively, and vice versa.
Pipeline Instance Count	Tracks the number of active request pipeline instances for the specified ASP.NET application. As only one execution thread can run within a pipeline instance, this number gives the maximum number of concurrent requests processed for a given application. Lowest the value signifies highest the performance of CPU.
Request Bytes In Total	Tracks the total size in bytes of all requests.
Request Bytes Out Total	Tracks the total size in bytes of the responses sent to a client. This does not include HTTP response headers.
Requests Executing	Tracks the number of requests currently in the process of execution.
Requests Failed	Tracks the total number of failed requests. Any status code greater than or equal to 400 increments this counter. For example, an unauthorized request that contains 401 as the status code increments the value of this counter.
Requests Not Found	Tracks the number of failed requests due to absence of required resources (status code 404 or 414).
Requests Not Authorized	Tracks number of requests that failed due to non-authorization (status code 401).
Requests Succeeded	Tracks the number of requests that executed successfully (status code 200).
Requests Timed Out	Tracks the number of requests that are timed out (status code 500).
Requests Total	Tracks the total number of requests made since the service was started.
Requests/Sec	Tracks the number of requests executed per second.
Sessions Active	Tracks the number of sessions currently active. This counter is supported only with in-memory session-state.
Sessions Abandoned	Tracks the number of sessions that have been explicitly abandoned. This counter is supported only with in-memory session-state.
Sessions Timed Out	Tracks the number of sessions that are timed out. This counter is supported only with in-memory session-state.
Sessions Total	Tracks the total number of sessions. This counter is supported only with in-memory session-state.
Transactions Aborted	Tracks the number of COM+ transactions cancelled for all active ASP.NET applications.
Transactions Committed	Tracks the number of transactions committed for all active ASP.NET applications.
Transactions Pending	Tracks the number of transactions in progress for all active ASP.NET applications.
Transactions Total	Tracks the total number of transactions for all active ASP.NET applications.
Transactions/Sec	Tracks the number of transactions per second for all active ASP.NET applications.

Health Monitoring with Web Events

In ASP.NET, you can monitor the health of a website by using the Web events. This feature provides a general framework for raising runtime events. Web events are instances of the Web event base class, which collects information related to the events of a website. The Web events provided by ASP.NET help you to track the performance of the website; and they can be raised at any time during the lifetime of the website. We show you how to use Web events as a monitoring tool in a website later in this chapter.

The different Web event base classes are:

- `WebBaseEvent`–Contains the required properties for all events, including the event code, the event detail code, the date and time the event was raised, the sequence number, the event message, and the rest.
- `WebManagementEvent`–Acts as a base class for management events, such as `lifetime`, `request`, `error`, and `audit`.
- `WebHeartbeatEvent`–Acts as a base class for events generated by a Web application at regular intervals. The interval of these events is defined by the `heartBeatInterval` attribute of the `healthMonitoring` configuration section of the Web application.
- `WebAuditEvent`–Acts as a base class for security audit events that allow you to determine the occurrence of certain conditions, such as authorization failure and decryption failure, related to a website.
- `WebRequestEvent`–Acts as a base class for all the informational request events in a website.
- `WebBaseErrorEvent`–Acts as a base class for all the events indicating error conditions in a website.

ASP.NET allows you to use default providers to process Web events. These providers are implemented by the following classes:

- `WebEventProvider`–Provides a base class for non-buffered event providers
- `BufferedWebEventProvider`–Provides the base functionality to create event providers that require buffering
- `SqlWebEventProvider`–Implements an event provider that saves event notifications to an SQL database

Debugging an Application

You may be familiar with the process of debugging applications in Windows. Programmatically, debugging is the process of finding and removing errors in a program. Debugging helps you identify logical errors in your application and ensure that your website exhibits the desired behavior, which is also indicative of a healthy website. Debugging ASP.NET websites is similar to debugging Windows applications, though the former is more complex. Visual Studio 2012 provides powerful tools to debug ASP.NET websites during the development and deployment stages. The objective behind debugging a website is to find logical errors contained in the code, which prevent the website from exhibiting the desired behavior. Debugging also allows you to know the cause of the errors. You learn how to debug a website by using the Debug mode and breakpoints of Visual Studio 2012 IDE in the *Immediate Solutions* section of this chapter.

Application Tracing Using ASP.NET Trace

The ASP.NET trace is used during the execution of an ASP.NET Web page. This feature allows you to collate all the information related to a particular website, such as request details, the page control hierarchy, or the execution of the various stages of the page lifecycle and controls. ASP.NET 4.5 integrates the .NET Framework standard tracing facility that contains the `System.Diagnostics.Trace` class. The `System.Diagnostics.Trace` class contains methods and events that allow you to view trace information produced by .NET components (such as a Web form, a control, an image, and a Web service) of your website. This class can also be used to view trace information of an ASP.NET website.

The `System.Diagnostics.Trace` class provides a variety of properties and methods that help in tracing the execution of code in a website. This class follows the concept of Instrumentation, which helps monitor the health of your website. Tracing enables you to isolate the problems of a running website and fix them separately, without conflicting with the running website. The inheritance hierarchy for the `System.Diagnostics.Trace` class is as follows:

```
System.Object
   System.Diagnostics.Trace
```

Noteworthy methods of the `System.Diagnostics.Trace` class are listed in Table 22.4:

Table 22.4: Noteworthy Methods of the System.Diagnostics.Trace Class

Method	Description
`Assert`	Checks a condition (specified as parameter) and displays a message if the condition is false. This method takes two parameters. The first parameter is of Boolean type (which is to be evaluated) and the second parameter is of String type (which is to be displayed as message).
`Close`	Closes the Listeners after flushing the output buffer. This method is used to get the output in a text file. A listener is a mechanism used to receive and store information. In tracing, listeners direct the tracing output to an appropriate target, such as a log, window, or text file.
`Fail`	Produces an error message for the current trace.
`Flush`	Flushes the output buffer and writes the data buffered to the Listeners.
`GetHashCode`	Acts as a hash function for a particular type of trace.
`GetType`	Obtains the type of the current instance of the `System.Diagnostics.Trace` class.
`Indent`	Increments the indent level for a trace by 1.
`Refresh`	Refreshes the configuration data of a trace.
`ToString`	Returns a string that represents the current instance of the `System.Diagnostics.Trace` class.
`TraceError`	Writes error information to trace listeners in the `Listeners` collection.
`TraceInformation`	Writes informational messages to trace listeners in the `Listeners` collection.
`TraceWarning`	Writes warning information to trace listeners in the `Listeners` collection.
`Unindent`	Decrements the indent level for a trace by 1.
`Write`	Writes information about a trace to a trace listener in the `Listeners` collection.
`WriteIf`	Writes information (one word at a time) about a trace to a trace listener in the `Listeners` collection if the condition is set to True.
`WriteLine`	Writes trace information to trace listeners belonging to the `Listeners` collection.
`WriteLineIf`	Writes trace information (one line at a time) to trace listeners belonging to the `Listeners` collection if the condition is set to True.

Noteworthy properties of the `System.Diagnostics.Trace` class are listed in Table 22.5:

Table 22.5: Noteworthy Properties of System.Diagnostics.Trace Class

Property	Description
`AutoFlush`	Obtains or specifies whether Flush method should be called on Listeners after every write on a file.
`CorrelationManager`	Obtains the `CorrelationManager` class object related to the thread of this trace. The `CorrelationManager` class contains methods used to save a thread-unique ID. This thread-unique ID is assigned to each trace event to differentiate the tracing information from other threads.
`IndentLevel`	Obtains or specifies the indent level of the instances of the `System.Diagnostics.Trace` class. The default indent level is zero.
`IndentSize`	Obtains or specifies the number of spaces in the indent for the current trace.
`Listeners`	Obtains the set of listeners monitoring the output of the current trace.

Table 22.5: Noteworthy Properties of System.Diagnostics.Trace Class

Property	Description
`UseGlobalLock`	Obtains or specifies a value that indicates whether a global lock should be used to lock tracing for a website to restrict access to authenticated users only.

Exception and Error Handling

ASP.NET also allows you to handle various types of errors and exceptions related to a particular website with the help of different error handling events, such as `Page_Error` and `Application_error`. These events allow you to track, report, and take appropriate corrective steps for the errors that occur while executing the website. For example, you can write the code to handle events, such as Page_Error and Application_error, to inform the user about an error, and display it in a customized error page. You learn how to handle exceptions and errors in a website later in this chapter.

The Application_Error Method

Sometimes, it is quite cumbersome to handle every error on each Web page. A simpler way is to handle the errors at the application level. To do this, we have to add the code inside the `Application_Error` method present in the `Global.asax` file of the website. The main functionality of the `Global.asax` file of the website is to catch all the errors that are not identified in a Try/Catch block. The code inside the `Application_Error` method is responsible for catching every unhandled exception that occurs in the website. ASP.NET examines the `Global.asax` file and compiles it into a .NET Framework class file, which inherits the `HttpApplication` class. This class defines the methods, properties, and events that are common to all the objects in an ASP.NET website. In this way, the `HttpApplication` class associates the `Global.asax` file with each page of the ASP.NET website. You should note to never set the `customErrors` attribute to Off in the `Web.config` file of your application, if you are not specifying the `Application_Error` handler in your `Global.asax` file. This is because, if you do so then the important information of your Web site can be exposed to anyone who can cause an error to occur on your site.

Monitor a Website Using Events

In ASP.NET, the Web event feature allows you to log information about built-in events at a specified source, in log files. These log files include information about unhandled exceptions and failed authentication attempts. The website administrator uses these log files to monitor the health of the website. Before implementing the Web event feature in a website, you need to specify the events in the event subscriptions section of the Web.config file. Adding a website in event subscriptions ensures that the website can log information about built-in events. You also need to specify the channels through which you want to deliver the event information. A channel is simply a medium of communication through which you receive the information collected by Web events related to a website. You can perform the following channel actions with the help of Web events:

- Saving events to Microsoft SQL Server
- Sending event reports through e-mail
- Writing events to Windows Event Log
- Forwarding events through Wireless Markup Language (WML)

You need to ensure that the health monitoring feature is enabled in the `Web.config` file of the website and the provider (used to provide information about events) is specified in this file, to monitor a website using events.

After learning the concepts related to application tracking, let's move on to the *Immediate Solutions* section.

Immediate Solutions

Using the Debug Mode

The Debug mode is the default mode used to execute websites in Visual Studio 2012. This mode helps you to identify errors that may occur while executing a website. These errors can be classified into the following categories:

- **Configuration errors**—Occur when there is an error in the syntax or structure of a `Web.config` file in the configuration hierarchy.
- **Parser errors**—Occur when the syntax of an `.aspx` page is not properly formed.
- **Compilation errors**—Occur when a page of a website written in a particular language contains incorrect program instructions.
- **Run-time errors**—Occur at the time of execution of a Web page. Run-time errors indicate problems that a Web developer can anticipate but can do nothing about it.

The error message displayed when a run-time error occurs is known as a Call Stack. It is a chain of procedure calls that generate a related exception, but it does not specify the exact location of the runtime error on the Web page. However, if you want to display the line number of the source code containing the runtime error, you have to enable the Debug mode in the website. ASP.NET supports the `Debug` attribute for a Web page, which allows you to display an error message in case of a run-time error. The value of the `Debug` attribute should be True to enable the Debug mode for the Web page.

Now, let's develop a website named `DebugExampleAppVB` (`DebugExampleAppVB` for VB and `DebugExampleAppCS` for C#) to understand the working of the `Debug` attribute.. You can find the code for the `Default.aspx` page in Listing 22.1:

Listing 22.1: Showing the Code for the `Default.aspx` Page

In VB

```
<%@ Page Language="VB" AutoEventWireup="false" CodeFile="Default.aspx.vb"
  Inherits="_Default" Debug="true"%>
<!DOCTYPE html>
<html xmlns="http://www.w3.org/1999/xhtml">
<head runat="server">
    <title>Debug Example</title>
</head>
<body>
   <form id="form1" runat="server">
   <div>
                          
                         
                         
                         
          <br />
       <br />
       Click the Click Me button to raise the Exception:<br />
       <br />
          
       <asp:Button ID="Button1" runat="server" Text="Click Me" OnClick="Button1_Click" />
       <br />
       <br />  
       <asp:Label ID="Label1" runat="server" Font-Bold="True" Font-Names="Verdana"
       Width="594px"></asp:Label>
                         
                         
                       
    <br />
       <br />
                         
```

```
                           
                           
        
        </div>
        </form>
</body>
</html>
```

In C#

```
<%@ Page Language="C#" AutoEventWireup="true" CodeFile="Default.aspx.cs"
    Inherits="_Default" Debug="true"  %>
<!DOCTYPE html>
<html xmlns="http://www.w3.org/1999/xhtml">
<head id="Head1" runat="server">
      <title>Debug Example</title>
</head>
<body>
        <form id="form1" runat="server">
        <div>
                               
                           
                           
                           
            <br />
            <br />
            Click the Click Me button to raise the Exception:<br />
            <br />
               
            <asp:Button ID="Button1" runat="server" Text="Click Me" OnClick="Button1_Click" />
            <br />
            <br />  
            <asp:Label ID="Label1" runat="server" Font-Bold="True" Font-Names="Verdana"
            Width="594px"></asp:Label>
                           
                           
                         
      <br />
            <br />
                           
                           
                           
        
        </div>
        </form>
</body>
</html>
```

Note that in the preceding listing, the value of the `Debug` attribute is set to True in the Page directive so that the error message is displayed when there is an error in the website. After creating the `Default.aspx` page, change the CodeFile file code. You can find the code for the CodeFile file of `Default.aspx` page in Listing 22.2:

Listing 22.2: Showing the Code for the CodeFile of the Default.aspx Page

In VB

```
Partial Class _Default
    Inherits System.Web.UI.Page
    Protected Sub Button1_Click(sender As Object, e As EventArgs) Handles Button1.Click
        Try
            Dim name As String = Nothing
            Response.Write(name.ToString())
        Catch ex As Exception
            Label1.Visible = True
            Label1.Text = "The Error Message is:  " & ex.Message
        End Try
    End Sub
    Protected Sub Page_Load(sender As Object, e As EventArgs) Handles Me.Load
```

```
        Label1.Visible = False
    End Sub
End Class
```

In C#

```
using System;
using System.Collections.Generic;
using System.Linq;
using System.Web;
using System.Web.UI;
using System.Web.UI.WebControls;
public partial class _Default : System.Web.UI.Page
{
    protected void Page_Load(object sender, EventArgs e)
    {
        Label1.Visible = false;
    }
    protected void Button1_Click(object sender, EventArgs e)
    {
        try
        {
            String name = null;
            Response.Write(name.ToString());
        }
        catch (Exception ex)
        {
            Label1.Visible = true;
            Label1.Text = "The Error Message is:  " + ex.Message;
        }
    }
}
```

Now, press the F5 key on the keyboard to run the application. The output is as shown in Figure 22.1:

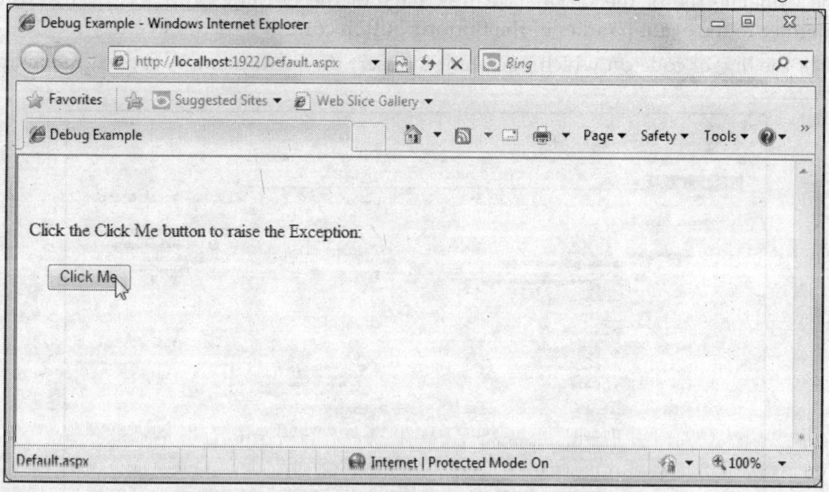

Figure 22.1: The DebugExampleAppVB Application

The message, The Error Message is: Object reference not set to an instance of an object is displayed when a user clicks the Click Me button in the `DebugExampleAppVB` website, as shown in Figure 22.2:

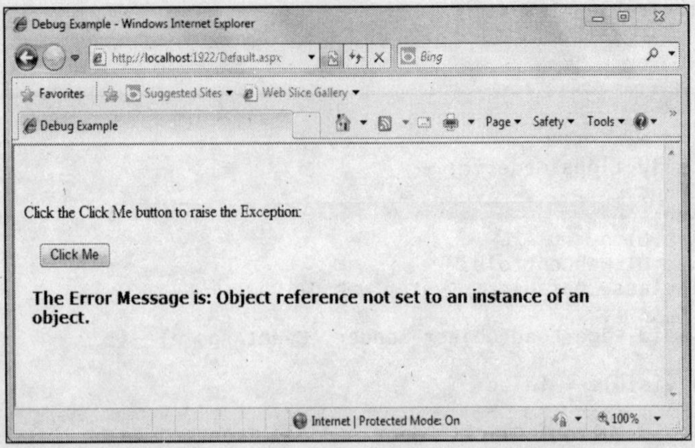

Figure 22.2: Displaying the Error Message

Let's now learn to use breakpoints in ASP.NET applications.

Using Breakpoints

While working with a website, you probably want to know about the execution flow of the CodeFile file. This file helps you to identify the problems when the code of the website is not working in the desired way. For this, you can use breakpoints in your application. Breakpoints allow you to know when a particular part of your code is executing. Now, let's learn how to use breakpoints in the website, named `DebugExampleAppVB (DebugExampleAppCS for C# and DebugExampleAppVB for VB),` which we just created, to show how an exception is caught. Perform the following steps to do this:

1. Open the CodeFile file of the `Default.aspx` page of the `DebugExampleAppVB` website and move the mouse-pointer to the event handler of the Button1 button control's `click` event.
2. Right-click the line of code on which you want to insert the breakpoint. A context menu appears, as shown in Figure 22.3:

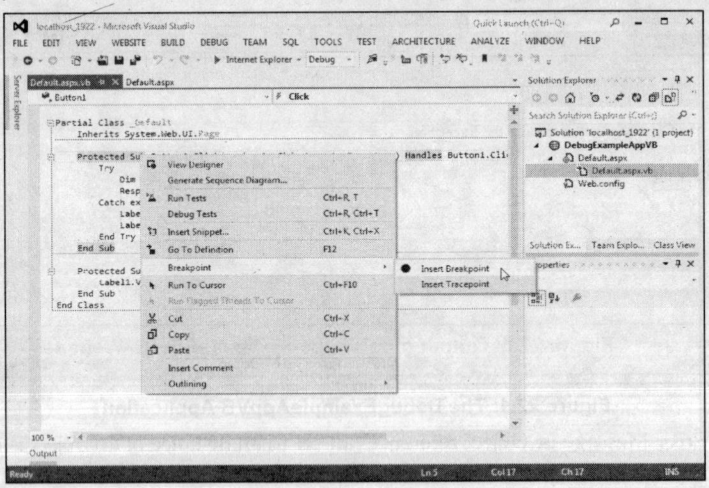

Figure 22.3: Inserting a Breakpoint

3. In the context menu, place the mouse-pointer on the Breakpoint option. A submenu appears (Figure 22.3).
4. Select the Insert Breakpoint option from the submenu (Figure 22.3). When you select the Insert Breakpoint option, a red circle appears in the left-side pane of the coding area (highlighted by the rectangular block), indicating the insertion of the breakpoint, as shown in Figure 22.4:

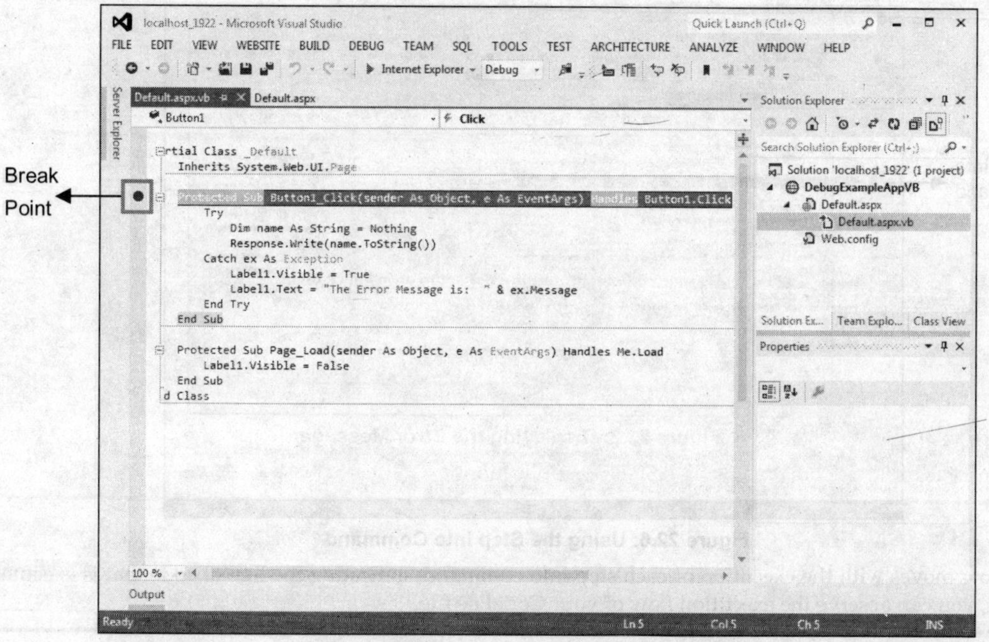

Figure 22.4: Showing an Inserted Breakpoint

5. Now, press the F5 key on the keyboard to run the application. The output is shown in Figure 22.5:

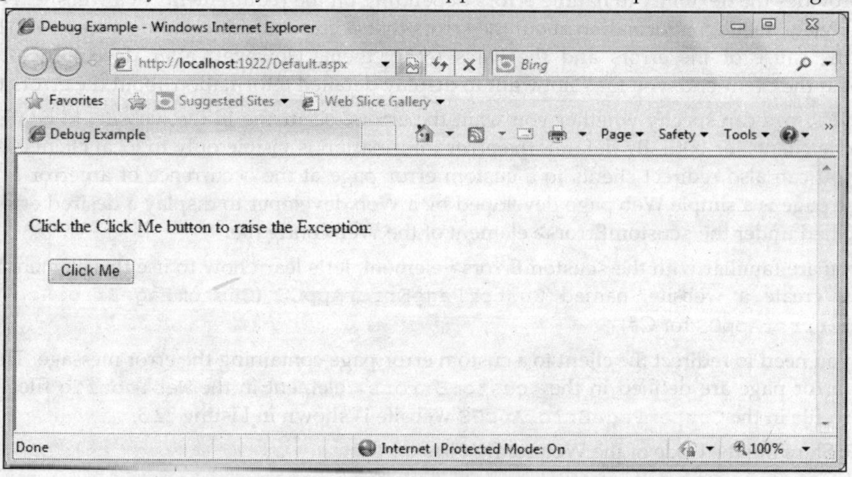

Figure 22.5: Output of the DebugExampleAppVB Website

6. Next, click the Click Me button on the Web page (Figure 22.5). This opens the CodeFile file where you have inserted the breakpoint.
7. Press the F11 key on the keyboard. The next line of the code is executed. This is called Step Into operation and is shown with a yellow arrow in Figure 22.6:

Step Into Command

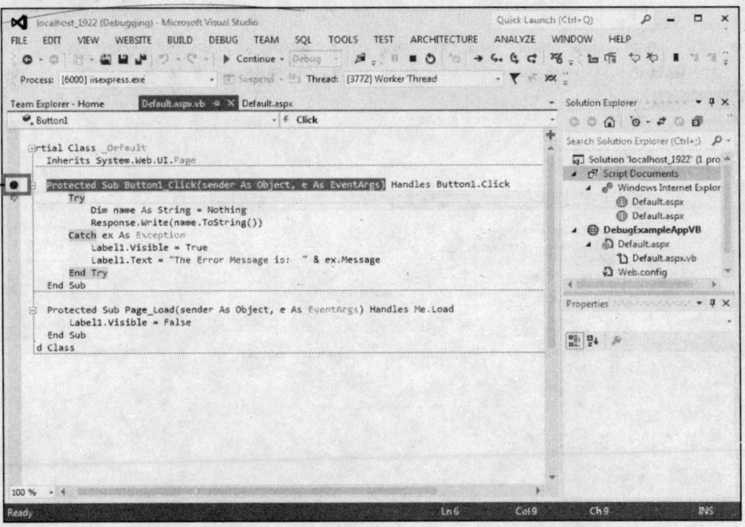

Figure 22.6: Using the Step Into Command

This arrow moves with the execution of each step into command, indicating the line of code that is executed. In this way, you can observe the execution flow of your CodeFile file.

Using the <customErrors> Element

ASP.NET provides the flexibility to handle errors depending on the requirements of a website. For example, you may want to view detailed information about the errors that occur while developing a website. This helps you to determine the cause of the errors and the ways to fix them. However, after developing the website and deploying it at the client-end, you may not want to display detailed information about the errors to the clients.

With ASP.NET, you can specify whether you want the errors, occurring in the website, to be displayed to local clients, remote clients, or both. By default, the error information is visible only to local clients. With the help of ASP.NET, you can also redirect clients to a custom error page at the occurrence of an error in the website. A custom error page is a simple Web page developed by a Web developer to display a desired error message. This page is specified under the <customErrors> element of the Web.config file.

Now that you are familiar with the <customErrors> element, let's learn how to use this element in a website. To do this, we create a website, named `CustomPageErrorAppCS` (`CustomPageErrorAppVB` for VB and `CustomPageErrorAppCS` for C#).

First of all, you need to redirect the client to a custom error page containing the error message. The parameters of the custom error page are defined in the `<customErrors>` element in the `Web.config` file. The code of the `Web.config` file in the `CustomPageErrorAppCS` website is shown in Listing 22.3:

Listing 22.3: Showing the Code of the Web.config File

In VB and C#

```
<?xml version="1.0"?>
<!--
  For more information on how to configure your ASP.NET application, please visit
  http://go.microsoft.com/fwlink/?LinkId=169433
  -->
<configuration>
  <system.web>
    <compilation debug="true" targetFramework="4.5"/>
    <httpRuntime targetFramework="4.5"/>
    <pages>
      <namespaces>
        <clear/>
```

```
            <add namespace="System"/>
            <add namespace="System.Collections"/>
            <add namespace="System.Collections.Specialized"/>
            <add namespace="System.Configuration"/>
            <add namespace="System.Text"/>
            <add namespace="System.Text.RegularExpressions"/>
            <add namespace="System.Web"/>
            <add namespace="System.Web.Caching"/>
            <add namespace="System.Web.SessionState"/>
            <add namespace="System.Web.Security"/>
            <add namespace="System.Web.Profile"/>
            <add namespace="System.Web.UI"/>
            <add namespace="System.Web.UI.WebControls"/>
            <add namespace="System.Web.UI.WebControls.WebParts"/>
            <add namespace="System.Web.UI.HtmlControls"/>
          </namespaces>
        </pages>
        <authentication mode="Windows"/>
        <customErrors mode="On" defaultRedirect="customErrorPage.htm"/>
      </system.web>
    </configuration>
```

The configuration defined in Listing 22.3 redirects local and remote clients to a custom error page customErrorPage.htm. This page can also be an .aspx page containing any common error message for any type of error in a website.

When you run the website, ASP.NET forwards the path of the Web page, on which the error has occurred, to the error page as a QueryString argument. The error page contains the description and the possible reasons for the error. The code for the CustomErrorPage.htm page, to which the remote and local clients are redirected in the CustomPageErrorAppCS website, is shown in Listing 22.4:

Listing 22.4: Showing the Code for the CustomErrorPage.htm Page

In VB and C#

```
<%@ Page Language="C#" AutoEventWireup="true" CodeFile="CustomErrorPage.htm.cs"
  Inherits="CustomErrorPage" %>
<html xmlns="http://www.w3.org/1999/xhtml">
 <head>
    <title>CustomError Page</title>
</head>
<body bgcolor="#cc9900">
  <strong><span style="text-decoration: underline"><em>You are on custom error page and
  the page you have requested doesn't exist</em></span></strong>
</body>
</html>
```

In the Default.aspx page of the CustomPageErrorAppCS website, a hyperlink is added at design time to redirect local and remote clients to the Default1.aspx page. If the Default1.aspx page is not found, then the clients are redirected to the CustomErrorPage.htm page. You can find the code for the Default.aspx page in Listing 22.5:

Listing 22.5: Showing the Code for the Default.aspx Page

In VB

```
<%@ Page Language="VB" AutoEventWireup="false" CodeFile="Default.aspx.vb"
  Inherits="_Default" %>
<!DOCTYPE html>
<html xmlns="http://www.w3.org/1999/xhtml">
<head id="Head1" runat="server">
    <title>CustomPageError Example</title>
</head>
<body>
    <form id="form1" runat="server">
    <div>
        <asp:HyperLink ID="HyperLink1" runat="server" NavigateUrl="~/Default1.aspx">go to
         Page Default1.aspx</asp:HyperLink>
        <div id="footer">
```

```
                     <p class="left">
        </div>
        </form>
    </body>
    </html>
```

In C#

```
    <%@ Page Language="C#" AutoEventWireup="true" CodeFile="Default.aspx.cs"
      Inherits="_Default" %>
    <!DOCTYPE html>
    <html xmlns="http://www.w3.org/1999/xhtml">
    <head runat="server">
        <title>CustomPageError Example</title>
    </head>
    <body>
        <form id="form1" runat="server">
        <div>
            <asp:HyperLink ID="HyperLink1" runat="server" NavigateUrl="~/Default1.aspx">go to
             Page Default1.aspx</asp:HyperLink>
            <div id="footer">
                     <p class="left">
        </div>
        </form>
    </body>
    </html>
```

Now, press the F5 key on the keyboard to run the application. The output is as shown in Figure 22.7:

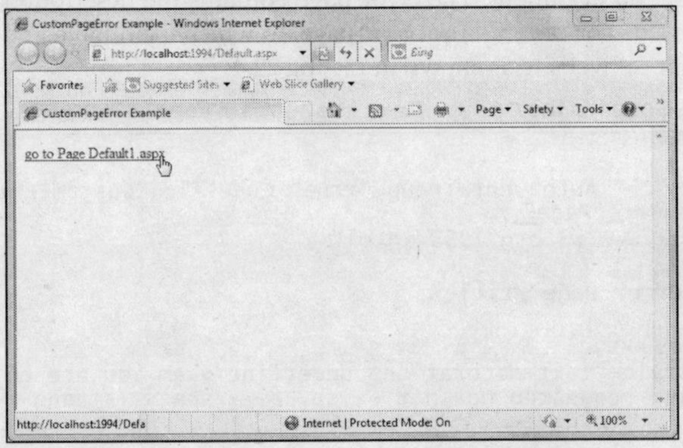

Figure 22.7: The Default.aspx Page of the CustomPageErrorAppCS Application

Now, click the `go to Page Default1.aspx` hyperlink. This takes you to the `Default1.aspx` page. However, if the `Default1.aspx` page is not found, you are redirected to the `customErrorPage.htm` page, as shown in Figure 22.8:

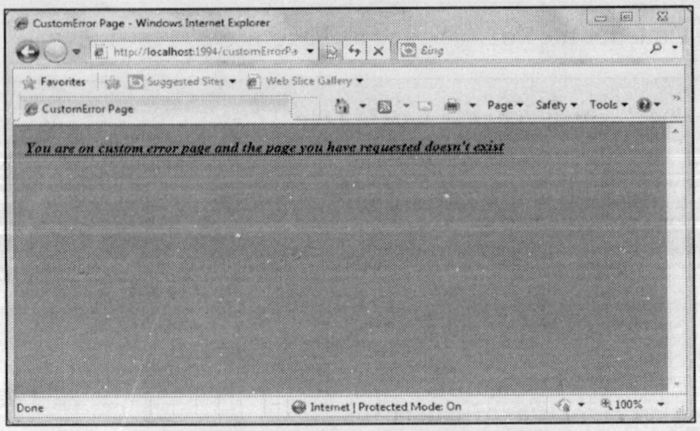

Figure 22.8: The CustomError Page

Now that you know how to use the <customErrors> element in a website, let's know about the various attributes of this element. Table 22.6 lists the attributes of the <customErrors> element:

Table 22.6: Attributes of the <customErrors> Element

Attribute	Description
defaultRedirect	Indicates the default Universal Resource Locator (URL) to which a browser should be redirected, if an error occurs. This is an optional attribute.
mode	Indicates whether the errors are displayed to local clients, to remote clients, or both. This is a mandatory attribute of the <customErrors> element.

The Mode attribute of the <customErrors> element assumes any one of the following three values:

- `RemoteOnly`—Indicates that the custom errors are displayed to remote clients only. This is the default mode, if no value is specified.
- `On`—Indicates that the custom errors are displayed to both local and remote clients.
- `Off`—Indicates that the custom errors are not displayed to any category of users, whether remote or local.

ASP.NET not only allows you to display a common error page for all types of errors, but it also assigns specific error pages to specific error status codes. For this, you need to use the inner <error> element inside the <customErrors> element, which associates HTTP status codes with custom error pages. The different attributes and values that you can use for the <error> element in a website are:

- `StatusCode`—Indicates the HTTP status code of errors, at the occurrence of which the custom error page is displayed. Some examples of the HTTP status codes are:
  - `403`—Access to specified file is denied
  - `404`—Specified file not found
  - `500`—Internal server error
- `Redirect`—Represents the URL of the error page to which the client browser should be redirected at the occurrence of an error

Using the Page_Error Method

You can handle exceptions or errors related to a website in different ways, either at the page level or at the application level. In page-level error handling, you monitor the errors related to each Web page of the website separately, whereas in application-level error handling, you monitor the errors related to the entire website. You can use the `Page_Error` method to handle the errors in a code, at the page level. The `Page` base class exposes the `Page_Error` method, which you can override in the CodeFile file of the Web page. The `Page_Error` method is called whenever an unhandled exception is thrown at runtime.

Now, let's create a website, named `PageErrorAppCS` (`PageErrorAppVB` for VB and `PageErrorAppCS` for C#), to show the use of the `Page_Error` method. You can find the code for the `Default.aspx` page in Listing 22.6:

Listing 22.6: Showing the Code for the `Default.aspx` Page

In VB

```
<%@ Page Language="VB" AutoEventWireup="false" CodeFile="Default.aspx.vb"
  Inherits="_Default" %>
<!DOCTYPE html>
<html xmlns="http://www.w3.org/1999/xhtml">
<head runat="server">
    <title>Pager_Error Method Example</title>
</head>
<body>
    <form id="form1" runat="server">
    <div>
    <asp:Label ID="Label1" runat="server" Text="This Button Generates an Error" Font-
        Bold="True" ForeColor="Fuchsia"></asp:Label>
```

```
                <br />
                <br /;
                <br />
                <asp:Button ID="Button1" runat="server" Text="Button" />
</div></form></body></html>
```

In C#

```
<%@ Page Language="C#" AutoEventWireup="true" CodeFile="Default.aspx.cs"
  Inherits="_Default" %>
<!DOCTYPE html>
<html xmlns="http://www.w3.org/1999/xhtml">
<head id="Head1" runat="server">
    <title>Pager_Error Method Example</title>
</head>
<body>
    <form id="form1" runat="server">
    <div>
    <asp:Label ID="Label1" runat="server" Text="This Button Generates an Error" Font-
        Bold="True" ForeColor="Fuchsia"></asp:Label>
                <br />
                <br /;
                <br />
                <asp:Button ID="Button1" runat="server" Text="Button"
                OnClick="Button1_Click" />
</div></form></body></html>
```

After creating the Default.aspx page, change the CodeFile file code. You can find the code for the CodeFile file of Default.aspx page in Listing 22.7:

Listing 22.7: Showing the Code for the CodeFile of the Default.aspx Page

In VB

```
Partial Class _Default
    Inherits System.Web.UI.Page
    Private Sub Page_Error(sender As Object, e As EventArgs)
        Response.Write("Error occurred: <br />" & Server.GetLastError().ToString())
        Server.ClearError()
    End Sub
    Private Sub PageLevelErrorTest()
        Dim array(8) As Integer
        For intCounter As Integer = 0 To 9
            array(intCounter) = intCounter
            Response.Write("The value of the counter is:" & intCounter & "<br />")
        Next intCounter
    End Sub
    Protected Sub Button1_Click(sender As Object, e As EventArgs) Handles Button1.Click
        PageLevelErrorTest()
    End Sub
End Class
```

In C#

```
using System;
using System.Collections.Generic;
using System.Linq;
using System.Web;
using System.Web.UI;
using System.Web.UI.WebControls;
public partial class _Default : System.Web.UI.Page
{
    protected void Page_Load(object sender, EventArgs e)
    {
    }
    void Page_Error(object sender, EventArgs e)
    {
        Response.Write("Error occured: <br />" + Server.GetLastError().ToString());
        Server.ClearError();
```

```
        }
        void PageLevelErrorTest()
        {
            int[] array = new int[9];
            for (int intCounter = 0; intCounter <= 9; intCounter++)
            {
                array[intCounter] = intCounter;
                Response.Write("The value of counter is: " + intCounter + "<br />");
            }
        }
        protected void Button1_Click(object sender, EventArgs e)
        {
            PageLevelErrorTest();
        }
    }
```

Now, press the F5 key on the keyboard to run the application. The output is as shown in Figure 22.9:

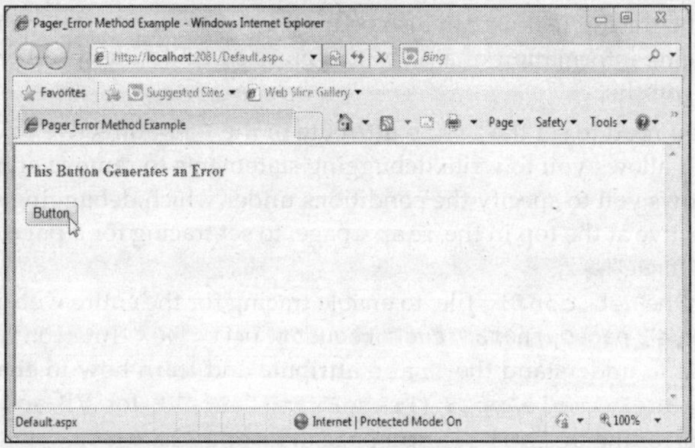

Figure 22.9: Default.aspx Page of PageErrorExample Application

Now, perform the following steps to understand the working of the Page_Error method:

1. Click the Button button (Figure 22.9). It generates a runtime exception named IndexOutOfRangeException.
2. Now, press the F11 key on the keyboard to continue with the execution of the website, till the time you view the output as shown in Figure 22.10:

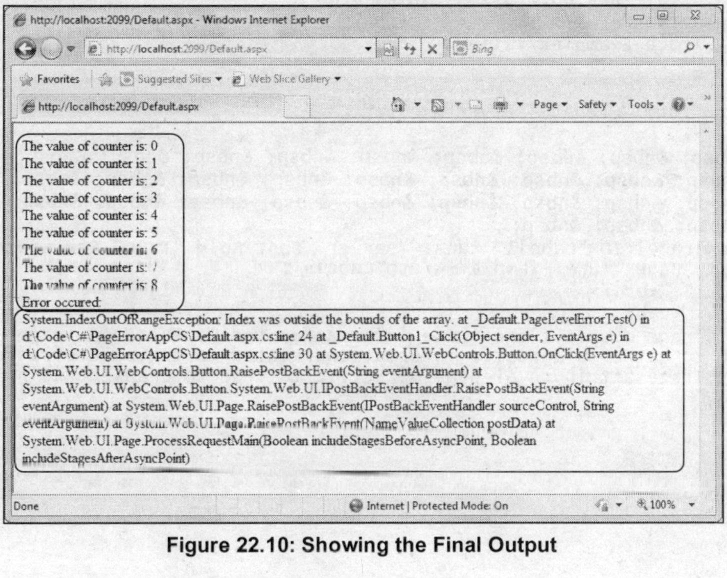

Figure 22.10: Showing the Final Output

Observe that instead of terminating the website, the `IndexOutOfRangeException` exception is caught by the `Page_Error` method, which is defined in the CodeFile file. The `Page_Error` method removes the exception by using the `Server.ClearError()` method and displays the output with the description of the exception. In Figure 22.10, the first circle displays the required output and the second circle displays the description of the exception.

NOTE

While using the Page_Error method, we cannot use controls to display dynamic content because this method is called before any control instance is created. When you run this application using F5, it will throw an exception in VS 2012 and not in the output page. To see the error in IE page, you have to run this application using start without debugging option

Using the Page Directive with the Trace Attribute

ASP.NET provides you with the tracing feature, which you can use to view diagnostic information related to an ASP.NET page request. The tracing feature can also be used to write debug statements in the code of a website. To obtain and display tracing information of a website, you need to decide whether you want information of a Web page or of the entire website.

To enable page tracing, you need to set the `Trace` attribute in the `Page` directive to True. This process is known as page-level tracing and it allows you to write debugging statements to remove errors in the `.aspx` page itself. Page-level tracing also allows you to specify the conditions under which debugging statements will be executed. Include the following directive at the top in the `.aspx` page, to set tracing for a page:

```
<%@ Page Trace="true"%>
```

Add the following code in the `Web.config` file, to enable tracing for the entire website:

```
<trace enabled="true" pageOutput="true" requestLimit="40" localOnly="false"/>
```

Now, let's create a website to understand the `Trace` attribute and learn how to enable tracing for a Web page. We name this website `TraceExampleAppCS` (`TraceExampleAppVB` for VB and `TraceExampleAppCS` for C#). You can find the code for the `Default.aspx` page in Listing 22.8:

Listing 22.8: Showing the Code for the `Default.aspx` Page

In VB

```
<%@ Page Language="VB" AutoEventWireup="false" CodeFile="Default.aspx.vb"
  Inherits="_Default" Trace="true"%>
<!DOCTYPE html>
<html xmlns="http://www.w3.org/1999/xhtml">
<head runat="server">
    <title>Trace Example</title>
</head>
<body>
    <form id="form1" runat="server">
    <div>
                         
                         
                         
         
        <asp:Label ID="Label1" runat="server" Font-Bold="True" Font-Names="Arial Black"
        Text="Page Trace Example"></asp:Label>
                <br />
                <br />
        This page displays the trace information for Default.aspx page. Tracing enables
        you to gather diagnostic information related to the page of a Web application.
        Set Trace attribute of page directive to true to enable tracing for a page.
        
    </div>
    </form>
</body>
</html>
```

In C#

```
<%@ Page Language="C#" AutoEventWireup="true" CodeFile="Default.aspx.cs"
  Inherits="_Default" Trace="true"%>
<!DOCTYPE html>
<html xmlns="http://www.w3.org/1999/xhtml">
<head id="Head1" runat="server">
     <title>Trace Example</title>
</head>
<body>
    <form id="form1" runat="server">
    <div>
                           
                         
                         
         
        <asp:Label ID="Label1" runat="server" Font-Bold="True" Font-Names="Arial Black"
        Text="Page Trace Example"></asp:Label>
               <br />
               <br />
        This page displays the trace information for Default.aspx page. Tracing enables
        you to gather diagnostic information related to the page of a Web application.
        Set Trace attribute of page directive to true to enable tracing for a page.
        
    </div>
    </form>
</body>
</html>
```

Now, press the F5 key on the keyboard to run the application. The output is as shown in Figure 22.11:

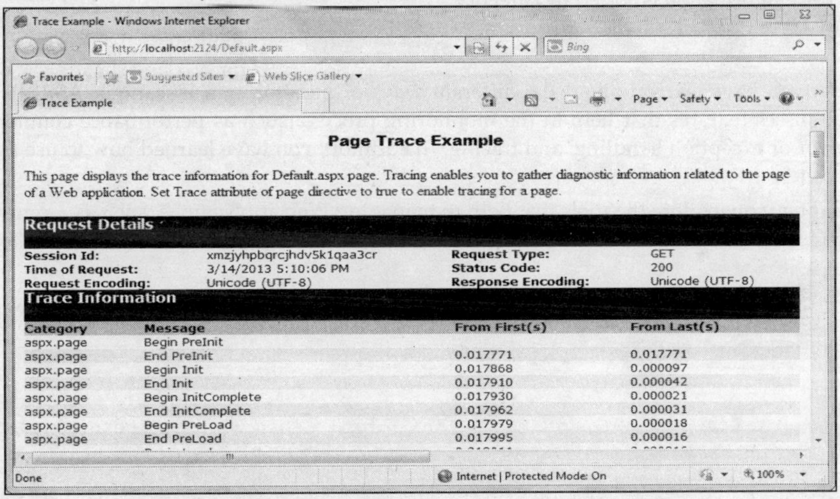

Figure 22.11: Output of the TraceExampleAppCS Website

NOTE

Trace information is always displayed at the end of the page, this is why you have to scroll the web page to view trace information.

Using the Trace Class Methods

ASP.NET provides the TraceContext property, which is present in the Trace class, to write debugging statements. The `Trace` class has two important methods, `Trace.Write()` and `Trace.Warn()`. You can use these methods to display a message on the output page whenever an action or error occurs in the website. Both the methods take a message string and category as arguments to display the desired message. The only difference between the two methods is that the output displayed using the `Trace.Warn()` method appears in red. The following is the syntax of the `Trace.Write()` method:

```
(For VB)
Trace.Write (Message) Or
(For C#)
Trace.Write (Message);
```

The syntax of the `Trace.Warn()` method is similar to the syntax of the `Trace.Write()` method. The syntax of the `Trace.Warn()` method is as follows:

```
(For VB)
Trace.Warn (Category, Message) Or
(For C#)
Trace.Warn (Category, Message);
```

In the preceding syntax of [Trace.Warn()], the `Category` argument specifies the category of the error.

If you want the code in the `Trace` class methods to be run only if the `Trace` attribute of the website is enabled, then you need to specify this condition by using a `Boolean` property `Trace.IsEnabled. This` is a property of a Web page that returns True if the `Trace` attribute for the Web page is enabled.

Include the following syntax in a Web page to ensure that the code in the `Trace` class methods executes only when the `Trace` attribute is enabled:

```
If Trace.IsEnabled Then
  Trace.Write("Category", Message)
End if
```

The preceding syntax shows the use of the `Trace.Write()` method to display the trace statements. In addition, note the use of the `Trace.IsEnabled` property to conditionally run the `Trace.Write()` method. In this example, the trace information is sorted by category.

Summary

In this chapter, you have learned about the different ways of monitoring a website in ASP.NET. This chapter specifically discusses features that help in the monitoring process, such as performance counters, Web events, debugging, error or exception handling, and tracing. In addition, you have learned how to use all these features in sample websites.

In the next chapter, you explore the tools that help in managing Web applications, such as `aspnet_regsql` and `aspnet_regiis`.

23 Managing Web Applications

In Depth

The Web application management ensures that the Web applications remain error-free for a long time and also meet the end-user requirements. In the previous versions of ASP.NET, such as 1.x and 2.x, managing a Web application was not an easy task. The developer was required to perform certain coding techniques to manage Web applications. However, performing coding techniques increases the work load and decreases the developer's productivity. Microsoft realized this fact and decided to introduce new tools, configuration files, and Application Programming Interfaces (APIs) for better management of Web applications.

In this chapter, you learn about the need for managing Web applications, ASP.NET configuration system, and Process model configurations. In addition, you learn about various tools for managing Web applications, such as the Web Site Administration Tool, the `aspnet_regiis` tool, and the `aspnet_regsql` tool. This chapter also describes how to verify configuration settings by using the ProtectSection method, and configure ASP.NET applications in Internet Information Services (IIS).

Need to Manage Applications

You need to manage the applications to make them error free and extend their usability. For instance, suppose you create a Web application and suddenly the application stops working due to some problem with the Web server and you are unable to connect to the SQL Server. What will you do? You will find these errors and rectify them.

When such a problem occurs at the user's end, the user will be unable to work till the time the website starts functioning again. What should then be done to resolve such errors so that a Web application runs for a long time and is able to fulfill the end-users' requirements? The only solution is to manage the Web applications on a regular basis with the help of the ASP.NET configuration files so as to remove the errors and fulfill the requirements of the end user.

The ASP.NET Configuration File

The ASP.NET configuration file is a tool that includes Extensible Markup Language (XML)-based files used to define settings for a Web application or an individual page of the application. The two types of configuration files present in the ASP.NET configuration system are:

- **machine.config**—Refers to a server-specific configuration file
- **Web.config**— Refers to an application-specific configuration file

The default configuration settings for all the Web applications of ASP.NET 4.5 are defined in the `machine.config` file. You can find the `machine.config` file at the following location on the hard drive:

```
C:\Windows\Microsoft.NET\Framework\v4.0.30319\Config
```

The application-specific configuration settings specified in the `Web.config` file are applied to all the child directories. If a `Web.config` file is present in the root directory of a Web application, then the configuration settings are applied to the entire Web application. ASP.NET Framework configures the IIS server in such a way that an error is returned when an attempt is made to open a `Web.config` file through a browser. You can find the `Web.config` file at the following location on the hard drive:

```
C:\Windows\Microsoft.NET\Framework\v4.0.30319\Config
```

A `Web.config` file consists of various elements, such as tags, comments, and text with the `<configuration>` tag as their root element. The configuration settings of ASP.NET applications are included within the `<configuration>` tag. You can include the `<pages>` section under the `<system.web>` section, which is nested inside the `<configuration>` tag. The `<pages >` section is used to define configuration settings for the ASP.NET compiler, as shown in the following code snippet:

```
<configuration>
  <system.web>
        <pages enableViewState="false" />
  </system.web>
</configuration>
```

In the configuration section, the collection settings, which are collections of elements, such as HTTP Handler and providers, are included. You can use the `<add>` and `<remove>` tags to add and remove elements from a configuration section, respectively. If you want to remove the entire collection settings, you can use the `<clear>` tag. In a `Web.config` file, the configuration settings defined within the `<configuration>` tag are applied to the entire current directory where the `Web.config` file is located and also to all the child directories within this current directory. The `<location>` tag defined in the `Web.config` file with the path attribute is used to apply configuration settings to a specific path directory only.

The `<location>` tag can also be used with the `allowOverride` attribute. This attribute is set to true by default. When you want to ensure that the configuration settings in the current `Web.config` file are not overridden by configuration settings specified in another configuration file, you can set the `allowOverride` attribute to false. Further, an error is generated if you try to override the settings of the current `Web.config` file in another configuration file.

The configuration settings specified within a `Web.config` file are processed by configuration section handlers, which are .NET Framework classes inherited from the `ConfigurationSection` class.

After discussing about the configuration file, let's discuss about the configuration of the process model in ASP.NET.

The processModel Configuration

In ASP.NET, the process model protects the processes running on the IIS Web server from being modified by the end user. The process model configuration settings determine the time for a new process to start serving the requests sent by the requesting client. The `<processModel>` configuration section in the `machine.config` file contains the process model configuration settings. The process recycling feature of process model allows configuring an ASP.NET process so that the process restarts on certain conditions, such as after a specific interval of time or after the performance of a process is degraded due to memory leaks or deadlock conditions. The process model supports two types of recycling, which determine the beginning of the new processes to replace the current processes. The types of recycling are as follows:

- Reactive process recycling
- Proactive process recycling

Let's discuss these in detail, one by one.

Reactive Process Recycling

Reactive process recycling restarts a process when the process is not able to complete requests sent by the client computer. Various conditions, such as deadlocks and access violations, might cause a process to restart. To control the conditions causing a process to restart, you can use the following configuration settings:

- **requestQueueLimit**—Manages deadlock conditions
- **memoryLimit**—Manages memory leak conditions
- **shutdownTimeout**—Specifies the time to shut down a worker process, which is the process under which all ASP.NET functionalities run

Proactive Process Recycling

Proactive process recycling restarts a process periodically even if there is no error in the process. In proactive process recycling, a process restarts after the completion of a specific number of requests or the time-out period. The various configuration settings that trigger the proactive process are defined in the `<processModel>` configuration section of the `machine.config` file. The various settings are as follows:

- **timeout**—Specifies a time limit in the hr:min:sec format that indicates the time after which a new worker process starts replacing the current process
- **idleTimeout**—Specifies a time limit in the hr:min:sec format that indicates the duration of inactivity after which the process shuts down
- **requestLimit**—Indicates the number of requests after which a new process replaces the current process

You can use the `logLevel` attribute in the `<processModel>` configuration section of the `machine.config` file, to write process model events to the Windows event log when the process cycling events occur. The values of the `logLevel` attribute can be any one of the following:

- **All**—Indicates that all the process cycling events are logged in the Windows event log
- **None**—Indicates that no process cycling events are logged in the Windows event log
- **Errors**—Indicates that only unexpected or error events are logged in the Windows event log

Now, let's discuss the various tools for managing the Web applications in ASP.NET. The first tool is ASP.NET Microsoft Management Console (MMC) Snap-In Tool.

The ASP.NET MMC Snap-In Tool

ASP.NET MMC Snap-In is a management tool that enables you to modify the settings of the `Web.config` and `machine.config` files. The MMC Snap-In tool helps in configuring the settings for the applications deployed on a Web server.

NOTE

Only the administrator can modify the settings of the Web.config and machine.config files.

In IIS 7, the MMC Snap-In tool is included in the admin tool. The new admin tool of IIS 7 basically modifies the settings of the `Web.config` and the `machine.config` files. This new IIS 7 admin tool has the following advantages:

- Does not require administrator authority to manage the individual sites
- Provides extensibility support so that you can extend the use of IIS 7 admin tool
- Provides better server health information, diagnostics, and more user information as compared to the information provided by the MMC Snap-In tool

After discussing the ASP.NET MMC Snap-In tool, let's move on to discuss another tool, `aspnet_regiis`.

The aspnet_regiis Tool

There are instances when on a single computer multiple versions of .NET framework are executing side-by-side. In such a situation the ASP.NET Internet Server Application Programming Interface (ISAPI) version determines the version of Common Language Runtime (CLR) that is to be used for an ASP.NET application. This is when the aspnet_regiis tool comes in use, which allows the administrator to update the script maps associated with an ASP.NET application to point to the ASP.NET ISAPI version that is associated with the tool. The `aspnet_regiis` tool is a command line tool in .NET Framework, which is available in the version-specific framework directory under the `Microsoft.NET\Framework` subdirectory of the Windows system folder. When multiple websites are hosted on a Web server and each of these websites is bound to a particular version of .NET Framework, the `aspnet_regiis` tool proves to be quite useful. This is because it is included with each version of the framework. To simplify the configuration process for an ASP.NET application, each version of ASP.NET comes with a linked version of the `aspnet_regiis` tool. The syntax of the `aspnet_regiis` tool is as follows:

```
aspnet_regiis [options]
```

Table 23.1 shows various options that can be used with the `aspnet_regiis` tool:

Table 23.1: Options for the aspnet_regiis Tool

Option	Description
`-disable`	Disables ASP.NET applications on the IIS Security Console, when used with the `-i`, `-ir`, or `-r` option.
`-?`	Lists all the options that can be used with the `aspnet_regiis` tool.
`-c`	Installs the client-side scripts for ASP.NET to the `aspnet_client` subdirectory of the IIS site directory

Table 23.1: Options for the aspnet_regiis Tool

Option	Description
`-e`	Removes the client-side scripts from the aspnet_client subdirectory of each IIS site directory for the current version of ASP.NET.
`-ea`	Removes the client-side scripts from the `aspnet_client` subdirectory of the IIS directory for all the versions available.
`-enable`	Enables ASP.NET applications in the IIS Security Console, when used with the `-i`, `-ir`, or `-r` option.
`-ga user`	Provides a user or a user group access to the IIS metabase and the directories used by ASP.NET.
`-i`	Installs the `aspnet_regiis` tool. It also updates the script maps of the applications that use previous versions of ASP.NET.
`-ir`	Installs and registers the version of ASP.NET that supports the `aspnet_regiis` tool. However, if you use the `ir` option with the `aspnet_regiis` tool, the script maps of the applications do not update. For this, you need to use the -i option.
`-k path`	Removes all the script maps from an ASP.NET application at a specified application path and the subdirectories of the root directory. This option is not supported by the Windows 7 operating system.
`-kn path`	Removes all the script maps from an ASP.NET application at a specified application root path and its subdirectories. This option is not supported by the Windows 7 operating system.
`-lk`	Lists the path and version of IIS metabase keys. The inherited IIS metabase keys are not displayed.
`-lv`	Lists the status and installation path of all the versions of installed ASP.NET applications.
`-norestart`	Restricts the restart of the World Wide Web Publishing Service after installing or updating ASP.NET script maps. Without using this option, all applications pools are recycled. This option is not supported by the Windows 7 operating system.
`-r`	Installs the script maps for the ASP.NET version, which is supported by the `aspnet_regiis` tool, at the IIS metabase root and for all script maps below the root. The existing script maps are changed to this version, regardless of the current installed version of ASP.NET.
`-s path`	Installs the script map for the current ASP.NET version at the specified path and updates the existing script maps of previous versions with this version..
`-sn path`	Installs the script map for a ASP.NET version at a specified IIS metabase path of an application.
`-u`	Uninstalls the version of ASP.NET that supports the `aspnet_regiis` tool.
`-ua`	Uninstalls all the versions of ASP.NET already installed on a computer.

Now let's discuss about the Web Site Administration Tool, which is another tool for ASP.NET that helps in managing Web applications.

The Web Site Administration Tool

The Web Site Administration Tool is used to configure the application and security settings of an ASP.NET Web application. You can use the Web Site Administration Tool to perform the following tasks:

- Configuring the application security settings, such as authentication and authorization
- Managing users and roles for an application

- Creating and managing application settings
- Configuring Simple Mail Transfer Protocol (SMTP) e-mail settings
- Making an application temporarily offline to update its content and data in a secure manner
- Adjusting the debugging and tracing settings
- Defining a default custom error page
- Selecting providers to use them with the site features, such as membership

Let's now learn about the Aspnet_regsql tool.

The Aspnet_regsql Tool

The `Aspnet_regsql` tool is a command line tool used to create a Microsoft SQL Server database. The Microsoft SQL Server database that is created with the help of the `Aspnet_regsql` tool is used by SQL Server providers in ASP.NET for adding or removing options from the existing database. The following is the syntax for using the tool:

```
Aspnet_regsql.exe <options>
```

The `Aspnet_regsql` tool provides various options, which are described in Table 23.2:

Table 23.2: Aspnet_regsql Tool Options

Option	Description
`-?`	Displays the Help text for the `Aspnet_regsql` tool
`-C <connection string>`	Specifies the connection string
`-E`	Authenticates the user currently logged in, with current credentials provided by Windows
`-P <password>`	Specifies the password for SQL server, with `-U` option
`-S <server>`	Specifies the name of the computer where the SQL server database is installed or need to be installed
`-sqlexportonly <filename>`	Generates an SQL script file that can be used to add or remove the specified features from an ASP.NET application
`-U <login ID>`	Specifies the user name for SQL Server, with `-P` option
`-W`	Runs the `Aspnet_regsql` tool in the wizard mode

Now, after discussing the various aspects of ASP.NET for managing Web applications, let's move forward and look at their implementations in the *Immediate Solutions* section of this chapter.

Immediate Solutions

Verifying the Configuration Settings

After configuring settings for your Web application, you can also verify these settings by defining a configuration object in the `.aspx` file. The configuration object allows you to collect information, such as the hierarchy of configuration sections and configuration section groups in a Web application. You can use the `Configuration.RootSectionGroup` property to obtain the root of the hierarchy in a configuration file. In addition, you can use the `Configuration.GetSection` method to access a configuration section to verify the configuration settings.

Let's, create a new Web application and name it as `VerifiedSettings` (also available as `VerifiedSettingsVB` in VB and `VerifiedSettingsCS` in C#), and add the code, shown in Listing 23.1, in the `Default.aspx` page of the `VerifiedSettings` Web application:

Listing 23.1: Showing the Code for the `Default.aspx` Page

In VB

```
<%@ Page Language="VB" AutoEventWireup="false" CodeFile="Default.aspx.vb"
  Inherits="_Default" %>
<!DOCTYPE html>
<%@ Import Namespace="System.Configuration" %>
<%@ Import Namespace="System.Web.Configuration" %>
<%@ Import Namespace="System.IO" %>
<%@ Import Namespace="System.Xml" %>

<script runat="server" language="VB">
  Public Sub Page_Load(source As Object,e As EventArgs)
        Label1.Visible = False
        ConfigSections.Visible = False
  End Sub
  Protected Sub Button1_Click(sender As Object,e As EventArgs)
        Label1.Text = TextBox1.Text
        Dim con As System.Configuration.Configuration =
        WebConfigurationManager.OpenWebConfiguration(TextBox1.Text)
        Dim textwriter As StringWriter = New StringWriter()
        Dim textXml As XmlTextWriter = New XmlTextWriter(textwriter)
        textXml.Formatting = Formatting.Indented
        textXml.WriteStartElement("configuration")
        Enumerate(con.RootSectionGroup, textXml)
        textXml.WriteFullEndElement()
        textXml.Flush()
        ConfigSections.Text = Chr(13) & Chr(10) &
        Server.HtmlEncode(textwriter.ToString())
        Label1.Visible = True
        ConfigSections.Visible = True
        Try
                Dim section As PagesSection = CType(con.GetSection("system.web/pages"),
                PagesSection)
                Label2.Text = section.SectionInformation.ToString()
                Label3.Text = section.EnableViewState.ToString()
                Dim sec As String = TextBox2.Text
                Dim settings As ConfigurationSection = con.GetSection(sec)
                Label6.Text = Chr(13) & Chr(10) &
                Server.HtmlEncode(Settings.SectionInformation.GetRawXml())
                Label5.Text = TextBox2.Text
                Catch
                TextBox1.Text = "invalid section name"
        End Try
  End Sub
  Sub Enumerate(grp As ConfigurationSectionGroup,writeXML As XmlWriter)
        Dim x As Integer
        Dim configsection As ConfigurationSectionCollection = grp.Sections
        For x = 0 To configsection.Count - 1
                writeXML.WriteStartElement(configsection(x).SectionInformation.Name)
```

```
                writeXML.WriteEndElement()
        Next
    End Sub
</script>

<html xmlns="http://www.w3.org/1999/xhtml">
<head runat="server">
    <title>Configuration Sections</title>
</head>
<body>
    <form id="form1" runat="server">
    <div>
    <h2>
                Enter the Virtual Path of the WebSite:</h2>
                <p>
                 <asp:TextBox ID="TextBox1" runat="server" BorderStyle="Double"
                Width="464px"></asp:TextBox></p>
                <p>
                Enter section you need to verify        <asp:TextBox
                ID="TextBox2"
                runat="server" BorderStyle="Double" Width="201px"></asp:TextBox>
                </p>
                <p>
                <asp:Button ID="Button1" runat="server" Text="Verify Settings"
                OnClick="Button1_Click" /> </p>
                <h2>
                <asp:Label runat="server" ID="Label1" /> </h2>
                <p>
                SectionInformation:   <asp:Label runat="server" ID="Label2"
                /> </p>
                <p>
                EnableViewState:      <asp:Label runat="server"
                ID="Label3" /></p>
                <p>
                        <asp:Label runat="server" ID="Label5" Width="111px" /> 
                        <asp:Label runat="server" ID="Label6" /></p>
                <p>
                        _______________________________________________</p>
                <p>
                         <asp:Label runat="server" ID="ConfigSections" /></p>
                <pre>
                </pre>
    </div>
    </form>
</body>
</html>
```

In C#

```
<%@ Page Language="C#" AutoEventWireup="true" CodeFile="Default.aspx.cs"
  Inherits="_Default" %>
<!DOCTYPE html>
<%@ Import Namespace="System.Configuration" %>
<%@ Import Namespace="System.Web.Configuration" %>
<%@ Import Namespace="System.IO" %>
<%@ Import Namespace="System.Xml" %>
<script runat="server" language="C#">
  public void Page_Load(object source, EventArgs e)
  {
        Label1.Visible = false;
        ConfigSections.Visible = false;
  }
  void Enumerate(ConfigurationSectionGroup grp, XmlWriter writeXML)
  {
        ConfigurationSectionCollection configsection = grp.Sections;
        for (int x = 0; x < configsection.Count; x++)
        {
              writeXML.WriteStartElement(configsection[x].SectionInformation.Name);
              writeXML.WriteEndElement();
        }
  }
```

```
    protected void Button1_Click(object sender, EventArgs e)
    {
        Label1.Text = TextBox1.Text;
        Configuration con = WebConfigurationManager.OpenWebConfiguration(TextBox1.Text);
        StringWriter textwriter = new StringWriter();
        XmlTextWriter textXml = new XmlTextWriter(textwriter);
        textXml.Formatting = Formatting.Indented;
        textXml.WriteStartElement("configuration");
        Enumerate(con.RootSectionGroup, textXml);
        textXml.WriteFullEndElement();
        textXml.Flush();
        ConfigSections.Text = "\r\n" + Server.HtmlEncode(textwriter.ToString());
        Label1.Visible = true;
        ConfigSections.Visible = true;
        try
        {
                PagesSection section = (PagesSection)con.GetSection("system.web/pages");
                Label2.Text = section.SectionInformation.ToString();
                Label3.Text = section.EnableViewState.ToString();
                String sec = TextBox2.Text;
                ConfigurationSection Settings = con.GetSection(sec);
                Label6.Text = "\r\n" +
                Server.HtmlEncode(Settings.SectionInformation.GetRawXml());
                Label5.Text = TextBox2.Text;
        }
        catch
        {
                TextBox1.Text = "invalid section name";
        }
    }
</script>

<html xmlns="http://www.w3.org/1999/xhtml">
<head runat="server">
    <title>Configuration Sections</title>
</head>
<body>
    <form id="form1" runat="server">
    <div>
        <h2>
                Enter the Virtual Path of the WebSite:</h2>
                <p>
                 <asp:TextBox ID="TextBox1" runat="server" BorderStyle="Double"
                Width="464px"></asp:TextBox></p>
                <p>
                Enter section you need to verify        <asp:TextBox
                ID="TextBox2"
                runat="server" BorderStyle="Double" Width="201px"></asp:TextBox>
                </p>
                <p>
                <asp:Button ID="Button1" runat="server" Text="Verify Settings"
                OnClick="Button1_Click" /> </p>
                <h2>
                <asp:Label runat="server" ID="Label1" /> </h2>
                <p>
                SectionInformation:   <asp:Label runat="server" ID="Label2"
                /> </p>
                <p>
                EnableViewState:      <asp:Label runat="server"
                ID="Label3" /></p>
                <p>
                        <asp:Label runat="server" ID="Label5" Width="111px" /> 
                        <asp:Label runat="server" ID="Label6" /></p>
                <p>
                        ________________________________________</p>
                <p>
                         <asp:Label runat="server" ID="ConfigSections" /></p>
                <pre>
                </pre>
</div></form></body></html>
```

Run the Web application by pressing the F5 key on the keyboard. The final output is shown in Figure 23.1:

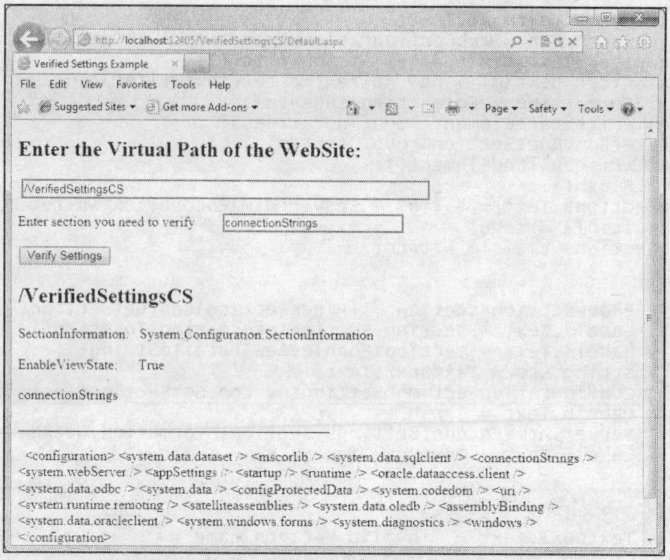

Figure 23.1: Showing Verified Settings

After verifying the settings that you have configured in the Web.config file, let's learn to use the aspnet_regiis tool of ASP.NET.

Using the Aspnet_Regiis Tool

To use the `aspnet_regiis` tool, you need to first open the Developer Command Prompt for VS2012 (as an administrator). After opening the command prompt, type and execute the following command to view the list of all the options of the `aspnet_regiis` tool:

```
aspnet_regiis -?
```

Figure 23.2 shows the output after executing this command:

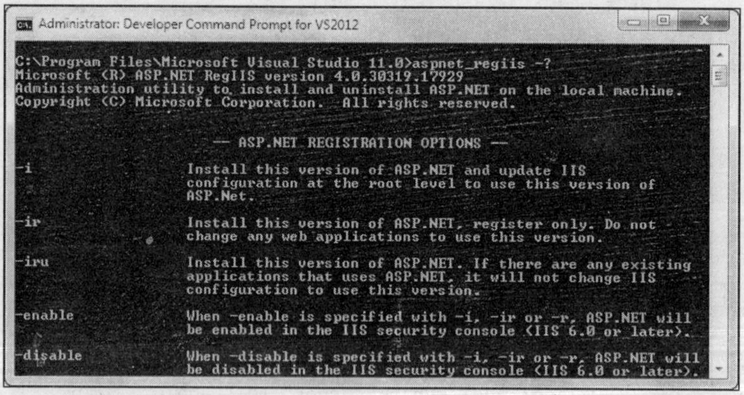

Figure 23.2: Displaying the Options of the aspnet_regiis Tool in the Command Prompt

Now, let's see the execution of another option, `-lk`, with the `aspnet_regiis` tool in the Visual Studio Command Prompt (2012) that allows you to view the path and version of the IIS metabase keys. Type and execute the following command on the command prompt

```
aspnet_regiis -lk
```

Figure 23.3 shows the output after executing this command:

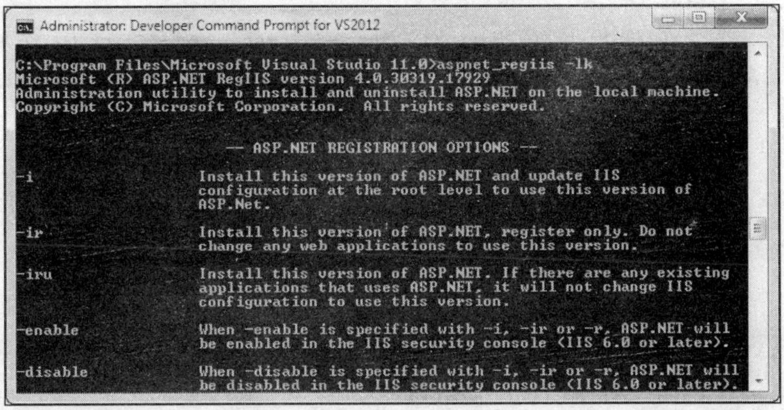

Figure 23.3: Displaying the Path and Version of the IIS Metabase Keys in the Command Prompt

Now, let's use the `ProtectSection` method to secure the configuration sections of the `Web.config` file.

Using the ProtectSection Method

You can use the `ProtectSection` method to encrypt the configuration sections of the `Web.config` file. This method is used with the `SectionInformation` property to retrieve the section information. Now, let's create an application named `ProtectedSection` (also available in `ProtectedSectionVB` in VB and `ProtectedSectionCS` in C#), in which we use the `ProtectSection` method. Perform the following steps to use the `ProtectSection` method in the Web application:

1. Add the code, shown in Listing 23.2, to use the `ProtectSection` method to encrypt a connection string section of the configuration file, in the `Default.aspx`.:

Listing 23.2: Showing the code for the `Default.aspx` Page

In VB

```
<%@ Page Language="VB" AutoEventWireup="false" CodeFile="Default.aspx.vb"
  Inherits="_Default" %>
<!DOCTYPE html>
<%@ Import Namespace="System.Configuration" %>
<%@ Import Namespace="System.Web.Configuration" %>
<script runat="server" language="VB">
  Protected Sub button1_Click(sender As Object,e As EventArgs)
  Handles button1.Click
        Const PROVIDER As String = "DataProtectionConfigurationProvider"
        Dim con As Configuration
        con = WebConfigurationManager.OpenWebConfiguration(Request.ApplicationPath)
        Dim sect As ConnectionStringsSection = con.ConnectionStrings
        sect.SectionInformation.ProtectSection(PROVIDER)
        con.Save()
        label1.Text = "Section of Web.config is now encrypted<br>"
        label1.Text = label1.Text & "Connection String you have provided is:" &
        ConfigurationManager.ConnectionStrings("Northwind").ConnectionString
  End Sub
</script>
<html xmlns="http://www.w3.org/1999/xhtml">
<head runat="server">
    <title>Using ProtectSection Method</title>
</head>
<body>
    <form id="form1" runat="server">
    <div>
        <br />
                <strong><span style="text-decoration: underline"><em>Use of
                ProtectSection Method
                <br />
```

```
                        </em></span></strong>
                        <br />
                        <br />
                        <asp:Button ID="button1" runat="server" Text="Click Me to Encrypt the
                        Connection String"
                        Width="481px" Height="35px" OnClick="button1_Click" Font-Size="Medium" />
                        <br />
                        <br />
                        <br />
                        <asp:Label ID="label1" runat="server" Height="19px"
                        Width="435px"></asp:Label>
    </div>
    </form>
</body>
</html>
```

In C#

```
<%@ Page Language="C#" AutoEventWireup="true" CodeFile="Default.aspx.cs"
  Inherits="_Default" %>
<!DOCTYPE html>
<%@ Import Namespace="System.Configuration" %>
<%@ Import Namespace="System.Web.Configuration" %>
<script runat="server" language="C#">
  const string PROVIDER = "DataProtectionConfigurationProvider";
  protected void button1_Click(object sender, EventArgs e)
  {
        Configuration con =
        WebConfigurationManager.OpenWebConfiguration(Request.ApplicationPath);
        ConnectionStringsSection sect = con.ConnectionStrings;
        sect.SectionInformation.ProtectSection(PROVIDER);
        con.Save();
        label1.Text = "Section of Web.config is now encrypted<br>";
        label1.Text += "Connection String you have provided is:" +
       ConfigurationManager.ConnectionStrings["Northwind"].ConnectionString;
  }
</script>
<html xmlns="http://www.w3.org/1999/xhtml">
<head runat="server">
    <title>Using ProtectSection Method</title>
</head>
<body>
    <form id="form1" runat="server">
    <div>
    <br />
                        <strong><span style="text-decoration: underline"><em>Use of
                        ProtectSection Method
                        <br />
                        </em></span></strong>
                        <br />
                        <br />
                        <asp:Button ID="button1" runat="server" Text="Click Me to Encrypt the
                        Connection String"
                        Width="481px" Height="35px" OnClick="button1_Click" Font-Size="Medium" />
                        <br />
                        <br />
                        <br />
                        <asp:Label ID="label1" runat="server" Height="19px"
                        Width="435px"></asp:Label>
    </div>
    </form>
</body>
</html>
```

2. Add the `<connectionStrings>` section in the `Web.config` file, as shown in the following code snippet:

```
<connectionStrings>
  <add name="Northwind" connectionString="Data Source=PUNEET-PC\\SQLEXPRESS;Initial
  Catalog=Northwind;Integrated Security=True"/>
</connectionStrings>
```

3. Run the Web application. A screen similar to Figure 23.4 is displayed:

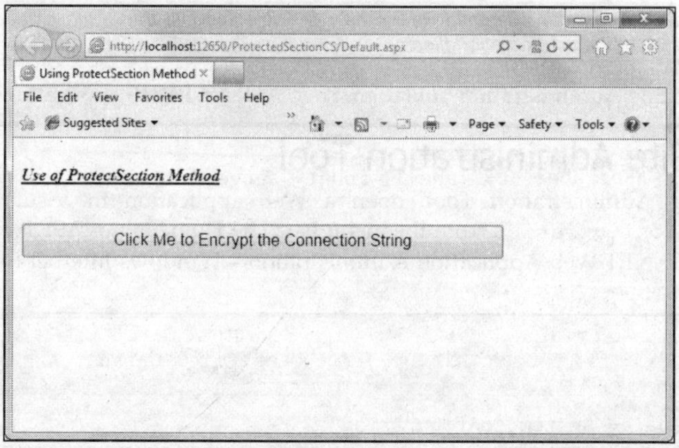

Figure 23.4: Displaying the ProtectedSection Example at Work

4. Click the Click Me to Encrypt the Connection String button on the `Default.aspx` page to encrypt the `Web.config` file connection string section. Figure 23.5 shows the output after clicking the button:

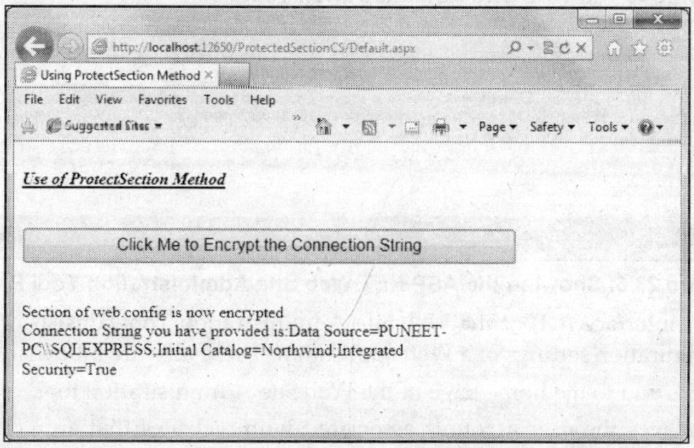

Figure 23.5: Displaying the Default.aspx with Connection String

Now, when you open the `Web.config` file, you are presented with the encrypted data in the `<connectionStrings>` section, as shown in the following code snippet:

```
    <connectionStrings configProtectionProvider="DataProtectionConfigurationProvider">
        <EncryptedData>
          <CipherData>
    <CipherValue>AQAAANCMnd8BFdERjHoAwE/Cl+sBAAAACu3nd2w47UyuzHVOo413tgQAAAACAAAAAAAQZgAAAAEAA
CAAAACxQT5dNPTDYHrNDotqR0hXvspU6Xp5l+9fvEUXM34YZAAAAAAOgAAAAIAACAAAAA+8flBMO91Injhy04p0bcrFqv
BADljw1TtQmw+9/d2wIABAAB0YlV5RsNE3qR4U0XUXwhIyTKHZTroMXQNjTfPGVwWDcdD78vwUF2ndXDBrq1QNnpLK1zcX
yk6AQJ6c4Apw4hO1Wjla8W17XrhQkzyyK75v4Xk+ggCh/TMjLCUILo4CjMjRxzIWQcog6uWfqCiBQcAC+Ct4e41sZtrCEu
XtyL8hf4dtG2kG9BFR2WwGRPNt4VJaAhCoqiENjEqQIu9tf5pidPE1pdqFzzkHdRz/UpKPtUNjhGmZhkIPc7++CWqkrK7T
4Z4XaghMZIT5YKHq9RZ2Gioz6KBSAhpYxcRGgkgtWjbt7t7UC0Tm+UVl9oO2kyZZcMEWLFvAg1q/fNjVzKg6Byo2GS9r2b
8oxv1ZIMpZtgZLMLnxk0hJjNzWaLHW0oc5G5Km9Xld6JmTTs1crUeVE8KUr3LCUQ7qFwo+9V4uvie31iGZI+wK7XNXY+Gt
/0iss9S1GjuyGSqRaQ1uH9TRCiwPQyx5DaACoMQ8UJHz2h61za77DHYUZf9zlKCvXxAAAAA0LyuuIBL8vZ/HvN+YnzpINl
QDi2LM/2v7Ac+kp3AjygeUCru8mLaWz424HRD8r2rBYsXclXP4WeMLFU8bsJ9cg==</CipherValue>
          </CipherData>
        </EncryptedData>
      </connectionStrings>
```

NOTE

You must give write permission to the Web.config file for the ASP.NET account to run the preceding code. You can also use the aspnet_regiis tool to encrypt the configuration files.

Now, let's use the Web Site Administration Tool to manage ASP.NET Web applications.

Using the Web Site Administration Tool

To use the Web Site Administration Tool, open a Web application in Visual Studio 2012 and select `WEBSITE→ASP.NET Configuration` from the menu bar. The Home tab of ASP.Net Web Site Administration Tool appears in the ASP.NET Web Application Administration - Windows Internet Explorer window, as shown in Figure 23.6:

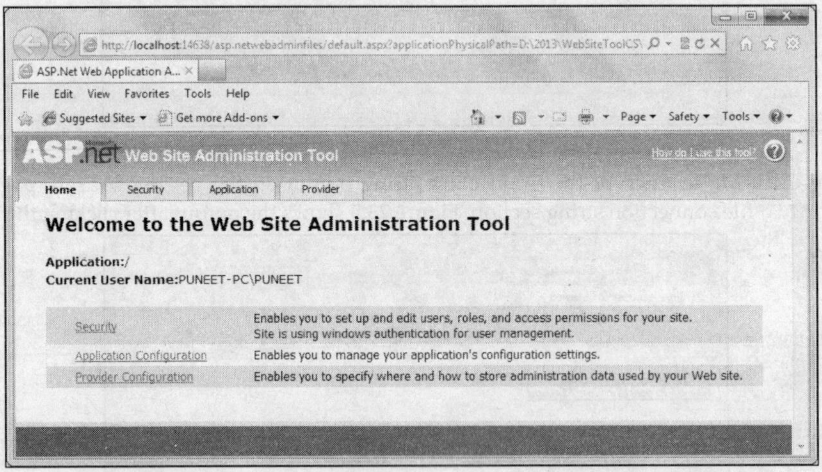

Figure 23.6: Showing the ASP.NET Web Site Administration Tool Page

In Figure 23.6, the user interface (UI) of the Web Site Administration Tool consists of different tabs that can be used to group the configuration settings of a Web application. These tabs are follows:

- **Home tab**—Returns you to the home page of the Web Site Administration tool.
- **Security tab**—Manages the user accounts associated with websites that are accessing a Web application, creates roles for the users, and provides different access rules for the users. For example, you might create roles, such as managers and members, and provide different access rights to specific folders.
- **Application tab**—Manages the settings to determine how a Web application sends an e-mail, such as SMTP. In addition, the settings also enable you to determine the online and offline settings of a Web application.
- **Provider tab**—Configures providers for storing website management data.

Let's discuss about these tabs in detail.

Using the Security Tab

The Security tab of the ASP.NET Web Site Administration Tool enables you to manage user accounts, roles, and rules for accessing Web applications. To open this tool for your ASP.NET Web site select the WEBSITE menu in Visual Studio 2012 IDE and click **ASP.NET Configuration option.** The page that opens when you select the Security tab of the Web Site Administration Tool is shown in Figure 23.7:

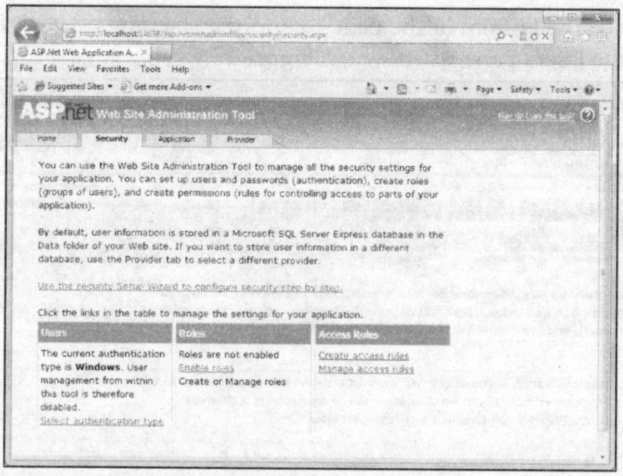

Figure 23.7: Showing the Security Tab of the Web Site Administration Tool

NOTE

By default, the Roles on the Security page are disabled and the authentication type is windows.

Various panes in the Security tab, as shown in Figure 23.7, are as follows:

- Users pane
- Roles pane
- Access Rules pane

The Users pane of the Security tab enables you to configure a Web application to use either the Forms-based authentication or Integrated Microsoft Windows authentication method. The Forms-based authentication method is used for Web applications that are accessed over the Internet. However, the Integrated Microsoft Windows authentication method is used to access the Web applications over a local network. When the Integrated Microsoft Windows authentication method is used, you can automatically log on to Web applications after logging on to a Windows-based network.

Now, let's perform the following steps to work with the Security tab:

1. Click the Select authentication type link in the Users pane of the Security page to open a page containing two radio buttons, From the internet and From a local network.
2. Select an option on the page to indicate if the Web application can be accessed over the Internet or from a local network. In our case, we have selected the From the internet option, as shown in Figure 23.8:

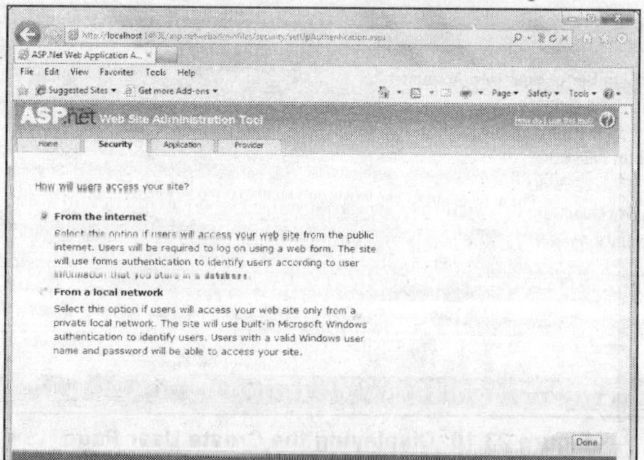

Figure 23.8: Showing the SetUpAuthentication page

3. Click the Done button at the bottom of the page to apply the settings. The Create user link and the Manage users link appears in the Users pane, as shown in Figure 23.9:

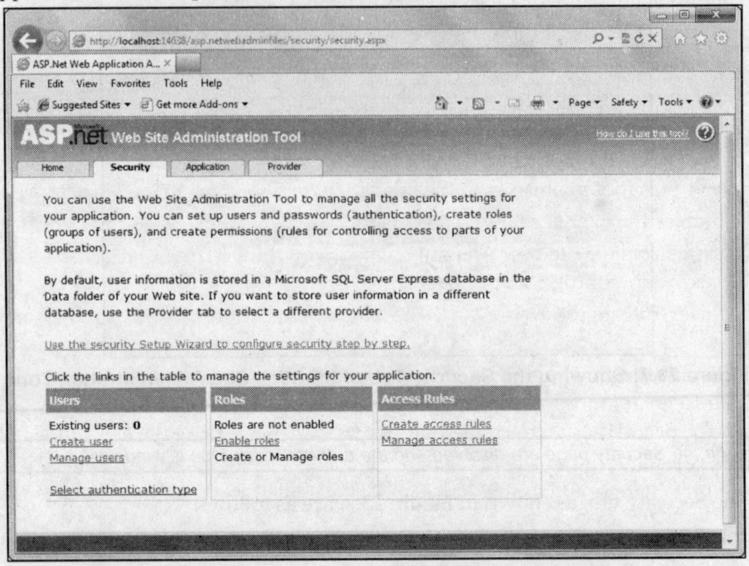

Figure 23.9: Showing the Create user and Manage users Link

> **NOTE**
> *You can click the Manage users link to manage (add, modify, or delete) the existing users.*

4. Click the Create user link on the Users pane of the Security page (Figure 23.9) to specify a user account for the new user of the Web application (Figure 23.10):

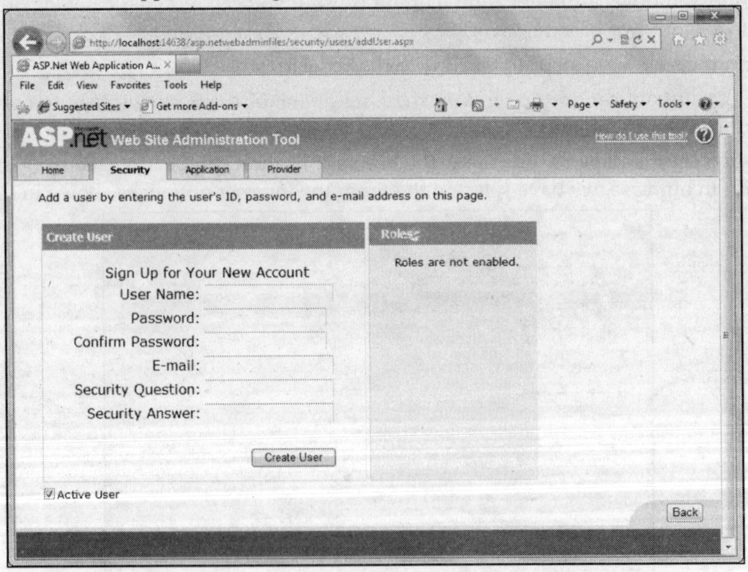

Figure 23.10: Displaying the Create User Page

Figure 23.10 shows the following fields that need to be filled:

- **User Name**—Specifies the name of a user for creating a user account.
- **Password**—Specifies a password for the user name. The password specified is case-sensitive.
- **Confirm Password**—Confirms the password again for the user.
- **E-mail**—Specifies the e-mail address of the new user.
- **Security Question**—Specifies a question that should appear when the user needs to reset or recover the password.
- **Security Answer**—Specifies an answer to the security question given in the Security Question text box.
- **Active User**—Enables the user account created as the active (current) user of the Web application.
- **Roles**—Indicates the role for the user account created. The roles for the user accounts are created separately by using the Roles section of the Security page.

5. Enter the new user information and click the Create User button to accept the new user information (Figure 23.10).

   A message is displayed which specifies that the account has been created successfully. You can click the Continue button to create more users or the Back button to go back to the Security page. You can use the Roles section of the Security page to create roles for the users accessing the Web application.

6. Click the Enable roles link under the Roles pane of the Security page. When you click the Enable roles link, the name of the link changes to Disable Roles and also enables the Create or Manage roles link, as shown in Figure 23.11:

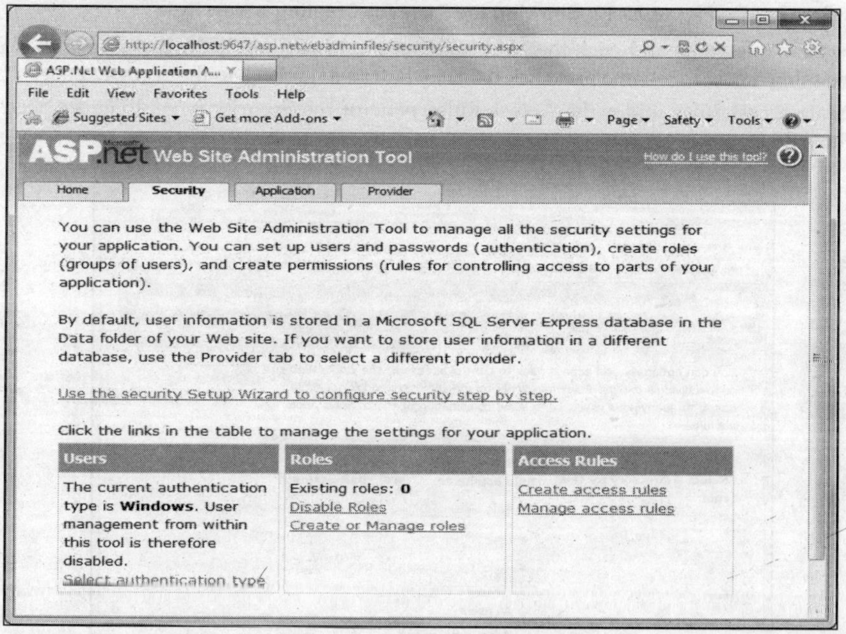

Figure 23.11: Showing the Disable Roles and Create or Manage Roles Links Under the Roles Pane

7. Click the Create or Manage roles link under the Roles pane of the Security page to display a page that allows you to create a new role, as shown in Figure 23.12:

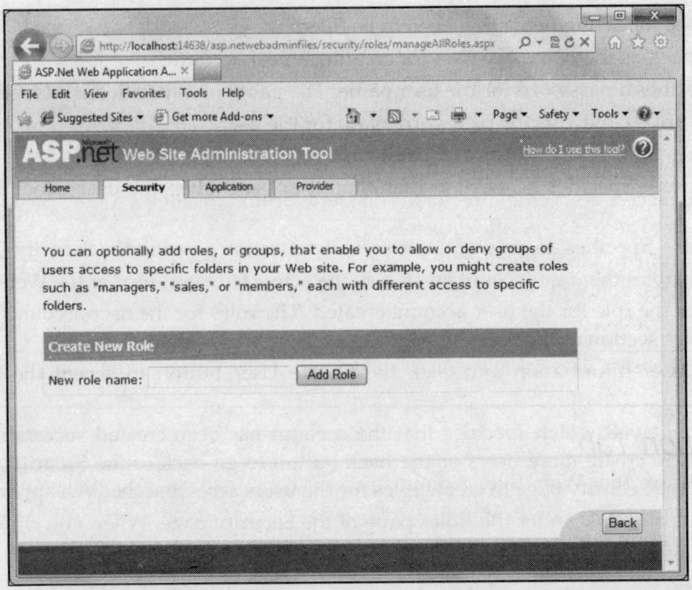

Figure 23.12: Showing the Page for Creating a New Role

8. Enter the new role name and click the Add Role button, to add a role for the user of the Web application after specifying a new role name and click the Back button to go back to the Security page.
9. Click Create access rules under the Access Rules pane of the Security page, to create access rules for the users. The Add New Access Rule group appears, as shown in Figure 23.13:

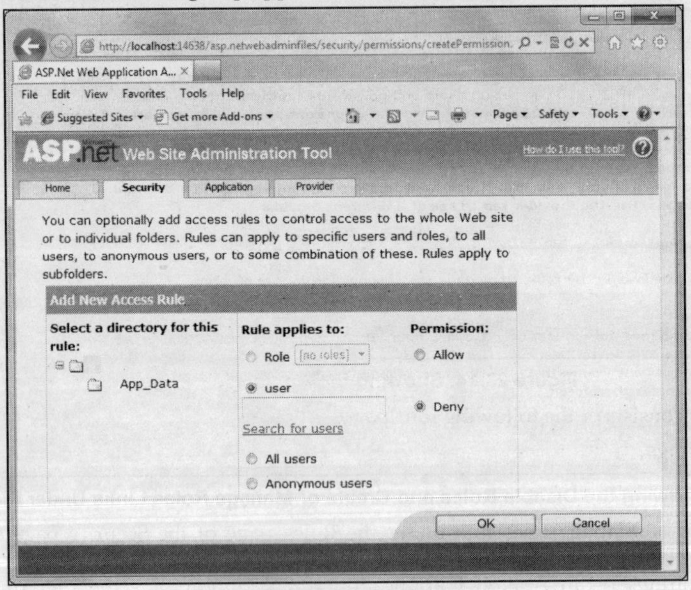

Figure 23.13: Adding New Access Rule

Figure 23.13 shows various panes in the Add New Access Rule group that assist in adding a new access rule. These fields are as follows:

- **Select a directory for this rule**—Enables you to select the rules that are created either for the entire Web application or for only a specific directory.

- **Rule applies to**—Enables you to select a role for which the access rules are applied. You can select the user radio button to enter the user account for which the access rules are specified. You can also select the All users radio button so that the access rules apply to all the users accessing the Web application. In addition, the Anonymous users radio button allows you to apply access rules to the non-registered user accounts only.
- **Permission**—Enables you to select either the Allow or Deny option. The Allow option helps a specified user account or role to access a specific directory. The Deny option disallows a user account or role indicated in the previous fields to access a specific directory.

10. Click the OK button to close the Add New Access Rule group and apply the settings specified. After applying the settings, you will be redirected to the Home tab.

NOTE

You can click the Manage access rules link in the Access Rules pane of the Security page to modify the access rules created earlier.

Using the Application Tab

The Application tab of the Web Site Administration Tool enables you to modify application-specific configurations, such as `appSettings`, `Debugging`, and `Tracing`. Figure 23.14 shows the Application tab of the Web Site Administration Tool:

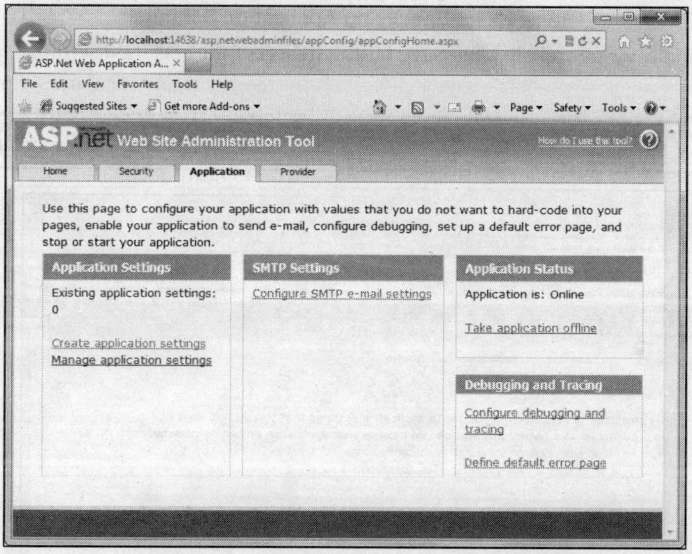

Figure 23.14: Showing the Application Page

The Applications tab consists of the following four panes:

- Application Settings
- SMTP Settings
- Application Status
- Debugging and Tracing

The configuration settings of an ASP.NET application can be modified using the Application page. In the Application Settings pane, click the Create application settings link. It opens a page that allows you to specify values for the Name and Value fields, as shown in Figure 23.15:

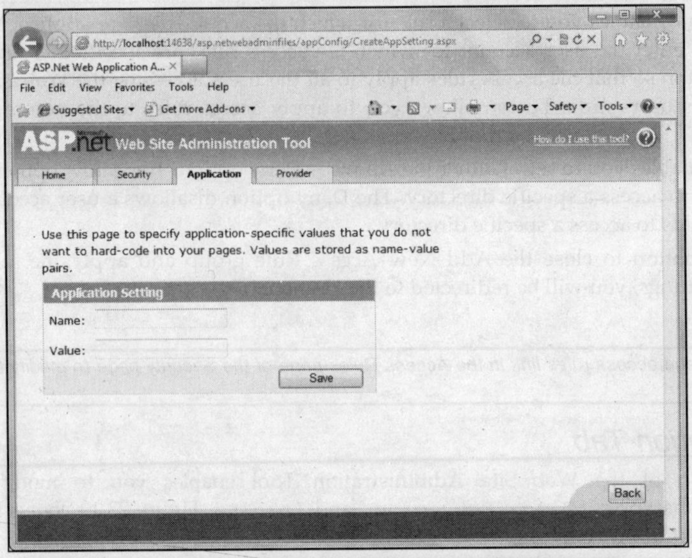

Figure 23.15: Specifying Application Settings

Specify the application settings and click the Save button to accept the specified settings.

NOTE

You can also manage the application settings by clicking the Manage application settings link in the Application Settings pane that allows you to view the existing settings and create new application settings, as shown in Figure 23.16:

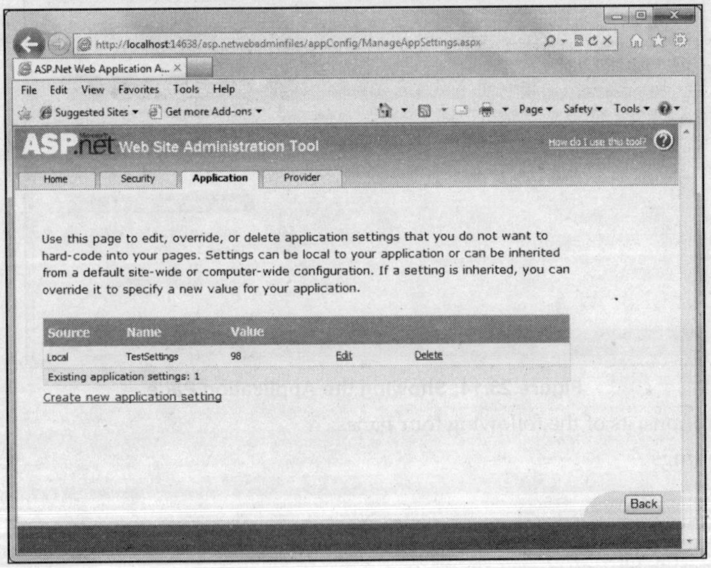

Figure 23.16: Managing Application Settings

In addition, the Application tab also allows you to create new settings. You can modify the application status by clicking the Take application link (offline link to take the Web application offline) in the Application Status pane.

The debugging settings of a Web application can also be edited by clicking the Configure debugging and tracing link to display a page in the Debugging and Tracing pane. The page that appears after you click Configure debugging and tracing link is as shown in Figure 23.17:

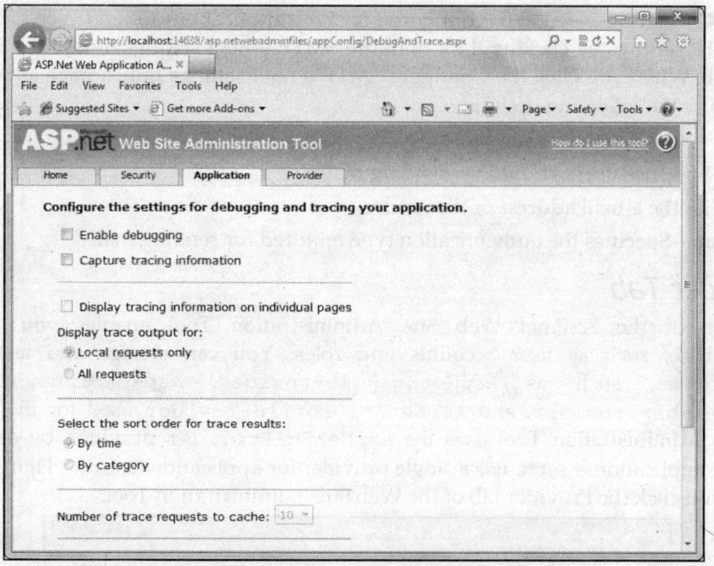

Figure 23.17: Configuring Settings for Debugging and Tracing Application

In Figure 23.17, select the Enable debugging check box to enable debugging. Select the Capture tracing information check box to display tracing information for the Web application. You can also define the default page that appears when an error occurs by clicking the Define default error page link in the Debugging and Tracing pane of the Application tab. The page that appears after you click the Define default error page link is shown in Figure 23.18:

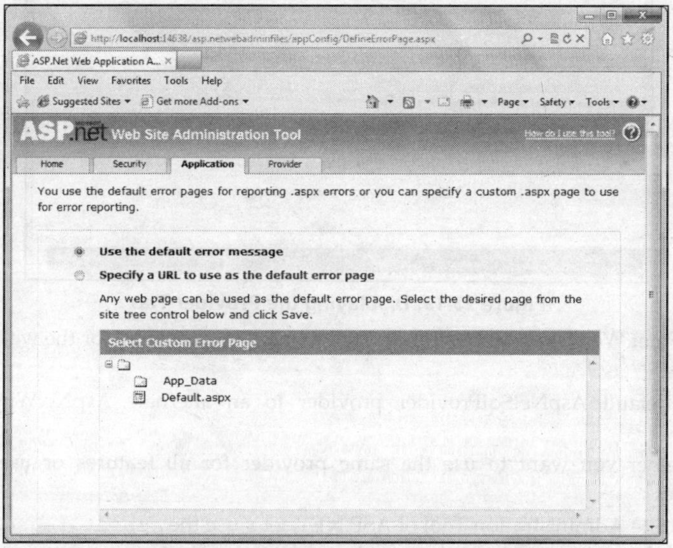

Figure 23.18: Displaying the Default Error Page

NOTE

In Figure 23.18, you can either specify a default error message by selecting the Use the default error message radio button or specify a Uniform Resource Locator (URL) by selecting the Specify a URL to use as the default error page radio button. The second option is used for redirection in case an error condition occurs.

Sometimes, the SMTP settings need to be configured for Web applications to send Web data by using SMTP. You can configure SMTP settings by clicking the Configure SMTP e-mail settings link in the SMTP Settings pane of the Application tab. When you click the Configure SMTP e-mail settings link, a page appears in which you will be asked to configure the following options:

- **Server Name**—Specifies the server name for the e-mail server
- **Server Port**—Specifies the port used for sending mails
- **From**—Specifies the e-mail address of the sender
- **Authentication**—Specifies the authentication type required for sending mails

Using the Provider Tab

The Provider tab of the ASP.net Web Site Administration Tool enables you to manage the data stored in a database, such as user accounts and roles. You can change and test providers by using the provider classes, such as `AspNetSqlRoleProvider`, `AspNetWindowsTokenRoleProvider`, `AspNetSqlMembershipProvider`, and `AspNetSqlProfileProvider` used for the Web application. The ASP.net Web Site Administration Tool uses the `AspNetSqlProvider` provider, by default, for all the Web applications, if the application is set to use a single provider for application features. Figure 23.19 shows the page that opens when you click the Provider tab of the Web Site Administration Tool:

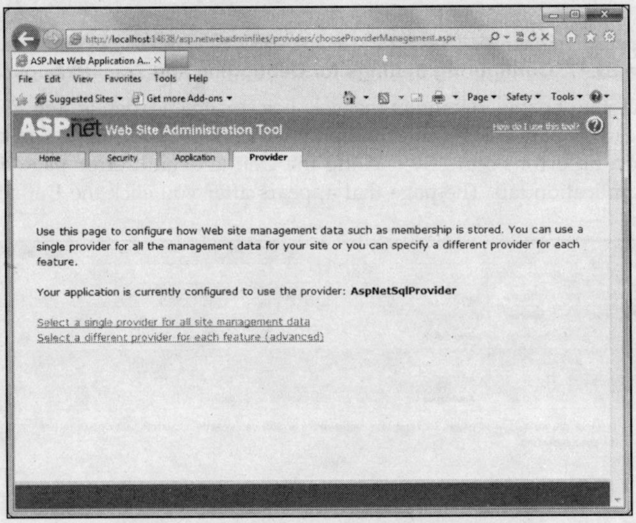

Figure 23.19: Displaying the Provider Tab

You can use the ASP.net Web Site Administration Tool to manage providers for the website in the following two ways:

- Changing the default AspNetSqlProvider provider to an alternate AspNetWindowsTokenRoleProvider provider
- Specifying whether you want to use the same provider for all features or use different providers for different features

After using the Web Site Administration Tool of ASP.NET, let's use the `Aspnet_regsql` tool.

Using the Aspnet_regsql Tool

To use the `Aspnet_regsql` tool, open the Developer Command Prompt for VS2012 window and type the following command to view the list of all options of the `Aspnet_regsql` tool and press Enter from the keyboard:

```
aspnet_regsql.exe -?
```

The output of the preceding command is shown in Figure 23.20:

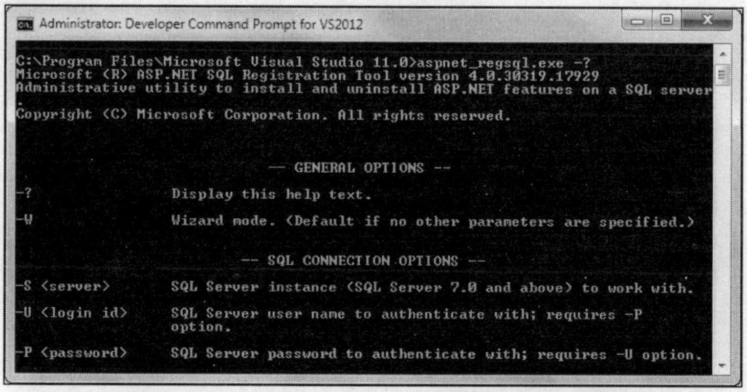

Figure 23.20: Displaying the Output of the aspnet_regsql Command

You can also run the `Aspnet_regsql` tool in the wizard mode by using the following command:

```
aspnet_regsql.exe -W
```

The output of the preceding command displays ASP.NET SQL Server Setup Wizard. This wizard enables you to configure the SQL Server database. The Welcome to the ASP.NET SQL Server Setup Wizard page of the ASP.NET SQL Server Setup Wizard is as shown in Figure 23.21:

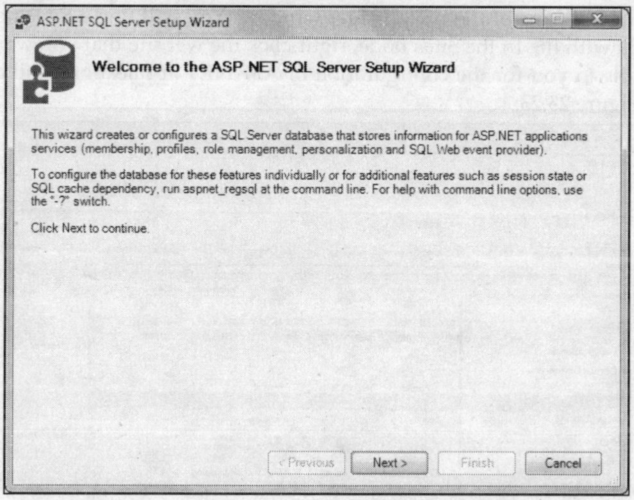

Figure 23.21: Showing the ASP.NET SQL Server Setup Wizard

The wizard displayed in Figure 23.21 can be used to configure the SQL Server database for the required application services. When you click the Next button, you are presented with two options, either to configure the SQL Server for application services or to remove the application services from an existing database. Select the options according to your requirement and configure the database for the required services.

After using the tools for ASP.NET for managing Web applications, let's learn how to configure ASP.NET applications in IIS.

Configuring ASP.NET Applications in IIS

Nowadays, configuring ASP.NET applications has become quite easy with the help of IIS Manager. You can open the IIS Manager window by entering `inetmgr` in the Run dialog box. Figure 23.22 shows the IIS Manager window:

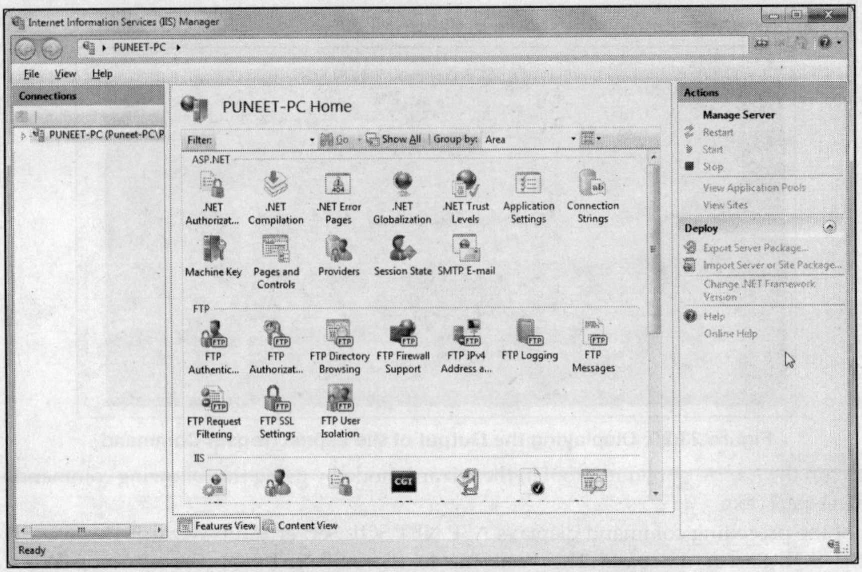

Figure 23.22: Displaying the IIS Manager Window

Expand the nodes on the left pane of the IIS Manager window. You will find a Sites node, which contains all the sites configured to work with IIS. In the Sites node, right-click the website that you want to configure. You notice that the options available to you for the configuration of ASP.NET applications will appear in the IIS Manager window, as shown in Figure 23.23:

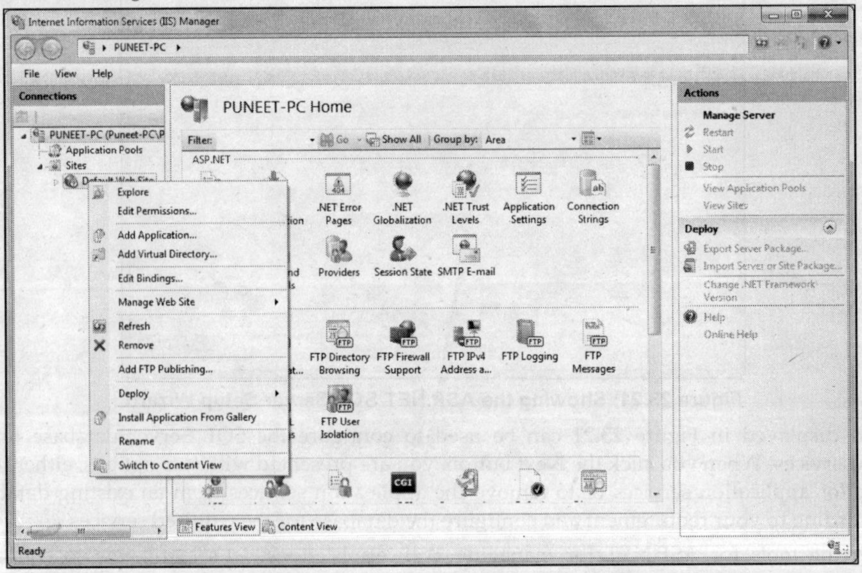

Figure 23.23: Displaying the Configuration Options in the IIS Manager Window

With the options available in the IIS Manager window, you can not only configure ASP.NET applications but also the IIS itself. You can also select the actions to be performed from the Actions pane on the right side of the IIS Manager window. You can even configure some of the basic settings of the sites by clicking the Basic Settings link in the Actions pane. The Edit Application dialog box appears, as shown in Figure 23.24:

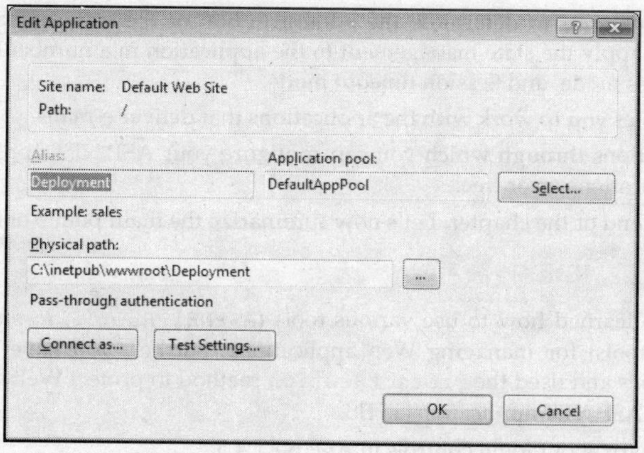

Figure 23.24: Showing the Edit Application Dialog Box

The Edit Application dialog box displays the following items:

- The name of the website.
- The Application pool, which is used for the application. There are four options in the Application pool, DefaultAppPool (which uses .NET Framework 2.0 and integrated pipeline mode) and Classic .NET AppPool (which uses .NET Framework 2.0 and classic pipeline mode), ASP.NET v4.0 which uses .NET Framework 4.0, and ASP.NET v4.0 Classic ASP.NET v4.0 Classic and classic pipeline mode.
- The Physical path, which contains the location of the ASP.NET application.

In addition to the basic settings of the applications, some options provided to you through the icons in the IIS Manager window are as follows:

- **.NET Compilation**—Specifies the compilation and running process of the application. You can also define the default language that is to be used in the compilation process, such as VB or C#.
- **.NET Globalization**—Allows you to specify the way in which the ASP.NET application is expected to deal with the culture and the encoding of the requests and responses, such as Unicode Transformation Format (UTF)-8, UTF-6, and US- American Standard Code for Information Interchange (ASCII).
- **.NET Profile**—Specifies the way in which the ASP.NET application is expected to deal with the ASP.NET personalization system. You can also specify the provider that is used by the system. By default, the AspNetSqlProfileProvider provider is used.
- **.NET Roles**—Adds roles to the ASP.NET application, which is used in the role-based management.
- **.NET Trust Levels**—Specifies the level of security applied to the application through specific, pre-generated configuration file, such as, web_hightrust.config, web_mediumtrust.config, and web_lowtrust.config. By default, the application uses the Web.config file.
- **.Net Users**—Enables the ASP.NET application to work with the ASP.NET membership system. You can add a user by providing certain details, such as username, password, security question and its answer, and the role of the user.
- **Connection Strings**—Adds connection strings to your ASP.NET application. The default connection string used by the ASP.NET application is LocalSqlServer. You can also modify or delete the existing connections strings.
- **Pages and Controls**—Specifys the settings that control ASP.NET pages (.aspx) and user controls (.ascx) in an application.
- **Providers**—Specifys the providers for an ASP.NET application. There are two providers, AspNetSqlRoleProvider and AspNetWindowsTokenRøleProvider, defined for the .NET Roles engine. The AspNetSqlMembershipProvider provider is defined for.NET users and the AspNetSqlProfileProvider provider is defined for the .NET profile. All these providers are specified by default.

- **Session State**—Enables you to determine the administration of the state management for the ASP.NET application. You can apply the state management to the application in a number of ways, including Session state mode, Cookieless mode, and Session timeout mode.
- **SMTP E-mail**—Enables you to work with the applications that deliver e-mails.

These are some of the options through which you can configure your ASP.NET application in IIS and manage and make your Web applications error free.

With this, we come to the end of the chapter. Let's now summarize the main points of the chapter.

Summary

In this chapter, you have learned how to use various tools (`ASPNET_REGIIS`, `ASPNET_REGSQL`, and ASP.net Website Administration tools) for managing Web applications. Further, you have verified the configuration settings of Web applications and used the `ProtectSection` method to protect Web applications. You have also learned how to configure ASP.NET applications in IIS.

In the next chapter, you learn about login controls in ASP.NET 4.5.

24

Working with Login Controls

If you need an Information on:	See page:

In Depth

In the present scenario, Internet is emerging as the most widely-used medium for performing various tasks, such as exchanging data and information as well as conducting online shopping and bank transactions. Apart from the common people, most of the governmental organizations and high business houses entirely depend on this medium for transmitting and receiving critical information and conducting their day-to-day business. All this information and data need to be secured against unauthorized access from illegal and malicious sources. Security is implemented in a website mainly through two processes, i.e. authentication and authorization. Authentication refers to the process of recognizing the identity of a user; whereas, authorization is the process of providing access to various resources, such as databases and printers, to the authenticated users.

Earlier, you need to write large pieces of code to create forms and user interfaces (UI) for authenticating the user, and displaying the desired page based on the roles or rights given to the user. However, creating such forms or user interfaces with the help of standard ASP.NET server controls is quite tedious and time-consuming. Microsoft realized the problem and developed a new series of server controls, called Login controls. To use Login controls in your website, you just need to drag-and-drop them on the Web form, which means there is no more need to write lengthy code in the codefile file. Login controls helps you to ensure that only authenticated users are allowed to access your website. The Login controls have built-in functionality (called Membership service) for all the tasks related to authentication and authorization of users. Login controls were introduced with ASP.NET 2.0 and are also available with later versions of ASP.NET, such as 3.0, 3.5, 4.0, and 4.5.

In this chapter, you first learn about the Membership service in ASP.NET 4.5. Next, you learn about various Login controls, which are used to provide a rich user interface to implement authentication and authorization of users logging on to a website.

Let's start the chapter by learning about the Membership service.

The Membership Service

The Membership service is one of the important features of ASP.NET that helps in validating and storing user credentials. To authenticate users, the Login controls make use of the Membership service, in which each user is provided with a unique username and password. A default Membership provider is configured automatically, while using the Login controls in a Web site. In short, ASP.NET Membership service and Login controls work simultaneously to achieve the goal of user registration and authentication.

The ASP.NET Membership service helps you implement the following functionalities:

- Helps in creating new users and passwords.
- Stores the membership information (such as username, password, e-mail address, and other supporting data) in data stores (such as Microsoft SQL Server database, Oracle database, or an XML file).
- Authenticates the visitors of a Web site.
- Helps in managing passwords by creating, changing, and resetting them. It also includes a password-reset system that takes a user-supplied question and response to reset the password of a user.
- Exposes a unique identification system for authenticated users that helps in role-management and personalizing Web sites.

Now, let's discuss all the Login controls provided by ASP.NET. The Login controls are available under the Login tab in the Toolbox of Visual Studio 2012 Integrated Development Environment (IDE). To use Login controls in your Web site, you can simply drag-and-drop the controls from the Toolbox on a Web Form. The Login tab provides the following controls:

- `Login`
- `LoginView`
- `LoginStatus`
- `LoginName`

- PasswordRecovery
- CreateUserWizard
- ChangePassword

Let's learn about these controls in detail.

The Login Control

The Login control provides a user interface that facilitates authentication of users of a Web site on the basis of username and password. This control can also be used for designing the home page of a Web site. By using the Login control on a Web page of any Web site, you can restrict access to other Web pages of the Web site to authenticated users only. It can be done by redirecting only authenticated users to other Web pages of the Web site.

The Login control is provided by the Login class. The class hierarchy of the Login class is as follows:

```
System.Object
   System.Web.UI.Control
         System.Web.UI.WebControls.WebControl
                System.Web.UI.WebControls.CompositeControl
                       System.Web.UI.WebControls.Login
```

The Login class contains various methods, properties, and events that are used to work with the Login control. These members enable you to customize Login control, such as displaying customized messages and creating links to change password or recover a forgotten password. The Login control contains built-in authentication logic; however, you can create your own logic by handling the Authenticate event. Noteworthy methods of the Login class are listed in Table 24.1:

Table 24.1: Noteworthy Methods of the Login Class

Method	Description
CreateChildControls	Creates individual controls of the Login control and associates event handlers with their events
OnAuthenticate	Raises the Authenticate event to authenticate users
OnLoggedIn	Raises the LoggedIn event when users log into a Web site after successful authentication
OnLoggingIn	Raises the LoggingIn event after users enter login information but before the authentication completes
OnLoginError	Raises the LoginError event when users fail to log in

Noteworthy properties of the Login class are listed in Table 24.2:

Table 24.2: Noteworthy Properties of the Login Class

Property	Description
BorderPadding	Retrieves or specifies the padding of borders of the Login control
CheckBoxStyle	Retrieves a reference to the Style object to define the display settings of the Remember Me check box
CreateUserIconUrl	Retrieves the location of an image to display the link for new users for registration
CreateUserText	Retrieves or specifies the text of a link to a registration page for new users
CreateUserUrl	Retrieves or specifies the Uniform Resource Locator (URL) of the new-user registration page
DestinationPageUrl	Retrieves or specifies the URL of the page displayed to a user when a login attempt is successful
DisplayRememberMe	Retrieves or specifies the value that indicates whether to display the Remember Me check box or not
FailureAction	Retrieves or specifies the action that occurs when a login attempt fails

Table 24.2: Noteworthy Properties of the Login Class

Property	Description
FailureText	Retrieves or specifies the text displayed when a login attempt fails
FailureTextStyle	Retrieves a reference to style properties to define the look of the failure text
HelpPageIconUrl	Retrieves the location of an image to display the link to the login help page
HelpPageText	Retrieves or specifies the text of a link to the login help page
HelpPageUrl	Retrieves or specifies the URL of the login help page
HyperLinkStyle	Retrieves a reference to a collection of properties that defines the look of hyperlinks in the Login control
InstructionText	Retrieves or specifies the login instruction text for a user
InstructionTextStyle	Retrieves a reference to the TableItemStyle object to define the style of the instruction text
LayoutTemplate	Retrieves or specifies the template to display the Login control
LoginButtonImageUrl	Retrieves or specifies the URL of an image to use as the login button
LoginButtonText	Retrieves or specifies the text for the Login control's login button
Orientation	Retrieves or specifies the value to indicate the position of elements of the Login control on the page
Password	Retrieves the password entered by a user
PasswordLabelText	Retrieves or specifies the text of the label for the Password text box
PasswordRecoveryText	Retrieves or specifies the text of a link of the password recovery page
PasswordRecoveryUrl	Retrieves or specifies the URL of the password recovery page
PasswordRequiredErrorMessage	Retrieves or specifies the error message that is displayed when the password field is left blank; this error message is also displayed in the ValidationSummary control
RememberMeText	Retrieves or specifies the text of the label for the Remember Me check box
RememberMeSet	Retrieves or specifies a value indicating whether to send a persistent authentication cookie to the user's browser or not
TitleText	Retrieves or specifies the title of the Login control
UserName	Retrieves the username entered by a user
UserNameLabelText	Retrieves or specifies the text of the label for the User Name text box

Noteworthy events of the Login class are listed in Table 24.3:

Table 24.3: Noteworthy Events of the Login class

Event	Description
Authenticate	Initiated when a user is authenticated
LoggedIn	Initiated when a user logs into the Web site and has been authenticated
LoggingIn	Initiated when a user submits the login information, before authentication takes place
LoginError	Initiated when a login error is detected

Login controls are made up of a combination of standard .NET controls, which are as follows:

- **Username Label and TextBox**—Get the string from a user, which is used to authenticate the user during the login process.
- **Password Label and TextBox**—Get the password as specified by a user. The TextBox control is always encrypted to hide the user's password from being displayed in the plain text.
- **Log In button**—Submits the user's request for authentication.

- **Remember Me check box**—Enables users to store their credentials (username and password) as a persistent cookie on their machines by selecting the displayed `CheckBox` control. It helps users to enter their credentials the next time they want to log in.
- **Title and Instruction**—Display a text usually to guide users while accessing `Login` controls. It provides information about the controls displayed below it.
- **Validators**—Display the required field validators for the validation of user credentials.

Figure 24.1 displays the Login control at design time:

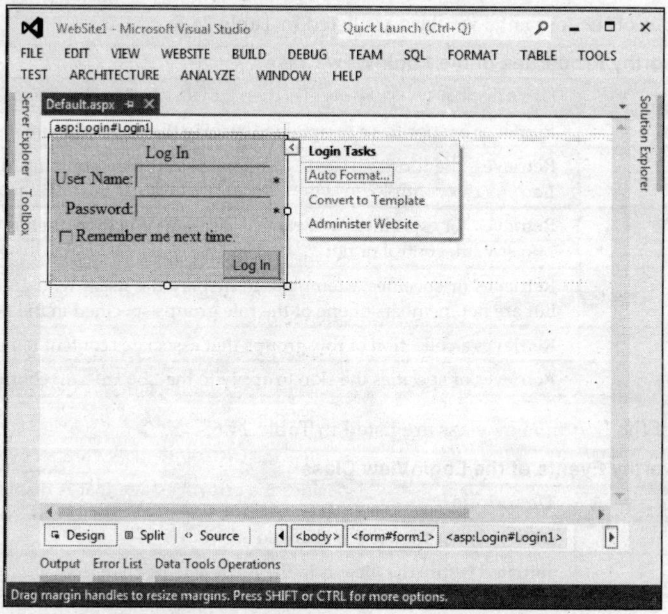

Figure 24.1: Displaying the Login Control

After discussing the `Login` control, let's learn about the `LoginView` control.

The LoginView Control

The `LoginView` control is a Web server control, which is used to display two different views of a Web page of any Web site, depending on whether a user has logged in to a Web page as a registered user or a visitor. This control provides a way of altering the look of the page or showing different content to different groups of users. This control has the built-in functionality to gather the current user's status and roles. If the user is authenticated, then the control displays the appropriate information to the user in three ways, which are as follows:

- **AnonymousTemplate**—Displayed when the user is not logged in
- **LoggedInTemplate**—Displayed when the user is logged in
- **RoleGroups**—Displayed when the user, who has logged in, is a member of a specific role associated with role-group templates

The `LoginView` control is provided by the `LoginView` class. The class hierarchy of the `LoginView` class is as follows:

```
System.Object
  System.Web.UI.Control
       System.Web.UI.WebControls.LoginView
```

The `LoginView` class contains various methods, properties, and events that are used to work with the `LoginView` control. Noteworthy methods of the `LoginView` class are listed in Table 24.4:

Table 24.4: Noteworthy Methods of the LoginView Class	
Method	**Description**
`DataBind`	Allows you to bind a data source with the `LoginView` control and all its child controls
`Focus`	Allows you to specify input focus to the `LoginView` control
`OnViewChanged`	Raises the `ViewChanged` event after the `LoginView` control changes its view
`OnViewChanging`	Raises the `ViewChanging` event before the `LoginView` control changes its view

Noteworthy properties of the `LoginView` class are listed in Table 24.5:

Table 24.5: Noteworthy Properties of the LoginView Class	
Property	**Description**
`AnonymousTemplate`	Retrieves or specifies a template to display the users who are not logged into the Web site
`Controls`	Retrieves the `ControlCollection` object that contains the child controls for the `LoginView` control
`EnableTheming`	Retrieves or specifies a value indicating whether themes can be applied to the `LoginView` control or not
`LoggedInTemplate`	Retrieves or specifies a template to display the users who are logged into the Web site, but are not members of one of the role groups specified in the `RoleGroups` property
`RoleGroups`	Retrieves a collection of role groups that associates content templates with particular roles
`SkinID`	Retrieves or specifies the skin to apply to the `LoginView` control

Noteworthy events of the `LoginView` class are listed in Table 24.6:

Table 24.6: Noteworthy Events of the LoginView Class	
Event	**Description**
`ViewChanged`	Initiated after the view is changed
`ViewChanging`	Initiated before the view is in the process to be changed

The `LoginView` control displays the AnonymousTemplate view by default; however, you can design a custom layout for the `LoginView` control as per your requirements. You can do so by adding any server control (such as `Label` and `TextBox`) to the empty region displayed on the `LoginView` control. You can simply drag-and-drop the `LoginView` control from the Toolbox to add it on a Web page. Figure 24.2 displays the `LoginView` control at design time:

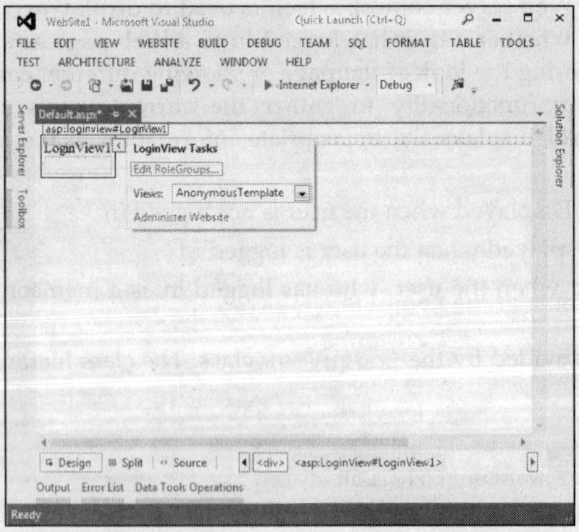

Figure 24.2: Displaying the LoginView Control

Let's discuss the LoginStatus control.

The LoginStatus Control

The LoginStatus control specifies whether a particular user has logged in to the Web site. The text displayed on this control changes according to the login status of the user. When the user is not logged in, the control displays the Login text as a hyperlink that facilitates the user in navigating to the login page. For this, the LoginStatus control uses the authentication section of the Web.config file and retrieves the URL of the login page. The LoginStatus control displays the Logout text as a hyperlink when the user is logged in to the Web site. As soon as the user clicks the Logout link, the LoginStatus control deletes the authentication information. The LoginStatus control provides the following two views:

- **Logged Out**—Displayed when a user is not logged in. In this view, it provides a link to the login page.
- **Logged In**—Displayed when a user is logged in. In this view, it provides a link to logout from the Web site.

The LoginStatus control is provided by the LoginStatus class. The class hierarchy of the LoginStatus class is as follows:

```
System.Object
   System.Web.UI.Control
        System.Web.UI.WebControls.WebControl
                  System.Web.UI.WebControls.CompositeControl
                            System.Web.UI.WebControls.LoginStatus
```

The LoginStatus class contains various methods, properties, and events that are used to work with the LoginStatus control. Noteworthy methods of the LoginStatus class are listed in Table 24.7:

Table 24.7: Noteworthy Methods of the LoginStatus Class

Method	Description
CreateChildControls	Creates the child controls to make the LoginStatus control
OnLoggedOut	Raises the LoggedOut event when a user clicks the logout link
OnLoggingOut	Raises the LoggingIn event when a user clicks the logout link on the LoginStatus control

Noteworthy properties of the LoginStatus class are listed in Table 24.8:

Table 24.8: Noteworthy Properties of the LoginStatus Class

Property	Description
LoginImageUrl	Retrieves or specifies the URL of the image used for the login link
LoginText	Retrieves or specifies the text used for the login link
LogoutAction	Retrieves or specifies a value to determine the action, when a user logs out of a Web site with the LoginStatus control
LogoutImageUrl	Retrieves or specifies the URL of the image used for the logout link
LogoutPageUrl	Retrieves or specifies the URL of the logout page
LogoutText	Retrieves or specifies the text used for the logout link

Noteworthy events of the LoginStatus class are listed in Table 24.9:

Table 24.9: Noteworthy Events of the LoginStatus Class

Event	Description
LoggingOut	Initiated after a user has sent a logout request to the server by clicking the logout link or button of the LoginStatus control
LoggedOut	Initiated by the LoginStatus class when the user's logout process completes

You can simply drag-and-drop the LoginStatus control from the Toolbox to add it on a Web page. Figure 24.3 displays the LoginStatus control at design time:

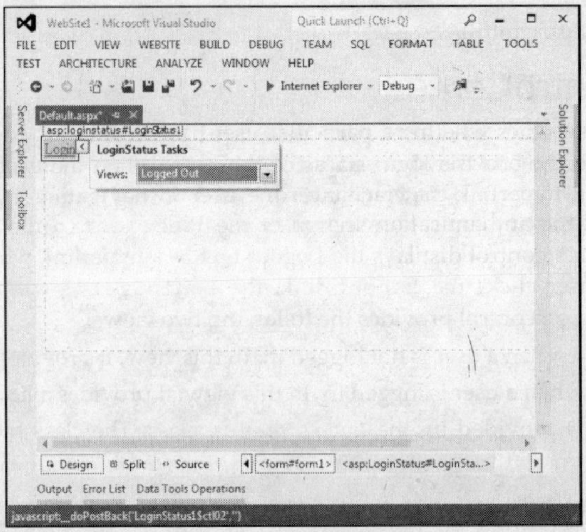

Figure 24.3: Displaying the LoginStatus Control

Now, let's discuss the LoginName control.

The LoginName Control

The LoginName control is responsible for displaying the name of the presently authenticated users. It uses Page.User.Identity.Name to return the value for the user's name. If there is no user logged in, then this control is not displayed on the Web page. This control is provided by the LoginName class. The class hierarchy of the LoginName class is as follows:

```
System.Object
  System.Web.UI.Control
       System.Web.UI.WebControls.WebControl
             System.Web.UI.WebControls.LoginName
```

The LoginName class does not contain any method, property, or event that is not inherited from any other class, such as the Control class. The only non-inherited property it contains is FormatString, which is used to display format item string in the LoginName control. You can simply drag-and-drop this control from the Toolbox to add it on a Web page. Figure 24.4 displays the LoginName control at design time:

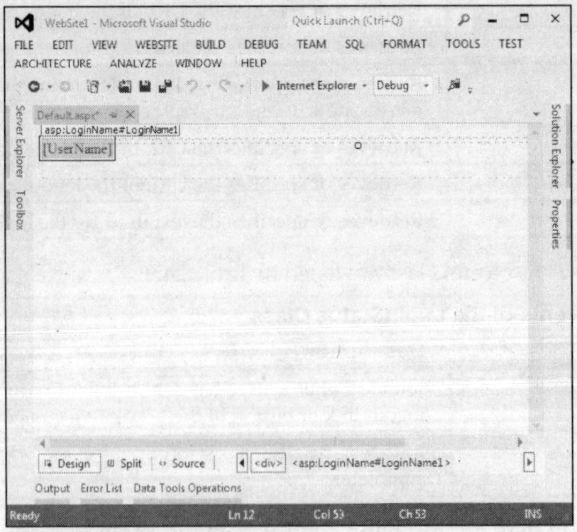

Figure 24.4: Displaying the LoginName Control

After discussing the LoginName control, let's learn about the PasswordRecovery control.

The PasswordRecovery Control

The PasswordRecovery control is used to recover or reset the forgotten password of a user. This control does not display the password on the browser, but sends the password as an e-mail message to the e-mail address specified at the time of registration. This control also uses the Membership service to create or reset the password. The PasswordRecovery control has the following three views:

- **UserName**—Refers to a view where a user is prompted to enter its username for its password to be recovered.
- **Question**—Refers to a view where a user is prompted to enter the answer for its security question.
- **Success**—Refers to a view where a message is displayed to a user. The message specifies that the retrieved password has been sent to the user.

To retrieve or reset a password, you must set some properties of the ASP.NET Membership service. The PasswordRecovery control uses the Membership service settings to retrieve or reset the password, which are given as follows:

- requiresQuestionAndAnswer—If this property is set to True, then users are required to answer a security question, which was specified at the time of creating the user accounts through ASP.NET configuration services.
- passwordFormat—If this property is set to Hashed, then the password is in the encrypted format. Therefore, this control will not be able to retrieve the password, but just reset the password.
- enablePasswordRetrieval—If this property is set to True, only then the Membership service allows any Web control to retrieve the password.
- enablePasswordReset—If this property is set to True, only then users are allowed to reset their passwords.

The PasswordRecovery control is provided by the PasswordRecovery class. The class hierarchy of the PasswordRecovery class is as follows:

```
System.Object
   System.Web.UI.Control
        System.Web.UI.WebControls.WebControl
              System.Web.UI.WebControls.CompositeControl
                    System.Web.UI.WebControls.PasswordRecovery
```

The PasswordRecovery class contains various methods, properties and events that are used to work with the PasswordRecovery control. Noteworthy methods of the PasswordRecovery class are listed in Table 24.10:

Table 24.10: Noteworthy Methods of the PasswordRecovery Class

Method	Description
OnAnswerLookupError	Raises the AnswerLookupError event when the user's answer does not match with the answer stored in the database
OnSendingMail	Raises the SendingMail event when a user is verified and the recovered password is sent to the user
OnSendMailError	Raises the SendMailError event when an e-mail message cannot be sent to a user
OnUserLookupError	Raises the UserLookupError event when the entered username does not match with any username stored in the database
OnVerifyingAnswer	Raises the VerifyingAnswer event before the user's answer is sent to the Membership service provider to recover the forgotten password
OnVerifyingUser	Raises the VerifyingUser event after submitting the username, but before sending it to the Membership service provider for verification

Noteworthy properties of the PasswordRecovery class are listed in Table 24.11:

Table 24.11: Noteworthy Properties of the PasswordRecovery Class

Property	Description
Answer	Retrieves the answer provided by a user to confirm the password recovery by the valid user
AnswerLabelText	Retrieves or specifies the label text for the password confirmation answer text box
AnswerRequiredErrorMessage	Specifies a custom error message for the PasswordRecovery control, in case a user leaves the answer field blank
BorderPadding	Retrieves or specifies the padding width inside the borders of the PasswordRecovery control
FailureTextStyle	Retrieves a reference to a collection of properties that defines the look of the error text
GeneralFailureText	Retrieves or specifies the error message to display when there is a problem with the Membership service provider for the PasswordRecovery control
HelpPageIconUrl	Retrieves the location of an image to display the link to the password recovery help page
HelpPageText	Retrieves or specifies the text of a link to the password recovery help page
HelpPageUrl	Retrieves or specifies the URL of the password recovery help page
HyperLinkStyle	Retrieves a reference to a collection of properties that defines the look of hyperlinks in the PasswordRecovery control
InstructionTextStyle	Retrieves a reference to the Style object to define the look of the explanatory text in the PasswordRecovery control
LabelStyle	Retrieves a collection of the Style objects to define the look of the TextBox control's labels in the PasswordRecovery control
MailDefinition	Obtains a reference to a group of properties that describe the features of e-mail messages that are used to send new or recovered passwords to users.
MembershipProvider	Gets a reference to the Membership service provider, which is used to gather user's identity
Question	Retrieves the password recovery question, which was provided by a user at the time of registration
QuestionFailureText	Specifies a custom message for the PasswordRecovery control to be displayed when a user provides an incorrect answer
QuestionTemplate	Retrieves or specifies the template used to set the look of the Question view of the PasswordRecovery control
QuestionTitleText	Retrieves or specifies the title of the PasswordRecovery control when the control is in the Question view
SubmitButtonImageUrl	Retrieves or specifies the image path that is used as the Button control
SubmitButtonStyle	Retrieves a reference to style properties that are used to define the look of the Button control
SubmitButtonText	Retrieves or specifies the text to be displayed on the Button control
SubmitButtonType	Retrieves or specifies the type of Button control that is used to render the PasswordRecovery control

Table 24.11: Noteworthy Properties of the PasswordRecovery Class

Property	Description
SuccessPageUrl	Retrieves or specifies the URL of the page to be displayed if the forgotten password is sent to the user's e-mail id successfully
SuccessTemplate	Retrieves or specifies the template for the PasswordRecovery control when it is in the Success view
SuccessText	Specifies a custom message for the PasswordRecovery control to be displayed in case the task of password recovery is accomplished successfully
SuccessTextStyle	Retrieves or specifies the style in which the Success text is to be displayed
UserName	Retrieves or specifies the text to be displayed in the User Name text box
UserNameFailureText	Retrieves or specifies the text when a user enters an invalid username
UserNameInstructionText	Retrieves or specifies the text in the PasswordRecovery control when it is in the UserName view
UserNameLabelText	Retrieves or specifies the label for the User Name text box
UserNameRequiredErrorMessage	Retrieves or specifies the error message that is displayed when a user does not enter any value in the User Name text box
UserNameTemplate	Retrieves or specifies the template used to display the UserName view of the PasswordRecovery control
UserNameTitleText	Retrieves or specifies the title of the PasswordRecovery control when it is in the UserName view
ValidatorTextStyle	Retrieves or specifies the style properties that are used to define the look of the error message of the Validator control

Noteworthy events of the PasswordRecovery class are listed in Table 24.12:

Table 24.12: Noteworthy Events of the PasswordRecovery Class

Event	Description
AnswerLookupError	Initiated when the user's answer to the question is found incorrect
SendingMail	Initiated when the server is sending an e-mail containing the password after the user's answer is found correct
SendMailError	Initiated when the SMTP Mail system throws an error while attempting to send an e-mail message
UserLookupError	Initiated when the Membership provider cannot find the username entered by a user
VerifyingAnswer	Initiated when a user has submitted the answer to the password recovery confirmation question
VerifyingUser	Initiated when the validation of username by the Membership provider is under process

You can simply drag-and-drop this control from the Toolbox to add it on a Web page. Figure 24.5 displays the PasswordRecovery control at design time:

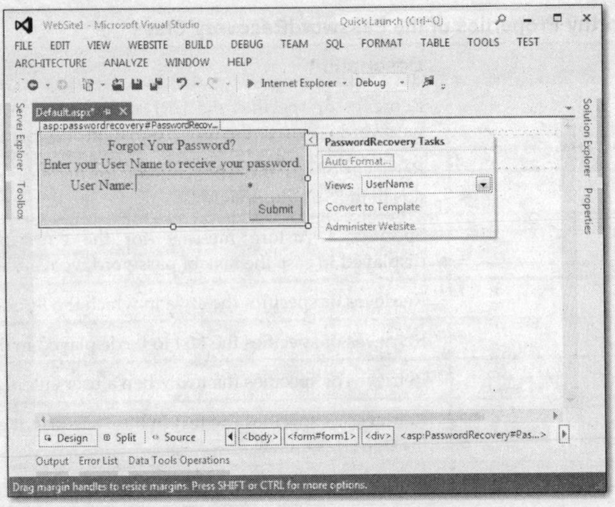

Figure 24.5: Displaying the PasswordRecovery Control

Let's learn about the `CreateUserWizard` control.

The CreateUserWizard Control

The `CreateUserWizard` control uses the Membership service to create a new user in the Membership data store. This control is an extended version of the already existing `Wizard` control. Being an extended control, the `CreateUserWizard` control can be customized by using templates and style properties. The `CreateUserWizard` control is provided by the `CreateUserWizard` class. The class hierarchy of the `CreateUserWizard` class is as follows:

```
System.Object
  System.Web.UI.Control
        System.Web.UI.WebControls.WebControl
               System.Web.UI.WebControls.CompositeControl
                      System.Web.UI.WebControls.Wizard
                             System.Web.UI.WebControls.CreateUserWizard
```

The `CreateUserWizard` class contains various methods, properties, and events. However, the methods of the `CreateUserWizard` class are mostly inherited and the other non-inherited methods are not of much use. Noteworthy properties of the `CreateUserWizard` class are listed in Table 24.13:

Table 24.13: Noteworthy Properties of the CreateUserWizard Class

Property	Description
`ActiveStepIndex`	Retrieves or specifies the step that is currently displayed to a user. This is an overridden property.
`Answer`	Retrieves or specifies the user's answer to the password recovery confirmation question.
`AnswerLabelText`	Retrieves or specifies the text of the label of the password confirmation answer text box.
`AnswerRequiredErrorMessage`	Retrieves or specifies the error message shown when a user leaves the password confirmation question unanswered.
`AutoGeneratePassword`	Retrieves or specifies a value indicating whether to generate a password automatically for the new user account.
`CompleteStep`	Defines the final step of the process to create a user account.
`CompleteSuccessText`	Retrieves or specifies the text displayed when a user account is created successfully.

Table 24.13: Noteworthy Properties of the CreateUserWizard Class

Property	Description
`CompleteSuccessTextStyle`	Retrieves a reference to a collection of properties that defines the look of the text displayed when a user account is created successfully.
`ConfirmPassword`	Retrieves the second password entered by a user.
`ConfirmPasswordCompareErrorMessage`	Retrieves or specifies the error message to be displayed when the passwords in the password text box and the confirm password text box do not match.
`ConfirmPasswordLabelText`	Retrieves or specifies the text of the label for the second password text box.
`ConfirmPasswordRequiredErrorMessage`	Retrieves or specifies the error message displayed when a user leaves the confirm password text box empty.
`ContinueButtonImageUrl`	Retrieves or specifies the URL of an image to display the Continue button. The Continue button is displayed as the final step of the process of creating a user account.
`ContinueButtonStyle`	Retrieves a reference to a collection of properties that defines the look of the Continue button.
`ContinueButtonText`	Retrieves or specifies the text caption displayed on the Continue button.
`ContinueButtonType`	Retrieves or specifies the type of button rendered as the Continue button.
`ContinueDestinationPageUrl`	Retrieves or specifies the URL of the page that a user will see after clicking the Continue button on the success page.
`CreateUserButtonImageUrl`	Retrieves or specifies the URL of an image displayed for the Create User button.
`CreateUserButtonStyle`	Retrieves a reference to a collection of properties that defines the look of the Create User button.
`CreateUserButtonText`	Retrieves or specifies the text caption displayed on the Create User button.
`CreateUserButtonType`	Retrieves or specifies the type of button rendered as the Create User button.
`CreateUserStep`	Retrieves a reference to the template, which will be used as a step in the process of creating a user account.
`DisableCreatedUser`	Retrieves or specifies a value indicating whether a new user should be allowed to log in to the Web site.
`DisplaySideBar`	Retrieves or specifies a value indicating whether to display the sidebar area of the control. This is an overridden property.
`DuplicateEmailErrorMessage`	Retrieves or specifies the error message displayed when a user enters an e-mail address that is already in use in the Membership service provider.
`DuplicateUserNameErrorMessage`	Retrieves or specifies the error message displayed when a user enters a username that is already in use in the Membership service provider.
`EditProfileIconUrl`	Retrieves or specifies the URL of an image to display beside the link to the user profile editing page.
`EditProfileText`	Retrieves or specifies the text caption for the link to the user profile editing page.
`EditProfileUrl`	Retrieves or specifies the URL of the user profile editing page.
`Email`	Retrieves or specifies the e-mail address entered by a user.
`EmailLabelText`	Retrieves or specifies the text of the label for the e-mail text box.
`EmailRegularExpression`	Retrieves or specifies a regular expression used to validate an e-mail address.
`EmailRegularExpressionErrorMessage`	Retrieves or specifies the error message displayed when the entered e-mail address does not pass the site's criteria for e-mail addresses.
`EmailRequiredErrorMessage`	Retrieves or specifies the error message shown to a user when an e-mail address is not entered in the e-mail text box.

Table 24.13: Noteworthy Properties of the CreateUserWizard Class	
Property	**Description**
`ErrorMessageStyle`	Retrieves a reference to a collection of style properties that defines the look of the error messages.
`HelpPageIconUrl`	Retrieves or specifies the URL of an image to display beside the link to the help page.
`HelpPageText`	Retrieves or specifies the text for the link to the help page.
`HelpPageUrl`	Retrieves or specifies the URL of the help page.
`HyperLinkStyle`	Retrieves or specifies a collection of properties that defines the look of hyperlinks.
`InstructionText`	Retrieves or specifies the help text to create a new user account.
`InstructionTextStyle`	Retrieves a reference to a collection of properties that defines the look of the instruction text.
`InvalidAnswerErrorMessage`	Retrieves or specifies the message displayed when the password retrieval answer is not valid.
`InvalidEmailErrorMessage`	Retrieves or specifies the message displayed when the entered e-mail address is not valid.
`InvalidPasswordErrorMessage`	Retrieves or specifies the message displayed when the password entered is not valid.
`InvalidQuestionErrorMessage`	Retrieves or specifies the message displayed when the password retrieval question is not valid.
`LabelStyle`	Retrieves a reference to a collection of properties that defines the look of labels.
`LoginCreatedUser`	Retrieves or specifies a value indicating whether a new user can login, after creating the user account.
`MailDefinition`	Retrieves a reference to a collection of properties that defines the characteristics of the e-mail message sent to new users.
`MembershipProvider`	Retrieves or specifies the Membership service provider called to create user accounts.
`Password`	Retrieves the password entered by s user.
`PasswordHintStyle`	Retrieves a reference to a collection of properties that defines the look of the text that describes password requirements.
`PasswordHintText`	Retrieves or specifies the text that describes password requirements.
`PasswordLabelText`	Retrieves or specifies the text of the label for the password text box.
`PasswordRegularExpression`	Retrieves or specifies a regular expression used to validate the provided password.
`PasswordRegularExpressionErrorMessage`	Retrieves or specifies the error message shown when the password entered does not conform to the specific pattern.
`PasswordRequiredErrorMessage`	Retrieves or specifies the text of the error message shown when a user does not enter a password.
`Question`	Retrieves or specifies the password recovery confirmation question entered by a user.
`QuestionLabelText`	Retrieves or specifies the text of the label for the security question text box.
`QuestionRequiredErrorMessage`	Retrieves or specifies the error message that is displayed when a user does not enter a password confirmation question.
`RequireEmail`	Retrieves or specifies a value indicating whether an e-mail address is required for a Web site user.

Table 24.13: Noteworthy Properties of the CreateUserWizard Class

Property	Description
SkipLinkText	Retrieves or specifies a value that is used to provide alternate text that notifies screen readers to skip the sidebar area's content. This is an overridden property
TextBoxStyle	Retrieves a reference to style properties that defines the look of TextBox controls.
TitleTextStyle	Retrieves a reference to style properties that defines the look of titles.
UnknownErrorMessage	Retrieves or specifies the error message displayed when an error returned by the Membership provider is not defined.
UserName	Retrieves or specifies the username entered by a user.
UserNameLabelText	Retrieves or specifies the text of the label for the User Name text box.
UserNameRequiredErrorMessage	Retrieves or specifies the error message displayed when the User Name text box is left blank.
ValidatorTextStyle	Retrieves a reference to the Style object that allows you to set the look of the validation error messages.
WizardSteps	Retrieves a reference to a collection containing all the WizardStepBase objects defined for the control. This is an overridden property.

Noteworthy events of the CreateUserWizard class are listed in Table 24.14:

Table 24.14: Noteworthy Events of the CreateUserWizard Class

Event	Description
ContinueButtonClick	Initiated when a user clicks the Continue button. The Continue button is displayed as the final step of the user account creation process.
CreatedUser	Initiated after the Membership service provider has created a new Web site user account.
CreateUserError	Initiated when the Membership service provider throws an error while creating a user account.
CreatingUser	Initiated before the Membership service provider is called to create a user account.
SendingMail	Initiated before sending a confirmation e-mail on successful creation of a user account.
SendMailError	Initiated when an SMTP error occurs while sending an e-mail to a new user.

The CreateUserWizard control has a default collection of steps to gather user information. However, you can also add additional steps to the wizard to collect additional user information. The following are some of the important components used to create the steps of the CreateUserWizard control:

- CreateUserWizardStep—Contains the user interface and the logic to create a new user account.
- CompleteWizardStep—Displays the information whenever a user account is created successfully.
- Collection of WizardSteps—Represents a collection of all the user-defined steps that are displayed one by one during the process of creating a user account. Although there can be multiple steps, only one step is displayed at a given time.
- Navigation Buttons—Refers to the buttons that are present in the navigation area below each WizardStep. The navigation buttons allow users to go to the next and previous steps in the CreateUserWizard control.
- SideBar—Refers to an optional component. It is responsible for listing all the WizardSteps steps; and therefore, it enables users to access any of the WizardSteps step randomly.

- `Header`—Refers to an optional component. It provides users with the information regarding each step. It is present at the top of the wizard.

You can simply drag-and-drop this control from the Toolbox to add it on a Web page. Figure 24.6 displays the `CreateUserWizard` control at design time:

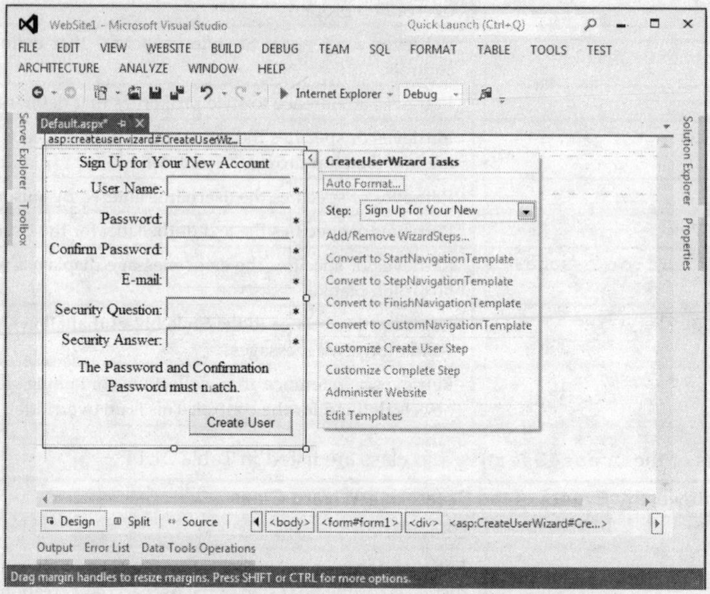

Figure 24.6: Displaying the CreateUserWizard Control

Let's now discuss the `ChangePassword` control.

The ChangePassword Control

The `ChangePassword` control allows users to change their password. This control prompts users to provide the current password first and then set the new password. If the old password is not correct, then the new password cannot be set. This control also facilitates in sending e-mails to users about the new password. The `ChangePassword` control is provided by the `ChangePassword` class. The class hierarchy of the `ChangePassword` class is as follows:

```
System.Object
  System.Web.UI.Control
       System.Web.UI.WebControls.WebControl
             System.Web.UI.WebControls.CompositeControl
                   System.Web.UI.WebControls.ChangePassword
```

The `ChangePassword` class contains various methods, properties, and events. However, the methods of the `ChangePassword` class are mostly inherited and the other non-inherited methods are not very useful. Noteworthy properties of the `ChangePassword` class are listed in Table 24.15:

Table 24.15: Noteworthy Properties of the ChangePassword Class

Property	Description
`BorderPadding`	Retrieves or specifies the amount of padding, in pixels, inside the border and the designated area for the `ChangePassword` control.
`CancelButtonImageUrl`	Retrieves or specifies the URL of an image to display with the Cancel button, if the Cancel button is configured by the `CancelButtonType` property to be an image button.
`CancelButtonStyle`	Retrieves a reference to style properties to define the look of the Cancel button on the `ChangePassword` control.

Table 24.15: Noteworthy Properties of the ChangePassword Class	
Property	**Description**
CancelButtonText	Retrieves or specifies the text displayed on the Cancel button.
CancelButtonType	Retrieves or specifies the type of button to be used for the Cancel button while customizing the ChangePassword control.
CancelDestinationPageUrl	Retrieves or specifies the URL of the page that a user is shown after clicking the Cancel button in the ChangePassword control.
ChangePasswordButtonImageUrl	Retrieves or specifies the URL of an image displayed next to the Change Password button on the ChangePassword control, if the Change Password button is configured through the ChangePasswordButtonType property to be an image button.
ChangePasswordButtonStyle	Retrieves a reference to a collection of style properties to define the look of the Change Password button.
ChangePasswordButtonText	Retrieves or specifies the text displayed on the Change Password button.
ChangePasswordButtonType	Retrieves or specifies the type of button to be used while rendering the Change Password button.
ChangePasswordFailureText	Retrieves or specifies a message that is shown when the user's password is not changed.
ChangePasswordTemplate	Retrieves or specifies the ITemplate object used to display the Change Password view of the ChangePassword control.
ChangePasswordTemplate Container	Retrieves the container that a ChangePassword control uses to create an instance of the ChangePasswordTemplate template. This provides programmatic access to child controls.
ChangePasswordTitleText	Retrieves or specifies the text displayed at the top of the ChangePassword control in the Change Password view.
ConfirmNewPassword	Retrieves the value of the Confirm New Password text box.
ConfirmNewPasswordLabelText	Retrieves or specifies the label text for the Confirm New Password text box.
ConfirmPasswordCompareErrorMe ssage	Retrieves or specifies a message that is displayed when the new password and the duplicate password are not identical.
ConfirmPasswordRequiredErrorM essage	Retrieves or specifies an error message that is displayed when the Confirm New Password text box is left blank.
ContinueButtonImageUrl	Retrieves or specifies the URL of an image to use for the Continue button on the Success view of the ChangePassword control, if the Continue button is configured by the ContinueButtonType property to be an image button.
ContinueButtonStyle	Retrieves a reference to style properties to define the look of the Continue button on the Success view of the ChangePassword control.
ContinueButtonText	Retrieves or specifies the text of the Continue button in the Success view of the ChangePassword control.
ContinueButtonType	Retrieves or specifies the type of button to be used when rendering the Continue button for the ChangePassword control.
ContinueDestinationPageUrl	Retrieves or specifies the URL of the page that a user will see after clicking the Continue button on the Success view.
CreateUserIconUrl	Retrieves or specifies the URL of an image to display next to the link of the Web page that contains a CreateUserWizard control for the Web site.
CreateUserText	Retrieves or specifies the text of the link to the Web page that contains a CreateUserWizard control for the Web site.
CreateUserUrl	Retrieves or specifies the URL of the Web page that contains a CreateUserWizard control for the Web site.
CurrentPassword	Retrieves the current password of a user.

Table 24.15: Noteworthy Properties of the ChangePassword Class

Property	Description
DisplayUserName	Retrieves or specifies a value indicating whether the ChangePassword control should display the UserName control and label.
EditProfileIconUrl	Retrieves or specifies the URL of an image to display next to the link to the user profile editing page.
EditProfileText	Retrieves or specifies the text of the link to the user profile editing page.
EditProfileUrl	Retrieves or specifies the URL of the user profile editing page.
FailureTextStyle	Retrieves a reference to style properties to define the look of error messages on the ChangePassword control.
HelpPageIconUrl	Retrieves or specifies the URL of an image to display next to the Change Password help page.
HelpPageText	Retrieves or specifies the link text to the Change Password help page.
HelpPageUrl	Retrieves or specifies the URL of the Change Password help page for the Web site.
HyperLinkStyle	Retrieves a reference to style properties that defines the look of hyperlinks on the ChangePassword control.
InstructionText	Retrieves or specifies the informational text that appears on the ChangePassword control.
InstructionTextStyle	Retrieves a reference to style properties that defines the look of the instructional text on the ChangePassword control.
LabelStyle	Retrieves a reference to style objects that defines the look of the text box labels on the ChangePassword control.
MailDefinition	Retrieves a reference to a collection of properties that defines the e-mail message that is sent to the users after they have changed their password.
MembershipProvider	Retrieves or specifies the Membership provider that is used to manage member information.
NewPassword	Retrieves the new password entered by a user.
NewPasswordLabelText	Retrieves or specifies the label text for the New Password text box.
NewPasswordRegularExpression	Retrieves or specifies the regular expression that is used to validate the passwords provided by users.
NewPasswordRegularExpressionErrorMessage	Retrieves or specifies the error message that is displayed when the password entered does not match with the regular expression defined in the NewPasswordRegularExpression property.
NewPasswordRequiredErrorMessage	Retrieves or specifies the error message that is displayed when a user leaves the New Password text box empty.
PasswordHintStyle	Retrieves a reference to style properties that defines the appearance of the hint text that appears on the ChangePassword control.
PasswordHintText	Retrieves or specifies the informational text about the requirements for creating a password for the Web site.
PasswordLabelText	Retrieves or specifies the label text for the Current Password text box.
PasswordRecoveryIconUrl	Retrieves or specifies the URL of an image to display next to a link of the Web page that contains the PasswordRecovery control.
PasswordRecoveryText	Retrieves or specifies the text of the link of the Web page that contains the PasswordRecovery control.
PasswordRecoveryUrl	Retrieves or specifies the URL of the Web page that contains the PasswordRecovery control.

Table 24.15: Noteworthy Properties of the ChangePassword Class	
Property	**Description**
PasswordRequiredErrorMessage	Retrieves or specifies the error message that is displayed when users leave the Current Password text box empty.
SuccessPageUrl	Retrieves or specifies the URL of the page that is shown to users after successfully changing the password.
SuccessTemplate	Retrieves or specifies the ITemplate object that is used to display the Success and Change Password views of the ChangePassword control.
SuccessTemplateContainer	Retrieves a container that a ChangePassword control uses to create an instance of the SuccessTemplate template. This provides programmatic access to child controls.
SuccessText	Retrieves or specifies the text that is displayed on the Success view between the SuccessTitleText property and the Continue button.
SuccessTextStyle	Retrieves style properties to define the look of text on the Success view.
SuccessTitleText	Retrieves or specifies the title of the Success view.
TextBoxStyle	Retrieves a reference to style properties that defines the look of TextBox controls on the ChangePassword control.
TitleTextStyle	Retrieves a reference to style properties that defines the look of titles on the ChangePassword control.
UserName	Retrieves or specifies the username for which the password is to be changed.
UserNameLabelText	Retrieves or specifies the label for the User Name text box.
UserNameRequiredErrorMessage	Retrieves or specifies the error message that is displayed when a user leaves the User Name text box empty.
ValidatorTextStyle	Retrieves a reference to style properties that define the look of error messages that are associated with any input validation used by the ChangePassword control.

Noteworthy events of the ChangePassword class are listed in Table 24.16:

Table 24.16: Noteworthy Events of the ChangePassword Class	
Event	**Description**
CancelButtonClick	Initiated when a user clicks the Cancel button to cancel the changing of a password
ChangedPassword	Initiated when the password is changed for a user account
ChangePasswordError	Initiated when there is an error in changing the password for the user account
ChangingPassword	Initiated before the password for a user account is changed
ContinueButtonClick	Initiated when a user clicks the Continue button
SendingMail	Initiated before a user is sent an e-mail confirmation that the password has been changed
SendMailError	Initiated when an SMTP error occurs while sending an e-mail message to a user

You can simply drag-and-drop the ChangePassword control from the Toolbox to add it on a Web page. Figure 24.7 displays the ChangePassword control at design time:

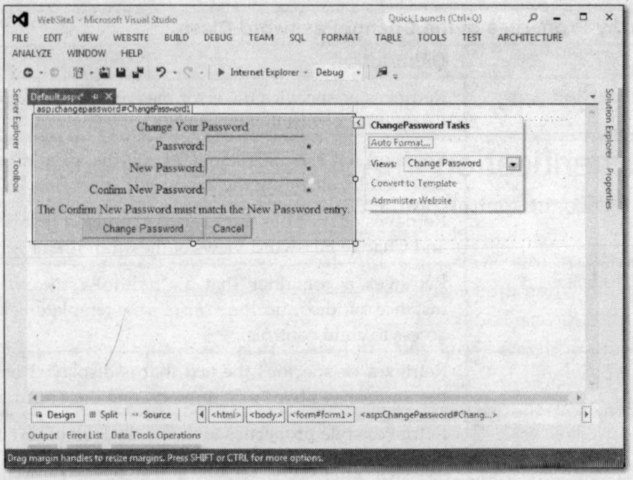

Figure 24.7: Displaying the ChangePassword Control

Now that you have become familiar with the Login controls and their respective methods, properties, and events, let's move ahead to learn the implementation of some of these controls in an application.

Immediate Solutions

Implementing Authentication in ASP.NET Using Login Controls

As already discussed, the Login controls are a new set of controls that allow you to easily create a well-functioning login page for a Web site. Let's create a simple Web site `LoginControlExampleApp` to depict the power of `Login` controls. In this Web site, add two Web Forms, `Login.aspx` and `Welcome.aspx`. The `Welcome.aspx` is accessible when a user successfully logs in through the `Login.aspx` page. You can find this example as `LoginControlExampleAppVB` (for VB) and `LoginControlExampleApp` (for C#). Let's now perform the following steps to learn about the implementation of authentication logic to validate users before allowing them to log on to the website:

1. Place a `Login` control on the `Login.aspx form` and change the `Auto Format style` property to `Classic` (Figure 24.8).
2. Click the Smart tag to open `Login Tasks` and select the `Administer Website` option, as shown in Figure 24.8:

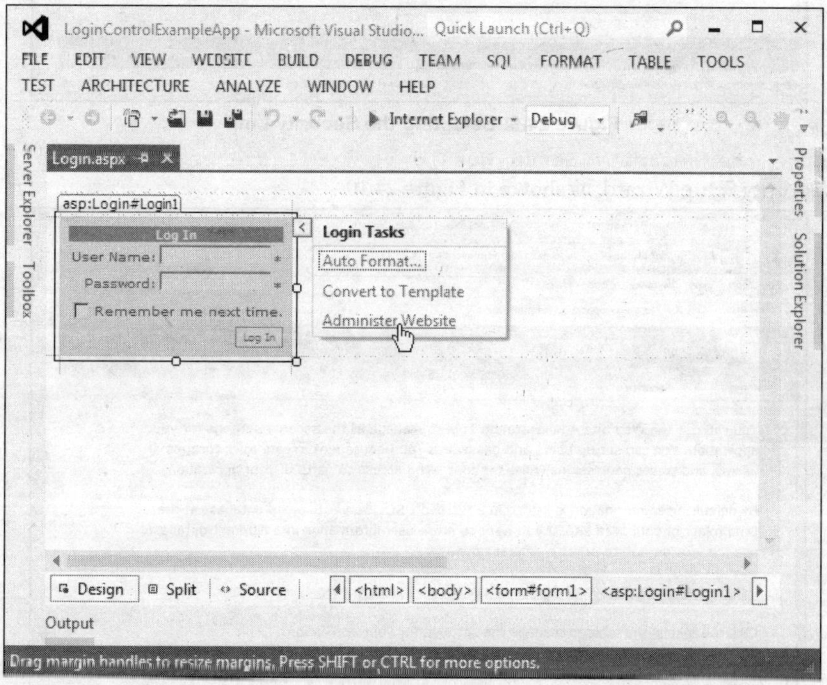

Figure 24.8: Selecting the Administer Website Option

`ASP.net Web Site Administration Tool` appears (Figure 24.9).

3. Click the `Security` link in the tool, as shown in Figure 24.9:

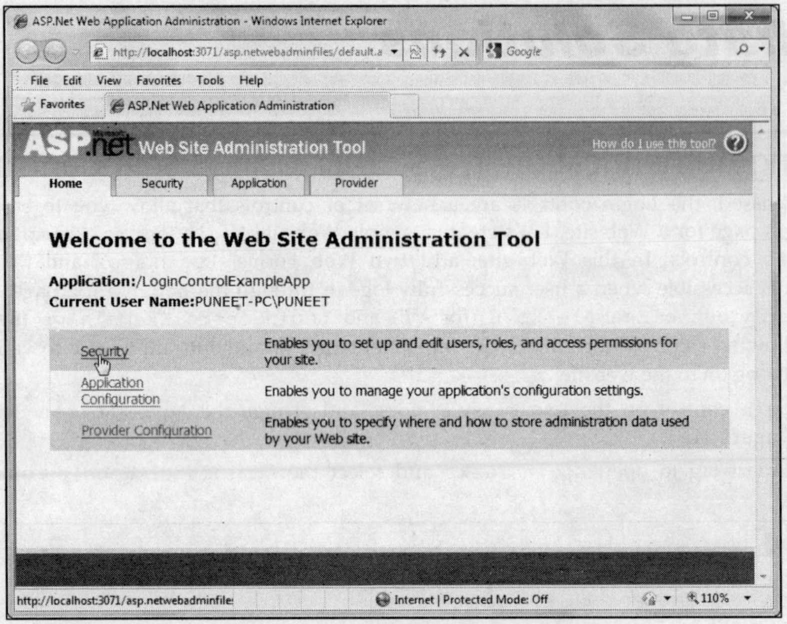

Figure 24.9: Selecting the Security Link

4. Click the `Use the security Setup Wizard to configure security step by step` link to open the Security Setup Wizard, as shown in Figure 24.10:

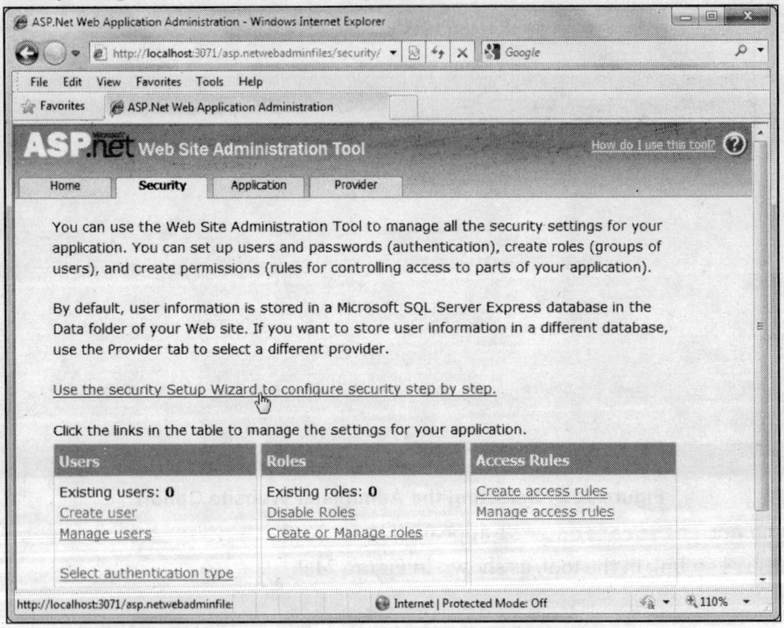

Figure 24.10: Clicking the Link

The Welcome to the Security Setup Wizard page appears (Figure 24.11).

5. Click the `Next` button in the Welcome to the Security Setup Wizard page, as shown in Figure 24.11:

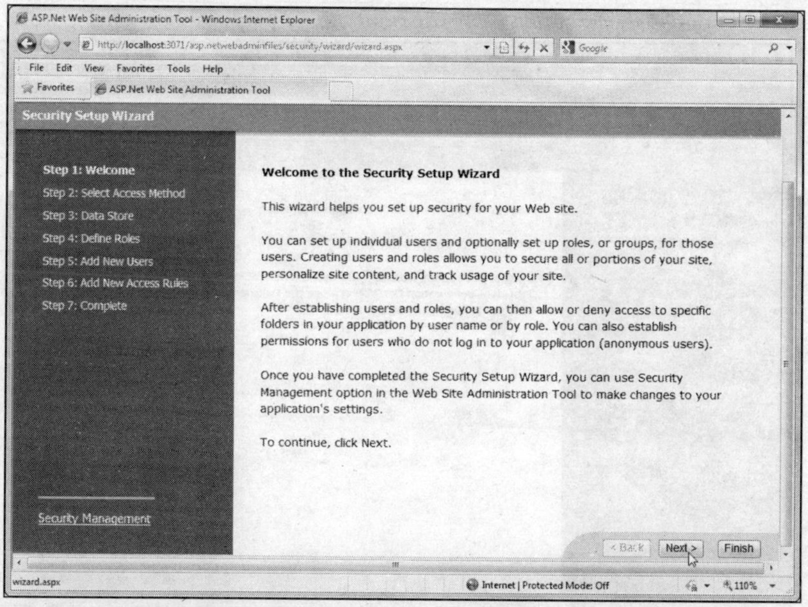

Figure 24.11: Displaying the Welcome to the Security Setup Wizard Page

The Select Access Method page appears (Figure 24.12).

6. Select the `From the internet` radio button and then click the Next button in the `Select Access Method` page, as shown in Figure 24.12:

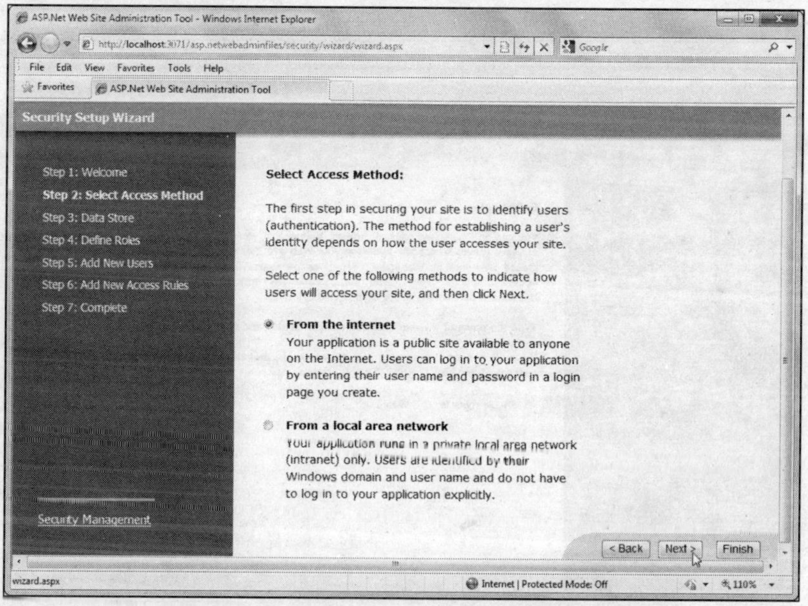

Figure 24.12: Selecting the From the internet Radio Button

The Advance provider settings page appears (Figure 24.13).

7. Click the `Next` button in the `Advance provider settings` page, as shown in Figure 24.13:

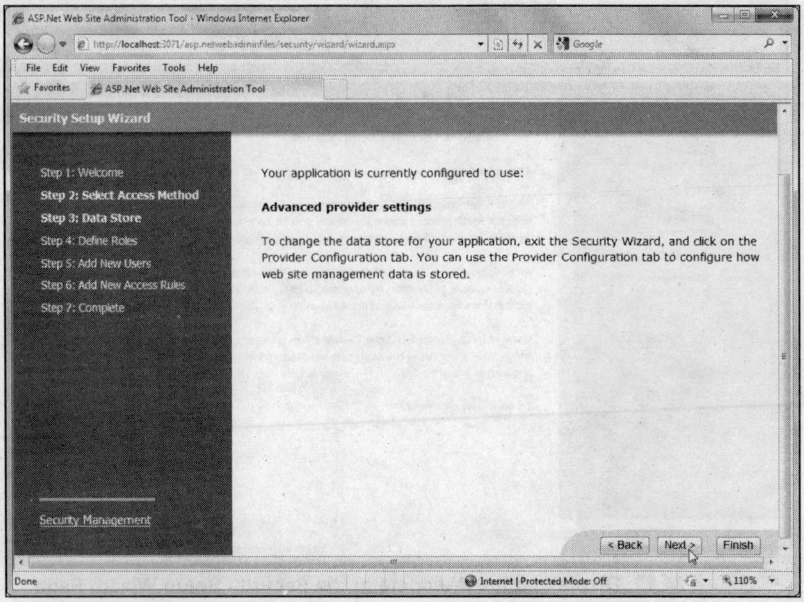

Figure 24.13: Displaying the Advance provider settings Page

The Define Roles page appears (Figure 24.14).

8. Select the `Enable roles for this Web site` check box and then click the `Next` button, as shown in Figure 24.14:

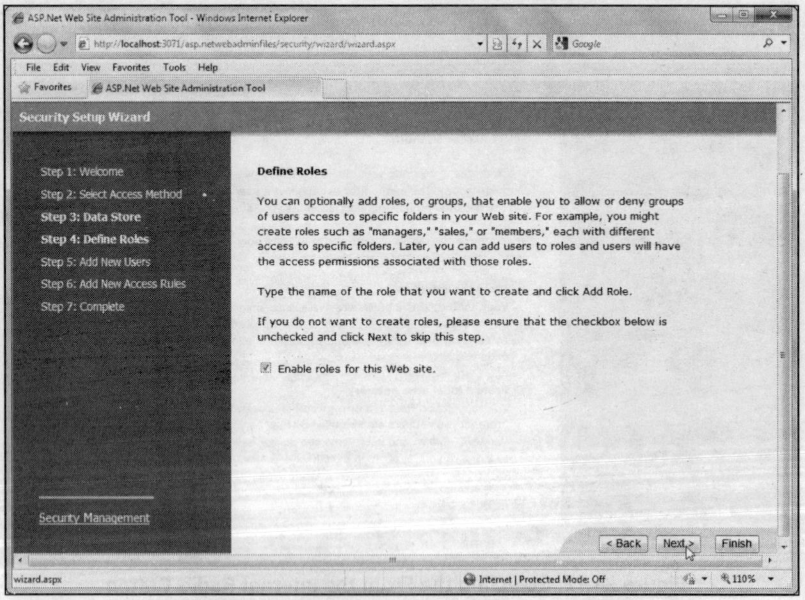

Figure 24.14: Enabling Roles for the Web Site

The Create New Role page appears (Figure 24.15).

9. Click the `Next` button in the `Create New Role` page, as shown in Figure 24.15:

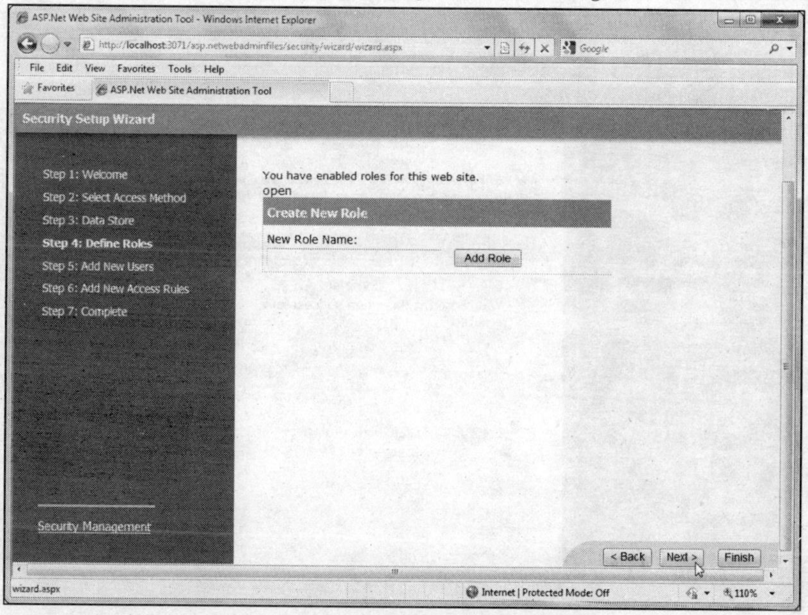

Figure 24.15: Clicking the Next Button

The Create User page appears (Figure 24.16).

10. Enter the details in the text boxes and click the `Create User` button to create the user account, as shown in Figure 24.16:

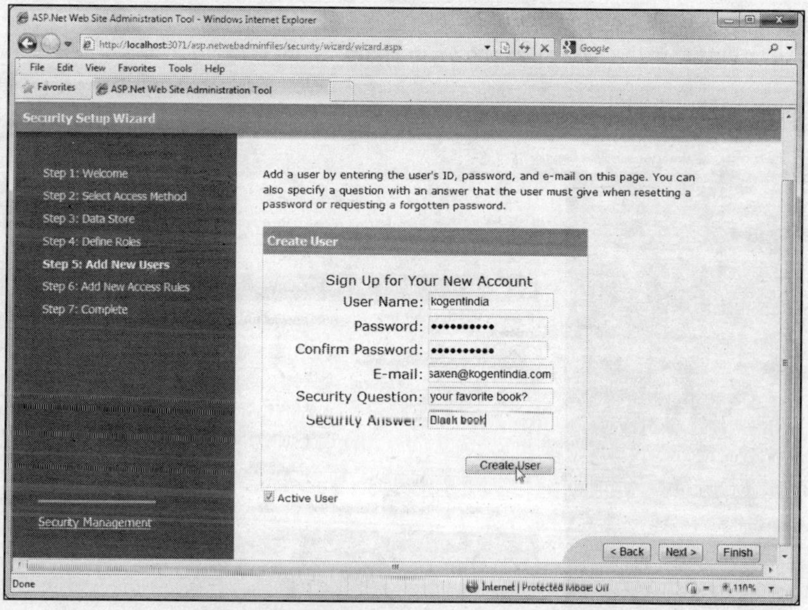

Figure 24.16: Creating the User Account

The message, `Your account has been successfully created,` appears in the `Create User` page (Figure 24.17).

11. Click the `Next` button in the wizard, as shown in Figure 24.17:

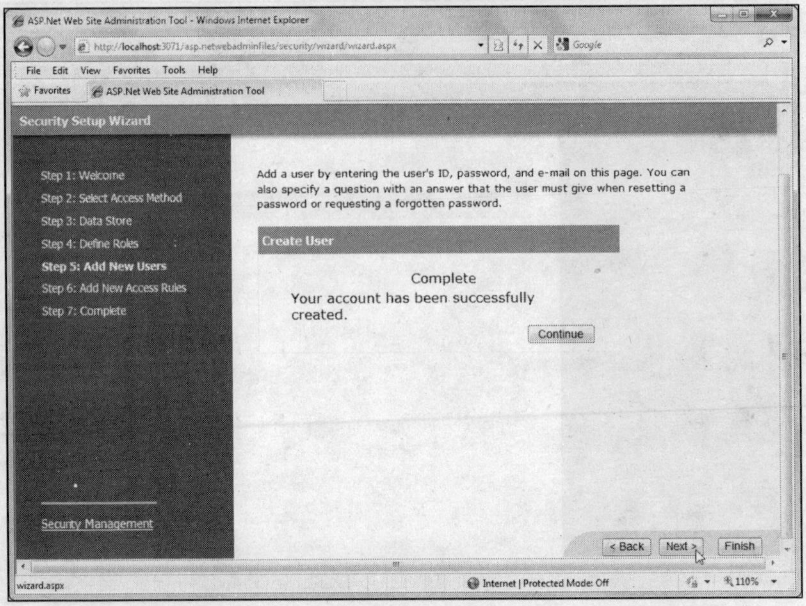

Figure 24.17: Displaying the User Account Complete Message

The Add New Access Rule page appears (Figure 24.18).

12. Select the `All Users` radio button in the `Rule applies to` section and the `Allow` radio button in the `Permission` section of the `Add New Access Rule` page (Figure 24.18).
13. Click the `Add This Rule` button (Figure 24.18).
14. Click the `Next` button in the wizard, as shown in Figure 24.18:

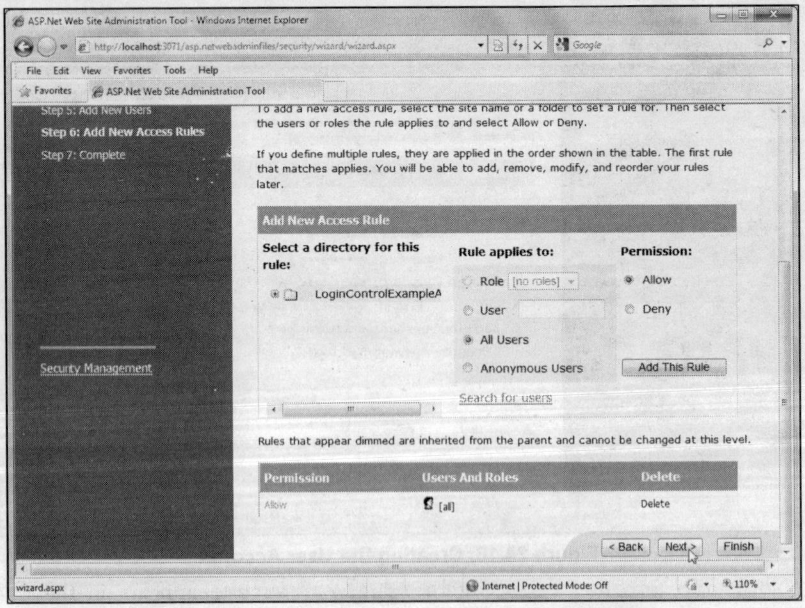

Figure 24.18: Adding the Access Rule in the Wizard

15. Click the `Finish` button, as shown in Figure 24.19:

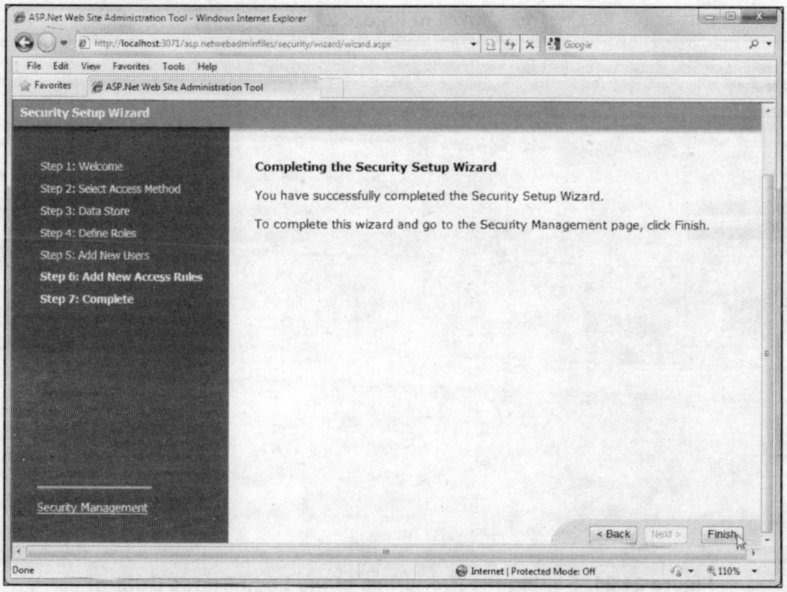

Figure 24.19: Finishing the Wizard

The `Security` tab appears displaying the `Existing user` as `1` (Figure 24.20).

16. Click the `Close` button (that is, the [X] button) on the top right corner of the window to close the tool, as shown in Figure 24.20:

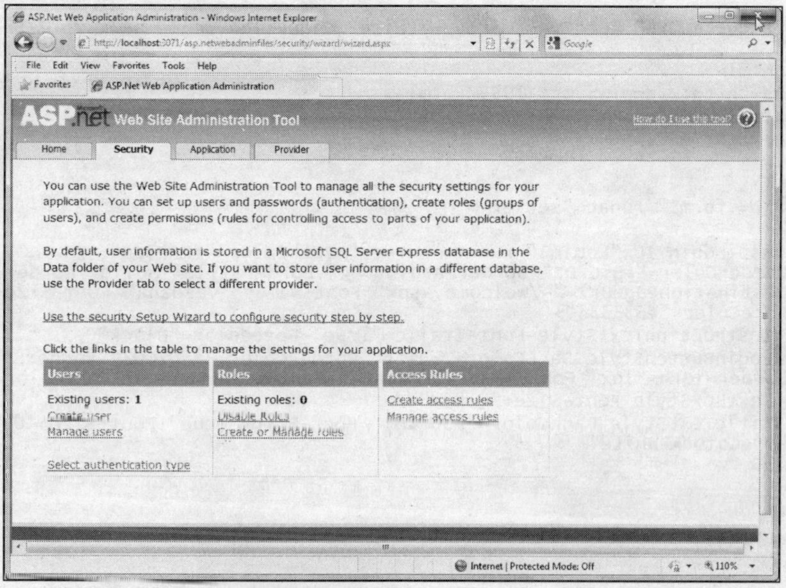

Figure 24.20: Displaying the Existing users

17. Add the `LoginName` and `LoginStatus` controls on the `Welcome.aspx` page (Figure 24.21).
18. Open the Properties window of the `LoginStatus` control and set the `LogoutAction` property to `Redirect` and the `LogoutPageUrl` property to `Login.aspx`.

19. Click the Smart tag of the `LoginStatus` control and select the `Logged In` option from the `Views` drop-down list in `LoginStatus Tasks`, as shown in Figure 24.21:

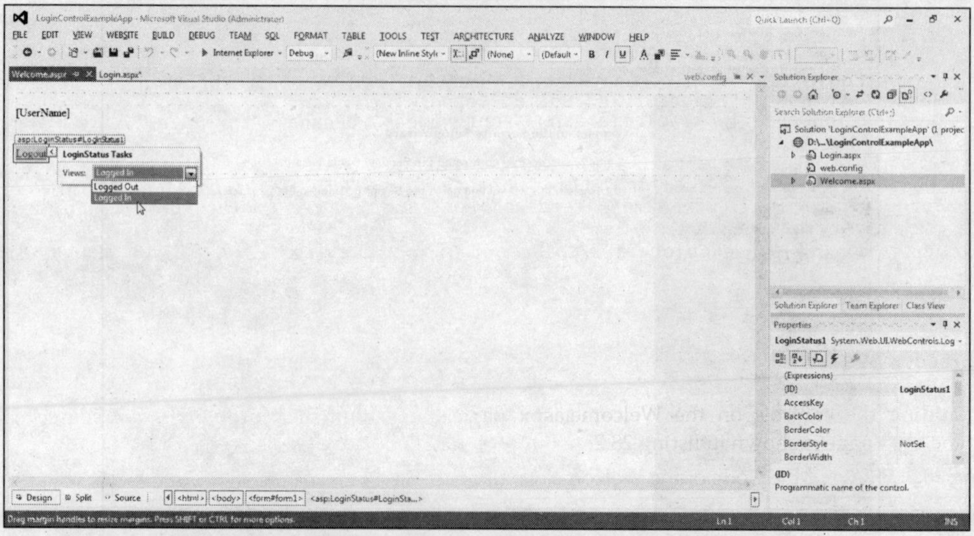

Figure 24.21: Setting the Properties of the LoginStatus Control

After adding the controls on the `Login.aspx` page and setting their properties, the source code of the `Login.aspx` page appears, as shown in Listing 24.1:

Listing 24.1: Showing the Code of the Login.aspx Page

In VB

```
<%@ Page Language="VB" AutoEventWireup="false" CodeFile="Login.aspx.vb" Inherits="Login"
  %>
<!DOCTYPE html>
<html xmlns="http://www.w3.org/1999/xhtml">
<head runat="server">
    <title></title>
</head>
<body>
    <form id="form1" runat="server">
    <div>
         <asp:Login ID="Login1" runat="server" BackColor="#EFF3FB"
         BorderColor="#B5C7DE" BorderPadding="4" BorderStyle="Solid" BorderWidth="1px"
         DestinationPageUrl="~/Welcome.aspx" Font-Names="Verdana" Font-Size="0.8em"
         ForeColor="#333333">
         <InstructionTextStyle Font-Italic="True" ForeColor="Black" />
         <LoginButtonStyle BackColor="White" BorderColor="#507CD1" BorderStyle="Solid"
         BorderWidth="1px" Font-Names="Verdana" Font-Size="0.8em" ForeColor="#284E98" />
         <TextBoxStyle Font-Size="0.8em" />
         <TitleTextStyle BackColor="#507CD1" Font-Bold="True" Font-Size="0.9em"
         ForeColor="White" />
</asp:Login>
    </div>
    </form>
</body>
</html>
```

In C#

```
<%@ Page Language="C#" AutoEventWireup="true" CodeFile="Login.aspx.cs" Inherits="Login" %>
<!DOCTYPE html>
<html xmlns="http://www.w3.org/1999/xhtml">
<head runat="server">
```

```
        <title></title>
    </head>
    <body>
        <form id="form1" runat="server">
        <div>
        </div>
        <asp:Login ID="Login1" runat="server" BackColor="#EFF3FB" BorderColor="#B5C7DE"
      BorderPadding="4" BorderStyle="Solid" BorderWidth="1px"
      DestinationPageUrl="~/Welcome.aspx" Font-Names="Verdana" Font-Size="0.8em"
      ForeColor="#333333">
      <InstructionTextStyle Font-Italic="True" ForeColor="Black" />
      <LoginButtonStyle BackColor="White" BorderColor="#507CD1" BorderStyle="Solid"
      BorderWidth="1px" Font-Names="Verdana" Font-Size="0.8em" ForeColor="#284E98" />
      <TextBoxStyle Font-Size="0.8em" />
      <TitleTextStyle BackColor="#507CD1" Font-Bold="True" Font-Size="0.9em" ForeColor="White"
      />
    </asp:Login>
    </div>
    </form>
    </body>
    </html>
```

After adding the controls on the Welcome.aspx page and setting their properties, the source code of the Welcome.aspx page is shown in listing 28.2:

Listing 28.2: Showing the Code of the Welcome.aspx Page

In VB

```
    <%@ Page Language="VB" AutoEventWireup="false" CodeFile="Welcome.aspx.vb"
      Inherits="Welcome" %>
    <!DOCTYPE html>
    <html xmlns="http://www.w3.org/1999/xhtml">
    <head runat="server">
        <title></title>
    </head>
    <body>
        <form id="form1" runat="server">
        <div>
        WELCOME!<asp:LoginName ID="LoginName1" runat="server" /><br />
            <asp:LoginStatus ID="LoginStatus1" runat="server" LogoutAction="Redirect"
                LogoutPageUrl="~/Login.aspx" />
        </div>
        </form>
    </body>
    </html>
```

In C#

```
    <%@ Page Language="C#" AutoEventWireup="true" CodeFile="Welcome.aspx.cs"
      Inherits="Welcome" %>
    <!DOCTYPE html>
    <html xmlns="http://www.w3.org/1999/xhtml">
    <head runat="server">
        <title></title>
    </head>
    <body>
        <form id="form1" runat="server">
        <div>

          WELCOME! <asp:LoginName ID="LoginName1" runat="server" /><br />
          <asp:LoginStatus ID="LoginStatus1" runat="server" LogoutAction="Redirect"
                LogoutPageUrl="~/Login.aspx" />
        </div>
        </form>
    </body>
    </html>
```

20. Open the `Login.aspx` page and press the F5 key on the keyboard to execute the application (Figure.24.22).

21. Enter the user name and password in the text boxes and select the `Remember me next time` check box (Figure 24.22).
22. Click the `Log In` button, as shown in Figure 24.22:

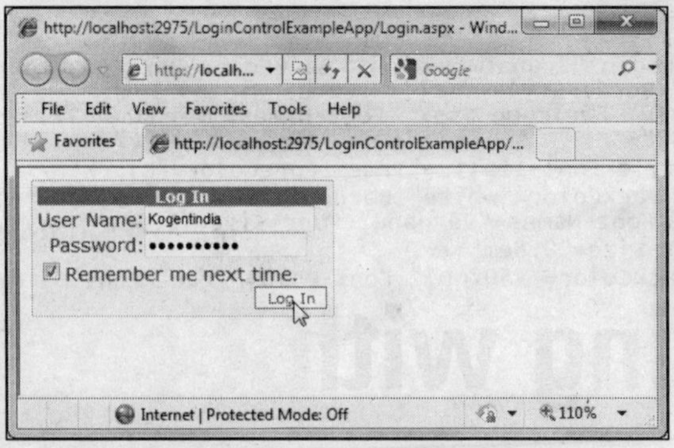

Figure 24.22: Entering the Details

The `Welcome.aspx` page appears displaying the user name (Figure 24.23).

23. Click the `Logout` link to return to the Login.aspx page, as shown in Figure 24.23:

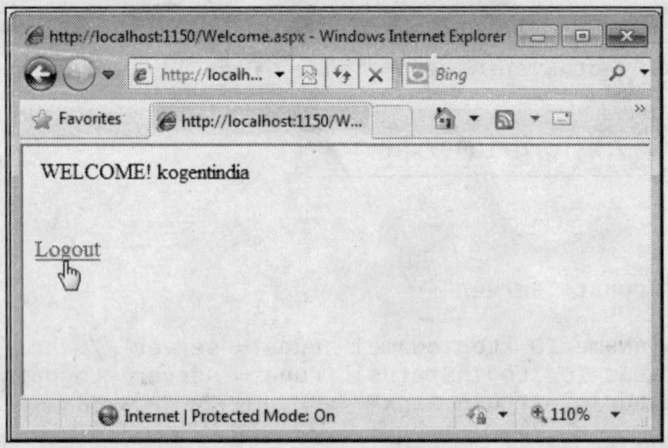

Figure 24.23: Displaying the Log in User Name

Let's now summarize the main points discussed in the chapter.

Summary

In this chapter, you have learned about the Membership service provider and the ASP.NET Login controls, which are used together for authentication and authorization of Web site users and enable you to create a secure Web site. Further, you have learned about the Login, LoginView, LoginStatus, LoginName, PasswordRecovery, CreateUserWizard, and ChangePassword controls. In addition, you have learned how to implement these Login controls in a Web site.

In the next chapter, you learn about various user profiles, such as anonymous user-profile and authenticated user-profile. You also learn how to create customized user profiles according to your requirements.

25

Working with User Profiles

In Depth

You have now been familiarized with the basic concept of personalization. In ASP.NET, websites can be personalized by using the concepts of user profiles and themes. Themes are used to enhance the look and feel of a Web page, but are incapable of storing and using the information of a specific user for personalization. In ASP.NET, you can use the concept of user profiles to display information of a specific user for personalization.

The `user profile` feature in ASP.NET allows you to define and store user-specific settings. In addition, a website can be more user-friendly if it is customized according to the preferences of a user. The ASP.NET profile feature connects information with an individual user and stores the information in a constant format. Profiles allow you to handle user information without requiring you to create and maintain separate database. In addition, the ASP.NET profile feature makes the user information available using an Application Programming Interface (API) that you can use anywhere in your application.

In order to use profiles, you have to first enable profiles by modifying the Web.config configuration file of your ASP.NET Web application. The ProfileProvider class performs the tasks of storing and retrieving profile data. You can use the profile provider class included with the .NET Framework, which stores profile data in SQL Server, or you can create and use your own profile provider class. You can create an instance of SqlProfileProvider class that connects to a database of your choice, or you can use the default instance of SqlProfileProvider class that stores profile data on the local Web server.

Let's understand the profiles by an example. Suppose there is a shopping cart website that consists of the items frequently purchased by the user. To induce such functionality, a website needs to retrieve and load the user's personal information when the request for a Web page is made for the first time. After the request is completed, the current settings, such as the address and phone number of a user, must be stored on the server. Consequently, when the same user requests for the same Web page, the respective settings stored on the server corresponding to a user are retrieved.

In this chapter, you learn how a website stores and utilizes user-specific information through user profiles. You also learn about the ProfileProvider class, and the Anonymous and Authenticated profiles.

Introducing User Profiles

A user profile is a collection of properties that describes the information you want to store for a specific user. You can store the properties associated with a user in a user profile. The data that is stored in a profile can be accessed programmatically.

The user's profile is defined in the `Machine.config` or `Web.config` file. The following code snippet of the `Web.config` file contains the description of a user profile:

```
<profile>
  <properties>
        <group name = “Contact”>
                <add name="Address" type="string" />
                <add name="Phone number" type="Integer" />
                <add name="Links" type="System.Collections.Specialized.StringCollection"
                serializeAs="Xml" />
        </group name>
  </properties>
</profile>
```

The preceding code snippet defines a profile by using properties in the Web.config file. The `<add>` element defines the properties of a profile. The properties of a user profile consist of both simple data types and complex data types. The `<group>` element allows you to group multiple properties in a common container. The `serializeAs` attribute defines the acceptable values for serialization, such as Extensible Markup Language (`XML`) and `Binary`. By default, the `String` type is assumed for the `serializeAs` attribute. When an application is executed, ASP.NET dynamically creates a profile object. All the properties that are defined through the `<add>` element become members of the dynamically created `Profile` class.

The following code snippet shows the way to use profiles defined in the configuration file (preceding code snippet):

In VB

```
Dim contactname as String = Profile.Contact.Address
```

In C#

```
string  contactname = Profile.Contact.Address;
```

The advantage of using user profiles is that it stores the information permanently. Therefore, information stored in the profile is not lost even when the user logs out of the website. For example, suppose a user makes some changes in the profile, such as a change in the current phone number, and logs out from the website. Next time, when the same user visits the website, the modified changes will be displayed.

The `System.Web.Profile` namespace contains classes that are used to implement ASP.NET user profiles in Web applications. Noteworthy classes of the `System.Web.Profile` namespace are listed in Table 25.1:

Table 25.1: Noteworthy Classes of the System.Web.Profile Namespace

Class	Description
`CustomProviderDataAttribute`	Sets the provider of profile property with a string of custom data
`DefaultProfile`	Declares a user-profile instance when the properties of the profile are not defined
`ProfileAutoSaveEventArgs`	Ensures the availability of the data for the ProfileAutoSaving event of the ProfileModule class
`ProfileBase`	Provides untyped accessing of values and information of the profile property
`ProfileEventArgs`	Ensures the availability of the data for the Personalize event of the ProfileModule class
`ProfileGroupBase`	Ensures untyped access of grouped ASP.NET profile property values
`ProfileInfo`	Provides information about a user profile
`ProfileManager`	Manages user profile data and settings
`ProfileMigrateEventArgs`	Ensures the availability of the data for the MigrateAnonymous event of the ProfileModule class
`ProfileModule`	Controls the creation of the user profile and its events
`ProfileProvider`	Provides profile services by using custom profile providers
`ProfileProviderAttribute`	Identifies the profile provider for a user-profile property
`SettingsAllowAnonymousAttribute`	Decides whether the profile property can be used for an anonymous user or not
`SqlProfileProvider`	Manages the user profile information stored in a SQL Server database

ASP.NET implements profile services using custom profile providers by using the ProfileProvider class. Now, let's explore the ProfileProvider class in the next section.

Understanding the ProfileProvider Class

The ProfileProvider class stores the values and information of a profile in the data source in such a manner that can be easily determined by the ProfileProvider implementation. The ProfileProvider abstract class inherits from the SettingsProvider abstract class, which already inherits from the ProviderBase abstract class or you can also use your own provider by defining a new class derived from the ProfileProvider abstract class.

The ProfileProvider class of the .NET Framework class library is available in the `System.Web.Profile` namespace, which resides in the `System.Web` assembly. The inheritance hierarchy for the `ProfileProvider` class is as follows:

```
System.Object
   System.Configuration.Provider.ProviderBase
        System.Configuration.SettingsProvider
              System.Web.Profile.ProfileProvider
```

Noteworthy public methods of the `ProfileProvider` class are listed in Table 25.2:

Table 25.2: Noteworthy Public Methods of the ProfileProvider Class

Method	Description
`DeleteInactiveProfiles`	Removes all user-profile data for profiles where the last activity date occurred before the specified date when this method is overridden
`DeleteProfiles`	Removes profile properties and information from the list provided
`FindInactiveProfilesByUserName`	Obtains the profile information for profiles, where the last activity date occurred on or before the mentioned date and the user name matches with the mentioned user name
`FindProfilesByUserName`	Obtains the profile information for profiles where the user name matches with the mentioned user names
`GetAllInactiveProfiles`	Obtains user-profile data from the data source for profiles, where the last activity date occurred on or before the mentioned date
`GetAllProfiles`	Obtains user profile data for all profiles stored in the data source
`GetNumberOfInactiveProfiles`	Returns the total number of profiles in which the last activity date occurred on or before the mentioned date

The following code snippet displays information about `providers` in the `Web.config` file:

```
<profile>
   <providers>
        <add name="AspNetSqlProfileProvider"
        connectionStringName="LocalSqlServer"
        applicationName="/"
        type="System.Web.Profile.SqlProfileProvider, System.Web,
        Version=4.0.0.0, Culture=neutral, PublicKeyToken=b03f5f7f11d50a3a"
        />
   </providers>
</profile>
```

Now, let's look into the different types of profiles that can be created in ASP.NET, which are anonymous profiles and authenticated profiles.

Anonymous Profiles

It is not necessary that users register to your website at their first visit. When a user visits your portal without logging in, that user is called an anonymous user. You may need to create and use user profiles for anonymous users, so that they are motivated to register on the website in future. Anonymous profiles are used to store information, such as Internet Protocol (IP) address of the system, of unregistered or anonymous users.

To create anonymous profiles, you need to enable the anonymous identification feature in the Web.config configuration file, as shown in the following code snippet:

```
<anonymousIdentification enabled="true"/>
```

The anonymous identification feature generates a unique identification number for each anonymous user visiting the website. A website can identify an anonymous user with the help of this unique identification number because this unique identification number and the other user-related information are stored in a `cookie` on the computer of the anonymous user. The following code snippet shows how to change the cookie name for anonymous identification through the Web.config configuration file:

```
<configuration>
  <system.web>
        <anonymousIdentification enabled="true"
        cookieName =".CkAnonymousidentification"/>
  </system.web>
</configuration>
```

A website can identify the anonymous user when the user visits the website the next time by using the preceding code snippet of the configuration file.

NOTE

By default, a cookie of a website expires after a time period of 100000 minutes or 69 days approximately. This time period is renewed every time a user visits the website.

In case the cookies are blocked on the computer of the anonymous user, the stored unique identification number in the Uniform Resource Locator (URL) is used by the anonymous user to send a request for the website on the Web server. The following code snippet shows how you can store a unique identification number in the URL through the Web.config configuration file:

```
<configuration>
  <system.web>
        <anonymousIdentification enabled="true"
        cookieless ="UseUri"/>
  </system.web>
</configuration>
```

The only problem with this method of storing the user information is that the identification number stored in the URL is lost when the user closes the browser on which the website is running.

NOTE

The anonymous identification feature for the profile properties is not enabled by default, because some properties store information, such as bank accounts or credit card numbers. These should not be made available to anonymous users.

Now, let's learn how to enable the anonymous identification feature. ASP.NET provides the `<anonymousIdentification>` element to enable the anonymous identification feature. The `<anonymousIdentification>` element is defined within the `<system.web>` element, which is defined in the `<configuration>` element.

The code snippet for the `<anonymousIdentification>` element is as follows:

```
<anonymousIdentification
  enabled="[true | false]"
  cookieless="[UseUri | UseCookies | AutoDetect | UseDeviceProfile]"
  cookieName=""
  cookiePath=""
  cookieProtection="[None | Validation | Encryption | All]"
  cookieRequireSSL="[true | false]"
  cookieSlidingExpiration="[true | false]"
  cookieTimeout="[DD.HH:MM:SS]"
  domain="cookie domain"
/>
```

Table 25.3 shows attributes of the `<anonymousIdentification>` element in detail:

Table 25.3. Attributes of the <anonymousIdentification> Element

Attribute	Description
`Cookieless`	Specifies whether to store the information of an anonymous user in a cookie on the user's computer. This attribute can take the following values: • `AutoDetect`—Determines whether the browser of an anonymous user's computer supports cookies. If the browser supports cookies, then the identification number of the anonymous user is stored in a cookie, otherwise, the identification number is stored in the URL using which the website is requested.

Table 25.3: Attributes of the <anonymousIdentification> Element

Attribute	Description
	• `UseCookies`—Stores the identification number of an anonymous user in a cookie. • `UseDeviceProfile`—Stores the identification number of an anonymous user either in a cookie or in a URL on the basis of the information provided by the `HttpBrowserCapability` class that specifies whether or not a browser supports cookies. • `UseUri`—Stores the identification number of an anonymous user in the URL by using which the anonymous user requests for the website. The default value of the `cookieless` attribute is `UseCookies`.
`cookieName`	Specifies the name of the cookie that stores information of an anonymous user. The default value is .ASPXANONYMOUS.
`cookiePath`	Specifies the location of the cookie that stores information of an anonymous user. The default directory is specified by"/".
`cookieProtection`	Secures the anonymous user information stored in the cookie. This attribute can take the following values: • `Encryption`—Encrypts the anonymous user information stored in the cookie. • `Validation`—Ensures that the anonymous user information is not modified while it is transmitted from the computer of the anonymous user to the server on which the website is running. • `All`—Encrypts as well as validates the anonymous user information stored in the cookies. • `None`—Specifies neither to encrypt nor to validate the anonymous user information stored in the cookie. The default value of the `cookieProtection` attribute is `Validation`.
`cookieRequireSSL`	Determines whether a Secure Socket Layer (SSL) connection is required to store the information of an anonymous user in a cookie. The default value of the `cookieRequireSSL` attribute is `false`.
`cookieSlidingExpiration`	Specifies the time after which the expiration time of the cookies is refreshed. If the `cookieSlidingExpiration` attribute is set to `true`, the expiration time of the cookie is refreshed when half of the expiration time is over. If the `cookieSlidingExpiration` attribute is set to `false`, the cookie expiration time is not refreshed and the cookie expires after the specified time. The default value of the `cookieSlidingExpiration` attribute is `true`.
`cookieTimeout`	Specifies the expiration time of a cookie. You need to specify the value for the `cookieTimeout` attribute in minutes. The default value of the `cookieTimeout attribute` is 100000 minutes.
`domain`	Specifies the name of the domain of a cookie. The default value of domain is an empty string " ".
`enabled`	Allows you to enable the anonymous identification feature. You need to set the enabled attribute to true to enable the anonymous identification feature. The default value of the `enabled` attribute is `false`.

Now, let's understand authenticated profiles.

Authenticated Profiles

When anonymous users register themselves, they become authenticated users. A registered user can access and view account-specific information when s/he logs on to the website. For example, if an anonymous user logs on to an online banking website, s/he would not be able to access account-specific information. However, in case of an authenticated user, the website will display account-specific information, such as the account number and the credit card number. The profiles that store the information about these users are known as authenticated profiles.

By default, all the profiles are authenticated profiles, because, as we have read earlier, the `enabled` attribute of the `<anonymousIdentification>` element is set to `false`.

NOTE

By default, the data type of the properties defined in a user profile is String. However, you can change the data type of properties that are used in user profiles.

The `<add>` element in the `Web.config` file supports various attributes that help you to specify the characteristics of a property. For example, you can set the `allowAnonymous` attribute of a property defined in the `<add>` element to `true` to allow the property to store information about anonymous users.

Now, you have become familiar with different types of profiles and their respective properties. Let's move ahead to the *Immediate Solutions* section. In this section, you learn how to implement profile in a Web application.

Immediate Solutions

Creating User Profile

You have learned that you need to define the properties for the user profile in the `Web.config` file. Now, let's learn how to create user profiles to personalize a website by performing the following steps:

1. Create a website and save it as ProfilesCS. You can find the code for this application in the ProfilesCS (for C#) and ProfilesVB (for VB) folders. Next, define the properties of the profile in the `Web.config` file, as shown in the following code snippet:

```
<?xml version="1.0"?>
<!--
  For more information on how to configure your ASP.NET application, please visit
  http://go.microsoft.com/fwlink/?LinkId=169433
  -->
<configuration>
  <system.web>
    <authentication mode="Forms"/>
    <anonymousIdentification enabled="true"/>
    <profile enabled="true">
      <properties>
        <add name="SName" allowAnonymous="true"/>
        <add name="Cname" defaultValue="ASP.NET 4.5" allowAnonymous="true"/>
        <add name="Rno" defaultValue="1001" allowAnonymous="true"/>
      </properties>
    </profile>
    <compilation debug="true" targetFramework="4.5"/>
    <httpRuntime targetFramework="4.5"/>
  </system.web>
</configuration>
```

In the preceding code snippet, we have created a user profile, where the `<anonymousIdentification>` element and the `allowAnonymous` attribute of the `<add>` element are set to `true`. Therefore, this user profile can be used for both, anonymous and authenticated users.

2. Replace the code for the Default.aspx file with the code, given in Listing 25.1, to add the controls required for the application:

Listing 25.1: Showing the Code for the `Default.aspx` Page

In VB

```
<%@ Page Language="VB" AutoEventWireup="false" CodeFile="Default.aspx.vb"
  Inherits="_Default" %>
<!DOCTYPE html>
<html xmlns="http://www.w3.org/1999/xhtml">
<head runat="server">
    <title></title>
    <script runat="server">
        Private Sub RevisePro(s As Object, e As EventArgs)
            Profile.SName = txtStudentName.Text
            Profile.Cname = txtCourseName.Text
            Profile.Rno = txtRollno.Text
        End Sub
</script>
</head>
<body>
    <form id="form1" runat="server">
    <div class ="itemContent">
                    <b>Welcome</b> <%= Profile.SName %>
                    <br />
                    <b>Roll number</b> <%= Profile.Rno %>
                    <br />
                    <b>Course undertaken by you</b> <%= Profile.Cname %>
```

```
                <hr />
                <b>Student Name:<span lang="en-us">     </span></b>
                 <asp:TextBox ID="txtStudentName" runat="Server" />
                <br />
                <br />
                <b>Roll number:</b>
                <span lang="en-us">       </span>
                <asp:TextBox ID="txtRollno" Runat="Server" style="margin-left: 5px" />
                <br />
                <br />
                <b>Course Name:</b>
              <asp:TextBox ID="txtCourseName" runat="Server" style="margin-left: 26px" />
                <br />
                <br />
                <br />
                <asp:Button ID="Button1" Text="Revise Profile"  OnClick="RevisePro"
                runat="server" />
    </div>
    </form>
</body></html>
```

In C#

```
<%@ Page Language="C#" AutoEventWireup="true" CodeFile="Default.aspx.cs"
  Inherits="_Default" %>
<!DOCTYPE html>
<html xmlns="http://www.w3.org/1999/xhtml">
<head runat="server">
    <title></title>
    <script runat="server">
        void RevisePro(Object s, EventArgs e)
        {
            Profile.SName = txtStudentName.Text;
            Profile.Cname = txtCourseName.Text;
            Profile.Rno = txtRollno.Text;
        }
</script>
</head>
<body>
    <form id="form1" runat="server">
    <div>
    <b>Welcome</b> <%= Profile.SName %>
         <br />
         <b>Roll number</b> <%= Profile.Rno %>
         <br />
         <b>Course undertaken by you</b> <%= Profile.Cname %>
         <hr />
         <b>Student Name:<span lang="en-us">     </span></b>
          <asp:TextBox ID="txtStudentName" runat="Server" />
         <br />
         <br />
         <b>Roll number:</b>
         <span lang="en-us">       </span>
         <asp:TextBox ID="txtRollno" runat="Server" style="margin-left: 5px" />
         <br />
         <br />
         <b>Course Name:</b>
         <asp:TextBox ID="txtCourseName" runat="Server" style="margin-left: 26px" />
         <br />
         <br />
         <br />
         <asp:Button ID="Button1" Text="Revise Profile"  OnClick="RevisePro"
         runat="server" />
    </div>
    </form>
</body></html>
```

3. Execute the application by pressing the F5 key on the keyboard. The output of the application is shown in Figure 25.1:

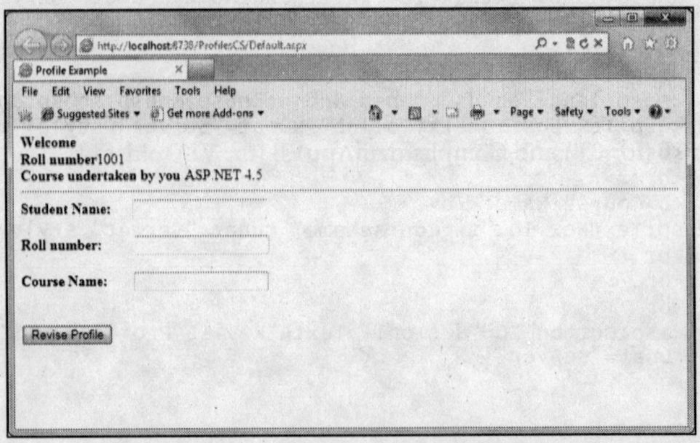

Figure 25.1: Displaying the Default Values

4. Specify the values for the Student Name, Roll number, and Course Name fields, and then click the Revise Profile button to store the information in a user profile (Figure 25.2).

The Default values are replaced by the new values on the Web page, as shown in Figure 25.2:

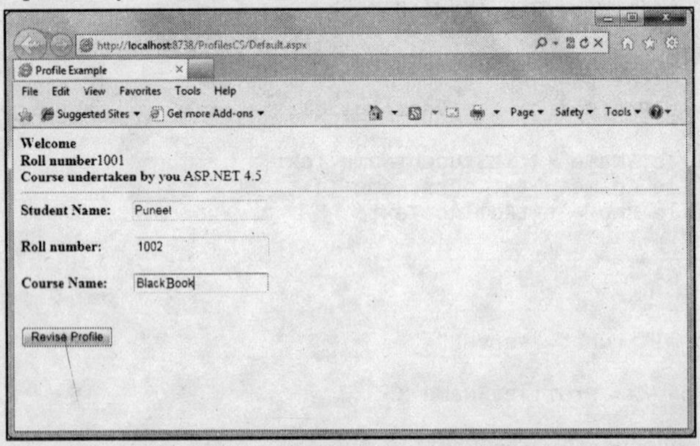

Figure 25.2: Displaying the New Values

5. After closing the website, when you visit it the next time, the Web page will automatically display the personalized information that you entered on your last visit to the website, as shown in Figure 25.3:

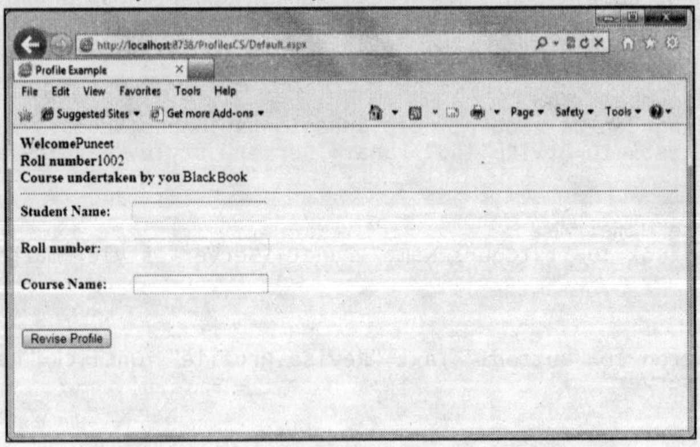

Figure 25.3: Displaying the Stored User Profile

Using Complex Data Types

In the preceding website, Profiles, we have used simple data types to define the properties of a user profile. Now, let's understand how you can use complex data types to define the properties of a user profile in the following steps:

1. Create a website and save it as ComplexdataAppCS. You can find the code for this application in the ComplexdataAppCS (for C#) and ComplexdataAppVB (for VB) folders.
2. The next step is to define the properties of the profile in the `Web.config` file, as shown in the following code snippet:

```
<?xml version="1.0"?>
<!--
  For more information on how to configure your ASP.NET application, please visit
  http://go.microsoft.com/fwlink/?LinkId=169433
  -->
<configuration>
  <system.web>
    <authentication mode="Forms"/>
    <anonymousIdentification enabled="true"/>
    <profile>
      <properties>
        <add name="StudentName" allowAnonymous="true"/>
        <add name="DOB" type="Classprofile" allowAnonymous="true"/>
      </properties>
    </profile>
    <compilation debug="true" targetFramework="4.5"/>
    <httpRuntime targetFramework="4.5"/>
  </system.web>
</configuration>
```

3. Replace the code for the Default.aspx file with the code, given in Listing 25.2, to add the controls required for the application:

Listing 25.2: Showing the Code for the `Default.aspx` Page

In VB

```
<%@ Page Language="VB" AutoEventWireup="false" CodeFile="Default.aspx.vb"
  Inherits="_Default" %>
<!DOCTYPE html>
<html xmlns="http://www.w3.org/1999/xhtml">
<head runat="server">
    <title></title>
    <script runat="server">
    Private Sub ReviseProfile(s As Object,e As EventArgs)
  Profile.StudentName = txtStudentName.Text
  Profile.DOB.Day = txtDay.Text
  Profile.DOB.Month = txtMonth.Text
  Profile.DOB.Year = txtYear.Text
  End Sub
    </script>
</head>
<body>
    <form id="form1" runat="server">
    <div>
    <b>Welcome</b> <%=Profile.StudentName%><br />
         <b>Date of Birth:</b> <%=Profile.DOB.Day%> <%=Profile.DOB.Month%>
        <%=Profile.DOB.Year%><br />
         <hr />
        <b>
        <br />
        Student Name:</b>
        <asp:TextBox ID="txtStudentName"  runat="server" />
        <br />
        <br /> <br />
```

```
            <b>Date:</b>
            <asp:TextBox ID="txtDay" runat="server" style="margin-left: 30px" />
            <br />
            <br />
            <b>Month:</b>
            <asp:TextBox ID="txtMonth"  runat="server" style="margin-left: 20px" />
            <br />
            <br />
            <b>Year:</b>
            <asp:TextBox ID="txtYear" runat="server" style="margin-left: 33px" />
            <br />
            <br />
            <asp:Button ID="Button1" Text="Revise Profile"  OnClick="ReviseProfile"
            runat="server" />
        </div>
        </form>
    </body></html>
```

In C#

```
<%@ Page Language="C#" AutoEventWireup="true" CodeFile="Default.aspx.cs"
  Inherits="_Default" %>
<!DOCTYPE html>
<html xmlns="http://www.w3.org/1999/xhtml">
<head runat="server">
    <script runat="server">
    void ReviseProfile(Object s, EventArgs e)
  {
        Profile.StudentName = txtStudentName.Text;
        Profile.DOB.Day = txtDay.Text;
        Profile.DOB.Month = txtMonth.Text;
        Profile.DOB.Year = txtYear.Text;
  }
    </script>
    <title></title>
</head>
<body>
    <form id="form1" runat="server">
    <div>
    <b>Welcome</b> <%=Profile.StudentName%><br />
         <b>Date of Birth:</b> <%=Profile.DOB.Day%> <%=Profile.DOB.Month%>
        <%=Profile.DOB.Year%><br />
         <hr />
        <b>
        <br />
        Student Name:</b>
        <asp:TextBox ID="txtStudentName"  runat="server" />
        <br />
        <br /> <br />
        <b>Date:</b>
        <asp:TextBox ID="txtDay" runat="server" style="margin-left: 30px" />
        <br />
        <br />
        <b>Month:</b>
        <asp:TextBox ID="txtMonth"  runat="server" style="margin-left: 20px" />
        <br />
        <br />
        <b>Year:</b>
        <asp:TextBox ID="txtYear" runat="server" style="margin-left: 33px" />
        <br />
        <br />
        <asp:Button ID="Button1" Text="Revise Profile"  OnClick="ReviseProfile"
        runat="server" />
    </div>
    </form>
</body></html>
```

4. Add a class file (Classprofile.cs in case of ComplexdataAppCS and Classprofile.vb in case of ComplexdataAppVB) to the Web application.
5. Add the following code in the class file, as shown in Listing 25.3:

Listing 25.3: Showing the Code for the Classprofile Class File

In VB

```
Imports Microsoft.VisualBasic
Public Class Classprofile
    Private Dy As String
    Private Mnth As String
    Private Yr As String
    Public Property Day() As String
        Get
            Return Dy
        End Get
        Set(value As String)
            Dy = value
        End Set
    End Property
    Public Property Month() As String
        Get
            Return Mnth
        End Get
        Set(value As String)
            Mnth = value
        End Set
    End Property
    Public Property Year() As String
        Get
            Return Yr
        End Get
        Set(value As String)
            Yr = value
        End Set
    End Property
End Class
```

In C#

```
using System;
using System.Collections.Generic;
using System.Linq;
using System.Web;
/// <summary>
/// Summary description for Classprofile
/// </summary>
public class Classprofile
{
  private string Dy;
  private string Mnth;
  private string Yr;
  public string Day
  {
        get { return Dy; }
        set { Dy = value; }
  }
  public string Month
  {
        get { return Mnth; }
        set
        {
                Mnth = value;
        }
  }
```

```
        public string Year
        {
                get { return Yr; }
                set
                {
                        Yr = value;
                }
        }
    }
```

6. Execute the application by pressing the F5 key on the keyboard. Enter your profile in the text boxes and click the Revise Profile button.The output of the application is shown in Figure 25.4:

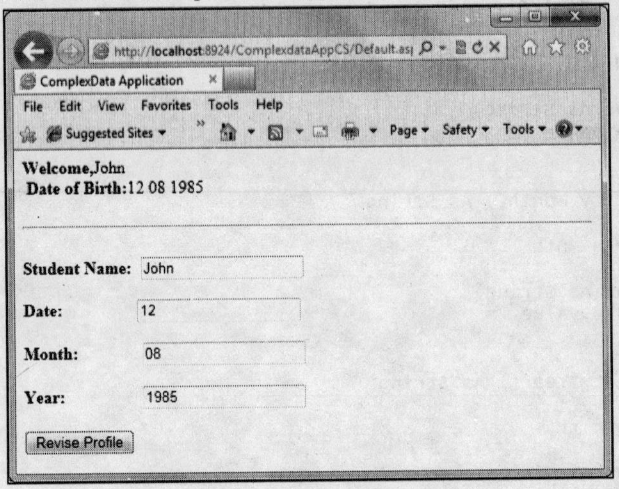

Figure 25.4: Entering the User Profile

After you close the website and visit it the next time, the Web page will display the personalized information that you entered on your last visit, as shown in Figure 25.5:

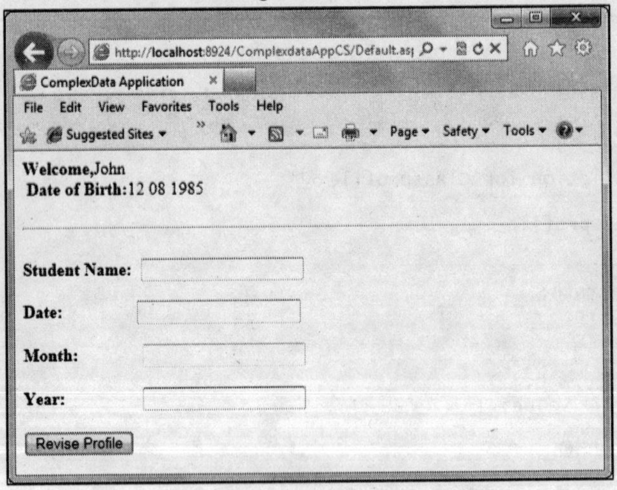

Figure 25.5: Displaying the Stored Profile

Creating Authenticated Profiles

Till now we have used anonymous profiles. Now, we understand and learn how to create authenticated user profiles in the following steps:

1. Create an application and save it as AuthenticatedProfilesCS. You can find the code for this application in the AuthenticatedProfilesCS (for C#) and AuthenticatedProfilesVB (for VB) folders.
2. Define the properties of the profile in the `Web.config` file. The code you need to write in the `Web.config` file of the `AuthenticatedProfilesCS` website to define the profile is as follows:

```
<?xml version="1.0"?>
<!--
  For more information on how to configure your ASP.NET application, please visit
  http://go.microsoft.com/fwlink/?LinkId=169433
  -->
<configuration>
  <system.web>
        <authentication mode="Forms"/>
        <roleManager enabled="true"/>
        <anonymousIdentification enabled="true"/>
        <profile>
                <properties>
                        <add name="Name"/>
                        <add name="Country" type="string"/>
                        <add name="Gender" type="string"/>
                </properties>
        </profile>
        <compilation debug="true" targetFramework="4.5"/>
  </system.web>
</configuration>
```

3. Add four Web forms in the Web application. In this application, we have named the forms as Createuser.aspx, Login.aspx, Manageprofiles.aspx, and Displayprofile.aspx.
4. Replace the code for the `Createuser.aspx` page with the code, given in Listing 25.4, to add the controls required for the application:

Listing 25.4: Showing the Code for the `Createuser.aspx` Page

In VB

```
<%@ Page Language="VB" AutoEventWireup="false" CodeFile="Createuser.aspx.vb"
  Inherits="Createuser" %>
<!DOCTYPE html>
<html xmlns="http://www.w3.org/1999/xhtml">
<head runat="server">
    <title></title>
</head>
<body>
    <form id="form1" runat="server">
    <div>
    <asp:CreateUserWizard ID="CreateUserWizard1" runat="server" BackColor="#F7F6F3"
         BorderColor="#E6E2D8" BorderStyle="Solid" BorderWidth="1px"
         Font-Names="Verdana" Font-Size="0.8em" Height="55px" Width="349px"
         oncreateduser="CreateUserWizard1_CreatedUser">
         <SideBarStyle BackColor="#5D7B9D" Font-Size="0.9em" VerticalAlign="Top"
         BorderWidth="0px" />
         <SideBarButtonStyle Font-Names="Verdana"
         ForeColor="White" BorderWidth="0px" />
         <ContinueButtonStyle BackColor="#FFFBFF" BorderColor="#CCCCCC"
         BorderStyle="Solid" BorderWidth="1px" Font-Names="Verdana"
         ForeColor="#284775" />
         <NavigationButtonStyle BackColor="#FFFBFF" BorderColor="#CCCCCC"
         BorderStyle="Solid" BorderWidth="1px" Font-Names="Verdana"
         ForeColor="#284775" />
         <HeaderStyle BackColor="#5D7B9D" BorderStyle="Solid" Font-Bold="True"
         Font-Size="0.9em" ForeColor="White"
```

```
HorizontalAlign="Center" />
<CreateUserButtonStyle BackColor="#FFFBFF" BorderColor="#CCCCCC"
BorderStyle="Solid" BorderWidth="1px" Font-Names="Verdana"
ForeColor="#284775" />
<TitleTextStyle BackColor="#5D7B9D" Font-Bold="True" ForeColor="White" />
<StepStyle BorderWidth="0px" />
<WizardSteps>
<asp:CreateUserWizardStep ID="CreateUserWizardStep1" runat="server"
Title="CreateUser">
<ContentTemplate>
<table border="0" class="style2" style="font-family:Verdana;font-size:100%;">
<tr>
<td align="center" colspan="2"
style="color:White;background-color:#507CD1;font-weight:bold;">
CreateUser</td>
</tr>
<tr>
<td align="right">
<asp:Label ID="UserNameLabel" runat="server" AssociatedControlID="UserName">User
Name:</asp:Label>
</td>
<td>
<asp:TextBox ID="UserName" runat="server"></asp:TextBox>
<asp:RequiredFieldValidator ID="UserNameRequired" runat="server"
ControlToValidate="UserName" ErrorMessage="User Name is required."
ToolTip="User Name is required."
ValidationGroup="CreateUserWizard1">*</asp:RequiredFieldValidator>
</td>
</tr>
<tr>
<td align="right">
<asp:Label ID ="lblName" runat="server" Text="Name">
</asp:Label>
</td>
<td align="left">
<asp:TextBox ID ="Name" runat ="server">
</asp:TextBox>
</td>
</tr>
<tr>
<td align="right">
<asp:Label ID="PasswordLabel" runat="server"
AssociatedControlID="Password">Password:</asp:Label>
</td>
<td>
<asp:TextBox ID="Password" runat="server" TextMode="Password"></asp:TextBox>
<asp:RequiredFieldValidator ID="PasswordRequired" runat="server"
ControlToValidate="Password" ErrorMessage="Password is required."
ToolTip="Password is required."
ValidationGroup="CreateUserWizard1">*</asp:RequiredFieldValidator>
</td>
</tr>
<tr>
<td align="right">
<asp:Label ID="ConfirmPasswordLabel" runat="server"
AssociatedControlID="ConfirmPassword">Confirm Password:</asp:Label>
</td>
<td>
<asp:TextBox ID="ConfirmPassword" runat="server"
TextMode="Password"></asp:TextBox>
<asp:RequiredFieldValidator ID="ConfirmPasswordRequired" runat="server"
ControlToValidate="ConfirmPassword"
ErrorMessage="Confirm Password is required."
ToolTip="Confirm Password is required."
ValidationGroup="CreateUserWizard1">*</asp:RequiredFieldValidator>
```

```
</td>
</tr>
<tr>
<td align="right">
<asp:Label ID="EmailLabel" runat="server" AssociatedControlID="Email">
E-mail:</asp:Label>
</td>
<td>
<asp:TextBox ID="Email" runat="server"></asp:TextBox>
<asp:RequiredFieldValidator ID="EmailRequired" runat="server"
ControlToValidate="Email" ErrorMessage="E-mail is required."
ToolTip="E-mail is required."
ValidationGroup="CreateUserWizard1">*</asp:RequiredFieldValidator>
</td>
</tr>
<tr>
<td align="right">
<asp:Label ID="QuestionLabel" runat="server"
AssociatedControlID="Question">Security
Question:</asp:Label>
</td>
<td>
<asp:TextBox ID="Question" runat="server"></asp:TextBox>
<asp:RequiredFieldValidator ID="QuestionRequired" runat="server"
ControlToValidate="Question" ErrorMessage="Security question is required."
ToolTip="Security question is required."
ValidationGroup="CreateUserWizard1">*</asp:RequiredFieldValidator>
</td>
</tr>
<tr>
<td align="right">
<asp:Label ID="AnswerLabel" runat="server" AssociatedControlID="Answer">Security
Answer:</asp:Label>
</td>
<td>
<asp:TextBox ID="Answer" runat="server"></asp:TextBox>
<asp:RequiredFieldValidator ID="AnswerRequired" runat="server"
ControlToValidate="Answer" ErrorMessage="Security answer is required."
ToolTip="Security answer is required."
ValidationGroup="CreateUserWizard1">*</asp:RequiredFieldValidator>
</td>
</tr>
<tr>
<td align="center" colspan="2">
<asp:CompareValidator ID="PasswordCompare" runat="server"
ControlToCompare="Password" ControlToValidate="ConfirmPassword"
Display="Dynamic"
ErrorMessage="The Password and Confirmation Password must match."
ValidationGroup="CreateUserWizard1"></asp:CompareValidator>
</td>
</tr>
<tr>
<td align="center" colspan="2" style="color:Red;">
<asp:Literal ID="ErrorMessage" runat="server"
EnableViewState="False"></asp:Literal>
</td>
</tr>
<tr>
<td align="right">
<asp:Label ID="lblcountry" runat="server" Text="Country"></asp:Label>
</td>
<td align ="left" colspan="2">
<asp:DropDownList ID="Country" runat="server" style="margin-left: 11px" >
<asp:ListItem>Others</asp:ListItem>
<asp:ListItem>India</asp:ListItem>
```

```
        <asp:ListItem>China</asp:ListItem>
        <asp:ListItem>Nepal
        </asp:ListItem>
        <asp:ListItem></asp:ListItem>
        </asp:DropDownList>
        </td>
        </tr>
        <tr>
        <td align="right">
        <asp:Label ID="Lblgender" runat="server" Text="Gender"></asp:Label>
        </td>
        <td align ="left" colspan="2">
        <asp:DropDownList ID="Gender" runat="server" style="margin-left: 9px" >
        <asp:ListItem>Male</asp:ListItem>
        <asp:ListItem>Female</asp:ListItem>
        </asp:DropDownList>
        </td>
        </tr>
        </table>
        </ContentTemplate>
        </asp:CreateUserWizardStep>
        <asp:CompleteWizardStep ID="CompleteWizardStep1" runat="server" >
        <ContentTemplate>
        <table border="0"
        style="font-family:Verdana;font-size:100%;height:212px;width:362px;">
        <tr>
        <td align="center" colspan="2"
        style="color:White;background-color:#5D7B9D;font-weight:bold;">
        Complete</td>
        </tr>
        <tr>
        <td>
        Your account has been successfully created.</td>
        </tr>
        <tr>
        <td align="right" colspan="2">
        <asp:Button ID="ContinueButton" runat="server" BackColor="#FFFBFF"
        BorderColor="#CCCCCC" BorderStyle="Solid" BorderWidth="1px"
        CausesValidation="False" CommandName="Continue" Font-Names="Verdana"
        ForeColor="#284775" Text="Continue" ValidationGroup="CreateUserWizard1" />
        <a href="Login.aspx">Login</a>
        </td>
        </tr>
        </table>
        </ContentTemplate>
        </asp:CompleteWizardStep>
        <asp:WizardStep ID="WizardStep1" runat="server" Title="Registerd">
        <asp:Label ID="Label1" runat="server"
        Text="You Are a Registered User now,You can login Into the website"></asp:Label>
        <a href="Login.aspx">Login</a>
        </asp:WizardStep>
        </WizardSteps>
        </asp:CreateUserWizard>
    </div>
    </form>
</body>
</html>
```

In C#

```
<%@ Page Language="C#" AutoEventWireup="true" CodeFile="Createuser.aspx.cs"
  Inherits="Createuser" %>
<!DOCTYPE html>
<html xmlns="http://www.w3.org/1999/xhtml">
<head runat="server">
    <title></title>
```

```
    </head>
    <body>
        <form id="form1" runat="server">
        <div>
        <asp:CreateUserWizard ID="CreateUserWizard1" runat="server" BackColor="#F7F6F3",
            BorderColor="#E6E2D8" BorderStyle="Solid" BorderWidth="1px"
            Font-Names="Verdana" Font-Size="0.8em" Height="55px" Width="349px"
            oncreateduser="CreateUserWizard1_CreatedUser">
            <SideBarStyle BackColor="#5D7B9D" Font-Size="0.9em" VerticalAlign="Top"
            BorderWidth="0px" />
            <SideBarButtonStyle Font-Names="Verdana"
            ForeColor="White" BorderWidth="0px" />
            <ContinueButtonStyle BackColor="#FFFBFF" BorderColor="#CCCCCC"
            BorderStyle="Solid" BorderWidth="1px" Font-Names="Verdana"
            ForeColor="#284775" />
            <NavigationButtonStyle BackColor="#FFFBFF" BorderColor="#CCCCCC"
            BorderStyle="Solid" BorderWidth="1px" Font-Names="Verdana"
            ForeColor="#284775" />
            <HeaderStyle BackColor="#5D7B9D" BorderStyle="Solid" Font-Bold="True"
            Font-Size="0.9em" ForeColor="White"
            HorizontalAlign="Center" />
            <CreateUserButtonStyle BackColor="#FFFBFF" BorderColor="#CCCCCC"
            BorderStyle="Solid" BorderWidth="1px" Font-Names="Verdana"
            ForeColor="#284775" />
            <TitleTextStyle BackColor="#5D7B9D" Font-Bold="True" ForeColor="White" />
            <StepStyle BorderWidth="0px" />
            <WizardSteps>
            <asp:CreateUserWizardStep ID="CreateUserWizardStep1" runat="server"
            Title="CreateUser">
            <ContentTemplate>
            <table border="0" class="style2" style="font-family:Verdana;font-size:100%;">
            <tr>
            <td align="center" colspan="2"
            style="color:White;background-color:#507CD1;font-weight:bold;">
            CreateUser</td>
            </tr>
            <tr>
            <td align="right">
            <asp:Label ID="UserNameLabel" runat="server" AssociatedControlID="UserName">User
            Name:</asp:Label>
            </td>
            <td>
            <asp:TextBox ID="UserName" runat="server"></asp:TextBox>
            <asp:RequiredFieldValidator ID="UserNameRequired" runat="server"
            ControlToValidate="UserName" ErrorMessage="User Name is required."
            ToolTip="User Name is required."
            ValidationGroup="CreateUserWizard1">*</asp:RequiredFieldValidator>
            </td>
            </tr>
            <tr>
            <td align="right">
            <asp:Label ID ="lblName" runat="server" Text="Name">
            </asp:Label>
            </td>
            <td align="left">
            <asp:TextBox ID ="Name" runat ="server">
            </asp:TextBox>
            </td>
            </tr>
            <tr>
            <td align="right">
            <asp:Label ID="PasswordLabel" runat="server"
            AssociatedControlID="Password">Password:</asp:Label>
            </td>
            <td>
```

```
<asp:TextBox ID="Password" runat="server" TextMode="Password"></asp:TextBox>
<asp:RequiredFieldValidator ID="PasswordRequired" runat="server"
ControlToValidate="Password" ErrorMessage="Password is required."
ToolTip="Password is required."
ValidationGroup="CreateUserWizard1">*</asp:RequiredFieldValidator>
</td>
</tr>
<tr>
<td align="right">
<asp:Label ID="ConfirmPasswordLabel" runat="server"
AssociatedControlID="ConfirmPassword">Confirm Password:</asp:Label>
</td>
<td>
<asp:TextBox ID="ConfirmPassword" runat="server"
TextMode="Password"></asp:TextBox>
<asp:RequiredFieldValidator ID="ConfirmPasswordRequired" runat="server"
ControlToValidate="ConfirmPassword"
ErrorMessage="Confirm Password is required."
ToolTip="Confirm Password is required."
ValidationGroup="CreateUserWizard1">*</asp:RequiredFieldValidator>
</td>
</tr>
<tr>
<td align="right">
<asp:Label ID="EmailLabel" runat="server" AssociatedControlID="Email">
E-mail:</asp:Label>
</td>
<td>
<asp:TextBox ID="Email" runat="server"></asp:TextBox>
<asp:RequiredFieldValidator ID="EmailRequired" runat="server"
ControlToValidate="Email" ErrorMessage="E-mail is required."
ToolTip="E-mail is required."
ValidationGroup="CreateUserWizard1">*</asp:RequiredFieldValidator>
</td>
</tr>
<tr>
<td align="right">
<asp:Label ID="QuestionLabel" runat="server"
AssociatedControlID="Question">Security
Question:</asp:Label>
</td>
<td>
<asp:TextBox ID="Question" runat="server"></asp:TextBox>
<asp:RequiredFieldValidator ID="QuestionRequired" runat="server"
ControlToValidate="Question" ErrorMessage="Security question is required."
ToolTip="Security question is required."
ValidationGroup="CreateUserWizard1">*</asp:RequiredFieldValidator>
</td>
</tr>
<tr>
<td align="right">
<asp:Label ID="AnswerLabel" runat="server" AssociatedControlID="Answer">Security
Answer:</asp:Label>
</td>
<td>
<asp:TextBox ID="Answer" runat="server"></asp:TextBox>
<asp:RequiredFieldValidator ID="AnswerRequired" runat="server"
ControlToValidate="Answer" ErrorMessage="Security answer is required."
ToolTip="Security answer is required."
ValidationGroup="CreateUserWizard1">*</asp:RequiredFieldValidator>
</td>
</tr>
<tr>
<td align="center" colspan="2">
<asp:CompareValidator ID="PasswordCompare" runat="server"
```

```
ControlToCompare="Password" ControlToValidate="ConfirmPassword"
Display="Dynamic"
ErrorMessage="The Password and Confirmation Password must match."
ValidationGroup="CreateUserWizard1"></asp:CompareValidator>
</td>
</tr>
<tr>
<td align="center" colspan="2" style="color:Red;">
<asp:Literal ID="ErrorMessage" runat="server"
EnableViewState="False"></asp:Literal>
</td>
</tr>
<tr>
<td align="right">
<asp:Label ID="lblcountry" runat="server" Text="Country"></asp:Label>
</td>
<td align ="left" colspan="2">
<asp:DropDownList ID="Country" runat="server" style="margin-left: 11px" >
<asp:ListItem>Others</asp:ListItem>
<asp:ListItem>India</asp:ListItem>
<asp:ListItem>China</asp:ListItem>
<asp:ListItem>Nepal
</asp:ListItem>
<asp:ListItem></asp:ListItem>
</asp:DropDownList>
</td>
</tr>
<tr>
<td align="right">
<asp:Label ID="Lblgender" runat="server" Text="Gender"></asp:Label>
</td>
<td align ="left" colspan="2">
<asp:DropDownList ID="Gender" runat="server" style="margin-left: 9px" >
<asp:ListItem>Male</asp:ListItem>
<asp:ListItem>Female</asp:ListItem>
</asp:DropDownList>
</td>
</tr>
</table>
</ContentTemplate>
</asp:CreateUserWizardStep>
<asp:CompleteWizardStep ID="CompleteWizardStep1" runat="server" >
<ContentTemplate>
<table border="0"
style="font-family:Verdana;font-size:100%;height:212px;width:362px;">
<tr>
<td align="center" colspan="2"
style="color:White;background-color:#5D7B9D;font-weight:bold;">
Complete</td>
</tr>
<tr>
<td>
Your account has been successfully created.</td>
</tr>
<tr>
<td align="right" colspan="2">
<asp:Button ID="ContinueButton" runat="server" BackColor="#FFFBFF"
BorderColor="#CCCCCC" BorderStyle="Solid" BorderWidth="1px"
CausesValidation="False" CommandName="Continue" Font-Names="Verdana"
ForeColor="#284775" Text="Continue" ValidationGroup="CreateUserWizard1" />
<a href="Login.aspx">Login</a>
</td>
</tr>
</table>
</ContentTemplate>
```

```
            </asp:CompleteWizardStep>
            <asp:WizardStep ID="WizardStep1" runat="server" Title="Registerd">
            <asp:Label ID="Label1" runat="server"
            Text="You Are a Registered User now,You can login Into the website"></asp:Label>
            <a href="Login.aspx">Login</a>
            </asp:WizardStep>
            </WizardSteps>
            </asp:CreateUserWizard>
        </div>
        </form>
    </body>
    </html>
```

5. Add the following code in the CodeFile of the `Createuser.aspx` page for authenticated profiles. Listing 25.5 shows the code for the CodeFile of the `Createuser.aspx` page:

Listing 25.5: Showing the Code for the CodeFile of the `Createuser.aspx` Page

In VB

```
    Partial Class Createuser
        Inherits System.Web.UI.Page
        Protected Sub CreateUserWizard1_CreatedUser(sender As Object, e As
      EventArgs) Handles CreateUserWizard1.CreatedUser
            Try
                Dim pc As ProfileCommon =
                CType(ProfileCommon.Create(CreateUserWizard1.UserName, True), ProfileCommon)
                pc.Country =
(CType(CreateUserWizard1.CreateUserStep.ContentTemplateContainer.FindControl("Country"),
DropDownList)).SelectedValue
                pc.Gender =
(CType(CreateUserWizard1.CreateUserStep.ContentTemplateContainer.FindControl("Gender"),
DropDownList)).SelectedValue
                pc.Name =
((CType(CreateUserWizard1.CreateUserStep.ContentTemplateContainer.FindControl("Name"),
TextBox)).Text)
                'save profile
                pc.Save()
            Catch ex As Exception
                Response.Write(ex.Message)
            End Try
        End Sub
    End Class
```

In C#

```
    using System;
    using System.Collections.Generic;
    using System.Linq;
    using System.Web;
    using System.Web.UI;
    using System.Web.UI.WebControls;
    using System.Web.Profile;
    public partial class Createuser : System.Web.UI.Page
    {
        protected void Page_Load(object sender, EventArgs e)
        {

        }
        protected void CreateUserWizard1_CreatedUser(object sender, EventArgs e)
        {
            try
            {

                ProfileCommon pc =
                (ProfileCommon)ProfileCommon.Create(CreateUserWizard1.UserName, true);
                pc.Country =
((DropDownList)CreateUserWizard1.CreateUserStep.ContentTemplateContainer.FindControl("Country"
)).SelectedValue;
```

```
                pc.Gender =
((DropDownList)CreateUserWizard1.CreateUserStep.ContentTemplateContainer.FindControl("Gender")
).SelectedValue;
                pc.Name =
(((TextBox)CreateUserWizard1.CreateUserStep.ContentTemplateContainer.FindControl("Name")).Text
);
                //save profile
                pc.Save();
            }
            catch (Exception ex)
            {
                Response.Write(ex.Message);
            }
        }
    }
```

6. Replace the code for the Login.aspx page with the code, given in Listing 25.6, to add the controls required for the application:

Listing 25.6: Showing the Code for the `Login.aspx` Page

In VB

```
<%@ Page Language="VB" AutoEventWireup="false" CodeFile="Login.aspx.vb" Inherits="Login"%>
<!DOCTYPE html>
<html xmlns="http://www.w3.org/1999/xhtml">
<head runat="server">
    <title></title>
</head>
<body>
    <form id="form1" runat="server">
    <div>
    <asp:Login ID="Login1" runat="server" BackColor="#FFFFCC" BorderColor="#E6E2D8"
        BorderPadding="4" BorderStyle="Solid" BorderWidth="1px" Font-Names="Verdana"
        Font-Size="0.8em" ForeColor="#333333" Height="332px" Width="351px">
        <TextBoxStyle Font-Size="0.8em" />
        <LoginButtonStyle BackColor="#FFFBFF" BorderColor="#CCCCCC" BorderStyle="Solid"
        BorderWidth="1px" Font-Names="Verdana" Font-Size="0.8em" ForeColor="#284775" />
        <LayoutTemplate>
        <table border="0" cellpadding="4" cellspacing="0"
        style="border-collapse: collapse;">
        <tr>
        <td>
        <table border="0" cellpadding="0" class="style1">
        <tr>
        <td align="center" colspan="2"
        style="color: White; background-color: #5D7B9D; font-size: 0.9em; font-weight:
        bold;">
        Log In</td>
        </tr>
        <tr>
        <td align="right">
        <asp:Label ID="UserNameLabel" runat="server" AssociatedControlID="UserName">User
        Name:</asp:Label>
        </td>
        <td>
        <asp:TextBox ID="UserName" runat="server" Font-Size="0.8em"></asp:TextBox>
        <asp:RequiredFieldValidator ID="UserNameRequired" runat="server"
        ControlToValidate="UserName" ErrorMessage="User Name is required."
        ToolTip="User Name is required."
        ValidationGroup="Login1">*</asp:RequiredFieldValidator>
        </td>
        </tr>
        <tr>
        <td align="right">
        <asp:Label ID="PasswordLabel" runat="server"
        AssociatedControlID="Password">Password:</asp:Label>
        </td>
```

```
            <td>
            <asp:TextBox ID="Password" runat="server" Font-Size="0.8em"
            TextMode="Password"></asp:TextBox>
            <asp:RequiredFieldValidator ID="PasswordRequired" runat="server"
            ControlToValidate="Password" ErrorMessage="Password is required."
            ToolTip="Password is required."
            ValidationGroup="Login1">*</asp:RequiredFieldValidator>
            </td>
            </tr>
            <tr>
            <td colspan="2">
            <asp:CheckBox ID="RememberMe" runat="server" Text="Remember me next time." />
            </td>
            </tr>
            <tr>
            <td align="center" colspan="2" style="color: Red;">
            <asp:Literal ID="FailureText" runat="server"
            EnableViewState="False"></asp:Literal>
            </td>
            </tr>
            <tr>
            <td align="right" colspan="2">
            <asp:Button ID="LoginButton" runat="server" BackColor="#FFFBFF"
            BorderColor="#CCCCCC" BorderStyle="Solid" BorderWidth="1px" CommandName="Login"
            Font-Names="Verdana" Font-Size="0.8em" ForeColor="#284775"
            onclick="LoginButton_Click" Text="Log In" ValidationGroup="Login1"
            Width="246px" />
            <br />
            <asp:Button ID="BtnCreateUser" runat="server" Height="22px"
            onclick="BtnCreateUser_Click" Text="Create New User" Width="247px"
            BackColor="#FFFBFF" BorderColor="#CCCCCC" BorderStyle="Solid"
            Font-Names="Verdana" Font-Size="Smaller" />
            </td>
            </tr>
            </table>
            </td>
            </tr>
            </table>
            </LayoutTemplate>
            <InstructionTextStyle Font-Italic="True" ForeColor="Black" />
            <TitleTextStyle BackColor="#5D7B9D" Font-Bold="True" Font-Size="0.9em"
            ForeColor="White" />
            </asp:Login>
    </div>
    </form>
</body>
</html>
```

In C#

```
<%@ Page Language="C#" AutoEventWireup="true" CodeFile="Login.aspx.cs" Inherits="Login" %>
<!DOCTYPE html>
<html xmlns="http://www.w3.org/1999/xhtml">
<head runat="server">
    <title></title>
</head>
<body>
    <form id="form1" runat="server">
    <div>
    <asp:Login ID="Login1" runat="server" BackColor="#FFFFCC" BorderColor="#E6E2D8"
        BorderPadding="4" BorderStyle="Solid" BorderWidth="1px" Font-Names="Verdana"
        Font-Size="0.8em" ForeColor="#333333" Height="332px" Width="351px">
        <TextBoxStyle Font-Size="0.8em" />
        <LoginButtonStyle BackColor="#FFFBFF" BorderColor="#CCCCCC" BorderStyle="Solid"
        BorderWidth="1px" Font-Names="Verdana" Font-Size="0.8em" ForeColor="#284775" />
```

```
<LayoutTemplate>
<table border="0" cellpadding="4" cellspacing="0"
style="border-collapse: collapse;">
<tr>
<td>
<table border="0" cellpadding="0" class="style1">
<tr>
<td align="center" colspan="2"
style="color: White; background-color: #5D7B9D; font-size: 0.9em; font-weight:
bold;">
Log In</td>
</tr>
<tr>
<td align="right">
<asp:Label ID="UserNameLabel" runat="server" AssociatedControlID="UserName">User
Name:</asp:Label>
</td>
<td>
<asp:TextBox ID="UserName" runat="server" Font-Size="0.8em"></asp:TextBox>
<asp:RequiredFieldValidator ID="UserNameRequired" runat="server"
ControlToValidate="UserName" ErrorMessage="User Name is required."
ToolTip="User Name is required."
ValidationGroup="Login1">*</asp:RequiredFieldValidator>
</td>
</tr>
<tr>
<td align="right">
<asp:Label ID="PasswordLabel" runat="server"
AssociatedControlID="Password">Password:</asp:Label>
</td>
<td>
<asp:TextBox ID="Password" runat="server" Font-Size="0.8em"
TextMode="Password"></asp:TextBox>
<asp:RequiredFieldValidator ID="PasswordRequired" runat="server"
ControlToValidate="Password" ErrorMessage="Password is required."
ToolTip="Password is required."
ValidationGroup="Login1">*</asp:RequiredFieldValidator>
</td>
</tr>
<tr>
<td colspan="2">
<asp:CheckBox ID="RememberMe" runat="server" Text="Remember me next time." />
</td>
</tr>
<tr>
<td align="center" colspan="2" style="color: Red;">
<asp:Literal ID="FailureText" runat="server"
EnableViewState="False"></asp:Literal>
</td>
</tr>
<tr>
<td align="right" colspan="2">
<asp:Button ID="LoginButton" runat="server" BackColor="#FFFBFF"
BorderColor="#CCCCCC" BorderStyle="Solid" BorderWidth="1px" CommandName="Login"
Font-Names="Verdana" Font-Size="0.8em" ForeColor="#284775"
onclick="LoginButton_Click" Text="Log In" ValidationGroup="Login1"
Width="246px" style="height: 18px" />
<br />
<asp:Button ID="BtnCreateUser" runat="server" Height="22px"
onclick="BtnCreateUser_Click" Text="Create New User" Width="247px"
BackColor="#FFFBFF" BorderColor="#CCCCCC" BorderStyle="Solid"
Font-Names="Verdana" Font-Size="Smaller" />
</td>
</tr>
</table>
```

```
            </td>
            </tr>
            </table>
            </LayoutTemplate>
            <InstructionTextStyle Font-Italic="True" ForeColor="Black" />
            <TitleTextStyle BackColor="#5D7B9D" Font-Bold="True" Font-Size="0.9em"
            ForeColor="White" />
            </asp:Login>
        </div>
        </form>
    </body>
    </html>
```

7. Add the code, shown in Listing 25.7, in the CodeFile of the `Login.aspx` page:

Listing 25.7: Showing the Code for the CodeFile of the `Login.aspx` Page

In VB

```
Partial Class Login
    Inherits System.Web.UI.Page
    Protected Sub LoginButton_Click(sender As Object,e As EventArgs)
        If Page.User.Identity.IsAuthenticated Then
            Response.Redirect("Displayprofile.aspx")
        End If
    End Sub
    Protected Sub BtnCreateUser_Click(sender As Object, e As EventArgs)
        Response.Redirect("CreateUser.aspx")
    End Sub
End Class
```

In C#

```
using System;
using System.Collections.Generic;
using System.Linq;
using System.Web;
using System.Web.UI;
using System.Web.UI.WebControls;
public partial class Login : System.Web.UI.Page
{
    protected void Page_Load(object sender, EventArgs e)
    {
    }
    protected void LoginButton_Click(object sender, EventArgs e)
    {
        if (Page.User.Identity.IsAuthenticated)
        {
            Response.Redirect("Displayprofile.aspx");
        }

    }
    protected void BtnCreateUser_Click(object sender, EventArgs e)
    {
        Response.Redirect("CreateUser.aspx");
    }
}
```

8. Replace the code for the `Displayprofile.aspx` page with the code, given in Listing 25.8, to add the required controls for the application:

Listing 25.8: Showing the Code for the `Displayprofile.aspx` Page

In VB

```
<%@ Page Language="VB" AutoEventWireup="false" CodeFile="Displayprofile.aspx.vb"
  Inherits="Displayprofile" %>
<!DOCTYPE html>
<html xmlns="http://www.w3.org/1999/xhtml">
<head runat="server">
```

```
    <title></title>
</head>
<body>
    <form id="form1" runat="server">
    <div>
    <asp:Literal ID ="Literal1" runat ="server" Text="<h1>Welcome</h1>"> </asp:Literal>
         <span><br />
        Name         </span>
         <asp:Label ID="Name" runat="server" Text="Label"></asp:Label>
                         <p>
         <span >Country       </span>
         <asp:Label ID="Country" runat="server" Text="Label"></asp:Label>
         </p>
         <p>
         <span >Gender        </span>
         <asp:Label ID="Gender" runat="server" Text="Label"></asp:Label>
         </p>
         <input id="Button1" type="button" value="Exit" onclick="window.close()"
         class="style2" />
        <br />
        <a href="Manageprofiles.aspx">ManageProfiles</a>
    </div>
    </form>
</body>
</html>
```

In C#

```
<%@ Page Language="C#" AutoEventWireup="true" CodeFile="Displayprofile.aspx.cs"
  Inherits="Displayprofile" %>
<!DOCTYPE html>
<html xmlns="http://www.w3.org/1999/xhtml">
<head runat="server">
    <title></title>
</head>
<body>
    <form id="form1" runat="server">
    <div>
    <asp:Literal ID ="Literal1" runat ="server" Text="<h1>Welcome</h1>">
         </asp:Literal>
         <span><br />
        Name         </span>
         <asp:Label ID="Name" runat="server" Text="Label"></asp:Label>
                         <p>
         <span >Country       </span>
         <asp:Label ID="Country" runat="server" Text="Label"></asp:Label>
         </p>
         <p>
         <span >Gender        </span>
         <asp:Label ID="Gender" runat="server" Text="Label"></asp:Label>
         </p>
         <input id="Button1" type="button" value="Exit" onclick="window.close()"
         class="style2" />
        <br />
        <a href="Manageprofiles.aspx">ManageProfiles</a>
    </div>
    </form>
</body>
</html>
```

9. Add the code, shown in Listing 25.9, in the CodeFile of the `Displayprofile.aspx` page:

Listing 25.9: Showing the Code for the CodeFile of the `Displayprofile.aspx Page`

In VB

```
Partial Class Displayprofile
    Inherits System.Web.UI.Page
    Protected Sub Page_Load(sender As Object, e As EventArgs) Handles
     Me.Load
        Country.Text = Profile.Country
        Gender.Text = Profile.Gender
        Name.Text = Profile.Name
    End Sub
End Class
```

In C#

```
using System;
using System.Collections.Generic;
using System.Linq;
using System.Web;
using System.Web.UI;
using System.Web.UI.WebControls;
public partial class Displayprofile : System.Web.UI.Page
{
    protected void Page_Load(object sender, EventArgs e)
    {
        Country.Text = Profile.Country;
        Gender.Text = Profile.Gender;
        Name.Text = Profile.Name;
    }
}
```

10. Replace the code for the `Manageprofiles.aspx` page with the code, given in Listing 25.10, to add the required controls to the application:

Listing 25.10: Showing the Code for the `Manageprofiles.aspx` Page

In VB

```
<%@ Page Language="VB" AutoEventWireup="false" CodeFile="Manageprofiles.aspx.vb"
  Inherits="Manageprofiles" %>
<!DOCTYPE html>
<html xmlns="http://www.w3.org/1999/xhtml">
<head runat="server">
    <title></title>
</head>
<body>
    <form id="form1" runat="server">
    <div>
    <asp:TextBox ID="Txtnumprofiles" runat="server"></asp:TextBox>
         <br />
         <br />
         <br />
         <span lang="en-us">Delete Inactive Profiles </span>
         <asp:Button ID="Btndelete" runat="server" onclick="Btndelete_Click"
         style="margin-left: 83px" Text="Delete" />
         <br />
         <br />
         <br />
         <asp:Label ID="Label1" runat="server" Text="Label"></asp:Label>
         <br />
         <br />
         <span lang="en-us">
         </span>
         <br />
         <a href="Displayprofile.aspx">Home</a>
           
```

```
            <a href="Login.aspx">Login</a>
              
            <a href="CreateUser.aspx">Create New User</a>
        </div>
        </form>
    </body>
    </html>
```

In C#

```
    <%@ Page Language="C#" AutoEventWireup="true" CodeFile="Manageprofiles.aspx.cs"
      Inherits="Manageprofiles" %>
    <!DOCTYPE html>
    <html xmlns="http://www.w3.org/1999/xhtml">
    <head runat="server">
        <title></title>
    </head>
    <body>
        <form id="form1" runat="server">
        <div>
        <asp:TextBox ID="Txtnumprofiles" runat="server"></asp:TextBox>
            <br />
            <br />
            <br />
            <span lang="en-us">Delete Inactive Profiles </span>
            <asp:Button ID="Btndelete" runat="server" OnClick="Btndelete_Click"
            style="margin-left: 83px" Text="Delete" />
            <br />
            <br />
            <br />
            <asp:Label ID="Label1" runat="server" Text="Label"></asp:Label>
            <br />
            <br />
            <span lang="en-us">
            </span>
            <br />
            <a href="Displayprofile.aspx">Home</a>
              
            <a href="Login.aspx">Login</a>
              
            <a href="CreateUser.aspx">Create New User</a>
        </div>
        </form>
    </body>
    </html>
```

11. Add the code in the CodeFile of the Manageprofiles.aspx page. Listing 25.11 shows the code for the CodeFile of the Manageprofiles.aspx page:

Listing 25.11: Showing the Code for the CodeFile of the `Manageprofiles.aspx Page`

In VB

```
    Imports System.Web.Profile
    Partial Class Manageprofiles
        Inherits System.Web.UI.Page
        Protected Sub Page_PreRender()
            Txtnumprofiles.Text =
            ProfileManager.GetNumberOfProfiles(ProfileAuthenticationOption.All).ToString()
        End Sub
        Protected Sub Btndelete_Click(sender As Object,e As EventArgs)
       Handles Btndelete.Click
            Try
                Dim del As Integer = 0
                del = ProfileManager.DeleteInactiveProfiles(ProfileAuthenticationOption.All,
                    DateTime.Now.AddMinutes(-4))
                Label1.Text = String.Format("{0} Profiles deleted ", del)
            Catch ex As Exception
```

```
            Label1.Text = ex.Message
        End Try
    End Sub
End Class
```

In C#

```
using System;
using System.Collections.Generic;
using System.Linq;
using System.Web;
using System.Web.UI;
using System.Web.UI.WebControls;
using System.Web.Profile;
public partial class Manageprofiles : System.Web.UI.Page
{
    protected void Page_Load(object sender, EventArgs e)
    {
    }
    protected void Page_PreRender()
    {
        Txtnumprofiles.Text =
        ProfileManager.GetNumberOfProfiles(ProfileAuthenticationOption.All).ToString();
    }
    protected void Btndelete_Click(object sender, EventArgs e)
    {
        try
        {
            int del = 0;
            del =ProfileManager.DeleteInactiveProfiles(ProfileAuthenticationOption.All,
            DateTime.Now.AddMinutes(-4));
            Label1.Text = String.Format("{0} Profiles deleted ", del);
        }
        catch (Exception ex)
        {
            Label1.Text = ex.Message;
        }
    }
}
```

12. Open the Solution Explorer window and right-click the Createuser.aspx page to open the context menu.
13. Select the Set As Start Page option from the context menu.
14. Execute the application by pressing the F5 key on the keyboard. Enter your details in the CreateUserWizard control (Figure 25.6).
15. Click the Create User button, as shown in Figure 25.6:

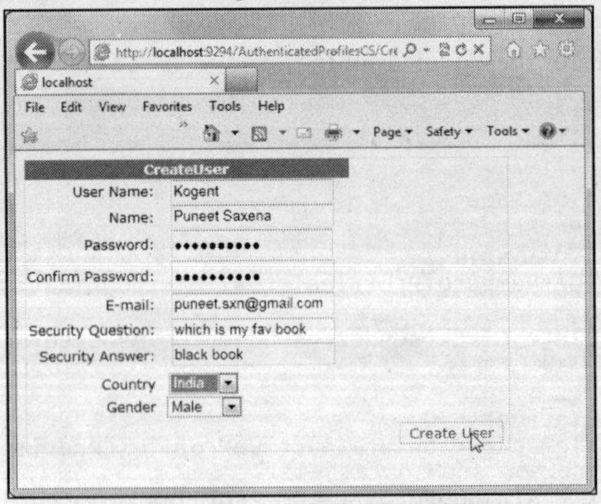

Figure 25.6: Creating the User

The message appears in the wizard as Your account has been successfully created (Figure 25.7).

16. Click the Login link, as shown in Figure 25.7:

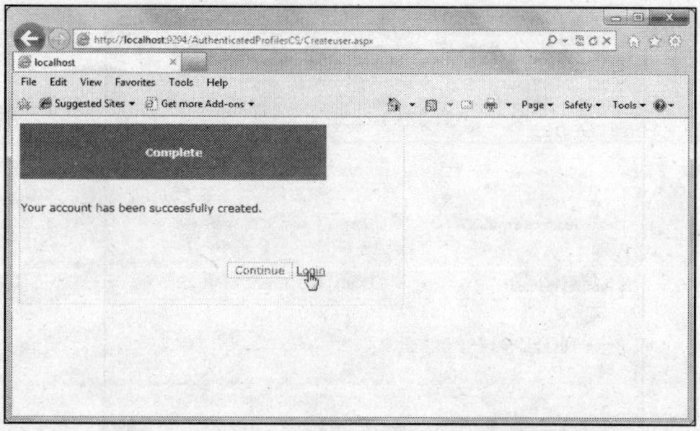

Figure 25.7: Displaying the Account Created Message

The Login.aspx page appears (Figure 25.8).

17. Enter the user name and password of your account in the User Name and Password text boxes, respectively (Figure 25.8).
18. Select the Remember me next time check box and click the Log In button, as shown in Figure 25.8:

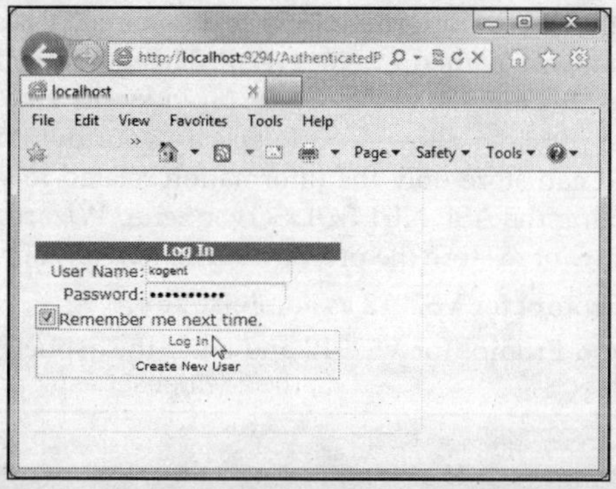

Figure 25.8: Displaying the Login.aspx Page

The Displayprofile.aspx page appears with your account details, such as Name, Country, and Gender (Figure 25.9).

19. Click the ManageProfiles link, as shown in Figure 25.9:

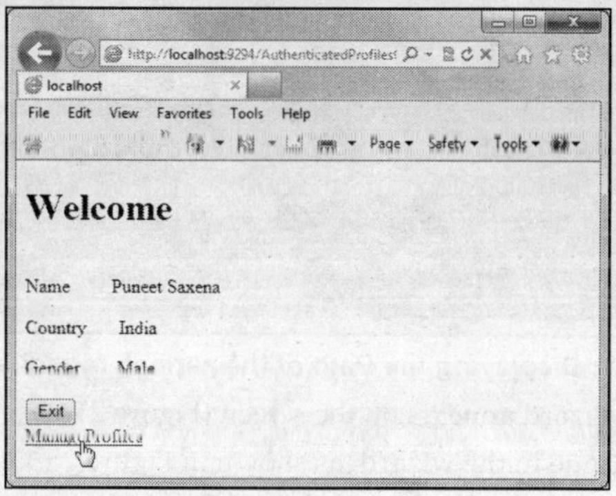

Figure 25.9: Displaying the User Information

The Manageprofiles.aspx page appears showing the total number of profiles in the text box (Figure 25.10).

20. Click the Delete button to delete the inactive profile, as shown in Figure 25.10:

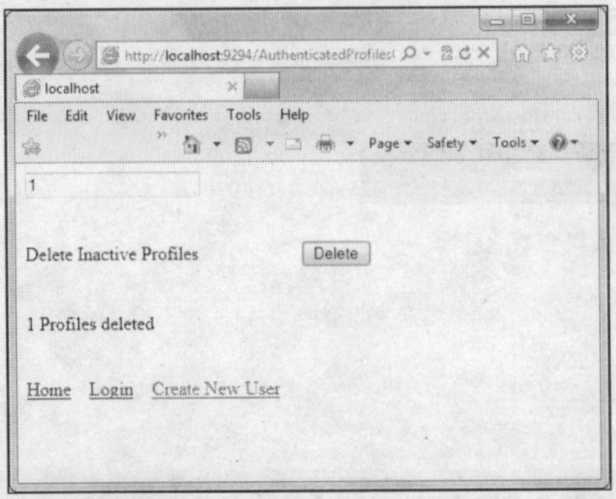

Figure 25.10: Displaying the Remaining Profiles after Deletion

Creating Custom Profile Providers

Now, let's discuss how to create a custom profile provider. You need to understand how and where the information associated with the profiles is stored first. ASP.NET stores profiles with the help of a provider that specifies the database in which the profile information is to be stored. By default, the profile information is stored in a SQL Server Express database named `ASPNET.MDF`. This database is located in the `App_Data` folder of a website. ASP.NET uses the `SqlProfileProvider` provider to store the profile information in this database. The configuration of the provider allows you to specify your own database for your website that can be shipped with your website and can store only the information related to your website. You can configure a database for your website by running the ASP.NET SQL Server Setup Wizard. The following steps guide you to specify the database in which you want to store the profile information of your website:

1. Open Developer Command Prompt for VS2012 as administrator.
2. Open the Developer Command Prompt for VS2012 and enter the aspnet_regsql.exe command, as shown in Figure 25.11:

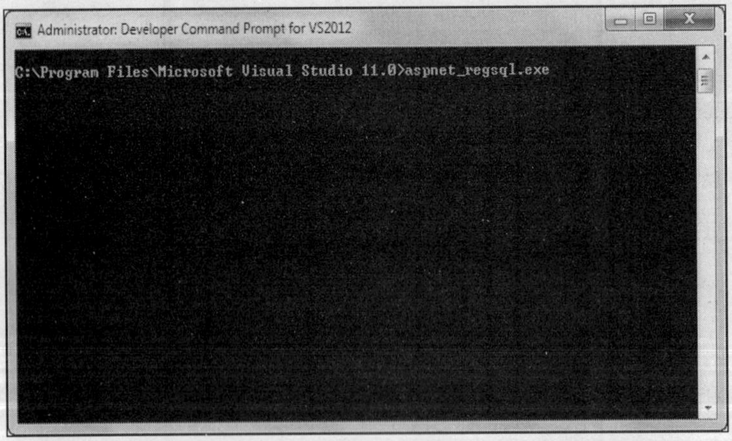

Figure 25.11: Displaying the Path of the aspnet_regsql.exe Tool

The ASP.NET SQL Server Setup Wizard appears on the screen (Figure 25.12).

3. Click the Next button to continue in the wizard, as shown in Figure 25.12:

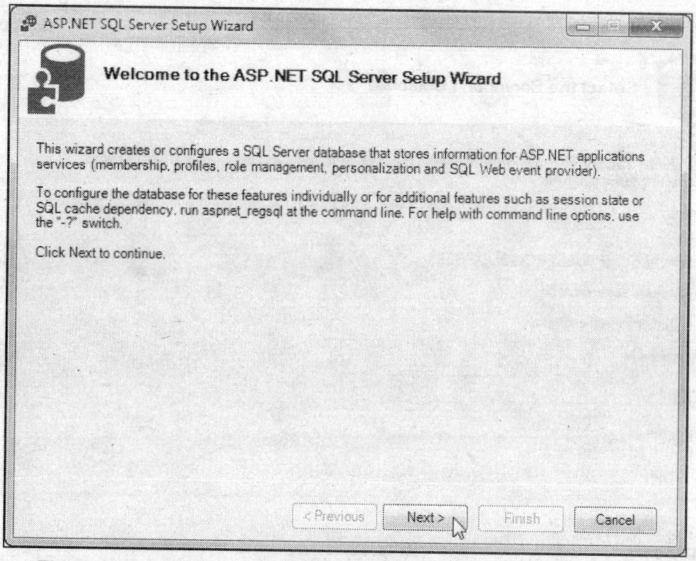

Figure 25.12: Initiating the ASP.NET SQL Server Setup Wizard

The Select a Setup Option page appears in the wizard (Figure 25.13).

4. Select the Configure SQL Server for application services radio button and click the Next button, as shown in Figure 25.13:

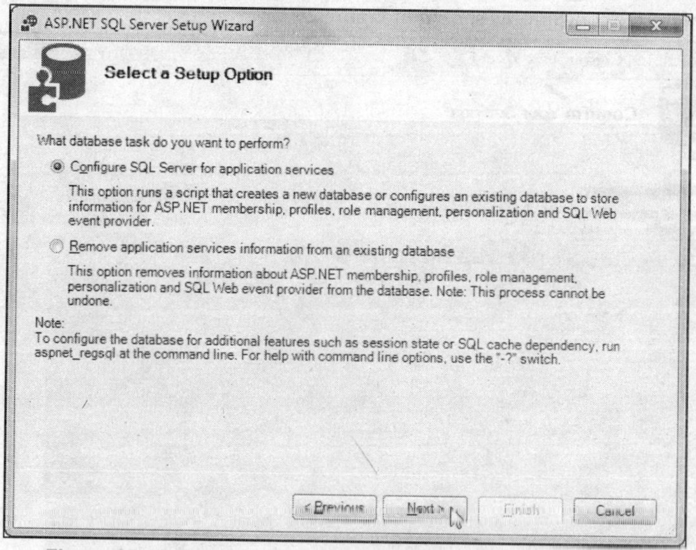

Figure 25.13: Selecting the SQL Server Application Services

The Select the Server and Database page appears in the wizard (Figure 25.14).

5. Enter the server name in the Server text box and select the name of the database from the Database drop-down list. In this application, we have used the Northwind database. Click the Next button, as shown in Figure 25.14.

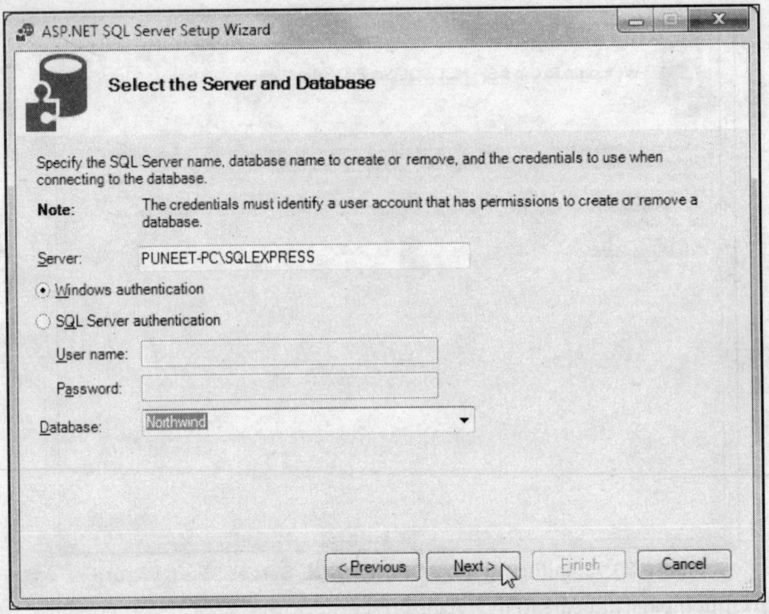

Figure 25.14: Selecting the Server and Database

The Confirm Your Settings page appears in the wizard (Figure 25.15).

6. Click the Next button to continue, as shown in Figure 25.15:

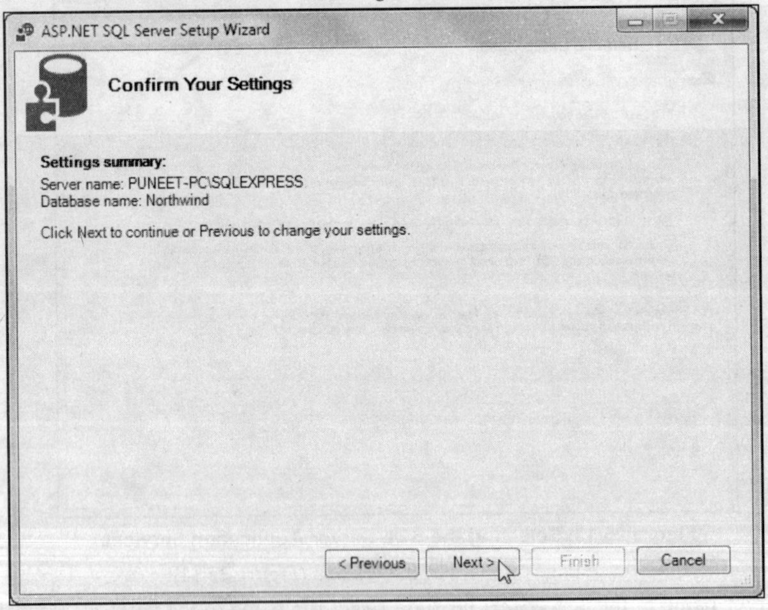

Figure 25.15: Confirming the Settings

The database has been created or modified page appears in the wizard (Figure 25.16).

7. Click the Finish button, as shown in Figure 25.16:

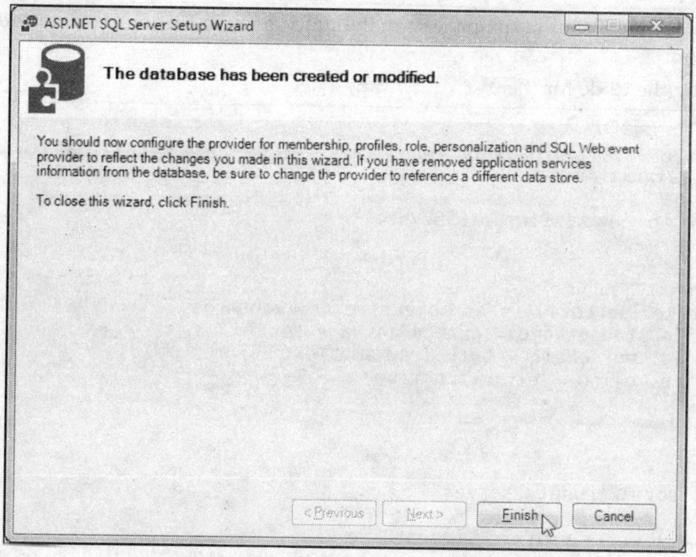

Figure 25.16: Closing the Wizard

8. After configuring the database (in which you want to store the profile information of your website), create a website and save it as ConfigureProfileProvidersCS. You can find the code for this application in the ConfigureProfileProvidersCS (for C#) and ConfigureProfileProvidersVB (for VB) folders. Now, modify the code in the `Web.config` file with the following code to associate the configured database with your application:

```
<?xml version="1.0"?>
<!--
  For more information on how to configure your ASP.NET application, please visit
  http://go.microsoft.com/fwlink/?LinkId=169433
  -->
<configuration>
  <connectionStrings>
    <add name="Constring" connectionString="Data Source= PUNEET-PC\SQLEXPRESS; Initial
  Catalog= Northwind; Integrated Security=True" providerName="System.Data.SqlClient"/>
  </connectionStrings>
  <system.web>
    <authentication mode="Forms"/>
    <anonymousIdentification enabled="true"/>
    <profile defaultProvider="ProfileProvider">
      <properties>
        <add name="StudentName" allowAnonymous="true"/>
        <add name="CourseName" allowAnonymous="true"/>
        <add name="Rollno" allowAnonymous="true"/>
      </properties>
      <providers>
        <add name="ProfileProvider" type="System.Web.Profile.SqlProfileProvider"
         connectionStringName="Constring"/>
      </providers>
    </profile>
    <compilation debug="true" targetFramework="4.5"/>
    <httpRuntime targetFramework="4.5"/>
  </system.web>
</configuration>
```

NOTE

You need to modify the connection string according to the system on which you want to run the application.

9. Replace the code for the Default.aspx page with the code, given in Listing 25.12, to add the controls required for the application:

Listing 25.12: Showing the Code for the `Default.aspx` Page

In VB

```
<%@ Page Language="VB" AutoEventWireup="false" CodeFile="Default.aspx.vb"
  Inherits="_Default" %>
<!DOCTYPE html>
<html xmlns="http://www.w3.org/1999/xhtml">
<head runat="server">
    <title></title>
    <script runat="server">
  Private Sub ReviseProfile(s As Object, e As EventArgs)
        Profile.StudentName = txtStudentName.Text
        Profile.CourseName = txtCourseName.Text
        Profile.Rollno = txtRollno.Text
  End Sub
</script>
</head>
<body>
    <form id="form1" runat="server">
    <div>
    <b>Welcome</b> <%= Profile.StudentName %>
         <br />
         <b>Roll number</b> <%= Profile.Rollno %>
         <br />
         <b>Course undertaken by you</b> <%= Profile.CourseName %>
         <hr />
         <b>Student Name:<span lang="en-us">     </span></b>
          <asp:TextBox ID="txtStudentName" runat="Server" />
         <br />
         <br />
         <b>Roll number:</b>
         <span lang="en-us">       </span>
         <asp:TextBox ID="txtRollno" runat="Server" style="margin-left: 5px" />
         <br />
         <br />
         <b>Course Name:</b>
         <asp:TextBox ID="txtCourseName" runat="Server" style="margin-left: 26px" />
         <br />
         <br />
         <br />
         <asp:Button ID="Button1" Text="Refresh Profile" OnClick="ReviseProfile"
         runat="server" />
         </div>
     </div>
     </form>
 </body>
 </html>
```

In C#

```
<%@ Page Language="C#" AutoEventWireup="true" CodeFile="Default.aspx.cs"
  Inherits="_Default" %>
<!DOCTYPE html>
<html xmlns="http://www.w3.org/1999/xhtml">
<head runat="server">
    <title></title>
    <script runat="server">
  void ReviseProfile(Object s, EventArgs e)
  {
        Profile.StudentName = txtStudentName.Text;
        Profile.CourseName = txtCourseName.Text;
        Profile.Rollno = txtRollno.Text;
  }
```

```
</script>
</head>
<body>
    <form id="form1" runat="server">
    <div>
    <b>Welcome</b> <%= Profile.StudentName %>
        <br />
        <b>Roll number</b> <%= Profile.Rollno %>
        <br />
        <b>Course undertaken by you</b> <%= Profile.CourseName %>
        <hr />
        <b>Student Name:<span lang="en-us">     </span></b>
         <asp:TextBox ID="txtStudentName" runat="Server" />
        <br />
        <br />
        <b>Roll number:</b>
        <span lang="en-us">       </span>
        <asp:TextBox ID="txtRollno" runat="Server" style="margin-left: 5px" />
        <br />
        <br />
        <b>Course Name:</b>
        <asp:TextBox ID="txtCourseName" runat="Server" style="margin-left: 26px" />
        <br />
        <br />
        <br />
        <asp:Button ID="Button1" Text="Refresh Profile" OnClick="ReviseProfile"
        runat="server" />        </div>
    </form>
</body>
</html>
```

10. Press the F5 key on the keyboard to execute the application and the output appears (Figure 25.17).
11. Enter your details in the Student Name, Roll number, and Course Name text boxes and click the Refresh Profile button (Figure 25.17).

The details appears on the Web page, as shown in Figure 25.17:

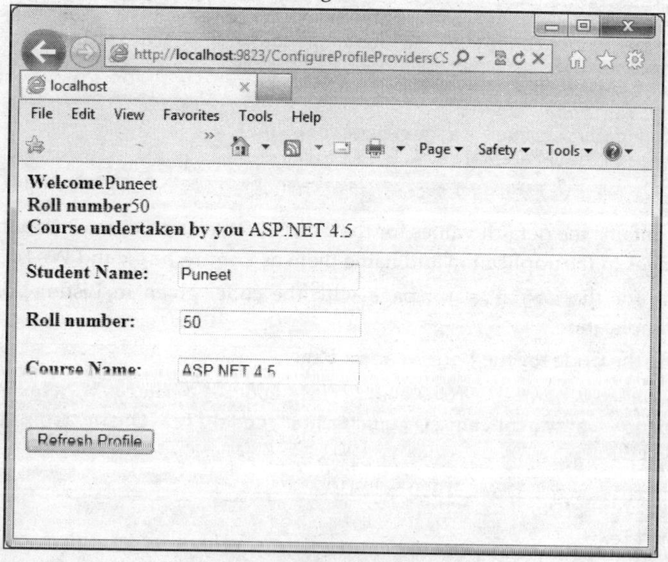

Figure 25.17: Creating the Profile

Migrating Profiles

Now, consider a situation in which an anonymous user visits your website and modifies his/her profile according to his/her preferences. After using your website for some time, the anonymous user becomes an authenticated user of your website. In such a case, the profile settings made by this user as an anonymous user will be lost and a new profile will be created for the user, now as an authenticated user. This is because an anonymous profile is stored on the basis of a unique identification number, which is lost when the anonymous user becomes an authenticated user of the website.

ASP.NET allows you to handle such situations by migrating the information of the anonymous profile to the authenticated profile. This prevents the user from creating the profile settings all over again, when he logs on to the website. Now, let's understand and learn how to migrate information from the anonymous profile to the authenticated profile of a user in the following steps:

1. Create a website and save it as MigrateProfile. You can find the code for this application in the MigrateProfileCS (for C#) and MigrateProfileVB (for VB) folders.
2. Incorporate the following changes in the `Web.config` file of the MigrateProfile application:

```
<?xml version="1.0"?>
<!--
  For more information on how to configure your ASP.NET application, please visit
  http://go.microsoft.com/fwlink/?LinkId=169433
  -->
<configuration>
  <appSettings>
    <add key="ValidationSettings:UnobtrusiveValidationMode" value="None"/>
  </appSettings>
    <system.web>
      <authorization>
      <deny users="?"/>
    </authorization>
    <anonymousIdentification enabled="true"/>
    <profile>
      <properties>
        <add name="CourseName" allowAnonymous="true" defaultValue="ASP.NET"/>
        <add name="CourseDuration" allowAnonymous="true" defaultValue="2      months"/>
      </properties>
    </profile>
    <authentication mode="Forms"/>
    <compilation debug="true" targetFramework="4.5"/>
    <httpRuntime targetFramework="4.5"/>
  </system.web>
</configuration>
```

The preceding code contains the default values for the CourseName and CourseDuration variables.

3. Add two Web pages in the application and name them as `Login.aspx` and `Welcome.aspx`.
4. Replace the code for the `Login.aspx` page with the code, given in Listing 25.13, to add the controls required for the application:

Listing 25.13: Showing the Code for the `Login.aspx` Page

In VB

```
<%@ Page Language="VB" AutoEventWireup="false" CodeFile="Login.aspx.vb"
  Inherits="Login" %>
<!DOCTYPE html>
<html xmlns="http://www.w3.org/1999/xhtml">
<head runat="server">
    <title></title>
</head>
<body>
    <form id="form1" runat="server">
    <div>
    <asp:Login ID="Login1" runat="server" BackColor="#F7F6F3" BorderColor="#E6E2D8"
        BorderPadding="4"
```

```
            BorderStyle="Solid" BorderWidth="1px" Font-Names="Verdana" Font-Size="Medium"
            ForeColor="#333333" Height="125px" Width="314px"
            DestinationPageUrl="~/Welcome.aspx">
            <TitleTextStyle BackColor="#5D7B9D" Font-Bold="True" Font-Size="0.9em"
            ForeColor="White" />
            <InstructionTextStyle Font-Italic="True" ForeColor="Black" />
            <TextBoxStyle Font-Size="0.8em" />
            <LoginButtonStyle BackColor="#FFFBFF" BorderColor="#CCCCCC" BorderStyle="Solid"
            BorderWidth="1px"
            Font-Names="Verdana" Font-Size="0.8em" ForeColor="#284775" />
            </asp:Login>
             
            <br />
            <br />
            Course name:<b> <%=Profile.CourseName%> </b>
            <br />
            <b>
            <br />
            Course duration:</b> <%=Profile.CourseDuration%>
        </div>
        </form>
    </body>
    </html>
```

In C#

```
    <%@ Page Language="C#" AutoEventWireup="true" CodeFile="Login.aspx.cs" Inherits="Login" %>
    <!DOCTYPE html>
    <html xmlns="http://www.w3.org/1999/xhtml">
    <head runat="server">
        <title></title>
    </head>
    <body>
        <form id="form1" runat="server">
        <div>
        <asp:Login ID="Login1" runat="server" BackColor="#F7F6F3" BorderColor="#E6E2D8"
            BorderPadding="4"
            BorderStyle="Solid" BorderWidth="1px" Font-Names="Verdana" Font-Size="Medium"
            ForeColor="#333333" Height="125px" Width="314px"
            DestinationPageUrl="~/Welcome.aspx">
            <TitleTextStyle BackColor="#5D7B9D" Font-Bold="True" Font-Size="0.9em"
            ForeColor="White" />
            <InstructionTextStyle Font-Italic="True" ForeColor="Black" />
            <TextBoxStyle Font-Size="0.8em" />
            <LoginButtonStyle BackColor="#FFFBFF" BorderColor="#CCCCCC" BorderStyle="Solid"
            BorderWidth="1px"
            Font-Names="Verdana" Font-Size="0.8em" ForeColor="#284775" />
            </asp:Login>
             
            <br />
            <br />
            Course name:<b> <%=Profile.CourseName%> </b>
            <br />
            <b>
            <br />
            Course duration:</b> <%=Profile.CourseDuration%>
        </div>
        </form>
    </body>
    </html>
```

5. Create a user using Login control as done earlier in the Chapter 24 Working with Login Controls. In this application, we have created a user with the name *Kogent*.
6. Add the code for the `Welcome.aspx` page with the code, given in Listing 25.14, to add the required controls for the application:

Listing 25.14: Showing the Code for the `Welcome.aspx` Page

In VB

```
<%@ Page Language="VB" AutoEventWireup="false" CodeFile="Welcome.aspx.vb"
  Inherits="Welcome" %>
<!DOCTYPE html>
<html xmlns="http://www.w3.org/1999/xhtml">
<head runat="server">
    <title></title>
</head>
<body>
    <form id="form1" runat="server">
    <div>
    <asp:Label ID="Label1" runat="server" Text="Welcome"></asp:Label> 
         <asp:LoginName ID="LoginName1" runat="server" FormatString="{0}!" />
         <br />
         <br />
         <asp:LoginStatus ID="LoginStatus1" runat="server"
         LogoutAction="RedirectToLoginPage"
         LogoutPageUrl="~/login.aspx" />
         <br />
         Course name:<b> <%=Profile.CourseName%> </b>
         <br />
         <b>
         <br />
         Course duration:</b> <%=Profile.CourseDuration%>
    </div>
    </form>
</body>
</html>
```

In C#

```
<%@ Page Language="C#" AutoEventWireup="true" CodeFile="Welcome.aspx.cs"
  Inherits="Welcome" %>
<!DOCTYPE html>
<html xmlns="http://www.w3.org/1999/xhtml">
<head runat="server">
    <title></title>
</head>
<body>
    <form id="form1" runat="server">
    <div>
    <asp:Label ID="Label1" runat="server" Text="Welcome"></asp:Label> 
         <asp:LoginName ID="LoginName1" runat="server" FormatString="{0}!" />
         <br />
         <br />
         <asp:LoginStatus ID="LoginStatus1" runat="server"
         LogoutAction="RedirectToLoginPage"
         LogoutPageUrl="~/login.aspx" />
         <br />
         Course name:<b> <%=Profile.CourseName%>  </b>
         <br />
         <b>
         <br />
         Course duration:</b> <%=Profile.CourseDuration%>
    </div>
    </form>
</body>
</html>
```

7. Add the Global.asax file in the application and add the following code, as shown in Listing 25.15:

Listing 25.15: Showing the Code for the `Global.asax` File

In VB

```
<%@ Application Language="VB" %>
<script runat="server">
    Sub Profile_MigrateAnonymous(s As Object, e As ProfileMigrateEventArgs)
        Dim anonProfile As ProfileCommon = Profile.GetProfile(e.AnonymousID)
        Profile.CourseName = anonProfile.CourseName
        Profile.CourseDuration = anonProfile.CourseDuration
    End Sub
    Sub Application_Start(sender As Object, e As EventArgs)
        ' Code that runs on application startup
    End Sub
    Sub Application_End(sender As Object, e As EventArgs)
        ' Code that runs on application shutdown
    End Sub
    Sub Application_Error(sender As Object,e As EventArgs)
        ' Code that runs when an unhandled error occurs
    End Sub
    Sub Session_Start(sender As Object,e As EventArgs)
        ' Code that runs when a new session is started
    End Sub
    Sub Session_End(sender As Object,e As EventArgs)
        ' Code that runs when a session ends.
        ' Note: The Session_End event is raised only when the sessionstate mode
        ' is set to InProc in the Web.config file. If session mode is set to StateServer
        ' or SQLServer, the event is not raised.
    End Sub
</script>
```

In C#

```
<%@ Application Language="C#" %>
<script runat="server">
    void Profile_MigrateAnonymous(object s, ProfileMigrateEventArgs e)
    {
        ProfileCommon anonProfile = Profile.GetProfile(e.AnonymousID);
        Profile.CourseName = anonProfile.CourseName;
        Profile.CourseDuration = anonProfile.CourseDuration;
    }
    void Application_Start(object sender, EventArgs e)
    {
        // Code that runs on application startup
    }
    void Application_End(object sender, EventArgs e)
    {
        //  Code that runs on application shutdown
    }
    void Application_Error(object sender, EventArgs e)
    {
        // Code that runs when an unhandled error occurs
    }
    void Session_Start(object sender, EventArgs e)
    {
        // Code that runs when a new session is started
    }
    void Session_End(object sender, EventArgs e)
    {
        // Code that runs when a session ends.
        // Note: The Session_End event is raised only when the sessionstate mode
        // is set to InProc in the Web.config file. If session mode is set to StateServer
        // or SQLServer, the event is not raised.
    }
</script>
```

8. Press the F5 key on the keyboard to run the application and the output appears (Figure 25.18).

9. Enter the user name and password in the Login control and select the Remember me next time check box (Figure 25.18).
10. Click the Log In button, as shown in Figure 25.18:

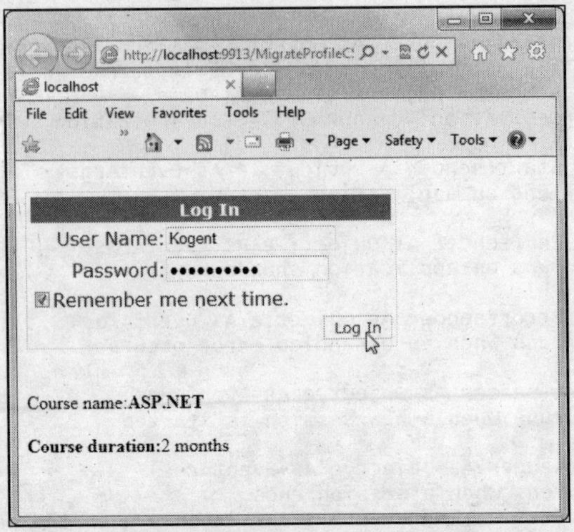

Figure 25.18: Displaying the Output

The Welcome.aspx page appears, as shown in Figure 25.19:

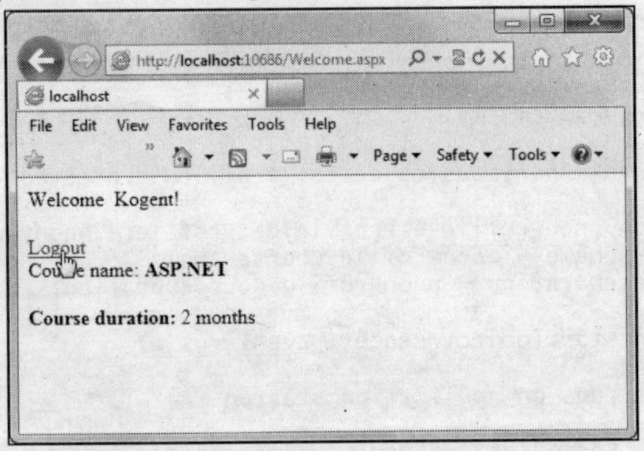

Figure 25.19: Displaying the User Name

Summary

In this chapter, you have learned about one of the aspects of personalization – user profiles. The two types of user profiles discussed in this chapter are anonymous and authenticated. In this chapter, you have also learned how to create and manage user profiles. In addition, you have learned how to configure a profile provider and create a custom profile in your ASP.NET application. Finally, you have learned to migrate an anonymous profile to an authenticated profile by using the user profile feature.

In the next chapter, you learn about security and cryptography in ASP.NET 4.5.

26

Security and Cryptography in ASP.NET

In Depth

Using the technologies and features of .NET framework and Visual Studio, you can develop different types of applications to suit different requirements. For example, you can develop desktop applications with Windows Forms and Windows Presentation Foundation (WPF), Web applications using Web Forms, ASP.NET AJAX, and Silverlight, or Web services using Windows Communication Foundation (WCF). An indispensable and common necessity in the design and development process of all these applications is the need to ascertain the security and reliability of these applications. Secure and reliable applications give users the assurance of a consistent and protected environment for running applications.

One of the primary security concerns for the developers and administrators is the level and kind of access to be given to the users or code to use a particular resource, such as a file, folder, or Web service. The resource may be present on either a local computer or accessible over a network (Internet or Intranet). The first step towards enforcing security is to decide the users to whom your application and other resources are accessible, i.e., to ensure that users do not have the permission to access any resource or code for which they do not have the authorization. Another cause of concern is to ensure proper behavior of your applications or code when they run on the users' computers. It means that the applications or code run without indulging in any memory trespassing or adversely affecting the running of other applications or code. In addition, you need to ensure that the applications that do not have the required permissions and privileges for accessing a resource are not inadvertently granted the same. In case you want to provide permissions to the applications, you need to do so based on the operations or actions that you want to allow for your applications.

In this chapter, you learn about various means of securing your ASP.NET 4.5 applications. You also learn about membership features of ASP.NET 4.5 to create and manage users. In addition, you learn about different authentication and authorization methods to secure a website. Finally, you learn about the cryptographic features for securing applications. Now, let's begin with the verification of the .NET code.

Introducing Code Verification and Security in .NET Framework

As learned earlier, when you compile a .NET application or code, the output generated is a machine-independent code called the Microsoft Intermediate Language (MSIL) code. The MSIL code is similar to the byte code in Java and needs to be converted to the self-executable machine (or native) code version at runtime. The MSIL code is packaged in a .NET assembly that is deployed when you deploy the application on different computers. Apart from the MSIL code, the assembly also contains the manifest, the metadata, and various other resources required for the application. The metadata consists of information about the types, classes, and methods used in the application. It also provides the type information or contract, that is, information about the types extended by the assembly to the Common Language Runtime (CLR) for running the application. The type information in the metadata and the MSIL are used by the CLR at the time of loading and running the .NET application for varied operations, such as allocating memory, referencing the namespaces and classes, and enforcing security.

At the time of running an application, the CLR loads the associated assembly and compiles the MSIL code with the just-in-time (JIT) compiler to change the MSIL code to native code. During JIT compilation at runtime, the CLR performs a verification process on the assembly. In this verification process, the metadata and the MSIL code in the assembly are checked if they are verifiably type-safe. The metadata inside the assembly is validated first, which is then followed by the verification of the MSIL code. Figure 26.1 gives you a pictorial view of the verification process:

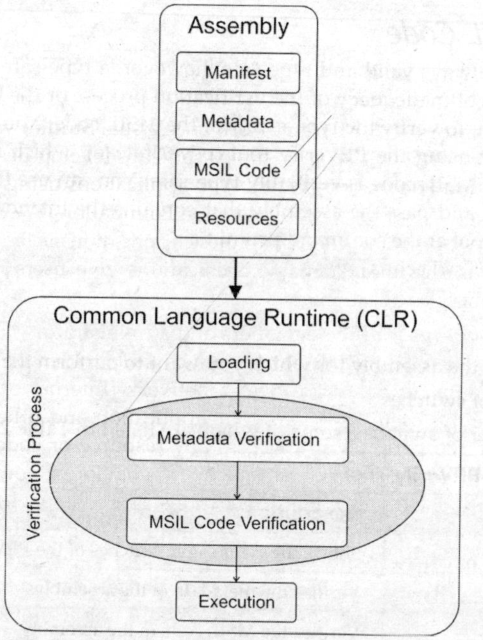

Figure 26.1: Displaying the Verification Process of a .NET Application

> **NOTE**
> *The metadata is validated not only at runtime, but also when you place the assembly in the Global Assembly Cache (GAC) or the download cache. This process ensures that the metadata is consistent without any buffer overflow.*

In .NET framework, the MSIL code can be considered as one of the four types of code – valid, invalid, type-safe, and verifiably type-safe code. Table 26.1 lists different types of MSIL code:

Table 26.1: Types of MSIL Code at Runtime

MSIL Code	Description
`Valid`	Refers to the MSIL code that follows the .NET syntax and conventions and therefore, can be converted to the native code. Valid MSIL code may use pointer arithmetic that is not type-safe.
`Invalid`	Refers to the MSIL code that cannot be converted to native code.
`Type-Safe`	Refers to the MSIL code in which types access and interact with one another only through their public contracts or methods.
`Verifiably Type-Safe`	Refers to the type-safe MSIL code that has passed the verification process.

Now, let's learn about type-safe and verifiably type-safe code in details.

Type-Safe Code

An MSIL code in which one type accesses the other types in the code only through a well-defined and authorized way is considered as a type-safe code. The well-defined and authorized means of access is by using the public methods and fields. If one or more types access the private fields or methods of another type, the MSIL code is not considered as type-safe. This implies that a type in the type-safe MSIL code cannot access the memory locations of another type unless it has the permission to do so. This memory segregation and type-safety of the MSIL code prevents infringement of types, which in turn ensures that there is no unwanted and malicious manipulation of one type by another. This eventually strengthens the security and reliability of the application.

Verifiably Type-Safe MSIL Code

A verifiably type-safe code is always valid and type-safe; however, a type-safe code may not be verifiably type-safe. This may happen because of inadequacy of the verification process or the language compiler. The CLR uses an inbuilt verification algorithm to verify the type-safety of the MSIL code. You can also check whether the MSIL code is verifiably type-safe by using the PEVerify tool (peverify.exe), which is a .NET framework utility that allows you to ensure that your MSIL code is verifiably type-safe. You can use the PEVerify tool at the Developer Command Prompt for VS2012 and pass the assembly that contains the intended metadata and MSIL code. The syntax for using the PEVerify tool at the command prompt is:

```
peverify assemblyname [switches]
```

In the preceding syntax:

- **peverify** – the PEVerify tool
- **assemblyname** – name of the assembly for which you want to perform the verification process
- **[switches]** – optional set of switches

The PEVerify tool has a number of switches, some of which are listed in Table 26.2:

Table 26.2: Switches of the PEVerify Tool

Switch	Description
`/help or /?`	Shows the syntax and switches of the PEVerify tool
`/md`	Verifies the metadata in the assembly
`/il`	Verifies the MSIL code in the assembly
`/clock`	Shows the time taken (in milliseconds) for verification
`/hresult`	Shows the error codes in hexadecimal format
`/unique`	Hides any repeating error codes
`/quiet`	Shows only the status of the verification, not the error codes
`/verbose`	Shows additional information about the verification process
`/ignore=hex.code [, hex.code]`	Ignores the specified error codes (in hexadecimal format)
`/ignore=@filename`	Ignores the error codes given in the specified response file
`/nologo`	Hides the product version and copyright information

Note that the PEVerify tool performs the verification in the absence of any or all of the switches listed in Table 26.2. The PEVerify tool validates the metadata first and if there are no errors, it verifies the MSIL code. In case of any error in the verification of the metadata, the MSIL code is not verified. However, if you specify the /md and /il switches, the MSIL code is verified irrespective of whether there are errors in the metadata.

If the MSIL code undergoes the verification process but does not pass the verification, then an exception occurs and the execution of the application is halted. In case you are certain that your code is completely trusted to be type-safe, then you can bypass the verification. You can also bypass the verification if you want to run a non-type-safe code. However, running a non-type-safe code is not recommended as it may lead to unpredictable results. To bypass the verification, you need to set the SkipVerification property of the SecurityPermissionAttribute to false at the assembly level.

NOTE

The verification process is performed by the CLR only on managed code; unmanaged code does not undergo the verification process and therefore, is run in a full-trust environment.

In this way, you can use the PEVerify tool to ensure the type-safety of your .NET application, making it secure and reliable to be run on the users' computers. With this, you learned to take the first step in securing your applications. Now, let's discuss the security changes in .NET Framework 4.5.

Security in the .NET Framework 4.5

Security is one of the key features of Web applications. The security prevents Web applications from unauthorized access or hacking. The hackers generally manipulate the functionality of the Web application and therefore, makes the Web application irrelevant for the user. Security also provides defense against threats or virus attacks. Without security, a developer cannot think of developing a Web application. Therefore, .NET Framework includes the security feature since its release which is widely used to secure the Web application. There are various types of security mechanism present in .NET related to identify the identity of the user that will be discussed later in this chapter. Now, Microsoft includes the security features in .NET Framework 4.5 by to make the Web application more secure from unauthorized access.

Let's discuss the security features in .NET Framework 4.5 one by one.

Enhanced Strong Naming

A strong name signature is used to identify assemblies in the .NET Framework. This signature is used as a unique identity for an assembly to ensure that references to the assemblies are not ambiguous in an application developed by using the .NET Framework. This signature also restricts unauthorized access and modification of assemblies in .NET Framework. In earlier versions of the .NET Framework, strong name signatures can be tracked; however, this shortcoming is removed in .NET Framework 4.5. Now, strong names include a signature key and an identity key. The signature key is used to sign assemblies and identity key is used to identify assemblies corresponding to their signature key values.

Security Policy Simplification

The .NET Framework provided Code Access Security (CAS) mechanism. This mechanism is used for controlling and configuring the ability of managed code. The CAS mechanism was powerful but was complicated, as this policy was applicable for native applications and therefore the security guarantee was limited. Therefore, developers look for alternating solutions, such as operating system-level solutions. This problem was solved in .NET Framework 4.5 by turning off the machine-wide security. The shared and hosted Web applications can now run more securely.

Security Transparency Level 2

The Security transparency feature was first introduced in .NET Framework 2.0 and was used basically for improving the efficiency of code validation. In .NET Framework 4.5, this mechanism is basically used to separate the code that executes as a part of the Web application from the code that executes as a part of infrastructure. The Security Transparency acts like an obstacle between the critical code and the transparent code. The critical code can do privileged things, such as modifications in the database, while the transparent code can run command within the limited permissions and cannot call critical code. The main aim of the security transparency is to provide effective mechanism to isolate code on the basis of privileges.

Obsolete Permission Requests

In .NET Framework 4.5, the runtime support is omitted that is used to implement the Deny, RequestMinimum, RequestOptional, and RequestRefuse permission requests. These requests are threat to security when they are not properly used. These set of permissions requests can easily be override, cannot be used outside the application, and cannot provide least privilege model. Therefore, .NET Framework 4.5 removed the runtime calling of these permission requests.

Conditional APTCA

In .NET Framework 4.5, the AllowPartiallyTrustedCallersAttribute (APTCA) allows the hosts to recognize those assemblies that they want to display to partial trust callers when used conditionally. The candidate assemblies are developed for partial trust, therefore, it must be APTCA or fully transparent. The APTCA uses the PartialTrustVisibilityLevel enumeration to specify the level of visibility for an APTCA assembly.

Evidence Objects

The object of any type that is identified by the security policy is known as evidence. The security policy consists of code groups. In the previous versions of .NET Framework, almost every object can be used as an evidence object if the hosting code applies it as evidence. At runtime, the evidence objects are considered as object references and type safety is not applied to them. This raised the problem in the .NET Framework because it applies implicit restrictions on which type can be used as evidence objects. The object which is going to be used as evidence has to be serialized and not null. If it is not so, then the CLR throws the exception.

To avoid the exception, the .NET Framework 4.5 includes the EvidenceBase class to apply constraints on those objects that may be considered as evidence and to add new requirements and features to the evidence objects. This class ensures that the evidence object should be serializable.

Evidence Collections

In the previous version of .NET Framework, the full set of evidence objects is generated by the CLR that are used with an assembly when it loads. The evidence objects are stored in the list, which can be used to search the specific object. Therefore, all the evidence objects are displayed whether they were used or not. This behavior was improved in the .NET Framework 4.5 as the evidence collection now acts like a dictionary. Now, there is no need to search a particular evidence object through iteration rather you can request for particular evidence and the collection returns the evidence. If the requested evidence object is not found then the evidence collection returns null. The dictionary model generates the evidence objects when they are requested.

Introducing Authentication and Authorization

The very first thing that comes to your mind while distributing your application or resource to the users is how vulnerable or strong it is. Depending on the vulnerability of the application or resource, you may want to limit its access to users. To limit the access and make the application or resource secure, you need to identify and allow access to only a certain set of people or users. Other people or users, who do not have the right to access, should not be able to use or access the application or resource. For this, you need to identify the people or users who are recognized by a valid system, such as the operating system on your computer. The process of identifying users of your application or resource is known as authentication. In general, a combination of the user name and the password is used to authenticate users. If the credentials (user name and password) of a user are valid, the user becomes an authenticated user; otherwise, the user is denied access to the requested application or resource.

After a user is authenticated, the next question that comes to the mind is whether or not to provide access to the requested application or resource. The access granted to an authenticated user depends on the operations or actions that the user is allowed or denied to perform on the requested application or resource. Many applications or resources may face a risk of misuse or unintentional manipulation by other users. Therefore, before deciding the actions that you allow an authenticated user to perform, you need to resolve what the user may gain from accessing the resource. After you resolve this matter, you can assign various actions to the authenticated users. This process of deciding whether an authenticated user can access the intended application or resource is known as authorization. The authorization of an authenticated user depends on the privileges that the user holds. Figure 26.2 shows a broad picture of the authentication and authorization process in .NET framework:

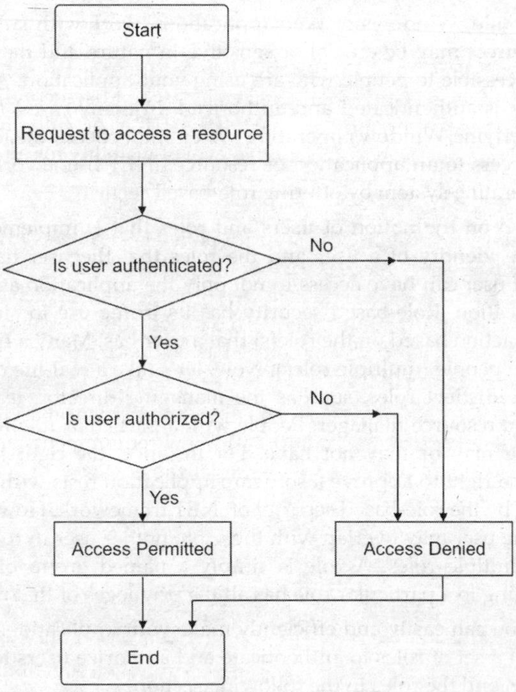

Figure 26.2: Pictorial Depiction of Authentication and Authorization in .NET Framework

Now, let's move on to learn about the first security mechanism, that is, role-based security.

Role-Based Security

The Web offers a great deal of services and features that can be used in diverse scenarios. Lately, there has been a steep increase in the number of Web applications in use and quality and speed of connectivity. Due to its connected and interactive nature (between server and clients), there is a myriad of threats that afflict the security and reliability of the Web applications. There are many ways in which a third-party user or application may gain access to the Web applications and then manipulate the functioning or data of the Web applications. Therefore, there is a dire need for a robust and impervious security mechanism for Web applications. It is imperative that Web developers have a thorough understanding of the potential security risks to the application and then accordingly incorporate the desired security. Some of the security risks to Web applications include phishing, hacking, and virus attacks.

The Web developer should keep the following things in mind while structuring the security system for a Web application:

- How does the Web application work?
- What is the nature and extent of communication between the server and the clients?
- What are the security threats to the Web application?
- How can these security threats affect the proper running of the Web application?
- What is the level of security that needs to be implemented?

Depending on the mentioned criteria, Web developers can implement the security system for Web applications. Web developers can secure applications in several ways, some of which include configuring firewalls on the Web server and encrypting data exchanged on the Web. Some of these, such as firewalls, may prove useful to only a certain extent. In .NET framework, there is more than one way in which you can secure the Web applications (ASP.NET Web applications).

The applications that you build, Windows or Web applications, work with large amount of data and resources. Some of the data and resources may be crucial or sensitive in nature and therefore, you would not want such data and resources to be accessible to people who are using your application. As you know, a user can access an application only if the user is authenticated and authorized. In many cases, the authentication is done by the security system of the underlying Windows operating system that checks the identity and the role of the person or user to allow or deny access to an application or resource. .NET framework and CLR leverages the security system of the Windows operating system by offering role-based security.

Role-based security is based on the notion of users and roles that is implemented in most modern operating systems. Depending on the identity of a user and the roles that the user has, the user is authenticated and authorized. The authorized user can have access to not only the application as a whole but also the classes and methods used in the application. Role-based security has its prime use in situations when the application or resource needs to verify an action based on the role(s) that a user has. Many a times, the intended action requires authorization from multiple people (multiple roles). Now, let's take a real-life example of an organization where there are people who have distinct roles, such as the managing director, team leaders, software developers, software testers, and human resource manager. People with a particular role have specific privileges and rights that people of another role may or may not have. For instance, the right to sanction leaves rests with the managing director, while the right to approve a software application rests with the team leaders. This concept of roles in real life is inherited by the role-based security of .NET framework. However, unlike the real-life scenario, the roles or privileges of one user may overlap with those of another user in role-based security. In other words, a single user may have multiple roles. A role is simply a named group of users that has the same set of privileges. Any user belonging to a particular role has all the privileges of that role.

With role-based security, you can easily and efficiently make your applications secure. Role-based security uses a principal, an identity, and a set of roles to authenticate and authorize users to use the applications. You learn about the principal, identity, and the roles in the following section.

Principal Object

Role-based security revolves around principal. A principal is an encapsulation of the identity of the user and the roles to which the user is affiliated. In .NET framework 4.5, identity of the user is represented through any of the available associated types; and roles of the user are represented by the permissions. The roles and the identity of a principal are taken into consideration by the application for authenticating and authorizing the user. Note that a principal can have only one identity but multiple roles.

Principal (or principal object) represents a user-specific environment in which your applications runs. Depending on the identity and roles of the user, the principal offers less or more security to your application. In .NET framework 4.5, role-based security allows you to work with three types of principals:

- **Windows Principals**—Refer to the users and roles of the Windows operating system
- **Generic Principals**—Refer to the users and roles other than the Windows principals
- **Custom Principals**—Refer to the users and roles that you create in the applications

NOTE

With Windows principals, the users and roles have to be linked with the user accounts on the Windows operating system. Therefore, you may need to create new user accounts on the operating system.

You can work with these three types of principals by using different classes available in the System.Security.Principal namespace in the .NET framework 4.5 class library. You can use the WindowsPrincipal class to work with a Windows principal or use the GenericPrincipal class to work with a principal not related to the Windows user accounts. For custom principals, you need to define your own principal class. Note that whether it is the WindowsPrincipal, GenericPrincipal, or a custom principal class, these classes implement the IPrincipal interface of the System.Security.Principal namespace. The IPrincipal interface offers a property and method for working with principals in the .NET applications. Table 26.3 lists the property and method extended by the IPrincipal interface:

Table 26.3: Property and Method of the IPrincipal Interface	
Property	**Description**
`Identity`	Retrieves the identity of the principal.
Method	**Description**
`IsInRole`	Returns a value that indicates whether the principal has the given role. For Windows principal, the role refers to the user group.

Both the WindowsPrincipal and GenericPrincipal classes include the Identity and the IsInRole() method. In case you are defining a custom principal class, you need to implement the IPrincipal interface.

When a user runs the application, it runs in a thread under some user account (or principal). Generally, it is the currently logged-in user of the computer, which is the current principal. Every thread in the application has a CallContext object that is linked with a principal. A single thread has exactly one principal. Figure 26.3 shows how the identity and roles of a principal are related with the thread:

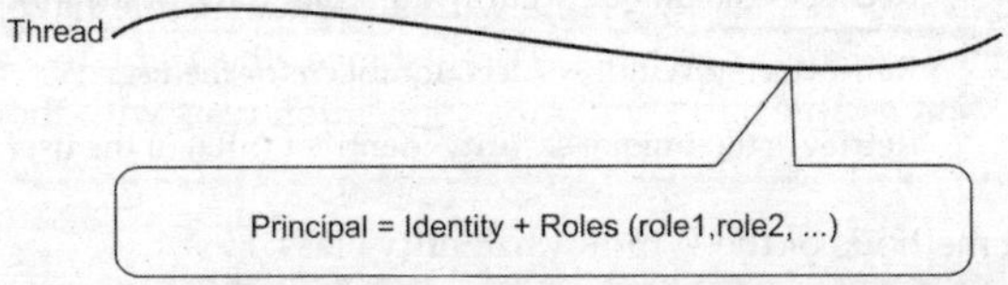

Figure 26.3: Showing the Relationship Between a Thread, Principal, Identity, and Roles

Note that by default, the principal (with identity and role) is created for an unauthenticated user. To create a Windows principal, you need to first set the principal policy of the current application domain to the WindowsPrincipal value of the PrincipalPolicy enumeration. You can do this by including the following code before creating the principal and identity:

```
AppDomain.CurrentDomain.SetPrincipalPolicy(PrincipalPolicy.WindowsPrincipal)
```

You need to add this code only for working with the Windows principals; you do not need this code for generic or custom principals.

Identity Object

As stated earlier, a principal object has an identity and a set of roles. You can consider identity to be a particular user (having a name) and principal to be the user account. An identity or identity object represents the user that needs to be authenticated and authorized to access your application.

Similar to principal objects, identity objects also represent Windows users or non-Windows users. Windows identities correspond to the existing users on the operating system and are available through the WindowsIdentity class. The non-Windows identities are those users that do not signify any users on the Windows operating system, for example, users created through the code. The non-Windows identities are available through the GenericIdentity class. Both these classes exist in the System.Security.Principal namespace and implement the IIdentity interface (also defined in the System.Security.Principal namespace). The IIdentity interface offers the essential functionality to work with identities. Table 26.4 lists the properties of the IIdentity interface:

Table 26.4: Properties of the IIdentity Interface	
Property	**Description**
`Name`	Retrieves the name of the user (identity)
`AuthenticationType`	Retrieves the type of authentication for the current user (identity)
`IsAuthenticated`	Retrieves a value that indicates whether the current user is authenticated

NOTE

You can create user or identity by creating an identity class that implements the IIdentity interface.

The properties offered by the IIdentity interface are a part of the WindowsIdentity and GenericIdentity classes. The WindowsIdentity class has several other properties and methods that pertain to a Windows user. Table 26.5 lists the properties of the WindowsIdentity class:

Table 26.5: Noteworthy Properties of the WindowsIdentity Class

Property	Description
`Groups`	Retrieves the groups or roles of the currently logged-in Windows user
`ImpersonationLevel`	Retrieves the level of impersonation for the current user
`IsAnonymous`	Retrieves a value that indicates whether the user is an anonymous user
`IsGuest`	Retrieves a value that indicates whether the user is a Guest user on the Windows operating system
`IsSystem`	Retrieves a value that indicates whether the user is a System user
`Owner`	Retrieves the unique security identifier (SID) of the token owner
`Token`	Retrieves the Windows account token for the user
`User`	Retrieves the unique security identifier (SID) of the user

Table 26.6 lists the important methods of the WindowsIdentity class:

Table 26.6: Noteworthy Methods of the WindowsIdentity Class

Method	Description
`GetAnonymous`	Retrieves an anonymous Windows user (identity)
`GetCurrent`	Retrieves the current identity object
`Impersonate`	Allows the impersonation of another Windows user

In most cases, an identity object has a name and an authentication type. With the Windows identities, the authentication type can be NT LAN Manager (NTLM) or Kerberos. You will learn more about the authentication types a little later. Now, let's discuss the role-based security checks.

Role-Based Security Checks

To incorporate authentication and authorization for role-based security, you need to add the necessary code in the application; that is, add the role-based security checks to authorize the user. You can include the role-based security checks in the following three ways:

- Accessing the Principal directly
- Using the imperative security check
- Using the declarative security check

You can directly access the principal object on the current thread and use the properties and methods to authenticate and authorize the user. You can also perform the imperative or declarative security check. Now, let's learn about the two frequently used security checks.

Imperative Security Check

You know that with the .NET framework security system, you can authenticate and authorize users not only at the holistic application (assembly) level but also at the class or method level. If you want to implement authorization in several methods in the application, you can employ the imperative security check. You may also use the imperative security check if you want other assemblies to authorize the user.

In the imperative security check, an imperative security demand is made to authorize the user. When the application runs, the current principal is checked to see if it has the minimum identity and roles required for authorization. This is done through a principal permission, which refers to a particular identity and role. You can use the principal permission to demand an imperative security check to validate the identity and role of the current principal. The identity and role of the current principal is checked against the specified identity and role of the principal permission. If both the identity and role are same, the user (principal) is authorized; else, the user is not authorized and an exception occurs.

The principal permissions are instances of the PrincipalPermission class that exists in the System.Security.Permissions namespace. The PrincipalPermission class inherits the System.Object class and implements the IPermission interface in the System.Security namespace and has various methods to allow you to work with the principal permissions. Table 26.7 lists the important methods of the PrincipalPermission class:

Table 26.7: Noteworthy Methods of the PrincipalPermission Class

Method	Description
`Copy`	Returns a duplicate copy of the current permission
`Demand`	Demands an imperative security check
`FromXml`	Creates a principal permission from an XML encoding
`GetHashCode`	Retrieves a hash code for the principal permission
`Intersect`	Returns a permission that is an intersection of the current and the given permissions
`IsSubsetOf`	Returns a value that indicates whether the current permission is a subset of the specified permission
`IsUnrestricted`	Returns a value that indicates whether the permission is unrestricted (that is, it matches any principal)
`ToXml`	Creates the XML encoding of the current permission
`Union`	Returns a permission that is a union of the current and the specified permissions

The Demand() method, given in Table 26.7, is called on the PrincipalPermission object to demand an imperative security check. The syntax to demand an imperative security check is:

```
principalPermissionObject.Demand()
```

The principalPermissionObject is the name of the PrincipalPermission object.

The identity and role against which the current principal is validated are passed as arguments to the constructor of the principal permission. Note that if you want to authorize based on only the role, then you can specify a null reference as the specified identity in the principal permission. In this case, the current principal can have any identity and need not be the same as specified in the principal permission. Similarly, when you want only the identity to be checked, you can specify a null value for the role. This implies that the current principal can have any role.

Declarative Security Check

You can use the declarative security check in role-based security when you want to implement authorization at the class, method, property, or event level. The declarative security check has the same functionality as the imperative security check, that is, to check the identity and role of the current principal against the specified identity and role given in the principal permission. In addition, the declarative security check is done every time the resource (class, method, or event) is requested. For instance, if you place a declarative security check at the class or method level, then every time an object of the class or a call to the method appears in the code, the current principal is checked against the specified identity and role in the respective principal permission. In case there is no match, an exception occurs; else, the current principal is authorized.

With declarative security check, you use attributes to mark the assembly, class, or method that you intend to protect. The attributes take various parameters that define the security check to be performed. The declarative security occurs at the compile-time and act as preconditions for accessing the assembly, class, or method.

In the declarative security check, you can create the principal permission by using the PrincipalPermissionAttribute class. The inheritance hierarchy of the PrincipalPermissionAttribute class is as follows:

```
System.Object
  System.Attribute
       System.Security.Permissions.SecurityAttribute
             System.Security.Permissions.CodeAccessSecurityAttribute
                   System.Security.Permissions.PrincipalPermissionAttribute
```

The PrincipalPermissionAttribute class has several properties and methods to allow you to specify the required identity and role that the current principal needs to match to access the class, method, or event. Table 26.8 lists the noteworthy properties of the PrincipalPermissionAttribute class:

Table 26.8: Noteworthy Properties of the PrincipalPermissionAttribute Class

Property	Description
Name	Sets or retrieves the name of the identity of the current principal.
Role	Sets or retrieves the role or membership of the principal.
Action	Sets or retrieves the security action(Inherited from SecurityAttribute).
Authenticated	Sets or retrieves a value that indicates if the current principal is authenticated or not.
TypeId	Retrieves the unique identifier for the current PrincipalPermissionAttribute object(Inherited from Attribute).
Unrestricted	Sets or retrieves a value that indicates whether the principal permission provides full access to the requested class or method. If this property is set to true, then the current principal is an authenticated user that can have any identity or role(Inherited from SecurityAttribute).

Table 26.9 lists the noteworthy methods of the PrincipalPermissionAttribute class:

Table 26.9: Noteworthy Methods of the PrincipalPermissionAttribute Class

Method	Description
CreatePermission	Returns a new PrincipalPermission
IsDefaultAttribute	Returns a value that indicates if the PrincipalPermissionAttribute object is the default principal permission for the derived classes(Inherited from Attribute).
Match	Returns a value that indicates if the principal permission is same as a given object (Inherited from Attribute).

You can specify the required identity and role by using the Name and Role properties of the PrincipalPermissionAttribute class. The syntax to use the PrincipalPermissionAttribute object in the code is as follows:

In VB:

```
'Declaration

<SerializableAttribute> _
<AttributeUsageAttribute(AttributeTargets.Class Or AttributeTargets.Method, AllowMultiple
  := True,  _
     Inherited := False)> _
<ComVisibleAttribute(True)> _
Public NotInheritable Class PrincipalPermissionAttribute _
     Inherits CodeAccessSecurityAttribute
'Usage

Dim instance As PrincipalPermissionAttribute
```

In C#:

```
[SerializableAttribute]
[AttributeUsageAttribute(AttributeTargets.Class|AttributeTargets.Method, AllowMultiple =
  true,
    Inherited = false)]
[ComVisibleAttribute(true)]
public sealed class PrincipalPermissionAttribute : CodeAccessSecurityAttribute
```

The brief explanation about the attributes is as follows:

- **PrincipalPermissionAttribute**—Refers to the PrincipalPermissionAttribute object
- **SecurityAction.Demand**—Refers to the Demand value of the SecurityAction enumeration
- **Name, Role**—Refer to the Name and Role properties of the PrincipalPermissionAttribute class
- **identityName**—Refers to the identity name that is required for the current principal to be authorized
- **principalRole**—Refers to the role that is required for the current principal to be authorized

Similar to the imperative security check, if you want to perform authorization based on only the identity or role of the current principal, then you can leave out the Role or Name property, respectively, in the PrincipalPermissionAttribute object.

NOTE

The PrincipalPermissionAttribute object is a security attribute stored in the metadata, which is used by the CLR to load and run the application. you should also note that the security attributes are used only for declarative security.

You can implement a declarative security check by using the SecurityAction enumeration. This enumeration has several flags that allow you to specify the kind of action you want to perform for declarative security check. Some of the common flags of the SecurityAction enumeration are listed in Table 26.10:

Table 26.10: Flags of the SecurityAction Enumeration

Flags	Description
`Assert`	Allows the current principal with the specified identity and/or role to access the class or method even when other calling code in the stack does not have the specified permission
`Demand`	Causes the CLR to check if the principal of all the calling code has the identity and/or role specified in the principal permission
`Deny`	Refuses access to the calling code even if the respective principals have the specified permission
`InheritanceDemand`	Causes the CLR to allow access if a derived class or overridden method has the specified permission
`PermitOnly`	Allows the calling code to access only a particular class or method even if the code has permission to access other classes and methods
`RequestRefuse`	Allows you to specify the permissions that you do not want to grant to the code (applicable only for assemblies, not for classes and methods)
`RequestMinimum`	Allows you to specify the minimum permission needed for the code (only applicable for assemblies, not for classes and methods)
`RequestOptional`	Allows you to specify additional permissions for the code (applicable only for assemblies, not for classes and methods)

Except for RequestRefuse, RequestMinimum, and RequestOptional, all other SecurityAction enumeration flags are applicable on classes and methods.

NOTE

The level or extent of the declarative security check depends on the location of the security check and the value of the SecurityAction enumeration. If you have specified a declarative security check at the class as well as the method level, then the security check at the method level overrides the security check at the class level.

Imperative Security Check Versus Declarative Security Check

Both imperative and declarative security checks serve the same purpose, only in a different way. Depending on your needs, you can select one or the other. Table 26.11 lists some of main differences between imperative and declarative checks:

Table 26.11: Difference Between Imperative and Declarative Checks

Imperative Security Check	Declarative Security Check
Allows only `Demand` and `Assert` security actions.	Allows all the security actions.
Executes at runtime and therefore, there is no way to know about the authorization status at compile time. It is useful when you do not want to disclose the permission requirement information.	Persists in the assembly at compile time; therefore, you can use tools, such as `permview` (using the /DECL switch), to see the check. This may help you to resolve security issues and configure the security policy while deploying.
Imperative checks are performed inside methods and evaluated every time the method is called so they usually provide inferior performance.	Security checks are evaluated once only at the load time, therefore, providing better performance.
Offers flexibility as it is used inside methods and allows checks for variables in the methods. However, the check is performed after accessing the method called and therefore, not as secure as the declarative check.	Allows checks at assembly, class, or method level and therefore, confirms authorization before the assembly, class, or method is accessed. This prevents any kind of potential invasion.

Now, let's move on to learn how role-based security provides a defense to ASP.NET applications.

The Roles Class

Role-based security plays a significant part in securing ASP.NET applications. With the help of principals, identities, and roles, you can easily and effectively protect your applications and other application-specific resources. A role is a group of similar type of users. For example, you can group all the users having administrative rights under the administrative role. Now, let's move on to the Roles class that allows you to create a role, assign users to a role, and manage a role. Managing role refers to assigning different permissions to the different roles for accessing an ASP.NET application. For example, you may need to restrict the users who are not the members of the Administrator role from accessing the membership data store.

The hierarchy of the Roles class is as follows:

```
System.Object
   System.Web.Security.Roles
```

A user can be a member of more than one role and enjoy privileges of multiple roles. For example, if you have created an online discussion forum in ASP.NET, you may need to assign single user to both, member role and moderator role. This user will enjoy privileges of both, member and moderator roles.

The `Roles` class is available in the `System.Web.Security` namespace, which resides in the `System.Web` assembly. The `Roles` class cannot be inherited.

You can use the members of the `Roles` class without qualifying them with the instance of the `Roles` class because `Roles` class is a static class.

NOTE

Roles work with authenticated users only.

Table 26.12 lists the noteworthy properties of the Roles class:

Table 26.12: Noteworthy Public Properties of the Roles Class

Property	Description
`ApplicationName`	Obtains or specifies the name of the application for which you want to store and retrieve the role information.

Table 26.12: Noteworthy Public Properties of the Roles Class

Property	Description
CacheRolesInCookie	Specifies whether or not to store the role information in a cookie.
CookieName	Obtains the name of the cookie that stores the role information.
CookiePath	Obtains the path of the cookie that stores the role information.
CookieProtectionValue	Specifies how to secure the role information stored in a cookie. The values of the CookieProtectionValue property can be Encryption, Validation, All, or None.
CookieRequireSSL	Determines whether the server requires a SSL connection to retrieve the role information stored in a cookie.
CookieSlidingExpiration	Specifies whether to refresh the expiration time of a cookie every time the server requests it.
CookieTimeout	Determines the amount of time left in expiration of a cookie.
CreatePersistentCookie	Specifies whether to store the role information in the cookie permanently.
Domain	Determines the domain name of the cookie storing the role information.
Enabled	Determines or specifies whether or not to manage roles for an ASP.NET application.
MaxCachedResults	Specifies the maximum number of roles that can be assigned to a user.
Provider	Obtains the default role provider of an ASP.NET application.
Providers	Obtains all the role providers that are configured for an ASP.NET application.

Table 26.13 lists the noteworthy methods of the Roles class:

Table 26.13: Noteworthy Public Methods of the Roles Class

Method	Description
AddUsersToRole	Assigns a role to users
AddUsersToRoles	Assigns specified roles to specified users
AddUserToRole	Assigns a role to a specific user
AddUserToRoles	Assigns multiple roles to a user
CreateRole	Creates a new role and add it to a data source
DeleteCookie	Removes the cookie storing the role information
DeleteRole	Deletes the specified role
GetAllRoles	Obtains a list of all the roles defined for an ASP.NET application
GetRolesForUser	Determines the roles that are assigned to a user
GetUsersInRole	Determines which users are the members of a specific role
IsUserInRole	Determines whether or not a user is a member of a specific role
RemoveUserFromRole	Deletes a user from a role
RemoveUserFromRoles	Deletes a user from multiple roles
RemoveUsersFromRole	Deletes multiple users from a role
RemoveUsersFromRoles	Deletes multiple users from multiple roles
RoleExists	Determines whether a role exists or not

In this section, you learn about the use of role-based security in ASP.NET applications, which includes the security architecture in ASP.NET, the authentication modes in ASP.NET, and impersonation and delegation.

Now, let's begin with the security architecture in ASP.NET.

ASP.NET Security Architecture

Securing ASP.NET applications involves an integrated synchronization between the Internet Information Services (IIS), the .NET Framework, and the underlying operating system. As you know, IIS is a part of the Windows operating system, such as Windows 7, and acts as a base for managing and organizing the Web applications on your computer. IIS offers a robust security system for safeguarding the Web applications and their resources. IIS can also make use of the security features of the Windows operating system.

Requests made by clients (Web browsers) for an ASP.NET Web application is first processed by the IIS. If a client is authenticated by IIS, then the request is forwarded to the ASP.NET application, else, the request is denied. The ASP.NET applications may use the security system of the .NET Framework to authenticate and authorize the clients.

In Figure 26.4, you can see how the IIS, .NET Framework, and the Windows operating system form the security architecture of ASP.NET applications:

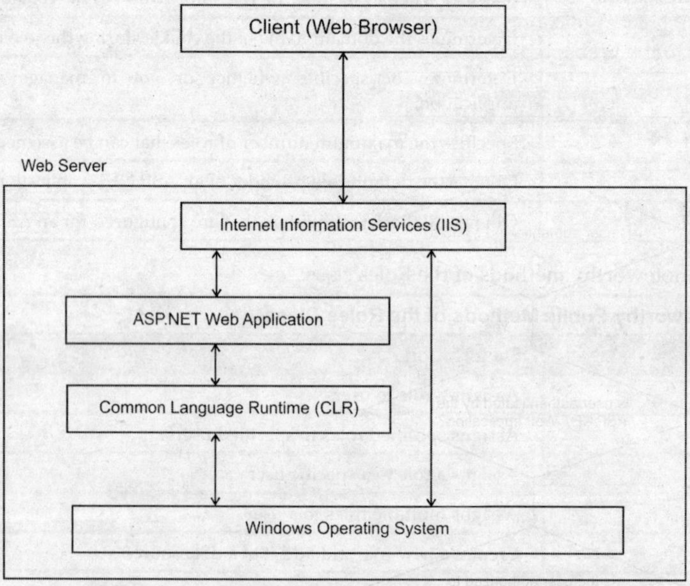

Figure 26.4: Security Architecture of ASP.NET Applications

The security of ASP.NET applications depends heavily on the security mechanism offered by IIS and .NET Framework. In IIS 6.0, 7.0, and 7.5 (packaged with Windows 7), the ASP.NET worker process (aspnet_wp.exe) runs under the Network Service account, which is the account under which the IIS worker process (w3wp.exe) also runs. The IIS worker process hosts the IIS Web server, while the ASP.NET worker process hosts the ASP.NET applications. The Network Service account is a built-in account that has certain limited privileges. This account provides security from malicious attacks by hackers and users who have the intention of damaging the Web server. The Network Service account is used to run the ASP.NET worker process and not the ASPNET user account as in previous versions of IIS and Windows (Windows XP).

There may be some situations when you want to run the ASP.NET worker process with lesser privileges as compared to the Network Service account. In such a situation, you can change the user account under which the ASP.NET worker process runs by changing certain relevant attributes in the machine.config file, which exists in the C:\Windows\Microsoft.NET\Framework\v4.0.30319\Config folder on your computer. The machine.config file is an XML file with various XML tags or elements that define the machine-level configuration settings for

.NET applications. You can open the machine.config file in the Notepad or Visual Studio 2012 and locate the <processModel> element in the <system.web> element. In the <processModel> element, you can set the userName and the password attributes. To make the ASP.NET worker process run under the TestUser user account, set the userName and password attributes as follows:

```
<processModel autoConfig="true" userName="TestUser" password="@kogent30"/>
```

The value of the password attribute is the password that you have specified for the TestUser account.

NOTE

Apart from the Network Service account, there are the Local System and Local Service built-in accounts. The Local System account belongs to the Administrators group and has the maximum privileges among the three. Therefore, the Local System account may prove to be unsafe for the Web server as well as the Web applications. The Local Service account has the least privileges and is useful when the application does not use any remote resources.

Authentication Modes

As you already know, authentication refers to the process of validating the identity of a user. The user may be a person, another application, or a service. The authenticity of the user of ASP.NET applications is collectively decided by the IIS and the ASP.NET application itself. When a user requests for a Web page, authentication is first performed by IIS. If IIS authenticates the user, then authentication is performed by the ASP.NET application. If the ASP.NET application also authenticates the user and the user has the authorization, then the user is granted access to the Web page, as shown in Figure 26.5:

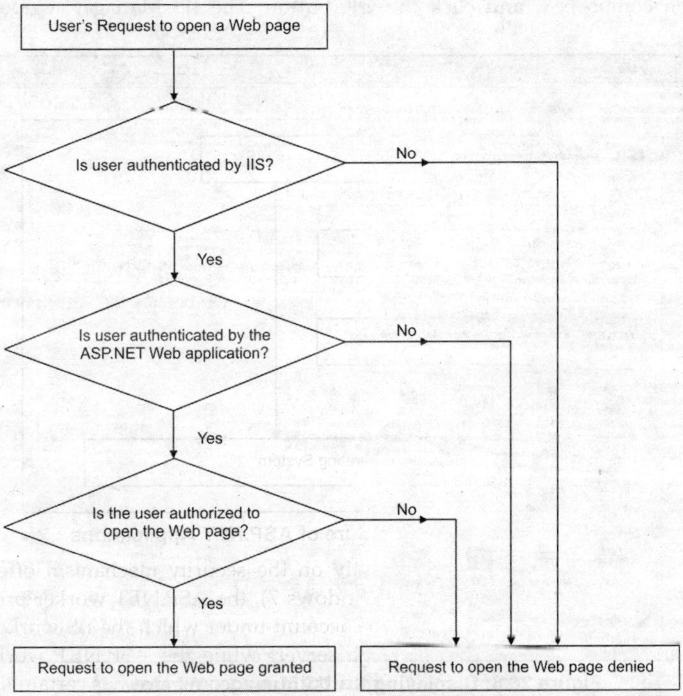

Figure 26.5: Displaying Authentication and Authorization for an ASP.NET Application

The authentication modes that are available for ASP.NET applications are:

- Anonymous authentication
- Windows authentication
- Forms authentication
- Passport authentication
- Federated authentication

Note that except for the passport authentication, all other authentication modes are supported by IIS 7.5 as well as ASP.NET. To allow authentication at the IIS-level, you need to use the IIS Manager and specify the desired authentication. If you want to allow authentication in the ASP.NET application, then you need to use an authentication provider. An authentication provider refers to the code module that contains the essential code to perform the desired authentication. ASP.NET offers authentication providers for Windows, Forms, and passport authentication; there is no authentication provider for anonymous authentication.

Now, let's learn about these authentication modes one by one.

Anonymous Authentication

Users that request an ASP.NET Web resource (for example, a Web page) are authenticated by default as anonymous users, that is, users with any random identity. When the users are authenticated as anonymous users, the process is referred to as anonymous authentication. In this type of authentication, credentials (user name and password) are not required to authenticate the user. This implies that any user attempting to access a Web resource is automatically authenticated, which is why anonymous authentication is useful when you want your ASP.NET application to be available to all the users or when you want better performance. Anonymous authentication provides least security and therefore, you need to be judicious about authenticating anonymous users for your ASP.NET applications.

Anonymous authentication is the default authentication mode of IIS. You can see this default setting by opening the IIS Manager. To view the IIS Manager, open the Run dialog box of the Windows operating system, type inetmgr in the Open combo box, and click the OK button. The IIS Manager window opens, as shown in Figure 26.6:

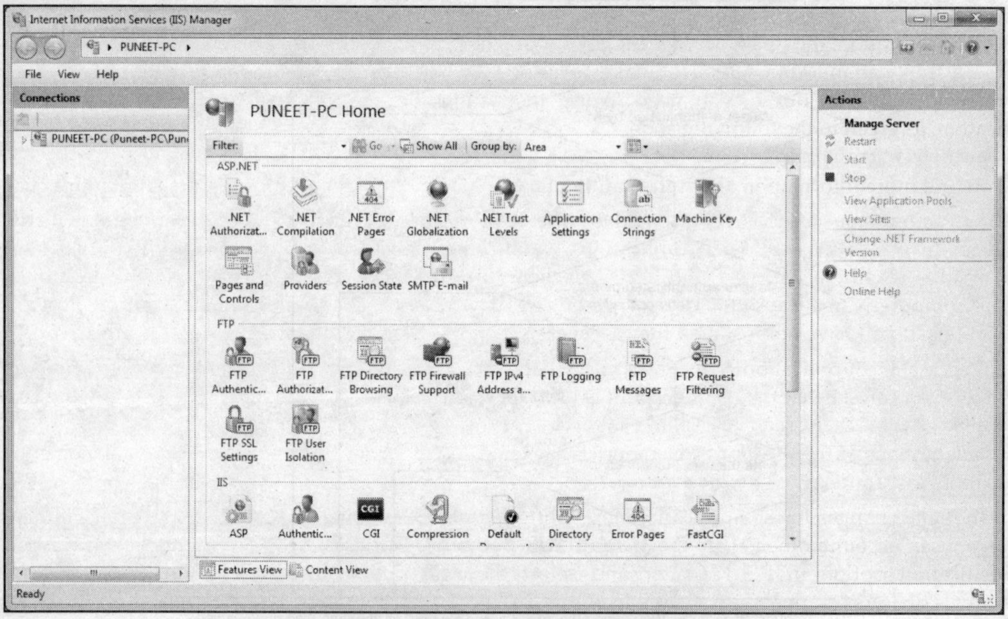

Figure 26.6: Displaying the IIS Manager Window

In the middle pane of the IIS Manager, double-click the Authentication icon. The different authentication modes available in IIS 7.5 appear in the IIS Manager, as shown in Figure 26.7:

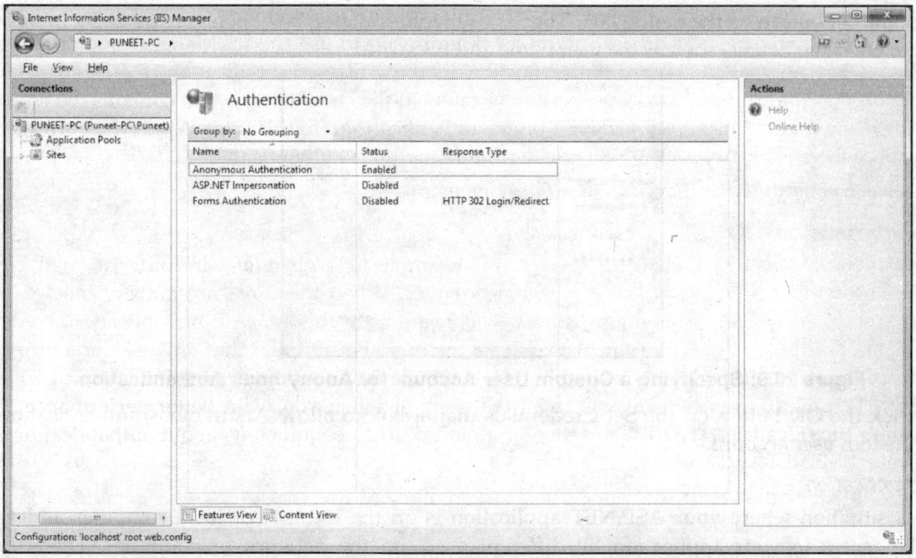

Figure 26.7: Displaying the Supported Authentication Modes in IIS 7.5

As shown in Figure 26.7, anonymous authentication is enabled by default in IIS 7.5. When a user requests for an ASP.NET application, the IIS recognizes the user as an anonymous user. The authentication then passes on to the ASP.NET application. You can also make an ASP.NET application to use anonymous authentication to authenticate users. To do so, you need to use the <authentication> element in the Web.config file of the application, as given in the following code:

```
<authentication mode="None" />
```

You can find more information about the <authentication> element in the Web.config file later in this chapter.

In IIS, an anonymous user is represented by the IUSR account, which is a built-in account with very less privileges to access the ASP.NET applications. Note that the IUSR substitutes the IUSR_<ComputerName> account, for example, IUSR_PUNEET-PC, where PUNEET-PC is the name of the computer. The IUSR_<ComputerName> account is also present in IIS 7.5, but is used only for File Transfer Protocol (FTP) applications. If you have not installed the FTP server, then this account does not exist.

If you access the applicationHost.config file in the C:\Windows\System32\inetsrv\config folder on your computer, you can see that the IUSR account is used for anonymous access, as shown in the following code:

```
<anonymousAuthentication enabled="true" userName="IUSR" />
```

The <anonymousAuthentication> element is a child element of the <authentication> element in the applicationHost.config file.

You can make changes in the applicationHost.config file or IIS Manager to process Anonymous authentication under a user account other than the default IUSR account. For this, you can right-click the Anonymous Authentication option in IIS Manager and select the Edit option. The Edit Anonymous Authentication Credentials dialog box appears, as shown in Figure 26.8:

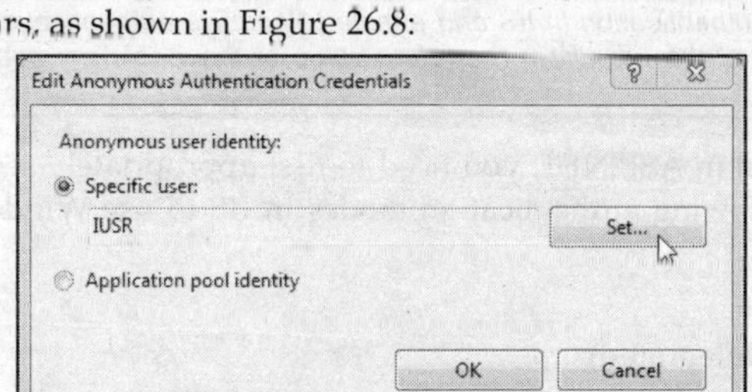

Figure 26.8: Editing the Account for Anonymous Authentication

Now, click the Set button on the dialog box. The Set Credentials dialog box opens(Figure 26.9). In this dialog box, you need to enter the details, such as the user name and password.

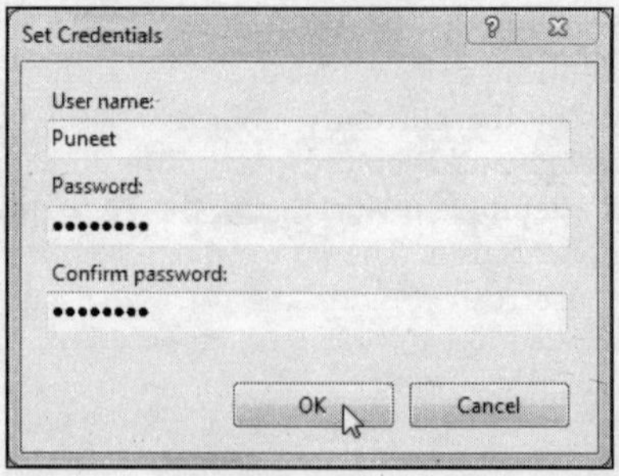

Figure 26.9: Specifying a Custom User Account for Anonymous Authentication

You can click the OK button on the Set Credentials dialog box to allow Anonymous authentication under the specified custom user account.

Windows Authentication

Consider a situation where your ASP.NET application is on the Intranet or local computer and you want to control the access to your application by different users on the network or computer. Therefore, granting anonymous access to the application may not be a feasible solution. In such a case, you can use Windows authentication to regulate access to your ASP.NET application. With Windows authentication, the identity of a user is checked against the Windows user accounts that are stored on the Web server. If the credentials of a user match with that of a Windows user account, then the user is authenticated. You can use Windows authentication in IIS as well as in the ASP.NET application. By default, all ASP.NET applications use Windows authentication. You can see the default setting of the <authentication> element in the following code:

```
<authentication mode="Windows" />
```

When you implement Windows authentication in an ASP.NET application, the application uses the authentication performed by IIS. If an unauthenticated user requests for a Web page of the ASP.NET application, then the IIS displays a dialog box to obtain the credentials of the user. After the user provides the Windows credentials, IIS validates the credentials against the existing Windows user accounts. If IIS finds a match, then the user is authenticated; otherwise, access to the Web page is denied. In case, IIS authenticates the user, identity of the authenticated user is passed on to the ASP.NET application.

In ASP.NET, the Windows authentication provider is responsible for implementing Windows authentication in the applications. The Windows authentication provider is an instance of the WindowsAuthenticationModule class that exists in the System.Web.Security namespace. A WindowsAuthenticationModule object refers to the identity of the authenticated Windows user in an ASP.NET application. When you enable Windows authentication in the ASP.NET application, the WindowsAuthenticationModule object creates a WindowsIdentity object to represent the authenticated user and assigns it to the User property of the HttpContext object.

NOTE

If you have selected anonymous authentication in IIS and enabled Windows authentication in the ASP.NET application, then the application obtains the identity of the user from the return value of the GetAnonymous() method of the WindowsIdentity class.

To use Windows authentication in ASP.NET, you need to first appropriately set the authentication mode at IIS. You can enable any of the following authentication modes in IIS to use Windows authentication in ASP.NET applications:

- Anonymous authentication
- Windows authentication (Integrated)
- Basic authentication
- Digest authentication

You have already learned that anonymous authentication is the default authentication mode of IIS. Now, let's learn about the Windows, Basic, and Digest authentication modes in IIS:

- **Windows Authentication (Integrated)**—In IIS, Windows authentication, also known as integrated Windows authentication, authenticates users based on the authenticity of their Windows credentials. IIS uses the Windows credentials of the currently logged-in user on the client to authenticate the user. Depending on the operating system and Web browser on the client, this first attempt of authentication may succeed or fail. In case the first attempt is unsuccessful, the Web browser on the client displays a dialog box prompting for the credentials of the user. The credentials provided in the dialog box are sent to the Web server for authentication. The user can provide the credentials up to three times to be sent to the Web server. If the user is unable to provide valid credentials on the third attempt, then an error appears in the Web browser. Figure 26.10 shows the process of integrated Windows authentication:

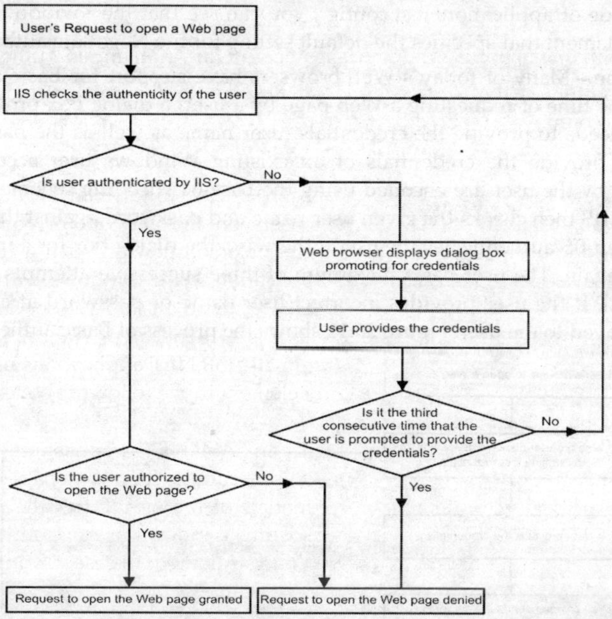

Figure 26.10: Displaying the Flow of Integrated Windows Authentication in IIS

When you enable Windows authentication in IIS, by default, the Negotiate authentication protocol is used. The Negotiate protocol negotiates with the Web browser to determine whether NTLM or Kerberos authentication is used. If both the Web server and browser support Kerberos, then the Kerberos authentication is used; else, NTLM authentication is used. The Kerberos authentication uses the Windows domain controller on the client, therefore, if the user has a Windows user account, then IIS may use Kerberos authentication. However, if the user is a non-Windows user or if there are no server proxies between the Web server and the client, then IIS may use NTLM authentication.

NTLM authentication is the default authentication for the Negotiate authentication protocol. You can see this default setting in the applicationHost.config file that is located in the C:\Windows\System32\inetsrv\config folder. In the applicationHost.config file, there is a <windowsAuthentication> element, as shown in the following code:

```
<configuration>
  .
  .
  <system.webServer>
     .
     .
     <security>
       .
```

```
        .
        <authentication>
            .
            .
            <windowsAuthentication enabled="false">
                <providers>
                    <add value="Negotiate" />
                    <add value="NTLM" />
                </providers>
            </windowsAuthentication>
        </authentication>
    </security>
  </system.webServer>
</configuration>
```

In the preceding code of applicationHost.config , you can see that the <windowsAuthentication> element has a <providers> element that specifies the default setting for the Negotiate authentication protocol.

- **Basic Authentication**—Many of today's Web browsers have support for Basic authentication. With Basic authentication, at the time of requesting a Web page by a user, a dialog box provided by the Web browser appears. The user needs to provide the credentials (user name as well as the password) in the dialog box. The user needs to provide the credentials of an existing Windows user account. The user name and password provided by the user are encoded using the Base-64 encoding scheme and then sent to the Web server as plain text. IIS then checks the given user name and password against the existing user accounts. If there is a match, then IIS authenticates the user; otherwise, the dialog box for supplying the user name and password appears again. The user has a maximum of three successive attempts to supply the correct user name and password. If the user provides incorrect user name or password at all the three times, then an HTTP error is displayed to the user. Figure 26.11 shows the process of Basic authentication:

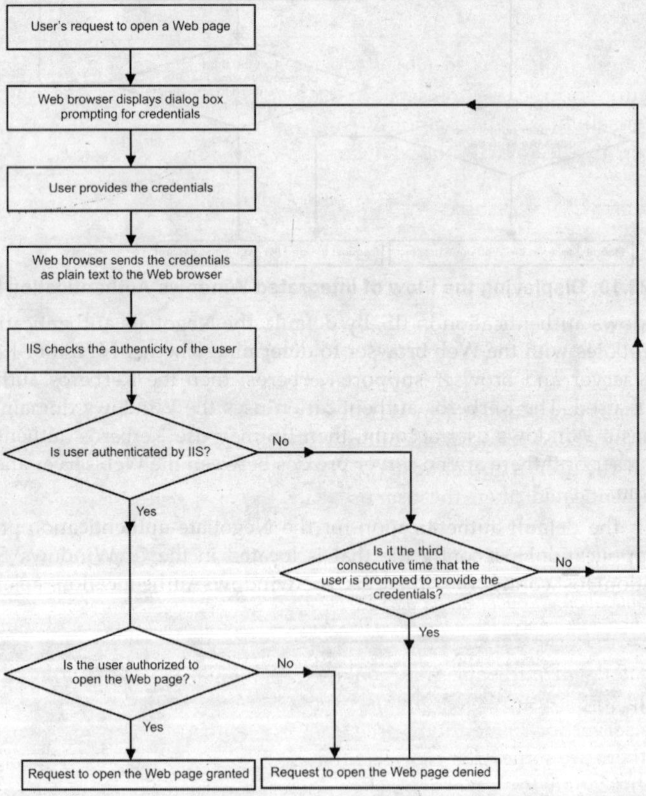

Figure 26.11: Displaying the Process of Basic Authentication in IIS

The Basic authentication transmits the user name and password in plain text across the network (Intranet), it is therefore, not advisable to use it, as there is a possibility of unauthenticated or unauthorized network users intercepting the request. Therefore, it is recommended that you use Basic authentication only when the network has a Secure Sockets Layer (SSL) connection, which is a communication protocol.

- **Digest Authentication**—It is same as Basic authentication, only with a better defence than Basic authentication. Unlike Basic authentication, in Digest authentication, the user name and password are not sent as plain text, rather they are sent as an MD5 message digest, which is a Message Digest 5 (MD5) hash. This MD5 hash makes it difficult for unauthenticated or unauthorized users to intercept. MD5 hash is an encrypted message that is sent in the HTTP header to the Web server. You will learn more about MD5 later in this chapter. The Web browser sends the MD5 hash to the Web server so that IIS can authenticate the user. The IIS furthers the MD5 hash to the Windows domain controller that then determines the authenticity of the user.

To implement the Digest authentication in IIS, you need to ensure that both the Web server and client are part of the same domain. In addition, the Windows domain controller needs to have the reversible encryption enabled to authenticate users through Digest authentication.

NOTE

Digest authentication works only for those Web browsers that support the HTTP 1.1 protocol. Some examples of HTTP 1.1-compliant Web browsers include Internet Explorer 6, 7, and 8.

Both the Basic and Digest authentication modes can provide security across proxy servers and firewalls. Moreover, to effectively implement Basic and Digest authentications, you need to first ensure that Anonymous authentication is disabled in IIS; otherwise, Anonymous authentication is used. Now, let's move on to learn about Forms authentication in IIS and ASP.NET.

Forms Authentication

Consider an ASP.NET application that provides functionality to buy and sell online (that is, through the Internet). To have a secure and reliable transaction, the application needs to uniquely identify the numerous users who want to buy or sell. In such a situation, creating Windows user accounts for each and every user may not be feasible. Moreover, the users may not be aware of which Windows credentials to use for accessing the application. In such cases, you may want to allow the users to subscribe or register with custom credentials. You can store the valid credentials in a database at the back-end or in the application itself. To authenticate such users (who have non-Windows credentials), you need to allow them to provide their credentials for authentication process, which is not possible with Anonymous and Windows authentication modes. ASP.NET provides an authentication mode known as Forms authentication that is suitable for such situations.

You can use Forms authentication to authenticate users who are independent of the Windows operating system. You can write your own code in the ASP.NET application to authenticate users. In Forms authentication, if a user attempts to access a Web page or resource, you can direct that user to another Web page (popularly known as the login page). The login page contains an HTML form on which the user needs to provide the credentials (user name and password) needed for authentication. When the login page is submitted to the Web server, the credentials are verified. If the user is authenticated, access to the requested Web page is granted to the user. In case the user is not authenticated, then the user is again directed to the login page to provide the correct credentials.

NOTE

When you use Forms authentication, the user name and password of the user are passed on to the Web server as plain text. Therefore, it is advisable to use SSL connections between the Web server and client while using Forms authentication.

If the user is authenticated, an authentication cookie containing a ticket that holds the credentials of the authenticated user is sent to the user. When the user makes any subsequent requests, then this authentication ticket is sent to the Web server for re-identifying the user. The authentication cookies are generated depending on the Web browser, as there are some Web browsers that do not support cookies. In such cases, you can employ a cookieless Forms authentication. In case of cookieless authentication, the authentication ticket is encrypted and then sent to the user in the URL itself.

When you are using Forms authentication in the ASP.NET application, you can enable Forms authentication in IIS. The Forms authentication in IIS facilitates authentication for both Windows and non-Windows users. Forms authentication in IIS allows security for even the non-ASP.NET content. Note that enabling Forms authentication alone in IIS results in an error as the user first needs to be authenticated by IIS, which is only possible through Anonymous, Windows (integrated), Basic, or Digest authentication modes. Therefore, you need to enable any of these four authentication modes in IIS. In most cases, Forms authentication is coupled with Anonymous authentication in IIS. This implies that the user is treated as an anonymous user by IIS. In case anonymous users are denied access in the Web.config file of the ASP.NET application and the authentication cookie is absent in the request, the login Web page appears. The users can then provide the credentials on the login page for authentication. Figure 26.12 shows the process of Forms authentication:

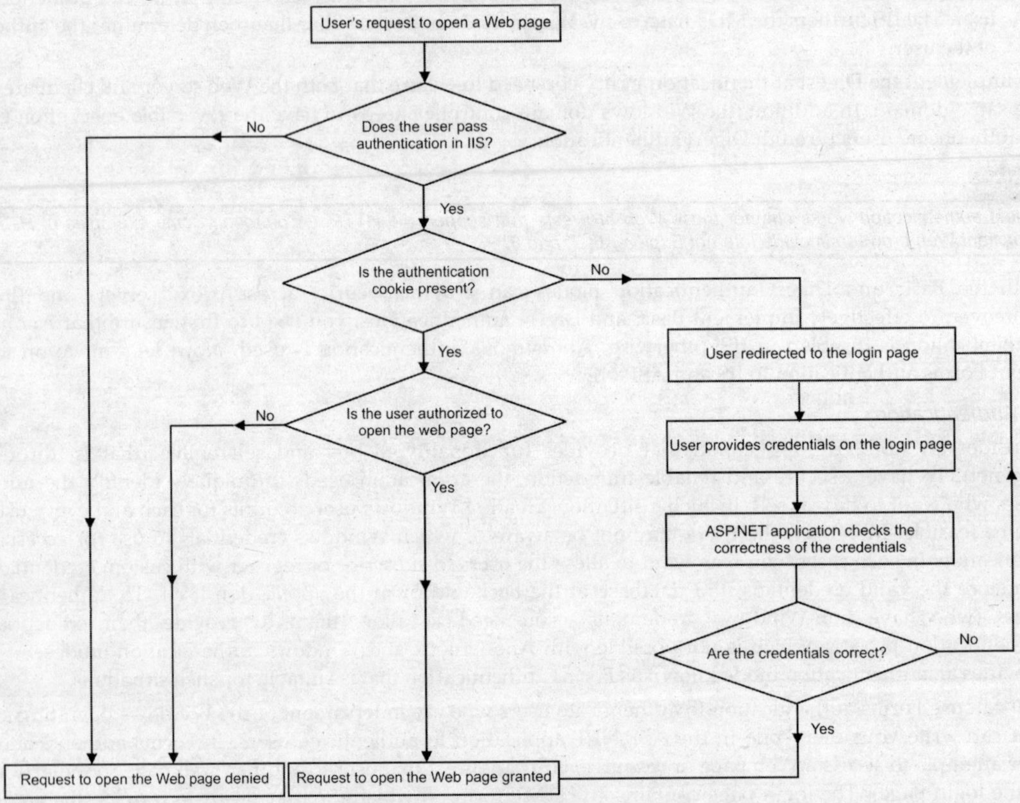

Figure 26.12: Displaying the Process of Forms Authentication

ASP.NET has a FormsAuthenticationModule class that facilitates the implementation of Forms authentication. A FormsAuthenticationModule object is responsible for searching the authentication ticket, redirecting the users to the login page, and authenticating the users. This object allows you to set the HttpContext.User property to the identity with which a user logs in. The identity of an authenticated user is represented by a FormsIdentity object. You can use the FormsIdentity object with the GenericPrincipal object to implement role-based security with Forms authentication.

The FormsAuthenticationModule class uses another class—FormsAuthentication to manage the process of Forms authentication. The FormsAuthentication class allows you to validate the credentials that users provide on the login page. This class has various properties and methods that you can use to specify the login page, redirect users to and from the login page, authenticate users, and create authentication cookies. Table 26.14 lists the noteworthy properties of the FormsAuthentication class:

Table 26.14: Noteworthy Properties of the FormsAuthentication Class

Property	Description
`CookieDomain`	Returns the name of the domain of the authentication cookie.
`CookieMode`	Returns a value that indicates whether the ASP.NET application supports cookies.
`CookiesSupported`	Returns a value that indicates whether the application allows cookieless Forms authentication.
`DefaultUrl`	Returns the default URL, that is, the URL to which users are redirected in the absence of a redirect URL.
`EnableCrossAppRedirects`	Returns a value that indicates if authenticated users can be redirected to Web pages of other ASP.NET applications.
`FormsCookieName`	Returns the name of the authentication cookie.
`FormsCookiePath`	Returns the path of the authentication cookie.
`LoginUrl`	Returns the URL of the login page to which unauthenticated users are redirected.
`RequireSSL`	Returns a value that indicates whether an SSL connection is required to send the authentication cookie to the Web server.
`SlidingExpiration`	Returns a value that indicates whether to use sliding expiration for the authentication cookie. If sliding expiration is enabled and if another request is made after half of the timeout interval, then the expiration time of the authentication cookie is reset.

Table 26.15 lists the noteworthy methods of the FormsAuthentication class:

Table 26.15: Noteworthy Methods of the FormsAuthentication Class

Method	Description
`Authenticate`	Checks the authenticity of the credentials provided by the user against the credentials stored in a database or application
`Decrypt`	Uses an encrypted Forms authentication ticket to create an authentication ticket
`Encrypt`	Creates a string object to hold the encrypted Forms authentication ticket
`GetAuthCookie`	Creates an authentication cookie for a particular user name
`GetRedirectUrl`	Returns the URL of the original request that causes a redirect to the login page
`HashPasswordForStoringInConfigFile`	Uses a given password and hash algorithm to generate a hash password that can be stored in a configuration file
`Initialize`	Initializes a FormsAuthentication object
`RedirectFromLoginPage`	Redirects an authenticated user back to the default or the originally requested URL
`RedirectToLoginPage`	Redirects an unauthenticated user to the login page
`RenewTicketIfOld`	Renews the authentication ticket by updating the date and time of issue of the ticket
`SetAuthCookie`	Creates an authentication ticket for a particular user name and adds the ticket to the cookies collection or the URL
`SignOut`	Removes the authentication ticket from the authentication cookie or the URL

Passport Authentication

With the Passport authentication, you can use the single logon service provided by Microsoft for multiple websites. The Passport authentication provides a single centralized hub for authenticating users. The users simply need to provide the credentials on a login page and if authenticated, can use the services of other member sites without the need to login again on each site. To implement Passport authentication in ASP.NET applications, you need to first download the .NET Passport SDK from the .NET Passport/Microsoft website (www.microsoft.com). You then need to install the Passport SDK after which you can use the classes that allow you to implement Passport authentication.

Federated authentication

Federated authentication is used to establish trust relationship between two domains. This authentication mode uses a Security Token Service (STS) in a domain to provide authentication information to an STS in another trust domain. This is a single sign-on authentication that removes the need for provisioning and managing duplicate accounts for users across applications and domains. In a federated authentication model, an Identity Provider (IdP) performs authentication and supplies security tokens as STS. These tokens contain information about the authenticated users including their identity, roles, and access rights.

Impersonation and Delegation

We have already discussed that all the ASP.NET applications run by default under the NETWORK SERVICE user account. This built-in Windows account provides the identity for the default application pool in which the ASP.NET applications exist. The NETWORK SERVICE account has limited rights and privileges on the Windows computer. This implies that the ASP.NET application can access only some files and perform specific operations on the computer. For example, the ASP.NET applications can read and write from databases on the computer but cannot delete database logs. In addition, with this low permission access to ASP.NET applications, the security and reliability of applications are preserved in case of any intrusion of the Web server.

There may be situations where you want your ASP.NET application to access a file, database, or any other local resource on the Web server but the NETWORK SERVICE account does not have the required permissions. In such situations, you can make your ASP.NET application to impersonate as a Windows user that has required privileges. For example, your ASP.NET application can impersonate as a user with administrative privileges to access a local resource.

In ASP.NET, impersonation refers to the process of acquiring the identity of an anonymous or authenticated user (Windows authentication) of an ASP.NET application and executing the application as that user. In this way, the ASP.NET application gets access to all the resources on the Web server to which the user has the permissions. You can implement impersonation in an ASP.NET application only when you are using Windows authentication in the application. You may recall that when Windows authentication is enabled in the ASP.NET application, authentication is only required at the IIS level; the application does not perform any authentication and uses the identity provided by IIS. In IIS, you can enable Anonymous, Windows, Basic, or Digest authentication mode to work with Windows users at the ASP.NET application level. This implies that based on the identity passed by IIS, ASP.NET applications can impersonate a Windows user. You can implement impersonation in the following three ways:

- **Impersonating an anonymous user whose identity is provided by IIS**—Occurs when you implement impersonation in an ASP.NET application and enable Anonymous authentication in IIS. In this case, the ASP.NET application runs as an anonymous user, which by default is IUSR.
- **Impersonating the currently logged-in Windows user who is authenticated by IIS**—Occurs when you implement impersonation in an ASP.NET application and enable any of Windows, Basic, or Digest authentication in IIS (with Anonymous authentication in IIS disabled). In this case, the ASP.NET application impersonates the Windows user whose credentials are used to log in to the application.
- **Impersonating a specific Windows user for all the anonymous and authenticated users**—Occurs when you implement impersonation in an ASP.NET application and provide the credentials of a particular Windows user. In this case, irrespective of the authentication enabled in IIS and the ASP.NET application, the application always runs as the impersonated user. Note that for this case, you need to use Access Control List (ACL) to ensure that the impersonated Windows user has permissions to write to the Temporary ASP.NET Files folder at the location C:\Windows\Microsoft.NET\Framework\v4.0.30319. The Temporary ASP.NET Files folder is the location where the compiled files of all the ASP.NET applications are stored.

To effectively implement impersonation in ASP.NET applications, you need to enable impersonation in IIS as well as in the application. To enable impersonation in IIS, double-click the Authentication icon, which opens the Authentication pane. Right-click the ASP.NET Impersonation option and select Enable.

You need to also enable ASP.NET Impersonation as it is disabled by default. You can do this by using the <identity> element in the Web.config file in the ASP.NET application. The <identity> element allows you to specify whether to enable or disable impersonation in the ASP.NET application. For example, to enable impersonation in an ASP.NET application, you can use the <identity> element as given in the following code:

```
<identity impersonate="true"/>
```

In case if you want an ASP.NET application to impersonate a particular user at all times, then you can use the <identity> element as given in the following code:

```
<identity impersonate="true"  userName="testuser" password="testuser"/>
```

In this code, the ASP.NET application impersonates the Windows user that has the same user name as well as password, which in this case is testuser.

When you want to disable impersonation in the application, you can use the <identity> element as given in the following code:

```
<identity impersonate="false"/>
```

NOTE

You will learn more about the <identity> element later in this chapter.

You can use impersonation in an ASP.NET application through code also. This is specifically useful when you want the ASP.NET application to impersonate a Windows user for temporarily accessing a particular resource and then change to the original account of the application. You can implement programmatic impersonation in ASP.NET by using the Impersonate() method of the WindowsIdentity class. As learned earlier, the WindowsIdentity class represents the identity of a Windows user. Therefore, you can use a WindowsIdentity object for the current Windows user and the Impersonate() method of the object to allow a specific ASP.NET code to impersonate the Windows user. Similar to the Web.config file, you can also specify the user name and password of a particular user to cause the code to run under the security context of that user for all the requests.

With impersonation, an ASP.NET application can use the identity of a Windows user and access the resources on the Web server. Now, suppose the ASP.NET application needs to access a resource on some other client (computer) on the network or a remote computer, such as an application requiring access to a network share. In such cases, you can use the identity of the same Windows user and access the resource on the remote computer. This process is known as delegation, which is just an extended form of impersonation. In delegation, the ASP.NET application impersonates as a Windows user and accesses the resources on another computer, that is, the credentials of the impersonated Windows user are delegated to the other computer on which the intended resource exists. Note that delegation is possible only with Basic and Windows (Kerberos) authentication.

NOTE

You need to exercise discretion while implementing delegation in ASP.NET applications, as improper user of delegation may compromise the network security.

Now, let's learn about the various elements in the Web.config file.

Security through the ASP.NET Configuration File

As stated earlier, you can implement security for an ASP.NET application in the application itself by using the configuration file of ASP.NET application. As you know, ASP.NET applications have a configuration file named as Web.config. It contains the settings for the directory in which the file exists. The settings applied to one directory apply to its child directories, provided the child directories do not have their own Web.config files. Note that apart from the individual Web.config file of different ASP.NET applications, there is a root Web.config file in the C:\Windows\Microsoft.NET\Framework\v4.0.30319\Config folder on your computer. This root Web.config file has the configuration settings that are common to all the ASP.NET applications. Some of the settings in this file are the same as those in the machine.config file.

The Web.config file has certain XML elements that you can use to incorporate security for the ASP.NET applications. The XML elements that pertain to the security of the ASP.NET applications include <authentication>, <authorization>, <identity>, and <location>. You may find these elements set in the machine.config file too. Note that the settings of these elements apply only to the ASP.NET resources. Therefore, you learn what these four elements signify and how you can use them to implement security in ASP.NET applications.

The <authentication> Element

The <authentication> element defines the authentication mode or scheme specified for an ASP.NET application. You can use this element in the machine.config file, root Web.config file, or the Web.config file of the Web application or site. Any attempt to use it in a Web.config file at the subdirectory or page-level results in an error. The <authentication> element appears within the <system.web> element, which itself is in the <configuration> element. The syntax of the <authentication> element is as follows:

```
<authentication mode="Federated|Windows|Forms|Passport|None">
   [<forms
   name="cookieName"
   loginUrl="loginURL"
   defaultUrl="defaultURL"
   protection="All|None|Encryption|Validation"
   timeout="30"
   path="path"
   requireSSL="true|false"
   slidingExpiration="true|false"
   enableCrossAppRedirects="true|false"
   cookieless="UseUri|UseCookies|AutoDetect|UseDeviceProfile"
   domain="domainName">
          <credentials passwordFormat="Clear|SHA1|MD5">
                 <user name="userName" password="password"/>
          </credentials>
   </forms>]
   [<passport redirectUrl="loginURL"/>]
</authentication>
```

In the preceding code, you can see that the <authentication> element has an attribute named mode. The mode attribute refers to the authentication mode specified for the ASP.NET application. There is a set of predefined values that can be set for the mode attribute. These values are given as follows:

- **Windows**—Refers to the Windows authentication for accessing the Web resource. It allows you to use any of the Windows authentication available in IIS, that is, with Basic, Digest, or Integrated Windows authentication. This is the default value for any Web resource.
- **Forms**—Refers to the Forms authentication for accessing the Web resource.
- **Passport**—Refers to the Microsoft Passport authentication for accessing the Web resource.
- **None**—Refers to the authentication when the user credentials (user name and password) are not required to access a Web resource. This value is useful for anonymous or custom authentication.

You can also notice from the syntax that the <authentication> element can have two child elements, <forms> and <passport>. The <forms> element is used when you use the Forms authentication, that is, when the mode attribute of the <authentication> element is set to Forms. The <forms> element has several attributes, which are listed in Table 26.16:

Table 26.16: Attributes of the <forms> Element

Attribute	Description
`Name`	Refers to the HTTP authentication cookie used for authentication of a user. The default value for this attribute is .ASPXAUTH.
`loginUrl`	Refers to the URL of the page where the user needs to provide the credentials for authentication. The default value for this attribute is login.aspx.

Table 26.16: Attributes of the <forms> Element

Attribute	Description	
`defaultUrl`	Refers to the URL of the page to which users are redirected after they are authenticated. The default value for this attribute is default.aspx.	
`protection`	Refers to the type of protection to be used for the authentication cookie. This attribute can have any of the following values:	
	All	Indicates that the cookie is protected by using both encryption and validation. This is the default value.
	None	Indicates that the application does not use encryption and validation to protect the cookie.
	Encryption	Indicates that the application uses the DES or 3DES to encrypt the cookie. No validation is performed on the cookie.
	Validation	Indicates that the application uses a validation mechanism to protect the cookie.
`timeout`	Refers to the time (in minutes) for which the authentication cookie exists. The cookie expires after the time specified by this attribute elapses. The default value for this attribute is 30 (minutes).	
`path`	Refers to the path for storing the authentication cookie. The default value for this attribute is /, which refers to the root folder of the application.	
`requireSSL`	Specifies whether a Secure Sockets Layer (SSL) connection is essential to pass the authentication cookie. The default value for this attribute is false.	
`slidingExpiration`	Specifies whether the expiration time for the authentication cookie resets on every request in the same session. The default value for this attribute is false.	
`enableCrossAppRedirects`	Specifies whether authenticated users can be redirected to Web pages in other Web applications. The default value for this attribute is false.	
`cookieless`	Refers to when and how the authentication cookie is generated. This attribute can have either of the following values:	
	UseUri	Indicates that cookies are not used at all.
	UseCookies	Indicates that cookies are always used.
	AutoDetect	Indicates that cookies are used only if the Web browsers support them. An attempt to use a cookie is through a probing mechanism.
	UseDeviceProfile	Indicates that cookies are used only for Web browsers that support cookies. There is no probing mechanism for Web browsers that support cookies. This is the default value.
`domain`	Refers to an optional domain for the outgoing authentication cookie. The default value for this attribute is an empty string.	

The <forms> element can have a <credentials> element that allows you to specify the credentials of users when they are authenticated using Forms authentication. The <credentials> element has an attribute named passwordFormat. This attribute refers to the format for storing the passwords in an encrypted state. This attribute can take the following values:

- **Clear**—Indicates that the passwords are not encrypted; instead, they are stored as plain text
- **SHA1**—Indicates that the passwords are encrypted using the SHA1 hash algorithm, which is the default value
- **MD5**—Indicates that the passwords are encrypted using the MD5 hash algorithm

The <credentials> element can have three child elements: <clear>, <remove>, and <user>. Table 26.17 lists these three child elements along with their syntax:

Table 26.17: Child Elements of the <credentials> Element

Child Element	Description	Syntax
`<clear>`	Allows you to clear all the references of any inherited connection strings. These elements allow you to use only those connection strings created by the current user.	`<clear/>`
`<remove>`	Allows you to remove a reference of a particular user from the available credentials.	`<remove name="userName"/>`
`<user>`	Allows you to define the users for the Web application.	`<user name="userName" password="password"/>`

Note that there can be several <user> elements in the <credentials> element. If a user requesting for the Web application has any of the user name and password combination, then that user becomes an authenticated user.

If you have specified Passport as the value for the mode attribute of the <authentication> element, then you need to define the <passport> element as the child of the <authentication> element. The <passport> element has only one attribute named redirectUrl. This attribute refers to the URL to which users are redirected for authentication with Microsoft Passport. The default value of this attribute is internal.

The <authorization> Element

As you know, after authentication, a user needs to be authorized to access and use an ASP.NET application. You can use the <authorization> element in the Web.config file to specify the kind of authorization you want to implement for the Web application. In the <authorization> element, you can specify the user names and/or roles that an authenticated user must have to perform an action in the Web application. Similar to the <authentication> element, you can define the <authorization> element in the machine.config or Web.config file of the Web application, website, Web page, or any subdirectory.

The <authorization> element also appears in the <system.web> element. The syntax of the <authorization> element is as follows:

```
<authorization>
  <allow users="comma-separated list of users"
         roles="comma-separated list of roles"
         verbs="comma-separated list of verbs"/>
  <deny users="comma-separated list of users"
        roles="comma-separated list of roles"
        verbs="comma-separated list of verbs"/>
</authorization>
```

In the preceding syntax, you can see that the <authorization> element does not have any attributes but can have two child elements, <allow> and <deny>. The <allow> element enable you to specify the users, roles, and HTTP transmission methods that have the permission to access the Web application. On the other hand, the <deny> element enable you to specify the users, roles, and HTTP transmission methods that are denied access to the Web application. Both these elements can have three attributes, as listed in Table 26.18:

Table 26.18: Attributes of the <allow> and <deny> Elements

Attribute	Description
`users`	Allows you to specify a comma-separated list of user names that are granted/denied access to the Web application. The default value for this attribute is an asterisk (*) indicating that all authenticated users have/do not have access to the Web application. You can also use a question mark (?) to allow/deny access only to anonymous users.
`roles`	Allows you to specify a comma-separated list of roles that are granted/denied access to the Web application. An empty string (" ") indicates that users that have no roles are granted/denied access.
`verbs`	Allows you to specify a comma-separated list of HTTP transmission methods that have/do not have access to the Web application. The HTTP transmission methods that you can specify include GET, POST, DEBUG, and HEAD.

NOTE

If you want to refer to the users or roles on the computer, then you can use the dot (.) to represent the current computer. This is only applicable for Windows user accounts.

TIP

It is advisable not to use the <deny> element prior to the <allow> element as the access is allowed or denied depending on the order in which elements are specified in the <authorization> element. For example, if you specify the <deny> element as follows:

```
<authorization>
   <deny users="*"/>
   <allow users="TestUser"/>
</authorization>
```

The <allow> element is rendered ineffective and no access is given to the TestUser user.

The <location> Element

You know how the use of the <authentication> and <authorization> elements in the Web.config file (at root-, application-, or directory-level) assists you to secure the whole ASP.NET Web application(s). Now, consider a situation where you want to secure only a particular range of Web pages in a Web application. In such a case, instead of using the <authentication> and <authorization> elements, you can use the <location> element. The <location> element allows you to apply certain configuration settings on a particular Web application or page (or a range of Web pages). You can also use the <location> element to secure a particular Web resource, such as a virtual directory or an image.

In the Web.config file, the <location> element can appear within the <configuration> element. The <location> element can contain any child element to specify the settings for the given Web application, page, or resource. The syntax of the <location> element is as follows:

```
<location allowOverride="true|false" path="Path" >
   <!--child elements-->
</location>
```

In the preceding syntax, the <location> element has two attributes:

- **path**—Refers to a particular Web application, page, or resource on which you want to secure or apply any other configuration settings. If this attribute is omitted or is set to an empty string, then the security (or configuration) settings apply to the current directory and all its child directories.
- **allowOverride**—Refers to whether the security (or configuration) settings can be overridden in the Web.config file of child directories. It can have either true or false as its value. If true, the settings can be overridden in the child directories; if false, the settings cannot be overridden. The default value is true for this attribute.

NOTE

You can use ~/ in the path attribute to represent the current application root directory. For example, consider the following code:

```
<location path="~/CustomerLists/Customer.xls">
   <system.web>
         <authorization>
               <deny users="TestUser"/>
         </authorization>
   </system.web>
</location>
```

In the preceding code, the TestUser user is denied access to the Customer.xls file in the CustomerList directory that exists in the root directory of the current Web application.

The <identity> Element

The <identity> element allows you to specify the identity of the Web application. It is helpful when you want to implement impersonation in Web applications. You can use the <identity> element in the Web.config file at root-

, application-, or directory-level. The <identity> element can appear within the <system.web> element in the Web.config file at the root-, application-, or directory-level. The syntax of the <identity> element is as follows:

```
<identity impersonate="true|false" userName="domain\userName" password="<secure
  password>"/>
```

In the preceding syntax, <identity> element has three attributes:

- **impersonate** – Refers to whether client impersonation is used. This attribute can have either true or false as its value. The default value for this attribute is false, which implies that impersonation is not used. If you set the attribute to true, then impersonation is used on every request.
- **userName** – Refers to the user name to be used in case you enable impersonation.
- **password** – Refers to the password to be used in case you enable impersonation.

NOTE

The values of the userName and password attributes of the <identity> element are stored as plain text in the Web.config file. However, you may choose to encrypt the values and save them in the registry. To store the encrypted values of the userName and password attributes in the registry, you need to first encrypt the values to the REG_BINARY format and then add the values in the registry by using the Aspnet_setreg.exe utility. After this, you need to use the registry keyword in the <identity> element to specify the registry key from which the values are read.

Membership Feature

The membership feature of ASP.NET provides a way for storing credentials of an authorized user in a data store. The two main advantages of using the membership feature to store the user credentials are:

- Abstracting the stored user credentials
- Reducing the complexities involved in verifying user credentials in Forms based authentication

Now, let's see how we can implement the membership feature in an application created using ASP.NET. The membership feature is implemented using the following two providers:

- ActiveDirectoryMembershipProvider
- SqlMembershipProvider

You can use both the providers with the ASP.NET Web applications that use Forms based authentication. You can also create your own custom provider to store user credentials in data stores other than Active directory and SQL Server, such as Lightweight Directory Access Protocol (LDAP) data store.

In addition to these two providers, you also need to use the `Membership` and `MembershipUser` class for implementing the membership feature in an ASP.NET application. Now, let's look into the details of these two providers and two classes one by one.

ActiveDirectoryMembershipProvider

`The ActiveDirectoryMembershipProvider` allows you to store user credentials either in an Active Directory or Active Directory Application Mode (ADAM) data store. In this topic, we learn to configure `ActiveDirectoryMembershipProvider` for a Web application.

You need to first define a connection string in the `<connectionStrings>` element of the `Web.config` file to configure `ActiveDirectoryMembershipProvider.`

The syntax used to define the connection string to an Active Directory data store is as follows:

```
LDAP://server/userdn
```

In the preceding syntax, server is the name of the computer on which the Active Directory data store resides and `userdn` is the name of the Active Directory data store in which user credentials are to be stored.

The code that allows you to create a connection string for an Active Directory data store is as follows:

```
<connectionStrings>
  <add name="ActiveDirectoryCS"
    connectionString=
    "LDAP://domain.testing.com/CN=Users,DC=domain,DC=testing,DC=com" />
</connectionStrings>
```

In the preceding syntax, the name of the connection string created is ActiveDirectoryCS. After creating the connection string, you need to create a membership provider of the type ActiveDirectoryMembershipProvider for your Web application. You can create the membership provider in the <provider> element of the Web.config file. The <provider> element is defined inside the <membership> element.

In addition to defining the <provider> element, you also need to set the defaultProvider attribute of the <membership> element to the name of the membership provider created in the <provider> element. This allows you to override the default provider settings, according to which default membership provider used for a Web application is SqlMembershipProvider.

Now, let's look at some of the common attributes of the <provider> element that you need to set, while defining the <provider> element for ActiveDirectoryMembershipProvider. Table 26.19 lists the attributes of the <provider> element:

Table 26.19: The Attributes of the <provider> Element

Attribute	Description
connectionPassword	Specifies the password using which you can access the Active Directory data store. This attribute ensures that the user accessing the Active Directory data store is an authenticated user.
connectionStringName	Specifies the name of the connection string created in the <connectionStrings> element of the Web.config file. This connection string allows you to perform create, update, get, and validate operations on the Active Directory data store.
connectionUsername	Specifies the user name using which you can access the Active Directory data store. This attribute ensures that the user accessing the Active Directory data store is an authenticated user.

NOTE

If you set the connectionUsername attribute, make sure that a value for the connectionPassword attribute is also specified. Similarly, if you set the connectionPassword attribute, make sure that a value for the connectionUsername attribute is also specified.

The following code illustrates the configuration of ActiveDirectoryMembershipProvider:

```
<membership defaultProvider="ADMembershipProvider">
  <providers>
     <add
     name="ADMembershipProvider"
     type="System.Web.Security.ActiveDirectoryMembershipProvider, System.Web,
     Version=2.0.0.0, Culture=neutral, PublicKeyToken=b03f5f7f11d50a3a"
     connectionStringName="ActiveDirectoryCS"
     connectionUsername="<domainName>\administrator"
     connectionPassword="pass"/>
  </providers>
</membership>
```

SqlMembershipProvider

The SqlMembershipProvider is used to store user credentials in an SQL Server data store. You need to first install an SQL Server membership data store and then configure SqlMembershipProvider to use SqlMembershipProvider in an ASP.NET application. An SQL Server membership data store is the one that is used to store user credentials. We will look at the details of installing the SQL Server membership data store and configuring SqlMembershipProvider in the subsequent topics.

Installing the SQL Server Data Store

Log on to the computer with an account that has the administrative permissions to use the computer, such as administrative account, to install an SQL Server membership data store on a computer. After logging on to the system, run the aspnet_regsql utility on the Developer Command Prompt for VS2012 and run it as administrator. The `aspnet_regsql` utility is used to install data stores for various features of ASP.NET, such as profiles, personalization, and membership. You need to understand its various options, which are as follows, to use the `aspnet_regsql` utility:

- `-E`—Facilitates authentication using the credentials of the currently logged on user
- `-S`—Specifies the name of the computer on which SQL Server data store is to be installed
- `-A m`—Generates tables and stored procedures required by `SqlMembershipProvider`

For example, you can use the following command to install a SQL Server membership data store on a computer:

```
aspnet_regsql.exe -E -S server -A m
```

In the preceding line of code, the name of the computer is server.

Configuring SqlMembershipProvider

By default, an instance of `SqlMembershipProvider`, `AspNetSqlMembershipProvider`, is defined in the `machine.config` file of your ASP.NET application. This instance connects your ASP.NET application to an instance of SQL Server data store running on the local computer. Therefore, if the SQL Server membership data store is installed on a local computer, you do not need to configure `SqlMembershipProvider` explicitly.

However, if you want to connect your ASP.NET application to an SQL Server data store running on a computer other than the computer on which your ASP.NET application is running, you need to configure `SqlMembershipProvider`. You can configure `SqlMembershipProvider` for an ASP.NET application by defining a connection string and an instance of `SqlMembershipProvider` in the `Web.config` file of the ASP.NET application.

Similar to `ActiveDirectoryMembershipProvider`, you need to define the `<provider>` element to create an instance of `SqlMembershipProvider`. Now, let's look at some of the common attributes of the `<provider>` element that you need to set, while defining the `<provider>` element for `SqlMembershipProvider` in Table 26.20:

Table 26.20: Attributes of the <provider> Element

Attribute	Description
`applicationName`	Specifies information of the users of a single application. You should qualify the user information with the value of the `applicationName`, while storing it in the SQL Server data store. This prevents conflicts between similar user names that may arise, while storing information of multiple applications in a single SQL Server data store. The default value of the `applicationName` attribute is `'/'`.
`EnablePasswordReset`	Specifies whether or not a user can modify its password. By default, the `enablePasswordReset` attribute is set to false. You can set this attribute to true only if the `requiresQuestionAndAnswer` attribute is set to true.
`PasswordFormat`	Specifies the format for storing a password in the SQL Server data store. This attribute can take the following values: • `Clear`—Stores the passwords in plain text. It is easy to store and retrieve passwords in this format; however, security of the passwords is compromised. • `Encrypted`—Stores the passwords in encrypted form. Decryption needs to be done to retrieve the passwords stored in this format. However, security of the passwords stored in the encrypted format is high. • `Hashed`—Hashes the password using a one-way hash algorithm while storing. The security of these passwords is high; however, you cannot retrieve the passwords stored in the hashed format.
`RequiresQuestionAndAnswer`	Specifies whether or not a user needs to provide a password question and answer to modify the password. The default value of this attribute is false.
`RequiresUniqueEmail`	Indicates whether or not e-mail address of the user of an ASP.NET application needs to be unique. The default value of this attribute is false.

The following code illustrates the configuration of SqlMembershipProvider using the preceding attributes:

```
<configuration>
  <connectionStrings>
    <add name="SqlServices" connectionString="Data Source=localhost;Integrated
  Security=SSPI;Initial Catalog=aspnetdb;" />
  </connectionStrings>
  <system.web>
    <authentication mode="Forms" >
      <forms loginUrl="login.aspx"
        name=".ASPXFORMSAUTH" />
    </authentication>
    <authorization>
      <deny users="?" />
    </authorization>
    <membership defaultProvider="SqlProvider"
      userIsOnlineTimeWindow="15">
      <providers>
        <add
          name="SqlProvider"
          type="System.Web.Security.SqlMembershipProvider"
          connectionStringName="SqlServices"
          applicationName="MyApplication"
          enablePasswordRetrieval="false"
          enablePasswordReset="true"
          requiresQuestionAndAnswer="true"
          requiresUniqueEmail="false"
          passwordFormat="Hashed"
          maxInvalidPasswordAttempts="5"
          passwordAttemptWindow="10" />
      </providers>
    </membership>
  </system.web>
</configuration>
```

The Membership Class

The Membership class allows you to create users for an ASP.NET application and manage these users. The users created for an ASP.NET application using the Membership class can access the ASP.NET application as authenticated users. The hierarchy of the Membership class is as follows:

```
System.Object
  System.Web.Security.Membership
```

Table 26.21 lists the noteworthy methods of the Membership class:

Table 26.21: Noteworthy Methods of the Membership Class

Method	Description
CreateUser	Creates a new user for an ASP.NET application.
DeleteUser	Deletes user of a specific user name. This method returns true if it deletes the user successfully and false if the user name of the user that is to be deleted does not exist.
FindUsersByEmail	Returns those e-mail addresses that matches with any part of the e-mail address passed to the method.
FindUsersByName	Returns the users, the user name of which matches with any part of the user name passed to the method.
GeneratePassword	Provides a password of specific length. The password returned by the GeneratePassword method contains specified number of non-alphanumeric characters.
GetAllUsers	Returns users on the basis of the page index and page size passed to the method.
GetNumberOfUsersOnline	Determines how many users are connected to the website currently. You cannot use this method if your application is using ActiveDirectoryMembershipProvider.

Table 26.21: Noteworthy Methods of the Membership Class

Method	Description
`GetUserNameByEmail`	Returns the name of the user, the e-mail address of which is passed to the method.
`UpdateUser`	Updates information of a user.
`ValidateUser`	Verifies the credentials of a user. This method returns true if the credentials of the user are valid, otherwise false.

MembershipUser Class

When an instance of the `MembershipUser` class is obtained, `the MembershipUser` class helps to perform the following task directly:

- Accessing the properties involved with the `MembershipUser` class
- Retrieving the user password, if membership is configured for the same
- Changing the password of a user
- Changing the password hint questions and answer, if membership is configured for the same
- Resetting the password of a user
- Unlocking the user account

Now, let's learn about another security mechanism known as cryptography.

Cryptography in .NET

Till now, you have learned how role-based security and CAS offer functionality to make .NET applications secure and reliable. You have also learned how role-based security allows you to control the security of the applications by granting or denying access to different users. In addition, you have learned how CAS allows users to authenticate an application before using it. Apart from the application, the data that is exchanged between the applications or computers on a network (Internet or Intranet) needs to be secured too. Consider a situation where there is a peer-to-peer ASP.NET application on the Intranet. Users of this application can communicate with one another by exchanging data through files. Now, one user named John intends to send an important file to another user named Harry on the same network. Although, John can send the file in its original form (in plain text), there is a risk of other users on the network who may intercept during the data exchange. Such an interception is not only unwarranted but also potentially harmful for the data. Therefore, to secure the data that is to be exchanged, it is advisable to use cryptography.

Cryptography, in literal sense, means hidden writing (or secret writing). It derives its name from the Greek words *krypto*, which means hidden, and *grafo*, which means to write. Cryptography is considered a branch of computer science that encapsulates mathematical algorithms and functions to allow you to secure data by modifying its original form such that it is incomprehensible to all users except the intended recipient. Cryptography is highly useful when you want to exchange data over a non-secure network and it serves three main purposes:

- **Confidentiality**—Implies that the data cannot be viewed or understood by any user other than the intended recipient. This is achieved by encrypting the data, i.e. modifying the original form of data such that only the intended recipient can read and understand the data by decrypting the encrypted data (also called ciphertext). In .NET framework, you can maintain the confidentiality of the data by using secret-key encryption or public key-encryption.
- **Data_Integrity**—Implies that the data that is received by the intended recipient is not modified or tampered by other users on the network. In .NET framework, this is achieved by using hash algorithms. A hash algorithm takes a piece of data and generates a fixed-length sequence of numeric/alphanumeric characters known as hash value (or simply hash). The hash value for one piece of data is uniquely distinct from hash values of other pieces of data. Therefore, if there is any change in the hash value of the data that reaches the intended recipient, then it can be concluded that the data may have been tampered with during the transmission.

- **Authenticity**—Implies that the received data is transmitted by the sender only and not by any other user on the network. In .NET framework, you can use digital signatures and hash algorithms to verify the identity of the sender. A digital signature is a block of code, which ensures that any data that is received originates from a specific user. It is used to simulate the security properties of a signature in digital form. Two algorithms are involved here, one for signing, in which the secret key of the user is used and other for verifying signatures, in which the public key of the user is used. The benefit of using digital signatures is that they provide authentication and integrity to the messages sent. Authentication of data ensures that it is received from a trusted source and integrity of data ensures that the received data has not been tampered with during transmission. In case of any tampering with the data, you can also reject the data.

In the following sections, you learn about the secret-key encryption, public-key encryption, and hash algorithms. However, prior to encryption and hash algorithms, let's learn about the System.Security.Cryptography namespace.

The System.Security.Cryptography Namespace

.NET framework 4.5 includes the `System.Security.Cryptography` namespace that contains numerous classes for various cryptographic services, such as encoding and decoding of data, encryption and decryption of data, generation of hashes, and authentication of sender. Table 26.22 lists some of the noteworthy classes contained in the `System.Security.Cryptography` namespace:

Table 26.22: Noteworthy Classes in the System.Security.Cryptography Namespace

Class	Description
`Aes`	Represents the abstract base class from which every implementation of the Advanced Encryption Standard (AES) inherits.
`AesCryptoServiceProvider`	Provides the facility to perform symmetric encryption and decryption by using the Cryptographic Application Programming Interface (CAPI) of the AES algorithm.
`AesManaged`	Provides a managed implementation of the AES symmetric algorithm.
`AsnEncodedData`	Represents Abstract Syntax Notation One (ASN.1)-encoded data.
`AsnEncodedDataCollection`	Represents a collection of objects of the `AsnEncodedData` class.
`AsnEncodedDataEnumerator`	Provides the ability to navigate through a collection of AsnEncodedData objects.
`AsymmetricAlgorithm`	Represents the abstract class that is the base class from which implementations of all asymmetric algorithms inherit.
`CngAlgorithm`	Contains the name of an encryption algorithm.
`CngAlgorithmGroup`	Contains the name of an encryption algorithm group.
`CngKey`	Provides basic functionality for working with keys of Cryptography Next Generation (CNG) objects.
`CngKeyBlobFormat`	Contains the name of a key BLOB format for CNG objects.
`CngKeyCreationParameters`	Contains various advanced properties for creating a key for CNG objects.
`CngPropertyCollection`	Provides a strongly typed collection of CNG properties.
`CngProvider`	Contains the name of a key storage provider (KSP) for the CNG objects.
`CngUIPolicy`	Contains optional parameters for configuring the UI that appears when a protected key is accessed.
`CryptoAPITransform`	Allows you to perform a cryptographic transformation of data
`CryptoConfig`	Allows you to access information about the cryptography configuration.
`CryptographicAttributeObject`	Contains a type and the collection of values associated with that type.

Table 26.22: Noteworthy Classes in the System.Security.Cryptography Namespace

Class	Description
`CryptographicAttributeObjectCollection`	Represents a collection of `CryptographicAttributeObject` objects
`CryptographicAttributeObjectEnumerator`	Provides the facility to enumerate through a `CryptographicAttributeObjectCollection` object.
`CryptographicException`	Represents an exception that occurs during a cryptographic operation.
`CryptographicUnexpectedOperationException`	Represents an exception that occurs when an unexpected operation occurs during a cryptographic operation.
`CryptoStream`	Provides a stream that connects data streams to cryptographic transformations.
`CspKeyContainerInfo`	Provides additional information (for example, the key number) about a cryptographic key pair.
`CspParameters`	Provides certain parameters that you can pass to the cryptographic service provider (CSP). The CSP performs various cryptographic computations.
`DeriveBytes`	Represents the abstract base class for all classes that have byte sequences of a given length.
`DES`	Represents the base class for all the implementations of the Data Encryption Standard (DES) algorithm.
`DESCryptoServiceProvider`	Provides a wrapper for accessing the CSP implementation of the DES algorithm.
`DSA`	Represents the abstract base class for all the implementations of the Digital Signature Algorithm (DSA).
`DSACryptoServiceProvider`	Provides a wrapper for accessing the cryptographic service provider (CSP) implementation of the DSA algorithm.
`DSASignatureDeformatter`	Provides the facility to verify a Digital Signature Algorithm (DSA) PKCS#1 v1.5 signature.
`DSASignatureFormatter`	Provides the facility to create a Digital Signature Algorithm (DSA) signature.
`FromBase64Transform`	Allows you to convert base-64 encoded data to a CryptoStream object.
`HashAlgorithm`	Represents the base class for all the implementations of cryptographic hash algorithms.
`HMAC`	Represents the abstract base class for all the implementations of Hash-based Message Authentication Code (HMAC).
`HMACMD5`	Represents a hash algorithm that is created using the Message Digest Algorithm 5 (MD5) hash function and is used as HMAC.
`HMACRIPEMD160`	Represents a hash algorithm that is created using the RACE Integrity Primitives Evaluation Message Digest 160 (RIPEMD160 hash function and is used as HMAC.
`HMACSHA1`	Represents a hash algorithm that is created using the Secure Hash Algorithm 1 (SHA1) hash function and is used as HMAC.
`HMACSHA256`	Represents a hash algorithm that is created using the Secure Hash Algorithm 256 (SHA256) hash function and is used as HMAC.
`HMACSHA384`	Represents a hash algorithm that is created using the Secure Hash Algorithm 384 (SHA384) hash function and is used as HMAC.

Table 26.22: Noteworthy Classes in the System.Security.Cryptography Namespace

Class	Description
`HMACSHA512`	Represents a hash algorithm that is created using the Secure Hash Algorithm 512 (SHA512) hash function and is used as HMAC.
`KeyedHashAlgorithm`	Represents the abstract base class for all the implementations of keyed hash algorithms.
`KeySizes`	Provides a set of key sizes for symmetric cryptographic algorithms.
`MACTripleDES`	Provides the facility to compute a Message Authentication Code (MAC) using the TripleDES hash algorithm for the input CryptoStream object.
`ManifestSignatureInformation`	Provides information for the manifest signature.
`ManifestSignatureInformationCollection`	Represents a read-only collection of objects of the ManifestSignatureInformation class.
`MD5`	Represents the abstract base class for all the implementations of the MD5 hash algorithm.
`MD5Cng`	Represents a CNG implementation of the MD5 128-bit hash algorithm.
`MD5CryptoServiceProvider`	Allows you to compute the MD5 hash value for the input data using the CSP implementation.
`Oid`	Represents an identifier for a cryptographic object.
`OidCollection`	Represents a collection of `Oid` objects.
`OidEnumerator`	Allows you to enumerate through an `OidCollection` object.
`PasswordDeriveBytes`	Provides the facility to use an extension of the PBKDF1 algorithm to get a key from a password.
`ProtectedData`	Provides the facility to make the data encrypting and decrypting.
`ProtectedMemory`	Provides the facility to make the memory protected and unprotected.
`RandomNumberGenerator`	Represents the abstract base class for all the implementations of generators of cryptographic random numbers.
`RC2`	Represents the base class for all the implementations of the RC2 algorithm.
`RC2CryptoServiceProvider`	Provides a wrapper for accessing the CSP implementation of the RC2 algorithm.
`Rfc2898DeriveBytes`	Provides the PBKDF2 functionality for password-based key derivation. This class uses a pseudo-random number generator that is based on HMACSHA1.
`Rijndael`	Represents the base class for all the implementations of the Rijndael symmetric encryption algorithm.
`RijndaelManaged`	Allows access to the managed implementation of the Rijndael algorithm.
`RijndaelManagedTransform`	Provides the facility to perform a cryptographic transformation of data by using the Rijndael algorithm.
`RIPEMD160`	Represents the abstract base class for all the implementations of the MD160 hash algorithm.
`RIPEMD160Managed`	Provides the facility to compute a RIPEMD160 hash of an input data using the managed library.
`RNGCryptoServiceProvider`	Implements a cryptographic Random Number Generator (RNG) by using the CSP implementation.

Table 26.22: Noteworthy Classes in the System.Security.Cryptography Namespace

Class	Description
`RSA`	Represents the base class for all the implementations of the Random Sequential Adsorption (RSA) algorithm.
`RSACryptoServiceProvider`	Provides the facility to perform asymmetric encryption and decryption using the CSP implementation of the RSA algorithm.
`SHA1`	Provides the facility to compute the SHA1 hash for an input data.
`SHA1Cng`	Provides the CNG implementation of the SHA1 hash algorithm.
`SHA1CryptoServiceProvider`	Provides the facility to compute the SHA1 hash value for an input data by using the CSP implementation.
`SHA1Managed`	Provides the facility to compute the SHA1 hash for an input data using the managed library.
`SHA256`	Provides the facility to compute the SHA256 hash for an input data.
`SHA256Cng`	Provides the CNG implementation of the SHA256 hash algorithm.
`SHA256CryptoServiceProvider`	Provides a wrapper for accessing the CSP implementation of the SHA256 hash algorithm.
`SHA256Managed`	Provides the facility to compute the SHA256 hash for an input data using the managed library.
`SHA384`	Provides the facility to compute the SHA384 hash for an input data.
`SHA384Cng`	Provides the CNG implementation of the SHA384 hash algorithm.
`SHA384CryptoServiceProvider`	Provides a wrapper for accessing the CSP implementation of the SHA384 hash algorithm.
`SHA384Managed`	Provides the facility to compute the SHA384 hash for an input data using the managed library.
`SHA512`	Provides the facility to compute the SHA512 hash for an input data.
`SHA512Cng`	Provides the CNG implementation of the SHA512 hash algorithm.
`SHA512CryptoServiceProvider`	Provides a wrapper for accessing the CSP implementation of the SHA512 hash algorithm.
`SHA512Managed`	Provides the facility to compute the SHA512 hash for an input data using the managed library.
`SignatureDescription`	Contains information about the various properties of a given digital signature.
`StrongNameSignatureInformation`	Contains information about the strong name signature of a manifest.
`SymmetricAlgorithm`	Represents the abstract base class for all the implementations of symmetric algorithms.
`ToBase64Transform`	Provides the facility to convert a CryptoStream object to base-64 encoded data.
`TripleDES`	Represents the base class for all the implementations of the Triple Data Encryption Standard algorithms.
`TripleDESCryptoServiceProvider`	Provides a wrapper for accessing the CSP implementation of the TripleDES algorithm.

NOTE

The Cryptography Service Provider (CSP) is a library that contains the Cryptographic Application Programming Interface (CAPI), which provides the cryptographic algorithms and functions.

Now, let's learn about the encryption and decryption processes in detail.

Encryption and Decryption

As stated earlier, encryption refers to the process of modifying a piece of data in plain text into another piece of data, known as encrypted data or ciphertext, such that no one other than the intended recipient can decipher the original data. When the recipient regenerates the data (in plain text) from the encrypted data, it is referred to as decryption. Encryption is done at the sender's end and decryption is done at the receiver's end. Note that it is essential that a lossless channel/network is used for successfully regenerating data after decryption. Figure 26.13 depicts a pictorial representation of encryption and decryption:

Figure 26.13: Displaying the Process of Encryption and Decryption

For encrypting and decrypting data, you need two things, a cryptography algorithm and a key. A cryptography algorithm is a sequence of instructions that encrypts and decrypts the data. Cryptographic algorithms use a particular value, known as key, to encrypt or decrypt data. The sender uses a given key to encrypt a piece of data, which is then transmitted to the intended recipient. When the intended recipient receives the encrypted data, the recipient decrypts the data using a given key. The key to encrypt and decrypt the data is decided prior to encrypting the data. This implies that if a user (including the recipient) does not have the predetermined key, then the user cannot decrypt the data. Therefore, it is essential for the intended recipient to have the right key; otherwise, it is almost impossible to decrypt the received encrypted data.

Depending on the key that is used for encryption and decryption, there are two types of encryption—secret-key encryption and public-key encryption. Now, let's first learn about the secret-key encryption.

Secret-Key Encryption

In secret-key encryption, a single key, also called the secret key, is used for both encryption and decryption of data. This secret key is shared between the sender and the intended recipient but is hidden from the remaining users on the network. The sender uses the secret key to encrypt the data and sends the encrypted data to the intended recipient over the network. When the intended recipient receives the encrypted data, the recipient uses the same secret key to decrypt the data. The recipient needs to use the same secret key that was used to encrypt the data; any other key will not serve the purpose. Note that the sender and the intended recipient need to know the secret key that is to be used for encryption and decryption. The sender and the intended recipient can share the secret key by generating the key at the sender's end, encrypting it using public-key encryption, and sending it to the intended recipient. Note that the length of the secret key determines the strength of the encryption, that is, encryption that uses a longer key is more difficult to break than the one that uses a smaller key.

Secret-key encryption is also known as symmetric encryption as encryption and decryption uses the same key. The cryptography algorithms used for secret-key (or symmetric) encryptions are known as symmetric algorithms. These algorithms are quite fast and, therefore, are suitable for encrypting and decrypting large amounts of data. Most of the symmetric algorithms are block ciphers as these algorithms encrypt a single block of data at a time. Block ciphers take a block of fixed number of bytes of the data and generate an output block of encrypted data. The fixed number of bytes that block ciphers take may differ from one block cipher to another. For example, one block cipher may take an input block of 8 bytes and another may take an input block of 16 bytes. If the entire data is larger than this fixed number of bytes, then a block cipher encrypts one block at a time. However, if the data is smaller than the fixed number of bytes, then the data is made larger to fit the fixed number of bytes.

The block ciphers provided by .NET framework 4.5 use an initialization vector (IV) along with the secret key to encrypt and decrypt data. An initialization vector initializes the first block of input data that is to be encrypted. For the remaining blocks of input data, a bitwise exclusive-OR is performed between the current block of input data and the previous block of encrypted data. This implies that except for the first block of encrypted data, a block of the encrypted data depends on its previous block of encrypted data. This process is known as cipher block chaining (CBC).

In .NET framework 4.5, there are various symmetric cryptography algorithms to implement secret-key encryption. All the symmetric algorithms inherit the SymmetricAlgorithm class defined in the System.Security.Cryptography namespace. The SymmetricAlgorithm class is an abstract base class that represents a symmetric algorithm. There are various properties and methods that the SymmetricAlgorithm class offers.

The syntax of the SymmetricAlgorithm class is as follows:

In C#:

```
[ComVisibleAttribute(true)]
public abstract class SymmetricAlgorithm : IDisposable
```

In VB:

```
<ComVisibleAttribute(True)> _
Public MustInherit Class SymmetricAlgorithm _
   Implements Idisposable
```

Table 26.23 lists some of the noteworthy properties of the SymmetricAlgorithm class:

Table 26.23: Noteworthy Properties of the SymmetricAlgorithm Class

Property	Description
`BlockSize`	Sets or retrieves the block size (in bits) used for the cryptographic operation
`FeedbackSize`	Sets or retrieves the feedback size (in bits) used for the cryptographic operation
`IV`	Sets or retrieves the Initialization Vector (IV) used in the symmetric algorithm
`Key`	Sets or retrieves the secret key for the symmetric algorithm
`KeySize`	Sets or retrieves the size (in bits) of the secret key used in the symmetric algorithm
`LegalBlockSizes`	Retrieves the block sizes (in bits) available for a symmetric algorithm
`LegalKeySizes`	Retrieves the key sizes (in bits) available for a symmetric algorithm
`Mode`	Sets or retrieves the operation mode (for example, CBC) of the symmetric algorithm
`Padding`	Sets or retrieves the type of padding (if the data is shorter than the fixed number of bytes) used for the symmetric algorithm

Table 26.24 lists the noteworthy methods of the SymmetricAlgorithm class:

Table 26.24: Noteworthy Methods of the SymmetricAlgorithm Class

Method	Description
`Clear`	Releases the resources used by the SymmetricAlgorithm class
`Create`	Allows the creation of a cryptographic object for a symmetric algorithm
`CreateDecryptor`	Creates an object for symmetric decryption
`CreateEncryptor`	Creates an object for symmetric encryption
`GenerateIV`	Generates a random IV for a symmetric algorithm
`GenerateKey`	Generates a random secret key for a symmetric algorithm
`ValidKeySize`	Allows you to determine if the given key size is acceptable by the current symmetric algorithm

The classes that inherit the SymmetricAlgorithm class correspond to the different symmetric algorithms. Figure 26.14 shows a pictorial representation of the inheritance hierarchy of the different symmetric algorithm classes:

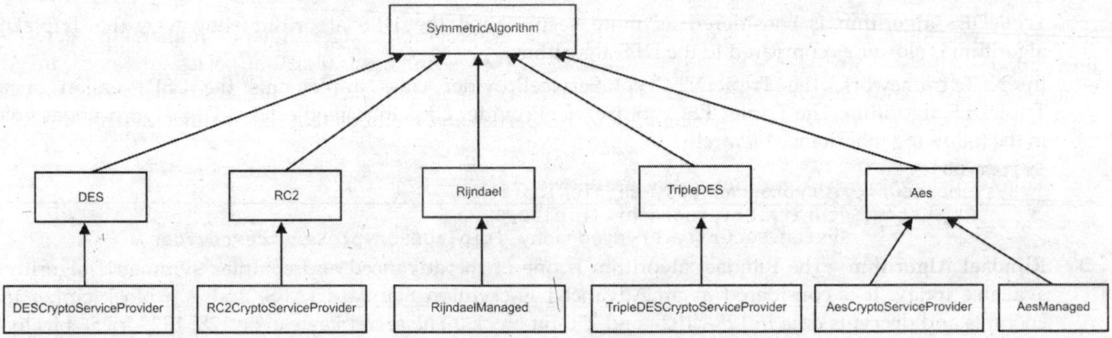

Figure 26.14: Inheritance Hierarchy of the Symmetric Algorithm Classes Used for Secret-Key Encryption

In Figure 26.14, you can see that the inheritance hierarchy has three tiers. At the root or top tier, the SymmetricAlgorithm class exists as the base class. In the middle tier, various abstract classes, such as DES, RC2, Rijndael, TripleDES, and Aes, implement the different symmetric algorithms. In the bottom tier, there are classes that provide the cryptographic service provider (CSP) or managed implementation of the respective algorithm.

The various symmetric algorithms and their description that are supported by .NET framework 4.5 are following:

- **Data Encryption Standard (DES) Algorithm**—The DES algorithm is one of the most common symmetric algorithms. This algorithm is a block cipher; and therefore, encrypts and decrypts data one block at a time. Each block is 8-bytes or 64-bit long. The DES algorithm uses a 64-bit secret key to encrypt and decrypt the blocks of data. Every eighth bit of the key is ignored by the algorithm, which implies that the key in effect is only 56-bit long. This 56-bit effective length of the DES secret key is smaller as compared to other symmetric algorithms, which makes it relatively less secure.

  In .NET framework, the DES algorithm is implemented through the DESCryptoServiceProvider Class. The `DESCryptoServiceProvider` class encapsulates CSP version of the DES algorithm to allow you to encrypt and decrypt using the DES algorithm. The inheritance hierarchy of the `DESCryptoServiceProvider` class is as follows:

```
System.Object
   System.Security.Cryptography.SymmetricAlgorithm
         System.Security.Cryptography.DES
                System.Security.Cryptography.DESCryptoServiceProvider
```

- **RC2 Algorithm**—The RC2 algorithm expands to Ron's Code or Rivest Cipher, which is named after its inventor, Ron Rivest. The RC2 algorithm is also a block cipher that encrypts and decrypts data in 64-bit blocks. The secret key has a variable length that can range from 8 bits to 64 bits. Due to the smaller key size, RC2 also does not prove to be a very secure symmetric algorithm. However, this algorithm is twice as faster as the DES algorithm and therefore, can be considered as a replacement for the DES algorithm.

  The RC2 algorithm is implemented in the RC2CryptoServiceProvider class that inherits from the RC2 class. The RC2CryptoServiceProvider class encapsulates the CSP implementation of the RC2 algorithm for performing encryption. The inheritance hierarchy of the RC2CryptoServiceProvider class is as follows:

```
System.Object
   System.Security.Cryptography.SymmetricAlgorithm
         System.Security.Cryptography.RC2
                System.Security.Cryptography.RC2CryptoServiceProvider
```

  The RC2CryptoServiceProvider class has a property named EffectiveKeySize that it inherits from the RC2 class. The EffectiveKeySize property allows you to set or retrieve the effective size or length (in bits) of the secret key that is used by the algorithm.

- **TripleDES Algorithm**—The TripleDES algorithm is an enhanced version of the DES algorithm. As the name suggests, the TripleDES algorithm performs three iterations of the DES algorithm to encrypt and decrypt 64-bit blocks of data. Every iteration may use three different secret keys where each key has a length of 64 bits; the effective length of the individual keys is 56 bits. Due to the three iterations, the

TripleDES algorithm is considered as more secure than the DES algorithm; however, the TripleDES algorithm is slower as compared to the DES algorithm.

In .NET framework, the TripleDESCryptoServiceProvider class implements the CSP version of the TripleDES algorithm. The TripleDESCryptoServiceProvider class inherits the TripleDES algorithm, as given in the following inheritance hierarchy:

```
System.Object
  System.Security.Cryptography.SymmetricAlgorithm
       System.Security.Cryptography.TripleDES
             System.Security.Cryptography.TripleDESCryptoServiceProvider
```

- **Rijndael Algorithm**—The Rijndael algorithm is one of the advanced and complex symmetric algorithms available today. It is considered as an Advanced Encryption Standard (AES) and is a block cipher that encrypts and decrypts data in 128-, 192-, and 256-bit blocks. The secret key can be 128, 192, or 256 bits long, which is quite large as compared to other symmetric algorithms, such as DES. Due to its long key length, it provides almost unbreakable encrypted data and therefore, it is one of the most secure symmetric algorithms till date. It is also one of the fastest symmetric algorithms.

  In .NET framework, the RijndaelManaged class contains the managed implementation of the Rijndael algorithm. The inheritance hierarchy of the `RijndaelManaged` class is as follows:

```
System.Object
  System.Security.Cryptography.SymmetricAlgorithm
       System.Security.Cryptography.Rijndael
             System.Security.Cryptography.RijndaelManaged
```

- **Advanced Encryption Standard (AES) Algorithm**—.NET framework 4.5 also allows you to use the AES algorithm that is actually a subset of the Rijndael algorithm. The secret key used in the AES algorithm is 128-, 192-, or 256-bit long and the data is encrypted and decrypted in blocks of 128 bits. With the AES algorithm, you cannot use the feedback mode.

  The Aes class in .NET framework is the abstract base class that extends the properties and methods for using the AES algorithm. This class is inherited by two other classes, AesCryptoServiceProvider and AesManaged that represent the CAPI and the managed implementations of the AES algorithm, respectively. The inheritance hierarchy of both these classes is as follows:

```
System.Object
  System.Security.Cryptography.SymmetricAlgorithm
       System.Security.Cryptography.Aes
             System.Security.Cryptography.AesCryptoServiceProvider
                   System.Security.Cryptography.AesManaged
```

Now that you have learned about the secret-key encryption, let's learn about the public-key encryption.

Public-Key Encryption

In public-key encryption, two keys are used to encrypt and decrypt data. The key used to encrypt the data is known as the public key and the key used to decrypt the data is known as the private key. You need to first generate the public and private keys to use public-key encryption. The public key is then made available to anybody who wants to send data. The sender can then use the public key to encrypt the data and send the encrypted data to you. When you receive the encrypted data, you need to use the private key, which remains hidden from the sender, to decrypt the data. The public and private keys are related to each other in such a way that data encrypted with a public key can be decrypted by using only the correct private key. Note that since you transmit the public key to the sender over the network, any user can intercept the transmission, access the public key, and use it to send encrypted data. Therefore, it is essential to first check the identity of the sender before decrypting the data. You also need to check if the data is encrypted with the same public key that you sent.

Public-key encryption is also known as asymmetric encryption as it uses one key to encrypt and another key to decrypt. The cryptography algorithms used to implement asymmetric encryption are known as asymmetric algorithms. This algorithm generates the private and public keys that are mathematically linked to each other. Public-key or asymmetric algorithms generate keys that are longer as compared to those generated in symmetric or secret-key algorithms. Due to the larger key lengths, asymmetric algorithms offer better security than symmetric algorithms. However, asymmetric algorithms are slow in comparison to the symmetric algorithms and therefore, are suitable only for exchanging small amounts of data. Asymmetric algorithms are primarily used for exchanging secret keys (in secret-key encryption) and creating digital signatures.

In .NET framework, all the asymmetric algorithms are inherited from the AsymmetricAlgorithm class, which is an abstract class representing an asymmetric algorithm. There are various properties and methods of the AsymmetricAlgorithm class. Table 26.25 lists the noteworthy properties of the AsymmetricAlgorithm class:

Table 26.25: Noteworthy Properties of the AsymmetricAlgorithm Class

Property	Description
`KeyExchangeAlgorithm`	Retrieves the name of the key exchange algorithm
`KeySize`	Sets or retrieves the size of the key used in the asymmetric algorithm in bits
`LegalKeySizes`	Retrieves the key sizes that are available for the asymmetric algorithm
`SignatureAlgorithm`	Retrieves the name of the signature algorithm

Table 26.26 lists the noteworthy methods of the AsymmetricAlgorithm class:

Table 26.26: Noteworthy Methods of the AsymmetricAlgorithm Class

Method	Description
`Clear`	Frees the resources used by the asymmetric algorithm
`Create`	Allows you to create a cryptographic object for the asymmetric algorithm
`FromXmlString`	Allows you to re-create an XML representation of the current asymmetric algorithm
`ToXmlString`	Creates and returns an XML representation of the current asymmetric algorithm

Several .NET classes allow you to work with the asymmetric algorithms. Figure 26.15 shows the inheritance hierarchy of these classes:

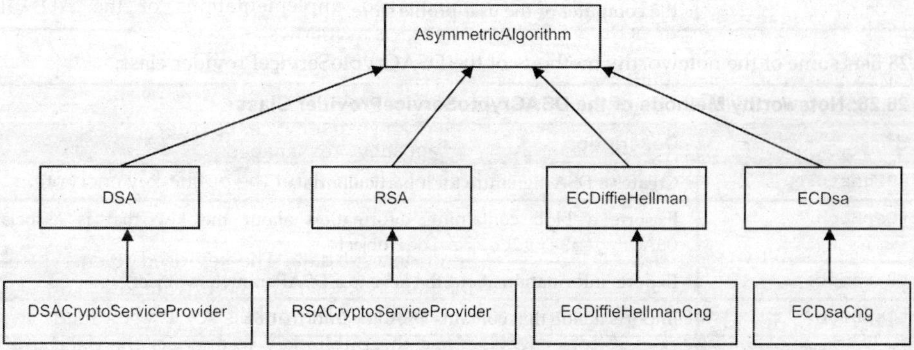

Figure 26.15: Inheritance Hierarchy of the Asymmetric Algorithm Classes Used for Public-Key Encryption

As shown in Figure 26.15, the inheritance hierarchy of the classes is divided into three tiers. The top tier consists of the AsymmetricAlgorithm class, which is the base class for all the asymmetric algorithms. The middle tier has abstract classes (for example, DSA, RSA, ECDiffieHellman, and ECDsa) that provide the properties and methods for a particular asymmetric algorithm. The classes in the bottom tier are the CSP or Cryptography Next Generation (CNG) implementation of the asymmetric algorithms.

NOTE

CNG is a Framework that encapsulates several managed APIs offering extensible cryptographic features and services. It is included in .NET framework to serve as an alternative to the CryptoAPI.

In .NET framework 4.5, the descriptions of various asymmetric algorithms are as following:

- **Digital Signature Algorithm (DSA)–** DSA was developed by National Institute of Standard and Technology (NIST) in 1991 for working with digital signatures. It is the United States Federal Government standard for digital signatures. The DSA algorithm is quite fast and can use keys that have lengths ranging from 512 bits to 1024 bits. The value of length can be incremented in the sets of 64 bits. This algorithm is not used to encrypt or decrypt data, but only to digitally sign the data. The algorithm uses a hash algorithm to create the digital signature of the sender, which is then used by the receiver to authenticate the sender.

  In .NET framework, the `DSACryptoServiceProvider` class contains the CSP implementation of the DSA algorithm. The inheritance hierarchy of the `DSACryptoServiceProvider` class is as follows:

```
System.Object
   System.Security.Cryptography.AsymmetricAlgorithm
         System.Security.Cryptography.DSA
                System.Security.Cryptography.DSACryptoServiceProvider
```

The `DSACryptoServiceProvider` class has several properties and methods that allow you to use the DSA algorithm in your applications. Table 26.27 lists some of the noteworthy properties of the DSACryptoServiceProvider class:

Table 26.27: Noteworthy Properties of the DSACryptoServiceProvider Class

Property	Description
`CspKeyContainerInfo`	Retrieves an object of the `CspKeyContainerInfo` class. A `CspKeyContainerInfo` object contains different types of information about the private and public key pair.
`PersistKeyInCsp`	Sets or retrieves a value that indicates whether a key should persist in the cryptographic service provider (CSP).
`PublicOnly`	Retrieves a value that indicates whether the `DSACryptoServiceProvider` object contains only a public key or both public and private keys.
`UseMachineKeyStore`	Sets or retrieves a value that indicates whether the key should persist in the key store of the computer or the user profile store.

Table 26.28 lists some of the noteworthy methods of the DSACryptoServiceProvider class:

Table 26.28: Noteworthy Methods of the DSACryptoServiceProvider Class

Method	Description
`CreateSignature`	Creates a DSA signature for a particular data
`ExportCspBlob`	Exports a blob containing information about the key that is associated with a `DSACryptoServiceProvider` object
`ExportParameters`	Exports information about the keys to a DSAParameters object
`ImportCspBlob`	Imports a blob that contains DSA key information
`ImportParameters`	Imports a given DSAParameters object
`SignData`	Allows you to compute the hash value of a given data and signs the data
`SignHash`	Allows you to create a digital signature for a given hash value by using the private key to encrypt the hash value
`VerifyData`	Returns a value that indicates whether the specified signature matches the signature computed for the given data
`VerifyHash`	Returns a value that indicates whether the specified signature matches the signature computed for the given hash value
`VerifySignature`	Returns a value that indicates whether the given DSA signature matches the signature computed for the specified data

- **Random Sequential Adsorption (RSA)**—The RSA algorithm is one of the most common public-key algorithms. It was introduced in 1977 by Ron Rivest, Adi Shamir, and Leonard Adleman and therefore, named after them. You can use the RSA algorithm for digitally signing and encrypting data. This algorithm can use keys with a minimum length of 384 bits.

In .NET framework, the `RSACryptoServiceProvider` class provides the CSP implementation of the RSA algorithm. The inheritance hierarchy of the `RSACryptoServiceProvider` class is as follows:

```
System.Object
  System.Security.Cryptography.AsymmetricAlgorithm
       System.Security.Cryptography.RSA
             System.Security.Cryptography.RSACryptoServiceProvider
```

The `RSACryptoServiceProvider` class has many properties and methods that you can use to work with the RSA algorithm. Table 26.29 lists some of the noteworthy properties of the RSACryptoServiceProvider class:

Table 26.29: Noteworthy Properties of the RSACryptoServiceProvider Class

Property	Description
`CspKeyContainerInfo`	Retrieves an object of the `CspKeyContainerInfo` class. A `CspKeyContainerInfo` object contains various information about the private and public key pair.
`PersistKeyInCsp`	Sets or retrieves a value that indicates whether a key should persist in the cryptographic service provider (CSP).
`PublicOnly`	Retrieves a value that indicates whether the `RSACryptoServiceProvider` object contains only a public key or both the public and private keys.
`UseMachineKeyStore`	Sets or retrieves a value that indicates whether the key should persist in the key store of the computer or the user profile store.

Table 26.30 lists some of the noteworthy methods of the RSACryptoServiceProvider class:

Table 26.30: Noteworthy Methods of the RSACryptoServiceProvider Class

Method	Description
`Decrypt`	Allows the decryption of data with the RSA algorithm
`Encrypt`	Allows encryption of data with the RSA algorithm
`ExportCspBlob`	Exports a blob containing information about the key that is associated with a `RSACryptoServiceProvider` object
`ExportParameters`	Exports information about the keys to an RSAParameters object
`ImportCspBlob`	Imports a blob that contains RSA key information
`ImportParameters`	Imports a given RSAParameters object
`SignData`	Allows to the computation of the hash value of a given data and signs the data
`SignHash`	Allows the creation of a digital signature for a given hash value by using the private key to encrypt the hash value
`VerifyData`	Returns a value that indicates whether the specified signature matches the signature computed for the given data
`VerifyHash`	Returns a value that indicates whether the specified signature matches the signature computed for the given hash value

- **Elliptic Curve Diffie Hellman Algorithm (ECDH)**—The ECDH algorithm is primarily used for the generation of private and public keys rather than encryption and decryption of data. The ECDH algorithm is provided by .NET framework 4.5 through the Cryptography Next Generation (CNG) classes. The ECDiffieHellmanCng class is the class that contains the implementation of the ECDH algorithm. The inheritance hierarchy of the ECDiffieHellmanCng class is as follows:

```
System.Object
   System.Security.Cryptography.AsymmetricAlgorithm
         System.Security.Cryptography.ECDiffieHellman
                System.Security.Cryptography.ECDiffieHellmanCng
```

The ECDiffieHellmanCng class has many properties and methods that you can use to work with the ECDH algorithm. Table 26.31 lists some of the noteworthy properties of the ECDiffieHellmanCng class:

Table 26.31: Noteworthy Properties of the ECDiffieHellmanCng Class

Property	Description
HashAlgorithm	Sets or retrieves the hash algorithm used to generate the keys. The default hash algorithm is SHA256.
HmacKey	Sets or retrieves the Hash-based Message Authentication Code (HMAC) key in use.
Key	Refers to a CngKey object that is used by the ECDH algorithm.
KeyDerivationFunction	Sets or retrieves the key derivation function used by the algorithm to convert the secret agreement to key information.
Label	Sets or retrieves the label used for deriving the key. By default, it is null.
PublicKey	Retrieves the public key used by one ECDiffieHellmanCng object to share the key with another ECDiffieHellmanCng object.
SecretAppend	Sets or retrieves a value that is appended to the secret agreement.
SecretPrepend	Sets or retrieves a value that is included at the very beginning of the secret agreement.
Seed	Sets or retrieves the seed value for generating the key. By default, it is a null reference.
UseSecretAgreementAsHmacKey	Retrieves a value that indicates whether the secret agreement is used as a HMAC key.

Table 26.32 lists the noteworthy methods of the ECDiffieHellmanCng class:

Table 26.32: Noteworthy Methods of the ECDiffieHellmanCng Class

Method	Description
DeriveKeyMaterial	Generates the key material from a given secret agreement
DeriveSecretAgreementHandle	Returns a handle for a secret agreement

- **Elliptic Curve Digital Signature Algorithm (ECDSA)**—The ECDSA algorithm has its use in digital signatures. The sender can digitally sign data with its private key and the receiver can validate the identity of the sender by using the sender's public key. The ECDSA algorithm is provided by .NET framework 4.5 through the ECDsaCng class that has the CNG implementation of the ECDSA algorithm. The inheritance hierarchy of the ECDsaCng class is as follows:

```
System.Object
   System.Security.Cryptography.AsymmetricAlgorithm
         System.Security.Cryptography.ECDsa
                System.Security.Cryptography.ECDsaCng
```

The ECDsaCng class has many properties and methods that you can use to work with the ECDSA algorithm. Table 26.33 lists some of the noteworthy properties of the ECDsaCng class:

Table 26.33: Noteworthy Properties of the ECDsaCng Class

Property	Description
HashAlgorithm	Sets or retrieves the hash algorithm used for digitally signing and validating the data
Key	Sets or retrieves the key used for digitally signing and checking the data

Table 26.34 lists the noteworthy methods of the ECDsaCng class:

Table 26.34: Noteworthy Methods of the ECDsaCng Class

Method	Description
SignData	Creates a digital signature
SignHash	Creates a digital signature for a given hash value
VerifyData	Verifies a given digital signature
VerifyHash	Verifies a given digital signature against a hash value

Hash Algorithms

Hash algorithms are hash functions that take a sequence of bytes of any length and convert it into smaller fixed-length sequence of bytes known as hash values. The hash values, also called message digest or digital fingerprint, represent the alphanumerical/numerical form of the data. The hash values are randomly generated and are unique for a particular piece of data (or message). That is, the hash values of two different pieces of data are also different. Even if two pieces of data or messages differ in a single letter, their hash values can be significantly different. Therefore, it can be considered that if two hash values are same, then the respective data or messages are also same. Due to this uniqueness of hash values, cryptographic hash algorithms are used for authenticating the sender and ensuring data integrity.

In .NET framework, the class that represents all the cryptographic hash algorithms is the HashAlgorithm class. This class is an abstract class that is inherited by any class that implements a hash algorithm. The HashAlgorithm class has several properties and methods to work with the hash algorithms.

Table 26.35 lists the noteworthy properties of the HashAlgorithm class:

Table 26.35: Noteworthy Properties of the HashAlgorithm Class

Property	Description
CanReuseTransform	Retrieves a value that indicates whether the current transform is reusable
CanTransformMultipleBlocks	Retrieves a value that indicates whether transformation can be performed on multiple blocks
Hash	Retrieves the hash value
HashSize	Retrieves the size (in bits) of the hash value
InputBlockSize	Retrieves the size of the input block
OutputBlockSize	Retrieves the size of the output block

Table 26.36 lists the noteworthy methods of the HashAlgorithm class:

Table 26.36: Noteworthy Methods of the HashAlgorithm Class

Method	Description
Clear	Frees all the resources used by the current HashAlgorithm object
ComputeHash	Computes the hash value for a given input data
Create	Creates a HashAlgorithm object
Initialize	Initializes an implementation of the HashAlgorithm class
TransformBlock	Computes the hash value for a particular portion of the input byte array and saves it in a given portion of the output byte array
TransformFinalBlock	Computes the hash value for a given portion of a given byte array

The various algorithms that are supported in .NET framework 4.5 are:

- Message-Digest Algorithm 5 (MD5)
- RACE Integrity Primitives Evaluation Message Digest-160(RIPEMD-160) Algorithm
- Secure Hash Algorithms (SHA)

MD5 Algorithm

The MD5 algorithm was introduced by Ron Rivest in the early 1990s to enforce data integrity and identity validation for data. It takes a message (or data) of any length and generates a hash value called message digest of 128 bits. .NET framework allows you to work with the MD5 algorithm through the MD5 base class, which is an abstract class that offers the properties and methods for the actual implementation of the algorithm. The MD5CryptoServiceProvider class provides the CSP implementation of the MD5 algorithm. The inheritance hierarchy of the `MD5CryptoServiceProvider` class is as follows:

```
System.Object
   System.Security.Cryptography.HashAlgorithm
        System.Security.Cryptography.MD5
                  System.Security.Cryptography.MD5CryptoServiceProvider
```

In .NET framework 4.5, another class, named MD5Cng, provides the CNG implementation of the algorithm. The inheritance hierarchy of the MD5Cng class is as follows:

```
System.Object
   System.Security.Cryptography.HashAlgorithm
        System.Security.Cryptography.MD5
                  System.Security.Cryptography.MD5Cng
```

RIPEMD-160 Algorithm

The RIPEMD-160 algorithm is an enhanced version of the MD5 algorithm. The RIPEMD-160 generates a 160-bit message digest as compared to the 128-bit message digest by MD5 algorithm. .NET framework provides the RIPEMD160 abstract class, which is the base class for all the classes that implement the RIPEMD-160 algorithm. The RIPEMD160Managed class is an in-built class that implements the algorithm using the managed library. The inheritance hierarchy of the RIPE160Managed class is as follows:

```
System.Object
   System.Security.Cryptography.HashAlgorithm
        System.Security.Cryptography.RIPEMD160
                  System.Security.Cryptography.RIPEMD160Managed
```

SHA Algorithms

The SHA algorithms refer to a set of hash algorithms developed by the National Institute of Standards and Technology (NIST). The SHA algorithms are based on the MD5 algorithm and are comparatively more secure due to their longer message digests. The various SHA algorithms supported by .NET framework are:

- **SHA1**—Generates a 160-bit message digest and is one of the most common SHA algorithms. The SHA1 class provided by .NET framework is the abstract class that facilitates the implementation of the SHA1 algorithm. The managed implementation of the SHA1 algorithm is provided by the SHA1Managed class. The inheritance hierarchy of the SHA1Managed class is as follows:

```
System.Object
   System.Security.Cryptography.HashAlgorithm
        System.Security.Cryptography.SHA1
                  System.Security.Cryptography.SHA1Managed
```

The `SHA1CryptoServiceProvider` class has the CSP implementation of the algorithm by inheriting the SHA1 class. The inheritance hierarchy of the `SHA1CryptoServiceProvider` class is as follows:

```
System.Object
   System.Security.Cryptography.HashAlgorithm
        System.Security.Cryptography.SHA1
                  System.Security.Cryptography.SHA1CryptoServiceProvider
```

In .NET framework 4.5, there is the SHA1Cng class that provides the CNG implementation of the SHA1 algorithm. The inheritance hierarchy of the SHA1Cng class is as follows:

```
System.Object
  System.Security.Cryptography.HashAlgorithm
       System.Security.Cryptography.SHA1
             System.Security.Cryptography.SHA1Cng
```

- **SHA256**—Generates a 256-bit message digest and is supported by .NET framework through the SHA256 abstract base class. The classes that implement the SHA256 algorithm inherit the SHA256 class. The managed implementation of the SHA256 algorithm is provided by the `SHA256Managed` class. The inheritance hierarchy of the `SHA256Managed` class is as follows:

```
System.Object
  System.Security.Cryptography.HashAlgorithm
       System.Security.Cryptography.SHA256
             System.Security.Cryptography.SHA256Managed
```

In .NET framework 4.5, the SHA256CryptoServiceProvider class provides the CSP implementation of the SHA256 algorithm. The inheritance hierarchy of the SHA256CryptoServiceProvider is as follows:

```
System.Object
  System.Security.Cryptography.HashAlgorithm
       System.Security.Cryptography.SHA256
             System.Security.Cryptography.SHA256CryptoServiceProvider
```

The CNG implementation of the algorithm is also provided in .NET framework through the SHA256Cng class. The inheritance hierarchy of the SHA256Cng class is as follows:

```
System.Object
  System.Security.Cryptography.HashAlgorithm
       System.Security.Cryptography.SHA256
             System.Security.Cryptography.SHA256Cng
```

- **SHA384**—Generates a 384-bit message digest and is supported by .NET framework through the SHA384 abstract base class. The classes that implement the SHA384 algorithm inherit the SHA256 class. The managed implementation of the SHA384 algorithm is provided by the `SHA384Managed` class. The inheritance hierarchy of the `SHA384Managed` class is as follows:

```
System.Object
  System.Security.Cryptography.HashAlgorithm
       System.Security.Cryptography.SHA384
             System.Security.Cryptography.SHA384Managed
```

In .NET framework 4.5, the SHA384CryptoServiceProvider class provides the CSP implementation of the SHA384 algorithm. The inheritance hierarchy of the SHA384CryptoServiceProvider is as follows:

```
System.Object
  System.Security.Cryptography.HashAlgorithm
       System.Security.Cryptography.SHA384
             System.Security.Cryptography.SHA384CryptoServiceProvider
```

The CNG implementation of the algorithm is also provided in .NET framework through the SHA384Cng class. The inheritance hierarchy of the SHA384Cng class is as follows:

```
System.Object
  System.Security.Cryptography.HashAlgorithm
       System.Security.Cryptography.SHA384
             System.Security.Cryptography.SHA384Cng
```

- **SHA512**—Generates a 512-bit message digest and is supported by .NET framework through the SHA512 abstract base class. The classes that implement the SHA512 algorithm inherit the SHA512 class. The managed implementation of the SHA512 algorithm is provided by the `SHA512Managed` class. The inheritance hierarchy of the `SHA512Managed` class is as follows:

```
System.Object
  System.Security.Cryptography.HashAlgorithm
       System.Security.Cryptography.SHA512
             System.Security.Cryptography.SHA512Managed
```

In .NET framework 4.5, the SHA512CryptoServiceProvider class provides the CSP implementation of the SHA512 algorithm. The inheritance hierarchy of the SHA512CryptoServiceProvider class is as follows:

```
System.Object
   System.Security.Cryptography.HashAlgorithm
         System.Security.Cryptography.SHA512
                System.Security.Cryptography.SHA512CryptoServiceProvider
```

The CNG implementation of the algorithm is also provided in .NET framework through the SHA512Cng class. The inheritance hierarchy of the SHA512Cng class is as follows:

```
System.Object
   System.Security.Cryptography.HashAlgorithm
         System.Security.Cryptography.SHA512
                System.Security.Cryptography.SHA512Cng
```

NOTE

The SHA256, SHA384, and SHA512 algorithms are collectively known as SHA2 algorithms.

Immediate Solutions

Managing Roles and Users

In ASP.NET, a role consists of a group of users. You will be able to assign users to a specified role, such as manager and admin, by managing a role,. A user can be assigned to more than one group with different permissions. Now, let's create a website and save it as RolesCS. You can find the code for this application in the RolesCS (for C#) and RolesVB (for VB) folders. Now, let's create a website to manage roles and corresponding users by performing the following steps:

In the Visual Studio 2012 IDE, select FILE→New→Web Site to open the New Web Site dialog box. In the dialog box, select the ASP.NET Empty Web Site option and specify RolesCS as the name of the website, and click the OK button.

Open the Web.config file and add the following line of code under the <system.web> tag in both C# and VB:

```
<roleManager enabled = "true" />
```

The preceding line of code enables `role manager` of a website. The role manager eases the task of managing roles and performing role-based authorization in your application. You can also perform the same function through Web Site Administration Tool (WAT). Under the Security tab of the Web Site Administration Tool, enable RoleManager (for more details on WAT, refer Chapter 24: *Working with Login Controls*). It will automatically add the preceding line of code into the Web.config file.

Add a Web page, Default.aspx, in the application and replace the code for the Default.aspx page with the code, given in Listing 26.1, to add the controls required for the application:

Listing 26.1: Showing the Code for the `Default.aspx` Page

In VB

```
<%@ Page Language="VB" AutoEventWireup="false" CodeFile="Default.aspx.vb"
  Inherits="_Default" %>
<!DOCTYPE html>
<html xmlns="http://www.w3.org/1999/xhtml">
<head runat="server">
    <title></title>
</head>
<body>
    <form id="form1" runat="server">
    <div>
    Enter Role Name:<br />
         <asp:TextBox ID="TextBox1" runat="server"></asp:TextBox>
         <asp:Label ID="Label1" runat="server" Text="Label" Visible="False"
           Width="304px"></asp:Label><br />
         <asp:Button ID="BtnCreate" runat="server"
         Text="Create Roles" />
          <asp:Button ID="BtnDelete" runat="server"
           style="margin-left: 81px"
         Text="Delete Roles" />
         <br />
         <br />
         <asp:DropDownList ID="Dropgetallroles" runat="server">
         </asp:DropDownList>

          <hr style="background-color:Black"/>
   <span style="color: #000000">
        <br />
        Enter user name:<br />
   </span>
<asp:TextBox ID="Txtusername" runat="server"></asp:TextBox><br />
         <span style="color: #000000">Enter Role:</span><br />
         <asp:TextBox ID="TxtRolename" runat="server"></asp:TextBox>
```

```
            <asp:Label ID="Label2" runat="server"></asp:Label><br />
            <br />
            <asp:Button ID="BtnAdd" runat="server"  Text="Add User"
            Width="103px" />
            <asp:Button ID="BtnDelUser" runat="server" style="margin-left: 63px"
            Text="Delete User" />
            <br />
            <br />
            <asp:GridView ID="GridView1" runat="server" BackColor="#DEBA84"
              BorderColor="#DEBA84"
            BorderStyle="None" BorderWidth="1px" CellPadding="3" CellSpacing="2"
            Height="100px" style="margin-left: 136px" Width="191px">
            <FooterStyle BackColor="#F7DFB5" ForeColor="#8C4510" />
            <RowStyle BackColor="#FFF7E7" ForeColor="#8C4510" />
            <PagerStyle ForeColor="#8C4510" HorizontalAlign="Center" />
            <SelectedRowStyle BackColor="#738A9C" Font-Bold="True" ForeColor="White" />
            <HeaderStyle BackColor="#A55129" Font-Bold="True" ForeColor="White" />
    </asp:GridView>
       </div>
       </form>
</body>
</html>
```

In C#

```
<%@ Page Language="C#" AutoEventWireup="true" CodeFile="Default.aspx.cs"
   Inherits="_Default" %>
<!DOCTYPE html>
<html xmlns="http://www.w3.org/1999/xhtml">
<head runat="server">
    <title></title>
</head>
<body>
    <form id="form1" runat="server">
    <div>

    Enter Role Name:<br />
         <asp:TextBox ID="TextBox1" runat="server"></asp:TextBox>
         <asp:Label ID="Label1" runat="server" Text="Label" Visible="False"
           Width="304px"></asp:Label><br />
         <asp:Button ID="BtnCreate" runat="server" OnClick="BtnCreate_Click"
         Text="Create Roles" />
          <asp:Button ID="BtnDelete" runat="server" OnClick="BtnDelete_Click"
           style="margin-left: 81px"
         Text="Delete Roles" />
         <br />
         <br />
         <asp:DropDownList ID="Dropgetallroles" runat="server">
         </asp:DropDownList>
        <br />
        <br />
        <br />
        <hr style="background-color:Black"/>
<span style="color: #000000">
        <br />
        Enter user name:<br />
</span>
<asp:TextBox ID="Txtusername" runat="server"></asp:TextBox><br />
         <span style="color: #000000">Enter Role:</span><br />
         <asp:TextBox ID="TxtRolename" runat="server"></asp:TextBox>
         <asp:Label ID="Label2" runat="server"></asp:Label><br />
         <br />
         <asp:Button ID="BtnAdd" runat="server" OnClick="BtnAdd_Click" Text="Add User"
```

```
Width="103px" />
<asp:Button ID="BtnDelUser" runat="server" style="margin-left: 63px"
Text="Delete User" OnClick="BtnDelUser_Click" />
<br />
<br />
<asp:GridView ID="GridView1" runat="server" BackColor="#DEBA84"
  BorderColor="#DEBA84"
BorderStyle="None" BorderWidth="1px" CellPadding="3" CellSpacing="2"
Height="100px" style="margin-left: 136px" Width="191px">
<FooterStyle BackColor="#F7DFB5" ForeColor="#8C4510" />
<RowStyle BackColor="#FFF7E7" ForeColor="#8C4510" />
<PagerStyle ForeColor="#8C4510" HorizontalAlign="Center" />
<SelectedRowStyle BackColor="#738A9C" Font-Bold="True" ForeColor="White" />
<HeaderStyle BackColor="#A55129" Font-Bold="True" ForeColor="White" />
</asp:GridView>
  </div>
  </form>
</body>
</html>
```

Now, add the following code in the code-behind file of the Default.aspx page. Listing 26.2 shows the code for the code behind file of the Default.aspx page of the application:

Listing 26.2: Showing the Code for the Code-Behind File of the Default.aspx Page

In VB

```
Imports System.Web.Security
Partial Class _Default
    Inherits System.Web.UI.Page
    Protected Sub BtnCreate_Click( sender As Object,  e As EventArgs)
    Handles
   BtnCreate.Click
        Try
            Label1.Visible = True
            Roles.CreateRole(TextBox1.Text)
            Dropgetallroles.DataSource = Roles.GetAllRoles()
            Dropgetallroles.DataBind()
            Label1.Text = "Role " & TextBox1.Text & "is Created"
        Catch
            Label1.Visible = True
            Label1.Text = "Unable to create role, as this role exists. Please try another
        role name."
        End Try
    End Sub
    Protected Sub BtnDelete_Click( sender As Object,  e As EventArgs)
  Handles
   BtnDelete.Click
        Label1.Visible = True
        Roles.DeleteRole(TextBox1.Text)
        Dropgetallroles.DataSource = Roles.GetAllRoles()
        Dropgetallroles.DataBind()
        Label1.Text = "Roles " & TextBox1.Text & " is deleted"
    End Sub
    Protected Sub Page_Load( sender As Object,  e As EventArgs) Handles
  Me.Load
        Dropgetallroles.DataSource = Roles.GetAllRoles()
        Dropgetallroles.DataBind()
    End Sub
    Protected Sub BtnAdd_Click( sender As Object, e As EventArgs)
  Handles
   BtnAdd.Click
        Try
            Label2.Visible = False
            Roles.AddUserToRole(Txtusername.Text, TxtRolename.Text)
```

```
            GridView1.DataSource = Roles.GetUsersInRole(TxtRolename.Text)
            GridView1.DataBind()
        Catch
            Label2.Visible = True
            Label2.Text = "User Already exist"
        End Try
    End Sub
  Protected Sub BtnDelUser_Click(sender As Object, e As EventArgs)
  Handles
   BtnDelUser.Click
        Try
            Roles.RemoveUserFromRole(Txtusername.Text, TxtRolename.Text)
            GridView1.DataSource = Roles.GetUsersInRole(TxtRolename.Text)
            GridView1.DataBind()
        Catch
            Label2.Visible = True
            Label2.Text = "User not exist"
        End Try
    End Sub
End Class
```

In C#

```
using System;
using System.Collections.Generic;
using System.Linq;
using System.Web;
using System.Web.UI;
using System.Web.UI.WebControls;
using System.Configuration;
using System.Web.Security;
public partial class _Default : System.Web.UI.Page
{
    protected void Page_Load(object sender, EventArgs e)
    {
            Dropgetallroles.DataSource = Roles.GetAllRoles();
        Dropgetallroles.DataBind();
    }
    protected void BtnCreate_Click(object sender, EventArgs e)
    {

        try
         {
                Label1.Visible = true;
                Roles.CreateRole(TextBox1.Text);
                Dropgetallroles.DataSource = Roles.GetAllRoles();
                Dropgetallroles.DataBind();
                //Label1.Visible = false;
                Label1.Text="Role " + TextBox1.Text+" is Created" ;
         }
         catch
         {
                Label1.Visible = true;
                Label1.Text = "Unable to create role, as this role exists. Please try
                another
                 role name.";
         }
    }
    protected void BtnDelete_Click(object sender, EventArgs e)
    {
        Label1.Visible = true;
        Roles.DeleteRole(TextBox1.Text);
        Dropgetallroles.DataSource = Roles.GetAllRoles();
```

```
            Dropgetallroles.DataBind();
            Label1.Text = "Roles " + TextBox1.Text + " is deleted";

        }
        protected void BtnAdd_Click(object sender, EventArgs e)
        {
            try
            {
                Label2.Visible = false;
                Roles.AddUserToRole(Txtusername.Text, TxtRolename.Text);
                GridView1.DataSource = Roles.GetUsersInRole(TxtRolename.Text);
                GridView1.DataBind();
            }
            catch
            {
                Label2.Visible = true;
                Label2.Text = "User Already exist";
            }
        }
        protected void BtnDelUser_Click(object sender, EventArgs e)
        {
            try
            {
                Roles.RemoveUserFromRole(Txtusername.Text, TxtRolename.Text);
                GridView1.DataSource = Roles.GetUsersInRole(TxtRolename.Text);
                GridView1.DataBind();
            }
            catch
            {
                Label2.Visible = true;
                Label2.Text = "User not exist";
            }
        }
    }
```

5. Press the F5 key on the keyboard to execute the application and to view the output.
6. Enter the role in the Enter Role Name text box and click the Create Roles button (Figure 26.16). The message appears displaying Role User is Created (Figure 26.16).
7. Click the drop-down list to view the role created, as shown in Figure 26.16:

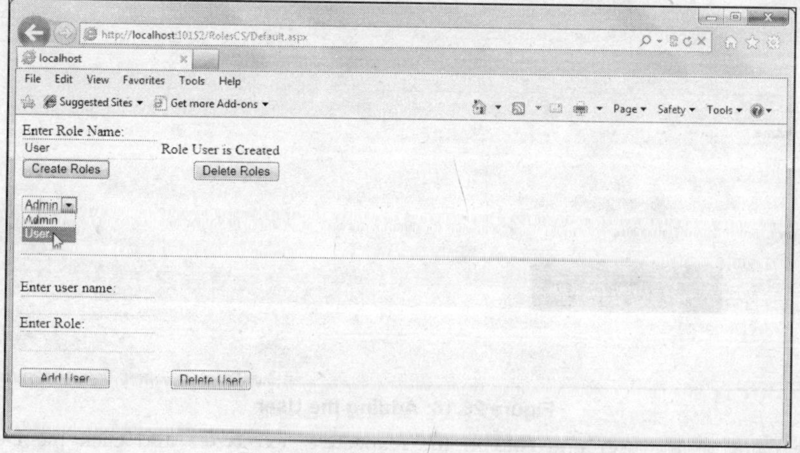

Figure 26.16: Creating the Roles

8. Enter the role name in the Enter Role Name text box and click the Delete Roles button (Figure 26.17).

The message appears displaying Roles User is deleted (Figure 26.17).

9. Click the drop-down list to view the role left, as shown in Figure 26.17:

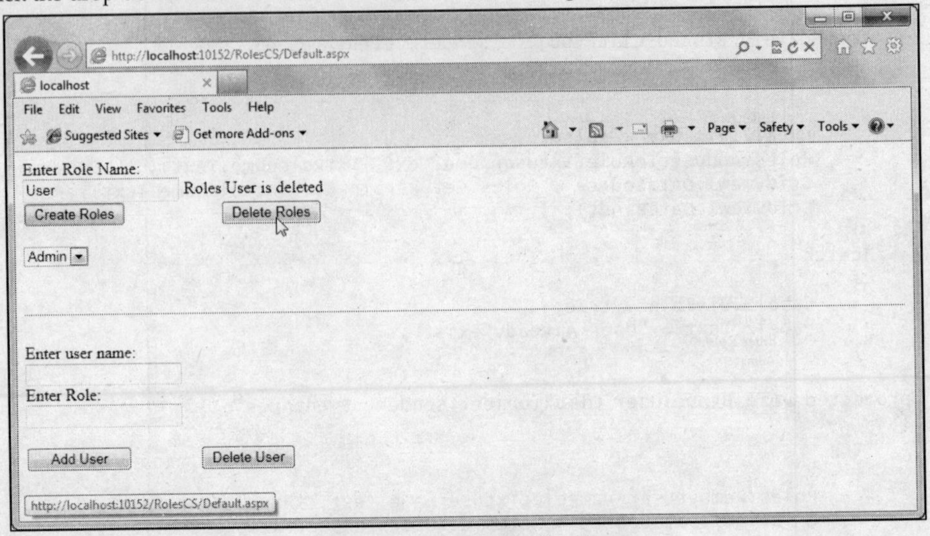

Figure 26.17: Deleting the User

10. Enter the user name in the Enter user name text box and also enter the role created in the Enter Role text box (Figure 26.18).
11. Click the Add User button to add the user and display it on the Web page for the Admin role, as shown in Figure 26.18:

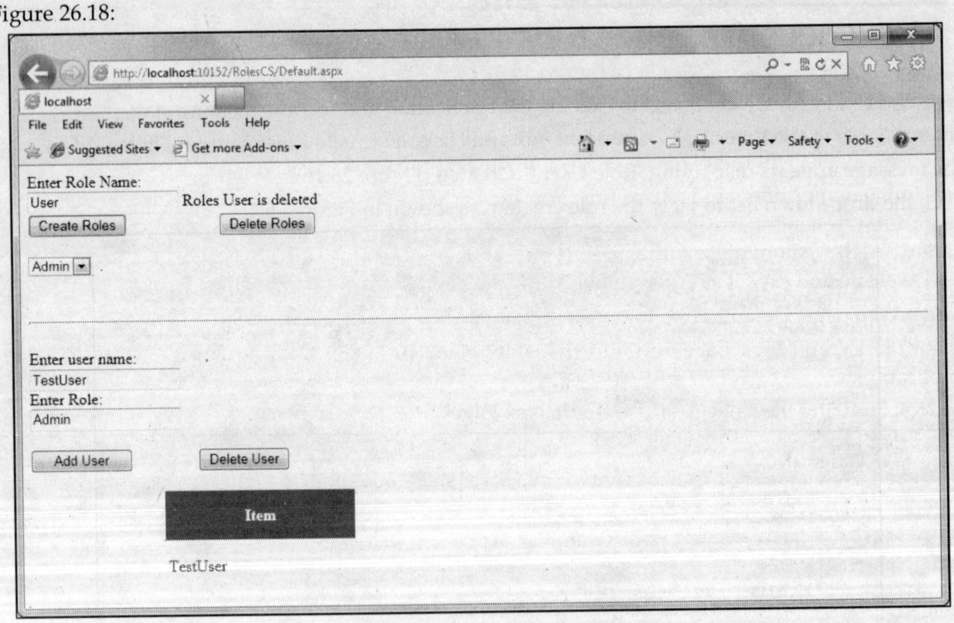

Figure 26.18: Adding the User

12. Enter the name of the user and role in the respective text boxes and click the Delete User button (Figure 26.19).

The Deleted user is not displayed on the Web page, as shown in Figure 26.19:

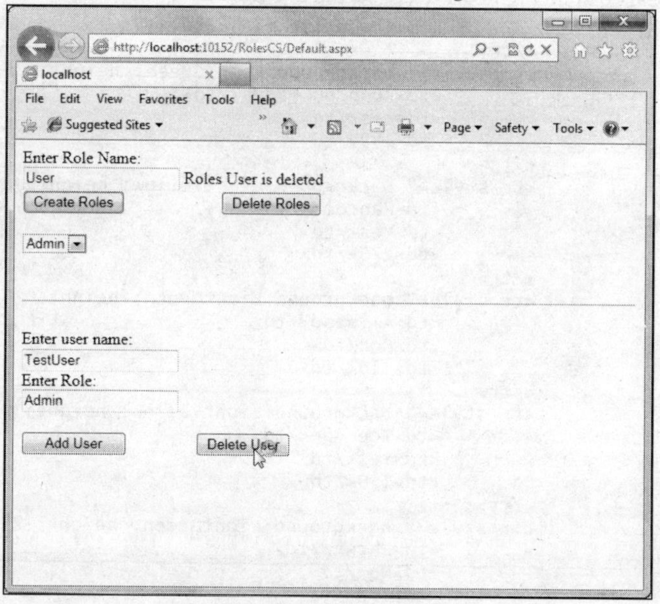

Figure 26.19: Deleting the User

In the application RolesCS, you learned to create and delete `Role` in a website. You also learned to create and delete users corresponding to a `Role. Now, let`'s learn the Anonymous authentication.

Using Anonymous Authentication in ASP.NET

Anonymous authentication is enabled in IIS by default. This implies that a user trying to access a Web page of an ASP.NET application is treated as an anonymous user by IIS. For an anonymous user, IIS does not require any kind of credentials. Many websites and Web applications allow users to access a majority of the Web content anonymously, that is, without the need of any authentication.

You can implement Anonymous authentication in ASP.NET application by setting the mode attribute of the <authentication> element in the Web.config file of the application or site. You can find the code for this application in the AnonymousAuthCS (for C#) and AnonymousAuthVB (for VB) folders. Let's create an ASP.NET website and save it as AnonymousAuthCS by performing the following steps:

1. Add a Web page, Default.aspx, to the AnonymousAuthCS Web application.

   Open the Default.aspx page and add the code, given in Listing 26.3, to add the required controls in the application:

Listing 26.3: Showing the Code for the Default.aspx Page

In VB

```
<%@ Page Language="VB" AutoEventWireup="false" CodeFile="Default.aspx.vb"
  Inherits="_Default" %>
<!DOCTYPE html>
<html xmlns="http://www.w3.org/1999/xhtml">
<head runat="server">
    <title></title>
</head>
<body>
    <form id="form1" runat="server">
    <div>
     <table style="z-index: 150; left: 250px; position: absolute; top:
                          75px; width: 361px; height: 114px;">
                       <tr style=" font-weight: bold">
```

```
                                <td >Movies</td>
                                <td>Available</td>
                                <td>Price (in Rs.)</td>
                        </tr>
                        <tr style=" background:LightGreen; height: 25px">
                                <td>Kung Fu Panda</td>
                                <td>Yes</td>
                                <td>150</td>
                        </tr>
                        <tr style=" background:LightYellow; height: 25px">
                                <td>Hancock</td>
                                <td>Yes</td>
                                <td>175</td>
                        </tr>
                        <tr style=" background:LightGreen; height: 25px">
                                <td>Amistad</td>
                                <td>No</td>
                                <td>110</td>
                        </tr>
                        <tr style=" background:LightYellow; height: 25px">
                                <td>Ice Age</td>
                                <td>Yes</td>
                                <td>150</td>
                        </tr>
                        <tr style=" background:LightGreen; height: 25px">
                                <td>Shrek</td>
                                <td>No</td>
                                <td>170</td>
                        </tr>
                        <tr style=" background:LightYellow; height: 25px">
                                <td>Jerry McGuire</td>
                                <td>Yes</td>
                                <td>155</td>
                        </tr>
                        </table>
        </div>
        </form>
    </body>
    </html>
```

In C#

```
    <%@ Page Language="C#" AutoEventWireup="true" CodeFile="Default.aspx.cs"
      Inherits="_Default" %>
    <!DOCTYPE html>
    <html xmlns="http://www.w3.org/1999/xhtml">
    <head runat="server">
        <title></title>
    </head>
    <body>
        <form id="form1" runat="server">
        <div>
        <table style="z-index: 150; left: 250px; position: absolute; top:
                              75px; width: 361px; height: 114px;">
                        <tr style=" font-weight: bold">
                                <td >Movies</td>
                                <td>Available</td>
                                <td>Price (in Rs.)</td>
                        </tr>
                        <tr style=" background:LightGreen; height: 25px">
                                <td>Kung Fu Panda</td>
                                <td>Yes</td>
                                <td>150</td>
                        </tr>
                        <tr style=" background:LightYellow; height: 25px">
                                <td>Hancock</td>
```

```
                    <td>Yes</td>
                    <td>175</td>
                </tr>
                <tr style=" background:LightGreen; height: 25px">
                    <td>Amistad</td>
                    <td>No</td>
                    <td>110</td>
                </tr>
                <tr style=" background:LightYellow; height: 25px">
                    <td>Ice Age</td>
                    <td>Yes</td>
                    <td>150</td>
                </tr>
                <tr style=" background:LightGreen; height: 25px">
                    <td>Shrek</td>
                    <td>No</td>
                    <td>170</td>
                </tr>
                <tr style=" background:LightYellow; height: 25px">
                    <td>Jerry McGuire</td>
                    <td>Yes</td>
                    <td>155</td>
                </tr>
                </table>
    </div>
    </form>
  </body>
  </html>
```

Anonymous authentication needs to be enabled to allow any user to access the Default.aspx page of the AnonymousAuthCS website. The Anonymous authentication is already enabled in IIS, you only need to enable it in the ASP.NET application.

Open the Web.config file of the application and change the settings of the <authentication> element, as given in the following code:

```
  <authentication mode="None" />
```

With this setting of the mode attribute of the <authentication> element, users are treated anonymously in IIS as well as in the application.

If a user tries to access the Default.aspx page in the Web browser, as shown in Figure 26.20, the IIS and the ASP.NET website do not require authentication to grant access to the user for viewing the page:

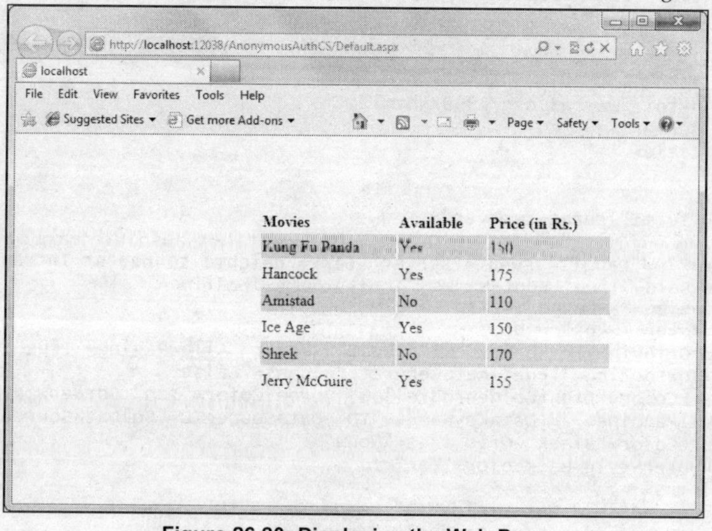

Figure 26.20: Displaying the Web Page

After learning the Anonymous authentication, let's learn the Windows authentication.

Using Windows Authentication in ASP.NET

As you know, Windows authentication is an ideal choice for authentication when you want to host an ASP.NET application on the local computer or Intranet. By default, ASP.NET applications are authenticated using the Windows credentials of the currently logged-in user. You can enable any of the following authentication modes in IIS to implement Windows authentication in an ASP.NET application:

- Anonymous authentication
- Windows authentication (Integrated)
- Basic authentication
- Digest authentication

In many cases, the default authentication, Anonymous authentication, in IIS is used with Windows authentication in ASP.NET. In such cases, IIS identifies users as anonymous and ASP.NET identifies users as Windows users. You can either disable Anonymous authentication in IIS or use the <authorization> element in the Web.config file to deny access to anonymous users.

Now, let's create an ASP.NET website and save it as WindowsAuthCS. You can find the code for this application in the WindowsAuthCS (for C#) and WindowsAuthVB (for VB) folders.

In this website, there are two Web pages, Default.aspx and AddEvent.aspx. The Default.aspx page displays the list of events and the AddEvent.aspx page allows you to add a new event. Perform the following steps to create the WindowsAuthCS website:

1. Add two Web pages, Default.aspx and AddEvent.aspx, in the Web application.
2. Open the Design view of the Default.aspx file and first add a GridView control in the Default.aspx page. Then, add an SQL Server Database item, named EventsData, in the project and specify a table, named events, in the database. Include five columns, named ID, EventName, Place, Time, and CreatedBy. Now, bind the GridView control to a new data source representing the events table in the EventsData database. In addition, enable paging and sorting by using the GridView Tasks.

Now, add the code, given in Listing 26.4, in the Default.aspx page to add the required controls:

Listing 26.4: Showing the Code for the Default.aspx Page

In VB

```
<%@ Page Language="VB" AutoEventWireup="false" CodeFile="Default.aspx.vb"
  Inherits="_Default" %>

<!DOCTYPE html>

<html xmlns="http://www.w3.org/1999/xhtml">
<head runat="server">
    <title></title>
</head>
<body>
    <form id="form1" runat="server">
    <div>
    <asp:Label ID="Label1" runat="server" Text="Welcome to Kogent Intranet"
         Font-Bold="True" Font-Names="Arial" Font-Overline="False"
         Font-Size="X-Large"></asp:Label>
         <br /><br /><br /><br />
         <asp:GridView ID="GridView1" runat="server" AllowPaging="True"
           AllowSorting="True" AutoGenerateColumns="False"
           BackColor="LightGoldenrodYellow" BorderColor="Tan" BorderWidth="1px"
           CellPadding="2" DataKeyNames="ID" DataSourceID="SqlDataSource1"
           ForeColor="Black" GridLines="None">
           <FooterStyle BackColor="Tan" />
         <Columns>
         <asp:BoundField DataField="ID" HeaderText="ID"
           SortExpression="ID" ReadOnly="True" />
```

```
            <asp:BoundField DataField="EventName" HeaderText="EventName"
              SortExpression="EventName" />
            <asp:BoundField DataField="Place" HeaderText="Place"
              SortExpression="Place" />
            <asp:BoundField DataField="SubmitTime" HeaderText="Time"
            SortExpression="SubmitTime" ControlStyle-Width="500px"/>
            <asp:BoundField DataField="CreatedBy" HeaderText="CreatedBy"
              SortExpression="CreatedBy" />
            </Columns>
            <PagerStyle BackColor="PaleGoldenrod" ForeColor="DarkSlateBlue"
              HorizontalAlign="Center" />
            <SelectedRowStyle BackColor="DarkSlateBlue" ForeColor="GhostWhite" />
            <HeaderStyle BackColor="Tan" Font-Bold="True" />
            <AlternatingRowStyle BackColor="PaleGoldenrod" />
            </asp:GridView>
            <asp:SqlDataSource ID="SqlDataSource1" runat="server"
              ConflictDetection="CompareAllValues"
               ConnectionString="<%$ ConnectionStrings:puneetConnectionString %>"
                     SelectCommand="SELECT [EventName], [Place], [SubmitTime], [CreatedBy],
            [ID] FROM [Events]" >
            </asp:SqlDataSource>
            <br /><br />
            <asp:HyperLink ID="HyperLink1" runat="server" NavigateUrl="~/AddEvent.aspx">
            Add New Event</asp:HyperLink>
        </div>
        </form>
    </body>
    </html>
```

In C#

```
    <%@ Page Language="C#" AutoEventWireup="true" CodeFile="Default.aspx.cs"
      Inherits="_Default" %>
    <!DOCTYPE html>
    <html xmlns="http://www.w3.org/1999/xhtml">
    <head runat="server">
        <title></title>
    </head>
    <body>
        <form id="form1" runat="server">
        <div>
         <asp:Label ID="Label1" runat="server" Text="Welcome to Kogent Intranet"
            Font-Bold="True" Font-Names="Arial" Font-Overline="False"
            Font-Size="X-Large"></asp:Label>
            <br /><br /><br /><br />
            <asp:GridView ID="GridView1" runat="server" AllowPaging="True"
              AllowSorting="True" AutoGenerateColumns="False"
              BackColor="LightGoldenrodYellow" BorderColor="Tan" BorderWidth="1px"
              CellPadding="2" DataKeyNames="ID" DataSourceID="SqlDataSource1"
              ForeColor="Black" GridLines="None">
              <FooterStyle BackColor="Tan" />
            <Columns>
            <asp:BoundField DataField="ID" HeaderText="ID"
              SortExpression="ID" ReadOnly="True" />
            <asp:BoundField DataField="EventName" HeaderText="EventName"
              SortExpression="EventName" />
            <asp:BoundField DataField="Place" HeaderText="Place"
              SortExpression="Place" />
            <asp:BoundField DataField="SubmitTime" HeaderText="Time"
            SortExpression="SubmitTime" ControlStyle-Width="500px"/>
            <asp:BoundField DataField="CreatedBy" HeaderText="CreatedBy"
              SortExpression="CreatedBy" />
            </Columns>
            <PagerStyle BackColor="PaleGoldenrod" ForeColor="DarkSlateBlue"
              HorizontalAlign="Center" />
            <SelectedRowStyle BackColor="DarkSlateBlue" ForeColor="GhostWhite" />
            <HeaderStyle BackColor="Tan" Font-Bold="True" />
```

```
            <AlternatingRowStyle BackColor="PaleGoldenrod" />
            </asp:GridView>
            <asp:SqlDataSource ID="SqlDataSource1" runat="server"
              ConflictDetection="CompareAllValues"
               ConnectionString="<%$ ConnectionStrings:puneetConnectionString %>"
                    SelectCommand="SELECT [EventName], [Place], [SubmitTime], [CreatedBy],
            [ID] FROM [Event]" >
            </asp:SqlDataSource>
            <br /><br />
            <asp:HyperLink ID="HyperLink1" runat="server" NavigateUrl="~/AddEvent.aspx">
            Add New Event</asp:HyperLink>
        </div>
        </form>
    </body>
    </html>
```

Now, add the code given in Listing 26.5 in the AddEvent.aspx page to add the required controls:

Listing 26.5: Showing the Code for the AddEvent.aspx Page

In VB

```
<%@ Page Language="VB" AutoEventWireup="false" CodeFile="AddEvent.aspx.vb"
   Inherits="AddEvent" %>
<!DOCTYPE html>
<html xmlns="http://www.w3.org/1999/xhtml">
<head runat="server">
    <title></title>
</head>
<body>
    <form id="form1" runat="server">
    <div>
    <asp:Label ID="Label1" runat="server" Text="Welcome to Kogent Intranet"
         Font-Bold="True" Font-Names="Arial" Font-Overline="False"
         Font-Size="X-Large"></asp:Label>
         <br /><br />
         <asp:Label ID="Label2" runat="server" Text="Please provide details of new event"
         Font-Bold="True" Font-Names="Arial"></asp:Label>
         <br /><br />
         <table width="100%" border="0">
         <tr>
                 <td class="style1">
                 <asp:Label ID="Label3" runat="server" Text="Event ID:" Font-Bold="True"
                 Font-Names="Arial"></asp:Label></td>
                 <td width="1%"> </td>
                 <td width="79%">
                 <asp:TextBox ID="ID" runat="server"></asp:TextBox></td>
         </tr>
         <tr>
                 <td class="style1"> </td>
                 <td width="1%"> </td>
                 <td width="79%"> </td>
         </tr>
         <tr>
                 <td class="style1">
                 <asp:Label ID="Label4" runat="server" Text="Event Name:" Font-Bold="True"
                 Font-Names="Arial"></asp:Label></td>
                 <td width="1%"> </td>
                 <td width="79%">
                 <asp:TextBox ID="name" runat="server"></asp:TextBox></td>
         </tr>
         <tr>
                 <td class="style1"> </td>
                 <td width="1%"> </td>
                 <td width="79%"> </td>
         </tr>
         <tr>
                 <td class="style1">
```

```
            <asp:Label ID="Label5" runat="server" Text="Event Time:" Font-Bold="True"
            Font-Names="Arial"></asp:Label></td>
            <td width="1%"> </td>
            <td width="79%">
            <asp:TextBox ID="time" runat="server"></asp:TextBox></td>
    </tr>
    <tr>
            <td class="style1"> </td>
            <td width="1%"> </td>
            <td width="79%"> </td>
    </tr>
    <tr>
            <td class="style1">
            <asp:Label ID="Label6" runat="server" Text="Event Location:" Font-
            Bold="True"
            Font-Names="Arial"></asp:Label></td>
            <td width="1%"> </td>
            <td width="79%">
            <asp:TextBox ID="location" runat="server"></asp:TextBox></td>
    </tr>
    <tr>
            <td class="style1"> </td>
            <td width="1%"> </td>
            <td width="79%"> </td>
    </tr>
    <tr>
            <td class="style1">
            <asp:Label ID="Label7" runat="server" Text="Created By:" Font-Bold="True"
            Font-Names="Arial"></asp:Label></td>
            <td width="1%"> </td>
            <td width="79%">
            <asp:TextBox ID="user" runat="server" Enabled="false" Height="111px"
            TextMode="MultiLine" Width="305px"></asp:TextBox></td>
    </tr>
    <tr>
            <td class="style1"> </td>
            <td width="1%"> </td>
            <td width="79%">
            <br />
                <asp:Button ID="Button1" runat="server" Text="Insert Record"
            Width="119px" />
            <asp:SqlDataSource ID="SqlDataSource1" runat="server"
            ConflictDetection="CompareAllValues" ConnectionString="<%$
             ConnectionStrings:puneetConnectionString %>"
            InsertCommand="INSERT INTO [Events] ([ID], [EventName], [Place],
            [SubmitTime],
            [CreatedBy]) VALUES (@ID, @EventName, @Place, @SubmitTime, @CreatedBy)" >

            <InsertParameters>
            <asp:ControlParameter ControlID="ID" Name="ID" PropertyName="Text"
             Type="Int32" />
                    <asp:ControlParameter ControlID="name" Name="EventName"
                    PropertyName="Text" Type="String" />
                    <asp:ControlParameter ControlID="location" Name="Place"
                     PropertyName="Text" Type="String" />
                    <asp:ControlParameter ControlID="time" Name="SubmitTime"
                    PropertyName="Text" Type="String" />
                    <asp:ControlParameter ControlID="user" Name="CreatedBy"
                    PropertyName="Text" Type="String" />
            </InsertParameters>
            </asp:SqlDataSource>
            <asp:Label ID="Label8" runat="server"></asp:Label>
            <br /><br />
            <asp:HyperLink ID="HyperLink1" runat="server"
              NavigateUrl="~/Default.aspx">Click
            here to see the list of events</asp:HyperLink></td>
    </tr>
```

```
            </table>
        </div>
        </form>
    </body>
    </html>
```

In C#

```
    <%@ Page Language="C#" AutoEventWireup="true" CodeFile="AddEvent.aspx.cs"
      Inherits="AddEvent" %>
    <!DOCTYPE html>
    <html xmlns="http://www.w3.org/1999/xhtml">
    <head runat="server">
        <title></title>
    </head>
    <body>
        <form id="form1" runat="server">
        <div>
         <asp:Label ID="Label1" runat="server" Text="Welcome to Kogent Intranet"
            Font-Bold="True" Font-Names="Arial" Font-Overline="False"
            Font-Size="X-Large"></asp:Label>
            <br /><br />
            <asp:Label ID="Label2" runat="server" Text="Please provide details of new event"
            Font-Bold="True" Font-Names="Arial"></asp:Label>
            <br /><br />
            <table width="100%" border="0">
            <tr>
                    <td class="style1">
                    <asp:Label ID="Label3" runat="server" Text="Event ID:" Font-Bold="True"
                    Font-Names="Arial"></asp:Label></td>
                    <td width="1%"> </td>
                    <td width="79%">
                    <asp:TextBox ID="ID" runat="server"></asp:TextBox></td>
            </tr>
            <tr>
                    <td class="style1"> </td>
                    <td width="1%"> </td>
                    <td width="79%"> </td>
            </tr>
            <tr>
                    <td class="style1">
                    <asp:Label ID="Label4" runat="server" Text="Event Name:" Font-Bold="True"
                    Font-Names="Arial"></asp:Label></td>
                    <td width="1%"> </td>
                    <td width="79%">
                    <asp:TextBox ID="name" runat="server"></asp:TextBox></td>
            </tr>
            <tr>
                    <td class="style1"> </td>
                    <td width="1%"> </td>
                    <td width="79%"> </td>
            </tr>
            <tr>
                    <td class="style1">
                    <asp:Label ID="Label5" runat="server" Text="Event Time:" Font-Bold="True"
                    Font-Names="Arial"></asp:Label></td>
                    <td width="1%"> </td>
                    <td width="79%">
                    <asp:TextBox ID="time" runat="server"></asp:TextBox></td>
            </tr>
```

```
<tr>
        <td class="style1"> </td>
        <td width="1%"> </td>
        <td width="79%"> </td>
</tr>
<tr>
        <td class="style1">
        <asp:Label ID="Label6" runat="server" Text="Event Location:" Font-
        Bold="True"
        Font-Names="Arial"></asp:Label></td>
        <td width="1%"> </td>
        <td width="79%">
        <asp:TextBox ID="location" runat="server"></asp:TextBox></td>
</tr>
<tr>
        <td class="style1"> </td>
        <td width="1%"> </td>
        <td width="79%"> </td>
</tr>
<tr>
        <td class="style1">
        <asp:Label ID="Label7" runat="server" Text="Created By:" Font-Bold="True"
        Font-Names="Arial"></asp:Label></td>
        <td width="1%"> </td>
        <td width="79%">
        <asp:TextBox ID="user" runat="server" Enabled="false" Height="111px"
        TextMode="MultiLine" Width="315px"></asp:TextBox></td>
</tr>
<tr>
        <td class="style1"> </td>
        <td width="1%"> </td>
        <td width="79%">
        <br />
            <asp:Button ID="Button1" runat="server" Text="Insert Record"
        Width="119px"
           OnClick="Button1_Click" />
        <asp:SqlDataSource ID="SqlDataSource1" runat="server"
        ConflictDetection="CompareAllValues" ConnectionString="<%$
         ConnectionStrings:puneetConnectionString %>"
   InsertCommand="INSERT INTO [Events] ([ID], [EventName], [Place], [SubmitTime],
        [CreatedBy]) VALUES (@ID, @EventName, @Place, @SubmitTime, @CreatedBy)" >

        <InsertParameters>
                <asp:ControlParameter ControlID="ID" Name="ID"
                PropertyName="Text"
                 Type="Int32" />
                <asp:ControlParameter ControlID="name" Name="EventName"
                PropertyName="Text" Type="String" />
                <asp:ControlParameter ControlID="location" Name="Place"
                PropertyName="Text" Type="String" />
                <asp:ControlParameter ControlID="time" Name="SubmitTime"
                PropertyName="Text" Type="String" />
                <asp:ControlParameter ControlID="user" Name="CreatedBy"
                PropertyName="Text" Type="String" />
        </InsertParameters>
        </asp:SqlDataSource>
        <asp:Label ID="Label8" runat="server"></asp:Label>
        <br /><br />
        <asp:HyperLink ID="HyperLink1" runat="server"
          NavigateUrl="~/Default.aspx">Click
        here to see the list of events</asp:HyperLink></td>
```

```
            </tr>
            </table>
        </div>
        </form>
    </body>
    </html>
```

3. Add the code given in Listing 26.6 in the code-behind file of the AddEvent.aspx page to use the WindowsPrincipal and WindowsIdentity objects:

Listing 26.6: Showing the Code for the Code-Behind File of the AddEvent.aspx Page

In VB

```
Imports System.Web.Security
Imports System.Web
Imports System.Security.Principal
Partial Class AddEvent
    Inherits System.Web.UI.Page
    Protected Sub Page_Load(sender As Object, e As EventArgs) Handles
         Me.Load
        time.Text = DateTime.Now.ToString()
        Dim WP As WindowsPrincipal = CType(HttpContext.Current.User, WindowsPrincipal)
        Dim WI As WindowsIdentity = CType(WP.Identity, WindowsIdentity)
        Dim winUser As String = "Name: " & WI.Name
        winUser &= Constants.vbLf & "Authentication Type: " & WI.AuthenticationType
        winUser &= Constants.vbLf & "Authenticated: " & (If((WI.IsAuthenticated), "Yes",
         "No"))
        user.Text = winUser
    End Sub
    Protected Sub Button1_Click(sender As Object, e As EventArgs)
         Handles Button1.Click
        SqlDataSource1.Insert()
        ID.Text = ""
        name.Text = ""
        time.Text = ""
        location.Text = ""
        Label8.Text = "1 new event created"
    End Sub
End Class
```

In C#

```
using System;
using System.Collections.Generic;
using System.Linq;
using System.Web;
using System.Web.UI;
using System.Web.UI.WebControls;
using System.Security.Principal;
public partial class AddEvent : System.Web.UI.Page
{
    protected void Page_Load(object sender, EventArgs e)
    {
         time.Text = DateTime.Now.ToString();
        WindowsPrincipal WP = (WindowsPrincipal)HttpContext.Current.User;
        WindowsIdentity WI = (WindowsIdentity)WP.Identity;
        string winUser = "Name: " + WI.Name;
        winUser += "\nAuthentication Type: " + WI.AuthenticationType;
        winUser += "\nAuthenticated: " + ((WI.IsAuthenticated) ? "Yes" : "No");
        user.Text = winUser;
    }
    protected void Button1_Click(object sender, EventArgs e)
```

```
        {
            SqlDataSource1.Insert();
            ID.Text = "";
            name.Text = "";
            location.Text = "";
            Label8.Text = "1 new event created";
        }
    }
```

4. Enable Windows authentication in IIS as well as in the ASP.NET application. For this, open the IIS Manager, select the application in the Connections pane on the left, and double-click the Authentication icon in the middle pane. Right-click the Anonymous Authentication option and select the Disable link to disable the Anonymous authentication. Right-click the Windows Authentication option and select Enable to enable Windows authentication. IIS will now authenticate only valid Windows users.

In the ASP.NET application, the mode of the <authentication> element is set to Windows by default; therefore, you do not need to explicitly enable it as you did in IIS.

NOTE

In case you have not disabled Anonymous authentication in IIS and have enabled the Windows authentication mode in the Web.config file, you need to use the <authorization> element, as given in the following code:

```
<authorization>
   <deny users="?" />
</authorization>
```

In the preceding code, the question mark (?) indicates that all the anonymous users are denied access to the application. If the user is not authenticated then the login fails and the application will not run.

5. Set the AddEvent.aspx page as a start page and press the F5 key on the keyboard to view the output.
6. Enter the values in the text boxes and click the Insert Record button to enter the records in the database, as shown in Figure 26.21:

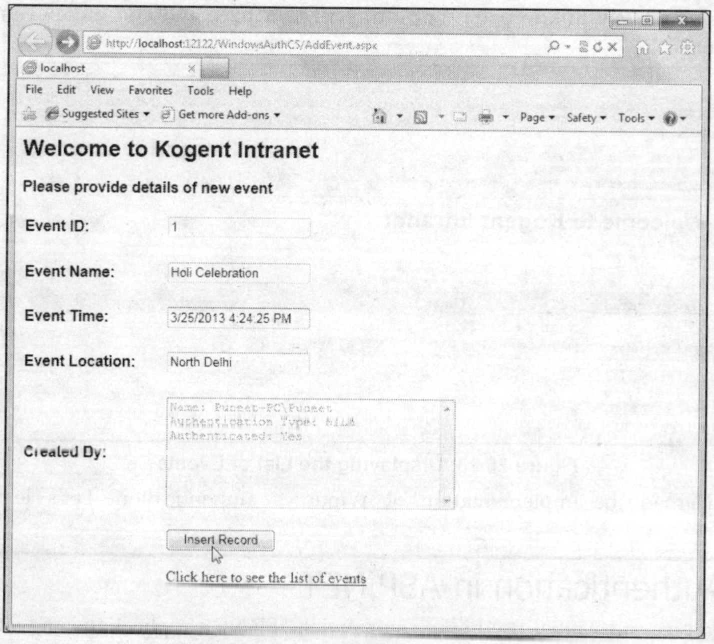

Figure 26.21: Inserting the Events

7. Click the Click here to see the list of events link to view the events from the database, as shown in Figure 26.22:

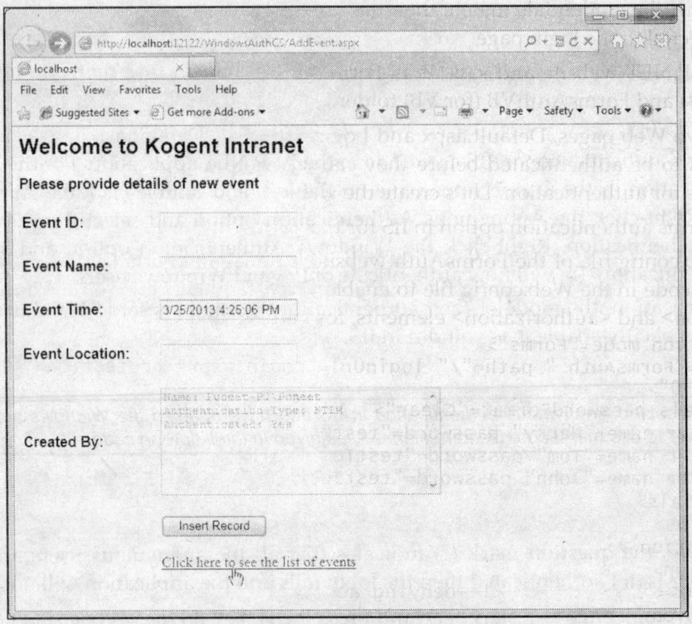

Figure 26.22: Clicking the Link

8. The Default.aspx page appears displaying the events entered in the database (Figure 26.23).
9. Click the Add New Event link to open the AddEvent.aspx page and add more events in the database, as shown in Figure 26.23:

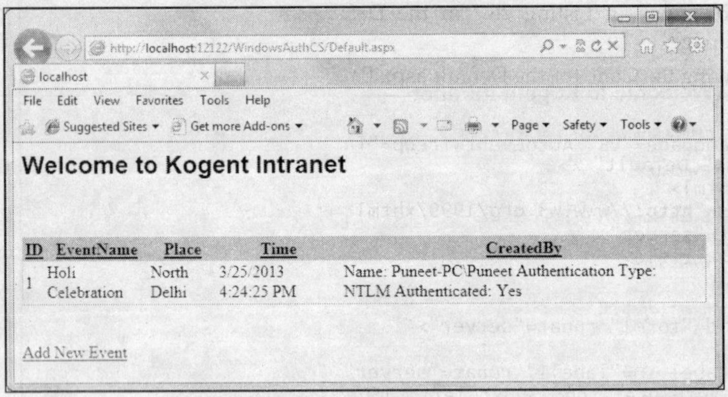

Figure 26.23: Displaying the List of Events

Now, you have learned the implementation of Windows authentication. Let's learn about the Forms authentication.

Using Forms Authentication in ASP.NET

Forms authentication has substantial use in the commercial ASP.NET applications and sites, such as those that pertain to online shopping, banking, and e-mailing. In Forms authentication, when a user requests for a protected Web page in the ASP.NET application or site and passes through IIS, the ASP.NET application checks if the user is unauthenticated. In the case of an unauthenticated user, the user is redirected to a login page where the user needs to provide the credentials (user name and password). The credentials provided by the user are then validated against the credentials stored in a given database or the Web.config file of the ASP.NET application or site. If the credentials match, then the user gets access to the requested Web page; otherwise, the user is again redirected to the login page.

Let's create an ASP.NET website and save it as FormsAuth. You can find the code for this application in the FormsAuth (for C#) and FormsAuthVB (for VB) folder.

The website has two Web pages, Default.aspx and Login.aspx. The Default.aspx page is the protected Web page that requires users to be authenticated before they can access it and Login.aspx is the login page where users provide credentials for authentication. Let's create the website by performing the following steps:

1. Enable the Forms authentication option in IIS for the FormsAuth website.
2. Open the Web.config file of the FormsAuth website for enabling Forms authentication in the website. Add the following code in the Web.config file to enable Forms authentication in the application, and change the <authentication> and <authorization> elements, for both VB and C#:

```
<authentication mode="Forms">
<forms name="FormsAuth " path="/" loginUrl="Login.aspx" protection="All"
  timeout="30">
  <credentials passwordFormat="Clear">
        <user name="Harry" password="testHarry" />
        <user name="Tom" password="testTom" />
        <user name="John" password="testJohn" />
  </credentials>
</forms>
</authentication>
<authorization>
  <deny users="?"/>          <!--denying access to anonymous users-->
</authorization>
```

The mode attribute of the <authentication> element is set to Forms. The <forms> element contains a <credentials> element that contains three <user> elements that specify the valid user names and passwords. In the <authorization> element, the <deny> element is used to deny access to the anonymous users. Therefore, only authenticated users have access to the Default.aspx page.

3. Add the code given in Listing 26.7 in the Default.aspx page to design the user interface (UI) of the Default.aspx page:

Listing 26.7: Showing the Code for the Default.aspx Page

In VB

```
<%@ Page Language="VB" AutoEventWireup="false" CodeFile="Default.aspx.vb"
  Inherits="_Default" %>
<!DOCTYPE html>
<html xmlns="http://www.w3.org/1999/xhtml">
<head runat="server">
    <title></title>
</head>
<body>
    <form id="form1" runat="server">
    <div>
     <asp:Label ID="label1" runat="server" style="z-index: 100; position:
          absolute; top: 30px; left: 150px; width: 200px"/>
        <br /><br /><br/>
        <asp:Label ID="label2" runat="server" Text="Conference in progress..."
        style="z-index: 100; position: absolute; top: 90px; left: 350px; width: 200px"/>
        <br/>
        <br/>
        <asp:Button ID="button1" runat="server" Text="Log out"
        style="z-index: 100; left: 350px; position: absolute; top: 200px; width: 200px;"
          />
    </div>
    </form>
</body>
</html>
```

In C#

```
<%@ Page Language="C#" AutoEventWireup="true" CodeFile="Default.aspx.cs"
  Inherits="_Default" %>
<!DOCTYPE html>
<html xmlns="http://www.w3.org/1999/xhtml">
<head runat="server">
    <title></title>
</head>
<body>
    <form id="form1" runat="server">
    <div>
    <asp:Label ID="label1" runat="server" style="z-index: 100; position:
           absolute; top: 30px; left: 150px; width: 200px"/>
         <br /><br /><br/>
         <asp:Label ID="label2" runat="server" Text="Conference in progress..."
         style="z-index: 100; position: absolute; top: 90px; left: 350px; width: 200px"/>
         <br/>
         <br/>
         <asp:Button ID="button1" runat="server" Text="Log out" OnClick="button1_Click"
         style="z-index: 100; left: 350px; position: absolute; top: 200px; width: 200px;"
           />

    </div>
    </form>
</body>
</html>
```

4. Add the code, given in Listing 26.8, in the code-behind file of the Default.aspx page:

Listing 26.8: Showing the Code for the Code-Behind File of the Default.aspx Page

In VB

```
Partial Class _Default
    Inherits System.Web.UI.Page
    Protected Sub button1_Click(sender As Object, e As EventArgs)
  Handles
  button1.Click
        Response.Redirect("Login.aspx")
    End Sub
    Protected Sub Page_Load(sender As Object, e As EventArgs) Handles
         Me.Load
        label1.Text = "Welcome, " & HttpContext.Current.User.Identity.Name
    End Sub
End Class
```

In C#

```
using System;
using System.Collections.Generic;
using System.Linq;
using System.Web;
using System.Web.UI;
using System.Web.UI.WebControls;
public partial class _Default : System.Web.UI.Page
{
    protected void Page_Load(object sender, EventArgs e)
    {
        label1.Text = "Welcome, " + HttpContext.Current.User.Identity.Name;
    }
    protected void button1_Click(object sender, EventArgs e)
    {
        Response.Redirect("Login.aspx");
    }
}
```

5. Open the Login.aspx file and add the code, given in Listing 26.9, to add the required controls for the application:

Listing 26.9: Showing the Code for the Login.aspx Page

In VB

```
<%@ Page Language="VB" AutoEventWireup="false" CodeFile="Login.aspx.vb" Inherits="Login"
   %>
<!DOCTYPE html>
<html xmlns="http://www.w3.org/1999/xhtml">
<head runat="server">
    <title></title>
</head>
<body>
    <form id="form1" runat="server">
    <div>
   <table style="z-index: 150; left: 250px; position: absolute; top: 75px; width:
           361px; height: 114px;">
        <tr>
                <td style="height: 25px">Enter User Name:</td>
                <td style="height: 25px"><asp:TextBox ID="textBox1" runat="server"
                  Width="126px"/></td>
                <td style="height: 25px;">
                <asp:RequiredFieldValidator ID="RequiredFieldValidator1"
                  ControlToValidate="textBox1" Display="Static" ErrorMessage="*"
                  runat="server"/>
                </td>
        </tr>
        <tr>
                <td style="height: 25px">Enter Password:</td>
                <td style="height: 25px"><asp:TextBox ID="textBox2" runat="server"
                  TextMode="Password"/></td>
                <td style="height: 25px;"><asp:RequiredFieldValidator
                  ID="RequiredFieldValidator2" ControlToValidate="textBox2"
                  Display="Static" ErrorMessage="*" runat="server"/>
                </td>
        </tr>
        <tr>
                <td style="height: 25px" colspan="3">
                <asp:CheckBox ID="checkBox1" runat="server" Text="Persistent
                  Cookie"/></td>
        </tr>
        <tr><td style="height: 25px"></td></tr>
        <tr>
                <td style="height: 25px"></td>
                <td style="height: 25px; left: 500px">
                <asp:Button ID="button1" Text="Login" runat="server"
                  Width="75px" />
                </td>
                <td></td>
        </tr>
        <tr><td style="height: 25px"></td></tr>
        <tr>
                <td colspan="3"><asp:Label ID="label1" runat="server" Text=""/></td>
        </tr>
        </table>
    </div>
    </form>
</body>
</html>
```

In C#

```
<%@ Page Language="C#" AutoEventWireup="true" CodeFile="Login.aspx.cs" Inherits="Login" %>
<!DOCTYPE html>
<html xmlns="http://www.w3.org/1999/xhtml">
```

```
<head runat="server">
    <title></title>
</head>
<body>
    <form id="form1" runat="server">
    <div>
    <table style="z-index: 150; left: 250px; position: absolute; top: 75px; width:
          361px; height: 114px;">
        <tr>
                <td style="height: 25px">Enter User Name:</td>
                <td style="height: 25px"><asp:TextBox ID="textBox1" runat="server"
                  Width="126px"/></td>
                <td style="height: 25px;">
                <asp:RequiredFieldValidator ID="RequiredFieldValidator1"
                  ControlToValidate="textBox1" Display="Static" ErrorMessage="*"
                  runat="server"/>
                </td>
        </tr>
        <tr>
                <td style="height: 25px">Enter Password:</td>
                <td style="height: 25px"><asp:TextBox ID="textBox2" runat="server"
                  TextMode="Password"/></td>
                <td style="height: 25px;"><asp:RequiredFieldValidator
                  ID="RequiredFieldValidator2" ControlToValidate="textBox2"
                  Display="Static" ErrorMessage="*" runat="server"/>
                </td>
        </tr>
        <tr>
                <td style="height: 25px" colspan="3">
                <asp:CheckBox ID="checkBox1" runat="server" Text="Persistent
                  Cookie"/></td>
        </tr>
        <tr><td style="height: 25px"></td></tr>
        <tr>
                <td style="height: 25px"></td>
                <td style="height: 25px; left: 500px">
                <asp:Button ID="button1" Text="Login" runat="server"
                  OnClick="login_Click" Width="75px" />
                </td>
                <td></td>
        </tr>
        <tr><td style="height: 25px"></td></tr>
        <tr>
                <td colspan="3"><asp:Label ID="label1" runat="server" Text=""/></td>
        </tr>
        </table>
    </div>
    </form>
</body>
</html>
```

Now, add the code, given in Listing 26.10, in the code-behind file of the Login.aspx page:

Listing 26.10: Showing the Code for the Code-Behind File of the Login.aspx Page

In VB

```
Partial Class Login
    Inherits System.Web.UI.Page
    Protected Sub login_Click(sender As Object, e As EventArgs) Handles
  button1.Click
        If FormsAuthentication.Authenticate(textBox1.Text, textBox2.Text) Then
            FormsAuthentication.RedirectFromLoginPage(textBox1.Text, checkBox1.Checked)
        Else
            label1.Text = "<b>Invalid Credentials! Please enter credentials again."
        End If
    End Sub
```

```
    Protected Sub Page_Load(sender As Object, e As EventArgs) Handles
  Me.Load
    End Sub
End Class
```

In C#

```
using System;
using System.Collections.Generic;
using System.Linq;
using System.Web;
using System.Web.UI;
using System.Web.UI.WebControls;
using System.Web.Security;
public partial class Login : System.Web.UI.Page
{
    protected void Page_Load(object sender, EventArgs e)
    {
    }
    protected void login_Click(object sender, EventArgs e)
    {
        if (FormsAuthentication.Authenticate(textBox1.Text, textBox2.Text))
        {
            FormsAuthentication.RedirectFromLoginPage(textBox1.Text, checkBox1.Checked);
        }
        else
        {
            label1.Text = "<b>Invalid Credentials! Please enter credentials again.";
        }
    }
}
```

6. Press the F5 key on the keyboard to execute the application and to view the output.
7. Enter the user name and password in their respective text boxes and select the Persistent Cookie check box (Figure 26.24).
8. Click the Login button to login, as shown in Figure 26.24:

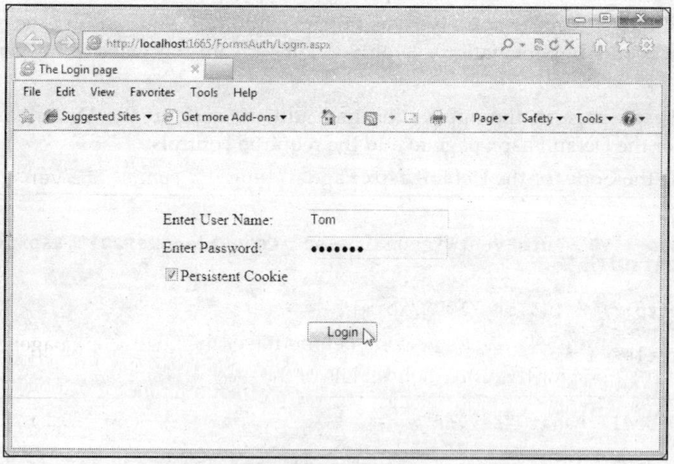

Figure 26.24: Entering the Credentials

Default.aspx page appears (Figure 26.25).

9. Click the Log out button to open the Login.aspx again, as shown in Figure 26.25:

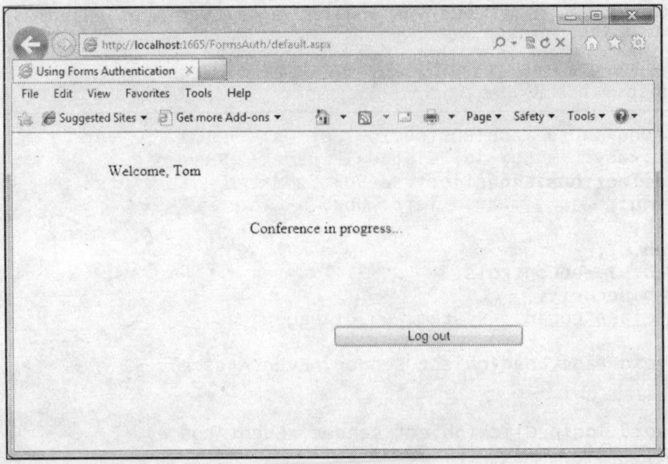

Figure 26.25: Displaying the Default.aspx Page to Authenticated Users

After learning the Forms authentication, let's learn Impersonation in ASP.NET applications.

Using Impersonation in ASP.NET Applications

Impersonation in ASP.NET is a process in which an ASP.NET application poses as an anonymous or authenticated user to gain access to a resource on the Web server. Impersonation is helpful when the account (NETWORK SERVICE in IIS 7.5 by default) under which the ASP.NET application runs does not have the necessary permissions to access the resource. The application can access the resource by impersonating as a Windows user that has the necessary permissions. In ASP.NET, you can implement impersonation either in the Web.config file or through code by using the WindowsIdentity.Impersonate() method. Now, let's demonstrate how to implement impersonation in an ASP.NET application. For this, create a folder, named MyFolder, in the D: drive of the computer and store some files in it.

Now, let's create an ASP.NET website and save it as ImpersonationCS. You can find the code for this application in the ImpersonationCS and ImpersonationVB folders. Let's create the website by performing the following steps:

1. Add the Default.aspx page in the application and add the code in the Default.aspx page. Listing 26.11 shows the code for the Default.aspx page to add the required controls:

Listing 26.11: Showing the Code for the Default.aspx Page

In VB

```
<%@ Page Language="VB" AutoEventWireup="false" CodeFile="Default.aspx.vb"
  Inherits="_Default" %>
<!DOCTYPE html>
<html xmlns="http://www.w3.org/1999/xhtml">
<head runat="server">
    <title></title>
</head>
<body>
    <form id="form1" runat="server">
    <div>
    <asp:Label ID="Label1" runat="server" Font-Bold="True" Font-Size="Large"></asp:Label>
          <asp:Label ID="Label2" runat="server" Font-Bold="True" Font-Size="Large"
         Font-Underline="True"></asp:Label>
         <br /><br />
         <strong>Click the button to fill the list box with file names</strong><br />
         <strong>
         <br />
         <br />
```

```
                  &nb
sp;               &
nbsp;               
;               &nb
sp;               &
nbsp; 
            </strong> <asp:Button ID="Button1" runat="server" Text="Fill the List" />
             <asp:ListBox id="ListBox1" runat="server"
            style="z-index: 100; left: 249px; position: absolute; top: 175px; height: 140px;
              width: 334px; margin-left: 0px;"></asp:ListBox>
            </div>
        </form>
    </body>
    </html>
```

In C#

```
    <%@ Page Language="C#" AutoEventWireup="true" CodeFile="Default.aspx.cs"
      Inherits="_Default" %>
    <!DOCTYPE html>
    <html xmlns="http://www.w3.org/1999/xhtml">
    <head runat="server">
        <title></title>
    </head>
    <body>
        <form id="form1" runat="server">
        <div>
            <asp:Label ID="Label1" runat="server" Font-Bold="True" Font-
            Size="Large"></asp:Label>
             <asp:Label ID="Label2" runat="server" Font-Bold="True" Font-Size="Large"
            Font Underline="True"></asp:Label>
            <br /><br />
            <strong>Click the button to fill the list box with file names</strong><br />
            <strong>
            <br />
            <br />
                  &nb
sp;               &
nbsp;               
;               &nb
sp;               &
nbsp; 
            </strong> <asp:Button ID="Button1" runat="server" Text="Fill the List"
              OnClick="Button1_Click" />
             <asp:ListBox id="ListBox1" runat="server"
            style="z-index: 100; left: 249px; position: absolute; top: 175px; height: 140px;
              width: 334px; margin-left: 0px;"></asp:ListBox>
        </div>
        </form>
    </body>
    </html>
```

2. Add the code, given in Listing 26.12, in the code behind file of the Default.aspx page:

Listing 26.12: Showing the Code for the Code-Behind File of the Default.aspx Page

In VB

```
    Imports System.IO
    Imports System.Web.Security
    Imports System.Security.Principal
    Partial Class _Default
        Inherits System.Web.UI.Page
        Protected Sub Button1_Click(sender As Object, e As EventArgs)
            Handles Button1.Click
            Label2.Text = "Impersonated account: " & WindowsIdentity.GetCurrent().Name
            Dim directory As New DirectoryInfo("D:\MyFolder")
            Dim files() As FileInfo = directory.GetFiles("*.*")
            For Each f As FileInfo In files
                ListBox1.Items.Add(f.FullName)
```

```
        Next f
    End Sub
    Protected Sub Page_Load(sender As Object, e As EventArgs) Handles
  Me.Load
        Label1.Text = "Welcome, " & HttpContext.Current.User.Identity.Name
    End Sub
End Class
```

In C#

```
using System;
using System.Collections.Generic;
using System.Linq;
using System.Web;
using System.Web.UI;
using System.Web.UI.WebControls;
using System.IO;
using System.Security.Principal;
public partial class _Default : System.Web.UI.Page
{
    protected void Page_Load(object sender, EventArgs e)
    {
        Label1.Text = "Welcome, " + HttpContext.Current.User.Identity.Name;
    }
    protected void Button1_Click(object sender, EventArgs e)
    {
        Label2.Text = "Impersonated account: " + WindowsIdentity.GetCurrent().Name;
        DirectoryInfo directory = new DirectoryInfo(@"D:\MyFolder");
        FileInfo[] files = directory.GetFiles("*.*");
        foreach (FileInfo f in files)
        {
            ListBox1.Items.Add(f.FullName);
        }
    }
}
```

In the preceding code for VB and C#, directives to the System.IO and System.Security.Principal namespaces are added. In the Page_Load() method, the value of HttpContext.Current.User.Identity.Name property is displayed in Label1. When the user clicks Button1, Label2 displays the impersonated account, i.e. the account under which the ImpersonationCS application runs. This account is retrieved from the Name property of the WindowsIdentity object that is returned by the WindowsIdentity.GetCurrent() method. The GetCurrent() method returns the current Windows user. The DirectoryInfo and FileInfo classes are used to retrieve and display the names of the files in the MyFolder folder. The file names are displayed in ListBox1.

3. Now, open the Web.config file in the ImpersonationCS application to enable impersonation in the Web.config file. Add the following code in the <system.web> element:

```
<identity impersonate="true"/>
```

In this code, the <identity> element is added to the Web.config file. The impersonate attribute of the <identity> element is set to true, allowing the application to impersonate a Windows user. The Windows user that the application impersonates is determined at run time, that is, when a user passes the authentication in IIS. To configure impersonation in IIS, open the IIS Manager, select the ImpersonationCS application in the Connections pane, and double-click the Authentication icon in the middle pane. Now, ensure that the ASP.NET Impersonation option is enabled. This option may be automatically enabled if impersonation is already enabled in the Web.config file. Now, let's use Anonymous authentication in IIS and see how impersonation takes place.

4. Press the F5 key on the keyboard to view the output (Figure 26.26).
5. Click the Fill the List button to view the impersonation, as shown in Figure 26.26:

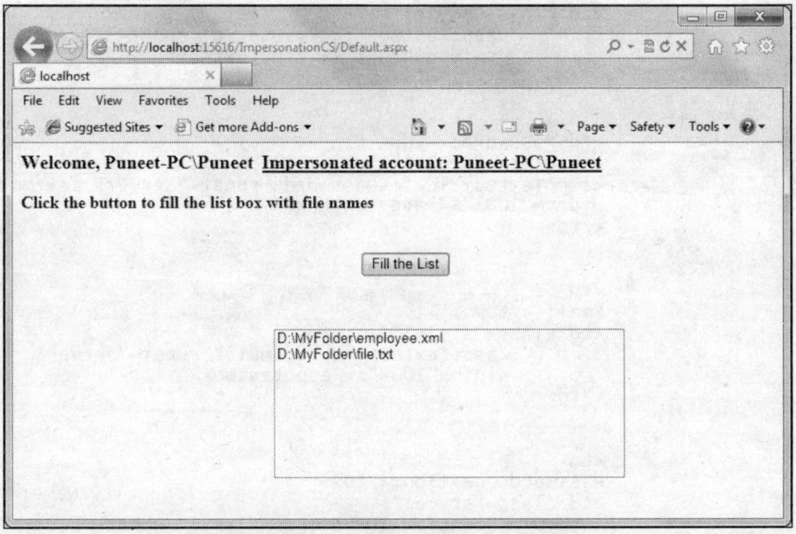

Figure 26.26: Displaying the Impersonated Account

After creating impersonation in Web application, let's learn to create user using the Membership class.

Creating User Using the Membership Class

You can create new users for a website or web application by using the Membership class,. The Membership class also enables a developer to provide more functionality such as deleting a user and generating passwords. Now, let's create a website and save it as MembershipCS. You can find the code for this application in the MembershipCS (for C#) and MembershipVB (for VB) folders. Now, let's create the website by performing the following steps:

1. Create the Web site MembershipCS and add a Web page, Default.aspx, in it.
2. Replace the code of the Default.aspx page with the code, given in Listing 26.13, to add the required controls for creating user using the `Membership` class:

Listing 26.13: Showing the Code for the Default.aspx Page

In VB

```
<%@ Page Language="VB" AutoEventWireup="false" CodeFile="Default.aspx.vb"
  Inherits="_Default" %>
<!DOCTYPE html>
<html xmlns="http://www.w3.org/1999/xhtml">
<head runat="server">
    <title></title>
</head>
<body>
    <form id="form1" runat="server">
    <div>
    <table id="tblLogin" cellspacing="1" cellpadding="1" style="border-right:
                blue thin solid; border-top: blue thin solid; border-left: blue thin
                solid; border-bottom: blue thin solid; width: 422px; height: 189px;"
                bgcolor="#cccc66">
            <tr>
                    <td colspan="2" >
                            <div style="text-align: center">
                            <strong><span style="text decoration: underline">
            Create User</span></strong>
                            </div>
                    </td>
            </tr>
            <tr>
                    <td width="40%">User ID:</td>
```

```
                <td class="style1">
                        <asp:TextBox id="myUserId" runat="server"
                          width="100%"></asp:textbox>
                </td>
        </tr>
        <tr>
                <td>Password:</td>
                <td class="style1">
                <asp:TextBox id="myPassword" runat="server" TextMode="Password"
                width="100%"></asp:textbox>
                </td>
        </tr>
        <tr>
                <td>
                Email:</td>
                <td class="style1">
                        <asp:TextBox id="myEmail" runat="server"
                        width="100%"></asp:textbox>
                </td>
        </tr>
        <tr>
                <td>
                Password Question:</td>
                <td class="style1">
                <asp:DropDownList ID="dropdownlist1" Runat="server" Width="100%">
                <asp:ListItem>Your favorite place?</asp:ListItem>
                <asp:ListItem>Your favorite color?</asp:ListItem>
                <asp:ListItem>Your role model?</asp:ListItem>
                </asp:DropDownList>
                </td>
        </tr>
        <tr>
                <td>
                Password Answer:</td>
                <td class="style1">
                        <asp:TextBox id="myPasswordAnswer" runat="server"
                        width="100%"></asp:textbox>
                </td>
        </tr>
        <tr>
                <td style="TEXT-ALIGN: center" colspan="2">
                <asp:Button ID="createbutton" runat="server" text="Click to
                Create User" />
                </td>
        </tr>
        </table>
        <br />
        <br />
    <asp:Label ID="lblresults" runat="server" Visible="false">Results:</asp:Label>
</div>
</form>
</body>
</html>
```

In C#

```
<%@ Page Language="C#" AutoEventWireup="true" CodeFile="Default.aspx.cs"
  Inherits="_Default" %>
<!DOCTYPE html>
<html xmlns="http://www.w3.org/1999/xhtml">
<head runat="server">
    <title></title>
    <style type="text/css">
        .style1
        {
            width: 324px;
        }
    </style>
</head>
```

```
<body>
    <form id="form1" runat="server">
    <div>

                <table id="tblLogin" cellspacing="1" cellpadding="1" style="border-right:
                  blue thin solid; border-top: blue thin solid; border-left: blue thin
                  solid; border-bottom: blue thin solid; width: 422px; height: 189px;"
                  bgcolor="#cccc66">
                <tr>
                        <td colspan="2" >
                                <div style="text-align: center">
                                <strong><span style="text-decoration: underline">
                        Create User</span></strong>
                                </div>
                        </td>
                </tr>
                <tr>
                        <td width="40%">User ID:</td>
                        <td class="style1">
                                <asp:TextBox id="myUserId" runat="server"
                                  width="100%"></asp:textbox>
                        </td>
                </tr>
                <tr>
                        <td>Password:</td>
                        <td class="style1">
                        <asp:TextBox id="myPassword" runat="server" TextMode="Password"
                         width="100%"></asp:textbox>
                        </td>
                </tr>
                <tr>
                        <td>
                        Email:</td>
                        <td class="style1">
                                <asp:TextBox id="myEmail" runat="server"
                                 width="100%"></asp:textbox>
                        </td>
                </tr>
                <tr>
                        <td>
                        Password Question:</td>
                        <td class="style1">
                        <asp:DropDownList ID="dropdownlist1" Runat="server" Width="100%">
                        <asp:ListItem>Your favorite place?</asp:ListItem>
                        <asp:ListItem>Your favorite color?</asp:ListItem>
                        <asp:ListItem>Your role model?</asp:ListItem>
                        </asp:DropDownList>
                        </td>
                </tr>
                <tr>
                        <td>
                        Password Answer:</td>
                        <td class="style1">
                                <asp:TextBox id="myPasswordAnswer" runat="server"
                                width="100%"></asp:textbox>
                        </td>
                </tr>
                <tr>
                        <td style="TEXT-ALIGN: center" colspan="2">
                        <asp:Button ID="createbutton" runat="server" text="Click to
                        Create User" OnClick="createbutton_Click"/>
                        </td>
                </tr>
                </table>
                <br />
                <br />
```

```
            <asp:Label ID="lblresults" runat="server" Visible="false">Results:</asp:Label>
        </div>
    </form>
</body>
</html>
```

3. Add the code, given in Listing 26.14, in the code-behind file of the Default.aspx page to add the functionality of creating user using the Membership class:

Listing 26.14: Showing the Code for the Code-Behind File of the Default.aspx Page

In VB

```
Imports System.Security.Principal
Partial Class _Default
    Inherits System.Web.UI.Page
    Protected Sub createbutton_Click(sender As Object, e As EventArgs)
         Handles createbutton.Click
        Dim status As MembershipCreateStatus
        Membership.CreateUser(myUserId.Text, myPassword.Text, myEmail.Text,
         dropdownlist1.SelectedValue, myPasswordAnswer.Text, True, status)
        Select Case status
            Case (MembershipCreateStatus.Success)
                myUserId.Text = Nothing
                myPassword.Text = Nothing
                myEmail.Text = Nothing
                dropdownlist1.SelectedIndex = -1
                myPasswordAnswer.Text = Nothing
                lblresults.Text = "User successfully created!"
                lblresults.Visible = True
                Exit Sub
            Case (MembershipCreateStatus.DuplicateUserName)
                lblresults.Text = "User already exist"
                lblresults.Visible = True
                Exit Sub
            Case Else
                lblresults.Text = "error creating users"
                lblresults.Visible = True
                Exit Sub
        End Select
    End Sub
End Class
```

In C#

```
using System;
using System.Collections.Generic;
using System.Linq;
using System.Web;
using System.Web.UI;
using System.Web.UI.WebControls;
using System.Web.Security;
public partial class _Default : System.Web.UI.Page
{
    protected void Page_Load(object sender, EventArgs e)
    {
    }
    protected void createbutton_Click(object sender, EventArgs e)
    {
        MembershipCreateStatus status;
        Membership.CreateUser(myUserId.Text, myPassword.Text, myEmail.Text,
          dropdownlist1.SelectedValue, myPasswordAnswer.Text, true, out status);
        switch (status)
        {
            case (MembershipCreateStatus.Success):
                myUserId.Text = null;
                myPassword.Text = null;
                myEmail.Text = null;
                dropdownlist1.SelectedIndex = -1;
                myPasswordAnswer.Text = null;
                lblresults.Text = "User successfully created!";
```

```
                break;
            case (MembershipCreateStatus.DuplicateUserName):
                lblresults.Text = "User already exist";
                break;
            default:
                lblresults.Text = "error creating users";
                break;
        }
        lblresults.Visible = true;
    }
}
```

4. Now, run the application by pressing the F5 key on the keyboard and enter the required information in the respective text boxes (Figure 26.27).
5. Click the Click to Create User button, as shown in Figure 26.27:

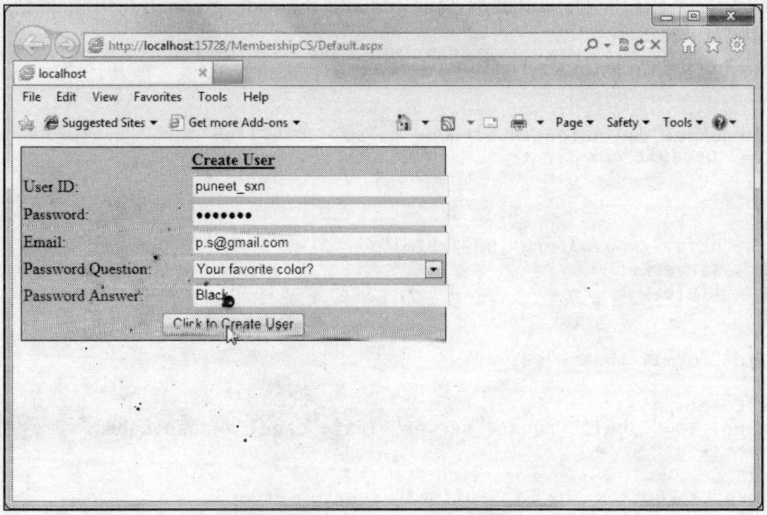

Figure 26.27: Creating the User

The message appears on the Web page displaying that the user is successfully created, as shown in Figure 26.28:

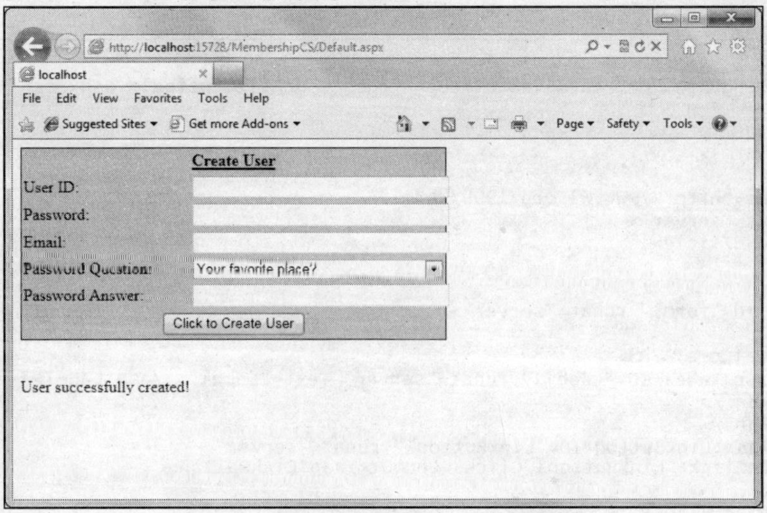

Figure 26.28: Displaying the Success Message

After creating the user, let's learn how to validate and retrieve the user.

Validating and Retrieving a User

We can validate the credentials of a user by using the membership feature in ASP.NET 4.5. The `Membership.ValidateUser` method is used to validate the credentials of a member. This method takes the username and password as parameters and returns true, if the credentials are correct. You can also retrieve the information of a user by using the `Membership.GetUser` method. We create a website and save it as ValidateUserCS. You can find the code for this application in the ValidateUserCS (for C#) and ValidateUserVB (for VB) folders. Now, let's create the website by performing the following steps:

1. Open the Web.config file and add the following line of code for both C# and VB:
```
<authentication mode="Forms"/>
```
2. Add two Web forms and name them as Default.aspx and Login.aspx.
3. Open the Source view of the Default.aspx page and add the code, given in Listing 26.15, to add the required controls for the application:

Listing 26.15: Showing the Code for the Default.aspx Page

In VB

```
<%@ Page Language="VB" AutoEventWireup="false" CodeFile="Default.aspx.vb"
  Inherits="_Default" %>

<!DOCTYPE html>

<html xmlns="http://www.w3.org/1999/xhtml">
<head runat="server">
    <title></title>
</head>
<body>
    <form id="form1" runat="server">
    <div>
    <h3>WelCome!</h3>
    <asp:Label ID="Label1" runat="server" Text="Label"></asp:Label>
         <br />
         <br />
         <asp:LinkButton ID="LinkButton1" runat="server"
           OnClick="LinkButton1_Click">Logout</asp:LinkButton></div>
    </form>
</body>
</html>
```

In C#

```
<%@ Page Language="C#" AutoEventWireup="true" CodeFile="Default.aspx.cs"
  Inherits="_Default" %>

<!DOCTYPE html>

<html xmlns="http://www.w3.org/1999/xhtml">
<head runat="server">
    <title></title>
</head>
<body>
    <form id="form1" runat="server">
    <div>
     <h3>WelCome!</h3>
        <asp:Label ID="Label1" runat="server" Text="Label"></asp:Label>
         <br />
         <br />
         <asp:LinkButton ID="LinkButton1" runat="server"
         OnClick="LinkButton1_Click">Logout</asp:LinkButton>
    </div>
    </form>
</body>
</html>
```

4. Add the code, given in Listing 26.16, in the code-behind file of the Default.aspx page to validate and retrieve a user:

Listing 26.16: Showing the Code for the Code-Behind File of the Default.aspx Page

In VB

```
Partial Class _Default
    Inherits System.Web.UI.Page

    Protected Sub Page_Load(sender As Object, e As EventArgs) Handles
  Me.Load
        Label1.Text = Convert.ToString(Membership.GetUser(User.Identity.Name))
    End Sub

    Protected Sub LinkButton1_Click(sender As Object, e As EventArgs)
         Handles LinkButton1.Click
        FormsAuthentication.SignOut()
        Response.Redirect("Login.aspx")
    End Sub
End Class
```

In C#

```
using System;
using System.Collections.Generic;
using System.Linq;
using System.Web;
using System.Web.UI;
using System.Web.UI.WebControls;
using System.Web.Security;
public partial class _Default : System.Web.UI.Page
{
    protected void Page_Load(object sender, EventArgs e)
    {
        Label1.Text = Convert.ToString(Membership.GetUser(User.Identity.Name));
    }
    protected void LinkButton1_Click(object sender, EventArgs e)
    {
        FormsAuthentication.SignOut();
        Response.Redirect("Login.aspx");
    }
}
```

5. Open the Source view of the Login.aspx page and add the code, given in Listing 26.17, to add the required controls:

Listing 26.17: Showing the Code for the Login.aspx Page

In VB

```
<%@ Page Language="VB" AutoEventWireup="false" CodeFile="Login.aspx.vb" Inherits="Login"
  %>

<!DOCTYPE html>

<html xmlns="http://www.w3.org/1999/xhtml">
<head runat="server">
    <title></title>
</head>
<body>
    <form id="form1" runat="server">
    <div>
    <strong><span style="color: #000099; text-decoration: underline">Enter your
           information</span></strong><br />
        <br />
        <table style="border-left-color: black; border-bottom-color: black; border-top-
        style:
  solid; border-top-color: black; border-right-style: solid; border-left-style: solid;
  border-right-color: black; border-bottom-style: solid"
```

```
          bgcolor="#ffcc99" id="TABLE1">
        <tr>
                <td style="width: 100px; height: 21px">
                <strong><span style="text-decoration: underline">User
                  Name:</span></strong></td>
                <td style="width: 100px; height: 21px">
                <asp:TextBox ID="TextBox1" runat="server"></asp:TextBox></td>
        </tr>
        <tr>
                <td style="width: 100px">
                <strong><span style="text-decoration:
                  underline">Password:</span></strong></td>
                <td style="width: 100px">
                <asp:TextBox ID="TextBox2" runat="server" TextMode="Password"
                  Width="151px"></asp:TextBox></td>
        </tr>
        <tr>
                <td style="width: 100px">
                </td>
                <td style="width: 100px">
                <asp:Button ID="Button1" runat="server" Text="Validate"
                  /></td>
        </tr>
        </table>
        <asp:Label ID="Label1" runat="server"></asp:Label>
    </div>
    </form>
</body>
</html>
```

In C#

```
<%@ Page Language="C#" AutoEventWireup="true" CodeFile="Login.aspx.cs" Inherits="Login" %>

<!DOCTYPE html>

<html xmlns="http://www.w3.org/1999/xhtml">
<head runat="server">
    <title></title>
</head>
<body>
    <form id="form1" runat="server">
    <div>
    <strong><span style="color: #000099; text-decoration: underline">Enter your
          information</span></strong><br />
        <br />
        <table style="border-left-color: black; border-bottom-color: black;
        border-top-style: solid; border-top-color: black; border-right-style: solid;
        border-left-style: solid; border-right-color: black; border-bottom-style: solid"
          bgcolor="#ffcc99" id="TABLE1">
        <tr>
                <td style="width: 100px; height: 21px">
                <strong><span style="text-decoration: underline">User
                  Name:</span></strong></td>
                <td style="width: 100px; height: 21px">
                <asp:TextBox ID="TextBox1" runat="server"></asp:TextBox></td>
        </tr>
        <tr>
                <td style="width: 100px">
                <strong><span style="text-decoration:
                  underline">Password:</span></strong></td>
                <td style="width: 100px">
                <asp:TextBox ID="TextBox2" runat="server" TextMode="Password"
                  Width="151px"></asp:TextBox></td>
        </tr>
        <tr>
```

```
                <td style="width: 100px">
                </td>
                <td style="width: 100px">
                <asp:Button ID="Button1" runat="server" Text="Validate"
                  OnClick="Button1_Click" /></td>
            </tr>
            </table>
            <asp:Label ID="Label1" runat="server"></asp:Label>
    </div>
    </form>
</body>
</html>
```

6. Now, add the code in the code-behind file of the Login.aspx page. Listing 26.18 shows the code for the code behind file of the Login.aspx page to validate and retrieve a user:

Listing 26.18: Showing the Code for the Code-Behind File of the Login.aspx Page

In VB

```
Partial Class Login
    Inherits System.Web.UI.Page
    Protected Sub Button1_Click(sender As Object, e As EventArgs)
  Handles
   Button1.Click

        If Membership.ValidateUser(TextBox1.Text, TextBox2.Text) Then
            FormsAuthentication.RedirectFromLoginPage(TextBox1.Text, False)
        End If
        Label1.Text = " you are not a registered user!!!"
    End Sub
End Class
```

In C#

```
using System;
using System.Collections.Generic;
using System.Linq;
using System.Web;
using System.Web.UI;
using System.Web.UI.WebControls;
using System.Web.Security;

public partial class Login : System.Web.UI.Page
{
    protected void Page_Load(object sender, EventArgs e)
    {
    }
    protected void Button1_Click(object sender, EventArgs e)
    {

        if (Membership.ValidateUser(TextBox1.Text, TextBox2.Text))
        {
            FormsAuthentication.RedirectFromLoginPage(TextBox1.Text, false);
        }
        Label1.Text = " you are not a registered user!!!";
    }
}
```

7. Press the F5 key on the keyboard to view the output.
8. Enter the user name and password in the User Name and Password text boxes, respectively, and click the Validate button, as shown in Figure 26.29:

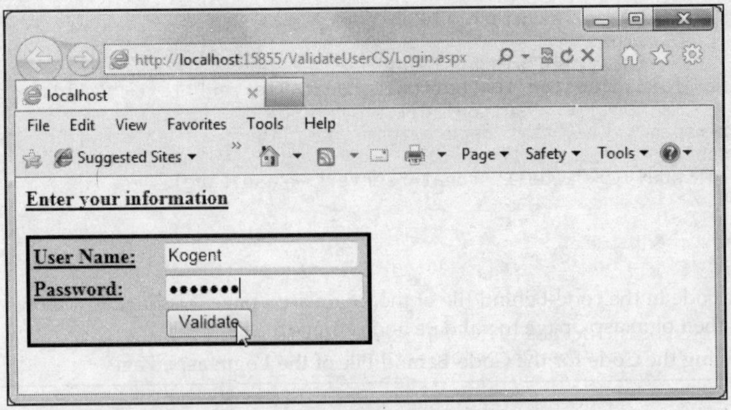

Figure 26.29: Validating the User

The Default.aspx appears displaying the user name (Figure 26.30).

9. Click the Logout link to open the Login.aspx page, as shown in Figure 26.30:

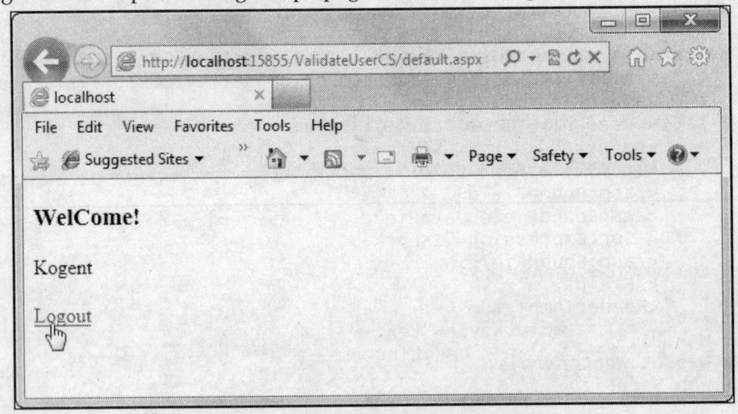

Figure 26.30: Displaying the Authenticated User

After learning the validation of the user, let's learn about the ItemUpdating event.

Using the ItemUpdating Event

The `ItemUpdating` event is used to modify and update the user account properties at runtime. You can also lock or unlock a user account. You can also modify the fields, such as e-mail and comments, by using the ItemUpdating event. Let's create a website and save it as ItemUpdateCS to understand the use of the ItemUpdating event. You can find the code for this application in the ItemUpdateCS and ItemUpdateVB folders. Now, let's create a website by performing the following steps:

1. Create the Web application, ItemUpdateCS, and add two Web forms, Default.aspx and Login.aspx.
2. Open the Source view of the Default.aspx page and add the following code, given in Listing 26.19, to add the required controls in the application:

Listing 26.19: Showing the Code for the Default.aspx Page

In VB

```
<%@ Page Language="VB" AutoEventWireup="false" CodeFile="Default.aspx.vb"
  Inherits="Default"
  %>
<!DOCTYPE html>
<html xmlns="http://www.w3.org/1999/xhtml">
<head runat="server">
```

```
        <title></title>
    </head>
    <body>
        <form id="form1" runat="server">
        <div>
        <strong><span style="text-decoration: underline"><em>Updating the users properties<br
            />
            </em></span></strong>
            <br />
            <br />
                
            <table id="update" cellpadding="0" cellspacing="0" >
            <tr>
                    <td style="width: 218px">
                    <asp:DetailsView AutoGenerateRows="False"
                      DataSourceID="ObjectDataSource1" Height="50px"
                    ID="DetailsView1" runat="server" Width="268px"
                      AutoGenerateEditButton="True"
                    OnItemUpdating="DetailsView1_ItemUpdating" BackColor="White"
                      BorderColor="#CC9966" BorderStyle="None"
                    BorderWidth="1px" CellPadding="4">
                    <Fields>
                    <asp:BoundField DataField="Email" HeaderText="Email"
                      SortExpression="Email"></asp:BoundField>
                    <asp:BoundField DataField="Comment" HeaderText="Comment"
                      SortExpression="Comment"></asp:BoundField>
                    <asp:BoundField DataField="UserName" HeaderText="UserName"
                      ReadOnly="True" SortExpression="UserName">
                    <HeaderStyle Font-Bold="True" />
                    <ItemStyle Font-Bold="True" />
                    </asp:BoundField>
                    <asp:BoundField DataField="IsLockedOut" HeaderText="IsLockedOut"
                      SortExpression="IsLockedOut" ReadOnly="True">
                    </asp:BoundField>
                    </Fields>
                    <HeaderTemplate>
                            <div style="text-align: center">
                                    Updating Properties
                            </div>
                    </HeaderTemplate>
                    <FooterStyle BackColor="#FFFFCC" ForeColor="#330099" />
                    <RowStyle BackColor="White" ForeColor="#330099" />
                    <PagerStyle BackColor="#FFFFCC" ForeColor="#330099"
                      HorizontalAlign="Center" />
                    <HeaderStyle BackColor="#990000" Font-Bold="True" ForeColor="#FFFFCC" />
                    <EditRowStyle BackColor="#FFCC66" Font-Bold="True" ForeColor="#663399" />
                    </asp:DetailsView>
                    <asp:ObjectDataSource ID="ObjectDataSource1" runat="server"
                    DataObjectTypeName="System.Web.Security.MembershipUser"
                      SelectMethod="GetUser"
                    TypeName="System.Web.Security.Membership"></asp:ObjectDataSource>
                    </td>
            </tr>
            </table>
            <hr />
            <asp:Button ID="Button1" runat="server" Text="Sign Out"
              /><br />
            <asp:LinkButton ID="LinkButton1" runat="server"
             OnClick="LinkButton1_Click">Delete Current Profile:</asp:LinkButton>
        </div>
        </form>
    </body>
    </html>
```

In C#

```
<%@ Page Language="C#" AutoEventWireup="true" CodeFile="Default.aspx.cs"
  Inherits="_Default" %>
<!DOCTYPE html>
<html xmlns="http://www.w3.org/1999/xhtml">
<head runat="server">
    <title></title>
</head>
<body>
    <form id="form1" runat="server">
    <div>
    <strong><span style="text-decoration: underline"><em>Updating the users properties<br
         />
         </em></span></strong>
         <br />
         <br />
             
         <table id="update" cellpadding="0" cellspacing="0" >
         <tr>
                 <td style="width: 218px">
                 <asp:DetailsView AutoGenerateRows="False"
                   DataSourceID="ObjectDataSource1" Height="50px"
                 ID="DetailsView1" runat="server" Width="268px"
                   AutoGenerateEditButton="True"
                 OnItemUpdating="DetailsView1_ItemUpdating" BackColor="White"
                   BorderColor="#CC9966" BorderStyle="None"
                 BorderWidth="1px" CellPadding="4">
                 <Fields>
                 <asp:BoundField DataField="Email" HeaderText="Email"
                   SortExpression="Email"></asp:BoundField>
                 <asp:BoundField DataField="Comment" HeaderText="Comment"
                   SortExpression="Comment"></asp:BoundField>
                 <asp:BoundField DataField="UserName" HeaderText="UserName"
                   ReadOnly="True" SortExpression="UserName">
                 <HeaderStyle Font-Bold="True" />
                 <ItemStyle Font-Bold="True" />
                 </asp:BoundField>
                 <asp:BoundField DataField="IsLockedOut" HeaderText="IsLockedOut"
                   SortExpression="IsLockedOut" ReadOnly="True">
                 </asp:BoundField>
                 </Fields>
                 <HeaderTemplate>
                         <div style="text-align: center">
                                 Updating Properties
                         </div>
                 </HeaderTemplate>
                 <FooterStyle BackColor="#FFFFCC" ForeColor="#330099" />
                 <RowStyle BackColor="White" ForeColor="#330099" />
                 <PagerStyle BackColor="#FFFFCC" ForeColor="#330099"
                   HorizontalAlign="Center" />
                 <HeaderStyle BackColor="#990000" Font-Bold="True" ForeColor="#FFFFCC" />
                 <EditRowStyle BackColor="#FFCC66" Font-Bold="True" ForeColor="#663399" />
                 </asp:DetailsView>
                 <asp:ObjectDataSource ID="ObjectDataSource1" runat="server"
                 DataObjectTypeName="System.Web.Security.MembershipUser"
                   SelectMethod="GetUser"
                 TypeName="System.Web.Security.Membership"></asp:ObjectDataSource>
                 </td>
         </tr>
         </table>
         <hr />
         <asp:Button ID="Button1" runat="server" Text="Sign Out" OnClick="Button1_Click"
           /><br />
         <asp:LinkButton ID="LinkButton1" runat="server"
          OnClick="LinkButton1_Click">Delete Current Profile:</asp:LinkButton>
```

```
    </div>
    </form>
</body>
</html>
```

3. Add the code, given in Listing 26.20, in the code-behind file of the Default.aspx to use the ItemUpdating event:

Listing 26.20: Showing the Code for the Code-Behind File of the Default.aspx Page

In VB

```
Partial Class _Default
    Inherits System.Web.UI.Page
    Protected Sub DetailsView1_ItemUpdating(sender As Object, e As
  DetailsViewUpdateEventArgs) Handles DetailsView1.ItemUpdating
        Dim updatesuser As MembershipUser = Membership.GetUser()
        updatesuser.Email = CStr(e.NewValues(0))
        updatesuser.Comment = CStr(e.NewValues(1))
        Membership.UpdateUser(updatesuser)
        e.Cancel = True
        DetailsView1.ChangeMode(DetailsViewMode.ReadOnly)
    End Sub
    Protected Sub Button1_Click(sender As Object, e As EventArgs)
         Handles Button1.Click
        FormsAuthentication.SignOut()
        Response.Redirect("Login.aspx")
    End Sub
    Protected Sub LinkButton1_Click(sender As Object, e As EventArgs)
  Handles LinkButton1.Click
        Membership.DeleteUser(User.Identity.Name)
        FormsAuthentication.SignOut()
        Response.Redirect("Login.aspx")
    End Sub
End Class
```

In C#

```
using System;
using System.Collections.Generic;
using System.Linq;
using System.Web;
using System.Web.UI;
using System.Web.UI.WebControls;
using System.Web.Security;
public partial class _Default : System.Web.UI.Page
{
    protected void Page_Load(object sender, EventArgs e)
    {
    }
    protected void DetailsView1_ItemUpdating(object sender, DetailsViewUpdateEventArgs e)
    {
        MembershipUser updatesuser = Membership.GetUser();
        updatesuser.Email = (string)e.NewValues[0];
        updatesuser.Comment = (string)e.NewValues[1];
        Membership.UpdateUser(updatesuser);
        e.Cancel = true;
        DetailsView1.ChangeMode(DetailsViewMode.ReadOnly);
    }
    protected void Button1_Click(object sender, EventArgs e)
    {
        FormsAuthentication.SignOut();
        Response.Redirect("Login.aspx");
    }
    protected void LinkButton1_Click(object sender, EventArgs e)
    {
        Membership.DeleteUser(User.Identity.Name);
        FormsAuthentication.SignOut();
```

```
            Response.Redirect("Login.aspx");
        }
    }
```

4. Open the Login.aspx page and modify the code from the code, given in Listing 26.21, in the Login.aspx page to add required controls:

Listing 26.21: Showing the Code of the Login.aspx Page

In VB

```
<%@ Page Language="VB" AutoEventWireup="false" CodeFile="Login.aspx.vb" Inherits="Login"
   %>
<!DOCTYPE html>
<html xmlns="http://www.w3.org/1999/xhtml">
<head runat="server">
    <title></title>
</head>
<body>
    <form id="form1" runat="server">
    <div>
    <strong><span style="text-decoration: underline"><em>Enter your login
           Information<br />
         </em></span></strong>
         <br />
         <br />
         <table id="tblLogin" cellspacing="1" cellpadding="1" style="border-right: black
           thin solid; border-top:
         black thin solid; border-left: black thin solid; border-bottom: black thin
           solid;" bgcolor="#ffffcc">
         <tr>
                 <td colspan="2" >
                         <div style="text-align: center">
                                 <strong><span style="text-decoration: underline">Login
                                   Form</span></strong>
                         </div>
                 </td>
         </tr>
         <tr>
                 <td width="40%">Enter Name:</td>
                 <td>
                 <asp:textbox id="textbox1" runat="server" width="100%"></asp:textbox>
                 </td>
         </tr>
         <tr>
                 <td>Enter Password:</td>
                 <td>
                 <asp:textbox id="textbox2" runat="server" textmode="Password"
                   width="100%"></asp:textbox>
                 </td>
         </tr>
         <tr>
                 <td style="TEXT-ALIGN: center" colspan="2">
                  <asp:Button ID="Button1" runat="server" Text="Login"
                  /></td>
         </tr>
         <tr>
         <td colspan="2" style="height: 21px">
         <asp:Label ID="label2" runat="server" Text=<%# "Application locking attempts:"
          & Membership.Provider.MaxInvalidPasswordAttempts %> />
                 </td>
         </tr>
         </table>
         <br />
         <br />
         <asp:label id="label1" runat="server" BackColor="#FFC080"
           Visible="false">Status:</asp:label> <br />
         <br />
```

```
        <br />
        <br />
        <br />
        <asp:label id="label4" runat="server" BackColor="#FFC080"
          Visible="false">Status:</asp:label> 
        <span style="color: #000099; text-decoration: underline"><strong>
        To unlock click here<br />
        </strong></span>
        <asp:Button ID="Button2" runat="server"
        Text="Unlock"/><br />
    </div>
    </form>
</body>
</html>
```

In C#

```
<%@ Page Language="C#" AutoEventWireup="true" CodeFile="Login.aspx.cs" Inherits="Login" %>
<!DOCTYPE html>
<html xmlns="http://www.w3.org/1999/xhtml">
<head runat="server">
    <title></title>
</head>
<body>
    <form id="form1" runat="server">
    <div>

    <strong><span style="text-decoration: underline"><em>Enter your login
          Information<br />
        </em></span></strong>
        <br />
        <br />
        <table id="tblLogin" cellspacing="1" cellpadding="1" style="border-right: black
          thin solid; border-top:
        black thin solid; border-left: black thin solid; border-bottom: black thin
          solid;" bgcolor="#ffffcc">
        <tr>
                <td colspan="2" >
                        <div style="text-align: center">
                                <strong><span style="text-decoration: underline">Login
                                  Form</span></strong>
                        </div>
                </td>
        </tr>
        <tr>
                <td width="40%">Enter Name:</td>
                <td>
                <asp:textbox id="textbox1" runat="server" width="100%"></asp:textbox>
                </td>
        </tr>
        <tr>
                <td>Enter Password:</td>
                <td>
                <asp:textbox id="textbox2" runat="server" textmode="Password"
                  width="100%"></asp:textbox>
                </td>
        </tr>
        <tr>
                <td style="TEXT-ALIGN: center" colspan="2">
                 <asp:Button ID="Button1" runat="server" Text="Login"
                  OnClick="Button1_Click" /></td>
        </tr>
        <tr>
        <td colspan="2" style="height: 21px">
        <asp:Label ID="label2" runat="server" Text=<%# "Application locking attempts:"
        + Membership.Provider.MaxInvalidPasswordAttempts %> />
```

```
                </td>
            </tr>
            </table>
            <br />
            <br />
            <asp:label id="label1" runat="server" BackColor="#FFC080"
              Visible="false">Status:</asp:label> <br />
            <br />
            <br />
            <br />
            <br />
            <asp:label id="label4" runat="server" BackColor="#FFC080"
              Visible="false">Status:</asp:label> 
            <span style="color: #000099; text-decoration: underline"><strong>
            To unlock click here<br />
            </strong></span>
            <asp:Button ID="Button2" runat="server" OnClick="Button2_Click"
            Text="Unlock"/><br />
        </div>
        </form>
    </body>
    </html>
```

5. Add the code, given in Listing 26.22, in the code-behind file of the Login.aspx:

Listing 26.22: Showing the Code for the Code-Behind File of the Login.aspx Page

In VB

```
Partial Class Login
    Inherits System.Web.UI.Page
    Protected Sub Button2_Click(sender As Object, e As EventArgs)
  Handles
  Button2.Click
        Dim memUser As MembershipUser = Membership.GetUser(textbox1.Text)
        If memUser IsNot Nothing AndAlso memUser.IsLockedOut = True Then
            memUser.UnlockUser()
        End If
        label1.Visible = False
    End Sub
    Protected Sub Button1_Click(sender As Object, e As EventArgs)
  Handles
  Button1.Click
        Dim userName As String = textbox1.Text
        Dim password As String = textbox2.Text
        If Membership.ValidateUser(userName, password) Then
            If Request.QueryString("ReturnUrl") IsNot Nothing Then
                FormsAuthentication.RedirectFromLoginPage(userName, False)
            Else
                FormsAuthentication.SetAuthCookie(userName, False)
                Response.Redirect("Default.aspx")
            End If
        Else
            label1.Visible = True
            label1.Text = "Unsuccessful login.  Please re-enter your information and try
                again."
        End If
        If (Membership.GetUser(userName) IsNot Nothing) AndAlso
           (Membership.GetUser(userName).IsLockedOut = True) Then
            label1.Text = " <b>Your account has been locked out.</b>"
        End If
    End Sub
    Protected Sub Page_Load(sender As Object, e As EventArgs) Handles
  Me.Load
        Me.DataBind()
    End Sub
End Class
```

In C#

```
using System;
using System.Collections.Generic;
using System.Linq;
using System.Web;
using System.Web.UI;
using System.Web.UI.WebControls;
using System.Web.Security;
public partial class Login : System.Web.UI.Page
{
    protected void Page_Load(object sender, EventArgs e)
    {
        this.DataBind();
    }
    protected void Button2_Click(object sender, EventArgs e)
    {
        MembershipUser memUser = Membership.GetUser(textbox1.Text);
        if (memUser != null && memUser.IsLockedOut == true)
            memUser.UnlockUser();
        label1.Visible = false;
    }
    protected void Button1_Click(object sender, EventArgs e)
    {
         string userName = textbox1.Text;
         string password = textbox2.Text;
         if (Membership.ValidateUser(userName, password))
         {
                 if (Request.QueryString["ReturnUrl"] != null)
                 {
                         FormsAuthentication.RedirectFromLoginPage(userName, false);
                 }
                 else
                 {
                         FormsAuthentication.SetAuthCookie(userName, false);
                         Response.Redirect("Default.aspx");
                 }
         }
         else
         {
                 label1.Visible = true;
                 label1.Text = "Unsuccessful login.  Please re-enter your information and
                 try
          again.";
         }
         if ((Membership.GetUser(userName) != null) &&
           (Membership.GetUser(userName).IsLockedOut == true))
         {
                 label1.Text = "  <b>Your account has been locked out.</b>";
         }
    }
}
```

6. Create the user using the ASP.net Web Site Administration Tool. (For more details, read chapter 24: Working with Login Controls).
7. Set the Login.aspx page as a start page and press the F5 key on the keyboard to execute the application.
8. Enter the user name and password in their respective text boxes and click the Login button, as shown in Figure 26.31:

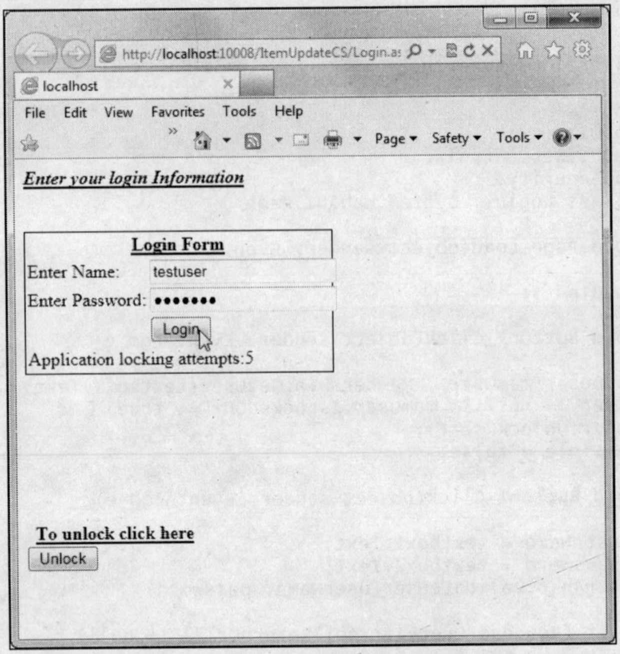

Figure 26.31: Displaying the Output

The Default.aspx page appears (Figure 26.32).

9. Click the Edit link to edit the comment, as shown in Figure 26.32:

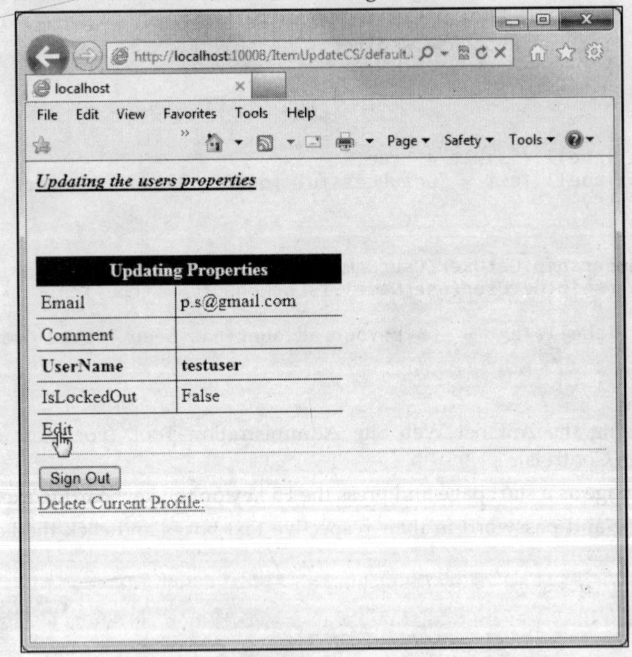

Figure 26.32: Editing the Information of the User

10. Enter the text in the Comment text box and click the Update link to update the comment, as shown in Figure 26.33:

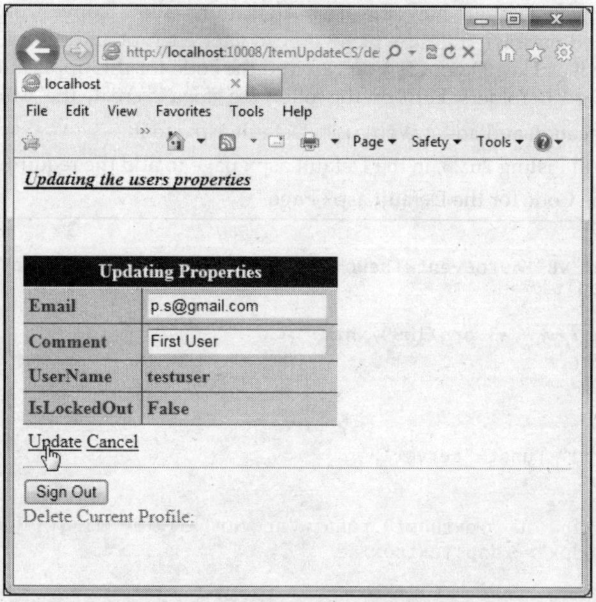

Figure 26.33: Updating the Information

11. Click the Sign Out button to log out from this page, as shown in Figure 26.34:

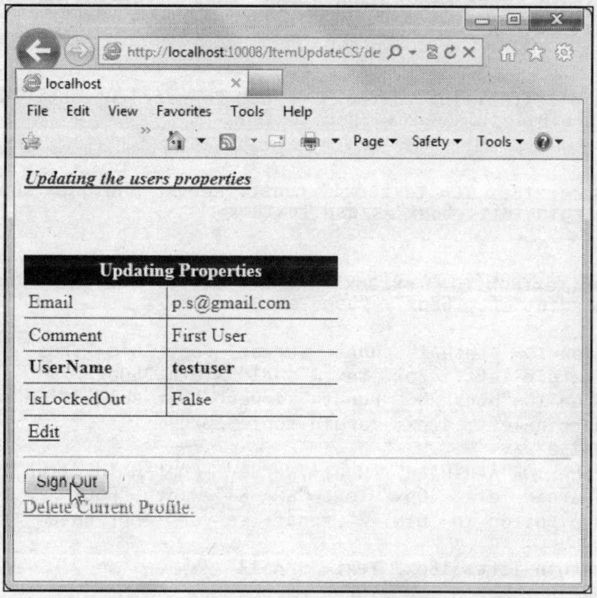

Figure 26.34: Displaying the Updating Information

After learning the ItemUpdating event to update the user information, let's now learn about the hash algorithm.

Using Hash Algorithms

In the In-Depth section, you learned how the hash algorithms allow conversion of data to a compressed, alphanumerical form called message digest, which you can later encrypt and send it to another user. Now, let's create a website and save it as HashDemoCS. You can find the code for this application in the HashDemoCS (for C#) and HashDemoVB (for VB) folders. Perform the following steps to create the website:

1. Create the Web application and add a Web page, Default.aspx, to it.
2. Add the code, given in Listing 26.23, in the Default.aspx page to add the required controls:

Listing 26.23: Showing the Code for the Default.aspx Page

In VB

```
<%@ Page Language="VB" AutoEventWireup="false" CodeFile="Default.aspx.vb"
  Inherits="_Default" %>
<!DOCTYPE html>
<html xmlns="http://www.w3.org/1999/xhtml">
<head runat="server">
    <title></title>
</head>
<body>
    <form id="form1" runat="server">
    <div>
   Type the text here
          <asp:TextBox ID="TextBox1" runat="server" style="margin-left: 25px"
          Width="169px"></asp:TextBox>
          <br />
          <br />
          SHA1     
          <asp:TextBox ID="TextBox2" runat="server" Height="20px"
          style="margin-left: 68px; margin-top: 66px" Width="310px"
             ></asp:TextBox>
          <br />
          <br />
         SHA256 <asp:TextBox ID="TextBox3" runat="server" Height="20px" Width="310px"
          style="margin-left: 68px"></asp:TextBox>
         <br />
         <br />
         SHA384<asp:TextBox ID="TextBox4" runat="server" Height="20px" Width="310px"
          style="margin-left: 68px"></asp:TextBox>
         <br />
         <br />
         SHA512<asp:TextBox ID="TextBox5" runat="server" Height="20px" Width="310px"
          style="margin-left: 68px"></asp:TextBox><br />
          <br />
          <asp:Button ID="Btnsha1" runat="server" Font-Bold="True"
           style="margin-left: 42px" Text="SHA1" Width="80px" />
          <asp:Button ID="btnsh256" runat="server" Font-Bold="True"
          style="margin-left: 42px; margin-top: 31px"
          Text="SHA256" />
          <asp:Button ID="Btnsh384" runat="server" Font-Bold="True"
           style="margin-left: 30px" Text="SHA384" Width="66px" />
           <asp:Button ID="BTN512" runat="server" Font-Bold="True"

          style="margin-left: 18px" Text="SHA512" />
    </div>
    </form>
</body>
</html>
```

In C#

```
<%@ Page Language="C#" AutoEventWireup="true" CodeFile="Default.aspx.cs"
  Inherits="_Default" %>
<!DOCTYPE html>
<html xmlns="http://www.w3.org/1999/xhtml">
<head runat="server">
    <title></title>
</head>
<body>
    <form id="form1" runat="server">
    <div>
    Type the text here
         <asp:TextBox ID="TextBox1" runat="server" style="margin-left: 25px"
         Width="169px"></asp:TextBox>
         <br />
         <br />
         SHA1     
         <asp:TextBox ID="TextBox2" runat="server" Height="20px"
         style="margin-left: 68px; margin-top: 66px" Width="310px"
            ></asp:TextBox>
         <br />
         <br />
        SHA256 <asp:TextBox ID="TextBox3" runat="server" Height="20px" Width="310px"
         style="margin-left: 68px"></asp:TextBox>
        <br />
        <br />
        SHA384<asp:TextBox ID="TextBox4" runat="server" Height="20px" Width="310px"
         style="margin-left: 68px"></asp:TextBox>
        <br />
        <br />
        SHA512<asp:TextBox ID="TextBox5" runat="server" Height="20px" Width="310px"
         style="margin-left: 68px"></asp:TextBox><br />
         <br />
         <asp:Button ID="Btnsha1" runat="server" Font-Bold="True"
         OnClick="Btnsha1_Click" style="margin-left: 42px" Text="SHA1" Width="80px" />
         <asp:Button ID="btnsh256" runat="server" Font-Bold="True"
         OnClick="btnsh256_Click" style="margin-left: 42px; margin-top: 31px"
         Text="SHA256" />
         <asp:Button ID="Btnsh384" runat="server" Font-Bold="True"
         OnClick="Btnsh384_Click" style="margin-left: 30px" Text="SHA384" Width="66px" />
          <asp:Button ID="BTN512" runat="server" Font-Bold="True"
         OnClick="BTN512_Click"
         style="margin-left: 18px" Text="SHA512" />
    </div>
    </form>
</body>
</html>
```

3. Add the code, given in Listing 26.24, in the code-behind file of the Default.aspx page to use hash algorithms:

Listing 26.24: Showing the Code for the Code-Behind File of the Default.aspx Page

In VB

```
Imports System.Security.Cryptography
Imports System.Text
Partial Class _Default
    Inherits System.Web.UI.Page
    Private hashValue(), MessageBytes() As Byte
    Private StringtoConvert As String
    Private MyUniCodeEncoding As UnicodeEncoding
    Protected Sub Btnsha1_Click(sender As Object, e As EventArgs)
  Handles
  Btnsha1.Click
        StringtoConvert = TextBox1.Text
```

```
        MyUniCodeEncoding = New UnicodeEncoding()
        MessageBytes = MyUniCodeEncoding.GetBytes(StringtoConvert)
        Dim SHhash As New SHA1Managed()
        hashValue = SHhash.ComputeHash(MessageBytes)
        For Each b As Byte In hashValue
            TextBox2.Text = TextBox2.Text + String.Format("{0:X2}", b)
        Next b
    End Sub
    Protected Sub btnsh256_Click(sender As Object, e As EventArgs)
  Handles
   btnsh256.Click
        StringtoConvert = TextBox1.Text
        MyUniCodeEncoding = New UnicodeEncoding()
        MessageBytes = MyUniCodeEncoding.GetBytes(StringtoConvert)
        Dim SHhash As New SHA256Managed()
        hashValue = SHhash.ComputeHash(MessageBytes)
        For Each b As Byte In hashValue
            TextBox3.Text = TextBox3.Text + String.Format("{0:X2}", b)
        Next b
    End Sub
    Protected Sub Btnsh384_Click( sender As Object,  e As EventArgs)
  Handles
  Btnsh384.Click
        StringtoConvert = TextBox1.Text
        MyUniCodeEncoding = New UnicodeEncoding()
        MessageBytes = MyUniCodeEncoding.GetBytes(StringtoConvert)
        Dim SHhash As New SHA384Managed()
        hashValue = SHhash.ComputeHash(MessageBytes)
        For Each b As Byte In hashValue
            TextBox4.Text = TextBox4.Text + String.Format("{0:X2}", b)
        Next b
    End Sub
    Protected Sub BTN512_Click( sender As Object,  e As EventArgs)
  Handles
   BTN512.Click
        StringtoConvert = TextBox1.Text
        MyUniCodeEncoding = New UnicodeEncoding()
        MessageBytes = MyUniCodeEncoding.GetBytes(StringtoConvert)
        Dim SHhash As New SHA512Managed()
        hashValue = SHhash.ComputeHash(MessageBytes)
        For Each b As Byte In hashValue
            TextBox5.Text = TextBox5.Text + String.Format("{0:X2}", b)
        Next b
    End Sub
End Class
```

In C#

```
using System;
using System.Collections.Generic;
using System.Linq;
using System.Web;
using System.Web.UI;
using System.Web.UI.WebControls;
using System.Security.Cryptography;
using System.Text;
public partial class _Default : System.Web.UI.Page
{
    byte[] hashValue, MessageBytes;
    string StringtoConvert;
    UnicodeEncoding MyUniCodeEncoding;
    protected void Page_Load(object sender, EventArgs e)
    {
```

```
    }
    protected void Btnsha1_Click(object sender, EventArgs e)
    {
        StringtoConvert = TextBox1.Text;
        MyUniCodeEncoding = new UnicodeEncoding();
        MessageBytes = MyUniCodeEncoding.GetBytes(StringtoConvert);
        SHA1Managed SHhash = new SHA1Managed();
        hashValue = SHhash.ComputeHash(MessageBytes);
        foreach (byte b in hashValue)
        {
            TextBox2.Text = TextBox2.Text + string.Format("{0:X2}", b);
        }
    }
    protected void btnsh256_Click(object sender, EventArgs e)
    {
        StringtoConvert = TextBox1.Text;
        MyUniCodeEncoding = new UnicodeEncoding();
        MessageBytes = MyUniCodeEncoding.GetBytes(StringtoConvert);
        SHA256Managed SHhash = new SHA256Managed();
        hashValue = SHhash.ComputeHash(MessageBytes);
        foreach (byte b in hashValue)
        {
            TextBox3.Text = TextBox3.Text + string.Format("{0:X2}", b);
        }
    }
    protected void Btnsh384_Click(object sender, EventArgs e)
    {
        StringtoConvert = TextBox1.Text;
        MyUniCodeEncoding = new UnicodeEncoding();
        MessageBytes = MyUniCodeEncoding.GetBytes(StringtoConvert);
        SHA384Managed SHhash = new SHA384Managed();
        hashValue = SHhash.ComputeHash(MessageBytes);
        foreach (byte b in hashValue)
        {
            TextBox4.Text = TextBox4.Text + string.Format("{0:X2}", b);
        }
    }
    protected void BTN512_Click(object sender, EventArgs e)
    {
        StringtoConvert = TextBox1.Text;
        MyUniCodeEncoding = new UnicodeEncoding();
        MessageBytes = MyUniCodeEncoding.GetBytes(StringtoConvert);
        SHA512Managed SHhash = new SHA512Managed();
        hashValue = SHhash.ComputeHash(MessageBytes);
        foreach (byte b in hashValue)
        {
            TextBox5.Text = TextBox5.Text + string.Format("{0:X2}", b);
        }
    }
}
```

4. Press the F5 key on the keyboard to execute the application
5. Enter the text in the Type the text here text box and click each button, such as SHA1,SHA256,SHA384, and SHA512 to view the text in various algorithm , as shown in Figure 26.35:

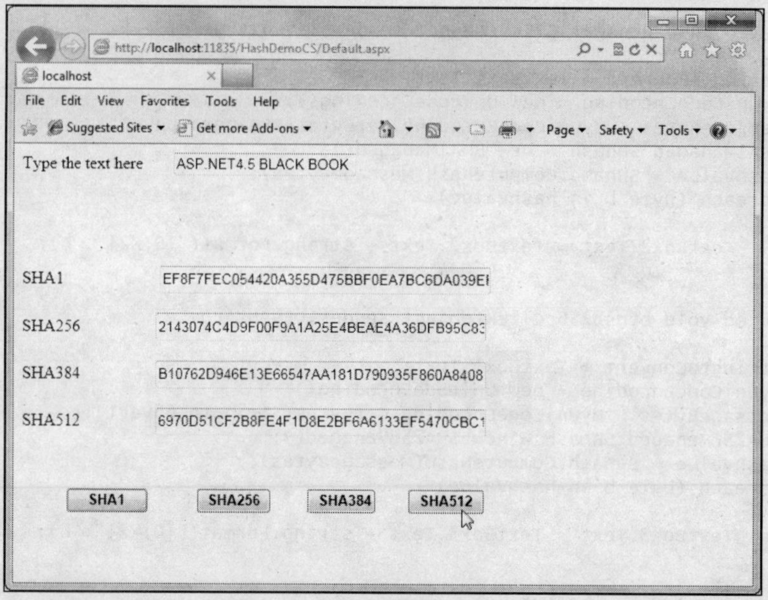

Figure 26.35: Converting the Text into Different Hash Algorithm

Let us now summarize the main points of the chapter.

Summary

In this chapter, you have learned that security is an essential design and development aspect of .NET applications. You have also learned about the code verification process performed by the CLR for .NET applications. In addition, you have learned about the concepts of authentication and authorization, which form the basis of role-based security.

This chapter also describes how to implement security in ASP.NET applications through various authentication modes, such as Anonymous, Windows, and Forms in IIS and the configuration files. You have also learned about impersonation and delegation in ASP.NET applications, membership feature in ASP.NET 4.5, and using membership features to create, delete, and manage users and roles. Furthermore, you have learned how to make .NET applications secure and reliable through cryptography by using hash algorithms.

In the next chapter, you learn how to develop mobile applications in ASP.NET 4.5.

27

Developing Mobile Applications

If you need an Immediate Solution to:	See page:

In Depth

In the previous chapters, you have learned how to create websites that are compatible with all modern desktop Web browsers, such as Internet Explorer 7.0 and later, Netscape Navigator 6 and later, Opera 7 and later, and Mozilla Firefox 1.0 and later. These websites appear the same and exhibit the same behavior on all desktop Web browsers. Now in the current scenario, websites can also be accessed through hand-held and resource-constrained devices, such as Personal Digital Assistant (PDA) and mobile phones. The browsers of these devices are not as powerful as desktop browsers. Moreover, the capacity of each hand-held device varies from the other in terms of memory and functional capability. Therefore, desktop browser-enabled Web forms might not always be accessible through hand-held devices. A website that is compatible with all hand-held devices differs from traditional desktop browser-enabled websites. The reason is that traditional desktop browser-enabled websites require more support in terms of memory and browsing speed as compared to the browsers of hand-held devices. Due to this reason, Microsoft launched .NET Compact Framework that enables you to create mobile Web applications. .NET Compact Framework inherits its architecture, classes, and runtime environment (Common Language Runtime (CLR) and managed code execution) from .NET Framework. The only thing that differentiates it from .NET Framework is some additional controls and classes that are specific to Mobile Web development.

In this chapter, you learn about the .NET Compact Framework and the Mobile Web application architecture. Next, you learn about the various Mobile Web form controls and the concept of adaptive rendering. In the end, you learn how to create a simple Mobile Web application.

Let's start by learning about .NET Compact Framework 4.5.

.NET Compact Framework 4.5

.NET Compact Framework provides an environment for running applications on mobile devices, such as Pocket PCs and mobile phones. This framework is integrated with the Windows CE .NET operating system and allows the applications to interact with the native components by calling the native functions. Figure 27.1 shows the architecture of .NET Compact Framework:

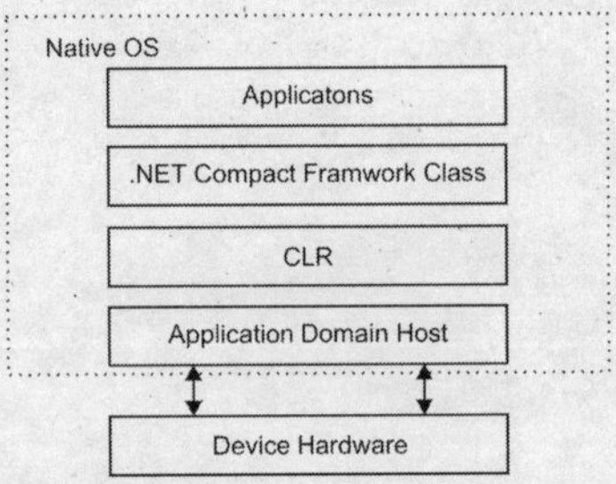

Figure 27.1: Showing the .NET Compact Framework Architecture

Each application created in .NET Compact Framework runs within a runtime construct called application domain. Restricting the execution of an application within the application domain provides several benefits, such as security and fault detection. The concept of application domain is implemented with the help of an application domain host, which resides as native system code in the system and initiates the CLR at runtime.

.NET Compact Framework does not support all the classes and namespaces of .NET Framework. It provides the following namespaces and classes:

- **Microsoft.WindowsMobile.DirectX**—Allows you to incorporate DirectX programming (DirectX programming requires more processing power than a computer and it can become complex because of the required mathematics) in your device applications. DirectX programming is commonly used in developing games.
- **Microsoft.WindowsMobile.DirectX.Direct3D**—Allows you to incorporate Direct3D programming in your device applications.

- **Microsoft.WindowsCE.Forms**—Provides classes, such as InputPanel and InputMethod, for creating device applications.
- **IrDAEndPoint**—Represents the end point of an infrared connection and provides information to a server for establishing a connection between the device and the server. This class exists in the System.Net namespace.
- **IrDACharacterSet**—Defines the character set supported by a mobile device. This class exists in the System.Net.Sockets namespace.
- **IrDAClient**—Provides services to the end point of an infrared connection to make new connections and exchange data streams. This class exists in the System.Net.Sockets namespace.
- **IrDADeviceInfo**—Provides information related to the mobile device, such as its name and type. This class exists in the System.Net.Sockets namespace.
- **IrDAHints**—Defines an enumeration for different types of devices, such as printer or modem. This class exists in the System.Net.Sockets namespace.
- **IrDAListener**—Sets a socket in the listening mode to monitor the connections from a specific source. This class exists in the System.Net.Sockets namespace.
- **Microsoft.ServiceModel.Channels.Mail**—Provides assistance to use Exchange Server Mail Transport of Windows Communication Foundation (WCF). The WCF Exchange Server Mail Transport is an e-mail-based transport that provides a queuing service to process requests.

Now, let's learn about the Mobile Web application architecture.

The Mobile Web Application Architecture

The Mobile Web application architecture is quite simple, but its implementation is complex. The architecture of a Mobile Web application is different for different types of devices. It can be explained by broadly classifying the device types into two categories, Pocket PC and Wireless Application Protocol (WAP)-enabled mobile device.

First, let's discuss the Mobile Web application architecture for Pocket PC. The sequence of tasks that are performed when a Pocket PC requests a Web page is as follows:

1. A Pocket PC sends a Hypertext Transfer Protocol (HTTP) request to the Web server over the Internet. The structure of an HTTP request is shown in Figure 27.2:

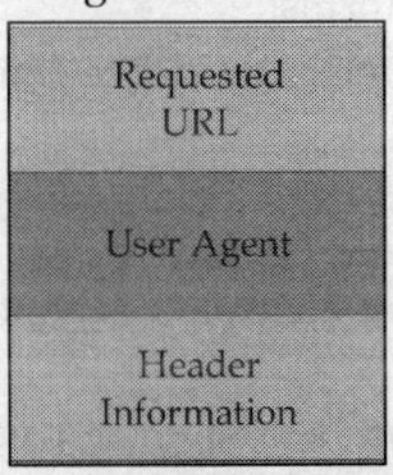

Figure 27.2: Showing the Structure of an HTTP Request

2. The Web server identifies the type of device that has sent the request (in this case, it is a Pocket PC). It also detects other information about the device, such as the markup and the browser that the device uses.
3. The User Agent string is matched with the entries in the `machine.config` file.
4. The Uniform Resource Locator (URL) present in the HTTP request is used to locate the requested mobile Web page.
5. If the mobile Web page is requested for the first time, it is compiled and stored in the assembly cache, and a new instance of the compiled Web page is used to process the request. Alternatively, if the compiled Web page is already present in the assembly cache, then an instance of the Web page is directly created to process the request. This process prevents recompilation of the Web page every time it is requested and results in enhanced performance of the Web page.
6. The business logic contained in the Web page is then executed and the device adapter corresponding to the requesting device is selected to generate the markup.

7. The generated HyperText Markup Language (HTML) is then sent back to the requesting browser inside an HTTP response object.

Now, let's move on to another type of device, a WAP-enabled mobile device. The sequence of steps in this case is as follows:

1. The Wireless Markup Language (WML) browser of the mobile device sends a WAP request to the WAP gateway to access a mobile Web page.
2. The WAP gateway converts the WAP request into an HTTP request and passes it to the Web server over the Internet.
3. The User Agent string is matched against the entries of the `machine.config` file and the compiled version of the requested page is instantiated.
4. The business logic is then executed and the appropriate WML device adapter is selected to generate WML for the requesting WML browser.
5. Generated WML is then encapsulated in an HTTP response object and sent to the WAP gateway.
6. The WAP gateway generates a WAP response object out of it and sends it back to the requesting WML browser.

In this way, a single Mobile Web application caters to the requests of different types of devices.

Let's now learn about the Mobile Web form controls.

Mobile Web Form Controls

Mobile Web forms controls are used to develop Mobile Web forms. They comprise a set of ASP.NET server controls and device adapters that render the controls onto the devices so that the control can be viewed on the display screen of the device. Some of the mobile controls are miniature versions of the Web form controls, such as `Label` and `TextBox`, while some of these controls are entirely new controls, such as the `DeviceSpecific` control introduced specifically for Mobile Web development. Now, let's take a quick look at the mobile control repository:

- **AdRotator**—Adds an advertisement banner to a Web page. You can also associate an image URL with this control to specify the location of the image that is to be displayed on the Web page.
- **Calendar**—Adds a calendar to the Web forms.
- **Command**—Adds an interactive User Interface (UI) element to a Web page. It takes the input from the users and passes it to the Web server.
- **CompareValidator**—Compares the field-value of one control with the field-value of another control. You can take the example of the Password and Confirm Password text boxes. To match the values of both the fields, you can use the CompareValidator control. It is almost the same as the ASP.NET CompareValidator Web form control.
- **CustomValidator**—Allows you to create a customized validation control. It is almost the same as the ASP.NET CustomValidator Web form control.
- **DeviceSpecific**—Uses device filter to detect which type of hardware device is displaying the current ASP.NET Mobile Web page. It is a container control and is always placed within a form or panel control.
- **Form**—Creates a form on the Mobile Web page to group different Mobile Web form controls together.
- **Image**—Specifies the location of multiple image files from which a specific image is selected and displayed depending on the type of target device. It is similar to the ASP.NET Image Web forms control and is used to display an image on the Web page.
- **Label**—Adds a Label control to display text on the Web page.
- **Link**—Adds a hyperlink to the Web page that points to a location within the same page or to some other URL.
- **List**—Displays a static or interactive list of items on the Mobile Web page.
- **ObjectList**—Enables you to add multiple fields to the items of an object list.

- **Panel**—Allows you to organize the mobile controls present on the Mobile Web page by grouping them together.
- **PhoneCall**—Allows end-users to dial a phone number.
- **RangeValidator**—Validates the value of a control to ensure that it falls within a specific range.
- **RegularExpressionValidator**—Validates the value of a control against a pre-specified regular expression.
- **RequiredFieldValidator**—Ensures that an end-user enters some value for a specific control. Actually, this control works by validating the control's value. It verifies whether the value of a control is different from that of its initial value.
- **SelectionList**—Specifies a list of controls with the capability of being viewed in different UIs.
- **StyleSheet**—Add a style-repository in the form of a stylesheet to the Mobile Web page. These styles are applied to the different controls present on the page.
- **TextBox**—Add a text box to the Mobile Web page similar to the ASP.NET TextBox Web form control.
- **TextView**—Displays a large amount of text on the Mobile Web page. Using TextView, you can also add optional markup tags with the text.
- **ValidationSummary**—Displays all the error messages generated from different validation controls at a single location.

Lets' now learn about adaptive rendering.

Adaptive Rendering

Adaptive rendering is a technique with the help of which a control is rendered according to the capabilities of a specific browser or markup. In the present scenario, there are different types of devices that possess different image capabilities and support different markups. Therefore, to support a framework in which you can develop a single application for all devices, adaptive rendering plays a key role. The various ways of implementing adaptive rendering in an application are as follows:

- **Default rendering**—Involves instantiation of the `HtmlTextWriter` class to create its object. The `RenderControl` method of the `HtmlTextWriter` class is then called recursively to append the markup of all the controls to the end of the `HtmlTextWriter` object, and then the `HtmlTextWriter` object is rendered on the target browser. The `HtmlTextWriter` class is not always instantiated in default rendering, but the instantiation depends on the type of target markup to be generated. In case of instantiating the `HtmlTextWriter` class, the ASP.NET Page Framework sends a query to the `TagWriter` property of the `Browser` object. For instance, if the target browser supports HTML 3.2, then the `Html32TextWriter` class is instantiated.
- **Custom TextWriter class**—Helps in specifying your own type of HTML markup, which is used to render controls. In addition to the default `TextWriter` classes, you can also create a custom `TextWriter` class by inheriting the `HtmlTextWriter` class.
- **Device Filtering**—Helps in customizing certain rendering aspects of Web server controls according to the browser. It works by applying filters to the Web server control's properties, attributes, and templates, and in some cases, to the attributes of the `Page` and `Control` directives. The device filter definitions are stored in the `App_Browsers` folder and are merged with the default browser definitions of the application to generate the appropriate device filter.
- **Control adapters**—Help in customizing the behavior of a page or control at different stages in the lifecycle of control. They are created by instantiating the `ControlAdapter` class. When the lifecycle of a control begins, ASP.NET Page Framework determines whether there is a control adapter associated with the control or not. If it is, then the method of adapter is called; however, if no adapter is associated, then the control's own method is called. The concept of control adapters differs from that of other methods of customized rendering as in that you can customize the control's behavior at any time in the control's lifecycle.

Let's now move to the Immediate Solutions section of the chapter to learn about developing mobile applications.

Immediate Solutions

Creating a Sample Mobile Web Application

Nowadays, mobile devices have a number of built-in applications, such as calculators, calendars, and To Do lists. In ASP.NET 4.5, a mobile application is created in a slightly different manner.

You need to install Microsoft WebMatrix2 and Windows Phone SDK 7.1 in your system. The Windows Phone SDK will install Windows Phone 7 emulator in your system.

Now, create a website and replace the default source code with the new code, as shown in Listing 27.1:

Listing 27.1: Showing the Code of the `Default.aspx` Page to be Replaced with the Default Source Code

In VB

```
<%@ Page Language="VB" AutoEventWireup="false" CodeFile="Default.aspx.vb"
  Inherits="_Default" %>
<%@ Register TagPrefix="mobile" Namespace="System.Web.UI.MobileControls"
  Assembly="System.Web.Mobile" %>

<!DOCTYPE html>

<html xmlns="http://www.w3.org/1999/xhtml" >
<body>
  <mobile:Form id="Form1" runat="server">
  </mobile:Form>
</body>
</html>
```

In C#

```
<%@ Page Language="C#" AutoEventWireup="true" CodeFile="Default.aspx.cs"
  Inherits="_Default" %>
<%@ Register TagPrefix="mobile" Namespace="System.Web.UI.MobileControls"
  Assembly="System.Web.Mobile" %>

<!DOCTYPE html>

<html xmlns="http://www.w3.org/1999/xhtml" >
<body>
  <mobile:Form id="Form1" runat="server">

  </mobile:Form>
</body>
</html>
```

After modifying the `Default.aspx` page, replace the code of code-behind file with the code shown in Listing 27.2:

Listing 27.2: Showing the Code of the Code-behind File

In VB

```
Partial Class _Default
    Inherits System.Web.UI.MobileControls.MobilePage

End Class
```

In C#

```
using System;
using System.Collections;
using System.ComponentModel;
using System.Data;
using System.Drawing;
using System.Web;
using System.Web.Mobile;
using System.Web.SessionState;
```

```
using System.Web.UI;
using System.Web.UI.MobileControls;
using System.Web.UI.WebControls;
using System.Web.UI.HtmlControls;
public partial class _Default : System.Web.UI.MobileControls.MobilePage
{
    protected void Page_Load(object sender, EventArgs e)
    {
    }
}
```

Now, your Web form is converted into a Mobile Web form. You can add Mobile controls to this form from the Toolbox. Mobile form controls are available under the tab named Mobile Web Forms. You can add the controls on the Mobile Web form through the source view only.

NOTE

Microsoft has removed the default support for Mobile Web pages in Visual Studio 2012. As a result, the template for Mobile Web form is not available in the Add New Item dialog box, and you have to convert your Web form to Mobile Web form manually.

In the following example, we create a mobile application of Grade Point Average (GPA) calculator to calculate the GPA score of students. The code of this application is available as `MobileApplicationVB(in VB)` and `MobileApplication(in C#)`. You can find the code for the `Default.aspx` page of the `MobileApplicationVB` and `MobileApplication` applications in Listing 27.3:

Listing 27.3: Showing the Code for the `Default.aspx` Page

In VB

```
<%@ Page Language="VB" AutoEventWireup="false" CodeFile="Default.aspx.vb"
  Inherits="_Default" %>
<%@ Register TagPrefix="mobile" Namespace="System.Web.UI.MobileControls"
  Assembly="System.Web.Mobile" %>

<!DOCTYPE html>

<html xmlns="http://www.w3.org/1999/xhtml" >
<body>
  <mobile:Form id="Form1" runat="server">
    <strong>
        Enter Credit Hours
        <br />
        </strong>
        <em>(Only Numeric Values)
        <br />
        <br />
        </em>
        <mobile:Panel ID="Panel1" Runat="server">
        <mobile:Label ID="Label3" Runat="server">
        Course 1 Credit Hours
        </mobile:Label>
        <mobile:TextBox ID="TextBox1" Runat="server">
        </mobile:TextBox>
        <mobile:Label ID="Label4" Runat="server">
        Course 2 Credit Hours
        </mobile:Label>
        <mobile:TextBox ID="TextBox2" Runat="server">
        </mobile:TextBox>
        <mobile:Label ID="Label5" Runat="server">
        Course 3 Credit Hours
        </mobile:Label>
        <mobile:TextBox ID="TextBox3" Runat="server">
        </mobile:TextBox>
        <mobile:Label ID="Label6" Runat="server">
        Course 4 Credit Hours
        </mobile:Label>
```

```
<mobile:TextBox ID="TextBox4" Runat="server">
</mobile:TextBox>
</mobile:Panel>
<br />
Enter Grades obtained
<br />
(Only grades A,B,C,D and E are allowed)
<br /><br />
<mobile:Panel ID="Panel2" Runat="server">
<mobile:Label ID="Label7" Runat="server">
Course 1 Grade
</mobile:Label>
<mobile:TextBox ID="TextBox5" Runat="server">
</mobile:TextBox>
<mobile:Label ID="Label8" Runat="server">
Course 2 Grade
</mobile:Label>
<mobile:TextBox ID="TextBox6" Runat="server">
</mobile:TextBox>
<mobile:Label ID="Label9" Runat="server">
Course 3 Grade
</mobile:Label>
<mobile:TextBox ID="TextBox7" Runat="server">
</mobile:TextBox>
<mobile:Label ID="Label10" Runat="server">
Course 4 Grade
</mobile:Label>
<mobile:TextBox ID="TextBox8" Runat="server">
</mobile:TextBox>
</mobile:Panel>
<br />
        
<mobile:Command ID="Command1" Runat="server" OnClick="Command1_Click">
Calculate
</mobile:Command>
</mobile:form>
<br />
<br />
<mobile:form id="Form2" runat="server">
<mobile:Label ID="Label2" Runat="server">
Your GPA Score Is
</mobile:Label>
<mobile:Label ID="Label1" Runat="server">
</mobile:Label>
 
<br />
<mobile:Command ID="Command2" Runat="server" OnClick="Command2_Click">
ReturnToGPACalc
</mobile:Command>
  </mobile:Form>
</body>

</html>
```

In C#

```
<%@ Page Language="C#" AutoEventWireup="true" CodeFile="Default.aspx.cs"
  Inherits="_Default" %>
<%@ Register TagPrefix="mobile" Namespace="System.Web.UI.MobileControls"
  Assembly="System.Web.Mobile" %>
<!DOCTYPE html>

<html xmlns="http://www.w3.org/1999/xhtml" >
<body>
  <mobile:Form id="Form1" runat="server">
    <strong>
```

```
Enter Credit Hours
<br />
</strong>
<em>(Only Numeric Values)
<br />
<br />
</em>
<mobile:Panel ID="Panel1" Runat="server">
<mobile:Label ID="Label3" Runat="server">
Course 1 Credit Hours
</mobile:Label>
<mobile:TextBox ID="TextBox1" Runat="server">
</mobile:TextBox>
<mobile:Label ID="Label4" Runat="server">
Course 2 Credit Hours
</mobile:Label>
<mobile:TextBox ID="TextBox2" Runat="server">
</mobile:TextBox>
<mobile:Label ID="Label5" Runat="server">
Course 3 Credit Hours
</mobile:Label>
<mobile:TextBox ID="TextBox3" Runat="server">
</mobile:TextBox>
<mobile:Label ID="Label6" Runat="server">
Course 4 Credit Hours
</mobile:Label>
<mobile:TextBox ID="TextBox4" Runat="server">
</mobile:TextBox>
</mobile:Panel>
<br />
Enter Grades obtained
<br />
(Only grades A,B,C,D and E are allowed)
<br /><br />
<mobile:Panel ID="Panel2" Runat="server">
<mobile:Label ID="Label7" Runat="server">
Course 1 Grade
</mobile:Label>
<mobile:TextBox ID="TextBox5" Runat="server">
</mobile:TextBox>
<mobile:Label ID="Label8" Runat="server">
Course 2 Grade
</mobile:Label>
<mobile:TextBox ID="TextBox6" Runat="server">
</mobile:TextBox>
<mobile:Label ID="Label9" Runat="server">
Course 3 Grade
</mobile:Label>
<mobile:TextBox ID="TextBox7" Runat="server">
</mobile:TextBox>
<mobile:Label ID="Label10" Runat="server">
Course 4 Grade
</mobile:Label>
<mobile:TextBox ID="TextBox8" Runat="server">
</mobile:TextBox>
</mobile:Panel>
<br />
        
<mobile:Command ID="Command1" Runat="server" OnClick="Command1_Click">
Calculate
</mobile:Command>
</mobile:form>
<br />
<br />
<mobile:form id="Form2" runat="server">
```

```
            <mobile:Label ID="Label2" Runat="server">
            Your GPA Score Is
            </mobile:Label>
            <mobile:Label ID="Label1" Runat="server">
            </mobile:Label>
             
            <br />
            <mobile:Command ID="Command2" Runat="server" OnClick="Command2_Click">
            ReturnToGPACalc
            </mobile:Command>
        </mobile:Form>
    </body>
    </html>
```

Now, replace the code of the code-behind file of the Default.aspx with the code given in Listing 27.4:

Listing 27.4: Showing the Code for the Code-behind File

In VB

```
Partial Class _Default
    Inherits System.Web.UI.MobileControls.MobilePage
    Protected Sub Command1_Click(sender As Object, e As EventArgs)
     Handles Command1.Click
        Dim Credit_Hr_1 As Integer = CType(TextBox1.Text, Integer)
        Dim Credit_Hr_2 As Integer = CType(TextBox2.Text, Integer)
        Dim Credit_Hr_3 As Integer = CType(TextBox3.Text, Integer)
        Dim Credit_Hr_4 As Integer = CType(TextBox4.Text, Integer)
        Dim Total_Crdt_Hr As Integer = Credit_Hr_1 + Credit_Hr_2 + Credit_Hr_3 +
        Credit_Hr_4
        Dim Grade1 As Char = CType(TextBox5.Text, Char)
        Dim Grade2 As Char = CType(TextBox6.Text, Char)
        Dim Grade3 As Char = CType(TextBox7.Text, Char)
        Dim Grade4 As Char = CType(TextBox8.Text, Char)
        Dim Grade_Value As Integer = 0
        Dim Temp_Grade_Value As Integer = 0

        If (Grade1 = "A") Then
            Temp_Grade_Value = Credit_Hr_1 * 4
        End If

        If (Grade1 = "B") Then
            Temp_Grade_Value = Credit_Hr_1 * 3
        End If

        If (Grade1 = "C") Then
            Temp_Grade_Value = Credit_Hr_1 * 2
        End If

        If (Grade1 = "D") Then
            Temp_Grade_Value = Credit_Hr_1 * 1
        End If
        If (Grade1 = "E") Then
            Temp_Grade_Value = Credit_Hr_1 * 0
        End If
        Grade_Value = Grade_Value + Temp_Grade_Value

        If (Grade2 = "A") Then
            Temp_Grade_Value = Credit_Hr_2 * 4
        End If

        If (Grade2 = "B") Then
            Temp_Grade_Value = Credit_Hr_2 * 3
        End If
        If (Grade2 = "C") Then
            Temp_Grade_Value = Credit_Hr_2 * 2
        End If

        If (Grade2 = "D") Then
            Temp_Grade_Value = Credit_Hr_2 * 1
        End If
        If (Grade2 = "E") Then
```

```
            Temp_Grade_Value = Credit_Hr_2 * 0
        End If

        Grade_Value = Grade_Value + Temp_Grade_Value

        If (Grade3 = "A") Then
            Temp_Grade_Value = Credit_Hr_3 * 4
        End If

        If (Grade3 = "B") Then
            Temp_Grade_Value = Credit_Hr_3 * 3
        End If

        If (Grade3 = "C") Then
            Temp_Grade_Value = Credit_Hr_3 * 2
        End If

        If (Grade3 = "D") Then
            Temp_Grade_Value = Credit_Hr_3 * 1
        End If

        If (Grade3 = "E") Then
            Temp_Grade_Value = Credit_Hr_3 * 0
        End If
        Grade_Value = Grade_Value + Temp_Grade_Value

        If (Grade4 = "A") Then
            Temp_Grade_Value = Credit_Hr_4 * 4
        End If

        If (Grade4 = "B") Then
            Temp_Grade_Value = Credit_Hr_4 * 3
        End If

        If (Grade4 = "C") Then
            Temp_Grade_Value = Credit_Hr_4 * 2
        End If
        If (Grade4 = "D") Then
            Temp_Grade_Value = Credit_Hr_4 * 1
        End If

        If (Grade4 = "E") Then
            Temp_Grade_Value = Credit_Hr_4 * 0
        End If
        Grade_Value = Grade_Value + Temp_Grade_Value

        Dim GPA As Decimal = Grade_Value / Total_Crdt_Hr

        Me.ActiveForm = Me.Form2

        Label1.Text = Grade_Value.ToString()

    End Sub
    Protected Sub Command2_Click(sender As Object, e As EventArgs)
     Handles Command2.Click
        Me.ActiveForm = Me.Form1
    End Sub
End Class
```

In C#

```
using System;
using System.Collections;
using System.ComponentModel;
using System.Data;
using System.Drawing;
using System.Web;
using System.Web.Mobile;
using System.Web.SessionState;
using System.Web.UI;
using System.Web.UI.MobileControls;
using System.Web.UI.WebControls;
```

```
using System.Web.UI.HtmlControls;

public partial class _Default : System.Web.UI.MobileControls.MobilePage
{
    protected void Page_Load(object sender, EventArgs e)
    {

    }
    protected void Command1_Click(object sender, EventArgs e)
    {
        int Credit_Hr_1 = Convert.ToInt32(TextBox1.Text);
        int Credit_Hr_2 = Convert.ToInt32(TextBox2.Text);
        int Credit_Hr_3 = Convert.ToInt32(TextBox3.Text);
        int Credit_Hr_4 = Convert.ToInt32(TextBox4.Text);
        int Total_Crdt_Hr = Credit_Hr_1 + Credit_Hr_2 + Credit_Hr_3 + Credit_Hr_4;

        string Grade1 = Convert.ToString(TextBox5.Text);
        string Grade2 = Convert.ToString(TextBox6.Text);
        string Grade3 = Convert.ToString(TextBox6.Text);
        string Grade4 = Convert.ToString(TextBox7.Text);

        int Grade_Value = 0;
        int Temp_Grade_Value = 0;
        if (Grade1 == "A")
            Temp_Grade_Value = Credit_Hr_1 * 4;

        if (Grade1 == "B")
            Temp_Grade_Value = Credit_Hr_1 * 3;

        if (Grade1 == "C")
            Temp_Grade_Value = Credit_Hr_1 * 2;

        if (Grade1 == "D")
            Temp_Grade_Value = Credit_Hr_1 * 1;

        if (Grade1 == "F")
            Temp_Grade_Value = Credit_Hr_1 * 0;

        Grade_Value = Grade_Value + Temp_Grade_Value;

        if (Grade2 == "A")
            Temp_Grade_Value = Credit_Hr_2 * 4;

        if (Grade2 == "B")
            Temp_Grade_Value = Credit_Hr_2 * 3;

        if (Grade2 == "C")
            Temp_Grade_Value = Credit_Hr_2 * 2;

        if (Grade2 == "D")
            Temp_Grade_Value = Credit_Hr_2 * 1;

        if (Grade2 == "F")
            Temp_Grade_Value = Credit_Hr_2 * 0;

        Grade_Value = Grade_Value + Temp_Grade_Value;

        if (Grade3 == "A")
            Temp_Grade_Value = Credit_Hr_3 * 4;
        if (Grade3 == "B")
            Temp_Grade_Value = Credit_Hr_3 * 3;

        if (Grade3 == "C")
            Temp_Grade_Value = Credit_Hr_3 * 2;

        if (Grade3 == "D")
            Temp_Grade_Value = Credit_Hr_3 * 1;
        if (Grade3 == "F")
            Temp_Grade_Value = Credit_Hr_3 * 0;

        Grade_Value = Grade_Value + Temp_Grade_Value;
        if (Grade4 == "A")
```

```
            Temp_Grade_Value = Credit_Hr_4 * 4;

        if (Grade4 == "B")
            Temp_Grade_Value = Credit_Hr_4 * 3;

        if (Grade4 == "C")
            Temp_Grade_Value = Credit_Hr_4 * 2;

        if (Grade4 == "D")
            Temp_Grade_Value = Credit_Hr_4 * 1;
        if (Grade4 == "F")
            Temp_Grade_Value = Credit_Hr_4 * 0;

        Grade_Value = Grade_Value + Temp_Grade_Value;

        float GPA = Grade_Value / Total_Crdt_Hr;
        this.ActiveForm = this.Form2;

        Label1.Text = Grade_Value.ToString();
    }
    protected void Command2_Click(object sender, EventArgs e)
    {
        this.ActiveForm = this.Form1;
    }
}
```

You can test this mobile application in a browser, but as this application is targeted towards a mobile device, you should use a mobile device emulator to run the application.

Now, add the application in the Microsoft WebMatrix2 software and run the application using the Windows phone 7 emulator. You can see the output, as shown in Figure 27.3:

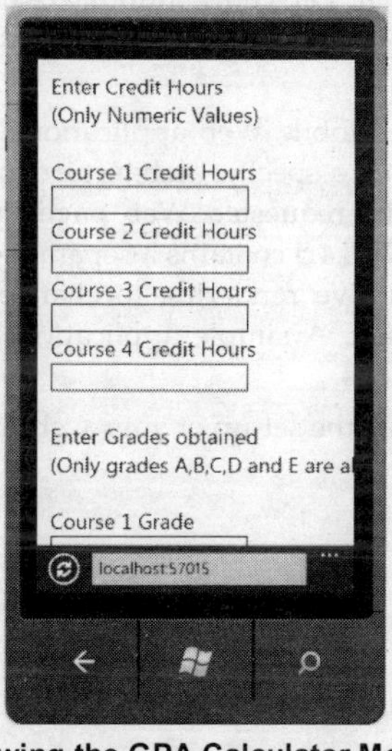

Figure 27.3: Showing the GPA Calculator Mobile Application

In Figure 27.3, there are several fields in which you need to enter credit hours and grades for different courses. Enter values in all the fields and scroll down the mobile screen to locate the Calculate button. Click the Calculate button to calculate the GPA score. The score appears, as shown in Figure 27.4:

Figure 27.4: Showing the Calculated GPA Score

You can click the ReturnToGPACalc link to return to the previous page and calculate the GPA score again.

With this, we come to the end of the chapter. Let's now summarize the main points of this chapter.

Summary

In this chapter, you have learned about Mobile Web applications and Mobile Web forms. You have learned about the .NET Compact Framework. It has a specific architecture to receive requests for Mobile Web pages and then to process the request and send the requested Web page. It is used for developing websites that are accessible through mobile devices. ASP.NET 4.5 contains a separate set of controls that are used to create Mobile Web pages. These controls support adaptive rendering to change their appearance according to the device through which the page is being accessed. A simple application is also given to make you understand the practical concept of Mobile Web applications.

In the next chapter, you learn how to create the set-up of your website and deploy it on the Web server.

28

Deploying Web Applications

In Depth

Deploying an application refers to the process of distributing an application among various end-users. You might wonder why to share an application with others. Let's consider an example to understand the need to deploy applications. Suppose you have developed an application that converts the values of one currency into another. You can use the application only for your company's benefit. However, if you choose to share the application with other companies, it will prove to be useful to them as well. In addition, other companies may contribute towards further improvement of the original application. You need to deploy the currency converter application to enable other companies to use and modify it. Traditionally, applications were deployed using scripted set-up programs. These set-up programs were based on the procedural model and focused on how to deploy the application. Now, things have changed. For example, take the case of Visual Studio, where the deployment of applications is much easier and flexible compared to the traditional approach of deploying applications.

This chapter describes the options available to deploy applications from both the Web server and the client perspectives. This chapter also describes the different deployment techniques, such as Web One Click Publish, Copy Web Site, and XCopy deployment. In the *Immediate Solutions* section, you learn how to deploy the applications using different deployment techniques.

Let's start with new features or enhancements in deployment techniques.

Web Deployment Features in Visual Studio 2012

When you have developed, tested, and debugged an application, the next step is to deploy it. The purpose of deploying an application is to ensure a simple and easy installation for application files and any other required files on a client computer. The .NET Framework provides you with some easy ways to deploy a Web application. You can deploy a Web application by copying its contents to the destination, by publishing it, or by using Web Installer. In addition, you need to perform some additional tasks on the target server that are given as follows:

- Perform the changes, such as settings for debugging or database connection strings in the Web.config file
- Configure the Internet Information Services (IIS) settings on the destination computer
- Install security certificates
- Set the values in the registry of the destination computer
- Install the application assemblies in the Global Assembly Cache (GAC) on the destination computer

Visual Studio 2012 enables you to deploy a Web application or a Web site on a target server by performing the following tasks:

- Transforming the Web.config file
- Deploying a SQL Server database
- Using the one-click publish feature
- Using the Copy Web Site tool

Web.config Transformation

Web.config is an XML document that contains settings for an ASP.NET Web application. It contains the information of control module loading, security configuration, session state configuration, application language, and compilation settings. A Web.config file can also include application specific items, for instance database connection strings. When you deploy a Web application on a different computer, you might need to change the following settings:

- Change a database connection string that points a production database
- Disable debugging

- Remove sensitive information, for instance the connection code when you have to provide a package to a community site

One of the solutions to set the preceding settings is to manually manage the changes in a Web.config file, by performing the following tasks:

- Modifying the Web.config file on a target server each time the project is deployed
- Creating and maintaining multiple versions of the Web.config file for each environment settings (in separate folders or with distinct names) and use the most appropriate on the basis of conditions
- Creating XSLT files to transform the Web.config files and apply them when the project is deployed.

Now in Visual Studio 2012, ASP.NET provides tools that automate the process of transforming a Web.config file when you deploy a Web application. For each environment, in which you want to deploy your Web application, you need to create a transform file that specifies the settings for the Web.config file on the basis of each environment.

A transform file includes the name of the destination environment with a prefix node, Web, and suffix node, Config. For example, the transform file for the Debug build configuration is Web.Debug.Config. A transform file is an XML file that uses XML attributes to specify how the Web.config file should be changed. Consider the following code snippet:

```
<connectionStrings>
  <add name="WebApplicationServices"
      connectionString="[ProductionDatabase]" />
</connectionStrings>
```

In the preceding code snippet, the transform file specifies that the connection string, named WebApplicationServices, would be converted to a production database when the Web application is deployed on the target server. Now, consider the following code snippet:

```
<?xml version="1.0"?>
<configuration xmlns:xdt="http://schemas.microsoft.com/XML-Document-Transform">
  <connectionStrings>
    <add name="WebApplicationServices"
        connectionString="[ProductionDatabase]"
        xdt:Transform="Replace" xdt:Locator="Match(name)"/>
  </connectionStrings>
</configuration>
```

In the preceding code snippet, the Locator attribute specifies that only the add element having the same name as WebApplicationServices should be changed. While, the Transform attribute specifies that the deployment process should replace the entire add element.

Database Deployment

In Visual Studio 2012, you can also deploy a Web application that use SQL Server database to store and maintain the data related to the application by creating script files (.sql files). You can create a custom .sql script file and specify the order in which the script should run on the target server, and then add this script file to a Web package. When a Web package is installed on a target server, it runs the script file and creates the same database on the server.

You specify SQL Server database scripting options in the Package/Publish SQL tab of the project properties window. You can access the project properties window by right-clicking the project name in Solution Explorer and selecting the Properties option. Figure 28.1 shows the Package/Publish SQL tab in the project properties window:

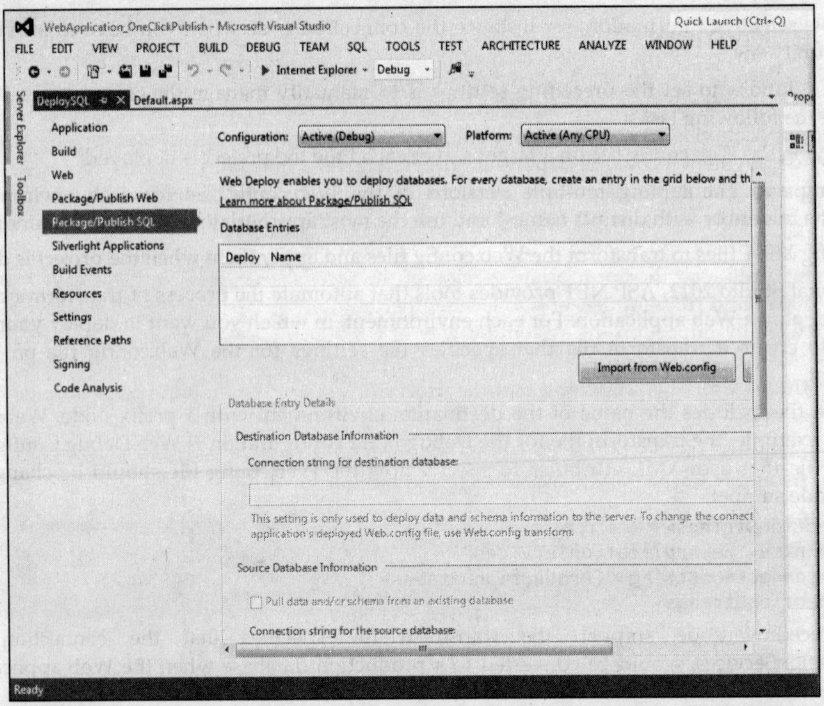

Figure 28.1: Displaying the Package/Publish SQL Tab in Project Properties

One-Click Publish for Web Applications

In Visual Studio 2012, the IIS remote management service is used to publish the Web application to the remote server. You have to create a publish profile for the testing or staging server to store the credentials securely to deploy a Web application on the server. After creating a publish profile, you can deploy the Web application to the target server with one click by using the Web One Click Publish toolbar.

Using the Copy Web Site Tool

The Copy Web Site tool is used to replace a final Web site with the previous Web site on a target server directly. It means you can open a folder on a target server, and then upload and download the files from the source Web site to the target Web site. The Copy Web Site tool synchronizes the files in both Web sites and keeps sites with updated files.

When the application files are copied from a source Web site to a target Web site, the Copy Web Site tool creates a file, named App_offline.htm, into the root directory of the target Web site. Till the App_offline.htm file exists, all requests to the Web site are redirected to this file. The App_offline.htm file shows a message to the clients that the Web site is being updated. After copying the application files, the Copy Web Site tool deletes the App_offline.htm file from the target Web site.

Some features of the Copy Web Site tool are given as follows:

- ❑ You can copy the .aspx and class files from a source server to a target server.
- ❑ You can open and copy files from any kind of Web site, such as Local IIS, Remote IIS, and File Transfer Protocol (FTP), supported by Visual Studio 2012.
- ❑ The synchronization feature of the Copy Web Site tool checks the files of both Web sites automatically and keeps them with the up-to-date versions of the files.

Now, let's learn how to deploy a WPF application.

XCopy Deployment

XCopy is used to deploy an application by copying a set of files to a folder on the target computer and then executing the application on the client. Regardless of the number of assemblies, if the files are copied to the same folder, the application is executed without editing the configuration settings and registry values. In other words, the XCopy deployment technique deploys a fully functional application by simply copying the assemblies to the target computer. The application starts using the assembly because the assembly is completely self-described, that is, the assembly contains all the information about the application. This is because the .NET compilers contain the identifiers and metadata into compiled modules and the Common Language Runtime (CLR) uses this information to load the appropriate version of the assemblies. The identifiers have the proper information required to load and run modules and to locate other modules referenced by the assembly. Though this process does not make any impact on the system by way of configuring the components and registry entries, it is also known as *zero-impact* installation. In the similar manner, uninstallation is also performed without making any impact on the system. The only thing that the process of uninstallation requires is to remove specific files from specific directories.

Users do not appreciate the XCopy deployment technique, as it does not have the ability to place assemblies in the Global Assembly Cache (GAC) and add icons to the Start menu.

In addition, the XCopy deployment technique can also work with Web applications with the exception of the folder structure, which means that the files are copied to a virtual directory that you have set up for your Web application. The Web application contains a couple of configuration files as well as images, determining which files must be included is a little bit tricky. When you open a C# project file, you can look at the `<Files>` element, which displays the attributes showing the files that make up the project, such as `BuildAction` and `RelPath`. You must copy these files if the `BuildAction` attribute contains the value `Content` out of the four values—`None`, `Content`, `Compile`, and `Embedded Resource`. We will know about the working procedure of XCopy deployment in the Immediate Solutions section later in this chapter.

The XCopy command can take a number of arguments. Noteworthy options are listed in Table 28.1:

Table 28.1: Noteworthy Options of the XCopy Command

Options	Description
/E	Copies directories, subdirectories, and files including empty ones
/S	Copies directories, subdirectories, and files excluding empty ones
/K	Copies attributes and normal XCopy will reset read-only attributes
/R	Overwrites read-only files
/O	Copies security-related information, such as file ownership and Access Control List (ACL) information
/H	Copies directories and subdirectories including hidden and system files
/I	Assumes the destination as a directory and creates if it does not exist
/C	Continues copying even if an error occurs

There are also a large number of arguments not included in the table. However, you can find them by using the following command at the command prompt:

```
xcopy /?
```

Immediate Solutions

Web Application Deployment

The deployment of Web application on the Web server is the last and important stage of the Web application development life cycle. The Web application is deployed on the server using various techniques or utilities present in .NET framework. We will learn each of the techniques one by one. Let's consider an example, where we create an installer for an application named `WebDeploymentTest`, which you can see under the Design view in Figure 28.2:

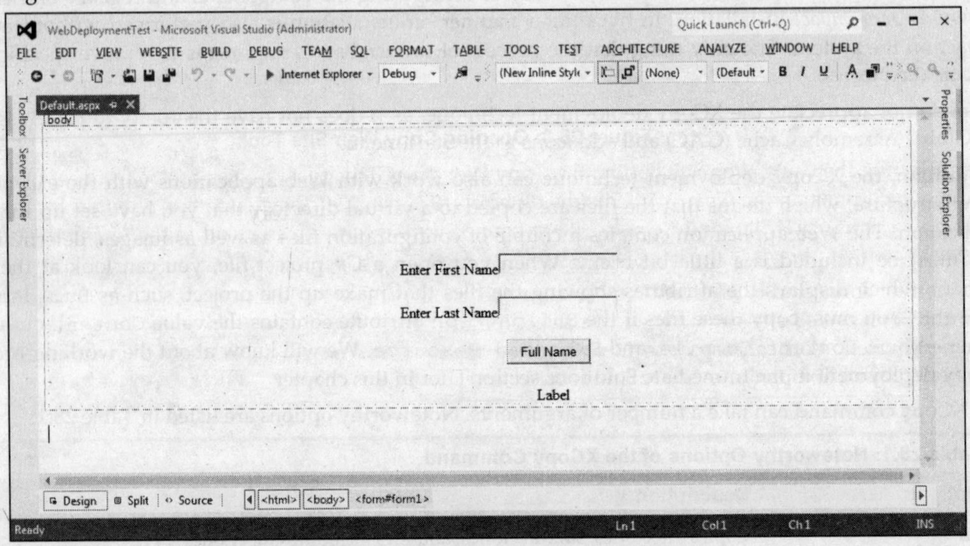

Figure 28.2: Displaying the Web Application

The `WebDeploymentTest` is a simple application that has three Label control, two TextBox controls, and a Button control.

When the user clicks the Full Name button, the contents of the `TextBox1` and `TextBox2` are joined and displayed on the Label1 control, according to the following instruction, which is written in the click event of the Button control:

The code for the click event of the Button control in VB is as follows:

```
Protected Sub Btnfullname_Click(sender As Object, e As EventArgs)
  Handles
  Btnfullname.Click
          Label1.Text = TextBox1.Text & " " & TextBox2.Text
End Sub
```

The code for the click event of the Button control in C# is as follows:

```
protected void Btnfullname_Click(object sender, EventArgs e)
{
  Label1.Text = TextBox1.Text + " " + TextBox2.Text;
}
```

Copy Web Site Deployment

After creating a Web application, you can deploy the Web application by using the Copy Web Site tool provided by Visual Studio 2012. You can open the Copy Web Site GUI by selecting the Copy Web Site option from the WEBSITE menu or by right clicking the application name in the Solution Explorer window, as shown in Figure 28.3:

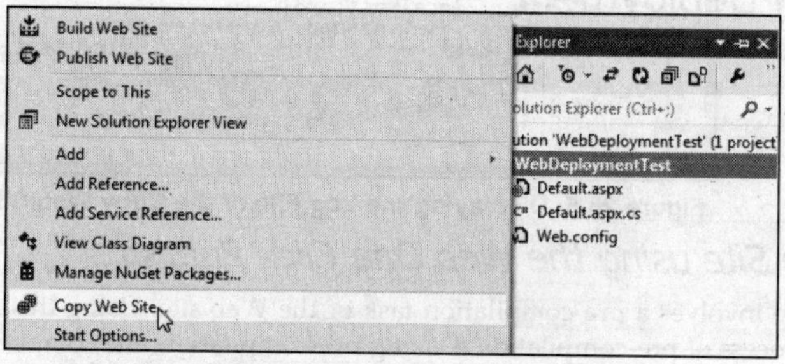

Figure 28.3: Opening Copy Web Site Tool

After selecting the Copy Web Site option, the Copy Web Site GUI appears. Click on the Connect to a remote site button, which pulls up the Open Web Site dialog box. The Open Web Site dialog box provides four options--File System, Local IIS, FTP Site, and Remote Site to connect to the server (discussed in the In Depth section of this chapter).

After getting connected to a server, you can copy the contents of your Web application to it by selecting the files from the Source Web site pane. When you select the files in the Source Web site pane, some movement arrows become enabled. You can copy the files by using these arrows placed in between the Source Web site and Remote Web site text panes, as shown in Figure 28.4:

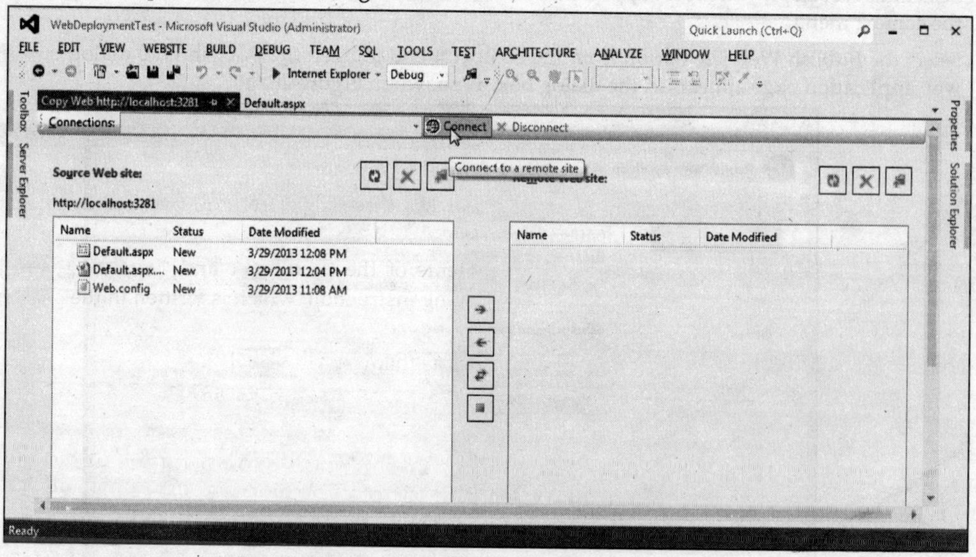

Figure 28.4: Copying the Files to Remote Location

After selecting a file, click the right-pointing arrow to copy the file to the Remote Web site pane. You can view the details of the copying actions that are recorded in a log file. You can view the log file by clicking the View Log button at the bottom of the Copy Web Site GUI as shown in Figure 28.5:

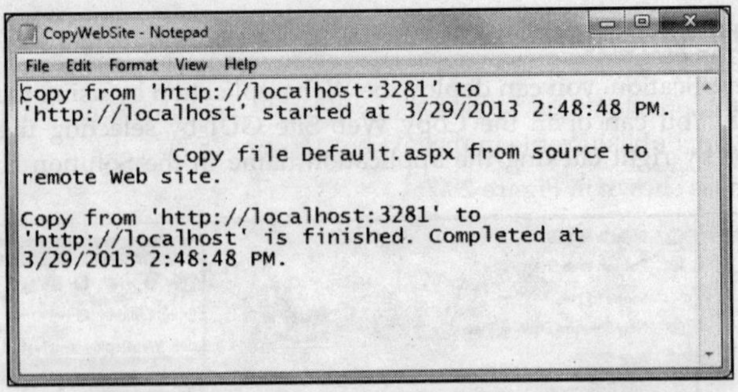

Figure 28.5: Displaying the Log File of the Copy Web Site

Deploying Web Site using the Web One Click Publish

Publishing a Web site involves a pre-compilation task of the Web site. Using this method, the Web site will be error free after the process of pre-compilation. During pre-compilation, the compiler checks out for all the errors involving syntax matching errors, type matching errors, variables transfer errors, and calling of sub routines across different application modules.

It also checks for the modules accessing application's global resources and the local computer resources. The pre-compilation process is the replica of the dynamic compilation of Web pages while rendering them in the browser. The output of the pre-compilation process is written in any directory of the local drives or external computer drives by using the FTP or HTTP. Any error(s) in the pre-compilation is visible as an error list in the Output window of the Visual Studio IDE. Now, perform the following steps to deploy a Web application using the one-click publish feature:

1. Select the WebDeploymentTest application name in the Solution Explorer window and right-click it to open the context menu.
2. Select the Publish Web Site option from the context menu to open the Publish Web dialog box. The Publish web application page appears in the dialog box, as shown in Figure 28.6:

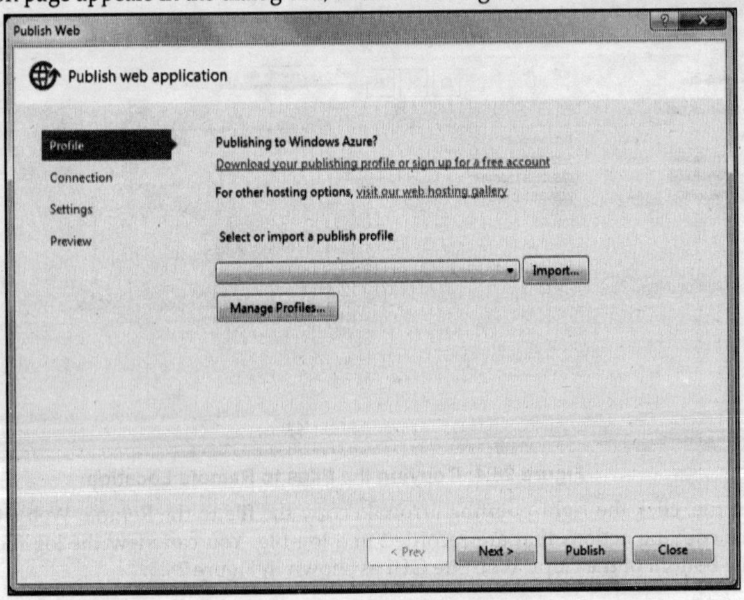

Figure 28.6: Showing the Publish web application Page

3. Select the <New> option from the Select or import a publish profile drop-down list. The New Profile dialog box appears (Figure 28.7).
4. Enter the name of the profile in the Profile Name text box to create a new publish profile. In our case, we have entered WebApp_PublishProfile in the text box (Figure 28.7).
5. Click the OK button, as shown in Figure 28.7:

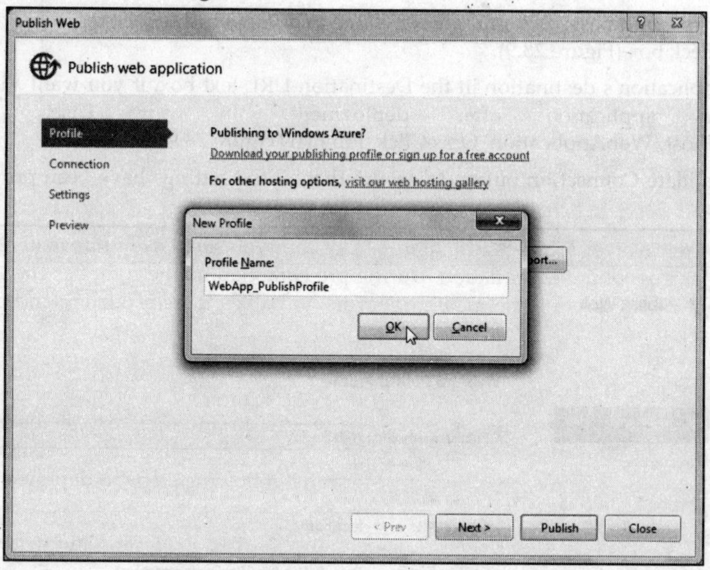

Figure 28.7: Creating a New Publish Profile

The Profile name appears next to Profile tab (Figure 28.8).

6. Select the Connection tab in the Profile web application page to open the settings in the tab, as shown in Figure 28.8:

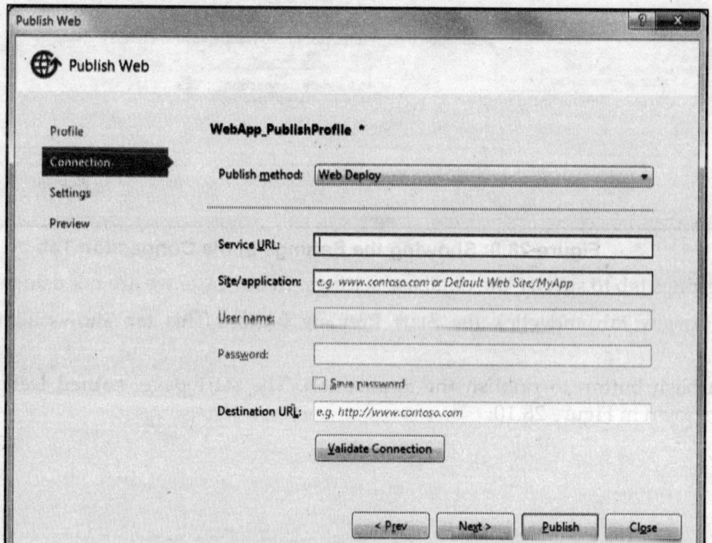

Figure 28.8: Showing the Settings in the Connection Tab

6. Select the Web Deploy option from the Publish method drop-down list (Figure 28.9).
7. Enter localhost in the Service URL text box, if you are publishing on your own computer. Otherwise, enter the address provided by the hosting company in the Service URL text box (Figure 28.9).
8. Enter Default Web site/application name in the Site/application text box. In our case, we have entered Default Web site/WebDeploymentTest (Figure 28.9).
9. Enter user name and password in the User Name and Password text boxes, respectively and click the Save password check box (Figure 28.9).
10. Enter the application's destination in the Destination URL text box, if you want Visual Studio to implicitly open the application after deployment. In our case, we have entered http://localhost/WebApplication_OnceClick_Publish (Figure 28.9).
11. Click the Validate Connection button to ensure that all the settings have been properly done, as shown in Figure 28.9:

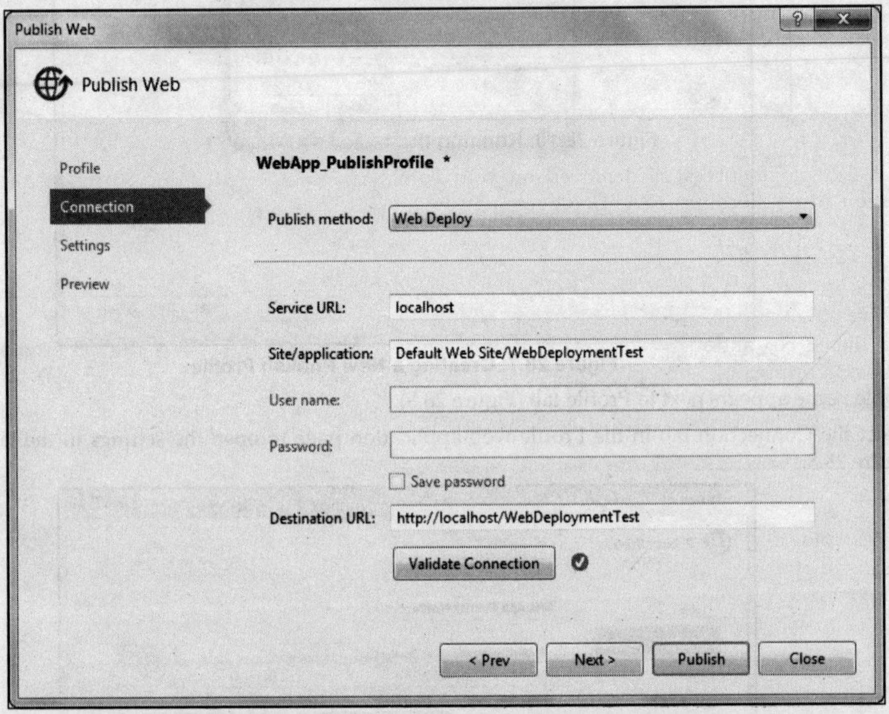

Figure 28.9: Showing the Settings in the Connection Tab

12. Select the Settings tab to specify the database settings. In our case, we are not using any database.
13. Select the Preview tab and click the Start Preview button. This tab shows all the pages in your Web application.
14. Click the Publish button to publish the application. The start page, named Default.aspx, appears in the browser, as shown in Figure 28.10:

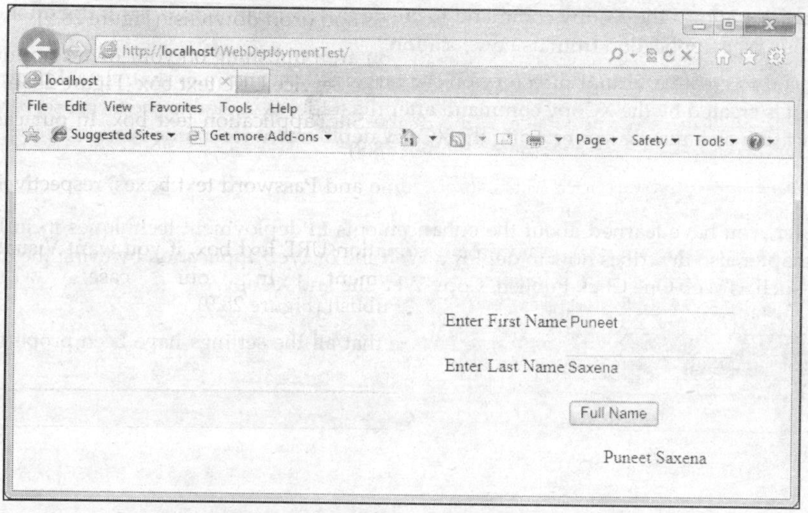

Figure 28.10: Running the Application in the Browser

Now, WebDeploymentTest is deployed on your computer. You can access it by typing the address of the application, http://localhost/WebDeploymentTest/, on your browser's address bar.

XCOPY Deployment

Now, let's see how a Web application is deployed using the XCopy deployment technique. Open the Run dialog box by pressing the WINDOWS and R keys simultaneously on your keyboard. Type cmd in the Open text box of the Run dialog box and then click the OK button. The command prompt opens. At the command prompt, type the following command:

```
xcopy /i /s C:\Users\Puneet\WebDeploymentTest D:\MyDeployment
```

NOTE

You need to provide the administrative rights to the Command Prompt.

The source folder WebDeploymentTest is placed under the C drive and the destination folder, MyDeployment, is placed in the D drive. When you execute this command, all the files and folders within the WebDeploymentTest folder are deployed in the target folder, as shown in Figure 28.11:

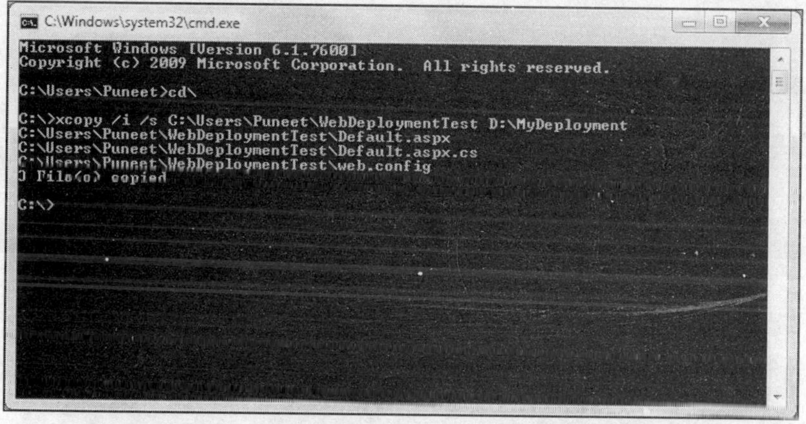

Figure 28.11: Using XCOPY Command in the Command Prompt

The /I parameter allows the XCopy command to create the destination folder if it does not exist. Now, you can easily run your Web application from its new location.

Now, you need to create a virtual directory on the target server and map that virtual directory to the physical directory that is created by the XCopy command after the folder is copied to the target server. We have deployed a Web application on a remote server using the XCopy deployment technique here.

Summary

In this chapter, you have learned about the enhancements in deployment techniques included in Visual Studio 2012. This chapter also describes how to deploy a Web site or Web application by using the different deployment techniques, such as Web One Click Publish, Copy Web site and XCopy.

29

Online Travel Agency

Bon Voyage Pvt. Ltd. is a travel agency established in Delhi with its branches spread all over India. The travel agency offers best rates on bus tickets, train tickets, and car rentals. This agency is receiving good response from the customers for the services it provides. To meet the expectations of customers, the management of the travel agency is looking forward to provide best travel experiences within the reach of the customers. However, while meeting the expectations of the customers, the agency is encountering the following problems:

- It is becoming difficult for the employees of the agency to handle the increasing number of customers
- It requires more time and effort to store and manage huge amount of bookings
- It is very difficult for the customers to search the office of the travel agency
- It is not able to receive proper feedback from the customers to improve its services

Therefore, the management of the Bon Voyage Pvt. Ltd. Travel agency decided to create a website through which it can provide the details of its services to the customers. In addition, the customers can book tickets online without standing in a queue. For this purpose, the management has contacted some software developers. The software developers recommend ASP.NET 4.5 to be used as the Web application Framework to develop the website, as it provides great functionality with minimal use of code.

The software developers have presented the agency with a complete flow chart of the website, which has been named as the Online Travel Agency portal. The flow chart of this project is shown in Figure 29.1:

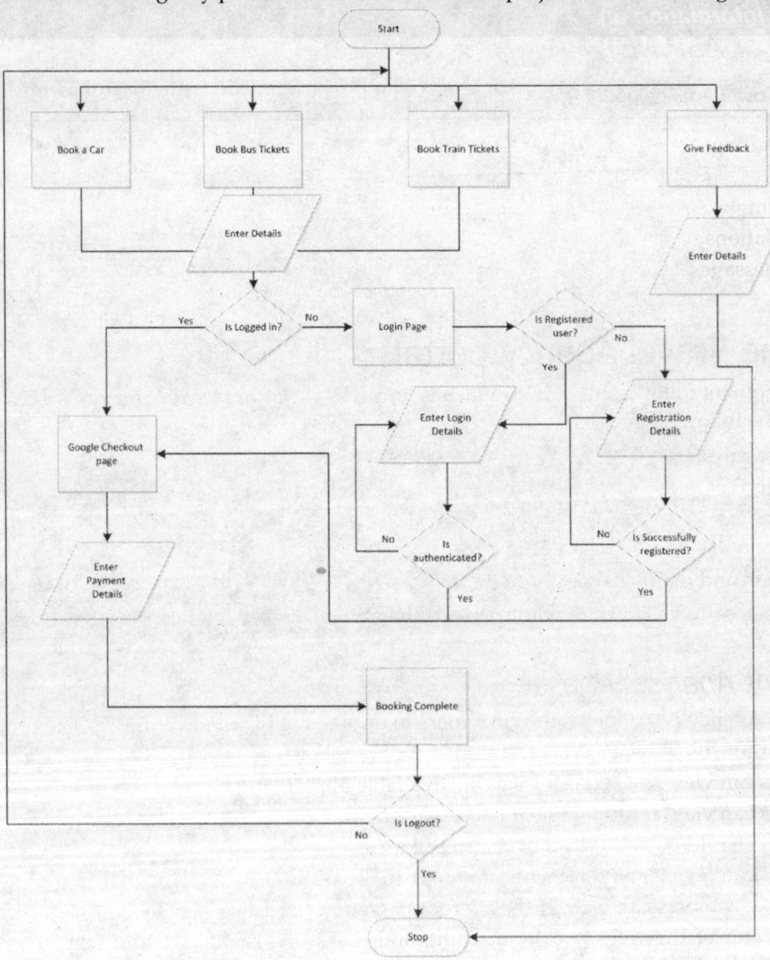

Figure 29.1: Showing the Flow Chart of Online Travel Agency portal

As shown in Figure 29.1, through the website, the customers can book a car, bus ticket, or train ticket and give feedback. The website is designed in such a manner that the customer (or the user) should be authenticated to make a booking. This implies that the customers have to login to the website for booking their mode of travel. If the user is not registered, then the user can register with the website by providing some registration details. After successfully logging on to the website, the user is redirected to the Google Checkout page, where the user can enter the payment details online and logout from the website. However, giving feedback does not require user authentication.

Project Requirements

Prior to development of the Online Travel Agency portal, you should ensure that your computer meets the basic software requirements and you are familiar with the basic concepts of C# or VB languages and ASP.NET 4.5.

Software Requirements

To develop the Online Travel Agency portal using C# and VB as languages and ASP.NET 4.5 Web application Framework, you must install the following software:

- Microsoft Visual Studio Ultimate 2012
- Microsoft SQL Server 2008

Basic Concepts of ASP.NET

To develop the Online Travel Agency portal, you should be familiar with the following basic concepts of ASP.NET:

- Database handling
- JavaScript
- Events handling
- Making validations
- Displaying messages
- Master page

SDLC of Online Travel Agency portal

A software development follows a life cycle, which is termed as Software Development Life Cycle (SDLC). SDLC generally entails the following phases:

- Requirement analysis
- Software design
- Development
- Testing
- Implementation and maintenance

Similar to any other software development project, the Online Travel Agency portal also has SDLC, which is discussed next.

The Requirement Analysis Phase

The Online Travel Agency portal helps the customers in organizing the mode of travel. The project should entail the following requirement:

- The customers can view the details of the cars available for booking
- The customers can view the schedule of particular bus and train routes
- The customers should be authorized or registered users
- The customers can register as a authenticated user to the website
- The registered customers can recover their forgot passwords and also change their passwords
- The administrator of the website can add, edit, and delete the car details and schedule of the buses and trains in the database of the project
- The customers can provide the feedback to the travel agency regarding their travel experiences

The Software Design Phase

The software design phase of the Online Travel Agency portal is divided into two sections, front end design or User Interface (UI) and the back end or database design.

Designing the Front End

The UI design of the Online Travel Agency portal is divided into the following three modules:

- Login Module
- Booking Module
- Administrator Module

Let's briefly examine these three modules.

The Login Module

The Login module is the first module of the Online Travel Agency portal, used to secure the website from unauthenticated users. In the Login module, you need to use the Login controls to provide security to the website. This ensures that only authenticated and authorized users can access all the links and navigation paths of the website. The unregistered or guest users can only view the schedule and fare charges of their mode of travel. Only a registered user can book the tickets for his or her journey. In this module, you need to perform the following tasks:

- Verify the user name and password of the customers who want to log in
- Recover forgot password of the existing customers
- Change the password of the logged in customers

The Booking Module

The Booking module is used by the customers of the Online Travel Agency project. In this module, customers can select any mode of travel from the available options that are car, bus, or train. All the customers can view the details and the fare of a particular car, bus, or train, but only the registered customer can book them.

The Administrator Module

The Administrator module can be accessed only by the administrator of the website. In this module, the administrator adds, updates, and deletes new records as well as schedules the travel date, after logging on to the website.

Designing the Back End Database

The database of this project acts as the back-end to store information, such as details of cars, buses, trains, booking details, and user details. In this project, we have used Microsoft SQL Server 2008 to create the database, named Travel for Online Travel Agency. The Travel database consists of multiple tables, which are as follows:

- aspnet_Applications
- aspnet_Membership
- aspnet_Paths
- aspnet_PersonalizationAllUsers
- aspnet_PersonalizationPerUser
- aspnet_Profile
- aspnet_Roles
- aspnet_SchemaVersions
- aspnet_Users
- aspnet_UsersInRoles
- aspnet_WebEvent_Events
- BusDetails
- CarDetails
- Feedback
- TrainDetails
- UserInfo

Let's look at the details of these tables.

NOTE

The tables prefixed with the aspnet_ keyword (such as aspnet_Applications and aspnet_Membership) are created automatically by the Login control using the membership service.

Table 29.1 gives an overview of the structure of the BusDetails table:

Table 29.1: The BusDetails Table

Column Name	Data type	Allow Nulls	Description
BusId	int - PK	No	Represents unique ID for buses
BFrom	varchar(50)	No	Represents the departing bus stop
BTo	varchar(50)	No	Represents the arrival bus stop
BDate	varchar(50)	No	Represents the departing date
SeatsAvailable	int	No	Represents the available seats ina particular bus
Fare	float	No	Represents the fare of a particular bus

Table 29.2 gives an overview of the structure of the CarDetails table:

Table 29.2: The CarDetails Table

Column Name	Data type	Allow Nulls	Description
CarId	int	No	Represents unique ID for cars
CarModel	varchar(50)	No	Specifies the car model
FullDayRent	varchar(50)	No	Represents the full day rent of the car
HalfDayRent	varchar(50)	No	Represents half day rent of the car
Price_ExtraKM	varchar(50)	No	Represents the price charged for extra Kilometers
Price_ExtraHour	varchar(50)	No	Represents the price charged for extra hours
CarCapacity	varchar(50)	No	Represents the capacity of the car
City	nvarchar(50)	No	Represents the destination city

Table 29.3 gives an overview of the structure of the Feedback table:

Table 29.3: The Feedback Table

Column Name	Data type	Allow Nulls	Description
Name	varchar(50)	No	Represents the name of the user submitting the feedback
EMail	varchar(50)	No	Represents the email of the user
Feedback	varchar(5000)	No	Represents the feedback submitted by the user

Table 29.4 gives an overview of the structure of the TrainDetails table:

Table 29.4: The TrainDetails Table

Column Name	Data type	Allow Nulls	Description
TrainID	int	No	Represents unique ID for train
DepartStation	varchar(50)	No	Represents the departure station
ArrivalStation	varchar(50)	No	Represents the arrival station
DepartureDate	varchar(50)	No	Represents the departure date
SleeperClass	int	No	Represents the seats available for sleeper class
ACFirstClass	int	No	Represents the seats available for first class
2Tier	int	No	Represents the seats available for 2 tier class
3Tier	int	No	Represents the seats available for 3 tier class

Table 29.4: The TrainDetails Table			
Column Name	**Data type**	**Allow Nulls**	**Description**
SleeperClassFare	int	No	Represents the fare of the sleeper class
ACFirstClassFare	int	No	Represents the fare of the first class
2TierFare	int	No	Represents the fare of the 2 tier class
3TierFare	int	No	Represents the fare of the 3 tier class
DepartureTime	varchar(6)	No	Represents the departure time of atrain

Table 29.5 gives an overview of the structure of the UserInfo table:

Table 29.5: The UserInfo Table			
Column Name	**Data type**	**Allow Nulls**	**Description**
UserId	varchar(100)	No	Represents the unique ID for users
UserName	varchar(50)	No	Represents the name of a user
FirstName	varchar(50)	No	Represents first name of a user
LastName	varchar(50)	No	Represents the last name of a user
ContactNumber	bigint	No	Represents the contact number of a user
Address	varchar(500)	No	Represents the address of a user
City	varchar(50)	No	Represents the city of a user
State	varchar(50)	No	Represents the state of a user
Nationality	varchar(50)	No	Represents the nationality of a user
Zip	bigint	No	Represents the zip code of the user address
Sex	varchar(2)	No	Represents the gender of a user

Let's now look at the development phase of this project.

The Development Phase

To develop the Online Travel Agency portal in Microsoft Visual Studio 2012, you need to perform the following tasks:

1. Design the interface
2. Validate the designed user interfaces
3. Create connection with the database

In the back-end, Microsoft SQL Server 2008 is required to store all the details.

The Testing Phase

After the development phase, the project should be tested for logical flaws and proper functioning of all operations. The project is also tested for proper functioning of all the methods and modules designed and developed along with the navigation links provided in the UI. Testing of the project ensures that the code and the connections created in the project function properly. You need to check that data is properly stored in the database as well as retrieved and updated whenever required.

The Implementation and Maintenance Phase

This is the last stage in the SDLC of the Online Travel Agency portal. The project is implemented for a client in real environment. The implementation phase includes proper execution of the project on client computers. The maintenance of the project entails updating the project for the required changes in the implemented system.

This completes the discussion on the Online Travel Agency portal, the complete code of which is provided on Web.

Glossary

@ Assembly Directive

It links an assembly to ASP.NET application files, such as a Web page, a user control, and a master page.

@ Control Directive

It defines control-specific attributes used by an ASP.NET page parser and a compiler.

@ Implements Directive

The @ Implements directive indicates that the Web page, user control, or master page must implement the specified .NET Framework interface.

@ Import Directive

It is used to explicitly import a namespace into ASP.NET application files, such as Web page, a user control, a master page, or a Global.asax file.

@ Master Directive

It defines attributes of a master page that are used by an ASP.NET page parser and compiler.

@ MasterType Directive

The @ MasterType directive provides a way to create a strongly typed reference to the ASP.NET master page when the master page is accessed from the Master property.

@ Outputcache Directive

This directive declaratively controls the output caching policies of a Web page or a user control.

@ Page Directive

It defines page-specific attributes used by an ASP.NET page parser and compiler.

@ PreviousPageType Directive

The @ PreviousPageType directive provides the means to get strong typing against the previous page as accessed through the PreviousPage property.

@ Reference Directive

This directive dynamically compiles and links the user control, page source file, or arbitrary file located at some virtual path with the current Web page.

@ Register Directive

It creates an association between the tag prefix and custom controls.

@ Webhandler Directive

It is used to identify an ASP.NET IHttpHandler page.

Accessibility Standards

Accessibility standards are set of rules used to create websites that can also be accessed by physically challenged or sensory impaired users.

ACID Properties

ACID is an acronym for Atomicity, Consistency, Isolation, and Durability. ACID properties are used with respect to databases. These properties were introduced with the purpose of safe sharing of data and keeping a check on inaccurate data from entering databases.

Action Methods

In MVC applications, action methods are usually used for one-to-one mapping with user interactions.

ActiveDirectoryMembershipProvider

ActiveDirectoryMembershipProvider allows you to store user credentials either in an Active Directory or in an Active directory Application Mode (ADAM) data store.

Adaptive Rendering

It is a technique to render a control according to the capabilities of a Web browser.

ADO.NET Data Services Framework

ADO.NET Data Services Framework is a Microsoft technology to create and consume data services, which makes it easy for developers to separate the presentation layer from the data layers while working with them.

ADO.NET Entity Framework

ADO.NET Entity Framework enables users to visually design models and map databases, tables, and views by using .NET Framework 4.5.

ADO.NET Metadata

ADO.NET Entity Framework uses ADO.NET metadata that provides infrastructure and type hierarchy to exhibit the conceptual entities, fundamental tables, and CLR classes according to Entity Data Model (EDM).

ADO.NET Metadata

ADO.NET Entity Framework uses ADO.NET metadata that provides infrastructure and type hierarchy to exhibit the conceptual entities, fundamental tables, and CLR classes according to the EDM.

AJAX

AJAX, an acronym for Asynchronous JavaScript and XML, updates the Web page content asynchronously.

AlwaysVisibleControlExtender

It allows you to fix an ASP.NET control, or a set of controls, to one of the page corners. This extender can target any of the control that you always want to make visible on the Web page.

Anonymous Methods

Anonymous methods allow you to handle an event directly instead of using a separate event handler.

Anonymous Profiles

Anonymous profiles are used to store information of unregistered users.

Application Lifetime

Application lifetime refers to the time-span for which an application domain persists.

Application Packages

When you compile Silverlight 3.0 applications, they are compiled into application packages. The application packages are files with the .xap extension.

Application Pool

It resides on the IIS in which the worker process of a Web application runs.

Application State

Application state is used to store data corresponding to all the variables of an ASP.NET Web application.

Application Tracking

It is the process of monitoring the health of a Web application or website to ensure effective working of the website.

Architecture of WCF

Architecture of WCF consists of various layers that help in developing distributed applications. These layers are: Contracts layer, Service Runtime layer, Messaging layer, and Activation and Hosting layer.

ASP.NET 4.5 Provider Model

The provider model illustrates the position of providers. Providers work as a bridge between Data Stores, such as SQL Server and ASP.NET Services, such as Membership, in ASP.NET applications.

ASP.NET AJAX Control Toolkit (ACT)

ACT consists of new controls that have AJAX functionalities and a variety of extenders to remove the limitation of ASP.NET controls and include new ideas and concepts.

ASP.NET Dynamic Data

ASP.NET Dynamic Data is used to create data-driven Web applications with minimal coding. ASP.NET Dynamic Data have the advantage of using all the capabilities of the Dynamic Data Framework.

ASP.NET Trace

This feature allows you to collate all the information related to a particular website, such as request details, the page control hierarchy, or the execution of the various stages of the page lifecycle and controls.

ASP.NET Web Service Infrastructure

The infrastructure of ASP.NET Web services provides a simple Application Programming Interface (API) for Web services to create and understand SOAP messages that, in turn, helps to invoke remote methods.

ASP.NET Web Service

An ASP.NET Web service may be defined as an independent and self-sustained unit of a software application hosted on the Internet.

ASP.NET Worker Process

The ASP.NET worker process allows ASP.NET Web applications to run on a Web server. It enables different assemblies of a program to work in conjunction with each other.

ASP.NET

ASP.NET is a Web development model, which is used to deliver interactive, data-driven Web applications over the Internet.

Assembly Manifest

The manifest, also known as assembly manifest, contains the assembly metadata needed for providing the assembly's version requirements and security identity.

Assembly

Assemblies are packaged into units containing programs and libraries. An assembly contains a self-describing binary file, which can be either Dynamic Link Library (DLL) or Executable (EXE).

Asynchronous call

The call to the server to update page content takes place in the background and is called an Asynchronous call.

Atom

Atom is a format based on XML language that is used for Web feeds developed by the Internet Engineering Task Force (IETF) Working Group.

Authenticated Users

When unregistered users register themselves, they become authenticated users.

Authentication

The process of identifying users of your application or resource is known as authentication.

Authorization

The process of deciding whether or not an authenticated user can access the intended application or resource is known as authorization.

Bindings

Binding is a process that specifies the communication protocols that are used to access services. Binding also specifies the details of transport, encoding, and protocols required by servers and clients to communicate with each other.

Breakpoints

Using Breakpoints allows you to know when a particular part of your code is executed.

Button Control

The Button control is used to create a button that sends a request to a Web page.

Cache Dependency

Cache dependency allows a cache item to be validated based on an external file or another cache item. If a cache dependency, such as an external file or another cache item is modified, then the cache item is not validated and is removed from the cache.

Cache Profile

A Cache profile allows you to define cache settings in the `web.config` file of an application and refers these settings on individual pages included in the application. By using cache profiles in an application, you can apply cache settings to multiple pages at one time.

Caching Modules

These modules perform tasks related to caching in the request-processing pipeline that, in turn, improves the performance of a website.

Caching

Caching is the process of temporarily storing the data either on a Web server or on the client-side. ASP.NET provides three kinds of caching techniques: Output caching (also called page level caching), Partial-page output caching, and Data caching.

Cascading Style Sheets (CSS)

CSS are designed to help you in defining the formatting styles once and using it multiple times. A CSS refers to a text file that defines formatting for the content of an HTML file.

Code Render Blocks

It is used to define the inline code or inline expressions that are executed when a Web page is rendered.

Code Sharing

It is a mechanism through which a common code is shared among different pages of a Web application.

Code-Behind Page Model

In the code-behind page model, the functionalities of a Web application and the HTML markup are implemented in two separate files. These two files are then linked together to run the Web application.

Coding Models

In ASP.NET 4.5, coding models refer to the methodologies used for writing code in a Web application.

CollapsiblePanelExtender

It enables you to hide or display the contents of a panel, alternatively. When you click the header of the collapsible section, the contents either appear or disappear.

Common Language Runtime

It provides functionalities, such as memory management, exception handling, debugging, security, thread execution, code execution, code safety, verification, and compilation.

Common Language Specification

The CLS is a specification that consists of rules to support language integration.

Common Type System

The Common Type System (CTS) specifies certain guidelines for declaring, using, and managing types at runtime. It is an integral part of the runtime for supporting cross-language communication.

Component Object Model (COM+) Service

COM+ services are referred to as Enterprise Services that help developers to build and develop robust server applications.

Compression Modules

These modules are used to compress the requested data in the request-processing pipeline.

Conceptual Model

A conceptual model defines the entities and relationships.

Conceptual Schema Definition Language (CSDL)

CSDL contains a design schema that provides a design template for an object model. An application uses an object model based on CSDL.

Consumer controls

Consumer controls are those controls that receive data from another control.

Content Modules

These modules are responsible for processing requests for static files and return a default page when a client does not specify a resource in a request.

Contexts

A context in .NET is a boundary that contains a collection of objects and provides runtime services to the objects that reside inside the process boundary.

Contracts

Contracts in WCF are the agreements between the services and their clients. The contracts of the services contain the information regarding the agreement, for example, contracts in WCF provide the interoperability they need to communicate with the client.

Control Adapters

It is used to customize the behavior of a page or control at different stages in the life-cycle of a control.

Controllers

Controllers are the components that handle all the Views associated to a Model, and ultimately select a View to render that displays the UI.

Control-state

Control-state holds information specific to a control, which is essential to be sent to the server at the time of postback. Control-state cannot be disabled like that in the case of view-state.

Copy Web Site Deployment

The Copy Web Site tool enables you to copy a website from your development server to either the same server or a remote server.

Cross-Page Postback

Cross-Page Postback is the process of receiving the response of a request by the server on another page.

Cross-platform Support

Specifies that any Windows platform that supports CLR can execute .NET application, that is, .NET application enables interoperability between multiple Windows operating systems.

Cryptography

Cryptography is considered a branch of computer science that encapsulates mathematical algorithms and functions that allow you to secure data by modifying its original form so that it is incomprehensible to all users except the intended recipient.

Crystal Reports

A Crystal Report is a standard yet powerful and dynamic tool used to create attractive and interactive reports, quickly and easily, that are ideal for formal presentations.

CrystalReportPartsViewer control

Displays report summary information in a small, portal-like window, with the ability to delve deeper into the report through a series of linked parts

CrystalReportViewer control

Displays the report in a page-based layout, with the ability to move between pages

Data Caching

Data caching is very useful when you need to cache custom data into the cache memory. Data caching supports six basic types of dependency models: File dependency, Key dependency, SQL dependency, Aggregate dependency, Time dependency, and Custom dependency.

Data Model

Data model is used to represent information about the data in a database and depict the relation between the items of a database.

Data Modeling

Data modeling is a technique to structure and organize data.

Databound Controls

The data bound controls are composite controls that are used with the data source controls to display and modify the data in a Web based application.

Debugging

It is the process of finding and removing logical errors from your application to ensure exhibition of the desired behavior by your website.

Disk Output Caching

Disk output caching is used to save cached responses in the disk as well as in memory.

Distributed Transactions

Enterprise Services offer distributed transactions, in which a transaction can be distributed across multiple database systems.

Document Type Definition (DTD)

It identifies the elements, attributes, and entities that are used to create and validate an XHTML document.

DOM

DOM an acronym for Document Object Model, represents a structured Web form in an object-oriented model, allowing programs and scripts to access and update the contents of a Web form.

DragPanelExtender

It targets the Panel control and enables you to drag the panel and drop it anywhere in the Web page.

Dynamic Compilation

The process of not compiling the same page again and again is called ASP.NET dynamic compilation. The .NET class, which has already been compiled, is executed.

Dynamic Data Framework

Dynamic Data Framework enables you to easily build data driven Web applications based on Entity Framework or LINQ to SQL data models.

Dynamic Language Runtime

The Dynamic Language Runtime (DLR) is a runtime environment that adds services to the CLR, to implement dynamic languages such as Python and Ruby, on the .NET Framework.

DynamicValidator Control
The ASP.NET Dynamic Data Framework provides the DynamicValidator control. This control catches the exceptions that are thrown from the data model during validation and raise those exceptions as a validation event on the Web page.

Empty Tags
The tags that do not contain any data or content within them are called empty tags, such as the line break tag (<br />).

Endpoint Behavior
Endpoint behaviors are used to customize the local behavior of the service endpoint.

Endpoint
An endpoint is simply a resource on the network to which messages can be sent. Endpoints of the services in WCF are responsible for all the communications between the client and the service. An endpoint of the WCF contains Address, Binding, Contract, and Behavior.

Extenders
The extenders add new and enhanced capabilities to ASP.NET server controls by using a block of JavaScript code.

File System
It allows you to keep the files of a Web application or website in a folder on the local hard drive or in a shared location on the local area network instead of the Internet Information Services (IIS).

FileUpload Control
The FileUpload control displays a text box control and a browse button that enable users to browse a file from the local or remote machine to upload it on a Web server.

FilteredTextBoxExtender
It enables you to apply filtering to a text box control, which prevents certain characters from getting inserted in the text box.

Filtering Operators
Filtering, as the name suggests, refers to the operation of filtering the result set so that it contains only those elements that satisfy a specified given condition.

FTP Server
This option enables you to actually store and update your applications while they reside on a server somewhere else in your enterprise.

Global Assembly Cache
Global Assembly Cache (GAC) is the central place for registering assemblies, so that different applications on the computer can use it later.

Global.asax File
The Global.asax file is a component of ASP.NET applications. This file contains code for the events that are raised at the execution time of the application.

Globalization
Globalization of Web applications is the process of designing and developing Web applications that can adapt to different languages and cultures.

Hash Algorithms
Hash algorithms are hash functions that take a sequence of bytes of any length and convert it into smaller fixed-length sequences of bytes known as hash values.

Hash function
A hash function is used to encrypt and decrypt data to make it secure while transferring it over the Internet.

HiddenField Control
The HiddenField control is used to store a value that needs to persist across posts to the server.

HoverMenuExtender
It enables you to display a pop-up menu when you move the mouse-pointer over the target control.

HTML Client Controls
When events of HTML controls are handled at the client-side, the HTML controls are called HTML client controls.

HTML Host Page
It is a Web page, also known as Test Page, used to host the Silverlight application.

HTML Server Controls
When events of HTML controls are handled at the server-side, the HTML controls are called HTML client controls.

HTTP Handlers

The HTTP Handlers handle user requests for Web application resources. For each user request type, there is a specific event handler to handle the request and send back the corresponding response object.

HTTP Modules

These modules perform tasks specific to Hypertext Transfer Protocol (HTTP) in the request-processing pipeline.

HTTP Request

A request made to the server by traditional applications or non-AJAX applications.

HTTP Server

This option allows you to develop and store your Web application on the IIS. An IIS can be a Local IIS or Remote IIS.

IIS

It is an acronym for Internet Information Services, used to host websites. It is also called a Web server.

Internationalization

The process of Internationalization involves identifying different contents for different locales, such as the date and time format.

JavaScript

JavaScript is a client-side scripting language that supports object-oriented programming. JavaScript is a dynamic language that provides tools to communicate with the back-end server.

Jquery library

The jQuery library is an open-source JavaScript library that can be used with both ASP.NET Web Forms and ASP.NET MVC

Label Control

The Label control is used to display static text on the Web page.

Lambda Expressions

A Lambda expression is an anonymous function that contains expressions and statements to create delegates or expression tree types.

LINQ Queries

A LINQ query specifies the information that you want to retrieve from a data source. LINQ queries can also perform additional functions, such as sorting and grouping the retrieved data.

LINQ to ADO.NET

LINQ to ADO.NET describes the database-centric aspects of LINQ. LINQ to ADO.NET consists of two separate technologies, LINQ to DataSet and LINQ to SQL.

LINQ to DataSet

LINQ to DataSet is an easier and faster way to query data cached in a DataSet object. LINQ to DataSet simplifies querying by allowing queries to be written in the programming language itself.

LINQ to Objects

LINQ to Objects refers to the use of LINQ queries with any IEnumerable or IEnumerable<T> collection directly, without the use of any intermediate LINQ provider or interface.

LINQ to SQL

LINQ to SQL is a component of .NET Framework, and is specifically designed to work with an SQL server database. It provides a runtime infrastructure for managing relational data as objects. It allows you to write queries to manipulate and retrieve data from the SQL server.

LINQ to XML

LINQ to XML is a new way to write and read XML data in .NET Framework.LINQ to XML supplements the standard XML classes in .NET Framework and makes working with XML easier.

Literal content

Literal content is a content that is in plain text only and not in the form of images, controls, etc.

Literal Control

The Literal control is used for displaying text on a Web page, similar to that done by a Label control.

Localization Expressions

The localization expressions enable you to access the local and global resources of the control programmatically to generate the localized content.

Localization

Localization refers to the process of making changes in a Web application to meet the language and cultural requirements of users from a specific physical location. The localization process involves configuring a Web application for a given culture.

Logging and Diagnostics Modules

Logging modules help in loading custom modules and passing information to the HTTP.sys component. Diagnostics modules keep track of and report events during request processing.

Logical Model

A logical model represents a relational model and a mapping between the conceptual and relational models.

Loosely Coupled Event (LCE)

An LCE helps in implementing COM+ services between the client and the server.

Managed Code

Managed code is the code that is executed directly by the Common Language Runtime (CLR). Applications created by using managed code automatically have CLR services, such as type checking, security, and automatic garbage collection.

Managed Modules

These modules are developed using the ASP.NET model. Generally, these modules are used to enhance the functionality of Native modules.

Mapping Specification Language (MSL)

MSL connects data types declared in CSDL to the database metadata. This metadata preserves data for an application that uses the defined object model.

Master Pages

Master Pages in ASP.NET help in defining the overall layout of a Web application and reusing the defined layout in all the pages derived from the master page. Two types of master pages are Simple Master Page and Nested Master Page.

Membership Service

The Membership service is used with ASP.NET Login controls and ASP.NET forms authentication to create a complete user authentication system.

Merge Tool

The Merge tool also called `Aspnet_merge.exe`, allows you to combine and manage assemblies created by the ASP.NET pre-compilation tool (`Aspnet_compiler.exe`).

Metadata

A metadata is binary information that describes your program, and is stored in a CLR Portable Executable (PE) file or in the memory.

Metadata

A metadata is binary information that describes your program, stored in a CLR Portable Executable (PE) file or the memory.

Model

A Model can be considered as the foundation of the MVC architecture, which is composed of business logic and data access code.

Model-View-Controller (MVC)

It is a design pattern that separates data access, business logic, and presentation logic and enables creation of a number of views accessing the same enterprise application model.

Module

It is an assembly that is used to implement specific functionalities.

.NET Compact Framework

It provides with an environment for creating applications that can be accessed through mobile devices, such as Pocket PCs and cell phones.

Navigation Controls

Navigation controls are used to navigate through the Web pages of an application. These controls are: `TreeView`, `Menu`, and `SiteMapPath`.

NumericUpDownExtender

It enables you to add an up and down button next to the TextBox control. These buttons are used to increment or decrement through a set of numeric values or other items.

Object Models

Object models show the objects that are associated with each other to perform some specific tasks.

Object Pooling

Object pooling enables increased performance and scalability of applications, and managing server resources by reusing the objects created.

Parallel Computing

When a large problem is divided into small parts that are addressed simultaneously, it is known as parallel computing. In other words, there are many computers that have multiple Central Processing Units (CPUs) attached so that multiple threads are executed simultaneously

Partial Updation

Partial updation updates only a particular portion of a Web page without affecting the rest.

Partial-Page Output Caching

Partial-Page Output caching is used to cache the specific part of a Web page, instead of caching the whole page.

PasswordStrengthExtender

It measures the strength of the password text entered within a text box by validating against different strength-specific parameters.

Personalization Data and Personalization Objects

Personalization data is used at the time of the initialization process. Personalization objects are used to personalize Web Parts controls.

PlaceHolder Control

The PlaceHolder control is used as a container to store server controls that are added to the Web page at runtime.

PLINQ

PLINQ is a parallel implementation of LINQ to Objects. This implies that PLINQ implements the standard query operators of LINQ as the extension methods and includes additional operators for implementing parallel operations

Postback

Postback is the process of sending the data back to the server for processing. ASP.NET provides a rich framework for handling postbacks from ASP.NET Web pages.

Principal Object

Principal (or principal object) represents a user-specific environment in which your application runs.

Private Assembly

When a single application uses an assembly, then it is called a private assembly.

Private Key

The key used to decrypt the data is known as the private key.

Proactive Process Recycling

Proactive process recycling restarts a process periodically even if there is no error in the process. In proactive process recycling, a process restarts after the completion of processing of a specific number of requests or the time-out period.

Process Model

The Process model in ASP.NET protects the processes running on the server from being modified by the end-user. The Process model configuration settings determine the time for a new process to start responding to the requests sent by the requesting client.

Provider Controls

Provider controls are those controls that send data to another control.

Public Key

The key used to encrypt the data is known as the public key.

Queued Components

Queued components help clients to run an application on the disconnected architecture.

Reactive Process Recycling

Reactive Process Recycling restarts a process when the process is not able to complete processing of the requests sent by the client computer.

ResizableControlExtender

It can be attached to an ASP.NET control to provide a graphical handle that enables users to dynamically resize the control.

RoundedCornersExtender

As the name suggests, RoundedCornersExtender is attached to any ASP.NET server control and makes the corners of the respective control round.

RSS

RSS is one of the Web feed formats used to keep you updated of the changes brought about in your website.

Security Modules

These modules perform tasks that are related to the security of the request-processing pipeline.

Serial Ports

A serial port is a physical interface used for serial communication to transfer information between a computer and a peripheral device.

Server Controls

Server controls are programmable objects that act as User Interface (UI) elements on a Web page. These controls are also known as server-side objects.

Session State

Session state stores session-specific information.

Shared Assembly

Shared assemblies are those assemblies that are placed in the global assembly cache so that they can be used by multiple applications.

Side-by-Side Execution

The process of executing multiple versions of an application or an assembly is known as side-by-side execution.

Silverlight

Silverlight allows you to develop Web applications that contain high-fidelity multimedia content and eye-catching visual effects. It supports XAML, 2-D vector graphics, animations, and multimedia in Web pages.

Simple Object Access Protocol (SOAP)

SOAP, one of the key elements in a Web service, is a protocol used for messaging. It is completely XML-based. SOAP specifications are standardized by World Wide Web Consortium (W3C) and are used by most companies that develop Web services.

Single-File Page Model

In the single-file page model, the functionalities of a Web application and the HTML markup are implemented in the same file.

SQLMemberShipProvider

SqlMembershipProvider is used to store user credentials in a SQL Server data store.

States

Refer to the status of a Web application at any instant of time. Preserving application state ensures that the changes made by a user are reflected whenever a page is reloaded.

Storage Schema Definition Language

The storage metadata schema is a formal description of the database that persists data for an application, based on the Entity Data Model (EDM).

TextBox Control

The TextBox control is an input control, which allows you to enter text.

TextBoxWatermarkExtender

It is used to provide a tip to the user that specifies the type of parameter entered within a text box.

The AccessDataSource Control

The AccessDataSource control is a data-source control that allows a Web server control to access a Microsoft Access database.

The Accessibility Checker Tool

This tool helps to verify the conformance of HTML markup of a Web page to the WCAG Priority 1 checkpoints, WCAG Priority 2 checkpoints, and Access Board Section 508.

The Accordion Control

The Accordion control is similar to CollapsiblePanelExtender. The Accordion control allows you to group multiple collapsible panels in a single control.

The ADO.NET Entity Data Model Designer

This designer enables us to open an .edmx file to create entities and map entities to database tables and columns through some visual tools included in the EDM Designer.

The ADO.NET Entity Data Model Item Template

This template is available for Visual Basic, C#, and ASP.NET website and Web application projects. It is basically used to launch the Entity Data Model Wizard.

The AdRotator Control

The AdRotator control displays a sequence of images, known as advertisements, on a Web page. The sequence in which the images appear can be predefined or random in nature.

The Aggregate Operators

The Aggregate operators compute a single value from a collection.

The AppearanceEditorPart Control

The AppearanceEditorPart control allows users to edit the properties associated with the appearance of a Web Parts control on the Web page. It is visible only when a Web Part control is selected for editing.

The ASP.NET MMC Snap-In Tool

The ASP.NET MMC Snap-In tool is a management tool that enables you to modify the settings of the `web.config` and `machine.config` files. It also helps in configuring the settings for applications deployed on a Web server.

The Aspnet_regsql Tool

The Aspnet_regsql tool is a command line tool used to create a Microsoft SQL Server database.

The BehaviorEditorPart Control

The BehaviorEditorPart control, as the name suggests, provides options that enable users to modify the behavior of Web Parts controls.

The BulletedList Control

The BulletedList control is a standard Web server control used to display items in the form of a bulleted list on a Web page.

The Calendar Control

The Calendar control displays a graphic calendar on which users can select dates.

The Canvas Control

It allows you to position and arrange the containing controls at given locations.

The CatalogZone Control

The CatalogZone control helps to create a catalog of Web Part controls and allow users to add or update the controls easily on a Web page.

The ChangePassword Control

It allows users to change their password. This control prompts users to provide the current password first and then allows them to set a new password.

The CheckBox Control

The CheckBox control creates a check box that can be selected by clicking it.

The CheckBoxList Control

You can use a CheckBoxList control to display a number of check boxes at once as a column of check boxes.

The CompareValidator Control

The CompareValidator control is used to compare the value entered by a user in one Input control with the value entered in another Input control or with an already existing value.

The ConnectionsZone Control

The ConnectionsZone control helps you to dynamically connect Web Parts controls.

The Content Control

It is used to contain only one piece of content of any type.

The Control Class

The Control class is the base class for all Web server controls. This class is derived from the Object class, which resides in the System namespace.

The Conversion Operators

The Conversion operators convert a collection into an array.

The CreateUserWizard Control

It is used to create a new user with the help of the Membership service in your Membership data store.

The CrystalReportPartsViewer Control

The CrystalReportPartsViewer control divides a report into different parts and displays its summary in a small, portal-like window, from where we can delve deeper into the report through a series of hyperlinks.

The CrystalReportSource Control

The CrystalReportSource control provides with the properties to modify or retrieve information that affects the appearance and functions of a report.

The CrystalReportViewer Control

The CrystalReportViewer control is a standard Form control used to view a report. This control displays a report in a page-based layout, providing with the ability to move between pages.

The CrystalReportViewer object model

In a Visual Studio Web form, the CrystalReportViewer object model is exposed as a .NET control that can be added to a Web Form to display a report.

The CustomValidator Control

The CustomValidator control is used to customize and implement data validation as per your requirement.

The DataList Control

The DataList control is a data-bound control that displays data by using templates. These templates define controls and HTML elements that should be displayed for an item.

The DataPager Control

The DataPager control is used to provide paging functionality to the data-bound controls, such as the ListView control.

The DeclarativeCatalogPart Control

The DeclarativeCatalogPart control displays a list of Web Parts controls and other server controls when the website is in the CatalogDisplayMode mode. A user can add controls from this catalog to a Web page.

The Deep Zoom Technology

The Deep Zoom technology allows you to easily, quickly, and smoothly zoom in or out multiple photographs simultaneously. Moreover, you can zoom in or out high-resolution images in applications.

The Description File

The description file is an XML file with a .WebPart extension. It contains property values, state data, and reference to the assembly or source file.

The DetailsView Control

The DetailsView control is a data-bound control that is used to display a single record from the associated data source in a table format, where each row of the table represents a field of the record.

The DeviceSpecific Control

It uses device filters to detect the type of hardware device that is displaying the current ASP.NET Mobile Web Forms page.

The Directory Class

The Directory class exposes static methods to create, move, and enumerate directories and subdirectories.

The DriveInfo Class

The DriveInfo class provides access to information related to a drive, such as space available on a drive, total storage space of the drive, and drive name.

The DropDownList Control

The DropDownList control displays the list of data as a drop-down list from where you can make a single selection.

The Dynamic Data Field Template

The Dynamic Data Field Templates are used to display, edit, and insert data into the data model.

The Dynamic Data Page Template

The Dynamic Data Page Templates are regular ASP.NET Web pages that are configured to display data from any table of a database connected with Dynamic Data.

The DynamicControl Control

The DynamicControl control helps in displaying the content that is defined in the data-bound controls, such as the FormView or ListView control, by using the ASP.NET Dynamic Data features.

The DynamicDataManager Control

The DynamicDataManager control helps in enabling a dynamic behavior for the Web controls that support dynamic data.

The DynamicEntity Control

The DynamicEntity control represents an entity for use by the ASP.NET Dynamic Data applications.

The DynamicFilter Control

The DynamicFilter control provides a UI that helps in filtering table rows using a specified column. The DynamicFilter control, which is referenced by the DynamicFilterExpression instance, can be used with the QueryExtender control.

The DynamicHyperLink Control

The DynamicHyperLink control helps in performing common tasks, such as edit, delete, and insert. The DynamicHyperLink control creates links that are based on table actions, which are defined in the Global.asax file.

The DynamicValidator Control

The `DynamicValidator` control of ASP.NET Dynamic Data is used to catch the exceptions that are thrown from the data model during validation and raise those exceptions as a validation event on the Web page.

The EditorZone Control

The EditorZone control is one of the primary editing controls used to change the appearance, format, and structure of Web pages containing Web Parts controls, at runtime.

The EDMGen.exe Tool

This command tool can be used to generate models and perform other functions on EDM metadata files, such as validating existing models.

The Element Operators

The Element operators in LINQ return just one element.

The Ellipse Control

It allows you to provide an elliptical shape.

The Embedded Crystal Reports Designer

The embedded Crystal Reports Designer is a graphical user interface (GUI) application that is used to create or modify reports. It defines the data source of the report, selects and groups the data records you want to use, and formats the objects and layouts of the report.

The Entity Data Model Wizard

This wizard generates an EDM from an existing database and also adds a connection string to the App.Config or Web.Config file and configures a single file generator to run on the conceptual model contained in the .edmx file, which encapsulates generated EDM through the wizard.

The EntityClient Provider

The EntityClient provider is an ADO.NET-managed provider that supports retrieving data described in an EDM.

The EntityConnection Class

This class represents a connection to an underlying data store.

The Extension Methods

The Extension methods allow you to recompile and modify the original data types.

The File and FileInfo Classes

The File and FileInfo classes allow you to perform various functions, such as creating, deleting, moving, renaming, and appending files.

The FormView Control

The FormView control displays a single record from the associated data source.

The Generation Operators

The Generation operators help in creating a new sequence of values.

The Grid Control

It allows you to arrange the child controls in rows and columns.

The GridSplitter Control

It allows you to provide a UI element that users can move to adjust the space between the rows and columns of a grid.

The GridView Control

The GridView control is a data-bound control that displays the values of a data source in the form of a table.

The Grouping Operators

The Grouping operators in LINQ are used to put data into groups so that the elements in each group share a common attribute.

The GZipStream or DeflateStream Class

We can compress or decompress the data in a file by using the GZipStream or DeflateStream class.

The HtmlControl Class

The HtmlControl class is the basis for all HTML server controls in ASP.NET.

The HttpHandler Components

These components are used to display dynamic contents on a Web page.

The HyperLink Control

The HyperLink control is used to create a link to another Web page that can be a page in your Web application or anywhere else on the World Wide Web (WWW).

The Image Control

The Image control is a standard Web server control, which is used to display an image on a Web page.

The ImageButton Control

The ImageButton control is a Button control, which displays an image instead of text.

The ImageMap Control

You can add an image map in a Web page by using the ImageMap control.

The ImportCatalogPart Control

The ImportCatalogPart control imports the description file of a Web Parts control or server control that can be used as a Web Parts control.

The InfoObject object model

The InfoObject object model provides with an enterprise-level object model for the SDK to represent a wide variety of information entities that can be both physical and network.

The Join Operators

The Join operators in LINQ are used to join objects in one data source with objects that share a common attribute in another data source.

The LinkButton Control

The LinkButton control is another standard Web server control used to link the current Web page to some other Web pages, similar to the HyperLink control. The only difference between the two is that the HyperLink control just allows the browser to navigate to a new Web page, whereas in the LinkButton control, we can also perform some other action by handling the Click and Command events of this control.

The LinqDataSource Control

The LinqDataSource control enables you to use LINQ in an ASP.NET Web page by setting the properties in the mark-up text.

The LinqDataSource Control

The LinqDataSource control is a data-source control that allows a Web server control to access data located in relational databases or in the memory data collection, such as an array and context objects. This control enables Web developers to use Language Integrated Query (LINQ), which simplifies the interaction between object-oriented programming and relational data by applying the principles of object-oriented programming to relational data.

The ListBox Control

The ListBox control is a standard Web server control used to select one or more items from a list of items on a Web page at runtime.

The ListView Control

The ListView control is a data-bound control used to display data from the associated data source. The ListView control enables a developer to display data in any format by using templates and styles.

The Localize Control

The Localize control is used to set a location on a Web page, where you can display localized text.

The Location Attribute

The `Location` attribute is used to define the location, where the data is to be cached. It can be on the server-side, client-side, or even a proxy server.

The Login Control

This control provides a UI to facilitate the authentication process carried out on users of a website on the basis of username and password.

The LoginName Control

It is responsible for displaying the name of an authenticated user.

The LoginStatus Control

It enables users to know whether a particular user is logged into a website or not. The text displayed on this control changes according to the login status of a user.

The LoginView Control

It is used to display two different views of a Web page of any website on the basis of whether or not a user is currently logged in.

The MediaElement Control

It allows you to host audio and video files.

The MetadataWorkspace Class

This class represents the ADO.NET metadata runtime service component that provides support for retrieving metadata from various sources.

The MicrosoftReportViewer Control

The MicrosoftReportViewer control is used to embed report functionalities in an ASP.NET Web application.

The MultiView Control

The MultiView control is a container for a group of View controls. It allows you to define a group of View controls, where each View control contains child controls.

The NoBot Control

The NoBot control prevents the spam/bot from filling the input forms automatically. The bots are techniques that ensure that users themselves are filling up the form instead of smart software.

The ObjectContext Class

This class represents a primary class for interacting with data in the form of objects that are instances of Entity Types defined in the EDM.

The ObjectDataSource Control

The ObjectDataSource control represents the business objects and allows you to use the ObjectDataSource control in conjunction with a data-bound control to display, edit, and sort the data on a Web page with little or no coding.

The ObjectStateManager Class

This class maintains the object state and identifies management for entity instances and relationship instances.

The Page Persistence Format

The page persistence format enables developers to retain property values of a control between browser sessions.

The PageCatalogPart Control

The PageCatalogPart control allows users to restore previously deleted Web Part controls on a Web page.

The Panel Control

The Panel control is one of the most frequently used controls. It creates a borderless division on the form; by using this division one can place controls inside the Panel control.

The Partitioning Operators

The Partitioning operators in LINQ are used to divide an input sequence into two sections, without rearranging the elements and then returning the result set with one of the sections that satisfies the given condition.

The PasswordRecovery Control

It is used to recover or reset the forgotten password of a user. This control does not display the password on the Web browser, but e-mails it at the e-mail address specified at the time of registration.

The PhoneCall Control

It allows end-users to dial a phone number.

The Popup Control

It allows you to temporarily display information on top of some other control.

The Postback model

In the postback model, with every request, the entire page is sent back to the server. The server then processes the request and performs modifications on the page, and sends the regenerated page to the viewer.

The Post-Cache Substitution Feature

The post-cache substitution feature of ASP.NET 4.5 allows caching of a Web page by substituting some of its content dynamically.

The Projection Operators

The Projection operators are used to transform an object into a new object of a different type.

The PropertyGridEditorPart Control

The PropertyGridEditorPart control provides a UI that allows users to edit the custom properties of a Web Part control on a Web page. This control is visible only when the Web page is in the edit mode.

The ProtectSection Method

The ProtectSection method is used to encrypt the configuration sections of the web.config file.

The ProxyWebPartManager Control

The ProxyWebPartManager control imitates the WebPartManager control of the master page in the content page.

The Quantifier Operators

The Quantifier operators return a boolean value if the elements of the sequence satisfy a specific condition.

The RadioButton Control

Similar to the CheckBox control, the RadioButton control creates a single radio button. The RadioButton controls can be grouped, where only one RadioButton control can be selected at a time.

The RadioButtonList Control

The RadioButtonList control displays data as a column of radio buttons and provides you with an easy way to display a single selection in the radio button group.

The RangeValidator Control

The RangeValidator control checks whether or not the value of an input control lies in the specified range.

The Rectangle Control

It allows you to display a rectangle.

The RegularExpressionValidator Control

Regular expressions are used to check whether or not the text matches a certain pattern. The RegularExpressionValidator control validates whether or not the value in the Input control (text box) matches the format specified by the regular expression, such as a US telephone number or a date format.

The RepeatButton Control

It allows you to provide a button that periodically raises its Click event until the mouse-button is released.

The Repeater Control

The Repeater control is a data-bound control that is used to display a repeated list of items from the associated data source. It is a single Web control that allows splitting mark-up tags across the templates. The Repeater control does not provide support to in-built layouts or styles. Therefore, while working with the Repeater control, you have to explicitly declare all layouts, formatting, and style.

The Report Viewer Control

The report viewer controls appear in the Toolbox and are used to view reports. Each control encapsulates complex report layout information into a GUI object within the Toolbox. The following are the two report viewer controls:

The ReportClientDocument object model

The ReportClientDocument object model provides with the capability to manipulate reports.

The ReportDocument object model

The ReportDocument model is the most extensive of all the models, which means that it has a wide range of functionalities to work with.

The RequiredFieldValidator Control

The RequiredFieldValidator control is the simplest control, and is used to ensure that the user has entered the data into the input control, such as TextBox, to which it is bound.

The ScriptManager Control

The ScriptManager control helps in implementing the AJAX functionality in an ASP.NET website. No other AJAX server controls can be added to the Web page in the absence of this control.

The ScriptManagerProxy Control

The content page uses the ScriptManagerProxy control to create a link to the Master page's ScriptManager control. The ScriptManagerProxy control works as a local object of the ScriptManager control in the content page.

The ServicedComponent Class

The ServicedComponent class is used as a base class for all the classes that need COM+ services.

The Set Operators

The Set operators in LINQ refer to the query operations that produce a result set.

The SiteMapDataSource Control

The SiteMapDataSource control allows you to work with the data stored in the SiteMap configuration file. This control also provides with the capability to customize site navigation by using site map data with data server controls, irrespective of the fact that controls are not navigation controls.

The Slider Control

It allows you to provide a slider that has a Thumb, which you can move to select a particular value from the given range of values.

The Sorting Operators

The Sorting operators in LINQ arrange the elements of a sequence based on one or more attributes. You can sort the data with one specific attribute and perform primary sorting on the elements.

The SqlDataSource Control

The SqlDataSource control is a data-source control that allows a server control, such as the GridView control, to access data located in a relational database, such as Microsoft SQL Server and Oracle. This control also generates a connection string to interact with data in an ASP.NET page.

The StackPanel Control

It allows you to arrange the containing controls in a horizontal or vertical stack.

The Stream Class

The Stream class is used to read, write, and query a file. The Stream class contains the FileStream class used to read from, write to, open, and close files on a file system.

The Substitution Control

The Substitution control is used to specify a section on an output-cached Web page, where you want to substitute the dynamic content for the control with the static content.

The System.Web.UI.WebControls.BaseValidator Class

The System.Web.UI.WebControls.BaseValidator class provides basic implementation required for all validation controls.

The TabContainer Control

The TabContainer control enables you to create a tabbed interface, where clicking each tab displays different contents. Switching from one tab to other does not need a postback.

The Table Control

The Table control helps create a table. This control is useful when you want to present data in a tabular format.

The TextBlock Control

It allows you to display text.

The Timer Control

The Timer control is used to update Web page content after a specific interval.

The ToggleButton Control

It allows you to provide a button that toggles between clicked and non-clicked states.

The UIHint Property

The `UIHint` property is used to specify a field template for a data field to display its UI.

The UpdatePanel Control

The UpdatePanel control helps to divide your Web page into parts and each part can be updated without depending on other controls.

The UpdateProgress Control

The UpdateProgress control is used to show the progress status of the requested data to refresh the content of a Web page.

The ValidationSummary Control

The ValidationSummary control collects all the Validation control error messages (known as summary) and displays it collectively on the screen.

The VaryByCustom Attribute

The `VaryByCustom` attribute is used to define custom strings to manage caching customized according to the requirements of a user.

The VaryByParam Attribute

The `VaryByParam` attribute is used to cache different copies of a Web page when it is generated dynamically, based on the parameters received in the form of `HTTP POST` or `HTTP GET`.

The View Control

The View control is a container for a group of controls. A View control must always be stored within a MultiView control.

The WCF Tools

WCF tools are designed to enable users to easily create, deploy, and manage WCF applications. The following are the tools of WCF:

- ServiceModel Metadata Utility Tool (Svcutil.exe)
- Find Private Key Tool (FindPrivateKey.exe)

- ServiceModel Registration Tool (ServiceModelReg.exe)
- COM+ Service Model Configuration Tool (ComSvcConfig.exe)
- Configuration Editor Tool (SvcConfigEditor.exe)
- Service Trace Viewer Tool (SvcTraceViewer.exe)
- WS-AtomicTransaction Configuration Utility (wsatConfig.exe)
- WS-AtomicTransaction Configuration MMC Snap-in
- WorkFlow Service Registration Tool (WFServicesReg.exe)
- WCF Service Auto Host (WcfSvcHost.exe)
- WCF Test Client (WcfTestClient.exe)

The Web Site Administration Tool

It is used to specify and manage all the security settings of a website, such as creating user and passwords, create roles, and assigning permissions.

The Web Site Administration Tool

The Web Site Administration Tool is used to configure the application settings and security settings of an ASP.NET Web application.

The WebPartManager Control

The WebPartManager control acts like a centralized hub that manages all other Web Parts controls on a Web page. This control coordinates the interaction between Web Parts and Web Parts zones.

The WebPartZone Control

The WebPartZone control is used to create a region where Web Parts or server controls can be relocated, maximized, or minimized. This region is called Web zone.

The WebService Directive

The WebService directive defines Web service-specific attributes, such as Namespace and Description attributes, used by the ASP.NET compilers and parsers.

The Wizard Control

The Wizard control provides navigation and a UI to collect related data across multiple steps. It also allows you to implement linear or non-linear navigation through the steps, such as skipping unnecessary steps or returning to a previously completed step to change a value.

The xhtmlConformance Tag

In ASP.NET 4.5, the xhtmlConformance tag helps you to specify the XHTML standards that your website needs to conform to. It is defined in the configuration file of the website.

The Xml Control

The Xml control displays an XML document without formatting or using Extensible Stylesheet Language Transformations (XSLT).

The XmlDataSource Control

The XmlDataSource control allows a data-bound control to bind the data with an XML document. This control also supports XPath expressions that allow to return only certain nodes from the XML document.

The XMLHTTP Protocol

This protocol is used in AJAX and sends data in the form of XML and JavaScript Object Notation (JSON) over the network.

The XMLHttpRequest Object

The XMLHttpRequest object is the core of ASP.NET AJAX as it is responsible for making requests to the server asynchronously, and it updates itself with the server response.

The XmlReader Class

The XmlReader class is used to read XML data in a fast, forward-only, and non-cached manner.

The XmlWriter Class

The XmlWriter class is used to write XML to a stream, a file, or a TextWriter object.

The XPathNavigator Class

The XPathNavigator class contains methods that are used to move and select elements from an XML document.

The XPathNodeIterator Class

The XPathNodeIterator class provides an iterator over a selected set of nodes.

The Zip Operators

The Zip operator is a new operator introduced in LINQ in ASP.NET 4.5, which helps in combining two collections into one.

Themes

Themes in ASP.NET help in maintaining a common look and feel across all or several pages of your website.

Transactions

A transaction can be defined as a set of executable statements that are executed as a single unit. Transactions help in maintaining consistency of data by ensuring that either all the statements within the transaction are executed or none of them is executed.

Transformers

Transformers are used to create connections between Web Parts controls.

Type-safe Code

An MSIL code in which one type accesses other types in the code only through a well-defined and authorized way is considered to be a type-safe code.

Unmanaged Code

Unmanaged code directly compiles to the machine code and runs on the machine, where it has been compiled.

Unmanaged Modules

These modules are assemblies with .dll extension and are also known as Native modules.

UpdatePanelAnimationExtender

It enables you to display animation while the UpdatePanel control is performing an asynchronous postback.

URL Routing

URL Routing validates variables used in the URL definition according to a pattern mentioned in the URL, and also automatically passes them as parameter arguments to a Controller action after validation.

User Agent

User agent is a device used to access a website, for example, a desktop graphical browser, voice browser, text browser, mobile phone, etc.

User Profiles

A user profile is a collection of various properties that describe the information you want to store for a user.

View state

View state stores page-specific information, when a page is posted back to the server.

View

A View provides the UI for the Model. Users interact with an application through a View.

Visual State Manager

Visual State Manager allows you to easily modify existing control templates and create new control templates.

W3C

It stands for World Wide Web Consortium, an international organization, responsible for framing the Web standards and techniques to be followed.

WCF Addresses

A WCF address consists of a URL that determines the protocols used by the services, the host on which it is running, and the path leading to it.

WCF Clients

A WCF client, also known as a WCF consumer, consists of a proxy that enables an application to communicate with the WCF service.

Web application

An application hosted on the Internet that can be accessed through a Web browser and used by multiple users simultaneously.

Web Events

This feature provides a general framework for raising runtime events and collects information related to the events of a website.

Web Feed

A Web feed is used to provide frequently updated content of a Web page. It is a document (often XML-based) that contains content items with Web links. Web feeds are designed to be machine-readable (computer) rather than human-readable.

Web Part Control Set

A Web Part control set is a group of components that enable users to modify the appearance and behavior of Web pages directly from the Web browser.

Web Parts Framework

Web Parts Framework enables users to directly customize a Web page from a Web browser as per users' requirements. These customizations are saved permanently in the data store and downloaded on the next visit of that particular user.

Web Service Description Languages

WSDL is an XML-based language that defines Web services. Every Web service consists of a corresponding WSDL document that specifies the location of the Web service and lists all the services that the Web service can perform.

Web Service Description

The Web service description provides the description of a Web service in the XML format, known as WSDL.

Web Service Directory

The Web service directory provides a central location for Web service providers. In other words, it is a place where Web service users (consumers) can easily locate services offered by other companies and organizations.

Web Service Discovery

The Web service discovery provides with the capability to locate Web services. This component locates documents that describe a particular Web service, through Web Service Description Languages (WSDL).

Web Service Wire Format

The Web service wire format provides with an interface to transmit data between a Web service and its users through protocols, such as HTTP-GET and HTTP-POST.

Web Standards

Web standards are recommendations given by W3C that define the guidelines and best practices for designing a website. Adherence to these Web standards helps Web developers to develop a more accessible, usable, and search engine friendly website.

Windows Authentication

In Windows authentication, the identity of a user is cross-checked against the Windows user accounts that are stored on the Web server.

Windows CardSpace (WCS)

WCS (formerly codenamed as InfoCard) is a client software provided by Microsoft that simplifies and improves the safety of accessing resources and helps in sharing personal information over the Internet.

Windows Communication Foundation (WCF)

WCF (formerly codenamed as Indigo) is one of the new technologies introduced by Microsoft in .NET Framework 3.0 for building and running connected systems.

Windows Communication Foundation (WCF)

WCF is a set of .NET technologies for developing and deploying services on Windows. WCF acts as a platform for creating and distributing connected applications. It also provides a unified framework for rapidly building service-oriented applications.

Windows Presentation Foundation (WPF)

Microsoft's WPF (formerly code-named as Avalon) provides the base for building applications and a clear separation between the user interface and the business logic.

Windows Workflow Foundation (WF)

WF is a technology introduced by Microsoft, which provides a programming model for building workflow-based applications on Windows.

Worker Process

A worker process is a process in which multiple application domains are hosted and ensures that each application works in its own application domain.

XAML Browser Applications

XAML browser applications (XBAP, pronounced as x-bap) are Web server-hosted WPF applications that run in a Web browser.

XAML Files

It is used to define the design and UI of a Silverlight application. Every Silverlight application has a few XAML files, such as App.xaml, App.xaml.cs or App.xaml.vb, Page.xaml, and Page.xaml.cs or Page.xaml.vb, which define the UI and basic behavior of a Silverlight application.

XCopy Deplyment

XCopy is a term used to deploy an application by copying a set of files to a folder on the target computer and then executing the application on the client-side.

Index

D

E

F

G

H

I

J

L

M

Q

R

S

T

U

V

W

X

Online Resource Available with the Book

The Online Resources available with ASP .NET 4.5 Programming *Black Book* contain elements specifically selected to enhance the usefulness of this book. The following elements are available on the http://www.dreamtechpress.com/ website:

- **Bonus chapters**—Five advance level chapters are provided on the website as bonus chapters.
- **Code from the book**—All executable applications provided in the book are provided on the website, so that you can run them without manually coding them line by line. You can find the code for these applications in C# and VB on the website.
- **Appendix**—Ten chapters are provided as appendices on the website.
- **Code for the project**—The complete code for the project, *Online Travel Agency*, is provided on the website. A ProjectReadMe file is also provided to help you work with the project.

System Requirements

You must be running Visual Studio 2012 and .NET Framework 4.5.

- To run the database examples, you should have access to a version of SQL Server, such as SQL Server 2008 or SQL Server 2008 R2.
- To run the Web application and service examples, you should have access to a Web server running Microsoft Internet Information Server (IIS) 7.5 that has the .NET Framework installed. IIS can be installed on the same machine on which you're running Visual Studio 2012.
- The supported operating systems are:
  - Windows 7 SP1 (x86 and x64)
  - Windows 8 (x86 and x64)
  - Windows Server 2008 R2 SP1 (x64)
  - Windows Server 2012 (x64)

Hardware Requirements

1.6 GHz or faster processor

1 GB of RAM (1.5 GB if running on a virtual machine)

10 GB of available hard disk space

600 MB of available hard disk space (language pack)

5400 RPM hard drive

DirectX 9-capable video card running at 1024 x 768 or higher display resolution

To access the Online Resources

1. Visit http://www.dreamtechpress.com/TitlePage.aspx?x=978-93-5119-080-6.
2. Click the Companion Content tab.
3. Enter the Download code: **ASP45-0806-BB-1264**.
4. Click the Download button.